THE BLUE G

*in preparation*

*Duncombe Park by John Sell Cotman*

BLUE GUIDE

# ENGLAND

Ian Ousby

*Maps and plans by John Flower*

**A & C Black**
London

**W W Norton**
New York

Tenth edition 1989

Published by A & C Black (Publishers) Limited
35 Bedford Row, London, WC1R 4JH

© Copyright A & C Black (Publishers) Limited 1989

Published in the United States of America by
W W Norton & Company, Incorporated
500 Fifth Avenue, New York, NY 10110

Published simultaneously in Canada by
Penguin Books Canada Limited,
2801 John Street, Markham, Ontario L3R 1B4

ISBN   0–7136–3028–0

A CIP catalogue record for this book
is available from the British Library.

ISBN 0-393-30608-9   USA

ISBN   0–7136–3163–5   Hardback

ISBN 0-393-02712-0   USA

**Ian Ousby** was educated at Cambridge and Harvard and has taught at universities in both England and America. His publications include *Bloodhounds of Heaven: The Detective in English Fiction from Godwin to Doyle*, (with L. Bradley) *The Correspondence of John Ruskin and Charles Eliot Norton, The Cambridge Guide to Literature in English* (editor) and *Blue Guide Literary Britain and Ireland*.

Typeset by CRB Typesetting Services, Ely, Cambs.
Printed and bound in Great Britain by
William Clowes Limited, Beccles and London

# PREFACE

In preparing this new edition of 'Blue Guide England' I have set myself the same task as my predecessors: to guide travellers through the vast wealth of England's cultural, historic and natural resources in a fashion that will help them better appreciate what they see and better judge what is most worth seeing. I have sought to include as much as a single volume could reasonably contain of the best or most characteristic in landscape, architecture, archaeology, art and history—all those aspects which, combined together in the present life of the nation, give England its distinctive flavour.

Since the Guide last appeared this distinctive flavour has changed enough to demand, if not a wholly new, at least a markedly different volume. Accordingly, the present Guide has been not merely 'updated' but substantially rewritten, reorganised and expanded. Much of the new material reflects the changes in taste which now make travellers take note of industrial sites and Victorian town centres (for example) as well as cathedrals, castles and picturesque villages. It has been particularly pleasant to record some excellent new museums and imaginative new displays in older museums, and to describe some of the smaller country houses which now open their doors to visitors. Considerably less welcome, though also duly noted, are the changes to the economy and appearance of our major cities and the pervasive effects of the rapid growth in tourism during the last decade.

Of course, the present Guide can no more claim to be comprehensive than previous editions did. I have not tried to catalogue every historic inn or Victorian mill or safari park, any more than I have tried to give, at the local level, detailed advice about where to eat, sleep, golf, swim, fish, sail, hang-glide or windsurf. Yet I hope that this book will prove full enough to grant readers the power of choosing for themselves, particularly in stepping aside from the well-beaten paths of the tourist trade and in discovering that England has more to offer than any single guide could capture.

My chief debt has been to the late Stuart Rossiter, whose previous edition of this guide invariably provided the firmest of starting-points and set the highest of standards for my own labours. I am also indebted to the specialised Blue Guides which cross the path of this one, and particularly to Ylva French, author of the London volume, for advising me about her territory. Throughout my work I have been given generous help by the staff at Tourist Information Centres and the places I describe: museums, galleries, cathedrals, churches, country houses, universities, schools and National Parks. Literally hundreds of them have noted changes, verified facts, pointed out details, rebuked or encouraged my opinions, and commented on my proposed descriptions. In addition, staff in virtually all the organisations mentioned or described in my opening sections have taken great pains in supplying information. The fact that they are too numerous to record by name here does not lessen my sense of gratitude. The staff of Cambridge University Library and Cambridge Public Library have helped me greatly in the desk work that forms a large part of travel writing. I would also like to thank the following for permission to reproduce their photographs as illustrations: Aerofilms Ltd; Anglian Water Board; Roman Baths and Museum, Bath; City of Bradford Metropolitan Council; Birmingham City Museum and Art Gallery; Resort and Conference Services Department, Brighton City Council; Britain on View, the British Tourist Authority; Trustees of the British Museum; BBC Hulton Picture Library; University of Cambridge Committee for Aerial Photography; Syndics of Cambridge University Library; Chester City Council; Dean and Chapter of Chester; Jeremy Davies; Dean Forest Studios; Dickens House, London; Dean and Chapter of Durham; Feathers Hotel, Ludlow; Financial Times; Gladstone Pottery Museum, Longton; Peter Hollings, Halifax; Borough of High Peak; Ironbridge Gorge Museum Trust; David Jones; Kershaw Studios, York; A.F. Kersting; Lancaster City Council; Dean and Chapter of Lichfield; Dean and Chapter of Lincoln; Lincoln City Council; Manchester City Art Gallery; National Trust Photographic Library; City Engineer's Department, Newcastle upon Tyne City Council; North York Moors National Park; Oxford County Library; Peak District National Park; Roberts Laurence Marketing, Liverpool; Royal Commission on the Historical Monuments of England; City of Salford Art Gallery and Museum; Shakespeare Birthplace Trust; Skipton Castle; Tate Gallery, London; York Civic Trust (Fairfax House, York). Thanks also to Ian Halcrow who undertook the picture research.

Lewis Braithwaite, David J. Breeze, Christopher Chippindale, Graham Coster, L.J.F. Keppie and Ann Stonehouse have been remarkably tolerant in allowing me to cover my ignorance by borrowing their expertise and even, in several cases, their very language. Finally, I count myself lucky in Tom Neville and the rest of the editorial staff who helped in the preparation of this book: Gemma Davies, David Jones and Ann Douglas. They have all been knowledgeable, patient and even, at times, optimistic.

# A NOTE ON BLUE GUIDES

The Blue Guide series began in 1918 when Muirhead Guide-Books Limited published 'Blue Guide London and its Environs'. Finlay and James Muirhead already had extensive experience of guide-book publishing: before the First World War they had been the editors of the English editions of the German Baedekers, and by 1915 they had acquired the copyright of most of the famous 'Red' Handbooks from John Murray.

An agreement made with the French publishing house Hachette et Cie in 1917 led to the translation of Muirhead's London Guide, which became the first 'Guide Bleu'—Hachette had previously published the blue-covered 'Guides Joanne'. Subsequently, Hachette's 'Guide Bleu Paris et ses Environs' was adapted and published in London by Muirhead. The collaboration between the two publishing houses continued until 1933.

In 1931 Ernest Benn Limited took over the Blue Guides, appointing Russell Muirhead, Finlay Muirhead's son, editor in 1934. The Muirheads' connection with Blue Guides ended in 1963 when Stuart Rossiter, who had been working on the Guides since 1954, became house editor, revising and compiling several of the books himself.

The Blue Guides are now published by A & C Black, who acquired Ernest Benn in 1984, so continuing the tradition of guide-book publishing which began in 1826 with 'Black's Economical Tourist of Scotland'. The Blue Guide series continues to grow: there are now more than 30 titles in print with revised editions appearing regularly and many new Blue Guides in preparation.

'Blue Guides' is a registered trademark.

# CONTENTS

## SOUTH MIDLANDS

**NORTHERN ENGLAND**

# Maps and Plans

# NOTES ON USING THIS GUIDE

The way this guide is organised will be familiar to readers of previous editions or other Blue Guides. It divides England into various regions (South-Eastern, South-Western and so forth), each of them defined and characterised in a brief introduction and then explored in routes for the motorist. These routes are not designed as 'suggested outings' with some particular tourist attraction or famous sight in view, but as journeys between major points on the map. Motorways are avoided in favour of long-established roads which have carried the traffic of history—usually not the fastest way but likely to be the most interesting. Many routes have alternative sections (labelled A, B, etc.) which offer different ways of making the trip between the same two places or touring the same general area. Detours from the main line of the routes and excursions from the stopping-points along the way further widen the scope of what is described.

Though it involves some overlapping of routes (duly indicated by cross-references), this system usually has the merit of grouping places close to each other on the map close to each other on the page. It serves the habitual traveller on the look-out for ways of relieving the journey and the leisurely tourist in search of places worth particular attention or detour. The very detailed index of place names (accompanied by a separate index of people) also encourages readers to follow their own plan.

**Type**. The main routes are described in large type. Smaller type is used for detours and excursions, for technical or historical background, and (generally speaking) for descriptions of greater detail or less importance.

**Abbreviations**. Most of the forms used are generally accepted and self-explanatory, but the following may require explanation:

| | |
|---|---|
| b. | born |
| C | century |
| c | circa (about) |
| cf. | compare |
| d. | died |
| Dec. | Decorated |
| DoE | Department of the Environment |
| EE | Early English |
| fl. | floruit (flourished) |
| ft | foot/feet |
| in | inch/inches |
| inhab. | inhabitants |
| m | mile/miles |
| NGS | National Gardens Scheme |
| No(s). | Number(s) |
| NT | National Trust |
| OS | Ordnance Survey |
| Perp. | Perpendicular |
| Rte(s) | Route(s) |
| St | Saint |
| St. | Street |
| Trans. | Transitional |
| yd | yard/yards |

**Asterisks**. Single asterisks indicate points of special interest or excellence. Double asterisks are used sparingly, for things worth travelling the length of the country to see.

**Distances** in miles are given cumulatively from the starting-point of the route or detour. Road straightening, one-way systems and bypasses ensure that they are at best approximate.

**Maps and plans**. The town plans and cathedral floor plans included in the text give detailed guidance. The road map of England at the back of the book is designed for general reference and planning only, not as a substitute for the motorists' maps now available in a bewildering variety of scales and formats. The paperbound Motoring Atlas (1:190,080 or 1in to 3m) published annually by Ordnance Survey is particularly useful. Those who prefer sheet maps can use the OS Routemaster series (1:250,000 or 1in to 4m) or the Michelin maps 402, 403 and 404 (1:400,000 or 1in to 6.30m).

Though useful for long-distance driving and planning, none of these maps is adequate to the local detail offered in the text. The headnote to each route lists the relevant sheet numbers in the OS Landranger series (1:50,000 or 1¼in to 1m), by far the best maps for getting to know an area of some size with proper intimacy. Where appropriate, the headnotes also recommend the relevant maps in other specialised series: the OS Tourist series (1:63,360 or 1in to 1m) or OS Outdoor Leisure series (1:25,000 or 2½in to 1m), for example.

**Population** figures, rounded off to the nearest hundred, are given as a rough indication of comparative sizes and hence of the facilities which the traveller can expect to find. They are taken from the census of 1981 if more recent local estimates are not available. Wherever possible, they refer to the town or city as historically defined rather than the amorphous modern borough into which it has been assimilated for the purposes of local government.

**Tourist Information Centres** are noted in the text, and street addresses given for those in major cities. The readily identifiable *i* symbol on local signposts usually makes them easy to find. They can provide information about local attractions, opening times, special events, transport and accommodation. Those in large or popular cities frequently offer walking tours in the company of accredited guides. Many centres can make provisional reservations at local hotels and guests houses, and many major ones are linked by the Book-a-Bed-Ahead-Service. Those described as 'seasonal' are in general open from Easter to the end of October, though a few close in September and also for a short period after Easter until May. (See also Useful Organisations: British Tourist Authority and English Tourist Board.)

**Opening times** for museums, galleries, historic buildings, country houses, etc., can vary from year to year, so that the arrangements specified by anything except an annual publication quickly become dated. This guide does not attempt to offer information that might well be misleading by the time the reader encountered it. It merely adds the word 'open' after sites to confirm that there is public access at certain times, if the description in the text does not otherwise make that fact clear. The phrase 'limited opening' (usually appearing in connection with privately owned country houses) warns that at the time of writing the building is open only one or two days a week during a short summer season, for a total of less than about 40 days a year.

Those intent on visiting a particular property are therefore urged to check in advance of any proposed trip. Tourist Information Centres can supply up-to-date information about opening times in the area they serve, and there are two useful annual index publications, 'Historic Houses, Castles and Gardens' and 'Museums and Galleries'. The National Trust issues an annual handbook to its properties.

Otherwise, a few general guidelines can be offered. The traveller will in general fare much better between Easter (or the beginning of April) and the end of October, dates which mark the outer limits of England's continually extending tourist season. In the winter months, the following are likely to be closed: many National Trust buildings (though not necessarily their grounds); most privately owned country houses; and some smaller museums, particularly those outside major centres or in areas heavily dependent on the tourist trade. Even in the tourist season smaller NT properties tend to close for one or two days a week, and only the largest privately owned country houses are open every day of the week. Public holidays add to the restrictions. Virtually all sites are closed on Christmas Day, Boxing Day and New Year's Day. Policy for Christmas Eve and and for the other Bank Holidays varies—Good Friday and the May Day Bank Holiday being especially unpredictable in their effect—but in general properties administered by national or local government are more likely to close and large privately owned tourist attractions to remain open.

English Heritage has a standardised system of opening times for its properties (except some in Greater London). It is indicated in the text by the following phrases:

*Standard opening*: 15 March to 15 October, Monday to Saturday 09.30–18.30 and Sunday 14.00–18.30. 16 October to 14 March, Monday to Saturday 09.30–16.00 and Sunday 14.00–16.00.

*Standard opening and summer Sunday mornings*: As above, but also open from 09.30 on Sundays from 1 April to 30 September.

*Summer standard opening*: 1 April to 30 September, Monday to Saturday 09.30–18.30 and Sunday 14.00–18.30.

*Summer standard opening and summer Sunday mornings*: 1 April to 30 September, daily 09.30–18.30.

Many smaller English Heritage properties are open at any reasonable time. Some otherwise open standard hours may in fact close one or two days a week, particularly in winter; some close for lunch, usually 13.00–14.00. All properties are closed on Christmas Eve, Christmas Day, Boxing Day and New Year's Day.

Parish churches, of course, rarely have official opening hours, but many are nowadays kept locked as a protection against vandalism. There is usually a notice outside giving instructions for obtaining the key.

See Useful Organisations for further details of English Heritage and the National Trust.

# PRACTICAL INFORMATION

The notes in this section are designed mainly for foreign visitors.

**Roads and driving**. Current driving licences issued by foreign countries are valid for up to 12 months. International Driving Permits can also be used. Car hire companies usually require that drivers have at least one year's driving experience and hold a licence free from endorsement; some companies also insist that drivers are at least 21 and not more than 65 years old.

Road regulations are summarised in 'The Highway Code', a booklet published by Her Majesty's Stationery Office (HMSO). The rule of the road is: drive on the left and overtake on the right. Drivers from countries which keep to the right should exercise particular care when entering roundabouts, remembering to go round clockwise rather than anti-clockwise and remembering also to give way to any traffic already on the roundabout. The wearing of seat belts is compulsory for the driver and front-seat passenger.

There are four types of road in Britain: motorways, 'A' roads, 'B' roads and 'unclassified' roads. All but the last are numbered on signs and maps. Motorways, labelled 'M' and signposted in white and blue, are modern communication arteries engineered for speed rather than interest; they usually have three lanes in each direction. Learner drivers, riders of small motorcycles, cyclists and pedestrians are forbidden. Drivers can stop in emergencies only, on the 'hard shoulder' to the left of the left-hand lane. 'A' roads generally follow more interesting and historic routes, though modern alterations in the form of dual carriageways, straightening of sharp bends, bypasses round town centres and ring roads round cities can make some almost as fast as motorways. 'B' roads, secondary routes used by local traffic, are narrower and more likely to wind—but also more likely to bring the motorist in contact with the real character of the landscape. Unclassified roads, identified on road signs only by their destination, vary from pleasantly empty country lanes to one-lane funnels cluttered with slow-moving tractors. The majority are too small to appear on motoring atlases but OS Landranger maps usefully subdivide them into categories which give the motorist some idea of what to expect.

Unless otherwise indicated, the speed limit is 30mph in built-up areas (i.e. those with street lighting), 60mph on single carriageways and 70mph on dual carriageways and motorways.

Two motoring organisations, the Automobile Association (AA) and the Royal Automobile Club (RAC), offer a wide range of useful services to members (particularly in the event of breakdown) as well as issuing many publications available to non-members. Temporary membership of one·or the other is often included in car hire terms. Members of the American Automobile Association (AAA) and of other clubs affiliated to the Alliance Internationale de Tourisme (AIT) receive membership benefits from the AA. Members of clubs affiliated to the AIT and the Féderation Internationale de l'Automobile (FIA) can use the RAC rescue services without charge. The AA headquarters is at Fanum House, Basingstoke, Hampshire RG21 2EA; phone 0256 201123. The RAC headquarters is at 49 Pall Mall, London SW1Y 5JG; phone 01–839 7050.

**Railways**. British Rail (BR) provides a quick and efficient service on its Inter-City network, with trains often departing at hourly intervals and reaching speeds of up to 125mph. Typical journey times from London are: less than 1 hour to Brighton; 1–1½ hours to Bath, Cambridge, Canterbury, Dover, Oxford and Salisbury; 1½–2 hours to Birmingham, Bournemouth, Bristol, Cardiff and Portsmouth; 2–3 hours to Chester, Exeter, Leeds, Lincoln, Liverpool, Manchester, Norwich, Sheffield and York; 3–4 hours to Plymouth and Penzance; and about 5 hours to Edinburgh. Inter–City trains have first-class and standard carriages, and restaurant and/or buffet cars. Inter-City trains with sleeping cars serve routes from London to Scotland and the South-West. The Motorail service enables travellers to transport their car by the same train.

Because the main railway network radiates from London like spokes from the hub of a wheel, journeys between provincial centres may be much slower and involve changing trains. The closure of branch lines in rural areas has reduced service to smaller places, and journeys sometimes have to be completed by bus.

BritRail passes are bargain tickets which allow unlimited travel for periods of 4, 8, 15 or 22 days or one month. They are available only to foreign visitors and must be bought before arrival in Britain. Rail-Rover tickets, which can be bought in Britain, allow unlimited travel for 7 or 14 days, either in specified regions or throughout the entire network.

**Coaches**. Long-distance coaches provide a cheaper but slower alternative to travel by rail. National Express, the largest operator, has the centre of its network at London's Victoria Coach Station and major interchanges at Bristol, Birmingham, Leeds and Manchester. Typical journey times are: London–Brighton 1¾ hours; London–Birmingham, the busiest route, 2½ hours; Leeds–Manchester 1½ hours; Newcastle–Penzance 12½ hours. Information can be obtained from National Express agents or, in London, by phoning 01–730 0202. The BritExpress card for foreign visitors, available from major agents, brings a reduction on all fares for periods of 8, 15 or 21 days.

**Accommodation**. The growth of tourist service industries means that England now offers a wide range of accommodation: hotels, inns, guesthouses, bed and breakfast (B&B), farmhouse accommodation, self-catering holiday accommodation, Youth Hostels, and camping and caravan sites. The best English hotels compare favourably with the best anywhere. Some of the 'country house' hotels and older inns in country towns occupy buildings that are themselves of architectural interest. It remains true, however, that by international standards the average hotel in the average provincial town charges too much and provides too little. Those who do not demand the full range of hotel facilities will appreciate the excellent value, as well as the friendly and informal atmosphere, offered by bed and breakfast and farmhouse accommodation.

The English Tourist Board operates a Crown Classification scheme for serviced accommodation, awarding from one to five crowns to indicate the range and sophistication of the facilities provided and placing simpler accommodation in a 'Listed' category. The services offered by Tourist Information Centres are described in Notes On Using This Guide.

A wide range of annual publications is issued by the English Tourist Board, the British Tourist Authority, the Automobile

Association and the Royal Automobile Club. Egon Ronay's guide to 'Hotels and Restaurants' and the Consumers' Association 'Good Hotel Guide' are reliable and demanding in their standards. The Youth Hostels Association and the annual accommodation guide issued by the Ramblers' Association are listed under Useful Organisations.

**Food**. Breakfast and tea are still the best meals to be had in England, and they are not hard to come by. Otherwise, travellers will find greater choice and higher standards than the poor international reputation of English food might lead them to expect. Many public houses (pubs) serve simple and inexpensive lunches. Italian, Chinese and Indian restaurants have introduced welcome variety in even the smaller towns.

Egon Ronay's 'Just a Bite' and 'Good Food in Pubs and Bars' are useful guides to simpler fare. (Connoisseurs of pubs for their own sake will appreciate the Consumers' Association 'Good Pub Guide' and the 'Good Beer Guide' published by CAMRA, the Campaign for Real Ale.) Egon Ronay's 'Hotels and Restaurants' and the Consumers' Association 'Good Food Guide' serve the needs of the gourmet.

**Money**. The pound sterling (£), the standard unit of currency, is divided into 100 pence (p). There are notes for £50, £20, £10 and £5; a small, gold-coloured coin for £1; 'silver' coins for 50p, 20p, 10p and 5p; and 'copper' coins for 2p and 1p. The ½p (halfpenny) is no longer legal tender.

Banks are open Monday to Friday 09.30 to 15.30 and, in some cases, Saturday 09.30 to 12.00. Outside these hours Bureaux de Change can also be found at airports, major railway stations, large hotels and department stores, and travel agencies.

**VAT**. Value Added Tax (popularly called 'vee-ay-tee' or 'vat') is a sales tax added to a wide range of goods and services, currently at a rate of 15 per cent. It should already be included in the prices quoted by hotels and restaurants. Major shops in London and other centres with a substantial tourist trade operate the Retail Export Scheme, which enables foreign visitors to get a refund for VAT paid on certain goods (but not hotel accommodation, car hire, etc.).

**Tipping**. Most hotels and many restaurants include a service charge in the bill. Add 10–15 per cent if it is not included. Taxi drivers and hairdressers expect a tip of 10–15 per cent, and porters 30–50p per suitcase. Cloakroom attendants and barmen in hotel cocktail bars expect some change to be left on the plate. Do not tip in pubs, cinemas or theatres.

**Post**. Post Offices are usually open Monday to Friday 09.00–17.30 and Saturday 09.00–12.30. Stamps are also available from the stamp machines outside major Post Offices and from some hotel desks. Inland letters can be sent at a first-class rate (90 per cent arrive the following day) or at a slower and cheaper second-class rate (usually delivered within three working days). European mail automatically goes airmail or by the quickest route, but airmail stickers and extra stamps are required for the service outside Europe.

**Telephones**. Britain's phone system is operated by a public company, British Telecom. The most useful coins for public phone booths are

10p and 50p pieces. Some new booths accept only 'phonecards', available from Post Offices and many newsagents and corner shops.

The cost of inland calls is governed by distance and by time of day: Monday to Friday 09.00 to 13.00 (very expensive); Monday to Friday 08.00 to 09.00 and 13.00 to 18.00 (expensive); and all other times including the weekend (less expensive, but still not cheap). International calls can usually be dialled directly. Rates to most countries are cheaper between 20.00 and 08.00 Monday to Friday and at the weekend.

**Summer Time**. British Summer Time, one hour ahead of Greenwich Mean Time, is adopted between the end of March and the end of October. The changes forward and back are always made at midnight on a Saturday, though the exact dates vary from year to year. They do not coincide with the changes that also take place on the Continent.

**Bank Holidays**. These public holidays fall on the following dates: New Year's Day; Good Friday; Easter Monday; the first Monday in May (May Day Bank Holiday); the last Monday in May (Spring or Whitsun Bank Holiday); the last Monday in August (Summer or August Bank Holiday); Christmas Day; and Boxing Day (26 December). If any of the moveable festivals or anniversaries should fall on a Sunday, the Monday afterwards is treated as a Bank Holiday instead.

**Medical services**. Visitors to Britain can use the accident and emergency services of the National Health Service free of charge. The National Health Service charges for hospital care and urgent treatment of visitors to Britain unless there is a reciprocal arrangement with their country of origin. Countries which have such an arrangement include EEC and most other European countries, Australia, New Zealand, Hong Kong and the USSR. All visitors should check their eligibility before they start their journey, and visitors from non-reciprocal countries (e.g. USA, Canada, Switzerland, Japan) should take out medical insurance.

# USEFUL ORGANISATIONS

**Automobile Association** (AA). See Practical Information: Roads and Driving.

**British Rail** (BR). See Practical Information: Railways.

The **British Tourist Authority** (BTA), the statutory agency responsible for encouraging tourism to Britain from overseas, maintains offices in 21 countries to provide information for prospective visitors. It also runs the British Travel Centre, 12 Regent St., Piccadilly Circus, London SW1Y 4PQ (phone 01–730 3400), which books rail, coach and air travel, sightseeing tours, theatre tickets and accommodation as well as providing information about the whole country. (For other information services in England, see English Tourist Board below.)

BTA overseas offices include:

*Australia*: 4th Floor, Midland House, 171 Clarence St., Sydney, New South Wales 2000; phone 29 8627.
*Canada*: 94 Cumberland St., Suite 600, Toronto, Ontario M5R 3N3; phone 416 961 8124/925 6326.
*Hong Kong*: Suite 903, 1 Hysan Avenue, Causeway Bay, Hong Kong; phone 5–764 366/764 371.
*New Zealand*: 8th Floor, Norwich Insurance House, CNR Queen and Durham Streets, Auckland 1; phone 9 31446.
*USA (Chicago)*: John Hancock Center, Suite 3320, 875 North Michigan Avenue, Chicago, Illinois 60611; phone 312 787 0492.
*USA (Dallas)*: Cedar Maple Plaza, 2305 Cedar Springs Rd, Dallas, Texas 75201–1814; phone 214 720 4040.
*USA (Los Angeles)*: World Trade Center, 350 South Figueroa St., Suite 450, Los Angeles, California 90071; phone 213 628 3525.
*USA (New York)*: 3rd Floor, 40 West 57th St., New York, New York 10019; phone 212 581 4700.

**British Waterways** (formally the British Waterways Board) are responsible for 2000 miles of inland waterways in England, Scotland and Wales. All general inquiries about canals and cruising are handled by the Information Centre at Melbury House, Melbury Terrace, London NW1 6JX (phone 01–262 6711).

The **Countryside Commission**, successor to the National Parks Commission, is an independent agency grant-aided by the government to protect the natural beauty of the countryside and to make it more accessible for public enjoyment. It is responsible for designating Areas of Outstanding Natural Beauty, Heritage Coasts and National Parks in England and Wales. The National Parks in England are: Dartmoor, Exmoor, the Lake District, Northumberland, the Peak District, the North York Moors and the Yorkshire Dales. Largely made up of privately owned land but subject to special planning control, they are administered by separate National Park Authorities which also provide special amenities for visitors.

The Countryside Commission is also responsible for creating and maintaining the Pennine Way and other long-distance paths for walkers: the Cleveland Way, Offa's Dyke Path, the Peddars' Way and Norfolk Coast Path, the Ridgeway Path, the North Downs Way, the South Downs Way, the South West Coast Path and the Wolds Way.

Further information is available from the Commission's headquarters at John Dower House, Crescent Place, Cheltenham, Gloucestershire GL50 3RA (phone 0242 521381).

**English Heritage** is the popular name for the Historic Buildings and Monuments Commission for England, which in 1984 took over responsibility from the Department of the Environment for protecting the country's architectural heritage and for administering nationally owned historic properties except royal palaces and parks. More than 350 such properties are open to the public, including prehistoric monuments (Stonehenge), Roman ruins (most of Hadrian's Wall), castles, abbeys, etc. Details of annual membership or life membership, which give free admission, are available at all staffed sites or from English Heritage Membership Department, PO Box 43, Ruislip, Middlesex, HA4 0XW. For opening times, see Notes On Using This Guide.

The head office is at Fortress House, 23 Savile Row, London W1X 2HE (phone 01–734 6010). Regional offices are as follows:

*Avon, Cornwall, Devon, Dorset, Gloucestershire, Isles of Scilly, Somerset, Wiltshire*: Bridge House, Clifton, Bristol BS8 4XA; phone 0272 734472 ext 205.
*Bedfordshire, Cambridgeshire, Essex except Tilbury Fort, Lyddington Bede House in Leicestershire, Norfolk, Northamptonshire, Suffolk*: Government

Buildings, Brooklands Avenue, Cambridge CB2 2BU; phone 0223 358911 ext 2967.
*Berkshire, Tilbury Fort in Essex, Greater London, Hertfordshire, part of Kent, Oxfordshire*: Thames House South, Millbank, London WS1P 4QJ; phone 01–211 8828.
*Cheshire, Humberside, Lancashire, North Yorkshire, South Yorkshire*: Duncombe Place, York Y01 2ED; phone 0904 58626.
*Cleveland, Cumbria, Durham, Northumberland, Tyne and Wear*: Carlisle Castle, Carlisle CA3 8UR; phone 0228 31777.
*Derbyshire, Hereford and Worcester, Leicestershire except Lyddington Bede House, Lincolnshire, Nottinghamshire, Shropshire, Staffordshire, Warwickshire*: Finchfield House, Castlecroft Rd, Wolverhampton WV3 8BY; phone 0902 765105.
*Hampshire, Isle of Wight, most of Kent, Surrey, East Sussex, West Sussex*: Spur 17, Government Buildings, Hawkenbury, Tunbridge Wells, Kent TN2 5AQ; phone 0892 48166.

The **English Tourist Board** (ETB), which works in conjunction with the British Tourist Authority (see above) to promote tourism, provides information services for visitors in England. Much of its operation is carried out through regional Tourist Boards and local Tourist Information Centres, where the wide range of ETB publications can be obtained. The regional Tourist Boards are as follows:

*Cumbria Tourist Board*: Holly Rd, Ashleigh, Windermere, Cumbria LA23 2AQ; phone 096 62 4444.
*East Anglia Tourist Board* (Cambridgeshire, Essex, Norfolk, Suffolk): Topplesfield Hall, Hadleigh, Suffolk IP7 5DN; phone 0473 822922.
*East Midlands Tourist Board* (Leicestershire, Lincolnshire, Northamptonshire, Nottinghamshire, part of Derbyshire): Exchequergate, Lincoln LN2 1PZ; phone 0522 531521/3.
*Heart of England Tourist Board* (Gloucestershire, Hereford and Worcester, Shropshire, Staffordshire, Warwickshire, West Midlands): 2–4 Trinity St., Worcester WR1 2PW; phone 0905 613132.
*London Tourist Board* (Greater London area): 26 Grosvenor Gardens, London SW1W 0ET; phone: 01–730 3450.
*Northumbria Tourist Board* (Cleveland, Durham, Northumberland, Tyne and Wear): Aykley Heads, Durham DH1 5UX; phone 091 3846905.
*North West Tourist Board* (Cheshire, Greater Manchester, Lancashire, Merseyside, the High Peak district of Derbyshire): The Last Drop Village, Bromley Cross, Bolton, Lancashire BL7 9PZ; phone 0204 591511.
*South East England Tourist Board* (Kent, Surrey, East Sussex, West Sussex): 1 Warwick Park, Tunbridge Wells, Kent TN2 5TA; phone 0892 40766.
*Southern Tourist Board* (Hampshire, Isle of Wight, part of Dorset): The Town Hall Centre, Leigh Rd, Eastleigh, Hampshire SO5 4DE; phone 0703 616027.
*Thames and Chilterns Tourist Board* (Bedfordshire, Berkshire, Buckinghamshire, Hertfordshire, Oxfordshire): The Mount House, Church Green, Witney, Oxfordshire OX8 6DZ; phone 0993 778800.
*West Country Tourist Board* (Avon, Cornwall, Devon, Isles of Scilly, Somerset, Wiltshire, part of Dorset): Trinity Court, 37 Southernhay East, Exeter EX1 1QS; phone 0392 76351.
*Yorkshire and Humberside Tourist Board* (Humberside, North Yorkshire, South Yorkshire, West Yorkshire): 312 Tadcaster Rd, York YO2 2HF; phone 0904 707961.

The **Forestry Commission** is the government department reponsible for carrying out Britain's forestry policy, through support and control of private development and through management of its own estates, which run to almost 700,000 acres in England. They include ancient woodlands like the New Forest, the Forest of Dean and Sherwood Forest as well as forests grown since the 1940s. The Commission provides a generous range of amenities for tourists: information centres, forest drives, walks and specialist trails, picnic sites, sports facilities, and cabin and camping areas. Publications and further information can be obtained from the three regional offices in England: 1a Grosvenor Terrace, York Y03 7BD (phone 0904 20221);

Avonfields House, Keynsham, Bristol BS18 2BD (phone 0272 869481); Tenison Rd, Cambridge CB1 2DU (phone 0223 314546). The Commission's headquarters are at 231 Corstophine Rd, Edinburgh EH12 7AT; phone 031 334 0303.

**National Express**. See Practical Information: Coaches.

The **National Gardens Scheme** (NGS) arranges the opening, on selected days each summer, of gardens not usually open to the public. All proceeds go to charity. A booklet published in March is available from booksellers and newsagents or directly from the NGS, 57 Lower Belgrave St., London SW1W 0LR (phone 01–730 0359).

**National Parks**. See Countryside Commission.

The **National Trust** (NT) is an independent charity dedicated to preserving places of historic interest or natural beauty in England, Wales and Northern Ireland. (There is a separate National Trust for Scotland.) Founded in 1895, it has grown into the largest conservation society and private landowner in Britain. About 190 historic houses, including 87 large country houses, are open to the public, together with prehistoric, Roman and industrial sites, churches, chapels and barns, gardens and landscaped parks, many acres of countryside and many miles of coastline. For opening times see Notes On Using This Guide. Annual membership or life membership, which give free admission to most properties, are available at all staffed sites or from PO Box 39, Bromley, Kent BR1 1NH (phone 01–464 1111). Members of the Royal Oak Foundation, the NT's membership affiliate in the USA, receive membership privileges; contact 285 West Broadway, Suite 400, New York, New York 10013.

The NT head office is at 36 Queen Anne's Gate, London W1X 2HE (phone 01–222 9251). Regional offices are as follows:

*Cornwall*: Lanhydrock Park, Bodmin, Cornwall PL30 4DE; phone 0208 4281.
*Devon*: Killerton House, Broadclyst, Exeter, Devon EX5 3LE; phone 0392 881691.
*East Anglia* (Cambridgeshire, Essex, Norfolk, Suffolk): Blickling, Norwich NR11 6NF; phone 0263 733471.
*East Midlands* (Derbyshire, Leicestershire, Lincolnshire, Northamptonshire, Nottinghamshire, South Humberside, and parts of Cheshire, Greater Manchester, Staffordshire, South Yorkshire, West Yorkshire): Clumber Park Stableyard, Worksop, Nottinghamshire S80 3BE; phone 0909 486411.
*Kent and East Sussex* (includes SE Greater London): Estate Office, Scotney Castle, Lamberhurst, Tunbridge Wells, Kent TN3 8JN; phone 0892 890651.
*Mercia* (Cheshire, Merseyside, Shropshire, most of Greater Manchester and Staffordshire, part of West Midlands): Attingham Park, Shrewsbury, Shropshire SY4 4TP; phone 074 377 343.
*Northumbria* (Durham, Northumberland, Tyne and Wear): Scots' Gap, Morpeth, Northumberland NE61 4EG; phone 067 074 691.
*Thames and Chilterns* (Bedfordshire, Berkshire, Buckinghamshire, Hertfordshire, London N of the Thames, Oxfordshire): Hughenden Manor, High Wycombe, Buckinghamshire HP14 4LA; phone 0494 28051.
*Severn* (Gloucestershire, Hereford and Worcester, Warwickshire, part of West Midlands): Mythe End House, Tewkesbury, Gloucestershire GL20 6EB; phone 0684 850051.
*Southern* (Hampshire, Isle of Wight, SW Greater London, Surrey, West Sussex): Polesden Lacey, Dorking, Surrey RH5 6BD; phone 0372 53401.
*North-West* (Cumbria, Lancashire): Rothay Holme, Rothay Rd, Ambleside, Cumbria LA22 0EJ; phone 0966 33883.
*Wessex* (Avon, Dorset, Somerset, Wiltshire): Stourton, Warminster, Wiltshire BA12 6QD; phone 0747 840224.
*Yorkshire* (Cleveland, North Humberside, North Yorshire, most of South York-

shire and West Yorkshire): Goddards, 27 Tadcaster Rd, Dringhouses, York YO2 2QG; phone 0904 702021.

The **Nature Conservancy Council** is the official body responsible for nature conservation in England, Scotland and Wales. Its functions include the management of some 234 nature reserves and about 4000 sites of special scientific interest. Further information is available from Northminster House, Peterborough PE1 1UA (phone 0733 40345).

The **Ramblers' Association** provides information about walking in the countryside. Members also receive a yearbook containing a useful guide to bed and breakfast accommodation near long-distance footpaths. Further details from 1–5 Wandsworth Rd, London SW8 2XX (phone 01–582 6878).

**Royal Automobile Club** (RAC). See Practical Information: Roads and Driving.

The **Youth Hostels Association** (YHA) for England and Wales maintains more than 260 hostels, in both urban and rural locations. Members of the YHA in their home country get world-wide access to hostels. Further details, including terms of membership, can be obtained from Trevelyan House, 8 St Stephen's Hill, St Albans, Hertfordshire AL1 2DY (phone 0727 55215).

# HISTORICAL INFORMATION

## Prehistoric Periods

| | |
|---|---|
| Neolithic | c 3500 BC–c 1700 BC |
| Bronze Age | c 1700 BC–c 650 BC |
| Iron Age | c 650 BC–AD 43 |

## Chronology of English History

| | |
|---|---|
| 55–54 BC | Julius Caesar makes two expeditions to Britain after subjugating Gaul. |
| c AD 10 | Cunobelin (Cymbeline), ruler of the Trinovantes, establishes his capital at Camulodunum (Colchester). |
| AD 43 | Roman conquest of Britain begins. |
| AD 50 | Caractacus, British leader, captured. |
| AD 60–61 | Unsuccessful rebellion by Boudicca (Boadicea), ruler of the Iceni. |
| 122 | Hadrian's Wall begun after the Emperor's visit to Britain. |
| 140–141 | Antonine Wall built in Scotland; abandoned c 163. |
| 209 | St Alban martyred. |
| 409 | Roman rule in Britain ends. |
| c 449 | Angles, Saxons and Jutes invade in force, establishing in the next 150 years the separate kingdoms of Kent, Sussex, Wessex, Mercia, Bernicia and Deira (merged as Northumbria), Essex and East Anglia. |
| 539 | Date which the 10C Welsh 'Annales Cambriae' gives for the death of the British leader Arthur at the Battle of Camlan. |
| 563 | St Columba founds a monastery on Iona (Hebrides). |
| 597–616 | Kent becomes the leading English kingdom under King Ethelbert. He is converted to Christianity by Augustine at the beginning of the Saint's mission to England. Augustine founds a monastery and later an archepiscopal see at Canterbury. |
| 617–685 | Supremacy of Northumbria, notably under Kings Edwin and Oswald (rulers in 616–632 and 633–641). Paulinus baptises Edwin at York in 627. Oswald helps St Aidan establish his monastery at Lindisfarne in 635. |
| 664 | Roman and Celtic churches meet at the Synod of Whitby, their decisions generally favouring Rome. |
| c 730–821 | Mercian supremacy, notably under Kings Ethelbald and Offa (rulers in 716–757 and 757–796). Offa's Dyke defines the Mercian boundary with Wales. |
| 731 | Bede completes his 'Historia Ecclesiastica' at Jarrow. |
| 793 | Lindisfarne sacked by Danish raiders. |
| 829 | Egbert, King of Wessex (802–839), establishes supremacy for the Wessex dynasty, which lasts during the next two centuries of Danish invasions. |
| 878 | After his great victory at Edington, Alfred the Great concedes much of Eastern England to Danish |

|  |  |
|---|---|
|  | control (the Danelaw). It is largely reconquered by his son Edward the Elder. |
| 991 | Ethelred the Unready introduces a tax, later known as Danegeld, to buy off the invading armies. |
| 1016 | Canute (Cnut), King of Denmark, becomes King of England. |
| 1042 | Wessex dynasty restored by Edward the Confessor. |
| 1066 | Norman Conquest. Harold II, after defeating the Norwegians at Stamford Bridge, is himself defeated by William of Normandy at Hastings. |
| 1085–1086 | 'Domesday Book' compiled. |
| 1087 | Death of William I (William the Conqueror); accession of William II (William Rufus). |
| 1100 | William Rufus dies, killed by an arrow while hunting in the New Forest; accession of his brother, Henry I. |
| 1135 | Death of Henry I; accession of his nephew Stephen. The challenge to his claim from Henry's daughter Matilda, leads to civil war. |
| 1154 | Death of Stephen; accession of Matilda's son, Henry II, inaugurates the Plantagenet dynasty. |
| 1167 | Expulsion of English students from Paris encourages the growth of universities at Oxford and, apparently slightly later, Cambridge. |
| 1170 | Thomas Becket murdered in Canterbury Cathedral. |
| 1171–1172 | Henry II lays claim to Ireland, awarding land to Norman knights. |
| 1189 | Death of Henry II; accession of Richard I (the Lionheart), largely absent on the Third Crusade and as a prisoner on the Continent. |
| 1199 | Death of Richard the Lionheart; accession of his brother John. |
| 1215 | King John compelled by barons to sign Magna Carta, designed to protect feudal rights and baronial privileges against royal abuse. |
| 1216 | Death of King John; accession of Henry III, with he Earl of Pembroke acting as Regent during his minority. |
| 1249 | University College, Oxford, founded; followed by Merton College (1264) and Balliol (before 1266) in Oxford and Peterhouse (1281–1284) in Cambridge. |
| 1265 | Defeat and death of Simon de Montfort at the Battle of Evesham ends the barons' rebellion. |
| 1272 | Death of Henry III; accession of Edward I. |
| 1277–1283 | Edward I conquers Wales. |
| 1290 | Edward's first queen, Eleanor of Castile, dies; Eleanor Crosses are built to mark the route of her funeral procession from Lincoln to Westminster Abbey. |
| 1307 | Edward I dies on his way to confront Scottish army led by Robert Bruce; accession of Edward II. |
| 1312 | Edward II's favourite Piers Gaveston is executed by the barons. |
| 1327 | Edward II deposed by his queen, Isabella of France, and her lover Mortimer and murdered at Berkeley Castle; accession of his son as Edward III. |
| 1337 | Hundred Years' War against France begins. |
| c 1343 | Geoffrey Chaucer born. |

| | |
|---|---|
| 1348–1349 | Black Death (mainly bubonic plague) reaches England. |
| 1351 | Statute of Labourers fixes wages in response to the labour shortage caused by the Black Death. |
| 1377 | Death of Edward III; accession of Richard II, son of Edward III's eldest son, the Black Prince. |
| 1381 | Peasants' Revolt, led by Wat Tyler, defeated. |
| c 1382 | First complete translation of the Bible into English, by the religious reformer John Wyclif, or his Lollard followers, appears; revised edition in 1388. |
| 1399 | Richard II deposed by John of Gaunt's son, Henry of Bolingbroke; he dies at Pontefract Castle in 1400. As Henry IV, Bolingbroke inaugurates the Lancastrian dynasty. |
| 1400 | Geoffrey Chaucer dies. |
| 1401–1417 | Persecution of the Lollards, followers of the religious reformer John Wyclif. |
| 1403 | Rebellion by the Earl of Northumberland and his son Henry Percy (Hotspur), joining with Owen Glendower of Wales, defeated at Shrewsbury. |
| 1413 | Death of Henry IV; accession of Henry V. |
| 1415 | Henry V resumes Hundred Years' War. English victory at Agincourt. |
| 1422 | Death of Henry V; accession of Henry VI. |
| 1450 | Jack Cade's rebellion defeated. |
| 1455 | First Battle of St Albans begins the Wars of the Roses, between the Lancastrian and Yorkist factions. |
| 1461 | Henry VI deposed; the Duke of York assumes the throne as Edward IV. |
| 1470–1471 | Henry VI briefly returns to the throne. Edward IV wins a decisive Yorkist victory over the Lancastrians at Tewkesbury. Henry VI murdered. |
| 1476 | William Caxton sets up his printing press at Westminster. |
| 1483 | Death of Edward IV. His child heir, Edward V, and his younger son Richard, Duke of York, are murdered in the Tower of London, possibly by their uncle, who assumes the throne as Richard III. |
| 1485 | Death of Richard III at Bosworth Field ends the Wars of the Roses. The victor, Henry VII, initiates the Tudor dynasty. |
| 1509 | Death of Henry VII; accession of Henry VIII. |
| 1513 | English army defeats and kills James IV of Scotland at Flodden. |
| 1534–1540 | English Reformation: Henry VIII breaks with the papacy, declaring himself head of the Church and dissolving the monasteries. |
| 1547 | Death of Henry VIII; his ten-year-old son by Jane Seymour succeeds to the throne as Edward VI, with Somerset as Lord Protector. |
| 1549 | 'Book of Common Prayer' issued; revised versions appear in 1552 and 1559, and a final text in 1662. |
| 1553 | Death of Edward VI; accession of Mary I, daughter of Henry VIII and Catherine of Aragon. She reunites the English church with Rome and persecutes Protestants. |
| 1558 | Protestantism restored with the death of Mary I and |

the accession of Elizabeth I, daughter of Henry VIII and Anne Boleyn.

| | |
|---|---|
| 1564 | Shakespeare born. |
| 1587 | Execution of Mary, Queen of Scots. |
| 1588 | Spanish Armada defeated. |
| 1599 | First Globe Theatre built in Southwark. |
| 1603 | Death of Elizabeth I without a direct heir. Accession of James I (James VI of Scotland and the son of Mary, Queen of Scots) unites the crowns of England and Scotland and initiates the Stuart dynasty. |
| 1605 | Gunpowder plot, Roman Catholic conspiracy to blow up the Houses of Parliament, discovered. Its anniversary, 5 November, enters the English calendar as Guy Fawkes Day. |
| 1611 | Authorised (King James) Version of the Bible issued. |
| 1616 | Shakespeare dies. |
| 1620 | 'Mayflower' sails from Plymouth. |
| 1625 | Death of James I; accession of Charles I. |
| 1629–1640 | Charles I rules without Parliament. |
| 1642 | Civil War, between the King and Parliament, begins. |
| 1644 | Royalists defeated at Marston Moor. |
| 1645 | Royalists defeated at Naseby. |
| 1646 | Charles I surrenders to the Scots. |
| 1649 | Charles I executed and the Commonwealth declared. |
| 1653–1658 | Oliver Cromwell rules as Lord Protector. |
| 1660 | Monarchy restored with the return of Charles II from exile. Royal Society founded. |
| 1665–1666 | Great Plague. |
| 1666 | Great Fire of London. |
| 1685 | Death of Charles II; accession of his Roman Catholic brother as James II. The Duke of Monmouth's Protestant rebellion is defeated at Sedgemoor. |
| 1688 | Glorious Revolution deposes James II in favour of his nephew William III, of the House of Orange, and daughter Mary II. |
| 1689 | The Bill of Rights consolidates the power of Parliament, reduces the power of the monarchy and debars Roman Catholics from the throne. |
| 1694 | Death of Mary II. Bank of England established. |
| 1701–1713 | War of the Spanish Succession. Duke of Marlborough defeats French at Blenheim, 1704. |
| 1702 | Death of William III; accession of Queen Anne, James II's second daughter. |
| 1707 | Parliamentary union of England and Scotland. |
| 1714 | Death of Queen Anne without immediate heir. The throne passes to the House of Hanover in the person of George I. |
| 1715 | Unsuccessful Jacobite rebellion in Scotland led by James II's son, the 'Old Pretender'. |
| 1720 | South Sea Bubble ruins many investors. |
| 1721–1742 | Whig ministry of Sir Robert Walpole, often described as the first Prime Minister. |
| 1727 | Death of George I; accession of his son, George II. |

| | |
|---|---|
| 1745–1746 | Unsuccessful Jacobite rebellion led by Charles Edward Stuart (the 'Young Pretender' or 'Bonnie Prince Charlie'), defeated at Culloden. |
| 1756–1763 | Seven Years' War. |
| 1759 | British Museum opened. James Brindley begins the Bridgewater Canal; Manchester–Worsley section opened in 1761. |
| 1760 | Death of George II; accession of his grandson, George III. |
| 1769 | James Watt patents his steam engine. |
| 1775–1783 | American War of Independence. |
| 1779 | World's first iron bridge built at Coalbrookdale in Shropshire. |
| 1800–1815 | Napoleonic Wars. Nelson defeats Franco-Spanish fleet at Trafalgar, 1805; Peninsula Campaign, 1808–1814; Wellington defeats Napoleon at Waterloo, 1815. |
| 1811 | Because of George III's insanity the future George IV becomes Prince Regent, with full royal powers. |
| 1811–1816 | Luddite riots by workers who attack the new machinery introduced in knitting and weaving. |
| 1819 | Peterloo massacre at mass meeting in Manchester. |
| 1820 | Regency ends with the death of George III and accession of the Prince Regent as George IV. |
| 1825 | Stockton and Darlington railway opened. |
| 1829 | Catholic emancipation. Metropolitan Police Force founded. |
| 1830 | Death of George IV; accession of his younger brother, William IV. Liverpool and Manchester railway opened. |
| 1831 | Captain Swing riots by agricultural workers. |
| 1832 | First Reform Act extends the franchise and redistributes parliamentary seats to give the new industrial towns greater representation. |
| 1834 | Tolpuddle Martyrs, six Dorset farmworkers, sentenced to transportation for trying to organise an illegal trade union. |
| 1837 | Death of William IV; accession of his niece, Queen Victoria. |
| 1838–1842 | Chartist agitation for extension of the vote to all adult males. |
| 1839 | 'Penny post' begins. |
| 1840 | Queen Victoria marries Prince Albert of Saxe-Coburg and Gotha. |
| 1846 | Corn Laws repealed. |
| 1847 | Factory Act limits the working day to ten hours. |
| 1851 | Great Exhibition. |
| 1854–1856 | Crimean War. |
| 1861 | Prince Albert dies. |
| 1867 | Second Reform Act extends the franchise. |
| 1868 | Trades Union Congress (TUC) formed in Manchester. |
| 1877 | Queen Victoria proclaimed Empress of India. Society for the Protection of Ancient Buildings formed. |
| 1882 | Ancient Monuments Protection Act, the first law of |

|          |                                                                                                                                                                        |
|----------|------------------------------------------------------------------------------------------------------------------------------------------------------------------------|
|          | its kind, gives a measure of protection to Stonehenge and 28 other prehistoric ruins.                                                                                   |
| 1895     | National Trust founded.                                                                                                                                                 |
| 1897     | Queen Victoria's Diamond Jubilee.                                                                                                                                       |
| 1899–1902 | Second South African (Boer) War.                                                                                                                                      |
| 1901     | Death of Queen Victoria; accession of Edward VII.                                                                                                                       |
| 1903     | Letchworth, the first 'garden city', begun.                                                                                                                             |
| 1908     | Herbert Asquith's Liberal government introduces old age pensions.                                                                                                       |
| 1910     | Death of Edward VII; accession of George V. In 1917 he renounces all German titles and adopts the name of Windsor for the royal family.                                 |
| 1914–1918 | First World War.                                                                                                                                                       |
| 1918     | Vote given to all men over 21 and all women over 30.                                                                                                                    |
| 1921     | Most of Ireland achieves independence as Irish Free State (Eire); as Northern Ireland, six counties of Ulster remain part of the United Kingdom.                        |
| 1922     | British Broadcasting Corporation (BBC) founded.                                                                                                                         |
| 1924     | First Labour government takes office, under Ramsay MacDonald.                                                                                                            |
| 1926     | General Strike.                                                                                                                                                         |
| 1929     | Vote given to all women over 21.                                                                                                                                        |
| 1932     | Green Belt established round London to control the spread of suburbs.                                                                                                   |
| 1936     | Death of George V. The Prince of Wales briefly succeeds as Edward VIII but abdicates before being crowned; his younger brother becomes George VI. Jarrow Hunger March to London by the unemployed. |
| 1939–1945 | Second World War.                                                                                                                                                     |
| 1945     | Election of Clement Attlee's Labour government, responsible for nationalising public service and other major industries, and for creating much of the Welfare State.    |
| 1949     | National Parks Commission (later the Countryside Commission) established, with the power to designate parks and outstanding areas of natural beauty in England and Wales. |
| 1952     | Death of George VI; accession of Elizabeth II.                                                                                                                          |
| 1956     | Calder Hall, the world's first industrial-size nuclear power station, opened at Windscale (Sellafield) in Cumbria.                                                      |
| 1959     | M1, Britain's first motorway, opened.                                                                                                                                   |
| 1969     | First significant discovery of North Sea oil; first supply brought ashore in 1975.                                                                                      |
| 1971     | Decimal currency introduced.                                                                                                                                            |
| 1973     | Britain joins the European Economic Community ('Common Market').                                                                                                        |
| 1982     | Falklands War.                                                                                                                                                          |

# Summary Table of English Sovereigns

**House of Wessex**

| | |
|---|---|
| Egbert | 802–839 |
| Ethelwulf | 839–855 |
| Ethelbald | 855–860 |
| Ethelbert | 860–866 |
| Ethelred I | 866–871 |
| Alfred the Great | 871–899 |
| Edward the Elder | 899–924 |
| Athelstan | 924–939 |
| Edmund I | 939–946 |
| Eadred | 946–955 |
| Eadwig | 955–959 |
| Edgar | 959–975 |
| Edward the Martyr | 975–979 |
| Ethelred II (the Unready) | 979–1016 |
| Edmund II (Ironside) | 1016 |

**House of Skjoldung**

| | |
|---|---|
| Canute (Cnut) | 1016–1035 |
| Harold I | 1035–1040 |
| Harthacnut | 1040–1042 |

**House of Wessex**

| | |
|---|---|
| Edward the Confessor | 1042–1066 |
| Harold II | 1066 |

**House of Normandy**

| | |
|---|---|
| William I (the Conqueror) | 1066–1087 |
| William II (Rufus) | 1087–1100 |
| Henry I | 1100–1135 |
| Stephen | 1135–1154 |

**House of Plantagenet**

| | |
|---|---|
| Henry II | 1154–1189 |
| Richard I (the Lionheart) | 1189–1199 |
| John | 1199–1216 |
| Henry III | 1216–1272 |
| Edward I | 1272–1307 |
| Edward II | 1307–1327 |
| Edward III | 1327–1377 |
| Richard II | 1377–1399 |

**House of Lancaster**

| | |
|---|---|
| Henry IV | 1399–1413 |
| Henry V | 1413–1422 |
| Henry VI | 1422–1461 and 1470 |

**House of York**

| | |
|---|---|
| Edward IV | 1461–1470 and 1471–1483 |
| Edward V | 1483 |
| Richard III | 1483–1485 |

**House of Tudor**

| | |
|---|---|
| Henry VII | 1485–1509 |
| Henry VIII | 1509–1547 |
| Edward VI | 1547–1553 |
| Mary I | 1553–1558 |
| Elizabeth I | 1558–1603 |

**House of Stuart**

| | |
|---|---|
| James I | 1603–1625 |
| Charles I | 1625–1649 |
| [Commonwealth and Protectorate | 1649–1660] |
| Charles II | 1660–1685 |
| James II | 1685–1688 |
| William III and Mary II | 1688–1694 |
| William III | 1694–1702 |
| Anne | 1702–1714 |

**House of Hanover**

| | |
|---|---|
| George I | 1714–1727 |
| George II | 1727–1760 |
| George III | 1760–1820 |
| [Regency | 1811–1820] |
| George IV | 1820–1830 |
| William IV | 1830–1837 |
| Victoria | 1837–1901 |

**House of Saxe-Coburg**

| | |
|---|---|
| Edward VII | 1901–1910 |

**House of Windsor**

| | |
|---|---|
| George V | 1910–36 |
| Edward VIII | 1936 |
| George VI | 1936–1952 |
| Elizabeth II | 1952– |

# ARCHITECTURAL INFORMATION

## Medieval Church Building Styles

**Saxon**: c 400–c 1066. Shares many characteristics with Norman, notably round arches and square towers, but is generally smaller in scale and simpler in detail. Narrow vertical strips of stone used for external decoration and 'long and short work' at the corners are distinctive features.

Examples: Barton-upon-Humber, Bradford-on-Avon, Brixworth, Cambridge (St Bene't), Deerhurst, Dover (St Mary de Castro), Earls Barton, Escomb, Greensted-juxta-Ongar, Hexham Abbey (crypt), Jarrow, Lastingham (crypt), Monkwearmouth, Repton, Ripon Cathedral (crypt), Wing. Crosses at Bewcastle, Gosforth, Sandbach.

**Norman**: c 1050–c 1150. The style called Romanesque on the Continent. It uses round arches, square towers and simple vaulting. Vigorous carving of detail relieves the bold, weighty masses.

Examples: Barfreston, Canterbury Cathedral (crypt), Durham Cathedral, Ely Cathedral (nave), Iffley, Kilpeck, Norwich Cathedral (tower, nave, transepts), Peterborough Cathedral (except W front), Rochester Cathedral (W front, nave), Romsey Abbey, Ruardean, Southwell Minster (nave, transepts, etc.), Winchester Cathedral (transepts).

## SECTION THROUGH CATHEDRAL

# TYPICAL CATHEDRAL PLAN

# TYPICAL ABBEY PLAN

**Transitional** (Trans.). The mid 12C style which combines elements of Norman and Early English, e.g. round and pointed arches.

Examples: Chichester Cathedral (retrochoir), Fountains Abbey (nave).

**Early English** (EE): c 1150–c 1280. The first phase of Gothic, which is distinguished from earlier styles by the pointed arch, the rib vault and the flying buttress. EE differs from later Gothic in its use of simple lancet windows and love of dogtooth moulding.

Examples: Beverley Minster (choir, transepts), Canterbury Cathedral (E end), Durham Cathedral (Chapel of the Nine Altars), Fountains Abbey (Chapel of the Nine Altars), Hexham Abbey (choir, transepts), Lincoln Cathedral (especially the Angel Choir), Rievaulx Abbey (especially the choir), Ripon Cathedral (W front), Salisbury Cathedral, Wells Cathedral (W front and nave), Winchester Cathedral (retrochoir), Worcester Cathedral (E end).

**Decorated** (Dec.): c 1280–c 1380. The second phase of Gothic, marked by the use of window tracery (developing from geometric to flowing patterns), the ogee curve and elaborately carved ornament (particularly striking on bosses, capitals and monuments).

Examples: Beverley Minster (Percy tomb), Bristol Cathedral (choir), Ely Cathedral (octagon, Lady Chapel), Exeter Cathedral, Gloucester Cathedral (tomb of Edward II), Howden, Norwich Cathedral (cloisters), Patrington, Selby Abbey (choir), Southwell Minster (chapter house), Wells Cathedral (especially the retrochoir, Lady Chapel and chapter house), York Minster (chapter house).

**Perpendicular** (Perp.): c 1380–c 1550. The last phase of Gothic, coinciding with the appearance of the Flamboyant style in France but markedly different in its stress on verticals and horizontals. Perp. enlarges windows, progressively flattening their arches, and reduces wall space. Lierne vaults and fan vaults make roof patterns more complex.

Examples: Beverley Minster (W front), Bristol (St Mary Redcliffe), Cambridge (King's College Chapel), Gloucester Cathedral (exterior and choir), Manchester Cathedral, Sherborne Abbey, Westminster Abbey (Henry VII's Chapel), Windsor (St George's Chapel), and many parish churches in Norfolk, Suffolk, the Cotswolds and Somerset.

# Later Building Styles

Two tendencies dominate English architecture from the 16C until the early 20C: Gothic, surviving or being revived in various forms, and classical, derived from the Continental Renaissance or directly from ancient models. The different styles that result are rarely pure or distinct, for several often flourish at the same time and are practised by the same architects. The characteristic approach is eclectic and the characteristic building hybrid.

**Renaissance**: late 16C–early 17C. Building energy goes mainly into country houses, which preserve the central hall from the medieval plan but celebrate their new freedom from the need for defence or fortification in a display of windows. Stylistically, they mix memories of Perp. with classical motifs from the French, Italian and Dutch Renaissance, commonly interpreted with more enthusiasm than sophistication.

Examples: Audley End, Blickling Hall, Burghley House, Burton Constable, Hardwick Hall, Hatfield House, Kirby Hall, Knole, Longleat, Montacute House, Parham, Wollaton Hall.

**Laudian Gothic**. 17C Gothic, as much survival as revival, tempered by classical detail. It is chiefly seen in church and university architecture, particularly at Oxford. The name refers to Charles I's archbishop but the style continues into the age of Baroque.

Examples: Cambridge (Peterhouse Chapel), Leeds (St John's), Oxford (All Souls College, Wadham College).

**Baroque**: late 17C–mid 18C. Marked by the use of curved forms to create spatial complexity and illusion and by exuberant decoration. In the hands of Wren, Hawksmoor and Vanbrugh, English Baroque is notably eclectic, often demonstrating its underlying classicism and periodically betraying its lingering fondness for Gothic.

Examples: Birmingham Cathedral, Blenheim Palace, Castle Howard, London (Royal Naval College at Greenwich, St Paul's Cathedral), Oxford (The Queen's College, Radcliffe Camera), Seaton Delaval Hall.

**Palladianism**: 17C–18C. An ideal of classical correctness and proportion derived from the work of Andrea Palladio (1508–80), introduced to England in the 1620s by Inigo Jones and revived in the 1720s by the 3rd Earl of Burlington, partly through his protégés Colen Campbell and William Kent. Its distinctive features, often assimilated into the looser vocabulary of English classicism, include the portico, the arcaded ground floor, the giant pilaster, and the open two-armed staircase.

Examples: Bath (work of John Wood the Elder and John Wood the Younger), Buxton (The Crescent), Cambridge (Senate House), Hagley Hall, Harewood House, Holkham Hall, Houghton Hall, London (Banqueting House in Whitehall, Chiswick House, Marble Hill House in Twickenham), Stourhead, Stowe, York (Assembly Rooms).

**Gothick**: mid 18C–early 19C revival of Gothic, sometimes called 'Strawberry Hill Gothic' (after the famous example of Horace Walpole's house) or 'Rococo Gothic'. Unlike its Victorian counterpart, it treats Gothic as a source of picturesque detail rather than a system of structural principles. Its inherent playfulness, manifest in the sham ruins and follies, connects it with the taste for Chinoiserie and Oriental fantasy which flourishes at the same time.

Examples: Arbury Hall, Ashridge, Audley End (chapel), Lacock Abbey, Stansted Park (chapel).

**Greek Revival**: mid 18C–mid 19C. A return to the Greek example of simplicity and dignity in reaction against the eclectic tendencies of 18C classicism. The textbook purity advocated by James 'Athenian' Stuart in the 1750s gave way to the freer approach of Sir John Soane and C.R. Cockerell. Like Palladianism, the Greek Revival extends the range of classicism in England rather than remaining an entirely distinct school.

Examples: Cambridge (Downing College), Chester Castle, Great Packington (church), Liverpool (St George's Hall, Bank of England), London (British Museum), Manchester (Bank of England), Oxford (Ashmolean Museum and Taylorian Institution), Shugborough.

**Gothic Revival**. The Victorian Gothic Revival followed Pugin and Ruskin in admiring medieval architecture for its purity as much as its picturesqueness and in finding it a source of moral values as well as structural principles. In practice, churches range from scholarly correctness (Scott) through eclecticism (Bodley, Pearson) to wilful,

creative eccentricity (Butterfield). Public buildings sometimes culti-
vate the Venetian Gothic praised by Ruskin, and country houses tend
towards the baronial.

Examples: Brighton (St Bartholomew's), Cambridge (St John's College Chapel),
Clumber Park (church), Hoar Cross (church), Knighthayes Court, Lancing
College (especially the chapel), Liverpool Cathedral, London (Houses of Parliament, Albert Memorial), Manchester Town Hall, Oxford (Keble College, University Museum), Rugby School, Scarborough (St Martin-on-the-Hill), Skelton
(church), Studley Royal (church), Truro Cathedral.

# FURTHER READING

In addition to the specialised guidebooks recommended in earlier sections, two useful digests appear annually: *Whitaker's Almanac* and *Britain: An Official Handbook*, the latter prepared by the Central Office of Information and published by Her Majesty's Stationery Office (HMSO).

Rather than attempting a systematic bibliography, the suggestions below record those books which the present editor has found interesting or useful. Standard general surveys or reference works are noted, but many specialist or local studies and all studies of individual figures have been omitted.

**Geology and Landscape**. Two books, taken together, make an ideal introduction: A.E. Trueman's *Geology and Scenery in England and Wales* (Pelican edition revised by J.B. Whittow and J.R. Hardy, 1971) and W.G. Hoskins's *The Making of the English Landscape* (Pelican edition 1970). *The Making of the English Landscape* also forms the first volume in, and gives the general title to, a series of county volumes edited by Professor Hoskins and Roy Millward.

**History and Archaeology**. The one-volume *Oxford Illustrated History of Britain*, edited by Kenneth O. Morgan (1984), makes a good general introduction. The Pelican History of England runs to nine volumes by different hands, many times reprinted and revised.

Frank Barlow, *The Feudal Kingdom of England 1042–1216* (3rd edition 1972); Peter Hunter Blair, *An Introduction to Anglo-Saxon England* (2nd edition 1977); Richard Bradley, *The Prehistoric Settlement of Britain* (1978); Asa Briggs, *The Age of Improvement 1783–1867* (1959); Barry Cunliffe, *Iron Age Communities in Britain* (2nd edition 1978); A.G. Dickens, *The English Reformation* (1964); Sheppard Frere, *Britannia: A History of Roman Britain* (2nd edition 1974); E.J. Hobsbawm, *The First Industrial Nation* (1969); J.P. Kenyon, *The Stuarts* (1958); J.H. Plumb, *The Growth of Political Stability in England 1675–1725* (1967) and *The First Four Georges* (revised edition 1974); F.M. Stenton, *Anglo-Saxon England* (3rd edition 1971); E.P. Thompson, *The Making of the English Working Class* (1963); Malcolm Todd, *Roman Britain 55 BC–AD 400: The Province Beyond Ocean* (1981); C.V. Wedgwood, *The King's Peace 1637–41* (1955) and *The King's War 1641–47* (1958); P. Williams, *The Tudor Regime* (1979); G.M. Young, *Victorian England: Portrait of an Age* (1936).

For urban, industrial and transport history: Asa Briggs, *Victorian Cities* (1963); Charles Hadfield, *English Canals* (5th edition 1974) and the ensuing series of regional canal histories; Michael Robbins, *The Railway Age* (1962); L.T.C. Rolt, *Victorian Engineering* (1970); H.J. Dyos and M. Wolff (editors), *The Victorian City* (1973).

**Architecture and Landscape Gardening**. The county volumes in the Buildings of England series, edited and largely written by Sir Nikolaus Pevsner, are indispensable. *A History of English Architecture*, by Peter Kidson, Peter Murray and Paul Thompson (revised Pelican edition 1979), makes a useful one-volume introduction.

Jean Bony, *The English Decorated Style: Gothic Architecture Transformed 1250–1350* (1979); R.W. Brunskill, *Traditional Buildings of Britain: An Introduction to Vernacular Architecture* (1981); Kenneth Clark, *The Gothic Revival: An Essay in the History of Taste* (3rd edition 1962); Alec Clifton-Taylor, *English Parish Churches as Works of Art* (1974) and *The Pattern of English Building* (3rd edition 1971); J. Mordaunt Crook, *The Greek Revival: Neo-Classical Attitudes in British Architecture 1760–1870* (1972); Gillian Darley, *Villages of Vision* (1975); Roger Dixon and Stefan Muthesius, *Victorian Architecture* (1978); Mark Girouard, *Life in the English Country House: A Social and Architectural History*

(1978) and *The Victorian Country House* (revised edition 1979); Christopher Hussey, *The Picturesque* (1927) and *English Gardens and Landscapes 1700–1750* (1967); Edward Hyams, *The English Garden* (1964); Robert Furneaux Jordan, *Victorian Architecture* (1966); Stefan Muthesius, *The English Terraced House* (1982); Roy Strong, *The Renaissance Garden in England* (1979); John Summerson, *Architecture in Britain: 1530–1830* (Pelican History of Art, 6th edition 1977); Geoffrey Webb, *Architecture in Britain: The Middle Ages* (Pelican History of Art, 1956).

**Painting and Sculpture**. *The Genius of British Painting*, ed. David Piper (1975), makes a good general introduction, while the Oxford History of English Art includes several notable volumes.

Martin Hardie, *Water-Colour Painting in Britain* (3 vols, 1966–68); Louis Hawes, *Presences of Nature: British Landscape 1780–1830* (1982); Andrew Hemingway, *The Norwich School of Painters 1803–1833* (1979); Luke Herrmann, *British Landscape Painting of the Eighteenth Century* (1973); Tim Hilton, *The Pre-Raphaelites* (1970); John Murdoch, Jim Murrell, Patrick J. Noon and Roy Strong, *The English Miniature* (1981); Ronald Paulson, *Emblem and Expression: Meaning in English Art of the Eighteenth Century* (1975); Sir Nikolaus Pevsner, *The Englishness of English Art* (1956); David Piper, *The English Face* (1957); Graham Reynolds, *A Concise History of Watercolours* (1971); Michael Rosenthal, *British Landscape Painting* (1982); Lawrence Stone, *Sculpture in Britain: The Middle Ages* (Pelican History of Art, 2nd edition 1972); Roy Strong, *The English Icon: Elizabethan and Jacobean Portraiture* (1969) and *The English Renaissance Miniature* (1983); Margaret Whinney, *Sculpture in Britain: 1530–1830* (Pelican History of Art, 1964).

**Literature**. The 5th edition of *The Oxford Companion to English Literature*, edited by Margaret Drabble (1985), is a standard reference book, though the present editor may be forgiven for preferring *The Cambridge Guide to Literature in English*, edited by Ian Ousby (1988). *The Country and the City* (1973) by Raymond Williams is worth singling out for its deeply felt attempt to connect literature with ideas of landscape and community.

**Travel books**. Very few books stand out from the vast list. William Cobbett's *Rural Rides* (1830) is matchless, and Henry James's *English Hours* (1905) deserves to be more widely read. Of modern books, John Hillaby's *Journey through Britain* (1968) has great charm and sense.

# LONDON

The capital lies about 40 miles inland from the mouth of the Thames, cut in two from E to W by the winding course of the river. In its full extent Greater London covers 625 square miles and consists of 33 separate boroughs, including the Cities of London and Westminster. It houses just under 7 million people. Though this number is regularly swollen by the influx of commuters and tourists, population density is still much lower than in many of the world's other major cities. Nearly one-third of London is still free of major building, and the visitor will quickly appreciate the parks and open spaces that relieve even the most crowded neighbourhoods.

The central part on which the tourist concentrates is a small fraction of Greater London: a strip less than two miles deep and about four miles wide as the crow flies, lying mainly on the N bank of the river and stretching from Kensington Gardens in the W to Tower Bridge and the Tower of London in the E. The West End, spreading from the political centre at Westminster, includes the shopping areas of Knightsbridge, Kensington High St., Oxford St., Piccadilly and the newly fashionable Covent Garden; the restaurant and theatre land of Piccadilly Circus and Leicester Square; and a host of museums and galleries, among them the South Kensington group, the Tate Gallery on Millbank, the National Gallery and National Portrait Gallery by Trafalgar Square, and the British Museum in Bloomsbury. The square mile of the City, dominated by banking and finance, is best known to tourists for St Paul's Cathedral and the Tower of London.

'Blue Guide London' and the 'Blue Guide Museums and Galleries of London' give a fuller description than the condensed and selective account below, which is intended for the stranger whose visit to the city is one stage in the exploration of England as a whole. It is divided into three sections: the West End; the City, the East End and the South Bank; and Outer London. These dispense with the walking tours used to describe cities elsewhere in this guide and list the main sights in alphabetical order. The asterisks and double asterisks which elsewhere mark items or places of special interest are not used, since inclusion in these lists constitutes a recommendation in itself. The nearest tube (underground railway) stations are indicated. For opening times, see the general remarks in Notes On Using This Guide; special peculiarities are noted in the text below. Since arrangements are liable to change, visitors with only limited time to spend in London are urged to check in advance.

The Tourist Information Centres managed by the London Tourist Board can advise about opening hours and many other matters. They are located at: Victoria Station Forecourt, SW1; Harrods, Knightsbridge, SW1; Heathrow International Airport; Selfridges, Oxford St., W1; and the West Gate of the Tower of London, EC3. The number of the Telephone Information Service is 01–730 3488. Written enquiries should be addressed to the London Tourist Board, 26 Grosvenor Gardens, SW1 0DU. The British Travel Centre run by the British Tourist Authority at 12 Regent St., Piccadilly Circus, SW1 (phone 01–730 3400) books rail, coach and air travel, sightseeing tours, theatre tickets and accommodation as well as providing information about the whole country. Of the Outer London boroughs described in Rte 3, Greenwich and Richmond also have Tourist Information Centres.

# 1   The West End

**Apsley House**: see Hyde Park and Kensington Gardens.

**Banqueting House**, Whitehall, SW1. Tube: Westminster (Circle, District), Charing Cross (Northern, Bakerloo, Jubilee). DoE monument. Closed Mondays and at short notice for government functions.

The one surviving relic of the old Palace of Whitehall, it was built for James I by Inigo Jones in 1625. Revolutionary for its date, his Palladian design exercised a lasting influence on English public buildings. The main hall has a magnificent painted ceiling (1629–34) by Rubens. Charles I was executed outside the hall in 1649—though not, perhaps, on the exact spot now marked with a plaque.

**British Museum**, Great Russell St., Bloomsbury, WC1. Tube: Tottenham Court Road (Central, Northern), Holborn (Central, Piccadilly).

Sir Robert Smirke's Greek Revival building (1823–47), with its great colonnaded entrance, houses the national collection of antiquities. Since the first bequest from Sir Hans Sloane in the 18C, its holdings of archaeology and art have grown to such size and variety that no single visit can begin to do them justice. The summary below lists the various departments, with a brief selection of their most famous items.

Greek and Roman: the Elgin Marbles, including the sculptures from the Parthenon. Western Asiatic: Assyrian reliefs and sculptures. Egyptian: the Rosetta Stone. Oriental: a matchless display of Chinese ceramics. Prints and Drawings: cartoons by Michelangelo and Raphael. Coins and Medals. Prehistoric and Romano-British: the Mildenhall Treasure. Medieval and later: the Sutton Hoo Treasure, and the Waddesdon Bequest of 14–17C objets d'art. The **British Library**, due to move to Euston Road in 1991/92, is still housed in the British Museum at present. There are tours of its domed Reading Room, not otherwise open to casual visitors. The public exhibition galleries display illuminated manuscripts (the Lindisfarne Gospels), historical and literary manuscripts (two of the four extant original copies of Magna Carta; Shakespeare's signature) and specimens of early printing (a Gutenberg Bible). The British Museum's ethnographic collection is displayed at the Museum of Mankind and the natural history collection at the Natural History Museum, both separately described below.

**Buckingham Palace** and **St James's Park**, SW1. Tube: Victoria (Circle, District, Victoria), St James's Park (Circle, District), Hyde Park Corner (Piccadilly), Charing Cross (Northern, Bakerloo, Jubilee). Royal Mews: open Wednesday and Thursday afternoons except Ascot Week and state occasions. Queen's Gallery: closed Mondays.

The Palace (not open) has been the London residence of the sovereign since 1837. The dull Edwardian façade which faces the Queen Victoria Memorial and the Mall does not deter the tourists, attracted particularly by the ceremony of Changing the Guard (11.30 every day from April to early August and on alternate days from August to March). On the Saturday nearest 11 June the Queen and other members of the royal household travel in procession along the Mall to Horse Guards Parade for the ceremony of Trooping the Colour, which marks the Queen's official birthday.

St James's Park, S of the Mall, is one of the most attractive London parks, charmingly laid out in an aristocratic surrounding of palaces and government buildings and commanding a famous view in the direction of Westminster. Ornamental wildfowl frequent the lake in the centre and Duck Island, at the E end, is reserved as their breeding ground. A band plays in the park from June to September.

In Buckingham Gate and Buckingham Palace Rd, around the corner from the Palace in the direction of Victoria Station, are: the *Royal Mews*, with the Queen's horses, state coaches, harnesses and liveries; and the *Queen's Gallery*, with changing displays drawn from the superb royal art collections.

**Carlyle's House**, 24 Cheyne Row, Chelsea, SW3. Tube: Sloane Square (Circle, District), South Kensington (Circle, District, Piccadilly). NT. Open from April to end of October; closed Mondays (except Bank Holiday Mondays) and Tuesdays.

Thomas Carlyle (1795–1881) and his wife Jane Welsh Carlyle (1801–66) lived in this Georgian terraced house from 1834 until their deaths. Filled with furniture, pictures and mementoes from the couple's long residence, its rooms still radiate the atmosphere of dignified simplicity they established.

**Chelsea Royal Hospital**: see Royal Hospital.

**Courtauld Institute Galleries**. Due to move in 1989 from Woburn Square, Bloomsbury, WC1, to Somerset House, The Strand, WC2, and then not likely to reopen until near the end of the year. Tube for Somerset House: Aldwych (Piccadilly, rush hour service only), Temple (Circle, District).

Part of the University of London, the galleries have notably strong collections of French Impressionism and Post-Impressionism, early Italian work, and paintings and drawings by Tiepolo and Rubens.

**Covent Garden**, WC2. Tube: Covent Garden (Piccadilly), Leicester Square (Northern, Piccadilly). Theatre Museum: closed Mondays.

Laid out in the style of an Italian piazza by Inigo Jones in 1631–39, Covent Garden was for centuries the site of London's main fruit and vegetable market. This moved to Battersea in 1974 but the 19C *Central Market Building*, with its iron and glass roofs, has been restored as the centrepiece of a lively, fashionable area of shops, restaurants, winebars and street entertainment. At the SE corner of the Piazza the *Flower Market Building* houses the *London Transport Museum*, with horse, motor and trolley buses, trams and railway rolling stock, and a superb collection of London Transport posters. The *Theatre Museum* displays the Victoria and Albert Museum's theatre collection. *St Paul's*, Inigo Jones's church (rebuilt to his original design in 1795) on the W side of the Piazza, contains monuments testifying to Covent Garden's long connection with artists and actors. E of the Piazza are the *Royal Opera House*, Bow St., the home of the Royal Ballet and Royal Opera companies, and the *Theatre Royal*, Drury Lane, on the site of the theatres managed by Garrick and Sheridan.

**Dickens House**, 48 Doughty St., Bloomsbury, WC1. Tube: Russell Square (Piccadilly). Closed Sundays.

Charles Dickens rented this terraced house in 1837–39, the period of 'Oliver Twist' and 'Nicholas Nickleby'. The fine collection of memorabilia—portraits, furniture, personal relics, letters,

*Westminster from the air, with the Houses of Parliament in the centre at the top*

manuscripts, and an extensive Dickens library—has not entirely banished the atmosphere of a family home.

**Geological Museum**, Exhibition Rd, South Kensington, SW7. Tube: South Kensington (Circle, District, Piccadilly).

Its highlights include: a magnificent collection of gemstones, in both their natural state and various stages of cutting; an excellent audio-visual display, 'The Story of the Earth'; exhibits illustrating the regional geology of Great Britain; and the world's largest display of metalliferous ores.

**Houses of Parliament**, Parliament Square, Westminster, SW1. Tube: Westminster (Circle, District).

The Houses of Parliament and Westminster Hall are no longer open for tours, except when organised by a Member of Parliament or peer. However, visitors are admitted to the Strangers' Galleries (public galleries) during debates. The House of Commons usually sits from 14.30 on Monday to Thursday and from 09.30 on Fridays; the House of Lords sits from 14.40 on Tuesdays, Wednesdays and some Mondays, from 15.00 on Thursdays and from 11.00 on some Fridays. Tickets can be obtained from the appropriate Member of Parliament, peer or foreign embassy in London; those without tickets should queue outside St Stephen's entrance. There are short recesses at Christmas and Easter and a summer recess from the end of July to the middle of October. The official State Opening of Parliament by the Queen usually takes place in late October or early November.

The handsome Gothic Revival buildings (1840–50; Sir Charles Barry and A.W.N. Pugin) are best seen from Westminster Bridge, the Thames or the Albert Embankment on the opposite side of the river. The stately façade is enlivened by rich decoration and three striking towers. The *Clock Tower* at the N end is recognised throughout the world as an emblem of London; strictly speaking, the name 'Big Ben' refers to the hour bell and not the clock. The *House of Lords* occupies the N half of the building and the *House of Commons* the S. A light in the Clock Tower by night and a flag on the *Victoria Tower*, at the SW end, by day indicate that Parliament is sitting.

The formal term, the Palace of Westminster, is a reminder that Parliament stands on a site used by monarchs as their chief London residence from the reign of Edward the Confessor (or perhaps earlier) until Henry VIII's time. The beautiful *Westminster Hall*, interrupting the Parliament Square façade, survived the fire which destroyed most of the medieval buildings in 1834. Originally built in 1097, the Hall was remodelled in 1394–1492, when the magnificent oak roof was added. It is particularly memorable as the scene of Richard II's deposition in 1399 and the trials of Sir Thomas More in 1535 and Charles I in 1649. Across the road from the Victoria Tower is another survival of the medieval palace, the low, moated *Jewel Tower* (English Heritage, standard opening but closed Sundays), which has fine original bosses and an exhibition which includes capitals from Westminster Hall. There are river views from *Victoria Tower Gardens*, where we also find memorials to the suffragettes Emmeline Pankhurst (1858–1928) and her daughter Christabel (1881–1958).

**Hyde Park and Kensington Gardens**, mainly W2. Tube: Marble Arch (Central), Hyde Park Corner (Piccadilly), Queensway (Central) and High Street Kensington (Circle, District) among others. Apsley House/Wellington Museum: closed Mondays.

Hyde Park merges with its western neighbour, Kensington Gardens, to form a large open space of more than 600 acres, still green and pleasant despite the tower blocks that now disfigure some of the skyline around its edges. The *Serpentine*, an artificial lake with waterfowl, and its continuation as the *Long Water* cut diagonally across.

**Marble Arch** (1828; John Nash) stands among the busy traffic islands at the NE corner of Hyde Park. Nearby is *Speakers' Corner*, where open-air orators gather on Sundays. **Hyde Park Corner**, at the SE end, is marked by Decimus Burton's *Wellington Arch* (1828). The Duke of Wellington lived from 1817 until his death in 1852 at *Apsley House* ('No. 1, London'), now handsomely restored as the **Wellington Museum**. Built by Robert Adam in 1771–78 and remodelled by Benjamin Wyatt in the 1820s, it contains portraits and relics of Wellington and his contemporaries which form a vivid record of the Napoleonic period, and superb paintings presented to the duke from the Spanish royal collection (Goya, Murillo, Rubens and Velasquez).

The famous sandtrack for riders known as *Rotten Row* leads from Hyde Park Corner through the park, between Knightsbridge and the Serpentine. The *Serpentine Gallery* holds exhibitions of modern art. Long Water stretches to the N, with a statue of J.M. Barrie's Peter Pan (1912) on its bank. Sir Gilbert Scott's massively elaborate *Albert Memorial* (1863–72) stands on the S edge of Kensington Gardens, looking across Kensington Gore to the domed **Royal Albert Hall** (1867–71). Though many types of public event take place here, the Hall is particularly famous for the season of Promenade concerts in July–September.

**Kensington Palace** (DoE monument), on the W side of the Gardens, was a residence of the reigning sovereign from 1689 until 1760. Queen Victoria, born here in 1819, lived at the palace until her accession in 1837. It is still the London home for various members of the Royal Family, though parts are open to the public. The original building of 1605 was altered by Sir Christopher Wren and Nicholas Hawksmoor in 1689–96. Externally, it is much as they left it, but the interior was sumptuously remodelled by Colen Campbell in 1718–21 and William Kent in 1722–24. The state apartments contain fine paintings and furniture from the royal collection, and there is a display of court dress and uniforms on the ground floor.

**Kensington Gardens**: see Hyde Park and Kensington Gardens.

**London Planetarium**: see Madame Tussaud's Waxworks.

**London Transport Museum**: see Covent Garden.

**Madame Tussaud's Waxworks**, Marylebone Rd, NW1. Tube: Baker Street (Circle, Metropolitan, Bakerloo, Jubilee). Open all day Sunday as well as weekdays.

The most famous waxworks in the world, it exhibits historical tableaux and figures of contemporary celebrities. Among the murderers and assassins in the Chamber of Horrors are death masks and historical items from the French Revolution. An inclusive ticket also admits visitors to the adjoining *London Planetarium*.

**Museum of Mankind**, 6 Burlington Gardens, Piccadilly, W1. Tube: Piccadilly Circus (Bakerloo, Piccadilly), Green Park (Victoria, Piccadilly, Jubilee).

The British Museum's ethnographic collection, particularly strong in material illustrating the tribal societies of West Africa, Oceania and North and South America, is shown in a series of imaginatively staged exhibitions. They are changed approximately every year.

**National Gallery**, Trafalgar Square, WC2. Tube: Charing Cross (Northern, Bakerloo, Jubilee), Leicester Square (Northern, Piccadilly).

William Wilkins's elegant building (1838), with one modern extension added and another planned for completion in the 1990s, houses the national collection of European art from the 15C to the early 20C. It is large and rich enough to defeat the visitor who attempts a single comprehensive tour. The brief selection below lists some of the most famous works usually on view; since pictures are often moved and rooms rearranged, they are given alphabetically by schools and artists.

British: Constable (The Haywain; Salisbury Cathedral); Gainsborough (Mrs Siddons); Hogarth (Marriage à la Mode); Turner (The Fighting Téméraire Tugged to her Last Berth; Rain, Steam, and Speed—The Great Western Railway). Dutch: Hobbema (The Avenue, Middleharnis); Rembrandt (Self-Portraits, aged 34 and 63); Vermeer (Young Woman Seated at a Virginal; Young Woman Standing at a Virginal). Flemish: Van Dyck (Equestrian Portrait of Charles I); Rubens (an outstanding collection, including The Rape of the Sabine Women). French, 17C: Claude (superb group of classical landscapes); Poussin (The Adoration of the Golden Calf). French Impressionists: Monet (The Thames below Westminster; Water Lilies); Renoir (The Umbrellas). German: Holbein (The Ambassadors). Italian, 13–15C: Giovanni Bellini (Doge Leonardo Loredan); Botticelli (Mystic Nativity; Venus and Mars); Leonardo da Vinci ('Virgin of the Rocks'); Piero della Francesca (Baptism of Christ); Uccello (Battle of San Romano; St George and the Dragon). Italian, 16C: Raphael (Pope Julius II); Titian (Bacchus and Ariadne). Netherlandish: Van Eyck (The Arnolfini Marriage). Spanish: Goya (Duke of Wellington); Velasquez (The 'Rokeby' Venus).

**National Portrait Gallery**, 2 St Martin's Place, WC2. Tube: Leicester Square (Northern, Piccadilly), Charing Cross (Northern, Bakerloo, Jubilee).

Here, around the corner from the National Gallery, the emphasis is on the sitters rather than the artists—though Holbein, Van Dyck, Hogarth, Reynolds and Gainsborough are all represented. Arranged chronologically (beginning on the second floor), the collection offers a pageant of famous people in all walks of life from the Middle Ages to the present century.

**Natural History Museum**, officially the *British Museum (Natural History)*, Cromwell Rd, South Kensington, SW7. Tube: South Kensington (Circle, District, Piccadilly).

Alfred Waterhouse's elaborate Romanesque building (1873–81), with its fine terracotta panels, is itself as impressive as the collections it houses. These consist of fossil and living plants and animals, minerals, rocks and meteorites, though the exhibitions on particular themes added in recent years show an increasing bias towards biology and man. The most popular exhibits are the dinosaurs in the vast Central Hall, dominated by the 85ft–long plaster-cast skeleton of *Diplodocus carnegii*, one of the largest land animals which ever lived.

**Palace of Westminster**: see Houses of Parliament.

**Queen's Gallery**: see Buckingham Palace and St James's Park.

**Regent's Park**, NW1. Tube: Regent's Park (Bakerloo), Baker Street (Circle, Metropolitan, Bakerloo, Jubilee) and, for the zoo, Mornington Crescent and Camden Town (both Northern). The London Waterbus Company runs a service along Regent's Park Canal from Camden Lock and Little Venice to the zoo (daily from April to October, weekends in winter).

Originally a royal hunting ground, Regent's Park was laid out in its present style as an aristocratic 'garden suburb' by John Nash from 1812 onwards, and named after the Prince Regent, who contemplated building a country house here. A road known as the Outer Circle runs around the outside; its S half is flanked by monumental Regency terraces, largely by Nash. The S part of the park itself contains a large artificial lake, the home of many wildfowl, and the pretty *Queen Mary's Gardens*, enclosed by the Inner Circle. The open-air theatre stages performances of Shakespeare during the summer. In the N part of the park lie the *Regent's Canal* and the **Regent's Park Zoo**, officially the *Gardens of the Zoological Society of London*. Founded in 1825 and opened to the general public in 1847, the zoo pioneered the exhibition of exotic animals. Part of its large collection has been transferred to the more spacious Whipsnade Zoo (Rte 39B).

**Royal Academy of Arts**, Burlington House, Piccadilly, W1. Tube: Piccadilly Circus (Bakerloo, Piccadilly), Green Park (Victoria, Piccadilly, Jubilee).

Although it maintains its school of art, the Royal Academy is now known above all for its exhibitions. The annual Summer Exhibition (May–August) shows contemporary British painting, sculpture, architecture and engraving which has not previously been exhibited; its tone is conservative. At other times of the year the Academy mounts loan exhibitions, often of great interest and popularity. The building is in origin a mid–17C house, remodelled by Colen Campbell for the art-loving 3rd Earl of Burlington in c 1717–20 and expanded in a grandiose Italianate style in the 19C.

**Royal Albert Hall**: see Hyde Park and Kensington Gardens.

**Royal Hospital**, Royal Hospital Rd, Chelsea, SW3. Tube: Sloane Square (Circle, District).

Sir Christopher Wren designed the handsome brick buildings of this refuge for old and disabled soldiers in 1682–92. It still houses about 420 pensioners, who wear scarlet uniforms in summer and dark blue ones in winter, but visitors are admitted to the grounds, chapel, hall and museum. The delightful *Ranelagh Gardens*, to the E, are the site of the Chelsea Flower Show in May.

**Royal Mews**: see Buckingham Palace and St James's Park.

**Royal Opera House**: see Covent Garden.

**St James's Park**: see Buckingham Palace and St James's Park.

**Science Museum**, Exhibition Rd, South Kensington, SW7. Tube: South Kensington (Circle, District, Piccadilly).

The museum displays a remarkable collection of machinery and industrial plant, working models, and scientific apparatus and instruments of virtually every kind. These include historic steam, oil, turbine and wind engines, railway locomotives (notably 'Puffing Billy', 1813) and rolling stock, motorcars and aircraft. A special exhibit is devoted to the fringes of present-day knowledge, including space flight. The top floors house the *Wellcome Museum of the History of Medicine*.

**Serpentine Gallery**: see Hyde Park and Kensington Gardens.

**Sir John Soane's Museum**, 13 Lincoln's Inn Fields, WC2. Tube: Holborn (Central, Piccadilly). Closed Sundays and Mondays.

The architect Sir John Soane (1753–1837) created this small museum in his home on the N side of Lincoln's Inn Fields, leaving the unmistakable imprint of his personality on the ingeniously contrived layout of the rooms and the richly varied collections which crowd them. Two series of paintings by Hogarth and the sarcophagus of Seti I are outstanding among the numerous items.

For the rest of Lincoln's Inn, see Rte 2, Inns of Court.

**South Kensington Museums**: see Geological Museum, Natural History Museum, Science Museum and Victora and Albert Museum.

**Tate Gallery**, Millbank, SW1. Tube: Pimlico (Victoria).

Opened in 1897 thanks to the generosity of the sugar magnate Sir Henry Tate, the gallery houses the national collection of British paintings from the 16C onwards, and of modern paintings and sculpture, both British and foreign, from the Impressionists to the present day. The recently opened Clore Gallery displays items from the matchless collection of Turner's work which the artist bequeathed to the nation, including 'Snow Storm: Hannibal Crossing the Alps' and 'Peace: Burial at Sea'. The main building contains a superbly representative collection of the British schools of landscape and portrait painting, with outstanding groups of work by Reynolds, Gainsborough, Stubbs, Blake, Samuel Palmer, Constable, the Pre-Raphaelites and Whistler. The almost comprehensive collection of 20C British art includes groups of work by the Bloomsbury Group and the Vorticists and, among sculptors, Moore and Hepworth. Of foreign schools and artists, the French Impressionists, Picasso and Braque are particularly well represented.

**Theatre Museum**: see Covent Garden.

**Victoria and Albert Museum**, Cromwell Rd, South Kensington, SW7. Tube: South Kensington (Circle, District, Piccadilly).

The V and A, as it is universally known, houses an unrivalled collection of applied and decorative art—probably the largest and certainly the most bewilderingly various in the world. The several miles of exhibition space contain paintings, sculpture, ceramics, woodwork, metalwork, jewellery, armour, textiles, carpets and furniture of most periods and many cultures. The displays are divided into two categories: the popular Primary Galleries, where works of art in different media are grouped together by period, style or nationality;

and, for the specialist or connoisseur, the Study Galleries which concentrate on works of the same type or medium. Exhibits include rooms reconstructed from demolished London buildings or designed especially for the museum (notably by William Morris and Philip Webb). The collections of paintings, prints, drawings and photographs, largely but not exclusively housed in the new Henry Cole Wing, are particularly notable for cartoons by Raphael; English and Continental portrait miniatures; and work by Constable.

**Wallace Collection**, Hertford House, Manchester Square, W1. Tube: Bond Street (Central, Jubilee).

Though not as well known to tourists as the National Gallery, the Tate Gallery or the Victoria and Albert Museum, the Wallace Collection is the single most important art collection in London. Remarkable for the choiceness and variety of its contents, it is particularly notable for 18C French painting (Boucher, Fragonard, Watteau), furniture and porcelain; works by Titian, Velasquez, Rubens, Van Dyck, Rembrandt, Hals (Laughing Cavalier), Poussin (Dance to the Music of Time), Hobbema, Canaletto and Richard Bonington; and European arms and armour. The setting is an 18C town house and the arrangement of the exhibition rooms gracefully exploits its atmosphere, juxtaposing the paintings with the furniture, sculpture and smaller works of art.

**Wellcome Museum of the History of Medicine**: see Science Museum.

**Wellington Museum**: see Hyde Park and Kensington Gardens.

**Westminster Abbey**, Broad Sanctuary, Westminster, SW1. Tube: Westminster, St James's Park (both Circle, District).

The Abbey has unique importance as the church where most English monarchs have been crowned and buried. Although Saxon and Norman monasteries stood on the site, the present building is largely EE, begun in 1245 by Henry III and continued after 1388 in harmony with the earlier work. The W towers and façade were built by Hawksmoor to Wren's design in c 1735. Inside, the grand proportions and delicate details of Henry Yevele's nave are almost overwhelmed by the vast array of monuments which makes the Abbey England's chief memorial to its famous dead. The tombs of sovereigns from Henry III (d. 1272) to George II (d. 1760) lie in the richest parts of the Abbey, at the E end: the *Chapel of Henry VII* (1503–19), a supreme example of late Perp. architecture, and the *Chapel of St Edward the Confessor*, built by Henry III to house the shrine, now mutilated, of the king who had rebuilt the Abbey in 1065. The S Transept is more famous as *Poets' Corner*, overflowing with graves and memorials of writers from Chaucer onwards. The monastic buildings off the cloister include the 12C *Chapter House* (English Heritage); the 11C *Pyx Chamber* (English Heritage), with an exhibition of Abbey treasures; and the *Norman Undercroft*, with an excellent small museum displaying the effigies used at royal funeral processions.

**Zoological Gardens**: see Regent's Park.

# 2    The City, East End and South Bank

**All Hallows by the Tower**: see the Tower of London.

**Barbican**, London Wall, EC2. Tube: Barbican (Circle, Metropolitan, closed Sundays), St Paul's (Central), Moorgate (Circle, Metropolitan, Northern). Museum of London: closed Mondays. Barbican Art Gallery: closed Mondays except Bank Holidays.

The 60-acre modern complex of public and residential buildings stands near the site of the N gate of a 2C Roman fort and the Roman city wall, repaired and heightened in the Middle Ages. Parts of the wall have been exposed, and a signposted walk follows its course along London Wall to the Tower of London (see below). The **Museum of London**, at the SW corner of the site, uses a series of imaginative displays to present the capital's history and its social and domestic life from earliest times to the most recent past. The **Barbican Centre**, beyond the partly medieval church of *St Giles without Cripplegate* to the N, includes the *Royal Shakespeare Company Theatre*, with its large main auditorium and the smaller Pit auditorium; the *Concert Hall* of the London Symphony Orchestra; and the *Barbican Art Gallery*, with changing exhibitions of modern art and selections from the City of London's outstanding collection.

**Bethnal Green Museum of Childhood**, Cambridge Heath Rd, E2. Tube: Bethnal Green (Central). Closed Fridays.

A branch of the Victoria and Albert Museum, it displays one of the world's largest collections of toys, dolls, etc., with a particularly fine group of dolls' houses.

**City churches**: see St Paul's Cathedral.

**Dr Johnson's House**, 17 Gough Square, EC4. Tube: Blackfriars (Circle, District), Chancery Lane (Central). Closed Sundays.

This early 18C building, in a little square off the N side Fleet St., is the only one of Samuel Johnson's many London addresses to survive. His home from 1749 to 1758, it contains portraits, letters and personal relics.

**Geffrye Museum**, Kingsland Rd, Shoreditch, E2. Tube: Liverpool Street (Central, Circle, Metropolitan), and then bus or 1m walk. Closed Mondays except Bank Holidays.

A small museum of domestic and interior design, with rooms furnished to illustrate the main changes of style from 1600 to the 1930s, it is well worth a visit despite its out-of-the-way location. It occupies a group of early 18C almshouses.

**George Inn**, Borough High St., Southwark, SE1. Tube: London Bridge (Northern).

Both a National Trust property and a working pub, the George is the only galleried inn still standing in London and the only survivor of the great coaching inns on Borough High St. which appear in the pages of Chaucer, Shakespeare and Dickens. In its present form the façade of the George dates from c 1676.

**Globe Theatre**: see Shakespeare Globe Museum.

**Gray's Inn**: see Inns of Court.

**Hayward Gallery**: see South Bank Centre.

**Imperial War Museum**, Lambeth Rd, SE1. Tube: Lambeth North (Bakerloo), Elephant and Castle (Northern, Bakerloo).
  Currently being redeveloped and expanded, the museum is devoted to all aspects of 20C warfare and to the part played by Britain and the Commonwealth in the two World Wars. As well as weaponry, military vehicles, uniforms, medals, documents, photographs and posters, the displays include an important collection of 20C art (Sargent, Paul Nash, Wyndham Lewis, Stanley Spencer, John Piper), shown in rotation.

**Inner Temple**: see Inns of Court.

**Inns of Court**, off Fleet St., EC4 and High Holborn, WC1. Tube: Temple (Circle, District), Chancery Lane (Central).
  The four great inns of court, which originated in the 13C, hold the exclusive right of conferring the rank of barrister in England and Wales. Each inn has a dining hall, library and chapel, set among squares, courts and gardens in a similar fashion to an Oxford or Cambridge college. Visitors are usually admitted freely to the precincts (except the Inner Temple and Middle Temple gardens) and to the Temple Church; inquire at the Porters' Lodges for details of admission to other buildings.
  The inns lie close to the boundary where the City of Westminster meets the City of London, marked by Temple Bar at the junction of the Strand with Fleet St. Immediately to the S are the **Middle Temple** and the **Inner Temple**, on a site that belonged to the Knights Templar. The **Temple Church** is one of five remaining round churches in England: its round part, with notable Templar effigies, was consecrated in 1185 and the chancel added in 1240. **Lincoln's Inn**, N of Fleet St. on Chancery Lane, has the dignified 17C *New Square*, restored 17C *Chapel* and 16C *Old Hall*. Beyond lie *Lincoln's Inn Fields*, central London's largest square; for Sir John Soane's Museum on the N side, see Rte 1. **Gray's Inn**, N of High Holborn, has gardens said to have been laid out by its most famous Treasurer, Sir Francis Bacon, whose statue stands in *South Square*. The heavily restored half-timbered façade of **Staple Inn**, on the S side of Holborn, is the most picturesque relic of the nine subordinate Inns of Chancery, dissolved in the 19C.

**Lincoln's Inn**: see Inns of Court.

**Middle Temple**: see Inns of Court.

**Monument**, Monument St., EC3. Tube: Monument (Circle, District). Closed Sunday afternoons in winter.
  Sir Christopher Wren designed this fluted Doric column topped by a flaming gilt urn to commemorate the Great Fire of 1666, which started in Pudding Lane nearby. A winding staircase leads to the upper gallery (202ft), worth the climb for the wide and striking view.

**Museum of London**: see Barbican.

**Museum of the Moving Image**: see South Bank Centre.

**National Film Theatre**: see South Bank Centre.

**National Theatre**: see South Bank Centre.

*The City of London from the air, with St Paul's Cathedral in the foreground*

**Royal Festival Hall**: see South Bank Centre.

**Royal Shakespeare Company Theatre**: see Barbican.

**St Paul's Cathedral**, EC4. Tube: St Paul's (Central), Mansion House (Circle, District).

Despite the tactless modern office blocks, Sir Christopher Wren's church still just manages to dominate the top of Ludgate Hill. Built in 1675–1710 to replace the medieval cathedral destroyed in the Great Fire of 1666, it combines a Gothic ground plan with classical details and baroque elements of which the most striking is the great central dome. Nicholas Stone's statue of John Donne survives from the old building. The *Crypt* contains the tombs of Nelson and Wellington and *Painters' Corner*. Wren lies beneath a terse epitaph in the N transept. A staircase leads up the dome to the *Whispering Gallery* and fine views from the *Stone Gallery* and *Golden Gallery*.

Visitors dismayed by the crowds St Paul's often attracts can seek out the City churches Wren and Hawksmoor built after the Great Fire. Many have been restored after wartime bomb damage. They include: to the E, *St Vedast* (Foster Lane), *St Mary-le-Bow* (Cheapside), *St Stephen* (Walbrook), Hawksmoor's *St Mary Woolnoth* (Lombard St. and King William St.), *St Michael* and *St Peter* (Cornhill); near the Thames to the S, *St Andrew-by-the-Wardrobe* (Queen Victoria St.), *St James Garlickhythe* (Upper Thames St.), *St Magnus the Martyr* (Lower Thames St.), and the shell of *St Dunstan-in-the-East* (off Lower Thames St.); and along Fleet St. to the W, *St Bride* (with an interesting crypt museum) and *St Clement Danes*. See also the Monument.

**Shakespeare Globe Museum**, Bear Gardens, Bankside, Southwark, SE1. Tube: London Bridge (Northern).

The museum is devoted to the history of Bankside in the Elizabethan and Jacobean eras, when it was centre of London's theatre district. Displays include a full working replica of the Cockpit theatre (1616), used for workshop productions.

A plaque on the wall in nearby Park St. marks the approximate site of Shakespeare's Globe Theatre, built in 1599. It burned down in 1613, and the second Globe was demolished in 1644. On the nearby riverfront the Shakespeare Globe Trust is building a replica of the first Globe, together with a small indoor theatre designed by Inigo Jones and an arts centre which will house the Globe Museum. Construction began in 1988, and visitors are welcome to watch the work in progress. A model of the project can be seen in the museum.

**South Bank Centre**, SE1. Tube: Waterloo (Northern, Bakerloo), Embankment (Circle, District, Northern, Bakerloo).

The post-war complex of cultural institutions which has grown up around the S ends of Waterloo Bridge and Hungerford Bridge includes: the **Royal Festival Hall** and two smaller concert halls, the *Queen Elizabeth Hall* and the *Purcell Room*; the **Hayward Gallery**, with changing exhibitions of contemporary art; the **Museum of the Moving Image**, devoted to the history of film and television; the **National Film Theatre**; and the **National Theatre**, with its three auditoria (the Olivier, the Lyttelton and the Cottesloe).

**Southwark Cathedral**, Borough High St., SE1. Tube: London Bridge (Northern).

This fascinating church (raised to cathedral status in 1905) lies at the S end of London Bridge, hemmed in by Borough Market, the railway and the river. Its choir and retrochoir, begun in 1207, are perhaps the earliest Gothic work in London. The monuments, which make a homely contrast to the grand collection in Westminster Abbey, include the tomb of John Gower (d. 1408). The 20C memorial to Shakespeare is a reminder of the church's close tie with the 16–17C theatres on neighbouring Bankside (see Shakespeare Globe Museum).

The cathedral was also connected with the Bishops of Winchester. A fragment of their 13C palace survives on nearby Clink St. (English Heritage, open at any reasonable time).

**Temple Church**: see Inns of Court.

**Tower Bridge**, EC3. Tube: Tower Hill (District, Circle).

Built in 1886–94, Tower Bridge spans the Thames immediately below the Tower of London. The road connecting its towers is formed by drawbridges which can be raised to allow vessels up the river. The high-level walkway, reached by lift or stairs from the N tower, offers panoramic views. The N and S towers contain exhibitions about the design of the bridge and the history of the City's bridges, and the steam engines which operated the bridge before electrification are on view in a museum outside the S tower.

**Tower of London**, Tower Hill, EC3. Tube: Tower Hill (District, Circle). DoE monument. Closed Sundays from November to February; Jewel House closed in February.

The Tower of London dates from about 1078, when William the Conqueror began to build the *White Tower* near the Roman E wall of the city. It contains *St John's Chapel*, the oldest example of Norman church architecture to survive in London. The castle was turned into a great concentric fortress in the reign of Henry III (1216–72); the outer curtain wall and the moat, now drained, were added by Edward I in 1275–85. The remarkably well-preserved buildings contain the Crown Jewels (among the most popular tourist attractions in London) and a uniquely important collection of European and Oriental arms and armour, as well as the *Regimental Museum of the Royal Fusiliers* and the *Heralds' Museum*.

In its time the Tower has been fortress, royal residence and state prison. Prisoners held here before their execution on Tower Green, outside the walls on Tower Hill or elsewhere in London have included: Sir William Wallace (d. 1305), Bishop St John Fisher (d. 1535), Sir Thomas More (d. 1535), Anne Boleyn (d. 1536), Catherine Howard (d. 1542), Lady Jane Grey (d. 1554), Sir Thomas Wyatt (d. 1554), the Earl of Essex (d. 1601), Sir Walter Raleigh (d. 1618), the Earl of Strafford (d. 1641), Archbishop Laud (d. 1645) and several spies during World War II. Those secretly murdered include Henry VI in 1471, the Duke of Clarence in 1478, and Edward V and his brother, 'the little Princes in the Tower', apparently in 1483. Guy Fawkes and his fellow conspirators in the Gunpowder Plot were tortured here in 1605–06. The long list of other prisoners stretches from David II of Scotland and John of France in Edward III's reign to Rudolf Hess in 1941.

The Tower is still maintained as an arsenal, with a garrison. The

Changing of the Guard takes place on Tower Green at 11.00 daily in summer and on alternate days in winter. Quite distinct from these soldiers are the Yeoman Warders, or 'Beefeaters', with their famous costume said to date from the time of Henry VII or Edward VI. They conduct guided tours on fine days.

A section of the Roman wall, heightened in the Middle Ages, stands near Tower Hill tube station in Wakefield Gardens (English Heritage, open at any reasonable time). A signposted walk follows its course to the Barbican (see above). Beyond Tower Hill, to the W, is the church of **All Hallows by the Tower**. Its 17C brick tower, from which Pepys watched the Great Fire in 1666, survived the bombs that destroyed much of the building in World War II. The undercroft contains an interesting museum of Roman and Saxon remains.

# 3   Outer London

**Chiswick**, W4. Tube: Hammersmith (Piccadilly, District), Ravenscourt Park (District). British Rail: Chiswick Station, from Waterloo. Hogarth's House: closed Tuesdays, also first two weeks of September and last three weeks of December. Chiswick House: English Heritage standard opening and Sunday mornings all year.

Like Richmond and Kew further upstream (see below), Chiswick became fashionable in the 18C as a suburb or country retreat from London. The Queen Anne and early Georgian houses make Chiswick Mall, by the river S of the Great West Rd, one of the most attractive streets of its period in London. William Hogarth (d. 1764) is buried in the churchyard of *St Nicholas*, with the 3rd Earl of Burlington's protégés Colen Campbell (d. 1729) and William Kent (d. 1748) and, from a later generation, James McNeill Whistler (d. 1903). *Hogarth's House*, his summer residence from 1749, survives on the busy Great West Rd beyond the Hogarth Roundabout. It contains a large collection of his engravings. *Chiswick House*, SW of the roundabout on Burlington Lane, is a lovely Palladian villa built by Burlington in 1725–29; much of the ornate decoration is by Kent, who also laid out the gardens.

**Greenwich**, SE10. British Rail: Greenwich or Maze Hill Stations, from Charing Cross. Docklands Light Railway from Tower Hill to Island Gardens. River launches from Westminster, Charing Cross or Tower Piers. Royal Naval College: grounds, Painted Hall and Chapel open afternoons, except Thursdays; hours liable to change at short notice.

On the S bank of the river downstream from central London, Greenwich has splendid buildings to remind the visitor of its royal and naval connections. The tea-clipper 'Cutty Sark' (1869) and Sir Francis Chichester's 'Gipsy Moth IV' (1966) are berthed by Greenwich Pier; both are open, and the 'Cutty Sark' contains a fine collection of ships' figureheads. The riverfront is dominated by the graceful baroque outline of the *Royal Naval College*, on the site of the palace which became a favourite residence of the Tudors. The present buildings were begun by John Webb in 1664 as a new palace for Charles II and continued by Wren from 1694 onwards as the Greenwich Hospital for disabled seamen. They include the Painted Hall, decorated by Sir James Thornhill, and the Chapel, rebuilt by

James 'Athenian' Stuart in 1779–89. Forming part of the same architectural group on the other side of Romney Rd are the buildings of the *National Maritime Museum*, including Inigo Jones's *Queen's House*, completed for Henrietta Maria in 1635 and extended by John Webb in 1662. Its collections illustrate virtually every aspect of Britain's naval history.

*Greenwich Park* climbs steeply to the top of the hill, where the *Old Royal Observatory* was the first headquarters of the Royal Observatory, founded in 1675 by Charles II and moved to Herstmonceux Castle in 1948 (Rte 10A). Outside the gate a 24-hour clock shows Greenwich Mean Time. The Greenwich Meridian, marking the earth's prime meridian (0° longitude), crosses the courtyard. The buildings include *Flamsteed House*, with its red time-ball, built by Wren for the first Astronomer Royal, Sir John Flamsteed. Now part of the National Maritime Museum, they house a collection of astronomical instruments. On the W side of the Park is *Ranger's House* (English Heritage), once the home of the Earl of Chesterfield, with musical instruments and a superb collection of portraits.

**Hampstead**, NW3. Tube: Hampstead (Northern). Fenton House (NT): open Easter to end of October, except Thursdays and Fridays.

Though now an affluent and fashionable suburb, Hampstead has been lucky in keeping much of its village charm and in keeping the high-lying *Hampstead Heath*, one of London's largest and most rugged open spaces. Flask Walk and Well Walk, leading E from Hampstead High St. towards the Heath, are famously picturesque streets; their names recall the village's brief popularity as a spa. *Keats House*, in Keats Grove to the S, was the poet's home from 1818 until he left England in 1820; it contains a large array of memorabilia. *Fenton House*, entered from Hampstead Grove N of the High St., is a late 17C house with collections of European and Oriental ceramics and musical instruments, often played by music students. Spaniards Rd and Hampstead Lane lead round the N edge of the Heath, passing the 16C *Spaniards Inn* on the way to *Kenwood* (English Heritage), remodelled by Robert Adam in 1767–69. It houses the Iveagh Bequest, principally of English, Dutch and Flemish paintings, with outstanding works by Rembrandt, Vermeer, Gainsborough, Reynolds and Romney. The grounds make a lovely venue for summer evening concerts.

**Highgate**, on the E side of Hampstead Heath, can be reached separately via Archway tube station (Northern line). *Highgate Cemetery*, though badly overgrown, is still one of the most impressive Victorian graveyards in England. It consists of a W part (guided tours only) with catacombs and an E part (more freely open) with the tombs of George Eliot and Karl Marx among other eminent people.

**Hampton Court Palace**, Surrey. British Rail: Hampton Court Station. River launches from Westminster Pier in summer. Also on Rte 36B, along the Thames from London to Oxford. DoE monument.

The Tudor and baroque buildings, art collection, beautifully planted gardens and riverside setting make the Palace one of the most popular tourist attractions in the London area.

A royal residence until the 18C, it was begun by Cardinal Wolsey in 1514 and surrendered after his fall in 1529 to Henry VIII. The Great Gatehouse in the mellow brick frontage, the large Base Court and the Clock Court beyond reflect the original layout of Wolsey's palace, as expanded and adapted by Henry VIII. His additions include the fan-vaulted ceiling of Anne Boleyn's Gateway and the curious astronomical clock. The E and S wings, replacing several Tudor courtyards, were built for William III by Sir Christopher Wren. The State Apartments on the first floor, keeping much of their original furniture and decorations, display works from the royal collection. The Italian schools (Tintoretto, Veronese) are particularly well represented among the c 500 paintings. The route continues via the Royal Chapel, built by Wolsey but embellished by Henry VIII; the Great Watching Chamber; and the Great Hall (1531–36), with a magnificent hammerbeam roof.

The gardens were laid out in their present formal style for William III, though the old Tennis Court (where Real Tennis is still sometimes played) was originally built for Henry VIII and the famous Maze planted in the reign of Queen Anne. The Lower Orangery contains a superb series of paintings by Mantegna.

**Richmond upon Thames** and **Kew**, Surrey. Tube: Richmond, Kew Gardens (both District). British Rail: Richmond, Kew Bridge, from Waterloo. River launches from Westminster Pier in summer. Ham House (NT, administered by the Victoria and Albert Museum): closed Mondays. Marble Hill House (English Heritage): closed Fridays. Syon House: open Good Friday to end September, except Fridays and Saturdays, and open Sundays in October.

The site of a royal palace from the 14C to the 17C and a fashionable country retreat in the 18C, Richmond is one of Greater London's most attractive suburbs. Richmond Green is made particularly handsome by the 17–18C houses that surround it, and Richmond Hill commands a famous view of the Thames valley. *Richmond Park*, enclosed as a royal hunting ground in the 17C, has 2500 acres of natural parkland with red and fallow deer. *Ham House*, by the river to the S and approached from Petersham Rd, is a 17C house which keeps its grand interior decoration, furniture and portraits.

Kew, to the N, is famous for the *Royal Botanic Gardens* which have grown from modest beginnings in 1759 to the present world-wide collection of plants. The buildings in the lovely 300-acre grounds include *Kew Palace* (DoE monument), built in 1631 and made a royal residence by George III; Sir William Chambers's *Orangery*, now housing a museum, and *Pagoda*, both built in 1761; and the famous greenhouses, notably Decimus Burton's *Palm House* (1844–48) and *Temperate House* (1860–99).

There are several points of interest on the opposite bank of the Thames from Richmond and Kew. *Marble Hill House*, reached via Richmond Bridge, is a wonderfully complete example of a Palladian villa, designed in 1723–29 by Roger Morris for George II's mistress Henrietta Howard, Countess of Suffolk. *Syon House*, reached via Kew Bridge, has a castellated Tudor exterior which contrasts with the state rooms grandly remodelled by Robert Adam in 1761, among the best surviving examples of his work. The collection of portraits include work by Van Dyck, Lely, Reynolds and Gainsborough. The grounds, laid out by Capability Brown, include the *British Heritage Motor Museum*.

**Windsor**: see Rte 36A.

# SOUTH-EASTERN ENGLAND

South-Eastern England stretches from London and the Thames Estuary down to the English Channel, its W boundary being defined for present purposes by the Southampton road. It includes the counties of Kent, Surrey, East and West Sussex, the greater part of Hampshire, and the Isle of Wight (now a separate county in itself). The region has thus a double aspect, facing towards both the capital and the sea. Its coastline is fringed with ports, fortresses, seaside resorts and retirement communities, and its centre crossed by the great arteries which have carried foreign invasion, pilgrimage, commerce and tourism over the centuries. In the N the shadow of London falls heavily across the landscape. Kent and Surrey, both 'Home Counties' sharing a border with the capital, lost ground to Greater London in the administrative changes of 1974 and the influence of the capital still reaches far beyond even these new boundaries. Surrey has suffered the sadder fate. Despised until the 19C as 'a barren county of heaths, firs and unprofitable soil', it owes much of its present appearance to the railway and the commuter. A pleasantly provincial atmosphere survives in only a few towns—like Farnham and Guildford—and only the occasional beauty spot among the otherwise suburbanised landscape can attract the visitor.

The major roads, and hence the routes suggested in this book, cross the region from N to S, but the basic contours of the land go from W to E. The great chalk belt centred in Wiltshire and the Salisbury Plain continues into Hampshire and separates into two distinct ranges of downland. The North Downs run between Farnham and Guildford as the narrow ridge of the Hog's Back and then achieve their greatest heights—the lovely Box Hill (596ft) near Dorking, for example—as they head towards Rochester and the Medway river. Here they swing toward the S coast, their ridge for part of the distance making the track known as the Pilgrims' Way, and finally confront the sea as the famous white cliffs of Dover. This cliff scenery extends S to Folkestone and N to Deal, appearing again in a modified form to enliven the tip of the Isle of Thanet around Ramsgate and Margate. The South Downs begin dramatically at Butser Hill (889ft) near Petersfield in Hampshire and end at the sea at Beachy Head and the Seven Sisters, near Eastbourne, with scenery that rivals the cliffs of Dover. But for much of their way across Sussex, particularly between Arundel and Lewes, they become the 'blunt, bow-headed, whale-backed downs' which for many people typify the look of South-Eastern England. It is a gentle landscape, with clean air and short, springy turf, inevitably suggesting 'mutton and pleasantness'.

The rivers cut through both ranges of downland, sometimes in quite steep and narrow valleys, running N into the Thames Estuary or S into the English Channel. Towns grew up at these junctions, where travellers along the chalk ridges had to descend to ford the water and where roads following the later routes along the valleys had to cross the downland. Thus, in the N, Guildford stands on the Wey, Leatherhead and Dorking on the Mole, Maidstone and Rochester on the Medway and Canterbury on the Stour. In the S, Winchester stands on the Itchen, Arundel on the Arun and Lewes on the Ouse.

The broad oval ring of the North and South Downs gives South-Eastern England its general character. The traveller from London to the coast—say, Brighton—is aware of crossing two distinctive chalk ridges, even on the most smoothly contoured of modern roads. The N outcrop overlooks the London Basin and the flat, often marshy countryside of the Thames Estuary, here very similar in character to the N shore in Essex. On the SW edge, in Hampshire, the Downs yield to the wide reaches of Southampton Water and the great heaths and woodlands of the New Forest. Offshore, on the Isle of Wight, the chalk reappears in some of the region's most dramatic scenery.

Between the North and South Downs lies the Weald, an area still thickly wooded in places and once covered by an immense forest, whose chief relic is at Ashdown. In the W its sandstone landscape gives South-Eastern England its highest point at Leith Hill (965ft) near Dorking. In Sussex the forest provided timber for shipbuilding and charcoal for smelting iron. Before it moved to the coalfields of the Midlands and the North in the 19C, the iron industry left its mark in the wealthy ironmasters' houses (like Bateman's, later Rudyard Kipling's home, at Burwash) and the occasional iron furnishings in the churches (like the grille in the Fitzalan Chapel at Arundel). In Kent the Weald makes the familiar—and charming—countryside of small farms and market gardens, of orchards and hop-fields with their distinctive cowled oast-houses. This region, sometimes called the Vale of Kent, trails down to the sea at the flat, changing coastline of Romney Marsh.

The Weald has also given South-Eastern England its best building materials. Otherwise, the area is not well endowed. Kentish ragstone, a limestone quarried near Maidstone, was used for Rochester Castle and the Westgate at Canterbury, and for parish churches, whose tall towers often combine the stone with knapped local flint in chequer-boarded patterns. Wealden sandstone made the churches around Tunbridge Wells, and the more attractive Horsham slates used for roofing. Yet both these stones are of limited and mainly local use, and leave South-Eastern England poor by comparison to its western neighbours. It is notable that for major buildings the materials did not come from the mainland at all: Caen stone was brought from Normandy for Canterbury Cathedral, Quarr stone from the Isle of Wight for Chichester and Winchester.

But the Weald had clay and timber. The clay made warm red bricks and tiles (often hung as cladding for outside walls) which give even the humbler buildings their sturdy and cheerful look. Oak and Spanish chestnut from the forest went into the abundance of half-timbered houses, confirming Kent in particular as a county that makes up for its comparative lack of great estates or country houses by the richness of its smaller farm buildings and the pleasing irregularity of its older townscapes. The so-called Wealden house, built from the 14C onwards, is a distinctive local feature. Here the central hall is open and two-storied, and only the upper floors at either wing are jettied outwards towards the front; the eaves of the roof are carried across the central gap by an overhanging brace.

The timber, brick and tile houses of the Weald, like the hop-fields and orchards of Kent or the soft contours of the South Downs, make for a cosily settled landscape, a peculiarly English kind of prettiness. Its small-scale charms attract the long-distance commuters, whose affluence has often helped to keep these pleasing effects well groomed. On the coast, alternating between chalk cliff and low-lying, sometimes marshy ground, we find a different atmosphere and a different sort of history. Our first impression is likely to be dominated by the resorts that grew up in the late 18C and 19C, when sea air and sea water were first thought fashionable and first alleged to be health-giving. There are points where it can seem that the coastline from Whitstable to Bognor has become merely a continuous chain of seaside amusements, man-made cliffs of boarding houses and depressingly regular blocks of retirement bungalows. These developments have long since crowded out the small packet stations and fishing villages that once fringed the coast: Brighthelmston has vanished beneath the Regency and Victorian splendours of Brighton. It is only in the occasional place—like the old part of Hastings—that we can still get an older, and more authentic, whiff of the sea.

Yet the resorts never erased reminders of the coast's fragile history of invasion and defence. At Richborough, where the Romans probably first landed in AD 43, and at Reculver the invaders built fortresses to guard the navigable channel which then separated the Isle of Thanet from the mainland. The Normans, who marked the scene of their victory with the splendid Battle Abbey, consolidated the sites their predecessors had chosen. Rochester Castle, emphatically commanding the Medway, is founded partly on the Roman city walls. Dover Castle has a Roman pharos (probably the oldest building to survive in England) as well as a Norman keep. At Pevensey, where William the Conqueror first landed, and at Portchester near Portsmouth the Norman work stands inside Roman fortifications.

The earliest parts of Southampton's fine city walls also belong to the Norman period, but the later additions and reinforcements speak of the continuing need for defence along the coast. In 1278 Edward I granted the first charter to the Cinque Ports, a system of maritime defence modelled on the 'Saxon Shore' of the Romans, naming Dover, Sandwich, Hythe, Romney and Hastings. Henry VII began Portsmouth's long history of royal dockyards and garrisons, while his successor performed the same service for Chatham. Fear of invasion by the Catholic powers of Europe also led Henry VIII to add to the coast's already impressive defences, most notably with the elegantly geometric Deal Castle. The threat of Napoleonic invasion created Martello towers—which can still be seen at Dymchurch on Romney Marsh and between Hastings and Eastbourne—and, later in the 19C, thoughts of the French again prompted Lord Palmerston's forts at Portsmouth.

Nor, alas, did the tradition stop in our own century. In Kent, which gained the sinister nickname of 'Bomb Alley' during the Second World War, Dover Castle provided shelter from cross-Channel shell fire. Portsmouth, like so many cities in the region a victim of heavy air raids, became one of the main D-Day assembly points. Hurst Castle, built by Henry VIII on a pebble spit guarding the W end of the Solent and already much altered in the 19C, again saw military service. So long a tradition makes present plans for a Channel tunnel (or 'fixed link', as politicians like cautiously to refer to it) a welcome change in how the English regard their neighbours across the narrow waters of the Channel, even despite fears about its effect on the surrounding region.

# 4    London to Dover via Rochester and Canterbury

Total distance 71m. In its main lines the route follows A2.—To (7m) Blackheath.—A207 to (16m) Dartford.—A2 to (28m) **Rochester** and (29m) **Chatham**.—To (39m) Sittingbourne.—To (46m) Ospringe for **Faversham** (bypassed).—To (56m) **Canterbury** (bypassed).—To (71m) **Dover**.

Maps: OS Landranger 177, 178 and 179.

A2 leaves London by the Old Kent Rd, (4m) *New Cross* and (7m) *Blackheath*. It then bypasses the centres of Bexleyheath and Dartford by the Rochester Way. A207 follows the line of Watling St., the old Dover road since Roman times, and offers a shorter route, up Shooter's Hill and down through Bexleyheath.—At (14m) *Crayford* we bear right.—16m. **Dartford** (42,000 inhab.), a busy town on the Darent, has a fine galleried inn of 1703. Wat Tyler's rising probably started in the town, and another inn (renamed after him) in the High St. claims to be a meeting place of his supporters. The *Church*, on the river, has a strong Norman tower with 14C upper storey.

Its spacious but over-restored interior contains a late 15C mural of St George and the Dragon. The Spilman tomb, with inscriptions in German, was erected to his wife (d. 1607) by Sir John Spilman or Spielmann (d. 1626), who came from Lindaü on Lake Constance and built at Dartford one of the earliest paper mills in England; according to popular belief 'foolscap' paper was so called from a jester ('Spielmann') forming part of his arms and used by him as a watermark. A tablet in the S aisle commemorates the Cornish engineer Richard Trevithick (1771–1833), who died in poverty at the Bull inn and was carried to his grave by his workmates at Hall's engineering works.

Beyond the town A207 passes over the approach to the Dartford–Purfleet tunnel and rejoins A2, here motorway in all but name and again following the Roman alignment.

An alternative road (A226) from Dartford to Rochester diverges left from Watling St., ¾m from the church. This follows the course known to both Shakespeare and Dickens when the Roman road had decayed.—2m. *Horns Cross*, in a region of chalk pits and cement works. A little to the left, looking out across the Thames is *Stone* •church, a beautiful building of c 1245 with a chancel higher than its nave. The richly sculptured interior of the chancel, with exquisite windows and blind arcading, has many features in common with contemporary work at Westminster Abbey. The Wylshire chantry (NE) is a 16C addition; the vault is a successful restoration by G.E. Street.—3m. *Greenhithe*, with a quaint riverfront, was the scene of the departure in 1845 of Sir John Franklin's ill-fated polar voyage. *Ingress Abbey* was enlarged in the 19C with stone from old London Bridge.—5m. *Northfleet* has a large 14C church on a bluff, with a contemporary rood screen.

7m. **Gravesend** (53,000 inhab.; Tourist Information), a famous Thames-side port, is the pilot station for vessels using the Port of London. It still maintains a traditionally maritime appearance with old inns and some weatherboarded houses in its narrow High St. The views of the river from near Town and Terrace Piers or (better) from Gordon Terrace, further E, are famous. The gardens here mark the site of Fort House, General Gordon's home in 1865–71. In one corner stands the *Milton Chantry* (English Heritage, summer standard opening), whose 18C exterior conceals a 14C building used as the chapel of a leper hospital and the chantry of the de Valence family. A statue (and windows in *St George's Church* W of the piers) commemorate the burial here of Pocohontas (d. 1617), the Indian princess who saved the life of Captain John Smith, the coloniser of Virginia. Leonard Calvert (son of Lord Baltimore, the founder of Maryland) set sail from Gravesend in 1633; so did the Quaker George Fox in 1671, and Charles and John Wesley in 1735 on their American journeys. A tablet recalls Strindberg's residence here in 1839.

At (10m) *Chalk* Dickens spent his honeymoon. The road descends *Gad's Hill* (wide view from the Sir John Falstaff inn), where Falstaff encountered the 'rogues in buckram' ('1 Henry IV', II, iv). At *Gad's Hill Place*, an 18C red-brick house now a school, Dickens lived from 1857 until his death in 1870. Part of the garden, known as the Wilderness, is reached by a tunnel under the road. The railway passes beneath the ridge in a tunnel originally built for a canal (1819–24). We rejoin the Roman road in Strood.—15m. *Rochester*, see below.

On the bleak peninsula lying between the Thames and the Medway to the E of Chalk are (3m) *Higham* church, with a 14C *door, screen and pulpit, and (5m) *Cooling Castle*, with a 14C gatehouse, the home of Sir John Oldcastle, the supposed original of Falstaff. In the churchyard nearby are the 18C gravestones commemorating the children of the Comport family which appear in the first chapter of Dickens's 'Great Expectations'. The marsh country where the opening scenes of the novel are laid stretches N to the Thames and is well seen from the remote village of *Cliffe*, 1½m NW of Cooling. The large 13C church has wall paintings of the martyrdom of St Edmund and of Christ in Majesty. The peninsula ends as the *Isle of Grain*.

A2 crosses the Gravesend–Wrotham road 4m N of *Meopham* (pronounced 'Meppam'), birthplace of the naturalist John Tradescant (1608–62), where the church of 1325 has a late 14C aisle and a pulpit (1682) from St Margaret's, Westminster. We skirt *Cobham Park*, on the right, finely landscaped by Repton.

**Cobham Hall** (now a girls' public school; limited opening) is an imposing, mainly Elizabethan mansion with a centre block of 1662–72 and archaising additions by the Reptons and James Wyatt. It was the home of the Duke of Richmond and his duchess, 'La Belle Stuart', and later the seat of the Earls of Darnley. At the SW entrance to the park is the delightful village of *Cobham*, whose church has the largest collection of *brasses in England (14–16C). Near the Leather Bottle inn, now pleasantly cluttered with Dickens .relics, Mr Pickwick discovered his wonderful inscribed stone. The New College Almshouses (open) evolved in 1598 from a college founded in 1362. At the W end of the village is Owletts (NT), a modest house of Charles II's reign.

At 26m the M2 diverges right and A2 continues into the centre of (28m) *Strood*, linked to Rochester by parallel bridges and now officially amalgamated with that city. In Knight Rd, S of the High St., is *Temple Manor*, a 13C hall of the Knights Templar with 16C additions (English Heritage, summer standard opening but closed Tuesday afternoons and Fridays).

A228 leads NE.—*Frindsbury*, right at ½m, has a flint church with Norman chancel and 13C wall paintings.—2m.*Upnor Castle* (English Heritage, summer standard opening) stands by the Medway on an unclassified road off A228. It was built in 1559–67 to protect Chatham dockyards on the opposite bank of the river. After the Dutch raid of 1667 proved its ineffectiveness, it became a magazine for Ordnance stores.—The 13C church of (4m) *Hoo St Werburgh*, right of A228, has a shingled spire.

28m. **ROCHESTER** (52,500 inhab.) owes its long history to its strategic position guarding Watling Street where it crosses the Medway. An important centre for Belgic civilisation, it was made a fortified camp, *Durobrivae*, by the Romans. The Saxon *Hroffeceaster* became a bishop's see in the 7C, and the Normans chose it as the site for a massive castle. The history of later centuries of travel along the London–Dover road is manifest in the varied and handsome buildings of the High St. Rochester is now officially united with Strood and Chatham, its neighbours to the W and E, as the city of Rochester upon Medway.

**Tourist Information Centre**: Eastgate Cottage, Eastgate, High St.

**Car Parks**: Esplanade, Corporation St., Boley Hill.

**Railway Stations**: Rochester and Chatham, ½m apart; the faster trains stop only at Chatham.

**Annual Events**: Dickens Festival in May/June; Admiral's Cruise in June/July; Admiralty Court in July; Medway Regatta in July.

**Famous visitors**. Charles II spent a night at Rochester in 1660 on his way from Dover, Pepys stayed in 1667 in the aftermath of the Dutch raid on the Medway and James II took ship from here on his escape in 1688. Dickens knew the city well from his childhood in Chatham and his later years at Gad's Hill; it appears in 'Pickwick Papers' and 'Great Expectations' and is the main location of 'The Mystery of Edwin Drood'.

A tour of Rochester naturally begins with its most distinctive landmark, the *Castle (English Heritage, standard opening and summer Sunday mornings). Perhaps the mightiest example of Norman military architecture in England, it occupies a site originally fortified by the Romans. The square five-storied keep, built c 1127 by William de Corbeuil, Archbishop of Canterbury, stands 120ft high with walls of coursed rubble averaging 12ft in thickness. Visitors can climb to the top for a panoramic view. The SE turret—round, while the others are square—was built to repair damage done when King John recaptured the castle from the rebellious barons in 1215. The keep is protected by a curtain wall following the line of the Roman wall in places; it was built c 1087 by Bishop Gundulf and partly rebuilt in the 14C.

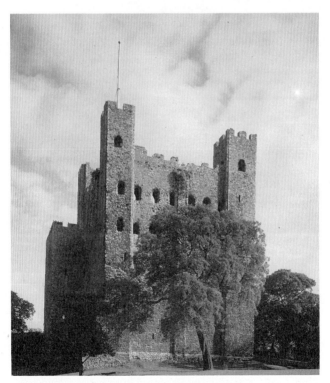

*Rochester Castle, the Norman keep*

The modestly sized **Cathedral** stands in stocky contrast to the castle keep. It dates mainly from the 11–14C and is like Canterbury in having double transepts, raised choir, and a presbytery with a large crypt underneath. Externally, the most striking feature is the Norman W front with its elaborate recessed *doorway, perhaps the best of its kind in England. The tympanum and figures on the shafts (Solomon and the Queen of Sheba) were added c 1175.

The first bishop was consecrated by Augustine of Canterbury in 604, making Rochester the second oldest see in England. The place where the apse of this original Saxon church stood is marked at the W end of the present nave; remains of a second Saxon church have been discovered beneath the N transept. Gundulf, the second Norman bishop (who built the White Tower at London), began a new church in 1082. His work can be seen in the nave, the crypt and the N tower bearing his name (originally detached and taller than it is now). The popularity of the shrine to St William of Perth, a pilgrim murdered in 1201, encouraged later rebuilding. Presbytery, E transepts and choir belong to the early 13C. The N transept dates from c 1250, the early Dec. S transept from c 1280, and the two E bays of the nave from c 1300. The central tower and spire were added c 1343, though it needed 20C rebuilding to restore their original appearance.

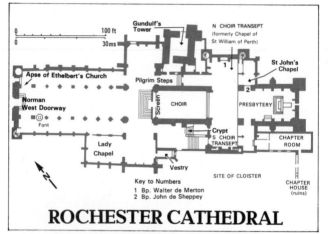

Key to Numbers
1 Bp. Walter de Merton
2 Bp. John de Sheppey

# ROCHESTER CATHEDRAL

The six W bays of the *Nave* are Norman, creating a sombre effect that is not relieved by the Perp. windows and clerestory. The elaborately adorned triforium passage opens on both nave and aisles. Remarkable, too, is the way that later builders reconstructed the triforium arches in the Norman style when the E bays and tower arch were altered. The *Lady Chapel* (c 1490) is off the S aisle, its great arch into the transept now closed by a modern altar screen. The *S Transept* has a brass memorial to Dickens, who wished to be buried in the cathedral, and a monument to Richard Watts (see below).

A peculiarity of the raised EE *Choir* is the lack of aisle arcades. The figures on the choir screen are a memorial to Dean Scott (1811–97), of Liddell and Scott's famous Greek lexicon. The details on the corbels and the lovely shafts of Purbeck and Petworth marble should be noted. The stalls and *monks' benches (with modern book desks) are early 13C and probably the oldest in England (cf. Winchester). Opposite the 19C bishop's throne is part of a 13C wall painting showing the Wheel of Fortune. The *N Choir Transept*, formerly the Chapel of St William of Perth, contains the heavily restored tomb of Bishop Walter de Merton (d. 1277), founder of the Oxford college, with an Elizabethan effigy in alabaster. In the arch between *St John's Chapel* at the E end and the *Presbytery* is the tomb, with coloured effigy, of Bishop John de Sheppey (d. 1360). The *S Choir Transept* has a remarkable Dec. *doorway (c 1340) leading to the Chapter Room.

From the S choir aisle a flight of steps descends to the *Crypt, one of the largest and most beautiful in England. It has fine EE vaulting, with great variety of spans, and some medieval graffiti on the piers. The two W bays, with piers of tufa and a white stone believed to be Barnack, and ribless quadripartite vaulting, are early Norman. The fragments of medieval glass in the E window came partly from Canterbury.

SE of the choir are the ruins of the *Chapter House* and remains of the Norman *Cloister* built by Bishop Ernulf (1115–24). The ruined 14C *Bishop's Gate* was the W entrance to the cloister.

The cathedral and castle confront each other across the charming little Boley Hill. The High St. lies immediately beyond Chertsey Gate at its N end, but it is worth following a much less direct route and heading in the opposite direction. On Bakers Walk, skirting the castle grounds to the right, are two notable buildings: the *Old Hall*, the home of Richard Watts (see below) visited by Elizabeth I in 1573, and *Satis House*, a 16C building with a Regency front which gave its name (but not its appearance) to Miss Havisham's home in 'Great Expectations'. From further up Boley Hill a lane leads left past the 15C *Prior's Gate* and the charming 18C *Minor Canon Row*, fictional home of Mr Crisparkle in 'Edwin Drood' and real home of the actress Dame Sybil Thorndike in her childhood. Beyond the 19C buildings of the *King's School*, refounded by Henry VIII after the Dissolution, the *Archdeaconry* (enlarged in 1661) and *Oriel House* (1758), we turn left into the splendid avenue of *The Vines*, whose name remembers the monks' vineyard once cultivated here. We emerge on Crow Lane opposite *Restoration House*, a handsome Tudor building so called because of the tradition that Charles II slept here on his way from Dover to London in 1660. Dickens apparently had it in mind for 'Satis House' in 'Great Expectations'.

Crow Lane descends to the High St., where we turn right. On the left is *Eastgate House*, an Elizabethan building in brick that became the 'Nuns' House' of 'Edwin Drood'. It now contains the *Charles Dickens Centre*, with audio-visual displays stressing the most popular aspects of the novelist's work. In the garden is the Swiss chalet which the actor Charles Fechter gave Dickens in 1865; it formerly stood in the grounds of Gad's Hill Place, where Dickens used it as his study. Opposite the museum is a gabled Tudor building claimed as the home of Mr Pumblechook in 'Great Expectations' and Mr Sapsea, the mayor in 'Edwin Drood'.

What Dickens calls 'the silent High Street—full of gables with old beams and timbers' leads NW back towards the river. The demolition of Free School Lane (on the right) revealed a long stretch of the old city wall with a corner bastion. An alley on the opposite side of the High St. leads to a garden alongside another stretch of the Roman and medieval wall. Beyond *La Providence*, on the right, a rebuilt group of almshouses now belonging to the Huguenot Society, is the gabled building known as *Watts' Charity* (open), founded in 1579 by the will of Richard Watts 'for Six Poor Travellers, who, not being rogues or proctors, may receive gratis for one night lodging, entertainment, and fourpence each' but discontinued in 1947. On the left is *Chertsey* (or *College*) *Gate*, the home of Jasper in 'Edwin Drood', leading to Boley Hill; the half-timbered building next to it is identified with the verger's house, where the mysterious Dick Datchery came to lodge, in the same novel. On the right of the High St., further on, are the old *Corn Exchange* (1706), 'oddly garnished with a queer old clock, as if Time carried on business there', and the *George Inn*, with a 14C undercroft. The 17C *Guildhall* (open), with a

fine plaster ceiling, has good portraits, including Queen Anne by Kneller and Sir Cloudesley Shovel (d. 1707), MP for Rochester. The panelled council chamber is outstanding. At the *Royal Victoria and Bull Hotel*, opposite, the Pickwickians stayed in the doubtful company of Mr Jingle, and Pip had a memorable encounter with Bentley Drummle in 'Great Expectations'.

The High St. ends at the bridge (1970), at least the sixth structure to have spanned the Medway at this point. On the Esplanade, in the shadow of the castle to the left, the balustrade uses stone from the 14C bridge demolished in 1857. Remains of the Roman walls are also visible along here. The *Bridge Chapel* (1387) was heavily restored in 1937 and is now used as the boardroom of the Bridge Wardens.

At *Borstal*, 1m S on the Maidstone Rd (B2097), is a prison reformatory (1902) for offenders under 21 which has given a generic name to others of its kind.

29m. **Chatham** (62,000 inhab.), Rochester's neighbour on the Medway, was for long one of the chief naval stations in Great Britain.

Henry VIII was the first to use Chatham for naval purposes, and by the time of Charles II it had become pre-eminent. In 1667 the Dutch fleet commanded by Admiral de Ruyter came up the Medway to Chatham, where it destroyed and captured ships but did not damage the town. The Great Lines were begun in 1715 to protect the dockyards from attack by land; their keypoint, Fort Amherst, was finished in 1782. The Royal Navy finally left Chatham in 1984. Dickens's childhood homes, after his family left Portsmouth, were in The Brook (now gone) and then at No. 2 (now 11) Ordnance Terrace, on a height above the railway station.

Chatham High St. continues Rochester High St. In it we find the *Sir John Hawkins Hospital*, founded in 1595 and rebuilt in the 19C; opposite is a restored Norman chapel, once part of a leper hospital. Medway St. bears left to the *Town Hall*, with lawns stretching to the river and a view of Rochester. Behind rise the derelict Great Lines, where a path climbs to the *Royal Naval Memorial* by Lorimer (1924) and Maufe (1952), giving a wide view of the Medway towns. Dock Rd continues above the Medway to *St Mary's*, a 19C church incorporating Norman details; it now houses the *Medway Heritage Centre*, whose exhibition traces the history of the river and the Medway towns. Opposite is a mounted statue of Lord Kitchener (d. 1916), removed from Khartoum in 1960. Further on is the former **Royal Naval Dockyard** (open), administered by the Chatham Historic Dockyard Trust since it was abandoned by the Navy in 1984.

The 85-acre site, first developed by the Navy in 1547, now holds about 60 buildings of historic interest. Particularly notable are: the *Main Gate* (1720) with huge Royal Arms added later on both sides; the *Dockyard Church* (1808); the *Ropery* (1785); the *Sail Loft* (1734); the steam *Saw Mills* by Sir Marc Brunel (1813–24); *Medway House* (1703) and the *Officers' Terrace* in the residential centre; and *No. 3 Slip* (1838), with a splendid timber roof. From the basins there are good views of Upnor Castle across the river.

In **Gillingham** (pronounced 'Jillingham'; 93,700 inhab.), on the hill above Chatham dockyard, are the *Brompton Barracks*, a well-designed early 19C quadrangle. It includes a statue of General Gordon (d. 1885) on camel-back, by Onslow Ford (1890), and the *Royal Engineers' Museum*, with relics of the General.

33½m. *Rainham* has a good 14C church tower.—36m. *Newington*, in a famous cherry-growing district, has a church with a handsome Perp. tower, a Tudor font cover and brasses. At *Lower Halstow*, 2m N, the Saxon church, remodelled in the 13C, has a leaden *font of c 1150.—37m. *Key Street* crossroads.

A249 diverges left for the Isle of Sheppey, via Kingsferry Bridge over the Swale, an arm of the Thames in which St Augustine baptised 10,000 people in 597. —7m. *Queenborough*, a decayed port, was named from Queen Philippa, wife of Edward III.—10m. **Sheerness** (33,400 inhab.; Tourist Information) a port at the mouth of the Medway, has the relics of a naval dockyard abandoned by the Admiralty in 1960. They include a dignified boatstore of 1861, one of the earliest iron-framed buildings. James II embarked here in an unsuccessful attempt to escape from England. A car ferry crosses to Flushing.—Offshore is the *Nore*, a sandbank buoyed for safety at least since the 16C. Here the pressed crews were brought to man the ships of the Royal Navy, and here they revolted in the Great Mutiny of 1797.

B2008 and B2231 run across the northern part of the island to (9m) *Leysdown*, on the estuary of the Thames. B2008 passes (3¼m) *Minster*, where the *abbey church of St Mary and St Sexburga, founded in 664, has a Saxon window in the N aisle. It contains the monument of Sir Robert Shurland (d. c 1300) and the fine brasses (c 1325) of Sir Roger de Northwode and his lady. The abbey gatehouse has been restored. The low clay cliffs to the E are rich in fossils.—At (5½m) *Eastchurch*, on B2231, the church has a Perp. rood screen and a memorial window (1912) to the first aviators killed in a flying accident. The ruins of the 16C manor house of *Shurland* lie ½m NE. The desolate marshland on the S of the island is given over to sheep and hares. *Harty*, on the SE corner, has a remote and touchingly simple church.

39m. **Sittingbourne** (33,600 inhab.) is a dull place but the ancient borough of *Milton Regis*, 1m N, has an old Court Hall and a good 17C building now serving as the Post ⊖ffice. The large 14C church, ¾m out on the Sheppey road, has a massive tower. On Crown Quay Lane to the E is the *Dolphin Yard Sailing Barge Museum. Bredgar*, 4m SW beyond the motorway, has a Dec. collegiate church and chantry cottages of c 1392.

Beyond Sittingbourne we enter orchard country, and (42m) *Teynham* is traditionally the first place where cherries and apples were grown in Kent.—46m. *Ospringe* has a 13C church with saddle-back Victorian tower, a vineyard nearby, and an early 16C building incorporating fragments of a 13C 'Maison Dieu' or pilgrims' shelter (English Heritage, summer season, Saturdays and Sunday afternoons). We diverge left 1m for Faversham.

**Faversham** (16,100 inhab.; Tourist Information) is an ancient town and port, a member of the Cinque Ports confederation (see Dover). James II was detained here after his abortive flight from Sheerness. Over 400 listed buildings remain, and the *Fleur de Lis Heritage Centre*, in a former 16C inn in Preston St., has colourful displays evoking the town's history. In the Market Place is a handsome *Guildhall* (1814) on timber arcades (1574). On either side of Court St. are Kent's only two major breweries, both in imposing 18–19C buildings. The splendid *Abbey St., largely 15–18C and restored with taste, runs parallel with the Creek. Near the end is *Arden's House*, the former abbey guesthouse (c 1520), where Thomas Arden was murdered at his wife's instigation in 1551, an event chronicled in the Elizabethan melodrama 'Arden of Feversham'. The site of the Cluniac abbey founded in 1147 by King Stephen, and the base of his tomb, were located in 1965. A path from Abbey Place leads back past the *Old Grammar School* (1567), now a Freemasons' Hall (open by appointment), to the *Parish Church*. The second biggest in Kent, it was enlarged with aisled transepts in 1315 (contemporary pillar *paintings), and given an unexpected Grecian nave in 1754 and a distinctive crown spire in 1797. The choir stalls have good misericords and poppyheads.

Westbrook Walk, at the end of West St. opposite Stonebridge Pond, leads to *Chart Gunpowder Mills* (1760), oldest of their kind in the world and restored as a memorial to 300 years of explosives manufacture (ended in 1935). Over looking the Pond is *Davington Priory*, comprising the plain Norman church and some domestic buildings of a nunnery founded here in 1153.—The church of *Preston*, just beyond the railway station, has a fine 13C chancel and alabaster monument (1629) to the grandparents of Robert Boyle, who formulated Boyle's Law).

48m. At *Brenley Corner* roundabout A2 is joined by M2.

For A299 NE to Whitstable and Herne Bay, see Rte 6.—An unclassified road leads right from Brenley Corner to (1m) *Boughton under Blean*, where Chaucer's pilgrims were joined by the Canon Yeoman. The Hawkins monument in the church has vigorous reliefs by Evesham (1618). 1¹/₂m beyond is *Selling*, with a church containing good EE glass.

Beyond Brenley Corner the present course of the A2 bypasses *Boughton Street*, on the left at 49m, its handsome main street once again peaceful, and *Dunkirk*, left at 50m, where the 19C church has a plaque commemorating the extraordinary Courtenay rebellion of 1838, which met its end in Bossenden wood to the N.—At (51¹/₂m) *Harbledown* the hilly road gives particularly good views. The Hospital of St Nicholas, founded for lepers by Archbishop Lanfranc, has an 11C chapel and rebuilt almshouses. The hill to the S is crowned by

*Barfreston church, the south doorway*

a Belgic fort. On St Thomas's Hill to the N (named after a vanished chapel dedicated to Becket) is the *University of Kent*, founded in 1961.—56m. **Canterbury** (bypassed), see Rte 5.

58m. *Patrixbourne*, left of the road, has a church with a *doorway of c 1175 and 16–17C Swiss glass.

At *Bekesbourne*, 1/2m beyond, are the remains of a palace of the Archbishops of Canterbury. It is worth continuing another 3m NE, beyond A257, to *Wickhambreaux*, which has a charming group of buildings around its village green. There is an Art Nouveau window (1896) by Arild Rosenkrantz in the church.

591/2m. *Bishopsbourne* church has a monument to the judicious Richard Hooker (1554–1600), rector here from 1595. Oswalds, now the rectory, was the home of Joseph Conrad (1857–1924) from 1919.—For the Elham Valley (B2065), see Rte 3.

At 631/2m B2046 leads left and an unclassified road branches right through *Womenswold* to (3m) **Barfreston**. The *church, probably built 1170–80, is perhaps the best and certainly the most ornate example of Norman work in Kent; the richly flowing carving of the S doorway is particularly notable.

641/2m. *Broome Park* (not open) is a fine house of 1635–38, once the seat of Lord Kitchener and probably the 'Tappington' of the 'Ingoldsby Legends'.—671/2m. The church at *Coldred* (left) has an EE bell gable.

From *Lydden*, right of A2, we may join B2060 for (2m) *Temple Ewell*, where King John met Pandulf, the Pope's legate, preparatory to resigning his throne at Dover. B2060 then runs W along the valley past the pleasant public parks of *Kearsney Abbey* (21/2m; left) and *Russell Gardens* to (41/2m) *Alkham*, where the beautiful 13C church has fine wall arcading in the N aisle.— From *River*, 1/2m S of Kearsney, we can make a similar trip down the next valley. At 11/2m are the remains of the Premonstratensian *St Radegund's Abbey* (not open).

71m. **DOVER** (32,800 inhab.) has for centuries been England's main gateway to the Continent as well as a crucial point in its defence against invasion. It lies on low ground at the mouth of the Dour and stretches up the narrow valley which here interrupts the line of the famous white cliffs, fortified to the E by Dover Castle, probably the best known of English coastal garrisons. The busy harbour includes the old Commercial Harbour, the Eastern and Western Docks and the Hoverport; the Admiralty Harbour was enclosed by massive breakwaters in 1898–1909 but abandoned as a naval base in 1923.

**Tourist Information Centre**: Townwall St.

**Car Parks**: Marine Parade, St James St., Ladywell St. and off Market Square. Multi-storey car park on Russell St.

**Buses**: from Pencester Rd to all destinations.

**Railway Stations**: Dover Priory, for all services; Marine (Western Docks) for cross-Channel services only.

**Ferry Services**: from the train-ferry berth at Marine Station (Western Docks) to Dunkerque, Ostend and Calais; also jetfoil service to Ostend. From the Car Ferry Terminal (Eastern Docks) to Boulogne, Calais, Zeebrugge and Ostend. Hovercraft from Hoverport (Western Docks) to Calais and Boulogne.

**History**. Dover (the Roman *Dubrae* or *Dubris*), in all ages a landing place of consequence, was the starting-point of Watling Street, the great Roman road to London via Canterbury, and in the 3–4C was a fortress guarding the 'Saxon Shore', which extended from The Wash to Spithead. Though there is evidence of an Iron Age settlement on the site, it has only a shadowy connection with Hengist and Horsa (or even, according to Camden, with King Arthur). It emerges into historical importance under the early Norman kings, and in 1190 Richard I assembled his knights here before starting on the Third Crusade. The castle came to be regarded as the 'Key of England', and in 1216, under Hubert de Burgh, successfully withstood a long siege by the Dauphin and King John's rebellious barons. About 1295, however, the town was pillaged by the French. During the Civil War, it was captured in 1642 by the Parliamentarians. Charles II landed here at the Restoration in 1660. Woodrow Wilson, the first President of the United States to visit England, landed at the Admiralty Pier in December 1918.

In the First World War Dover was the headquarters of the Dover Patrol, the naval organisation in which British and American destroyers combined to protect navigation against German submarines and mines. In the Second World War it played a prominent part in the evacuation from Dunkirk, and was one of the first places to be bombed in the Battle of Britain. From 1940 to 1944 the town was under continual shell fire, the casemates of the Castle providing shelter for the population.

The **Straits of Dover**, 17m wide between Dover and Cape Gris Nez, are the narrowest part of the Channel. Here, within sight of the town, the Spanish Armada of 1588 received its first shattering blow. Captain Webb swam from Dover to (21m) Calais in 1875 in 21³/4hrs, and more recently the Straits have been swum many times, mostly in the reverse direction. Louis Blériot was the first man to fly an aeroplane across the Channel (25 July 1909), and the Hon. C.S. Rolls the first to cross and recross in a single flight (1910), but they were preceded by François Blanchard, who flew from Dover to Guines in his dirigible balloon (7 January 1785).

Dover is the chief of the **Cinque Ports**, a system of maritime defence modelled on the 'Saxon Shore' ports of the Romans. The name (pronounced 'Sink') dates back to the 11C or earlier, and the first charter was granted by Edward I in 1278. It named five ports—Dover, Sandwich, Hythe, Romney and Hastings—which, in return for various privileges and immunities, were bound to supply ships for the royal fleet when required. Rye and Winchelsea were added as 'Ancient Towns', and various other places as 'Limbs' or 'Members'. The Cinque Ports are under the nominal jurisdiction of a Lord Warden, whose official residence is at Walmer Castle; the post has been held by William Pitt, the Duke of Wellington and Sir Winston Churchill, and is now held by HM the Queen Mother. Dover is the only original Cinque Port to survive as a flourishing harbour.

**\*Dover Castle** (English Heritage, standard opening and Sunday mornings all year) commands the summit of the cliff E of the town. Motorists reach it from Castle Hill Rd, through *Constable's Tower* (1227). The route passes 'Queen Elizabeth's Pocket Pistol', a bronze cannon 23ft long, presented by Charles V to Henry VIII; it was cast in Utrecht in 1544 and bears a Low Dutch inscription. Pedestrians approach from the bombed Norman church of *St James* at the beginning of Castle Hill Rd and enter through *Canon Gate*. The *Pharos*, perhaps the oldest standing building in England (c AD 50), is a relic of the original Roman fortress; its octagonal belfry was added by Humphrey of Gloucester. The ancient church of *St Mary de Castro*, built of Roman bricks, is Saxon but suffered bad restoration in 1860. The *Keep* was built by Henry II (1181–87), with walls 17–22ft thick. It contains an armoury and a late Norman chapel. Many of the rooms have inscriptions scratched by prisoners of war during Marlborough's campaigns. From the top storey a well descends into the thickness of the wall and down into the cliff for 289ft. There is a fine \*view.

The town is best explored from Market Square, from which Cannon St. leads N. On New St. (left) is the *Roman Painted House* (open), a well-preserved town house with \*wall paintings and an underfloor heating system. *St Mary's Church*, on the right-hand side of Cannon St., has a Norman tower. It contains memorials to the actor Samuel Foote (1720– 77) and the poet Charles Churchill (1732–64), 'the comet of a season', who died at Boulogne. Further N, in Biggin St., is the *Town Hall* incorporating the fine *Maison Dieu Hall* (open), a 14C enlargement of the pilgrims' hostel founded in c 1221 by

Hubert de Burgh; the restored 13C chapel at the E end was changed in the 19C into a Sessions Hall. St Richard of Chichester died in the Maison Dieu. *Maison Dieu House* adjoining, now a public library, is an attractive mansion built in 1665 for the Agent Victualler of the Navy. The *Museum* beside the Town Hall contains local history displays and changing exhibitions.

In Priory Rd, the tiny restored *Chapel of St Edmund*, consecrated in 1253 by St Richard, was formerly attached to the Maison Dieu; dissolved in 1544, it was reconsecrated in 1968. Near Priory Station is *Dover College*, whose buildings include the refectory, dormitory and gatehouse of *St Martin's Priory*, a Benedictine foundation of 1132.

S of Market Square, the main street reaches the harbour at the Promenade. The well laid-out *Marine Parade* (maintained by the Dover Harbour Board) leads in front of *The Gateway* (1961), a long block of flats with interesting garden-mosaic, and continues to the *Eastern Docks*, passing monuments to Captain Webb and C.S. Rolls. Waterloo Crescent, with the White Cliffs Hotel, leads W to the *Prince of Wales Pier*. Beyond the *Commercial Harbour* lies the *Admiralty Pier*, housing the Marine Station; it reaches 1300yd out to sea and its raised promenade commands fine views.

From Marine Parade a path climbs to the *Eastern Heights*, which give an excellent view of the harbour and hoverport. On *North Fall Meadow*, E of the Castle, a memorial marks the spot where Blériot landed. A cliff walk continues past a conspicuous radar station to (3m) the *South Foreland*, with its lighthouse, and (4m) *St Margaret's Bay* (Rte 6).
    The *Western Heights* are occupied by the *Citadel* (now a borstal) and other Napoleonic fortifications. Left of the road near the summit are the foundations of a 12C *Church of the Knights Templar* (English Heritage, open at any reasonable time). Here King John made submission to Pandulf, the Pope's legate, in 1213. A deep cleft separates the Western Heights from *Shakespeare Cliff* (350ft; footpath), so called from traditional association with a famous passage in 'King Lear' (IV, vi). It is approached direct from the town via Limekiln St. and Archcliff Rd; the return from its W end can be made by the beach at low tide.
    From Dover to *Deal*, *Sandwich* and *Ramsgate*, see Rte 6.

# 5  Canterbury

**CANTERBURY** (34,400 inhab.) is not the county town of Kent nor even its largest population centre, but it is certainly its most important ancient city. Its situation on the banks of the Stour at a convenient staging point between London and England's traditional port of entrance at Dover made the growth of a major settlement inevitable. The Roman town became the capital of a Saxon kingdom and, with the arrival of Augustine in 597, this in turn developed into a centre for Christianity in England. With the martyrdom of Thomas Becket in 1170 the importance of both city and cathedral increased, and they became the goal for the most famous of all English medieval pilgrimages. Modern Canterbury has suffered wartime bombing and almost equally disastrous post-war city planning; pedestrianisation of the central streets has done only a little to relieve the congestion caused by the large numbers of tourists. Yet for all this, Canterbury still keeps a prosperous market atmosphere that dates back to Roman times; the cathedral that dominates the visitor's first impression of the city is only the most conspicuous of many buildings, domestic as well as ecclesiastical, which bear witness to its status in the Middle Ages.

**Tourist Information Centre**: 13 Longmarket.

**Car Parks**: Castle Row, Rosemary Lane, Broad St., Watling St. Multi-storey car parks in Castle St. and Gravel Walk.

**Bus Station**: St George's Lane.

**Railway Stations**: Canterbury East, for London via Faversham and for Dover; Canterbury West, for London via Ashford, and for Maidstone and Ramsgate.

**Theatre**: Marlowe Theatre, The Friars.

**Annual Event**: Festival of music and drama in September/October.

**History**. The Roman *Durovernum*, a commercial post at the junction of military roads from Lympne, Dover and Richborough, was renamed *Cantwarabyrig* (borough of the men of Kent) by the Saxons, and about 560 became the capital of Ethelbert, King of Kent. To this court, where the Frankish Queen Bertha was already a Christian, St Augustine and his fellow missionaries were welcomed in 597; the king granted to them and to Bertha the use of a church, and was himself baptised with many of his subjects. In 598 Augustine founded a Benedictine monastery, which became the revered burial place of the kings and early sainted archbishops, afterwards named St Augustine's Abbey. On his later return to England as 'bishop of the English' he established another church which became the first cathedral; a monastery was afterwards organised as the priory of Christ Church by Lanfranc. It was not until the murder of Archbishop Thomas Becket in 1170 and his canonisation three years later that the fame of the cathedral eclipsed that of St Augustine's Abbey and that the ecclesiastical supremacy of the archbishops was definitely established. As 'the holy blissful martyr', St Thomas drew all England and many foreign pilgrims to his miracle-working shrine until its demolition by Henry VIII in 1538. Louis VII of France made the pilgrimage in 1179. The holiday aspect of the pilgrimages is immortalised in Chaucer's 'Canterbury Tales'. The latest reckoning makes the present archbishop, the Most Reverend Robert Runcie DD, the hundred and second in a series including many famous names.

Canterbury was attacked by German aircraft in May and June 1942. The cathedral escaped serious damage, but a large area SE of the centre was destroyed. This quarter was replanned disastrously in the styleless manner of the 1950s with the eccentric conservation of a few church towers. Excavations in the bombed area unearthed the foundations of a Roman theatre (only the second to be identified in Britain). A pre-Roman settlement of c 200 BC and a Saxon colony of the 5C have also been traced, proving a continuous occupation of 2000 years.

**Famous natives, residents and visitors**. Geoffrey Chaucer (c 1343–1400) did not live to complete the poem that would have brought his pilgrims to Canterbury, but he himself was a visitor in his capacity as Clerk of Works to the King when the cathedral nave was being rebuilt. The birthplace of Christopher Marlowe (1564–93) at No. 57 St George's St. was destroyed by bombs in 1942 but the tower of the nearby church where he was baptised still stands. Izaak Walton (1593–1683), of 'The Compleat Angler', was married at St Mildred's Church. The Rev. R.H. Barham (1788–1845), author of 'The Ingoldsby Legends', was born at No. 61 Burgate (destroyed; plaque). Dickens, a frequent visitor, sent David Copperfield to Dr Strong's school in Canterbury and made the Wickfields and Uriah Heep natives of the city; the former Sun Inn, near Christ Church Gate, has been identified with the hotel where the Micawbers stayed. Joseph Conrad (1857–1924) was buried in the Roman Catholic cemetery.

THE CATHEDRAL AND ITS PRECINCTS. The modern approach diverges from the old Dover road, which passed through the city from NW to SE, becoming the High St. in the centre. Rheims Way now channels traffic round the S walls, giving a good view of the cathedral and passing on the left, *St Mildred's Church* and the *Castle* (both described under Stour St. below). We reach the city centre through its rebuilt section.

The best way to reach the cathedral is by following the traditional pilgrims' route from the High St. along Mercery Lane, a little alley

0 — 100 feet
0 — 30 metres

Corona

Henry IV's Chantry

St Andrew's Chapel

Infirmary

Treasury

Trinity Chapel

St Martin's Chapel

St Anselm's Chapel

LIBRARY (over)

St John's Chapel
St Gregory's Chapel

WATER TOWER

N E TRANSEPT

S E TRANSEPT

LIBRARY

LIBRARY PASSAGE

CHAPTER HOUSE

Lady Chapel

St Michael Chapel

N W TRANSEPT

Screen

S W TRANSEPT

SOUTH PORCH

CLOISTER

Font

**Key to Numbers**
1 Abp Benson
2 Orlando Gibbons
3 Abp Peckham
4 Abp Warham
5 Margaret Holland
6 Abp Langton
7 St Augustine's Chair
8 Abp Chichele
9 Abp Bourchier
10 Abp Lang
11 Site of Becket's Shrine
12 Henry IV
13 Dean Wotton
14 Black Prince
15 Abp Courtenay
16 Cardinal Coligny
17 Abp Walter
18 Cardinal Pole
19 Abp Temple
20 Abp Sudbury
21 Abp Kempe

# CANTERBURY CATHEDRAL

once lined with shops and booths selling healing water from Becket's Well in the cathedral crypt, medallions of St Thomas and other souvenirs of pilgrimage. In Butter Market stands the War Memorial of 1921 and the main entrance to the cathedral precincts, *Christ Church Gate*, a beautiful Perp. structure commemorating Arthur, Prince of Wales (1486–1502). It was built in 1517—not 1507, the date mistakenly carved when it was restored in the 1930s. The gates themselves are of c 1662.

The *Cathedral* is the mother church of Anglican Christianity and the seat of the Archibishop of Canterbury, Primate of All England. Its architectural importance, however, does not quite match its ecclesiastical rank. The grandest aspect of the building, undoubtedly, is the exterior. The silhouette of its two low W towers and tall central *tower, all in lovely grey Caen stone, makes a commanding view whether it is seen at close quarters from Christ Church Gate or from the outskirts of the city (Rheims Way or the walls by the Dane John Gardens, for example). The inside of the cathedral lacks any feature as striking and its interest lies mainly in details, like the excellent stained glass and the profusion of tombs. Unfortunately, appreciation of them is made difficult by the crowds of visitors and the distinctly commercial atmosphere.

Despite its long history and continuous importance, the cathedral as it stands today is largely the creation of two distinct periods: 1070–1184 and 1391–1505. The oldest parts are fragments of the church raised by Lanfranc, the first Norman archbishop (1070–89), on the ruins of Augustine's original church. This hasty reconstruction quickly proved too small and was replaced with a grander building, supervised by Priors Ernulf and Conrad, between 1096 and 1130. The next stage in the cathedral's history came in the wake of Thomas Becket's murder in 1170 and his canonisation three years later. The French mason William of Sens and his successor, William the Englishman, added the E transepts and remodelled the E end in honour of the saint (1175–84). For some 200 years the cathedral remained in this state, until 1391, when Henry Yevele began to replace the unambitious nave and W transepts which had survived from Lanfranc's time. The work was finished with the completion of Bell Harry, the noble Perp. central tower, by John Wastell in 1505.

The main entrance is by the *S Porch* (1418), probably built to commemorate the English victory at Agincourt in 1415, but a tour of the interior best starts from the W end. Yevele's *Nave* has lost its original stained glass but still impresses by its lightness, its stately simplicity and by the vista it offers towards the E, where a flight of steps ascends to the choir screen and a second flight approaching the altar can be glimpsed beyond. Under the NW tower is the 'Corinthian Throne' (1704) carved by Grinling Gibbons. In the N aisle are the ornate font (1639) and Nicholas Stone's monument to the organist and composer Orlando Gibbons, who died suddenly on his way through Canterbury in 1625. An elaborate 15C screen, with the crowned figures of six monarchs and its original iron gates, separates the nave and choir.

From this spot we get a good view of Yevele's *West* (or *Nave*) *Transepts* with their great *windows. The NW window was donated by Edward IV (d. 1483), who is portrayed in the glass; the SW window has 15C tracery and glass, with some 12C glass from the clerestory of the choir. The NW transept was the scene of Becket's martyrdom. The four knights who murdered him entered by the door from the cloisters, and a slab in the pavement marks the spot where the archbishop is believed to have fallen. The adjoining *Lady Chapel* is late Perp. (1449–68) with rich fan vaulting. St Michael's Chapel, the corresponding chapel in the SW transept, has a fine group of monuments, notably those to Margaret Holland (d. 1437) and Archbishop Stephen Langton, who helped the barons persuade King John to sign Magna Carta in 1215.

The *Choir*, among the longest in England, was built by William of Sens in a mixture of Norman and EE styles. It narrows at the E end to preserve the Norman side chapels, and is separated from the aisles by beautiful and unusual *screens alternating with canopied tombs. The *Choir Aisles* and the *East* (or *Choir*) *Transepts* are mainly the work of Ernulf and Conrad, altered by William of Sens. They are rich in stained glass and monuments. A 15C fresco of the life of St Eustace can be seen on the wall by the NE transept, while St Anselm's Chapel (off the S choir aisle) has a 12C wall painting of St Paul on Malta.

The part of the cathedral E of the choir was built wholly in honour of St Thomas. Until its destruction in 1538 his shrine stood behind the High Altar in the *Trinity Chapel*, with lovely columns of coloured marble. The stained-glass *windows (1220–30) depict miracles performed by the saint. Immediately behind the High Altar is the so-called *'St Augustine's Chair', probably dating from Langton's time, in which Archbishops of Canterbury have traditionally been enthroned. Between the N piers is the resplendent *tomb of Henry IV (d. 1413) and his second wife, Joan of Navarre (d. 1437); between the piers on the S side are the tomb and effigy of Edward, the Black Prince (d. 1376), with modern reproductions of his armour. At the extreme E end of the building is the delightful circular *Corona*, added by William the Englishman, with a fine 13C window.

The lofty and spacious *Crypt*, entered from the SW or NW transept, is the main survival of Ernulf and Conrad's work, with vigorous Norman carving on the capitals of the pillars and their ornamental shafts. Especially fine is the central pillar of St Gabriel's Chapel in the SE corner; the apse preserves its *paintings of c 1130. A chapel in the S aisle is walled off to form a 'Temple' for French Protestants, who have worshipped here since 1568; it includes the beautiful Black Prince's Chantry, donated in thanks for the dispensation of 1363 that allowed him to marry his kinswoman Joan, the 'Fair Maid of Kent'. Of the same period and perhaps from the same donor is the exquisite stone screen in the adjoining chapel of Our Lady of the Undercroft. The late 12C *Crypt* beneath the Trinity Chapel and the Corona includes the site of the chapel where St Thomas was first buried; on 12 July 1174 Henry II completed his penance for the murder here. It now houses *remains from the Saxon church at Reculver (see Rte 6), two 7C columns and fragments of a stone cross.

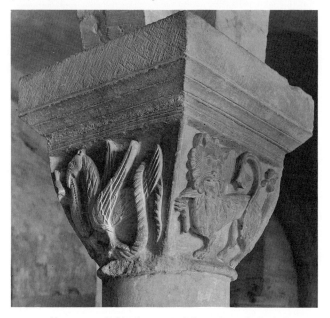

*Norman capital in the crypt of Canterbury Cathedral*

On the N side of the cathedral are the extensive monastic buildings. The Benedictine monastery founded by St Augustine was enlarged and converted into a priory by Lanfranc, and much altered and rebuilt by later archbishops. The *Great Cloister* (1397–1414) is entered from the NW transept. Though mainly Perp., it incorporates some fine Norman work and beautiful EE arcading in the N walk, cut into by the Perp. vaulting. The painted vault *bosses, which include over 800 shields, are superb; one, in the E walk, portrays Yevele, the architect. Opening off the E walk is the spacious *Chapter House*, whose lower part is the work of Prior Eastry (1304– 20), completed by Chillenden when he began the cloisters. T.S. Eliot's 'Murder in the Cathedral' was commissioned for performance here in 1935. To the NE is the rebuilt *Chapter Library* (1954), replacing a building destroyed in 1942. In the *Dark Entry*, between this and the chapter house, are two fine ranges of pillars of Lanfranc's time, some with incised decoration; these and the pillar bases in the lawn beyond the modern arcade of the library were part of the sub-vault of the *Dormitory*. We emerge in the *Infirmary Cloister*, passing on the right a door into the crypt and a stair to the NE transept. On the left is the elaborate Norman sub-vault of the *Lavatory Tower*, part of the ingenious water-supply system of Prior Wibert (1151–67); the upper floor is Perp. The cloister is continued by the 13C sub-vault of the *Prior's Chapel*; the chapel itself was replaced after 1660 by the brick Howley Library.

The infirmary cloister is prolonged N by a passage below the Wolfson Library (1966) to *Prior Sellingegate* (c 1480) and the Green Court. On the E side of this square stands the *Deanery*, mixed medieval and 16C; in the SW corner is the *Archdeaconry* with a curious wooden pentice (or lean-to) of 1390 in its garden. To the E of this the *Larder Gate Building* (1951) incorporates a 15C archway and part of the monastic kitchens. This, with all the remaining buildings in the square, belongs to the **King's School**, a monastic foundation of the 7C, installed on this site by Henry VIII as a grammar school for boys. Christopher Marlowe, William Harvey, Walter Pater and Somerset Maugham were pupils here. The monastic *Brewhouse* and *Bakehouse* (1303) are incorporated in the N range. In the NW corner of the Green Court the exterior *Norman Staircase* (1151–67) leading to the hall is unique and still supremely beautiful, despite the modern roof. Through the adjacent *Court Gate* we enter the *Mint Yard*, the former Almonry. Hence the North Gate opens on Palace St., named from the Archbishop's Palace destroyed by Puritans c 1643. From then until the completion of the present modest palace on the old site in 1901, the archbishops had no official residence in Canterbury.

Returning to the Prior's Chapel, we turn E where a stately row of Norman arches marks the hall of the *Infirmary*. The more ornate arches, still further E are remains of the 14C *Infirmary Chapel*. On the right of the hall is the arcaded Norman *Treasury*, while the *Choir School* on the left incorporates a refectory of 1343. Passing round the unfinished exterior of the Corona, we join the path skirting the S side of the cathedral. This leads across the former lay cemetery, which extended from the S Porch to the exquisitely arcaded *St Anselm's Tower* and was there divided by a wall from the monks' cemetery. The grandeur and fine colouring of the SE transept are very striking from this point. Opposite the E end of the cathedral is an old walled garden, now the site of the *Kent War Memorial* (by Sir Herbert Baker). On its E side is a bastion of the old city wall, transformed into a chapel of silence, with a cenotaph, flags and inscriptions. A gate opens into Broad St., where a fine stretch of the medieval city wall still stands.

FROM THE CATHEDRAL TO ST AUGUSTINE'S ABBEY AND LONGPORT. Lady Wooton's Green leads from the opposite side of Broad St. to *St Augustine's College* (not normally open), founded for missionaries in 1848 and now occupied by the King's School. It covers part of the site of **St Augustine's Abbey**, incorporating *Fyndon's Gate* (1300–09), the great gate of the monastery, as its main entrance, as well as parts of the guest hall and, further S, the badly restored *Cemetery Gate* (1390). The remaining college buildings follow the medieval plan and are the first major work of William Butterfield. The excavated *ruins of the abbey churches and cloister (English Heritage, standard opening) are reached from Longport.

The original Abbey of St Peter and St Paul, founded by St Augustine in 598 had three separate 7C churches in line. In 978 St Dunstan rededicated the abbey to the founder, and in 1049–59 Abbot Wulfric began to link the two W churches by a rotunda on the model of St-Bénigne at Dijon. All this work was demolished by the first Norman abbot, who in 1073 started a new church, completed c 1120.

The abbey, which to the time of Becket ranked as the second Benedictine house in Europe, was destroyed in 1538 and a royal posting house built on the site. This was visited by Elizabeth I, Charles I (who received his bride here in June 1625) and Charles II.

The N part of the first church (*St Peter and St Paul*) lies beneath a low protective roof. King Ethelbert, Queen Bertha, St Augustine and at least eight of his early successors were buried in it, and the empty tombs of St Lawrence, St Mellitus and St Justus have been identified. The massive octagonal foundations of *Abbot Wulfric's Rotunda* are prominent to the SE. Of the *Norman church* the NW wall of the nave still stands, with Tudor additions of the 'King's House', and much of the crypt of the apsidal choir. *St Pancras*, the easternmost of the three 7C churches, built of Roman bricks, had its E end altered c 1387.

Longport continues E past, on the left, the *County Gaol* of 1808 and, on the right, the *Hospital of John Smith* (1657). After ½m we reach **˙St Martin's Church**, in use for Christian services before the coming of St Augustine, possibly on the site of a Romano-British church.

St Martin's Hill was occupied by Roman villas in the 4C, and possibly part of a pre-Christian building exists in the W part of the chancel S wall, especially the square-headed archway; the round-headed doorway is probably early Saxon. The nave, of Kentish rag, is plastered in the Roman fashion; the tower is 14C. Within, the 13C chancel arch and subsequent restorations obscure the antiquity of what is one of the earliest extant churches in Europe. A Norman piscina at the SE corner of the nave is beautiful in its simplicity, but most interesting is the tub-shaped ˙font, the lower part possibly of Saxon origin, but too late to be that in which Ethelbert was baptised. On the N wall is a 16C carving of St Martin.

FROM BURGATE TO WESTGATE. We re-enter the walls by Burgate. On the left is the tower of the ruined *St Mary Magdalene*, which preserves a striking memorial to John Whitfield (d. 1691). To the left, further on, the Longmarket shopping precinct covers the remains of a *Roman House* (open), with a fine mosaic pavement. On St George's St. beyond stands the tower of the bombed church of *St George*, where Marlowe was baptised (tablet). St George's St. continues as High St. On the left side is *Queen Elizabeth's Guest Chamber*, a splendid Tudor house of 1573 with colourful pargetting, now a restaurant. Further, on the right, is the *Beaney Institute*, housing the *Royal Museum and Art Gallery*.

The disused church in St Margaret's St., leading to the left, houses the *Canterbury Pilgrims' Way*, an exhibition which seeks to bring Chaucer's 'Canterbury Tales' to life with the same gimmicks of presentation used by the Jorvik Viking Centre in York.

Further on, Stour St. also leads left from High St. The picturesque *Greyfriars* (not open at time of writing) was the first Franciscan friary in England, founded in 1267 and consecrated in 1325. In the 17C the Cavalier and poet Richard Lovelace lived here for a time. Further along Stour St. are the greatly altered 14C buildings of the *Poor Priests' Hospital*, now the *Museum of Canterbury's Heritage*. It displays treasures from excavations in the Roman, Saxon and medieval town, among them a Roman hoard of silver spoons, a Saxon cross and badges worn by medieval pilgrims. A more recent exhibit is Stephenson's *Invicta* steam engine (1830), used on the Canterbury–Whitstable railway. Stour St. continues to *St Mildred's Church*, still showing its Saxon origins despite 19C restoration. Izaak Walton was married here in 1626.

The detour can be lengthened by following Gas St., opposite the church, to the keep of the *Castle* (c 1175). Beyond, in the angle of the city walls, here offering a fine ˙view of the cathedral, are the gardens of the *Dane John*. The obelisk on the Dane John itself (an unexplained tumulus 80ft high) commemorates the laying out of the grounds in 1790.

Best Lane, a right turn from the High St. opposite the junction with Stour St., leads to the 13–14C refectory and undercroft of *Blackfriars*, now a Christian

Science church (occasionally open). The refectory was for a time used as a Baptist chapel, in which Defoe is said to have preached in 1724.

Beyond the Post Office is the *Hospital of St Thomas*, or *Eastbridge Hospital* (open), a well-preserved hostel founded in 1180 for poor pilgrims, with a fine chapel and crypt, and a hall with an early 13C Christ in Majesty, painted in tempera. The street crosses a branch of the Stour and changes its name to St Peter's St. Overlooking the river on the right are the *Weavers' Houses*, heavily restored Tudor buildings now converted into shops, once occupied by the Huguenots who settled in Canterbury after the revocation of the Edict of Nantes (1685). At the end of St Peter's St., with the 13C *St Peter's Church* on the right, we see the imposing **Westgate**, only

*Westgate, Canterbury*

survivor of the seven city gates, which was built probably by Henry Yevele (1375–81). The guard chamber (open) contains a collection of arms and armour, fetters, a scold bridle, etc., and there is a good view from the top of the tower. The church of the *Holy Cross* (c 1380), just inside the gate, is now the *Guildhall*; to the left are the attractive *Westgate Gardens*, with a tower of the city wall.

Outside the gate the old London road, here called St Dunstan's St., passes on the right the old *Falstaff Inn* (now a restaurant), which was a hostelry for pilgrims arriving after the city gates were closed. On the left, beyond, a 16C house claims to be the home of Agnes Wickfield in Dickens's 'David Copperfield'. Further on is the 13C *St Dunstan's Church*, with the Roper vault containing the head of the sainted Sir Thomas More (1478–1535), given to his daughter Margaret Roper after 14 days' exposure on London Bridge. A brick archway opposite is the only relic of the Ropers' house.

FROM CANTERBURY TO FOLKESTONE by the Elham Valley, 20m via B2065, a winding but pretty road.—To (5½m) *Bishopsbourne*, see Rte 4. B2065 skirts Charlton Park as it branches right from A2.—7½m. *Barham*, a pleasant little village.—12½m. *Elham* (pronounced 'Eelam') has a pretty square with a fine 12–15C church. Among the interesting contents are: a 15C alabaster triptych (one panel restored), 15C and 16C stained glass, and some good 20C fittings. The Abbot's Fireside (1614; now a hotel) has an elaborate carved fireplace of 1624.—At (13½m) *Lyminge* the church (c 965) adjoins the foundations of a 7C nunnery founded by Eadburg (Ethelburga), daughter of Ethelbert.—20m. *Folkestone*, see Rte 7.—The direct road from Canterbury to Folkestone (A260; 17m) diverges from the Dover road beyond Broome Park and crosses the pleasant upland common called *Swingfield Minnis*. A sideroad leads left to *St John's Commandery*, a medieval chapel of the Knights Hospitallers later converted into a farmhouse (English Heritage, access for pre-arranged parties only).

FROM CANTERBURY TO MARGATE (16m; A28) and RAMSGATE (16½m; A28 and A253).—To the S of (2½m) *Sturry* is *Fordwich*, the old port of Canterbury when the Stour was navigable, where the Caen stone for the cathedral was landed. The ancient town hall has a ducking stool.—At (9m) *Sarre* A253 diverges right for *Ramsgate* (Rte 6), passing 1m N of *Minster*, where the grand *church has a fine Norman tower and nave and an EE chancel. Nearby is Minster Abbey (now occupied by Benedictine nuns; open). The W range dates from the late 11C or early 12C, and this incorporates the W end of the abbey church (with a spiral staircase in the tower); excavations have revealed the plan of the church, which can be seen marked out in the ground. A groin-vaulted passage and chapel are also shown. From Sarre the Margate road, A28, continues NE.—(10m) *St Nicholas-at-Wade* and (16m) *Margate*, see Rte 6.

From Canterbury to *Ashford*, see Rte 7.

# 6   London to Dover via Margate, Ramsgate and the Isle of Thanet

Total distance 98m. A2, A207 and A2 again to (46m) Faversham (bypassed) and (48m) Brenley Corner, see Rte 4.—A299 to (56m) Whitstable and (60m) Herne Bay (both bypassed).—A299, A28 to (72m) **Margate**.—A255 to (75m) Broadstairs and (76½m) **Ramsgate**.—A253, A256 to (83½m) Sandwich (bypassed).—A258 to (89½m) Deal and (8m) **Dover** (Rte 4).

Maps: OS Landranger 178, 179.

This alternative to Rte 4 reaches Dover by a longer and less direct route, avoiding Canterbury and instead following the 'Saxon Shore' round the Kent coast. The roads approaching Margate and Ramsgate are crowded in summer, particularly at weekends.

We begin by following Rte 4 to (46m) *Faversham* (bypassed) and the roundabout at (48m) *Brenley Corner*, where we diverge NE towards the coast on A299.

Some interesting villages flank the road. *Hernhill*, ³/₄m to the right at 48¹/₂m, has a charming little green with a typical Wealden house, the Red Lion, on one side and a Perp. church on the other. At *Graveney*, 2m left at 53m, the church is mainly 14C, with a Norman chancel, oak roof, early 16C rood screen and several brasses, among them a large one to John Martyn (d. 1436).

A299 skirts the seaside resorts of (56m) *Whitstable* and (60m) *Herne Bay*. Whitstable (27,900 inhab.; Tourist Information), noted for its oysters, faces the Isle of Sheppey. Herne Bay (27,500 inhab.; Tourist Information) has a more attractive seafront with an esplanade of 1830. The pier was wrecked by a storm in 1978. At *Reculver*, on the coast 2m off our road at 62m and approached by an ugly caravan site, we enter the **Isle of Thanet**.

This exposed NE corner of Kent, the vulnerable tip of the 'Saxon Shore' which the Romans defended against pirates, is called an isle because its western boundary, the river Wantsum, joins the Stour in the S and once formed a continuous navigable channel linking Reculver and Richborough. The Romans used it as part of the regular water route from Boulogne (*Bononia*) to London, and built forts at Reculver (*Regulbium*) and Richborough (*Rutupiae*).

Inside the walls of the Roman fort at Reculver stand the bleak but impressive 12C towers that survive from the church established here in 669 (English Heritage, standard opening hours from June to August). The rest of the Saxon church was demolished in 1809, though its ground plan is marked.

*The towers of Reculver church*

A299 joins A298 near (66m) *St Nicholas-at-Wade*, whose church has EE carvings on Norman arches.—68m. *Birchington* is a resort now joined to Margate. The 13–14C church has brasses in the Quex chapel; also the Crispe mural monument (1651) with its six busts by J. Marshall, and a bust of Anna Crisp (d. 1708) by William Palmer. Dante Gabriel Rossetti, who died here in 1882 at a house pulled down in 1963, is commemorated by a Celtic cross in the churchyard (by Ford Madox Brown) and a window in the S aisle (by Frederic James Shields).

½m SE lies *Quex House* (open), a building of 1813 replacing the one that William III used as a stage on his journeys to and from Holland. Its grounds contain two 19C tower follies and the *Powell-Cotton Museum* of natural history and ethnography. At *Acol*, ½m further S, is the chalk pit of 'The Smuggler's Leap' ('The Ingoldsby Legends').

72m. **MARGATE** (53,300 inhab.) is one of the most popular seaside resorts in England, enjoying fine sands and fresh breezes off the North Sea.

**Tourist Information Centre**: Marine Terrace.

**Car Parks**: Seaview Terrace, Marine Terrace, Cecil Square, The Parade, Trinity Square.

**Buses**: bus stops in Canterbury Rd (Westbrook), The Harbour and Eastern Esplanade (Cliftonville).

**Railway Station**: Station Rd, S of Marine Terrace.

**Amusements**: Winter Gardens Theatre and Queens Hall (holiday shows); amusement park in Marine Terrace.

**History**. Once a packet station for Flushing, Margate saw the embarkation of the Elector Frederick V (King of Bohemia) and Elizabeth Stuart after their marriage in 1613. William III and the Duke of Marlborough frequently used its harbour. In 1588 Lord Howard of Effingham and Sir Francis Drake wrote despatches from 'Meregate' after the defeat of the Spanish Armada. Margate grew into a resort in the 18C, when sea-bathing first became fashionable. The bathing-machine was invented in 1753 by Benjamin Beale, a local Quaker. Until the coming of the railway visitors from London made the journey down the Thames estuary in 'Margate hoys', ships modelled after the Thames sailing barges.

The handsome quarter on the cliffs E of the old town is known as *Cliftonville*, while to the W is *Westbrook*. A favourite spot, beside the sands and seafront, is the *Jetty* (1240ft long). The pier by Rennie (1810–15) was totally destroyed in the great storm of January 1978. In the old town is the flint church of *St John* (partly 12C) rich in brasses, of which the most striking is the skeleton commemorating Richard Notfelde (d. 1446). In King St. is a restored Tudor house (open). King St. continues inland as Dane Rd, where, at the foot of Grotto Hill, we find the *Grotto* (open), fantastically decorated with shells. Despite the claims made for its great antiquity, it is apparently a late 18C or early 19C folly.

*Kingsgate*, 3m E via B2052, is where Charles II landed in 1683 on his way from London to Dover. An imitation Norman castle (now flats) was built here by Lord Holland in 1760. Beyond, across the bay, is the *North Foreland* (lighthouse), the *Promontorium Acantium* of the Romans, off which Monk defeated De Ruyter in 1666.
From Margate to *Canterbury*, see Rte 5.

A254 leads directly to Ramsgate. Our route takes A255 SE via (75m) **Broadstairs** (Tourist Information), a quiet resort but also an expanding residential town (23,400 inhab.). Harbour St. leads down to the charming bay through *York Gate*, a flint arch built in 1540 to protect the 'stair' or gap in the low white cliffs.

Dickens described Broadstairs as 'one of the freest and freshest little places in the world'; tablets mark the houses associated with him. In one of them, *Archway House* spanning Harbour St., he wrote part of 'Barnaby Rudge'. At *Bleak House*, on top of the cliff above the pier and commanding a fine view, he planned the novel after which it was renamed and wrote much of 'David Copperfield'. Now the *Dickens and Maritime Museum*, it has a good collection of Dickensiana, including the lectern he used for public readings. *Dickens House* (open), at the W end of Victoria Parade, has been identified with the home of Betsey Trotwood, though 'David Copperfield' locates it near Dover. Its exhibition traces Dickens's connection with Broadstairs. At *Pierremont Hall* Queen Victoria stayed in 1829.

76½m. **RAMSGATE** (38,200 inhab.), a port and resort spreading over two chalk cliffs and the 'gate' or valley between them, faces S and so is more sheltered than Margate.

**Tourist Information Centre**: Argyle Centre, Queen St.

**Car Parks**: Harbour Parade, Victoria Parade and off High St.

**Railway Station**: off the Margate road (A254).

**Ferry Terminal**: daily sailings to Dunkerque.

**Amusements**: Granville Theatre, on the E Cliff; Argyle Centre, Queen St.; casino and amusement park on seafront.

**History**. Here Heine stayed in 1827, Elizabeth Fry died in 1845, and Van Gogh taught in a school in 1876. In 1914–18 Ramsgate came next after Dunkirk and Calais as a target for German bombardment (119 air raids), while in 1940 it was one of the chief bases for the evacuation of the British Army from Dunkirk.

The *Harbour*, with an obelisk (1821) recording the departure from Ramsgate of George IV to Hanover, is of growing commercial importance, especially for the import of cars. The yacht marina has berths for 500 craft.

At the end of W Cliff is the RC church of *St Augustine*, now part of a monastery, which A.W.N. Pugin paid for and considered his best work (1845–50). The interior, in Whitby stone, is one of the finest of its date. It has a monument to Pugin, who is buried here. The church stands next to the house he designed for himself, the *Grange*, where he died in 1852. On E Cliff is the early 19C Wellington Crescent, the gigantic Granville Hotel by E.W. Pugin and, at the end of the seafront, the King George IV memorial park. *St George's Church* (1824–27), off High St., has a conspicuous tower and light interior.

From Ramsgate we take A253 W, passing the suburb of *St Lawrence*, with a 13–15C church and Norman tower. At 78½m we follow A256 S, which skirts *Pegwell Bay*, famous for its fossils and the subject of a celebrated Victorian painting by William Dyce.

Beside the road is a Danish longship which was built and sailed in 1949 to celebrate the 1500th anniversary of the landing of Hengist and Horsa at Ebbsfleet (see below). ½m further, a sideroad leads right to (1m) *St Augustine's Cross* (English Heritage, open at any reasonable time), erected in 1884 to commemorate his landing in 597. However, the exact landing place may have been at the now vanished *Stonar* across the Stour from Sandwich.

Beyond (80½m) *Ebbsfleet* the skyline is dominated by the huge power station (1963) of *Richborough*, in a loop of the Stour, now an industrial estate but originally created in 1916 as a war-transport depot. At 82½m we leave A256 to cross the Stour by a toll bridge of 1797 into (83½m) **Sandwich** (4200 inhab.; seasonal Tourist Information). This charming medieval town, still largely contained within its ancient limits, was one of the original Cinque Ports (see Dover, Rte 4), though it now lies 2m from the sea. Becket landed here in 1170 after his self-imposed exile in France, as did Richard Coeur de Lion in 1194 after his Austrian imprisonment. Thomas Paine lived in New St. for a year as a master stay-maker.

On the Quay are the *Fisher Gate* and part of the town walls, continued further W with a fine raised promenade. The Tudor gate-tower gave its name to the *Barbican* theatre. The attractive Upper Strand St. has the Old Customs House and, at the end, a large house (1911) designed by Lutyens. We may turn right to reach *St Clement's*, on higher ground, an EE church with a low arcaded Norman tower and many interesting internal features. The fine High St. leads back towards the centre and (left) *St Peter's*, which dates from the end of the 13C, with later additions. Beyond is the Cattle Market with the *Guildhall*, much extended in 1910. It contains a 17C courtroom and a museum. Further N, in Strand St., is *St Mary's* founded in the early 12C (restored). The *King's Arms* is a timber-framed house of 1592. Beyond is *Manwood Court* (c 1580), the fine former grammar-school building.

A257 leads W out of Sandwich and, in half a mile, a sideroad leads right to (1m) *Richborough Castle*, on the Stour (English Heritage, standard opening). This is probably where the Romans landed in AD 43. A fort was built here to guard *Rutupiae*, the chief Roman port on the E coast of England until the end of the occupation. In the late 3C it became an important fort of the 'Saxon Shore'. The ruins include the S, W and N walls of the Saxon Shore fort, in places 25ft high. At the W Gate, Watling St., the Roman road from Canterbury, enters the fort. Within the walls are remains from Roman and Saxon times (1–3C AD), including the cruciform foundations of a large monument built to commemorate the final conquest of England in AD 81–96, a Saxon church dedicated to St Augustine, and defensive ditches, etc. A small museum contains interesting objects found during excavations. To the S is the site of a Roman amphitheatre (also English Heritage, open at any reasonable time).

Among the sandhills overlooking *Sandwich Bay*, 2½m E of the town, are the magnificent *Royal St George's* and the *Prince's Golf Links*. Further N, at the mouth of the Stour, is *Shellness* nature reserve.

89½m. **Deal** (26,000 inhab.; Tourist Information), a 'limb' of the Cinque Ports, is a quiet coastal town with excellent streets of 18C houses parallel to the sea. *Old* or *Upper Deal* lies inland; St Leonard's Church has a late Norman aisled nave. Deal or its immediate vicinity is believed to be the scene of Julius Caesar's landing in 55 BC, and William Penn sailed from here in 1682 on his first voyage to America. *Deal Castle* (English Heritage, standard opening) is the most intricate of the three castles built by Henry VIII to protect the safe anchorage of the Downs (see below). It is well preserved with good vaulted chambers and galleries. The scant remains of *Sandown Castle* lie to the N, and beyond, the famous *Royal Cinque Ports Golf Course*.

Off the coast lie the *Goodwin Sands*, a series of dangerous sandbanks about 10m in length, marked by lightships and exposed at low water. According to the legend, these were once the fruitful island of Lomea, which was submerged by a furious storm in the 11C, owing to the fact that the stones intended to strengthen its sea-wall were used by the abbot of St Augustine's for the tower of Tenterden church. The *Downs*, the famous roadstead between the Goodwin Sands and the coast, form a natural refuge, not too safe in strong gales from the S, when the traditional hardihood of the Walmer lifeboatmen is often called upon to help ships in distress. In the great storm of November 1954, the South Goodwin lightship was lost and in that of January 1978 Deal was extensively flooded.

90½m. *Walmer* adjoins Deal to the S. *Walmer Castle*, the third built in this area by Henry VIII, was converted c 1730 into the official residence of the Lord Warden of the Cinque Ports (English Heritage, standard opening but closed Mondays and when Lord Warden is in residence). The Duke of Wellington, who succeeded Lord Liverpool in the office in 1829, died here in 1852; his furnished apartments have been preserved.

At 92½m B2058 diverges left for (1¾m) *St Margaret's at Cliffe*, on steep wooded cliffs in the lee of the South Foreland. The old church in the landward part of the village is a good example of Norman work. On the E horn of *St Margaret's Bay* stands the Dover Patrol Monument, a tall granite obelisk unveiled in 1921. Companion monuments have been erected at Cap Blanc Nez and in New York Harbour. There is a pleasant walk along the cliffs, part of the Saxon Shore Way, back to (4m) Walmer via *Kingsdown*.

98m. **Dover**, see Rte 4.

# 7 London to Dover via Maidstone and Folkestone

Total distance 78m. The route starts on A2 and quickly changes to A20, which is followed for the rest of the way.—To (4m) New Cross.—To (19m) Farningham.—To (27m) Wrotham Heath.—To (35m) **Maidstone**.—To (54m) **Ashford**.—To (71m) **Folkestone**.—To (78m) **Dover** (Rte 4).

Maps: OS Landranger 177, 188, 189 and (briefly) 179.

M20 offers a fast but uninteresting alternative to A20 from (17m) Swanley, at M25, to Folkestone.

We leave London by A2 (Old Kent Rd), turning right on to A20 at (4m) *New Cross* and passing through suburbs.—19m. *Farningham*, just beyond M25, is a pleasant village on the Darent. Its EE church has a Perp. tower.

A225 runs S from Farningham to (9m) Sevenoaks through typical Kentish scenery. At (1m) *Eynsford* are the ruins of a small Norman castle of c 1100, with a high curtain wall but no keep (English Heritage, open at any reasonable time). Opposite the partly Norman church a sideroad crosses the Darent by a stone bridge and leads under a graceful railway viaduct to (½m) **Lullingstone Roman Villa** (English Heritage, scheduled to reopen in 1989, opening hours not announced). It is one of the most spectacular Roman villas in England. Excavations have disclosed fine mosaic pavements in the reception rooms (as well as three marble busts now in the British Museum). The painted wall plaster which has been pieced together reveals the existence of the earliest known place of Christian worship in Britain (4C). On a hillside above the site an important Romano-British pagan funerary temple of AD 300 was uncovered in 1958. A private road continues to *Lullingstone Castle* (open). The large brick gatehouse (c 1497) announces the Tudor origins of the house, though they are concealed beneath very elegant remodelling of the Queen Anne period. The church in the grounds has fine tombs of the Hart Dyke family.—A225 continues S, passing (on the right at 4m) *Shoreham*, with a late Perp. church.—At (5½m) *Otford* are the remains of a 16C manor house of the Archbishops of Canterbury. To the left runs the so-called *Pilgrims' Way*, originally a British track, following the S slope of the Downs and giving fine views.—9m. *Sevenoaks*, Rte 9A.

N of Farningham A225 descends the Darent valley to (4m) *Dartford* (Rte 4).—At (2m) *Sutton-at-Hone* the church has a monument to Sir Thomas Smyth (1558?–1625), grandly remembered as 'Governor of the East Indian and Other Companies, Treasurer of the Virginian Plantation and sometime Ambassador to the Emperor and Great Duke of Russia and Muscovy'. The house of St John's Jerusalem (12–18C) incorporates the 13C chapel of a Commandery of the

*Mosaic pavement at Lullingstone Roman villa*

Knights Hospitallers (NT, chapel and garden open). The 10–12C church of *Darenth* (³/₄m NE), partly constructed of Roman materials, has a priest's chamber above the vaulted chancel and a curious font of c 1140.

A20 passes near (21¹/₂m; left) *Brands Hatch* motor-racing circuit and at 25m descends the notorious Wrotham Hill.—26m. *Wrotham*, pronounced 'Rootam', is an attractive village with an early 14C church.

A227 leads right to (1m) *Borough Green* railway station and A25 continues to (2m) *Ightham* (pronounced 'Item'), with interesting monuments in its church. *Oldbury* (NT), ¹/₂m W on the N side of A25, is a large Iron Age hill-fort. Off A227 2¹/₂m S of Ightham is *Ightham Mote* (NT). Built in the early 14C, it is everything a picturesque manor house should be: a comfortable square of timber and stone enclosing a court and surrounded by a moat. We enter by the gatehouse, whose lower part is 14C but whose upper floors, like the S and W wings, were built in the mid 15C. On the opposite side of the cobbled yard stands the Great Hall, which dates from the 14C, though its large Perp. window was added c 1521 and the oak panelling was designed by the 19C architect Norman Shaw. To the N are more Tudor additions, notably the chapel with a fine painted roof.—We return to A227, where a sideroad leads E in ³/₄m to the pleasant village of *Plaxtol*. 1m E is *Old Soar Manor* (English Heritage, summer standard opening), a fine example of the solar end of a knight's manor house of c 1290, now attached to an 18C house.—A227 continues S to (5m) *Shipbourne*, a village of considerable character and a birthplace of the poet Christopher Smart (1722–71).—For (8m) *Tonbridge*, see Rte 9A.

A20 passes M20 and M26 and reaches (27m) *Wrotham Heath*, where it is joined by A25 from Sevenoaks. 2m S via B2016 are *Great Comp Gardens* (open) laid out since the 1950s by the owners of the 17C house.—29m. *West Malling*, a pleasant 18C village, preserves the ruins of a Benedictine abbey, founded in 1090 by Bishop Gundulf of

Rochester (open on request, but with the restrictions of a closed Order); a new abbey church was consecrated here in 1966. *St Leonard's Tower*, beyond the end of the High St., dates from c 1080 (English Heritage, open at any reasonable time). About 1m W is *Offham*, where the green has a quintain (or post used as a mark in tilting practice), the only one to survive in England.

*Leybourne Castle* (now the wing of a 20C house), 1/2m N on A228, was the home of William de Leybourne (d. 1310), England's first admiral; he is remembered by a tablet in the church.— *Clare House* (1793), in an attractive park, is on the old road linking West Malling with (2m) *East Malling*, which has a 14–15C church, and an important Fruit Research Station (open by appointment) in Bradbourne House (rebuilt 1715).

31 1/2m. *Ditton*. A sideroad (narrow bridge) leads left for Aylesford (see below). Just beyond, the M20 may be joined to bypass Maidstone.

35m. **MAIDSTONE** (71,800 inhab.), the congested county town and agricultural centre of Kent, with paper mills and breweries, lies on both banks of the Medway. It is an important shopping centre; some of the streets off the High Street, all with interesting old houses, have been closed to traffic.

**Tourist Information Centre**: The Gatehouse, Old Palace Gardens, Mill St.

**Car Parks**: King St., Stoneborough Centre, Medway St., College Rd, Mote Rd.

**Bus Station**: Palace Avenue.

**Railway Stations**: Maidstone East, off Sandling Rd (A229), and Maidstone West, off Tonbridge Rd (A26).

**River Cruises**: Undercliffe Boathouse (near the Tourist Information Centre) down the Medway to Allington Lock (see below), from Easter to October.

**Theatre**: Hazlitt Theatre, Earl St.

**Annual Event**: Kent County Show in July at Detling Showground, 2m NE via A249.

On the E bank of the Medway, a little S of the bridge, is the fine large church of *All Saints* (Perp.), chiefly built by Archbishop Courtenay (d. 1396) in connection with a secular *College* (suppressed in 1547), which can be seen to the S through a vaulted gate-tower. The church contains good sedilia and stalls (with misericords), a carved chancel screen (1886), the canopied tomb of Dr Wotton, first Master of the College (1417), with a wall painting of him being presented to the Virgin by Saints and a memorial (S wall) to Laurence Washington (d. 1619), a collateral ancestor of George Washington. The existing *Palace*, N of the church, is Perp. with an Elizabethan E front. Near the road is a small 13C house, now the Tourist Information Centre. Across Bishop's Way is a 14C *Tithe Barn* (open), with a fine roof, now housing a splendid collection of 17–19C carriages, many of them royal. In the 18C *Town Hall* on the High St. hangs a portrait of Disraeli who held Maidstone as his first parliamentary seat. In St Faith's St., near the East Station, the fine 16C Chillington Manor is now the *Museum and Art Gallery*, with relics of William Hazlitt (a native of Maidstone) and important collections of Kentish and natural history, costumes, ceramics and paintings.

*Otham*, 3m SE, has good timber-framed houses, notably Wardes and Stoneacre, a mainly 15C manor house (NT) with great hall and crownpost roof.—Off B2163 4 1/2m S of Maidstone is *Boughton Monchelsea Place* (open), an Elizabethan mansion (1567) of Kentish ragstone, with some interesting later alterations, including Regency Gothic in the E range. The church in the handsome park was heavily restored in the 19C but has a monument by Scheemakers to Sir

Christopher Powell (d. 1742). The lychgate (1470) is one of the oldest in England.

Off A20 2m NW is *Allington Castle* (open), a heavily restored building of the late 13C, with Tudor additions. It was the early home of Sir Thomas Wyatt (1503–42), the poet, and from here his son Sir Thomas (1521–54) set out on the ill-starred rebellion against Queen Mary's Spanish marriage. Allington now belongs to the Carmelites, and is used for religious conferences and retreats.—About 2m NE of Maidstone via *Penenden Heath*, the assembly ground of the Men of Kent since Saxon times, is *Boxley*. The partly Norman church has a memorial to Sir Francis Wyatt, who became Governor of Virginia in 1621.

FROM MAIDSTONE TO CHATHAM, 8m via A229. At *Sandling*, on the outskirts of the town just before the junction with M20, a sideroad leads left to (¼m) *Allington Lock*, with a view across the Medway to Allington Castle, and the *Museum of Kent Rural Life*, with oast-house, hop garden, orchard, etc.—*Aylesford*, 1¼m beyond, has a fine river frontage, a 14C bridge, a lovely old inn and the noble monument to Sir Thomas Colepeper (d. 1604) in its church. Sir Charles Sedley (1639– 1701), the poet and wit, was born in *The Friars* (½m W), which incorporated much of one of the earliest Carmelite foundations in England (1240). In 1949 the Carmelites reoccupied the buildings, this being the first occasion in England for a dispossessed Order to regain its old home; the relics of St Simon Stock (d. 1265), the first prior, were translated from Bordeaux, and in 1958–61 a new Shrine Church (for open-air services) was built by Adrian Gilbert Scott on the site of the sanctuary of the priory church (open).—Left of A229 at 2m is *Kit's Coty House* (English Heritage, open at any reasonable time), a huge dolmen with a capstone 11ft long; its long barrow survived up to the 18C. It stands in a magnificent position.—A229 now follows a Roman course, climbing Bluebell Hill and the North Downs, and crossing M2 to enter (8m) *Chatham* (Rte 4).

FROM MAIDSTONE TO TONBRIDGE, 14m via A26 and a pleasant reach of the Medway valley.—2m. *East Barming* has a Norman church with sculptured bench-ends c 1300.—4m. *Teston*, with a medieval bridge, was the home of Admiral Lord Barham (1726–1813). *West Farleigh*, on the S bank, has a well-preserved early Norman church and some large 18C houses.—5m. *Wateringbury*. 1m left at *Nettlestead*, the tiny church has a fine series of windows.—6 ½m. *Mereworth Castle* (not open) was built in 1720–23 by Colen Campbell, modelled on Palladio's Villa Rotonda near Vicenza.—10m. *Hadlow* has a church with a Saxo-Norman W end, and the remains of a castle built by Walter Barton May (c 1830), including a tower 170ft high.—14m. *Tonbridge*, see Rte 9A.

A20 runs E out of Maidstone and through the large village of *Bearsted*, where the poet Edward Thomas lived in 1901–04, to (40m) the junction with B2163. Immediately to the N is *Eyhorne Manor* (not open at time of writing), a typical Wealden house built for a yeoman farmer in the 15C and overlaid with 17C and 18C additions. *Hollingbourne*, 1m beyond, is a charming village on the Pilgrims' Way, with the fine tomb of Lady Elizabeth Culpeper (d. 1638) in its church. By taking B2163 S we come quickly to **\*Leeds Castle** (open), picturesquely sited in the middle of a lake and looking from a distance like the typical medieval castle of romance.

The original Norman castle, begun c 1120, was greatly extended by Edward I and his queen, Eleanor of Castile, after it was conveyed to the crown in 1278. To this period belong part of the Gloriette (the keep rising sheer from the lake at the N tip of the castle), the revetment wall surrounding the island and the additions to the gatehouse. The charming Fountain Court in the Gloriette was added in the reign of Edward III, while Tudor contributions included the Maiden's Tower to the SE. The main part of the castle, however, was rebuilt in 1822 and most of the interiors shown are 19C or 20C reconstructions. Among the happier importations are the wood panelling from Thorpe Hall, Peterborough, in the main building and the 16C oak staircase brought from France and installed in the Gloriette.

42m. *Harrietsham* has a church with a Norman font and, in East St., a fine 16C Wealden House.—44m. *Lenham* is nicely grouped round the church, which has a rare armchair sedile. Sir Henry Wotton

(1568–1639), poet, diplomat and wit, was born at *Boughton Malherbe*, 2½m SW beyond *Chilston Park*, praised by Evelyn in 1666.—48m. *Charing* has a noble church and the remains of a manor house of the archbishops of Canterbury.

*Otterden Place* (not open), 3½m N, is a pleasant Tudor and Georgian house beside a church rebuilt in 1753 but preserving a fine monument of 1620.—B2077 leads SW from Charing through pleasant countryside and villages, notably (3m) *Pluckley* and (8m) *Smarden*, particularly rich in timber-framed houses. At 11m the road joins A274 and heads S to (12m) *Biddenden* (Rte 8B).

At 52m a sideroad leads right to (⅓m) *Godinton Park* (limited opening, and by appointment). Built mainly in 1628–31, it is notable for its fine woodwork, especially the staircase and the Great Hall, which survives from the 14C building on the site.

54m. **Ashford** (40,000 inhab.; Tourist Information), an ancient market town, was an important centre for building steam locomotives. The church, surrounded by charming old houses, has a Perp. tower and contains monuments and brasses, including that of Elizabeth, Countess of Atholl (1375). Replanning has not been kind to the rest.

FROM ASHFORD TO CANTERBURY, 14m. A28 leads NE along the Stour valley.—3m. *Kempe's Corner*. 1m to the right is *Wye*, a pretty little town that may have been the birthplace of Aphra Benn (1640–89), dramatist, novelist and spy. Among the good houses of several periods, the timber-framed Yew Trees (16–17C) on Scotton St. is notable. Wye College (1892), the agricultural school of London University, has inherited the buildings of a school and college founded in 1447 by Archbishop Kempe. The crown cut in the chalk downs (right) commemorates the coronation of Edward VII. *Brook*, 2¾m SE, has a Norman church containing wall paintings.—4m. *Boughton Aluph*, left of the road, has a recently restored church with 14C nave arcades and contemporary stained glass. In the beautiful surrounding country stands *Eastwell Park* (2000 acres; lake), crossed by the Pilgrims' Way. Richard Plantagenet, natural son of Richard III, lived here after his father lost the crown at Bosworth Field, working as a bricklayer until his death in 1550.—6m. *Godmersham* has an unusual apsidal church with a Norman tower and a 12C relief of an archbishop. At Godmersham Park, backed by fine woods, Jane Austen often visited her brother Edward Knight (monument in church).—9m. **Chilham**, perched on a hill to the left of the road, is a conspicuously pretty village built in feudal fashion with its square of timber-framed houses standing between the flint church and the gates of the *Castle*. A keep of the original 12C building survives but the rest of the castle is a mansion built in 1616 for Sir Dudley Digges. The park, landscaped by Capability Brown, is open and 'medieval banquets' are held in the keep.—11m. *Chartham* church has a fine chancel, windows with 'Kentish' tracery and good brasses (the one to Sir Robert de Septvans, d. 1306, being the oldest in Kent). The timber roof is original.—14m. *Canterbury*, see Rte 5.

A20 passes between (57m) *Mersham* (pronounced 'Merzam'), where the church has monuments by Evesham and Nicholas Stone, and *Mersham le Hatch*, an Adam house of 1766 (not open).—60m. *Sellindge* church has a Norman door.—At (63m) *Newingreen* a road climbs right to *Lympne Castle* (Rte 8A). The Roman Stone St. leads N to Canterbury, passing on the left *Westenhanger* racecourse and the remains of a fortified manor house. A20 bears left and passes the entrance to (65½m) *Sandling Park* (gardens open under NGS).

71m. **FOLKESTONE** (43,700 inhab.) is an ancient town, once a 'limb' of the Cinque Ports, now a seaside resort and a major point of departure for the Continent. *Cheriton*, near the M20 3m NW of the centre, has been chosen as the site for the British terminal of the Channel Tunnel. An ambitious programme of construction, costing the British and French companies involved an estimated £5.2 billion, is scheduled for completion in 1993.

**Tourist Information Centre**: Harbour St., with a seasonal kiosk in the pedestrian precinct, Sandgate Rd.

**Car Parks**: The Leas, Bouverie Rd West, Forresters Way, Harbour St.

**Bus Station**: Bouverie Square.

**Railway Stations**: Folkestone Central, the main station; Harbour, for cross-Channel ferry passengers only; West, for local traffic.

**Ferry Services**: to Boulogne.

**Amusements**: repertory theatre at Leas Pavilion, concerts and other entertainments at Leas Cliff Hall and Marine Hall.

The chief attraction for visitors is the *Leas, a wide grassy promenade extending along the top of the cliff for over a mile, with views of the sea and the coast of France, 22m distant. Striking new buildings are being added to the impressive mid 19C terraces. More sheltered walks are afforded by the shrub-grown paths on the face of the beautifully planted cliff (lift). At the W end of the Leas the *New Metropole Arts Centre* holds temporary exhibitions of painting and sculpture. A *Road of Remembrance* planted with rosemary, descending to the harbour, commemorates the First World War, and a toll road runs along the base of the cliff to Sandgate. Near the E end of the Leas is the church of *St Mary and St Eanswyth*, largely rebuilt since its foundation in 1137 on the site of an 11C nunnery church. The Harvey Aisle (added in 1874) and the W window, presented by over 3000 medical men, as well as a statue (1881) on the Leas, commemorate William Harvey (1578–1657), discoverer of the circulation of the blood, who was born at Folkestone. In the chancel is a 14C canopied tomb with effigy. The site of Folkestone's ancient castle may be determined by *The Bayle* and *Bayle Pond*, near the church. In Grace Hill is the *Museum* with collections of local interest, including finds from two Roman villas excavated near the road to the Warren. Only a few narrow streets leading down to the lively harbour survived the bombing of 1941–44 but the district has kept its nautical atmosphere.

To the E beyond the harbour is the East Cliff, with a sandy beach and pleasant gardens. Further on (1¹/₂m E) is the *Warren*, a rough expanse of tumbled chalk between the cliffs and the shore, of interest to the botanist, entomologist, and fossil-gatherer.—On the N rise the *Sugar Loaf, Caesar's Camp*, and other chalk hills.

From Folkestone to *Canterbury*, see Rte 5; to *Hastings*, see Rte 8A.

The Dover road climbs steeply above the Warren and crosses open downland, stormy in winter.—71m. **Dover**, see Rte 4.

# 8    Folkestone to Hastings

The first route keeps near the coast and crosses Romney Marsh; the second makes the journey by heading inland through the towns and villages of the Weald.

# A.   Via Rye and Winchelsea

Total distance 37m. **Folkestone**, see Rte 7.—A259 is followed
throughout.—To (5m) **Hythe**.—To (14m) New Romney.—To (26m)
**Rye**.— To (29m) **Winchelsea**.—To (37m) **Hastings** (Rte 9A).

Maps: OS Landranger 189, 199.

**Folkestone**, see Rte 7.—We follow A259 past the inconspicuous
remains of Sandgate Castle, one of Henry VIII's coastal defences, to
(2m) *Sandgate*, Folkestone's western neighbour. Shorncliffe Camp,
on the plateau above the small resort, first became an important
military barracks in the Napoleonic era.— 5m. **Hythe** (12,700 inhab.),
one of the Cinque Ports, is divided in two by the Royal Military Canal
of 1804–06, beginning its 23m course to Rye. The unpretentious
seafront has three Martello towers, built in the same period to
counter the threat of invasion by Napoleon. The old village on the
hillside has some interesting houses, particularly the Old Manor
House at the top. The EE church has a raised chancel above a vaulted
processional path, containing over 500 skulls and other human
bones, believed to have been brought from the old churchyard
(14–15C). Lionel Lukin (1742–1834), who invented the lifeboat in
1785, is buried in the church. A Light Railway runs from Hythe to
Dymchurch and New Romney.

1m N of Hythe is *Saltwood Castle* (open by appointment for parties only), a
handsome building dating mainly from the 14C. Becket's murderers are
traditionally said to have met here on their way to Canterbury, while the
naming of Thorpe's Tower remembers the long imprisonment of William
Thorpe, a prominent Lollard. In recent years the castle was the home of Lord
Clark (1903–83), the art critic and historian.

10m. *Dymchurch* has a sea-wall 3m long protecting the marshes,
where the Romans also built a dyke and barrier. Two Martello towers
have been restored and one is now a museum (English Heritage,
summer standard opening). It is the 24th of 74 which originally
extended along the coast from Folkestone to Seaford. The 12C
church at *Burmarsh*, 1m N in Romney Marsh, still has three of its
medieval bells.—14m. **New Romney** (4600 inhab.) was one of the
original Cinque Ports, though its harbour was destroyed in the 13C.
The beautiful Norman and EE church has a memorial to the
children's writer E. Nesbit (1858–1924). She is buried at *St Mary in
the Marsh*, 2m N, where the 13C church keeps its Norman tower.

About 3m S of A28 at 15m is *Lydd* (4700 inhab.), whose EE and Dec. church is
sometimes known as 'the cathedral of Romney Marsh'. The chancel was
destroyed by German bombs. The Perp. tower is particularly fine, with good
vaulting. The interior incorporates remains of a Saxon church. The explosive
lyddite takes its name from its development at experimental ranges here. A
road goes over the shingle flats to (3m) *Dungeness*, on a bleak promontory with
rough seas and good deep-sea fishing. It has a bird sanctuary, two nuclear
power stations and two lighthouses; the older one (1904) is open in summer.

A259 swings inland through the marsh via (16m) *Old Romney*, which
has an unrestored 13C church with later additions.—At 18m the road
branches sharply left.

A sideroad leads right to (2m) *Ivychurch*, where the church has a handsome
tower and two-storied S porch.— A2070 and B2080 lead straight ahead from
A259 to (1¹/₂m) the tiny village of *Snargate*. Its EE and Perp. church has a
curious wall painting at the W end. *Appledore*, on the bank of the Royal Military
Canal 2m further, has a good 14C church. *Horne's Place Chapel*, 1¹/₂m N, is the
14C domestic chapel of a manor house (English Heritage, Wednesdays only
10.00–17.00).

19m. *Brookland* •church has a detached weatherboarded steeple in the shape of a pyramid, and a Norman lead font.—The road zigzags through the irrigation system of the marshes, passing (on the right) the complex of waterways feeding into the sea from Rye.

26m. **Rye** (4300 inhab.; Tourist Information), the larger of the two 'Ancient Towns' added to the Cinque Ports, stands on a hill looking across the salt marshes toward its neighbour, Winchelsea. The cobbled streets, narrow and sometimes hilly, have many attractive buildings of the 15–18C.

Rye has lost most of its former importance through alteration of the coast, but keeps part of its trade and in summer is often crowded with visitors. The Rye potteries are well known. The town was twice burned down by the French (1377 and 1448), and many of its inhabitants still bear the names of the Huguenot

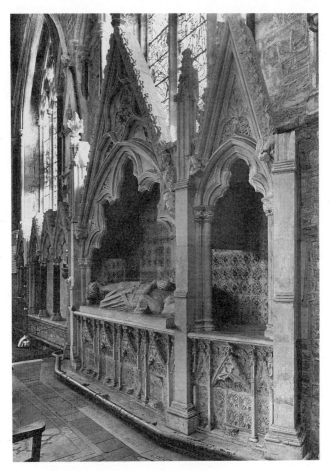

*The Alard tombs in Winchelsea church*

fugitives who took refuge here. John Fletcher, the dramatist, was born here in 1579 in a house in Lion St., now a tea-shop.

The approach at the N end of the town is through *Land Gate*, the last of three in the wall erected by Edward III. On top of the hill is *St Mary's*, a Norman and EE church with Dec. and Perp. windows and good flying buttresses. The mahogany altar table is alleged (wrongly) to have been made with wood from the Armada. The pendulum of the great clock is probably the oldest in England still at work with its original mechanism (1561–62). The W window commemorates Archbishop Benson (1829–96). No. 40 Church Square, a small building of c 1263, was a house of the *Friars of the Sack*, and to the SE is the turreted *Ypres Tower* (locally 'Wipers', a pronunciation made familiar by British soldiers in Flanders), built c 1250 by Peter of Savoy and sold in 1430 to one John de Ypres. It now houses a museum of local history. *Flushing Inn*, in a square N of the church, has an interesting cellar and 16C mural painting. *Lamb House* (NT) in West St., facing the W end of St Mary's, was the home of Henry James (1843–1916) from 1898 onwards, and afterwards of E.F. Benson (1867–1940), author of the 'Lucia' and 'Dodo' novels. In the romantic Mermaid St., which leads off West St., is the early 16C *Mermaid Hotel*. In High St. is the building of *Peacocke's School* (1636), where Thackeray's Denis Duval was a pupil. The *Monastery* in Conduit Hill, off High St., was originally part of a late Dec. Augustinian Friary.

*Rye Harbour*, 1½m S, is now a quiet fishing port at the mouth of the Rother. Across the river towards *Camber* is the famous Rye Golf Course. At the beginning of the harbour road a footpath leads over the marshes to *Camber Castle*, one of Henry VIII's coastal defences, made irrelevant by the changed course of the river and dismantled in 1642.

29m. **Winchelsea**, the companion 'Ancient Town' of Rye, lies on a knoll rising over the marshes and the river Brede. The original town and harbour were destroyed by the encroachments of the sea, and this 'new' Winchelsea was founded by Edward I in 1283, and rebuilt on the regular lines of a French 'bastide'. It has long since shrunk to the dimensions of a village but its buildings still 'plead haughtily for honours gone'. It is the opening scene of Thackeray's 'Denis Duval'.

The *Church of St Thomas Becket*, occupying one of the 'squares' laid out by Edward I, is the most important Dec. building in Sussex (begun c 1300). The nave has vanished or was never built. The church contains beautiful sedilia and some very fine 14C tombs of the Alards. Part of the window tracery is of the so-called 'Kentish' pattern. The modern glass is by Douglas Strachan (1928–33). The old *Court Hall* opposite contains a museum of Winchelsea's history and the history of the Cinque Ports. Of the wall that once surrounded the town, *Strand Gate* is at the beginning of the road to Rye, and *Pipe Well* (or *Land Gate*) is to the NW; *New Gate* is now some distance S.

31m. *Icklesham* has a fine Norman *church with 14C chancel.—37m. **Hastings**, see Rte 9A.

# B.   Via Tenterden

Total distance 48m. **Folkestone**, see Rte 7.—A259 to (5m) **Hythe**.—A261, B2067 to (7½m) Lympne.—B2067 to (27m) **Tenterden**.—A28 to (48m) **Hastings** (Rte 9A).

Maps: OS Landranger 189, 188 (briefly) and 199.

**Folkestone**, see Rte 7.—To (2m) *Sandgate* and (5m) *Hythe*, see Rte 8A.—We leave Hythe on A261 and turn left at 6m on B2067 for (7½ m) *Lympne*, pronounced 'Lim'. S of the road and the village, on the edge of the escarpment overlooking Romney Marsh, stands *Lympne Castle* (open), once a residence of the Archdeacons of Canterbury. The original 13–15C buildings, two towers connected by a central hall block, were incorporated into a larger house by the architect Sir Robert Lorimer in 1906. Only the medieval parts, of which the most impressive is the Great Hall, are shown. The fine views from the towers and the gardens include the scanty remains of *Stutfall Castle*, the castrum of the Roman Portus Lemanis. The nearby church, probably built by Archbishop Lanfranc (d. 1089), has been much restored. *Port Lympne* (open), to the W of the village, is an early 20C country house by Sir Herbert Baker. Its grounds are now a popular zoo park.

B2067 continues W along the line of the escarpment, with the Royal Military Canal and Romney Marsh to the left and woodland to the right.—For a brief period in 1511–12 Erasmus held the living of *Aldington*, a mile N of the road at 11½m.—Beyond (17½m) *Ham Street* we leave the marshes behind and head further into the countryside of the Weald.

27m. **Tenterden** (6200 inhab.; seasonal Tourist Information) is a dignified little town still displaying the prosperity brought in successive centuries by shipbuilders, clothmakers and ironmasters. Its broad High St. is flanked by handsome houses in brick, tile, timber and white-painted weatherboarding and by several old inns. The church has a noble Perp. tower and a roof of wood shingles. The resuscitated Kent and East Sussex Light Railway runs steam locomotives along the old track to Hexden Bridge, 5m SW.

*Tenterden*

*Smallhythe Place* (NT), 2m S on B2082, is an early 16C timber-framed building, once the harbourmaster's house when Smallhythe was the port for Tenterden and later the home of Ellen Terry from 1899 until her death here in 1928. It is preserved as a memorial to the actress.

FROM TENTERDEN TO CRANBROOK, 13m. We head N on A28. 1m to the right of the junction with A262 is *High Halden*, where the church has a splendid timber belfry.—A262 goes left to (6m) *Biddenden*, with a picturesque half-timbered street. *Headcorn*, 5m further N, also has some fine old houses.—A229 leads W from Biddenden to (10m) *Sissinghurst Castle* (NT), a mellow fragment of a Tudor mansion where Gibbon once served as an officer in charge of French prisoners. It was later the home of Victoria Sackville-West (1892–1962) and her husband, Sir Harold Nicolson. Her study and the long library are shown, but the chief attraction of Sissinghurst is the lovely garden she created. Richard Church (1893–1972), poet and novelist, lived in the grounds.—A229 continues to the little town of (13m) **Cranbrook** (seasonal Tourist Information), with a steep High St. and the largest working windmill in England (1814). The grammar school, founded in 1576, was the birthplace of the poet Phineas Fletcher (1582–1650); the present buildings are 18–20C. The Perp. church has some 16C stained glass, and wooden bosses (c 1300) on the W wall.

The main route follows A28 W from Tenterden to (31m) *Rolvenden*, with a fine 14C church. *Great Maytham Hall* (limited opening), on the outskirts, is a mansion of 1909 by Sir Edwin Lutyens. The greater part of the house has been converted into flats and only the main rooms on the ground floor are shown. Between 1898 and 1907 Frances Hodgson Burnett was tenant of the Georgian house that stood on the site; the walled garden claimed as the inspiration of 'The Secret Garden' can still be seen. 2¹/₂m W of Rolvenden, along B2086 and past two windmills, is *Benenden*, with its famous girls' public school built in the Elizabethan style in 1859.—At (33m) *Newenden* the tiny church has a carved late Norman font.—We cross the Rother valley into East Sussex.— 35m. *Northiam*, with weatherboarded houses, has a church with a fine Perp. spire and elegant piers carrying EE nave arcades. *Great Dixter* (open), ³/₄m NW, is a half-timbered 15C house restored and enlarged with great sensitivity by Lutyens in 1910. He was also responsible for the gardens.

*Bodiam Castle* (NT) is 5m W of Northiam. Built by Sir Edward Dalyngruge in 1385 and dismantled during the Civil War, the fortress keeps its strikingly neat and unified appearance even though it is now a mere shell. A wide moat protects a rectangle of stone walls, with round towers at the corners and square ones in the middle, and this in turn surrounds a square inner courtyard. The great gateway on the N side is flanked by machiolated turrets; the outer portcullis is still visible, and there are grooves for two more beyond. The building was carefully restored by Lord Curzon in 1919.

At (40m) *Brede* the church has the well-carved tomb of Sir Goddard Oxenbridge (1537).—A28 descends the wide open valley of the Brede and climbs again to (42m) *Westfield*, which has a Norman church.—48m. **Hastings**, see Rte 9A.

# 9  London to Hastings

## A.  Via Sevenoaks

Total distance 63m. In its main lines the route follows A21, but diverges periodically for the towns and sights A21 bypasses.—A2 to (4m) Lewisham.—A21 to (10m) Bromley.—A21, A224 to (24m) **Sevenoaks**.—A225, B245 to (30m) **Tonbridge**.—A21 to (53m) John's Cross.—A2100 to (56m) Battle.—A2100, A21 to (63m) **Hastings**.

Maps: OS Landranger 177, 188, 199.

We leave London by the Old Kent Rd for New Cross and (4m) *Lewisham*, where A21 diverges right for (10m) *Bromley*.

At 15m an unclassified road on the right leads through pleasant country to (3m) *Downe*. The Georgian *Down House* (open), ½m S, was the home of Charles Darwin from 1842 until his death in 1882. It contains the study where 'The Origin of Species' was written, innumerable personal possessions, and a display about the scientist's grandfather, Erasmus Darwin (1731–1802); also paintings by Stubbs and by Joseph Wright of Derby.

A21 joins A224, which climbs the North Downs to Badger's Mount and then descends into the valley of the Darent. At 20m, after crossing M25 and M26, the road branches right to bypass Sevenoaks, but we continue S for the town centre.

The sideroad leading SW (right) from this junction skirts *Chevening Park* (not open), a mid 17C house, perhaps by Inigo Jones, altered in the 18C. In the fine wooded park is a lake where the inventive 3rd Earl Stanhope (d. 1816) launched 'the first craft ever propelled by steam'. His daughter, the eccentric Lady Hester Stanhope (1776–1839), was born here.

22m. *Riverhead*, with some pleasant 18C houses.

Here A25 diverges left for (2m) *Seal*, where the interesting church has a 16C tower, a brass of 1395 and a bronze sculpture of a child (1908).—6m. *Ightham* and *Ightham Mote*, 2½m S, see Rte 7.

24m. **Sevenoaks** (17,100 inhab.; Tourist Information) is pleasant but unexciting except for the handsome High St. at the S end of the town. This has an array of good 17–18C houses and the church of *St Nicholas*, with 13C nave arcades and a Perp. chancel notable for its monuments. Donne was pluralist rector in 1616–31. *Sevenoaks School* was founded in 1432 and still inhabits 18C buildings designed by Lord Burlington. The triangular *Vine* is said to be the oldest cricket ground in England, and William Pett (1710–86), the earliest known maker of cricket bats, lived at Sevenoaks.

At the S end of Sevenoaks, E of A225, is **\*Knole** (NT), one of the finest as well as the largest mansions in England.

The core of the present house was built by Archbishop Thomas Bourchier (d. 1486) as a palace for himself and succeeding Archbishops of Canterbury. In 1532 Cranmer resigned it to Henry VIII, who proceeded to enlarge it, most strikingly by the addition of the Green Court through which visitors approach the building. Elizabeth I granted the lease of the estate to her cousin, Sir Thomas Sackville, later Earl of Dorset. When he acquired it permanently in 1603 he undertook a grand remodelling which still largely determines the visitor's impression of Knole today.

Behind Henry VIII's Green Court is the front courtyard of Bourchier's palace, the Stone Court, remodelled in the 17C. One side is occupied by the Great Hall, also remodelled, with a vigorously carved screen and portraits by Van Dyck.

The Great Staircase, another of Sackville's alterations to the house, is among the very best of its date. The upper rooms keep their original fittings, and their collection of 17C *furniture is outstanding. We first tour a series of small rooms: the Brown Gallery (early English furniture and historical portraits); Lady Betty's Rooms (English carpets); the Spangle Bedroom (17C Brussels tapestries); the Venetian Bedroom; and the Leicester Gallery (with a surviving 15C fireplace). Next follow the state rooms, with fine 17C plasterwork ceilings and fireplaces: the Ballroom (portraits of the Sackvilles by Van Dyck, Kneller, Gainsborough, etc.); the Crimson Drawing Room (portraits by Reynolds); the Cartoon Gallery; and the King's Bedroom, fitted up for James I, with magnificent Carolean furniture. The park (open free to pedestrians every day) extends to about 1000 acres and commands a famous view of the Weald of Kent.

Victoria Sackville-West (1892–1962), born at Knole, wrote a history of the house and made it the setting for her novel 'The Edwardians'. In 'Orlando' her friend Virginia Woolf offered a deliberately fanciful evocation of Knole through the centuries.

A225 continues S from Sevenoaks to (26m; on the left) *Riverhill House* (limited opening), a small Queen Anne building enlarged by successive generations; it stands in gardens with fine trees.—A225 converges with A21 at the roundabout shortly beyond. The village of *Sevenoaks Weald*, ³/₄m W, was home of Edward Thomas and W.H. Davies in 1904–06. Caxton is reputed to have been born at the Long Barn. Sir Harold Nicolson and Victoria Sackville-West made the 15–16C building a meeting place for the Bloomsbury Group in 1915–30; here Virginia Woolf started 'Orlando' and Roy Campbell wrote 'The Georgiad'.—We follow B245 south.

30m. **Tonbridge** is a market town (30,400 inhab.) on the Medway. Among the ancient timbered buildings to survive are the 15C *Chequers Inn* in the High St. and the 16C *Portreeve's House* in East St. The remains of the Norman *Castle* (open), built by William the Conqueror's kinsman Richard de Clare and enlarged in the 13C, stand above the river. *Tonbridge School* (off the High St.) was founded in 1553 by Sir Andrew Judd but the buildings it now occupies are 19C. Jane Austen's father, Rev. George Austen, was a master here and E.M. Forster an unhappy pupil.—*Tudeley* church, 3m E, has a stained-glass window by Marc Chagall (1967).

We rejoin A21 S of Tonbridge as it climbs to (35m) *Pembury*.—37m. B2160 leads left for *Matfield*, 1¹/₂m, with a fine group of early Georgian houses on the green.—39m. To the right are *Owl House Gardens* (open), with woodland walks extending to 12 acres.

A262 diverges left, passing (1m) *Finchcocks* (limited opening), a baroque house of 1725 with a collection of keyboard instruments. Concerts and courses are held here.— *Goudhurst* (3m) is a hilltop village commanding fine views. Its church has monuments to the Culpeper (or Colepeper) family, including one in coloured wood to Sir Alexander Culpeper (d. 1537). 1¹/₂m NW, in an area famous for oaks, is *Horsmonden* church, early 14C, with a fine brass to Henry de Grofhurst (c 1340). *Bedgebury National Pinetum* (open), off B2079 2¹/₂m S, belongs to the Royal Botanic Gardens.—A262 continues E from Goudhurst for *Cranbrook* and *Sissinghurst Castle* (Rte 8B).

40m. *Lamberhurst*, once the centre of the Wealden iron-smelting industry. 1¹/₂m W is *Bayham Abbey*, a ruined 13C Premonstratensian house (English Heritage, summer standard opening).—A21 continues SE, passing *Scotney Castle* (NT) on the left. The grounds were beautifully laid out in the Picturesque manner in the 1830s, making cunning use of the ruined 14C castle (with 17C additions). The new house (by Salvin) added at the same time is not open.—At (45m) *Flimwell* we enter East Sussex. About 3m E on A268 is *Hawkhurst*, where William Penn once owned the ironworks. The good late Dec. church in the old village to the S has been kindly treated in successive restorations. For *Rolvenden*, 8m further NE, and *Bodiam Castle*, 4m SE of Hawkhurst, see Rte 8B.—48m. *Hurst Green*.

A265 leads SW past the 17C *Haremere Hall* (gardens open; house, limited opening and by appointment for parties), pleasantly sited on the steep hillside, to (2m) *Etchingham*, with a Dec. church with fine window tracery and fragments of the original stained glass. It also contains good stalls, a screen and brasses.—6m. *Burwash* has a pleasant High St. and a church with a Norman tower. *Bateman's* (NT), a 17C ironmaster's house, was the home of Rudyard Kipling (d. 1936). Exhibits include his Nobel Prize citation (1907), the first time the award for literature was won by an Englishman. The surrounding country, with low undulating hills, is the scene of 'Puck of Pook's Hill'. At *Brightling*, 2m S, is the pyramid tomb of Mad Jack Fuller (d. 1834).

At (53m) John's Cross we take the right fork, A2100, which leads due S.—56m. **Battle** (Tourist Information), a pleasant little town, takes its name from the Battle of Hastings (1066), fought to the SE. The fine 12–15C *Church* has interesting pier capitals and fragments of 15C stained glass. There is also the handsome tomb of Sir Anthony Browne (see below) and his wife, a few brasses, and a memorial to Edmund Cartwright (1743–1823), inventor of an early power loom, who died at Hastings and is buried here. The Market Square is dominated by the gatehouse of *Battle Abbey* (grounds and ruins English Heritage, standard opening and summer Sunday mornings; Abbot's House, now a school, not normally open).

Battle Abbey was founded by William the Conqueror, in fulfilment of a vow made before the fateful battle, on the spot where Harold erected his royal standard and afterwards fell. The abbey was colonised by Benedictines from Marmoutier, near Tours, and the church was consecrated to St Martin in 1094. At the Dissolution (1539), the richly endowed abbey was given by Henry VIII to Sir Anthony Browne, Master of the Horse, who destroyed the church.
The imposing *Gatehouse* (1339) is battlemented and turreted with Dec. arcading; the E wing is 16C. In front as we enter are the inhabited parts of the abbey, including the *Abbot's House*, remodelled by Browne, and two towers (1540), all that remains of *Princess Elizabeth's Lodgings*. The *Abbey Church*, 224ft long, has practically disappeared except for part of the undercroft of the 14C E extension, which had five chapels. The high altar was erected on the spot where Harold's body was found. The most impressive remains are those of the *Dormitory*, to the S of the church, with its fine S wall and lancet windows. The undercroft is intact, with three beautiful EE vaulted chambers. The lower floor formed the E side of the *Cloister*; the arcading of the W side with Perp. tracery is incorporated into the school house (Abbot's House). Scant remains of the *Parlour* may be seen adjoining the Dormitory to the N. Beyond these to the right, we reach a broad walk commanding a view of the battlefield, including the heights of Senlac and of Telham (across the valley), where the Normans encamped the night before the battle.
At *Sedlescombe*, an attractive village 2m NE, a Pestalozzi Village for refugee children was founded in 1960. *Ashburnham* church (1665), 3m W of Battle, contains interesting tombs and ironwork from a local industry that flourished until 1825. The Place, for about 800 years until 1935 the home of the Ashburnham family, is now a Church of England College.

63m. **HASTINGS** (74,800 inhab.) has two aspects to its history and its present character. The first is the old harbour town to the E, fortified by William the Conqueror to become the leading Cinque Port in the 12C; even after it lost its harbour to the encroaching sea, it remained a lively fishing port. The second Hastings is the seaside resort to the W, first attracting fashionable attention in the late 18C and, with the development of adjoining **St Leonards** in the 19C, growing into a byword for genteel propriety. The Duke of Wellington spent his honeymoon here in 1806, and Charles Lamb came to do 'dreary penance' and complain of the 'heterogeneous assemblage of sea-mews and stockbrokers'.

**Tourist Information Centre**: 4 Robertson Terrace; (seasonal) The Fishmarket.

**Car Parks**: along the seafront and between the High St. and The Bourne in the Old Town.

**Railway Stations**: Hastings Central, at the W end of Havelock Rd; St Leonards Warrior Square, at the end of King's Rd; West St Leonards, at the W end of the double town; Ore, 1m NE, the terminus of the electric line.

**Bus station**: Queen's Rd.

**Amusements**: White Rock and Pier Pavilions (concerts, dancing, etc.); Stables Theatre, The Bourne.

**Annual Event**: Music Festival in March.

The *Old Town* of Hastings, the fishing port between the West Hill and the East Hill, keeps its narrow streets and ancient houses though less and less of its old atmosphere. Here are *The Fishmarket*, the tall black storing-sheds for nets (a unique survival), and the *Fishermen's Church*, now a fishing museum, on Rock-a-Nore Rd. The Perp. church of *St Clement*, near the S end of the High St., contains two brasses (1563 and 1601) and was the scene of Dante Gabriel Rossetti's marriage in 1860. Nearby is the *Old Town Hall*, now a museum of local history. At the other end of the attractive High St., with many fine houses, is the RC church of *St Mary Star of the Sea* (1882), built mainly by the poet Coventry Patmore, who lived at Old Hastings House nearby. Beyond are the old *Stables* of c 1700, now a theatre. To the E is *All Saints'*, another Perp. church, where Titus Oates (baptised here in 1660) was for a short time curate under his father (rector 1660–90). All Saints' St. contains more fine houses: No. 125 was often visited by Sir Cloudesley Shovel and Garrick frequently stayed in a house at the sea end.

The scanty ruins of the Norman *Castle* (open) on West Hill can be reached by lift from George St. or by walking up Castle Hill Rd, from near the early 19C Wellington Square. *St Clement's Caves* (open), excavated on the E slope of the West Hill, are said to have been used by smugglers and were certainly used as air-raid shelters during the Second World War.

From the centre of Hastings, between the central station and the seafront, Queen's Rd leads past the 19C *Town Hall* to the pleasantly wooded *Alexandra Park* (100 acres). Cambridge Rd leads W past *White Rock Gardens* to the *Museum and Art Gallery*, with collections of Wealden pottery and Sussex ironwork and an Indian pavilion of 1886.

The seafront from the W end of Hastings to St Leonards gives an interesting picture of 19C development. E of Harold Place is Pelham Crescent (1824) by Joseph Kay, with the church of *St Mary* as its centrepiece. W of Queen's Hotel is the White Rock Pavilion and crowded pier. St Leonards was laid out by James and Decimus Burton (1828–34), with the Royal Victoria Hotel, altered now in more than name, forming the centre of a composition extending inland.

The most attractive short walk from Hastings is that from the East Hill along the cliffs to (³/4m) *Ecclesbourne Glen* and (1³/4m) *Fairlight Glen*, where the cliffs rise to a height of 400ft and the luxuriant trees descend almost to the sea. Beyond the head of the glen, ¹/2m from the sea, we may join the road and return to (2¹/4m) Hastings via the suburb of *Ore*, high up on St Helen's Down.

FROM HASTINGS TO EASTBOURNE, 17m via A259. The coast is lined with Martello towers.—5m. *Bexhill* (35,500 inhab.; Tourist Information), a seaside resort with an esplanade and good public park, the De La Warr pavilion (1935), and a golf course. The church of *St Peter* at Old Bexhill dates back to 1070 and contains a unique Saxon tombstone. The *Manor House* was once a residence of the Bishops of Chichester. J.L. Baird (1888–1946), the pioneer of television, lived at No. 1 Station Rd (plaque) from 1941.—12½m. *Pevensey*, on Pevensey Bay, the landing place of William the Conqueror in 1066. Beyond the EE church is *Pevensey Castle (English Heritage, standard opening), a Norman castle, consisting of a keep begun c 1080 and a gatehouse and inner bailey added in the 13C. It stands in the SE angle of an enclosure of about ten acres, surrounded by a Roman wall, strengthened by round towers and still at places 20ft high. This was the Roman *Anderida*, one of the great fortresses of the 'Saxon Shore', which was taken in 491 by the Saxons, who 'slew all that dwelt therein, nor was there one Briton left'. Opposite is the *Old Minthouse* (14C).—17m. *Eastbourne*, see Rte 10A.

From Hastings to *Folkestone*, see Rte 8.

# B. Via Westerham

Total distance 69m. To (10m) Bromley, see Rte 9A.—A233 to (19m) **Westerham**.—B2026 to (25m) Edenbridge.—B2027, B2167 to (31m) Penshurst.—B2176, A26 to (36m) **Tonbridge** (Rte 9A).—To (69m) **Hastings**, see Rte 9A.

Maps: OS Landranger 177, 188, 199.

We follow A2 and A21 to (10m) *Bromley* (see Rte 9A), where A233 diverges right.—14½m. *Biggin Hill* airfield was a vital fighter station in the Battle of Britain. The road climbs (16m) *Westerham Hill* (809ft; view), the highest point in Kent, and then descends to cross the Pilgrims' Way and M25.

19m. **Westerham** is pleasantly situated near the source of the Darent. General Wolfe (1727–59) was born in the vicarage and spent his early boyhood in what is now known as *Quebec House* (NT). Some of his relics are displayed in the house, and also at *Squerryes Court* (open), a 17C mansion by A25 W of the town. Although Wolfe left Westerham at the age of eleven, Harry Warrington in Thackeray's 'The Virginians' is represented as visiting him here. On the village green is a statue of the General by Derwent Wood (1911). That of Churchill by Oscar Nemon (1969) stands on a marble plinth given by Marshal Tito of Yugoslavia. *Pitt's Cottage*, now a restaurant, was for a time the country retreat of the younger Pitt. The parsonage of Mr Collins, in Jane Austen's 'Pride and Prejudice', was at 'Hunsford, near Westerham'.

We leave Westerham by B2076, passing on the left wooded sandy hills stretching to *Brasted* (NT; 600 acres, with pleasant walks and drives).—21m. *Chartwell* (NT), the country home of Sir Winston Churchill in 1922–65, is now preserved as a memorial to him.— 22m. *Crockham Hill*, with a good view over the Weald. We cross the railway and the junction with B2027 into (25m) *Edenbridge*, with some old buildings near the bridge.—B2027 leads E, passing at 27m an unclassified road leading right for (2m) *Hever*, where the church with a fine shingled spire has the beautiful tomb of Sir Thomas Boleyn (d. 1538), father of Anne, and a brass of Margaret Cheyne (d. 1419).

**Hever Castle** (open) is a fortified 14C house surrounded by a square moat, elaborately restored after it was bought by the American, William Waldorf Astor, in 1903. Historically, it is interesting as the reputed meeting place of Anne Boleyn (perhaps born here) and Henry VIII, who afterwards granted it to Anne of Cleves. Architecturally, it is notable for the rich Edwardian woodwork. It has an Italian garden and a neo-Tudor village built for Mr Astor by Frank L. Pearson to provide offices and guest rooms.

28m. An unclassified road leads right for *Chiddingstone* (1¹/₂m), a charming group of half-timbered houses (NT). The *Castle* (open), a 17C house remodelled as a Gothic castle c 1805, is notable for its 17C woodwork and its collection of Stuart and Jacobite relics, among them Prince Charles Edward's last letter before the 1745 rebellion and Monmouth's plea for his life written the day before his execution.

29¹/₂m. *Penshurst Station.* From here B2176 leads S to (31m) *Penshurst*, a delightful village with many buildings in the local vernacular tradition by George Devey (c 1850). We follow the path past the church (with Sidney monuments) to *Penshurst Place (open), which, despite various enlargements during its long history, is still a wonderfully complete specimen of a medieval manor house.

It was originally built by Sir John de Pulteney, several times Lord Mayor of London, in the 1340s. His *Great Hall is still the most striking feature of the house, 64ft long, with chestnut roof, 'Kentish' tracery and open hearth (though the louvre in the roof through which the smoke escaped does not survive). The arrangement of the screens passage is original but the screen itself is Elizabethan. From that period, too, is the Long Gallery in the SW wing. Penshurst has been in the possession of the Sidneys since 1552 and its most interesting contents are probably the portraits of that distinguished family, including Sir Philip Sidney (born here in 1554) and Algernon Sidney (1663); in the armoury are personal relics of Sir Philip. Ben Jonson was the first of many visiting poets who praised the charms of Penshurst and the hospitality of its owners. An avenue in the beautiful park is named 'Sacharissa's Walk' from Lady Dorothy Sidney (d. 1684), the Sacharissa of Edmund Waller's poetry.

34m. *Bidborough*, a pleasant village with a well-sited church.—36m. **Tonbridge**, and on to (69m) **Hastings**, see Rte 9A.

# 10   London to Eastbourne

## A.   Via Tunbridge Wells

Total distance 66m. To (30m) **Tonbridge**, see Rte 9A.—A26 to (35m) **Tunbridge Wells**.—A267 to (43m) Mayfield.—A267, A22 to (61m) Polegate.—A22 to (66m) **Eastbourne**.

Maps: OS Landranger 177, 188, 199.

From London to **Tonbridge**, see Rte 9A. We leave the town by A26.—32¹/₂m. B2176 leads right for Penshurst (Rte 9B).— 33¹/₂m. *Southborough* (10,000 inhab.), with a pleasant common. *Speldhurst*, 2m W, has windows by William Morris and Burne-Jones in the church.

35m. **TUNBRIDGE WELLS** (44,800 inhab.), a town with a history as an inland health resort, lies in an attractive district of hills and moorland where Kent and Sussex meet. It was officially named 'Royal Tunbridge Wells' by Edward VII.

**Tourist Information Centre**: Town Hall.

**Car Parks**: Major Yorks Rd and Eridge Rd (near the Pantiles), and Mount Pleasant Rd.

**Buses**: from Mount Pleasant.

**Railway Station**: Central Station, Mount Pleasant.

**Theatre**: Assembly Hall, Crescent Rd.

**Annual Events**: Cricket Week in June; Pantiles Festival in June/July; Carnival in July; Lawn Tennis Tournament in July.

**History**. The mild chalybeate waters of Tunbridge Wells were first brought to notice by the hypochondriac Dudley, Lord North, in 1606 and enjoyed a great vogue after the Restoration, reaching their height of fashion in 1735–61, when Beau Nash came here from Bath to preside as Master of Ceremonies. Local names such as Mount Sion, Mount Ephraim and perhaps Calverley (Calvary?) suggest a Puritanical strain in the patrons of the place, and Tunbridge Wells long had the reputation of being the watering place of the serious-minded. 'Tunbridge Ware' is a kind of wood mosaic produced, originally at Tonbridge, from the 17C until 1934.

At the town centre is an imposing group of buildings including the *Town Hall*, *Assembly Hall*, *Library* and *Museum*, with the largest public collection of Tunbridge Ware, as well as domestic and agricultural bygones, dolls, etc. But the chief centre of interest is the \***Pantiles**, a short promenade first laid out in 1638 and named from its

*Tunbridge Wells, the Chalybeate Spring in the Pantiles*

original square tile paving (later replaced with Purbeck stone). On one side is a colonnade, and some fine houses were added in the 18C and 19C. A recent development to the S blends well with the curve of the shop facades; another development, housing craft work, specialist shops and studios, opened in 1988. At the Chalybeate Spring water can be bought from the 'dipper', a traditional service dating back to the discovery of the Spring. Opposite the N entrance to the Pantiles is the church of *King Charles the Martyr* (1684) with a contemporary plaster ceiling. The Calverley estate to the NE was laid out by Decimus Burton in 1828–52. To the W and N stretches the Common (170 acres) with its gorse and bracken.

Short walks may be taken to *Rusthall Common*, 1m NW, with the fantastic Toad Rock, and to the *High Rocks*, 1¹/₂m SW, a curious sandstone formation. From the High Rocks a path leads near the Medway to the pretty village of (3¹/₂m) *Groombridge*, with a chapel of 1625. The charming moated *Groombridge Place* (mid 17C; footpath through the park) lies to the left of the road. ³/₄m NW is *Burrswood*, by Decimus Burton (1831–38), now the Dorothy Kerin Home of Healing.

Groombridge can also be reached via A264 and B2188. *Withyam*, 3m further SW, has monuments of the Sackville family including the baroque *tomb of the 13-year-old Thomas Sackville (d. 1677) by C.G. Cibber. To the S are *Old Buckhurst*, the former seat of the Sackvilles (now flats), and *Duckings*, a fine timbered farmhouse.

*Crowborough*, on A26 7m SW of Tunbridge Wells, has an 18C church and vicarage. Sir Arthur Conan Doyle (1859–1930) died here at the house called Windlesham, and Richard Jefferies lived at Downs Cottage.—For Bayham Abbey, 6m SE of Tunbridge Wells, and Scotney Castle, on A21 2m beyond, see Rte 9A.

A267 ascends into the Weald, crossing from Kent into East Sussex.—43m. **Mayfield** is a pleasant village standing on high ground. The Middle House Hotel dates from 1575. The convent school (open by appointment) includes part of the 14C *Old Palace*, a favourite residence of the Archbishops of Canterbury from the time of St Dunstan (d. 988). The medieval *Hall, carefully restored as a chapel by E.W. Pugin in 1863–66, has three huge stone arches on exquisitely carved corbels, carrying a timber roof. The chapel contains a 14C crucifixion, a Madonna (c 1460) and the decorated back to the original Archbishop's throne. *St Dunstan's Church* (13–15C) has some iron tomb slabs from local foundries in its pavement.—48¹/₂ m. *Cross-in-Hand* is 1¹/₂m W of *Heathfield*, an untidy village whose church has the cenotaph of Lord Heathfield (d. 1790), defender of Gibraltar. A pillar in the neighbouring hamlet of *Cade Street* marks the spot where the rebel Jack Cade was mortally wounded by Alexander Iden, sheriff of Kent, in 1450.—At 57m. we join the A22.

A271 leads E to (4m) *Herstmonceux*. About 1¹/₂m S of the village is *Herstmonceux Castle*, the present home of the Royal Greenwich Observatory, which will be moved to Cambridge before about 1990. An astronomical exhibition in the Equatorial Group of Telescopes, the gardens and the grounds are open from Easter to the end of September. The moated 15C brick-built castle was partially rebuilt this century. The fine S gatehouse is mainly original. Except for two rooms with exhibitions of local history and wild life, the interior is not normally open. Opposite the W entrance to the grounds is a 12– 13C church with a magnificent late 15C monument and fine brass of William Fiennes (d. 1402).

2m SW of the junction of A267 and A22 is *Michelham Priory* (open), the attractive moated remains of an Augustinian house founded in 1229. A rebuilt refectory, the washing place on the cloister wall and a vaulted room that may have been either buttery or parlour survive from the 13C. The Tudor wing, added by Herbert Pelham after 1587, has interesting old furniture. In the grounds are a watermill and a Tudor barn. The fine gateway tower over the moat dates from c 1395.

61m. *Polegate* stands at the junction with A27, leading E to (5m) Pevensey (Rte 9A) and W to Lewes (Rte 10B). A sideroad leads S to (1½m) *Wannock*, on the left, with its glen and its old mill, and (3m) *Jevington*, which has a restored church with a massive tower.—A22 continues S via (65m) *Willingdon*, left of the main road, where the 13C church has monuments and brasses.

66m. **EASTBOURNE** (79,000 inhab.) is sheltered by the South Downs and the steep, magnificent headland of Beachy Head. Beneath the town's present amorphous appearance is a history of development common among South coast resorts. The old village lies about 1m inland, its centre announced by the medieval church. The seafront, now 2½m long, first became fashionable with visitors at the end of the 18C and was systematically developed by the Duke of Devonshire in the 1850s, without much architectural distinction but with a generous number of parks and gardens.

**Tourist Information Centres**: 3 Cornfield Terrace; (seasonal) The Pier, Marine Parade.

**Car Parks**: Hyde Gardens. Multi-storey car parks in Trinity Trees, Ashford Rd, and the Arndale Centre.

**Buses**: from Terminus Rd.

**Railway Station**: Terminus Rd.

**Annual Events**: Pre-Wimbledon Ladies Tennis Championships at Devonshire Park in June; Cricket Week at the Saffrons in August; Eastbourne Show two days in August.

**Famous residents and visitors**. Dr John Bodkin Adams (d. 1983) was a local practitioner. Lewis Carroll spent his summer holidays at No. 7 Lushington Rd. Debussy finished his symphonic sketches, 'La Mer', at Eastbourne.

In the old village are the 18C *Manor House*, now containing the *Towner Art Gallery* with a good collection of Sussex pictures and 20C art, and *St Mary's*, a Trans. church with Dec. windows and Perp. tower. Beneath the 16C *Lamb Inn*, opposite, is an EE vaulted chamber. Between the old and new towns stands *Compton Place* (1726–27) by Colen Campbell, now a school but until 1954 a seat of the Dukes of Devonshire.

The *Parade* or *Esplanade* skirts the seafront in terraces at different levels. It extends eastwards past the *Pier* of 1872 to (¾m) the *Redoubt*, built to resist the threat of Napoleonic invasion and now accommodating two military museums. Westwards it leads to (1½m) *Holywell*, near the foot of Beachy Head, passing the *Wish Tower* (1804), a restored Martello tower—the 73rd of 74 along the coast—with a small museum. Just inland from this point is *Devonshire Park* (13 acres), famous for its tennis tournaments, and nearby is *Eastbourne College*, a well known boys' school.

Fully 3m SW of the pier by the zigzagging Duke's Drive, beginning just beyond Holywell, is **'Beachy Head** ('Beauchef'; 575ft). The ruined *Belle-Tout Lighthouse*, erected in 1831 about 1m W and rebuilt after war damage, was superseded in 1902 by a new lighthouse at the foot of the cliff.—The walk may be continued to (¾m) *Birling Gap*, where the cable from France comes ashore, beyond which are the cliffs known as the *Seven Sisters* (NT; 632 acres).—The Downs to the NW are good for walking.—For other places of interest W of Eastbourne, see Rte 10B.

# B.  Via East Grinstead and Lewes

Total distance .70m. A23 to (14m) Purley.—A22 to (31m) **East Grinstead**.—To (36m) Wych Cross.—A275 to (52m) **Lewes**.—A27 to (65m) Polegate (Rte 10A).—A22 to (70m) **Eastbourne** (Rte 10A).

Maps: OS Landranger 176, 187, 198.

We take A23 (Rte 11A) out of London and change to A22 at (14m) *Purley*, to bypass (19m) *Caterham* and leave the suburbs behind.—21m. *Godstone*, just beyond M25, has a fine 16C inn.

A25 leads W to (1¹/₂m) *Bletchingley*, a pretty village where the 12–15C church has a huge monument to Sir Richard Clayton, Lord Mayor of London (d. 1707). To the N, at *Brewer Street*, is a half-timbered 15C farmhouse and Pendell Court, a brick gabled mansion of 1624.—For Redhill, 2m W of Bletchingley, see Rte 11A.

A25 leads E to (4m) *Limpsfield*, an attractive village below a pleasant common. The church has a Norman tower and three lancet windows in the chancel. The composer Frederick Delius (1863–1935) is buried in the churchyard. *Detillens* (limited opening) is a 15C hall house behind an 18C brick front; its contents include a collection of chivalric orders and decorations.—For Westerham, 3m further E on A25, see Rte 9B.

27m. *Newchapel*, with the first Mormon Temple in Europe (1958).

*Lingfield*, 2m E, has a large church rebuilt in the Perp. style by Sir Reginald Cobham (d. 1446); it contains a good collection of brasses, as well as the monument to Sir Reginald and his wife. The church at *Crowhurst*, 2m N of Lingfield, has a wooden steeple, brasses and a cast-iron tomb slab of local type.

Beyond (29m) *Felbridge* we cross from Surrey into Sussex.—31m. **East Grinstead** (22,300 inhab.) is a pleasant town with a wide High St. flanked by good buildings, including several timber-framed houses. *Sackville College (open) is a Jacobean almshouse of 1619.

*Standen* (NT), 2m S, is a house of 1891–94 by Philip Webb. Its interior is a fine example of the work of the Arts and Crafts movement, including textiles and wallpaper by Morris and Co.—*Hammerwood Park* (open), 3¹/₂m E of East Grinstead on A264, is a Greek Revival house of 1792, one of only two in England by Benjamin Latrobe, who emigrated to America and left his mark on Philadelphia, Baltimore and Washington DC. It is currently being rescued from years of neglect.

34m. *Forest Row* lies in *Ashdown Forest*, a beautiful region of wood and moorland. Ashdown House here is the second of Latrobe's English houses. On the bank of the infant Medway are the ruins of *Brambletye*, a mansion built in 1631 but still Jacobean in spirit. Further W is the large *Weir Wood Reservoir* and 1¹/₂m SW the *Spring Hill Wildfowl Park* (open).

36m. *Wych Cross*, at the junction of A22 and A275, is in the heart of the forest.

An unclassified road leads 3m W to the isolated village of *West Hoathly*, with a 13C church and 15C Priest's House (open), now a folk museum of the Sussex Archaeological Society. Nearby is *Gravetye Manor* (now a hotel), with a late Elizabethan S front, famous for the gardens by William Robinson (1838–1935), a pioneer of modern gardening.

From Wych Cross A22 bears left, offering an alternative route to Eastbourne via the small town of (45m) *Uckfield*, with the Maiden's Head, a fine Georgian inn. 1¹/₂m W is *Pilt Down*, site of a famous archaeological hoax.

The main route follows A275 to (40m) *Danehill*, where a road leads right to (1¹/₂m) *Horsted Keynes*, with a Norman church and miniature 13C effigy. The station on the Bluebell Railway (see below) is further W.—At 41½m the road passes close to *Sheffield Park*, the mansion of Edward Gibbon's friend, the 1st Earl of Sheffield. The *Gardens* (NT) are by Capability Brown.

Just beyond is *Sheffield Park Station*, from which the Bluebell railway runs for 5m through charming scenery to Horsted Keynes.
  Gibbon (1737–84) is buried in the church of *Fletching*, 2m E, which also contains the Dalyngridge brass (c 1380) and a unique brass of a glover (1450).

At 44m we cross the A272. To the W lies *Chailey North Common*, once owned by Anne of Cleves (now a nature reserve), with a windmill and the Heritage Crafts School for Crippled Children.

52m. **LEWES** (13,800 inhab.) straddles the gap in the South Downs where the Ouse makes its way towards the sea at Newhaven. A 17C visitor found it 'a place of good antiquity, large well built and well inhabited ... beautified with divers handsome streets', and so it still is.

**Tourist Information Centre**: Corner of High St. and Fisher St.

**Car Parks**: West St., Westgate St., Railway Yard, North St., Brook St.

**Bus Station**: Eastgate St.

**Railway Station**: Station Rd (S of Southover Rd).

**Theatre**: Lewes Little Theatre, Lancaster St.

**Annual Event**: Guy Fawkes's Day (5 November) is an occasion of great bonfires and firework displays, a tradition probably dating from before the Gunpowder Plot of 1605.

**History**. The name derives from the Old English 'hlaew', meaning hill, and indicates the strategic value of the place to the Saxons, who made it one of the capitals of the South Saxon kings and established two mints here. The importance of Lewes was increased when William de Warenne, a powerful friend of William the Conqueror, and his wife founded the castle and the Cluniac priory (c 1075–88). Henry III built the town walls, but in 1264 he was defeated by Simon de Montfort at the Battle of Lewes, fought on the slope of the Downs to the W. The thoroughness with which the priory was dismantled at the Reformation suggests a local Protestant fervour, and in 1555–57, during the reign of Mary Tudor, 17 Protestant martyrs were burnt at the stake near the present Town Hall. They are commemorated by an obelisk (1901) on Cliffe Hill to the E.

**Famous residents**. The diarist John Evelyn (1620–1706) attended the Grammar School in 1630–37 (see Southover Grange below). Tom Paine (1737–1809) lived here in 1768–74 (see below).

The Norman **Castle** (open) stands on a height near the middle of the town, almost blocking the pass through the Downs. It was built, unusually, with a motte at each end of an oval bailey. Warenne's keep is now a ruin, though it offers one of several good views from the town into the surrounding countryside. The fine barbican (1334) is well preserved. At the corner of Castle Gate is the *Barbican House Museum* of the Sussex Archaeological Society.

The unusually handsome *High St.*, reaching down towards the Ouse in the E and up the hill to the W, displays a medley of different periods and local building styles: timber-framing, tile-hanging, weatherboarding, and red and grey brickwork. On or just off the stretch E of the castle are: *Pelham House*, 16C with an 18C facade in St Andrew's Lane; the Georgian *White Hart Hotel* opposite the old *County Hall* (now the Law Courts) of 1812; and the *Town Hall* (1893), unappetising outside but with an Elizabethan staircase from Slaugham Manor inside (Rte 11B). The *Market Tower* (1792) is unusual. The road continues beyond the Ouse as the charming, narrow Cliffe High St.

Returning to the Castle and continuing W up the High St., we pass the round tower of *St Michael's* on the right. The 15C *Bull House* opposite was Tom Paine's home. Another 15C building, now a bookshop, stands at the corner of Keere St. (see below). *Shelley's Hotel* dates from the 16C and has a flagged hall. Beyond more good houses further up is *St Anne's Church*, mainly 12C, with a fine Norman font.

The suburb of *Southover* can be reached by following Keere St. to the S, passing fragments of the *Town Wall*. Beyond, on the right-hand side of Southover High St., stands *Southover Grange* (1572), the childhood home of John Evelyn; its pleasant gardens are open. The street bears right to the church of *St John*, which preserves the lead coffins of William de Warenne (d. 1088) and his wife, and her carved tomb slab. The so-called *Anne of Cleves House* (open), further on, is an interesting patchwork of the medieval, the early 16C and the Elizabethan. Its collection of local history includes good Sussex ironwork.

Behind the church, and bisected by the railway, lie the extensive but rather formless ruins of the *Priory of St Pancras*, once the most important Cluniac house in Britain, founded in 1075 and systematically demolished by Thomas Cromwell in 1539. The coffins of the founders (see above) were discovered beneath the site of the high altar in 1845. A monument in the form of a medieval helmet by Enzo Plazzotta was placed here in 1965 to mark the 700th anniversary of the Battle of Lewes. The remains are best viewed from the recreation ground in Mountfield Rd.

On the Ouse bank, 1m N, is *South Malling* church (1627), where John Harvard, 'founder' of Harvard University, was married in 1636. Walks may be taken on the Downs: to *Mount Harry* (640ft), 2¹/₂m NW, above the racecourse; *Cliffe Hill* (golf course); *Mount Caburn* (490ft; with a good British fort), 2¹/₂m SE.

B2192 leads NE to (3m) *Ringmer*, with a village signpost recording its connection with the wives of John Harvard and William Penn. **Glyndebourne** (1m S) is a mansion in lovely grounds and a famous opera house. 1¹/₂m further S is *Glynde*, with the 16C *Glynde Place* (open), which has Rubens's original sketch for the ceiling of the Banqueting House in Whitehall.—B2192 continues from Ringmer to (7¹/₂m) *Halland*, where *Bentley* (open) is a modest house with formal gardens created by Mary Askew in 1942–70, a wildfowl reserve and a motor museum.

FROM LEWES TO EASTBOURNE VIA NEWHAVEN (20m).—We follow an unclassified road S to (3¹/₂m) *Rodmell*, where the little 17C *Monk's House* (NT) was the home of Leonard and Virginia Woolf; she committed suicide in the nearby Ouse in 1941.—The road passes the round church towers of *Southease* and *Piddinghoe*.—7m. **Newhaven**, a small port (9900 inhab.) at the mouth of the Ouse. The 'new' haven dates from 1570, when the Ouse mouth shifted from the E to the W side of the valley. The fugitive Louis-Philippe landed here in 1848 and put up at the Bridge Hotel. The apsidal 12C church, high above the town, is a relic of the medieval village of Meeching. A car ferry crosses from Newhaven harbour to Dieppe.—A259 crosses the Ouse and passes *Bishopstone*, on the left, with its little Norman church (partly Saxon) and remains of a Saxon village and cemetery discovered in 1968.—11m. *Seaford* (17,800 inhab.; Tourist Information), a bathing and golfing resort. The church has Norman portions and a remarkable capital by the S door, and a relief of St Michael and the Dragon (c 1130–40). A fine cliff walk leads E over Seaford Head to *Cuckmere Haven* (2¹/₂m) while the road to Alfriston (3¹/₂m; see below) runs via 'High and Over' (or Hindover), with a fine *view.—At (13³/₄m) *Exceat* the road crosses the Cuckmere valley near the charming village of *Westdean*. The church here has two bronze busts: one of the painter Sir Oswald Birley (1880–1952) by Clare Sheridan, the other of Lord Waverley (d. 1958) by Epstein.—16¹/₄m. *Friston* church has a Saxon window.—17m. *Eastdean*, ¹/₂m to the right, has a church with a Norman tower.—20m. *Eastbourne*, see Rte 10A.

The main route takes A27 from Lewes, passing beneath Mount Caburn (see above).—55m. Turning on the left for Glynde and Glyndebourne, see above. To the right, beyond, is *Firle Place* (open), seat of the Gage family since the 16C. General Gage was commander of the British forces at the beginning of the American War of Independence. The house contains good paintings, including the Cowper collection from Penshanger, and some notable Sèvres china. Behind rises *Firle Beacon* (718ft; *view), peppered with Neolithic and Bronze Age barrows, and in *West Firle* church are Gage monuments, including three made in 1595 by Gerard Johnson (or Janssen).—58m. A lane on the right leads to *Charleston Farmhouse* (open), where Vanessa Bell lived from 1916, making it a gathering place for the Bloomsbury Circle and, with Duncan Grant, decorating it in a distinctive fashion.—61½m. *Berwick* church (EE) has wall paintings (1942–43), including a Crucifixion by Duncan Grant.

On the Cuckmere 2m S is **Alfriston**, with an interesting Perp. church (the 'Cathedral of the Downs') and the shaft of a market cross. The 14C timber-built parsonage (open) was the first building acquired by the NT in 1896. The 16C Star Inn has quaint carvings. *Lullington*, beyond the river, has one of the smallest churches in England, only 16ft square, in fact the chancel of a larger building.

63½m. *Wilmington* has the scanty ruins of a 14C Benedictine priory (open). A small museum has a collection illustrating rural life. In the face of the chalk downs on our right is the *Long Man of Wilmington*, a figure 240ft tall, with a staff in each hand. Its origin and purpose are uncertain; but its age is at least medieval.—65m. *Polegate* and A22 to (70m) **Eastbourne**, see Rte 10A.

# 11 London to Brighton

## A. Via Redhill

Total distance 51m. A23 to (14m) Purley.—A23 to (21m) **Redhill**. —A23 to (25m) Horley.—B2036 to (37m) Cuckfield.—A272, A273 to (44½m) Clayton.—A23 to (51m) **Brighton**.

Maps: OS Landranger 176, 187, 198.

Slower but more attractive than Rte 11B. For the motorway (M23), see Rte 11B.

We leave London via Vauxhall Bridge Rd, Streatham High Rd and Purley Way (the Croydon bypass).—14m. *Purley.*—15¼m. *Couldson*. The road on the right ascends to the still rural village of *Chipstead* (2m) with a 12–13C church. The isolated church of *Chaldon*, 3m SE, has a large and remarkable tempera painting of the 'Ladder of Human Salvation' (c 1200).—Beyond the M23 and M25 we cross the North Downs, which separate the London basin from the Weald.

21m. **Redhill**, an important railway junction, is an eastern extension of Reigate (Rte 11B).

The road to Godstone leads E via (3m) Bletchingley (Rte 10B).—At *Outwood*, 3m SE of Redhill, is a windmill of 1665 and 2000 acres of NT property.

On approaching (25m) *Horley* we take B2036 left and soon after

wards enter Sussex and the attractive countryside of the Weald.
—27m. *Burstow* church (1m E) is partly 12C, and has a memorial to
John Flamsteed (d. 1719), the Astronomer Royal, who was rector here
from 1684.—29¹/₂m. A sideroad leads left to *Worth*. The large Saxon
\*church retains its original plan and masonry, with an imposing
chancel arch and rare two-light windows. The font is 13C.—On the
left beyond (33m) *Balcombe* we see the lofty viaduct which carries
the railway across the Ouse valley.—37m. *Cuckfield* (28,300 inhab.)
lies on the Southern Forest Ridge. Henry Kingsley (1830–76) is
buried in the churchyard. As it leaves the town, the road passes the
delightful gatehouse of *Cuckfield Place*, a fine mansion of c 1574
(altered in 1848), described in Harrison Ainsworth's novel 'Rookwood'. Legh Manor, beyond *Ansty* 2m SW, is a small 16C mansion
with interesting furniture and lovely gardens (limited opening).
—A272 leads E from Cuckfield to (38¹/₂m) the junction with A273.

1m further E is the pleasant town of *Haywards Heath*. To the N, *Lindfield* has
some fine old houses in the well-preserved village street. *Wakehurst Place
Garden* (open), on B2028 3¹/₂m NW, is owned by NT and administered by the
Royal Botanic Gardens, Kew. The 460-acre park, created by the first Lord
Wakehurst, a President of the Royal Horticultural Society, combines scenic
beauty with botanic interest.

We take A273 S through (41m) *Burgess Hill* (23,500 inhab.) and
(43¹/₂m) *Hassocks*. To the E is *Ditchling* (2m), a village where the
artist Sir Frank Brangwyn (1867–1956) died. About 1¹/₂m SW of
Hassocks is the Elizabethan house of *Danny* (limited opening).—At
(44¹/₂m) *Clayton* we reach the South Downs. On the right rises
*Wolstanbury Hill* (677ft), on the left *Ditchling Beacon* (812ft; NT),
with a \*view and two windmills. Clayton church has an 11C chancel
arch and well-preserved \*wall paintings (c 1140).—At 46m we rejoin
A23.

51m. **BRIGHTON** (146,100 inhab.) is the largest town and most
famous seaside resort in southern England. Its buildings reach 3¹/₂m
inland towards the South Downs, while the seafront stretches 7m
from Hove in the W (an independent borough with 66,600 inhab.) to
beyond Rottingdean in the E. Its nickname of 'London by the Sea'
aptly sugests its urban liveliness and its variegated seaside charms,
ranging from Regency elegance to cheerful 20C vulgarity.

**Tourist Information Centres**: Marlborough House, Old Steine; (seasonal)
Seafront, King's Rd; Town Hall, Norton Rd, Hove.

**Car Parks**: West St., Town Hall, Bread St., Trafalgar St., Pelham St. Multi-storey
car parks in Cannon Place, Churchill Square, Church St., North Rd, Blackman
St. Underground car parks at the Metropole, Regency Square and High St.

**Bus Station**: Pool Valley.

**Railway Stations**: Central, at the N end of Queen's Rd, for all trains; Hove, for
Worthing, Portsmouth and London trains; Preston Park, for the N side of town;
and London Rd.

**Entertainments**: Theatre Royal, New Rd; Dome (variety), by the Royal Pavilion;
Gardner Centre for the Arts, University of Sussex; and all the usual seaside
amusements in abundance along the seafront.

**History**. Brighton is mentioned in Domesday Book under the name of *Brighthelmston* or *Brithelmeston*, after a more or less mythical Bishop of Selsey; and
the fishing village of Domesday seems to have remained a fishing village for
about seven centuries. The one gleam of interest in its history is that Charles II
spent a night here before his escape to France in 1651. The foundation of its
modern prosperity was laid in the middle of the 18C by Dr Richard Russell of
Lewes, who strongly recommended its bracing air and sea-bathing (tablet on

the Albion Hotel). Fanny Burney, Mrs Thrale and Dr Johnson were among the early visitors (1770). A decisive cachet of fashion was added when George IV, then Prince of Wales, came to live here in 1786 and built the Pavilion. Its growth was then rapid, towards Kemp Town in the E and Hove in the W; the coming of the railway confirmed Brighton's popularity, while making it less exclusively fashionable.

**Famous natives, residents and visitors.** Aubrey Beardsley (1874–98; born in Buckingham Rd) and Roger Quilter (1877–1953) were natives of Brighton; Herbert Spencer (1820–1903), who lived at No. 5 Percival Terrace, Kemp Town, R.S. Surtees (1803–64), Hablot K. Browne ('Phiz'; 1815–82), Thomas Hughes (1822–96), and G.J. Holyoake (1817–1906), the social reformer, all died here. The list of distinguished residents includes George Canning (1770–1827; tablet on the Royal Crescent Hotel), Harrison Ainsworth (1805–82) and Richard Jefferies (1848–87). Rowland Hill (1795–1879), the originator of penny postage, was also chairman of the Brighton Railway, and was responsible for the introduction of express and excursion services. Lewis Carroll spent his Christmas holiday for 25 years at No. 11 Sussex Square, Kemp Town. William Friese-Greene (1855–1921), a pioneer of the cinema, had his workshop in Middle St.; Gladstone frequently spent his holidays at the former Lion Mansion Hotel; and Metternich stayed at No. 42 Brunswick Terrace in 1848–49. Sir Hamilton Harty (1880–1941) died at Hove, and Sir Winston Churchill was at school at Lansworth House, Brunswick Rd, in 1883–85.— Thackeray's 'Vanity Fair', Dickens's 'Dombey and Son' and Graham Greene's 'Brighton Rock' all feature Brighton in their pages.

The centre of the town is the *Old Steine* (pronounced 'Steen'), an open space with gardens, believed to take its name from the stone where fishermen used to dry their nets. On the W side, No. 55 was the residence of George IV's mistress and secret wife, Mrs Fitz-herbert (d. 1837, and buried in St John's, Kemp Town). The Steine is dominated by the *Royal Pavilion (open), the palace which George built for himself while Prince of Wales.

The Prince first rented a 'superior farmhouse' on the site in 1786; the next year Henry Holland enlarged it into a symmetrical neo-classical composition. In 1815–22, after many plans and possible architects had been debated and rejected, John Nash transformed Holland's building into the exotic fantasy whose distinctive outline now startles and delights the visitor. Nash's pagodas and balconies are Oriental only in the loosest sense, mixing Indian, Chinese and even Gothic with happy freedom; they surrender everywhere to the possibilities of ornate invention rather than to the requirements of scholarly accuracy. The result captures the spirit of the Regency at play more completely than any other building of the age. The rich interiors range from the deliberately dramatic Banqueting Room to the restrained sophistication of the Prince's private apartments.

Queen Victoria, not somebody who could be expected to appreciate the Pavilion's charms, sold the building to the town of Brighton and moved her seaside home to Osborne in 1845. It has been excellently restored in recent years and again has much of its original furniture. It is fully furnished during the annual Regency exhibition, between early June and the end of September.

William Porden's royal stables with their distinctive dome (1804–08) have been converted into the *Dome Theatre*. Round the corner in Church St. is the *Public Library, Museum and Art Gallery*.

The Museum is interesting for its Sussex Room, illustrating the archaeology and history of Sussex, and contains the well-known Willett Collection of English pottery. The Art Gallery, with 18C furniture (made for Stanmer House) and silver (by Lamerie and Paul Storr), has a representative collection of British painting of the 19C and early 20C, fine watercolours, and some Old Masters.

The old town between the Old Steine, West St., and North St. (the main shopping street), contains The Lanes, a quarter of narrow alleys, with many antique shops. Brighton Square is a successful new

# BRIGHTON

| 0 | 300 yards |
| 0 | 300 metres |

*Pelmet in the Music Room of the Royal Pavilion, Brighton*

addition to this pedestrian precinct. The area to the N right up to Trafalgar St. and bounded W and E by Queen's Rd and the Victoria Gardens is developing a similar character.

A broad Esplanade stretches the whole length of the seafront. E of the Old Steine and Palace Pier runs Marine Parade, with attractive early 19C terraces, squares and crescents, to (1m) *Kemp Town*, the Regency development begun by Thomas Read Kemp in 1823 with Wilds and Busby as his architects and Thomas Cubitt among the builders. Sussex Square and Lewes Crescent, fronting the sea, make a handsome centrepiece. On the level of the beach is the wide and well-sheltered Madeira Drive, skirted by Volk's Electric Railway, and bordered by a covered walk ½m long, above which is a sheltered promenade on the cliff-side. The drive ends at *Black Rock*, where a large marina caters for pleasure boats. An undercliff walk continues to Rottingdean and Saltdean (see below).

The *Palace Pier*, immediately S of the Old Steine, replaces the Chain Pier, the first of its kind (1823), which stood a few yards further E until it was destroyed by a December storm in 1896. For many years it was the terminus of the cross-Channel service to Dieppe, and Queen Victoria and the Prince Consort disembarked here in 1843. The *West Pier* (1866) is now closed.

W of Palace Pier, King's Rd runs to (1m) **Hove**, and is prolonged to Kingsway, separated from the beach by well-kept lawns and skirting charming squares and terraces. Regency Square and Brunswick Square and Terrace are notable examples of early 19C architecture. Adelaide Crescent (1830–50) and Palmeira Square are also attractive. Hove *Museum* is in Brooker Hall, New Church Rd.

At the start of the London Rd, N of the Old Steine, is *St Peter's*, the parish church of Brighton since 1873, a conspicuous Perp. building by Barry (1824). In Ann St., a left turn off the London Rd, is another and better 19C church, the magnificent plain brick *St Bartholomew (1872–74) by the local architect Edmund Scott.

London Rd continues as Preston Rd to (1m) *Preston Park* and *Preston Manor* (open). Built in 1758 on the foundations of a medieval building, the house was given to Brighton by Sir Charles and Lady Thomas-Stanford in 1932. Most of the contents remain, and the atmosphere is still that of an Edwardian family home.

The collections include good porcelain and silver and, in the library, the Macquoid Bequest of furniture and decorative arts.

On Dyke Rd, running NW from the centre, is the original parish church of *St Nicholas*, built in 1380 but largely rebuilt in 1853. The font (c 1170) has good carvings of the Last Supper, the Baptism of Christ and the Legend of St Nicholas. The font cover is an elabrate memorial to the Duke of Wellington (1853). On the N wall, near what used to be the Thrale pew, is a tablet recording that Dr Johnson used to worship here. In the churchyard (S of chancel) lies Nicholas Tettersell, captain of the ship that bore Charles II from Shoreham in 1651 (see below). Nearby (E) is the tomb of Martha Gunn (1727–1815), most famous of Brighton 'bathing-women'.

Dyke Rd continues past (1m) the *Booth Bird Museum* to (5¹/2m) the *Devil's Dyke, a deep and narrow hollow in the Downs. The top of the dyke hill (697ft), since 1928 the property of Brighton, gives a wide view. The Dyke is a good starting-point for walks on the Downs. A pleasant descent can be made NE via the pretty hamlet of *Saddlescombe* to (1¹/2m) Poynings (Rte 11B).
    The road from Brighton to Lewes (9m) via (4¹/2m) *Falmer*, skirts *Stanmer Park*, occupied since 1961 by the **University of Sussex**, with buildings designed by Sir Basil Spence; the Gardner Centre for the Arts holds music and drama events. The public still have access to the beautiful park (535 acres).

FROM BRIGHTON TO NEWHAVEN, 9m. Marine Parade leads E to Black Rock (see above), where A259 continues past *Roedean*, a famous school for girls founded in 1885.—3m. **Rottingdean** lies at the mouth of a 'dean' (or combe) in the chalk cliffs and still preserves its old village street. The church has windows by Sir Edward Burne-Jones (1833–98), who is buried in the churchyard at the SW corner of the church and who lived at North End House in the village. Rudyard Kipling stayed for a time at The Elms. The *Grange* (open) contains a good collection of toys, Sussex antiquities and Kipling relics. *Ovingdean*, 1m SW, has a church with an 11C chancel and a manor house which appears in Harrison Ainsworth's 'Ovingdean Grange'.—The cliff road goes on to (4¹/2m) *Saltdean* and (6m) the dreary *Peacehaven* (Tourist Information).—9m. *Newhaven*, see Rte 10B.

FROM BRIGHTON TO WORTHING, 10¹/2m, A259 or A57.—1m. **Hove.**—2m. *Portslade* and (3¹/2m) *Southwick* are connected by a line of wharves. At the foot of the Downs above Southwick is an interesting Roman villa.—5m. **Shoreham-by-Sea** (20,800 inhab.; Tourist Information) is still important as a port. From the small harbour Charles II escaped to Fécamp in 1651. *St Mary de Haura* (i.e. 'of the harbour') has a fine Trans. choir with EE vaulting. The tower arches have unusually large capitals. In the nearby High St. is *The Marlipins*, a small medieval house now open as a museum. In Old Shoreham, 1m up the Adur, just below the new bridge, is the Norman church of *St Nicholas*, with a contemporary tower and a partly Saxon W end. To Horsham, see Rte 12.—We cross the Adur.—7¹/4m. *Lancing* has a partly Norman church. *Lancing College*, on the right, has an impressive Gothic Revival *chapel, begun in 1868 and completed with a huge rose window in 1977. It is open to the public.—10¹/2m. Worthing, see Rte 12.

# B.  Via Reigate

Total distance 52m. A217 to (21m) **Reigate.**—A217, A23 to (30m) Crawley (bypassed).—A23 to (34m) Handcross.—A23 to (46m) Pyecombe.—A23 to (52m) **Brighton** (Rte 11A).

Maps: OS Landranger 176, 187, 198.

Quicker but less interesting than Rte 11A. The fastest way from London to Brighton uses the well-landscaped M23, either from its beginning on A23 S of Coulsdon or from the interchange with M25, to bypass Reigate/Redhill and Crawley.

To leave London we cross the Thames by Putney Bridge and take A217 through Wandsworth. In Mitcham the road swings right to bypass Sutton via (15m) *Banstead*. Beyond (16m) *Burgh Heath* we cross the interchange with M25 (access to M23) and descend Reigate Hill (*view).

21m. **Reigate** (52,600 inhab. with Redhill), on the southern edge of the North Downs, does not have much to detain the visitor. In the High St. is the old *Town Hall* (1728). To the N are the earthworks marking the site of the *Castle* destroyed in the Civil War; the gateway was built in 1777 out of the old stones. The large parish church of *St Mary Magdalene* at the E end of the town has a fine nave arcade of c 1200. Lord Howard of Effingham (1536–1624), victor over the Spanish Armada in 1588, is buried beneath the chancel.

W of the town is *Reigate Priory*, on the site of an Augustinian foundation of the 13C and once the seat of Lord Howard. To its S is the finely wooded ridge of *Reigate Park*.—*Reigate Hill* (700ft) and *Colley Hill* (763ft), 1¹/₂m N and NW of the town, include about 150 acres of NT land and command wide views of the Weald.—In easy reach are the churches of *Leigh* (3¹/₂m SW; pronounced 'Lye'), with brasses, and *Charlwood* (6¹/₂m S), with 13–15C wall paintings and a 15C screen.—A25 to (6m) *Dorking* (Rte 12) leads via (2m) *Buckland*, where the rebuilt church has an old wooden belfry.

26¹/₂m. *Gatwick*, with London's second airport, has a spur from M23. We enter Sussex and change to A23.—30m. **Crawley**, a 'satellite' town (72,800 inhab.), is bypassed to the W. Right of the road is St Leonard's Forest.—34m. *Handcross*. ¹/₂m SE are the noted gardens of *Nymans* (NT). At *Slaugham Manor* (1m SW), now a hotel and country club, are the ruins of a mansion probably built for the ironmaster Richard Covert (d. 1579) and dismantled in 1735; it is perhaps by Flynton, who carved Richard's tomb in the church.—45m. *Newtimber Place* (limited opening), right of the road, is a moated 17C house with a Georgian dovecote and Etruscan-style wall paintings in the hall.—46m. *Pyecombe* lies in a gap of the South Downs between Wolstanbury Hill on the left (Rte 11A) and Newtimber Hill (660ft; NT). In the church the central chancel arch is Norman and the interesting lead font dates from the late 12C. On the W side of Newtimber Hill is *Poynings* (2m) where the 14C church is on the plan of a Greek cross; and there is another lead font at *Edburton*, 2m further W. For Devil's Dyke, see Rte 11A.—54m. **Brighton**, Rte 11A.

# 12  London to Worthing

Total distance 57m. A3 to (14m) Hook Corner.—A243 to (20m) Leatherhead (bypassed).—A24 to (23¹/₂m) Burford Bridge (Box Hill).—A24 to (25m) **Dorking** (bypassed).—A24 to (38m) **Horsham** (bypassed).—A24 to (50m) Washington.—A24 to (57m) **Worthing**.

Maps: OS Landranger 176, 187, 198.

A route more interesting for scenery than for towns.

We leave London by Putney Bridge and take A3 as it bypasses Kingston to the S. At (14m) *Hook Corner* we turn left on A243.

An alternative way from London (A24) runs via Morden to (15m) **Epsom** (69,200 inhab. with Ewell). At *Epsom Downs*, 1¹/₂m NW, the Derby and the Oaks (started in 1780 and 1779) are run in May or June. The parish church has monuments by Flaxman and Chantrey.—At (17¹/₂m) *Ashtead* the writer George

MacDonald died in 1905. The church has a stained glass window of c 1500 from Herck in Belgium.—A24 joins the main route at (19¹/2m) Leatherhead.

15¹/2m. *Chessington*, on the right, is a popular zoo and amusement park.—20m. **Leatherhead** (40,500 inhab.) has become one of the most featureless towns in Surrey. Anthony Hope (Sir Anthony Hope Hawkins; 1863–1933) is buried in ₁the churchyard. The Council Offices stand on the site of Kingston House, where John Wesley preached his last sermon on 23 February 1791.

FROM LEATHERHEAD TO GUILDFORD, 11¹/2m via A246, along the N ridge of the Downs.—From (2m) *Great Bookham* a sideroad leads S for 1¹/2m to *'Polesden Lacey* (NT). The house was built by Thomas Cubitt in 1824 on the site of a mansion once owned by Sheridan, but owes most of its present character to the handsome Edwardian alterations by Ambrose Poynter. The first-rate collection of paintings includes 17C Dutch works and British portraits (Reynolds, Raeburn). The grounds give lovely views across the North Downs, and there is a pleasant walk S to *Ranmore Common.*—At (5m) *East Horsley* the church has an 11C tower and good brasses.— 7m. Between *West Horsley* and *East Clandon* is *Hatchlands* (NT), a neat brick house in the Palladian style built for Admiral Boscawen in 1756–57. The interior is by Robert Adam, though lacking its original furniture and rather the worse for later alterations.—8¹/2m. *Clandon Park* (NT), built by Giacomo Leoni in the 1730s, has fared considerably better. The magnificent interior, with plasterwork by Artari and chimneypieces by Rysbrack, has been well restored and redecorated (by John Fowler). The contents include the Gubbay collection of Chinese porcelain birds.—11¹/2m. *Guildford,* see Rte 13B.

We leave Leatherhead by A24.—22m. *Mickleham*, left of the road, lies in the valley of the Mole between the chalk downs. At the church Fanny Burney was married in 1793 and George Meredith in 1864. A path leads across the Mole and through *Norbury Park*, famous for its beeches and for the yews in the 'Druids' Grove', rejoining the road near Burford Bridge. *Juniper Hall*, 1m SE, now a study centre, was once occupied by a group of French refugees, including General d'Arblay, who married Fanny Burney.—23¹/2m. *Burford Bridge* spans the Mole at the foot of Box Hill. At the hotel Keats finished 'Endymion' and R.L. Stevenson stayed several times in 1878–86.

*'Box Hill* (596ft), including c 900 acres of NT property, is a spectacular expanse of down and woodland with numerous box trees from which it takes its name. A fine walk leads along the S face following the **Pilgrims' Way**, via Pebble Coombe to (6m) Reigate (Rte 11B); or the ridge may be followed N across Mickleham Downs (NT) to 4m Leatherhead.—A little above Burford Bridge is *Flint Cottage*, the home from 1867 of George Meredith (1828–1909), who is buried in Dorking cemetery. At the top of the steep garden is the chalet built by Meredith as a study and bedroom in 1877. A later occupant of the cottage was Max Beerbohm, a refugee in the Second World War from Rapallo, and from his bombed cottage at Abinger.

25m. **Dorking** (21,700 inhab.) has little intrinsic interest but makes a good centre for walks. Ralph Vaughan Williams lived here for 20 years.

A pleasant walk to the NW leads over *Ranmore Common* to (3m) *Polesden Lacey* and (5m) *Great Bookham* (see above).
*'Leith Hill*, 4¹/2m SW of Dorking, is at 965ft the highest point in SE England. On a clear day the *'view includes St Paul's in London and the Channel, with ships passing Shoreham Gap. The surrounding woods (NT; 750 acres) are rich in bluebells and rhododendrons. Walkers can approach the hill from the Guildford road (A25) between Westcott and Wotton Hatch, or from Holmwood Station, off A24. From the summit a pleasant path leads N to Friday Street and then down the W bank of the brook to Wotton House on the A25. Motorists take the road climbing to (3¹/2m) *Coldharbour*, a hamlet at the foot of *Anstiebury Camp* (not open), the finest prehistoric camp in Surrey, with double trenches. Beyond (4m) Coldharbour church the road crosses a beautifully wooded stretch

and passes just below the conspicuous tower on the top of the hill. Further on, we turn right for (7½m) *Abinger*, with a restored 11C church, a manor house with Jacobean porch, and the old stocks on the green. About ¾m E is *Friday Street*, a picturesque hamlet of red cottages facing a large mere. 2m SW the charming village of *Holmbury St Mary* lies beneath *Holmbury Hill* (857ft). We join the A25 to Guildford due N of Abinger at (8½m) *Manor Farm*.

FROM DORKING TO GUILDFORD, 12m via A25.—Beyond (1¼m) *Westcott* and The Rookery (left), birthplace of Malthus (1766–1834), A25 climbs to (23/ 4m) *Wotton*. Below the road, on the right, we see the church where the diarist John Evelyn (1620–1706) is buried in the family chapel. On the left is Evelyn's home, *Wotton House* (not open); some of the surrounding woods date from his planting. Shortly before the second sideroad on the left (leading to Leith Hill, see above), we pass *Crossways Farm* (George Meredith's 'Diana of the Crossways') and (4½m) *Abinger Hammer*, a village named after an old iron furnace. E.M. Forster (1878–1969) lived at West Hackhurst (not open) and left the adjoining Piney Copse ('Forster's Wood') to the NT on his death.—5m. *Gomshall Station.* An attractive road leads S to *Peaslake* (2½m) and almost to the top of *Coneyhurst Hill* (844ft), the W summit of the Leith Hill greensand ridge. The thickly wooded ridge to the N (*Hackhurst Downs, Netley Heath;* 270 acres NT) is crossed by steep and remote lanes, some of them accessible by car.—6½m. A25 bypasses **Shere**, on the Tillingbourne, perhaps the prettiest village in Surrey, with a well-restored 12–15C church.

At the fork in the road beyond Shere A248 (left) offers an alternative way to Guildford. At 1m is *Albury Park* (now flats; limited opening), an originally Tudor house remodelled several times, most thoroughly by A.W.N. Pugin in 1846–52, without impressive result. The gardens laid out by John Evelyn are not open to the public. The old village church, redundant since the 1840s, has traces of Saxon and Norman work. *Chilworth* (2½m) lies N of *Blackheath* (NT), a tract of open heath. 1m N of the village is *St Martha's Hill* (720ft), with the lonely *Chapel of St Martha* (*view) on the Pilgrims' Way. The Norman fabric was largely rebuilt in 1848.

A25 ascends to (8½m) *Newlands Corner* (500ft), on the summit of the chalk ridge, affording a famous *view. Part of the Pilgrims' Way is traceable on the Downs, and to the S appears St Martha's Chapel. The road goes on, over *Merrow Downs*, to (10m) *Merrow*, and then left to (12m) *Guildford* (Rte 13B).

A pleasant walk leads back from Newlands Corner to (8m) Dorking along the crest of the North Downs, via Netley Heath and Ranmore Common.

S of Dorking A24 skirts *Holmwood Common* (NT; 630 acres) and enters Sussex. About 1½m SW of (35m) *Warnham* is *Field Place* (not open), where the poet Shelley (1792–1822) was born.

38m. **Horsham** (bypassed) is a congested market town (25,400 inhab.). Many old houses are to be seen in The Causeway, at the end of West St., among them the gabled 16C *Museum* with the old stocks, bullring, and whipping-post. At the end is the EE *Church*, with Perp. windows and a shingle spire, containing interesting monuments. Horsham stone, easily split, is a traditional material for roofslabs throughout Sussex.

About 2m SW, are the large but somewhat ineffective red-brick buildings of **Christ's Hospital**, the famous 'Blue Coat School', founded in London by Edward VI in 1552 and removed here in 1902. The boys still wear the ancient costume of blue gowns, knee breeches, and yellow stockings. This was the school of Charles Lamb, Coleridge,. Leigh Hunt and Constant Lambert, and among earlier pupils were Camden, Stillingfleet and Middleton. In the dining hall is a large painting by Verrio depicting the Endowment of the Royal Mathematical School in 1672; in the chapel are paintings by Brangwyn.

FROM HORSHAM TO SHOREHAM, 21m.—A281 leads S to (7m) *Cowfold*. The Perp. church, surrounded by pretty cottages, has a fine tower and contains the splendid brass, 10ft long, of Prior Nelond (1433).—Beyond (8¼m) *St Hugh's Charterhouse*, established by monks from the Grande-Chartreuse (1877–83), we turn right on B2116 for (9½m) *Partridge Green*, where we take B2135 S and cross the Adur.—At (12m) *Ashurst* 'Michael Fairless' (Margaret Fairless Barber; d. 1901), author of 'The Roadmender', is buried. She died at Mock Bridge

House, near Shermanbury, 1¹/₂m E on the Henfield road.—16m. **Steyning**, a pleasant little town with an old grammar school at the foot of the Downs, has a *Church founded by St Cuthman. Its most striking feature is the series of enriched late Norman arches in the nave (c 1150). The plain E arches of the nave and aisles are 100 years older. Near the Purbeck marble font is the 'Steyning Stone', probably of pre-Christian origin, rediscovered in 1938 in the churchyard. In the house on Chantry Green Yeats wrote many of his later poems. About 2m W rises *Chanctonbury Ring* (783ft), a conspicuous summit crowned with ancient entrenchments and a circle of beeches. Glorious walks may be taken from Steyning along the Downs to (5m) the Devil's Dyke (Rte 11A) on the E, or to (10m) Amberley (Rte 13A) on the W.—A283 heads S to (17m) *Bramber*, where the little Norman church with interesting capitals. It stands beside fragments of a castle (English Heritage, open at any reasonable time) including part of a tower keep 76ft high, erected to guard the estuary of the Adur. St Mary's (open) is a handsome medieval house with later panelling and leather wall-hangings. The House of Pipes is a museum of smoking. At *Botolphs* and at *Coombes*, 1m and 2m S, are quaint little churches of 11C foundation, with wall paintings of c 1100.—21m. *Shoreham*, see Rte 11A.

From Horsham to *Guildford*, see Rte 13B; to *Arundel*, etc., see Rte 13A.

44m. *West Grinstead*, on the left, has a partly Norman church. In West Grinstead Park is 'Pope's Oak', under which the poet is said to have written 'The Rape of the Lock' at the suggestion of his host, John Caryll. On the right of A24 are the ruins of *Knepp Castle* and *Knepp Park*, with a lake 1m long. At *Shipley*, on B2224 1m further W, is a restored early 19C mill (open), once owned by Hilaire Belloc (1870–1953) who lived in the house nearby.—50m. *Washington*, where John Ireland died in 1962, lies below Chanctonbury Ring (see above) and a fine road leads W beneath the South Downs to (2¹/₂m) *Storrington* (2¹/₂m) and (6m) Amberley (Rte 13A).—53m. *Findon* (bypassed) is the nearest village to Cissbury Ring (see below). A280, the 'Long Furlong' with splendid views, leads right for Arundel.

57m. **Worthing** (91,700 inhab.; Tourist Information) is a resort with a mild climate, a shingly beach and an atmosphere made sedate by the large number of retired people. It has little of interest apart from the *Museum* in Chapel Rd, with a good collection of Roman remains, English watercolours, dolls, etc.

Worthing, however, makes a good centre for touring the South Downs and its churches.—The Trans. Norman church of *Broadwater*, a suburb 1m N, has old brasses and monuments. In the nearby cemetery lie Richard Jefferies (see below) and W.H. Hudson (1841–1922), the naturalists.—The *church at *Sompting*, 2m NE, has been called 'the greatest architectural curiosity in the county', largely because the Saxon tower has the single example in England of a 'Rhenish helm' roof. Inside are fragments of Saxon carving and a vaulted chapel built on the S side of the nave by the Templars (c 1184). Nearby is the cottage where Edward Trelawny, friend of Byron and Shelley, died in 1881.—*Tarring*, 1¹/₄m NW of Worthing's centre, has a charming High St. which includes the Parsonage Row Museum of Sussex Folklore, and a famous fig garden said to have been planted by Becket. The EE church, with a Perp. tower, contains a tablet to the antiquary John Selden (1584–1654), born at *Salvington*, 1m further N. *High Salvington*, another 1m N beyond A24, has a restored post mill of 1700.—*Cissbury Hill* (602ft; NT), 3m N of Worthing, is crowned by *Cissbury Ring* (c 300 BC), the largest entrenchment on the South Downs.

FROM WORTHING TO CHICHESTER, 25m by the coast road (A259) past a succession of seaside resorts.—At (2¹/₄m) *Goring-by-Sea* Richard Jefferies died in 1887.—10m. *Littlehampton* (22,200 inhab.; seasonal Tourist Information), with good sands at the mouth of the Arun.—12m. *Climping* has a 13C church with a tower of 1170. To the N is *Ford*, with an open prison and a tiny Norman church.—At (16¹/₂m) *Felpham*, now a suburb of Bognor, are the cottage where William Blake lived in 1801-04 and the house of his patron and fellow poet William Hayley (1745–1820), who is buried in the church.—18m. **Bognor Regis** (39,500 inhab.; Tourist Information), a resort favoured by Queen Victoria, became 'Regis' after George V spent a convalescent holiday in 1929 at *Aldwick*, 1¹/₂m W.—We join A259 for (25m) *Chichester*, see Rte 13A.

# 13  London to Portsmouth

## A.  Via Arundel and Chichester

Total distance 84½m. To (25m) Dorking, see Rte 12.—A24 to
(29½m) Beare Green.—A29 to (42½m) Billingshurst.—A29 to
(47½m) Pulborough.—A29 to (54½m) Whiteways Lodge.—A284
to (56½m) **Arundel**.—A27 to (66½m) **Chichester** (bypassed).
—A27 to (84½m) **Portsmouth** (bypassed).

Maps: OS Landranger 176, 187, 197, 196 (briefly).

Longer and less direct than Rte 13B but more interesting for
architecture.

From London to (25m) *Dorking*, see Rte 12.—At (29½m) *Beare Green*
we take A29 to the right.—Near (33m) *Ockley* the Danes were
defeated by Ethelwulf of Wessex in 851. Leith Hill (Rte 12) rises on
the right.—At (38½m) *Roman Gate* begins a long section of the
Roman Stane Street, leading from London to Chichester.— 42½m.
*Billingshurst*, with a 16C half-timbered inn. At *Coolham*, 3m SE, is
the curiously named 'Blue Idol', an old Quaker meeting house (now a
guest house) associated with William Penn. For Shipley, 2m further,
see Rte 12. *Wisborough Green*, 2m W of Billingshurst on the Petworth
road, is a charming village on the verge of some of the best country in
Sussex. Its church has late 13C wall paintings.—47½m. **Pulborough**,
on the Arun, has a large EE and Perp. church with brasses.

At *Bignor*, 7m SW (2m W of Bury, see below), in a pleasant position at the foot of
the Downs, is a fine *Roman Villa* (open). It was inhabited in the 2–4C and first
excavated in 1811–19, when the rustic buildings covering important mosaics
(mostly 4C) were erected. A museum has finds from later excavations.—A
footpath leads along the Arun from Pulborough to *Wiggonholt*, 2m SE, while
*West Chiltington*, 3m E, has its stocks and whipping-post and a good 12C
church with contemporary wall paintings.
   4m SE of Pulborough is *Parham* (open), nicely set in a deer park at the foot of
the Downs. Built for the Palmer family in 1577, it is a substantial yet restrained
building of grey stone, with a roof of Horsham slate. The handsome interior
includes a Great Hall and Long Gallery. The Green Room has items connected
with the naturalist and explorer Sir Joseph Banks (1743–1820), among them
portraits by Reynolds and Romney, and a charming little kangaroo by Stubbs.

FROM PULBOROUGH TO MIDHURST, 12m via A283 and A272.—1m. *Stopham*,
with a narrow 14C bridge on the Arun.—5m. *Petworth* has narrow tangled
streets and good buildings of almost every period. Close to the centre stands
**Petworth House** (NT), built between 1688 and 1696 in the French grand style.
The Marble Hall has woodcarving by John Selden, while the small dining room
(or Carved Room) is rich with the work of Grinling Gibbons. The *art collection
is outstanding, with Greek and Roman sculpture, portraits by Van Dyck and
Kneller, and works by Turner, a frequent guest here. The Chapel is a pleasing
mixture of 13C (from the original house on the site) and 17C (carvings by
Selden). The *grounds (open all year) are among the finest achievements of
Capability Brown.—12m. **Midhurst**, a charming old town on the Rother, is
interesting for the imposing ruins of *Cowdray House*, a Tudor mansion
destroyed by fire in 1793, in Cowdray Park (open). Richard Cobden
(1804–65) and H.G. Wells were pupils at the 17C Grammar School (altered in
18C). The church of *Easebourne* (pronounced 'Ezburn'), 1m NE, contains an
effigy of Sir David Owen (d. 1535), uncle of Henry VII, and adjoins the buildings
of a 13C priory of Augustinian nuns (now the church hall and vicarage). About
1m S of Midhurst an obelisk commemorates Cobden, who is buried at *West
Lavington*, ¾m SE. *Trotton*, 3½m W of Midhurst, was the birthplace of the
dramatist Thomas Otway (1652–85). The church has a wall painting of the Last

Judgement (c 1380) and impressive brasses to members of the Camoy family; one of 1310 is the earliest brass in England to a woman.

*The ruins of Cowdray House*

We cross the Arun, which meanders through rich water meadows.—48¹⁄₂m. *Hardham* has a church with 12C wall paintings.—52¹⁄₂m. *Bury*, 2m from Bignor (see above), where the novelist John Galsworthy (1867–1933) had his country home, lies opposite *Amberley*, a charming *village with a ruined castle of the Bishops of Chichester (not open) and a late Norman church. The Amberley Chalk Pits Museum has an open-air display of industrial history in a former limeworks and quarry.—54¹⁄₂m. *Whiteways Lodge* commands a fine *view, with Arundel Park on the left. A284 leads S.

56¹⁄₂m. **Arundel** (2400 inhab.; Tourist Information), a country town in the gap made by the Arun in the South Downs, clusters round the base of its *Castle* (open).

Besieged by Henry I in 1102 and by Stephen in 1139, the Norman castle was finally laid in ruins by the Parliamentarians in 1643–44. The present building is mainly a baronial exercise of the 1790s and 1890s. The late Victorian chapel and the Library (1801) are interesting speciments of the Gothic Revival. Of medieval architecture, only the Fitzalan Chapel (see below), the lower stages of the 12C Keep and the 13C Bevis Tower survive relatively unscathed.

The parish church of *St Nicholas* (c 1380) has a rare pre-Reformation pulpit and 14C wall paintings. The *Fitzalan Chapel*, behind the altar and separated from the rest of the building by an ancient iron grille protected by plate glass, is the property of the Duke of Norfolk (who is a Roman Catholic). It was originally founded in 1380 as the chapel of the College of the Holy Trinity and contains fine *monuments of the Fitzalans, previous holders of the earldom of Arundel, which passes with the property and was acquired by the Howards through marriage in 1580. The 15th Duke (1847–1917) restored the chapel and also built the conspicuous Roman Catholic cathedral church of *St Philip Neri*, with a slender flèche (1869–76; J.A. Hansom). The writer George MacDonald was pastor of the Tarrant St. chapel in 1850. In the High St. is *Potter's Museum of Curiosity*, a Victorian museum of taxidermy.

Charming walks ascend both banks of the Arun to (3m) *Amberley Bridge* on the W bank and to (2m) *Burpham* on the E bank, at the foot of the South Downs, with a Norman and EE church and a notable promontory-fort, probably built to resist Danish sea-raiders.—For *Littlehampton*, 4m S of Arundel on A284, see Rte 12.

A27 runs W from Arundel, crossing the Bognor road (A29) near (60¹/₂m) *Fontwell*. To the right is (¹/₂m) *Slindon*, where Archbishop Stephen Langton died in 1228 (memorial in church), with 3500 acres of NT land above it. To the left is Fontwell Park racecourse (steeplechases).—63¹/₂m. Opposite *Tangmere* is *Boxgrove*, ¹/₄m N of the main road. The interesting Benedictine \*priory church here is notable for late Norman and EE work recalling Bishop Seffrid's contributions to Chichester cathedral. The W end of the nave is now in ruins. The pretty ceiling was painted by Lambert Barnard in 1530. The De La Warr chantry is an elaborate work of 1532. Of the monastic buildings to the N, only the ruined guest house (c 1300) and a fragment of the cloister remain.

66¹/₂m. **CHICHESTER** (24,200 inhab.), a charming cathedral city and the administrative centre of West Sussex, preserves an unusual number of 18C houses, both large and small. It is the ancient *Noviomagus*, called *Cisseceaster* in the Saxon Chronicle, and betrays its Roman origin in its four main streets, meeting at right angles in the centre of the town.

**Tourist Information Centre**: St Peter's Market, West St.

**Car Parks**: Avenue de Chartres, Southgate, South Pallant, Friary Lane, Little London, Cattle Market, Festival Theatre.

**Bus Station**: A286, beyond Southgate.

**Railway Station**: A286, beyond Southgate.

**Theatre**: Chichester Festival Theatre, Oaklands Park.

**Annual Events**: Festival Theatre Season May–September. Chichester Festivities (music, drama, exhibitions) in the first half of July. Racing at Goodwood Park for 15 days each year, including the Goodwood Cup in July. The Southern Cathedrals Festival of music is held annually (in July) in rotation with Winchester and Salisbury.

The \***Cathedral** is mainly Norman, and most later additions conform with the spirit of its original builders. The result may not be among the grandest English cathedrals but is certainly one of the most quietly satisfying. The exterior, a mixture of greenish limestone from the Isle of Wight and Caen stone, blends informally with the busy West St. The graceful spire, said to be the only English cathedral spire visible from the sea, dominates the town and makes a constant focus of views from the flat countryside around Chichester.

The cathedral was begun by Bishop de Luffa after the see of Selsey was moved here in c 1075. Work continued throughout the next century, interrupted by a serious fire in 1114, and the building consecrated in 1184 embodied the main structure of the present church. A second fire in 1187 prompted Bishop Seffrid II (1180–1204) to sympathetic alterations: renewing the inside of the clerestory, vaulting the roof in stone and converting the Norman apse into a square retrochoir. The three porches and sacristy are of the EE period. The outer aisles

SOUTH STREET

Canon Gate

WEST STREET

0 —— 100 feet
0 —— 30 metres

Vicars College

Lady Chapel

St John Baptist's Chapel

St Mary Magdalene's Chapel

GRAVE YARD

13

CLOISTER

RETRO-CHOIR

12

Small Sacristy

Treasury (Chapel of the Four Virgins)

Piper Tapestry

10
11
9

BURIAL

PRESBYTERY

GROUND

('Paradise')

8
7

RITUAL CHOIR

6

5

GRAVE YARD

Bell-Arundel Screen

4

St RICHARD'S WALK

Pulpit

3

SOUTH PORCH

CLOISTER

St Clement's Chapel

St George's Chapel

2

BELL TOWER

NORTH PORCH

Font

1

Bishop's Palace Gate →

Sailors' Chapel (NW Tower)

SW TOWER

WEST PORCH

Key to Numbers

1 William Collins
2 William Huskisson
3 Fitzalan Tomb
4 Maud of Arundel (?)
5 Bp Langton
6 Bp Stratford (?)
7 Thomas Weelkes
8 Gustav Holst
9 Romanesque Sculptures
10 Bp Sherburne
11 Dean Hook
12 St Richard's Altar & Shrine
13 Bp Luffa

# CHICHESTER CATHEDRAL

were added and the Lady Chapel enlarged in the Dec. style in about 1300. The spire, cloister and detached belfry (unique to an English cathedral apart from the modern one at Chester) were built soon after 1400.

Visitors enter by the EE W porch, from which the sober and harmonious proportions of the interior are immediately apparent. The arcades and gallery of Bishop de Luffa's *Nave* contrast effectively with Bishop Seffrid's light and graceful clerestory (in which Purbeck marble is freely used) and the Dec. tracery of the aisles. The monuments include two by Flaxman, to the poet William Collins (1721–59) in the SW tower and to Agnes Cromwell (d. 1797) in St Clement's Chapel. In the N aisle are: a statue of William Huskisson, the MP killed at the opening of the Liverpool and Manchester Railway in 1830; the fine tomb of Richard Fitzalan, Earl of Arundel (d. 1376) and his wife; and the tomb ascribed to Maud, Countess of Arundel (c 1300).

The *S Transept* has a fine seven-light window (c 1330). Below is the tomb of Bishop Langton (1305–37); opposite, under a fine Dec. canopy, is an expressive effigy, probably of Bishop Stratford (d. 1362), on a tomb chest dating from 1846. Here also are two unusual paintings (c 1519, restored) by Lambert Barnard, a local artist employed by Bishop Sherborne (1508–36). The EE *Sacristy* W of this transept has vaulting on exquisite corbels. The *N Transept*, long used as the parish church, has pictures of bishops by Lambert Barnard. The composer Gustav Holst (1874–1934) is buried here. On the W wall is a memorial to Thomas Weelkes, composer of madrigals and cathedral organist in 1602–23. The *Treasury* adjoins the transept to the E; above is the *Library* (open by appointment).

The nave is separated from the *Choir* by the Bell–Arundel Screen, a three-aisled structure attributed to Bishop Arundel (1459–78) and restored to its original position in memory of Bishop Bell (1929–58). The choir stalls, partly modernised, date from c 1335 and have good misericords. The most striking feature of the choir is the enormous tapestry by John Piper (1966) covering the altar screen. In the S aisle are two sculptured stone *panels (c 1140) of great refinement, showing Christ at the Gate of Bethany and the Raising of Lazarus. The vista of this aisle is closed by the Chapel of St Mary Magdalene, with a painting by Graham Sutherland over the altar.

The *Retrochoir* is a charming example of the final transition from the massive Norman to the lighter Gothic style. The interval between the Purbeck marble piers and their detached shafts is wider than in any other known example. The sculptural decoration in the triforium is noteworthy. On the N side is a window by Marc Chagall (1978). On the S side is a fragment of 2C Roman mosaic, discovered under the foundations in 1969. Of the long, narrow *Lady Chapel* the two W bays belong to the original Norman church while the two E bays were added between 1288 and 1304. The first two bays show traces of the paintings by Lambert Barnard which once covered the vaults throughout the church. The simple tomb of Bishop de Luffa is in the first bay.

The *Cloisters*, entered by the beautiful EE S porch, are 15C and irregular in both register and form. They were not built for monastic purposes, and have no N walk; originally they surrounded the cathedral's 'paradise', or burial ground. From the S walk a passage called St Richard's Walk leads to Canon Lane. In front is the *Deanery* (1725); to the right the lane ends at the 14C gateway of the *Bishop's Palace*, half of which is now a theological college. Its chapel and kitchen walls are of the 13C, the remainder 14–18C. The chapel (entered opposite the SW tower) has fine vaulting and corbels, and an exquisite painted tondo (c 1250). At the other end of the lane, beyond the 15C Vicar's Close, is the 16C *Canon Gate* into South St. By another entrance to the precincts, a few yards to the left along South St., is a 12C vaulted undercroft (now a café) beneath the 14C *Vicar's Hall and Parlour*.

At the centre of the town stands the rich *Market Cross* (1501), surmounted by a cupola put up in 1724. On the E side is a good bronze bust of Charles I. North St., the finest in the city and predominantly Georgian, leads past (right) *Market House* (1807) by Nash and the former church of St Olave (now a bookshop), with early Norman features. On the outside wall of the *Council Chambers* (1731–33; interior shown when not in use) is a Roman inscription recording the erection of a temple to Neptune and Minerva. The stone was dug up in 1723 on this site. We follow Lion St. (right) to the quiet St Martin's Square, a delightful group of houses. Here is

*St Mary's Hospital (open), founded c 1158 for the care of the sick but since 1528 an almshouse for the aged. The *Great Hall*, formerly the infirmary but since 1680 occupied by small dwellings, has a magnificent timber roof reaching at the sides to within 6ft of the floor. So that patients could hear mass from their beds, the hall is separated from the *Chapel* only by a carved oak screen (a unique arrangement in England, though it is also adopted at Beaune in France). Except for the partitions and chimneys, the whole dates from c 1290; the chapel has good stalls and misericords. To the N is the well-kept *Priory Park*, with the EE choir of the *Grey Friars' Church*, later used as an assize court, and now the *Guildhall Museum* (open). Here William Blake was tried for sedition in 1804 after he had ejected a soldier from his garden at Felpham. The park also contains the motte of Chichester Castle, and is surrounded by part of the *City Walls*. These rest on Roman foundations and indicate the extent of the Roman town. The N and E walls have raised footpaths.

Further N, in Broyle Rd (the continuation of North St.), is the cantilevered *Festival Theatre* (1969; Powell and Moya), with an open stage, famous for its season of drama in the summer months.

In Little London, leading S from Priory Rd, the *Chichester District Museum* is housed in an 18C corn store.

Exhibits include: prehistoric remains; Roman finds from the town cemetery; woodcarving from The Grange, a mansion demolished in 1962, and from the Oliver Whitby School (founded in 1712, merged in Christ's Hospital in 1951); and rooms devoted to the Royal Sussex Regiment. Frequent exhibitions are held. The fitting sculpture by John Skelton, outside, dates from 1964.—If we continue S across East St., and then turn right, we reach St John's Church (1812) with an interesting octagonal Low Church plan and monumental three-decker pulpit. At No. 11 Eastgate Square, further on, Keats began 'The Eve of St Agnes' in 1819.

The area SE of the Market Cross is known as *The Pallant*, with four streets intersecting the Palatinate or Archbishop's 'Peculiar', a sort of miniature city within the city. It contains some very fine 18C and 19C buildings, among them *Pallant House* (c 1712), now open as a gallery with pictures, porcelain and furniture.

West St., opposite the cathedral, has more 18C houses. Leading from it is Chapel St., where further Roman remains came to light in 1971. West St. continues past a well-placed church by R.C. Carpenter (1848–52) to the striking *Westgate House* (1696), now the county record office. The modern *County Hall* behind is inoffensive, although recent extensions in Tower St. are far less harmonious. Westgate Fields, further W, gives good views of the cathedral and the walls, despite the intrusion of a new College and the bypass.

Just 1¼m W is *Fishbourne Roman Palace (open), excavated in 1961–69. The largest Roman building so far found in Britain, it rivals the imperial palaces of Rome itself in size and grandeur. The museum houses many objects found during the excavations.

The palace is believed to have belonged to Cogidubnus, a Roman citizen, who was ruling as king in the Chichester area at the time of the Roman invasion by Vespasian. It is thought that Fishbourne could have been the base and supply depot for the Roman army in c AD 43. Two large wooden storehouses of this period have been discovered, and evidence of a harbour. Although a large house was built in AD 50–59, the main palace and gardens were constructed c AD 75. Remains of the N wing of this palace are now covered by a pleasant protective building, and mosaics of this period are the finest examples yet discovered in Britain. Parts of the W and E wings have also been uncovered, and the extensive garden has been replanted on the lines of the bedding trenches found during excavations. The S part of the garden and S wing lie under modern houses and the A29 road. Early in the 2C, part of the palace was demolished, new mosaics were laid, and central heating installed. In c AD 285 the whole palace was destroyed by fire, evidence of which can be seen in the N wing.

For several weeks in the summer Chichester becomes a starting-point for the races at *Goodwood Park (views), 4½m N; there is also an airfield, motor circuit, and golf course. **Goodwood House** itself (open), the seat of the Duke of Richmond, was built by James Wyatt (1780– 1800). It contains a fine collection of portraits by Van Dyck, Lely and Kneller and pictures by Stubbs and Canaletto. The park (open daily) is noted for its cedars. Overlooking it is the *Trundle*, a prehistoric earthwork on *St Roche's Hill* (667ft). On A286 beyond is the *Weald and Downland Open Air Museum*, with a fine display of 14–19C buildings rescued from southern England and reconstructed on the site. Further N is *Singleton*, a secluded village with a Norman church, containing an unusual pulpit incorporated into the side of the chancel arch with two lancet openings.—The chancel of the church at *Apuldram*, 1½m SW of Chichester, has triple-lancet windows with Purbeck marble shafts, a rare feature it shares with Brecon Priory in Wales.

*A Wealden house, reconstructed at the Weald and Downland Open Air Museum*

FROM CHICHESTER TO SELSEY, 8m. B2145 crosses the fertile peninsula of Selsey ('seal's island'), mainly interesting because St Wilfrid established Christianity among the South Saxons here in 681. The saint was followed by a long line of bishops, until the Conqueror transferred the see to Chichester.—4m. *Sidlesham*. At *Pagham*, an untidy seaside village 2m E by footpath (the approach by road is from Hunston, 3m N), is a finely proportioned EE church with lancet windows, dedicated to St Thomas Becket.—6½m. A sideroad leads left for *Church Norton* (1m). Overlooking Pagham Bay and its nature reserve (700 acres) is the romantic St Wilfrid's Chapel. The simple 13C chancel is all that remains of the church which was moved to Selsey.—8m. *Selsey* church, built in 1865, incorporates the fine nave arcades of the old church. To the S projects the headland of *Selsey Bill*, and along the sandy shore to the W are the bungalow resorts of *Bracklesham* and *East Wittering*.

From Chichester to *Bognor* and *Worthing*, see Rte 12.

69½m. *Broadbridge*. About ½m S is *Bosham* (pronounced 'Bozzam'), a pretty village and yachting centre on Chichester Harbour. The small *church of singular interest appears in the Bayeux Tapestry, where Harold is shown on his way to hear mass before his ill-starred visit to Normandy. The tower, the W part of the chancel with the fine chancel arch, and possibly the nave date from the time of Edward the Confessor; the aisles are later. The chancel, with a good lancet E window, was extended in the early Norman period and again in the EE period.

Tradition alleges that a young daughter of King Canute was buried here, and a small stone coffin was found at the required spot in 1865. Some think Bosham the scene of Canute's command to the waves (cf. Southampton, Rte 14A). From here a road leads to a ferry for *West Itchenor*, a picturesque yachting village.

At (73½m) *Emsworth* we enter Hampshire. The Isle of Wight comes into view on the left. Among fine woodland 4m N is *Stansted Park* (open), originally built by Talman in 1686 and rebuilt in the same style by Sir Reginald Blomfield after a fire in 1900. Most interesting is the Gothick chapel added by Lewis Way. Keats was present at its consecration in 1819, and the stained glass influenced 'The Eve of St Agnes'.—75½m. *Havant*, a rapidly developing town, has trebled its population to 116,650 inhabitants (with Waterloo) in 30 years.

To the S lies *Hayling Island* (seasonal Tourist Information), 4m long and 2m broad, with (2½m) *North Hayling* and the resort of (4½m) *South Hayling*. The EE church of St Mary at South Hayling has good sculptures and lancet windows. In the churchyard is a yew 31ft in circumference. The defunct branch line from Havant to Hayling is remembered at the Hayling Billy Inn, named from the locomotive preserved outside. A ferry connects the western tip of the island with Portsmouth.

84½m. **PORTSMOUTH** (179,400 inhab.) occupies most of Portsea Island, a narrow peninsula flanked by Langstone Harbour to the E and the magnificent Portsmouth Harbour to the W. This ideal position has made it England's chief naval base since the time of the Tudors, a history commemorated by a wealth of local museums and exhibits. In addition to the naval base and dockyard, the city includes Old Portsmouth and the attractive resort and residential district of Southsea. *Gosport*, on the other side of Portsmouth Harbour, though an independent borough, is closely associated with the city.

**Tourist Information Centres**: The Hard; (seasonal) Clarence Esplanade, Southsea; (seasonal) Continental Ferry Port.

**Car Parks**: Southsea Common, Southsea Castle, Portsmouth and Southsea Station, Victoria Park, Spring St.

**Bus Station**: Winston Churchill Avenue.

**Railway Stations**: Portsmouth and Southsea Station; Portsmouth Harbour Station (for the Isle of Wight ferry).

**Ferry Services**: from Continental Ferry Port to Guernsey, Jersey, Caen, Cherbourg, Le Havre and St Malo; from Portsmouth Harbour Station to Gosport and to Ryde (Isle of Wight); from Gunwharf Rd, Old Portsmouth, to Fishbourne (Isle of Wight); from Ferry Rd, Eastney, to Hayling Island. Hovercraft service from near Clarence Pier, Southsea, to Ryde.

**Theatres**: Kings Theatre, Albert Rd, Southsea; Portsmouth Drama Centre, Reginald Rd, Eastney; The Hornpipe, Kingston Rd, Portsmouth.

**Annual Event**: Southsea Show on Southsea Common during the first weekend in August.

**History**. A small town existed at the mouth of Portsmouth Harbour soon after the Conquest, but the real history of Portsmouth began during the reign of Henry VII, who established the first dry dock and declared Portsmouth a Royal dockyard and garrison. Remains of the later Tudor fortifications are still an outstanding feature. Charles II was married in Government House to Catherine of Braganza in 1662. The city suffered heavily from air raids in 1941–44, and was one of the main D-Day assembly areas.

**Famous natives, residents and visitors**. Those born at Portsmouth include: Charles Dickens (1812–7), whose father was a clerk in the dockyard; George Meredith (1828–1909); the novelist Sir Walter Besant (1835–1901); Isambard Kingdom Brunel (1806–59); Jonas Hanway (1712–86), the philanthropist; and John Pounds (1766– 1839), the crippled cobbler who founded the first 'ragged school' (1812). Fanny Price, the heroine of Jane Austen's 'Mansfield Park', had her first home here. Conan Doyle wrote his first Sherlock Holmes story, 'A Study in Scarlet', while practising as a doctor here. In 'Kipps' H.G. Wells describes his years in Portsmouth. The city's associations with Lord Nelson and other naval heroes are innumerable.

In the middle of Portsmouth, near the main railway station, is the civic centre with the Central Library, Tourist Information Centre and the restored Victorian *Guildhall*. To the N is the chief shopping area. To the SW lies Old Portsmouth; to the SE, Portsea. To the W is the Naval base, Dockyard and Harbour. Between Old Portsmouth and the Naval base is the United Services Recreation ground, entered by two former town gates, the *King James Gate* (1687) in Burnaby Rd and the *Land Port* (1698) in its original position in St George's Rd (both English Heritage, exteriors open at any reasonable time).

The *Charles Dickens Birthplace Museum* is at No. 393 Old Commercial Rd, N of the centre. The modest house has been restored and refurnished in a style appropriate to the year (1812) when the novelist was born here; items on display include the couch from Gad's Hill Place (Rte 4) on which he died in 1870.

**HM Naval Base** is entered from Portsea Hard by the Victory Gate. A town in itself, it covers an area of over 300 acres and comprises 15 dry docks, 62 acres of fitting and repairing basins, 6000 yards of wharf-age, 10 miles of railways and some fine 18C houses, including the former Navigation School ('HMS Dryad') and Admiralty House (the office of the Commander-in-Chief). In 1987 *HMS Warrior*, an iron-hulled warship launched in 1860, was permanently berthed near the Hard and Portsmouth Harbour Station. Just inside the entrance to the Base is the *Exhibition* of objects retrieved from the 'Mary Rose' (see below). To the left is the *Royal Naval Museum*, occupying three Georgian storehouses and dealing with naval history from the 16C to the Falklands Campaign. In the *Old* or *King Charles's Dock* (1648) is **\*HMS Victory**, restored and fitted out almost to her appearance as at Trafalgar. Visitors can see the spot where Nelson fell and the cockpit where he died. Before Trafalgar the 'Victory' was the flagship of Keppel, Kempenfelt, Howe, Hood and Jervis, and afterwards of Saumarez; she still flies the flag of the Commander-in-Chief, Naval Home Command. Nearby, in a roofed-over dry dock, is the **\*Mary Rose** (open). This flagship, the pride of Henry VIII's navy, sank off Portsmouth in 1545; the hull was raised in 1982 and is now the object of a lengthy conservation programme. Visitors view it from an aluminium footbridge.

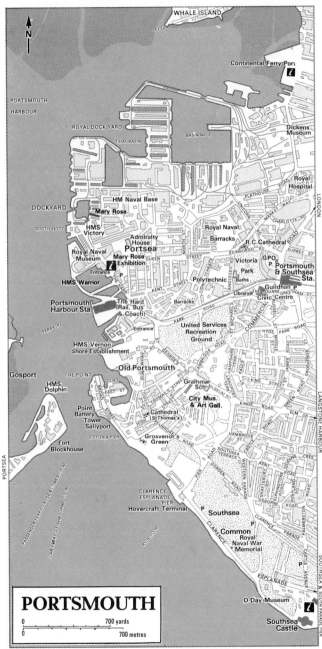

# PORTSMOUTH

| 0 | | | | | | | 700 yards |
| 0 | | | | | | | 700 metres |

At the S end of Portsea Hard is the castellated entrance to the *Gun Wharf*, with the Torpedo and Anti-Submarine School ('HMS Vernon').

High St., the main street of Old Portsmouth, was devastated in 1941. The *Grammar School* founded in 1732 is largely contained in a former barracks with a fine Georgian façade. Among the few surviving old houses is *Buckingham House* (plaque), formerly the Spotted Dog Inn, where the 1st Duke of Buckingham was assassinated by John Felton in 1628. Later (1634–35) the house belonged to John Mason, founder of New Hampshire and captain of Southsea Castle. A plaque on a new building marks the site of the George Hotel, where Nelson spent the night before embarking on his last voyage. The unfinished **Cathedral**, founded in 1927, incorporates the original chancel and transepts of the church of *St Thomas of Canterbury*, dating from 1188–96, with the nave and tower rebuilt c 1693. The cupola was added in 1703. The old church now forms the sanctuary and choir; the nave and aisles, begun in 1935 by Sir Charles Nicholson, are still incomplete.

The S Presbytery aisle (c 1185) contains a monument by Nicholas Stone (1631) to the Duke of Buckingham (see above), and the S choir aisle, known as the Navy Aisle (rededicated 1938), serves as a memorial to the many Royal Naval heroes. The choir, with a W gallery of 1708, contains the Corporation Pew of 1693. On the NE wall of the N transept is a mural of the Last Judgement (c 1250). In the nave is the 'Golden Barque', which served as a weather vane on the tower from 1710 to 1954. The new N tower transept contains a plaque of the Madonna by Andrea della Robbia plaque of the Madonna.
Several old houses survive in St Thomas's St. N of the Cathedral, and in Lombard St. The *City Museum and Art Gallery* in Museum Rd has a collection of local paintings, including work by Clarkson Stanfield, George Smith of Chichester and the Cole family, and of modern and contemporary work.

Broad St., passing on the left the *Sally Port*, the classic point of embarkation for England's naval heroes, and the 15C *Round Tower*, runs NW to the *Point*, on the narrow entrance to the harbour. Here a few alleys characteristic of the old town remain. **Portsmouth Harbour**, less than 300yd wide at its entrance, expands into a vast basin 4m long and 2m broad, giving secure anchorage to the largest vessels. A raised rampart and sea-wall walk extend E from the Round Tower towards Clarence Pier. Below the ramparts, on Governor's Green, is the *Garrison Church* (English Heritage, summer standard opening). The EE building was originally a hospital ('Domus Dei'), with the patients in the nave and a chapel in the choir; the nave was gutted in 1941. Further on, in Pembroke Gardens, is a statue of Nelson (1951).

Beyond Clarence Pier we reach **Southsea**, a seaside resort commanding views of the Isle of Wight and the shipping in Spithead. *Southsea Common*, laid out with ˙gardens, extends the length of the Esplanade. Among the memorials here are the anchor of the 'Victory' and the large *Naval War Memorial*. The *D-Day Museum* has as its centrepiece the Overlord Embroidery, 270ft long (longer than the Bayeux Tapestry), telling the story of the Normandy landings. *Southsea Castle*, built by Henry VIII and now restored, houses a museum with local archaeology, blockmaking machinery by Sir Marc Brunel and the BBC Tudor costume exhibition. Beyond are the Tourist Information Centre, the Rock Garden Pavilion and the *South Parade Pier*, a centre of holiday activity. Near the Canoe Lake is *Cumberland House Museum*, mainly of natural history, with a freshwater aquarium. The former Officers' Mess (1868) of Eastney Barracks houses the *Royal Marines Museum*. On Henderson Rd, further E, the *Eastney Pumping Station* (open) has machinery of 1887.

**Gosport** (77,300 inhab.; seasonal Tourist Information), on the W side of the harbour, can be reached by ferry from Portsmouth (see above) or by A32 from Fareham (see below). Near Gosport Hard is the church of the *Holy Trinity*, containing an organ brought from the demolished mansion of Canons in Middlesex, where Handel may have played on it. Haslar Bridge (no vehicles) leads to *Haslar Hospital* (façade of 1746–62), with accommodation for 2000 patients. The sea-wall leads to *Fort Blockhouse* at the entrance to the harbour and opposite Portsmouth's Round Tower. The submarine base at 'HMS Dolphin' includes the *Royal Navy Submarine Museum*. Off A32 to the N is *Fort Brockhurst* (English Heritage, summer standard opening), part of the elaborate defensive system built by Lord Palmerston in the 1850s to counter the threat of French invasion.

*Fort Widley* (open), on A333 5m N of Portsmouth centre, is another part of Palmerston's system of fortification. It has fine views over the Solent.

FROM PORTSMOUTH TO SOUTHAMPTON, 21m by A27.—We skirt the foot of Portsdown, with Portsmouth Harbour on the left.—7¹/₄m. **Portchester** (i.e. *Portus Castra*) has a magnificent *Castle* (English Heritage, standard opening and summer Sunday mornings). The Roman *fortress, Portus Adurni*, was placed here to guard the Saxon Shore; its bastions are superb. Recent excavation has revealed extensive Saxon occupation. In the NW angle of the Roman fortress Henry II built a *castle in 1160–72, extended by Edward II and Richard II; here Henry V mustered his Agincourt expedition. The roof of the keep commands the entire harbour. The *church in the SE angle was founded by Austin Canons in 1133. On Portsdown is a *Nelson Monument* (150ft) erected by his comrades at Trafalgar.—10¹/₂m. **Fareham** (88,300 inhab.; Tourist Information) is a busy market town with a fine High St.; it stands at the junction with A32, leading S to (5m) Gosport (see above) and N to the Meon Valley and Alton (Rte 14A). *Boarhunt*, with a late Saxon church, is 3m NE.—11m. *Titchfield* has a large church (Saxon to Perp.) with a splendid monument to the Southampton family by Gerard Johnson (1594). *Titchfield Abbey* (English Heritage, summer standard opening but closed on Mondays and on Tuesday afternoons) was built by the 1st Earl of Southampton in 1542 on the site of the abbey church (1232–38) and incorporates its nave. Here Margaret of Anjou, just landed at Southampton, was married to Henry VI in 1445 and Charles I was arrested in 1647 before his imprisonment at Carisbrooke.—21m. *Southampton*, see Rte 14A.

# B.  Via Guildford and Petersfield

Total distance 69m. We follow A3 most of the way.—To (29m) **Guildford** (bypassed).—A3100 to (33m) Godalming.—A3100 to (35m) Milford.—A3 to (41m) **Hindhead**.—To (53m) **Petersfield**.—To (69m) **Portsmouth** (Rte 13A).

Maps: OS Landranger 176, 187 (briefly), 186, 197, 196 (briefly).

Shorter and more scenic than Rte 13A.

Leaving London by Putney Bridge, we join the A3 at Putney Heath. The modern course of the road bypasses Kingston, Esher and Cobham, meeting the old Portsmouth road again at (20m) *Pain's Hill*, near M25.

The old Portsmouth road, now labelled A308 and A307, passes through *Kingston upon Thames* (see 'Blue Guide London') and, beyond *Sandown Park* racecourse, becomes the High St. of (16m) *Esher* (61,400 inhab.). Of the original Esher Place built by Bishop Waynflete in 1477–86 and occupied by Wolsey the only relic is the gatehouse (Wolsey's Tower), altered by William Kent. From Esher A244 runs W towards the Thames at Walton, Weybridge and other places described in Rte 36B. Off A244 ¹/₂m S of Esher lies *Claremont*, a mansion built in 1769–72 for Clive of India by Capability Brown with Henry Holland and Holland's young pupil, John Soane. The house is now a school run by Christian Scientists (limited opening). *Claremont Landscape Garden* (NT), reached by a separate entrance from A307, is one of the earliest examples of English landscaping to survive. It was begun by Sir John Vanbrugh and Charles Bridgeman before 1720 and developed by William Kent; there is a lake with an island and temple, and a curious turf amphitheatre.

From Pain's Hill A245 runs SE to (6¼m) Leatherhead (Rte 12). It passes through *Cobham* village, where Cedar House (NT, open by appointment) has a 15C hall.—At (2¹/₃m) *Stoke d'Abernon* the church, with Saxon and EE work and too much restoration, contains the earliest *brass in England (to Sir John d'Abernon, 1277), a brass to his son (d. 1327) and 14–16C Flemish glass.

22m. *Wisley Common*, with the pretty Bolder Mere to the left of A3 and, to the right, the *Gardens of the Royal Horticultural Society* (open). *Ockham*, 1m S, has a distinctive Victorian village centre built by the first Lord Lovelace. In the church is a lovely seven-light E window and a monument to the 1st Lord King (d. 1734) by Rysbrack.—24m. *Ripley* is bypassed by the A3. Off the old road (B2215) lie the 13C ruins of *Newark Priory* (Augustinian, founded c 1190) on the banks of the Wey (see Rte 36B).

A247 leads NW from B2215 through *Old Woking*, with an interesting church near the river, to (4m) **Woking** (81,400 inhab.), created by the coming of the railway and still mainly a dormitory town for London commuters.

29m. **GUILDFORD** (56,700 inhab.), the county town of Surrey, stands where the Wey cuts through the chalk ridge of the North Downs. Its pleasant hilly streets and river scenery make Guildford a more interesting place than most Surrey towns.

**Tourist Information Centre**: Civic Hall, London Rd.

**Car Parks**: Bright Hill, Civic Hall, Farnham Rd, North St., Millbrook, Upper High St., Guildford Park Rd. Multi-storey car parks in Bedford Rd, Leapale Rd, Sydenham Rd and York Rd. Underground car park in Tunsgate.

**Bus Station**: near The Friary and North St.

**Railway Stations**: Guildford Main Line Station, W of the river near the centre; London Rd Station off A3100.

**Theatres**: Yvonne Arnaud Theatre, Millbrook; Bellerby Theatre, Leapale Lane.

**Annual Event**: Surrey County Show in Stoke Park each May.

The steep *High St., descending to the river in the W, has a handsome medley of old houses. Near the top the *Royal Grammar School* keeps its 16C main building, with a library founded in 1573 by Bishop Parkhurst and containing 89 chained books (open by appointment). Beyond the junction with Chertsey St. lower down is a fine group of buildings, beginning with the Jacobean brick *Abbot's Hospital* (guided tours avaialble), founded in 1619 for a master, twelve brethren and ten sisters. The massive gatehouse is outstanding. Inside are some fine carved oak, stained glass of 1621 in the chapel, a portrait group by the local painter John Russell (1745–1806) and portraits of Calvin, Wyclif and Foxe. Beyond are the wonderfully exuberant *Guildford House* of 1660, now open as an art gallery, and the *Guildhall* (open by appointment), with a Restoration frontage and clock added to a Tudor structure. *Trinity Church*, opposite, was rebuilt in the 18C; it contains the monument of Archbishop Abbot (d. 1633) from an earlier church and the cenotaph of Speaker Onslow (d. 1768), buried at Merrow. The *Angel Hotel*, a coaching inn further down the hill, has groined 13C cellars.

Quarry St., a left turn from the High St. as it nears the river, has more old houses and the unusual church of *St Mary*. Most of the building is late Norman (1160–80) but the tower is Saxon, as the splayed openings above the tower arches inside show. A little way beyond the church is the *Castle Archway*, leading to the public gardens where the keep of the Norman *Castle* (c 1150) stands on an artificial mound. Near the archway is a small *Museum* of Surrey antiquities, ironwork, needlework and relics of Lewis Carroll (C.L. Dodgson; 1832–98). He frequently visited his sisters' home, 'The Chestnuts', on Quarry St. and is buried in Guildford cemetery.

Millbrook, another left turn from the High St., descends to the *Yvonne Arnaud Theatre*, in meadows by the Wey overlooked by the picturesque backs of Quarry St. The church of *St Nicholas* on the other side of the river incorporates the 15C Loseley Chapel, with monuments to the Mores of Loseley.

On Stag Hill, about ³/₄m NW of the town centre, stands the **Cathedral** of the diocese of Guildford, created in 1927, by Sir Edward Maufe.

Begun in 1936, the building was consecrated in 1961 and finished in 1964. The plain exterior is made of local brick, relieved only by sculptured allegorical figures. The interior, austerely effective in a modern Gothic style, is faced in stone with concrete vaults. The furnishings throughout are designed with consistent simplicity.

The N side of the hill is occupied by the *University of Surrey*, constituted in 1966 from the former Battersea Polytechnic and moved to this site.

On the Wey just S of Guildford is *St Catherine's Hill*, crowned with the ruins of an early 14C chapel and offering a good view.—*Loseley House* (open), in a finely wooded park 2m SW, is an admirable example of an Elizabethan manor house (1560–69). The so-called 'Nonsuch' panels of Henry VIII's reign in the great hall were probably painted for the king's tents. The Norman *church of Compton*, 1¼m W of Loseley and 3m from Guildford, has Saxon cells and tower and a unique chapel above its low vaulted sanctuary. The wooden rail of this chapel is probably the oldest woodwork in England. On the chancel arch is the incised figure of a Norman soldier. The painter G.F. Watts (1817–1904) lived at Limnerslease, ½m N of Compton, and his memory is kept green here by the *Watts Gallery*. The Mortuary Chapel in the new graveyard is adorned with symbolic terracotta work made by the villagers under the direction of Mrs Watts (d. 1939).

FROM GUILDFORD TO HORSHAM, 22m.—A281 leads to (1½m) *Shalford* with an 18C watermill and, near the church, the village stocks and whipping-post. We can make the entire journey on A281 but a more interesting route follows B2128 at (3m) *Bramley*, passing through (4m) *Wonersh*, with its old manor house, and (9m) *Cranleigh*, with a fine 14C church and a boys' school (1863).—22m. *Horsham*, see Rte 12.

From Guildford to *Leatherhead* and to *Dorking*, see Rte 12; to *Farnham*, *Alton* and *Winchester*, see Rte 14A.

S of Guildford A3100 ascends the Wey.—33m. **Godalming** (18,200 inhab.), an old town formerly a centre of the Surrey wool trade, has narrow streets, an elegant little market house and 17C half-timbered and decorated brick buildings. Aldous Huxley (1894–1963) was born here. The large church of *St Peter and St Paul* near the station is mainly Norman and 13C.

N of the town are the imposing buildings of *Charterhouse School* by Hardwick and others. Founded in London by Thomas Sutton in 1611, it was moved here in 1872. An old archway carved with the names of former Carthusians was brought from London. Among famous pupils are: Crashaw, Lovelace, Isaac Barrow, Roger Williams (of Rhode Island), Steele, Addison, Wesley, Blackstone, Thomas Day (author of 'Sandford and Merton'), Grote, John Leech, Thackeray, Baden-Powell, Vaughan Williams and Max Beerbohm. The library contains many of Leech's drawings for 'Punch' and the manuscript of Thackeray's 'The Newcomes'.

*Eashing Bridges* (NT), over the Wey near the A3 1½m W of Godalming, are said to date from King John's time.—On the attractive B2130

*'The Pepperpot', the old town hall and market house
(1841), Godalming*

leading from Godalming to *Hascombe*, 3m SE, is (2m) the *Winkworth
Arboretum* (NT), a hillside planted with rare trees and shrubs.

At (35m) *Milford* the Victorian church has stained glass by Morris
and Co. Milford and Witley commons include 377 acres of NT land.
A3100 here joins A3.

FROM MILFORD TO PETWORTH, 14m by A283.—1½m. *Witley*, where George Eliot
lived from 1877 until 1880, the year of her death, at The Heights (now
Rosslyn Court).—3m. *Hambledon*, left of the road, lies beneath *Hydon's Ball*
(593ft; NT), a wooded hill crowned with a monument to Octavia Hill (1838–
1912), the social reformer.—4m. *Chiddingfold* is a typical Wealden village, once

engaged in making glass and iron. The Crown Inn is medieval.— 14m. *Petworth*, see Rte 13A.

FROM MILFORD TO MIDHURST, 16m by A286.—7m. **Haslemere** is agreeably situated between the heathery heights of Blackdown and Hindhead. A market town (13,900 inhab.) which still boasts two 18C coaching inns, it has become the centre of a diffuse residential district. Its popularity dates from 1877, when the scientist John Tyndall (1820–93) came to live on Hindhead. Another resident, Arnold Dolmetsch (1858–1940), is commemorated by the festival of medieval music held in July. The *Educational Museum* in High St. has exhibits of British birds, geology, zoology, botany and local industries. **Blackdown** (918ft) rises 2¹/₂m S of Haslemere and commands a wide view of the Weald. To reach it we leave the town by Tennyson's Lane (NT) and climb to the right. Tennyson died in 1892 at *Aldworth*, a house built by him on the E slope in 1868–69 and named from his wife's ancestral connection with Aldworth in Berkshire.—16m. *Midhurst*, see Rte 13A.

The A3 rises through heathy country.—38m. *Thursley*, to the right of the road, has a church with a fine timber-framed belfry, three windows of c 1030 and a font which may be Saxon.—41m. **Hindhead** rises N of Haslemere. The summit at *Gibbet Hill* (895ft) is marked by a granite cross and a pillar with an indicator showing the chief points in the magnificent *view. The spot, and the surrounding common which includes over 2000 acres of NT property, get very crowded at weekends.

The name of Gibbet Hill refers to the murder of a sailor in 1786 on the old road skirting the edge of the *Devil's Punch Bowl*, a curious depression on the N side, where a memorial stone records the crime and the fate of the assassins—an inscription listened to 'with greedy interest' by Dickens's Smike when Nicholas Nickleby read it to him.—From Hindhead to *Farnham*, see Rte 14A.

From Hindhead to Petersfield the road winds either side of the border between Hampshire and West Sussex.—45m. *Liphook* is a good centre for walks (e.g. in *Wolmer Forest* to the NW). The Fabian philosopher Sidney Webb, later Lord Passfield (1859–1947), died here at Passfield Corner.—53m. **Petersfield** (9000 inhab.; Tourist Information) is a country town with a restored partly Norman church and a statue of William III on horseback (1724).

*Bedales*, 1m N, is a well-known co-educational school. 1¹/₂m N is *Steep*, with the cottage of the poet Edward Thomas (1885–1917); there is a memorial to him on the hill opposite. About 2¹/₂m S of Petersfield is *Buriton*, where the manor house was Gibbon's early home, and 4m SE is *Harting*, where Cardinal Pole was rector in 1526– 51 and Anthony Trollope lived in 1880– 82. *Elsted* church, 2m further E, has a 13C chancel built on a Saxon nave with herringbone masonry. Roofless for 100 years, it was skilfully restored in 1952.
On B2146 about 1¹/₂m S of Harting is *Uppark* (NT), a neat box of a house designed by William Talman in 1685–90. The main rooms keep their mid 18C appearance. The Victorian servants' quarters in the basement are of particular interest, since the mother of H.G. Wells (1866–1946) was housekeeper here and in 'Tono-Bungay' the novelist recalled his boyhood impressions of life at Uppark.

We cross the South Downs beside *Butser Hill* (887ft) and beyond (61m) *Horndean* and *Waterlooville* reach the boundary of Portsmouth. A333 leads (right) across the steep ridge of Portsdown (400ft) towards Southwick.—At (67m) *Hilsea* we pass the M27 and reach Portsea Island, on which the main part of the city stands.—69m. **Portsmouth**, see Rte 13A.

# 14  London to Southampton

## A.  Via Alton and Winchester

Total distance 80m. A3 to (29m) Guildford (bypassed), see Rte 13B.
—A31 to (39m) Farnham.—A31 to (48m) **Alton** (bypassed).—
A31 to (68m) **Winchester** (bypassed).—A333, A33 to (80m)
**Southampton**.

Maps: OS Landranger 176, 187 (briefly), 186, 185, 196.

We follow A3 and the course of Rte 13B to the beginning of the
Guildford bypass. After a further 3m the A31 leads W along the chalk
ridge known as the *Hog's Back* (350–500ft), a favourite spot with
weekend tourists.

39m. **Farnham** (35,500 inhab.; Tourist Information) is a pleasant,
thriving place with good Georgian houses and the *Castle* of the
Bishops of Winchester dominating the town. The ruined moated
keep (English Heritage, summer standard opening) was built in
1160–75 by Bishop Henry de Blois on the site of an earlier tower
whose deep well-shaft has been exposed. The Centre for International Briefing occupies the domestic buildings (limited opening).
They include the Norman great hall, chapel and kitchen but owe
much of their present form, particularly the fine staircase and chapel,
to Bishop Morley (1662–84). Fox's Tower, in fact built by William of
Waynflete (1404–75), is a lovely example of early brickwork.

The handsome Castle St. descends into the town. In the churchyard of the large *St Andrew's* is the tomb of William Cobbett
(1763–1835), probably born at the house now the *Jolly Farmers Inn*.
The *Willmer House Museum* in West St., with more good Georgian
buildings, is devoted to Cobbett relics and local history. Charles I
spent a night at the house which has become the *Library* on the way
to his trial in London.

Off B3001 2m SE, in the lovely valley of the Wey, stands *Waverley Abbey*
(English Heritage, open at any reasonable time). It was the first Cistercian
house in England, founded in 1128, though the surviving ruins date from early
13C rebuilding. The name is said to have given Sir Walter Scott the title of his
first novel. Beyond the river is *Moor Park* (now an Anglican education centre),
where Swift worked as secretary to Sir William Temple and met Esther Johnson
(Stella).

The attractive A287 runs SE from Farnham across *Frensham Common* (922
acres; NT), passing (4½m) *Frensham Pond*. The three low heather hills about
2m E are known as the *Devil's Jumps*.—6m. *Churt* was the home of Lloyd
George in 1925–44.— 8½m. Hindhead, see Rte 13B.

About 3m N of Farnham lies **Aldershot**, an inconsiderable village before the
establishment of the military camp in 1855, but now having a population of
32,700, including the troops. The camp covers about 10 square miles, with its
'Lines' barracks and military institutions of all kinds. Its history is traced by the
*Military Museum* on Queen's Avenue. On the W of the town is an equestrian
statue of Wellington, brought from London in 1885.—Beyond A287 1m N of
Farnham is the height known as *Caesar's Camp*.—*Crondall*, off A287 4m NW of
Farnham, has a fine Norman church with a good brass of a priest (1381).

We leave Farnham on A31, passing on the left the turning for A325,
which crosses *Alice Holt Forest* (200 acres), with the Forestry Commission's research station, and leads to the large artillery camp at
(10m) *Bordon*.—A31 follows the course of the Wey as we enter

Hampshire.—At (46m) *Holybourne* the novelist Elizabeth Gaskell died in 1865.

48m. **Alton** (14,600 inhab.) has a long and attractive main street, with the *Curtis Museum*, displaying a remarkable collection of farm implements, craftsman's tools and domestic utensils. The *Allen Gallery* in Church St. opposite, is devoted to paintings and English pottery. *St Laurence* is a large town church, mainly Perp., with a Norman crossing, Saxon font and 15C pillar painting of Henry VI. The S door was riddled with bullets when the Parliamentarians shot the Royalist Colonel Boles in 1643.

The charming village of *Selborne*, on B3006 5m SE, was made famous by Gilbert White (1720–93) in 'The Natural History of Selborne'. The Wakes (open), the house where he was born and died, is preserved as a memorial to him; there 'are also relics of Captain Oates, the Antarctic explorer. The church has a Norman font and piers; there is a fine old yew in the churchyard, where White is buried. Selborne Hill (NT), W of the village towards Newton Valence, was the scene of many of White's observations.

At (49m) *Chawton* is the simple red-brick house (open) where Jane Austen lived in 1809–17, the period of her chief works.

FROM CHAWTON TO FAREHAM, 25m via A32.—We reach the lovely Meon Valley at (12½m) *West Meon*, where Thomas Lord (1755–1832) of the London cricket ground is buried. *East Meon*, a delightful village 3m E, has a *church with a black Tournai marble font like those in Winchester Cathedral and St Michael's, Southampton. The Norman tower makes a splendid group with the Court House of c 1400 opposite. A ridge road running from West Meon to the Royal Naval signal school 5m SE passes the Iron Age fort known as *Old Winchester Hill* and offers good *views.—15½m. *Corhampton* has a remarkable late Saxon church with a plain Norman font and an old stone chair in the sanctuary.—17m. *Droxford* has a partly Norman church and an 18C rectory. Its railway station was headquarters of the War Cabinet immediately before D-Day in 1944. *Hambledon*, 3½m SE, claims to be the birthplace of cricket (1774). Its church is of peculiar plan and many periods.—21½m. *Wickham*, birthplace of William of Wykeham (1324– 1404), has a fine square and a flour mill made from the timbers of the 'Chesapeake'.—25m. *Fareham*, see Rte 13A.

59m. **New Alresford** still keeps the plan laid out in 1200 by Bishop Lucy of Winchester, with *Broad St., surely the most attractive village street in Hampshire, rising towards the church tower from an artificial reservoir created by the bishop. A plaque marks the birthplace of Mary Russell Mitford (1787–1855), author of 'Our Village'. In summer, steam trains run along a reopened stretch of the old 'watercress' line.

2m SW is *Tichborne*, a pleasant village with a partly Saxon church and the seat of the family embroiled in the 19C law suit involving the 'Tichborne Claimant'.—Admiral Rodney (d. 1792) is buried at *Old Alresford*, 1m N of New Alresford on B3046. At *Northington*, 3m further N, The Grange is an ambitious exercise in the Greek Revival style (c 1809) by William Wilkins (English Heritage, exterior viewing only, at any reasonable time).
    From New Alresford B3047 leads W on an alternative route (12m) into Winchester. Just S of the bridge at (4m) *Itchen Abbas* is Avington Park (limited opening). Its main frontage was created by George Brydges, a favourite of Charles II, when he remodelled an earlier house on the site in about 1700; the 3rd Duke of Chandos added improvements in the 1780s. Admiral Rodney spent part of this youth here. The house is now divided into flats and only the main state rooms, with some handsome decorations, are open.

68m. **WINCHESTER** (35,500 inhab.) is one of the great historic cities of England. Now a county town with a cathedral and a famous boys' public school, it was once the capital of the Saxon kingdom and continued to vie with London in administrative importance until the

Middle Ages. Fragmentary relics of its ancient greatness survive among the handsome 18C buildings which testify to Winchester's later, more modest status as a market centre.

**Tourist Information Centre**: Guildhall, The Broadway.

**Car Parks**: Middle Brook St., Chesil St., Worthy Lane. Multi-storey car park in Tower St.

**Bus Station**: The Broadway.

**Railway Station**: off Stockbridge Rd (A272).

**Theatre**: Theatre Royal, corner of Jewry St. and City Rd.

**Annual Events**: Folk Festival in May; Carnival Week in mid July. The Southern Cathedrals Festival of music is held annually (in July) in rotation with Chichester and Salisbury.

**History**. In 1897 Winchester celebrated the 1000th anniversary of its civic institutions. It is the successor to the British settlement of *Caer Gwent*, the Roman town of *Venta Belgarum*, and the Saxon *Wintanceaster*, which became the capital of Wessex and saw Egbert crowned as first king of all England in 829. Christianity was introduced by Bishop Birinus in 634, though the bishopric was not founded till 40 years later. Winchester was the capital of Alfred and of many of his successors, including Canute and the Danish kings; Edward the Confessor was crowned in the Old Minster in 1043; and William the Conqueror made the city a joint capital with London and was crowned in both, an example followed by several of his successors. In commerce Winchester was long the rival of London, reaching its zenith in the 12C, but by the time of Henry VIII its famous wool industry had died out. Here Henry III (Henry of Winchester) was born in 1207, and here in 1100 Henry I, in 1402 Henry IV, and in 1554 Mary and Philip of Spain were married. In 1213, at the door of the cathedral, Archbishop Stephen Langton absolved King John from excommunication. Winchester was captured by Cromwell in 1645, after the Battle of Naseby.

Since 1953 demolition and rebuilding in Winchester have encouraged an important programme of excavation. The course of the Iron Age defences has been traced; part of the Roman forum has been excavated on the Cathedral Green; virtually the entire site of the Old Minster, the Saxon cathedral, has been revealed; and parts of the Castle and Bishop's Palace at Wolvesey have been investigated. Work continues on the city defences and on the large Roman cemeteries which extended N and E of the walls.

**Famous residents and visitors**. Izaak Walton (1593–1683), author of 'The Compleat Angler', died at No. 7 The Close. Jane Austen died at No. 8 College St. in 1817. Keats wrote his 'Ode to Autumn' and may have finished 'The Eve of St Agnes' on a visit in 1819. See also the list of famous Wykehamists under Winchester College below.

The sharp curves of Magdalen Hill descend to Soke Bridge across the Itchen, where the *City Mill* of 1744 is now a youth hostel (NT; open). The Broadway, beyond, is dominated by Hamo Thornycroft's bronze statue of King Alfred. The *Abbey Grounds* on the left occupy the site of a convent for Benedictine nuns founded by Alfred's wife, Alswitha. *St John's Hospital* preserves a 13C chapel and an early 15C building with twin infirmaries. Further on is the High St., now partly pedestrianised, rising towards the West Gate. The tower of the demolished *St Maurice's Church* on the left preserves a Norman doorway. The colonnaded *Pentice* has overhanging gables, barge boards and moulded ridge tiles. The *Butter Cross* dates from the 15C but was drastically restored in the 19C. The nearby church of *St Laurence* probably occupies the site of the Conqueror's Chapel Royal. S of it stands The Square and the *City Museum*. Its display of archaeological finds from Winchester and Hampshire includes: Belgic pottery; Roman mosaic floors and painted wall plaster; the fragment of a carved Saxon cross shaft; Saxon coins minted in the city; painted stone from the Saxon New Minster; and a 12C inscription

# WINCHESTER

| | | |
|---|---|---|
| 0 | | 500 yards |
| 0 | | 500 metres |

commemorating King Alfred from Hyde Abbey. A path leads from The Square to the cathedral precincts.

At first sight the *Cathedral may disappoint, for it stands on low ground and its squat nave is unrelieved by a tower of commanding height. Yet it impresses on closer view, both by its size—at 556ft it is the longest medieval church in Europe—and by the richness of its interior.

In 1971 excavations N of the present cathedral located the Saxon Old Minster built by Cenwalh, King of Wessex, in 643–48 as cathedral of all Wessex. In 862 St Swithun (always spelt this way in Winchester, never 'Swithin') was buried outside its W door. On 15 July 961 his remains were moved inside the church; rain began to fall as soon as the grave was opened and continued for 40 days, thus starting the legend of the saint's control over the English summer climate. To the N was the New Minster, an abbey founded by King Alfred and built by Edward the Elder in 903; it moved to Hyde outside the N gate of the city (see below) c 1110. To the W lay the Royal Palace. Of all this complex nothing is visible above ground, though the plan of the Old Minster has been marked out.

The present cathedral was begun by Bishop Walkelin in 1079 and consecrated in 1093. This superb Norman building was altered and extended by Bishop Godfrey de Lucy (1189–1204) in the EE style. Bishop Edington (1346–66) rebuilt the W front and began the transformation of the nave from Norman to Perp. The task was continued by the great Bishop William of Wykeham (1367–1404)—architect, statesman and founder of Winchester College and New College, Oxford—and finished by Bishop Waynflete (1447–86). In 1905–12 Sir T.G. Jackson and Sir Francis Low used concrete to underpin the foundations, which the original builders had not carried down to sufficiently firm ground.

The core of the *Nave, with its thick walls, bold vaulting and massive piers, is the Norman work of Walkelin. The two W bays on the N side and the W bay on the S side were rebuilt by Edington, and the remainder, including the arcades, transformed by Wykeham in the Perp. style. The ceiling bosses of the magnificent lierne vault include the arms of Edington and Wykeham. Against the W wall are statues of James I and Charles I by Hubert Le Sueur. In the W end of the N aisle is a stone Cantoria, or minstrels' gallery, where silverware from the treasury is displayed. On the wall of this aisle are a brass tablet and window to Jane Austen, buried beneath the pavement at this spot. In the next bay stands the 12C *font, one of only seven fonts in England of black Tournai marble, with rich carvings of Belgian workmanship. In the S arcade of the nave opposite Jane Austen's memorial is *Wykeham's Chantry, commemorating the bishop (d. 1404), one of the cathedral's unrivalled series of chantries reflecting the development of architecture from 1366 to 1555. Edington's Chantry stands further E in the same arcade; opposite it is the Jacobean pulpit.

The *Transepts remain much as Walkelin left them (1079–98), showing the vast scale of his design, except for later Norman rebuilding made necessary by the fall of the central tower in 1107. In the N transept the 12C Chapel of the Holy Sepulchre has *wall paintings and the W aisle, the Epiphany Chapel, has windows by Burne-Jones. In the S transept is the Venerable Chapel, with elaborate ironwork, and Prior Silkstede's Chapel (1524), with the grave of Izaak Walton and a famous modern window (1914) in his memory. The S choir aisle is entered through a 12C iron *grille which may come from St Swithun's shrine (see below).

The *Choir* is distinguished by magnificent *stalls (1305–10) with vigorous misericords, the oldest surviving cathedral stalls in England except for some fragments at Rochester; the desks and stools of the upper tier date from 1540. The pulpit was given by Prior Silkstede (c 1520); its carved skeins of silk make a rebus on his name. Under the tower is the marble tomb traditionally thought to be that of William Rufus. The piers, arches and clerestory of the Presbytery, prolonging the choir to the E, were rebuilt early in the 14C. Bishop Fox (1501–28) rebuilt the outer walls of its aisles, inserted the tracery of the clerestory and W window, and added the wooden lierne vault with superb bosses. To him also are due the screens betwen presbytery and aisles, which now bear six elaborate mortuary chests (four of 1525, two copied in 1661) made to contain the bones of Egbert, Canute and other pre-Conquest monarchs. The great Reredos, almost certainly dating from c 1840, was mutilated at the reformation but repaired in the 19C; there is, however, some fine original work in the spandrels of the doors. On the E side of the reredos is the Feretory, a place for the 'feretra' or

Key to Numbers

1 Jane Austen
2 Bp William of Wykeham
3 Bp Edington
4 Field-Marshal Lord Wavell
5 Izaak Walton
6 William Rufus
7 Bp Gardiner
8 Bp Fox
9 Shirine of St Swithun
10 Bp Waynflete
11 Cardinal Beaufort
12 Earl of Portland

# WINCHESTER CATHEDRAL

shrine for saints' relics. To its N is the Chantry of Bishop Gardiner (1555) and to its S the Chantry of Bishop Fox (1528), with a remarkable memento mori.

The large *Retrochoir* by Bishop Lucy (1189–1204) is, with the Chapel of the Holy Sepulchre, the earliest Gothic work in the building. (Except for the choir of Lincoln Cathedral, it may be the earliest pure Gothic work in England.) The shrine of St Swithun stood in its centre, where a new shrine was placed in 1962. On the feretory wall at the W end are nine exquisite niches and below is the entrance to the 'Holy Hole', or vault. On either side of the retrochoir are (N) the Chantry of Bishop Waynflete (1486) and (S) the Chantry of Cardinal Beaufort (1447). The late 12C Chapel of the Guardian Angels (N) has painted *bosses of c 1240 in the roof and the effigy of Richard Weston, Earl of Portland (d. 1635), a masterpiece attributed to Francesco Fanelli. In the Lady Chapel, extended in the 15C, are late 15C woodwork and wall paintings, as well as the chair used by Mary Tudor at her wedding to Philip II of Spain in 1554. The chapel to the S, fitted up as a chantry by Bishop Langton (1501), has remarkable woodwork.

The impressive *Crypt* (subject to flooding and open only in the dry summer months), entered from the N transept, is in three parts. The first two are Norman, of the same date and character as the transepts. In the first and larger, under the high altar, is a well which would have been outside the original Saxon church and was probably the ancient Holy Well. The rectangular E crypt below the Lady Chapel is EE (1189– 1204).

Over the passage between the S transept and the Norman arches of the old Chapter House is the *Library* (12C, reconstructed in 1668), containing 4000 printed books and some rare manuscripts. Its chief treasure is the 12C *Winchester Bible, a magnificent illuminated Vulgate.

From the SW corner of the nave we reach the Close through the *Slype*, a passage made in 1636 as a substitute for the right of way through the cathedral. The large and beautiful *Close* itself is partly surrounded by the ancient monastery walls. The Norman *arcade of the demolished Chapter House links the S transept to the *Deanery*, which is approached by a vestibule of three arches (c 1225–50). The 14C *Pilgrims' Hall* (open), with an early hammerbeam roof, stands next to the main building of the *Pilgrims' School* (1687), where the choristers' classrooms occupy the picturesque 16C Priory stables. We leave the close by the 13C *King's Gate*, over which is the church of *St Swithun* (rebuilt in the 16C).

Kingsgate St. is lined with old houses, mostly belonging to the College. On No. 9 is a tablet to the composer Samuel Sebastian Wesley, cathedral organist in 1849–64.

In College St. is the house where Jane Austen died (plaque). Further on is the great gateway (1394–97) of ***Winchester College** or *St Mary's College*, founded by William of Wykeham in 1382 and the model for the great public schools of England. The first stone of the chapel was laid in 1387 and the buildings were occupied in 1394. The school is allied with New College, Oxford, founded by Wykeham in 1379. Besides the 70 foundation scholars, who live in college, there are about 570 'commoners' living in boarding houses.

The chapel, war memorial cloister and, during term, the old cloisters and chantry are open. Guided tours are available in summer.

To the left of Outer Court are the *Warden's Lodgings*, with a frontage of 1833. Within the Middle Gate is Chamber Court. The *Chapel* here still has its original fan-tracery ceiling of wood (by Hugh Herland, who designed the roof of Westminster Hall) and some original *glass portraying Richard II from the E window (now in the late 15C S chapel). The *Dining Hall* has a fine oak roof, renewed in 1819. In the passage to the *Kitchen* is a curious figure of the 'Trusty Servant', placed here in the 16C and repainted in 1809; in the *Beer Cellar* further along the passage is a *Treasury*. In the middle of Wykeham's *Cloisters* is *Fromond's Chantry* (1420–45), with an E window incorporating seven figures from the original glass of the chapel. In the garth Lord Wavell (1883–1950) is buried, while the cloister is carved with the names of Bishop Ken (1656) and many other famous Wykehamists. On the wall of '*School*' (1683–87; not shown during term), sometimes ascribed to Wren, is the inscription 'aut disce, aut discede, manet sors tertia caedia' ('learn, leave, or be licked'). To the E, beyond the mill stream, is the *New Hall* (1958–60) by P. Shepheard, lined with the oak panelling and screen (1680–82) from the chapel. Sir Herbert Baker's beautiful *War Memorial Cloister* (entered from Kingsgate St.) commemorates over 500

Wykehamists who died in 1914–18 and 270 who died in 1939–45. The Victorian buildings in the area include the quincentenary memorial (1897) by Basil Champneys, formerly a theatre, and a gymnasium and sanatorium recently converted by E. Cullinan into a theatre and art school. The *College Sickhouse* dates from 1656.

Famous Wykehamists include Sir Henry Wotton, Sir Thomas Browne, the dramatist Thomas Otway, Sydney Smith, Trollope, Dr Arnold and his son Matthew, Lord Wavell, Sir William Empson, Hugh Gaitskell and Richard Crossman.

On the left (N) side of College St. are the ruins of *Wolvesey Castle* (English Heritage, summer standard opening), a bishop's palace begun by William of Gifford (c 1110) and developed in its fullest form by Henry de Blois (1129–71). Of the medieval building, only the Perp. chapel survives, though excavation has shown that four ranges, including two great halls, enclosed a central courtyard. A wing of the neighbouring *Palace*, rebuilt by Sir Thomas Fitch for Bishop Morley in 1684, is now the bishop's residence; the rest was pulled down in 1800.

A path leading S from College Walk along the Itchen makes a pleasant route to the Hospital of St Cross (see below).

From the end of College St. another path goes between the City Wall and the river back to Soke Bridge (see above). Beyond the bridge, at the corner of Chesil St., is a mid 15C house claiming to be the oldest in Winchester. The 13–14C church of *St Peter* on Chesil St. has been converted into a theatre club. There are good views from *St Giles Hill* to the E. *St John's Church*, 1/4m N, dates from various periods between the 12C and the 16C and has aisles wider than its nave. It contains 13C wall paintings in the embrasures of two lancet windows in the N aisle, uncovered in 1958.

We resume the main course of the walking tour at the Butter Cross, from which High St. climbs towards the West Gate. It passes, on the left, *God Begot House* (open), a Tudor building with a display of jewellery, silver, china and crystal. On the left is the *Old Guildhall* of 1713, now a bank, with the curfew bell-tower and a clock commemorating the Treaty of Utrecht. The *West Gate* (open) is a good specimen of medieval military architecture, the archway being 13C and the upper part c 1380; it houses a small museum with a fine array of medieval weights, the 13C moot horn and the city champion's costume.

Castle Hill leads left to the *Great Hall* (open) of the castle begun by William the Conqueror and enlarged and altered by Henry III in 1222–36. Here Sir Walter Raleigh was tried in 1603 beneath its clustered columns of Purbeck marble and beautiful two-light windows. At the W end, above the remains of the royal dais, hangs the romantically named 'Round Table of King Arthur', 18ft in diameter, known to have been here in 1400 and scientifically dated in 1976 to the 14C; it was painted in 1522 for a visit of the Emperor Charles V and repainted in 1789. Next to the great Hall rise the new *Law Courts* and to the N are the buildings of *County Hall* (1959–60).

The *Royal Greenjackets Museum* is in Romsey Rd. Tower St. or Jewry St. and their prolongation Hyde St., with some fine 17C houses, lead N for 1/2m to the gatehouse which is all that remains of *Hyde Abbey*. This foundation, originally known as the New Minster (see the Cathedral above), moved here c 1110. The monks brought the body of King Alfred with them, but its final resting place is unknown. Nearby is *St Bartholomew's Church*, with some Norman fragments.

Southgate St., opposite Jewry St., still has an 18C appearance. *Serle's House* (c 1732) is now the *Royal Hampshire Regiment Museum*; nearby stands the *Royal Hussars Museum*. In St Cross Rd about 1m further S is the **\*Hospital of St Cross** (open), though a more pleasant approach (suggested above) comes along the river from College Walk.

The Hospital was founded by Bishop Henry de Blois for 13 poor brethren in 1136, and a second foundation (of 'Noble Poverty') was added by Cardinal Beaufort in 1446. The brethren of the first foundation wear a black gown with a Jerusalem cross, while the others have a red gown bearing a cardinal's hat. Passing through the outer court, we take our tickets at the *Beaufort Tower*, where the 'Wayfarer's Dole' of bread and ale is still supplied on request. In the inner court are the *Brethren's Houses* (c 1445), the *Refectory*, the *Kitchen*, the *Master's House*, the *Infirmary* and the *\*Church*, a fine example of its period (1136–c 1250). The unusual lectern dates from 1510, and in front of the altar is a brass of the Master of the Hosptial (1410). The triptych in the S chapel is attributed to Mabuse (d. c 1533). Trollope's 'The Warden' undoubtedly refers to St Cross. ·

Across the river to the E rises *St Catherine's Hill* (255ft), commanding a fine view. At the top are a clump of trees, an Iron Age fort, the foundations of a medieval chapel and a 'mizmaze' cut in the turf. *Chilcomb*, in the valley 1m to the NE, has a small, very early Norman church.

FROM WINCHESTER TO NEWBURY, 25m on A34.—At (3m) *Worthy Down* we bear right. 2m W is the village of *Crawley*, said to be the 'Queen's Crawley' of 'Vanity Fair'.—11m. *Tufton*, on a charming reach of the Test ¹/₂m W of A34, has an 11–12C church with a 15C mural of St Christopher.—At (12m) *Whitchurch* the church has an inscribed Saxon headstone and a 17C Ten Commandments board.

At Clap Gate we cross the line of the Roman *Portway*, and beyond (15m) *Litchfield* we see the tumuli known as the *Seven Barrows* and *Beacon Hill* (858ft), both to the left. The 5th Earl of Carnarvon (1866–1923), who with Howard Carter discovered the tomb of Tutankhamen, is buried on top of Beacon Hill.—19m. *Highclere Castle* (open), the seat of the Carnarvon family, was remodelled in the Gothic style by Charles Barry in 1842. The large park was landscaped in the 18C but much altered by Victorian planting.—At (20m; right) *Burghclere* the Sandham Memorial Chapel (NT), built as a First World War Memorial, has remarkable murals of war scenes by Stanley Spencer (1927–32).—25m. *Newbury*, see Rte 20.

FROM WINCHESTER TO FAREHAM, 20m.—We take A333 and B3354 to (3¹/₂m) *Twyford*, where Benjamin Franklin wrote part of his autobiography. Beyond the village A335 branches right on an alternative route to (9m) Southampton via (3 ¹/₂m) *Eastleigh* (53,100 inhab.; Tourist Information), a 19C railway town which heavy industries and Southampton's airport.—B3354 and B2177 continue to (11¹/₂m) *Bishop's Waltham*, with the ruins of a moated Palace built by Bishop Henry de Blois of Winchester in c 1135 and extended in the 15C (English Heritage, standard opening). William of Wykeham died here in 1404. *Botley*, 4m SW, was William Cobbett's home in 1805–17.—16¹/₂m. *Wickham*, where we join A32, see the route from Chawton to Fareham above.—20m. *Fareham*, see Rte 13A.

FROM WINCHESTER TO SOUTHAMPTON VIA ROMSEY, 17¹/₂m on A3090, A31 and A3057.—We head SW from Winchester on A3090 with Pitt Down rising to our right.—In the churchyard at (5m) *Hursley* is the grave of John Keble (1792–1866), leader of the Oxford Movement and vicar of Hursley for about 30 years. He rebuilt the church, on strict Ecclesiological principles, from the proceeds of 'The Christian Year'; it has stained glass whose design was supervised by William Butterfield. Merdon Manor (no longer standing) was the home of Richard Cromwell (d. 1712), buried in the church with several members of his family.—Beyond the village we join A31.

10m. **Romsey** (12,900 inhab.; seasonal Tourist Information), a small town on the Test, is famous for its *\*Abbey Church*. A nunnery was first founded here in 907 by Edward the Elder for his daughter, St Elfleda. Remains of a later Saxon church (c 1000) have been discovered beneath the floor of the present building and can be seen through a trapdoor in the N transept. The church that survives is mainly Norman, built from 1120 onwards, with only a few later additions: the EE bays (1230–50) at the W end of the nave, and the two 14C E windows. Indeed, Romsey keeps the character of a Norman conventual church more completely than any other building of equal size in England. The choir aisles end in apses (squared externally); the E sides of the transepts are adjoined by circular chapels. The N aisle and transept were long used as the parish church, and the reredos has paintings on wood of the Resurrection and saints (c 1500). Monuments in the S transept include a simple floor slab to Earl Mountbatten of Burma (1900–79) and an elaborate memorial of the 1650s to John St Barbe and his wife. The beautiful mouldings and original Norman triforium and clerestory of the choir are worth special attention. At the E end of the S choir aisle is a carved Saxon crucifix (c 940). Outside the S or Abbess's Door is another Saxon crucifix, the famous *Romsey Rood, ascribed to the first half of the 11C. The foundations of the Lady Chapel can be seen beyond the E end.

The so-called *King John's Hunting Box*, just E of the abbey, is a small 13C hall house. In the market place are a wrought-iron sign bracket from which two of Cromwell's soldiers were hanged and a statue of Lord Palmerston (1784–1865).

His home, *Broadlands* (open), lies just S of the town and the A31. It is now popular with visitors mainly for its connection with Lord Mountbatten, profusely remembered in the exhibits, and with the Prince and Princess of Wales who, like the Queen and Prince Philip, started their honeymoon here. The building itself, originally dating from the 16C, was converted into a pleasant Georgian mansion in 1766 by Capability Brown, who also landscaped the grounds. The collection of paintings includes several Van Dycks.

*Mottisfont*, off A3057 4¹/₂m NW, has a church with a Norman chancel arch and 15C stained glass. Mottisfont Abbey (NT) is a mainly 18C house built in and around the nave and cloisters of a 12C Augustinian priory. Only a few rooms are open, notably the monks' cellarium and a drawing room decorated by Rex Whistler in 1938. The river Test runs by the pleasant gardens.—Florence Nightingale (1820–1910) is buried at *East Wellow*, 3m W of Romsey. Embley House (now a school), on the way from the town, was her family home in winter in 1825–96.

From Romsey A3057 heads SE to (17¹/₂m) Southampton, passing the suburb of *Maybush*, headquarters of the Ordnance Survey, established in 1741 and moved to Southampton in 1841.

The direct route from Winchester to Southampton follows A333 S to join A33.—72m. *Otterbourne*, on A31 to the left, was the lifelong home of the novelist Charlotte M. Yonge (1823–1901), who is buried outside the church her father built. There is also a memorial to John Keble, who held this parish with Hursley (see above).—Passing (74¹/₂m) *Chandler's Ford*, we enter Southampton through the leafy suburb of *Bassett*.

80m. **SOUTHAMPTON** (204,400 inhab.) stands at the head of Southampton Water, the estuary of the Test, on a peninsula bounded to the E by the river Itchen. This fine natural harbour, one of the best in England, has made it a great seaport, the starting-point for famous ventures like Henry V's French expedition, the emigration of the Pilgrim Fathers and the maiden voyage of the 'Titanic'. Of the history that goes with such events, Southampton still has important reminders—particularly the fine stretches of medieval city wall—though they are dispersed among modern development alternating between the unsuccessfully bold and the effortlessly bland.

**Tourist Information Centre**: Above Bar Shopping Precinct.

**Car Parks**: Central Station, West Park Rd, Grosvenor Square, Western Esplanade, Gloucester Square, Eastgate St., College St., Lime St.

**Bus Station**: Windsor Terrace (S of Civic Centre) Coach station in Bedford Place (N of Civic Centre).

**Railway Stations**: Central Station, Blechynden Terrace (W of Civic Centre). Several local stations, including Southampton Airport, are served by London trains and there are special trains to the docks for some liner sailings.

**Ferry services**: ferry and hydrofoil to Cowes, Isle of Wight. Local ferry between Town Quay and Hythe Pier. Cruises around harbour.

**Airport**: Southampton Airport, Eastleigh (on A335 3¹/₂m N of the city centre). Flights to Exeter, Gatwick, Alderney, Guernsey, Jersey, Amsterdam, Cherbourg, Paris.

**Theatre**: Nuffield Theatre, University of Southampton. Concerts etc. in the

Turner Sims Concert Hall, The University; The Guildhall, West Marlands Rd; and Gaumont Theatre, Commercial Rd.

**Annual Events**: International Boat Show in Mayflower Park (September). The Knighthood Contest, a bowling competition dating from 1776, is held every August at the Old Green in Platform Rd, which claims to be the oldest in the world (1299).

**History**. The Saxon town of *Hamwith* superseded the Roman *Clausentum* (now Bitterne) on the other side of the Itchen. Both already had overseas trade, and it is said that at Hamwith Canute administered the famous rebuke to his courtiers (though Bosham has a rival claim). After the Norman Conquest the Continental trade of Southampton became of great importance. Part of Richard Coeur de Lion's crusading fleet sailed from Southampton in 1189; in 1345 and 1415 the armies that conquered at Crécy and Agincourt took ship here; and in modern times it has continued to be the principal port of embarkation for troops on foreign service down to 1914 and again in 1944. The most notable of many hostile descents was that of 1338, when a large French, Spanish, and Genoese fleet plundered the town. In the 15C it was the chief centre of trade wth Mediterranean ports. The Pilgrim Fathers initially sailed for America from Southampton in 1620 in the 'Speedwell' (which had brought some of them from Holland) and the 'Mayflower'. The rise of Portsmouth and a terrible visitation of the plague (1665) conspired with other causes to diminish the prosperity of Southampton, but a new era of advance was ushered in by the creation of a spa and the Napoleonic wars. This was confirmed by the coming of the railway and the building of the docks in the 1840s, when Southampton replaced Falmouth as mail-packet station for the Mediterranean and (later) North America. In 1940–41 the town suffered heavily from air raids. In the 1930s it was in the forefront of flying-boat design and operation, and more recently the hovercraft was invented here.

**Famous natives, residents and visitors.** Natives of the city include Isaac Watts (1674–1748), writer of hymns; Charles Dibdin (1745–1814), composer of sea songs; Sir John Everett Millais (1829–96), Pre-Raphaelite painter; George Saintsbury (1845–1933), historian and critic; and Lord Jellicoe (1859–1935), naval commander. John Alden (1599–1686), the Pilgrim Father whom Longfellow made the hero of his poem 'The Courtship of Miles Standish', was an artisan of Southampton. Jane Austen lived here after her return to Hampshire from Bath in 1806. The American humorist 'Artemus Ward' (C.F. Browne) died here in 1867; and here R.J. Mitchell worked on the Schneider seaplanes which led to the Spitfire.

We begin at the **Civic Centre** (1932–39; E.B. Webber), a group of municipal buildings with a tall clock tower that is Southampton's most distinctive landmark. The *Art Gallery* in the N wing has an excellent collection.

It includes works by Reynolds, Romney, Gainsborough, Richard Wilson, John Opie and Burne-Jones. The exhibit of 20C English art is outstanding; the Camden Town Group and Graham Sutherland are particularly well represented, but there are also good examples of John Piper, Paul Nash, Matthew Smith, Augustus John and Stanley Spencer. The earliest Continental painting is a 14C triptych by Nuzi, and there is another triptych by Goossen van der Weyden and works by Van Dyck, Jordaens and Maes. Later painters represented include Utrillo, Renoir, Corot, Sisley, Camille Pissarro, the surrealist Delvaux, and the French 'Primitive' painters Rousseau and Vivin. The sculpture includes small bronzes by Maillol, Degas, Gaudier-Brzeska and Epstein.

N of the gallery stretches *West Park*, the first of several green spaces that are a pleasant feature of the city, with a statue of Isaac Watts. Sir Edwin Lutyens's Cenotaph looks across the road to *East Park*, where we find a memorial to the engineers killed in the 'Titanic' (1912). The lawns continue S and E with *Palmerston Park*, *Houndwell Park* and *Hoglands Park*.

From the Civic Centre we walk S on the unimaginatively rebuilt Above Bar St. At the head of the High St. stands ***Bargate** (open), the old N gate of the city and the most elaborate city gate to survive in England. The N side still has its 13C drum towers, as well as the 15C

# SOUTHAMPTON

0 _____ 700 yards

0 _____ 700 metres

projection with machiolated parapet. This is enlivened by 17C armorial decorations and guarded by leaden lions of 1743. The battlemented S front has three 13C arches; the taller flanking arches were pierced in 1764 and 1774. The statue above is of George III. The windows were gothicised in 1865, after the Guildhall (c 1400) on the upper floor had been made a court of justice.

It now houses a museum of local history. Among the exhibits are the oak panels, repainted in the 17C, of Sir Bevis of Southampton, the legendary hero of the town, and the giant Ascupart whom he conquered.

Bargate now stands cruelly isolated by modern traffic from the old city walls (described later), warning visitors what 20C development has done to Southampton's High St. A few good buildings do survive, however, beginning (on the E side) with the *Star* and the bow-windowed *Dolphin*, rebuilt as Georgian coaching inns but both 15C in origin.

To the right of the High St. lies St Michael's Square, originally the centre of the Norman-French quarter. *St Michael* is the only medieval parish church to survive in the city, though it was altered by Francis Goodwin in 1828–29. The low central tower rests on early Norman arches but bears a disproportionately tall 18C spire. The 12C font of black Tournai marble is like the ones at Winchester Cathedral and East Meon. The screens are excellent modern ironwork and the Lady Chapel has a 14C Flemish brass lectern from the bombed church of Holy Rood (see below). *Tudor House* (open), a handsome timber-framed house with a banqueting hall on the W side of the square, is now a period museum. In the garden, by the ramparts of the city wall, is a rare example of a Norman merchant's house, built c 1150–75 and popularly known as *King John's House*. (We encounter it again in the course of touring the city walls.) In the fine Bugle St., leading S, is the *Duke of Wellington Inn*, rebuilt c 1490 on 12C foundations and admirably restored in 1963. Further S is the Wool House, described later in the walking tour.

Beyond the Dolphin in High St., the ruined *Holy Rood* church has been made a memorial to men of the Merchant Navy killed in 1939–45. Philip II of Spain heard his first mass in England here in 1554 before riding to his wedding at Winchester. Further S in Lower High St. is the *Red Lion*, with a Norman cellar and 'King Henry V's courtroom'. Further on, in Porter's Lane to the right, are the remains of a long Norman house misleadingly known as *Canute's Palace*. To the left in Winkle St. stands *God's House* or the *Hospice of St Julian*, founded in the 12C, granted to The Queen's College, Oxford in 1343 and now housing four 'brothers' and four 'sisters' in cottages rebuilt in 1861.

The drastically restored chapel was assigned to Walloon refugees in 1567 and still has a congregation using the Anglican service in French. It contains the remains of Lord Scrope, Sir Thomas Grey and Richard, Earl of Cambridge, executed for treason outside Bargate in 1415 (see Shakespeare's 'Henry V', II, ii). Against the S wall is a strange memorial to the first Walloon minister (1569).

At the SE angle of the walls beyond are *God's House Tower* and *God's House Gateway*. The early 15C tower is now an excellent *Museum of Archaeology* (open) with local prehistoric, Roman, Saxon and medieval finds, and pottery of later periods.

We pass beneath the gateway to Town Quay. Platform Rd, to the left, skirts *Queen's Park* to reach the main gates of the Docks which occupy the lower end of the town's peninsula.

Opened in 1842, they are less busy now than in their first century of traffic, though ocean-going liners like the QEII still berth here. The harbour enjoys the advantage of a double tide, first via the Solent and then, two hours later, via Spithead. The docks can be visited on a bus tour leaving from the Civic Centre, and there are cruises round the harbour in summer.

Canute Rd continues E from the Docks to the Itchen Bridge, passing Albert Rd South with the *Southampton Hall of Aviation* (open). Its display includes the Sandringham Flying Boat and an exhibit tracing the work of R.J. Mitchell, designer of the Schneider seaplanes and the Spitfire.

To the W Town Quay passes the entrance to French St., preserving a 13C merchant's house (English Heritage, standard opening). The *Wool House*, further W, is a fine 14C warehouse later used as a jail for prisoners of the Napoleonic wars. It still has its original Spanish chestnut roof, and has been restored as a maritime museum. Exhibits include model ships carved in bone by the French prisoners. Beyond are the *Royal Pier* and *Mayflower Park*. On Western Esplanade, opposite, stands the *Pilgrim Fathers'* Memorial (1913) commemorating the sailing of the 'Mayflower' on 15 August 1620.

On reclaimed land further W extend the *New Docks* (1934), with the King George V Graving Dock, 1200ft long, 135ft wide and 59ft deep, the largest commercial dry dock in England. Behind lies a huge factory estate with much of Southampton's heavy industry.

Western Esplanade makes a good starting point for a tour of the surviving stretches of *Walls.

Dating from Norman times but much altered in later centuries, they formed a circuit of about 1¼m enclosing and defending the old town. About 25–30ft high, they were strengthened at intervals by towers and had seven principal gates. The N and E sides were defended by a double moat, while the S and W sides looked over the tidal estuary of the Test, since largely reclaimed at these points. The W side of the walls is the best preserved.

A flight of steps leads to a rampart walk, soon blocked by the 17C *Guard Room* (in fact, probably a merchant's storehouse). This stands next to the 14C *West Gate*, once giving directly on to West Quay, embarkation point for the Pilgrim Fathers in 1620 and probably also for Henry V's army in 1415. To the N begin the external arcades, recessed arches with holes for showering missiles on attackers, added to the defences after the French raid of 1338. The conspicuous gunports in the walls of *King John's House* (see Tudor House above) are reputedly the earliest of their kind in Great Britain. A medieval postern opens into Blue Anchor Lane. Opposite the Swimming Baths is Simnel St., with an early 14C *Undercroft*. To the N are the mutilated *Castle Watergate* and the *Castle Vault*. A tall block of flats (1963; Eric Lyons) marks the site of the Castle, whose curtain wall formed part of the town defences. The Forty Steps mount to the rampart walk between the 15C *Catchcold Tower* and the *Arundel* (or *Windwhistle*) *Tower* at the NW corner.

Bargate St. follows the N course of the town moat, though only fragments of wall survive and the magnificent Bargate itself is stranded amid modern traffic. The NE corner of the walls is marked by the ruined *Polymond Tower*. The line of the E wall, with a few remains, is indicated by the street named Back of the Walls, leading S to God's House Tower and God's House Gate.

London Rd and The Avenue lead N to *Southampton Common*, a natural park of 350 acres, with a *Zoo*, a cemetery and the County Cricket Ground.—At *Highfield*, about 1m E of the Common, is the *University of Southampton*. The educational institute opened here in 1862 as the result of a bequest from H.R. Hartley, a local wine merchant, was incorporated as a university college in 1902 and received its charter as a university in 1952. There are now about 5000 students, and an associated School of Navigation (at Warsash, see below). The most striking building is the copper-covered *Nuffield Theatre* (1961; Sir Basil Spence) used for both lectures and drama.

Facing Southampton Water 7m SE of the city centre is *Netley Abbey**

(English Heritage, summer standard opening and weekends in winter), a Cistercian foundation of 1239 originally occupied by monks from Beaulieu. The picturesque ruins include the church, cloisters, chapter house and some domestic buildings. *Netley Castle*, built in the 16C to guard the Solent, was radically transformed in the 19C and is now a convalescent hospital.—*Hamble*, 1¹/₂m further SE, a yachting centre on the W side of the Hamble estuary, has a good Norman and EE church. On the E side of the estuary is *Warsash*.

The tip of land reaching out into Southampton Water from the opposite shore is occupied by *Calshot Castle*, one of Henry VIII's coastal defences (English Heritage, summer standard opening). 12m from Southampton, it is reached by following A326 past (9¹/₂m) *Fawley*, with its oil refinery, and B3053.

From *Portsmouth* to Southampton, see Rte 13A.

# B.   Via Basingstoke and Winchester

Total distance 75m. A4, A30 to (18m) Staines (bypassed).—A30 to (26¹/₂m) Bagshot (bypassed).—A30 to (29m) **Camberley** (bypassed).—A30 to (46m) **Basingstoke** (bypassed).—A30, A33 to (63m) **Winchester** (bypassed), see Rte 14A.—A333, A33 to (75m) **Southampton**, see Rte 14A.

Maps: OS Landranger 176, 186, 185, 196.

M3 provides a quick alternative way as far as Winchester. It can be reached at the start of the journey from A316 in Sunbury or joined from M25 S of Egham.

We take A4 and then A30 W from London.—18m. We bypass *Staines* to the N. From the first roundabout on the bypass M25 leads S to M3. From the second, A308 leads NW past Runnymede to Windsor (Rte 36A) and another road leads into the centre of (20m) **Egham**. The early 19C church of *St John The Baptist* preserves the remarkable monuments of Sir John Denham (d. 1638) and his two wives; the boy with the second Lady Denham grew up to be the poet Sir John Denham (1615–69). *Great Fosters*, an Elizabethan mansion further S, is now a hotel.—On A30 beyond Egham stands (21m) *Royal Holloway College*, a wonderfully extravagant brick building of 1879–87 by W.H. Crossland. It was endowed by Thomas Holloway, who made his fortune from Holloway's Pills, as a college for women and later incorporated into the University of London. The picture gallery (open by appointment only) has a good collection of 19C art.—22m. *Virginia Water*, an artificial lake 1¹/₂m long, laid out in 1746 by Paul Sandby for the Duke of Cumberland, forms the S boundary of Windsor Great Park. The ruined colonnade was brought by George IV from Lepcis Magna, near Tripoli.

FROM VIRGINIA WATER TO READING, 18¹/₂m on A329.— 3¹/₂m. **Ascot** is the scene of the most fashionable race meeting of the year, with the Gold Cup in June.—5m. *Bracknell* (48,800 inhab.; Tourist Information) is a 'satellite' town, headquarters of the Meteorological Office since 1961.—10¹/₂m. *Wokingham* (24,300 inhab.), bypassed to the N by A329(M), has the picturesque Lucas Almshouses of 1665. *Finchampstead Ridges* (60 acres; NT), 4m S, give a magnificent view to the south.—18¹/₂m. *Reading*, see Rte 20.

23m. *Sunningdale*, famous for its golf course, is a residential district among fir and beech woods in the heart of the affluent 'stockbroker belt'.—26¹/₂m. We bypass *Bagshot*.

To the S are *Bisley* (3¹/₂m) with the camp and ranges that are the meeting place in July for the National Rifle Association; *Brookwood* (5¹/₂m) and the London Necropolis, a huge cemetery with a memorial (1958) to the Commonwealth forces of the last war; and *Pirbright* (6¹/₂m), with the grave of Sir Henry Morton

Stanley (1841–1904), the journalist and explorer famous for his meeting with Livingstone.

From A30 beyond Bagshot A325 leads SW to (8½m) *Aldershot* (Rte 14A). It passes (3m) *Frimley*, where the American humorist Bret Harte (1839–1902) is buried in the churchyard.—7m. *Farnborough* (45,500 inhab.; Tourist Information) is home of the Royal Aircraft Establishment. The Farnborough International Exhibition and Flying Display is held here every two years in the first week of September. Near the station is the church built in 1887 by the Empress Eugénie (1826–1920) as a mausoleum for her husband Napoleon III, their son the Prince Imperial and herself. The adjoining abbey is occupied by Benedictines from Prinknash. On the other side of the railway is Farnborough Hill, now a convent, where the Empress died.

29m. **Camberley** (52,000 inhab. with Frimley) lies in a heathy district largely devoted to military pursuits. On the right of A30 is the *Royal Military Academy, Sandhurst* for army officers, in beautiful grounds with a lake.

Founded in 1799 as the Royal Military College, it was merged in 1946 with the Royal Military Academy, Woolwich. The Mons Officer Cadet School was also moved here from Aldershot. The Indian Army Room in the main building contains uniforms, portraits, and medals. The *War Memorial Chapel* (1922) commemorates 4000 former cadets who fell in the First World War, and a roll of honour is dedicated to 19,781 officers of the Commonwealth who fell between 1939–46. The Victory Memorial from Lüneburg Heath was brought to Sandhurst in 1958.—About 2m further N is *Crowthorne* with the public school of *Wellington College*, established in 1853, primarily for the sons of deceased officers. In the vicinity is *Broadmoor*, an institution for the criminally insane.

We cross the Blackwater into Hampshire.—33½m. *Blackbushe Airport* is 3m N of *Fleet* (26,000 inhab.). Fleet Pond (130 acres) once provided fish for the monks of Winchester.—Beyond (36m) *Hartley Wintney* B3016 leads left to *Winchfield* (1¾m), with a beautiful little church, partly robust Norman.

2m S of Winchfield is **Odiham**, with a fine High St. and the old stocks and whipping-post near the church. The town stands on the Basingstoke Canal, which runs E and N to connect with the Wey and the Thames at Weybridge. Substantial stretches of the decayed waterway have been reclaimed since the mid 1970s, and Odiham now makes a good starting-point for walks along the banks, as well as for public and charter cruises. *Odiham Castle*, 1m NW, has only the shell of its 13C keep. David II of Scotland was held here after the Battle of Neville's Cross in 1346.—About 2m N of Hartley Wintney stands *Bramshill House* (now the Police Staff College, not open), a striking Jacobean mansion in brick (1612) with good gardens. Bramshill lies in the parish of *Eversley*, where Charles Kingsley was curate and then rector from 1842 until his death in 1875; he is buried in the churchyard, 1½ NE.— *West Green House*, N of A30 beyond Hartley Wintney, is a small 18C building with a walled garden (NT; limited opening of garden, house open by appointment only).

40m. **Hook** has a brick church of 1937–38 by Sir Edward Maufe. —We next pass, on the left at 42m, the tiny Norman church of *Nately Scures* and, on the right at 43½m, the village of *Basing* (or *Old Basing*). Its large Perp. church has 16C monuments to the Paulet family. *Basing House* (open) was built by Sir William Paulet, 1st Marquess of Winchester (d. 1572), on the site of an earlier castle. During the Civil War it resisted the Parliamentarians for two years, finally yielding to Cromwell himself in 1645, when Inigo Jones was among the prisoners taken. Little remains intact except a gatehouse, dovecote and tithe barn; there is an exhibition showing the history of the site.—A30 bypasses the centre of Basingstoke.

46m. **Basingstoke**, a London 'overspill' town, has grown from a population of 25,000 in the 1960s to 67,400. *St Michael's* is a good 16C town church. The Old Town Hall in Market Place houses the

*Willis Museum and Art Gallery*, with local collections and touring exhibits. In the old graveyard near the station are the ruins of the *Holy Ghost Chapel*, 13C and 16C.

*The Vyne (NT)*, off A340 4m N, is a splendid house with distinguished work of several periods. It was built by Lord Sandys in c 1520 and twice altered on a major scale, first by John Webb in c 1655 and then during the ownership (1754–76) of John Chute, friend to Horace Walpole. Externally, the brick entrance front belongs to the original Tudor mansion; the window surrounds, large N portico and garden pavilion are Webb's work. Inside, the most interesting features are the dramatic staircase by Chute, Lord Sandys' chapel with the original stalls and 16C Flemish glass and tiles, and the Long Gallery with linenfold panelling. There are some good chimneypieces by Webb, and the house is handsomely furnished throughout.

An alternative route to (23m) Winchester follows B3046 S, passing through (9m) *Chilton Candover*, where the crypt of the demolished Norman church has been excavated.—For (10m) *Northington*, (13m) *Old Alresford* and (14m) *New Alresford*, where we turn W on A31, see Rte 14A.

The main route follows A30 and A33.—Beyond (61m) *King's Worthy* the Winchester bypass leads left. *Headbourne Worthy* (right) has important Saxon work in its church, particularly a fine but damaged *rood.—For (63m) **Winchester** and the continuation of the route to (75m) **Southampton**, see Rte 14A.

# 15  Isle of Wight

Map: OS Landranger 196. Walkers need the OS Outdoor Leisure map (1:25,000 or 2¹/₂in to 1m).

The **Isle of Wight** (120,000 inhab.) lies off the Hampshire coast opposite Southampton and Portsmouth. Separated from the mainland by the straits of the Solent on the NW and Spithead on the NE, it is shaped like an irregular lozenge about 23m wide and about 13m from N to S. Within this small compass the scenery is both beautiful and impressively varied. The landscape of the north, for the most part low lying and often wooded, yields to the ridge of chalk downs running across the centre of the island. This is bisected by the river Medina as it flows past Newport, the island's capital, from the wide and undulating plains in the south. The scenery grows more dramatic near the southern fringes of the island, achieving a series of wonderful geological surprises on the coastline: the distinctive Needles and the coloured sandstone of Alum Bay in the west, the Undercliff near the southern tip and the heights of Culver Cliff in the east. Most of this fine landscape has been well preserved. The National Trust owns more than 3000 acres and protects another 1600. Well-signposted footpaths and nature trails abound, and hardy walkers can follow the coastline almost continuously for its circuit of about 65 miles.

This natural beauty, together with the mild climate and the presence of several well-established seaside resorts, attracts many visitors, and the island gets crowded during the summer.

**History**. The Isle of Wight was conquered without difficulty in AD 43 by the Romans, who called it *Vectis* or *Ictis*, and after 449 it seems to have been settled by the Jutes. Relics of both these occupations have been found. Annexed to the Saxon kingdom of Wessex in 661 and converted to Christianity during the next

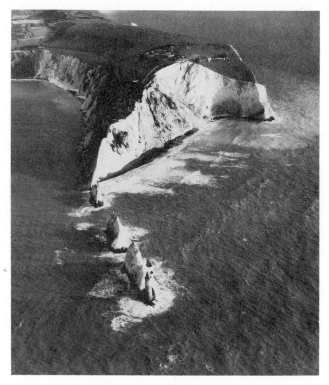

*The Needles, at the western tip of the Isle of Wight*

half century, it had become the headquarters of the Danes by the end of the 10C. William the Conqueror bestowed the lordship of the island on William Fitz-Osbern, from whom it passed to the family of Redvers, Earls of Devon. In 1293 it was repurchased by the Crown and ruled for the next several centuries by locally appointed wardens and English peers with hereditary rights. The island was still vulnerable to attack, however, and the most serious of several French raids occurred in 1377 and 1545. Henry VII put the management of the island in the hands of a Captain, a title later changed to Governor. Charles I was imprisoned here in 1647–48, for most of the time at Carisbrooke Castle.

The 19C brought happier royal connections. The island's popularity with the fashionable began during the Regency, when the Prince's patronage of the yacht club gave it the title 'Royal', and was confirmed by Queen Victoria's decision to move her summer residence from Brighton to Osborne House. Ryde had already achieved some status as a resort by the 1820s, and was followed in the 1840s and 1850s by Ventnor, Sandown and Shanklin. Such developments brought distinguished Victorians to the island: Tennyson, the photographer Julia Margaret Cameron and the family which produced the poet Swinburne were residents, while Dickens, the painter G.F. Watts and his wife Ellen Terry were among the visitors.

Long included in Hampshire administratively, the Isle of Wight is now a county in itself.

**Ferry services**. From Portsmouth to Ryde or Fishbourne (3m W of Ryde): passenger ferry from Portsmouth Harbour Station to Ryde; car ferry from Gunwharf Road, Old Portsmouth, to Fishbourne; hovercraft from Clarence Pier, Southsea, to Ryde. From Southampton to Cowes: car ferry and hydrofoil. From

Lymington to Yarmouth: car ferry. Booking is advisable on all these routes during the summer.

The usual port of entry is **Ryde** (24,700 inhab. with Seaview and St Helens), on a hillside overlooking Spithead.

**Tourist Information Centre** (seasonal): Western Esplanade.

**Car Parks**: beyond W end of Western Esplanade, George St.

**Railway Stations**: Pier Head, Western Esplanade and St John's Rd.

**Bus Station**: Western Esplanade.

**Amusements**: Variety shows, concerts, etc. In Esplanade Pavilion; summer concerts in the Bandstand Enclosure.

**Annual events**: Yacht racing at Fishbourne and Seaview in June, July and August.

The *Pier*, nearly ¹/₂m long, gives a magnificent view of Spithead and its shipping. The town still has many Regency and Victorian buildings to remind the visitor of its first development as a resort in the 19C. The most conspicuous of several churches is *All Saints'* (1868–72) by Gilbert Scott, with a tall steeple added later.

At *Binstead*, off A3054 1m W, the church was mainly rebuilt in the 19C but keeps its EE chancel. The fine wood panelling comes from the chapel at Winchester College, and the carved altar panelling is late 16C Flemish work. The Norman doorway rebuilt as a gateway outside the church has a grotesquely carved beast. 1m further on are the scanty remains of *Quarr Abbey*, a Cistercian house founded by Baldwin de Redvers for Savigny monks in 1131. It took its name from the nearby quarries which supplied limestone for Winchester and Chichester Cathedrals. The estate was sold to the Benedictines of Solesmes in 1907, and Dom Paul Bellot built a remarkable brick *church in 1911–12 (open to the public and reached from the Fishbourne road).—We may continue to (3m) *Fishbourne*, with the car ferry slip, on the attractively wooded Wootton Creek; 1m beyond the opposite bank is *Wootton* church, with a Norman door.

2¹/₂m E of Ryde is the attractive yachting village of *Seaview*, reached by the sea-wall and a footpath or a toll road. 2m beyond is another sailing centre, *St Helens*, with the tower of its old church overlooking the sea and the Duver (NT), a spit of sand and shingle reaching into Bembridge Harbour. Bembridge (see below) is reached by ferry or toll road.

FROM RYDE TO NEWPORT, 8m. A3054, the main road, is dull beyond (3m) *Wootton Bridge* and a better route, with some splendid views, goes S and W from Ryde on unclassified roads via (4m) *Mersley Down* (413ft) and (5¹/₂m) *Arreton Down* (444ft). For Arreton Manor, Haseley Manor and Newchurch, below the downs, see the route from Newport to Sandown below.

FROM RYDE TO VENTNOR, 12m by A3055.—3m. *Brading* is a quaintly decayed little town at the foot of Brading Down (407ft; view) and at the head of a once navigable inlet. The fine church (1150–1250) has a tower with an open lower stage. The many monuments include the *effigy in oak of Sir John Oglander (d. 1655) in the Oglander Chapel. On the chancel floor is an incised slab to John de Cherewin (d. 1441). The 16C rectory opposite now houses Osborn-Smith's Wax Museum, devoted to the history of the island. In the High St. is the Lilliput Museum of Antique Dolls and Toys. Under the old Town Hall are kept the stocks and whipping-post, and at the crossroads is the ring once used in bull-baiting.

About 1m SW are the remains of a *Roman Villa* (open), including mosaic pavements, heating arrangements and objects unearthed during excavation in 1880.—On the Down about 1m W of Brading is *Nunwell House* (open), once the seat of the Oglander family, a Jacobean and Georgian building with period furniture.

FROM BRADING TO BEMBRIDGE, 3¹/₂m.—1m. *Yaverland*, right of the road, has a Jacobean manor house next to a church with a late Norman door and chancel arch, and a well-carved modern reredos.—3¹/2m. **Bembridge**, a yacht-ing resort, lies at the mouth of a shallow harbour. The *Ruskin Galleries* at Bembridge School contain a large collection of pictures and manuscripts by Ruskin and his contemporaries (open by appointment only). The windmill (NT) of c 1700 is the last to survive on the island. Bembridge airport is used by private aircraft and charter services.—A charming coast walk leads to (5m) *Sandown* past the *Foreland* (the E point of the island), *Whitecliff Bay* (geologically interesting) and *Culver Cliff* (254ft), the seaward end of *Bembridge Downs* (343ft; view), with its old fort and monument to Lord Yarborough (d. 1846).

7m. **Sandown**, a resort with a long esplanade and a pier, lies between the white Culver Cliff and the dark red promontory of Dunnose. It is now administratively combined with Shanklin (16,000 inhab.).

**Tourist Information Centre**: The Esplanade.

**Car Parks**: Fort St., Sandown Bay Leisure Centre on The Broadway, St John's Rd, Station Avenue.

**Railway Station**: Station Avenue.

**Amusements**: Concerts and shows in Pavilion Theatre; band concerts in Ferncliffe Gardens.

The sands are particularly fine, while the cliff walk to Shanklin commands an excellent view of the bay. The Public Library in High St. houses the *Museum of Isle of Wight Geology*, with a large and unique collection of rocks and fossils.

9m. **Shanklin**, one of the best known resorts on the island, is built mainly on high ground away from the sea but has an esplanade, a good sandy beach and a pier (damaged in the gale of October 1987). A lift operates between town level and the esplanade.

**Tourist Information Centre**: No. 67 High St.

**Car Parks**: Esplanade, Regent St., Atherley Rd.

**Railway Station**: Regent St.

**Amusements**: Shanklin Theatre in Steephill Rd off High St.; band concerts in Rylstone Gardens.

At the S end of High St. is the 'Old Village', with a few thatched cottages and rich vegetation. Above a fountain, near the Crab Inn, are some lines written by Longfellow when staying here in 1868. Keats's visit in 1819 is recorded by a plaque on Eglantine Cottage. Close by is the upper entrance of *Shanklin Chine*, a narrow wooded fissure in the sandstone, above which are the attractive *Rylstone Gardens* with splendid views from the cliffs. The Chine is floodlit on summer evenings.

A pleasant walk leads 3m to Ventnor past (¹/3m) the head of the small *Luccombe Chine*, (1¹/2m) the *Landslip* and (2¹/4m) *Bonchurch*.

The road climbs sharply over Shanklin Down and then descends, with the Landslip on the left.—11m. *Bonchurch* is a pretty village beneath the towering downs. The tiny old church has some slight Norman remains of c 1170. In the new churchyard, higher up, is the grave of A.C. Swinburne (1837–1909), who used to spend his boyhood holidays at nearby East Dene, now a hostel.

12m. **Ventnor** (6500 inhab.) was developed as a resort in the 1840s, when visitors began to seek it out for its mild winter climate. The centre of the town is laid out on a series of terraces above the sea and under *St Boniface Down* (787 ft; NT), the highest point of the island.

**Tourist Information Centre** (seasonal): No. 34 High St.

**Car Parks**: High St., Marlborough Rd, Dudley Rd.

**Bus Station**: Albert St Coach station in Pier St.

**Amusements**: Band concerts on summer Sundays in the Park.

The road descends steeply to the little esplanade and pier. From the charming Park, reached by the St Lawrence road, there is a cliff walk along the **•Undercliff**, a natural terrace consisting of a huge mass of chalk and limestone which has slipped off the blue clay beneath.

FROM VENTNOR TO FRESHWATER VIA CHALE, 17m via A3055 or 19m via A3055 and B3339.—2m. *St Lawrence*, see below. The road is bordered on the right by steep cliffs (200ft) with a fine walk along the top; the Undercliff proper is below us.—The road turns inland to (4m) *Niton*, a pleasant village with a 13C church, and a good centre for walking. On the S extremity of the island is *St Catherine's Lighthouse*, with one of the most powerful coast-lights in the world (open afternoons in season at the discretion of the keeper).—From (5½m) *Blackgang* a footpath leads up the prominent *St Catherine's Hill* (781ft; NT), crowned by *St Catherine's Oratory*, a 14C tower used as a lighthouse or beacon (English Heritage, open at any reasonable time). *Hoy's Monument*, near the N end of the Down, celebrates the visit of Tsar Alexander in 1814. *Blackgang Chine*, left of A3055, is 400ft deep and practically bare of vegetation.—From the EE church at (6m) *Chale* A3055 continues straight along the coast to (17m) Freshwater, one of the few roads on the island commanding wide sea views. A more varied route follows B3399 inland through (7½m) *Chale Green*, (8½m) *Kingston* and (10½m) *Shorwell*, a pretty village with thatched, stone-built houses. The 15C church, with an early 13C door, is rich in contents: a delightful wall painting of St Christopher (c 1440); a Perp. stone pulpit entered through a pillar, with a canopy of 1620 and an hour-glass; a 16C brass of a priest; and many 17C Leigh monuments. Nearby are three great manor houses (not open): *Northcourt* (1615), with beautiful terraced grounds; *Westcourt* (1579), ½m W; and *Wolverton* (c 1600), ½m SW. *Yafford*, 1m SW of Shorwell, has a restored 19C watermill and farm park (open).—At (12m) *Brighstone*, another stone-built village, the church has a late 13C chancel and Jacobean pulpit.—13½m. *Mottistone* has a church with coloured pillars, and a manor house of 1567 (not open). The adjoining woods, as well as the cliffs to the S and SW, are NT.—19m. *Freshwater*, see below.

FROM VENTNOR TO FRESHWATER AND ALUM BAY VIA NEWPORT AND YARMOUTH, 24½m.—Beyond (2m) *St Lawrence*, with one of the smallest churches in England, we follow an unclassified road inland.—3½m. *Whitwell* church has two chancels, originally separate chapels.—We join A3020 at (6m) *Godshill*, an attractive old village on a hill. The stately Perp. church has a rare **•wall painting of Christ hanging from a lily cross and a painting of Daniel in the lions' den, a composition by Rubens probably executed by a member of his school. The monuments include a rich one to Sir John Leigh (d. 1529) and several to the Worsleys of Appuldurcombe, including Sir Richard (d. 1805), historian of the island.

The remains of *Appuldurcombe House* (English Heritage, standard opening) lie 2m SE near *Wroxall*. Begun in 1701, and designed for the Worsleys by an unknown architect, it was clearly intended to be the noblest house on the island. Today it is only a roofless shell, though there is a small museum on the site and the grounds landscaped by Capability Brown in the 1780s survive.

We follow A3020 to (8m) *Rookley*. To the right is *Merstone*, with a Jacobean manor house (not open). In Gatcombe Park to the left is *Gatcombe* church, a 13C building with the wooden effigy of a knight. The stained **•glass** (1865–66) in the chancel windows is by Morris, Rossetti, Burne-Jones and Ford Madox Brown. Whitecroft Hospital, with its conspicuous tower, lies ½m N.

11m. **Newport** (23,600 inhab.), the capital of the island, is a busy and attractive town built where the river Medina cuts through the central chalk ridge to flow northwards into the sea at Cowes.

**Tourist Information Centre** (also Isle of Wight Tourist Board headquarters): No. 21 High St.

**Car Parks**: Chapel St., Church Litten, Coppins Bridge, Lugley St., Medina Avenue and International Stores, Pyle St.

**Bus station**: South St.

**Theatres**: Apollo Theatre, Pyle St., and Medina Theatre, Mountbatten Centre, Fairlee Rd.

Although the port is no longer the centre of trade that originally gave Newport its importance, some of its former character has been conserved. The *Quay Arts Centre* inhabits a restored warehouse in Little London. The High St. to the S has some charming 18C houses—notably the Red House—and the *Guildhall* (1819) by Nash. The Jacobean *Grammar School* (not open) in St James St. was the lodging of King Charles when he left Carisbrooke Castle for the conference in 1648; the Parliamentary Commissioners were housed at the Bugle Inn. The church of *St Thomas* (1854) preserves its Victorian interior, and contains a monument commissioned by Queen Victoria to Princess Elizabeth (see Carisbrooke Castle below), who is buried in the vault beneath. This, and a plaque to Prince Albert, are fine works by Marochetti. Relics from the old church include the elaborate pulpit (1636), an alabaster effigy of 1582 and a 17C font. Behind, in St Thomas Square, is *God's Providence House* (1701), now a restaurant. Beyond, in Pyle St., is the former Victoria Methodist Church with a fine façade, now the Apollo Theatre. In Cypress Rd, to the right of A3056 towards Sandown, is a *Roman Villa* of 2–4C (open).

FROM NEWPORT TO SANDOWN, 8m by A3056. The road passes two country houses.—4m. *Arreton Manor* (open) is a 17C house with fine panelling and period furniture, as well as a museum of childhood and an adjoining 'country craft village'. The nearby church has a beautiful late 13C S chapel.—5m. *Haseley Manor* (open) is a Tudor house remodelled in the 18C.—*Newchurch*, 1m left of our road at 5¹⁄₂m, has a church with an 18C wooden tower and a gilded 'pelican' lectern.

From Newport to *Cowes*, see below.

About 1m SW of Newport is **\*Carisbrooke Castle** (English Heritage, standard opening and summer Sunday mornings), on a hill about ¹⁄₂m S of the village.

The castle was founded on the site of a Roman fort in early Norman times for the defence of the island, and was always important as a fortress. Its chief interest, however, is the imprisonment here of Charles I from November 1647 to September 1648, when he was removed to Newport Grammar School and then to Hurst Castle on the mainland. His daughter Elizabeth (1635–50) died a prisoner here.

The outer entrance is an archway of 1598, beyond which we cross a stone bridge and pass through a noble 14C *Gatehouse* with a 15C upper stage and inner doors. To the right stands the rebuilt *Chapel of St Nicholas*. The former *Governor's Lodging*, the heavily restored range of domestic buildings facing the gatehouse, consists of the *Great Hall* (with a chimneypiece of 1390), the remains of a chapel of c 1270 (with an interesting wall painting) and the *Great Chamber*. An upper room houses the *Isle of Wight County Museum*, with an archaeological collection, local antiquities and relics of Charles I. Among the pottery are some very early Neolithic examples. There is a section devoted to children (16–19C), and the oldest chamber organ in working order in Britain (1602). To the S of the Governor's Lodging is the 16C *Well House*, where water is drawn from the well by a donkey treading inside a large wheel. Beyond is the lofty mid 12C *Keep*, with a well 160ft deep. From the 12C *Ramparts* Roman earthworks can be seen to the S.

*Carisbrooke* has a Priory Church with the finest tower in the island (1474). The 12C arcade survives but the chancel was pulled down by

Sir Francis Walsingham, Elizabeth I's Secretary of State. The 16C tomb of Lady Margaret Wadham, aunt of Jane Seymour, has interesting carvings.—We follow B3401 to (15m) the *Calbourne* crossroads. In the village, to the left, the pleasant rebuilt church contains a brass of a knight (1379). The road continues over the downs (516ft) to Brighstone (2½m, see above).—We turn right at the Calbourne crossroads for (17½m) *Shalfleet*, where the church has a huge square Norman tower, a Norman doorway with tympanum, a good roof and unusual window tracery. The remarkable S arcade is 13C. *Newtown*, 1¼m NE, is a silted former port with a little 18C town hall (NT) and a chapel of 1835 by A.F. Livesay. In the estuary is a nature reserve (NT).

A3054 continues W to the tiny but ancient port of (21m) **Yarmouth** (seasonal Tourist Information) on the estuary of the Yar. Near the car ferry terminal are the remains of *Yarmouth Castle*, built by Henry VIII (English Heritage, summer standard opening). The 17C *Church* contains a statue of Admiral Sir Robert Holmes (d. 1692), who took New York from the Dutch in 1664. The figure was begun as Louis XIV by a French sculptor and was captured at sea.

A3054 continues past (2m) *Colwell Bay* to (3m) **Totland**, a pleasant little resort with a pier. B3322 continues a further 1½m to Alum Bay (see below).

An unclassified road leads left from A3054 to (23½m) *Freshwater*. The rebuilt church has a Norman doorway, and memorials to Thackeray's daughter, Lady Ritchie (d. 1919), and to Tennyson (1892). The poet's wife (d. 1896) is buried in the churchyard. Freshwater was also the birthplace of the physicist Robert Hooke (1653–1703).—24½m. **Freshwater Bay** is a resort where G.F. Watts and Ellen Terry spent their honeymoon in 1864.

About ¾m NW is *Farringford*, now a hotel, the mansion leased by Tennyson in 1853 and bought in 1855 out of the profits from 'Maud'. He wrote 'Crossing the Bar' on one of his annual journeys across the Solent between Farringford and Aldworth, his Surrey home.—There are fine walks E of Freshwater Bay, across *Afton Down* to (3m) *Brook*, with its lifeboat station and submerged forest. The coastline along this stretch is NT property.

Between Freshwater Bay and (3m) the Needles are the impressive *Freshwater Cliffs*, rising to a height of about 400ft. They are best seen from the sea, and motor boats from Yarmouth and Totland piers make the trip to the Needles and Alum Bay, passing the cave known as *Lord Holmes's Parlour* and the recessed arch at *Scratchell's Bay*. The walk along the top of the downs above the cliffs gives a series of grand views, and *Tennyson Down* (485ft; NT) is crowned by a monument to the poet. The view near the *Needles Old Battery* (NT), a Palmerstonian fort of 1862, is very striking, but the remarkable contrast between the white cliff of the S side of Alum Bay and the many-coloured sands toward its centre should be seen from a boat. *Alum Bay*, named after the alum formerly extracted from its clay, is famous for the brilliant colours of its vertical strata of sandstone. A granite memorial marks the site of the first permanent wireless station (1897–1900), from which Lord Kelvin sent the first paid marconigram in 1898. At the S extremity of the bay are the three isolated, pointed masses of chalk 100ft high known as the *Needles*, with a lighthouse on the outermost.

FROM NEWPORT TO COWES, 4½m by A3020. The road keeps to high ground W of the Medina, passing *Parkhurst Prison*.—At (2½m)

*Northwood* is the mother church of Cowes, with a Norman doorway and Jacobean pulpit.

**Cowes** (19,700 inhab.), a busy little port with the island's best harbour, is the chief yachting centre in England. In the days of sail it was an important packet station, and it is still a boat-building centre.

**Tourist Information** (seasonal): High St.

**Car Parks**: Parade, Medina Rd, Park Rd. In East Cowes: Well Rd and Esplanade.

**Annual Events**: Yacht racing April to September with regattas each weekend, Round-the-Island Race in May and Cowes Week in the first week of August.

The older part, *West Cowes*, on the left bank of the Medina, has a winding and hilly High St. (one way N to S) running parallel to the shore, with some quaint old shops. At its N end is the Parade, where a table commemorates the departure of the 'Ark' and the 'Dove' with the founders of Maryland on 22 November 1633. Thomas Jefferson landed here in 1784 and 1789 on his way to and from his embassy in Paris. *Cowes Castle*, further N, has been rebuilt but was originally one of Henry VIII's defences; since 1856 it has been the headquarters of the *Royal Yacht Squadron*, the most exclusive yacht club in the world. Hard by is the Royal London Yacht Club. At the other end of High St. and in its continuation as Birmingham Rd are shipbuilding and engineering works, and Westbourne House, where Dr Thomas Arnold of Rugby was born. The newer part of West Cowes, along the Solent, has a long esplanade opened in 1926 by Edward VIII, when Prince of Wales; it extends W beyond *Egypt Point* to the resort of (1m) *Gurnard*. At *East Cowes*, on the other side of the Medina (ferry; toll), are *Norris Castle* (1799; James Wyatt), where Queen Victoria spent some youthful holidays, and the church of *St James*, with the grave of the architect John Nash (d. 1835).

Overlooking the bay about 1m SE is *'**Osborne House** (DoE, open), built in an Italaniate style in 1845–51 by Prince Albert and Thomas Cubitt, and long the seaside home of Queen Victoria, who died here in 1901. King Edward presented it to the nation the following year as a memorial of his mother, and one wing was made into a convalescent home for officers and civil servants. It is one of the most complete, as well as the best preserved, examples of High Victorian taste in England.

The State Apartments include the Durbar Room, added in 1890 and decorated in an elaborate Indian style by J. Lockwood Kipling, father of the writer. The private suite on the first floor, kept much as it was at the death of the Queen, richly evokes her domestic life with Albert. The park, much of it planted by the Prince Consort, is not open to the public but visitors may see the *Swiss Cottage* used by the royal children, 1/2m E of the house. Nearby is a museum of objects collected by the Royal family on their travels and Victoria's bathing-machine.

On the bank of the river, 3/4m S of Osborne, stands *Whippingham* church (1854–62), a strange medley of styles, said to have been designed by Prince Albert.

# 16  The New Forest

Maps: OS Landranger 195 and 196, or OS Tourist map (1:63,360 or
1in to 1m). Walkers need the OS Outdoor Leisure map (1:25,000 or
2½in to 1m).

The *New Forest occupies the SW corner of Hampshire, between
Southampton Water and the Avon. It existed as such in 1016 but was
formally established and given its present name c 1079 by William
the Conqueror. 'Forest' was a legal term implying an area subject not
to common law but to the forest law, designed to safeguard wild deer
for the king's hunting (just as 'chase' was a similar tract not
belonging to the Crown). It was then a sparsely inhabited, infertile
region of woods, thickets and open heaths, and still largely retains
that aspect; indeed, its continued survival may have depended as
much on the paucity of its soils as on the protection of the forest laws.
Hunting gradually became less important, and from the 16C onwards
tracts of land were enclosed for the growing of timber. Today the
Forest encompasses some 93,000 acres, of which 67,000 are managed
by the Forestry Commission, comprising 45,000 acres of Open Forest
waste where ponies and cattle graze by common right and 22,000
acres of Inclosure woodland; villages and farmland occupy the
remainder.

Through a series of historical accidents the radical changes which
have taken place in the English countryside over the last 200 years
passed the Forest by, and its Open Waste is now the largest stretch of
semi-natural vegetation in lowland Britain. For the scientist its
ecological importance is immense. The heaths are among the few
remaining areas large enough to support a complete spectrum of
heathland flora and fauna; the bogs are among the finest of their
kind, with rare species of plants, birds and insects. The unenclosed
woods are the best relics of relatively undisturbed deciduous forest in
Britain, being mainly of oak, beech and holly; the oak and beech
grown for timber in the Inclosure woodlands enjoy longer rotations
than elsewhere. Both areas are rich in characteristic wildlife, providing refuges for deer, badger and foxes and habitat for breeding birds
like crossbills, goldcrests and firecrests. By far the most familiar
inhabitants, however, are the hardy and active New Forest ponies,
descended from an indigenous wild breed.

The visitor will find many car parks and picnic places, crowded in
summer. Waymarked trails lead into the Forest's attractive inner
recesses and the many gravel tracks are open without restriction to
the walker. Wild camping is not permitted. Details of camp sites can
be obtained from the Forestry Commission, The Queen's House,
Lyndhurst, Hants SO4 7NH.

**Lyndhurst** (seasonal  Tourist  Information),  on  A35  between
Southampton and Bournemouth, is the best headquarters for visitors.
Its elaborate *Church* of 1858–70 contains a painting by Lord Leighton
and windows by Morris and Burne-Jones; the churchyard has the
grave of Mrs Reginald Hargreaves, the original of 'Alice in Wonderland'. To the W is the *Queen's House*, former manor house of the
Royal manor of Lyndhurst and now the office of the Deputy Surveyor,
the Forestry Commission official in charge of the Forest. It adjoins the
*Verderers' Hall*, where the Verderers of the New Forest sit in open
court every two months to hear presentments about the Forest and
adjudicate on matters affecting the exercise of grazing rights. The

hall is open to the public only when the court is in session. Contents include a hatchment of the arms of Charles II, a Tudor dock and other furniture, and an early Tudor stirrup popularly but wrongly supposed to have belonged to William Rufus, killed in the Forest in 1100 (see Rufus Stone below).

A ROUNDTRIP SOUTH FROM LYNDHURST THROUGH BROCKENHURST AND BEAULIEU, 17m.—A337 leads S to (4m) **Brockenhurst**, a popular starting-point for excursions.

An unclassified road, for part of its way the Rhinefield Ornamental Drive, leads W and then N to (4½m) A35 and (6½m) *Bolderwood* (see below). The forest walks leading from its car parks include (at 2m) the Ober Water Walk and (at 3½m) the Tall Trees Walk.

From Brockenhurst A337 continues S to (4¾m) **Lymington** (38,700 inhab.), a picturesque old port and yachting station at the mouth of the Lymington river, which flows into the Solent. King Henry II landed here in 1154 on the way to his coronation. Paul Verlaine was an usher in 1879 at a school next to the church, his last post in England. From the pier car ferries cross to Yarmouth on the Isle of Wight. In the isolated church of *Boldre*, 2m NE, which has a wide nave with simple Norman arcades, Southey married his second wife in 1839. William Gilpin (1724–1804), author of 'picturesque' travel books, was vicar here.

From *Keyhaven*, 4m SW of Lymington, a ferry goes to *Hurst Castle* (English Heritage, summer standard opening and summer Sunday mornings; weekends only in winter), built by Henry VIII on a pebble spit to guard the W entrance to the Solent. In 1648 Charles I was brought from the Isle of Wight and confined here for 18 days before being moved to Windsor. The castle was extensively modernised in the 19C and 20C.

B3055 and B3054 run E from Brockenhurst through attractive woodland and heath to (10m) *Beaulieu* (Tourist Information), pronounced 'Bewley', a pleasant village in a lovely situation at the head of the tidal Beaulieu river.

*Beaulieu Abbey, a wealthy and powerful Cistercian house, founded by King John in 1204, stood on the E side of the river. The chief relic of its buildings is the EE refectory, now the *Parish Church*, with fine lancet windows, roof bosses and a beautiful reader's *pulpit. Other remains (open) are the ruined cloisters, three arches of the chapter house and the lay brothers' dormitory; the frater and cellarium house an exhibition of monastic life. Only the S wall of the large church survives; its foundations are marked out by stones. Margaret of Anjou, wife of Henry VI, sought sanctuary here with her son Prince Edward in 1471 after the Battle of Barnet, and Perkin Warbeck found a brief refuge here in 1497.

The *Palace House* (open), originally the gatehouse, is the residence of Lord Montagu. The *National Motor Museum*, approached from the Lyndhurst road, has a superb display of motoring history from 1894 to the present; the collection of veteran and vintage cars and motor cycles is among the finest in the world.—A pleasant walk can be taken down the creek to (2¼m) *Buckler's Hard*, a pretty waterside hamlet on the Beaulieu estate, famous for its shipbuilding yard in the 18C and now much developed as a tourist attraction. There is a Maritime Museum, and several cottages contain tableaux illustrating the history of the village.— *Exbury Gardens* (open), on the opposite side of the river and 4m SE of Beaulieu, have 200 acres of woodland gardens and a fine display of rhododendrons, azaleas and camellias.

B3056 leads NW from Beaulieu back to (17m) Lyndhurst.

A ROUNDTRIP NORTH FROM LYNDHURST TO BOLDERWOOD, RUFUS STONE AND MINSTEAD, 17m.—We climb Lyndhurst Hill to the W on A35. At the top we bear right through *Emery Down*, with its large village green, and then left on an unfenced road to (4m) *Bolderwood*, with the King Oak and many fine fir trees.

An unclassified road, for part of the way an Ornamental Drive, leads S and E to

(2½m) A35, where it meets the sideroad from Brockenhurst (see above). It passes through (1m) *Mark Ash Wood*, with the finest beeches in the Forest, and (2¼m) *Knightwood Inclosure*, with the Knightwood Oak, one of the oldest pollarded trees in the Forest.

At 4½m we pass under the A31, here dual carriageway, and at 5½m turn right to cross the old aerodrome before turning right again to rejoin A31 at (8½m) *Stoney Cross* as it heads left towards the Cadnam roundabout.— Left of the road is (9½m) the *Rufus Stone*, marking the spot where it is said William Rufus was killed by an arrow glancing from a tree in 1100. According to one account the king was accidentally killed by Sir Walter Tyrrel, according to another he was murdered by a dispossessed Saxon; all that is known for certain is that he was killed by an arrow in the Forest and hastily buried at Winchester.—At (11½m) the *Cadnam* roundabout we briefly return on the other carriageway of the A31 before turning left for the pretty village of (15m) *Minstead*, where Conan Doyle is buried in the churchyard. Nearby are the fine gardens of *Furzey* (open), with a 16C cottage and a gallery displaying local crafts.—We complete the return to (17m) Lyndhurst by joining A337 E of Minstead.

# SOUTH-WESTERN ENGLAND

South-Western England, as defined for the purposes of this guide, stretches W from the Hampshire border and fringes of the New Forest and S from the A4, the old way from London to Bath and Bristol. It thus includes Wiltshire; Dorset; Somerset and that part of the new county of Avon (created in 1974) which formerly belonged to Somerset; Devon; and Cornwall.

No other English country is dominated by chalk as completely as Wiltshire is. Its centre, Salisbury Plain, is also the centre from which the chalk downs of England radiate—running E to become the North and South Downs of Surrey, Kent and Sussex, SW through Dorset to the coast, and NE through the Marlborough Downs to the Berkshire Downs, the Chilterns and the Lincolnshire and Yorkshire Wolds. In Wiltshire itself the downs make a wide landscape of gently rolling hills, covered by short springy turf (ideal for grazing sheep) with few trees—though sometimes a copse on top of a down makes a fine silhouette against the skyline. Salisbury Plain has been too much invaded by military camps and manoeuvres to show these efects at their characteristic best, and the traveller needs to go N into the Marlborough Downs around Avebury, where several of the chalk figures of horses cut into the hillsides can also be seen. The great stone circles at Avebury and Stonehenge are the most conspicuous reminders of the prehistoric culture that once flourished here.

The builders of Avebury and of the larger circle and horseshoe at Stonehenge used sarsen (grey wether), a sandstone which outcrops naturally in the region. For Salisbury Cathedral the masons could quarry their stone at nearby Chilmark. Otherwise, Wiltshire is like all chalk regions relatively poor in suitable building stone—which may be why some of the uprights at Stonehenge are 'blue' stones brought all the way from the Presely Hills in Wales, and why the county has so little distinguished church architecture. For domestic buildings, the characteristic materials are flint and the local red bricks and tiles which make so handsome a show in, for example, the High St. of Marlborough.

Dorset, Somerset and the southern half of Avon, Wiltshire's western neighbours, are more varied in their geology, and hence their landscape and architecture, too. Of the three, Dorset presents the simplest face, its central strip made by the chalk downs continuing from Salisbury Plain. Like the Wiltshire downs, they have their prehistoric monuments (Maiden Castle, by the Dorchester–Weymouth road, must surely be the finest hill fort in England) and their chalk hill figures, including the figure of George III near Osmington and the much older giant at Cerne Abbas, perhaps the most interesting of all these West Country carvings. To the SE of the downs is the unremarkable heathland made memorable by Thomas Hardy's Egdon Heath in 'The Return of the Native'. To the NW of the downs are fertile, clayey vales which, since the spirit of Hardy pervades Dorset, inevitably remind the visitor of the Vale of the Great Dairies in 'Tess of the d'Urbervilles'. Dorset's coastline, less commercialised than the coastline of its immediate neighbours, springs several interesting surprises: the Isle of Purbeck, where the shelly limestone called Purbeck marble is quarried; the Isle of Portland, that large lump of white limestone reaching out into the Channel; the curious shingle barrier known as Chesil Bank; and the blue lias cliffs, famous for their fossils, around Lyme Regis.

The coastline of Avon and N Somerset can seem disappointing by comparison, with only the cliffs around Clevedon and Weston-super-Mare to relieve the flatness of the Severn Estuary. The variety and interest of the region lie inland: in the Mendip Hills, with their gorges and caverns, stretching from near Frome to Weston; in the Somerset Levels, with islands like Glastonbury Tor rising from the marshland; and in the Quantock Hills, eastern outlier of Exmoor, above Taunton. The fertile, orchard-growing valleys further inland, like the Vale of Taunton Deane, can seem to some eyes the quintessential Somerset landscape. From such variety comes one of the best ranges of building stone that any English region can boast. Particularly beautiful are the Bath stone which gives lightness yet dignity to that city's Georgian streets and the stone quarried at Ham Hill in the S, seen to its best effect at Montacute House. Throughout Somerset the churches are conspicuous for their tall, ornate Perp. W towers.

Where Dorset and Somerset can still at times seem blessedly free of tourists and the worst effects of the tourist trade, Devon and Cornwall bear all too clearly the scars inflicted by the crowds of summer visitors who crawl their way down the congested A30 to the SW peninsula in search of caravan sites, clotted-cream teas, Devon cider, Cornish fudge and souvenirs of Land's End. The real attractions of the peninsula have not disappeared, but the traveller needs to pick his time and place warily. This is particularly true of the long coastline, where seaside amusements alternate with historic ports (Plymouth in the S, Barnstaple and Bideford in the N) and with a landscape rich and varied in its natural beauty: the serpentine rock of the Lizard and the wide sweep of Mount Bay in the S, for example, or the contorted granite and slate near Boscastle and Tintagel and the headland from Barnstaple (or Bideford) Bay around to Minehead.

Inland Devon has several distinct regions. Old Red Sandstone makes up the smooth plateau of Exmoor in the N, lying partly in Somerset but belonging to Devon in character. Red rock and red earth appear again in the S as part of what seems to most visitors the typically Devonian countryside—with deep lanes through wooded hills and combes (valleys) generously watered by a network of rivers. The houses and cottages here are sometimes made of cob, or unbaked earth, whose presence beneath the whitewash or pinkwash is betrayed by the slightly rounded corners of the buildings and the use of thatch rather than a heavier roofing material. Near the centre of the county rises the bleak plateau of Dartmoor, the first and largest of the chain of granite outcrops which continues westward with Bodmin Moor and Land's End and resurfaces again as the Scilly Isles.

Together with slate, granite epitomises one side of the paradoxical nature of Cornwall, a place alternately if not simultaneously harsh and friendly. Granite and slate make the wild coastline and the dreary industrial hinterland of tin and copper mines, slate and china-clay quarries—a landscape made all the more depressing by the decline and near collapse of several of these industries since the 19C. Granite makes the square unadorned outlines of the parish churches, where the only decorative flourishes are carved on the woodwork inside, and the squat outlines of the low, thick-walled cottages. And yet, at the same time, Cornwall is also a place with mild climate and rich vegetation, a place where the Gulf Stream brings an early spring and makes palm trees a fashionable adornment to suburban gardens. Neither granite nor palm trees are particularly English, let alone the conjunction of the two, and their presence helps underline the foreignness of Cornwall, reminding the visitor that this is a Celtic place linked by history to Brittany across the Channel as well as to its English neighbours. The ancient Cornish language, which died out in the 18C, survives in the place names. Of the most frequent Cornish prefixes, 'Tre' means 'dwelling', 'Ros' 'heath', 'Pol' 'pool', 'Lan' 'church', 'Caer' 'town' or 'fort', and, 'Pen' 'summit' or 'headland'.

# 17 London to Salisbury and Weymouth

## A. Via Dorchester

Total distance 131m. A4, A30 to (46m) Basingstoke (bypassed), or alternative way by M3, see Rte 14B.—A30, M3, A303, A30 to (67m) Stockbridge.—A30 to (82m) **Salisbury**.—A354 to (105m) Blandford Forum.—A354 to (117m) Puddletown.—A35 to (122m) **Dorchester**.—A354 to (131m) **Weymouth**.

Maps: OS Landranger 176, 186, 185, 184, 195 (briefly), 194.

From London to (46m) *Basingstoke*, see Rte 14B. A30 bypasses the town and joins M3, which we follow for 2m before branching right on A303 towards Andover (Rte 19). At *Steventon*, 2½m NW of this roundabout, Jane Austen (1775–1817) was born and spent her first 25 years.—60m. At the junction with A34 we leave A303 for A30 again. The road crosses rich agricultural downland to (66m) *Woolbury Ring* (NT), an Iron Age hill-fort with good views, and drops into the valley of the Test at (67m) *Stockbridge*, centre of the fishing on this famous stream.

*Danebury*, another Iron Age hill-fort with good views, is 3m NW. Finds from recent excavation are displayed at Andover (Rte 19).—A3057 follows the Test S from Stockbridge via (6½m) *Mottisfont* to (10m) *Romsey* (both Rte 14A).

71m. A30 crosses a tributary of the Test. At *Nether Wallop*, 1m right, the church has a 15C painting of St George and the Dragon.—At (74½m) *Lopcombe Corner* we enter Wiltshire.—At (76m) the Pheasant Inn, formerly The Hut, about 2m N of *Winterslow*, Hazlitt wrote the 'Winterslow Papers' and was visited by Charles and Mary Lamb.—Just beyond (79m) *Figsbury Ring*, an Iron Age camp with a view of Salisbury, we cross the prominent line of the Roman road from Winchester to Old Sarum (a splendid walk of 21½m).

**SALISBURY** (36,000 inhab.) began its prosperous but uneventful history in 1220, when the bishop's see was moved from the dry uplands of Old Sarum to this fertile spot in the valley where the Avon, the Bourne and the Nadder meet. The cathedral is famous for its Close, the largest in England, and its spire, the tallest in England. Seen from the water meadows, the graceful silhouette of the spire has long been a favourite subject of painters. The area round the Market Place, to the N, preserves its medieval layout of squares known as 'chequers'. Now mainly an agricultural centre, Salisbury was once known for its cloth trade.

**Tourist Information Centres**: Fish Row and City Hall, Malthouse Lane.

**Car Parks**: Central Car Park (off Castle St. and the ring road), Churchill Way, New St.

**Bus Station**: Endless St. **Coach Station**: by Central Car Park, off Castle St.

**Railway Station**: W of the city centre, reached via Fisherton St.

**Theatre**: Playhouse, Malthouse Lane.

**Annual Events**: the Southern Cathedrals Festival of Music is held annually (in July) in rotation with Chichester and Winchester. Salisbury Festival in September.

**Famous residents**: George Herbert (1593–1633) spent his last years at Bemerton nearby. Henry Fielding (1707–54) eloped from Salisbury with Charlotte Cradock, his first wife. Thomas Hardy portrays the city as 'Melchester' in his novels; in 'Jude the Obscure' Sue Brideshead studies at the training college in the Close, while the hero works on the restoration of the cathedral.

The most striking approach to the cathedral is by the 14C *St Ann's Gate*, which leads into the North Walk of the precincts and gives us our first complete view from the NE. The tranquil **•Close**, with its spacious lawns, trees and dignified old houses, makes a fine setting for the great church.

The Avon marks the W boundary of the precincts; the other three sides are enclosed by a 14C wall of stone from Old Sarum. Many houses deserve attention. The *Deanery*, in Bishop's Walk off North Walk, is mainly 13C. In Choristers' Square, beyond the end of North Walk, are the gabled, mainly 15C *Wardrobe* (housing the *Duke of Edinburgh's Royal Regimental Museum*), the *Wren Hall* (1714) and *•Mompesson House* (NT), with handsome plasterwork, panelling, staircase and furniture as well as a garden bounded by the N wall of the close. The riverside gardens of *North Canonry*, in West Walk, are open in summer. The late 14C *King's House*, beyond, contains the *Salisbury and South Wiltshire Museum*; among the exhibits are archaeological finds from Stonehenge and other local sites, the Pitt-Rivers Collection, a display illustrating the history of Salisbury and Old Sarum, and prints, drawings and photographs of local scenes. The old 13–18C *Bishop's Palace*, now housing the Cathedral School, is SE of the cathedral.

The **•Cathedral** was begun by Bishop Poore in 1220, when the cathedral at Old Sarum had become untenable, and consecrated in 1258. It was built on a virgin site and, alone among English medieval cathedrals, is of uniform design (EE). Although the graceful **•spire** was the daring addition of a century later (c 1320), it fulfils the original pyramidal conception. Its apex (at 404ft the tallest in England) is 2$\frac{1}{2}$ft out of perpendicular. The lovely stone used in both phases of building came from the Chilmark quarry, 12m W of Salisbury.

The interior is not as satisfying as the exterior, despite its fine proportions and the harmony of the design. The chilliness of the effect was increased by the ruthless way James Wyatt (1788–89) removed screens and chapels and tidied the monuments into rows. Sir Gilbert Scott's restoration (begun in 1859) tried to minimise the damage, and some colour has ben restored to the aisles by the repainting of tombs.

The *Nave*, perhaps rather narrow for its height, is divided into ten bays by clustered columns of polished Purbeck marble. The fine triforium has characteristic EE plate tracery. In the W triple lancet window is a patchwork of 13–15C glass, some from Dijon, and the third window from the W in the S aisle has a 14C **•Tree of Jesse**. At the W end of the aisles is some lovely 13C grisaille glass. The **•clock movement** at the W end of the N aisle, probably the oldest surviving mechanism in Europe (1386), has been put in working order.

Among the monuments the following may be mentioned (beginning at the W end of the S aisle): 1. Oldest monument in the church, brought from Old Sarum (possibly Bishop Herman, d. 1078); 2. Bishop Roger of Old Sarum (d. 1139); 3. Bishop Jocelin of Old Sarum (d. 1184); 4. Bishop Beauchamp (d. 1482); 5. Robert, Lord Hungerford (d. 1459), an elaborate effigy; 6. Base of the 13C shrine of St Osmund (the holes are the 'foramina' into which the sick were thrust to be healed); 7. Bishop de la Wyle (d. 1271); 8. **•William Longespée** (d. 1226), 1st Earl of Salisbury and son of Henry II (the earliest English military effigy, once brilliantly coloured). We cross to the N aisle. 9. **•Sir John Cheney** (d. 1509), a gigantic knight of the bodyguard of Henry VII, who fought against Richard III at Bosworth; 10. Walter, Lord Hungerford (d. 1449), a hero of Agincourt, and his wife. 11. Sir John de Montacute (d. 1390), a hero of Crécy, wearing elaborate gauntlets; 12. William Longespée, 2nd Earl of Salisbury, killed by the Saracens near Cairo (1250); 13. Diminutive effigy, probably enclosing the heart of Bishop Poore (d. 1237).

The *W Transepts* resemble the nave. The Perp. arches at the crossing were inserted by Bishop Beauchamp (1450–81) to strengthen the original arches against the lateral thrust of the tower and spire. In the NW arm is a bust of the naturalist and writer Richard Jefferies (d. 1887); in the SW arm is a War Memorial chapel.

In general design the *Choir* and *Presbytery* differ little from the nave. They suffered from drastic clearing by Wyatt, bent on creating a vista from end to end of the church. The paintings on the vault are repaintings (c 1870) of defaced 13C originals. The stalls have been freely restored. The throne is by Scott,

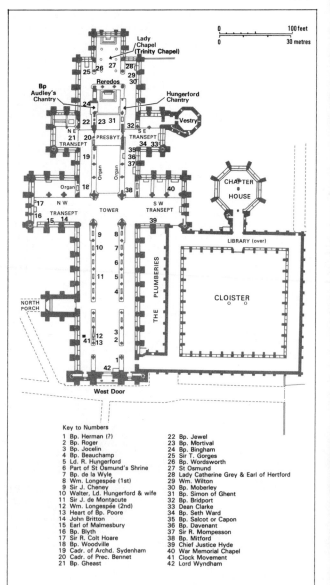

**SALISBURY CATHEDRAL**

Key to Numbers

1 Bp. Herman (?)
2 Bp. Roger
3 Bp. Jocelin
4 Bp. Beauchamp
5 Ld. R. Hungerford
6 Part of St Osmund's Shrine
7 Bp. de la Wyle
8 Wm. Longespée (1st)
9 Sir J. Cheney
10 Walter, Ld. Hungerford & wife
11 Sir J. de Montacute
12 Wm. Longespée (2nd)
13 Heart of Bp. Poore
14 John Britton
15 Earl of Malmesbury
16 Bp. Blyth
17 Sir R. Colt Hoare
18 Bp. Woodville
19 Cadr. of Archd. Sydenham
20 Cadr. of Prec. Bennet
21 Bp. Gheast

22 Bp. Jewel
23 Bp. Mortival
24 Bp. Bingham
25 Sir T. Gorges
26 Bp. Wordsworth
27 St Osmund
28 Lady Catherine Grey & Earl of Hertford
29 Wm. Wilton
30 Bp. Moberley
31 Bp. Simon of Ghent
32 Bp. Bridport
33 Dean Clarke
34 Bp. Seth Ward
35 Bp. Salcot or Capon
36 Bp. Davenant
37 Sir R. Mompesson
38 Bp. Mitford
39 Chief Justice Hyde
40 War Memorial Chapel
41 Clock Movement
42 Lord Wyndham

though most of his furnishings were replaced in 1959 by Lord Mottistone. In front of the altar are buried the Earls of Pembroke. On the N side of the second bay from the E is the fine late Perp. Chantry of Bishop Audley (d. 1524), and opposite is the Hungerford Chantry (c 1429), an important example of early ironwork. In the *NE Transept* are portions of the original 13C screen and the unusual 14C *brass of Bishop Wyville (d. 1375). In the N choir aisle near Audley's chantry is the cenotaph of Bishop Bingham (d. 1246) and further E are the lavish monuments to Sir Thomas Gorges (d. 1610) and his wife. The *Lady Chapel*, to the E, is the earliest part of the building (1220–25). It is divided into nave and aisles by graceful clustered shafts and slender single pillars. Some of the glass is 13C and 14C. In the centre stood the shrine of St Osmund (d. 1099), Bishop of Old Sarum; his grave slab, on the S side, marks the spot where his body was first reburied after the rebuilding of the cathedral. At the E end of the S choir aisle is the imposing monument of Edward, Earl of Hertford (d. 1621) and his wife Lady Catherine (d. 1568), sister of Lady Jane Grey. Also in the S choir aisle are the finely sculptured tomb of Bishop Bridport (d. 1262) and the Mompesson tomb (1627); two windows here are Pre-Raphaelite, and in the *SE Transept* is some 13C grisaille glass. The tomb of Bishop Mitford (d. 1407), further W, has some delicate sculpture.

From the SW transept we enter the well-preserved *Cloisters (c 1270), begun by Bishop de la Wyle, unusually large for a non-monastic church. They are separated from the cathedral itself by a passage known as the Plumberies. Above the E side is the *Library* (open), built in 1446 and devoted to its present purpose in 1756. It contains almost 200 manuscripts, including an Anglo-Saxon liturgy with finely drawn capitals and a late 11C St Augustine, perhaps written by St Osmund. The octagonal *Chapter House*, entered from the E walk, was built a little after the cloisters. The late 13C sculptures illustrate scenes from Genesis and Exodus.

We leave the close by the *North* or *High St. Gate*, with the charming *College of Matrons* (1682) to its right. The Crane Bridge leads left to *Queen Elizabeth Gardens*, by the Nadder, which give a good view of the cathedral. On the right of the High St., leading N from the close, is the *Old George*, with a remarkable roof tree and a room where Pepys slept. Old George Mall, behind, is a cleverly harmonised pedestrian precinct. Silver St., further on to the right, ends at the hexagonal 15C *Poultry Cross*. Nearby is the large civic church of *St Thomas*, also 15C, with a carved roof and a restored painting of the Last Judgement over the chancel arch. In the Market Place to the E stands a statue of Lord Herbert of Lea (1810–61) by Marochetti; another, of the blind statesman Professor Fawcett (1833–84), faces Blue Boar Row, where he was born. The *Guildhall* (1788–95), by Taylor and Pilkington, contains a portrait of the Duke of Queensberry by Raeburn.

From the NE corner Endless St. leads N to Salt Lane, on the right, with the 16C *Shoemakers' Hall* and the 15C *Pheasant Inn*.

Queen St. leads S from the Market Place. In New Canal, to the right, a cinema façade masks the *Hall of John Halle*, built by a wealthy woolstapler in 1470–83. In Milford St., to the left, is the *Red Lion Hotel*, with a picturesque courtyard. Queen St. is continued S as Catherine St. and St John St., passing the 18C *White Hart Hotel* (American associations) and the old *King's Arms*, where faithful Royalists arranged the escape of Charles II after the Battle of Worcester. In St Ann's St., to the left, stands the old *Joiners' Hall* (c 1550), with a fine timbered front. Exeter St., beyond St Ann's Gate, leads to the pleasant *Riverside Walk* (left), while St Nicholas Rd (right) goes on to the Harnham Bridge, passing the remains of *St Nicholas Hospital*, founded, like the bridge, by Bishop Bingham.

*Britford* church, 1¼m SE of Harnham Bridge, has Saxon sculptures on the NE arch of the nave.—At *Bemerton*, 1½m W of Salisbury, George Herbert spent the last three years of his life; he is buried in the old 14C church.—For *Wilton House*, 3m W of Salisbury by A30, see Rte 18A.

FROM SALISBURY TO STONEHENGE, 10½m. A345, the direct road, is 1m shorter but less pretty than the secondary road preferred here, which follows the Avon valley. We leave Salisbury by Castle St.—1½m. *Stratford-sub-Castle* has a manor house once occupied by the elder Pitt, who first entered Parliament in 1735 as member for Old Sarum.

*Old Sarum* (English Heritage, standard opening and summer Sunday mornings) stands on a low hill E of the village. It is the site successively of an Iron Age British hill-fort known to the Romans as *Sorviodunum*, a Saxon town, and a Norman fortress and cathedral. The bishopric of Sherborne was translated to Sarum about 1075. The cathedral begun by Bishop Herman and continued by Bishop St Osmund was consecrated in 1092, and later enlarged by Osmund's successor, Bishop Roger. Conflict with the military authorities in the castle, and a water shortage, caused the transference of the see to Salisbury in 1220. Sarum cathedral was razed in 1331 to provide building material for the close at Salisbury and the town gradually emptied, though a chapel survived until the 16C and the 'rotten borough' of Old Sarum returned two members to Parliament until 1833.

*Old Sarum*

Almost no traces of Roman occupation have been found, and the remains excavated are chiefly Norman. NW of the central mound where the Norman castle stood the foundations of the cathedral have been marked out. They show Bishop Roger's enlargement of the E end of the original church.

To the right of the road as we pass through (5½m) *Woodford* is *Heale House*, where Charles II hid after the Battle of Worcester. Only the gardens are open. A bridge crosses the Avon to *Durnford* (1½m), where the Norman and EE church adjoins an early earthwork known as *Ogbury Camp*.—Beyond (7m) *Lake*, reputedly the home of Sir Lancelot , is *Wilsford*, with a Norman church tower. —At 9m we turn left on A303 to (10½m) *Stonehenge* (Rte 19).

A354, the Weymouth road, leads SW from Salisbury. At (85m) *Coombe Bissett* we cross the Ebbe.

An unclassified road goes W along the valley to join the A30, passing through the pleasant villages of (1m) *Stratford Tony*, (5m) *Broad Chalke* where John Aubrey (1626–97) lived at the manor house, and (11m) *Berwick St John*, beneath the heights of *White Sheet Hill* (794ft) to the N and *Winkelbury Hill* (earthwork) and *Win Green* (908ft) to the S.

92m. We enter Dorset, crossing Bokerley Dyke, where we briefly join the line of the Roman road, leaving it again before (94m) *Handley Hill*, where we cross B3081 from Shaftesbury to Ringwood (Rte 18A).—105m. **Blandford Forum** (3900 inhab.; Tourist Information), a market town on the Stour, was burned down four times between 1579 and 1731, and has some fine buildings of 1735–40 by John and William Bastard, notably the town hall and the church. The pulpit is from the destroyed Wren church of St Antholin in London. The sculptor Alfred Stevens (1818–75) was a native.

*Tarrant Crawford*, 3m SE of Blandford, has an unspoilt 13C church with *wall paintings, mainly 14C, illustrating the life of St Margaret of Antioch, and the coffin slab of Bishop Poore of Salisbury, a native.

A350 leads N from Blandford to (13m) Shaftesbury (Rte 18A).—At 1m it gives a good view across the Stour to *Bryanston*, built by Norman Shaw as a country house in 1889–94 and now a boys' school.—*Hod Hill*, left of the road at 3m, is an important example of a prehistoric summit fort, enclosing a permanent Roman fort in its NW corner.—The church at *Iwerne Courtney* or *Shroton* (4½m) has work of 1610 still in the Gothic style. *Hambledon Hill* (622ft), W of the village, is a neolithic earthwork enjoying a fine view.—*Iwerne Minster* (6m) has a church with a good spire and Norman details, and Clayesmore School, built as a country house by Alfred Waterhouse (1878).

Off A354 about 9m SW of Blandford is *Milton Abbas*, a 'model' village dating from 1780, when the 1st Earl of Dorchester cleared the old village from beside his mansion, *Milton Abbey*, ³/₄m NW. The house, designed in the Gothic style by Sir William Chambers stands on the site of a monastery founded by Athelstan in 938 and incorporates the Abbot's Hall of 1498. It is now a school (open during spring and summer holidays). Beside it is the *Abbey Church*, still noble despite being reduced to its 14C choir and transepts and its 15C pinnacled tower. Inside are a rich altar screen of 1492, an elaborate 15C wooden tabernacle, two paintings referred to in the reign of Edward IV, interesting tombs and a brass of Sir John Tregonwell (1565). The tiny chapel of St Catherine on the hillock above was begun by Athelstan, and restored under the Normans and again in the 16C. The *Park Farm Museum* deals with local history and agriculture.

A354 joins A35 at (117m) *Puddletown*. The church is rich in details: gargoyles, Norman font, three-decker pulpit, 17C W gallery and a fine group of 14–16C monuments. The village is the 'Weatherbury' of Hardy's 'Far from the Madding Crowd', and *Waterston Manor* (not open), 2m NW on B3142, was Bathsheba's home.

On A35 ½m E of Puddletown stands *Athelhampton* (open), its main battlemented wing built by Sir William Martyn in the 1480s and the W wing added by his son in the next century. It stands on the legendary site of King Athelstan's palace and is the 'Athelhall' of Hardy's writing. The *Great Hall keeps its original dimensions, linenfold panelling, timber roof and oriel window. The Dining Room has good 18C furniture. The beautiful formal gardens were laid out in the 1890s.

119m. In the hamlet of *Higher Bockhampton*, S of A35, stands *Hardy's Birthplace* (NT, interior open by appointment). The writer spent his childhood in this low, thatched cottage and returned in 1867, writing 'Under the Greenwood Tree' and 'Far from the Madding Crowd' here.—120m. *Stinsford*, also S of the road, is the 'Mellstock' of Hardy's work. His heart is buried in the churchyard; the rest of him lies in Westminster Abbey.

122m. **DORCHESTER** (14,000 inhab.), the county town of Dorset,
has been luckier than many county towns in keeping its character
despite modern development and expansion. It preserves the market
atmosphere and many of the specific features described by Hardy,
who calls it 'Casterbridge'. Dorchester's appeal lies not so much in
individual buildings as in the general effect of its lively but dignified
streetscapes.

**Tourist Information Centre**: No. 7 Acland Rd.

**Car Parks**: Charles St., Weymouth Avenue, Bridport Rd.

**Railway Stations**: Dorchester South and Dorchester West, both S of the centre,
off Weymouth Avenue.

**History**. The site of an Iron Age settlement, Dorchester became the Roman
*Durnovaria* after about AD 70. It is rich in Roman remains (eg. Maumbury
Rings) and the course of the old walls is marked by the tree-lined avenues
known as 'The Walks'. In the Civil War the town was staunchly Parliament-
arian, though it suffered one period of Royalist occupation. After the Battle of
Sedgemoor in 1685 it was the scene of the notorious Bloody Assizes, where
Judge Jeffreys sentenced 74 of the Duke of Monmouth's supporters to death
and 175 to transportation. The Tolpuddle Martyrs were tried here in 1834.

**Famous residents**: The Dorset poet William Barnes (1801–86) and Thomas
Hardy (1840–1928).

A35 becomes High East St. as it enters Dorchester. It climbs from the
water meadows of the river Frome past (all on the right) the *King's
Arms*, an important location in 'The Mayor of Casterbridge', made
conspicuous by its handsome portico with bow window above, and
the 19C *Town Hall and Corn Exchange* to the 15C church of **St Peter**,
with a statue of William Barnes outside. The church has two 14C
effigies in the Hardy Chapel, a monument to the politician Denzil
Holles (d. 1680) and an effective 19C reredos. From the junction
outside the church Cornhill leads S, passing on the right the *Ante-
lope Hotel*, which contains the Oak Room where Judge Jeffreys
presided over the Bloody Assizes. Cornhill continues as South St.,
with (on the left) the 18C house, now Barclays Bank, which Hardy
made Michael Henchard's home and *Napper's Mite*, a 17C almshouse well restored and adapted as shops. On the opposite side of the
street a plaque marks the home of William Barnes, next to the
architect's office where the young Hardy worked.

Weymouth Avenue leads from the junction at the bottom of South St. to
*Maumbury Rings*, the largest and most perfectly preserved Roman amphitheatre in the country.

High West St. leads from St Peter's Church, beginning with the
**\*Dorset County Museum** on the right. It contains fine collections of
natural history, agricultural equipment, fossils and British and
Roman antiquities, including a hoard of 22,000 silver coins, a figure
of a Thracian horseman and a late 4C \*mosaic pavement with a head
of Christ (discovered at Hinton St Mary in 1963). There are also relics
of William Barnes and Hardy, among them Hardy's reconstructed
study from Max Gate and the manuscript of 'The Mayor of Casterbridge'. On the opposite side of the street is the traditional lodging of
Judge Jeffreys, now a café. Further up on the right is the *Old Shire
Hall*, containing the *Old Court* (open) where the Tolpuddle Martyrs
were tried. The Top o' Town beyond is marked b a roundabout and a
statue of Hardy (1931; Eric Kennington).

From the roundabout the Bridport road leads straight ahead to the *Dorset
Military Museum*, with an unusually good collection. Poundbury Rd, by the
museum, leads right to (1m) *Poundbury Camp*, an Iron Age earthwork later
used by the Romans.—The Grove leads right from the Top o' Town roundabout,

passing a fragment of the Roman W wall on the right near the bottom of the hill.
It continues as A37 to (1¹/2m) *Wolfeton House* (open), an early 16C and
Elizabethan house with an irregular gatehouse, fine woodwork, fireplaces and
plaster ceilings in the Parlour and Dining Room, and a stone staircase.

A352, the Wareham road, runs SE from Dorchester and passes, after about
1m, *Max Gate* (not open), the house Hardy designed for himself in the 1880s
and lived in until his death.—A right turn ¹/2m beyond leads to the little village
of *Winterbourne Came*, where William Barnes was rector from 1862 until his
death.

Off A354, the Weymouth road, on a conspicuous hill about 2m S of Dorchester
stands *Maiden Castle (English Heritage, open at any reasonable time). It is
perhaps the finest prehistoric fort in England, covering 115 acres and at one
point showing eight lines of defence. Excavations in 1934–37 and 1985–86 have
shown that the hill was occupied first as a neolithic camp and again from about
500 BC. The majority of the earthworks were built in the first century BC, only
to be stormed by the Roman general Vespasian in AD 43. The latest building
was a Roman temple of the 4C near the top of the hill.

From Dorchester to *Wimborne* and *Bournemouth*, see Rte 17B; to *Sherborne*,
see Rte 18A; to *Exeter*, see Rte 18B.

A354, the Weymouth road, climbs to the Ridgeway, with Maiden
Castle on the right, and then descends through (127m) *Upwey*.

131m. **WEYMOUTH** (46,300 inhab.), an old harbour town and
popular seaside resort, stands on both sides of the river Wey, the
older part to the S and the newer part (once known as Melcombe
Regis) to the N. The town is notable for its handsome late Georgian
buildings and its beautiful bay, divided by the harbour into
Weymouth Bay (N) and Portland Roads (S).

**Tourist Information Centres**: Pavilion Theatre Complex, Esplanade; (seasonal)
near the king's statue, also on the Esplanade.

**Car Parks**: Preston Beach Rd, The Swannery on Radipole Park Drive, Ferry
Terminal and Pavilion Esplanade, Municipal Offices on North Quay.

**Bus Station**: Edward St.

**Railway Stations**: at junction of King St. and Queen St., and at Ferry Terminal.

**Amusements**: Seaside amusements at Alexandra Gardens, Pier Bandstand,
Bowleaze Cove (2m NE); summer shows, etc. in Pavilion Theatre; concerts at
Harbour Pleasure Pier.

**Ferry services**: to Guernsey, Jersey and (summer only) Cherbourg.

**History**. Weymouth's natural situation has given it a long history as a port and
military base. John Endicott sailed in 1628 to found the plantation of Salem in
Massachusetts, and the American assault force was launched from here on
D-Day in 1944. The town's popularity as a resort began in 1789, when
George III paid the first of many visits. Hardy's 'The Trumpet-Major' gives a
good picture of Weymouth ('Budmouth') as a 'royal watering-place' during the
Napoleonic era.

**Famous natives**: The painter Sir James Thornhill (1675–1734), who represented
Melcombe Regis in Parliament for 12 years; Thomas Love Peacock (1785–1866).

The most striking landmark N of the river and the landlocked
harbour is the elaborately painted and gilded *statue of George III
(1810) on the Esplanade. Among the good Georgian buildings to the
N is the *Gloucester Hotel*, the king's summer home during his visits.
Beyond the fanciful *Jubilee Clock* (1887) are, both on the left,
*Greenhill Gardens* and *Lodmoor Country Park*, 70 acres of salt
marshland kept as a nature reserve.

Westham Rd leads W from the king's statue to Westham Bridge and *Weymouth
Museum*, with an exhibit of local history including George III's
bathing-machine. *Radipole Lake*, an extension of the Wey to the N, has a bird
sanctuary and swannery.

The attractive St Mary St. leads S from the king's statue to the 19C church of *St Mary*, with an altarpiece by Thornhill. The street continues to Custom House Quay, where the Town Bridge leads to the old town. In Trinity St., to the left, is *Tudor House* (limited opening), restored and fitted with appropriate furnishings. The headland to the E ends with *Nothe Gardens*, *Nothe Fort* and the old stone pier of 1824.

S of Weymouth is the **Isle of Portland** (10,900 inhab.), a limestone peninsula 4¹/2m long and 1³/4m wide. Its rocky and almost treeless surface is pitted by the quarries that have yielded white stone for many fashionable buildings since Wren chose it to face St Paul's Cathedral. The bleakness of the landscape is relieved by the fine views out to sea and, particularly, across Portland Harbour. The peninsula is connected to the mainland by *Chesil Beach*, a remarkable bank of shingle about 30ft high and 200yd wide, extending 18m W to Bridport. The pebbles gradually decrease in size from E to W.

A354 passes through the suburban village of *Wyke Regis* as it leaves Weymouth and reaches Portland at (4m) *Fortuneswell*. A road branches left to *Castletown*, with a Royal Navy base and *Portland Castle* (English Heritage, summer standard opening, but closed on Tuesdays and on Wednesday mornings), built by Henry VIII in 1520. *Sandsfoot Castle*, his other blockhouse on the opposite shore, is in ruins. *Portland Breakwater*, built by convicts in 1849–72, is c 6000ft long and encloses the largest harbour in the kingdom (2107 acres); an inner harbour was added in 1947.—A354 climbs past quarries to (5¹/2m) *Easton*, the chief village on the island (Tourist Information). *St George's church, W of the centre, was built in 1744–66 by a local mason, Thomas Gilbert. The Borstal institution on the coast to the E incorporates the buildings of the 19C prison. On Wakeham Rd to the S is the *Portland Museum*, devoted to local history; the 17C building is also known as *Avice's Cottage*, from its connection with Hardy's 'The Well-Beloved'. *Pennsylvania Castle* (now a hotel) here was built c 1800 by James Wyatt for John Penn, governor of the island and a grandson of the founder of Pennsylvania; its grounds include the ruins of the late 11C *Rufus Castle*. A footpath descends to *Church Ope Cove*, where there is good swimming and a ruined watch-tower contemporary with Portland Castle.—7m. *Southwell* is the last village before the small hamlet of (8¹/2m) *Portland Bill*, a fine mass of rock with a bird observatory and an old lighthouse overlooking the dangerous race offshore. Much of the area belongs to the Ministry of Defence.

FROM WEYMOUTH TO BRIDPORT, 18m by B3157, with good views of Chesil Beach.—9m. *Abbotsbury* is a charming village, popular with visitors. It has the ruins of a Benedictine abbey, with a fine 15C barn (not open) and a gable near the churchyard (English Heritage, open at any reasonable time), as well as a swannery and sub-tropical gardens (both open in summer). On a height to the S stands the 15C *St Catherine's Chapel*, with a stone vault (English Heritage, open at any reasonable time).—18m *Bridport*, see Rte 18B.

# B.   Via Bournemouth

Total distance 142m. A4, A30 to (46m) Basingstoke (bypassed), or alternative way by M3, see Rte 14B.—A30, M3, A303, A30 to (82m) **Salisbury**, see Rte 17A.—A338 to (98m) Ringwood.—A31, A338 to (109m) **Bournemouth**.—A35, A350 to (115m) Poole.—A350, A35, A351 to (124m) Wareham.—A352, A353 to (142m) Weymouth.

Maps: OS Landranger 176, 186, 185, 184, 195 or 194; OS Outdoor Leisure map (1:25,000 or 2¹/2in to 1m) for Purbeck.

From London to (46m) *Basingstoke*, see Rte 14B, and on to (82m) **Salisbury**, see Rte 17A. From Salisbury we follow A338 down the Avon valley.—88m. *Downton* has a partly Norman church and a moot, or mound, where Saxon assemblies were held (not open). *Trafalgar House* (1¹/2m N; not open), built in 1733 and extended later in the same century, was given to Nelson's family by the nation after the Battle of Trafalgar.—Over the Hampshire border at (90m) *Breamore* (pronounced 'Bremmer') the 10–11C *church has a stone rood and an Anglo-Saxon inscription over the archway to the S transept. The church stands in parkland near *Breamore House* (open), an Elizabethan mansion in rose-red brick. Built for the Hulse family in 1583, it needed substantial rebuilding after a fire in 1856.

The Great Hall overlooks the Avon valley. The Dining Room has a carved stone Renaissance fireplace and (like the bedrooms) good 16–17C furniture. Among the portraits by Thomas Hudson in the West Drawing Room is one of the earliest paintings to show cricketing equipment. The grounds contain a *Carriage Museum* and a *Countryside Museum* with agricultural machinery.

92m. *Fordingbridge*, where Augustus John died in 1961, has a 13–15C church.— From (98m) *Ringwood*, near the W fringes of the New Forest, B3347 continues down the Avon valley to approach Bournemouth through Christchurch; the faster route follows A31 and then A338.

109m. **BOURNEMOUTH** (144,800 inhab.) stands at the mouth of the little Bourne valley overlooking Poole Bay. Its cliffs are inter- rupted by beautiful 'chines', or ravines, while its inland scenery is rich in pinewoods, well preserved in about 2000 acres of public parks and gardens. Bournemouth's popularity as a resort began c 1810 and by the end of the century its reputation for elegance led Thomas Hardy to describe it (under the name of 'Sandbourne') in 'Tess of the d'Urbervilles' as a 'Mediterranean lounging-place on the English Channel'.

**Tourist Information Centre**: Westover Rd.

**Car Parks**: Bath Rd South, Bath Rd North, St Peter's Rd, Cotlands Rd, Madeira Rd, Upper Terrace Rd, Undercliff Drive.

**Coach Station**: Oxford Rd. Local buses from the Square, country services from the Triangle.

**Railway Station**: off Holdenhurst Rd.

**Amusements**: Pier Theatre; Pavilion (theatre, ballroom, etc.) on Westover Rd; Bournemouth International Centre (with two concert halls, used by the Bourne- mouth Symphony Orchestra).

**Airport**: at Hurn (off A338 5m N). Flights to Alderney, Guernsey and Jersey.

**Famous natives and residents**: Sir Hubert Parry (1848–1918) was born and John Keble (1792–1866) died at Bournemouth. Paul Verlaine taught at St Aloysius' College in 1875–76. Robert Louis Stevenson lived in 1884–87 in a house on Alum Chine Rd whose site is now occupied by a memorial garden.

In the graveyard of *St Peter's*, E of The Square, are the tombs of William Godwin (d. 1836), his wife Mary Wollstonecraft (d. 1797), and their daughter Mary Shelley (d. 1851), author of 'Frankenstein'. Shelley's heart, retrieved from his funeral pyre at Viareggio, is buried in his wife's grave. The *Russell–Cotes Art Gallery and Museum*, on East Cliff Promenade S of the church, is housed in a late Victorian villa. Its collections include 17–20C paintings (works by Morland and Richard Wilson and Rossetti) , ceramics, three rooms of Japanese art, an Irving room of theatrical relics and five period rooms.

The banks of the Bourne are attractively laid out with gardens and behind the large *Meyrick Park*, N of The Square, stretch the remains of *Talbot Woods*, with fragrant pine trees. On the coastline to the W are *Darley Chine*, *Middle Chine*, *Alum Chine* and *Branksome Chine*, while *Boscombe Chine* lies to the E.

6m W on A35 is **Christchurch** (33,300 inhab.; Tourist Information), an ancient town at the head of Christchurch Harbour, between the Avon and the Stour.

Once known as 'Twineham', the town takes its present name from the magnificent *Priory Church*, now the longest parish church in England (312ft).

The late 15C W tower (120ft high) offers a fine view from the top. There is beautiful Norman work (c 1090–1120) on the outside of the N transept. We enter by the N Porch (c 1300), the largest in the country; under the tower is a monument to Shelley by H. Weekes (1854). The *Nave, built by Bishop Flambard of Durham about 1093, is a fine example of Norman architecture, especially the triforium; the clerestory is EE and the vaulting is by William Garbett (1819). The aisles are Norman, re-cast in the 13C. The 14C rood screen was drastically restored in 1848. The Choir is for the most part late 15C; the stalls have fanciful misericords (1200–1500), but the chief feature is the stone *reredos (Dec.) representing the Tree of Jesse. The Chantry of the Countess of Salisbury (beheaded 1541), the Lady Chapel (c 1405), St Michael's Loft (with a museum), the Draper Chantry (1529) at the E end of the S aisle, and Flaxman's monument to Viscountess Fitzharris (d. 1815) should not be overlooked.

Opposite the King's Arms, N of the church, are the ruins of *Christchurch Castle and Norman House* (English Heritage, open at any reasonable time). The Georgian *Red House* in Quay Rd contains a small museum of local interest. —About 2m S is *Hengistbury Head*, with fine sea views, and 2m SE is *Mudeford*, with a sandy beach.

We leave Bournemouth to the W through the suburban districts of *Branksome* and *Parkstone*, where the imposing Italianate church of St Osmund (1905) has 17C ironwork from St Mary-le-Bow in London. B3369 leads left to (2m) *Canford Cliffs* and the magnificent gardens of *Compton Acres* (open), established in the 1920s, with seven individual gardens (Japanese, Italian, Rock and Water, Heather, Roman, English and Palm Court).—115m. **Poole** (118,900 inhab.; Tourist Information) is an ancient and still active seaport. On the Quay, lined with old warehouses, are the *Custom House* and *Poole Pottery* (open for tours). The *Maritime Museum*, around the corner in Paradise St., is housed in a late 15C building. *Scaplen's Court* (open) in the High St. is another 15C house, arranged as a museum of domestic history and local archaeology. The 18C *Guildhall* (open) on Market St., off High St., has displays of local history. The Quay faces *Poole Harbour*, a large and almost landlocked bay fringed with heathland. Near its narrow mouth is *Brownsea Island* (NT), reached by passenger ferry from Poole Quay and Sandbanks; it includes a nature reserve, with a heronry and waterfowl sanctuary, and gives fine views of the Dorset coast. The Boy Scout movement began at a trial camp here in 1907.

FROM POOLE TO DORCHESTER VIA WIMBORNE, 27m on A349, A31 and A35.—5m. **Wimborne** (5500 inhab.; Tourist Information), an ancient market town on the river Allen where it meets the Stour, has good Georgian houses and a fine *Minster*, or collegiate church. The crossing tower, in red sandstone, is Trans. Norman and the W tower (1448–64) is Perp. The most interesting features of the rather crowded interior, with much Norman work, are: the early 16C Flemish glass of the E window, the monument to the Duke of Somerset (d. 1444) and his wife in the choir, the chained library, and the late 16C clock in the W tower. S of the church is the *Priest's House Museum*. Near the Allen is *Deans Court Garden* (limited opening).

*Canford Magna*, 1½m SE, has a 12C church with the tomb of Sir Henry Layard (1817–94), excavator of Nineveh, and Canford School, built as a country house by Barry in the 1840s.—In *West Moors*, 7m NE of Wimborne, is *Highbury Garden* (limited opening). On B3082 1½m NW of Wimborne stands **Kingston Lacy**, acquired by the NT in 1982 and officially opened to the public in 1986 after a major campaign of restoration. Originally built by Sir Roger Pratt in 1663–65, the house was transformed in 1835–40 by Charles Barry, who encased the brick exterior in Chilmark stone. Inside, his fine marble staircase is notable; so is the Library added by Robert Brettingham in the 1780s. Much of the splendid interior decoration was acquired or commissioned in Italy by William John Bankes (1786–1855), the collector and traveller. The furniture in the Saloon includes items from William Beckford's Fonthill Abbey. The *art collection has Bankes family portraits by Van Dyck, Lely, Lawrence, Romney and Salvator Rosa. Many of the other pictures were collected by William Bankes; they include works by Sebastiano del Piombo (in the Dining Room), Giulio Romano, Jan Brueghel the Elder, Titian and Rubens (all in the Saloon), and Zurbaran and Murillo (in the Spanish Room). The landscaped grounds, with fine cedars, have an Egyptian obelisk and sarcophagus, and a restored Victorian fernery.—B3082 continues beyond Kingston Lacy to (4m) *Badbury Rings*, an Iron Age hill-fort with good views, reputed to be the site of Arthur's last battle, Mons Badonicus; the Romans made it one of their main road junctions. B3082 ends at (9m) *Blandford Forum* (Rte 17A).

A31 leads W from Wimborne along the valley of the Stour, passing (10m) the prominent Lion and Stag Gate of *Charborough Park*.—At (13m) *Winterbourne Tomson* the tiny apsidal church has beautiful 18C oak fittings.—We join A35 at (16m) *Bere Regis*, the 'Kingsbere' of Hardy's 'Tess'. The interesting church has a good carved timber ceiling and the burial chapel of the Turbervilles. *Woodbury Hill*, nearby, is the scene of 'Greenhill Fair' in Hardy's 'Far from the Madding Crowd'.—At (19m) *Tolpuddle* the line of the Roman road from Badbury Rings crosses A35. The village is famous for the Tolpuddle Martyrs, five agricultural workers sentenced to transportation in 1834 for 'forming an illegal union' and now regarded as pioneers of the Trade Union movement.—For (21½m) *Athelhampton*, (22m) *Puddletown* and (27m) *Dorchester*, see Rte 17A.

The main route follows A350 and A35 from Poole around Hole's Bay, a branch of the harbour with a huge power station. At (120m) *Lytchett Minster* we bear left on A351.—124m. **Wareham** (4600 inhab.), an ancient and interesting little town on the navigable Frome, is built within an enceinte of massive Anglo-Saxon earthworks ('the Walls'), with its four main streets intersecting at right angles. *Lady St Mary's Church* contains a stone coffin traditionally connected with King Edward the Martyr; the unusual shape may derive from Saxon burial customs. There is also an hexagonal lead font, and two remarkable little chapels. *St Martin's*, a small church on the walls, is partly Saxon and has Norman wall paintings (badly damaged). The fine monument to T.E. Lawrence (see below) is by Eric Kennington.

The **Isle of Purbeck**, SE of Wareham, is a bold promontory of downs and heath yielding potter's clay and the shelly limestone known as Purbeck marble. Access to some of the lovelier stretches of its scenery is restricted because of use by the army. We follow A351 down the centre of the headland.—From (1m) *Stoborough* an unclassified road leads right to a ridge of the *Purbeck Hills* 2m away, with a *view from the summit. Kimmeridge and its bay (see below) lie beyond.—5m. *Corfe Castle* is a pretty village, boldly placed on an isolated hill in the middle of a gap in the Downs. Above it stand the striking ruins of *Corfe Castle* (NT), famous for its gallant defence for six weeks in 1643 by Lady Bankes against 600 Parliamentary troops. In 1646, however, it was seized by stratagem and deliberately reduced to its present curiously shattered condition by gunpowder. The castle, dating mainly from the Norman period, occupies the site of a 10C Saxon stronghold of King Edgar, at the gate of which King Edward the Martyr was murdered by his stepmother Elfrida in 979 to clear the way to the throne for her son Ethelred. It was a favourite residence of King John, and Edward II was imprisoned here in 1326 just before his death at Berkeley Castle.

*Kingston*, in a fine position high on the downs 2m S of Corfe Castle, has a sumptuous church by G.E. Street (1880). Chancellor Eldon, buried in the old parish church, died in 1838 at *Encombe*, 1½m SW. The area abounds in small Purbeck marble quarries. *Church Knowle*, 1½m SW of Corfe, has a painted triple chancel arch and a wall tomb of 1572. The tiny village of *Kimmeridge* lies 2½m further SW, near *Smedmore House* (limited opening), built mainly in the 18C, with marquetry furniture, paintings (David Cox and Copley Fielding), antique dolls and a walled garden. A private road (toll) runs to the secluded *Kimmeridge Bay*.

A351 continues to (11m) **Swanage** (8600 inhab.; Tourist Information), a pleasant seaside resort on a fine bay. The façade of the *Town Hall* was designed by Wren and originally belonged to the Mercers' Hall in London; the clock tower near the pier was first erected in honour of the Duke of Wellington at the S end of London Bridge.

*Corfe Castle*

A road runs on to (½m) *Peveril Point* and the coastguard station. Another road goes S to (1¼m) *Durlstone Head* and on to the *Tilly Whim Caves*, once used by smugglers. From here a spectacular walk can be taken W along the cliffs past (1½m) *Dancing Ledge*, so called from the motion of the waves of the making tide, to (4½m) *St Aldhelm's Head*, with a Norman chapel, and (5½m) the lovely little bay of *Chapman's Pool*. The Dorset Coast Path (see below) continues W to Weymouth. The return to (6m) Swanage can be made through *Worth Matravers*, where the Norman church has an impressive S door and chancel arch, and *Langton Matravers*, with a church tastefully rebuilt in 1875. —About 3m N of Swanage is the charming village of *Studland*, with a tiny Norman church, on a pretty bay with good bathing. On the moor 1m NW of Studland is a curious perched block of ferruginous sandstone known as the *Agglestone*. The road (toll) continues 3m further to the floating bridge for Sandbanks and Bournemouth.

The main route follows A352 W from Wareham along the valley of the Frome.—129m. The pretty village of *Wool* has Woolbridge Manor (now a hotel), approached by a fine bridge, a home of the Turbervilles where Tess and Angel Clare spent their wedding night. The romantic but scant ruins of *Bindon Abbey* (not open), founded by Robert de Newburgh in 1172, lie about ½m E.

About 2m N is *Bovington Camp*, the original headquarters of the Royal Tank Corps, with a Tank Museum. On the Puddletown road further N is *Clouds Hill* (NT), the cottage belonging to T.E. Lawrence (Lawrence of Arabia; 1888–1935). He is buried at *Moreton*, near B3390 to the W.
*Lulworth Cove*, 5m S of Wool, is a remarkable circular bay about 500yd in diameter, almost completely landlocked by tall oolite and chalk hills. The ˙Dorset Coast Path leads W along the cliffs to (10m) Weymouth; to the E, on the way to the Isle of Purbeck, it passes through military firing ranges and is closed most weekdays.

At 136m the Weymouth road, A353, leaves the Dorchester road and crosses the Downs.—To the right beyond (139m) *Osmington* is a figure on horseback cut into the chalk, supposed to represent George

*The chalk figure of George III cut into the Downs near Osmington*

III (see 'The Trumpet Major').—Left of the road at (140m) *Overcombe* are the foundations of the small *Jordan Hill Roman Temple* (English Heritage, open at any reasonable time).—142m. **Weymouth**, see Rte 17A.

# 18  London to Exeter

## A.  Via Salisbury and Yeovil

Total distance 170m. A4, A30 to (46m) Basingstoke (bypassed), or alternative way by M3, see Rte 14B. —A30, M3, A303, A30 to (82m) Salisbury, see Rte 17A. Then A30 throughout.—To (86m) Wilton.
—To (102m) **Shaftesbury**.—To (118m) **Sherborne**.—To (123m) **Yeovil**.—To (132m) Crewkerne.—To (141m) Chard.—To (154m) Honiton (bypassed).—To (170m) **Exeter**.

Maps: OS Landranger 176, 186, 185, 184, 183, 194 (briefly), 193, 192.

An excellent route for country houses, but A30 is congested during summer weekends and other holiday periods. At such times A303, though not without its problems, is preferable: follow the main line of Rte 19 to Sparkford and then the Sparkford–Exeter detour.

From London to (46m) *Basingstoke*, see Rte 14B, and on to (82m)*Salisbury*, see Rte 17A.—86m. *Wilton* (4000 inhab.) is a carpet-making town with a remarkable church (1844) by T.H. Wyatt in Italian Romanesque style, lavishly adorned with marble and mosaics and with 12–16C stained glass from various sources. The magnificent 16–17C mansion of **Wilton House** (open) is particularly interesting for the *work of Inigo Jones and for its *art collection.

Of the house built by the 1st Earl of Pembroke in the 1540s on the site of a former abbey, only the general plan and the Holbein Porch (since removed to the grounds) remain. The Elizabethan house that succeeded it was provided with an Italianate S front by Isaac de Caus (c 1633), superbly restored after a fire by Inigo Jones and his nephew-in-law John Webb (1649–52). James Wyatt's Gothic alterations (1801–14) have been modified externally but can still be seen inside. The Front Hall has a statue by Peter Scheemakers (1743) of Shakespeare, who may have acted in a performance of 'As You Like It' at Wilton in 1603. The Single Cube Room, the first of Inigo Jones's splendid state rooms, has a dado by de Critz illustrating scenes from Sir Philip Sidney's 'Arcadia', which was partly written here. The elaborately decorated Double Cube Room has a fine display of Van Dycks, among them a portrait of Charles I and one of his children. Paintings elsewhere in the house include works by Andrea del Sarto, Pieter Brueghel the Younger, Jan Brueghel the Elder, Rembrandt, Wouwermans, Rubens, Lely, Poussin, Teniers and Richard Wilson; there are also terracotta busts by Roubiliac, and furniture by Chippendale and William Kent. Apart from various amusements, the grounds contain the Palladian Bridge built by the 9th Earl (d. 1751).

FROM WILTON TO WARMINSTER AND LONGLEAT, 20m by A36 and A362.—A36 follows the valley of the Wylye. Though close, the river is largely hidden from view, and the prettier scenery along the S bank can be seen from a little unclassified road. At (11m) *Codford St Peter* the church has an excellently carved 9C cross shaft.—At (14m) *Heytesbury* are an imposing 12–15C church restored by Butterfield and a Tudor almshouse faithfully rebuilt c 1769. Siegfried Sassoon died at Heytesbury House in 1967. *Scratchbury* and *Battlesbury*, two Iron Age forts to the right of the road further on, both give wide

*The Palladian bridge at Wilton House*

views.—18m. **Warminster** (15,100 inhab.; seasonal Tourist Information) lies just below the Downs at the junction with A350, the Chippenham–Shaftesbury road (Rte 20). The Georgian main street has good coaching inns, and there is an organ formerly at Salisbury Cathedral in the 14C parish *Church*. *Lord Weymouth School*, founded in 1707 by the Thynne family of Longleat, has a portal by Wren. Dr Arnold of Rugby was a pupil.

A362 runs W to Frome (8m, see Rte 24). Below (2m) *Cley Hill*, another conspicuous Iron Age hill-fort, is the entrance to **Longleat** (open). Built for Sir John Thynne in 1559–80, with Robert Smythson among the architects, the house breaks with older traditions in the regularity of its plan and the uniform handling of all four main fronts. Inside, only the Great Hall belongs substantially to Thynne's time, with stone floor and hammerbeam ceiling. The corridors and main staircase are part of Sir Jeffrey Wyatville's alterations (1801–11) and the Italianate decoration in many of the rooms, including the former Long Gallery, was added by J.D. Crace in the 1870s. The Old Library where Bishop Ken (1637– 1711) wrote his hymns is not open. Most striking of the many paintings are the portraits and, in the State Drawing Room, a Holy Family attributed to Titian. The grounds were landscaped by Capability Brown (1757–62) and Repton (c 1790). Their atmosphere is not improved by the various amusements housed in the former outbuildings or by the Safari Park, attractions which also make Longleat crowded in summer.—At *Horningsham*, 1m S, the thatched Meeting House is said to have been built in 1566 by Thynne for his Scottish Presbyterian masons and is claimed as the oldest Dissenting place of worship in England.

FROM WILTON TO MERE, 25m. From *Barford St Martin*, on A30 3m W of Wilton, we follow B3089 along the Nadder valley.—7m *Dinton*. Near the church is Hyde's House (NT but not open), a building of 1725 on the probable site of the house where Edward Hyde, Earl of Clarendon (1609–74) and historian of the Civil War, was born. Philipps House (NT, open by appointment only) is a neo-Grecian building of 1813–16 by Sir Jeffrey Wyatville. Little Clarendon (NT, open by appointment only) is a late 15C house; the adjoining cottage (NT but not open) was the birthplace of Henry Lawes (1596–1662), composer and friend of Milton.—10m. *Teffont Magna* is a pretty village. The gardens of Fitz House are open on limited days in summer.—S of (15m) *Fonthill Bishop* stood Fonthill Abbey, the extravagant and insecurely founded Gothick mansion built by James Wyatt in 1796–1812 for William Beckford (1759–1844), author of 'Vathek'. *Tisbury*, 3m S of B3089, has a large 12–13C cruciform church with a fine 15C roof. *Wardour Castle*, 2m SW of Tisbury, is a country house by James Paine (1769–76), with a fine staircase and a chapel enlarged by Sir John Soane (1788). It is now a school (open in summer holidays). The earlier home of the Lords Arundell of Wardour is ³/₄m SE, near A30, at *Wardour Old Castle* (English Heritage, summer standard opening and weekends only in winter). Built c 1393, it was badly damaged in the Civil War but preserved for its picturesque appeal.—At 20m B3089 crosses A350, the Chippenham–Shaftesbury road (Rte 20).—At 21m we join A303 4m E of *Mere* (Rte 18).

The main route follows A30 W from Wilton, through Barford St Martin and (94m) *Fovant*, where the chalk downs are carved with the emblems of the troops quartered here in 1914–18.—101m. We cross the border into Dorset.

102m. **Shaftesbury** (4900 inhab.; Tourist Information), wonderfully placed on a spur 700ft high, is the picturesque relic of a town whose ancient grandeur included a castle, twelve churches and four market crosses. The house for Benedictine nuns founded by King Alfred in 880 became the wealthiest nunnery in England. The scanty *Abbey Ruins* (open) are beautifully laid out; the ground plan of the church has been revealed by excavation; and there is an interesting little museum. The empty tomb of Edward the Martyr (d. 978) was found in 1861 on the N side of the altar, and in 1931 a casket containing what may be his bones was unearthed nearby. King Canute died here in 1035. *St Peter's Church* has a good 15C N parapet and 16C W porch. The formidably steep *Gold Hill commands a lovely view. At the top is the *Local History Museum*, with a collection of buttons (once the town's chief manufacture).

FROM SHAFTESBURY TO RINGWOOD, 25m on B3081, a fine scenic road across Cranborne Chase. A zigzag climbs Charlton Down to 862ft.—8m. *Tollard Royal* was King John's seat for the hunting of Cranborne Chase.—Beyond (13m) *Sixpenny Handley*, where the ancient church has 13C wall paintings, we cross A354, the Salisbury–Blandford road (Rte 17A), and then the prominent line of the Roman Ackerley Dyke.—18m. *Cranborne*, to the left, is a small town with a charming Tudor and Jacobean manor house. The *gardens (limited opening) were originally laid out in the 17C by John Tradescant. *Knowlton Church and Earthworks* (English Heritage, open at any reasonable time) consist of a ruined Norman church surrounded by the remains of a henge monument.—We cross Ringwood Forest and turn left on A31 to (25m) *Ringwood* (Rte 17B), on the Avon and near the W fringes of the New Forest (Rte 16).

From Shaftesbury to Chippenham, see Rte 20.

Beyond Shaftesbury A30 crosses the fertile *Vale of Blackmore*, watered by the Stour and the Cale, familiar to readers of Hardy's 'Tess of the d'Urbervilles'.

From (108m) *East Stour* B3092 leads S via (4m) *Marnhull*, the 'Marlott' of 'Tess', to (9m) *Sturminster Newton*, a quiet market town on the Stour, where Hardy lived in 1876–78. The Dorset poet William Barnes (1801–86) was born at *Rushay*, 1¹/₂m W. Off A357 1m E of Sturminster Newton is *Fiddleford Mill House* (English Heritage, summer standard opening), the hall and solar block of a 14C house altered in the early 16C; the roofs are superb.—From (112m) *Henstridge*, on the A30, A357 goes 3m S to *Stalbridge*, with a tall market cross.

114m. *Purse Caundle Manor* (open), on the left, is a picturesque medieval manor house in grey stone, with Tudor additions and an attractive garden.—The church of (115m) *Milborne Port* is notable for its early Norman crossing and other details.

118m. **Sherborne** (7600 inhab.; seasonal Tourist Information) is a lively and handsome stone-built town with many ancient buildings and a magnificent *Abbey Church*. As it stands, this is one of the best surviving examples of Perp. architecture, but it also incorporates considerable remains from earlier periods.

A bishopric was established at Sherborne in 705 and moved to Old Sarum in 1075. The abbey attached to the cathedral was occupied after 998 by Benedictine monks. The 11C doorway at the W end and the four piers that support the crossing survive from the last Saxon church on the site. Of the Norman church that replaced it after 1122, there remain the S porch, the crossing arch and parts of the N and S transepts. The Lady Chapel followed in the 13C. The 15C brought an almost complete rebuilding in the Perp. style, beginning with the choir and continuing with the nave, both of which have *fan vaulting of exceptional richness.

There are a number of striking monuments. The Wykeham Chapel off the N transept has the tomb of Sir John Horsey (d. 1546); in the N transept a stone marks the probable grave of the poet Sir Thomas Wyatt (d. 1542). In the S transept is the vast baroque memorial (1698) by John Nost to John Digby, 3rd Earl of Bristol, and his two wives; St Katherine's Chapel, on the W side, contains the tomb of John Leweston (d. 1584) and some good 15C heraldic glass. The peal of eight bells in the tower is said to be the heaviest in the world.

*Sherborne School*, an important public school for boys refounded by Edward VI in 1550, incorporates the 15C Abbot's Hall and other monastic buildings. The *Almshouse of St John the Baptist and St John the Evangelist*, on Trendle St. nearby, is a two-storied medieval hospital (1437). Among the pleasant row of old buildings on Half Moon St., heading E from the abbey church, is the *Museum*, with collections of local history and a Victorian dolls' house. The street ends at the early 16C *Conduit*. Cheap St. runs N, passing Newland with *Lord Digby's School* (c 1720) on the right, to The Green, where we find a charming 16C building known as *The Julian*.

On the S side of the Yeo ½m E are the ruins of the bishop's *Castle* built in the early 12C and briefly inhabited by Sir Walter Raleigh (English Heritage, standard opening and summer Sunday mornings). On the opposite side of the lake stands the present *Sherborne Castle* (open), built by Raleigh in 1594. Most of the interior was remodelled in 1859–60, though there is a 17C plaster ceiling in the Red Drawing Room, a Gothick Library of c 1760 and a fine collection of Digby family portraits. The park has lovely walks and views.—The Tudor manor house (open) at *Sandford Orcas*, off B3148 4m N, has good stained glass and furniture, and an attractive garden.

FROM SHERBORNE TO DORCHESTER, 19m by A352, through the countryside of Hardy's 'The Woodlanders'.— 8½m. An unclassified road leads right, across *Batcombe Down* (*views). The remote church of *Melbury Bubb*, 4m N of the road, has a very early Norman carved *font.—9m. *Minterne Magna* with the Edwardian Minterne House (gardens open).—11m. *Cerne Abbas* is a charming village, popular with visitors, preserving the beautiful 15C gatehouse of a Benedictine abbey. The church has 14C wall paintings and a 15C screen. Above it is the *Cerne Giant* (NT), a figure 180ft long cut in the chalk.—19m. *Dorchester* (Rte 17A).

*The Cerne Giant*

121m. *Compton House* (open), N of A30, houses exotic butterflies and the Lullingstone Silk Farm. At *Bradford Abbas*, S of the road, the church has a notable W front, stone screen, font and 15C bench ends.—We cross the Yeo and enter Somerset.—123m. **Yeovil** (27,300 inhab.; Tourist Information) is a busy town, badly served by modern development but keeping its old character round the beautiful Perp. *church.

T.S. Eliot (1888–1965) is buried and the navigator William Dampier (1652–1715) was born at *East Coker*, 3m SW.

FROM YEOVIL TO ILMINSTER, 14m by A3088 and A303.—2m. *Brympton d'Evercy (open), built of the local Ham Hill stone, is a satisfying mixture of styles and periods, early 16C and Elizabethan on the main front, and 1670s on the garden front. The interiors are mainly 18C. There is also a vineyard and a museum of crafts and agriculture. *Odcombe*, 1m SW, was the home of the eccentric traveller Sir Thomas Coryate (?1577–1617).—4m. *Montacute* has a Norman and Perp. church with a fine tower. *Montacute House* (NT), built for Sir Edward Phelips in the 1590s, is a masterpiece. The exterior, in Ham Hill stone weathered to a lovely gold, is delicately enriched with balustrades, shaped gables, niches holding sculptured figures and, on the N and S sides, oriel windows marking either end of the Long Gallery. The Great Hall has a carved screen and a lively plaster frieze showing, among other scenes, a skimmington ride. Much of the panelling in the house has been renewed but the fireplaces and heraldic glass survive. Good collections of appropriate furniture and portraits (on loan from the National Portrait Gallery) have been

*One of the two oriel windows at the north and south ends of the Gallery, Montacute House*

assembled.—5¹/₂m. *Stoke-sub-Hamdon*, a charming village, has a church of outstanding interest and a 15C Priory (NT, hall open). The Fleur-de-Lis inn has a fives court built in 1760. *Ham Hill*, with famous limestone quarries, has been a fort since neolithic times. *Norton-sub-Hamdon*, 1m S, is dominated by its Perp. church tower.—At 7m we join A303 (Rte 19) for (14m) *Ilminster.*

132m. **Crewkerne** (5300 inhab.) is a market town with a richly decorated 15C church, a grammar school founded in 1499 and almshouses of 1604 and 1707.

The pretty village of *Hinton St George*, 3m NW, has 16–19C monuments of the Poulett family in its church.—The gardens (open) of *Clapton Court* are near B3165 3m SW of Crewkerne.

FROM CREWKERNE TO DORCHESTER, 21m by A356 and A37, a hilly route.—We leave Somerset for Dorset and make the steep ascent to (4m) *Winyard's Gap*, with NT woodland and a wide view.—The road crosses *Toller Down*, where 'Far from the Madding Crowd' opens, and descends to (13m) *Maiden Newton*, where the church has a carillon of 35 bells cast in Louvain in 1882.—16m. We join A37.—21m. *Dorchester* (Rte 17A).

FROM CREWKERNE TO BRIDPORT, 12m by A356 and A3066. We leave A356 beyond (1¹/₂m) *Misterton*.—6m. **Beaminster** (pronounced 'Bemminster') is a handsome little place; its church has a stately Perp. tower adorned with sculptures. Thomas Fuller (1608–61) was rector of *Broadwindsor*, 3m NW. To the W of Beaminster rise *Lewesdon Hill* (894ft; NT) and *Pilsdon Pen* (909ft; *view), the highest hill in Dorset. Wordsworth lived in 1795–97 at *Racedown Lodge* (not open) below Pilsdon Pen, on B3165 (the Lyme Regis road) N of its junction with B3164 from Broadwindsor.—7m. *Parnham House* (open) is a Tudor mansion in lovely grounds. Later alterations to its exterior include the battlements and pinnacles added by Nash in 1810. The interior, including the Great Hall, is mainly the result of 20C reconstruction, though there is a carved 17C overmantel in the Strode Bedroom. Parnham also houses a furniture workshop and school for craftsmen in wood.— 12m. *Bridport* (Rte 18B).

A30 climbs above 750ft (view), then descends *Windwhistle Hill* between a noble avenue of beeches, skirting the grounds of *Cricket House*, built in 1804 for Admiral Hood and now having a wild-life park.—141m. **Chard** (9400 inhab.) is a lace-making town with the former Court House of 1590 where Jeffreys sat at the 'Bloody Assizes'. Margaret Bondfield (1873–1953), the first woman cabinet minister, was born here; the painter Lucien Pissarro (1863–1944) died at *South Chard*, 2m S.

In the rich green valley of the Axe, off B3162 3¹/₂m SE, is *Forde Abbey* (open). The house rose from the beautiful remains of a Cistercian abbey founded in 1138 and reconstructed in the Perp. style by the last abbot. Sir Edmund Prideaux's additions in the classical style (1649–59) blend remarkably well with the earlier work. They are seen at their best in the splendid Saloon, where the famous Mortlake tapestries from Raphael's cartoons hang. The Chapel was formerly the abbey's chapter house. The lovely grounds extend to 25 acres. Jeremy Bentham rented Forde Abbey in 1814–17.

**Axminster** (seasonal Tourist Information), a pleasantly situated little town on A358 7m S of Chard, is known for its carpet industry, re-established in 1937 after a lapse of a century. At *Musbury*, 2m SW, the church has the *Drake monument, with three pairs of polychrome stone figures (1588–1636), including the grandparents of the Duke of Marlborough.

The Exeter road grows very hilly, rising to 733ft beyond Snowdon Hill. Entering Devon, we cross the Yarty valley and climb past (146¹/₂m) *Yarcombe* to 874ft before being joined by A303.—154m. **Honiton** (6600 inhab.; seasonal Tourist Information) is known for its lace, now chiefly made in the neighbouring villages, and its trout fishing. The harmonious 18C High St. has coaching inns. A375 diverges left for Sidmouth (Rte 18B).

161m. A30 passes 1m N of **Ottery St Mary** (7000 inhab.; seasonal Tourist Information), the birthplace of S.T. Coleridge (1772–1834) and the occasional childhood home of Thackeray, who made it the 'Clavering St Mary' of 'Pendennis'. The town is chiefly interesting for its EE and Dec. collegiate *church. Much of the exterior, including the transeptal towers, was copied from Exeter Cathedral by Bishop Grandisson in 1338–42. The Dorset aisle (1504–30) has fine fan vaulting, and the *clock keeps its original Elizabethan works. The weather vane (1335) is the oldest still working in England; the stocks still stand in the churchyard. 1m NW of Ottery is *Cadhay Manor* (limited opening), a 16C manor house behind an 18C entrance front. Its most striking feature is the courtyard, in sandstone and flint chequerboarding with statues of the Tudor monarchs over the doorways.—165m. We pass *Clyst Honiton* and Exeter Airport (see below).

170m. **EXETER** (95,600 inhab.), the county town of Devon, stands on rising ground on the NE bank of the Exe and is connected with the tidal estuary at Topsham by a ship canal, 5m long, begun in 1563. Despite damage from heavy wartime bombing, it remains a historic city, with a cathedral, substantial remains of its medieval walls and streets following their Roman course.

**Tourist Information Centres**: Civic Centre, Paris St. and (seasonal) Exeter services area of M5 at Sandygate.

**Car Parks**: Dix's Field, Southernhay East, Guildhall Shopping Centre, Paul St., Mary Arches St.

**Bus Station**: Paul St.

**Railway Stations**: St David's, off A377 NW of the centre; Central, near the Castle, 1/2m from St David's; St Thomas, off B3212 1/2m SW of centre, for local (south Devon) trains.

**Airport**: at Clyst Honiton, on A30 5m E. Flights to Belfast, Gatwick, Plymouth, Southampton, Guernsey, Jersey.

**Theatres**: Barnfield, Barnfield Rd; Northcott, Exeter University.

**Annual Events**: Devon County Show on Thursday–Saturday nearest to 16–18 May; Exeter Festival, last week in May and first week in June.

**History**. Exeter was the *Isca Dumnoniorum* of the Romans and the *Escancestre* of the Saxons. The city has often been attacked or besieged. It was stormed by the Danes in 876 and, though walls were built by Athelstan c 932, it was plundered again in 1003. In 1068 it submitted to William the Conqueror only after a long siege, and the castle was begun. Though occupied by Parliament at the onset of the Civil War, it was later held for the king until 1646. The city was attacked from the air in 1942, when 40 acres, including many old buildings, were destroyed.

**Famous natives**: Sir Thomas Bodley (1545–1613), Princess Henrietta (1644–70), daughter of Charles I, Archbishop William Temple (1881–1944) and, probably, Nicholas Hilliard (1537–1619) were born here. Richard Hooker (1554– 1600) was a native of Heavitree, now a suburb to the E.

The High St., continued down to the Exe Bridge by Fore St., keeps its Roman course but has been largely rebuilt since the German bombing. Broadgate, on the left beyond the Guildhall (see below), makes the best approach to the cathedral.

The *Cathedral, though comparatively small, is one of the most attractive in England. Except for the Norman towers, it is built mainly in the Geometric Dec. style.

A Saxon monastery existed here by 680. The bishopric of Devon and Cornwall was moved from Crediton to Exeter in 1050, for its greater security. The conventual church founded by Athelstan c 932, which probably served as the earliest cathedral, was replaced by a Norman building (1112–1206). Of this the

BARNSTAPLE

University

PRINCE OF WALES ROAD

**St David's Station**

NEW NORTH ROAD

STRATHAM RISE

VELWELL ROAD

**Fire Station**

HOWELL ROAD

HOWELL ROAD

DANES ROAD

HOOPERN STREET

Tech. Coll.

Bury Meadow

**H.M. Prison**

HELE ROAD

ELM GROVE ROAD

NEW NORTH ROAD

BONHAY ROAD

LOOE ROAD

ST DAVIDS HILL

RICHMOND ROAD

QUEENS TERRACE

**Central Station**

Northernhay

Assize Court

ROAD

Rougemont

HALDON ROAD

QUEEN STREET

Albert Memorial

Museum University

Museum

Library

Art Gallery

LOWER NORTH STREET

River Exe

BONHAY ROAD

NORTHERNHAY STREET

Information Bureau

Bus Station

Market

PAUL STREET

GOLDSMITH STREET

HIGH STREET

QUEEN STREET

MUSGRAVE

St Stephen's

IRON BRIDGE

**St Michael's**

Mount Dinham

Exe Old Cemetery

BARTHOLOMEW ST EAST

NORTH STREET

MITRE LANE

MARY ARCHES STREET

**Guildhall Shopping Centre**

WATERBEER STREET

**Guildhall**

**St Mary Arches**

**St Petrock's**

**St Martin's**

CATHEDRAL YARD

THE CLOSE

BARTHOLOMEW ST WEST

BARBICAN STEPS

FORE STREET

St Olave's

St Nicholas Priory

**Cathedral**

FOOT PATH

MINT

KING STREET

SMYTHEN STREET

Market

SOUTH STREET

GEORGE'S STREET

Bishop Palace

R.C. Church

BEAR STREET

PALACE GATE

Tuckers Hall

**Bonhay Pleasure Ground**

TUDOR STREET

WEST STREET

PRESTON STREET

Trinity

**Exe Island**

**St Mary Steps**

NEW BRIDGE STREET

EDMUND ST

CHICKLERY

WESTERN WAY

P

FRIARS GATE

THE QUAY

COLLETON CRESCENT

OKEHAMPTON STREET

ALBION STREET

COWICK STREET

**Exe Bridge**

GERVASE AVENUE

COMMERCIAL ROAD

GREAT SHILHAY

**Custom House**

**Maritime Museum**

ALPHINGTON STREET

**St Thomas Station**

**EXETER**

| 0 | 300 yards |
| 0 | 300 metres |

St John the Evangelist's Chapel

St Gabriel's Chapel

Chap. of St. George or Speke's Chantry

Lady Chapel

RETRO CHOIR

Bp.Oldham's Chantry or St Saviour's Chapel

St Andrew's Chapel

St. James' Chapel

Pulpit

Bishop's Throne

Vestry

St John the Baptist Chapel

St Paul's Chapel

Sylke Chantry

St Paul's Tower (over)

Clock Mechanism

3  Great Screen (Organ over)

Nave Choir Stalls

St John's Tower (over)

Organ Pipes

CHAPTER

HOUSE

Choristers' Vestry

LIBRARY

Pulpit

Minstrel's Gallery

NORTH PORCH

CLOISTER

Font

St. Edmund's Chapel

DEANERY

West Door

Bp. Grandison's Chantry

**Key to Numbers**

1  R.D. Blackmore tablet
2  Hugh Courtenay, Earl of Devon
3  St Mary's Altar (Henry de Bracton)
4  Bp Marshall
5  Bp Stapeldon
6  Bp Bronescombe
7  Bp Quivil
8  Bp Leofric (?)
9  Bp Stafford
10  HMS *Exeter* Window
11  Sir Peter Courtenay (brass)

# EXETER CATHEDRAL

only important remains are the massive transeptal towers, unique in England except for the copies at Ottery St Mary. Bishop Bronescombe began to transform the Norman church c 1270; work continued under his successors until the time of Bishop Grandisson (d. 1369).

The many flying buttresses contrast effectively with the solid austerity of the Norman towers, to which the battlements and turrets were added in the 15C. The W façade is decorated with sculptured figures, the lower ones (with the Enthronement of the Virgin as their central subject) apparently added by Grandisson, the upper ones possibly as late as the 15C.

The most striking characteristic of the *interior is its uniform design, each detail marked by purity of style (Dec.) and answering to its counterpart with unfailing symmetry. The roof, with good bosses, forms the longest continuous stretch of Gothic vaulting in the world (over 300ft). There is a lofty clerestory but the triforium is represented by a small blank arcade. On the N side of the *Nave*, with its fine Purbeck marble pillars, is the *Minstrels' Gallery (by Bishop Grandisson). The *Transepts*, with beautiful window tracery and exquisite triforium galleries, were rebuilt by Bishops Bronescombe and Quivil (d. 1291) under the Norman towers. In the N transept are the Sylke Chantry (1508), a 15C wall painting of the Resurrection, a *clock of 1423 and a statue by Chantrey of the painter James Northcote (1746–1831). The S transept has the tomb of Hugh Courtenay, Earl of Devon (d. 1377), and his wife. From its SW corner a vestry leads to the *Chapter House*, EE and Perp. with a ceiling of 1465–78. Its N and S niches contain polyester resin sculptures by Kenneth Carter (1974).

The *Choir* is separated from the nave by a triple-arched screen erected by Bishop Stapledon (d. 1326), with 17C paintings. Monuments include those of Bishops Marshall (d. 1206) and Stapledon on the N side. The stalls and reredos are 19C, though the former have EE misericords; the oak *Bishop's Throne and the stone sedilia are exquisite early 14C work. St James' Chapel (S), destroyed by bombing, has been beautifully rebuilt. St Andrew's Chapel (N) has a memorial window to the men of 'HMS Exeter', sunk in 1942. Bishop Oldham's Chantry (1519), in the SE corner, is decorated with owls in punning reference to the founder's name ('Owldham'). At the S side of the Lady Chapel entrance is a *wall painting (c 1500) of the Assumption and Coronation of the Virgin. The *Lady Chapel* is mainly the work of Bishop Bronescombe and includes his tomb (1329), intricately decorated, with the gilding and colour well restored.

On the S side of the cathedral part of the *Cloister* has been rebuilt in the original Dec. style. A wing of the rebuilt Bishop's Palace houses the *Cathedral Library* (open), entered from Palace Gate, which contains some Anglo-Saxon charters, the Exeter Domesday MS and the 10C Exeter Book, a famous Anglo-Saxon collection of poetry.

The **Cathedral Close** has several interesting old houses. By the 15C and 17C church of *St Martin* in the NE corner is *Mol's Coffee House* (1596), now a jeweller's. No. 5 has a 15C hall, while the *Law Library* at No. 8 occupies a 14C hall. Further on, a stone archway with a Jacobean oak door leads to a charming little quadrangle. A statue of Richard Hooker (by Alfred Drury) stands N of the cathedral.

We return to High St., leaving on the left the much altered church of *St Petrock*, with a pre-Norman tower. The ***Guildhall**, dating from 1330 and thus one of the oldest civic buildings to survive in England, has a pillared façade of 1593 projecting over the pavement. The Hall (open) has a fine roof of 1464, with corbels showing the bear and ragged staff of Warwick the Kingmaker, and panelled walls of 1595 ornamented with the arms of guilds, mayors, etc.

In Waterbeer St. behind the Guildhall is a tessellated pavement (covered) which may mark the site of the Roman Praetorium. Nearby is *St Pancras' Church*, with an EE chancel and piscina, Norman font and Jacobean pulpit.

Further up High St. is *St Stephen's*, rebuilt c 1665 with an elevated chancel on an old arch called 'Stephen's Bow'. From the quiet little square behind, Bedford St. leads to Southernhay, a charming street with Georgian houses. On its W side is a fine section of the **City Wall** with bastions, revealed by bombing. In Eastgate, at the N end of Southernhay, is the entrance to the *Underground Passages* (open), probably medieval conduits for the city's water supply.

We regain High St. at its NE end. In Castle St. to the right are the *Rougemont House Museum*, a Georgian building with collections of costume and lace, and the beautiful **Rougemont Gardens**, which contain the scanty remains of the *Castle* erected by William the Conqueror. Beyond Castle Yard (with the *County Assize Court* of 1774) stretch *Northernhay Gardens*, where another part of the old city wall can be seen. The *Prison* (1853) is prominent beyond the railway to the N.

The W part of the wall is reached via Northernhay St. and Bartholomew St. A footpath runs along the top, above the *Old Cemetery* (opened in 1637).

Queen St. leads from Northernhay's W exit back to the High St., passing the *Royal Albert Memorial Museum and Art Gallery*, with natural history and anthropology, Exeter silver, ceramics, glass, costumes from 1750 and an important collection of English paintings (works by Reynolds, Turner and Opie).

We go down High St. to Fore St. A turning on the right leads to the church of *St Mary Arches*, with Norman nave and Jacobean monuments. *St Olave's* in Fore St. has an unorthodox plan. In The Mint, leading to the right, is the guest wing of the Benedictine •**Priory of St Nicholas** (open), with a Norman undercroft, 13C and 15C kitchen, 15C guest hall and the Prior's solar. In the garden is a 7C Celtic cross, attached for 200 years to a pier of the Exe Bridge. The Mint takes its name from the small assay furnaces once in the undercroft. Lower down Fore St., on the right, is *Tucker's Hall* (open), the guildhouse of the 'weavers, fullers and shearmen', with a fine roof (1471) and oak panelling (1634).

We descend the steep West St., to the left, to the interesting church of *St Mary Steps*, with its Norman font, fine rood screen and curious clock (c 1656). Next door are some 16C houses, including one moved on rollers from further W in 1961. Opposite the church stood the West Gate and a little further on was the Water Gate. On the Quay is the *Custom House* (1678–81). Beyond is the *Maritime Museum*, with a large collection of full-size boats, some of them afloat in the Canal Basin.

From the Custom House the line of the old city wall runs NE to the South Gate (removed in 1819) and along Southernhay (see above). In Magdalen St., branching right, is *Wynard's Hospital*, built c 1430, with a courtyard and a chapel sympathetically restored in the 19C. It is now a centre for voluntary organisations.

The *University of Exeter* occupies several fine mansions with beautiful grounds and new buildings by Holford in Prince of Wales Rd, about 1m N of the centre. Founded as a school of art in 1855 and incorporated as the University College of South-West England in 1922, it received its charter in 1955. The Northcott Theatre was opened in 1967.

FROM EXETER TO EXMOUTH, 11m.—Leaving by South St. and passing (1m) the County Hall, we cross the bypass just above the Exe and the 16C *Countess of Wear Bridge* (widened 1937).—4m. *Topsham*, now a yachting centre, used to be the port of Exeter. The charming Strand has several houses in the Dutch style and a museum of local history. A ferry runs to Exminster and Turf.—5½m. We join A376 S of *Clyst St George*. The sculptor Nicholas Stone (1586–1647) was born at *Woodbury*, 2m SE.—9m. *A La Ronde* (open) is a polygonal house built in 1795.—11m. **Exmouth** (28,800 inhab.; seasonal Tourist Information) is a seaside resort with a sandy beach, an esplanade and a view across the mouth of the Exe. A ferry runs to *Starcross* on the opposite bank, and there are excursion steamers in summer. A376 continues to Budleigh Salterton (Rte 18B).

FROM EXETER TO BARNSTAPLE, 40m on A377.—We follow the Creed valley, passing (5m) *Newton St Cyres*, where the church has good monuments.—8m. **Crediton** (6200 inhab.), the birthplace of St Boniface or Winfrid (680– 755), was the seat of the episcopal see of Devon and Cornwall from 909 until its removal to Exeter in 1050. A statue of the saint (by Alan Durst) was unveiled in 1960. The sandstone church once collegiate, was founded in the 12C but dates mainly from the 15C; it contains two good 17C tombs.—At (14½m) *Morchard Road Station* B3220 for Bideford branches left. We keep to A377 and enter the beautiful valley of the Taw (good fishing).—17m. *Lapford* church, on the right, has a wealth of fine woodwork.—21m. *Eggesford* has fine Chichester monuments in its church, while *Chawleigh*, 2m NE, and *Chulmleigh*, 2½m N, have good rood screens.—32m. *Umberleigh* lies between two villages with interesting churches: *Atherington*, 1¼m W, has a 16C rood loft and *Chittlehampton*, 2¼m NE, dedicated to the local virgin martyr Urith, has a noble *tower of 1520. *Cobbaton*, 3m N of Umberleigh, has a Combat Vehicle Museum.—At 36m, where our road crosses the Taw, a lane goes straight on to (1½m) *Tawstock*, where the 14C *church has good monuments and one of the most elaborate pews in the country.— 40m. *Barnstaple* (Rte 26).

From Exeter to *Taunton* and *Bristol*, see Rte 23; along the Exe to *Bampton*, see Rte 26; to *Plymouth*, see Rte 28; to *Tavistock*, see Rte 29A; to Plymouth via *Princetown*, see Rte 29B; to *Bodmin* and *Penzance*, see Rte 32; to *Bude*, see Rte 35.

# B.  Via Dorchester, Lyme Regis and the Coast

Total distance 177m. A4, A30 to (46m) *Basingstoke* (bypassed) or alternative way via M3, see Rte 14B.—A30, M3, A303, A30 to (82m) Salisbury and A354, A35, to (122m) Dorchester, see Rte 17A.—A35 to (137m) **Bridport**.—A35, A3052 to (146m) **Lyme Regis**.—A3052 to (161m) Sidford.—A3052 to (177m) **Exeter** (Rte 18A).

Maps: OS Landranger 176, 186, 184, 194, 193, 192.

From London to (46m) *Basingstoke*, see Rte 14B, and on to (82m) *Salisbury* and (122m) *Dorchester*, see Rte 17A. We leave Dorchester on A35, running W across downland.—126½m. The ruined prehistoric circle known as the *Nine Stones* (English Heritage, open at any reasonable time) lies S of A35 as it leaves *Winterbourne Abbas*.

The countryside S of Winterbourne Abbas is rich in prehistoric remains. About 3m SW, on the Downs beyond the pretty village of *Littlebredy*, is *Kingston Russell Stone Circle* (English Heritage, open at any reasonable time). *Blackdown Hill* (776ft), 2m S of Winterbourne Abbas, is crowned by a monument of 1846 to Admiral Sir Thomas Hardy (1769–1839), flag-captain of the 'Victory' at Trafalgar; he was born at *Kingston Russell* manor house, NW of Littlebredy.

128m. *Winterbourne Poor Lot Barrows*, S of A35, are a Bronze Age group (English Heritage, open at any reasonable time).—137m. **Bridport** (6900 inhab.; seasonal Tourist Information) is an agreeable little town 1½m N of its harbour and beach at *West Bay*. The attractive main street has an 18C *Town Hall*. In South St., near the mainly Perp. *Church*, a 16C stone building houses the small *Museum and Art Gallery*; one of its displays illustrates the ancient local trade of net- and rope-making (a 'Bridport dagger' is a hangman's halter).—The road grows very hilly, with some gradients of 1 in 5.— 140m. *Chideock* is a charming village, with fine cliff scenery (NT) to the S.—144m. *Charmouth* is a pleasant little resort with a steep street. Both here and at Bridport Charles II was nearly taken by Parliament men on his flight from Worcester.

At *Whitchurch Canonicorum*, 2½m NE, the Norman to Perp. church contains the little shrine of St Candida, the only shrine in England (apart from that of Edward the Confessor at Westminster) to survive the Reformation unplundered.

A35 bears right for Axminster (Rte 18A); we follow A3052 towards the coast.

146m. **LYME REGIS** (3400 inhab.) is a charming old fishing town and resort overlooking Lyme Bay and ringed by blue lias cliffs rich in fossils. The hilly streets, with many picturesque buildings, keep their Regency atmosphere.

**Tourist Information Centre**: The Guildhall, Bridge St.

**Car Parks**: junction of Bridge St. and Broad St.; Broad St.; Pound St.

**Coach Stop**: Pound St.

**Annual events**: Carnival and regatta in the first full week of August.

**History, natives and visitors**. In 774 Cynewulf granted the land to the monks of Sherborne, so that they could distil salt from sea-water. The town received its royal charter from Edward I. Staunchly Parliamentarian, it withstood a two-month siege by the Royalists during the Civil War; among its defenders was the future Admiral, Robert Blake. The Duke of Monmouth landed here with three ships and 80 men on 11 June 1685 to begin his abortive rebellion against James II. Natives of Lyme include: Captain Thomas Coram (1668–1751), who established the London Foundling Hospital; Eleanor Coade (1733–1821), inventor of Coade Stone; and the geologist Mary Anning (1799– 1847), who discovered the ichthyosaurus in the neighbouring cliffs in 1811. Among the visitors attracted by Lyme's popularity as a resort were Jane Austen and the artist Whistler. The town is the setting for John Fowles's novel 'The French Lieutenant's Woman' and the film derived from it.

The stone pier known as the *Cobb*, where the Duke of Monmouth disembarked, is perhaps more famous as the scene of Louisa Musgrove's accident in 'Persuasion'. Marine Parade leads NE from the Cobb to Bridge St. and the town centre, where the pleasant medley of buildings includes the *Philpot Museum*, notable for its collection of fossils. The *Church*, a much altered Norman building to the N, contains a 16C tapestry commemorating the marraige of Prince Arthur and Catherine of Aragon.

About 3½m W is the *Dowlands Landslip*, where some 40 acres of ground slipped down from the cliff in 1839.

In the hilly country immediately W of Lyme A3052 crosses the border into Devon.

6m W of Lyme B3172 leads S from the main road, following the bank of the Axe and passing (1½m) *Axmouth*, with the unusual 15C tower house of *Bindon* 1m E. The breezy little resort of **Seaton** (5000 inhab.; seasonal Tourist Information) lies 1½m further S. Delightful walks lead along the coast E to the Landslip (see above) and W via (1m) *Beer*, a fishing village with old quarries, and (3m) *Branscombe Mouth*. The good church of the romantic village of *Branscombe* lies 1½m from the sea. Over 300 acres of the Branscombe estate, including medieval farmhouses, a forge and a bakery, are NT property.

153m. *Colyford*, 1m S of *Colyton*, has a fine church with a 15C octagonal lantern, good monuments and an early 10C cross.—157m. *Blackbury Castle*, on the right, is an Iron Age hill-fort (English Heritage, open at any reasonable time).—At (161m) *Sidford* we cross the Honiton–Sidmouth road.

*Sand* (limited opening), in a valley off A375 2m NE, is a Tudor manor with a medieval outbuilding.
   **Sidmouth** (12,400 inhab.; seasonal Tourist Information), a dignified resort with many Regency villas, is delightfully situated between reddish cliffs and protected to the N by a circle of hills. Queen Victoria lived at Woolbrook Cottage (now Royal Glen Hotel) as a baby, and her father died here in 1824.

The *Norman Lockyer Observatory* (1912) was attached to Exeter University in 1948.

A pleasant road leads SW from Sidmouth to (4m) *Otterton*, near the popular beach at *Ladram Bay*, (4³/4m) *East Budleigh* and (6¹/4m) **Budleigh Salterton** (4400 inhab.; seasonal Tourist Information), once occupied in salt extraction from the Otter and now a resort. Near East Budleigh are (1m W) *Hayes Barton*, the farmhouse where Sir Walter Raleigh (1552–1618) was born, and (1m N) *Bicton Park*, with fine gardens, arboretum, countryside museum and miniature railway. For Exmouth, 4m W of Budleigh Salterton, and an alternative way into Exeter, see Rte 18A.

A3052 crosses the Otter at (164m) *Newton Poppleford.*—177m. **Exeter**, see Rte 18A.

# 19 London to Taunton

Total distance 144m. A30 to (46m) Basingstoke (bypassed), or alternative way by M3, see Rte 14B.—A30, M3, A303 to (65m) Andover (bypassed).—A303 to (79m) Amesbury (bypassed).—A303 to (110m) Wincanton (bypassed).—A303, A372 to (131m) Langport.—A378, A358 to (144m) **Taunton**.

Maps: OS Landranger 176, 186, 185, 184, 183, 193.

Less interesting for the towns listed above than for the landscapes, historic places (Stonehenge, Stourhead, etc.) and Somerset churches along the way. The main route as far as Sparkford and then the detour to Exeter provide a somewhat easier alternative to Rte 18A, which follows the often congested A30.

From London to (46m) *Basingstoke*, see Rte 14B. A30 bypasses the town and joins M3, which we follow for 2m before branching right on A303.—65m. **Andover** (31,000 inhab.; seasonal Tourist Information), well bypassed to the S, is an ancient town unattractively redeveloped. The local museum incorporates a *Museum of the Iron Age*, with finds from Danebury Ring (Rte 21).

A much prettier way from Basingstoke, 1m shorter, follows B3400 along the upper Test valley.—7m. *Overton* is in the rolling chalk hills praised by Cobbett.—8¹/2m. *Laverstoke* is a model village where the paper for banknotes was made for over 200 years.—11m. *Whitchurch*, on the Winchester–Newbury road, see Rte 14A.—18m. *Andover*.

FROM ANDOVER TO DEVIZES, 26m by A303 to (3¹/2m) *Weyhill* and then A342 along the NE margin of Salisbury Plain (see below).—8m. *Ludgershall*, just across the border with Wiltshire, has a medieval cross in the main street and a fine monument to Sir Robert Brydges (d. 1558) in the church. Ludgershall Castle (English Heritage, open at any reasonable time) is the scanty ruin of an early 12C royal castle.—17m. *Upavon*, at the head of the Avon valley, has a church with a restored Norman chancel and font. The village is headquarters of RAF Air Support Command.—At (21m) *Chirton*, on the right, the church has a Norman doorway.—22m. We pass B3098 from Westbury.—24m. *Stert*, on the left, is a pleasant hamlet.—26m. *Devizes*, see Rte 24.

A303 leads across the chalk ridges on the edge of **Salisbury Plain**, an undulating, almost treeless expanse about 20m long by 10m wide, lying within an area roughly defined by Andover (E), Salisbury (S), Warminster (W) and Devizes (N). It is divided from N to S by the Avon, flowing from Upavon through Amesbury to Salisbury.

The Plain is the focal point from which the great chalk belts of Southern England radiate. One outcrop reaches SW through Wiltshire to the Dorset coast; another goes NE as the Marlborough Downs, the Berkshire Downs and the Chilterns. To the E lie the Hog's Back and the North Downs, the Hampshire Downs and the South Downs. This natural position at the meeting point of hills

and their ridgeway paths made Salisbury Plain an important centre of prehistoric settlement; it is still rich in monuments and remains. The bleak and
lonely appearance of the landscape, only a little altered by modern agriculture,
has not been improved by the firing ranges and permanent military camps that
abound; these include *Bulford* (artillery), *Netheravon* (RAF), *Upavon* (RAF),
*Larkhill* (artillery) and *Tidworth*.

**79m. Amesbury** (Tourist Information) lies S of A303. The large,
flint-built *Abbey Church* is Norman and EE. Legend makes its
predecessor, a Saxon nunnery founded in 980, the 'holy house at
Almesbury', where the penitent Queen Guinevere sought refuge. At
*Amesbury Abbey* (not open), since rebuilt, John Gay wrote 'The
Beggar's Opera' in 1727 while a guest of the Duke of Queensberry.

*Earl's Farm Down Barrows* or *Ratfyn Barrows*, by A303 NE of the town, are
Bronze Age burial mounds (English Heritage, open at any reasonable time). By
A303 to the NW are the prehistoric earthworks, known as *Vespasian's Camp*.
Near *Durrington*, off A345 1½m N, is *Woodhenge*, a Bronze Age monument
with six concentric rings of wooden posts, now replaced by concrete stumps,
inside a mound and ditch (English Heritage, open at any reasonable time).
—A345 continues N along the valley of the Avon to (7½m) *Upavon* (see above).
It passes *Netheravon*, with an 18C dovecote (English Heritage, exterior only,
open at any reasonable time).

**81m.** ***Stonehenge** ('Stanhenges', 'hanging stones'), the most
famous monument of prehistoric Europe, is a circular setting of
massive standing stones (English Heritage, standard opening and
summer Sunday mornings; admission free to NT members). A
surprisingly small structure, the main central ruin is only 110ft in
diameter; it originally contained just 162 stones, mostly undecorated

*Stonehenge*

and arranged in a straightforward way. It stands isolated on the open chalk down—Emerson thought it 'like a group of brown dwarfs on the wide expanse'—but, when seen close to, the mass of its monoliths can make the most striking impact.

Stonehenge is not a single-period site, but the ruins of a series of earthen monuments, now heavily eroded, and of stone structures, dating from before 3000 BC to about 1000 BC. The central portion (about 2000 BC) is unique among the relics of ancient Europe; it includes the famous trilithons, pairs of huge upright stones with a third laid crossways across their tops and held in place by mortice-and-tenon joints.

The early features at Stonehenge include a circular bank and ditch, now only a foot deep where it is crossed by the visitors' path, and the Heel Stone, an unshaped upright stone by the access road on the NE. The main ruin consists of five concentric features. From the outside they are:
(1) A circle of 30 uprights, standing about 13½ft above the ground, and once supporting a continuous run of lintel stones. 16 uprights and five lintels remain in place.
(2) A circle of about 60 small uprights, about 5ft above the ground. Six still stand, while others are fallen and broken.
(3) A horseshoe arrangement of five trilithons, open to the NE, the tallest standing about 24ft above the ground. Three are intact; only one upright of each of the other two stands.
(4) A horseshoe arrangement of small uprights. Six of the original 19 remain.
(5) A central stone, once erect but now lying flat, called the 'Altar Stone'.
The large circle and horseshoe are built of sarsen, a sandstone which outcrops naturally in the Avebury region to the N. It is of exceptional hardness, which both accounts for the superb preservation of elements of Stonehenge and emphasises the engineering achievements of its builders. The upper surface formed by the lintels of the sarsen circle was made level to an accuracy of a very few inches, although the ground slopes; the uprights are of differing heights and the lintels of differing thicknesses. Some sarsens bear carvings of prehistoric axes and (perhaps) daggers, difficult to see unless the light is good. The small uprights are of igneous rock, brought about 200m from the Presely Hills of South-West Wales.

Stonehenge belongs, like Avebury (Rte 20) and the Rollright Stones (Rte 40), to the class of prehistoric monuments called 'stone rings' or 'stone circles'. It is quite exceptional in its complex plan, in the precision with which its stones have been shaped, and in its provisions of lintels. Accordingly, it has always presented grave difficulties of interpretation, and has been attributed in different centuries to giants, Romans, Danes, Phoenicians, Druids, Mycenaean Greeks and—in our own time—to UFOnauts. Current archaeological opinion emphasises its comparability, in terms of the physical labour involved, with other massive sites in the region, such as Avebury, Silbury Hill (Rte 20) and Durrington Walls (a huge banked enclosure 2m N, but without standing stones and now ploughed down to near-invisibility). The symmetrical layout of Stonehenge, oriented towards the NE where the sun rises on Midsummer Day, indicates that it was positioned to a solar alignment. Secure evidence for other astronomical features, or its use as a prehistoric observatory-cum-computer, is very slight.

Because of the crowds Stonehenge attracts, the centre is normally closed and visitors kept at a distance which makes it hard to see the monument properly. It is better to visit it on those winter days when the centre is open (check in advance with English Heritage), or to follow the waymarked paths that show some of the many hundred ancient, though less spectacular, sites of the Stonehenge environs.

Beyond Stonehenge A360 leads NW across the Plain to (4m) *Shrewton*, where B390 goes to (14m) *Heytesbury* and (17m) *Warminster*, both on Rte 18A.—A360 continues to (18m) *Devizes* via (8m) *Tilshead*, where the church has flint and chalk banding characteristic of the local architecture. White Barrow, a neolithic long barrow ¾m S, is NT property.

87m. *Yarnbury Castle*, on the right, is a prehistoric hill-fort. The road descends to (89m) *Wylye*, in its river valley, where the church has a 17C pulpit.—99m. For B3089, leading SE to Wilton, see Rte 18A.—

We descend to (103m) **Mere** (Tourist Information), where Charles II rested at the Talbot Inn on his flight after the Battle of Worcester, and the Dorset poet William Barnes kept school for 12 years. The large Dec. church has 15C stalls and screens.—150½m. *Zeals*.

In the attractive village of *Stourton*, 1½m N, is **Stourhead** (NT), one of the most completely satisfying expressions of 18C culture in England. The house was built in 1721–24 for the banker Henry Hoare by Colen Campbell, pioneer of the Palladian movement. The wings were added by Thomas Atkinson in 1790–1804 and the portico was built, to Campbell's original design, in 1840; the central block was reconstructed after a fire in 1902. The interior contains furniture designed for the house by the younger Chippendale; the library has a striking 19C Wilton carpet, and a plaster panel, brought from elsewhere, attributed to Grinling Gibbons. The severe restraint of the building serves as foil to the magnificent Picturesque landscaping of the *grounds. They were begun by Henry Hoare but owe their final appearance to the work of his son, another Henry, from 1741 onwards. A walk round the lake provides a series of artfully contrived vistas which combine nature with man's work: the parish church, the 14C High Cross of Bristol (erected here in 1780), temples by Flitcroft and a famous rustic Grotto. The rhododendrons are a later addition. On the ridge about 2m N of the park stands *Alfred's Tower*, built in 1772 to mark the supposed site where Alfred the Great rallied his army to repel the Danes in 879.

Beyond Zeals A303 crosses the northern tip of Dorset before entering Somerset.—110m. The road bypasses **Wincanton** (Tourist Information), an old coaching town famous for its racecourse, at the head of the *Vale of Blackmore*. In the church porch is a curious relief of the legend of St Eligius, patron saint of smiths.

Two roads run N from Wincanton to Shepton Mallet.—On B3081 lies (4½m) **Bruton**, a charming old town with a Perp. church (18C chancel), the King's School dating from 1519 and a packhorse bridge (Bruton Bow). Sexey's Hospital (1638) adjoins the Court House (1684), now a school. The road continues via (8m) *Evercreech*, with one of the best church towers in Somerset, to (11½m) *Shepton Mallet* (Rte 22).—A371, 1½m longer, goes from Wincanton via (4m) the modern gardens (open) of the 18C *Hadspen House* and (5m) *Castle Cary*, where the diarist James Woodforde served as curate of his father's parish in 1771–76. There are fine churches at *Alford*, 1½m W, and *Ditcheat*, 2m NW of Castle Cary.

At 115½m we pass between *North Cadbury* (right), with a fine church and manor house, and *Cadbury Castle* (left), a hill-fort covering 18 acres and a claimant to be the Camelot of Arthurian legend. Excavations in 1966–70 have proved that it was occupied almost continuously for nearly 4000 years, from Neolithic to Saxon times.—117½m. *Sparkford*, at the junction of the road from Frome to Yeovil. *Queen's Camel*, 1½m SW, has another fine church, late 14C.

FROM SPARKFORD TO EXETER, 54m by A303 and A30.—We follow the main route (see below) W from Sparkford but after 5m bear left on A303.—7m. *Ilchester*, left of the road, once an important town on the Foss Way, was the Roman Lendiniae and the birthplace of Roger Bacon (1214– 94).—9m. *Tintinhull*, left of the road. Tintinhull House (NT, only garden open) is early 17C with 18C additions and a famous formal garden laid out in the early 20C—11m. *Martock*, 2m N on B3615, has a big church with Perp. tower and perhaps the best tie-beam *roof in Somerset. Among the attractive buildings nearby is the 13–14C *Treasurer's House* (NT, open by appointment).—12m. For A3088, leading left to Yeovil via Montacute House, see Rte 18A.—13½m. *South Petherton*, N of the road, has a good church.—20m. At *Ilminster* (3700 inhab.; seasonal Tourist Information), a pleasant little town, the noble Perp. church contains the tombs of Nicholas and Dorothy Wadham (d. 1609 and 1618), founders of Wadham College, Oxford. The former boys' school nearby is a restored building of 1586. *Dillington House*, 1m NE, a 16C building with 19C alterations, was the home of Lord North while Prime Minister; it is now the Somerset College for Adult Education. *Barrington Court* (NT), off B3168 3½m NE, is an E-shaped 16C mansion built of the local Ham Hill stone, with a lively roofline. Most of the panelling inside, though appropriate, is not original to the house. The walled gardens were partly designed by Gertrude Jekyll. The neighbourhood has interesting churches: at *Stocklinch, Stocklinch Ottersey* (18C W gallery) and *Shepton Beauchamp* (Perp. tower), S and SE of Barrington Court; at *Dowlish Wake*, 1½m SE of Ilminster, with the tomb of J.H. Speke (1827–64), who discovered the source of the Nile; and at *Donyatt*, 2m W.—We enter hilly country and cross the border into Devon, joining A30 at 30m and following Rte 18A to (54m) *Exeter*.

121½m. At *Yeovilton*, about 1½m S of A303, is the Royal Naval Air Station. The *Fleet Air Museum (seasonal Tourist Information) has Concorde 002 and over 50 planes illustrating the history of aviation at sea.—122½m. We change from A303 to A372. *Lytes Cary* (NT), about 1m N, is a small manor house built from the 14C onwards. The oldest part is the chapel, originally detached from the house; the 15C hall has a good timber roof. The furniture throughout is 17–18C.

*Keinton Mandeville*, off A37 2m N, was the birthplace of Sir Henry Irving (1838– 1905).—From *Barton St David*, 1m beyond, the first member of the

*The tower of Huish Episcopi church*

presidential family of Adams emigrated to the United States.

162½m. *Long Sutton* has an interesting church and court house. *Somerton*, 2½m NE, is an old-fashioned little town with a fine Dec. church and a 17C market cross. It was once the capital of Somerset and residence of the West Saxon kings.—At (129½m) *Huish Episcopi* the church has one of the finest towers in Somerset, a Norman doorway, and glass by Burne-Jones (1899). *Kingsbury Episcopi*, 4m S, has another lavishly decorated tower.—131m. **Langport**, overlooking the marshes of the Parrett, has a fine Perp. church with good stained glass and an interesting Norman carving over the S door. The so-called Hanging Chapel, an ancient Perp. chapel above an archway near the church, is now a masonic temple. Walter Bagehot (1826–77) was a native of Langport.

At *Muchelney Abbey* (English Heritage, summer standard opening but closed on Tuesdays and Wednesday mornings), 2m S, the foundations of the church, the early 16C abbot's house and part of the S cloister survive. To the W is a 15C Priest's House (NT, open by appointment).—*Low Ham* and *High Ham*, 1¾m and 3m N of Langport, both have notable churches, the one a 17C Gothic work with many strange features, the other containing splendid woodwork.

We leave Langport on A378.—133m. At *Curry Rivel* the Perp. church has good parclose screens. To the N, *Red Hill* (NT) looks out over the marshland of West Sedgemoor.—136m. *Fivehead*.

The ˙church of *Ile Abbots*, 2m S, has a fine tower with original sculptures, and beautiful sedilia and piscina.—For the villages to the N, see Rte 24.

140m. We change from A378 to A358. *Hatch Court* (limited opening), 2m SE of the junction, is a Palladian house of 1755 by Thomas Prowse, an amateur architect and friend of Sanderson Miller. The square central block with corner turrets is relieved by curved wings and an arcade on the S front. The interiors include a dramatic staircase hall, and there is a good collection of chinaware.

144m. **TAUNTON** (35,300 inhab.), the county town of Somerset and a flourishing market centre, lies in the beautiful valley of Taunton Deane, famous for its apples and cider.

**Tourist Information Centre**: The Library, Corporation St.

**Car Parks**: The Crescent, Paul St., Canon St.

**Bus Station**: W of the castle.

**Railway Station**: ¾m N of the town centre.

**Theatre**: Brewhouse Theatre and Arts Centre, Coal Orchard.

**Annual Events**: Music and Drama Festival in November.

**History**. Founded c 705 by Ine, King of the West Saxons, to guard the river crossing against the Celts, Taunton remained a fortified seat of the Bishops of Winchester for more than a thousand years. The castle dates from the early 12C. In 1497 the unsuccessful rebel Perkin Warbeck was examined here by Henry VII, the castle withstood three sieges by Royalist forces in 1644–45; much of the town was destroyed by fire. On 20 June 1685, James, Duke of Monmouth, was proclaimed king in the market place. After the Battle of Sedgemoor swift retribution fell on the inhabitants, who suffered the cruelties of 'Kirke's Lambs' and Judge Jeffreys's Bloody Assize. The later prosperity and character of Taunton's merchant class are reflected in the town's surviving 18C buildings and Dissenting chapels; Queen's College (1843) and Taunton School (1847) are both important Dissenting foundations.

**Famous natives**: A.W. Kinglake (1809–91), historian and author of 'Eothen', was born at Wilton House in Vivary Park.

The centre of town is the triangular, traffic-congested market place, now called Fore St., with the *Market House* of 1770–72. From the NE side Hammet St., its Georgian symmetry recently and unpardonably spoiled, leads to *St Mary Magdalene*, one of the largest and richest Perp. churches in England. The magnificent, richly sculptured tower, 163ft high, was reconstructed in 1858–62. The church has double aisles, figures of angels between the clerestory lights, and a glorious oak roof. To the N are Middle St., with the former *Methodist Chapel* opened by John Wesley in 1776, and the church of *St James*, with a good font and a fine tower rebuilt in 1870. On the NW side of the market, opposite Hammet St., Castle Bow leads to Castle Green and the much restored 12C *Castle*, now housing the *Somerset County Museum*. Exhibits include a good prehistoric collection (with finds from the Iron Age lake villages at Glastonbury and Meare), Roman *mosaics from Low Ham and East Coker, and a portrait of Judge Jeffreys.

On the S side of the market place is *Tudor House* (1578), where Jeffreys lodged. High St. nearby leads S to *Vivary Park* and (left) Mary St., where the *Unitarian Chapel* has an interior of 1721. East St., leading from the market place, has *Gray's Almshouses* (1635); in East Reach, beyond, are the thatched *St Margaret's Almshouses* (rebuilt), formerly a leper hospital.

*Kingston St Mary*, 3m N, has a fine Perp. church tower.—The gardens of *Hestercombe House* (now owned by the Somerset County Fire Brigade), 3m NE, were laid out in 1905 by Sir Edwin Lutyens and Gertrude Jekyll.—*Trull*, 2m S of Taunton, has a small church with 16C woodcarving, including a remarkably fine pulpit. *Poundisford Park* (open), near *Pitminster* 1½m further S, is a Tudor house; the great hall has a fine 16C plaster ceiling and a gallery above the screen.

From Taunton to *Bristol* and *Exeter*, see Rte 23; to *Marlborough*, see Rte 24; to *Minehead*, see Rte 25B; to *Barnstaple*, see Rte 26.

# 20 London to Bath and Bristol

Total distance 199m. M4, A308 to (26m) Maidenhead, see Rte 36A. We then follow A4 throughout.—To (38½m) **Reading**.—To (56m) Newbury.—To (74m) Marlborough.—To (93m) Chippenham.—To (106m) **Bath** (Rte 21).—To (119m) **Bristol**.

Maps: OS Landranger 176, 175, 174, 173, 172.

M4, the fast alternative to A4, passes S of Maidenhead and Reading, heads N towards Swindon and approaches Bristol by M32 spur.

The detours from Newbury, Chippenham and Bristol make useful connections between SW England and the Cotswolds (particularly Rte 38B).

From London to (26m) *Maidenhead*, see Rte 36A.—34½m. Near *Twyford*, S of the road, is *Ruscombe*, where William Penn died in 1718.

38½m. **READING** (138,000 inhab.; Tourist Information), the county town of Berkshire, stands on the Kennet and is cut off by the railway from the nearby Thames. A centre of the medieval cloth trade, it became known for beer, bulbs and biscuits; nowadays it is the administrative headquarters for many large companies. There is little to delay the tourist.

In the old centre of town is the 12C church of *St Laurence*, rebuilt

but still imposing. Archbishop William Laud (1553–1645), a native of
Reading, was baptised in the font. The *Museum and Art Gallery* is
notable for *finds from nearby Silchester, a unique collection
illustrating the everyday life of a country town in Roman Britain, and
for finds of all ages from the Thames, including a magnificent gold
*torc of the mid Bronze Age from Moulsford. The Forbury leads to
the ruins of the Benedictine *Abbey*, founded by Henry I in 1121 and
once ranking as third in all England. A tablet in the chapter house
commemorates the fact that 'Sumer is icumen in', the earliest known
round for several voices, was written by a monk here c 1240. A
memorial stone marks the grave of Henry I (d. 1135). The heavily
restored gatehouse was once a school, where Jane Austen was a
pupil in 1786. In *Reading Gaol*, adjoining the ruins, Oscar Wilde
wrote 'De Profundis' (1897); the 'Ballad of Reading Gaol' is later. At
Blake's Lock, on the Kennet further E, is a *Museum* dealing with
Reading's industrial history and waterways.

The churches of *Greyfriars* in Friar St. and *St Mary* in The Butt,
both W of the old town centre, have some medieval work. Watlington
St. leads SE from the centre, past the 18C *Watlington House* (with a
garden front of 1688), to the *Royal Berkshire Hospital*, with an Ionic
façade of 1839. Mary Russell Mitford (see below) lived between 1789
and 1804 at the house in London Rd marked with a tablet.

*Whiteknights Park*, on Shinfield Rd 1½m S, is the site of the *University of
Reading* (4400 undergraduates), which began in the centre of town in 1902,
received its charter in 1926 and moved here in 1957. The campus includes the
*Museum of English Rural Life*, the *Ure Museum of Greek Archaeology* and the
*Cole Collection* of zoological specimens.
   *Three Mile Cross*, 3½m S of Reading, is the scene of 'Our Village' by Mary
Russell Mitford (1787–1855). She is buried at *Swallowfield*, 2½m further SE.
Swallowfield Park (limited opening) is a much altered late 17C house by
William Talman, the architect of Chatsworth.—From Three Mile Cross an
unclassified road leads SW to (8m) **Silchester**, identified with *Calleva
Atrebatum*, a flourishing Roman (and pre-Roman) town which seems to have
contained several dyeworks. The site of the ancient town is enclosed by 2–3C
walls fully 1½m in circuit and at places on the S side still 12–14ft high (English
Heritage, open at any reasonable time). A building, almost certainly a 4C
church, has been excavated. The little *Calleva Museum* serves as an excellent
introduction to the greater collection at Reading. The interesting parish church
(1m E by footpath, 2m by road) lies just inside the E gate; 150yd from the NE
corner of the enceinte are the earth banks of a Roman amphitheatre.—3½m E of
Silchester church and 1½m S of Swallowfield is *Stratfield Saye House* (open),
presented by the nation to the Duke of Wellington in 1815. He altered and
extended the 17C house but never fulfilled his ambition of creating a Waterloo
Palace to equal Blenheim Palace. Contents include portraits, mosaic pavements
from Silchester (set into the hall floor) and relics of the duke: the Wellington
Exhibition in the stables has his funeral carriage, and his favourite charger,
Copenhagen, is buried in the paddock nearby. On the E side of the park is the
Wellington Monument, with a bronze statue by Marochetti (1866).
   From Reading to *Virginia Water* via *Wokingham* and *Ascot*, see Rte 14B; to
*London* and *Oxford* by river, see Rte 36B.

We leave the Thames valley and follow the tributary valley of the
Kennet.—42½m. *Theale* has a large church of 1820–22 modelled on
Salisbury Cathedral. About 3¼m NW, beyond *Englefield*, is
*Bradfield College*, a public school founded in 1850 and noted for the
Greek plays performed by the boys every third year.—47m.
*Aldermaston* railway station.

An unclassified road on the left leads to (1¼m) *Padworth*, with a small Norman
church; *Ufton Court* (not open), an Elizabethan mansion ¾m E, was the home of
Arabella Fermor, heroine of Pope's 'The Rape of the Lock'.—*Aldermaston*, 1½m
SW of its station, has a 14C wall painting and a fine monument to Sir

George Forster (d. 1526) in its church. The Atomic Weapons Research Establishment has been the starting-point of a famous political protest, the Aldermaston march, since the 1950s.

From (48½m) *Woolhampton* a road climbs N to *Douai Abbey*, a Benedictine house (1903) with a boys' school transferred from Douai in France, and to (3m) *Bucklebury Common*, an open sandy heath. The Old Vicarage gardens contain sculptures by Moore and other contemporary artists.

56m. **Newbury** (26,400 inhab.; Tourist Information), once a centre of the cloth trade, is a thriving town known for its racecourse, about ½m SE. The Jacobean Cloth Hall, with an 18C galleried granary, is now a *Museum*; it contains collections of local history, etc. and Civil War relics. Jack of Newbury—John Smallwood, afterwards Winchcombe (d. 1520)—was a patriotic clothier who lead 150 men to Flodden in 1513; his brass can be seen in the church of *St Nicholas*, which he rebuilt. Benjamin Woodridge, the first graduate of Harvard, was rector of Newbury. The disused *Kennet and Avon Canal* has been restored for pleasure cruising some miles W of the town.

The N end of Newbury, on the main road, called *Speenhamland*, gave its name to the allowance system of poor relief to supplement wages, first practised here in 1795.
During the Civil War two indecisive battles were fought near Newbury. A monument 1m SW marks the scene of the first (1643). The second took place the following year 1m NW of the town, near the 14C gatehouse of *Donnington Castle* (English Heritage, open at any reasonable time).

FROM NEWBURY TO ANDOVER, 15m by A343.—4½m. *Highclere Castle*, see Rte 14A.—10m. *Hurstbourne Tarrant* has early 14C wall paintings. At *St Mary Bourne*, 3½m SE, is a Tournai marble font.—15m. *Andover*, see Rte 19.

FROM NEWBURY TO OXFORD, 25m by A34. We cross the downs and, beyond (9m) *East Ilsey*, once an important sheep market, descend into the *Vale of the White Horse* (Rte 38B).—For (15½m) *Steventon*, (19m) *Abingdon* and on to Oxford, see Rte 36A.

FROM NEWBURY TO SWINDON. The fast way is by M4, reached via A34 N of Newbury. A more interesting alternative (26m) follows B4000 up the beautiful valley of the Lambourn.—11m. *Lambourn*, separated from the Vale of the White Horse by the Lambourn Downs, is an old town with important training stables. The late Norman church has an alabaster relief of Charles I.—15m. *Ashdown House* (NT) is a tall building of unusual design, built by Lord Craven in 1660. The monumental staircase leads from ground floor to roof, where there is a view of the Downs. Above the park is *Alfred's Castle*, an Iron Age fort. Alfred fought the Danes nearby in 871.—17½m. *Ashbury* has a Norman and EE church.— At (20m) *Shrivenham* we change to A420.—26m. *Swindon*, see Rte 38B.
From Newbury to *Winchester*, see Rte 14A.

57m. *Speen* stands on the site of the Roman station of *Spinis*.—62m. *Avington*, a quiet village on the Kennet, has a Norman church. —64m. *Hungerford*, made sadly famous by the shooting massacre of August 1987, is otherwise known as a centre for antique shops and for angling on the Kennet.

The pretty village of *Inkpen*, 3½m SE, has a church used by the Templars, who are reputed to have introduced the tulips and lilies that now grow wild in the area. Le Nôtre (1613–1700) stayed at the rectory and designed its gardens. *Inkpen Beacon* (954ft) and *Walbury Hill* (974ft), the highest chalk down in England, lie to the S; both give fine views.—*Littlecote* (open), 3m NW of Hungerford, is a mansion of c 1500 in red brick and flint. The great hall has oak panelling and a fine collection of Cromwellian armour; the 17C chapel replaces the altar by a pulpit. The grounds contain a Roman villa excavated in 1976, with a mosaic floor depicting Orpheus.—*Ramsbury*, 3m further NW, was the seat of the Bishops of Wiltshire in the 10C. It has an unusually large 13C church. The unclassified road continues up the valley to (11½m) *Marlborough* via (10m)

*Mildenhall* (pronounced 'Minall'), the Roman *Cunetio*, where the church has Saxon and Norman details and notable early 19C woodwork.

Beyond (67m) *Froxfield* we skirt the N edge of *Savernake Forest*, a beautiful tract of oaks and beeches.

74m. **Marlborough** (5,800 inhab.; seasonal Tourist Information) has a broad old *High St., largely colonnaded and tile-hung on one side and closed at either end by church towers. Spanning the main road to the W of the town is *Marlborough College*, a public school founded in 1843. William Morris was a pupil. Castle House sets the graceful architectural style of the well-grouped buildings. Built c 1700–20 for the 6th Duke of Somerset, it was for a century a famous coaching inn (see Stanley Weyman's 'The Castle Inn'); in this house the poet Thomson wrote part of his 'Spring' (1727) while the guest of the Countess of Hertford. In the grounds is Castle Mound, identified by legend as the burial place of Merlin. The White Horse to the S was cut by schoolboys in 1804.

An attractive walk of 6m from Marlborough to Avebury (see below) leads via *Manton*, famous for its training stables, and (3m) the great dolmen known as the *Devil's Den*, and then over the Downs, sprinkled with 'grey wethers' or sarsen stones, curious boulders left isolated by the denudation of softer strata.

A346 leads S to Andover (Rte 19) via (5¹/₂m) *Burbage*, where Jane Seymour (1509?–37) was born and celebrated her marriage feast with Henry VIII at Wolf Hall.

A345 runs S across the Vale of Pewsey. Along the N side of the Downs runs the *Wansdyke*, probably a post-Roman border entrenchment, stretching with many gaps from beyond Savernake Forest to Dundry Hill, S of Bristol. The *White Horse*, NW of (7m) *Pewsey*, was first cut on the Downs in 1785.—9¹/₂m. *Manningford Bruce* has an early Norman church.—11m. *Upavon*, on the N edge of Salisbury Plain, see Rte 19.

From Marlborough to *Glastonbury* and *Taunton*, see Rte 24.

The *Wansdyke* runs parallel to A4 on the Downs to the S.—79¹/₂m. The Ridgeway path, here running N to S, crosses our road.—At (80m) *West Kennett*, where B4003 leads right for Avebury, we approach one of the most important groups of prehistoric antiquities in England. (They are all in the care of English Heritage and, except for the Avebury Museum, open at any reasonable time.)—80³/₄m. *Silbury Hill*, constructed c 2660 BC, is at 130ft high the largest artificial mound in Europe (no access to the hill itself). A footpath leads ¹/₂m S of the road to *West Kennett Long Barrow*, a chambered tomb of c 3250 BC, with about 46 burials contemporary with the use of Windmill Hill. The finds from the 1955–56 excavations are in the Devizes museum.—81¹/₂m. *Beckhampton* stands at the junction of A4 with the Swindon–Devizes road (Rte 24). Some 400yd of Roman road are preserved alongside the Devizes road, to the SW.

Just to the N, the village of *Avebury* (seasonal Tourist Information) stands in the centre of **Avebury Stone Circles**, a henge monument of c 2450–2200 BC 'as much surpassing Stonehenge', says Aubrey 'as a cathedral doth a parish church'.

Visitors should first turn down the village street to the *Church*, which has a reworked Saxon nave, a Saxo-Norman tub font, a rood loft of 1460 and a squint. The late 16C *Avebury Manor* (not open at time of writing) has good panelling and plasterwork. At its gates is the *Avebury Museum* (standard opening and summer Sunday mornings), with finds from Avebury and Windmill Hill, providing a superb introduction to the monuments.

The remains of Avebury consist mainly of a massive circular earthwork, ³/₄m round and about 15ft high, with a fosse originally 30ft deep on its inner side, thus suggesting a religious rather than a defensive purpose for the entrenchment. Fringing the inner edge of the fosse stands, in part, a gigantic circle of unhewn megaliths; there were two smaller concentric circles in the centre of the enclosed area. The largest stones weigh about 60 tons. From the circle an avenue of smaller stones (many re-erected) led SE along B4003, beyond West Kennett, to a group of small stone and timber circles called *The Sanctuary*, long since vanished but now marked out on the ground.—1½m NW via *Avebury Trusloe* is *Windmill Hill*, with a neolithic causewayed enclosure built c 3250 BC and used until c 2000.

A4 climbs the Downs; on the left are the Lansdowne Column (c 1843) and a White Horse cut in the turf in 1780.—87½m. *Calne* (10,300 inhab.; Tourist Information), noted for its Wiltshire bacon since the first factory was set up here c 1770, has a much altered 12C church.

Off A4 2½m SW is *Bowood* (open), a mansion first built in 1625 and several times altered in the 18C. The main house was demolished in 1955–56 but the surviving part includes the S range by Robert Adam (1768– 70). It contains an Orangery now serving as a picture gallery, the laboratory where Dr Joseph Priestley discovered oxygen in 1774, and a chapel by C.R. Cockerell (1821); among the exhibits are Lord Byron's Albanian costume and watercolours by Bonington and Turner. The handsome grounds were laid out by Capability Brown (1761–68) and others. A separate garden (open in season), entered from A342, has rhododendron walks and a mausoleum by Adam. At Sloperton Cottage near *Bromham*, off A342 3m S of Bowood, the poet Thomas Moore (1779–1852) passed most of the last 35 years of his life; a Celtic cross marks his grave in the churchyard.

93m. **Chippenham** (19,300 inhab.; Tourist Information) is a busy country town on the Avon.

John Wood the Younger built the church of *Hardenhuish* (pronounced 'Harnish'), 1m NW, in 1779. *Kington St Michael*, off A429 about 2½m NW, was the birthplace of John Aubrey (1626–97). *Castle Combe*, 6m further W, is a pretty village with a 13C market cross and the ruins of a Saxon castle. The church has the fine tomb of Walter de Dunstanville (d. 1270).

FROM CHIPPENHAM TO SHAFTESBURY, 34m by A350.—3½m. *Lacock* (NT) is a pretty village, popular with tourists. The church has a fine late Perp. chapel. *Lacock Abbey* (NT), on the Avon, is a pleasing amalgamation of several periods. Founded in 1232 for Augustinian canonesses, it was dissolved in 1539. The new owner, Sir William Sharington, demolished the church but incorporated the fine 13– 14C cloisters into his new house. Sanderson Miller added the hall and dining room to the W side in the 1750s, contributing much to the abbey's present Gothick appearance. William Henry Fox Talbot carried out his early photographic experiments here in the 1830s; the medieval barn houses a museum of the history of photography.—7m. *Melksham* (9600 inhab.; Tourist Information) is an agricultural town with a restored church, originally Norman.—11m. An unclassified road leads left to (1½m) *Steeple Ashton*, once an important wool market, which still has its lock-up and charter cross, and a restored wool merchant's house. The church has a late Perp. *nave of 1480 with curious corbels and fine vaulting.—16m. **Westbury** (7300 inhab.; Tourist Information) is an old town, now an important railway junction with a handsome Perp. church. On the downs 2m E are *Bratton Camp*, an Iron Age hill fort enclosing a neolithic long barrow, and the *White Horse of Westbury*, dating in its present form from the 18C (both English Heritage, open at any reasonable time). Off A3098 2m W of Westbury is *Chalcot* (limited opening), a classical house of c 1680, recently well restored, with a collection of modern pictures. —20m. *Warminster*, see Rte 18A.—29m. *East Knoyle* was the birthplace of Sir Christopher Wren (1632–1723). *Pyt House* (limited opening), near *Newtown* 2m SE, is an early 19C building designed by its owner.—34m. *Shaftesbury*, see Rte 18A.

A420, running W over the Cotswolds from Chippenham, provides an alternative route direct to (22m) Bristol.—1½m. *Sheldon Manor* (open) was largely rebuilt in the 17C but keeps its remarkable 13C porch. There is also the site of a deserted medieval village to the W.—We cross the border with Avon before reaching the high-lying town of (9m) *Marshfield*. **Dyrham Park** (NT), beyond A46 3m NW, is a mansion with a garden front of 1692 and an Italianate main extension by Talman, architect of Chatsworth, in 1698–1704. It contains a Renaissance chimneypiece, and paintings by Murillo and the Dutch masters.

From Chippenham to *Faringdon* and also to *Cirencester*, see Rte 38B.

97m. *Corsham* has good 17–18C houses, a large church and *Corsham Court* (open), a mansion of 1582 altered in 1760–65 by Capability Brown for Paul Methuen. Part of the building now houses the Bath Academy of Art.

The state rooms, sumptuously furnished, contain Paul Methuen's remarkable *collection of paintings by Italian, Flemish, Dutch and English masters. Outstanding among the more than 300 works exhibited are The Betrayal (Van Dyck), The Annunciation (studio of Filippo Lippi) and St John the Baptist in the Wilderness (Andrea del Sarto). The guidebook contains an excellent catalogue.

A long hill leads down to (100m) *Box*, past the entrance to *Box Tunnel*, the longest railway tunnel in the world when it was built by Brunel in 1837. The underground quarries of Bath stone were used in 1939–45 both as an aircraft factory and to house treasures from the national museums. *Colerne*, 2m N, has a broken 9C cross shaft in its 13–14C church.

106m. **Bath**, see Rte 21.—A4 crosses the Avon. A431, an alternative road to Bristol, stays on the N bank and passes (112½m) *Bitton*, with a notable church. The church at *Oldland Common*, just to the NW, has an Ecce Homo by Murillo.

119m. **BRISTOL** (399,600 inhab.), on the Avon 7m from the Bristol Channel, is an old cathedral city, seaport and manufacturing centre. It has imported wine from Bordeaux since the 12C and from Spain since the 15C. In the 17C and 18C it grew rich on trade with the Americas, and is still a major importer of goods from across the Atlantic, though larger vessels now dock at Avonmouth. The City Docks, from which John and Sebastian Cabot set sail for North America in 1497, have taken on new life with leisure and recreation centres. Long known for its tobacco, confectionery and aircraft industries, the city produced the Bristol Boxkite in 1910 and the Anglo-French Concorde in 1969. Despite war damage and strenuous redevelopment, Bristol preserves a few 17C houses, some gracious 18C and early 19C terraces and some splendid examples of Victorian industrial architecture.

**Tourist Information Centre**: Narrow Quay.

**Car Parks**: Canons Rd, Prince St., Redcliffe Way, Park Row, Lewins Mead.

**Bus and Coach Station**: Marlborough St.

**Railway Stations**: Temple Meads Station (Inter-City services), SE of the centre; Parkway Station (Inter-City), near Mangotsfield, 5m NE, with access to M4 and M5.

**Airport**: at Lulsgate, on A38 8m SW. Flights to Isle of Man, Newquay, Scilly Isles, Jersey, Cardiff, Belfast, Dublin, Amsterdam.

**Theatres**, etc.: Theatre Royal, King St.; Little Theatre, Colston St.; Hippodrome, St Augustine's Parade; Colston Hall (concerts); Arnolfini, Narrow Quay (arts complex with cinema, gallery, etc.); Watershed, Canons Rd (media centre with cinemas, galleries, etc.).

**Annual Events**: North Somerset Agricultural Show (May); Bristol Powerboat Grand Prix (June); World Wine Fair and Festival (July); Harbour Regatta and Rally of Boats (August); Bristol Flower Show (August).

**History**. Probably of late Saxon foundation, Bristol was the centre of the pre-Conquest trade in English slaves—as it later became, in the 18C, the centre of the African slave trade. At the time of the Domesday survey it already ranked next after London, York, and Winchester. In the 12C the town is described by William of Malmesbury as full of ships from every part of Europe, which ascended the tidal Avon to the very doors of the merchants. The castle, at the junction of the Avon and Frome, was rebuilt in 1126 by Robert, Earl of Gloucester; King Stephen was held prisoner here for nine months in 1141. The summary execution of Richard II's followers before the castle was to give Bristol its only scene in Shakespeare. The growing trade in cloth and wine favoured maritime daring and led to the founding of the Merchant Venturers' society. On 24 June 1497, John Cabot and his son Sebastian, who had sailed from Bristol in the 'Matthew', discovered the mainland of America, and in the following year Sebastian Cabot explored the American coast from Newfoundland to Florida. During the Civil War, Bristol was captured by Prince Rupert in 1643 and became the chief Royalist stronghold in the West; but in 1645 it was stormed by the Parliamentarians under Fairfax and in 1655 its castle was slighted by order of Cromwell. During the Reform riots of 1831 two sides of Queen Square, with the Mansion House, custom house, bishop's palace, and gaol, were burned. In 1838 the 'Great Western', Isambard Kingdom Brunel's first steam ship and pioneer of the transatlantic steam traffic, was launched at Bristol. In 1940–41 the city was heavily attacked from the air, amid great loss of life and property.

**Famous natives, residents and visitors**: Defoe is believed to have met Alexander Selkirk, the original of Robinson Crusoe, or to have heard his story in Bristol. Thomas Chatterton (1752–70), the 'marvellous Boy', was born near St Mary Redcliffe. The actress and novelist 'Perdita' Robinson (1758–1800) was born in a house by the cathedral and attended the school in Park St. kept by Hannah More (1745–1833) and her sisters. The painter Sir Thomas Lawrence (1769–1830) was the son of an innkeeper in Redcross St. Robert Southey (1774–1843), the son of a mercer, was born in Wine St.; he returned to Bristol with Coleridge in 1794–95, when they were planning to found their 'Pantisocratic' society in America. Samuel Plimsoll (1824–98), 'the sailors' friend', was born at No. 9 Colston Parade and John Addington Symonds (1840–93) at No. 7 Berkeley Square. The cricketer W.G. Grace (1848–1915) was born at Downend, near Mangotsfield, 3m NE and lived at No. 15 Victoria Square. College St., now demolished, was the birthplace of W. Friese-Greene (1855–1921), pioneer of the cinema. Cary Grant was born here (as Archibald Leach) in 1904.

The focus of movement in modern Bristol is The Centre, an ornamental open space formed in 1893 by covering over part of an arm of the Floating Harbour. The statues are of Edmund Burke, MP for Bristol in 1774–80, and Edward Colston (1636–1721), benefactor of the city. At the S end is a figure of Neptune. Baldwin St. leads E to Bristol Bridge, but we turn S through a Georgian quarter, partly rebuilt, bounded on three sides by the Floating Harbour. In King St. are the *Merchants' Almshouses* (1699), well restored after the bombing that destroyed the adjoining Hall. The Merchant Venturers' society is traceable back to the reign of Henry II. Also in this street are: an employment centre occupying the old *Free Library*, founded in 1613 but removed to the Central Library in 1906; the *Theatre Royal*, modelled on Wren's Drury Lane theatre in London, opened in 1766, the home of the Bristol Old Vic since 1946; *Coopers Hall*, with a classical front (1744) by Halfpenny; the *St Nicholas Almshouse* (1656; rebuilt 1961); the splendid *Llandoger Trow* inn and other fine 17C houses. The *Old Granary* in Little King St. is an entertaining piece of Victorian architecture. The new Redcliffe Way runs diagonally across Queen Square, scene of the riots of 1831, past an equestrian statue of William III by Rysbrack. At No. 16 David Hume was a merchant's clerk in 1734; No. 37 was the first American Consulate in Europe (1792).

We cross the *Floating Harbour*, formed in 1803–09 by diverting a 2m stretch of the tidal Avon into a new channel. On the opposite bank stands *St Mary Redcliffe*, called by Queen Elizabeth I 'the fairest, the goodliest, and most famous parish church in England'. Replacing a 12C church, it was built in a magnificent and harmonious Perp. style mainly between 1325 and 1375, the S side being older than the N; the tower is mid 13C in its lower stages, early 14C above. The church owes much to the generosity of William Canynge the elder (d. 1396) and his grandson William Canynge the younger

**BRISTOL**

0 _____ 300 yards
0 _____ 300 ms

Severn Bridge & GLOUCESTER

N

CLIFTON Suspension Bridge & Zoo

CLEVEDON & WESTON-S-MARE

Victoria Rooms

ST. PAUL'S ROAD
WHITELADIES ROAD
ELMDALE ROAD
PRIORY RD.
ST. MICHAEL'S PARK
WOODLAND ROAD
SOUTHWELL ROAD
ALFRED PL.
ST. MICHAEL'S HILL
TERRELL
MARLBOROUGH STREET

Academy

ELTON ROAD
Grammar School
TYNDALL AVENUE
HOREFIELD ROAD
UPPER MAUDI

QUEEN'S AV.
Tyndalls Park
ROAD
ROYAL FORT ROAD
University
Almshouses

RICHMOND HILL
QUEEN'S RD.
ELMDALE ROAD
UNIVERSITY ROAD
WOODLAND ROAD
UNIVERSITY WALK

PARK PL.
TRIANGLE
QUEEN'S ROAD
University
St Michael's

R.C. Church
RUYSDAEL PL.
City Art Gallery & Museum
ROAD
PERRY
STEPS
Foster Almsh

Queen Elizabeth Hospital (City School)

BERKELEY
PARK
ROW
LODGE
ST.
Red Lodge
ELTON LANE
COLSTON STREET
HOEBURN
COLSTON

JACOBS WELLS
BERKELEY SQUARE
CHARLOTTE STREET
PARK STREET
Car Park
Colston Hall
Centre

Cabot Tower
St George's
PIPE LA.

Brandon Hill
GREAT GEORGE STREET
Georgian Ho.
FROGMORE STREET
Entertainment Centre
DENMARK ST.
ST. AUGUSTINE'S PARADE
BROAD
QUAY

JACOBS WELLS ROAD
Hippodrome
St Marks
Statue

New Council House
COLLEGE ST.
P
College Green
Watershed

Baths
Cabot House
DEANERY ROAD
Library
COLLEGE SQUARE
Cathedral

HOT WELL ROAD
ST. GEORGES ROAD
ANCHOR
School
ROAD
Narrow Quay
Arnolfini

SS Great Britain
Coach Park
ROAD
CANONS ROAD
PRINCE STREET
Princes St. Bridge
National Lifeboat Museum

WAPPING DOCK
GASFERRY ROAD
BUTTS ROAD
Bristol Indust. Mus

FLOATING HARBOUR

CUMBERLAND ROAD

CORONATION ROAD
PARK ROAD
ALLINGTON ROAD

(1399?–1474), two famous mayors of Bristol. It was extensively restored in 1930–33.

The massive tower, richly decorated with pinnacles and ballflower ornaments, is crowned by a spire 285ft high (the upper part is recent). The hexagonal late 13C *N Porch, most unusual in ground plan and execution, has an intricately carved door and an inner porch of 1180. The S Porch dates from c 1325.

The interior is light and spacious, with elaborate vaulting and stellate tomb recesses. There is no triforium or horizontal string course. The aisled transepts are an unusual feature in parish churches, rare even in cathedrals. The American Chapel under the tower has some old stained glass, a fine grille (1710) by William Edney, and the so-called rib of the dun cow slain by Guy of Warwick (really a whalebone, said to have been presented to the church by Cabot in 1497). Here too is a wooden figure of Elizabeth I (c 1574). In the S transept are the monuments of Canynge the younger and his wife, and another Canynge, as Dean of Westbury College. The tomb slab of Admiral Sir William Penn (d. 1670), captor of Jamaica and father of the founder of Pennsylvania, is at the entrance to this transept; his classical monument, with his armour, is high up at the W end of the nave. The canopied monuments of the Medes (c 1475), and an interesting brass of their son, are in the N choir aisle. The Lady Chapel has two bays, one 25 years older than the other (1375–1400) and modern stained glass.

There are good brasses (kept covered) to Sir John Inyn (d. 1439), in the Lady Chapel, and, in front of the high altar, to John Brooke (d. 1512) and his wife Johanna.

Above the N porch is a muniment room where the boy poet Thomas Chatterton pretended to have discovered the Rowley MS in an old chest. Chatterton, nephew of the sexton of St Mary's, was born in Redcliffe Way nearby (house open by application to the Director, City Museum). A poor statue in the churchyard shows him in the school uniform of Colston's Hospital. In 1795 Southey and Coleridge were married to the Fricker sisters at St Mary Redcliffe.

E of the church are *Temple Meads Station* and the ruined *Temple Church*, a large Perp. building with a tower 5ft out of the perpendicular, on the site of a church of the Knights Templar (English Heritage, exterior viewing only, at any reasonable time). Close by is the church of *St Thomas* by J. Allen (1792–95), with an earlier reredos (1716) and *organ loft (1730).

Much of the *City Docks* W of St Mary Redcliffe is being redeveloped for leisure and recreation. In Prince's Wharf are the *National Lifeboat Museum* and the *Bristol Industrial Museum*. In Great Western Dock, further W, lies Brunel's *SS Great Britain* (open), the first ocean-going ship with screw propulsion. She made her maiden voyage to New York in 1845. In 1970 she was towed home from the Falkland Islands, where she had been wrecked in 1886, to be restored in the docks where she was built. On the dock is a museum of relics of her history.

Redcliffe St. leads N from St Mary Redcliffe to (½m) *Bristol Bridge*, built in 1768 to replace the original structure of 1247. On the left, in Baldwin St., is *St Nicholas*, a Gothick church of 1762 with a 14C crypt and an altarpiece by Hogarth, now a local museum.

N of the bridge lies the old centre of the city. The Cross, the junction of High St., Wine St., Broad St. and Corn St., was marked until 1733 by the medieval High Cross now at Stourhead (Rte 19). At the corner of Wine St. is *Christ Church*, rebuilt by Paty in 1786–90, with two Quarter Jacks of 1728 from the old church, a striking rood screen, and a 17C font from St Ewen's (now replaced by the Old Council House) in which Southey was baptised.

On the corner of Corn St. stood the bookshop of Joseph Cottle, friend and publisher of Coleridge, Wordsworth and Southey, while on the opposite corner is the *Old Council House* by Smirke (1827). In *All Saints*, a good 15C church with two Norman bays, is the monument to Edward Colston by Gibbs and Rysbrack. The

Exchange, by the elder Wood (1743), is now a market; in front are the 'Nails', four bronze tables once used by local merchants for their cash transactions (hence, perhaps, 'to pay on the nail'). Corn St. is continued by Clare St., with the elaborate tower (133ft) of *St Stephen's*, a church of 1450–90. Inside are some good late medieval tomb recesses and two monuments of 1617 and 1627. The iron gates and *sword rest, by Edney, are from St Nicholas'.

Beyond the Cross, High St. is continued by Broad St. On the left is the *Guildhall* (1843), now used as law courts. The *Bank of England* (1845) is by C.R. Cockerell. Further down, on the right, the façade of a 19C printing house is decorated with brightly coloured tiles. Spanning the end of the street is *St John's Gate*, with statues of Brennus and Belinus, mythical founders of Bristol, topped by the spire of St John's, a 14C church on two levels.

Wine St., greatly rebuilt, leads NE from the Cross. On the right a new block masks the tower of *St Mary-le-Port*; in *Castle Park* beyond is the ruined church of *St Peter*.

Union St. leads N to the church of *St James*, the nave of a late Norman priory church built in 1130 by Robert, Earl of Gloucester (d. 1157), whose tomb it contains. The W front has a rose window of unique design.

Newgate, straight on, keeps the name of the former prison where the poet Richard Savage died in 1743. The Broadmead Shopping Centre, to the left, includes *Quakers' Friars*, a square with relics of a 13C Dominican priory. Rebuilt to serve as the *Cutlers' Hall* and *Bakers' Hall*, the upper floor (open) houses a Planning Exhibition. The *Register Office*, adjoining on the E, occupies the Old Friends' Meeting House (1747), on a site first occupied by the Quakers in 1670. Here Penn married his second wife in 1696. Further N we find the oldest Methodist Chapel in England, the '*New Room*' built by John Wesley in 1739 and well restored in 1930. Wesley himself used the living quarters upstairs. His statue, by A.G. Walker (1933), stands in the courtyard.

Nelson St. leads back from Broadmead to The Centre. On the right Christmas St. has the 13C porch of the vanished *St Bartholomew's Hospital*. The quaint Christmas Steps climb up to Colston St. from the opposite side of Rupert St. At the top are some stone seats, an old inscription, and *Foster's Almshouses* (rebuilt 1861–84), with a 16C chapel dedicated to the Three Kings of Cologne. Higher up is *St Michael's*, of 1744 with a 15C tower; and above that again are the more attractive *Colston's Almshouses*, founded in 1691.

St Augustine's Parade leads S from The Centre to College Green, the former burial ground of the abbey.

The *Cathedral* stands on the traditional site of St Augustine's Oak, where the saint is said to have conferred with the British Christians in 603. It was originally the church of an abbey founded in 1148 for Augustinian canons by Robert Fitzhardinge, Provost of Bristol; after the Dissolution it became the cathedral of the new see of Bristol, created in 1542.

The chapter house and two gateways in the precincts survive from the Norman buildings. The choir was rebuilt in 1298–1363, mainly by Abbot Knowle (1306–32), connecting with the previously detached Elder Lady Chapel erected by Abbot David c 1215. The transepts were largely rebuilt after 1463, on the model of the older work. The Norman nave, half rebuilt at the Dissolution, was allowed to fall into ruin and the church remained naveless until 1868–88, when the present nave and its two W towers were added by G.E. Street. The central tower dates from c 1450.

# BRISTOL CATHEDRAL

Key to Numbers

1 Sir John Young
2 Bp Butler Monument
3 Maurice, Lord Berkeley & mother
4 Bp Bush
5 Bust of Robert Southey
6 Abbot Newbury
7 Abbot Hunt
8 Abbot Newland
9, 10, 11 Berkeley Tombs
12 Harrowing of Hell coffin

The cathedral is a rare example of a 'hall church'—that is, the aisles, nave and choir are all the same height, without triforium and clerestory, and the pier arches reach the full height of the building. In the aisles the *Nave* Street copied the extraordinary vaulting of the choir; at the W end is the tomb of Sir John Young (d. 1603) and his wife Joan. The *N Transept* has rich lierne vaulting, a beautiful window and a monument to Bishop Butler (d. 1752) with an inscription by Southey. The *Elder Lady Chapel* is pure EE, with Dec. vaulting and E window and a beautiful arcade with grotesque carvings. On the S side is the tomb of the 9th Lord Berkeley (d. 1368) and his mother.

The *Choir*, in an early Dec. style unparalleled elsewhere, has the earliest lierne vaulting in England and beautiful foliage capitals. The canopied stalls (given by Abbot Elyot, 1515–26) have been restored; the misericords and pew ends deserve attention. The organ case and front pipes date from 1685. The reredos (1899) is by Pearson. The choir aisles are noteworthy for two features: the skeleton vaulting, which recalls timber rather than stone construction, and the stellate tomb recesses (cf. St Mary Redcliffe, above, and St David's Cathedral in Wales). The enamelled glass in the E windows was presented by Dean Glemham (1661–67). In the N choir aisle, the earlier of the two, are: a tablet to Hakluyt, prebendary here in 1586–1616; a 13C coffin cover with Lombardic inscription; the tomb of Bishop Bush (d. 1558) with a 'cadaver'; and a bust of Southey by Baily. The *Eastern Lady Chapel* behind the chancel has a beautiful Dec. *E window, with original glass of c 1340, and other glass of the same date in the ÷W window. The reredos is partly Knowle's but with cresting added by Abbot Burton (1526–71). The chapel contains beautiful sedilia (restored) and the tombs of Abbots Newbury (1428–73), builder of the tower, Hunt (1473–81) and Newland (1481–1515), coloured according to their original scheme. A tablet marks the grave of Bishop Butler. In the S choir aisle, with Berkeley monuments in the tomb recesses, is the beautiful Dec. entrance to the monastic *Sacristy*; off it opens the *Berkeley Chapel*, with a gilt brass *chandelier of 1450 from the Temple Church. The late Dec. *Newton Chapel*, at the W end of the S choir aisle, has 17–18C tombs of the Newton family.

The *S Transept*, with a groined roof by Abbot Hunt (1473–81), contains a sculptured coffin lid (c 1000) of the Hereford school showing the Harrowing of Hell. In the Norman S wall is the entrance to the night stair.

A door in the W wall of the S transept leads to the scanty remains (restored) of the *Cloisters* (c 1480). Off the E walk is the late Norman *Chapter House*, rectangular and enriched with zigzag and cable mouldings and interlaced arches. The E wall was rebuilt after the 1831 riots. The series of vestries, etc. built in 1923 as a memorial to H.O. Wills, founder of Bristol University, occupy the site of the Dorter. The doorways of the slype and day stair are preserved. At the end is the 14C doorway of the former bishop's palace (not open).

W of the cathedral, leading from College Green to College Square, is the *Abbey Gateway*, late Norman with a Perp. upper part. In Cloister Court, inside the gate to the left, a 13C gateway was the entrance to the Refectory, now part of the Cathedral School (refounded 1542); lower down, in College Square, is another Norman gateway which led to the abbot's lodgings. Next to it, the *Central Library* (1906; Holden) has a chimneypiece by Grinling Gibbons from the old King St. library.

On the W side of the Green is the *Council House* (1933–55; Vincent Harris). The statue of an Elizabethan seaman, by Wheeler, commemorates John Cabot. On the NE side is the lovely *St Mark's*, or the Lord Mayor's Chapel.

Founded c 1230 by Maurice de Gaunt as the chapel of a hospital for the support of a chaplain and the relief of 100 poor daily, it was taken over by the Corporation in 1541. The hospital became a school; the chapel was used by a Huguenot congregation from 1687 until 1722, when it became the official chapel of the Corporation.

The nave, except for the 16C roof, and the transept arches belong to the original 13C chapel; the N transept dates from 19C rebuilding. The aisle, with its wagon-shaped roof, was added c 1260, the chancel, chapels and tower in the late 15C. The 16–17C French and Flemish stained glass came mostly from Fonthill Abbey (Rte 18A) and Ecouen. The fine monuments include those of the founder; his nephew Robert de Gournay (d. 1269); his brother Henry, first Master of the hospital; and Sir Maurice Berkeley (d. 1464). The reredos and *sedilia were restored c 1500; the sword rest (1702) was made by Edney for the Temple Church. The *Poyntz Chapel*, in the SE, is a notable late Perp. chantry (c 1520), with early glass and 16C Spanish tiles.

Park St. climbs from College Green towards Clifton. At No. 43 Hannah More and her sisters kept a boarding school (1767–74) where 'Perdita' Robinson was a pupil. At No. 7 Great George St. (left) is the *Georgian House* (open), a dignified merchant's house of 1789 with appropriate furnishings; Coleridge and Wordsworth probably first met here in autumn 1795. The classical *St George's*, opposite, is by Smirke (1823). *Brandon Hill* (260ft), beyond, is crowned with the *Cabot Tower* (105ft; open), built in 1897–98 to mark the quatercentenary of Cabot's expedition. On the NW slope of the hill is *Queen Elizabeth's Hospital*, a blue-coat school founded in 1590.

The *Red Lodge* (open) in Park Row, E of Park St., was built in 1578–90 and contains fine carved woodwork and stonecarving of the 16C and 18C, as well as an interesting museum with contemporary furnishings.

Among the imposing group of public buildings in Queen's Rd, at the top of Park St., is the **City Museum and Art Gallery**. Behind the street-front Art Gallery building (1905) lies an extension given by the Wills family in 1930.

The Museum and Art Gallery contains broadly based local and regional collections, some of national and international significance. The natural sciences, represented by major mineral and fossil specimens and by world-wide natural history material, are mostly housed in recently modernised galleries which feature aquaria and an audio-visual programme. Besides extensive British archaeology illustrating South-West England, there is an important display on ancient Egypt and a gallery devoted to pre-Roman and Roman glass from the Mediterranean, which complements major holdings of Bristol and British 17–20C drinking glasses and containers, and the largest collection of *Chinese glass outside China. The Museum's chief treasure is the *series of 8C BC Assyrian relief carvings from Nimrud (Iraq); above them hangs a modern replica of the Bristol Aircraft Company's first commercial aircraft, the 1910 Boxkite. Here too are local coins, medals and awards, and a fine series of historic maps of the city.
  The art collection has a broad coverage of European paintings, with a *portrait of Martin Luther by Lucas Cranach, Giovanni Bellini's 'Descent into Limbo' and a fine diptych by Taddeo Gaddi. The later schools include works by Vuillard, Delacroix, Redon and Renoir. The local Bristol school is strongly represented by Francis Danby, Samuel Jackson and other Bristol painters. The largest collection of English delftware is held in Bristol and the English porcelain is particularly strong in Bristol ware. There is a fine Oriental collection which includes bronzes, porcelain, lacquer, glass and Japanese prints.

On the right rises the commanding Gothic tower (1925) of the **University of Bristol Wills Memorial Building**. The university was founded through the generosity of the tobacco tycoon H.O. Wills in 1909.

In Tyndall's Park, behind, are the *Grammar School*, founded by Robert and Nicholas Thorne in 1532 and transferred here in 1879, and many new buildings of the university, which has extended E beyond Woodland Rd. In this road is the *Baptist College*, originally established in 1720 in Stokes Croft; it owns a miniature of Cromwell and a unique copy of Tyndale's New Testament (1526). In Cotham Rd, a little to the NE, is the *Western Congregational College*, founded by the Independents in 1752 and transferred from Plymouth in 1901.

Further on in Queen's Rd opposite the Garden Centre and the *Victoria Rooms* (1840), a well-proportioned classical building by Dyer, now the University Club Rooms, is the *Royal West of England Academy*.
  We are now in **Clifton**, the high-lying residential quarter at the W end of Bristol with a few 18C mansions and many gracious early 19C villas and terraces. Queen's Rd and Clifton Down Rd climb to (½m) *Clifton Down* and, further N, *Durdham Down*, which together form a

limestone plateau (250–300ft above the rest of the city. They are bounded on the W by the impressive *Avon Gorge*, spanned by the graceful *Clifton Suspension Bridge* (toll), begun by Brunel in 1831 but not completed till 1864. The chains were once part of the old Hungerford Bridge in London. It is 1352ft long (702ft between the piers), 31ft wide and 245ft above high tide. The bridge commands a splendid *view of the gorge, marred at low water by the muddy bed of the river. On the opposite side are the beautiful *Nightingale Valley* and the hanging *Leigh Woods* (159 acres; NT).

*The Clifton Suspension Bridge, Bristol*

On the hill above the E end of the bridge is an *Observatory* (open) with a camera obscura.—From the E end of the bridge a zigzag footpath descends to the *Hotwells*, a spa which attracted crowds of fashionable visitors in the 18C (see Smollett's 'Humphry Clinker' and Fanny Burney's 'Evelina'). The long Hotwell Rd leads back to (1m) College Green, passing *Holy Trinity*, a church by C.R. Cockerell (1828–30), gutted in 1941 and charmingly refitted by T. Burrough (1959).

In Clifton Park, ³/₄m NE of the bridge, is the boldly contemporary *Clifton Cathedral* (RC), a hexagonal building in reinforced concrete, completed in 1973.

Clifton Down Rd continues N from near the bridge to (³/₄m) *Bristol Zoo*. Close by is *Clifton College*, a public school founded in 1862. Earl Haig (statue in the quadrangle), Sir Henry Newbolt, Sir A. Quiller-Couch, Robert Hichens, Roger Fry, Joyce Cary and I.A. Richards were pupils.

At *Westbury-on-Trym*, off A4018 3m N of central Bristol, is the 15C gatehouse (NT) of a college of secular clerks where Wyclif was a prebend. The former collegiate church is mainly Perp. but has some EE features. The monument of Bishop Carpenter (d. 1477), responsible for the rebuilding, lies near the sanctuary. Another 15C building, in Church Rd, was probably part of the college. Mrs Indira Gandhi attended Badminton School here. Near *Henbury*, 1¹/₂m N, is *Blaise Castle House Museum* (open), a plain mansion of 1795 now containing exhibits of everyday urban and rural life. The park, landscaped by Repton, has the 18C Stratford Mill (from the 'drowned' Chew valley) and garden buildings (including a thatched dairy) by John Nash. *Blaise Castle* itself, on Henbury Hill, is a sham ruin built in 1766. *Blaise Hamlet* is a 'model' village of Picturesque cottages designed by Nash in 1810–12 (NT, but cottages not open).

The fine Perp. church tower built by the Merchant Venturers in 1483 on *Dundry Hill*, 4¹/₂m S of Bristol, commands a wide *view.

FROM BRISTOL TO THE SEVERN BRIDGE. The quick route (13m) simply follows M32 spur to M4. A slower but slightly more interesting route (14m) leaves the city by A4, along the N bank of the Avon.—3¹/₂m. *Shirehampton* has a fine public park (NT).—6m. **Avonmouth**, where the Avon flows into the Severn, has the major docks of the Corporation of Bristol.—We follow A402 up the Estuary, passing on the left at 10¹/₂m the *Severn Tunnel* (railway), the longest tunnel in Britain (4m 638yd), built in 1873–86 by Brunel's pupil, Charles Richardson. —From (14m) *Aust* we get a good view of the *Severn Bridge* (toll), carrying M4 across to *Chepstow* and the Welsh bank of the Estuary (Rte 45A).

FROM BRISTOL TO CLEVEDON, 13m by A369 and B3124. We leave the city by the Clifton Suspension Bridge and Leigh Woods (see above) and follow the pleasant Gordano valley.—6m. *Portbury* (left) has a large partly Norman church. We cross M5.—8¹/₂m. *Portishead*, on the Severn Estuary, is the third limb of Bristol Docks. We take B3124.—8³/₄m. At *Weston-in-Gordano* the church has a unique 'Palm Sunday' gallery.—13m. *Clevedon* (17,900 inhab.) is a quiet resort, well sited on the Estuary at the foot of *Dial Hill* (296ft; view). In Old Church Rd, near the station, is a cottage (plaque) doubtfully identified as the 'pretty cot' to which Coleridge brought his bride, Sara Fricker, in 1795. In the old church of *St Andrew* are buried Arthur Hallam (1811–33), subject of Tennyson's 'In Memoriam', and his father, the historian Henry Hallam (1777–1859). *Clevedon Court* (NT), on B3130 1¹/₂m NE, is a lovely house built in 1320 but including the tower and old hall from an earlier building. Despite Elizabethan and later additions, it keeps its medieval plan of rooms. There are good collections of Eltonware and the local Nailsea glass. Thackeray, a guest of the Elton family in 1848, used the house as model for 'Castlewood' in 'Henry Esmond'.—An alternative way from Bristol to Clevedon follows B3128 and B3130 along the Yeo valley. At 9m the road passes between (left) *Tickenham* and (right) a hill crowned by *Cadbury Camp*, an entrenchment of 7 acres with a double rampart.

FROM BRISTOL TO WESTON-SUPER-MARE, 21m by A370.—12¹/₂m. *Congresbury* (pronounced 'Commsbury') has a vicarage built in 1445 and an EE church with a fine stone spire. At *Yatton*, 1¹/₄m N, is another good church (12–15C) and at *Claverham* adjoining on the NE, a Friends' Meeting House of 1729.—We cross M5 and enter (21m) **Weston-super-Mare** (58,000 inhab.; Tourist Information), a resort on the Bristol Channel with an esplanade, a sandy beach and two piers, one leading to the rocky islet of *Birnbeck*. It is built partly on the slopes of *Worlebury Hill* (357ft; views) encircled by a toll road. On top are the remains of a British camp. Off the coast are the islets of *Steep Holme* and *Flat Holme*. On the opposite shore of the Axe is *Brean Down*, a bird sanctuary.—About 4m N are the remains of *Woodspring Priory*, founded as an expiatory chapel in honour of Thomas Becket by a grandson of Reginald Fitzpurse, one of his murderers. The land extending to the N is NT (access from Sandy Bay).—2m S is the ruined *Uphill Old Church*.

FROM BRISTOL TO GLOUCESTER, 35m by A38. We cross M5 and M4.— 10¹/₂m. *Thornbury* (left), the early home of the cricketer W.G. Grace (1848–1915) and his brothers, has a Perp. church.—For *Berkeley*, left at 18m, and (35m) *Gloucester*, see Rte 38A.

FROM BRISTOL TO CIRENCESTER, 38m. B4058 leads to (6¹/₂m) *Winterbourne*, where the heavily restored church has interesting effigies and a brass of 1370. —9¹/₂m. *Iron Acton* has a 15C memorial cross in the churchyard.—17¹/₂m. *Wotton-under-Edge* is a pleasant little town. In *Kingswood*, off B4060 1m SW, is a late 14C gatehouse, sole remnant of a Cistercian abbey founded in 1139

(English Heritage, summer season daily 10.00–18.00, winter daily 10.00–16.00).—We climb the wooded slopes of the Cotswolds. On the right is *Newark Park* (NT), with a footpath to *Ozleworth*, where the early Norman church has a hexagonal tower. The substantial houses of *Alderley*, 2m down the valley, recall the prosperous wool traders of the 16–18C. At the top of the ridge (21¹/₂m) we join A4135 for (28m) *Tetbury*. Thence to *Cirencester*, see Rte 38B.

From Bristol to *Exeter*, see Rte 23.

# 21  Bath

**BATH** (85,000 inhab.) is one of the most beautiful cities in England, though nowadays its beauty is all too often overwhelmed by the crowds of visitors. Its long and distinguished history stems almost entirely from the natural hot springs which gush to the surface here at a constant temperature of 46.5°C. Their medicinal properties were first exploited by the Romans, whose excavated baths now make one of the chief landmarks for visitors. The city again rose to prominence as a fashionable spa in the 18C, when it was visited by almost everyone of account in literature, politics and society. The architect John Wood the Elder and his successors made Bath an enduring monument to Palladian elegance with the squares, terraces and crescents, built of the honey-coloured local stone, which rise tier on tier up the steep wooded sides of the Avon valley.

**Tourist Information Centre**: Abbey Churchyard.

**Car Parks**: Broad St., Charlotte St., Kingsmead Square, Manvers St., Sawclose. Multi-storey car parks in Avon St., Ham Gardens, Walcot St.

**Bus Station**: Manvers St.

**Railway Station**: Spa Station, facing the S end of Manvers St.

**Theatre**: Theatre Royal, Sawclose.

**Music**: a trio plays chamber and light music in the Pump Room during morning coffee and Sunday afternoon tea. Brass and military bands give concerts in Parade Gardens on summer Sunday afternoons.

**Annual Events**: Bath International Festival of Music (May and June); West of England Antiques Fair (May); Contemporary Art Fair (May and June); Royal Bath and West Country Show (May and June); County Cricket Festival (June).

**History**. According to legend, the city was established by the British swineherd-prince Bladud (father of King Lear) who, expelled from court as a leper, cured himself by imitating his swine and rolling in the warm mud where the mineral waters stagnated. In about AD 44–60 the Romans built a fort here, at the junction of the Foss Way and the route from London to the Welsh frontier. Their city, with its baths and temple, dates from after AD 60. They called the settlement *Aquae Sulis*, from the local Celtic god Sulis, but added the name of their own healing deity, Minerva. The Saxons, who captured Bath in 577, renamed it *Hat Bathum*. The see of Wells was moved here between 1090 and about 1206, and its bishops are still known as Bishops of Bath and Wells. In the Middle Ages Bath was a centre of the cloth trade, as Chaucer's portrait of his 'Wife of Bath' testifies. The zenith of Bath's prosperity as a fashionable watering-place was reached during the 18C. Beau Nash (Richard Nash; 1674–1761), appointed Master of Ceremonies in 1704, introduced order and method into the social life of the place. The wealthy, self-made Ralph Allen (1693–1764) exploited the rich quarries of Bath stone, and a new, Palladian city was designed and built by John Wood the Elder (1704–54) and his son, John Wood the Younger (1728–81). Thomas Baldwin, John Palmer, John Eveleigh and Robert Adam were among the architects who carried on the tradition until about 1800. Portraits of Bath at the height of its popularity have been given by Smollett ('Humphry Clinker'), Sheridan ('The Rivals'), Fanny Burney ('Evelina'), Jane Austen ('Northanger Abbey', 'Persuasion') and, for a

Beckford's Tower

Sion Hill

SOMERSET CRESCENT

LANSDOWN CRESCENT

High Common

Golf Course

VIA JULIA (ROMAN ROAD)

WESTON ROAD

Botanic Gardens

Royal Victoria Park

ROYAL CRESCENT

Museum

Lower Common

GRAVEL WALK

ROYAL AVENUE

THE CIRCUS

Assembly Rooms

Crescent Gardens

Car Park

BRISTOL ROAD

Libr. & Geology Mus.

QUEEN SQUARE

Herschel Museum

Theatre Royal

Cross Bath

Hetling House

Tech. Coll.

River Avon

Cemetery

WESTMORLAND STATION RD.

Oldfield Park

St Mary Magdalen

Beechen Cliff

WELLS WAY

WELLS

N

**BATH**

| 0 | 400 yards |
| 0 | 400 ms |

later period, Dickens ('Pickwick Papers'). Christopher Anstey's amusing satire, 'The New Bath Guide' (1766), should not be forgotten. In the 19C, when Bath became respectable rather than fashionable, the city's character was changed but not destroyed by the arrival of Brunel's Great Western Railway and the decline of the Kennet and Avon Canal (though this is being well restored). The Bath Festival, now internationally famous for its music, was started in 1947 and the University of Bath was founded at Claverton Down in 1965.

The city has given its name to Bath chairs, Bath stone, Bath buns, Bath Oliver biscuits and Bath chaps (cooked pigs' cheeks rolled in breadcrumbs and made into cones) but not to Bath brick, which was developed at Bridgwater and called after its maker.

**Famous natives, residents and visitors**. Few English cities can boast connections with so many distinguished people. They are listed here (not exhaustively) by the streets where they lived or stayed, and the streets are given in the order they are passed in the walking tours suggested below.

WEST AND NORTH FROM THE CENTRE. *Kingsmead Square*: Bishop Butler died at Rosewell House in 1752. *Sawclose*: Beau Nash died at the house, now a restaurant, next to the Theatre Royal. *Trim St.*: General Wolfe left No. 5 in 1759 to take command of the assault on Quebec. *Queen Square*: No. 15, now replaced by the Reference Library, was the home of John Wood the Elder. *New King St.*: No. 9 was home of the Sheridan family, No. 22 of the naturalist W.H. Hudson. At No. 19 (now a museum) Sir William Herschel first observed the planet Uranus in 1781. *Gay St.*: No. 8 is associated with Mrs Piozzi (Mrs Thrale) and No. 30 with the potter Josiah Wedgwood. No. 34 was in 1874–84 the first studio of William Friese-Greene who, with John Rudge, originated cinematography in England; they are also remembered by a plaque at No. 10 New Bond St. *The Circus*: William Pitt, Earl of Chatham and MP for Bath, stayed at Nos. 7 and 8; the explorer David Livingstone at No. 13; Clive of India at No. 14; Thomas Gainsborough, who won his early fame in Bath, at No. 17; Parry, the Arctic voyager, at No. 27. Admiral Phillip (1738–1814), first Governor of New South Wales, spent his last years at No. 19. *Royal Crescent*: George Saintsbury died at No. 1 in 1933, Frederic Harrison at No. 10 in 1923. No. 5 was the home of Christopher Anstey, author of 'The New Bath Guide', and No. 17 of Sir Isaac Pitman, inventor of modern shorthand. From No. 11 Elizabeth Linley eloped with the dramatist Sheridan in 1772. *St James's Square*: at No. 35 Dickens, Forster and Maclise were guests of the poet Walter Savage Landor in 1840.

NORTH AND EAST OF THE CENTRE. *Great Pulteney St*: the historian Lord Macaulay is associated with No. 1, the novelist Bulwer-Lytton with No. 2, the architect Thomas Baldwin with No. 6, the anti-slavery campaigner William Wilberforce with No. 36 and the evangelical writer Hannah More with No. 76. *Sydney Place*: Jane Austen lived with her parents at No. 4.

EAST OF THE CENTRE: *North Parade*: No. 11 was the residence of Edmund Burke, and Goldsmith stayed here in 1771; No. 9 was visited by Wordsworth. *Pierrepont St.*: Nelson came to No. 2 in 1780 after the expedition to Central America; at No. 4 the actor James Quin was visited by Handel. *South Parade*: at No. 6 the young Sir Walter Scott lived in 1777 with his uncle; at No. 14 Mrs Thrale was visited by Dr Johnson and Fanny Burney. *Old Orchard St*: Sarah Siddons achieved her first real stage success in 1775 at the Bath Theatre (now the Masonic Hall).

NORTH-EASTERN OUTSKIRTS. *Lansdown Crescent*: William Beckford moved to No. 20 in 1823, extending his residence to adjoining houses before his death in 1844.

The centre of Bath is formed by the Abbey, the Pump Room and the Roman Baths and Museum.

The **Abbey Church**, standing in the attractive paved piazza called *Abbey Churchyard*, is the last of the great English pre-Reformation churches, built in a consistent late Perp. style. Externally, its most striking features are the flying buttresses and the W front, with a magnificent window of seven lights flanked by turrets on which are carved ladders with angels ascending and descending.

A nunnery founded at Bath in 676 was converted into a Benedictine monastery by King Edgar, crowned there in 973. The Norman church built by Bishop John de Villula (c 1107) fell into ruin after the bishopric was restored to Wells. The smaller present church was begun in 1499 by Bishop Oliver King, but its completion was delayed by the dissolution of the monasteries and it was not consecrated until 1616. It was heavily restored in 1864–74, by Sir Gilbert Scott, and again in the 1950s.

The spacious interior is remarkable for the size and number of its windows; there is no triforium and the clerestory windows are unusually high. The glass is nearly all modern. Bishop King's original plan for the rich fan-tracery roof was completed when Scott extended it over the nave. At the SE angle of the choir is the small chantry of Prior Bird, notable for its carving, begun in 1515 but finished only in recent years. Apart from the altar tomb of Bishop Montagu (d. 1618) on the N side of the nave, there are no big monuments. Most of the wall tablets commemorate the fashionable society who came to Bath in the 18C. Notables include: Beau Nash (d. 1761) in the S aisle; Sir Isaac Pitman (d. 1897) in the N aisle; James Quin (d. 1766), with a poem by Garrick, in the N choir aisle; and the political economist Thomas Malthus (d. 1834) in the porch.

The covered cloisters against the S side of the nave were built in 1923.

On the S side of Abbey Churchyard stands the **Pump Room** (open; inclusive ticket for Roman Baths and Museum and Assembly Rooms). Rebuilt in the classical style by Thomas Baldwin and John Palmer in 1792–96, it bears on its architrave the motto 'water is best' in Greek. The handsome interior has a statue and a portrait of Beau Nash, and a longcase clock presented to the city in 1709 by its maker, Thomas Tompion. Windows overlook the King's Bath. Coffee (with a morning concert) and tea (concert on Sunday afternoons) are served, and a fountain supplies mineral water.

The adjoining *'**Roman Baths and Museum** embody the substantial remains of the temple and complex of baths built at the centre of Aquae Sulis, some 20ft below the present street level, between the 1C and the 4C AD. Fragments of Roman Bath were turned up during Georgian rebuilding of the city, but excavation did not begin in earnest until 1878; it has continued to yield important discoveries up to the present day.

The first major exhibit is the reconstructed pediment of the temple to Sulis Minerva, with a charming Romano-Celtic Gorgon's head as its centrepiece. Underground staircases and corridors lead past the *King's Bath*, named from the medieval structure placed on top of the reservoir which the Romans built to harness the hot spring. The display cases nearby contain a remarkable assembly of votive offerings recovered from the spring: coins, personal jewellery, pieces of pewter scratched with prayers and curses, as well as vessels used in religious ceremonies. A walkway leads across the excavated site of the temple precinct, with part of the entrance steps. On display are: a superb head of Minerva, found beneath Stall St. in 1727; sculptured fragments later used as paving stones; two corners of the sacrificial altar, showing Hercules Bibax and Bacchus; carved reliefs of a mastiff carrying a roe deer and a hound chasing a hare; and the Façade of the Four Seasons, with its Luna pediment.

Near the impressive Roman overflow from the spring we enter the baths. The *Great Bath* is now roofless, and its pillars, terrace and statues of famous Romans are 19C, but the bath itself and the surrounding pavement are in a fine state of preservation. At the edge we can see the bases of the piers that once supported the roof; the flight of steps by which the bath was entered is visible in the murky, steaming water; and the bottom still has its flooring of lead from the Mendips. Architectural fragments displayed around the sides

*Gorgon's head on the pediment of the temple of Sulis
Minerva, Roman Baths and Museum, Bath*

include part of the roof vaulting constructed in the 3C with hollow
tiles.

The *East Baths*, several times altered by the Romans, include: the
Lucas Bath, where the water was cooler than in the Great Bath, with
two different floor levels; a little semicircular bath probably used for
curative treatment; and part of the hypocaust serving a suite of
Turkish baths, a later addition to the complex. The *West Baths* have a
circular bath of cold water, added in the 2C. The hypocaust, flues and
stoking holes used to heat adjoining rooms also survive.

WEST AND NORTH FROM THE CENTRE AND BACK. Bath St., a perfect
colonnaded thoroughfare, leads W from the Roman Baths and Stall
St. to the delightful *Cross Bath*, originally medieval but rebuilt by
Baldwin and Palmer (1784). The *Hot Bath* (or Old Royal Bath) to the
left is by John Wood the Younger. We continue on Hetling Court,
past the back of *Hetling House* (now the Abbey Church House), one

of the city's few Elizabethan houses (1570, restored 1954). A right turn on Westgate Buildings takes us past Kingsmead Square, where the baroque *Rosewell House* is by John Strahan (1736). Sawclose, heading N, has the *Theatre Royal*, with a façade of 1804–05 by George Dance the Younger, and the house (now a restaurant) where Beau Nash died. We continue N to Queen Square (1728–34), the first of John Wood the Elder's major contributions to the city. He lived and died not at No. 24, where his memorial plaque is placed, but at a house on the site now occupied by the *Reference Library* on the W side. The building also contains the *Geology Museum*, based on the North Somerset collection of Charles Moore (1814–81).

In New King St., off the SW corner of the square via Chapel Row and Charles St., the *Herschel Museum* was home of the astronomer and musician Sir William Herschel (1738–1822). The dramatist Sheridan lived at No. 9 at the time of his elopement with Elizabeth Linley (1772).
    From Queen's Parade, off the NW corner of the square, a flight of steps leads to a footpath curving past the back of the Circus to a superb view of the Royal Crescent (see below).

Gay St., also by the elder Wood, climbs N from Queen Square to his masterpiece, the *Circus, begun in 1750 and planned so that a true crescent faces each of its three approaches. In Bennett St., to the right, are the **Assembly Rooms** (open; inclusive ticket with Pump Room and Roman Baths and Museum), built by the younger Wood in 1769–71, gutted by fire in 1942 and since restored. They now house a lively *Museum of Costume with exhibits from 1850 to the present. Along Brock St. to the left of the Circus is the younger Wood's masterpiece, the *Royal Crescent (1767–74). Its leisurely, majestic sweep is both the perfect foil to the enclosed space of the elder Wood's Circus and the final realisation of the Palladian grace to which the architects of Bath aspired. No. 1, beautifully restored and furnished by the Bath Preservation Trust, is open to the public.

The charming *Royal Victoria Park*, W of the Crescent, is the largest of the city's many green spaces, with a botanic garden.—At No. 35 St James's Square, behind the Crescent, Dickens conceived the character of Little Nell while visiting the poet Walter Savage Landor.
    See North-Western Outskirts below for an extension of the walk N from the Crescent to Lansdown Crescent and Lansdown Hill.

NORTH AND EAST FROM THE CENTRE. High St. leads N from the abbey to Bridge St. The attractive alleyways of shops on the left include the Corridor (1825), Northumberland Place and Union Passage. On the right are municipal buildings whose nucleus is Baldwin's *Guildhall* of 1768–75, containing a great Adam-style *Banqueting Room* (open unless otherwise booked) with Whitefriars chandeliers of 1778 and portraits of George III and Queen Charlotte. In the N wing is the *Public Library* and the **Victoria Art Gallery**.

Many portraits from its permanent collection are hung in the other public buildings of Bath. The gallery's own temporary displays (supplemented by travelling exhibitions) draw from a rich stock of items connected with the city, including works by the local Barker family, Rowlandson, Thomas Malton and Sickert. The European collection includes a 15C Flemish 'Adoration of the Magi' attributed to Hugo van der Goes.

Bridge St. leads to the charming little *Pulteney Bridge*, flanked with shops. Built by Robert Adam in 1769–74, it is his one major contribution to the city's architecture. On the other side of the river Laura Place, with a fountain and a Victorian pillar-box, marks the

start of the long Great Pulteney St., designed by Baldwin (1788) and
unbroken on the left except for a terrace overlooking Henrietta Park.
Beyond the *Postal Museum*, on the right, the street ends at the
**Holburne of Menstrie Museum**.

Housed in a building of 1796–97, originally a hotel, the collections grew from
the bequest of Sir Thomas Holburne (d. 1874). Particularly strong is the
collection of English paintings, among them portraits by Gainsborough, Allan
Ramsay and Raeburn and works by Stubbs, Henry and George Morland, and
the Barkers of Bath. European works include 17C Italian and French as well as
Flemish and Dutch paintings. Also exhibited are English and continental silver
and porcelain, Italian majolica, and Italian Renaissance bronzes. The Crafts
Study Centre (opened in 1977) concentrates on 20C British work.
Jane Austen lived in youth with her parents at No. 4 Sydney Place, to the right
of the museum.—Behind the museum lie the shady *Sydney Gardens*, laid out in
1795 as the 'Vauxhall' of Bath. They are crossed by Brunel's Great Western
Railway and the Kennet and Avon Canal.
See Eastern Outskirts below for Sham Hill.

EAST FROM THE CENTRE. On York St., immediately S of the Pump
Room and Abbey Churchyard, is the picturesque cobbled square of
Abbey Green, with *Sally Lunn's House*, reputedly the oldest house in
Bath (now a tea shop), around the corner on North Parade Passage.
We follow York St. E to North Parade, passing *Ralph Allen's Town
House*, built for the self-made magnate by the elder Wood in 1727. It
originally enjoyed a clear view eastward to his folly, Sham Castle
(see Eastern Outskirts below). North Parade and South Parade
(reached by Pierrepont St. or Duke St.), begun in 1740, belong to one
of the elder Wood's earliest grand designs for the city. To the N are
the pleasant *Parade Gardens*. Near *North Parade Bridge* is the
so-called *Sheridan's Grotto*, a stone alcove once used as a 'post
office' for lovers' secret letters.

NORTH-WESTERN OUTSKIRTS. About 1m NW of the centre, beyond the Royal
Crescent and St James's Square, is Lansdown Crescent (1789–93; John Palmer).
William Beckford, author of 'Vathek', lived at No. 20 and adjoining houses from
1823, when he left Fonthill Abbey, until his death in 1844. Somerset Place
(c 1790) and Camden Crescent (c 1788), both by John Eveleigh, also command
fine views of the city. On Lansdown Hill, another 1m NW, stands the
neo-classical *Beckford's Tower*, built for the writer by E.H. Goodridge in 1827. It
contains a small museum, and the belvedere on top has one of the best views in
the West of England. The site of the Battle of Lansdown (1643), 2¹/2m N, is
marked by and 18C monument to the Royalist victor, Sir Bevil Grenville, killed
on the battlefield (English Heritage, open at any reasonable time). From
*Prospect Stile*, 2m W of the tower and situated on a well-defined Roman road,
both Bath and Bristol are visible.

NORTH-EASTERN OUTSKIRTS. We take A4, the London road, along the N bank of
the Avon. Above (2m) *Bailbrook* rises Little Solsbury Hill (NT) with an Iron Age
hill-fort. A left turn just before we enter *Batheaston* leads in a little over 2m to *St
Catherine's*, with the remains of a 16C grange and a church of 1490 with
contemporary glass.

SOUTH-WESTERN OUTSKIRTS. The village of *Englishcombe* near the Wansdyke,
off A367 4m SW of the centre, has a tithe barn and a church with grotesque
Norman sculpture on its N side and a figure of a swaddled child above the
chancel arch.

SOUTHERN OUTSKIRTS. *Beechen Cliff*, rising above the Avon just S of the
railway station, gives the best near view of the city. It is reached by crossing the
Southgate Footbridge and then following either Holloway or the steps climbing
from Lyncombe Hill.

SOUTH-EASTERN OUTSKIRTS. Prior Park Rd climbs steeply from Claverton Rd, S
of the river by the railway station. After about ¹/2m the narrow Church St. leads
left to *Widcombe*, with the lovely Widcombe Manor (not open) opposite the
church. At Widcombe Lodge nearby Henry Fielding wrote part of 'Tom Jones'.
The hill continues beyond the turning for Church St. to (1m) **Prior Park**

(grounds and chapel open), the magnificent Palladian mansion John Wood the Elder built for Ralph Allen in 1743. Allen's friendship with Pope, Fielding and other writers of the age makes it rich in literary associations. Altered, damaged by fire and now in use as a Catholic school, the house still has its fine chapel, and there is a lovely Palladian bridge in the grounds. From *Combe Down*, above Prior Park, a pleasant footpath leads down into Widcombe.

EASTERN OUTSKIRTS. On Bathwick Hill, about 1m beyond Sydney Gardens, is *Sham Castle*, an artificial ruin built for Ralph Allen in about 1760, with good views. *University of Bath* lies on Claverton Down beyond. For Claverton, see the route to Bradford-on-Avon below.

FROM BATH TO BRADFORD-ON-AVON, 9m by A36 and B3108. A36, the Warminster road, follows the S bank of the canal.—2m. *Bathampton*, to the left, was the home of the painter Walter Sickert from 1938 until his death in 1942. He is buried in the churchyard.—3½m. *Claverton*, right of A36, has the grave of Ralph Allen. The manor house of 1820 by Sir Jeffry Wyatville is an **American Museum** with 17–19C domestic interiors imported from America (Shaker room, Pennsylvania Dutch room, etc.) and folk art. A plaque records that Sir Winston Churchill made his first political speech here in 1897.—4½m. Just short of *Limpley Stoke* we branch left on B3108, crossing the river and the canal and climbing tortuously to the lovely stone-built little town of (9m) **Bradford-on-Avon** (8800 inhab.; Tourist Information). *St Laurence's* is perhaps

*The Saxon church of St Laurence at Bradford-on-Avon*

the best Saxon church in the country. The lower part probably dates from Aldhelm's foundation in c 705, the arcading above from the end of the 10C. The flying angels over the chancel arch are particularly noteworthy. The *Town Bridge* is 17C, with two 13C arches and an almost unique lock-up made from an old bridge chapel (cf. Wakefield). The *Parish Church* is Norman, Dec. and Perp. with some good details. *Barton Farm*, to the S, has a remarkable early 14C tithe barn. *South Wraxall*, 3¹/₂m N, has a fine 15C manor, and at *Great Chalfield*, 3m NE, there is another house of the same period (NT) and a church with 15C wall paintings. *Westwood*, 1¹/₂m SW of Bradford, has another good manor house (NT), built in 1400–1620, and a church with a notable tower and glass of c 1520.

The return to Bath can be made via *Farleigh Hungerford*, on A366 3¹/₂m SW, where the late 14C *Castle* (English Heritage, standard opening but closed on Tuesdays and Wednesday afternoons in winter) has the tomb of its builder and the church (1443) has his stained-glass portrait, and, (2m further) *Norton St Philip*, where the 15C inn occupies the former guest house of the abbot of Hinton Charterhouse.

For *Dyrham Park*, off A46 8m N of Bath, see Rte 20.

From Bath to *London* and *Bristol*, see Rte 20; to *Wells*, see Rte 22.


# 22  Bath to Wells and the Mendip Hills

Total distance 23m. **Bath**, see Rte 21.—A367 to (8m) Radstock.—A367, A37 to (17m) **Shepton Mallet**.—A371 to (23m) **Wells**.

Maps: OS Landranger 172, 183, 182.

A39, the direct road from Bath to Wells via Farrington Gurney and Chewton Mendip, is shorter (20m) but less interesting.

**Bath**, see Rte 21. We leave Bath on A367, following the line of the Foss Way.—5¹/₂m. From *Peasedown St John* unclassified roads lead left to (2m) *Wellow*, the probable birthplace of the composer John Bull (?1562–1628), which has a faithfully restored church of 1372 with a fine roof and unique fresco of c 1500. About 1m S is *Stoney Littleton Long Barrow*, a neolithic chambered burial mound (English Heritage, open at any reasonable time).—8m. *Radstock*, with the neighbouring town of *Midsomer Norton* (18,300 inhab. together), was the chief centre of the Somerset coalfield; the last pit closed in 1973. Beyond the town A367, now on a markedly Roman alignment, leaves B3139, a more direct road to Wells, on the right.—At (11m) *Stratton-on-the-Fosse* a community of Benedictine monks expelled from Douai in 1793 founded *Downside Abbey* in 1814. It includes a boys' public school and a massive church (open to the public) built between 1874 and 1938, with the shrine of St Oliver Plunkett.—We climb the Mendip Hills to (14m) *Oakhill*.—17m. **Shepton Mallet** (6300 inhab.; seasonal Tourist Information) has a market place with 15C shambles and a restored 16C cross. Old houses survive in the adjoining network of lanes. There is a superb panelled wagon ⁺roof in the church. The grounds of the Bath and West Agricultural Show, held in early June, lie to the SE.—A371 runs W along the pretty valley of the Sheppey.—19¹/₂m. *Croscombe* church has good Jacobean woodwork.

23m. **WELLS** (9000 inhab.; Tourist Information), with its great cathedral, is a quiet market town at the foot of the Mendip Hills. Wholly ecclesiastical in origin and development, it keeps much of its medieval character; market place, cathedral, Bishop's Palace and the old buildings of the clergy form a harmonious group.

The irregular market place is enclosed by the 17C *Crown Hotel*, the *Town Hall* of 1779 and a N side built c 1450 by Bishop

Wells Close

# WELLS CATHEDRAL

Key to Numbers

1 Bp. Haselshawe
2 Bp. Ergum
3 Bp. Wm. of March
4 Viscountess Lisle
5 Thomas Boleyn (?)
6 Chan. Milton
7 Bp. Harewell
8,9,10 Saxon Bishops
11 Bp. Wm Bytton II
12 Bp. Ld. Arthur Hervey
13 Bp. Lake
14 Bp. Beckington
15 Bp. Duduc
16 Dean Gunthorpe
17 Bp. Drokensford
18 Canon John Martel
19 Dean Godelee
20 Dean Creighton
21 Chan. Biconyll
22 Bp. Giso
23 Bp. Ralph of Shrewsbury
24 Bp. Berkeley
25 26 Saxon Bishops
27 Bp. Still
28 Bp. Kidder
29 Bp. Cornish

Beckington. The *Bishop's Eye* leads to the Bishop's Palace (see below) and the *Penniless Porch* (where alms were distributed) to the cathedral close, known as Cathedral Green, rivalled in its calm beauty only by the close at Salisbury. This, however, is best entered by *Browne's Gate* (or the *Dean's Eye*) in Sadler St., where the whole astonishing façade of the cathedral bursts on the view. All these gates were built by Bishop Beckington.

The **∗∗Cathedral**, famous for its W façade and its 'scissors arches', is wonderfully complete in all its parts. Certainly among the most beautiful English cathedrals, it may also be simply the most beautiful.

Tradition says that a church of St Andrew was founded by King Ine c 705 near the springs which have given the city its name. In 909 Wells became the seat of the new bishopric of Somerset, but Bishop John de Villula (1088–1122) transferred the see to the walled town of Bath. Under Bishop Savary (1192–1205) the title of the see was 'Bath and Glastonbury'. Bishop Jocelin (1206–42) returned to Wells and in 1219 surrendered the claim to Glastonbury, retaining the title 'Bath'. His successors ever since 1244 have been Bishops of 'Bath and Wells', and the monks of Bath and the canons of Wells had equal voices in the election of the bishops until the suppression of the abbey of Bath in 1539.

The present cathedral was begun c 1180 under Bishop Reginald. The three W bays of the choir, the transepts, and the E bays of the nave were probably finished soon after 1200. The N porch was built for Bishop Jocelin, who also saw completed the nave, and the famous W front designed by Thomas Norreys (fl. 1229–49). The church was consecrated in 1239. To the Dec. style belong the chapter house (1293–1306), with its staircase and earlier undercroft (1286), and the central tower, raised to its present height in 1321. The present 'Lady Chapel behind the high altar' (as it was called to distinguish it from an earlier 'Lady Chapel next to the cloister'), the three E bays of the choir, and the retrochoir were rebuilt under Dean Godelee and completed c 1325. The Perp. W towers, designed by William de Wynford (d. 1405), were largely paid for by two bishops: the SW tower by Bishop Harewell (d. 1386) in his lifetime, and the NW tower by Bishop Bubwith (d. 1424) in a legacy. The cathedral suffered at the hands of Puritans and Monmouth's rebels. It was restored in the 19C by Benjamin Ferrey and by Anthony Salvin; further restoration of the W façade was carried out in 1975–86.

The ∗∗W façade is pure EE work that challenges comparison with Reims or Amiens. Its vast screen, divided vertically by six buttresses, is made unusually wide (147ft) by placing the W towers (Perp. in their upper stages) not at the end of the aisles but outside them. This provides the framework for a superb display of ∗∗statues and sculptural detail by a local school of craftsmen. There were originally over 400 figures in full colour, carried in six tiers across the whole façade and round the sides of the towers. Nearly 300 remain, about half of them life-size or larger, making the finest collection of medieval sculpture in England. The damage done by weather and iconoclasm prevents identification in many cases. In the tympanum of the main portal are the Virgin and Child; in the niche above, the Coronation of the Virgin. The gable has the nine orders of angels, the apostles and the Saviour (a replacement figure by David Wynne, 1985).

Also on the exterior, the N side of the nave has an elegant Dec. parapet (c 1326) and Perp. window tracery. The ∗N Porch, now even more exquisite carving, was built c 1213. On the N transept is a clock (15C dial repainted in the 19C) with two ∗figures in armour striking the quarters with their battle axes (c 1470). The Chain Gate, an elegant Perp. bridge (1443–65), connects the chapter house with Vicars' Close.

When we enter the cathedral from the W end, our attention is immediately caught by the remarkable double straining ∗arch, or 'scissors arch', one of three added c 1338–48 to support the weight of the tower (completed by the addition of a spire c 1322). Like the octagon at Ely, these arches are at once a bluntly technical solution to an engineering problem and a wonderful visual coup. The rich architecture of the *Nave* makes it look taller than it is (67ft), and the unbroken row of lancets in the triforium greatly increases its apparent length. The chief decorations are the elaborate ∗capitals, and the medallions and carvings in the spandrels of the lancets in the triforium. The S clerestory has an early Perp. gallery. On the N side is the hexagonal Perp. chantry of Bishop

*The 'scissors arches' in Wells Cathedral*

Bubwith (d. 1424), with an alabaster panel of the Ascension; opposite is the chantry of Treasurer Hugh Sugar (d. 1489), with a stone pulpit of 1547 attached. The imposing lectern (1661) was a gift of Bishop Creighton; the sidelights of the W window have remains of enamel-painted glass (1670–72) presented by him.

The space beneath the tower, which is EE with fan-tracery vaulting, is bounded on three sides by the scissors arches; on the fourth is a 14C screen adapted to carry the organ. The aisled transepts (c 1190) have carved *capitals. In the *N Transept* is the *clock (1386–92) with its contemporary astronomical indications and tournament of knights; the original works are at the Science Museum in London. In the *S Transept* are the Chapel of Calixtus, containing a tomb (c 1440) with unique representations of medieval choir vestments and alabaster *panels of the Annunciation and the Trinity, and the Chapel of St Martin, with the tomb of Chancellor William Biconyll (d. 1448). By the S wall of the transept are a 19C copy of the brass of Viscountess Lisle (d. 1464) and the tomb of Bishop William of March (d. 1302). The Saxon font comes from the earlier cathedral.

In the S choir aisle are the tombs of Bishop William Bytton II (d. 1274), with the oldest incised slab in England, and Bishop Beckington (d. 1465), with an exquisite canopy, iron screen and 'memento mori'. The effigies of Saxon bishops were probably set up c 1205 to vindicate the priority of the see of Wells over that of Bath. Both aisles keep some 14C glass, while the *SE Transept* has glass (1500–25) from Rouen by pupils of Arnold of Nijmegen, acquired in 1812 and 1953, and also the effigy of Bishop Drokensford (d. 1329). Adjoining the SE chapel is the lofty tomb of Canon John Martel (d. c 1350).

Of the *Choir*, the first three bays (EE, end of 12C) formed the original presbytery, the ritual choir then extending from the space under the tower to the first bays of the nave. The E portion of the choir is in a rich Geometric Dec. style; its lierned stone vaulting recalls the wooden roofs common in Somerset. The 14C stalls, backed by a Victorian stone canopy, have 61 *misericords. The E end of the choir is formed by three arches surmounted by the E window, with *glass of c 1340 depicting a Tree of Jesse. Over the low screen behind the altar we get a charming view of the *Retrochoir* and *Lady Chapel*. Both are Dec. but the retrochoir was added later, uniting the Lady Chapel with the presbytery by four supporting pillars and some ingenious vaulting. The Lady Chapel itself, finished before 1326, is an irregular octagon; its large windows are filled with fragments of superbly coloured glass (c 1320). We now pass the *NE Transept*, with a sculpture of the Ascension and the monuments of Bishop Creighton (d. 1672) and Chancellor Milton (d. 1337). In the N choir aisle are the fine alabaster effigy of Bishop Ralph of Shrewsbury (d. 1363), the monument of Bishop Berkeley (d. 1581) and more effigies of Saxon bishops.

From the N transept an exquisite early Dec. staircase leads to the octagonal **Chapter House**, in the full Dec. style and the finest of its period in England. Probably finished c 1306, it has 32 delicate vaulting ribs springing from the central pier. The double-arched doorway, the old glass in the lights of the beautiful windows, the corbels of the vaulting and the carved heads on the springers of the arcade formed by the 51 stalls are all worth attention. The staircase continues over the Chain Gate to Vicars' Close (see below).

From the S transept a doorway leads to the *Chapter Library*, built over the E walk of the cloisters in 1425. It contains 6000 books, original charters from 968 onwards and a crozier with 13C Limoges enamelling. The three-sided *Cloisters*, also entered from the S transept, were rebuilt c 1425–1508. A Perp. Lady Chapel adjoining the E walk was destroyed in 1552. The walls are lined with tablets removed from the cathedral, including one on the E side to the Wells composer Thomas Linley (1732–95) and his daughters, one of whom married the dramatist Sheridan. The central space is known as the 'Palm Churchyard', probably because of the Palm Sunday procession which passed through it.

The ***Bishop's Palace**, S of the cathedral, is still used by the bishop; the grounds and part of the buildings are open on limited afternoons in summer. The surrounding walls and moat were added by Bishop Ralph of Shrewsbury (1329–63). The swans in the moat are summoned by bell at 11.00 and 16.00 each day; they find the bell-rope let down and ring the bell themselves to demand bread. Beyond the 14C gatehouse are the ruins of the magnificent *Great Hall*, built by Bishop Burnell (1274– 92) and dismantled under Bishop Barlow (1549–54). Bishop Burnell's *Chapel* is a beautiful piece of Dec. work. The *Palace* itself was built by Bishop Jocelin in 1230–40. To the SW is the long, buttressed *Bishop's Barn*, a perfect specimen of the early 15C. A path leads round the S side of the moat and back to the road, giving a good view of the finest E end in England, with the Dec. central tower, octagonal chapter house (fine gargoyles) and octagonal Lady Chapel standing clear of the choir.

On the N side of the Cathedral Green is the *Old Deanery*, partly rebuilt by Dean Gunthorpe in 1472–98. Adjoining it is the *Museum*, the rebuilt Chancellor's House, with finds from Wookey Hole and other local antiquities. Next comes the *Music School* of Wells Cathedral School, incorporating the hall of the Archdeaconry (now used as a concert hall), modernised but dating from c 1280 and with a 15C timber roof.

Further E and connected with the N side of the cathedral by the bridge over the Chain Gate lies the unique 14C ***Vicars' Close**, built by Bishop Ralph and his successors for the College of Vicars Choral, the deputies of the canons. It consists of two rows of 21 houses, altered but keeping their original charm. Between the Chain Gate and the close is the Vicars' Hall, or refectory (completed 1348), where the members of the college ate together. At the further end of the close is the tiny chapel, altered by Bishop Beckington. Beyond is the 14–18C *Tower House* and, opposite, the *Prebendal House*, a 15C building with a superb porch, assigned to the principal of the college.

In East Liberty and North Liberty handsome domestic buildings of many periods are now part of Wells Cathedral School.

The civic church of *St Cuthbert is the largest parish church in Somerset. It has an assertive Perp. tower of the local type, ornate roofs, a carved pulpit of 1636 and, in the transepts, two well-carved though mutilated reredoses (one a Jesse Tree). Close by are *Bishop Bubwith's Almshouses* (1436, with 17C additions).

Wells makes a good centre for touring the **Mendip Hills**. This limestone chain, about 25m long and never more than 6m wide, stretches from near Frome (Rte 24) in the SE to meet the coast at Weston-super-Mare (Rte 20). Its southern edge, now marked by the course of A371, rises out of the Somerset marshes. The central plateau, most prominent between Shepton Mallet and Shipham, reaches 1066ft at Blackdown, between Cheddar and Burrington Combe. The hills are known for their gorges, caves and 'swallow-holes', though the most famous caves are now sadly commercialised. Some show traces of prehistoric settlement, while the uplands have open trenches (or 'scruffs') and spoil heaps from Roman lead mining.

A 35m circuit of the Mendips from Wells begins by taking a sideroad 2m NW to *Wookey Hole* (open), where the river Axe gushes to the surface. Three caves are open; twelve more have been explored. Bone remains found in the Hyaena Den show occupation from c 35,000 BC to c 12,000 BC. The caves are now owned by Madame Tussaud's, who have added a museum as well as less appropriate amusements (restored 19C paper mill, traditional fairground, penny arcade, history of waxworks exhibition). A steep unclassified road climbs the hills to (5m) *Priddy* (789ft), where the Romans mined lead. A little higher up we join B3135. The road descends *Cheddar Gorge*, a narrow cleft winding more than 2m between dramatic limestone cliffs which rise to 430ft. The cliffs are perforated by caves with wonderfully delicate stalactites. *Cox's Cave* and the larger *Gough's Cave* are both open. Gough's Cave was inhabited from the Stone Age to Romano-British times; finds are displayed in the museum at the cave mouth.—11½m. *Cheddar* (Tourist Information) is a large village, crowded in summer, at the mouth of the gorge. The cheese for which it is famous is now widely made and imitated elsewhere.

*Wedmore*, in the marshland 4m S, gave its name to the peace concluded in 878 between King Alfred and Guthrum the Dane after the Battle of Ethandune (see Edington, Rte 24). The church has a fine 12C portal and a 15C St Christopher overpainted c 1520.

A371 leads W to (13½m) *Axbridge*, the centre of a strawberry-growing area. King John's Hunting Lodge is, despite its name, a Tudor merchant's house; owned by the NT, it now contains a small local museum. The commanding Perp. church has a nave roof of 1636.—We join A38 for about 1m (see Rte 23), before branching left to (15½m) *Winscombe* and (17m) *Banwell*, where the churches both have fine Perp. towers and good glass. At Banwell there are also fine roofs, W gallery, pulpit and a screen of 1522.—A368 now runs E along the N flank of the Mendips to (23m) *Burrington*.

An alternative way back to Wells from Burrington continues along A368 through woodland to (1m) *Blagdon*, overlooking a lake-reservoir. The village gave its name to the 'Blagdon Controversy' (1800–03), provoked by charges of Methodism against Hannah More's early experiments in Sunday School education. A368 then continues along the foot of the hills, with fine views and good churches at (4½m) *Compton Martin* and (10m) *Chewton Mendip*. A39 runs directly from here to (16m) Wells.

From Burrington B3134 climbs *Burrington Combe*, smaller and less plagued with tourists than Cheddar Gorge. While sheltering from a thunderstorm here, Augustus Toplady (1740–78) was inspired to write 'Rock of Ages'. The road passes just below *Blackdown*, highest point of the Mendip Hills, and the centre of Roman lead mining at *Charterhouse*.—At (31m) *Green Ore* we turn S on A39 for (35m) *Wells*.

# 23   Bristol to Exeter

Total distance 76m. **Bristol**, see Rte 20.—A38 to (32m) Bridgwater.—A38 to (44m) **Taunton** (Rte 19).—A38 to (51m) Wellington.—A38 to (58m) Waterloo Cross.—B3181 to (63m) Cullompton.—B3181 to (67m) **Exeter** (Rte 18A).

Maps: OS Landranger 182, 193, 181, 192.

M5 follows a roughly similar line.

**Bristol**, see Rte 20. We leave the city by Redcliffe Hill and Bedminster. Dundry Hill and tower are on our left as A38 climbs.—5½m. *Barrow Gurney*, with reservoirs.

B3130 leads left to (4½m) *Chew Magna*, a pretty place with Georgian houses and a Perp. church with tall tower. Near the charming village of *Chew Stoke*, 1m SW, is a huge reservoir formed by flooding the Chew valley.—*Stanton Drew*, 1½m further E, has *three neolithic stone circles, two avenues of standing stones, and the Cove, the remains of a burial chamber (English Heritage, standard opening but closed Sundays).

8m. *Lulsgate*, with Bristol airport, on the right.

*Wrington*, about 1½m NW of the road 3m further on, has one of the best Perp. church towers in the region. It was the birthplace of John Locke (1632–1704), remembered by a tablet in the churchyard wall, and the resting place of Hannah More (1745–1833). Barley Wood, her home in 1802–28, lies about 1m NE; she had previously lived at *Cowslip Green*, on the A38.

Between (13m) *Churchill* and (17m) *Axbridge*, we cross the W outliers of the Mendip Hills, explored in Rte 22. A38 then descends into the rich grazing flats, or 'levels', of North Somerset between the Axe and the Parrett.—23m. The isolated *Brent Knoll* (457ft; NT) breaks the monotony of the landscape; there is a fine *view from the Iron Age hill-fort on the summit. The church in the village on its further side is Norman with Perp. additions; it has satirical bench ends and a monument to John Somerset (d. 1663).

At (25m) *Highbridge* a road leads right for (1¾m) **Burnham-on-Sea** (14,900 inhab. with Highbridge; Tourist Information), a resort at the mouth of the Parrett. Its church has a white marble altarpiece carved by Grinling Gibbons as part of Wren's refurbishing of the chapel at Whitehall Palace in 1686.

32m. **Bridgwater** (30,300 inhab.; seasonal Tourist Information) is a busy town on the Parrett, here tidal. The local red brick—called 'Bath brick' after its maker, not the city—was manufactured from the clay and sand deposited by the river. A statue of Admiral Blake (1599–1657) stands in the Cornhill outside the *Market House* (1834), with a handsome curved colonnade. The Wednesday market includes an auction still conducted in pounds, shillings and pence. Blake's birthplace, in Blake St. to the S, is now the *Museum*, with relics of the admiral, the Duke of Monmouth and the Battle of Sedgemoor, and exhibits of old Bridgwater shipping and other local industries. The church of *St Mary*, in a quiet setting beind the Market Hall, has a slender spire built in 1366 by Nicholas Waleys. Inside are wide Dec. transepts (Jacobean screen in S transept), 15C chancel roof, Perp. pulpit, and a painting captured from a French ship of the Armada and given to the town in the 18C. West Quay has Dutch-gabled buildings and The Lions, a fine house of c 1730. *Castle Street is one of the best Georgian townscapes in Somerset, begun in 1723 by the Duke of Chandos.

In the marshes 3m SE of Bridgwater and 1m N of *Westonzoyland* is **Sedgemoor**, where the Duke of Monmouth's rebellion against James II was crushed on 6 July 1685, less than a month after he had landed at Lyme Regis and a fortnight after he had been proclaimed king at Bridgwater. A flagstaff and memorial stones mark the field where the dead lie buried. Westonzoyland church, notable for its lovely *roof of c 1500, has a memorial recalling the temporary imprisonment here of 500 rebel peasants, some score of whom were hanged in chains from the belfry battlements.

From Bridgwater to *Minehead* along the NE fringes of the Quantock Hills, see Rte 25A.

*The Somerset marshes: looking south-east over King's Sedge Moor from Greylake, near Westonzoyland*

36m. *North Petherton* church has a fine tower. It contains a replica of the 9C Alfred Jewel, found in nearby Parker's Field in 1693 and now in the Ashmolean Museum at Oxford (see also Burrow Mump and Athelney, Rte 24).—The church of (38m) *Thurloxton*, to the right, has wood furnishings of 1634.

44m. **Taunton**, Rte 19.—We cross the fertile valley to the smaller town of (51m) *Wellington* (10,600 inhab.; seasonal Tourist Information), from which the great duke took his title. The church has the tomb of Sir John Popham (d. 1607), the judge who tried Raleigh.

*Nynehead*, 2m N, has a church with sculptures by the della Robbia and other Italian artists, beside a manor house of 1675 (not open).—*Cothay Manor* (not open), near *Thorne St Margaret* 5m W of Wellington, survives largely unaltered as a 15C manor house.—To the S of Wellington rise the *Black Down Hills*, crowned by (2½m) the *Wellington Monument* (NT; 900ft). *Culmstock Beacon* (819ft), at their W extremity, has a stone fire turret.

We soon enter Devon. At (58m) *Waterloo Cross* A373 leads past the junction with M5 towards Tiverton (Rte 26). We continue S on B3181, the old A38. To the left is the Culm valley, leading to (7m) *Hemyock* at the foot of the Black Down Hills. We descend the river past (63m) *Cullompton*, where the fine Perp. ˙church has a richly carved roof, a magnificent tower and the beautiful 16C vaulted Lane aisle.—At the hamlet of (68½m) *Beare* we enter a large and finely wooded stretch of NT property. It includes *Killerton House*, reached by taking B3185 right at *Budlake*, a plain Georgian building by John Johnson (1778–79) that now contains the Paulise de Bush costume collection. The lovely hillside gardens, which have a chapel of 1841 by C.R. Cockerell, were first laid out in the late 18C.—71m. *Broadclyst* has a notable church.—At (73m) *Pinhoe* we reach the outskirts of (76m) **Exeter** (Rte 18A).

# 24  Marlborough to Taunton via Glastonbury

Total distance 74m. **Marlborough**, see Rte 20.—A4 to (7m) Beckhampton, then A361 throughout.—To (14m) Devizes.—To (24m) Trowbridge.—To (32m) Frome.—To (43m) Shepton Mallet (Rte 22).—To (52m) **Glastonbury**.—To (74m) **Taunton** (Rte 19).

Maps: OS Landranger 173, 183, 182, 193.

A361, running N from Beckhampton to Swindon, Lechlade, Burford, Chipping Norton and Banbury, makes an attractive link between the West Country and the Midlands.

**Marlborough**, see Rte 20. We follow A4 and Rte 20 to (7m) *Beckhampton*, just S of Avebury, where we turn S on A361. At 10m the road crosses the line of the *Wansdyke* and at 12m passes by *Roundway Hill*, to the right. In 1643 the Parliamentarian army was defeated at Roundway Down, on the other side of the hill.—14m. **Devizes** (10,600 inhab.; seasonal Tourist Information) stands at the mouth of the Vale of Pewsey. Once called *Ad Divisas* ('on the borders'), it owes its existence to the castle, since replaced, built by Bishop Roger of Sarum c 1150. It is now a busy market town with a *Town Hall* (1806–08) by Thomas Baldwin of Bath, a *Market Cross* (1814) by Benjamin Wyatt bearing an interesting inscription, and many handsome 18C buildings. The painter Sir Thomas Lawrence was son of the landlord at the Bear, one of several coaching inns that survive. The churches of *St John's*, with a fine tower, and *St Mary's* were founded by Bishop Roger, the former for the castle and the latter for the town; both were enlarged in the 15C. The *Museum* of the Wiltshire Archaeological and Natural History Society in Long St. has an outstanding collection of *prehistoric finds from the Wiltshire barrows, including the 'Marlborough Bucket', a Belgic wooden vat with bronze reliefs of the 1C BC. There are also exhibits from the Roman, Saxon and medieval periods, and a natural history display. The picture gallery has a window by John Piper.

Parallel to A361 W of the town the Kennet and Avon Canal descends by a series of 29 locks, like a gigantic flight of stairs.
    An alternative way from Devizes to Frome begins by taking A360 S.—2m. *Potterne* has a good EE church and the late 15C timber-framed Porch House. The church at *Urchfont*, 3m SE, has a fine chancel.—5m. B3098 leads W, along the edge of Salisbury Plain.—10m. *Edington* is probably the Saxon Ethandune, where King Alfred defeated the Danes in 878. The 14C *priory church is a beautiful example of the transition from Dec. to Perp. Among the monuments are two from the abandoned church at *Imber*, now in the military zone of Salisbury Plain to the SE. An annual festival of church music takes place in August.—We pass the White Horse of Westbury and reach (14) *Westbury*, on the Chippenham–Shaftesbury road (Rte 20). A3098 continues to (20m) *Frome*.
    From Devizes to *Andover*, see Rte 19.

At 21m we cross A350, the Chippenham–Shaftesbury Road (Rte 20).—24m. **Trowbridge** (23,000 inhab.; seasonal Tourist Information) is the most modest of English county towns, though the handsome Georgian and Regency houses in Fore St., The Parade and Round-stone St. testify to the wealth and taste of its cloth merchants. The poet George Crabbe, a reluctant exile from the Suffolk coast, was rector of the restored 15C church from 1813 until his death in 1832; his tomb is in the chancel. *Bradford-on-Avon* (Rte 21) lies 3m NW. —27½m. *Rode*, just over the Somerset border, was the home of Constance Kent, who confessed in 1865 to the murder of her infant half-brother here five years earlier. Rode Manor has tropical bird gardens (open).

32m. **Frome** (pronounced 'Froom'; 14,500 inhab.; seasonal Tourist Information) is solidly built in stone, with steep, narrow streets and a thriving market. The paved Cheap St. has a central water course. The 13C and late 14C parish church has suffered from restoration. Outside its E end is the tomb of the outspoken Bishop Ken (1637–1711).

The bishop died at *Longleat*, 4½m SE (Rte 18A). Other places in easy reach of Frome include *Lullington*, 2½m N, where the church has a Norman font and N doorway, and the attractive village of *Mells*, 3½m W, where the beautiful Perp. *church has monuments by Burne-Jones and Sir Alfred Munnings. The restored 16C manor house (not open) belongs to the Horner family, of which 'Little Jack Horner' is said to have been a member. *Witham Friary*, 5m SW of Frome, was the site of the first Carthusian monastery in England, founded in 1178–79 by Henry II in expiation of Becket's murder. The lay brothers' chapel, still in use as the parish church, was probably built by the third prior, St Hugh of Lincoln.

33½m. A361 skirts Marston Park. The church of *Marston Bigot* has 16C German glass and a monument probably by Westmacott.—35m. *Nunney*, N of our road where it is joined by A359, has a small moated castle of 1393 (English Heritage, open at any reasonable time). *Cloford* church, off A359 1m SW, has 17C monuments to the Horner family.—41½m. *Doulting* provided the stone for Wells Cathedral.

The heavily restored church has good timber roofs in the transepts.
—43m. **Shepton Mallet**, see Rte 22. We rejoin A361 SW of the town
just before (45m) *Pilton*, built on a steep hill, with a fine partly
Norman church and a Georgian manor house.

52m. **GLASTONBURY** (6800 inhab.), an ancient town at the base
of Glastonbury Tor, is famous for the ruined abbey where history and
legend combine to create a uniquely powerful atmosphere. Once the
most important pilgrim shrine in England, it now attracts summer
tourists in large numbers.

**Tourist Information Centre:** (seasonal) Northload St.

**Car Parks:** High St., Magdalene St., Northload St., Archer's Way and George
St., all near the market place; Bere Lane, near the Abbey Barn.

**Buses:** leave from opposite the Town Hall in Magdalene St.

**Annual Events:** Anglican pilgrimage on the last Saturday in June; the Roman
Catholic pilgrimage usually takes place on the previous Sunday. Carnival in
mid November.

The ***Abbey** (open) represents the earliest Christian foundation in
England. It survived Saxon, Danish and Norman conquests, and
presents a continuity of religious life unparalleled elsewhere.

According to the romantic legend, St Joseph of Arimathea and eleven companions brought the chalice of the Last Supper (or, according to another tradition,
the phials that held the blood of the Crucifixion) to Glastonbury in about AD 60.
Here, in the Druidic Isle of Avalon or Ynyswytryn, the 'Blessed Isle', they built
the 'Vetusta Ecclesia', or primitive church of wood and wattle. Refounded by
Pope Eleutherius in 166, the settlement was visited by St Patrick (who,
according to one legend, died here in 463) and by St Bridget (488). Larger
churches, always carefully including the Vetusta Ecclesia, were raised by Ine,
King of the West Saxons, in 708; by St Dunstan (d. 988), who was born and
educated at Glastonbury; and by Thurstin and Herlewin, the first Norman
abbots after the Conquest. Under Dunstan, who became abbot c 940 and
introduced the Benedictine rule, the abbey became a centre of learning and
gave England many great churchmen. The Saxon kings Edmund I (d. 946),
Edgar (d. 975), and Edmund Ironside (d. 1016) were buried here. Until 1154,
when precedence was given to St Albans, the mitred abbot of Glastonbury was
the premier abbot of England. The remains of King Arthur and Guinevere,
reputed to have been discovered here in 1191, were finally reinterred in front of
the high altar in 1276, in the presence of Edward I.
   In 1184 the whole abbey, including the Vetusta Ecclesia, was burned to the
ground. Rebuilding began at once and, except for a few later additions, was
completed in 1303. The first part to be finished was the Lady Chapel (often
called St Mary's Chapel), on the exact site of the old wooden chapel and, so it is
said, in strict fidelity to the ancient plan. The abbey was suppressed in 1539; the
last abbot, Richard Whiting, was executed on the Tor. After the Reformation the
buildings were neglected, and until about 1830 were used as the stone quarry of
the neighbourhood. The ruins were bought for the Church of England in 1908.

We enter from the market place by the *Abbot's Gate*, which contains
a museum. Of the vast *Church* the only remains are: the two E piers
of the central tower, with portions of the transeptal walls attached;
one of the N transeptal chapels, with groups of floor tiles; parts of
the S aisle walls of the nave and choir; and the W door. This leads into
the 13C Galilee connecting the church with the late Romanesque
*Lady Chapel (walls still standing), with rich carvings and interlac-
ing arcades. Beneath is a 15C crypt connecting with an ancient well.
The length of the whole range of buildings was shown to be about
590ft by the discovery in 1909 of the apsidal Edgar Chapel, built by
Abbot Bere, at the extreme E end. The foundations of St Dunstan's
Chapel at the extreme W, and of the N porch and the Loretto Chapel
on the N side of the nave, are marked on the ground, as well

as the sites of the chapter house, cloisters and the sub-vaults of the refectory and dormitory. To the SW is the 14C *Abbot's Kitchen*, with a high octagonal stone roof and lantern; it contains a small display illustrating monastic life.

In High St. are the *George and Pilgrims' Inn* of 1470 (now a hotel) and the *Abbot's Tribunal* (English Heritage, standard opening), with fine old woodwork. It houses a museum with interesting finds from the Iron Age lake villages of Meare and Glastonbury. The church of *St John the Baptist* (1465) has a fine tower and a 15C sarcophagus from the abbey. *St Benedict's*, built on older foundations by Abbot Bere, lies W of the market place.

In Bere Lane is the late 14C *Abbey Barn* (open), with emblems of the Evangelists and a fine collar-beam roof; together with the adjoining farmhouse, it is now a museum of Somerset rural life. In the garden of *Chalice Well*, at the base of the Tor nearby, is the chalybeate spring once venerated for its healing powers.

The **Tor** (NT; 521ft) E of the town commands a famous *view of Glastonbury, Wells and the Bristol Channel. It is crowned by the tower of the ruined chapel of *St Michael*.—On *Wearyall Hill* W of the town grew the original 'Glastonbury Thorn' (*Crataegus praecox*) which, according to the legend, sprang from St

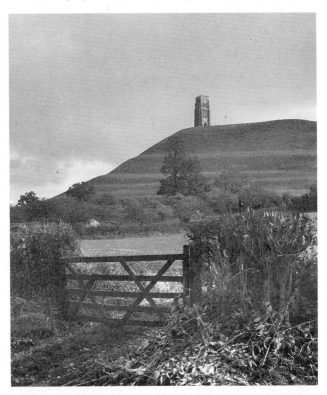

*Glastonbury Tor*

Joseph's staff. The tree was cut down by the Puritans but offshoots, which blossom at Christmas, can be seen in the abbey grounds and St John's churchyard.

*Meare*, on B3151 3½m NW, once stood by a large lake. It has the 14C Fish House of the abbey (English Heritage, open at any reasonable time) and the abbot's summer palace. Finds from the Iron Age lake village ½m NW are in the museums at Glastonbury and Taunton.— *Butleigh*, 4m S of Glastonbury, was the birthplace of Admiral Hood (1724–1816); his monument in the church has an epitaph by Southey.

A39 runs together with A361 to (53½m) *Street* (8800 inhab.), a little town dominated by Clark's shoe factory; there is a museum of shoemaking history. Off our road about 1½m NW lies *Sharpham Park* (not open), a manor house built by Abbot Bere and the scene of Abbot Whiting's arrest in 1539; the novelist Henry Fielding (1707–54) was born here.—57m. We follow A361 when it separates from A39, and cross King's Sedge Moor to (62m) *Othery*, where the church has a Perp. central tower. Westonzoyland and Sedgemoor (Rte 23) lie NW. In the drained marshes to the S King Alfred gathered his forces for the final struggle against the Danes in 878. The scene of his adventure with the burned cakes is laid here, and the 9C Alfred Jewel was found at nearby North Petherton (Rte 23).—64m. *Burrow Mump* (NT), an isolated hill rising above the fens near *Burrow Bridge*, is the probable site of Alfred's fort. *Athelney*, 1½m SW, has a memorial pillar.

Unclassified roads run S and W from Burrow Bridge to (4m) *Stoke St Gregory*, where the church has an early 14C octagonal crossing tower and some fine Perp. additions. We can continue along the S bank of the Tone to (5½m) *North Curry*, with an imposing church framed by a handsome medley of buildings, and (9m) *Creech St Michael* church, with a wagon roof and interesting 13C details. We rejoin the main road 1½m N.

At (70m) *Walford Cross*, near M5, A361 is joined by A38. When they divide 1m further on, A361 leads into Taunton from the N, A38 from the S.—74m. **Taunton**, see Rte 19.

# 25  The Quantock Hills

The **Quantock Hills** extend from near A38 and M5 between Bridgwater and Taunton towards the sea. Formed of the Old Red Sandstone characteristic of Devon rather than Somerset geology, they are an isolated outpost of Exmoor and the Devon moorland to the W. With their clear streams, wild red deer, heather and wortleberries, and their sheltered wooded combes, they rise gently from the Vale of Taunton Deane in the S, reaching their greatest height at Will's Neck (1261ft) 2m SE of Crowcombe, and fall steeply to the narrow coastal plain and the Bristol Channel. The officially designated Area of Outstanding Natural Beauty covers about 36 square miles, of which 750 acres are NT.

The two routes suggested below are primarily for the motorist and follow major roads around the fringes of the hills. A magnificent •walk of about 7m can be taken along the ridge from Lydeard Hill car park (½m NE of West Bagborough) to the Staple Plain car park (NT) at West Quantoxhead. It passes by Will's Neck and gives views of Dartmoor and the Black Down Hills to the S and W, Exmoor and the Brendon Hills to the W, the Mendip Hills to the E and the Somerset and Welsh coasts to the N.

Further information can be obtained from the Quantock Information Centre, Castle St., Nether Stowey and from Fyne Court, headquarters of the Somerset Trust for Nature Conservation, in Broomfield, 4¹/₂m N of Taunton.

# A.   Bridgwater to Minehead

Total distance 27m. **Bridgwater**, see Rte23. We follow A39 throughout.—To (8¹/₂m) **Nether Stowey**.—To (15m) West Quantoxhead.—To (18m) Williton.—To (25m) **Dunster**—To (27m) **Minehead**.

Maps: OS Landranger 182, 181.

**Bridgwater**, see Rte 23. We take A39 along the NE fringe of the Quantocks, with flat Somerset marshland to our right.—3¹/₂m. *Cannington* is home of the Somerset College of Agriculture and Horticulture, in an Elizabethan mansion on the site of a Benedictine priory, with a collection of tropical plants in its Court Gardens (open). *Combwich*, 1¹/₂m N, is a quaint village on the banks of the Parrett. The tidal mud flats and salt marshes of *Bridgwater Bay*, another 3m NE, are a nature reserve (restricted access via the Warden).—5m. An unclassified road leads S to (1¹/₂m) *Spaxton*, where the church has lovely carved bench ends, including one showing a fuller, or clothmaker, with his tools.—8¹/₂m. **Nether Stowey** (Quantock Information Centre) has the cottage (NT) where Coleridge lived from winter 1796 to 1798. Wordsworth came to live at Alfoxton (see below) in 1797, and the association of the two poets led to the publication of 'Lyrical Ballads'.

A fine scenic road leads across the hills to Crowcombe (Rte 25B).—At *Ramscombe*, about 2m SW of Nether Stowey, the Forestry Commission provides a forest trail.—*Stogursey*, 3m N of Nether Stowey, has a Norman priory church. There are plans to extend the nuclear power station at *Hinkley Point*, 3m further N.

10m. *Dodington*, right of A39, has a beautiful Elizabethan manor house (not open).—Near (11¹/₂m) *Holford*, a good centre for walks, is *Alfoxton* (or *Alfoxden*) *House*, Wordsworth's home in 1797 and now a hotel.—By the sea N of (13m) *Kilve* is a ruined 15C chantry.—14m. *East Quantoxhead* is a charming village.—From (15m) *West Quantoxhead*, at the end of the walk along the hills suggested above, we descend to the coastal plain and (18m) *Williton*, where our road is joined by A358 from Taunton (Rte 25B). The Orchard Hill Museum, with agricultural tools etc., is housed in a 17C watermill. *Watchet*, 2m N, is a small port on the Bristol Channel. The Market House Museum by the harbour has exhibits of local history and geology.—19¹/₂m. *Washford* lies just N of *Cleeve Abbey, founded for Cistercian monks in 1188 (English Heritage, standard opening). The abbey church has largely disappeared, but surviving buildings include the gatehouse of c 1530, cloisters, excellently preserved EE dormitory and the 15C *refectory, with a timber roof; there are also several fine doorways and tiled pavements.—22¹/₂m. *Carhampton* church has a lovely rood screen. The little resort of *Blue Anchor* lies 1m NE.

25m. **Dunster**, just inside the Exmoor National Park (with a seasonal National Park Information centre), is an immensely attractive old place. Its many interesting buildings include the 17C *Yarn Market* in the High St., the medieval *Butter Cross* NW of the church and *Gallox Bridge*, a medieval packhorse bridge of A396 to the S (all English Heritage, open at any reasonable time). The large *Priory Church* of 1150, enlarged in the 13C and 15C, has a good roof, a *screen of 1500 and Luttrell monuments. *Dunster Castle* (NT) was built by Mohun, Earl of Somerset, c 1070 and held by the Luttrells from 1376. It owes much of its present, emphatically romantic appearance to the embellishments by Anthony Salvin in 1867. The interior, with halls and library by Salvin, has late 17C plasterwork and woodcarving, and a unique series of mid 17C Dutch embossed leather hangings. Outstanding among the collection of family portraits is Hans Eworth's painting of Sir John Luttrell (1550). On the river Avill near the grounds is the restored 18C *Castle Mill* (NT).

A396 goes up the wooded valley of the Avill to (7m) *Wheddon Cross* (see Rte 27B).

27m. **MINEHEAD** (11,200 inhab.; Tourist Information) is a seaside resort. The picturesque quay and harbour at its W end lie beneath the old village, where steep lanes lead up to the 14C church (good screen inside). In the centre of the lower town is a statue of Queen Anne (1719). There is a large holiday camp at the E end. In summer there are daily excursions from the seafront along the old West Somerset Railway to Bishop's Lydeard (Rte 25B).

There is a nature trail on the cliffs to the NW, and a fine stretch of the Somerset and North Devon Coast Path to the W, leading past *North Hill* (*view) to (3½m) *Selworthy Beacon*. For this and other parts of Exmoor, see Rte 27A.


# B.   Taunton to Minehead

Total distance 24m. **Taunton**, see Rte 19.—A361 to (2m) Norton Fitzwarren.—A358 to (5m) Bishop's Lydeard.—A358 to (10½m) Crowcombe.—A358 to (15m) Williton.—A39 to (22m) **Dunster**.—A39 to (24m) **Minehead** (Rte 25A).

Maps: OS Landranger 193 (briefly) and 181.

**Taunton**, see Rte 19. We take A361 to (2m) *Norton Fitzwarren* (Rte 26), then branch right on A358 through part of the Vale of Taunton Deane and along the SW fringe of the Quantocks.—5m. *Bishop's Lydeard*, on the right, has a Perp. church with good woodcarving and a 14C churchyard cross. The old West Somerset Railway runs to Minehead (Rte 25A).

From the car park at *Lydeard Hill*, beyond *West Bagborough* 3m N, we start the walk along the ridge of the Quantocks suggested above.

At (6¾m) *Combe Florey*, on the left, Sydney Smith was rector from 1829 to 1845 and Evelyn Waugh (1903–66) spent his last years. *Gaulden Manor* (open), near *Tolland* 3m further W, is partly 12C, with good plasterwork. It was once the home of the Turbervilles. The *Brendon Hills* appear to the left of A358.—9m. *Crowcombe*, to the right, has a Perp. church with good bench ends and two crosses, 12C and 14C. Opposite is the 15C Church House (open), a rare survival. A fine scenic road crosses the Quantocks to Nether Stowey (Rte 25A).

—11m. *Halsway Manor*, on the right, is partly medieval and partly 19C. Now a centre for folk music and dance, it is open by prior appointment.—13m. *Bicknoller* church has a carved screen and Tudor bench ends.

*Stogumber*, 2m SW, has attractive cottages and a Perp. church with a good 17C monument to Sir George Sydenham (d. 1597). The priest who prosecuted Joan of Arc came from Stogumber. *Combe Sydenham Hall* (open), in a pleasant valley 2m further W, is a mainly Elizabethan building, recently restored.

At (15m) *Williton* we join A39 and follow Rte 25A to (24m) **Minehead**.

# 26 Taunton to Barnstaple and Ilfracombe

Total distance 64m. **Taunton**, see Rte 19. We follow A361 throughout.—To (20m) Bampton.—To (38m) South Molton. —To (50m) **Barnstaple**.—To (64m) **Ilfracombe**.

Maps: OS Landranger 193, 181, 180.

**Taunton**, see Rte 19. A361 winds through magnificent scenery S of the Brendon Hills and Exmoor (explored in Rte 27).—2m. *Norton Fitzwarren*, a centre of cider making, has a good church screen of 1509. A358 branches right, past the Quantocks to Minehead (Rte 25B).—7m. *Milverton*, to the left, has a Georgian main street and a fine Perp. church with carved woodwork.—11m. *Wiveliscombe*.—We enter Devon before (20m) *Bampton*, a small town with Georgian houses. It makes a good starting-point for excursions into Exmoor (Rte 27B).

FROM BAMPTON TO EXETER, 21$\frac{1}{2}$m, following A396 down the valley of the Exe.—7m. **Tiverton** (16,500 inhab.; seasonal Tourist Information) is an old market town on the Exe. *Tiverton Castle* (open) was begun in 1066 and keeps its 14C gatehouse, two towers and the ruins of its walls amid much later addition and restoration. The fine *Church*, 15C but freely restored, contains the richly carved Greenway Chapel (1517) and an organ of 1696 by Father Smith. The *Museum* near the Town Hall has a folk collection and relics of Tiverton's lace-making industry. The old buildings of *Blundell's School* (NT, only the forecourt open), founded in 1604, stand on the bank of the Loman. R.D. Blackmore (1825–1900) was a pupil, and sent John Ridd of 'Lorna Doone' to school here. There are trips along the Grand Western Canal from Canal Hill in summer. *Knightshayes Court* (NT), 1$\frac{1}{2}$m N, is a spirited piece of Victorian Gothic begun in 1869 by William Burges. The richly decorated interiors, now being restored, are by Burges and Crace. The garden has extravagant topiary.—11$\frac{3}{4}$m. *Bickleigh Bridge* dates from 1640. *Bickleigh Castle* (open), $\frac{1}{2}$ m S on the W bank of the Exe, has a Norman chapel and 15– 17C gatehouse.—21$\frac{1}{2}$m. *Exeter*, see Rte 18A.

A361 crosses the Exe valley.—38m. *South Molton* (seasonal Tourist Information) has a pleasant old centre with a Guildhall of 1743 and a Victorian covered market. From B3226 3m N, a sideroad leads across Exmoor to (11m) *Simonsbath* (Rte 27B). At *Charles*, left of B3226 another 3m N, is the rectory where the novelist R.D. Blackmore spent his boyhood.—Just before (42m) *Filleigh* we pass, on the right, the splendid mansion of *Castle Hill*, built in 1684, enlarged c 1730–40 and rebuilt after fire in 1934 (open by appointment in summer). It has a good collection of 18C furniture, tapestry, porcelain and pictures.—45m. *Swimbridge* church has a notable rood screen.

50m. **BARNSTAPLE** (19,000 inhab.), at the head of the Taw estuary, has many handsome old buildings to remind the visitor of its long history as a seaport and market town. It makes a good centre for exploring North Devon.

**Tourist Information Centre**: Cattle Market.

**Car Parks**: Cattle Market, Castle St., Vicarage St., Coronation St. Multi-storey car park off Queen St.

**Bus Station**: The Strand.

**Railway Station**: off A39 on the SW bank of the Taw.

**Theatre;** Queen's Hall Theatre, Boutport St.

**Annual Events**: Barnstaple Fair on the Wednesday before 20 September.

**History**. One of the four original burghs of Devon and the westernmost port in the Saxon kingdom of Wessex, *Beardastaple* received its first charter in 930. Athelstan established a mint and garrison here and a priory at nearby Pilton. The Normans fortified the town and built the castle and keep now marked by the mound on the NE bank of the Taw. The 'staple' in Barnstaple's name shows its early importance as a market centre and this, together with its position on the estuary, assured its continuing prosperity from the 16C to the 18C. The town contributed five ships to the fleet Drake used to defeat the Spanish Armada in 1588, and thrived on the trade with North America, particularly in woollen goods and pottery. The local Barum ware is still made.

**Natives and residents**: John Gay (1685– 1732) and the architect W.R. Lethaby (1857–1931) were Barumites. The martyr St Cuthbert Mayne (1544–77) was born at *Shirwell*, 4m NE. 'Saki' (H.H. Munro, 1870–1916) spent an unhappy childhood with his grandmother and maiden aunts at *Pilton*, 1/2m N.

The bridge of 16 arches spanning the Taw was originally built in the 13C but widened in 1796 and 1962. There is a pleasant riverside promenade. *Queen Anne's Walk* is a colonnade of 1796–98 with a statue of Queen Anne (1708). *St Peter's Church*, restored but dating in part from the 14C, has a crooked spire and interesting monuments. The former *St Anne's Chapel* (1330), now open as a local museum, served as the Grammar School; its pupils included St Cuthbert Mayne, Bishop Jewel of Salisbury (1522–71) and John Gay. High St. and Boutport St. have good 17C and 18C buildings, while *Horwood's Almshouses* and the *Maids' School* nearby, and the *Penrose Almshouses* in Litchdon St. E of the Square, are typical of 17C Barnstaple.

The church at *Pilton*, 1/2m N, has good woodwork.—The gardens (open) of Marwood Hill in *Marwood*, 4m N, are notable for their camellias.

A39 leads NE from Barnstaple to (7m) *Arlington Court* (NT), a Regency house with a collection of objets d'art. The building is perhaps less interesting than the grounds (museum of horse-drawn vehicles) and the beautiful wooded setting, with nature trails and walks to the Yeo valley. A39 continues to (10m) *Blackmoor Gate* and crosses Exmoor to (21 1/2m) *Lynton* and *Lynmouth* (Rte 27A).

From Barnstaple to *Exeter*, see Rte 18A.—To *Okehampton*, see Rte 29A.—To *Penzance* via the N coast, see Rte 35.

A361 follows the right bank of the Taw estuary, passing the RAF station at (53 1/2m) *Chivenor* on the left. The church of *Heaton Punchardon*, 1/2m to the right, has the sumptuous tomb of Richard Coffin (d. 1523).— 56 1/2m. *Braunton* has a large church dedicated to the Celtic St Brannock, with an early tower, good bench ends and other woodwork. Nearby is a local museum. To the SW is the 'Great Field', over 300 acres still cultivated on the medieval strip system. From *Saunton*, on B3231 2m W, the Somerset and North Devon Coast Path bisects the flat peninsula to the S, with *Braunton Burrows* nature reserve occupying one of the largest sand dunes in Britain. To the N, the path follows the headland round to Ilfracombe.—A361 follows the valley and then climbs to 662ft at (61½m) *Mullacott Cross*. Woolacombe (see below) lies on B3343 3½m W.

64m. **ILFRACOMBE** (10,100 inhab.) is the most popular seaside resort of North Devon, with good sands and a wide range of holiday amusements. Its chief merit, however, is its natural setting among spectacular cliff scenery, with pleasant woods and glens inland.

**Tourist Information Centre**: Promenade.

**Car Parks**: off High St. and Wilder Rd, and at the Pier.

**Bus Depot**: junction of Fore St. and Broad St.

**Amusements**: Victoria Pavilion, on the Promenade.

**Steamers**: to Lundy in summer, and cruises along the coast.

*Holy Trinity*, beyond the W end of High St., is a Norman church enlarged in 1322; it has richly carved wagon roofs. The steep turnings on the seaward side of High St. leads to *Wildersmouth Beach*, with *Capstone Hill* (181ft; view) and the *Victoria Pavilion* at its base. To the W are the *Tunnels Beaches*, approached through tunnels in the rock. To the SE of the Capstone are the *Harbour* and *Pier*, sheltered on the N side by *Lantern Hill*, with the remains of the 13C *Chapel of St Nicholas* (open) on its crest. Further SE is the sheltered *Rapparee Cove* beneath the lofty *Hillsborough* (447ft; view). At *Hele Bay*, on the other side of Hillsborough and reached from A399, is a restored 16C watermill (open). *Chambercombe Manor* (open), 1m SE of the town centre, is a small, mainly 16–17C house.

The scenery of the headland W of Ilfracombe is superb. Much of the land is owned by the NT and crossed by the Somerset and North Devon Coast Path. Immediately W of the town is the **'Torrs Walk**, a zigzag 'corniche' path giving lovely views of the sea. We continue past *Flat Point* to (3m) *Lee*, a pretty village famous for its fuchsias, a little inland from *Lee Bay*. From the bay a hilly footpath leads to (5m) *Bull Point Lighthouse*, and from here we may follow the road to (6½m) **Mortehoe**. The EE church, with a 14C tower, contains the tomb of William de Tracey (1321), a former vicar sometimes confounded with the murderer of Thomas Becket. *Morte Point*, a rock-bound headland 1m W, commands a wild and wide view. The road goes on S past (7m) *Barricane Bay*, with its beach of minute shells, to (7½m) **Woolacombe** (seasonal Tourist Information), with a sandy beach. The Somerset and North Devon Coast Path continues S, round (11m) *Baggy Point*, to join B3231 at (12¾m) *Croyde* for (14½m) *Saunton* (see above).

For Exmoor and the coastal route to *Minehead*, see Rte 27A.—For *Lundy*, see Rte 35.

# 27 Exmoor

Maps: OS Landranger 180 and 181, or OS Exmoor Tourist map (1:63,360 or 1in to 1m).

**'Exmoor** is today defined by the extent of the National Park which straddles Somerset and Devon. It reaches along the N coast from near Minehead in the E to Combe Martin, just short of Ilfracombe, in the W. Its southernmost point is beyond Dulverton near the confluence of the Barle and the Exe. Inside the 265 square miles enclosed by these boundaries lies some of the finest countryside in England, over 16,000 acres of it owned and protected by the National Trust. There are only about 10,000 inhabitants, most of them in small villages, and only four places large enough to qualify as towns:

Dunster, Porlock, and Lynton with Lynmouth in the N, and Dulverton in the S. Major roads are few, but there are more than 600 miles of public footpaths.

The region is given its distinctive character by the plateau of Old Red Sandstone and slate on which it stands, regularly reaching 1300ft and rising to its highest point at Dunkery Beacon (1704ft) S of Porlock. Its contours, at their gentlest in the Brendon Hills to the E, are everywhere less rugged than the granite tors of Dartmoor. The scenery is at its most spectacular on the coast, where the plateau abruptly meets the sea in a series of headlands interrupted only by the Vale of Porlock. England has few, if any, more beautiful stretches of coastline. The moors lie inland, including the tract known as Exmoor Forest, about 30 square miles centred on the village of Simonsbath and entirely in Somerset. (Here as elsewhere in England, the term 'forest' is merely a legal one. The region was mentioned as a royal forest in a charter of King John but lost this status in 1819). The countryside is sometimes boggy, with colourless tussocky grass, grey furze, bracken and heather. This bare hill pasture supports a hardy race of horned sheep. The characteristic wildlife includes the buzzard and the wild red deer. Two herds of the native Exmoor ponies have been established in recent years by the National Park Authority to maintain the numbers of this ancient breed.

The rivers that drain the plateau to both N and S add much to its beauty, creating rich green pasture in the wider valleys and thickly wooded clefts in the smaller ones. The West Lyn and East Lyn, with their many tributaries, flow N to make their dramatic joint exit into the Bristol Channel between Lynton and Lynmouth. To the W is Heddon's Mouth, while to the E the lovely little valley of the Avill runs down to the sea at Dunster. The Exe, flowing S past Exeter to the English Channel at Exmouth, is joined by the Haddeo and the Barle between Dulverton and Bampton in some of the region's most delightful scenery.

The Exmoor National Park Visitor Centre at Dulverton is open all year round; there are seasonal National Park Information Centres at Dunster, County Gate, Lynmouth and Combe Martin.

## A.  Minehead to Ilfracombe

Total distance 37½m. **Minehead**, see Rte 25A.—A39 to (6m) Porlock.—A39 to (16½m) **Lynmouth** and **Lynton**.—A39 to (28m) Blackmoor Gate.—A399 to (33m) **Combe Martin**.—A399 to (37½m) **Ilfracombe** (Rte 26).

This route is for motorists, but walkers can follow the magnificent scenery of the *Somerset and North Devon Coast Path all the way between Minehead and Ilfracombe.

**Minehead**, see Rte 25A. A39 undulates along the N verge of Exmoor, passing just S of (3½m) *Selworthy*, a pretty village with a green, tithe barn and fine Perp. church below *Selworthy Beacon* (1012ft), and (4m) *Allerford*, which has a two-arched packhorse bridge, a Museum of Rural Life and a Farm Park with rare breeds of animals.—6m. **Porlock** (the 'enclosed port') is a charming place in a fertile vale. The little 13C church of *St Dubricius* has the sumptuous tomb of Baron Harington (d. 1418) and his wife.

About 1½m W is the pretty little harbour of *Porlock Weir*, from which footpaths lead another 1¾m to *Culbone* church, the smallest parish church with nave and chancel in England.

**Dunkery Beacon** (1704ft; NT), a dark brown moorland hill and the highest on Exmoor, rises about 4m S of Porlock. Motorists can drive nearly all the way to the top, either by *West Luccombe* or by \*Horner Woods and Cloutsham. On a clear day the view from the Beacon extends from Brown Willy in Cornwall (S) to the Malvern Hills (N), and includes about 120m of the Bristol Channel. The descent can be made SE to (3½m) *Wheddon Cross* (Rte 27B) or NE to (3m) *Wootton Courtenay*; the narrow, winding road S of Cloutsham goes on to (4m) *Exford* (Rte 27B).

The long ascent of *Porlock Hill* by A39 (1 in 4 gradient with dangerous bends) can be avoided by an easier toll road to the right, which rejoins A39 just before (9m) *Oare Post*. Here an unclassified road branches left to (1½m) Oareford (see below). A little further on we reach the summit (1378ft) and begin a gentle descent through the woods of *Culbone Hill*, with fine views of the sea.

A sideroad on the left leads S to the countryside associated with R.D. Blackmore's 'Lorna Doone'. At (1m) *Oare* church the heroine was married to John Ridd and shot by Carver Doone. We continue W to (2m) *Malmshead*, with a Natural History Centre illustrating local wildlife. From here we walk S on a track that quickly becomes a footpath, following the course of *Badgworthy Water*. After 1m we reach the memorial erected by Blackmore's admirers in 1969; the stream nearby has been identified with the waterslide up which John Ridd struggles in the novel. Shortly beyond is the **Doone Valley** itself, less wild and romantic than readers of 'Lorna Doone' may have been led to expect. According to tradition, the Doones were a little clan of outlaws who made their headquarters here at the end of the 17C, terrorising the local countryside until a particularly atrocious act of cruelty goaded the inhabitants to crush them. The only trace of their settlement is the foundations of some huts. Blackmore, whose grandfather was rector of the adjoining parish of Oare, adapted and embellished the legend. The Doone valley lies 5m from Simonsbath (Rte 27B) by a rough moorland route. Good walkers who wish to see a really wild bit of Exmoor may continue SE from the Badgworthy valley for 1½m, turn E for (2½m) the *Chalk Water* and make their way down this stream to (6½m) *Oareford*; from here the road goes downstream to Oare and (8½m) Malmshead.

At (12m) *County Gate* (1059ft; seasonal Exmoor National Park Information) we enter Devon. Malmshead (see above) is about ¾m S by footpath. To the N are the beautiful grounds of \*Glenthorne and the *Old Barrow* (1135ft).—Beyond (15m) *Countisbury* (866ft) the road descends *Countisbury Hill* (1 in 4 gradient), with fine views. A path branches right to *Sillery Sands*.

16½m. **LYNTON** and **LYNMOUTH** (seasonal Exmoor National Park Information at Lynmouth; Tourist Information at Lynton) are picturesque and popular resorts. Lynmouth lies on the shore where the deep valleys of the East and West Lyn converge—a vulnerable position that made it the victim of devastating floods in August 1952. Lynton stands on the edge of the cliff 430ft above. Steep roads and a cliff railway connect the two. The best general views of the villages are from *Hollerday Hill*, W of Lynton, and *Summerhouse Hill* (850ft), climbed by a zigzag path beginning by the parish church in Lynmouth. Near the bridges in Lynmouth is the entrance to *Glen Lyn*, revealing the romantic cascades and fern-clad banks of the lower course of the West Lyn.

FROM LYNMOUTH TO WATERSMEET AND ROCKFORD, a walk of 4m. Leaving Lynmouth by Tors Rd, we quickly reach the path on the right bank of the East Lyn, which forces its way through the narrow Watersmeet valley, thickly wooded or strewn with rocks on either side. At (1¾m) \*Watersmeet (NT) the East Lyn is joined by Hoar Oak Water; a 19C fishing lodge now serves as NT shop, information centre, etc. Our path follows the left bank of the valley, rising considerably above the stream. Passing through Nutcombe Wood, we emerge (3m) on the hillside, but soon re-enter the woods by a small gate. Various paths lead right to the *Long Pool*, with its fall. Regaining the main path, we soon reach (4m) a bridge across the stream to *Rockford*. Hardy walkers may continue another 5m to the Doone valley (see above) by following the S bank of the river past (1m) *Leeford* to (3m) *Malmshead*. The return from Rockford to (3¾m) Lynmouth leads W to (½m) *Brendon* church and (1¼m) *Hillsford Bridge*, near A39.

FROM LYNTON TO COMBE MARTIN ALONG THE COAST ROAD, 12½m. The toll road runs inland off Hollerday Hill into the *Valley of the Rocks (walkers may take the cliff path called the *North Walk on the seaward side of the hill). Passing *Lee Abbey* and *Lee Bay* (superb views), the road drops steeply above (3½m) *Woody Bay*, a tiny resort enclosed by abrupt and richly wooded cliffs. A wide sweep, high above the sea (views), follows through (4½m) *Martinhoe*, then a steep descent to (6¾m) the *Hunter's Inn*, delightfully situated in the valley of the Heddon, about 1m above its mouth. From here a path on either side of the Heddon leads in 1½m to *Heddon's Mouth* (NT), a small cove ringed with cliffs and connected by a beautiful cliff path with Woody Bay (2m more, see above). The road (*views) now winds up above *Trentishoe* (1m; to the right), with a full view of the sea, to reach (9½m) a summit (989ft) between *Trentishoe Down* (1060ft; NT) to the left and *Holdstone Down* (1145ft; NT) to the right, before descending to (10¾m) *Stony Corner* (844ft), where several roads meet. On the coast to the right are the *Great Hangman* (1043ft; NT) and the *Little Hangman* (716ft), the E pillar of Combe Martin Bay. A steep hill joins A399 at the SE end of (12½m) *Combe Martin*.

As it leaves Lynton A39 climbs the East Lyn by *Hillsford Bridge*, crosses *Beggars Roost* (947ft), and drops down to (22½m) *Barbrook Mill* to meet the more direct road from Lynton and Lynmouth up the charming valley of the West Lyn. By *Dean Steep* we climb again to a summit of 1013ft at *Martinhoe Cross.*—26m. *Parracombe*, bypassed by A39 at the foot of a steep hill, has a disused church with Georgian interior.—At (28m) *Blackmoor Gate* we turn right on A399.

A39 continues to (10m) *Barnstaple* (Rte 26).—B3226 heads left, with *Wistlandpound Reservoir* on the right. From it B3358 branches left across Exmoor to (8½m) *Simonsbath* (Rte 27B).

33m. **Combe Martin** (seasonal Exmoor National Park Tourist Information), popular with tourists, straggles for 1½m along the road where the deep valley of the Umber makes its way to the sea. The 15C *Church*, with an EE chancel, has a fine tower and contains a sculptured effigy of 1634. The *Pack of Cards Inn* was reputedly built by a gambler. Further on, a road leads left to (½m) *Berrynarbor*, the birthplace of Bishop Jewel of Salisbury (1522–71), with a beautiful Perp. church tower.—34¾m. *Watermouth* has a 19C Gothic castle (open), much commercialised, and two caves.—We pass (36½m) *Hele Bay* and enter (37½m) **Ilfracombe** (Rte 26).

# B. Bampton to Lynton and Lynmouth

Total distance 35½m. **Bampton**, see Rte 26.—A396, B3222 to (5¾m) Exbridge.—B3222 to (8½m) **Dulverton**.—B3222 to (9¾m) Hele Bridge.—A396 to (17m) **Wheddon Cross**.—B3224, B3223 to (27m) **Simonsbath**.—B3223 to (33m) Hillsford Bridge.—A39 to (35½m) **Lynton** and **Lynmouth** (Rte 27A).

A devious cross-country route from the S of Exmoor to the coast, with several inviting detours and alternatives.

**Bampton**, on A361 between Taunton and Barnstaple, see Rte 26. The picturesque village of *Exebridge* can be reached directly by B3222

(2½m), but it is worth taking the longer route (5¾m) that follows A396 along the winding course of the river Exe and then branches left on B3222.

A396 continues up the valley of the Exe directly to (2¼m) Hele Bridge (see below). At 1¼m a turning on the right follows the side valley of the Haddeo E to (1m) *Bury* with its narrow hump-backed bridge.

B3222 continues NW from Exebridge up the valley of the Barle, which here marks the S boundary of Exmoor National Park, passing (6½m) *Brushford* on the left. At 8½m we reach **Dulverton** (Exmoor National Park Visitor Services), a fishing resort and a good centre for walks in the valley.

B3223 clings to the wooded banks of the Barle for ¾m and then begins to climb the hills. At 4m an unclassified road descends left into the valley where the river is crossed by (1½m) *Tarr Steps*, an ancient clapper bridge 180ft long, rebuilt after the floods of 1952. At 4¾m B3223 gives a fine view from the summit of *Winsford Hill* (1399ft; NT). At 6m another sideroad to the left descends into the valley at *Withypool*. At (8½m) *White Cross* we reach the junction with B3224 just W of Exford (see below).

From Dulverton B3222 runs E to (9¾m) *Hele Bridge*, where A396 heads N up the Exe valley.—12m. A sideroad leads left to (2m) *Brompton Regis* and, beyond, the large *Wimblehall Reservoir*.—At (14m) *Exton*, a typical Exmoor lowland settlement, the *Brendon Hills* begin to rise on our right.—14½m. *Coppleham Cross* marks the confluence of the Exe and the Quarme. A sideroad leads left to (1½m) *Winsford*, a hunting and fishing centre in charming surroundings on the banks of the Exe. The politician Ernest Bevin (1881–1951) was born here.—A396 continues to (17m) **Wheddon Cross**.

A396 continues NW, down the wooded valley of the Avill, past (3½m) *Timberscombe* to (7m) *Dunster* (Rte 25A).—A sideroad leads SE from Wheddon Cross through the Brendon Hills, with particularly fine views at ¾m and 1½m.—*Dunkery Beacon* (Rte 27A) lies 3m NW of Wheddon Cross.

B3224 runs W to (22m) *Exford*, a fishing resort on the Exe, with the kennels of the Devon and Somerset stag hounds.—At (23m) *White Cross* we are joined by B3223, which has come over Winsford Hill from Dulverton (see above). Shortly afterwards we enter *Exmoor Forest* proper.—27m. **Simonsbath** is named from a pool in the Barle above the bridge.

B3358 runs W to (5m) *Challacombe*, where it passes between *Chapman Barrows* (1574ft) to the N and *Shoulsbarrow Castle* (1553ft), a prehistoric hill-fort to the S. At 6¼m it joins B3226, which follows the edge of the National Park to (8½m) *Blackmoor Gate* (Rte 27A).—A minor road heads SW from Simonsbath past (3m) *Span Head* (1618ft) to (11m) *South Molton* (Rte 26).

B3223 continues N from Simonsbath through the open moorland of Exmoor Forest. *Chains Barrow* (1561ft) lies to the left.—29½m. *Brendon Two Gates* (1379ft) marks the boundary with Devon and the N limit of Exmoor Forest. To the right is *Brendon Common*, with the *Doone Valley* beyond (Rte 27A).—The road drops down to (33m) *Hillsford Bridge*, where we pick up A39 and follow the river valley to (35½m) **Lynton** and **Lynmouth** (Rte 27A).

# 28 Exeter to Plymouth

## A.  Via Ashburton

Total distance 43m. **Exeter**, see Rte18A. We follow A38, dual
carriageway throughout and bypassing the towns.—To (9½m)
Chudleigh.— To (19m) Ashburton.—To (21½m) Buckfastleigh.
—To (32m) Ivybridge.—To (43m) **Plymouth**.

Maps: OS Landranger 192, 191, 202, 201.

**Exeter**, see Rte 18A. We leave the city to the SW, passing (1½m)
*Alphington* where the church has a notable font of c 1140, and join
A38.—3½m. *Kennford.*—6m. A380 branches left to Newton Abbot
(Rte 28C). We keep on A38.—9½m. *Chudleigh*, with the picturesque
*Chudleigh Rocks* to the S. For *Ugbrooke House*, near A380, see Rte
28C.

B3193, a pleasant road, goes up the Teign valley to (7½m) *Dunsford* (Rte 29B).
On the opposite side of the valley are *Higher Ashton* (6m from Chudleigh),
where the 15C *church has fine rood and parclose screens, and
*Doddiscombsleigh* (8m from Chudleigh), with a wealth of 14C stained glass in
its church.

A38 crosses the Teign and Bovey and becomes the S boundary of
Dartmoor National Park (Rte 29).—19m. **Ashburton**, a good
starting-point for excursions across the moor, see Rtes 29C and
D.—We cross (20¾m) *Dart Bridge* and turn right for (½m) **Buckfast
Abbey**, founded by Canute in 1018, refounded for Cistercians by
Stephen in 1147 and colonised by French Benedictines in 1882.

Nothing remains of the original building but a 12C undercroft and the 14C
Abbot's Tower. The present cruciform church (open), modelled on Kirkstall and
Fountains, with a square central tower, was built by the monks with their own
labour in 1907–38 on the old foundations. The dignified interior has a magnificent mosaic pavement; an altar, font, and corona modelled on German Romanesque works; two candelabra; and a plaque to Abbot Vonier (d. 1938) by Benno
Elkan.—*Hembury Castle*, an Iron Age camp, lies 1m NW, surrounded by NT
woodland.

From Dart Bridge the road goes on to (21½m) *Buckfastleigh* (2900
inhab.), a small market town once famous for woollens. The late
Perp. church has good monuments.—The poet Robert Herrick is
buried at (23½m) *Dean Prior*, where he was rector in 1629–47 and
again in 1662–74.—The road passes (25m) *Syon Abbey*, a Bridgettine
nunnery since its foundation by Henry V in 1414 (formerly at
Isleworth), to reach (26½m) *South Brent*, on the right, with a Norman
church tower and font. *Brent Hill* (1019ft), 1m N, gives a good view
and the romantic scenery of the *Dean Burn Valley*, 3m N, repays a
visit. For the upper Avon valley, see Rte 29C.

32m. **Ivybridge**, a beautifully situated village loved by Turner,
takes its name from the 13C bridge over the Erme. It makes a good
starting-point for excursions on S Dartmoor.

Pleasant walks may be taken in the beautiful *Ivybridge Woods* and to (2m)
*Hanger Down*, (1½m) *Western Beacon* (1088ft), or (2m) *Harford Bridge*. From
*Harford* church (Perp.) a fine moorland walk leads along the right bank of the
Erme to (3m) the *Stall Moor Circle*. Higher up the valley are some good
examples of hut circles.—The road from Ivybridge to (8m) *Shaugh Prior* (Rte
29B) leads to (3m) *Cornwood* and thence NW, via (5m) *Tolch Moor Gate*, with

the fine heights of *Pen Beacon* (1407ft) and *Shell Top* (1546ft) on the right.—To *Two Bridges* over the moor, see Rte 29C.

38m. *Plympton*, 4m NE of A38, is a 'Stannary' town (see introduction to Rte 29) and the birthplace of Sir Joshua Reynolds (1723–92), with the old grammar school (1664) where he and his fellow artists Benjamin Haydon and James Northcote were pupils. The Guildhall where Reynolds presided as mayor, rebuilt in the 19C, is open on written application. The church of St Mary is noteworthy. Sir Christopher Wren was MP for Plympton.

*Hemerdon House* (limited opening), 2m NE, is an early 19C building with a collection of West Country paintings and prints.—At *Sparkwell*, 3m NE of Plympton, is the Dartmoor Wild Life Park.
  *Saltram* (NT), 2m W of Plympton, is the largest country house in Devon, a Tudor building greatly extended in the 1740s. The exterior is plain but the interior is notable for the grand saloon and dining room by Robert Adam (1768), with ceilings by Zucchi, furniture and china, and 14 portraits by Reynolds, a frequent visitor to the house. The kitchen remains in full working order. The landscaped park, uncomfortably close to A38, has an orangery and chapel (1776).

After crossing the Plym, we leave A38 (the Plymouth bypass) on the right.
  43m. **PLYMOUTH** (244,000 inhab.) stands in a dramatic position at the mouths of the Plym and the Tamar and at the head of Plymouth Sound, a splendid natural haven hemmed in with islands and promontories. A major seaport and naval garrison with a long history, Plymouth is also a resort and centre for holidaymakers in SW England.

**Tourist Information Centre**: Civic Centre, Royal Parade; (seasonal) No. 12 The Barbican.

**Car Parks**: Charles Cross, Mayflower St. West, Mayflower St. East, Derry's Cross, Theatre Royal, Leigham St., Elphinstone, Lambhay Hill.

**Bus Station**: Bretonside for all country services; suburban services from city centre.

**Railway Station**: North Rd, N of the centre.

**Theatres**: Theatre Royal, Royal Parade; Athenaeum Theatre, Derry's Cross; Serenade Theatre, opposite Mayflower Steps.

**Ferries**: to Roscoff and Santander. Local ferry service from Ferry Rd, Devonport, to Torpoint (for Antony House) and from Admiral's Hard, Stonehouse, to Cremyll (for Mount Edgcumbe). Pleasure cruises from the Barbican to Cawsand and Drake's Island, and from Phoenix Wharf round the warships and dockyard to the Yealm and the Tamar.

**Airport**: 4m N of city centre, off A386. Flights to Aberdeen, Cork, Exeter, Gatwick, Guernsey, Heathrow, Jersey, Newquay, Scilly Isles.

**Annual Events**: Lord Mayor's Day (May); Naval Base Fair at HMS Drake (June); Sutton Harbour Regatta (July); Plymouth Week (sailing, July); Bristol and West Drake Open Bowls Tournament (August).

**History**. Plymouth, known to Domesday Book as Sutton, received its charter and its present name in 1439, was fortified soon after, and has ever since played an important part in the maritime history of England. Catherine of Aragon landed here in 1501. The town supplied seven ships to fight the Armada (1588), and in Plymouth Sound the English fleet awaited the arrival of the Spaniards. The starting-point for many expeditions by Drake, Sir Humphrey Gilbert and Sir John Hawkins (a native of the town), Plymouth was also the last port touched by the Pilgrim Fathers on their way from Southampton to America in 1620. In the Civil War it sided with Parliament, and was the only town in SW England to escape capture by the Royalists. Air raids in 1941–45 destroyed many historic buildings, though the city centre has been thoughtfully rebuilt.

# PLYMOUTH

| 0 | 800 yards |
| 0 | 800 metres |

American troops embarked from Plymouth on D-Day in 1944, and the Falklands Task Force began and ended its expedition here in 1982.

**Famous natives**: Sir John Hawkins (1532–95); the theologian Joseph Glanvill (1636–80); the painters James Northcote (1746–1831) and Benjamin Haydon (1786–1846); the eccentric poet and parson R.S. Hawker (1830–75); Emma Lavinia Gifford (1840–1912), first wife of Thomas Hardy; the writers Henry Austin Dobson (1840–1921), Sir John Squire (1884–1958) and L.A.G. Strong (1896–1958). The Antarctic explorer Captain R.F. Scott (1868–1912), born in Devonport, is commemorated by monuments on Mount Wise and St Mark's Church, Ford (Keyham), where he served as a choirboy.

Royal Parade, the main thoroughfare of the new city centre, runs from St Andrew's Cross in the E to Derry's Cross in the W. Halfway along, where the broad Armada Way cuts a swathe S to the Hoe, stands a flagstaff based on a bronze representation of Drake's drum. The restored *Guildhall* immediately to the E (open when not in official use), built in 1870–74 and reopened in 1959, has a hall with windows by F.H. Coventry representing the city's history and a huge but incongruous Gobelins tapestry showing the Miraculous Draught of Fishes. Opposite, across the Great Square with ornamental pools, rises the *Civic Centre* of 1962 (open); a lift goes up to the belvedere on the 14th floor (*view). To the N is a modern shopping centre with the colourful *Pannier Market* (1960). Armada Way leads down to the Hoe between the Council House and the *Law Courts* (1963), with a striking entrance panel by P. Fourmaintreaux.

The *Hoe is a raised esplanade with wide lawns, overlooking the Sound. A well-loved legend has Sir Francis Drake playing bowls here when the Spanish Armada was first sighted. Among the monuments are a replica (1884) of Drake's statue at Tavistock and *Smeaton's Tower* (open in summer), the upper part of the third Eddystone Lighthouse. The top of the tower gives the best view from the Hoe, which in clear weather reaches 14m S to the Breakwater and the Eddystone Lighthouse (see below). To the E is the *Royal Citadel* (English Heritage, guided tours in summer), built in 1666, with a fine gateway and a statue of George II in Roman costume; the buildings are now used by a commando regiment of the Royal Artillery. Below their walls is the *Plymouth Aquarium* (open), part of the research laboratory of the Marine Biological Association.

N of the Citadel lies the old quarter of Plymouth, with the quay known as the *Barbican*. The *Mayflower Stone and Steps* commemorate the departure of the Pilgrim Fathers in 1620. Nearby plaques remember the homecoming of the Tolpuddle Martyrs (1838) and the first seaplane flight across the Atlantic (1919). Among the historic buildings are the *Old Custom House* (1586) to the N, the *Elizabethan House* (open) on New St. and the *Island House*, where the Pilgrim Fathers are said to have spent their last night in England, at the head of Southside St.

We follow Southside St. and Notte St. to St Andrew's St., with the *Merchant's House Museum* (open), a 16–17C building now containing exhibits of Plymouth's history. **St Andrew's**, the mother church of Plymouth, is 15C with a good tower.

The nave, burned by enemy action in 1941, was reconsecrated in 1957, with a W window by John Piper and Patrick Reyntiens. The head, by Chantrey, of Zachariah Mudge (d. 1769) survived the fire. The entrails of Sir Martin Frobisher (d. 1594) and of Admiral Blake (1599–1657) are buried in or near the chancel. Captain William Bligh of the 'Bounty' was baptised here.

Behind St Andrew's is *Prysten House* (open), with a galleried courtyard, built in 1498 as a merchant's house and not, as used to be believed, a monastic hostel.

From St Andrew's Cross Exeter St. leads NE, carried over the Bus Station by a viaduct, to the ruined 17C *Charles Church.*

In Drake Circus, N of St Andrew's Cross, are the *Public Library* and the *Museum and Art Gallery*, notable for works by Sir Joshua Reynolds, James Northcote and Benjamin Haydon (all local men), Old Master drawings, Plymouth and other silver, and William Cookworthy's Plymouth and Bristol porcelain.

Union St. leads W from Derry's Cross through *Stonehouse*. On the promontory to the S are the quay at *Admiral's Hard*, the *Royal Marine Barracks* (begun 1784) and the vast *Royal William Victualling Yard* laid out by Rennie in 1826–35, with a colossal statue of William IV over the gate. Beyond (1¼m) *Stonehouse Bridge* lies **Devonport**, famous for its Navy dockyard. On *Mount Wise*, to the left, stand the official residences of the General in Command and the Port Admiral, and the Scott Monument of 1925 (view). Richmond Walk, below, leads to *Mutton Cove.*

The *Devonport Column*, adjoining the former *Guildhall* (1821–23), commemorates the change of name from 'Plymouth Dock' to Devonport in 1824; both are by a local architect, John Foulston. Since 1960 much of the old centre has been lost to the S dockyard. The *Sailors' Rest*, founded by Agnes Weston (d. 1918) with accommodation for 1000 men, is now used by the Polytechnic.

The *Dockyard* covers 300 acres and fronts on the Hamoaze, or estuary of the Tamar, which is reserved as a harbour for warships, including nuclear submarines. The S Dockyard and the *Gun Wharf*, built by Vanbrugh (1718–25), are connected with the *Keyham Steam Yard* in the N by railway tunnel. The largest ships can be refitted here.

The return to the city centre can be made across *Devonport Park*. *St Andrew's, Stoke Damerel*, the mother church of Devonport, was enlarged in 1750 with ships' masts as roof piers. Immediately opposite, Devonport and Tamar High Schools occupy the former *Station Hospital* (1797). We leave Victoria Park and North Rd on the left. The *Royal Naval Hospital* dates from c 1762. In Wyndham St. stands the *Roman Catholic Cathedral* (1858; Joseph Hansom), a Gothic Revival building with a tall spire.

The granite *****Breakwater** (1812–41) protecting the entrance of Plymouth Sound may be visited on a pleasure cruise from the Barbican. The trip passes *Drake's Island*, where Cromwell's general John Lambert was confined from 1664 until his death in 1683. The island is now an Adventure Training Centre.

The *****Eddystone Lighthouse**, 14m S, was built by Sir James Douglas in 1878–82; its light, flashing twice every ½ minute, is visible for 17m. Of its predecessors, the first (1696–99; Winstanley) was swept away by a storm in 1703; the second, of wood (1706–08; Rudyard), was destroyed by fire in 1755; and the third, Smeaton's lighthouse of 1759, was removed in 1882 because the sea had eroded the rock on which it stood.

**Mount Edgcumbe** (open), on the Cornish peninsula, is best reached by taking the pedestrian ferry from Admiral's Hard in Stonehouse to *Cremyll*. The 16C mansion, gutted by fire in 1941 and rebuilt in 1960, is far less interesting than the varied and finely wooded *****grounds** laid out between 1761 and 1800, with deer park, temples, amphitheatre and French, English and Italian gardens. They enjoy magnificent views over Plymouth Sound. From Cremyll the road climbs to (2½m) the twin fishing villages of *Kingsand* and *Cawsand*. A fine cliff walk continues past *Penlee Point* to (2½m) *Rame Head*, with the 15C chapel of St Michael.

The ferry crossing the Hamoaze from Ferry Rd in Devonport to the Cornish coast at *Torpoint* (8400 inhab.) gives access to *Antony House* (NT), off A374 1m inland. Standing in pleasant grounds leading down to the banks of the Lynher, the house (1711–21) has a central block of grey Pentewan stone flanked by colonnades and red-brick wings. The well-preserved interior has original panelling, furniture and portraits of the Carew family.—A374 continues W to (4½m) *Sheviock*, where the 13C church has Courtenay monuments. *Portwrinkle*, 1m SW, has a long sandy beach stretching E to Rame Head (see above).—7m. *Polbathic*. 1m NE is *St Germans*, where the striking church, with two W towers and a deep-set Norman *porch, served as the cathedral of Cornwall until c 1409. Nearby is the early 19C mansion of Port Eliot, and to the W are the 17C Moyle almshouses. About 3m SW of Polbathic is the resort of *Downderry*.—12m. The road forks, A387 heading W to Looe (7m) and A374 continuing N to join A38 for Liskeard (6m), both in Rte 30.

The attractive excursion up the *Tamar* to (19m) *Weir Head* takes c 5½hr by boat from Phoenix Wharf. Steering through the *Hamoaze* between Devonport (right) and Torpoint (left) we leave the mouth of the Lynher on the left, and enter the Tamar proper, the boundary between Devon and Cornwall. We pass under the *Royal Albert Bridge* of the railway (built by Isambard Kingdom Brunel in 1859; nearly ½m long, 100ft clearance) and then the *Tamar Suspension Bridge* (Rte 30). At the W or Cornish end of these lies (4m) *Saltash*. Above the bridges the river expands into a lake ¾m wide, with the Tavy estuary to the right and Great Mis Tor visible in the distance to the N. At *Landulph* (left) is the tomb of Theodore Palaeologus (d. 1636), a descendant of the Byzantine emperors. On the same side, round the next bend, is *Pentillie Castle*, with its charming grounds.—14m. *Calstock* and *Cotehele House*, see Rte 29A. The river makes a wide loop (3m) to the right to (17m) *Morwellham Quay*, about 1m short of the *Morwell Rocks* (300ft), on the right.—At (19m) *Weir Head* we are within 4m of Tavistock (Rte 29A). The fine scenery higher up is accessible by small boat only.

Among the pleasant bays SE of Plymouth are *Bovisand*, *Heybrook* and *Wembury*, where the 15C church with 17C Hele and Calmady tombs overlooks the Great Mew Stone. The Hele almshouses date from 1682. The coast W to *Warren Point* is NT property.

From Plymouth to *Princetown* and *Dartmoor*, see Rte 29B; to *Truro* and *Penzance*, see Rte 30.


# B.   Via Torquay and the Coast

Total distance 70m. **Exeter**, see Rte 18A. We follow A379 throughout.—To (13m) Dawlish.—To (16m) Teignmouth.—To (24m) **Torquay**.—To (27m) Paignton.—To (35m) **Dartmouth**.—To (50m) Kingsbridge.—To (58m) Modbury.—To (70m) **Plymouth** (Rte 28A).

Maps: OS Landranger 192, 202, 201.

A380, the direct road from Exeter to (20m) Torquay, runs via Newton Abbot (Rte 28C).

**Exeter**, see Rte 18A. We leave the city to the SW, passing (1½m) *Alphington* (Rte 28A), and briefly follow A38 to A379, which runs down the W bank of the Exe estuary.—At (7¾m) *Kenton* the 14C church has a wonderful rood screen of c 1480; part of its loft is modern. In a large deer park to the left is *Powderham Castle* (open), with the fortified mansion built by the Courtenays in 1390–1420 at its core, though much of its present appearance dates from 18C and 19C alterations. The staircase hall (1754), with elaborate carving and plasterwork, and the music room by James Wyatt (1794–96) are particularly notable.—From (9m) *Starcross* a ferry runs to Exmouth (Rte 18A). The tower of a pumping house of Brunel's experimental atmospheric railway survives here.—13m. **Dawlish** (10,800 inhab.; Tourist Information) is a resort laid out in 1803, sheltered by the Haldon range (821ft), with the successor to Brunel's atmospheric railway skirting the beach on a viaduct. Dickens made it the birthplace of Nicholas Nickleby. *Dawlish Warren*, 1½m NE, has a good sandy beach.—16m. **Teignmouth** (pronounced 'Tinmouth'; 13,300 inhab.; Tourist Information), well situated at the mouth of the

Teign, has been a resort since the 18C. Andrew Patey of Exeter built the fine classical *Den Crescent* (1826) and *St Michael's* (1823), in an extravaganza of styles. Keats stayed here in 1819.

The walk N by the Sea Wall to (2m) the curiously formed red rocks known as the *Parson* and the *Clerk* is worth taking, and also the walk to (2m) *Little Haldon* (811ft).—A381 follows the Teign to (6m) Newton Abbot (Rte 28C), passing on the right (2¹/₂m) *Bishopsteignton*, where the Perp. church has a Norman doorway and 13C tympanum.

A long bridge crosses the estuary to *Shaldon*, with some charming Regency houses, under a bold headland called the *Ness*. The hilly Torquay road skirts the cliff above Babbacombe Bay (see below).

24m. **TORQUAY** is the largest and most popular of the three resorts (the others are Paignton and Brixham) which overlook Tor Bay. Now administratively combined as the county borough of Torbay (115,600 inhab.), they have also been labelled the 'English Riviera' because of their mild climate and semi-tropical vegetation. Torquay itself stands on several hills rising from the N shore of the bay.

**Tourist Information Centre**: Vaughan Parade.

**Car Parks**: Union St., Shedden Hill, Victoria Parade, Meadfoot Rd.

**Bus Station**: Lymington Rd.

**Railway Stations**: Torquay Station, off Torbay Rd (A379); Torre Station, off Newton Rd (A380).

**Amusements**: Pavilion Entertainments Centre and Princess Theatre, both in Princess Gardens; Coral Island Leisure Complex, on E side of the harbour; Babbacombe Theatre, Babbacombe Downs Rd.

**Ferries**: Services to Alderney, Guernsey and Jersey; local service to Brixham.

**Annual Events**: Bowls Tournament (June), Carnival (July) and Regatta (August).

**Famous natives and residents**: Elizabeth Barrett Browning made a long convalescent stay at Torquay in 1838–41. Agatha Christie (1890–1976) was born here, and Sean O'Casey lived here from 1954 until his death in 1964.

Torbay Rd leads from Torquay Station at the SW end of the town, past the fine grounds of *Torre Abbey* (open), a 17–18C house built on the remains of a Premonstratensian abbey founded in 1196. Of the monastic buildings, the chapter house doorway (c 1200), 14C gate-house, guest hall and a fine tithe barn survive. The house now contains the municipal art gallery. The road ends at (c 1m) the lively *Inner Harbour*. The *Outer Harbour*, bounded on the N by Princess Gardens, is protected from the sea by Princess Pier and Haldon Pier. Near Haldon Pier are *Aqualand*, with local and exotic marine life, the *Coral Island Leisure Complex* and the *Royal Torbay Yacht Club*. The Strand is continued NW by Fleet St. and Union St., the main thoroughfare of the town. The characteristic terraces of Torquay were designed by Jacob Harvey and his sons John and William in 1811–53. *St John's* (1861–71) is a striking church by G.E. Street, decorated by Burne-Jones.

From the Strand, Torwood St. and Babbacombe Rd lead NE past the *Museum*, which contains finds from Kent's Cavern. After about 1m, at *Wellswood*, we turn right on Ilsham Rd to *Kent's Cavern* (open), a stalactite cave inhabited between 100,000 and 8000 BC. Flint and bone implements have been discovered here.

From the cavern we make our way N to (¹/₂m) **Anstey's Cove**, a pretty little bay, and return by the Bishop's Walk (cliff path; *view) and Marine Drive. Passing below *Lincombe Gardens* we descend to (2m) *Meadfoot Beach*, whence we may reach (³/₄m) the harbour across the elevated *Daddy Hole Plain* (view).

Nearly 2m N of the harbour, by the winding Babbacombe road or over *Warberry Hill* (448ft), lies the suburb of **Babbacombe**, above *Babbacombe Bay*, notable for its lovely colouring. The splendid church of All Saints (1865–74) is by Butterfield. A good view of the coast is obtained from Babbacombe Down. Near a miniature *Model Village* (open), a cliff railway (summer only) descends to Babbacombe and Oddicombe beaches. Beyond Babbacombe is *St Marychurch*, where the old parish church, retaining a 12C font, has been well restored after bomb damage in 1943. From *Petitor* a fine walk leads along the cliffs to (1¼m) *Watcombe*, with its *Giant Rock*, and to (2m) *Maidencombe*, going on to (3m) *Labrador*, and Shaldon.

Among the points of interest W of Torquay are (1m) *Cockington* with its Perp. church, 16–17C manor house, old forge and thatched cottages; *Marldon* (3m), where the Perp. church has monuments of the Gilberts of Compton, including Sir Humphrey Gilbert, half-brother of Sir Walter Raleigh and coloniser of Newfoundland (1583); and (4m) *Compton Castle* (NT), a fortified house of the 14–16C with courtyard, great hall, chapel and kitchen.

27m. **Paignton** (Tourist Information) is almost continuous with Torquay. The *Church* has a Norman doorway, the Kirkham Chantry (c 1526) with a fine *screen, and an old stone pulpit. The 14C *Coverdale Tower* is a fragment of a palace of the Bishops of Exeter and has no connection with the Protestant reformer Miles Coverdale. Nearby is the 15C *Kirkham House* (English Heritage, summer standard opening but closed on Tuesdays and on Wednesday mornings). *Oldway Mansion* (gardens and some rooms open), now the offices of Torbay Borough Council, was built by the 19C American sewing-machine millionaire Isaac Singer and further aggrandised by his son, Paris. The *Torbay and Dartmouth Steam Railway* runs from Paignton Station to (7m) Kingswear in summer. The famous *Zoo and Botanical Gardens* are on the Totnes Rd; 2m further W is the *Torbay Aircraft Museum*. S of Paignton are *Goodrington Sands*.— 30½m. The church at *Churston Ferrers* has an E window donated by Agatha Christie.

**Brixham** (Tourist Information), 1½m E of Churston, is a resort and fishing port with an attractive harbour known for its busy fish market and trawlers (Trawler Race in June). The Old Market House on the Quay contains the *British Fisheries Museum*. A statue commemorates William of Orange's landing near here in 1688. *Brixham Museum*, next to the town hall, is devoted to local and maritime history and the history of the Coastguard Service.

From (34½m) *Kingswear* we cross the Dart by ferry to **Dartmouth** (6300 inhab.; seasonal Tourist Information), an ancient port on a beautiful land-locked *estuary, famous for the *Royal Naval College* (in buildings by Aston Webb) on Mount Boone to the N. Crusaders embarked from Dartmouth in 1147 and 1190, and American troops in 1944. Thomas Newcomen (1663–1729), inventor of the atmospheric steam engine, was born here; one of his engines (1725, altered in 1821) is displayed in Royal Avenue Gardens. The church of *St Saviour*, altered c 1630, has a handsome 15C rood screen, a carved stone pulpit, and a gallery of 1633 bearing the arms of the merchant families. A brass of 1408 to John Hawley (identified with Chaucer's Shipman) and the ironwork on the S door are noteworthy. The fine restored *Butterwalk* (1635–40), with carved overhangs, includes a small maritime museum. *Bayard's Cove Fort* (English Heritage, open at any reasonable time), now ruined, was built in 1509–10 to guard the inner haven. Further S, at the narrow mouth of the harbour, are *St Petroc's Church*, with a Norman font, and *Dartmouth Castle* (English Heritage, standard opening and summer Sunday mornings), built in 1481 and enlarged in the 16C. It stands opposite *Kingswear Castle* (1491–1502).

In summer there are steamer cruises up the river Dart to (10m) Totnes (Rte 28C). Opposite (3m) *Dittisham* on the right bank is *Greenway*, the birthplace of Sir Humphrey Gilbert (1539?–83). The *Anchor Rock*, where (according to tradition) Sir Walter Raleigh used to smoke his pipe, is visible at low water. Beyond (6m) *Stoke Gabriel*, on the left bank, we skirt the hanging woods of *Sharpham*, on the right bank.

Beyond Dartmouth A379 climbs steeply, passes (36³/₄m) *Stoke Fleming* with its conspicuous church, and reaches the shore at (38m) *Blackpool*. Beyond (39m) *Strete* the road follows a strip of shingle separating the sea from *Slapton Ley*, a narrow freshwater lagoon and nature reserve. *Slapton*, ¹/₂m N of the lagoon, has the scanty remains of a chantry (1372).—At (42¹/₂m) *Torcross* the road turns abruptly inland.

From Torcross the Devon South Coast Path leads through fine cliff scenery to (4m) *Start Point*, (9m) *Prawle Point* and (14¹/₂m) *Portlemouth*, where a ferry crosses to Salcombe (see below). Portlemouth can also be reached by sideroads (about 8m) from *Chillington*, on A379 W of Torcross, via the charming village of (4m) *South Pool* or (4m) *Chivelstone*, both of which have interesting churches.

50m. **Kingsbridge** (4100 inhab.; Tourist Information), at the head of the land-locked Kingsbridge Estuary, is a busy little market town. The colonnaded *Shambles* of 1585 have an upper storey added in 1796. There is a good monument by Flaxman in the church.

**Salcombe** (2400 inhab.; seasonal Tourist Information), on A381 6¹/₂m S, is a delightful resort with charming scenery and rich vegetation. Once an important shipbuilding port, it has since become a sailing centre. J.A. Froude (born at Dartington near Totnes) is buried in the churchyard. The Devon South Coast Path leads along a magnificent stretch of scenery (NT), past (2m) *Bolt Head* to (8m) *Bolt Tail* and *Hope Cove*.—About 4m W of Kingsbridge is the little resort of *Thurlestone*.

A379 crosses the Avon at (53¹/₂m) *Aveton Gifford*, where the fine church was almost destroyed in the Second World War.—58m. *Modbury* (seasonal Tourist Information) is a severe little town with steep streets and slate-hung houses.

Off *Bigbury-on-Sea*, at the mouth of the Avon 5m S, is the tidal *Burgh Island.*

At 59m we cross the Erme. The churches of *Ermington* (1m N) and *Holbeton* (1¹/₂m S) have similar twisted spires and good screens. —63¹/₂m. *Yealhampton* (pronounced 'Yampton') stands at the head of the Yealm estuary. *Newton Ferrers* is attractively situated on the estuary 2m SW. The coastal scenery to the S, with the ruined church of *Revelstoke*, is magnificent.

70m. **Plymouth**, see Rte 28A.


# C.   Via Newton Abbot and Totnes

Total distance 47m. **Exeter**, see Rte 18A.—A38, A380 to (15m) **Newton Abbot** (bypassed).—A381 to (24m) **Totnes**.—A385 to (30m) junction with A38.—A38 to (47m) **Plymouth**, see Rte 28A.

Maps: OS Landranger 192, 191 (briefly), 202, 201.

**Exeter**, see Rte 18A. We leave the city to the SW, gain A38 (Rte 28A) and at 6m bear left on A380, climbing the steep *Telegraph Hill* (1 in 7). —10m. To the right of the road stands *Ugbrooke House* (open), an ancient house remodelled by Robert Adam in a castellated style in the 1760s, when Capability Brown landscaped the park. The

handsome interior has good 18C furniture and portraits by Lely in the
drawing room. Adam's chapel is claimed as the oldest Roman
Catholic parish church in SW England.—15m. **Newton Abbot** (21,000
inhab.; Tourist Information) is a busy market town and railway
centre. In the centre is the 14–15C *St Leonard's Tower*, where
William of Orange is said to have been first proclaimed king after his
arrival at Paignton (Rte 28B) in 1688. Off A381 to the W, by the banks
of the Lemon, is *Bradley Manor* (NT), a well-preserved 15C house
with a Perp. chapel.

B3195 leads E to the coast at (4¹/₂m) Shaldon (Rte 28B) via (2¹/₂m)
*Combeinteignhead*, in pleasant country. At *Haccombe*, 2m SW of
Combeinteignhead, the EE church has interesting 15–17C effigies and brasses
of the Carew family.—A382 goes up the Teign valley to (6m) Bovey Tracey and
(12¹/₂m) Moretonhampstead (Rte 29D), making a good approach to Dartmoor
from the Torbay coast.

From Newton Abbot A380 continues to Torquay (Rte 28B). We take
A381 S to (19m) *Ipplepen*, on the right, with a 15C church. *Torbryan*,
1m W, has the Church House Inn of 1500 and a *church with old
glass and a screen of c 1430.—22¹/₂m. *Littlehempston*, on the right,
has a 14C parsonage, now a farmhouse.

24m. **Totnes** (5600 inhab.; seasonal Tourist Information) is one of
the oldest and most handsome towns in England. It lies on the side of
a hill with the Dart at its base, and consists mainly of one long
congested *street with many Elizabethan houses. Approaching the
town from the river, we walk up the hill and reach on our left the
*Elizabethan House Museum*, built c 1575, with a collection of
furniture and domestic objects. Just beyond, the street is spanned by
the arch of the *East Gate*, rebuilt c 1500. On the right stands the
church of *St Mary* (1432–60), in red sandstone, with a noble tower, a
splendid coloured and gilt stone *rood screen, good parclose screens
and a stone pulpit. Behind it stands the charming *Guildhall* (open), a
pillared 16–17C building; its interior preserves the old court room
and mayor's parlour. High St. continues up the hill to *Totnes Castle*
(English Heritage, standard opening but closed on Tuesdays and on
Wednesday mornings in winter), with a 14C keep on the Norman
motte. A walk round the circular upper storey gives a fine *view.

Off A384 about 2¹/₂m E is the picturesque ruin of *Berry Pomeroy Castle* (English
Heritage, not open at time of writing), dating largely from the 16C but with a
14C great gateway.—*Bowden House* (open), 1m S of Totnes, is a small building
of several periods, though the visitor's first impression is dominated by the
Queen Anne façade (1704). Beyond the house sideroads continue 1¹/₂m SE to
the attractive village of *Ashprington*.—The historian J.A. Froude (1818–94) was
born at *Dartington*, 2m N of Totnes. *Dartington Hall* is a restored 14C manor
house. The estate is now a trust with agricultural and other commercial
enterprises. Here, too, are a school, a College of Arts and an Adult Education
Centre. The fine grounds include terraces overlooking the old tiltyard; one of
them has a statue by Henry Moore.
For river cruises from Totnes down the Dart to Dartmouth, see Rte 28B.
—Sideroads follow the pretty upper valley of the Dart to (7m) Buckfastleigh (Rte
28A) via (3m) *Staverton*, noted for its picturesque bridge. In summer the journey
can be made by the steam service of the *Dart Valley Railway*.

A385 leads W from Totnes to (30m) the junction with A38, where we
follow Rte 28A to (47m) **Plymouth**.

# 29 Dartmoor

Maps: OS Landranger 191, 202 and (briefly) 201, or OS Dartmoor Tourist map (1:63,360 or 1in to 1m). Walkers need the OS Outdoor Leisure map (1:25,000 or 2½in to 1m).

**Dartmoor National Park** lies between A30 and A38 in Devon, covering 365 square miles (24m from N to S and 23m from E to W). At its core is Dartmoor proper (300 square miles), once a royal forest and still sometimes called by that title. This tableland is the easternmost of the granite masses which punctuate the surface of SW England. Further W, they form Bodmin Moor, the Downs above St Austell, the countryside between Redruth and Helston, and the Land's End peninsula. The Scilly Isles are the remnant of the westernmost outcrop.

Dartmoor is the highest as well as the largest of these formations. Its mean elevation is about 1200ft, but some of the hills rise over 1800ft and, near Okehampton in the N, they exceed 2000ft. The characteristic grey 'tors' that crown many hills are piles of granite broken and weathered to look oddly like the ruins of human habitation. The slopes beneath these heights are covered by gorse and heather, while the low-lying country has tracts of dark peat and dangerous bog marked by the bright green of its grass. This moorland provides rough grazing for the semi-wild breed of Dartmoor ponies, and for cattle and sheep—some of which, like the ponies, are pastured all year round. The many streams that criss-cross the region flow into rivers draining the tableland to the S: the Bovey and the Teign (meeting S of Bovey Tracey to reach the sea at Teignmouth); the Dart (running past Buckfastleigh to Totnes and Dartmouth); the Avon (meandering SW after it leaves the moor at South Brent); the Erme (heading due S beyond Ivybridge); the Plym (which eventually gives its name to Plymouth); and the Tavy (running through Tavistock into the Tamar estuary at Plymouth).

In the valleys to the S the countryside grows wooded and friendly; the centres of population here, joined by the course of A38, cling to convenient river crossings. But to the N, Dartmoor can be as bleak as it is isolated. The heart of the moorland is crossed by only two roads of any consequence, meeting at Two Bridges, and boasts only one town of any size, Princetown. The long-term prison here, together with the unfriendly contours of the landscape, the treacherous bogs, the frequent mists and penetrating rain, have contributed much to the moor's forbidding reputation. Its grimly romantic atmosphere is well evoked by Conan Doyle's 'The Hound of the Baskervilles'.

Yet the region is also rich in historic and, especially, prehistoric remains. With its abundance of water, building stone and pasture, and its lack of the forests which then densely covered much of the surrounding lowland, Dartmoor attracted Bronze Age and Iron Age settlers. Evidence of their presence survives in stone circles and rows, hut circles, cairns and trackways. Several of the chief sites are now administered by English Heritage. Rude stone bridges ('clapper' bridges) and stone crosses marking the way to the religious houses on the borders of the moor survive from medieval times. There are also vestiges of the mining for tin, copper and manganese that once flourished here. Tavistock, Chagford, Ashburton and Plympton are the four 'Stannary' towns appointed by a charter of Edward I for the weighing and stamping of tin and the holding of monthly mining courts.

*Sherlock Holmes on Dartmoor: an illustration by Sidney Paget to Sir Arthur Conan Doyle's 'The Hound of the Baskervilles'*

Walkers need to take special precautions: carrying a map and compass; avoiding swampy spots (bright green grass); making for a valley if overtaken by mist; and remembering that recent rain can make the streams impassable. There is a large military training area in the N of Dartmoor which includes three firing ranges (marked by red and white posts, and by noticeboards at the main approaches). Maps showing these areas can be seen at local post offices, inns, etc. For information about access restrictions, write to or telephone the Range

Liaison Officer, Devon Training Areas, Seaton Barracks, Tavistock Rd, Plymouth (Plymouth 772312, extension 249).

The headquarters of the Dartmoor National Park Authority is at Parke, Haytor Rd, Bovey Tracey (Rte 29D), and there are information centres (open from Easter to the end of October) at Okehampton and Tavistock (Rte 29A), Steps Bridge, Postbridge and Princetown (Rte 29B), and New Bridge (Rte 29C).

# A. Exeter to Tavistock via Okehampton

Total distance 39m. **Exeter**, see Rte 18A.—A30 to (23m) **Okehampton** (bypassed).—A30, A386 to (39m) **Tavistock**.

Maps: OS Landranger 192 (briefly), 191.

This route follows the N and W boundaries of the National Park.

**Exeter**, see Rte 18A. We take A30 W from the city.—At (11m) *Cheriton Bishop* on the left, where the church has a good font and woodwork, we reach the edge of the National Park.

Sideroads lead SW through (1½m) *Crockernwell* and (3m) *Drewsteignton* to (4m) *Castle Drogo (NT)*, one of the last English country houses in the grand style, built in 1910–30 by Sir Edwin Lutyens for Julius Drewe, founder of the Home and Colonial Stores. Made of local granite, it is dramatically massed on a superb site overlooking the Teign. The comfortably grand interior, with bare stone walls and high windows, is particularly notable for the main staircase and for the kitchen and service rooms. We can rejoin the main route by continuing to A382, which heads NW to meet A30 near *Whiddon Down*.

18½m. *South Zeal*, a former copper-mining village with a 16C inn, lies beneath *Cosdon* or *Cawsand Beacon* (1799ft; view). *South Tawton*, 1m N, one of John Wesley's regular preaching stations, has a 15C granite church beside a 16C church house.

Sideroads lead SE from South Zeal to (1½m) *Throwleigh*, a remote parish with a fine 15–16C church and old farmhouses. Beyond the many hut circles on the moor above is a spectacular stone circle about 90ft in diameter. For *Chagford*, 5m SE of Throwleigh, see Rte 29D.

At (19½m) *Sticklepath* the Finch Foundry Museum of rural industry has water-powered machinery in working order. A sideroad goes up the pretty valley of the Taw to the village of (1¾m) *Belstone*, with tors to the S.

23m. **Okehampton** (4200 inhab.; seasonal National Park Information), at the confluence of the East and West Okement, is popular as a base for exploring N Dartmoor. The *Museum of Dartmoor Life* on West St. offers a good introduction to the region. The *Castle* (English Heritage, standard opening but closed on Tuesdays and on Wednesday mornings in winter), in a fine position on the river 1m SW, has some late Norman work in its keep.

In the military zone to the S are (1½m) *Okehampton Camp*, (4½m) *Yes Tor* (2028ft; view) and (4¾m) *High Willhays* (2039ft), the highest point on Dartmoor. A red flag on Yes Tor indicates danger from artillery practice.—The remote but lovely 14C church of *Bratton Clovelly* lies 7½m W of Okehampton, off B3128 (the Holsworthy road).

FROM OKEHAMPTON TO BARNSTAPLE, 29m. B3217 goes N along the West Okement valley to (12m) *Dowland*, where the little church has an early 16C oak arcade.—13½m. *Dolton* church contains a strange font made from two blocks of a 10C cross. We climb to cross B3220.—20½m. *High Bickington* is notable for the *bench ends* in its partly Norman church.—Beyond (22½m)

*Atherington* (Rte 18A) we join A377 for (29m) *Barnstaple* (Rte 26).—An alternative route (39m) follows A386 to (20m) *Great Torrington* and (27m) *Bideford* and A39 to Barnstaple; see Rte 35.

From Okehampton to *Launceston, Bodmin* and *Penzance*, see Rte 32.

We leave Okehampton on A30.—25½m. Beyond *Meldon*, left of the road, is *Meldon Reservoir*, formed in 1970–71 by flooding much of the steep West Okement valley.—27½m. We follow A386 as it branches left from A30.—31m. A sideroad leads 1m W to **Lydford**, now a mere village but an important town with a mint in Saxon times. The late 12C keep of its *Castle* (English Heritage, open at any reasonable time) was used as a 'Stannary' prison. Here the Forest Courts were believed to act in accordance with the maxim 'first hang and draw, and then hear the cause, is Lydford Law'. In the 16C the town imprisoned their MP, Richard Strode, for introducing an unpopular bill; the incident led to the establishment of Parliamentary privilege. From *Lydford Gorge* (NT) a steep walk leads to the spectacular waterfall known as the *White Lady*.

For the walk from Lydford to *Merrivale* via *Mary Tavy* and *Peter Tavy*, see Rte 29C.

To reach ***Tavy Cleave**, a deep rocky valley with bold tors on its W side, we follow the footpath leading E from A386 at the junction with the turning for Lydford. At 2¼m we cross the Lyd by stepping stones (beware danger signals) and walk E to (3m) *Doe Tor* and SE to (3¾m) *Hare Tor*, from which we descend to (4½m) the Cleave.—Another pleasant walk starting from the same spot goes NE, crossing the Lyd by stepping stones and climbing to (1m) *Brat Tor*, in full view from the stream. We can continue another 1m NE to *Great Links Tor* (1924ft).

As we pass through (35m) *Mary Tavy* the conical *Brent Tor* (1100ft; view), with a 13C chapel of St Michael, rises on the right.

39m. **TAVISTOCK** (seasonal National Park Information), a grim stone-built 'Stannary' town, stands on the Tavy just beyond the W boundary of Dartmoor. The heavy Victorian Gothic benefactions of the 7th Duke of Bedford overshadow the chief remains of Tavistock's Benedictine *Abbey*, founded in 981: the restored main gatehouse, a fragment of the cloister (in the churchyard), the infirmary hall (now the Unitarian chapel) and the wall by the river. The W gateway stands in the vicarage garden, which also has three inscribed stones (possibly 6C), one with Oghams. The 15C church of *St Eustachius* contains the fine monument of Sir John Glanville (d. 1600).

About ½m S on the Yelverton road is a statue by Boehm of Sir Francis Drake (1542–96), who was born at *Crowndale*, ½m further down the Tavy.

FROM TAVISTOCK TO LISKEARD, 18½m by A390. We follow the road across the Tamar by the medieval New Bridge to (14½m) *Gunnislake. Calstock*, by the river 2¼m S, has a graceful railway viaduct. The noble church of *Bere Ferrers* lies about 3½m further SE, near the Tavy estuary. ***Cotehele House** (NT), 2m S of Gunnislake via *Albaston*, is a finely preserved medieval manor, around several courtyards, built in 1485–1627. It still has original furniture, armour, 17–18C tapestries and needlework. The chapel has a clock of 1489. The watermill and cider press in the grounds have been restored. The quay by the Tamar has pleasant 18C and 19C buildings and a small shipping museum.—Passing *Kit Hill* (1094ft) on the right, we reach (10m) *Callington*, with a noble church. *Dupath Well* (English Heritage, open at any reasonable time), off A388 1m E, is a well house of c 1500.—18½m. *Liskeard*, see Rte 30.

# B.   Exeter to Plymouth via Princetown

Total distance 41m. **Exeter**, see Rte 18A.—B3212 to (12m)
Moretonhampstead (Rte 29D).—To (24m) Two Bridges (Rte 29C).
—To (25½m) **Princetown**.—To (31m) Yelverton.—A386 to (41m)
**Plymouth** (Rte 28A).

**Exeter**, see Rte 18A. We leave the city to the SW on B3212.—The
road dips down into the valley of the Teign, here marking the E edge
of Dartmoor National Park, with the pretty village of (6m) *Dunsford*
on the right, and crosses the river at (6¾m) *Steps Bridge* (seasonal
National Park Information).—12m. **Moretonhampstead**, see Rte 29D.
We cross the Bovey before (15m) *Beetor Cross*, where roads go S to
Bovey Tracey and N to Chagford, both in Rte 29D. One mile further
on B3212 climbs the shoulder of *Shapley Common* (1075ft), rising on
our left, and gives a fine **·**view.

A track leads S to (1½m) **·***Grimspound*, a good example of a late Bronze Age
settlement (English Heritage, open at any reasonable time). A wide dry-stone
wall encloses about 4 acres with the remains of 24 huts; the old field pattern can
be traced outside the pound. Across the valley, ½m due W, is *Challacombe
Stone Row*, a triple row with what may be the remains of a stone circle. It can
also be approached from Warren House Inn.

B3212 passes between tors with stone circles, stone rows and disused
mines; footpaths lead from (18m) *Warren House Inn*.—20m.
*Postbridge* (seasonal National Park Information) has a fine example
of a 'clapper' bridge over the East Dart. There is another at *Bellever*,
about 1m downstream.

The valley is rich in prehistoric remains. *Broadun Ring*, a group of huts inside an
enclosure, is about 1½m N on the W bank of the river. The **·***Grey Wethers*, the
two largest stone rings on the moor, are across the valley about 2m further N.
For the footpaths from *Chagford*, see Rte 29D.

We cross B3357 at (24m) *Two Bridges* (Rte 29C).—25½m. **Princetown**
(seasonal National Park Information) owes its existence to the *Prison*
opened in 1809 by the Lord Warden of the Stannaries for prisoners of
the Napoleonic wars. American prisoners were added after the war
of 1812, the total number at one point being over 9000. The church
was built by the men in 1814; a memorial window (1910) and a
gateway (1928) commemorate the 218 Americans who died on the
moor. In 1850 the building was reopened for English convicts, and in
a mutiny of 1932 part of the prison was burned down. Some of the
surrounding moorland was cultivated by convicts before the system
of hard labour was abolished.—28½m. *Yennadon Down*, to the left,
commands a view with a particularly fine grouping of the tors round
Burrator Reservoir, visited in the detour below.—29m. *Dousland*.

*Walkhampton*, ½m N, has a conspicuous church tower and a 16C church
house.—A sideroad leads 1m S from Dousland to *Meavy*, with an old village
cross. *Sheepstor*, 1¼m E, has an ancient bullring, a 15C priest's house and the
tomb of Rajah Brooke of Sarawak (d. 1868). In the S side of the tor (845ft) that
gives its name to the village is the *Pixies' Cave*. About 2m SE are the
*Drizzlecombe* prehistoric remains (Rte 29C). NW of Sheepstor is the beautiful
*Burrator Reservoir*, the largest in Devon (150 acres).

31m. **Yelverton** stands on the edge of *Roborough Down* just inside
the W boundary of the National Park.

\***Buckland Abbey** (NT) is 3m W. Built by the Cistercians in 1278, it was acquired by the Grenvilles after the dissolution of the monasteries and converted into a private house by Sir Richard Grenville in 1576. Sir Francis Drake bought the property in 1581. The tower of the abbey church is incorporated into the house. Sir Richard Grenville's Great Hall has panelling and a fine plaster ceiling and friezes. Later additions include a handsome Georgian staircase (1772). The house is now a museum of folk art, naval history and Drake relics, of which Drake's Drum is the most famous. The grounds include the huge 14C tithe barn, now containing a display of horse-drawn vehicles.—About 1m N is *Buckland Monachorum*, where the fine Perp. church has a monument to Lord Heathfield (d. 1790), the defender of Gibraltar.

We take A386 S towards Plymouth.—35m. *Bickleigh*, on the left.

About 1½m NE is \**Shaugh Bridge*, at the junction of the Meavy and the Plym, with the beautiful wooded *Bickleigh Vale* (part NT). Above Shaugh Bridge is the fine cliff on the Plym known as the *Dewerstone Rock* (NT). For the way from *Shaugh Prior*, 1m SE, to *Ivybridge* (8m), see Rte 28A.

37m. *Plymouth Airport.*—41m. **Plymouth**, see Rte 28A.

# C.  Ashburton to Tavistock

Total distance 20m. Unclassified road to (7m) Dartmeet.—B3357 to (11m) **Two Bridges**.—B3357 to (20m) **Tavistock** (Rte 29A). \*

Maps: OS Landranger 202, 191.

The route cuts across Dartmoor from SE to W with several good detours, particularly for walkers.

**Ashburton** (3600 inhab.), on the S boundary of the National Park, lies by A38 between Exeter and Plymouth (Rte 28A). It is a 'Stannary' town with many old houses, a 14–15C *Church* and a *Museum* of local antiquities and geology. We leave on the unclassified road signposted for Tavistock and cross the Dart at 1¼m by the medieval *Holne Bridge*.

About ½m beyond, when the woods of *Holne Chase* are on our right, a sideroad leads left to (1m) the picturesque village of *Holne*, birthplace of Charles Kingsley (1819–75).—A good walk leads SW from Holne across the common to (2m) the Mardle. We cross the stream and strike S to (2½m) *Pupers Hill* and (4m) *Hickaton Hill*, with hut circles and pounds. To the S of the hill, crossing the Abbot's Way (see below), flows the Avon, here dammed to form a small reservoir. We take the river as our guide to (6m) \**Shipley Bridge*. A lane continues down the valley to (8½m) *South Brent* on A38 (Rte 28A).

We cross the Dart again, by (2½m) *New Bridge* (seasonal National Park Information).

A sideroad leads N along the bank of the Dart and the Webburn to (1½m) *Buckland-in-the-Moor*, where the EE church has a Perp. screen and Norman font, at the foot of *Buckland Beacon* (1282ft; view).

7m. The East and West Dart rivers unite at \**Dartmeet*. Hexworthy, 1¼m S, is a fine viewpoint.—B3357 leads W from Dartmeet.

11m. **Two Bridges**, at the junction of the two main roads across the moor, lies just below the confluence of the West Dart and the Cowsic. The Cowsic valley is particularly charming, and a Lich Way may be followed from Lydford Tor (2½m up the valley) to Peter Tavy (c 6m W; see below). On the Dart, 1¾m N, is *Wistman's Wood*, one of the few old groves of stunted oaks that still linger on the Moor. About ¾m NE is *Crockern Tor* (1391ft), where the Tinners' Parliament was attended until 1730 by representatives of the four original 'Stannary' towns.

Another excursion may be made from *Tor Royal*, 1½m SW, to *Nun's Cross*, 3½m S, thought to have been used as a boundary mark for the Forest of Dartmoor in 1204 (mentioned in 1240), and bearing the inscriptions 'Siward' and 'Boc Lond'. Good walkers may proceed by (4½m) an old mine on *Harter Tors*, to (5¼m) the prehistoric remains on the Plym at *Drizzlecombe*, which include circles, rows, cairns and standing stones, and on W to (7m) *Sheepstor* (Rte 29B).

From Nun's Cross an old track known as Abbot's Way, running first SE and thence SW, leads to (1¼m) a ford on the Plym. The path on the other side is ill defined, but a SE course will bring us to (2½m) *Erme Head* (c 1530ft), with its mining remains. Descending the left bank of the Erme, we reach (3½m) a stream coming from some clay-works. Crossing this and keeping SE, we reach the old railway track, which we follow S to (6m) the slope of *Three Barrows* (1522ft; view) and (8m) a point c ¾m E of Hartford church. About ¼m further on we descend SSW to a gate, from which a lane leads in the same direction to (10m) *Ivybridge* (Rte 28A).

From Two Bridges to *Princetown* and *Plymouth*, see Rte 29B.

At (13m) *Rundlestone* the road from Princetown joins B3337.—15m. *Merrivale Ancient Village*, before the modern village of that name, is an early Bronze Age settlement with hut circles, stone rows and cairns (English Heritage, open at any reasonable time).

An easy walk to Lydford (9m) leaves the Tavistock road c 1m W at a point where a watercourse runs under the road. We strike NNW over the common for (2m) *Cox Tor* (1452ft; view). A lane on the N side of the hill on which the tor stands leads to (2¾m) a farmhouse whence a path runs W to (3¼m) *Peter Tavy Combe*, with its charming cascades. About ½m from the lower end of the combe is the village of *Peter Tavy*; from the church a lane runs N to (4¾m) *Mary Tavy*. Beyond this village we follow A386 N through Blackdown for c 1¼m and then take a rough track to the left, which crosses the shoulder of *Gibbet Hill* (1159ft) to (7½m) a sideroad running NE to (9m) *Lydford* (Rte 29A).

Tors rise on either side of the road before it drops down to (20m) **Tavistock** (Rte 29A).

# D.  Ashburton to Chagford and back

Total distance 35m. **Ashburton**, see Rte 29C.—Unclassified roads to (6½m) Haytor Vale and (10m) **Bovey Tracey**.—A382 to (17m) **Moretonhampstead**.—A382 and unclassified roads to (21½m) **Chagford**.—Unclassified roads and B3344 to (29m) Widecombe-in-the-Moor.—Unclassified roads back to (35m) **Ashburton**.

Maps: OS Landranger 202 (briefly) and 191.

A tour of E Dartmoor, partly on steep and narrow roads.

**Ashburton**, see Rte 29C. We head NW on an unclassified road to (2m) *Ausewell Cross* and continue N past *Buckland Beacon* (1281ft; view to the W) to (4½m) *Hemsworthy Gate*, where *Rippon Tor* (1563ft), studded with cairns, stands on the right.—We head right and pass the double-headed *Hay Tor* (1490ft; good views), where the tracks of a horse-operated railway opened in 1820 to serve the granite quarries can still be seen.—6½m. **Haytor Vale**.

The 14–15C parish church is at *Ilsington*, 1½m SE. The dramatist John Ford (1586–1640?) was baptised here.—N of Haytor Vale are (3m) *Becka Falls* and (4m) *Manaton*, a delightful village near Lustleigh Cleave (see below). At *Hound Tor*, 1½m SE of Manton, are the remains of a medieval village inhabited from late Saxon times until c 1300 (English Heritage, open at any reasonable time).

We continue W from Haytor Vale, with the road dropping down past the nature reserve of *Yarner Wood* on the left to (10m) **Bovey Tracey** (headquarters of the Dartmoor National Park Authority), a good centre for excursions in SE Dartmoor and the lower Teign valley to the E. The Perp. church, dedicated to St Thomas Becket, has a remarkable coloured stone screen and pulpit.

*John Cann's Rocks*, 1m NW, and *Bottor Rock*, 1¹/₂m NE, are two good points of view.

From Bovey Tracey we follow A382 NW and turn left for (13¹/₂m) **Lustleigh**, with an interesting church and the *Cleave*, a moorland valley about 1m W.—Returning to A382 we follow the valley to (17m) **Moretonhampstead**, a pleasant little town with a colonnaded almshouse of 1637. It makes a good starting-point for the moorland near the Teign. *North Bovey*, 1³/₄m SW, is a lovely village above the Bovey with an oak-shaded green. For B3212, the Exeter–Tavistock road, see Rte 29A.—At (20m) *Easton Cross* we turn left from A382 for (21¹/₂m) **Chagford**, a quiet and charming old 'Stannary' town which makes a good starting-point for excursions on N or E Dartmoor.

A pleasant walk of about 8m can be taken via *Teigncombe*, 2¹/₂m W, to (4m) the stone remains at *Kestor* (1433ft), then N to the *Wallabrook Clapper* and (5m) the *Scorhill Circle*. We return to Chagford via (6m) *Gidleigh*, with a fortified mansion of c 1300.—From *Batworthy*, about ¹/₂m SW of Teigncombe, we can walk another ¹/₂m to *Shovel Down*, with a stone circle and several stone rows. The walk can be extended SW, keeping W of *Fernworthy Forest*, via the *Grey Wethers* to *Postbridge* on B3212 (both Rte 29B).—Other places of interest near Chagford are: the Iron Age hill-fort at *Cranbrook Castle*, 3m NE; *Fingle Bridge* over the Teign, 4m NE; and *Castle Drogo*, 2¹/₄m NE (Rte 29A).

We turn S over Meldon Hill to (24m) *Beetor Cross*, where we continue S.—At 26m we turn right on an unclassified road which passes some fine tors to reach (29m) **Widecombe-in-the-Moor**, a beautifully situated village made famous by the song 'Widdicombe Fair'. It is now popular with tourists. The 14–16C church has a commanding tower; the church house (NT but not open) is early 15C. The fair is still held on the second Tuesday in September.—We head E across the Webburn, turn right for (30¹/₂m) *Hemsworthy Gate* and go S back to (35m) *Ashburton*.

# 30  Plymouth to Truro and Penzance

Total distance 79m. **Plymouth**, see Rte 28A.—A38 to (17m) Liskeard (bypassed).—A38, A390 to (28m) St Austell (bypassed).—A390, A39 to (49m) **Truro**.—A39, A394 to (66m) Helston.—A394. A30 to (79m) **Penzance**.

Maps: OS Landranger 201, 200, 204, 203.

**Plymouth**, see Rte 28A, where an alternative way of starting the journey from the city (via Torpoint) is described. The main route heads NW from the centre to join A38 at the large suburb of (4m) *St Budeaux*. Its church (1563) saw the marriage of Sir Francis Drake in 1569 and contains the tomb of Sir Ferdinando Gorges (d. 1647), first governor of Maine. The old village lay 1¹/₄m N on the creek leading to *Tamerton Foliot*, still with attractive waterside scenery.—We cross the river by the *Tamar Suspension Bridge* (toll) of 1959–61 by Mott,

Hay and Anderson; The *Royal Albert Bridge* (see Rte 28A) runs alongside. *Saltash* (12,700 inhab.), an old borough on the Cornish bank, is bypassed by A38. *Trematon Castle* (open by written application), with 13C keep and gatehouse, lies 1½m SW and 2½m further on is *Ince Castle* of c 1550 (limited opening of gardens only), overlooking the beautifully wooded Lynher.—A38 crosses the Lynher and then the Tiddy, and at 11m is joined by A374 from Polbathic, the end of the alternative route from Plymouth via Torpoint (Rte 28A).

17m. **Liskeard** (6300 inhab.) is a market town with a spacious square and a large Perp. church. It is one of Cornwall's four 'Stannary' towns, with Lostwithiel, Truro and Helston (cf. introduction to Rte 29). The historian Edward Gibbon became its MP in 1774.

About 2½m N lies *St Cleer*, with a holy well, giving a good view of the S part of Bodmin Moor (Rte 32). The area is rich in ancient monuments (all English Heritage, open at any reasonable time): the *Doniert Stone* (1m NW), probably a memorial to Durngarth, King of Cornwall in the 9C; the *Trevethy Quoit* (1m NE), a burial chamber of standing stones built c 3200–2500 BC; and the *Hurlers* (2m N of the Trevethy Quoit), three imperfect circles of c 2200–1400 BC. The *Cheesewring*, a striking pile of weathered granite slabs about 30ft high, lies ½m beyond the Hurlers.—The fine church of *St Neot*, about 5m NW of Liskeard, has good stained glass of 1400–1532, partly restored. For *Dozmary Pool*, about 4m N of St Neot, see Rte 32.

FROM LISKEARD TO LOOE AND POLPERRO, 13½m by B3254 and A387 down the Looe valley.—3m. *St Keyne* has a Mechanical Music Centre with fair organs etc.—4½m. *Duloe*, with a 13C church and a stone circle.—9m. **Looe** (4500 inhab.; seasonal Tourist Information), on both banks of its river, is a historic little port and a former haunt of smugglers, now a popular resort and centre for shark fishing.—13½m. **Polperro**, further W, a picturesque and popular fishing village in a narrow ravine, was also known for smuggling. A road leads W to (10½m) *Bodinnick Ferry* opposite Fowey (see below). A hilly road goes NW from Polperro via (6m) *Lanreath*, with good stalls in its church and a farm museum, to (11m) Lostwithiel (see below).

From Liskeard to *Tavistock*, see Rte 29A.

19m *Dobwalls* has a museum devoted to the wildlife painter Archibald Thorburn (1860–1935).—We branch left on A390 and cross the Fowey at (28m) **Lostwithiel** (Tourist Information), the 13C capital of Cornwall, once represented in Parliament by Joseph Addison. The *Church* has a striking 14C spire, a fine Dec. E window and *font. The medieval *Fowey Bridge* and *Stannary Court*, and the *Guildhall* of 1740, are of interest. *Restormel Castle* (English Heritage, standard opening and summer Sunday mornings, but closed on Tuesdays and on Wednesday mornings in winter), high above the river 1½m N, has a circular keep of c 1200 and the ruins of a Great Hall added a century later.

About 2m beyond Lostwithiel B3269 branches S from A390, passing (after another 3m) the hill-fort of *Castle Dore*, which legend identifies as the palace of King Mark. *Golant*, by the river 1m E, is associated with Tristram and Iseult; the church has good woodwork.—5¼m. **Fowey** (pronounced 'Foy'; Tourist Information), a characteristically Cornish little place at the mouth of the estuary, was once a major seaport. It has a charming square and many old houses. The 13–15C church of St Finnbarus has a rich tower, Norman font, good monuments and a wagon roof. Above is the 19C Place House. The ruined *St Catherine's Castle* (English Heritage, open at any reasonable time), ¾m SW, was built by Henry VIII to defend the harbour. Ferries cross the river to *Polruan* and to *Bodinnick*. From Bodinnick we should climb to *Hall Walk* (NT) on the N bank of Pont Creek, with a *view and memorials to the Second World War dead and to Sir Arthur Quiller-Couch ('Q'; 1863–1944), who spent much of his life at Fowey. From Hall Walk we can follow the river to Pont and then head S to the old church of *Lanteglos*, returning to Fowey via Polruan (3½m in all). Much of the cliff scenery from Polruan E to Polperro (see above), including *Lantic Bay*, *Pencarrow Head* and *Lantivet Bay*, is NT.

At (31m) *St Blazey* we approach the rather dreary china-clay country. To the N, however, is the wooded *Luxulyan Valley*, rich in ferns and spanned by the Treffry Viaduct (c 1830). S of St Blazey are *Par*, a china-clay and granite shipping port, and *Carlyon Bay*.—36m. **St Austell** (36,600 inhab. with Fowey) is the centre of the china-clay industry whose refuse heaps mar the adjoining district. The church has a good Perp. tower embellished with statues, and a Norman font.

*Carthew*, 2m N, has the Wheal Martyn Museum, devoted to the china-clay industry. The handsome harbour village of *Charlestown*, 1½m SE on A3061, has a Shipwreck Museum. Nearby *Duporth Bay* has a holiday resort.—B3273 runs S from St Austell to (5½m) *Mevagissey*, an attractive fishing port with cottages and a fine harbour; the church has a 17C monument with an amusing epitaph. A sideroad continues to (8m) *Gorran Haven*, pretty and unspoilt, and *Dodman Point*, a lovely gorse-covered promontory (400ft; NT). The Cornwall Coast Path leads W to (2½m) *Caerhays Castle* (limited opening of gardens only), a Gothick castle of 1808 by John Nash overlooking *Veryan Bay*.

FROM ST AUSTELL TO ST MAWES, 18m. Following A390, the Truro road, for 3m we then turn left on B3287 and on A3078. Lanes on the left lead to (11½m) *Portloe* and (12m) *Veryan*, with its early 19C 'round houses'. Between them on the coast is *Nare Head* (NT).—11½m. *Ruan High Lanes.*—At (14m) *Trewithian* the road on the left leads to (18m) *St Anthony-in-Roseland*, with an attractive 12–13C church, via (15½m) the seaside village of *Portscatho*. The right branch continues via (16¼m) *St Just-in-Roseland*, with a lovely churchyard set in a cove off the Fal estuary, to (18½m) **St Mawes**, with one of Henry VIII's coastal castles (English Heritage, standard opening and summer Sunday mornings) looking across the Fal estuary to Pendennis Castle. A ferry connects St Mawes with Falmouth (see below).

The road on the right at Ruan High Lanes makes a pleasant alternative route (14¼m) to Falmouth. We cross the Fal estuary by (4½m) *King Harry Ferry* (cars; toll). On the W bank is *Trelissick Garden* (NT) beyond which a lane leads left to the pretty village of *Feock* (1½m) and the Friends' Meeting House (1709) in the form of a thatched cottage at *Come-to-Good*.—At 7¼m we join A39 about 4m S of Truro and follow the route to Falmouth suggested below.

49m. *Grampound*, on the Fal, has a wide and dignified high street. Once notorious as a 'rotten borough', it was John Hampden's first parliamentary seat (1621).—42½m. *Trewithen* (open), on the left, is a mansion of c 1715 by Thomas Edwards of Greenwich. Particularly notable are the gardens laid out by George Johnstone in the 1920s, with camellias, magnolias and rhododendrons.—44m. *Probus* church has a beautiful late Perp. tower.

49m. **TRURO** (16,300 inhab.) is pleasantly situated on a branch of the Fal river. Historically important as a market centre and port, it became a cathedral city in the 19C and, though not the county town, is now the home of Cornwall County Council.

**Tourist Information Centre**: Municipal Buildings, Boscawen St.

**Car Parks**: Lemon Quay, Lower Lemon Quay, Castle St., Old Bridge St.; multi-storey car parks in Moorfield and St Clement St.

**Bus Station**: Station Rd, W of the centre.

**Railway Station**: Station Rd, W of the centre.

**River excursions**: to Falmouth via Malpas.

**Famous natives**: the actor Samuel Foote (1720–77) and the missionary Henry Martyn (1781–1812).

The Georgian terraces in Boscawen St. and Lemon St. and the fine houses in Prince's St. and Trafalgar Row reflect Truro's prosperity in the 18–19C. The *Museum and Art Gallery* has a fine collection of Cornish minerals and antiquities, as well as paintings by the local painter John Opie (1761–1807). The **Cathedral** (1880–1910) was built by J.L. Pearson in the EE style after the diocese of Cornwall was

Key to Numbers
1 Abp Benson Brass
2 King Edward VII Tablet
3 Robartes Monument
4 Abp Benson's Pastoral Staff
5 'Cornubia, Land of the Saints'

OLD BRIDGE ST

All Saints Chapel

Sedilia

Sedilia

Bishop's Throne

Organ

Old Parish Church

CHAPTER HOUSE

CATHEDRAL SCHOOL

Pulpit

VICTORIA

Lectern 4

PORCH

3    5

TOWER

ST MARY'S STREET

Baptistery

1

Font

CLOISTER COURT

NORTH PORCH

SOUTH PORCH

ALEXANDRA TOWER

EDWARD VII TOWER

2

WEST PORCH

0    100 feet
0    30 metres

HIGH CROSS

# TRURO CATHEDRAL

separated from the diocese of Devon in 1876. It stands largely on the site of Truro's 16C parish church, whose graceful Perp. S aisle was incorporated in the new building as an additional S aisle to the choir. The tall circular *Baptistery is a memorial to Henry Martyn. The N aisle has a tablet to the writer Sir Arthur Quiller-Couch. The panoramic painting by John Miller in the N transept was unveiled in 1980.

A pleasant riverside drive leads S to (1³/4m) *Malpas* (pronounced 'Mopus'; ferry), overlooking the confluence of the Truro and Tresilian rivers. We can continue on foot to (2¹/2m) *St Clement*, where there is a stone with Latin and Ogham inscriptions S of the 13C church. A lane leads back to (4m) Truro.

FROM TRURO TO FALMOUTH. BY ROAD (A39), 11m. Beyond (4m) *Carnon Downs* we cross Restronguet Creek and ascend a side valley to (5m) *Perranarworthal.* —8¹/4m. *Penryn* (5100 inhab.), an ancient town at the head of

Penryn Creek, is built of the granite for which it is famous.—BY RIVER, 11m in about 1hr. The boat descends Truro river to (1³/4m) *Malpas* and enters the Fal proper. To the left are the grounds of the mainly 19C *Tregothnan House* (not open). Below is *King Harry Reach*, with a ferry and the woods of Trelissick (see above) on the left. Further down we reach the wide *Carrick Roads*. *Restronguet* and *Mylor Creeks* are on the right, and beyond *Trefusis Point* the boat enters Falmouth harbour.

11m. **FALMOUTH** (18,500 inhab.; Tourist Information) overlooks its beautiful sheltered harbour opening off Carrick Roads. It is both a well-equipped port and a popular seaside resort, with three sandy beaches on Falmouth Bay, facing S. The numerous creeks are ideal for boating excursions, offering a great variety of scenery. Oysters are cultivated in several places on the estuary.

**Ferries** (weekdays only in winter) to *St Mawes* and to *Flushing* from Prince of Wales pier. Daily cruises in summer to *Helford* and to *Truro*.

**History.** Falmouth was the chief Atlantic packet station from 1689 to 1840, at first serving Corunna and, after 1702, the West Indies. The road from Exeter via Okehampton, Launceston, St Columb and Truro was devised in 1704 for the Falmouth mails.

The most interesting part of the town is by the harbour, where Market St. and Church St. have many old houses. The *Church of King Charles the Martyr*, built by Sir Peter Killigrew in 1662–65, has a fine classical interior and a tablet to the 14th Earl of Glencairn (d. 1791), friend and patron of Robert Burns. Further on, an obelisk of 1738 commemorates the powerful but extinct Killigrew family; the remains of their home, *Arwenack House*, stand opposite. At the end of the peninsula, looking across to St Mawes Castle, is **Pendennis Castle** (English Heritage, standard opening and summer Sunday mornings), built by Henry VIII and taken by the Parliamentarians in 1645 after a five months' siege. A beautiful road leads round the promontory. The *Custom House* is one of several early 19C buildings in the Doric style; near it is the 'King's Pipe', the chimney used for burning contraband tobacco.

The lovely peninsula of *Roseland* (visited on the detour from St Austell to St Mawes above) can be reached by the ferry to St Mawes; motorists must go round by the ferry over King Harry Reach.—The ferry trip from Falmouth to *Flushing* (see above) is also recommended. *Mylor* church (1¹/2 NE of Flushing) has Norman details, a good screen and the tallest cross in Cornwall.

The *Lizard* peninsula (Rte 31), to the SW, is reached by unclassified roads passing through or near the villages of (6¹/2m) *Constantine*, (9m) *Gweek*, at the head of the Helford river, and (10¹/2m) *Mawgan*, with a Perp. church. To the E of Mawgan is *Trelowarren*, the beautifully wooded estate of the Vyvyans; the 17–19C house, with a Gothick chapel, is now mainly used as an ecumenical centre (limited opening).—The Cornwall Coast Path, the walkers' route to the Lizard (c 23m), goes via (3¹/2m) *Rosemullion Head* (NT) and (5m) the subtropical *Glendurgan Gardens* (NT) to (6m) *Helford Passage*, where a ferry crosses the river to Helford.

We follow A39 from Truro, branching right after 7m on A394.—66m. **Helston** (10,700 inhab.), once one of Cornwall's 'Stannary' towns, is a lively and attractive little place above the Loe valley. We reach the Lizard peninsula (Rte 31) from here. The church of 1756–62 is by Thomas Edwards. On 8 May each year large crowds are attracted by the Furry Dance (or Floral Dance) in which couples, moving to a tune probably as old as the fête itself, solemnly dance along the streets and through the houses and gardens.

At *Wendron*, on B3297 3m NE, part of the Poldark Mine has been reopened as a museum to the Cornish tin-mining industry.

B3304 leads SW from Helston to (3m) the charming village of *Porthleven*, with a considerable harbour. At 1½m the road passes the beautiful grounds of *Penrose* (open) on the bank of *Loe Pool*, which disputes the possession of King Arthur's sword Excalibur with Dozmary Pool on Bodmin Moor (Rte 32). The pool is closed to the sea at its SW end by *Loe Bar*.

The strenuous coast walk to (17½m) Penzance leads via (3m) Porthleven, (5m) *Trewavas Head*, the fine bathing beach at (6½m) *Praa Sands* near the ruined *Pengersick Castle*, (10½m) *Cudden Point* and (14m) Marazion. On the E side of Cudden Point is *Prussia Cove*, once a haunt of smugglers.

A394 continues to (69½m) *Breage*, where the church has late 15C mural paintings of St Christopher and a 3C Roman milestone. *Godolphin House* (limited opening), 2¼m NW, has a fine colonnaded front of 1635 and good Tudor work inside.—The road follows the curve of Mount's Bay round to (75½m) *Marazion*, deriving its name from 'marghas', the old Cornish word for 'market'. Several hundred yards out to sea rises ˙**St Michael's Mount**, a steep crag of granite and slate resembling a smaller Mont St Michel. It is connected to the shore by a causeway uncovered for 3hr at low tide, and reached at other times by boat from Marazion or Penzance. The island is NT; the castle that crowns it still belongs to the St Aubyn family but is open to visitors.

*St Michael's Mount*

Identified with the Roman *Ictis*, from which Cornish tin was exported, St Michael's Mount became an early centre of Christianity, possibly in the 5C. There was a Celtic monastery here from the 8C, and in 1047 Edward the Confessor established a chapel and placed it under the Benedictine abbey of Mont St Michel in Normandy. The monastery was later absorbed into the castle built by the St Aubyns. Despite considerable alterations, the buildings keep their romantic appearance from the shore. The most interesting features are the

14–15C chapel, the Gothick rococo drawing room formed from the Lady Chapel, and the medieval refectory, now called the Chevy Chase Room because of the hunting scenes on its 17C plaster frieze.

The church of *St Hilary*, 2m E of Marazion, has a Dec. spire and two inscribed stones, one 4C Roman and the other 6–7C.

Beyond Marazion we join A30.

79m. **PENZANCE** ('holy headland'; 19,500 inhab.) stands on the curve of Mount's Bay. Popular as a resort and a base for excursions in the Land's End district, it still keeps some of the atmosphere of a seaport. The mild climate favours market gardening.

**Tourist Information Centre**: Alverton St.

**Car Parks**: Esplanade, Wharf Rd and Alverton Rd.

**Bus Station** and **Railway Station**: by Albert Pier beyond the E end of Market Jew St.

**Ferry Service**: to Scilly Isles by RMV 'Scillonian III'. Helicopter service from the heliport off A30 E of the centre. Boat trips to St Michael's Mount.

**Famous natives and residents**: Sir Humphry Davy (1778–1829), pioneer of electro-chemistry and inventor of the miners' safety lamp, was born in Penzance. The Scottish poet John Davidson (1857–1909) drowned himself here.

Market Jew St. ('Marghas Yow' or 'Thursday Market') climbs from the railway station and harbour in the E to the former *Market House* (1836), now a bank, with a statue of Sir Humphry Davy outside. Of the several interesting streets leading down toward the sea, Chapel St. is particularly notable for its Georgian and Regency buildings, and for the eccentric *Egyptian House* of 1830 (now a National Trust shop). The first announcement of the English victory at Trafalgar was made from the minstrel gallery of the *Union Hotel*. Off Morrab Rd, to the W, are: the *Library*, with rare Cornish books and prints; *Penlee Park*, with the ancient market cross and the interesting *Museum* of natural history and Cornish antiquities; and *Morrab Gardens*, with subtropical plants. St John's Hall in Alverton St. has the *Royal Geological Society Museum* (closed at time of writing but likely to reopen).

The Esplanade goes on to (1m) **Newlyn**, a fishing village which gave its name to a school of local artists headed by Stanhope Forbes (1857–1948), responsible for the fittings (1937–41) of *St Peter's Church*. Their work can also be seen in the *Art Gallery*. The road ends at (3m) **Mousehole** (pronounced 'Mowsal'), a picturesque fishing village with the fine Elizabethan Keigwin Arms (no longer an inn). *Paul* church, ½m inland, is the burial place of Dolly Pentreath (d. 1777), usually described as the last person who spoke Cornish.—From Mousehole we may follow the coast footpath to (5½m) *Lamorna Cove*. By B3315 near *Boleigh*, 1½m inland, are the *Tregiffian Burial Chamber* of the 3C BC (English Heritage, open at any reasonable time) and two standing stones and a stone circle, known as the *Pipers* and the *Merry Maidens*. The cliff walk can be continued to (13m) the *Logan Rock* (Rte 33).

For other places of interest N and W of Penzance, see Rte 33.

# 31 The Lizard

Maps: OS Landranger 203 and 204.

The Cornish peninsula S of Helston (Rte 30) and the Helford river is generally known as the **Lizard**, from the headland at its tip. It stands 200–350ft above sea level, formed largely of serpentine, a greenish rock which can also be seen in many local buildings. In the centre are the breezy *Goonhilly Downs*, where the Cornish heath (*Erica vagans*) grows abundantly, with the radio telescope and satellite communications centre making prominent landmarks. The striking cliff scenery and fine beaches of the coastline (much of it NT) are more interesting.

The peninsula is bisected from N to S by A3083, running from Helston past the naval air station at *HMS Seahawk* to (10½m) *Lizard Town*, a straggling village ¾m inland from *Lizard Point*, the southernmost point of England (49° 57′ 32″ N lat.), marked by two powerful lighthouses. B3292 runs from the main road to St Keverne and Coverack on the E coast, and B3296 runs to Mullion on the W coast; the smaller villages and coves around the coastline are reached by unclassified roads. Walkers will prefer to take at least part of the coastal route of about 24m suggested below, which goes down the W coast to Lizard Point and back up the E coast.

We leave *Helston* to the SW and skirt the W side of *Loe Pool*, by the gardens of *Penrose*, to reach the sea at (2½m) *Church Cove* (Rte 30), where we follow the coastguard path to the left.—5½m. The 15C parish church of *Gunwalloe*, with a detached belfry, is beautifully situated in *Church Cove*. Granite boulders have been placed to protect it from further encroachment by the sea.—6½m. At *Poldhu Cove* a monument set up by the Marconi Co. marks the site of the wireless station which in 1901 transmitted the first wireless signal across the Atlantic.

A road runs inland to (1m) *Mullion*, where the Perp. church has elaborately carved *bench ends.

The next point on the coast is (6¾m) *Polurrian Cove*, with a good sandy beach. This is followed by (7½m) *Mullion Cove* (NT), a beautiful little fishing harbour with serpentine rocks, caves and a view of *Mullion Island* (NT).—The path goes on via *Predannack Head*, *Vellan Head* and *Gew Graze* to (12½m) *Kynance Cove* (NT), with its richly coloured serpentine cliffs, fantastic rock formations and silvery sands. On the W side is *Asparagus Island*, where, when the tide is making, clouds of spray rise from the *Devil's Bellows*. The cave here is called the *Devil's Throat* or *Drawing Room*, while the two on the shore are known as the *Kitchen* and *Parlour*.—We may now turn inland for (14m) *Lizard Town* (see above) or continue along the coast past *Yellow Carn Cliff*, *Caerthilian Cove* and *Pistol Meadow*, where the bodies washed ashore from the wreck of the 'Despatch' were buried in 1809, to (14m) *Lizard Point* and its lighthouse (see above).

The coast walk goes on beyond the *Bumble Rock*, the W horn of *Housel Bay*, with the huge cavity known as the *Lion's Den*. Rounding *Bass Point*, we begin to follow the E side of the peninsula. Beyond *Hot Point* we pass *Kilcobben Cove*, with the Lizard lifeboat station. *Landewednack*, with the parish church of Lizard Town, lies inland. The *Dolor Hugo* and other caves on this part of the coast are best explored by boat.—16m. The *Devil's Frying Pan* is another circular hollow like the Lion's Den.—16¼m. *Cadgwith* is a picturesque little fishing village.—Beyond the glade of *Poltesco* and (3½m) the broad *Kennack Sands* we round (21m) *Black Head*, famous for its serpentine, and reach (22½m) *Coverack*, a charming little place.—In the cove beyond *Manacle Point* is (25½m) the dreary *Porthoustock*.

Offshore are the dangerous *Manacle Rocks* and 1m inland is *St Keverne*, with the largest church in W Cornwall. The buff, green and rose-coloured stones in the pillars of its arcade are not local but may have been brought from Brittany. Many victims of shipwrecks are buried in the churchyard.

From the little fishing village of (13m) *Porthallow* or from (14½m) *Gillan*, further N, sideroads lead via (19½m) *Mawgan* (Rte 30) to A3083 and (about 24m) *Helston*. The latter route passes (16½m) *Manaccan*, with an interesting church.

A road runs N from Manaccan to (1½m) *Helford*, where a ferry crosses the river to join the Falmouth road at Helford Passage (Rte 30).


# 32   Exeter to Bodmin and Penzance

Total distance 113m. **Exeter**, see Rte 18A. We follow A30 throughout.—To (23m) **Okehampton**, see Rte 29A.—To (42m) **Launceston** (bypassed).—To (64m) **Bodmin** (bypassed).—To (95m) Redruth (bypassed).—To (98m) Camborne (bypassed).—To (113m) **Penzance** (Rte 30).

Maps: OS Landranger 192 (briefly), 191, 201, 200, 204 (briefly), 203.

A more direct way from Exeter to Penzance than Rtes 28 and 30 but less interesting, and congested in summer.

**Exeter**, see Rte 18A. To (23m) **Okehampton**, see Rte 29A.—32m. At *Lewtrenchard*, on the left, the writer Sabine Baring-Gould was both squire and rector from 1881 until his death in 1924.—Beyond (37m) *Lifton* we cross the Tamar and enter Cornwall.

42m. **Launceston** (6200 inhab.; Tourist Information), a pleasant town anciently known as *Dunheved* ('hill-head'), rises between two hills. One is crowned by the fine cylindrical keep of the ruined Norman *Castle* (English Heritage, standard opening but closed on Tuesdays and on Wednesday mornings in winter). George Fox, the Quaker, was imprisoned here in 1656. On the other hill is a public park; both command views. The *South Gate* is the only remaining town gate. *St Mary Magdalene's Church*, with a 14C tower, has elaborate carving of 1511–24 on the exterior, particularly on the S porch. *St Thomas'* preserves a Norman font. A Norman arch from the Augustinian priory is now the entrance to the White Hart Hotel, while the large Georgian *Lawrence House* (NT) in Castle St. is now the local museum. The Kensey is crossed by two fine old bridges, one a footbridge 1m E.

46m. *Polyphant*, to the right of A30, is a small quarrying village which has supplied stone for many Cornish churches.—49m. *Altarnun*, again to the right, has a pretty village street and the 15C *church of St Nonna, one of the best in Cornwall. The Norman font and early 16C bench ends are outstanding. There are more good bench ends at *Leaneast*, across the river Inny 2m N.

We cross the wild **Bodmin Moor**, one of the granite masses which punctuate the SW peninsula, but smaller and lower than its eastern neighbour, Dartmoor. The region is dotted with ancient stones, circles and crosses; for those near A38 to the S, see Rte 30.—At (54m) *Bolventor* we pass the famous Jamaica Inn of Daphne du Maurier's novel. *Dozmary Pool*, about 1½m SE, is sometimes identified with the lake into which Sir Bedivere threw King Arthur's sword Excalibur (cf. Loe Pool, Rte 30). About 3m NW of Bolventor rise *Brown Willy* ('Bryn Whelli'; 1377ft), the highest point in Cornwall, and its twin summit, *Rough Tor* (1311ft; NT).—59m. A road leads right to (1½m)

*Blisland*, with a pleasant village green and the *church of St. Protus and St. Hyacinth, partly Norman, with a 15C tower and an interior richly restored by F.C. Eden and Sir Ninian Comper. There is fine scenery on the moor to the N, in (2m) the valley of the De Lank river, E of the quarries, and near the *Devil's Jump* (3m further).

64m. **Bodmin** (12,100 inhab.; Tourist Information) is the county town of Cornwall, though the county council offices are now in Truro. Its 15C church is the largest medieval church in Cornwall; it has a *font of c 1200, a movable piscina of 1495, interesting woodwork and the remarkable tomb of Prior Vivian (d. 1533).

*Lanhydrock* (NT), overlooking the Fowey valley 2½m SE, is a 17C house largely rebuilt after a fire in 1881. The exterior is a convincing facsimile but most of the interior is Victorian in atmosphere. The gatehouse and *Long Gallery*, with a richly decorated plaster ceiling, survive from the original building.—At *Washaway*, 4m NW of Bodmin by A389, is *Pencarrow* (open), a Palladian house of the 1760s by Robert Allanson of York. The rich interior has good furniture and pictures, including family portraits by Reynolds. —*Cardinham*, about 4m NE of Bodmin, has a good 15C church, with bench ends, and a Celtic cross.

We now enter the china-clay country centred on St Austell to the S (Rte 30) and the conical white waste dumps are seen on all sides. —67m. *Lanivet* has 6–10C carved and inscribed stones in its churchyard.—69m. *Victoria* (seasonal Tourist Information) is 1m N of *Roche*, where a chapel of 1409 is built into an outcrop of granite. *Hensbarrow* (1027ft; view) rises to the S.—We pass the large Iron Age hill-fort of *Castle-an-Dinas* (703ft) on the right, and reach (76½ m) *Indian Queens*, where the road for Newquay (Rte 35) branches to the right. At (77m) *Fraddon* A30 is joined by A39, which bears left after another mile for Truro (Rte 30).—79m. *Summercourt* has a traditional fair in September.

95m. **Redruth** became the Cornish mining centre in the 19C, when the tin and copper industries flourished. It is now incorporated with (98m) **Camborne** (46,500 inhab. together). In Redruth the house of William Murdock (1754–1839), who first exploited gas as a source of light, has been restored as a memorial to him and to Richard Trevithick (1771–1833), the engineer who pioneered the use of high-pressure steam. Trevithick spent much of his life at *Penponds*, SW of Camborne, and was born at *Pool*, between Redruth and Camborne. The *Cornish Engines Museum* (NT) at Pool preserves beam engines used in tin mining.

SW of Redruth is *Carn Brea* (738ft), occupied from neolithic times to the Middle Ages. At *Gwennap Pit*, a grassy hollow 1¼m SE of Redruth, John Wesley preached to large congregations of miners.

From *Portreath*, a small resort NW of Redruth, B3301 runs SW to (5½m) *Gwithian*, skirting a fine stretch of cliffs owned by NT, including *Godrevy Point*, the E horn of St Ives Bay.

105m. *Hayle* is a small port on the estuary at the head of St Ives Bay, opposite Lelant.

About 1m beyond Hayle A3074 heads round the bay to St Ives.—1m. *Lelant* is a resort, with the mother church of St Ives.—3m. *Carbis Bay*, another resort, lies to the right. The triangular monument on the hill to the left was erected in 1782 by John Knill, mayor of St Ives and a smuggler turned lawyer, who intended it as his tomb.—4½m. **St Ives** (11,000 inhab.; Tourist Information), a popular resort on one of the most charming bays in England, is known for its connection with artists. The potter Bernard Leach established his workshop here, with Shoji Hamada, in 1920. Ben Nicholson and Dame Barbara Hepworth moved to St Ives in 1939, forming the centre of a group which included the local painter Peter

Lanyon (1918–64). Barbara Hepworth's house and studio are now a museum of her life and work, administered by the Tate Gallery. The 15C church is dedicated to St Ia, an Irish saint believed to have suffered martyrdom here in the 5C. It contains good bench ends and a Madonna by Hepworth; there is a 15C cross by the S porch.—The conspicuous *Trencrom Hill* (NT; view) lies 3m S. —*Towednack*, 3m SW on a lane off the Zennor road, has a plain little church with a 13C chancel arch. There are fine points on the coast SW but the road via (4m) *Zennor*, (8m) *Morvah* and (12m) *St Just* to (18m) *Land's End*, all in Rte 33, is hilly and not very interesting.

113m. **Penzance**, see Rte 30.

# 33  The Land's End District

Map: OS Landranger 203.

The SW peninsula of Cornwall leading to **Land's End** is a granite mass, part of the chain which starts with Dartmoor and Bodmin Moor to the E and ends with the Scilly Isles to the SW. It rises from the lowlands connecting St Ives Bay and Mount's Bay in the E to an average height of about 400ft, though some hills exceed 800ft. On the coastline the rocks have been broken and weathered by Atlantic rollers to create, particularly in the S, some of the most dramatic cliff scenery in England. The interior abounds in ancient stone monuments. The district is described below in a series of short routes from Penzance (Rte 30). St Ives makes an alternative starting-point for excursions through the N.

FROM PENZANCE TO LAND'S END, 10m by A30. We leave Penzance by Alverton St. and follow A30 past the junction with A3071 for St Just to (2½m) *Drift*, with a reservoir to the right.

The unclassified road on the right leads to (1½m) *Sancreed*, where the churchyard has two crosses. 1¼m SW is the Iron Age village of *Carn Euny* (English Heritage, open at any reasonable time), occupied from before 400 BC until the end of the Roman period, with the relics of several huts and a superb *fogou, or underground chamber.

At (3¼m) *Catchall* A30 keeps to the right. Just before the top of Tregonebris Hill, on the right, is a standing stone known as the *Blind Fiddler*, while about ¼m to the left stands *Boscawen-noon*, a stone circle about 75ft in diameter.—At (5½m) the village of *Crows-an-Wra* is an old cross. A sideroad leads to the right past *Carn Brea* (657ft; NT), said to enjoy the widest sea view from the mainland of the British Isles. A medieval chapel once stood on the largest of several neolithic barrows. Further on we are joined by B3306 from St Just and beyond (8¾m) *Sennen* we reach (10m) *Land's End*.

The westernmost point of England (5° 41′ 31″ W long.), known to the ancients as *Bolerium* and in Cornish as *Penwith*, Land's End is a huge, turf-topped mass of granite, 60ft in height, from which a narrow ridge juts out into the sea. The *view extends 25m W to the Scilly Isles and is bounded on the N by Cape Cornwall and the Brisons rocks. Immediately in front is the *Longships Light-house*. To the right (N) and left (S) are the rocks known as the *Irish Lady* and the *Armed Knight*. About 9m SW is the *Wolf Rock Lighthouse*.

FROM PENZANCE TO THE LOGAN ROCK, 9m. We follow A30 from Penzance to (3¼m) *Catchall*, where we branch left on B3283.—5¼m. *St Buryan* has a large collegiate church with a tall granite 15C tower and a good rood screen, partly restored.—From (8¼m) *Treen* we can reach the coast at the rocky *Penberth Cove*, the headland fort of *Treryn Dinas* and the *Logan Rock* (NT), ³/₄m S.

This huge mass of stone (65 tons) is so delicately balanced that it can easily be moved, but it has never rocked or 'logged' so well since it was idly overset in 1824, with the aid of a friend, by Lieutenant Goldsmith (the writer's nephew), who had to replace it at a cost of about £125.

*Porthcurno*, ³/₄m W of the Logan Rock, has the open-air Minack Theatre. *Porthcurno Cove* is the main landing station of deep-sea cables. *St Levan*, 1¹/₄m beyond, has a small EE and Perp. church with a good screen and bench ends.—The coastal walk continues westward to (3¹/₂m) *Land's End* past some magnificent rock scenery, including *Tol Pedn Penwith* and *Pordenack*.

FROM PENZANCE TO ZENNOR, 7m. The obvious route, by B3311 to the outskirts of St Ives and then SW on B3306, is not very interesting, though at ¹/₂m B3311 passes W of the pleasant village of *Gulval*, a centre of market gardening, and at (2¹/₂m) *Castle Gate*, near the hill fort of *Castle-an-Dinas*, it gives a splendid view of Mount's Bay. A better route takes the unclassified road which branches left from B3311 at ¹/₄m and follows the Trevaylor valley NW. On the right we pass (1¹/₂m) *Bleu Bridge*, a slab bridge with an inscribed stone, possibly 7C.—Beyond (3m) *Newmill* we can turn right to (4¹/₂m) the Iron Age village of *Chysauster* (English Heritage, standard opening but closed on Thursday afternoons and on Fridays in winter). The best excavated and most expressive site of its kind in SW England, it has four pairs of houses on either side of a main street.—To the left of our main road, 1m beyond the turning for Chysauster, is the *Mulfra Quoit* dolmen. A path on the left, just short of (5¹/₂m) B3306, leads to the fine beehive hut at *Bosporthennis*.—*Gurnard's Head*, a bold promontory, lies ³/₄m straight ahead from the junction with B3306. We turn right, passing a half-fallen dolmen of unusual size of the moor to the S.—7m. *Zennor* has a 15C church with a mermaid carved on one of its bench ends, and the Wayside Museum of local history. D.H. Lawrence completed 'Women in Love' while living here during the First World War. St Ives (Rte 32) is 4m NE.

FROM PENZANCE TO MORVAH AND ST JUST, 10m. We take B3312 NW from Penzance to (2m) *Madron*, overlooking Mount's Bay, with the mother church of Penzance. There is a ruined baptistery and well 1m N. *Trengwainton Garden* (NT), ³/₄m SW, also has a view of the bay. We follow the unclassified road NW for Morvah.—Beyond (4m) *Lanyon Quoit* dolmen (NT) a path leads in ³/₄m to the *Ding Dong Mine*, almost certainly worked before the Christian era. On the moors to the NW are the *Mên-an-Tol* ('holed stone') and the *Mên Scryfa* ('written stone'). A little further E are the remains of a stone circle called the *Nine Maidens* (1m W of Mulfra, see above). From our road, 1m beyond the Lanyon Quoit, a track on the left brings us in 1¹/₄ m to the late Iron Age hill-fort known as *Chûn Castle*, with two concentric walls and a fine dolmen of earlier date.—We turn left on B3306 for (6m) *Morvah*. *Portheras Cove* is ³/₄m NW.— 10m. **St Just** (4000 inhab.), the centre of a once important mining area, has a 15C church and an amphitheatre where the old Cornish miracle plays were staged.

About 1¹/₄m W is *Cape Cornwall* (view), with an unusual Bronze Age tomb, *Ballowall Barrow* (English Heritage, open at any reasonable time), to its S. Good walkers can follow the coast to (6¹/₂m) Land's End.

# 34  The Isles of Scilly

Maps: OS Landranger 203, or OS Outdoor Leisure map (1:25,000 or 2½in to 1m).

An archipelago of about 150 islands, islets and rocks 28m SW of Land's End, the **Scilly Isles** form an outlying part of the granitic mass of Cornwall. Their name—taken from Scilly Isle, one of the smallest of the group—is something of a mystery, and they are no longer exclusively identified with the Cassiterides, or 'Tin Islands', of Herodotus. According to legend they are the only visible relic of Lyonesse, the land of Arthurian romance, which lies forty fathoms deep between them and Cornwall. The inummerable passage graves and other *Bronze Age remains give colour to the supposition that the isles were the highlands adjoining the low alluvial plain of Lyonesse. Since 1337 they have belonged to the Duchy of Cornwall, but are administered by their own all-purpose local authority, the Council of the Isles of Scilly.

The climate is very mild (mean winter temperature 8°C, summer 14°C). The permanent population is some 1900, confined to the five islands of *St Mary's, St Martin's, Tresco, Bryher* and *St Agnes*. The chief occupations are tourism (from April to October) and the growing of early flowers (from the beginning of December onward) and early potatoes for the mainland market. Some fishing continues. Seals and seabirds abound on the many uninhabited islands, and the autumn migration of both sea and land birds in October is renowned.

**Tourist Information Centre**: Town Hall, St Mary's.

**Transport to the Isles**: The RMV 'Scillonian III' of the Isles of Scilly SS Co. crosses from Penzance Dock to Hugh Town, St Mary's in about 2½hr. Daily sailings from April to mid October, except Sundays, with double sailings on Saturdays and some Wednesdays from mid May to the end of August. Winter service twice weekly.

Frequent helicopter service (in about 20 min.) by British Airways Helicopters Ltd from Penzance Heliport to St Mary's Airport throughout the year and to Tresco Heliport from April to September inclusive.

Air passenger services from Plymouth, Exeter and Newquay. Connecting services to Channel Islands, Cork, Gatwick and Heathrow.

Charter air passenger service from St Just (Land's End) by Isles of Scilly Skybus Ltd.

**Transport between the Isles**: Passenger launches connect St Mary's (Quay) with the off-islands of St Agnes, Bryher, Tresco and St Martin's daily from April to October inclusive, weather permitting. From November to March a freight launch provides a less frequent service.

**St Mary's**, the largest island (2½m by 2m), contains about three-quarters of the population. *Hugh Town*, the capital of the group, lies on the isthmus between the Garrison and the main landmass. It has a pleasant main street and a good museum. The *Garrison* has fortified walls built in 1715–46 (English Heritage, open at any reasonable time) and *Garrison Hill*, with a good view and the *Star Castle* of 1593 (now a hotel). On the W coast are the incomplete 16C fort known as *Harry's Walls* (English Heritage, open at any reasonable time), *Carn Morval* (view), and the Bronze Age burial mound and village of the Roman period at *Bant's Carn* (English Heritage, open at any reasonable time). *McFarlands Down* in the N has a good view. On the E coast are the Bronze Age passage grave and burial mound at *Innisidgen* (English Heritage, open at any reasonable time) and *Porth Hellick Point*, near the best preserved Bronze Age burial site on the islands (English Heritage, open at any reasonable time) and the cliff fort of *Giant's Castle*. In the S are *Old Town Bay*, with the graves of 120 people lost in the wreck of the 'Schiller' in 1875, and *Peninnis Point*, with a lighthouse and a good view. Near the Point is a 'logan rock' weighing over 300 tons.

**Tresco** lies about 1m NW of St Mary's. *Tresco Abbey* has wonderful subtropical *gardens (open), with the few remains of a Benedictine priory and the Valhalla Museum of figureheads of ships lost on the Scilly rocks. Near the N end of the island beyond *New Grimsby* is the so-called *King Charles's Castle* (English Heritage, open at any reasonable time), in fact probably built by Edward VI. The name of *Cromwell's Castle* (English Heritage, open at any reasonable time) nearby commemorates the fact that the Isles, the last stronghold of the Royalists, were subdued by the Cromwellians under Admiral Blake.—On the N coast is *Piper's Hole*, a narrow shaft running underground for 600ft. The harbour at *Old Grimsby* on the E coast has a 16C gun battery (English Heritage, open at any reasonable time).—**Bryher**, W of Tresco, repays a visit by its rocky coast, especially at *Shipman Head* and *Hell Bay*.—**Samson**, Bryher's southern neighbour, is now uninhabited.—**St Helen's**, NE of Tresco and uninhabited since the 19C, has the scanty remains of a medieval church and a Celtic monastery, probably connected with St Elidius. The island's name is apparently a corruption of the saint's name.—**St Martin's**, NE of Tresco, is known for its fine beaches. The island abounds in Bronze and Iron Age remains, and has an early navigation mark—the Day Mark of 1685—on *Chapel Down*, at the E tip.—**St Agnes**, SW of St Mary's, has some good barrows, a curiously perched boulder called the *Punch Bowl*, and the old sacred well of *Sancta Warna*. On the Downs is an ancient maze, set in pebbles and known as 'Troy Town'. The disused early 18C lighthouse is the second oldest purpose-built lighthouse in the country to survive; its fire basket is now in Tresco Abbey gardens.

The lighthouse at *Bishop Rock*, some 4m SW of St Agnes (boat trips on calm days only), guards the *Western Rocks* and particularly the *Gilstone Ledge*, where Admiral Sir Cloudesley Shovel's flagship 'Association' foundered in 1707 with the loss of 2000 men, including the Admiral. The wreck was rediscovered in 1967. In 1971 treasure from the 'Hollandia', which foundered off *Gunners Rock* in 1743, yielded previously unknown Spanish-American coins and many Mexican 'pieces of eight'. Many other wrecked ships have been rediscovered in recent years in the treacherous waters around the Western Rocks and the *Nor'rard Rocks* (off Bryher's W coast), and investigation continues.

# 35 Penzance to Barnstaple: The North Coast of Cornwall and Devon

Total distance 117m. **Penzance**, see Rte 30.—A30 to (15m) Camborne and (18m) Redruth, see Rte 32.—A30, A3075 to (34m) **Newquay**.— A392, A3059 to (41m) St Columb Major.—A39 to (49m) **Wadebridge**.—A39 to (60m) Camelford.—B3266, B3314, B3263 to (65m) **Tintagel**.—B3262 to (68m) **Boscastle**.—B3262, A39 to (82½m) Stratton (**Bude**).—A39 to (98m) Clovelly Cross (**Clovelly**).—A39 to (108m) **Bideford**.—A39 to (117m) **Barnstaple** (Rte 26).

Maps: OS Landranger 203, 204 (briefly), 200, 190, 180.

An excellent way for tourists who have reached Land's End by the S coast to make the return journey, this route loosely follows the course of A30 and A39. The excursions to the coast (Tintagel, Boscastle, etc.) are well worth the extra miles, for the cliff scenery of N Cornwall and N Devon is among the most romantic in England.

**Penzance**, see Rte 30.—A30 to (15m) *Camborne* and (18m) *Redruth*, see Rte 32. We continue on A30 for a further 5m and then branch left on A3075 for Newquay.

From the same roundabout B3277 leads left to (3m) *St Agnes*. The painter John Opie (1767–1807) was born at the hamlet of *Mithian*, 1½m E. *St Agnes Beacon* (629ft; view) and much of the coastline leading to the popular little bay of *Porthtowan*, 2½m SW, are NT.— B3285 continues NE from St Agnes to (7m) **Perranporth**, on Perran Bay. About 1½m N are the remains of the small *Oratory of St Piran*, restored to the light of day in 1835 after having been buried in *Penhale Sands* for over 700 years. It is believed to have been built over the tomb of St Piran in the 7C. The 11C church with its cross, a little inland, was also engulfed by the sands. About 1½m E of Perranporth is the ancient amphitheatre of *St Piran's Round*.

**34m. NEWQUAY** (17,500 inhab.) lies on a magnificent coast. The combination of sandy beaches and Atlantic rollers have made it a centre for surfing.

**Tourist Information Centre**: Cliff Rd.

**Car Parks**: Fore St., Manor Rd, Mount Wise, Tolcarne Rd.

**Bus Station**: off East St.

**Railway Station**: off Cliff Rd.

**Entertainments**: Cosy Nook Theatre on Towan Promenade and other seaside amusements.

**Airport**: off 3059 4m NE. Passenger services to Aberdeen, Bristol, Heathrow, Plymouth, Scilly Isles.

The town lies parallel with the coast, at the landward end of the promontory ending in *Towan Head*, which separates *Newquay Bay*, with its pleasant little harbour and beaches, from *Fistral Bay*, overlooked by the golf course and *Pentire Point*.

*Trerice* (NT), 3m SW via A392 and A3058, is a small, well-preserved manor house of 1571.—A good walk leads S and W from Newquay across the Gannel river to (2m) *Crantock*, where the church has a font recarved in 1473, and (4m) *Kelsey Head* (NT). *Holywell Bay*, 1m beyond, lies near the N edge of Penhale Sands (see above). *Cubert*, 1½m S of Crantock, has a curious church in a wild, windswept setting above the Sands.

FROM NEWQUAY TO PADSTOW, 13m by B3276, a winding, hilly and often narrow road. It leaves Newquay to the N via *Porth*, the original settlement, and hugs the coast along *Watergate Bay*.—From (5m) *Mawgan Porth* a sideroad leads up the beautiful *Vale of Mawgan* to *St Mawgan* (2m), a lovely village where the 13–15C church has a fine tower and a wealth of woodcarving (1450–1550) and a 14C cross in the churchyard. The nearby manor house of *Lanherne*, with a façade of 1580 and a 10C cross at its gate, is now a nunnery.—The rock *scenery at (7½m) *Bedruthan Steps* is particularly impressive in rough weather.—B3276 follows the coast to (9m) *Porthcothan Bay* and then turns inland to (11m) *St Merryn*. Sideroads and lanes lead NW to *Trevose Head* (2½m), with a lighthouse and a good view. *Constantine Bay* lies on its W side. *Harlyn Bay*, on the E side, has a cemetery of 400–300 BC with several graves preserved near the museum.—13m. **Padstow** ('Petrock's Stow'), a decayed port on the Camel estuary, has an attractive cluster of cottages on its quay. The church has an EE tower, a 15C font and the 17C Prideaux monument. Prideaux Place, with an Elizabethan façade, stands opposite. The town is known for its Hobby Horse festivities on May Day. A ferry crosses the estuary to Rock (see below).—*Stepper Point*, 2½m N (footpath via St George's Well), has a fine view of the coast.—A389 leads SE to (7m) Wadebridge (see below) via (3½m) *St Issey*, where the church has a fine carved reredos of c 1400 in catacleuse stone;

much shorter and more attractive is the footpath following the derelict railway line along the Camel.

From Newquay we take A392 and pass just S of (36m) *St Columb Minor*, with a late Dec. church tower, and then branch left on A3059, skirting the airport.—We join A39 at (41m) *St Columb Major*, which has a prominent Dec. and Perp. church with a crudely carved font of c 1300. *Castle-an-Dinas* (Rte 32) lies 2m SE. The high-lying road, commanding wide views down to the sea, crosses the St Austell–Padstow road at (43¹/₂m) *Winnard's Perch*.—At 44¹/₂m we pass, on the right, the line of standing stones called the *Nine Maidens* and at 46¹/₂m a path leads 2m across *St Breock's Downs* to a prehistoric standing stone (English Heritage, open at any reasonable time). On the Downs to the N are the *Pawton* dolmen and the inscribed stone of *Nanscow*.

49m. **Wadebridge** (Tourist Information), a market town on the Camel estuary, has a fine bridge dating from 1485, widened several times since. *Egloshayle*, on the opposite bank, has an EE and Perp. church.

FROM WADEBRIDGE TO DELABOLE, 12m by B3314. We join B3314 on the N bank of the estuary and, after 1¹/₂m, cross the river Amble.—2¹/₂m. A sideroad leads left to *Rock* (3m), connected with Padstow by ferry, and *Polzeath* (6m), a sandy seaside resort with *Pentire Point* (NT) to the N and *Trebetherick* and *Daymer Bay* to the S. On the *St Enedoc* golf course, between Trebetherick and Rock, is a 15C church recovered from the sand in 1863. Sir John Betjeman (1906–84) is buried here.—B3314 continues N, then turns parallel to the coast to (6¹/₂m) *St Endellion*, where the church has a shrine carved in catacleuse by the same hand as the St Issey reredos. *Port Isaac*, 2m N, is a delightful fishing village on a little cove, popular with visitors. A magnificent stretch of coast (NT and Cornwall North Coast Path) goes W past *Portquin* to (c 6m) Pentire Point.—From (8m) *Pendogget* B3267 leads right to St Teath and Camelford. Our road passes below *Tregeare Rounds*, an Iron Age fort with three rings of earthworks (view).—12m. *Delabole*, where slate has been quarried for four centuries, lies 2m S of the road from Camelford to Tintagel (see below).

52m. *St Kew Highway*. The village church, over 1m N, has 15C stained glass and an Ogham stone.—60m. **Camelford** (seasonal Tourist Information), once regarded as the site of Camelot, is in fact a dull place. Its mother church, with another inscribed Saxon stone, is at *Lanteglos*, 1¹/₂m SW.

A39 climbs to 1000ft, with wide but dreary views towards the highest point in Cornwall, Brown Willy (Rte 32).

About 1m short of Camelford we branch left on B3266, passing the turning on the right for *Slaughterbridge*, the scene of a battle between Britons and Saxons in 823, but not of Arthur's death. We then follow B3314 and B3263 towards the coast.—63¹/₂m. *Trewarmett* lies inland of *Trebarwith Strand*, where Gull Rock rises out of the fine bay.

65m. **Tintagel** is deservedly one of the most famous places in Cornwall. The little village (once called *Trevena*) is now horribly commercialised, though the *Old Post Office* (NT), a 14C building, deserves a visit. Even the crowds of summer visitors cannot destroy the grandeur of *Tintagel Head*, a promontory connected to the mainland by a rocky neck. The scanty remains of the *Castle* (English Heritage, standard opening and summer Sunday mornings) perilously straddling mainland and promontory have only slight architectural interest but complete the romantic charm of the scene. Early chroniclers and later poets have conspired to accept it as the birthplace of King Arthur, son of Uther Pendragon and Ygrayne. The castle was a stronghold of the Earls of Cornwall from c 1150 and the keep on the mainland dates from c 1236–72, but excavations have revealed traces of a Celtic monastery occupied from c 500 to c 850. A steep railed path mounts to the summit, with the remains of a small 13C chapel (perhaps incorporating some Saxon work), a freshwater spring and a natural cavern. The *view from the headland takes in the wild and rocky shore from Trevose Head in the S to Hartland Point in the N.

The *Parish Church*, dedicated to St Materiana and St Marcelliana, on the cliffs W of the village has a curious Norman font and a stone altar in the little Lady Chapel; the N wall of the nave and chancel may be Saxon work.—*Bossiney*, adjoining the village to the N, had Sir Francis Drake as its MP. Just to the N is *Rocky Valley*, leading left to the sea and right to *St Nectan's Kieve*, a pretty waterfall.

68m. **Boscastle** has an intricate little *harbour (NT), now disused, flanked by steep cliffs. The name is a corruption of the vanished Bottreaux Castle.

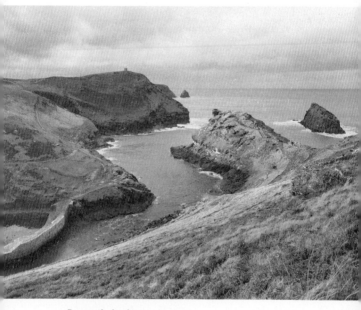

*Boscastle harbour*

The magnificent walk along the coast to the N (much of it NT) goes to (5½m) *Crackington Haven* via (1m) *Pentargon Bay*, with its waterfall, and (1½m) *Beeny Cliff*, both associated with the poetry of Thomas Hardy. He met his future wife, Emma Gifford, in 1870 at *St Juliot*, 2½m E of Boscastle in the valley of the Valency river, when he was restoring the little church.

B3263 continues NE from Boscastle to rejoin A39.—78m. At *Poundstock*, W of A39, the church and 14C Guildhall make an attractive group. The Elizabethan Penfound Manor (not open) has origins in a manor of Edith, wife of Edward the Confessor.—81½m.

The road divides. A39 continues straight ahead for (82½m) *Stratton* (seasonal Tourist Information at Stamford Hill), where the fine Perp. church contains the tomb of Sir John Arundell (1561).

At *Stamford Hill*, just to the NW, the Parliamentarians were defeated in 1643. —*Launcells*, 1m E, has a lovely church with 15C woodwork and tiles, Norman font and Gothick pulpit.

From the road junction A3073 heads left to (82½m) **Bude** (6800 inhab. with Stratton; seasonal Tourist Information), a popular resort with magnificent coastal scenery to both N and S. *Bude Haven*, with good sands, is protected by a breakwater ending in the *Chapel Rock*. *Compass Point*, S of the town, and *Efford Beacon*, SW, have good views.

A pleasant walk leads S along the coast to (4m) *Widemouth Bay* (via (1½m) *Upton*.
   **Morwenstow**, where the eccentric poet R.S. Hawker was vicar from 1834 to 1875, lies on the coast about 8m N of Bude. To reach it we follow the coast past *Menachurch Point* to (4½m) the *Duck Pool* at the mouth of the *Coombe Valley* (see below) and either continue along the coast via (1m) the *Lower* and (1½m) *Higher Sharpnose Point* or turn inland for ½m and then take the road. Morwenstow church has an early Norman font and Norman arches with beautiful zigzag moulding. There is quaint rhymed inscription over the door of Hawker's vicarage. *Tonacombe* (not open), a Tudor house just to the S, is the home of Eustace Leigh in Charles Kingsley's 'Westward Ho!'—Good walkers can continue N to (7m) *Hartland Quay* and (9m) *Hartland Point* (see below). —From Duck Pool, on the way to Morwenstow, we may follow the *Coombe Valley* to (3½m) Kilkhampton (see below), passing the site of Sir Richard Grenville's mansion (NT) and *Stowe Wood*.

FROM BUDE TO EXETER, 50m. A3072 runs E, crossing A39 at (2m) Stratton (see above).—Further on we cross the Tamar and the disused Bude Canal (1825), with inclined planes instead of locks, and enter Devon.—9m. *Holsworthy*, at the junction with A388 from Launceston to Bideford, has a massive Perp. church tower. 11m. *Stapledon*, on the left, was the birthplace of Walter de Stapledon (1261–1326), founder of Exeter College, Oxford.—14m. Sideroads lead N to *Thornbury* (3m) with the Devon Museum of Mechanical Music.—22m. *Hatherleigh*, on the river at the junction with A386 from Okehampton to Torrington. The church of *Northlew*, 4½m SW, has good 16C woodwork.—We follow B3216, rejoin A3072 and cross the Okement 5m N of Okehampton. —28½m. *Sampford Courtenay*, a charming village, has a Perp. church with good roofs. The Western Rising of 1549 against the Reformation began here. —We cross the Taw, bypassing *North Tawton*, and join A377 at (38m) *Copplestone*. For the rest of the way, via (42m) *Crediton* to (50m) *Exeter*, see Rte 18A.

We follow A39 N from Stratton.—87m. **Kilkhampton** church has a Norman S doorway and carved *bench ends.—At 91m we enter Devon.—At (98m) *Clovelly Cross*, with the site of an Iron Age fort, we turn left on B3237 for **Clovelly**, a village whose picturesque charms have made it overwhelmingly popular with visitors.

It lies in a narrow rift between superbly wooded cliffs with magnificent sweeping views of Barnstaple or Bideford Bay. The main street, far too steep for cars, descends in steps and stages past neat whitewashed cottages to the little cove and pier (1587).—The lovely *Hobby Drive extends SE. To the NW are the grounds of *Clovelly Court*, whose main beauty spot is *Gallantry Bower* (c 1¼m), rising sheer from the sea and giving a fine view. The rocky cove of *Mouth Mill* lies ½m beyond. On the way back we can pass the surviving 14C wing of Clovelly Court. The *Church*, near B3237 and the visitors' car park, has monuments of the Carys and the Hamlyns and a memorial to Charles Kingsley (1819–75), who spent his boyhood at the rectory.
   From Clovelly Cross we turn W for (4m) the village of *Hartland* and (5½m) *Stoke*, where the large 14C church has a striking rood screen, font and roof. We reach the coast at the secluded hamlet of (6½m) *Hartland Quay*, with

contorted slate rocks. Just over ½m S is the waterfall at *Speke's Mill Mouth*.
The splendid *Hartland Point*, 4½m N, is the NW tip of Devon.

A39 continues E, passing the entrance to Hobby Drive (see above), a
lovely alternative approach to Clovelly.—From (100m) *Buck's Cross* a
lane leads down to the hamlet of *Buck's Mill* (1m).—104½m. B3236
leads left to (3m) *Westward Ho!* (see below) through *Abbotsham*,
where the small 13C church has a Norman font and good bench
ends.

108m. **Bideford** (pronounced 'Biddyford'; 12,200 inhab.; seasonal
Tourist Information) stands on two hills rising from the Torridge. Still
a working port, it enjoyed its heyday in the 16C when the Grenvilles
obtained the town charter (1573) and Bideford men made up the
crew of the 'Revenge' on the Azores expedition. This era was
celebrated in Kingsley's 'Westward Ho!' (1855), partly written at
Bideford. The *Bridge* of 24 arches across the Torridge is medieval in
origin, though it has since been widened. The *Church*, rebuilt in
1864, keeps its Norman font and a monument to Sir Thomas Grayn-
fyldd (d. 1513). The Quay and Bridgeland Rd have prosperous
merchants' houses of c 1690. Facing the quay is a statue of Kingsley,
and eight old Spanish cannon stand in the nearby park.

**Lundy** (about 40 inhab.) is a granite island 3m long and ¼–¾m broad in the
Bristol Channel, 12m off Hartland Point. Owned by NT and administered by the
Landmark Trust, it is served by steamers from (25m) Bideford all year round and
from (23m) Ilfracombe (Rte 26) in the summer. It has some curious rock
formations and is the breeding place of innumerable puffin, etc. The island
remained a nest of pirates down to the reign of Queen Anne; the ruined *Marisco
Castle* near the quay was the stronghold of one such ruling family. The *Shutter
Rock*, off the SW end, so called because it is believed that it would exactly fill
the rifted opening of the adjacent *Devil's Lime Kiln*, was the scene of the wreck
of the 'Santa Catharina' in Charles Kingsley's 'Westward Ho!' The 19C
buildings include a church, an inn and three lighthouses.

A386 leads N from the quay via (1½m) *Northam* to (3m) *Appledore*, a quaint
little port still with shipyards, or to (3m) **Westward Ho!**, a resort named after
Kingsley's novel. The Royal North Devon Golf Course lies to the N, separated
from the sea by the curious *Pebble Ridge*. Rudyard Kipling attended school
here.
   To the S A386 follows the Torridge.—General Monk (1608–70) was baptised
at the Norman font in the church of (2m) *Landcross*.—4m. *Weare Giffard*, a
former port on the opposite bank of the river, has an interesting church and 15C
manor house.—7m. **Great Torrington** (4100 inhab.; seasonal Tourist Information), with some good Georgian houses, stands high above the river. *Rosemoor
Garden* (open), started in 1959, lies ¾m S of the centre on B3220. *Merton*, 6m
SE on A386, was the birthplace of Walter de Merton, founder of the Oxford
college; it is also associated with Henry Williamson's 'Tarka the Otter' (1927).
   There are several churches worth visiting in the lonely country SW of
Bideford, notably at *West Putford* (11½m) and *Sutcombe* (16½m).

A39 crosses Bideford bridge and follows the river N, passing *Tapeley
Park* (open), home of the Christie family of Glyndebourne, a much
altered 18C house with Italian plaster ceilings and an Italian terraced
garden.—111m. *Instow*, facing Appledore at the confluence
of the Torridge and the Taw, has wide sands at low water.—117m.
**Barnstaple**, see Rte 26.

# SOUTH MIDLANDS

Of all the regional labels with which the English make do in the absence of officially designated provinces, the term 'Midlands' is the vaguest, as well as the least appetising, stopping unpromisingly short at telling us that the area in question lacks a coastline. Yet it is still preferable to the emptily colourful coinages of the tourist industry—the Heart of England, the English Shires, and so on—even if it does require special, and to some extent arbitrary, definition. In the present guide central England has been divided into the North Midlands, described in the next section, and South Midlands, described here. Its southern boundary is the valley of the Thames, and its eastern boundary the course of the A1. The third side of the triangle is formed by a line drawn roughly from the Severn and the Wye in the SW to the Wash in the NE—a rather less arbitrary boundary than it might at first sight appear. Its course begins with Gloucester, Worcester and Hereford in the W, passes through Coventry and Leicester, and ends by the A1 at Stamford. The bulk of the area thus enclosed is filled by Gloucestershire, Oxfordshire, Warwickshire, Buckinghamshire, Northamptonshire and Bedfordshire, though parts of several other counties are included at the fringes: Hereford and Worcester in the W, Berkshire in the S, Hertfordshire in the E and Leicestershire in the N.

A bird's eye viewpoint looking N and W from London would show the land falling into an alternating rhythm of hill and plain, hill and valley, usually running crosswise to the major roads that radiate from the capital like the spokes of a wheel. The first major outcrop is of chalk, spreading N and E from the great centre of chalkland on Salisbury Plain. In the S, on the Berkshire Downs near Wantage, chalk creates the landscape of smooth, turfy contours and wide, breezy views which is familiar throughout so much of Southern England. Along its top a section of the Ridgeway Path, dotted with prehistoric monuments, overlooks the Vale of the White Horse with its ancient chalk figure cut into the soil. Further N, the gentle ridge of the Chiltern Hills runs through Buckinghamshire and into Bedfordshire before it merges into the broad swath of chalk that continues through Eastern England. The Chilterns were once densely wooded, as Burnham Beeches can still remind us, and they can still have a remote upland atmosphere, as in the villages N of High Wycombe or S of Stokenchurch. Yet the distinctive local character is best shown by the comfortable brick-built high streets of High Wycombe or Wendover—townscapes ready-made for the process of affluent suburbanisation which has largely overtaken them.

Beyond the Chilterns lie the vales of Oxfordshire, with the limestone ridge of the Cotswold Hills rising in the W. While the Chilterns traditionally depended on their beech forests for the local furniture industry, the Cotswolds grew rich off the lamb's back. Places like Burford, Stow-on-the-Wold, Chipping Camden, Broadway and Cirencester still testify to the prosperity the wool trade once brought. Their beauty comes from the honey-coloured local stone, a worthy rival to the Bath stone and Ham stone produced from the southern extension of the same limestone belt. Cotswold stone gives dignity to the houses and particularly to the handsome Perp. churches of the region; elsewhere, its warm tones can be seen in many Oxford buildings.

Approached from the E, the landscape of the Cotswolds is gentle. Its dramatic effects lie on the sharp W edge, where a series of famous viewpoints (Cleeve Hill, Birdlip and Broadway) overlook the flat country beyond. The Vale of Evesham, in the N, is a broad, fertile plain watered by the Avon and its many tributaries as its winds down from Stratford to join the Severn at Tewkesbury. By comparison to this pleasant fruit-growing country, the expanses of the Severn Vale around and, particularly, below Gloucester can seem dull and unvaried to the eye.

Where the Chilterns are chalk and the Cotswolds limestone, the Malverns, the last range of hills encountered on the journey W from London, are of hard pre-Cambrian rock. They rise with surprising suddenness from the W edge of the vale beyond Worcester, giving a foretaste of the Welsh scenery to come. Much the same can be said of the Wye valley, which marks the border with Wales as it winds down from Monmnouth to Chepstow. Its tightly looping course through cliff and forest is among the most beautiful—and dramatic—inland scenery in the country.

This view of the region has so far looked more W than N from London and, in doing so, it has merely followed the preference shown by generations of tourists. The Wye valley, at the W extremity, was among the first 'beauty spots' established on the itinerary of English travellers in the 18C, when lovers of the picturesque and the first Romantic poets came down the river to admire the lovely ruins of Tintern Abbey. Their spring waters made the Malvern Hills a fashionable spa resort. As for the country closer to London, the routes to Oxford and Stratford-upon-Avon via Blenheim and Woodstock or to Oxford and Cotswold villages like Bourton-on-the-Water follow a path beaten by thousands of coach tours every summer.

At first glance, it is not difficult to see why the country N of London has been less favoured. The capital has certainly left its ugly mark to the W, laying waste the scenery of the Thames valley well beyond Heathrow Airport and making the Buckinghamshire countryside of the Chilterns suburban, but even this damage can seem mild by comparison to what the traveller encounters on the routes N through Hertfordshire and Bedfordshire. Here the major roads run past an apparently endless sprawl of new towns, satellite towns and garden cities that are neither gardens nor cities. Even beyond the influence of London the region is still the graveyard of modern town planning, with Corby (in the ironstone part of Northamptonshire) a monument to yesterday's mistakes and Milton Keynes (blandly spreading over north Buckinghamshire) a reminder of how little we have learned.

Nor is the picture any more cheering in the region's historic centres. In the W, Oxford has a charm that can survive even the growth of the motor industry around it, while Warwick, as Nikolaus Pevsner says, is a 'perfect county town'. Further W, Gloucester and Worcester have been insensitively redeveloped but, like Hereford, at least have their cathedrals to commend them. In contrast, Bedfordshire, Northamptonshire and Leicestershire—lacking an ancient cathedral within their boundaries—have dull county towns. Bedford, with least to be proud of, has treated itself the best; Northampton and Leicester have all but submerged the modest historic character they possessed beneath inner ring roads and shopping centres.

The real interest of these counties will elude the traveller who sticks to major roads and heads for major destinations. Ampthill, in Bedfordshire, and Olney, in the northern tip of Buckinghamshire where it meets Bedfordshire and Northamptonshire, are just two examples of the many smaller places whose appeal belies their immediate surroundings and stands in pleasant contrast to their larger neighbours. Northamptonshire, and the country bordering it to the N and E, is particularly rich in this respect. The limestone belt which continues up from the Cotswolds may not create scenery to rival the Cotswolds, but it produces an equally handsome building material. Traditionally quarried at Barnack and Ketton or as roofing slabs at Collyweston, this elegant stone has helped make North-amptonshire extraordinarily rich in architecture. The county's traditional reputation for 'spires and squires' is fitting tribute to the beauty and abundance of its parish churches and country houses. The list of the handsome stone-built towns and villages would begin with Oundle, Higham Ferrers, Rockingham and Duddington but have difficulty completing itself in decent compass. Stamford, just outside Northamptonshire at the junction of several counties, is a fitting climax to the region, for here the local stone and the local style have created one of the finest provincial townscapes England can boast.

# 36  London to Oxford: The Thames Valley

## A.  By road via Windsor and Henley

Total distance 60m. M4 to (21m) Slough, for **Windsor**.—A308 to (26m) Maidenhead.—A4, A423 to (35m) **Henley**.—A423 to (51m) Dorchester (bypassed).—A423 to (60m) **Oxford** (Rte 37).

Maps: OS Landranger 176, 175, 164.

Windsor makes a popular day-trip from London, and so is often unpleasantly crowded. Alternative ways by coach and rail are described in 'Blue Guide London'.

We leave London on M4, passing (junction 4) *Heathrow Airport*, the M25, and, to our N, the dreary wasteland of (21m) *Slough* (87,000 inhab.). At junction 6 (Slough West) we leave the motorway for Windsor, about 1m S.

  **WINDSOR** (28,300 inhab.; Tourist Information), on the S bank of the Thames, is famous for the castle where English kings and queens have lived for 900 years.

  Thames St. climbs from the river and car park to the High St., which continues between the Castle bastions and 18C houses, now shops. The statue of Queen Victoria at Castle Hill is by Sir Edgar Boehm (1887).

  Castle Hill leads to the entrance to **··Windsor Castle**.

Precincts and castle open daily except Garter Day (June); State Apartments, Dolls House and Exhibition of Drawings closed when royal family is in residence (usually April and parts of March, May, June and December). All or part of the castle may be closed at short notice. The ceremony of the Changing of the Guard takes place every day except Sunday by the entrance.

  Saxon kings first settled at Old Windsor but their palace of Kingsbury was allowed to crumble after William the Conqueror built a wooden fortress at New Windsor in 1066. This was rebuilt in stone by Henry II in 1165–79 and then improved and extended by Edward III, preserving, however, the original plan of two baileys and a mote-hill. Henry I's marriage to Adeliza of Louvain (1121) was the first royal wedding to be celebrated here; Edward III was born in the castle in 1312 and Henry IV in 1421. Three kings—David II of Scotland, John of

**Key to State Apartments**

1. Grand Staircase
2. Grand Vestibule
3. Waterloo Chamber
4. Garter Throne Room
5. Grand Reception Room
6. St George's Hall
7. Queen's Guard Chamber
8. Queen's Presence Chamber
9. Queen's Audience Chamber
10. Queen's Ballroom
11. Queen's Drawing Room
12. King's Closet
13. King's Dressing Room
14. State Bedchamber
15. King's Drawing Room
16. King's Dining Room

WINDSOR CASTLE

France and James I of Scotland—have been imprisoned within its walls; from his cell window James first saw his future wife, Jane Beaufort. Edward III's queen, Philippa of Hainault, died here in 1369. The present appearance of the building dates from extensive restoration by Sir Jeffry Wyatville for George IV.

We enter the *Lower Ward* by *Henry VIII's Gateway*. In front is the entrance to the *Horseshoe Cloisters*, built during Edward IV's reign; at their NW corner stands the *Curfew Tower*, with a 13C interior, eight bells and an unusual clock which chimes every three hours. On the right are the houses of the Military Knights of Windsor, an order founded by Edward III as the 'Poor Knights of Windsor' at the same time as the Order of the Garter and given its present name by William IV in 1833. The central tower (1359) bears the arms of Philip and Mary.

**'St George's Chapel** is a superb Perp. building, ranking with King's College Chapel in Cambridge and Henry VII's Chapel at Westminster. It was begun in 1478 by Henry Janyns for Edward IV and continued by William Vertue in 1503–11.

We enter by the S door. The *Nave* has a fine lierne vault with carved bosses. At the SW corner is the *Beaufort Chapel*, where the tomb of the Earl of Worcester (d. 1526) has a Flemish bronze grating, unusual in Britain. The great W window contains fine glass of 1503–09. In the NW corner is the tomb of George V (d. 1936) by Lutyens and Reid Dick, and of Queen Mary (d. 1953), with the theatrical tomb of Princess Charlotte (d. 1817) in the Urswick Chapel behind.

The *Choir* is separated from the nave by a Gothic screen (c 1785) by Henry Emlyn. The organ, originally placed centrally (as in King's College Chapel), was rebuilt in flanking sections to give a better view of the fan vaulting. In the *North Choir Aisle* is (left) the *Rutland Chapel* (1481) with effigies of George Manners (d. 1513) and his wife. To the right is the *Chantry Chapel of William, Lord Hastings* with contemporary paintings of his execution in 1483. To the left is the memorial chapel of George VI (1969). To the N of the high altar a superb pair of gates (1482) fronts the tomb of Edward IV. Above is the royal pew, a splendid wooden oriel provided by Henry VIII for Catherine of Aragon. A vault in the centre of the floor contains the remains of Henry VIII, Jane Seymour and Charles I. The stalls, in three tiers, are surmounted by the helmets, crests and banners of the 26 Knights of the Garter, whose installations have taken place at Windsor since 1348. The reverse stalls are those of the royal family, the sovereign's stall marked by the royal standard.

We turn left after the screen. The *Bray Chapel* contains the cenotaph of the Prince Imperial, son of Napoleon III, killed in South Africa in 1879. In the *South Choir Aisle* the *Chantry of John Oxenbridge*, on the left, contains paintings of 1522, the great sword of Edward III and a simple slab marking Henry VI's tomb. On the S side of the altar is the tomb of Edward VII and Queen Alexandra (by Mackennal). The SE chapel, with the tomb of the Earl of Lincoln (d. 1585), is called the *Lincoln Chapel* or *John Schorne's Tower*, from the relics of Sir John Schorne (d. 1314), brought in 1478 from North Marston in Buckinghamshire.

The E wall of the ambulatory once formed the W front of Henry III's Chapel (1240–48) and retains its original doors. Beyond the floor slab of Sir Jeffry Wyatville the NE door leads through a slype, or passage, to the *Dean's Cloister*, preserving arcading of Henry III's Chapel and a piece of fresco. To the N is the picturesque *Canon's Cloister* of 1353–56.

The **Albert Memorial Chapel** was rebuilt by Henry VII as a burial place for Henry VI, completed by Wolsey and converted by Queen Victoria into a memorial for Prince Albert (d. 1861), buried at Frogmore. Albert's cenotaph is by Baron Triqueti. The chapel also contains the tombs of the Duke of Clarence (d. 1892), the elder son of Edward VII, by Alfred Gilbert, and of the Duke of Albany (d. 1884), Queen Victoria's youngest son. Beneath the chapel George III, Queen Charlotte and six of their sons (including George IV and William IV) are buried.

To the left of the entrance to the North Terrace is the *Winchester Tower*, where Chaucer may have lived in 1390 when Master of Works at Windsor. From the North Terrace there is a view of the Home Park, Eton and Stoke Poges church.

Below is St George's School, the choir school in the building (1802) of Travers College, founded in 1795 from the bequest of Samuel Travers (d. 1725) for 'Naval Knights', an order corresponding to the Military Knights (see above) but disbanded in 1892.

From the North Terrace we enter the room displaying *Queen Mary's Dolls House* and the *Exhibition of Old Master Drawings*. The dolls house was designed for Queen Mary by Lutyens; details include books and paintings by contemporary authors and artists, working plumbing and electric lighting. The exhibition of drawings displays a changing selection from the royal collection, including works by da Vinci and Holbein.

Nearby is the entrance to the **·State Apartments**, occupying the N wing of the Upper Ward. Used mainly for royal functions, they contain a superb collection of paintings, furniture, sculpture and other treasures. Visitors with limited time should note that, on the whole, the finest works of art are in the rooms toward the end of the present circulation order. The position of some items is liable to change: a brochure on sale gives up-to-date details.

From the *China Gallery* we climb the *Grand Staircase*, with a statue of George IV by Chantrey, and armour made for Henry VIII and the sons of James I. The *Grand Vestibule* has relics of Napoleon and the Japanese surrender sword (early 16C) of 1945. The large *Waterloo Chamber*, constructed in 1830 inside a 12C court, contains portraits, mostly by Lawrence, of those instrumental in the downfall of Napoleon. The *Garter Throne Room* has portraits of sovereigns in their Garter robes; the *Grand Reception Room* has fine Gobelins tapestries. The noble *St George's Hall*, 185ft long, where the Garter festivities are held, bears the coats of arms of the knights since 1348 on the walls and ceiling. The portraits of English sovereigns from James I to George IV are by Van Dyck, Kneller, etc., while the parallel range of busts includes work by Rysbrack, Roubiliac, Nollekens and Chantrey. The *Queen's Guard Chamber* displays a fine suit of armour (1585) made for Sir Christopher Hatton and busts by Leone Leoni. The *Queen's Presence Chamber* and the *Queen's Audience Chamber* both have Gobelins tapestries and ceilings by Verrio glorifying Queen Catherine of Braganza. In former is a bust of Handel by Roubiliac, in the latter portraits of the Princes of Orange (by Honthorst) in frames carved by Grinling Gibbons. The *·Queen's Ballroom* contains an unequalled array of portraits by Van Dyck (Charles I, Henrietta Maria, their children and members of the court) with 17C French and English furniture.

The *·Queen's Drawing Room* has several works by Holbein and a portrait of Elizabeth I, when Princess, by an unknown artist. In the *King's Closet* are views of Venice by Canaletto and a portrait of Garrick and his wife by Hogarth. The *·King's Dressing Room* contains Van Dyck's painting of Charles I from three points of view and portraits by Clouet, Memling, Dürer, Andrea del Sarto, Rembrandt, Holbein and Rubens (of himself and of Van Dyck). The *King's State Bedchamber* contains a Louis Seize bed and several Canalettos. The *·King's Drawing Room* contains works by Rubens (Holy Family, etc.) and a St Martin by Van Dyck. the *King's Dining Room* has a ceiling by Verrio and carvings by Grinling Gibbons.

The elliptical **Round Tower** (or Keep) provides a magnificent view. Its lower half (1170) was heightened by Wyatville.—The *Queen's Private Apartments* (not open) are on the E side of the Upper Ward. The passage between the Round Tower and the Upper Ward leads through St George's Gateway to Castle Hill, near the entrance to the *Royal Stables*.

N and E of the Castle is the *Home Park*, where the Royal Windsor Horse Show is held annually in mid May. In the S part are *Frogmore House* and *Mausoleum*. The latter contains the remains of Queen Victoria and the Prince Consort; also buried here are the Duke of Windsor, Edward VIII (d. 1972), and the Duchess of Windsor, the former Mrs Simpson (d. 1986). It is usually open on the first Wednesday and Thursday in May and on the Wednesday nearest to 24 May, Queen Victoria's birthday.

We return from the Castle down Castle Hill to Queen Victoria's statue. The *Guildhall*, immediately S, was designed by Sir Thomas Fitch in 1687 and finished by Wren in 1707. It is adorned with statues of Queen Anne and Prince George of Denmark. The parish church of *St John the Baptist* in the High St. was rebuilt in 1822; it contains a Last Supper ascribed to Franz de Cleyn (1588–1658) and carvings by Grinling Gibbons and others. Market St. and Church St. are both cobbled, with attractive houses.

The *Royal Mews* (open) in St Alban's St. display the Queen's horses and carriages, including the Scottish State Coach used at the 1981 royal wedding, and a selection of gifts presented to the Queen for her Silver Jubilee in 1977.

Opposite Castle Hill is *Windsor and Eton Central Station*, half of which has been converted into *Madame Tussaud's Royalty and Railways Exhibition*.

The original Royal Waiting Room and large Jubilee Glass Canopy built for the present station by the Great Western Railway Co. to celebrate Queen Victoria's Diamond Jubilee have been restored. Madame Tussaud's have added life-like figures of all the personalities involved; they have restored railway carriages and built a full-size replica of the Queen-class locomotive, one of the most powerful engines of the time, which pulled the train in which foreign royal guests arrived to be received by Queen Victoria.

In Thames St. is the *Theatre Royal, Windsor*, founded in 1792 with George III as its patron. The present building dates from 1815. It is the centre of the Windsor Festival, held annually in September with concerts in St George's Chapel and Eton College.

The *Household Cavalry Museum*, Combermere Barracks, is in St Leonard's Rd, just S of central Windsor on the way to Windsor Safari Park. It contains one of the country's largest collections of arms, saddlery, standards and uniforms.

S of Windsor is **Windsor Great Park** (nearly 2000 acres), crossed by the road to Ascot and the Long Walk. The latter, planted with elms by Charles II and replanted after 1945 with horse chestnut and plane trees, stretches straight from the Castle to (2³/4m) *Snow Hill*, where there is a huge statue of George III by Westmacott. Still within the park, best approached via Old Windsor village along the winding Crimp Lane, is (4m) the *Savill Garden* (open), 20 acres of lovely woodland named after a former park ranger. S of the garden is Smith's Lawn, a polo ground, and beyond that the *Valley Gardens* (open). These lie on the N side of Virginia Water (Rte 14B).—For Runnymede to the E, see Rte 36B.

*Windsor Safari Park* (open), SW of central Windsor, includes a drive-round section with wild animals, children's zoo, picnic areas, dolphinarium, etc.

Across Windsor Bridge (no cars) begins the long street forming the small town of **Eton** (3500 inhab.) and leading to **Eton College**, founded by Henry VI in 1440 and perhaps the most widely known of all English schools. It is open to visitors during afternoons in term, and from 10.30 in the Easter and summer holidays.

The main block of fine mellow brick includes two courts or quadrangles. The larger—School Yard—contains a statue of Henry VI (1719). A frieze commemorates 1157 Etonians who fell in the First World War and 748 killed in the Second. Above is the *Upper School* (1689–94) with busts of eminent Etonians, damaged in 1941 but restored; the panelled walls and staircases are covered with names of boys going on to King's College, Cambridge (earliest 1577), with wooden pillars of c 1625. The *Chapel, a Perp. structure begun in 1441 and completed in 1483, has a fan vault added in 1958 by Sir William Holford. A superb series of wall paintings (1479–88) of British workmanship was discovered in 1847 and has been restored; the stained-glass E window is by Evie Hone (1952) and the clerestory windows are by John Piper. A museum opened in 1985.

A fine gatehouse of c 1517 erected by Provost Lupton leads to the second court, or *Cloisters*, with the Collegers' *Dining Hall* (1450) and the *College Library* (1725–29) above it.—In the playing fields beyond is the 'wall' which gives it name to the 'wall game', a style of football peculiar to Eton.

Famous old Etonians include Fielding, Dr Thomas Arne, Charles James Fox, Richard Porson, the elder and younger Pitt, Sir Robert Walpole and his son Horace, Gray, Shelley, Wellington, Canning, Gladstone, Swinburne, Sir Leslie Stephen, Sir Hubert Parry, Robert Bridges, Captain Oates, Sir Steven Runciman, J.B.S. Haldane, M.R. James, Aldous Huxley, Cyril Connolly, George

*Stanley Spencer, Swan Upping at Cookham (1914–19)*

Orwell, Anthony Eden, Harold Macmillan, Ian Fleming, Lord Hailsham, Lord Carrington, Humphrey Lyttelton.

*Dorney Court* (open), off B3026 3m W of Eton, is a pleasant house of c 1500 in timber and brick, with a well-preserved interior.

The main route follows A308 W from Windsor to (26m) **Maidenhead** (49,000 inhab.; Tourist Information), a resort on the Thames at the beginning of a beautiful stretch extending about 7m to Marlow. Oldfield, by the river, houses the *Henry Reitlinger Bequest* (open), notable for Oriental ceramics and drawings.

FROM MAIDENHEAD TO HIGH WYCOMBE. There are two routes, by A4094 (11½m) from the bridge or by A308 and A404 (10½m) from the centre.—A4094 passes Boulter's Lock (Rte 36B) and (3½m) **Cookham**, a pretty riverside village where Sir Stanley Spencer (1891–1959) was born and spent most of his life, putting local scenes and people into many of his paintings. A gallery in the High St. is devoted to his work and life, and there is a copy of his Last Supper in the church. A4094 crosses the river to the large residential village of (4½m) *Bourne End*.—The alternative way by A308 and A404 crosses the river between (4¾m) Bisham, pronounced 'Bizzum', and (5½m) Marlow. *Bisham Abbey* (not open), now the National Sports Centre, is a Tudor house incorporating the remains of an Augustinian priory. The church has a monument to Sir Philip and Sir Thomas Hoby (d. 1558 and 1566) and a fine armorial window of enamelled glass. **Marlow** (14,100 inhab.) is a pleasant old place, with attractive houses and a suspension bridge across the Thames (1831–36; William Tierney Clark). Shelley and his wife visited Thomas Love Peacock here in 1815, and in 1817–18, when they lived at Albion House in West St., Shelley wrote 'The Revolt of Islam' and Mary Shelley 'Frankenstein'. The parish church has a curious monument to Sir Miles Hobart (d. 1632), paid for by Parliament, depicting the accident that killed him. The RC church (1845–48) is by A.W.N. Pugin.

FROM MAIDENHEAD TO BEACONSFIELD. The direct route follows the way to High Wycombe via A4094 and Bourne End described above. An interesting alternative (8m) goes via *Taplow*, off A4 2m NE of the centre of Maidenhead. Sir Stanley Spencer (see above) died here, and the church has 14–15C brasses. From the village the road climbs steeply and soon skirts, on our left, the beautiful woods of **Cliveden** (NT, open). The house, designed in 1849 by Sir Charles Barry, lies further N. It is let to Blakeney Hotels Ltd, and only three rooms are open. On the right is the estate of *Dropmore* (not open) and, beyond, *Dorneywood* (NT), presented to the nation as an official residence for a Secretary of State; only the gardens are open, by written appointment. Further E is the fine wooded common of *Burnham Beeches* (Rte 38A).—Beyond (5m) *Hedsor* we descend to join A4094, the High Wycombe road, at (6m) *Wooburn*, but keep right on B4440 for *Beaconsfield* (Rte 38A).

We take A4 out of Maidenhead to Maidenhead Thicket, with the *Courage Shire Horse Centre* (open), and bear right on A423.—At *Hurley*, ½m from the river, the partly Saxon and partly Norman church, restored in the 19C, was the nave of a Benedictine priory church. Remains of the cloisters and domestic buildings are incorporated in nearby houses.

35m. **Henley-on-Thames** (11,000 inhab.; Tourist Information) is a pleasant and prosperous town with some timber-framed houses and many 18C ones. It is famous for the Royal Regatta in June/July (see headnote to Rte 36B). At its E end stands a handsome bridge of 1786, with sculptured masks of the Thames and Isis over its central arches. The big *Church*, with a Perp. tower, has flint and stone chequer-boarding outside, and a monument to Dame Elizabeth Periam (d. 1621) inside. The *Chantry House* and the *Red Lion*, both nearby, are 14C.

*Fawley Court* (open), off A4155 1m N, is a country house by Wren (1684) with alterations and additions by James Wyatt in the 1770s, when Capability Brown also landscaped the handsome gardens. The drawing room has a plasterwork ceiling by Grinling Gibbons. The building is now the Divine Mercy College, a

boys' school run by the Marian Fathers, who have added a museum largely
devoted to their Order's connection with Poland.—In the Chilterns 5m N of
Henley, off A423 and B480, is *Stonor Park* (open), a pleasant medley of most
architectural periods from the 13C onwards and for much of its history an
important centre of Roman Catholicism. The 12–14C chapel, with its interior
made Gothick in 1757, has been in use for Mass without break for eight
centuries. The Jesuit martyr Edmund Campion (1540–81) set up his printing
press here.—*Greys Court* (NT), 3m W of Henley, is a Jacobean house enclosed
by the ruins of a fortified mansion of c 1350. It has a Tudor donkey-wheel like
the one at Carisbrooke.

On A321 3¼m S of Henley, on the Berkshire bank of the Thames, is the pretty
village of *Wargrave*. The church, burned down by suffragettes in 1914, was
rebuilt in 1916, when some fine Norman masonry was discovered beneath the
17C brick casing of the tower. It contains a S window by John Hayward (1962)
and the monument of Thomas Day (1748–89), author of 'Sandford and
Merton'.—Tennyson was married in 1850 at *Shiplake*, on the opposite bank of
the river.

Beyond Henley A423 leaves the Thames valley and climbs the
Chilterns to (40½m) *Nettlebed*. The countryside to the N is explored
in Rte 38A.—Beyond the summit, we descend past (42m) *Nuffield*, on
the left, from which the Oxford car magnate William Robert Morris
(1877–1963) took his title. His home at Nuffield Place (limited
opening) keeps its atmosphere of the 1930s.

At 43½m A423 bears left from its natural course, blocked by RAF Benson, to
(46½m) *Crowmarsh Gifford*, with its little Norman church, on the Thames
opposite Wallingford. It then heads right, along the E bank of the river, to (48m)
*Benson*. Jethro Tull (1674–1741), the pioneer of mechanised farming, lived at
Howbery Park, between Crowmarsh and Benson.

It is more attractive and no further to leave A423, continue on the old
road for 1½m and then turn right for (46m) **Ewelme**, prettiest of the
Chiltern villages, with its 15C *Church, almshouse and school
making a lovely group. In the church is the *tomb of Alice, Duchess
of Suffolk (d. 1475), one of only three effigies showing a woman
wearing the Order of the Garter (cf. Stanton Harcourt, Rte 36B).
Among the 15 brasses are those of her father, Thomas Chaucer (d.
1434), supposed to be the son of the poet, and his wife. The screens
and roofs are notable, and the font has a magnificent pyramidal
*cover of carved wood; the head on the corbel above may represent
Edward III. Jerome K. Jerome (1859–1927), author of 'Three Men in a
Boat', is buried here.—The large village of (48m) *Benson* was once a
seat of the kings of Mercia. The airfield lies to the SE.

We rejoin A423, leading to (49m) *Shillingford*. The pleasant village
of *Warborough*, adjoining Shillingford to the N, has a 13C lead font in
its church.

On A329 2m S of Shillingford is **Wallingford** (6300 inhab.; Tourist Information),
a historic town with narrow streets on a medieval plan, remains of the earth
ramparts that encircled it, and an old bridge gracefully widened in 1809. The
Town Hall dates from 1670. The legal historian Sir William Blackstone (1723–
80) is buried in the church.

A329 heads down from Wallingford to (15m) Reading, keeping to the S bank
of the Thames through one of the loveliest stretches of its valley, visited by river
in Rte 36B. Agatha Christie (1890–1976) is buried at *Cholsey*, off A329 3m SW of
Wallingford. From *Streatley*, on A329 5m S of Wallingford and at the foot of the
Berkshire Downs, B4009 heads 3m W to *Aldworth*, with the remarkable series of
14C De la Beche *effigies in its church.

*North Moreton* church, 3m W of Wallingford, has fine 14C glass in the
Stapelton chantry.—From Wallingford W to Wantage, see Rte 38B.

Beyond Shillingford A423 crosses the Thame, a tributary of the
Thames, and bypasses (51m) **Dorchester**. Now merely a village of

pleasant houses, it was a Roman military centre and an important Saxon town, the cathedral city of Wessex (634–705) and of Mercia (869–1072). A priory of Augustinian canons was founded on the site of the cathedral c 1140 and, though the other monastic buildings were destroyed at the Reformation, the *Abbey Church* survives as the parish church.

The nave and W end of the choir belong to the original Norman church, probably begun before the abbey and completed c 1180. The S nave aisle and both choir aisles are in the Geometric Dec. style (1280–1320), while the E end dates from the close of the Dec. period. The low W tower and round transept arches were added in the 17C.

The three *windows at the E end are the chief glory of the building, unique in being traceried throughout and ornamented with sculptured figures. The great E window, divided in two by a massive buttress, contains much 14C glass. On the N side is the Jesse window, growing from a stone figure of Jesse on the windowsill. Under the S window are the canopied sedilia and piscina, with 12C glass in the little triangular windows behind. Note also the lead font (1170–80), decorated with figures of the Apostles.

An 'Anglo-American' garden has been laid out on the site of the cloisters, N of the church.

*Overy*, ¼m SE, has some attractive cottages.

A423 runs directly from Dorchester to Oxford, but a diversion (about 4m longer) can be made on A415, following the loop of the Thames to the W.—3m. *Clifton Hampden* (Rte 38B).—7m. **Abingdon** (22,700 inhab.; Tourist Information) is a pleasant old town. It sprang up round a powerful Benedictine abbey founded in 675, and was the

*The County Hall, Abingdon*

county town of Berkshire until 1870. Appropriate modern building has enhanced its character. The rebuilt bridge gives a striking view, with the former *Gaol* (1811), now a leisure centre, prominent in the foreground. On the N bank of the Thames are the remains of the *Abbey* (open), so closely integrated with later buildings that it is hard to distinguish them. We enter through the impressive 15C gatehouse, next to the 12–15C church of *St Nicholas*. The abbey church has disappeared, and the main survivals are a range of ancillary buildings by the mill stream to the S. They include the large square 14C hall known as the Checker (i.e. Exchequer), now fitted up as the Unicorn Theatre, and the early 16C Long Gallery. The 18C *Guildhall*, S of the abbey gatehouse, contains an art gallery with civic plate, etc. (open by appointment only). It preserves traces of the abbey hospital and includes the old grammar school of 1563. Just down Bridge St., the *Crown and Thistle* has a picturesque courtyard. In the market place stands the *County Hall* of 1677–80 by Christopher Kempster, Wren's master mason (English Heritage, open afternoons except Bank Holidays). It contains a local museum. A shopping precinct runs NW, while the attractive East St Helen St. leads to *St Helen's*, a noble Perp. church with a fine spire, double aisles and a Jacobean pulpit. The churchyard is surrounded by almshouses, including the picturesque *Christ's Hospital*, founded in 1553 in direct succession to the ancient Guild of the Holy Cross (hall open by appointment).

At *Drayton*, on B4017 2½m S, the church has 16C alabaster carvings. —*Steventon*, 1½m further on B4017, has a street with medieval buildings, now private houses, once belonging to a Benedictine priory. South Cottage (NT), one of the Priory Cottages, is open by written application to the tenant.—*Milton Manor* (open), beyond A34 1½m E of Steventon, is a modest 17–18C house in red brick, notable for its Gothick chapel and library.—*Sutton Courtenay*, by the river 2m E of Drayton, see Rte 36B.—*Radley*, 2½m NE of Abingdon, has a boys' public school founded in 1847.—At *Sunningwell*, beyond A34 3m N of Abingdon, the church has a classical seven-sided porch added by Bishop Jewel of Salisbury when he was rector here in 1552. The medieval Oxford philosopher Roger Bacon is said to have used the tower for astronomical calculations.—For *Kingston Bagpuize*, 6m W of Abingdon on A415, see Rte 38B.

A423, the direct road from Dorchester to Oxford, passes through (57m) *Nuneham Courtenay*. The village was moved to its present position by Earl Harcourt in 1765. *Nuneham Park* (left), with its beautiful wooded grounds, is now a conference centre (limited opening).—At 57m we reach the Oxford ring road. A4144, to the W, enters the city via Folly Bridge, A4158 (E) via Magdalen Bridge. *Iffley*, on the river between these two roads, has perhaps the best-preserved small Norman parish *church in England, built c 1170. The low, square tower has fine carving on its top storey, and the W front has a beautifully ornamented doorway. The last bay of the chancel is EE, and many of the windows were inserted in the 14–15C. The doorways to the former rood loft reveal elaborate groined archways.—60m. **Oxford**, see Rte 37.

# B.   By River

Maps: OS Landranger 176, 175, 174 (briefly) and 164, or Stanford's
River Thames map (published by E. Stanford Ltd, 12–14 Long Acre,
London WC2).

Rising in the Cotswolds and eventually joining the sea through its
broad estuary E of London, the Thames has a total course of about
210 miles. The Thames Valley extends from Kingston-upon-Thames,
near the edge of SW London, to (91½m) Oxford. The river here is
ideal for boating—and hence apt to get crowded with pleasure craft
in summer. Its commercial traffic is slight, its current gentle (except
after floods) and its scenery unsurpassed for quiet, typically English
beauty: low hills and wooded cliffs, small towns and villages,
meadows and country houses with gardens and lawns sloping down
to the water. The finest reaches are between Maidenhead and
Marlow, Henley and Sonning, Mapledurham and Goring. Reading is
the only industrial town.

**Passenger boats** run between most of the major points along the river. Salter
Brothers Ltd of Oxford operate a twice daily service in summer between Staines
and Windsor, Windsor and Marlow, Henley and Reading, Abingdon and
Oxford. Kingston and Hampton Court are both connected with central London
by the regular service (every day in summer, weekends in spring and autumn)
from Westminster Pier. A full list of companies and their locations is given in the
useful pamphlet, 'Cruising on the River Thames', obtainable from Customer
Services (River Division), Thames Water, Nugent House, Vastern Rd, Reading
RG1 8DB. For further information, write to: The Secretary, Upper Thames
Passenger Boat Association, Turk Launches Ltd, Thames Side, Kingston-upon-
Thames.

**Boats for hire**. Rowing boats, punts, canoes, etc. are available by the hour or
day at many points, and cruisers by the day or week from the many hire firms.
The best punting waters are at Staines, Maidenhead and Goring. For
companies and their locations, see 'Cruising on the River Thames'.
    All pleasure boats must be registered with Thames Water before being used
in any way on the river upstream of the Teddington boundary. Application
forms are obtained from and handled by Finance Directorate (Income Section),
Thames Water, address as above.

**Regattas**. Henley Royal Regatta is held on five days in the first week of July,
over a course of about 1¼m between Temple Island and Poplar Point, just N of
Henley Bridge. Founded in 1839 and now the leading amateur regatta in the
world, it is a crowded and fashionable occasion. Other rowing regattas are held,
mostly in July and early August, at Molesey, Marlow, Kingston, Staines,
Walton, Reading, Bourne End and Goring.

**Kingston-upon-Thames** (see 'Blue Guide London') is 10m SW of
central London, reached by British Rail from Waterloo or steamer
service from Westminster Pier. We go upstream.—3m. *Hampton
Court* (see Rte 3 and 'Blue Guide London'), with the palace on the
right and the mouth of the Mole on the left. Above Tagg's Island is
*Hampton* (right), with Garrick's Villa.—We leave Greater London for
Surrey and, beyond a series of reservoirs, reach (6m) *Sunbury Lock*.
Sunbury lies on the N bank.—7½m. *Walton Bridge*. *Walton-on-
Thames* is on the S bank, with St George's Hill. At the bend in the
river we pass *Cowey Stakes*, which disputes with Brentford the claim
to be where Julius Caesar crossed the Thames in 54 BC. The straight
Desborough Channel here cuts off c 1m, but the river runs more
pleasantly by *Lower Halliford*, with Thomas Love Peacock (1785–
1866) buried in Halliford churchyard, and *Shepperton*, with a
pleasant 17–18C village centre.—9½m. *Shepperton Lock*.

On the left, at the mouth of the Wey, is **Weybridge** (49,200 inhab. with Walton), which preserves the column (1794) from London's Seven Dials on its green. Between Weybridge and (19½m) Godalming the *Wey Navigation* (NT) is open to pleasure boats. It passes through a charming stretch of country at *Pyrford*, near Newark Priory and Old Woking (Rte 13B), and skirts the grounds of Sutton Place.

Beyond Chertsey Bridge (1780–85) is (11½m) *Chertsey Lock*. Abbey Mead (left) recalls the famous Benedictine abbey at *Chertsey*, founded in the 7C and refounded in 1110, of which almost nothing survives. It was known especially for its floor tiles, which adorn many English churches.—At (12½m) *Laleham*, on the right, Matthew Arnold (1822–88) was born and is buried beside the partly Norman church. Laleham Abbey was the home of Lord Lucan of Crimean War fame.—13½m. *Penton Hook Lock*, with a marina.—15½m. **Staines** (53,800 inhab.), with two bridges across the Thames.—Just short of (16½m) *Bell Weir Lock* we pass under the M25; the Colne enters the Thames from the right. The right bank here belongs to Berkshire, though for most of the way to Henley it is Buckinghamshire. On our left is *Egham* (Rte 14B) and, beyond, the level meadow of **Runnymede** (NT), with (18m) *Magna Carta Island*, probably the actual place where King John signed Magna Carta in 1215. The entrance pavilions were designed by Lutyens (1932). Above, on *Cooper's Hill*, rises the Commonwealth Air Forces Memorial (1953) by Sir Edward Maufe; beyond are the Magna Carta Memorial (1957) and the John F. Kennedy Memorial (1965). The S bank of the river becomes Berkshire. Just within the boundary is Beaumont College, a Roman Catholic public school founded in 1861, in a house once occupied by Warren Hastings.—19½m. *Old Windsor Lock* is at the entrance to one of three artificial cuts on the way to Oxford.—21½m. *Datchet* (left) faces the Home Park of Windsor. William Herschel moved here after receiving a pension from George III; Haydn's visit is supposed to have inspired 'The Creation'.—22½m. *Romney Lock*, with a good view of Eton College and its playing fields.—23m. *Windsor Bridge* connects **Windsor** with **Eton** (Rte 36A).

Most of the riverside towns and villages between Windsor and Oxford are described more fully in the road routes: see particularly Rte 36A but also the index.

Above Windsor is (24m) *Clewer*, on the left, with the headquarters of the Clewer Sisterhood and a partly Norman church.—25m. *Boveney Lock*.—27m. *Down Place*, left, was home of the publisher Jacob Tonson (d. 1736) and a meeting place of the Kit-Cat Club. —At (27½m) *Monkey Island* the stream is very swift. We pass under a bridge carrying the M4.—28m. *Bray Lock*. The large village of *Bray*, ½m further, has the picturesque Jesus Hospital (1627). In the 18C song, the time-serving Vicar of Bray boasts that he has three times changed his creed to keep his living.

Passing under Brunel's railway bridge (1837–38) and Maidenhead Bridge (1772–77) we reach (29½m) **Maidenhead**, opposite *Taplow*. One of the most beautiful (and popular) reaches of the river begins here.—30¼m. *Boulter's Lock*, with \**Cliveden Woods* stretching along the right bank for about 2m beyond.—*Hedsor* stands on high ground E of (32¼m) *Cookham Lock*. *Cookham* lies ½m beyond the lock on the left bank; on the right, 1m farther, is *Bourne End*.—The fine *Quarry Wood* begins on the left just short of (36½m) *Marlow Lock*. **Marlow** is on the right bank, with the grounds of Bisham Abbey opposite. Bisham church can be reached from the river bank.—38m. *Temple Lock.*—38½m. *Hurley Lock*. About 1m further, on the right, is *Medmenham Abbey* (not open), a ruined 13C Cistercian monastery rebuilt as a country house in the 18C.

Sir Francis Dashwood's Hell-Fire Club met here from 1745, adopting from Rabelais the motto 'Fay ce que voudras' ('Do what you please') and becoming notorious for blasphemous orgies, probably exaggerated in the telling. John Wilkes (a guest only), the poet Charles Churchill and the playwright Paul Whitehead were among the leading spirits.

42m. *Hambleden* stands 1m N of its lock. The 17C mansion of *Greenlands* (not open), further along on the right, is now an administrative staff college. Then come *Temple Island* and the Henley Regatta Course. *Fawley Court* (open), to the right, stands opposite *Remenham*, on the boundary between Buckinghamshire and Oxfordshire.

44½m. **Henley** is on the right (Oxfordshire) bank.—45½m. *Marsh Lock*. On the left is a pretty backwater. Then comes *Wargrave* on the Berkshire bank.—At (48m) *Shiplake Lock* the little river Loddon joins the Thames. *Shiplake* is on the right; on the left is St Patrick's Stream, another pleasant backwater.—50½m. The charming village of *Sonning*, on the left, has an ancient bridge and a church with eight 15–17C brasses. *Sonning Lock*, just beyond the bridge, is one of the prettiest on the river.—53½m. *Caversham Lock*, near the bridges connecting **Reading** with *Caversham*, its suburb on the N bank.

About ½m before the lock the Thames is joined by the Kennet, linked with the Kennet and Avon Canal to the W but not yet navigable all the way to (18½m) *Newbury*.

At (57m) *Tilehurst* the church has the splendid monument of Sir Peter Vanlore (d. 1627).—58m. *Mapledurham Lock*, with a much painted mill and weir, inspired some of E.H. Shepard's drawings for Kenneth Grahame's 'The Wind in the Willows'. Close by is **Mapledurham House** (open), a manor house of 1588–1612 in patterned red brick.

Pope frequently visited Teresa and Martha Blount here. The oak Tudor staircase and some early 17C plaster ceilings survive, with some unusual 17–18C carved wooden heads of animals in the entrance hall, and good furniture and portraits throughout the house. The chapel of 1797 is in the Gothick style. The lovely grounds, which Pope may have helped to lay out, include the remains of the earlier manor house and a restored watermill.

The pretty village has almshouses of 1629 and a church restored by Butterfield in 1863, with its S aisle reserved as a Roman Catholic chapel for the owners of the manor.

We now enter one of the finest reaches of the Thames. *Hardwick House* (not open), on the right, is delightfully situated.—60½m. *Whitchurch Lock*, with a toll bridge connecting *Whitchurch* (right) to *Pangbourne* (left), where Kenneth Grahame lived at Church Cottage from 1924 until his death in 1932. Further along, also on the left, is *Basildon*, with a low-lying church, the *Child Beale Wildlife Trust* (open) and, set on the hill, **Basildon Park** (NT), a Palladian house in Bath stone by John Carr of York (1770). It keeps its octagon room and grand staircase, as well as much of the original plasterwork. On the opposite bank is the lovely Hartslock Wood.—64½m. *Goring Lock*, with a rebuilt bridge. The ancient Icknield Way crosses the Thames at *Goring*, on the right bank. The church, with a tourelle on its Norman tower and Roman (?) tiles in the S porch, contains remnants of the chapel of an Augustinian nunnery. Beyond the pretty

Berkshire village of *Streatley* both banks are in Oxfordshire.—65m.
*Cleeve Lock.*—Opposite (76m) *Moulsford* is *South Stoke*, with an EE
church. *North Stoke*, further on, was the home of the singer Dame
Clara Butt (1873–1936).

70½m. *Wallingford Bridge*, leading from **Wallingford** to
*Crowmarsh Gifford.*—71½m. *Benson Lock.* The twin *Sinodun Hills* or
*Wittenham Clumps*, with an Iron Age earthwork, come into view and
remain in sight for the next 8m.—72½m. *Shillingford.* 2½m further
on is the mouth of the Thame. Above this point the Thames is also
known, poetically but not locally, as the Isis.—75½m. *Day's Lock.*
From *Little Wittenham*, on the left bank, we can climb the Sinodun
Hills. From the right bank a footpath leads to (1m) **Dorchester** past
the Dyke Hills, an old fortification stretching from the Thame to the
Thames.—On the right are (76¾m) *Burcot* and (78m) *Clifton
Hampden*, with a heavily restored 12–14C church on a low cliff.
—78½m. *Clifton Lock.* On the backwater is the pretty village of *Long
Wittenham*, where the church has a late Norman lead font and a
unique piscina which doubles as the founder's monument.—We next
pass *Appleford*, on the left, near the railway bridge. Didcot power
station dominates the scene.—81½m. *Culham Lock. Culham*, on the
right, is connected by a bridge with *Sutton Courtenay*, a delightful
village on a pretty backwater reached from the far end of Culham
Cut. The Liberal Prime Minister Herbert Asquith (1852–1928) and
George Orwell (Eric Blair, 1905–50) are buried here.—*Old Culham
Bridge*, on another backwater, dates from 1430.—**Abingdon** has a
rebuilt bridge, ¼m before (84m) *Abingdon Lock.*—Beyond the
railway bridge we pass, on the right, the beautiful woods of
*Nuneham Park.*—88½m. *Sandford Lock*, the deepest on the Thames,
with the Radley College boathouse.—89½m. We pass under the
railway and the Oxford ring road, with Hinksey Stream branching
left.—90m. *Iffley Lock*, with Iffley church on the right. The stretch
from here to Folly Bridge is the scene of the 'Eights' and 'Torpid'
boatraces. Opposite the New Cut, an artificial mouth of the Cherwell,
is the Oxford University boathouse, on the left. Christ Church
Meadow appears on the right.—91½m. *Folly Bridge*, the landing
place for **Oxford** (Rte 37).

THE THAMES ABOVE OXFORD. Known at Oxford as the 'Upper River',
it is much less crowded, despite its beauty, since the headroom at
Osney Bridge is only 7½ft.—1m. *Osney Lock.* On the right is the
entrance to the *Oxford Canal*, originally projected by Brindley in
1769, which runs via *Banbury* to (49m) the *Napton* junction with the
Grand Union Canal (Rte 39B) and continues N from (54m) the
*Braunston* junction to (77m) the *Hawkesbury* junction with the
Coventry Canal.—2m. On the left is *Binsey*, with St Frideswide's
Well by its little 12–13C church. On the right is Port Meadow, where
the burgesses of Oxford have enjoyed the right of free pasture since
the time of Edward the Confessor.—3¼m. *Godstow Lock*, with the
Trout Inn and the remains of the Benedictine nunnery where 'Fair'
Rosamond, mistress of Henry II, was educated and buried (c 1176)
after her death at Woodstock. The little village of *Wytham*, with its
woods, lies ¾m W.—We go under a bridge carrying the Oxford ring
road and reach (4¼m) *King's Lock*, near another entrance to the
Oxford canal. At 6m we pass the mouth of the Evenlode (right).—7m.
*Eynsham Lock*, with Swinford Bridge (1777) leading to *Eynsham*,
¾m to the right.—8½m. *Pinkhill Lock.*—11½m. *Bablock Hythe*,
celebrated in Matthew Arnold's 'The Scholar Gipsy'. On the left a

path leads to (1m) *Cumnor*, the scene of Amy Robsart's death. Cumnor Place is gone but the church is interesting, with one of two known contemporary statues of Elizabeth I and a memorial to Amy Robsart.

2m NW is **Stanton Harcourt**, with the remains of the 15C manor house (limited opening) abandoned when the Harcourt family seat was moved to Nuneham Courtenay in 1750. The picturesque group includes the gatehouse, kitchen and Pope's Tower, so called because the poet stayed here in 1717–18 while translating the 'Iliad'. The church has a rare mid 13C chancel screen and the monument of Margaret Harcourt (d. 1471), one of the three known effigies of ladies wearing the Order of the Garter (cf. Ewelme, Rte 36A).

12½m. From *Northmoor Lock* a footpath runs S to (1m) *Appleton*, with a manor house of c 1190 (not open).—15m. *New Bridge*, where the Windrush flows in, is medieval. R.D. Blackmore (1825–1900) was born at the pretty village of *Longworth*, 1½m SW. For *Kingston Bagpuize*, 1½m S of New Bridge, see Rte 38B.—17m. *Shifford Lock* is at the entrance to a cut, which is crossed by a ford.—21m. *Tadpole Bridge*.—21½m. *Rushey Lock*.—24m. *Radcot Lock*.—26m. *Radcot Bridge* (14C) is the best surviving medieval bridge over the Thames. Stone quarried near Burford for St Paul's Cathedral was shipped from here.—27m. *Grafton Lock*. On the left, beyond, is the church of *Eaton Hastings*; for *Buscot Park*, see Rte 38B. On the right is *Kelmscott*, the 16–17C manor that William Morris made his country home from 1871 until his death in 1896. It gave its name to the Kelmscott Press in Hammersmith. Now owned by the Society of Antiquaries, it is open by written appointment only. Morris is buried in the churchyard, with a tomb designed by Philip Webb.—We pass the boundary between Oxfordshire and Gloucestershire on the right bank before (29½m) *Buscot Lock*.—30¼m. *St John's Lock*, the last on the journey upstream. The left bank belongs briefly to the N tip of Wiltshire. —31m. **Lechlade** (Rte 38B) marks the present limit of navigation. On the Thames to the W lie: (32¼m) *Inglesham*, at the entrance of the derelict Thames and Severn Canal, with a fine 14C tomb of Purbeck marble in its church; (37m) *Kempsford*, with a beautiful church tower; and (42¼m) *Cricklade* (Rte 38B). See Rte 38B also for the river's source at *Thames Head*, near Cirencester.

# **37** Oxford

**OXFORD** (116,400 inhab.) is famous for its ancient university. The grouping of its towers and spires makes a beautiful sight in the distance. On closer view, the college buildings prove rich in examples, often excellent examples, of every period from the medieval to the present, and of most major English architects since the Renaissance. Their combined effect—seen at its best in High St., Broad St. and the square where the Radcliffe Camera stands—is sometimes skilfully planned and sometimes happily accidental.

These charms attract tourists in large numbers, encouraged by Oxford's convenient position on the route of coach tours from London to Stratford-upon-Avon. The city suffers, too, from rapid 20C expansion. Oxford today, emphatically a city even apart from the university and the tourists, is a lively but often congested place with much modern development near its historic centre and industry among its suburban sprawl.

Several days are needed to get to know the place properly. Even the most cursory tour should include Christ Church (with Oxford Cathedral), Merton, Queen's, Magdalen and New College, as well as the Sheldonian Theatre and the Ashmolean Museum. The four walks from the centre suggested below take in all the chief points of interest; the tours of the outskirts that follow them are for the more leisurely visitor.

**Tourist Information Centre**: St Aldate's.

**Car Parks**: There is a sensible Park and Ride system, with car parks served by buses to the centre at Thornhill (A40, E), Red Bridge (Abingdon Rd, S), Seacourt (Botley Rd, W) and Pear Tree (Woodstock Rd, N), all near the ring road. City centre car parks at Westgate shopping centre (surface and multi-storey), Gloucester Green, the railway station, Worcester St., Abbey Place, Oxpens Rd and St Clement's St.

**Coach Station**: Gloucester Green.

**Railway Station**: Botley Rd, about 1/2m W of Carfax.

**Theatres**: Apollo Theatre, George St.

**Annual Events**: Eights Week (late May), with college balls, plays, concerts and boat races on the Isis (Thames) between Iffley and Folly Bridge. Torpids, also boat races, take place in February. For the celebration of May Day, see Magdalen College.

**Access to Colleges**: In recent years the pressure of tourism has made the colleges adopt more stringent policies about opening to the public. Many are closed in the morning, but most are open for at least a few hours in the afternoon. Some colleges limit access to quads and grounds; chapels, halls, old libraries and other features of interest may or may not be open. Visitors should not enter staircases or working libraries without a prior appointment. Precise details, which vary from college to college and year to year, can be obtained from the Tourist Information Centre.

**History.** Oxford's name (the 'ford for oxen' over the Thames at Hinksey) shows that it first owed its existence to a convenient river-crossing. Yet there was no Roman or British settlement, and the city is not mentioned in written records until the Anglo-Saxon Chronicle of 912. By then it was an important trading centre with several religious foundations (the priory of St Frideswide's may date from the early 8C), where kings several times held councils of state.

Despite picturesque legends that the university was founded by the mythical British king Memphric or, at least, by Alfred the Great, nobody knows when or how it began. It is first mentioned in the 12C, when its growth was encouraged by the influx of English students expelled from Paris in 1167. The teaching body was in due time recognised as a 'studium generale', or university, with all the powers of a corporation. In 1214 it received from the papal legate Pandulf its first legal privilege, conferring immunity from lay jurisdiction—the first stage in the long and often riotous struggle between Town and Gown. The first colleges to be endowed as separate bodies with their own rules and privileges were University College (1249), Merton (1264) and Balliol (before 1266). They were reserved for graduates only, and until the time of Elizabeth I most students lived in the numerous halls (or hostels kept by graduate principals).

Fondly called the 'home of lost causes', the university acquired a long history of ideological turbulence. The teachings of John Wyclif and his Lollard followers caused controversy in the 14C. The Reformation brought first the Calvinist iconoclasm of Edward VI's reign and then the Catholic reaction under Queen Mary, when the Protestant martyrs Cranmer, Latimer and Ridley were burnt at the stake in Broad St At the outbreak of the Civil War the university supported the Royalist cause while the city declared for Parliament. Oxford became the headquarters of the king and court in 1642, but in 1646 yielded to General Fairfax. After the Restoration the university settled down into the ease of the 18C, interrupted only by political disputes and the Methodist movement. Religious controversy of another kind was caused in the 1830s by the High Church tendency known as the Oxford (or Tractarian) Movement under the leadership of Pusey, Keble and Newman.

The process of democratising the university was started by the 'Extension' movement and the foundation of Ruskin College in the 19C. The academic year

1919–20 brought three particularly important changes: the admission of women to university degrees, the dethroning of Greek as a necessary part of a university education and (after 700 years of independence) the acceptance of a government grant. Recent years have seen previously all-male colleges becoming co-educational.

Yet perhaps the most important 20C changes have come with the rapid expansion and industrialisation of the city itself. In the 19C the university was able to resist the encroachments of the Industrial Revolution, remaining famous for the pastoral beauty of its immediate surroundings. That changed in the 1920s when William Robert Morris, later Viscount Nuffield (1877–1963), began production of the Morris car at Cowley to the SE, still the headquarters of the Austin–Rover group. The university today has become an oasis in a busy, traffic-congested city that is as much England's Detroit as its Athens or Florence.

**The University**. Oxford has 35 colleges, of which 28 admit both undergraduates and graduates, with undergraduates predominating and making up a total population of about 9500. The undergraduate colleges vary both in their date of foundation, with Balliol, University College and Merton (see above) being the oldest and St Catherine's (1963) the newest, and in their size. St Catherine's is presently the largest (410 undergraduates) and Corpus Christi (200) the smallest. All the colleges originally founded for men now admit women as well. Of the colleges founded for women (Lady Margaret Hall, Somerville, St Hugh's, St Hilda's and St Anne's), only Lady Margaret Hall and St Anne's now admit men. In the undergraduate population at large men outnumber women by about two to one.

The six graduate colleges—Linacre, Nuffield, St Antony's, St Cross, Wolfson and the newest, Green—have all been founded since 1937. All Souls, a much older foundation, admits only fellows.

In addition, there are five permanent private halls, whose students are subject to the statutes of the university, partake in its privileges and are admitted to its degrees: Campion Hall, Greyfriars, Mansfield, Regent's Park and St Benet's. Campion Hall, Greyfriars and St Benet's are primarily for members of religious Orders (Jesuit, Franciscan and Benedictine respectively) and admit men only.

Not incorporated with the university, but enjoying a special relation to it, are Ruskin College (now primarily for students sponsored by their trade unions) and five theological institutions: Ripon, St Stephen's, Wycliffe, Manchester and Blackfriars.

**The Oxbridge system**. A distinguishing mark of Oxford and Cambridge, often perplexing to visitors, is their combination of the college and university systems. The colleges are self-governing bodies with their own endowments and statutes, responsible for admitting undergraduates, accommodating them, supervising the progress of their studies, regulating their behaviour and in general providing the focus of their social life. The university, which has no campus and no building as such, is in effect all the members of the colleges organised into another corporate body, also self-governing. It awards degrees and establishes general policy. Through the various faculties, or subject groups, into which its research and educational activities are divided, it is also responsible for providing lectures and laboratory work and for conducting examinations.

Physically, the colleges consist of rooms with communal functions (hall, chapel and library) and private rooms where the members live and work, arranged around quadrangles which are called quads at Oxford and courts at Cambridge. The college community is made up of a head, fellows and undergraduates, together with honorary fellows, graduate students and service staff of whom the most visible are the porters stationed in the lodge by the main entrance. The head is known as Master (the almost invariable term at Cambridge), Warden, Principal, Provost, Rector, Dean (at Christ Church) or President (though at Cambridge this title occasionally denotes the Vice-Master). The fellows (popularly known as dons) are selected from distinguished graduates, not necessarily of the university or college where they hold their fellowship. Apart from assisting the adminstrative life of the college, their function is to teach students either individually or in small groups (at tutorials in Oxford, supervisions in Cambridge). Undergraduates live in college for part of their career and in one of its hostels or approved lodgings for the remainder. They are usually expected to dine in Hall a given number of times during each term. The old rules governing the time by which they had to be in their rooms in the evening, when the gates were closed, have been greatly relaxed in recent years. So, too, have the regulations about wearing gowns, though some colleges still require them at formal Hall. At Cambridge gowns are short black robes (except at Caius and Trinity, where they are dark blue). At Oxford, scholars (undergraduates singled out for certain privileges because of academic distinction) have longer gowns than the rest (commoners), whose gowns are little more than loose black jackets.

The ceremonial head of the university is the Chancellor, elected for life and usually an eminent public figure. (At Oxford the position is currently held by Lord Jenkins of Hillhead, at Cambridge by His Royal Highness The Prince Philip, Duke of Edinburgh.) The executive head is the Vice-Chancellor, normally (though at Oxford not necessarily) the head of one of the colleges, who holds office for four years at Oxford, two at Cambridge. The ultimate governing authority, consisting of all holders of the MA or higher degrees, is known as Convocation at Oxford and the Senate at Cambridge. In the past these bodies had wide voting rights but now their function is largely confined to formal duties, such as electing the Chancellor and (at Oxford) the Professor of Poetry. In practice, legislative authority rests with Congregation (Oxford) and the Regent House (Cambridge), composed of all resident doctors and MAs holding teaching or administrative posts in the university or colleges. Administrative authority lies with the smaller elected bodies known at Oxford as the Hebdomadal (or weekly) Council and at Cambridge as the Council of the Senate.

The General Board of the Faculties co-ordinates educational policy and oversees the work of the various Faculty Boards, which organise courses of study, appoint teachers and conduct examinations in their separate fields. Most undergraduates read for an honours degree, usually the BA, which takes three or four years, depending on the subject. No further examination is required for an MA, which can be obtained for a small fee six or more years after acceptance into the university. Full details of courses of study, first and higher degrees, etc. are given in the university handbooks, calendars and prospectuses.

The academic year, which occupies less than seven months, begins in October and is divided into three terms: Michaelmas, Hilary and Trinity at Oxford; Michaelmas, Lent and Easter at Cambridge. Examinations are held in late May and June. Degree ceremonies take place at intervals throughout the year, at Oxford in the Sheldonian Theatre, at Cambridge in the Senate House. The main ceremony at Oxford is Commemoration, or Encaenia, on the Wednesday following the end of Trinity term (early July); at Cambridge it is General Admission (two days in late June).

From 1603 until 1950 the universities of Oxford and Cambridge each returned two members to Parliament, thus giving graduates the privilege of voting in their university as well as their home constituency. Members for Oxford University have included Peel and Gladstone, and for Cambridge University William Pitt the Younger.

The centre of the old city is **Carfax** (possibly from the Latin 'quadrifurcus' or the French 'quatre voies'), where four main streets join: St Aldate's, leading S to Folly Bridge over the Thames; High St., leading E to Magdalen Bridge over the Cherwell; Cornmarket, leading N and finally broadening out into St Giles; and Queen St., leading W to the modern Westgate shopping centre and the railway station.

The 14C tower (open) with clock jacks, at the NW angle of Carfax, is all that remains of *St Martin's Church*. The composer Orlando Gibbons (1583–1625) was baptised here, and Shakespeare is said to have stood sponsor to the infant William Davenant (1606–68), whose father was landlord of the Crown Tavern. At No. 3 opposite is the guest chamber of the inn, now known as the Painted Room (open), where John Davenant may have entertained Shakespeare. The wall paintings date from 1450 and 1550, the panelling from 1630.

SOUTH AND EAST FROM CARFAX. We go down St Aldate's, passing (right) the Tourist Information Centre and the Post Office and (left) the Town Hall, housing the *Museum of Oxford*. Behind the largely 19C *St Aldate's Church*, on the right, is Pembroke College; opposite is the main front of Christ Church.

In Brewer St. (right) are the *Cathedral Choir School*, where Dorothy L. Sayers was born in 1893, and *Campion Hall*, for Jesuits (1936; Lutyens). In Rose Place, further on, is the *Old Palace*, built in the 16C by Robert King, last Abbot of Osney and first Bishop of Oxford, but dating in its present form from 1628 (restored 1952) and now, with its stark modern extension, the home of the Roman Catholic Chaplaincy to the university.

No. 83 St Aldate's, opposite the entrance to Christ Church Meadow, is the original of the shop in Lewis Carroll's 'Through the Looking Glass'. St Aldate's descends to (1/4m) *Folly Bridge*, rebuilt in 1825–27 by Ebenezer Perry, where the gatehouse once stood which Roger Bacon is said to have used as his observatory.

**Pembroke College** (300 undergraduates), founded in 1624 to supersede Broadgates Hall, is named after the Earl of Pembroke, Chancellor of the university at the time.

Dr Johnson, who studied here in 1728–29, had second-floor rooms over the gateway. The old refectory of Broadgates Hall, now the *Senior Common Room* (not open), has his desk, his teapot and his portrait by Reynolds. The *Chapel*, originally 18C, was redecorated by C.E. Kempe in 1884 to make the most lavish neo-Renaissance interior in Oxford. The Besse Building, Beef Lane (now a paved footpath) and reconstructed 16C houses of Pembroke St. form a delightful *North Quad* (1954–62), reminiscent of a square in a small country town. The new *Library* (1974) was the gift of a family of America alumni; the *Macmillan Building* (1976) was erected to house more undergraduates.

FAMOUS MEMBERS: of Broadgates Hall: Bishop Bonner, Francis Beaumont, William Camden, John Pym and Sir Thomas Browne, whose undergraduate years spanned the change to Pembroke. Of Pembroke: Samuel Johnson, William Shenstone, George Whitefield, Sir William Blackstone, John Lemprière (of the 'Classical Dictionary'), James Smithson (founder of the Smithsonian Institute in Washington DC), Senator William Fulbright, Patrick Campbell, Michael Heseltine.

**\*Christ Church** (390 undergraduates), familiarly known as 'the House', is built on the largest and most aristocratic scale of any Oxford college. It was first founded by Wolsey as Cardinal College in 1525, on the site of St Frideswide's Priory. After Wolsey's fall Henry VIII refounded it as Henry VIII College, an ecclesiastical establishment only, in 1532. At the Reformation this was suppressed in turn, to be refounded yet again in 1545 as Christ Church. By a unique arrangement, the remains of the old priory church became Oxford Cathedral as well as the college chapel, and the Dean (appointed by the Crown) head of both the cathedral chapter and the college.

The usual visitors' entrance is by the wrought-iron gates of the War Memorial Gardens and along the Broad Walk of the spacious *Christ Church Meadow* to the *Meadows Building* (1863). The buildings facing us beyond the Meadow Gate are the remains of St Frideswide's Priory: the original frater (later the Old Library, now undergraduate rooms), the cloister and the cathedral. The Perp. *Cloister* (1499) was destroyed on the W side in 1525; in the E walk is the late Norman doorway of the *Chapter House*, a beautiful rectangular EE chamber, now used for exhibitions of church plate.

The **\*Cathedral**, the smallest in England, owes its present, mainly Norman appearance to rebuilding in 1140–80. Of the many later alterations, the most conspicuous are the squat 13C spire and the W front and E end by Sir Gilbert Scott (1870).

The visitors' entrance leads into the S aisle. In the *Nave*, the massive Norman pillars of the arcades are alternately round and octagonal, and an illusion of height is given by the unusual placing of the triforium inside the main arches, with secondary arches below. The roof is 16C timberwork, the pulpit and organ screen are 17C, the stalls 19C. The N aisle has a W window with spectacular glass by Abraham van Linge (c 1630) depicting Jonah and Nineveh; the S aisle has a W window by Morris and Burne-Jones, the first of several in the cathedral. There are monuments to the philosopher Bishop Berkeley (1685–1753) and to the Tractarian leader Edward Pusey (1800–82).

# OXFORD

University Parks

River Cherwell

Laboratory

Pitt Rivers Mus.

University Museum

Radcliffe Science Library

Zoological Dept.

New College Playing Fields

St Catherine's College

Rhodes House

Mansfield College

St Cross

John's Gardens

Gardens

MANOR ROAD

Trinity Gardens

Wadham College

SAVILE RD

School of Geography

JOWETT ROAD

Kettell Hall

Old Music Room

Manchester Coll.

HOLYWELL STREET

Magdalen Grove

New Bodleian Library Ext

Clarendon Building

Hertford College

Sheldonian Theatre

Exeter Coll.

Divinity School

Bodleian Library

New College

City Wall

New College Gardens

St Peter's in the East

Radcliffe Camera

QUEEN'S

Lincoln Coll.

Brasenose Coll.

All Souls College

Queen's College

St Edmund Hall

New Building

St Mary's

St Swithin's Quad.

Market

All Saints

Magdalen College

Mitre

HIGH STREET

University College

Examination Schools

Magdalen Water Walks

Town Hall

Oriel College

Magdalen Bridge

Peckwater Quad

MERTON STREET

Waynflete (Magd Coll.)

Library

Corpus Christi College

Merton College

Botanic Gardens

Magdalen Coll. School

Christ Church

Tom Quad

Cathedral

Merton Field

St Hilda's College

BROAD WALK

NEW WALK

Christ Church Meadows

Playing Fields

IFFLEY ROAD

COWLEY

ST CLEMENTS

Folly Bridge & ABINGDON

The *Choir* has a gloriously vaulted late 15C *roof. The E end is by Scott. Like the lantern, the *Transepts* have early 16C roofs. The S end of the S transept is a conjectural restoration by Scott. St Lucy's Chapel, in the former E aisle of this transept, has a flamboyant *E window with old glass (c 1330) including a representation of Becket's martyrdom from which the saint's head has been struck out. Opening from the N transept are three parallel aisles: the N choir aisle, the Lady Chapel and the Latin Chapel. Between the first two is the fragmentary base of the late 13C shrine of St Frideswide, once the goal of pilgrims, and opposite, between the Lady Chapel and the Latin Chapel, is the Perp. watching chamber from which the treasures of the shrine were guarded. The Latin Chapel has massive 14–16C oak stalls, some 14C glass in the N windows and interesting monuments, including one to Robert Burton (1577–1640) of 'The Anatomy of Melancholy'. Two of these three N aisles have E windows by Morris and Burne-Jones, while the Latin Chapel has an earlier window (1858) by Burne-Jones.

The W end of the cathedral opens into the *Great Quadrangle* (or *Tom Quad*), the largest in Oxford, begun by Wolsey as a cloister and not completed until the 1660s. The pool in the centre is known as the 'Mercury' from its statue, now a modern copy of the original 17C one by Giovanni da Bologna. On the W side is the *Great Gate* (1526), the main college entrance from St Aldate's, below the famous *Tom Tower*, added by Wren in 1681 to house 'Great Tom', the huge bell from Osney Abbey. It sounds 101 times at 21.05 every evening, once for each member of the original foundation, formerly the signal for the closing of all college gates.

The college *Hall* (open) is entered from the bell tower (1879) near the cathedral in the SE corner of the quad. We climb a staircase (1805; James Wyatt) whose beautiful fan-tracery *roof (1640) is a very late example of the style in England. The hall itself, the largest in Oxford, was completed in Wolsey's time. It has a richly carved hammerbeam roof and portraits by Lely, Kneller, Reynolds, Gainsborough, Romney, Lawrence, Millais, Watts, Herkomer and Graham Sutherland. Henry VIII (by Sonmans) dominates, flanked by Elizabeth I (perhaps by Zuccero) and Wolsey (perhaps by Robert Greenbury). Wolsey's vast kitchen below is still in use (not open).

In the NE corner of the quad is Dr Fell's Tower, with statues of Dean John Fell (1660–86; 'I do not like thee, Dr Fell') and Dean Liddell (1855–91). Beneath it Kill Canon Passage, so called because of its cold draughts, leads to *Peckwater Quad*, built in 1706–11 on the site of the Peckwater Inn. On its S side is the splendid *Library* of 1717–72 (open by special appointment) with beautiful plasterwork ceilings, woodwork and furnishings, and some of the earliest wall bookcases to be built. Its collection includes the manuscript of John Evelyn's diary and memorabilia of Wolsey and Lewis Carroll. On the W side of Peckwater is the entrance to the modern *Blue Boar Quad* (1968; Powell and Moya); on the E is *Canterbury Quad*, built in 1773–83 on the site of the old Canterbury College. The *Picture Gallery* (open) has the finest collection in Oxford of paintings and drawings, mostly 14–17C Italian.

FAMOUS MEMBERS include many politicians and Prime Ministers (Canning, Peel, Gladstone, Salisbury, Halifax, Eden, Douglas-Home). Among other notables are: Richard Hakluyt, Sir Philip Sidney, Robert Burton, Thomas Otway, William Penn, John Locke, John and Charles Wesley, 'Monk' Lewis, Edward Pusey, John Ruskin, Lewis Carroll (C.L. Dodgson), Sir Adrian Boult, Sir William Walton, Lord David Cecil, W.H. Auden. Charles I made the Deanery his residence during the Civil War.

We leave Christ Church either by the gate of Canterbury Quad or by the path in Christ Church Meadow leading N from the Broad Walk across Merton Field. Both routes bring us to Merton St. and a group of three colleges: Oriel on the N side (entered from Oriel St. around the corner), Corpus Christi and Merton on the S.

**Oriel College** (280 undergraduates) was first founded as St Mary's College in 1324 by Adam de Brome, almoner to Edward II and rector of St Mary the Virgin, which was used as the college chapel in the Middle Ages. In 1326 the college was refounded by Edward II and renamed the King's College. Its present name comes from La Oriole, a building on the site acquired in 1329.

The picturesque front quad, built between 1619 and 1642, is a good example of 17C Gothic. The *Hall* has a fine hammerbeam roof and, over the porch outside, statues of the Virgin Mary and two kings, perhaps Edward II and James I or Charles I. The *Chapel* has good woodwork. The quad to the left is 18C, with a handsome Palladian *Library* by James Wyatt (1788). St Mary's Quad incorporates the hall and chapel (c 1640) of St Mary Hall, absorbed by Oriel in 1902. The new front in the High St. was built by Basil Champneys (1909–11) from a bequest by Cecil Rhodes, whose statue it bears.

FAMOUS MEMBERS: Sir Walter Raleigh, William Prynne, Bishop Butler, Gilbert White, Bishop Samuel Wilberforce, Dr Arnold, Mark Pattison, Thomas Hughes, J.A. Froude, Matthew Arnold, A.H. Clough, Cecil Rhodes, Richard Hughes, A.J.P. Taylor. The leaders of the Oxford Movement were fellows: John Keble, John Henry Newman, Edward Pusey and Richard Hurrell Froude.

**Corpus Christi College** (190 undergraduates) was founded in 1517 by Bishop Richard Foxe.

The gateway, with its fine oriel window and fan-vaulted roof, and the front quad date from the founder's time. The tall sundial was erected in 1581, and the perpetual calendar round its plinth added in 1616. The small but attractive *Hall* has a hammerbeam roof, the *Chapel* a striking E window and an altarpiece of the school of Rubens. The rich *Library* is one of the most picturesque in Oxford. Beyond, to the SE, is a small quad with cloisters on one side and the *Turner Buildings* (1706) on the other.

FAMOUS MEMBERS: Nicholas Udall, Richard Hooker, Thomas Day, John Keble, Dr Arnold, Sir Henry Newbolt, Robert Bridges, Sir Isaiah Berlin.

**\*Merton College** (250 undergraduates) is in all essentials the oldest college in Oxford, though both University College and Balliol were endowed a few years earlier. It was founded by Walter de Merton in 1264 as a special training school for the secular as opposed to the monastic clergy. Its organisation was the model for subsequent Oxford and Cambridge colleges.

The buildings are among the oldest and most interesting in Oxford. The gateway tower was built in 1418. Opposite the gate, on the S side of the front quad, is the *Hall*, virtually rebuilt by Scott in 1874 but with original 13C ironwork on its door. On the W side, past the old *Treasury* or *Muniment Room* (1274) with high-pitched stone roof, is the entrance to the picturesque *\*Mob Quad* (c 1308). The Dec. *\*Chapel* (1294–97), with a conspicuous Perp. tower added in 1450, is the oldest in Oxford. It never had a nave, and the 14C transepts now form an antechapel, which contains a fine Dec. piscina, old glass, and the monuments of Sir Henry Savile (d. 1622), Sir Thomas Bodley (d. 1613) by Nicholas Stone and Anthony à Wood (d. 1695). Three arches of the screen designed by Wren are in the crossing. The beautiful windows of the choir are filled with painted glass of c1300. There are two fine brasses (1387 and 1471) in front of the high altar. The *Library*, in Mob Quad, is perhaps the most interesting medieval library in England. Built in 1371–78, it was the first to store books upright in shelves instead of lying them flat in presses, and it keeps many of its old fittings. In addition to manuscripts, its treasures include Chaucer's Astrolabe. Two adjoining rooms display memorabilia of Sir Max Beerbohm.

The *Fellows' Quad*, built in 1608–10, is in the elegant late Gothic style copied at Oriel, Wadham and University Colleges. To the E of the front quad is *St Alban's Quad* (rebuilt by Basil Champneys, 1904–10), on the site of St Alban's Hall, which was founded in 1220 and amalgamated with Merton in 1881.

FAMOUS MEMBERS: Thomas Bradwardine and other notable 14C philosophers and mathematicians, and John Wyclif. Other notables include Sir Thomas Bodley, Anthony à Wood, Thomas Carew, Sir Richard Steele, Lord Randolph Churchill, George Saintsbury, Sir Max Beerbohm, T.S. Eliot, Louis MacNeice, Robert Byron, Sir Angus Wilson, Sir Lennox Berkeley and Robert Morley. William Harvey was Warden during the Civil War, and Henrietta Maria lodged here while the king was at Christ Church. Philip Massinger attended St Alban Hall, and Newman was its Vice-Principal.

Oriel St., Magpie Lane, Logic Lane and the E end of Merton St. all join the High St., explored in the next walking tour.

EAST FROM CARFAX. We follow *High St. (the High), leading in a gentle curve and a splendid series of changing vistas to (½m) Magdalen Bridge. The beauty of the streetscape is usually obscured by traffic and shoppers during the business week and can best be appreciated early on a Sunday morning.

The first points of interest, both on the left, are the covered market and the Mitre, a much altered 17–18C coaching inn. On the opposite corner of Turl St. stands the classical *All Saints' Church* (probably by Dean Aldrich, 1706–08), with a distinctive spire, now used as the library of Lincoln College (visited in the walk N and E from Carfax, below).

Beyond the High St. front of Brasenose, on the same side, is the church of **St Mary the Virgin**, whose Dec. *tower and spire make a familiar Oxford landmark. The tower (open) gives perhaps the best view of the city. Facing the High is an Italianate baroque porch (1637), designed by Nicholas Stone and given by Dr Morgan Owen, chaplain to Archbishop Laud. The image of the Virgin and Child inspired one of the charges against Laud at his trial in 1644. The main entrance is around the corner in Radcliffe Square.

Since at least the 14C St Mary's has been used as the university church, where the University Sermons are preached by 'select preachers' every Sunday morning and where the Bampton lectures are given. Cranmer, soon to become one of Oxford's Protestant martyrs, publicly repudiated his recantation here in 1556. John Wesley worshipped and preached here, as in the 19C did the leaders of the Oxford Movement. Newman was vicar from 1828 to 1843.

The tower, spire, Brome chapel and Congregation house, all on the N side, date from the early 14C. Otherwise the church was largely rebuilt in the Perp. style at the university's expense in c 1463–90. The many monuments include: a slab in the choir recording the burial of Amy Robsart (d. 1560); the tomb of Adam de Brome (d. 1328), vicar of the church and founder of Oriel College; and plaques to Dr John Radcliffe and the antiquary John Aubrey (1626–97).

Radcliffe Square is worth exploring further before we return to the High. Its centrepiece is the *Radcliffe Camera**, a handsome baroque rotunda with a dome rising from an octagonal base, built by James Gibbs (1737–49) to house Dr Radcliffe's science library. It has long been part of the Bodleian.

On the W side of the square is **Brasenose College** (320 undergraduates), founded in 1509 by William Smyth, Bishop of Lincoln, and Sir Richard Sutton. The name probably derives from the brazen knocker (a lion's head) of an older hall on the site, carried off to Stamford in the migration of Oxford students in 1333 and recovered only in 1890. Another derivation is from a supposed 'brasenhus', or brewery, on the site.

A handsome gateway tower leads into the front quad, begun in the founder's time but given its third storey in the early 17C. The *Library* and *Chapel* in the adjoining quad were both built in 1656–66, the latter in an interesting combination of the classical and Gothic styles. Its plaster fan-tracery ceiling hides the hammerbeam roof brought from the dissolved St Mary's College. There is a pretentious monument to Walter Pater (1839–94) in the antechapel. The High St. front is by Sir T.G. Jackson (1886–1909); cleverly inserted W of Jackson's quad are sets of rooms by Powell and Moya (1959–61), the first of their many buildings in both Oxford and Cambridge.

FAMOUS MEMBERS: John Foxe, Robert Burton, Elias Ashmole, John Marston, Thomas Traherne, R.H. Barham of the 'Ingoldsby Legends', Walter Pater, Earl Haig, John Buchan, Charles Morgan, John Middleton Murry, Robert Runcie (Archbishop of Canterbury), William Golding, John Mortimer.

On the N side of Radcliffe Square stands the *Old Schools Quad-rangle*, built in 1613–19. Over the doorways are the names of the disciplines formerly studied here. The gate tower on the E side, by Thomas Holt, is ornamented with columns of the five classical orders and a statue of James I. The building is now part of the **Bodleian Library**. The only part open to the public is the former *Divinity School*, entered through the vestibule, or *Proscholium*, on the W side of the quadrangle near Le Sueur's statue of the Earl of Pembroke. A noble room with an elaborately vaulted and arched ˙roof, it now houses changing exhibitions of manuscripts and rare books. Cranmer, Latimer and Ridley, the Protestant martyrs, were examined here in 1555. Readers are admitted to the rest of the library by ticket and must be either members of the university or suitably sponsored. Visitors' passes for viewing the glorious Duke Humphrey's Library are issued only to: senior and resident members and their guests; visiting librarians; members of the Friends of the Bodleian, and members of the American friends of the Bodleian, and their guests.

*Nicholas Hawksmoor's North Quad at All Souls College, Oxford*

One of the oldest and most important libraries in the world, the Bodleian was first endowed by Humphrey, Duke of Gloucester (1391–1477), whose collection was dispersed in the reign of Edward VI. In 1602 the library was refounded by Sir Thomas Bodley, fellow of Merton and Ambassador to the Netherlands. From his collection of 2000 books, the library has grown to more than 4½ million volumes, as well as over 50,000 manuscripts. It is one of the six copyright libraries, which receive a copy of every book published in the UK.

Hertford College, by the NE corner of Radcliffe Square, is visted on the walk N and E from Carfax (below). To reach the main entrance of All Souls College, on the E side of the square, we return to the High.

**All Souls College** was founded in 1438 by Henry Chichele, Archbishop of Canterbury, both as a college of higher theological and legal studies and as a chantry for the souls of those killed in the French wars. It has a Warden and over 60 fellows but no undergraduates—a unique arrangement until the foundation of Nuffield College in 1937.

The fine front and gateway, facing the High, and the front quad are carefully restored 15C work. From the NW corner of the quad an exquisitely vaulted passage leads to the Perp. *Chapel*, with 15C *glass in the antechapel, a 15C carved oak roof, an 18C screen and a beautiful stone *reredos, restored in 1872–79 after being walled up for over 200 years. The statues are 19C but the painting is original. The *North Quad* is a remarkable exercise in Gothic by Nicholas Hawksmoor (1715–40). The *Codrington Library* (not open), on its N side, contains 150,000 volumes and many drawings from Wren's office, including some for St Paul's.

FAMOUS MEMBERS: Thomas Linacre, Jeremy Taylor, Sir Christopher Wren, Sir William Blackstone, Max Müller, W.P. Ker, T.E. Lawrence, and a host of other distinguished scholars and politicians too numerous to detail.

**University College** (310 undergraduates) lies a little further down the High, almost opposite All Souls. Though it nominally claims Alfred the Great as its founder, it received its first endowment from the bequest of William of Durham in 1249, and was administered by the university until 1280. It moved to its present site about 1332.

The long curved front of the college, with its oriels, gables and two gateway towers, is a good example of 17C Gothic. The W gateway, with statues of Queen Anne outside and James II inside, leads to the larger *Front Quad* (1634–77). The E gateway, with statues of Queen Mary outside and Dr Radcliffe inside, leads to the smaller quadrangle built in 1716–19 from a bequest by Dr Radcliffe. In Front Quad is the *Chapel*, heavily remodelled by Scott in 1862 but with 17C panelling, stalls and screens, and stained glass (1641) by Abraham van Linge. A passage from the NW corner of the quad leads to the *Shelley Memorial*, a domed chamber containing a realistic figure of the drowned poet by Onslow Ford (1893).

Later additions to the college include the *New Building* (1842; Barry), the *Library* (1861; Scott) and, in Logic Lane, the *Goodhart Building* with copper roof and spire (1960–61; Robert Matthew and Johnson-Marshall).

FAMOUS MEMBERS: Lord Herbert of Cherbury, Roger Newdigate (founder of the Newdigate Prize for Poetry), Shelley (sent down after only 11 months for publishing his pamphlet on 'The Necessity for Atheism'), Prince Felix Youssoupoff (Rasputin's assassin), Clement Attlee, Lord Beveridge (Master), C.S. Lewis, Stephen Spender, Harold Wilson (fellow), Lord Goodman (Master), V.S. Naipaul.

Beyond University College are the *Examination Schools* (1876–82; Sir T.G. Jackson), now used for lectures as well. By the corner of Queen's Lane, opposite, is the graceful façade of *The Queen's College* (290 undergraduates). It was founded in 1340 by Robert de Egglesfield, chaplain to Queen Philippa, wife of Edward III; she was the first of a long line of Queens consort to take an interest in the college. The founder provided for a Provost and 12 fellows to represent Our Lord and Apostles, and 70 'poor boys' as disciples, the first formal arrangement in Oxford for the education of undergraduates.

The college was mainly rebuilt in the baroque style between 1682 and 1765, though the identity of its architects is far from clear. The *Front Quad*, separated from the street merely by a screen and gatehouse with a cupola, owes something to Nicholas Hawksmoor, though his design was greatly altered in the building. On either side of the passage leading into the *North Quad* are the *Hall* and the *Chapel*, the latter with a decorated ceiling (the painting in the apse is by Sir James Thornhill), a magnificent baroque screen, and glass by Abraham van Linge. The North Quad, built before the Front Quad and with Wren playing a part in the early designs, has the magnificent *Library* on its W side.

FAMOUS MEMBERS: Thomas Middleton, William Wycherley, Edmund Halley, Joseph Addison and William Collins (who both migrated to Magdalen), Jeremy Bentham, Walter Pater, Leopold Stokowski, Sidney Keyes and Lord Florey (Provost).

It is worth following Queen's Lane to **St Edmund Hall** (360 undergraduates), the last survivor of the medieval halls, dating from the 13C. It is dedicated to St Edmund of Abingdon, Archbishop of Canterbury, who taught at Oxford c 1195–1200. Controlled by Queen's College from 1557 to 1937, it has enjoyed full collegiate status since 1957.

Three sides of the charming front quad were built in the 16C and 17C; the S side, on the right, was added in 1932–34. The tiny panelled *Chapel* has windows by Morris and Burne-Jones and a striking altarpiece by Ceri Richards (1958). The old church of *St Peter in the East*, further up Queen's Lane, is now the college library; only the late Norman crypt is open to visitors.

FAMOUS MEMBERS: Thomas Hearne, Sir Robin Day, Terry Jones.

Beyond St Edmund Hall, Queen's Lane winds round to join New College Lane, explored in the walking tour N and E from Carfax (below).

The remainder of the walk along the High is dominated by the view of **\*Magdalen College** (pronounced 'Maudlin'; 380 undergraduates), one of the most beautiful and spacious as well as richest colleges. It was founded on the site of a former Hospital of St John in 1458 by William of Waynflete, successively headmaster of Winchester, Provost of Eton, Bishop of Winchester and Lord Chancellor.

The chief feature of the High St. front is the graceful Perp. \**Tower*, built in 1492–1505 (tradition says by Wolsey, then the bursar) as the bell tower of the college chapel, though detached from it. It has recently been magnificently restored. A hymn is sung from the top at 06.00 on May morning.

We enter by St John's Gateway (1885). To the left are the Victorian Gothic *St Swithun's Buildings* and, beyond them, *Longwall Quad* (1932; Giles Gilbert Scott) and the *New Library*, built in 1851 as a hall for Magdalen College School. Ahead are the *President's Lodgings*, also Victorian, and the *Grammar Hall* (1614), a restored fragment of the vanished Magdalen Hall. Immediately to the right are the open-air pulpit, where a University Sermon is preached on the Sunday after St John the Baptist's Day (24 June), and the narrow entrance to the *Chaplain's Quad*, with remains of St John's Hospital and the blocked-up Pilgrim's Gate into the High.

The buildings on the E side (right) of *St John's Quad* are those planned and largely completed by William of Waynflete. The *Founder's Tower* (not open) contains state apartments and is still part of the President's Lodgings. Under the Muniment Tower is the entrance to the *Chapel*, finished before 1483, though its interior is now practically 19C work. The fine Lyttleton monument (1634) is by Nicholas Stone. The choir is famous for its singing, and visitors are welcome to choral services (18.00 on Monday and Wednesday–Friday, 17.15 on Saturday, 11.30 and 15.15 on Sunday in term). A passage beneath the Muniment Tower leads to the \**Cloisters*, with grotesque carvings on the buttresses, dating from the founder's time but heavily restored in the 19C. A flight of stairs at the SE corner leads to the *Hall* (1474), altered but keeping its beautiful panelling, oriel, musicians' gallery on top of a Jacobean screen; the oak roof is modern. The *Old Library* (not open) on the W side contains illuminated manuscripts and Wolsey's copy of the Gospels.

A passage on the N side leads across a wide lawn to the elegant *New Building* (1733). On the left is Magdalen's deer park, the *Grove* (not open). On the right a bridge crosses the Cherwell to a meadow with the delightful *Water Walks.

FAMOUS MEMBERS: Bishop Richard Foxe, John Colet, Cardinal Wolsey, Cardinal Pole, John Foxe, Sir Thomas Bodley, John Hampden, Joseph Addison and William Collins (who both migrated from Queen's), Edward Gibbon (sent down for converting to Catholicism and later contemptuous of the academic standards he found at Magdalen), John Wilson (Christopher North), Charles Reade, Oscar Wilde, Compton Mackenzie, C.S. Lewis, Sir John Betjeman, Gilbert Ryle, Sir Rupert Cross, A.J.P. Taylor, Lord Florey, Desmond Morris, Peter Brook, Dudley Moore.

Just beyond the college the stately *Magdalen Bridge*, built by John Gwynn in 1772–79 and widened in 1883, crosses the Cherwell.

Opposite Magdalen is the **Botanic Garden** (open), the oldest in England, founded in 1621, with a gateway by Nicholas Stone. Rose Lane, to the right of the garden, leads into Merton Field and Christ Church Meadow.

Across Magdalen Bridge, immediately to the left, are Magdalen's *Waynflete Building* (1960–61; Booth, Ledeboer and Pinckheard) and the startling *Florey Building* of Queen's College (1968–70; James Stirling). *Stone's Hospital*, an almshouse of 1697–1700, is in St Clement's St. On the right after we cross the bridge are *Magdalen College School* and, on a pleasant riverside site, **St Hilda's College**, founded for women in 1893 and still admitting women only (340 undergraduates). Famous members include Dame Helen Gardner and Barbara Pym. In Iffley Rd is *Greyfriars*, a permanent private hall for Franciscan students.

NORTH AND EAST FROM CARFAX. Cornmarket St. is mainly a shopping street but we should note, on the right, *St Michael's Church*, whose Saxon tower was once part of the city's defences. The church was restored after a fire in 1953. The four figures in the E windows are the oldest stained glass in Oxford (c 1290). William Morris married Jane Burden here in 1859.

In St Michael's St., to the left, are the mid Victorian buildings of the *Oxford Union Society*, founded as a social and debating club in 1823. The frescoes added by Rossetti, Morris and other Pre-Raphaelites in 1857 have since faded.

We turn right into the wide, handsome *Broad St. On the opposite side stands **Balliol College** (350 undergraduates), founded before 1266 by John de Balliol, father of the Scottish king, as a penance for insulting the Bishop of Durham,. The first statutes were given by his widow, Dervorguilla, in 1282. The college achieved its high academic reputation in the 19C under a series of distinguished Masters, of whom Benjamin Jowett (1817–93) was the most famous.

The college was also virtually rebuilt in the 19C, by Alfred Waterhouse (the Broad St. front and E side of the front quad, and the Hall in *Garden Quad*, 1867–77), William Butterfield (the chapel, 1856–57) and Anthony Salvin (part of the W side of Garden Quad, 1852–53). In the front quad, the *Library* and reading room (originally the Hall) are in fact 15C but were altered beyond recognition by Wyatt in the 1790s. The interior of Butterfield's *Chapel* has been toned down in the 20C. Some Anglo-Flemish glass of 1529, discarded by Butterfield, has been reset in the E window; other windows have glass of 1637 by Abraham van Linge. In the NW corner of the front quad a passage leads, by way of an ancient wooden door originally at the Broad St. entrance to Garden Quad. Here Waterhouse's *Hall* sits uneasily between two 1960s additions (by Oxford Architects Partnership).

Coffee was probably first drunk in England by N. Conopios, a Cretan student in 1637.

FAMOUS MEMBERS: John Wyclif (Master in 1364), John Evelyn, Adam Smith, Robert Southey, J.G. Lockhart, Cardinal Manning, both Archbishops Temple (father and son), A.P. Stanley, Matthew Arnold, A.H. Clough, Algernon Swinburne (persuaded to leave in 1860), T.H. Green, Gerard Manley Hopkins, Andrew Lang, Arnold Toynbee, A.C. Bradley, Lord Curzon, Lord Asquith, Hilaire Belloc, Monsignor Ronald Knox, King Olav of Norway, Lord Beveridge, Harold Macmillan, Julian Huxley, Aldous Huxley, Graham Greene, Anthony Powell, Nevil Shute, Edward Heath, Denis Healey, Lord Jenkins of Hillhead.

The *Oxford Story*, on the opposite side of Broad St., is an exhibition which seeks to bring the history of the university to life with the same gimmicks of presentation used by the Jorvik Viking Centre in York.

**Trinity College** (250 undergraduates), E of Balliol, lies some way back from Broad St. It was founded in 1555 by Sir Thomas Pope, a wealthy Oxfordshire landowner, but incorporates part of the much older Durham College, founded c 1286 for students from the Benedictine monasteries at Durham and elsewhere in the north. The varied yet harmonious buildings and the spacious grounds are among the most attractive in Oxford.

We enter the large and irregular front quad through iron gates of 1737. To the right, facing Broad St., are some old cottages converted into college rooms and, beyond them, *Kettell Hall*, built for himself by Dr Kettell, President in 1618–20. The E range and the *President's Lodgings* are by Sir T.G. Jackson (1883–87). We continue straight ahead to the main gateway, built by President Bathurst in 1691–94. He was also responsible for the *Chapel*, to the right, which has a superb baroque interior marred only by the Victorian stained glass. The carved lime and juniper wood reredos may be the work of Grinling Gibbons. The E range of *Durham Quad*, including the *Old Library* (not open), is a 15C fragment of Durham College. The *Hall*, on the W side, is a modest building of 1618–20 with a fine collection of portraits. In *Garden Quad*, beyond, the N range is a much altered building by Wren (1665); the E side opens out into pleasant gardens. On their S side, also reached by the gate between Jackson's buildings in the NE corner of the front quad, are the college's 20C additions: the neo-classical *War Memorial Library* (1928; J. Osborne Smith) and *Cumberbatch Quad* (1964–68; Maguire and Murray), built over the underground showrooms of Blackwell's bookshop.

FAMOUS MEMBERS: Lord Baltimore (founder of Maryland), Henry Ireton, John Aubrey, Sir John Denham, William Pitt, Lord North, Walter Savage Landor (sent down in 1793 for firing at the rooms of the man opposite), Cardinal Newman, Sir Richard Burton, Sir Arthur Quiller-Couch, James Elroy Flecker, Laurence Binyon, Monsignor Ronald Knox, Lord Goddard, Lord Clark, Terence Rattigan, Anthony Crosland.

We now follow Turl St. (the Turl) from the S side of Broad St. opposite Trinity. On the left stands **Exeter College** (280 undergraduates), founded by Walter de Stapledon in 1314 and refounded by Sir William Petrie in 1566.

The college has been much rebuilt at various periods. The Turl St. front and main quad are essentially 17–18C but owe their present look to Victorian alterations. The *Hall*, on the S of the quad, dates from 1618 and originally faced a chapel of the same date, demolished to make way for the present, inappropriate *Chapel* (1857) by Sir Gilbert Scott. It contains a tapestry by William Morris and Edward Burne-Jones, who first met as undergraduates here. *Palmer's Tower* (1432), facing the E end of the chapel, is the oldest part of the college. From here passages lead right to the *Library* (1856; Scott) and pleasant garden, and left into the small *Margary Quad*, with the *Thomas Wood Building* (1964; Brett and Pollen) on its W side.

FAMOUS MEMBERS: John Ford, the first Earl of Shaftesbury, Sir Charles Lyell, J.A. Froude, F.D. Maurice, William Morris, Edward Burne-Jones, Sir Hubert Parry, J.R.R. Tolkien, Richard Burton, Alan Bennett.

On the opposite side of the Turl is **Jesus College** (300 undergraduates), the first post-Reformation college in Oxford, founded in 1571, nominally by Elizabeth I but really by Hugh Price,

Treasurer of St David's. For many years the college had a close connection with Wales.

The oldest part is the Turl St. front, rebuilt in the Perp. style in 1856 by Buckler, who also restored the Market St. front. The S side of the front quad and the N side, with the Principal's house and the chapel, were built by Sir Eubule Thelwall, Principal in 1621–30. The *Chapel*, extended eastwards in 1636, has a barrel-vaulted roof, late 17C screen and early 17C pulpit; other features date from G.E. Street's restoration in 1864. The *Hall* (c 1617), opposite the main entrance, has a carved Jacobean screen and portraits of Elizabeth I, Charles I (by Van Dyck), Charles II (attributed to Lely) and the architect John Nash (by Lawrence). In the *Senior Common Room* (not open) is a fine original portrait of Elizabeth I by Zucchero and one of Canon Jenkins by Holman Hunt. The charming inner quadrangle was mainly the work of Sir Leoline Jenkins, Principal in 1661–73. The *Library* has 17C fittings. A passage on the N side leads to the college's 20C additions, including a block (by J. Fryman) to commemorate the college's quatercentary in 1971.

FAMOUS MEMBERS: Lancelot Andrewes, Richard (Beau) Nash, J.R. Green, Sir John Rhys, T.E. Lawrence, Harold Wilson, Magnus Magnusson.

Further down the Turl, also on the left, is **Lincoln College** (250 undergraduates), one of the best preserved of the late medieval colleges. It was founded in 1427 by Bishop Fleming of Lincoln for training clergy to refute the Wycliffite or Lollard heresy.

The attractive N quadrangle keeps its 15C appearance. The *Hall* (1437) has its original 15C timbers and smoke louvre, and a screen and wainscoting of 1696–1700. On the right are the rooms in which John Wesley, a fellow of the college, is said to have lived and members of the Holy Club or Methodists first met (open on application to the porter). The S quadrangle (1608–31) contains the *Chapel* built by Bishop Williams of Lincoln (1629–31), notable for its painted glass attributed to Bernard van Linge, its cedar wainscoting and carved bench ends.
    *All Saints Church*, at the corner of the Turl and the High, passed in the walk E from Carfax (above), was part of the college's original endowment and has been used as its library since 1975.

FAMOUS MEMBERS: Bishop Sanderson of Lincoln, Sir William Davenant, Dr John Radcliffe, John Wesley, Mark Pattison, Edward Thomas, Robert Speaight, Sir Osbert Lancaster, Lord Florey, Sir John Beazley, Egon Wellesz, John le Carré (David Cornwell).

We return to Broad St. and continue E. The street ends on the left with the inexpressive block of the *New Bodleian*, begun by Sir Giles Gilbert Scott in 1935, but on the right there is a handsome group of university buildings. The lovely *Old Ashmolean Museum* (open), the first public museum in the world, was built in 1678–83 for Elias Ashmole's collection of natural curiosities (see the Ashmolean, on the walk N and W from Carfax, below). It is now the *Museum of the History of Science*, with a fine collection of scientific instruments. The *Sheldonian Theatre* (open), the first work of Sir Christopher Wren, was built in 1663–69 at the expense of Archbishop Sheldon as a venue for university occasions. Degree-giving ceremonies are held here. The plan of the building, semi-circular in front and rectangular behind, imitates the Theatre of Marcellus in Rome. It is partly surrounded by railings whose stone plinths carry 13 busts, renewed in 1972. The octagonal cupola, a reconstruction of 1832 which is larger than Wren's original one, gives a famous view over the city. The ceiling inside has an allegorical painting by Robert Streeter (1669). Beyond the Sheldonian is the *Clarendon Building*, designed by Hawksmoor under Vanbrugh's influence in 1713, partly from the profits of Clarendon's 'History of the Great Rebellion'. It used to house the Clarendon Press but is now part of the Bodleian.

A short way along Parks Rd, N from the end of Broad St., is **Wadham College** (360 undergraduates), facing the gardens of Trinity. It was founded by Nicholas Wadham of Somerset and built in 1610–13 on the site of an Augustinian friary by his widow Dorothy.

The well-preserved buildings are a fine example of Jacobean Gothic. Between the hall and chapel, on the E side, is a Jacobean porch with statues of Nicholas and Dorothy Wadham. The *Chapel*, altered inside in the 19C, has a Jacobean screen and an E window by Bernard van Linge (1622). The *Hall* has a hammerbeam roof, a Jacobean screen and a large portrait collection. The secluded *Gardens* give a lovely view of the garden front. The S quadrangle has a pleasant copper-roofed block (1954; Henry Goddard) and, E of the Foundation Building, the imposing *Library* (1977; Gillespie, Kidd and Coia).

FAMOUS MEMBERS: Admiral Blake, John Wilmot (Earl of Rochester), Sir Charles Sedley, Sir Christopher Wren, Speaker Onslow, Sir T.G. Jackson, Lord Birkenhead, Sir Thomas Beecham, Maurice Bowra (Warden), Cecil Day-Lewis, Rex Warner, Michael Foot, Melvyn Bragg, Alan Coren. The ingenious Dr John Wilkins was Warden in Wren's time.

We return down Parks Rd to the junction with Broad St. The handsome Holywell St., on our left, is the starting point for a tour of the Eastern Outskirts (below). We continue S on Catte St., quickly coming to **Hertford College** (320 undergraduates), with its distinctive bridge spanning New College Lane and linking its old and new buildings. The college began life as Hart Hall, founded in 1282, which afterwards became Hertford College (1740–1805) but was absorbed by Magdalen Hall in 1822. On the dissolution of Magdalen Hall in 1874, the college was refounded through the bequest of Thomas Charles Baring, the banker.

The oldest part of the main quad is the NE corner, where the *Old Hall* dates from the late 16C. The E range, containing the *Old Library* and *Senior Common Room*, was built early in the 17C, the present *Library*, (formerly the chapel) in the 18C. Most of the rest of the college is the work of Sir T.G. Jackson, including the *Hall* and staircase (1877), the present *Chapel* (1910), the bridge (1913) and the *Octagon* (1923–26). The new *Holywell Quad* was completed in two phases between 1976 and 1981.

FAMOUS MEMBERS. Of Hart Hall: John Donne, John Selden, Lord Henry Pelham. Of the original Hertford College: Charles James Fox. Of Magdalen Hall: William Tyndale, Thomas Hobbes, Lord Clarendon, Sir Matthew Hale, Sir Henry Vane and Dr John Wilkins. Of the refounded Hertford College: W.R. Inge, Evelyn Waugh.

The handsome buildings of Radcliffe Square are visited in the walk E from Carfax (above).

New College Lane goes on to **\*New College** (380 undergraduates), founded in 1379 by William of Wykeham, also the founder of Winchester College. Behind its modest entrance, it is one of Oxford's grandest colleges, and its buildings (completed about 1386) remain a superb example of Perp. architecture.

The front quad was marred by the addition of a third storey (1675) and the modernisation of its windows (1711). The noble *Chapel*, on the N, was restored in 1879 by Sir Gilbert Scott who, unfortunately, raised the roof. The antechapel has its original 14C *glass, except for the insipid W window painted by Thomas Jarvis to the designs of Sir Joshua Reynolds (1777), a fine series of 23 brasses dating from 1403 to 1619, and Epstein's statue of Lazarus (1951). In the chapel itself the reconstructed stalls retain their old arm rests and misericords, including one of the founder (first stall on the S side). On the N side of the altar are the founder's *crozier and a painting of St James by El Greco. The choral services rival those at Magdalen. The *Hall*, adjoining the chapel, is the oldest and one of the finest in Oxford, with early 16C linenfold panelling and a roof by Scott (1877).

W of the chapel are the detached *Bell Tower* and the quiet *Cloisters*, with remarkable wood vaulting, memorial tablets and eight statues from the steeple of St Mary the Virgin.

A passage in the E side of the quad, under the *Founder's Library* (1778; Wyatt), leads to the handsome *Garden Quad* of 1684–1708, enclosed on its E side by a lovely wrought-iron screen (1711). The chief feature of the spacious *Gardens* is a well-preserved remnant of the old city wall, dating from the time of Henry III.

The range of buildings facing Holywell St. to the N is by Scott (1872) and Basil Champneys (1896 and 1885). The *Sacher Building* (1961–62; David Roberts) faces E to Longwall St.

FAMOUS MEMBERS: William Grocyn, William of Waynflete, Sir Henry Wotton, Bishop Ken, Sydney Smith, John Galsworthy, A.P. Herbert (last independent MP for the University, 1935–50), Maurice Bowra, Lord Longford, Lord David Cecil, Hugh Gaitskell, George Woodcock, E.F. Schumacher, Len Murray, Tony Benn, John Fowles.

From the end of this walk we can join the High (on the walk E from Carfax, above) via New College Lane and Queen's Lane, passing St Edmund Hall, or via Catte St., running S from the head of New College Lane through Radcliffe Square, or via Longwall St.

NORTH FROM CARFAX. We begin by following the course of the previous walk up Cornmarket St. but, instead of turning right into Broad St., continue straight ahead into Magdalen St. and past the church of *St Mary Magdalen*, largely rebuilt by Scott. He was also responsible for the prominent *Martyrs' Memorial* (1841) outside, modelled on the medieval Eleanor Crosses, with statues of Cranmer, Ridley and Latimer, burned at the stake in 1556 in nearby Broad St.

The memorial stands at the beginning of the broad, tree-lined thoroughfare called St Giles, with the side of Balliol College on the

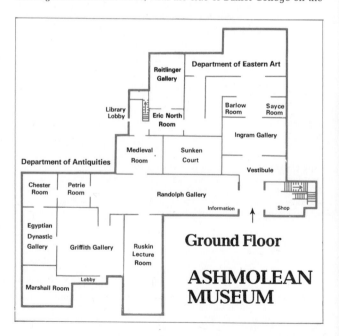

right. At the corner of Beaumont St., on the left, is a Greek Revival building by C.R. Cockerell (1841–45). Its E wing, facing St Giles, is occupied by the *Taylor Institution* (the 'Taylorian'), founded for the study of modern languages from the bequest of Sir Robert Taylor (d. 1788).

The central range and W wing house the **··Ashmolean Museum**, one of the best museums in England outside London, with the university's magnificent art and archaeological collections.

Their nucleus was 'Tradescant's Ark', collections of rarities formed by John Tradescant the Elder (d. 1638) and his son, and settled on Elias Ashmole. He offered them to the university, which built the Old Ashmolean on Broad St. to receive them. When they outgrew this building, the natural curiosities were transferred to the University Museum and the ethnographical exhibits to the Pitt-Rivers Museum, both visited later on this walking tour, and the remainder housed here.

GROUND FLOOR. The bookstall is to the right of the entrance and the information desk is in the Randolph Gallery to the left. The *Randolph Gallery* contains classical sculptures, Greek, Hellenistic and Roman originals, and Roman copies, mainly from the Arundel or Pomfret marbles, including a torso of c 480–60 BC, a pedimental sculpture embodying two linear measures (Aegean of the 5C BC), and the fragment of a frieze of an Athenian temple. In the showcases are fine temporary displays of individual aspects of archaeology. To the W are: the *Petrie Room* containing Egyptian predynastic material, mainly from Sir Flinders Petrie's excavations; the *Chester Room*, with fine scarabs, beads, seals, papyri, etc.; and the *Egyptian Dynastic Gallery*, which includes pottery, faience, jewellery, bronzes and glass, mostly from excavated sites. The *Griffith Gallery* of Egyptian sculpture contains: the *shrine of Taharqa from Kawa (7C BC) decorated in bas-relief; finds from the Oxford excavations in Nubia; reliefs, stelae and sculpture; mummy cases and funerary furnishings; wall paintings and fragmentary reliefs from Tell el-Amarna; and Coptic textiles. From here a passage leads to the *Marshall Room*, with coloured Worcester porcelain (1750–83).

N of the Randolph Gallery, the *Medieval Room* contains: the *Alfred Jewel (9C AD; cf. North Petherton, Rte 23), perhaps the head of an 'aestel', or pointer, for following the lines of illuminated manuscripts; the similar Minster Lovell Jewel; Viking antiquities; local pottery; brooches; medieval tiles; the Odda Stone, the foundation stone (1056) of the Saxon chapel at Deerhurst (Rte 42); and objects of historical interest. To the right of the Medieval Room is the *Sunken Court* (open to students on request) containing the reserve collection of Greek vases.

Opposite the main entrance is the well-arranged *Department of Eastern Art. The vestibule has examples of Gandhara sculpture and other early Asian cultures to one side and early Chinese bronzes to the other. The *Ingram Gallery* of Chinese ceramics (400 BC–14C AD) contains also pottery tomb figures (AD 618–906), a Song gilt bronze Bodhisattva and 16C cast-iron heads. The following rooms to right and left show 14–20C Chinese porcelains and Chinese decorative arts. A large seated polychromed wooden Buddha dominates the end of the gallery. The room beyond is devoted mainly to Japanese ceramics and other decorative arts. The *Screen Gallery* houses Japanese fine arts and leads through a display of Indian and South Asian decorative arts to the *Tibetan Room*. On the left are stone, metal and terracotta works from India and South Asia. To the right is the *Eric North Room*, where exhibitions are usually changed monthly. The *Reitlinger Gallery*, connecting with both the Eric North Room and the Screen Gallery, displays the arts of Islam.

FIRST FLOOR. Passing through the small *Founder's Room*, exhibiting portraits of Elias Ashmole and his contemporaries, we descend a few steps into the **Department of Antiquities**, the many superb finds arranged for expert study rather than aesthetic appreciation. The *Tradescant Room* has objects from the original 17C collections, and historical relics such as Guy Fawkes's lantern, Bradshaw's hat, Powhatan's mantle, etc. Opposite is a room illustrating the timescale of Old World archaeology from the palaeolithic through the periods covered by specialist displays in adjacent galleries. Displayed in the *John Evans Room* are objects of the European Neolithic, Bronze and Iron Ages, including gold ornaments, fine collections of bronze implements, Celtic art, and a large alcove of Italian and Etruscan antiquities. The *Cretan collection in the *Arthur*

Heberden Coin Room — Department of Antiquities — Drapers Gallery — Myres Room — Leeds Room — Beazley Room — Arthur Evans Room — Hill Music Room — John Evans Room — Fox-Strangeways Gallery — Weldon Gallery — Gordon Childe Room — Tradescant Room — Landscape Room — Mallett Gallery — Fortnum Gallery — Hindley Smith Gallery — McAlpine Gallery — Founder's Room — Porcelain Room — Eldon Gallery — Farrer Gallery — Staircase to second floor / Department of Western Art / Chambers Hall Gallery / Combe Gallery / Ward Gallery — Warren Room — **First Floor** — Department of Western Art

*Evans Room*, principally from the excavations of Sir Arthur Evans at Knossos, is of special importance, and includes Minoan pottery, seals, Linear B tablets, swords, jewellery and finds from the Dictaean Cave. Fine Cycladic marble figurines, lead boat models and finds from excavations at Phylakopi on Melos are also displayed here. Beyond is the *Myres Room* of Cypriot antiquities, with pottery, jewellery, sculpture, etc. To the right is the *Drapers' Gallery*, exhibiting material from the pre-Islamic Near East, notably finds from Jericho and Jerusalem, and 'Luristan Bronzes'. To the left the *Beazley Room* is devoted to Greek antiquities, including silver, bronzes, terracottas, gems, jewellery and Geometric, Orientalising and Black-and-Red figure pottery. The *Leeds Room* houses finds from the Roman Empire and from Europe during the Dark Ages, with particular reference to Britain. A staircase descends to the Byzantine lobby. The *Heberden Coin Room* contains rich collections of Greek, Roman, Oriental, medieval European and modern coins, and medals from all periods. (Students may consult the main part of the collection by appointment only.) Nearby is the *Hill Music Room*, which contains 16–18C Italian and English stringed instruments, including 'Le Messie' by Stradivarius.

This room is part of the **Department of Western Art**, which occupies the rest of the upper floors. Beyond the Founder's Room (see above) is the *Fortnum Gallery*, containing many of the Fortnum collection of bronzes, as well as a remarkably representative collection of 13–16C Italian *paintings. These include two of the most celebrated Florentine paintings in this country, 'The Hunt in a Forest' by Uccello and 'The Forest Fire' by Piero di Cosimo, and major works by Giovanni di Paolo, Orcagna, Pintoricchio, Lorenzo di Credi, Filippo Lippi, Crivelli, Bronzino, Giovanni Bellini, Veronese, Giorgione, Tintoretto and Jacopo Bassano.

At the end is the *Mallett Gallery* with tapestries, sculpture and a display of drawings by Michelangelo and Raphael. The *Fox-Strangeways Gallery* has works by 17C Dutch and Flemish painters, including Rubens, Van Dyck, Salomon van Ruysdael and Jacob van Ruisdael, Koninck, Drost and Bril. The *Weldon Gallery* is devoted mainly to 17C–early 18C Italian art, though several other schools are also represented here, together with baroque sculpture in silver, bronze and marble, and a collection of 13–18C rings. Of the paintings, 'The Deposition' by Van Dyck, 'The Judgement of Hercules' by Paolo de

Matteis and 'The Exposition of Moses' by Nicolas Poussin are outstanding. The adjoining *Landscape Room* brings together work by Gaspard Poussin, Claude Lorrain, Corot, Richard Wilson and Constable.

The *Hindley Smith Gallery* displays French 19–20C painting and sculpture. Camille Pissarro is particularly well represented, and there are works by Toulouse-Lautrec, Van Gogh, Monet, Manet, Renoir, Cézanne, Bonnard, Rodin, Matisse and Picasso. The adjoining room contains 18C European porcelain. Beyond this is the *Eldon Gallery*, where a changing selection from the Department's rich collection of drawings, watercolours and prints, and sometimes loan exhibitions, are displayed. Approached through the Eldon Gallery is the *McAlpine Gallery* devoted to temporary exhibitions, often of modern art. A vestibule at the far end of the Eldon Gallery containing drawings by the great school of Russian stage design gives access to the *Fine Art Library* (ticket holders only), the *Print Room* (open on application) and the small *Warren Room* with English Delft ware.

In the *Farrer Gallery* are the Fortnum ceramics, mainly Hispano-Moresque, Turkish and Italian, and collections of silver, including pieces by Huguenot craftsmen working in London c 1705–50 (Lamerie, Platel and the Courtaulds); also examples of Italian sculpture, including works by the Della Robbia. Among the smaller works of art here are: ivories and plaquettes; 13–16C Limoges enamel, including a reliquary depicting the martyrdom and burial of St Thomas Becket in champlevé enamel; and a fine display of 16–17C timepieces.

The Farrer Gallery leads back into the Mallett Gallery, from which a staircase showing examples of tapestry and needlework and a case of French 18C porcelain leads to the second floor. On the landing is a fine collection of German 18C porcelain.

The SECOND FLOOR begins with the *Chambers Hall Gallery* devoted to 18C paintings and sculpture, including works by Tiepolo, Guardi, Canaletto, Batoni, Panini, Reynolds, Gainsborough, Hogarth and Roubiliac. The collection of 19–20C British art in the *Combe Gallery* is notable for work by Samuel Palmer and the Pre-Raphaelites, including Rossetti, Holman Hunt, Millais and Arthur Hughes. The *Ward Gallery* has Dutch 17–18C paintings of flowers and still life, together with Dutch earthenware and glassware.

The *Cast Gallery* lies to the N of the museum, approached from St John's St. It contains over 250 casts of Greek and Graeco-Roman statuary, arranged in historical sequence.

The dignified Georgian Beaumont St. leads W, past the *Playhouse* (1938; Sir Edward Maufe). At the end is **Worcester College** (320 undergraduates), once known from its remoteness as 'Botany Bay'. It was founded in 1714 by Sir Thomas Cookes, but the site had been occupied first by Gloucester College (founded in 1283), the general house of studies for English Benedictines, and after the Reformation by Gloucester Hall.

The main buildings (1746–91) are in the classical style. The *Chapel*, originally by Wyatt, was elaborately redecorated—and made very dark—by Burges in 1866 with paintings and mosaics recalling his work at Cardiff Castle. On the left side of the quadrangle is a row of five small *monastic houses, relics of the medieval Gloucester College, with the arms of Benedictine abbeys over the doorways. The large and beautiful *Gardens contain a lake. On the S and E sides of the gardens are the *Nuffield Block* (1931) and *New Building* (1961; Sir Hugh Casson).

FAMOUS MEMBERS. Of Gloucester College: Thomas Walsingham. Of Gloucester Hall: Richard Lovelace, Sir Kenelm Digby. Of Worcester College: Thomas De Quincey, Richard Adams, Rupert Murdoch.

Along Walton St. beyond Worcester is *Ruskin College*, founded in 1899 by Walter Vrooman and Charles Beard, American admirers of John Ruskin, to enable working men to study history, sociology and economics in the academic atmosphere of Oxford. It is not officially connected with the University. Further N are the buildings of the *Oxford University Press.*

For Nuffield College and other sites S of Worcester College, see Western Outskirts below.

We return to St Giles. Opposite the Taylorian is **St John's College** (350 undergraduates), founded in 1555 by Sir Thomas White, a Reading clothier and Lord Mayor of London, on the site of the old Cistercian college of St Bernard, which had been founded in 1437 by Archbishop Chichele.

The front quad is the oldest part, being on three of its sides the remains of St Bernard's College, with a third storey added in the 17C. Over the gateway are statues of St Bernard, Chichele and White, with a statue of St John the Baptist by Eric Gill (1936) on the inner side. The *Chapel* and *Hall*, on the left, are both 16C but much altered, the chapel in the 19C and the hall in the 18C. A handsome doorway and passage opposite the main entrance lead into *'Canterbury Quad,*' begun in 1596–97 but completed by Archbishop Laud in 1631–36. His elegant colonnades and baroque decoration make an interesting contrast with the traditional Oxford Jacobean-Gothic style elsewhere in the quad. The bronze statues of Charles I and Henrietta Maria on the gate towers are by Le Sueur. The *Old Library* (open by written appointment only) has a portrait of Charles I, partly composed of minutely written psalms, and memorabilia of Laud.

To the S (right) of the front quad is *Dolphin Quad*, partly 18C and partly by Sir Edward Maufe (1948). In the N quadrangle, left of the front quad, the most striking building is the bold series of interlocking polygons (1958–60; Michael Powers and the Architects Co-Partnership).

The *'Gardens,* laid out in the 18C, are among the best in Oxford.

FAMOUS MEMBERS: Edmund Campion, Archbishop Laud, Archbishop Juxon, James Shirley, A.E. Housman, Gilbert Murray, Sir Tyrone Guthrie, Robert Graves, Philip Larkin, Kingsley Amis.

Opposite St John's College, as we continue N along St Giles, are *Blackfriars*, established in the 1920s for Dominican monks studying in Oxford, and *Pusey House*, a theological centre named after the Tractarian leader, with a chapel and library. Since 1981 it has also been the headquarters of **St Cross College**, a graduate college founded in 1965. In Pusey St. is *Regent's Park College*, a permanent private hall of the university and training centre for Baptist clergy. Opposite *St Benet's Hall*, another permanent private hall, stands *Queen Elizabeth House*, a 17C building used as a centre for Commonwealth studies. St Giles ends with *St Giles's Church*, mostly 12C and 13C, isolated in the fork of Woodstock Rd and Banbury Rd. These are explored in Northern Outskirts, below.

Little Clarendon St., on the left, leads to a large complex of university and faculty buildings.

The present tour heads right on Keble Rd, with science faculty buildings on the left, and around the corner into Parks Rd, where Keble College and the University Museum face each other.

**Keble College** (390 undergraduates) opened in 1870 as a memorial to the Tractarian leader John Keble (1792–1866) and to provide an Oxford education for 'gentlemen of slender means'. From the start, William Butterfield's *'buildings* (1868–82) provoked controversy by their tense, angular shapes and bold use of polychromatic brick ('streaky bacon'); they still have the power to call forth widely differing reactions.

The vast *Chapel*, dominating the main quad, has a splendidly rich interior. A small sidechapel houses Holman Hunt's 'The Light of the World', excluded from the main chapel because Butterfield believed it inappropriate to a place of worship. The *Hall*, the longest in Oxford, has George Richmond's portrait of Keble among its collection of paintings. The *Library* has a remarkable collection of illuminated medieval manuscripts, incunabula, and early printed books as well as Keble and Newman letters.

*Keble College, Oxford, by William Butterfield*

The **University Museum**, opposite, houses the natural science collections of the university, including some impressive prehistoric skeletons. The *building was designed in 1855 by Benjamin Woodward with the active participation of Ruskin. Its cathedral-like interior of iron and glass is rich with decorative detail. Behind it is the *Pitt-Rivers Museum of Ethnology and Pre-History*, with exhibits from around the world, including those collected by Captain Cook.

The *University Science Area*, with a medley of 19–20C buildings, extends down South Parks Rd to the University Parks (see Eastern Outskirts, below).

Parks Rd goes N round the edge of the University Parks towards Lady Margaret Hall (see North-Eastern Outskirts, below). To the S, it passes Wadham College and joins Broad St., on the walk N and E from Carfax (above).

WESTERN OUTSKIRTS. Queen St. leads W from Carfax, away from the older colleges and into a more recently developed area. Near the entrance to the large new Westgate shopping centre on the left, New Inn Hall St. leads right to **St Peter's College** (280 undergraduates), founded as a private hall in 1928 and granted full collegiate status in 1961. It incorporates a much altered fragment of New Inn Hall, one of the oldest medieval halls. Its chapel is the church of *St Peter-le-Bailey* (1874; Basil Champneys), with an E window by John Hayward (1964). Opposite St Peter's is the old gateway of St Mary's Hall, an Augustinian house dissolved by Elizabeth I. Erasmus prepared his edition of the Greek Testament here in 1498. The site is now occupied by *Frewin Hall*, belonging to Brasenose College.

New Rd continues W from the shopping centre and the end of Queen St. On its right stands **Nuffield College**, founded in 1937 by Lord Nuffield (William Robert Morris), the car manufacturer, for graduate studies and research. It has some 38 resident fellows and about 60 students working for higher degrees. The buildings (by Austen Harrison, with Thomas Barnes and Piers Hubbard) follow the founder's preference for a traditional Cotswold style. The Chapel was planned with the help of John Piper, who also designed the altar and (with Patrick Reyntiens) the stained-glass windows. Across the road from Nuffield, the County Hall, Assize Court and prison occupy the site of the Norman and medieval *Castle*,.claimed as the birthplace of Richard I in 1157.

The area S and W of New Rd and the castle was once the site of several religious houses: Osney Abbey, Rewley Abbey, and the Franciscan house to which the medieval philosopher Roger Bacon belonged.

Worcester St. leads N from New Rd to Worcester College (see the walk N from the city centre, above).

Park End St. leads W from the end of New Rd to (1/4m) the railway station.

EASTERN OUTSKIRTS. We begin at the E end of Broad St., on the walk N and E from Carfax (above). The old and dignified Holywell St. runs E, past (right) Bath Place and a back entrance to New College, and (left) the *Old Music Room* of 1748, the first room in Europe to be built solely for musical purposes.

On Mansfield Rd, also to the left, is *Manchester College*, a Unitarian training college which began at Manchester in 1786 and moved to Oxford in 1888. The buildings (1891–93; T. Worthington) are Victorian Gothic; the chapel has windows by Morris and Burne-Jones. Beyond is *Mansfield College*, founded in Birmingham in 1838 as a Congregationalist training college but now a permanent private hall of the university. Its fine Victorian Gothic buildings are by Basil Champneys (1887–89). Mansfield Rd ends at South Parks Rd, met again near the end of this tour.

Holywell St. continues E to meet Longwall St., running right to the High, and St Cross Rd, which we follow left. On the right is the church of *St Cross*, with a 12C chancel arch and 13C tower, and *Holywell Manor*, a much altered 15C building now used as a graduate centre by Balliol and St Anne's. The extension of Balliol opposite is named after its architect, Sir Leslie Martin, who also designed the *English Faculty*, *Bodleian Law Library* and *Institute of Statistics* (1964) at the fork of St Cross Rd and Manor Rd.

We follow Manor Rd to the right and cross the Cherwell to reach **St Catherine's College** (410 undergraduates), founded in 1868 as a society for non-collegiate students and raised to collegiate status in 1963. Its buildings, gardens and (notably) furnishings were all designed by the Danish architect Arne Jacobsen (1960–64). A.A. Milne and Edward Thomas were both members of the earlier society.

We retrace our steps down Manor Rd and turn right into St Cross Rd, which continues between playing fields to join South Parks Rd. On the lefthand corner is the huge *Zoology and Psychology Building* in stilted concrete (1965–70; Sir Leslie Martin). Beyond are the University Science Area, the University Museum and Keble College (on the walk N from Carfax, above). On the righthand corner is **Linacre College**, founded as a graduate society in 1926 and raised to the status of graduate college in 1965. Ahead, to the N, are the *University Parks*, with playing fields (including the university cricket ground) and a network of pleasant footpaths. To the right is an attractive walk along the Cherwell, and from the SE corner a footpath leads between two branches of the river to join (c 1m) the Marston Rd.

NORTH-EASTERN OUTSKIRTS. **Lady Margaret Hall** is beautifully situated on the N side of the University Parks. It can be reached by footpath through the Parks; alternative approaches take Parks Rd and Norham Gardens from Keble College (on walk N from Carfax, above) or Banbury Rd (Northern Outskirts, below). The first place of higher education for women in Oxford, it was founded for Anglican students in 1878 and achieved full collegiate status in 1960. It now admits men as well (340 undergraduates). Its main buildings—by Basil Champneys (1881–83), Reginald Blomfield (1896–1915) and Raymond Erith (1961)—make a harmonious neo-Georgian group. The Chapel (1931; Sir Giles Gilbert Scott) has a painting of the flagellation of Christ attributed to Taddeo Gaddi and a beautiful triptych by Burne-Jones (c 1863). The gardens stretch down to the Cherwell. Famous members include Barbara Hammond, Dame C.V. Wedgwood, Georgina Battiscombe, Lady Antonia Fraser.

Also by the Cherwell, N of Lady Margaret Hall, is **Wolfson College**. It can be reached by taking Dragon School Lane from Lady Margaret Hall, or by taking Bardwell Rd from Banbury Rd (Northern Outskirts, below). Starting as a graduate society, Iffley College, in 1965, it grew into a graduate college the following year with the help of grants from the Wolfson and Ford Foundations. The first President was Sir Isaiah Berlin. The handsome white and grey concrete buildings are by Powell and Moya (1971–74).

NORTHERN OUTSKIRTS. We begin at the N end of St Giles (on the walk N from Carfax, above), where Woodstock Rd and Banbury Rd fork.

On the lefthand side of Woodstock Rd is **Somerville College**, a college for women only (350 undergraduates) founded in 1879 as a non-denominational alternative to the Anglican Lady Margaret Hall. The original building, Walton House, dates from 1826; subsequent buildings are ranged around a large central quadrangle. The main entrance is through the Darbishire Quad (1932). Famous members include Vera Brittain, Rose Macaulay, Dorothy L. Sayers, Margaret Kennedy, Dorothy Hodgkin, Dame Janet Vaughan, Winifred Holtby,

Indira Gandhi, Marghanita Laski, Margaret Thatcher, Shirley Williams, Iris Murdoch.

Immediately N of Somerville is the *Radcliffe Infirmary*, a teaching hospital founded in 1770 from the bequest of Dr John Radcliffe. Its original building is by Henry Keene. Beyond lies another of the doctor's bequests, the lovely *Radcliffe Observatory* (open by appointment), built by James Wyatt and Henry Keene in 1772–94. Since 1979 it has been the centrepiece of **Green College**, a new foundation named after Dr and Mrs Cecil Green of Dallas, Texas, and devoted to advanced scientific studies.

Opposite is **St Anne's College**, founded in 1879 as a society for women studying in Oxford and granted full collegiate status in 1952. It now admits men as well (380 undergraduates). The varied buildings, dating from the 1930s onwards, include the graceful Hall (1959; Gerald Banks) and the Wolfson Building (1966; Howell, Killick, Partridge and Amis).

On the corner of Bevington Rd, beyond St Anne's, is *St Antony's College* for graduates, founded in 1948. Bevington Rd leads into Banbury Rd opposite *Wycliffe Hall*, an Anglican theological college. About ¼m N is **St Hugh's College**, founded for women in 1886 by Elizabeth Wordsworth, who also founded Lady Margaret Hall, and granted full collegiate status in 1959. It still admits women only (330 undergraduates). The main buildings (1914–36) are brick neo-Georgian; the Wolfson Building (1966) is by David Roberts.

Bardwell Rd leads E from Banbury Rd to Wolfson College (see North-Eastern Outskirts, above).

Banbury Rd leads S from Wycliffe Hall back to St Giles, passing the turning for Lady Margaret Hall (North-Eastern Outskirts, above) and the buildings of the science faculties.

OUTSKIRTS: VIEWS. The low hills around Oxford offer some good views of the city, worth hunting out among the suburbs.—*Shotover Plain*, with its very steep approach road, is a large open common about 3m E of Magdalen Bridge, just beyond the ring road.—*Boar's Hill*, 4m SW and also beyond the ring road, has *Jarn's Mound*, a wild garden and wood made by the archaeologist Sir Arthur Evans (d. 1941).—*Raleigh Park* is by the ring road and *North Hinksey*, about 1½m W.

OUTSKIRTS: RIVER SCENERY. There is a pleasant trip up the Cherwell from Magdalen Bridge to (c 4½m) *Water Eaton* and (c 6½m) *Islip*, also visited in the routes to Banbury and Bicester below.—Good walks can also be taken beside the Thames upstream toward Stanton Harcourt and downstream toward Abingdon, both described in Rte 36B. For the splendid church at *Iffley*, passed on the way downstream, see Rte 36A.

FROM OXFORD TO BANBURY, 23m by A423. From St Giles we follow the Banbury Rd. through the N outskirts of the city and cross the A40. Just over ½m beyond a lane leads right for (1m) *Water Eaton* on the Cherwell and, after another ½m, A43 branches right for Bicester (see below).—Beyond (4½m) *Kidlington* we cross the Oxford Canal (Rte 36B).—From (12½m) *Hopcroft's Holt* B4030 leads right for (1½m) *Rousham*, a charming little village on the Cherwell. The church has interesting Norman and Dec. features. **Rousham Park** (open) is a 17C house altered in 1738 by William Kent, of less interest than the *gardens he laid out, among the best surviving examples of Picturesque landscaping in England. Horace Walpole found 'the sweetest little groves, glades, porticos, cascades and river imaginable' and thought Rousham 'the most engaging of Kent's works'. —13¼m. *Steeple Aston*, on the right, remains an attractive place despite recent development. The church includes a baroque monument of 1730.—16½m. *Deddington*, once an important market town, has mounds marking the site of its castle (English Heritage, open at any reasonable time). The church at *Somerton*, on the Cherwell 4m SE, has some remarkable 16C monuments.—At (19½m) *Adderbury* we join Rte 39A and the road from London.

FROM OXFORD TO BICESTER, 12m by A423, A43 and A421. We follow the route to Banbury (above) for 4m and branch right on A43.—5m. A road leads right for (1m) *Islip*, birthplace of Edward the Confessor (1004). The church at *Wood Eaton*, 1¾m S, has a painted 14C rood beam in its roof. The church at *Charlton-on-Otmoor*, 2½m NE of Islip, is a well-preserved example of the transitional style between Dec. and Perp., with a fine early 16C rood screen and loft.—7½m. *Weston-on-the-Green* stands at the fork of A43 to Northampton and A421 for Bicester. Weston Manor, now a hotel, is a much altered 15–16C building.—12m. *Bicester*, Rte 39A.

From Oxford to London via *Henley* and *Windsor*, see Rtes 36A and 36B; to

London via *High Wycombe*, and to *Gloucester* via *Cheltenham*, see Rte 38A; to *Stratford-upon-Avon*, see Rte 40; to *Worcester*, see Rte 41.

# 38   London to Gloucester: The Cotswolds

## A.   Via the Chilterns,
## Oxford and Cheltenham

Total distance 104m. We follow A40 throughout.—To (25m) *Beaconsfield*.—To (29m) **High Wycombe**.—To (36½m) *Stokenchurch*.—To (55m) **Oxford** (bypassed; Rte 37).—To (66m) *Witney* (bypassed).—To (73m) *Burford* (bypassed).—To (82m) *Northleach*.—To (95m) **Cheltenham**.—To (104m) **Gloucester**.

Maps: OS Landranger 176, 175, 165, 164, 163, 162.

M40 covers the 40m stretch from Denham to just short of Wheatley, bypassing Beaconsfield, High Wycombe and Stokenchurch, and offering a quick way through the Chilterns. The present route cuts through the centre of the Cotswolds. The hills to the S are described in Rte 38B, and their N fringe in the journeys from Oxford to Stratford (Rte 40) and Oxford to Worcester (Rte 41).

A40 heads NW from central London.—Beyond (18m) *Uxbridge Common* it crosses the Grand Union Canal in the Colne valley and enters the **Chiltern Hills**.

This range of chalk downs runs from near Reading through the SE corner of Buckinghamshire, at 700–850ft for much of the way, reaching its highest point at Coombe Hill (852ft) near Wendover (Rte 39A) and gradually petering out further N, beyond Luton. The dense beech forests of the Chilterns encouraged the local industry of furniture-making ('Windsor' chairs), now largely centred on High Wycombe.
   The only way that a member of Parliament may vacate his seat is by accepting the stewardship of the Chiltern Hundreds (Stoke, Desborough and Burnham), or that of the Manor of Northstead in Yorkshire, which are both offices of profit under the Crown and hence incompatible with Parliamentary duties. The nominal duty of the Steward of the Chiltern Hundreds is to protect wayfarers from bandits, who once lurked in the forests.

19m. The roundabout at *Denham* marks the start of M40. The busy A412 heads SW to (6½m) *Slough*. Just beyond the roundabout, on the right, is the old village street of Denham. The church contains the brass of Dame Agnes Jordan, Abbess of Syon (c 1540), one of only two extant brasses of an abbess. Denham Place is a notable 17C house.—We pass M25 on the way to (21m) *Gerrards Cross*, a residential suburb stretching N to Chalfont St Peter.

Off A413 4½m N is **Chalfont St Giles**, with the little cottage (open) where Milton lived in 1665–66 while the plague was raging in London. 'Paradise Lost' was finished and 'Paradise Regained' begun here. The church has medieval wall paintings. A413 goes on to join Rte 39A at *Amersham*.—Newland Park, about 2½m E of Chalfont St Giles, has the imaginative *Chiltern Open Air Museum*, with reconstructed old buildings from the Chilterns.—*Jordans*, about 2m S of Chalfont St Giles, has a group of historic Quaker buildings: the meeting house built in 1688, with the graves of William Penn (1644–1718), founder of Pennsylvania, and of Milton's friend Thomas Ellwood (d. 1713) in its burial ground; Old Jordans, the 17C farmhouse (now a guesthouse of the Society of Friends) where Penn and his fellow Quakers gathered before the meeting house was built; and the barn allegedly built from the timbers of the 'Mayflower'.

2m S of Gerrards Cross, just beyond M40, is the pretty village of *Fulmer*, where the church of 1610 has a rare contemporary wooden font. **Stoke Poges**, 2m further S, is famous for its connection with the poet Thomas Gray (1716–71) and for the picturesque churchyard where his 'Elegy' was probably written. There is a monument to him by James Wyatt (1799) E of the churchyard, and he is buried with his mother near the E wall of the church. The church itself dates mainly from the 14C. The 'Bicycle Window' (1643), showing a hobby horse, is a curiosity which attracts tourists. Gray's 'Ode on a Distant Prospect of Eton College' is said to have been written in his mother's garden at *Stoke Court* (not open) to the NW.—We can rejoin A40 at Beaconsfield via A355, W of Stoke Poges, skirting the magnificent forest tract of *\*Burnham Beeches* (444 acres).

25m. **Beaconsfield** (11,000 inhab.) is much developed to the N but keeps its wide high street of Georgian brick. The town boasts several famous residents. The poet Edmund Waller (1606–87), born at Coleshill to the N, is buried in the churchyard. Edmund Burke (1729–97), who lived here from 1768, is buried in the church. G.K. Chesterton (1874–1936), who came here in 1909 and wrote many of his Father Brown stories at Beaconsfield, is commemorated in St Theresa's RC church. For Disraeli, who derived his title from the town, see Hughenden Manor below. In Warwick Rd, N of the railway station, is the *Bekonscot Model Village* (open).

From Beaconsfield to *Maidenhead*, see Rte 36A.

29m. **High Wycombe** (60,500 inhab.; Tourist Information), known for its furniture industry, has suffered badly from redevelopment. The lofty 13–16C *Church* is the largest in the county. The *Guildhall* (1757), close by, is by Henry Keene and the *Market Hall* (1761) by Robert Adam.

*Penn*, on B474 about 2½m NE, is claimed to be the ancestral home of William Penn's family. The church has a good nave roof, a 15C painted Doom and Penn brasses.

FROM HIGH WYCOMBE TO AYLESBURY. The direct route runs via West Wycombe (see below). A more attractive way (18½m), giving a much better flavour of the Chiltern countryside, begins by taking A4128 N from the centre of High Wycombe.—1½m. *Hughenden Manor* (NT) was Disraeli's country seat from 1847 until his death in 1881. He is buried in the churchyard, and the church has a monument erected by Queen Victoria.—At (2m) *Hughenden Valley* the road forks. The sideroad continues straight ahead through hilly country via (5m) *Speen* and (7m) *Lacey Green* to join A4010, the West Wycombe–Aylesbury road, at (9m) *Princes Risborough*. A4128 continues from Hughenden valley to (5½m) *Prestwood* and a region closely associated with John Hampden (1594–1643), MP for Buckinghamshire and a leading supporter of the Parliamentarian cause in its conflict with Charles I. On the sideroads leading N and W of Prestwood are (6½m) the stone cross marking the parcel of land for which Hampden refused to pay the illegal 'ship money' tax and (7½m) *Hampden House* (not open), his home, rebuilt in the 18C. Close by is the church of *Great Hampden*, where he is buried; it contains the tomb of his first wife (d. 1634), with a touching epitaph, and several re-used brasses of the Hampdens. A well-preserved stretch of *Grim's Dyke*, an ancient bank and ditch of uncertain purpose, runs between Great Hampden and Lacey Green (see above). Sideroads continue N from Hampden House to join A4010 and reach Aylesbury via Stoke Mandeville. We pass, on the left, (9½m) *Chequers* (not open), the Tudor mansion used as the Prime Minister's country residence, and on the right, *Coombe Hill* (852ft; NT), the highest point of the Chilterns.—18½m. *Aylesbury*, see Rte 39A.

From High Wycombe to *Maidenhead*, see Rte 36A.

31½m. *West Wycombe* is a fascinating place, dominated by the work of Sir Francis Dashwood (1708–81), best known for his Hell-Fire Club (cf. Medmenham Abbey, Rte 36B). On the hill S of A40 lies his house, *West Wycombe Park* (NT), rebuilt in a mixture of classical styles between 1740 and 1771. It has several painted ceilings, and some good 18C furniture. The *grounds are landscaped with temples around an artificial lake. The village has some charming 16–18C houses (most of them NT but not open). On the hill N of A40 is the church, originally medieval but eccentrically rebuilt by Sir Francis, with a huge gilded ball on top of its tower. At the E end is a huge hexagonal mausoleum (1765; John Bastard). Below are artificial caves (open), quarried 1750–52 and used, it is said, for the revels of the Hell-Fire Club.

FROM WEST WYCOMBE TO AYLESBURY, 16m by A4010.—1½m. *Bradenham* church has a Saxon doorway and the grave of Isaac Disraeli (1766–1848), Benjamin's father, who lived in the manor house from 1829 until his death. —7m. **Princes Risborough** is a small town below the Chiltern Hills. Opposite the church is the 17–18C *Manor House* (NT, limited opening by written appointment with the tenant). *Monks Risborough*, to the N, has an interesting EE and Perp. church. Cut into the hillside opposite the village is the *Whiteleaf Cross* (NT), probably marking the junction of the Icknield Way with another important road running N to Oxford; there is a good view across the Vale of Aylesbury. *Bledlow*, a finely placed village 2m SW of Princes Risborough, has a Norman font in the church and, on the hill further SW, another chalk cross.—For (12m) *Stoke Mandeville* and (16m) *Aylesbury*, see Rte 39A.

Beyond (36½m) *Stokenchurch* we reach the crest of the Chiltern ridge (787ft), with a good view, and descend the long hill into Oxfordshire.—40m. *Aston Rowant*, ¾m to the right, has a church with early Norman details and a Purbeck marble font.

Some of the best Chiltern scenery is reached by the sideroads running S from A40 between Stokenchurch and Aston Rowant. The Hambleden road gives fine *views as it crosses *Ibstone Common*, with its little Norman church and windmill, before descending to (4m) *Fingest*, where the Norman church has a unique twin-gabled tower.—7m. *Hambleden*, a charming village, is 3m from the Thames and about 2m from Henley by road or footpath (Rtes 36A and 36B).—Another road from A40, further W, follows the crest of the Chilterns to (8m) *Nettlebed* (Rte 36A) via *Christmas Common* and (6m) *Cookley Green*. Just before Cookley Green a road branches left through *Pishill* to (3m) *Stonor* (Rte 36A).

From Aston Rowant B4009 heads SW to (3m) *Watlington*, with a 17C market house. *Chalgrove*, 4m NW of Watlington, was scene of the battle where John Hampden was mortally wounded in 1643; he is commemorated by a stone obelisk.

45½m. *Milton Common*, near the end of the M40.

A329 leads NW, passing on the left (1m) *Rycote Chapel* (English Heritage, standard opening but closed on Fridays and alternate Thursdays in winter), a private chapel of 1449 with both original and 17C furnishing.—4m. **Thame** (8500 inhab.; Tourist Information) is a market town with a pleasant High St. The large church has a fine early 14C screen and the monument of Lord Williams (d. 1559) and his wife. Nearby are the original Grammar School buildings (1575) where Hampden, Dean Fell and Anthony à Wood were educated.

49m. **Wheatley.**

*Waterperry*, 2½m NE, has the former gardens of Waterperry Horticultural School (open) and a charming little church with a three-decker pulpit, 18C box pews, the late 14C effigy of a knight and a palimpsest brass of c 1440 re-used c 1540 for Walter Curson and his wife.—*Garsington Manor* (gardens open under NGS), 3m S of Wheatley, was in 1915–29 the home of Philip and Lady Ottoline Morrell, who made it an important literary gathering place. Yeats, Rupert Brooke, D.H. Lawrence, T.S. Eliot, Aldous Huxley and members of the Bloomsbury group were all visitors.

50½m. *Forest Hill* was the scene of Milton's unhappy first marriage.—55m. **Oxford**, see Rte 37.

A40 bypasses the city to the N.—61½m. *Eynsham*, to the left, has

an old village cross and a few fragments of its once famous abbey.
—66m. *Witney* (14,100 inhab.; Tourist Information), to the right of
A40 on the Windrush, has a 17C butter cross, an 18C town hall and
many other good Georgian buildings, including some used for the
local industry of blanket-making. The large and handsome church
has an EE tower and spire, animal carvings on the porch, a large Dec.
N window and 14–17C monuments.

*Minster Lovell* is charmingly situated on the Windrush 3m W of Witney. Near its
good Perp. church are the picturesque ruins of the 15C *Minster Lovell Hall*
(English Heritage, standard opening), with great hall, solar, kitchens and a
well-preserved dovecote.—At *North Leigh*, on A4095 3m NE of Witney, the
church contains the lovely Wilcote Chapel (c 1440). About 2m N of the village is
a 4C *Roman Villa* (English Heritage, summer standard opening but closed on
Thursdays and alternate Fridays) with baths and *mosaics.
   There are many interesting churches in the lowlands S of Witney. *Brize
Norton* (4m SW) has a Norman door and a fine screen. *Black Bourton* (6m SW),
the birthplace of the novelist Maria Edgeworth (1767–1849), has another
Norman door and wall paintings of c 1275. *Broadwell* church (8m NW) is
11–13C, and at *Langford* (³/₄m further) the *church has a largely Saxon tower
and a Saxon carving of the Crucifixion set in the 13C porch.—*Bampton*, 5¹/₂m S
of Witney and 2m N of Tadpole Bridge (Rte 36B), is a large stone-built village
with good 17–18C houses. Its church has Norman work and an EE *spire.—At
*South Leigh*, 2³/₄m SE of Witney, the church is notable for its 14–15C wall
paintings. John Wesley preached his first sermon here in 1725.

A40 runs parallel to the Windrush as it approaches the **Cotswold
Hills**, the narrow limestone ridge running NE to SW across
Gloucestershire.

In the E the Cotswolds rise by easy stages from the valleys of Oxfordshire, on a
line marked roughly by Chipping Norton, Burford and Cirencester. Their W
edge, running past Chipping Campden, Broadway, Cheltenham and Stroud,
drops abruptly away into the Vale of Evesham and the Severn Vale, with
famous viewpoints at Broadway, Cleeve Hill and Birdlip. At 1031ft, Cleeve Hill
is the highest point of the Cotswolds; few places are above 1000ft, and most are
between 500 and 600ft. These gently wooded hills make ideal sheep pasture.
The region's long connection with wool is shown by the discovery of a fulling
establishment at Chedworth, one of several important Roman sites hereabouts,
and by the frequency with which 'ship'—a corruption of 'sheep'—turns up in the
names of towns, villages and streets. The equally common prefix, 'chipping',
comes from 'cheapening' and indicates a market centre. The prosperity enjoyed
by the Cotswold wool trade in the 14–16C has left its permanent mark in the
many handsome churches, towns and villages built of local stone weathering
into rich yellows and browns. Tourists have now replaced wool as the region's
staple, making much of its picturesque charm dangerously self-conscious.

73m. **Burford** (Tourist Information), on the Windrush to the N, is an
attractive little place, once one of the chief Cotswold wool towns. The
High St., with medieval and Renaissance merchants' houses, drops
steeply to cross the river by a fine old bridge. The *Tolsey Museum* is
devoted to local history. The church of *St John the Baptist, a mixture
of Norman, EE and Perp., contains many chapels and monuments,
notably those of Edmund Harman (d. 1569) and his wife (N aisle), and
and Lord Chief Justice Tanfield (d. 1625) and his family (N chapel),
perhaps by Gerard Christmas. A memorial in the S transept to
Christopher Kempster (1626–1709), one of Wren's master masons,
reminds us of the nearby stone quarries at Taynton, Great Barrington, etc.

*Swinbrook*, on the N bank of the Windrush 2¹/₂m E, has a church with
grotesquely carved stalls and 17C monuments of the Fettiplaces arranged in
tiers. *Asthall*, across the river, has a good church and manor house.—*Shilton*, in

a valley 2¹/₂m SE of Burford, has a partly Norman church with an interesting carved font.—The *Cotswold Wildlife Park* (open) is off A361 2m S of Burford.

FROM BURFORD TO STOW-ON-THE-WOLD AND BACK THROUGH BOURTON-ON-THE-WATER. A424 heads NW from Burford across the border with Gloucestershire. —(10m) **Stow-on-the-Wold** (seasonal Tourist Information) is the highest settlement in Gloucestershire—'Stow on the Wold/ Where the wind blows cold'—and probably originated as a look-out post on the Foss Way. Later a Cotswold wool town, it is now popular with visitors, as the many antique shops bear witness. Horse fairs are held in May and October. A 14C cross stands in the large market place and the old church contains a Crucifixion by Caspar de Crayer (1610). *Oddington*, off A436 2¹/₂m E, has a restored old church with wall paintings and Norman details. The *Cotswold Farm Park* lies 6¹/₂m W of Stow off B4077. —B4068, continued by A436, goes SW to rejoin A40 and the main route at (21¹/₂m) *Andoversford*. On A436 1¹/₂m E of its junction with B4068 is *Notgrove Long Barrow* (English Heritage, open at any reasonable time).

A more interesting way back from Stow-on-the-Wold takes A429, following the straight Roman course of the Foss Way over the hills.—14m. Left of our road is the pretty **Bourton-on-the-Water**, with the Windrush flowing down its main street. The *Birdland Zoo Garden*, the *Cotswolds Motor Museum*, the *Model Railway Exhibition*, the *Model Village* and the *Village Life Exhibition* cater to the large numbers of tourists. The picturesque villages of *Lower Slaughter* and *Upper Slaughter*, 1¹/₂m and 2¹/₄m N, are also overrun with visitors in summer. Their curious name comes from the Anglo-Saxon word meaning 'slough', or muddy place. —We rejoin A40 just W of (19m) *Northleach* (see below). A429 continues SW, still following the line of the Foss Way, another 10m to *Cirencester* (Rte 38B). From (3m) *Fossebridge*, on the Coln, sideroads lead left (E) to the partly Saxon church of *Coln Rogers* and the Norman church of *Coln St Dennis*. **Chedworth**, 3m W of Fossebridge, has a partly Norman church and the best *Roman Villa* (NT) in England, with well-preserved baths and pavements. The local tradition is that the countless lilies of the valley growing here were originally planted by the Romans.

For Bibury, SW of Burford, see Rte 38B.

The main route follows A40 W from Burford.—78m. A sideroad on the right leads to *Sherborne*. The Dutton family monuments in the church include work by Rysbrack and the elder Westmacott and the striking effigy of Cromwell's friend John Dutton (d. 1657). He built the beautiful hunting lodge, *Lodge Park* (not open), beyond the A40 2m SW.—At (82m) *Northleach* the 15C church has a splendid *porch and brasses of local wool merchants. By the junction with A429 W of the town the well-presented *Cotswold Countryside Collection* (including seasonal Tourist Information) is housed in a former prison of 1789–91. See above for A429 NE to Stow-on-the-Wold via Bourton-on-the-Water and SW to Cirencester via Chedworth.—At (88m) *Andoversford* we meet A436 from Stow (see above). There is a good view at *Kilkenny*, on A436 1¹/₂m SW. *Withington*, 3m S of Andoversford, has picturesque cottages and a church with Perp. tower, Perp. clerestory windows and Norman work.—89¹/₂m. *Whittington*, N of A40, has a church with 14C effigies and a 16C manor house (not open).

95m. **CHELTENHAM** (86,600 inhab.) lies between the steep W edge of the Cotswolds and the Severn Vale. It still keeps many Regency buildings from its days as a fashionable spa, as well as its 19C public schools and a lingering reputation as a favourite place for army officers and civil servants to retire to. In recent years it has also become the home of several important annual festivals, a conference venue and a tourist centre for the Cotswolds.

**Tourist Information Centre**: Municipal Offices, The Promenade.

**Car Parks**: Portland St., St James St., High St., St George's Rd, Rodney Rd, Bath Rd (all short stay); Sherborne Place, St James Square, Winchcombe St. (all long stay). Multi-storey car parks in Grosvenor Terrace and Regent Arcade.

**Coach Station**: St Margaret's Rd.

**Bus Station**: (country and town services) Royal Well Rd.

**Railway Station**: Lansdown Road Station, about 1m W of the centre.

**Airport**: Gloucester and Cheltenham Airport at Staverton, 4m W. Passenger services to Guernesey and Jersey.

**Theatres**: Everyman, Regent St.; Playhouse, Bath Rd.

**Annual Events**: Steeplechasing at Prestbury Park, off A435 1m N, from October to May, with National Hunt Festival in March, including the Cheltenham Gold Cup. Competitive Festival of Music, Speech, Drama and Dancing (May). International Festival of Music (July). Cricket Festival (August). Flower Show (September). Festival of Literature (October).

**History**. Cheltenham remained a small market town until the 18C, when a well with medicinal waters was discovered on the site now occupied by Cheltenham Ladies' College. Captain Henry Skillicorne founded the spa by enclosing the well and building an assembly room in 1738–40. The seal of fashionable approval was set by George III's five-week visit in 1788 (described in the diary of Fanny Burney, a member of Queen Charlotte's entourage), and Cheltenham's popularity was further encouraged by the Duke of Wellington's belief that its waters were good for his liver disorder. He opened the new assembly room (now destroyed) in High St. in 1816 and took an interest in the construction of the Pittville Pump Room during the 1820s. As spa towns began to go out of fashion during the 19C, Cheltenham found a new and equally respectable identity with the foundation of the Gentlemen's College (1841) and the Ladies' College (1853).

**Famous natives and residents**. Edward Jenner (1749–1823), discoverer of smallpox vaccine, lived in St George's Rd. The Australian explorer Charles Sturt (1795–1869) died and the composer Gustav Holst (1874–1934) was born here. Visitors to the spa included Lord Byron, who first proposed to his future wife Annabella Milbanke in the old assembly room, Macready and Tennyson.

Just off the High St. in the centre of town is the old parish church of *St Mary*, with a 14C broach spire. Inside are a beautiful rose window of c 1320, a brass of 1513 on the N side of the chancel, and a tablet to Henry Skillicorne, developer of the spa, with a lengthy epitaph. The *Art Gallery and Museum* in nearby Clarence St. is notable for its collections of 17C Dutch paintings (Brouwer, Ostade, Steen, Wouwermans, etc.), 17–20C English paintings and work by Ernest Gimson and the Arts and Crafts Movement. Also on display are Chinese porcelain, pottery, costumes, furniture, local archaeological finds and Cotswold prints.

The tree-lined Promenade, leading SW from the High St., is the most handsome survival of Regency Cheltenham. The buildings have splendid ironwork balconies. A ∙terrace of c 1823 on the right now houses the *Municipal Offices* and the *Tourist Information Centre*. In front is a statue by Lady Scott of Dr Edward Wilson, who died with Scott in the Antarctic in 1912. On Oriel Rd to the left is the *Town Hall* (1903). On St George's Rd to the right are the buildings of *Cheltenham Ladies' College*, founded in 1853; its former pupils include the novelist Margaret Kennedy. Beyond the *Imperial Gardens* and the fine *Queen's Hotel* by the Jearred brothers (1837–38), the Promenade continues as Montpellier Walk, with *Montpellier Gardens* and, opposite, a row of shops (1836–38) separated by caryatid figures copied from the Erechtheion at Athens. The street ends at the *Rotunda* (1825–26) of the original Montpellier Spa, now Lloyds Bank.

Montpellier Terrace leads left to Bath Rd and *Cheltenham College*, founded in 1841. The poet James Elroy Flecker was son of the first headmaster and another poet, Cecil Day-Lewis, a teacher here. Old Cheltonians include Lord Morley, W.E. Lecky, A.C. Bradley and the Australian novelist Patrick White.

Clarence Rd, NE of the High St. beyond the coach station, has the *Gustav Holst Birthplace Museum*, a Regency house with memorabilia of the composer and a refurbished Victorian kitchen and servants' quarters. Evesham Rd runs N from Clarence Rd to *Pittville Park*. The *Pittville Pump Room* (open), built in 1825–30 and restored in 1960, houses the Gallery of Fashion, a museum recreating the history of Cheltenham from the 18C.

*Leckhampton Hill* (978ft), on B4070 2m S, has a view and a striking outcrop of rocks nicknamed the Devil's Chimney. *Seven Springs*, 1½m further SE, is the source of the Churn and considered by some the true head of the Thames (cf. Thames Head, Rte 38B).

FROM CHELTENHAM TO BROADWAY, 15m by A46 along the edge of the Cotswolds.—Beyond (2¼m) *Southam* we climb *Cleeve Hill* (1031ft), the highest point in the Cotswolds, with a popular view W over the Vale of Severn. *Bishop's Cleeve*, 2m NW, has a Norman *church with a well-decorated W front, a massive nave and a superb Jacobean musicians' gallery. The fine monuments include one to Richard de la Bere (d. 1636) and his wife.—7m. *Winchcombe* is a pleasant old market town with a fine late Perp. church, freely restored but keeping some good gargoyles. There is also a museum in the Old Town Hall, and a Railway Museum. *Sudeley Castle* (open), 1m SE, was built c 1450 but slighted in the Civil War and made habitable again in the 19C. The 19C interiors are interesting chiefly for the collection of paintings (Rubens, Van Dyck, Constable, Turner). The Dungeon Tower has a large exhibition of toys. In the pleasant Victorian gardens is the Chapel, with the tomb of Catherine Parr (1512–48), Henry VIII's widow and wife of Sudeley's owner, Lord Seymour. 2m S of Winchcombe, on the way to *Charlton Abbots*, is the neolithic *Belas Knapp Long Barrow* (English Heritage, open at any reasonable time).—9m. *Hailes Abbey* (English Heritage, standard opening and summer Sunday mornings, but closed Tuesday–Thursday in winter) is a ruined Cistercian monastery, founded in 1246 and later famous with pilgrims for its relic of Christ's blood, mentioned in Chaucer's 'Pardoner's Tale'. Only a fragment of the 15C cloister survives but there is an excellent *museum with roof bosses, tiles, etc. The parish church is outstanding for its *wall paintings of c 1300.—10m. B4077 heads E towards Stow-on-the-Wold. At 1m it passes *Stanway*, with a picturesque group formed by the church, the 16–17C Stanway House (limited opening) and its striking gatehouse, once thought to be by Inigo Jones but probably the work of a local master mason. The house has a Great Hall, some 18C rooms and a 14C tithe barn.—15m. *Broadway*, see Rte 41.

103m. **GLOUCESTER** (pronounced 'Gloster'; 92,100 inhab.) lies in the Severn Vale on the E bank of the river. It attracts visitors mainly by the relics which survive from its medieval past, particularly the great cathedral whose tower makes so elegant a landmark in the surrounding countryside. Otherwise, Gloucester is an important commercial centre which in recent years has lost some of its traditional industry but gained new businesses, notably in computer technology. The city centre has been badly redeveloped.

**Tourist Information Centre**: St Michael's Tower, The Cross.

**Car Parks**: outside the cathedral, Royal Oak Rd, Blackfriars and Longsmith St., St Michael's Square, Wellington St., Nettleton Rd, Park St. Multi-storey and roof-top parking at Eastgate Shopping Centre and bus station.

**Bus Station**: off Market Parade and Bruton Way, about ½m E of the cathedral.

**Railway Station**: off Bruton Way, beyond the bus station.

**Airport**: Gloucester and Cheltenham Airport at Staverton, 4m NE. Passenger services to Guernsey and Jersey.

**Theatre**: King's, King's Barton St., New Olympus, Barton St.

**Annual Events**: The Three Choirs Festival (August) rotates annually between Gloucester, Worcester and Hereford cathedrals. It is next held at Gloucester in 1989 and 1992. Founded c 1715 and continuous since 1724, it has given first performances to works by Elgar and Vaughan Williams and is one of the finest choral festivals in the world.

**History**. In the 1C AD the Romans established a fortress here, at the lowest point where the Severn could conveniently be crossed. It quickly grew into *Glevum*, one of England's four coloniae, with walled fortifications and a street pattern (still apparent today) based on a central cross. After the Norman Conquest the city became a favourite with several generations of kings, receiving its first charter in 1155 and witnessing the coronation of Henry III in 1216. Gloucester sided with Parliament in the Civil War and successfully withstood a Royalist siege in 1643. At the Restoration it was punished by having its Roman walls dismantled and its boundaries greatly reduced. The Industrial Revolution transformed Gloucester into an inland port with its own dock basin (1810) and canal (1827) linked directly to the Severn estuary. Known particularly for its trade in imported timber, it also numbered railway carriage workshops and the Gloster Aircraft Company among its local industries. The 1960s and early 1970s saw major redevelopment of the crowded city centre. More is threatened, and there are schemes to find new uses for the decayed 19C docks.

**Famous natives.** John Taylor (1580–1653), the Water Poet; Robert Raikes (1735–1811), the virtual founder of Sunday Schools; George Whitefield (1714–1770), the evangelical preacher, born at the Bell Inn on Southgate St.; Sir Charles Wheatstone (1802–75), inventor of the electric telegraph; W.E. Henley (1849–1903), poet and essayist, born at No. 2 Eastgate St.; Ivor Gurney (1890–1937), poet and composer, born on Constitution Walk.

The centre of the city is formed, in Roman fashion, by the junction at the Cross of four streets: Northgate, Southgate, Eastgate and Westgate. The Perp. tower of *St Michael's* at the SE corner is now the Tourist Information Centre.

We reach the cathedral by Westgate St. and College St. Our route along Westgate passes *Maverdine House*, on the right, turning a quaint façade towards a sidelane. The little College Court, beyond, has a building, now shop and museum, claimed as the original of the Tailor of Gloucester's house in Beatrix Potter's story and the *Pilgrims' Arch* leading to College Green. Opposite College St. is the *Shire Hall* by Robert Smirke (1816), with its huge modern extension. Westgate St. continues with the interesting *Folk Museum* in a group of medieval timbered buildings on the left, including one known as Bishop Hooper's Lodging from the belief that Hooper spent his last night here in 1555 before his martyrdom in nearby St Mary's St. Opposite is the church of *St Nicholas*, with a Perp. spire and Norman S door.

The •**Cathedral** stands on College Green, the central tower, W façade and S entrance porch immediately proclaiming it a major achievement of Perp. architecture.

The plan of the present building was established by Serlo, whom William the Conqueror made abbot of a new Benedictine foundation replacing the Order which had flourished here in various forms since the 7C. Serlo's Norman church was begun in 1089 and finished soon after 1100. In 1327 the abbey accepted the body of Edward II, murdered at Berkeley Castle and refused burial at Bristol and Malmesbury. His shrine quickly began to attract pilgrims and, from the vast income which resulted, the monks rebuilt both church and abbey. Work started in 1337 and continued throughout the next hundred years. Because Gloucester's wealth enabled it to employ a court mason, the church became the first great success in the new Perp. style. The exterior is largely Perp. and in the choir a Perp. casing effectively disguises the Norman core. The central tower was added in 1450, and the beautiful Lady Chapel (1457–98) closed the work of the Gloucester masons. At the Dissolution Henry VIII raised the church to cathedral rank.

The *Nave* is predominantly Norman, apart from the two W bays built in 1421–37. Its great cylindrical pillars overpower the triforium and the timid EE clerestory and vaulting (1242–45). Their exceptional height was made necessary by the original cloister outside the N wall, preventing low aisle windows and allowing light into the nave only through a lofty pier arcade. The cloister supported the N aisle when the S aisle became unsafe and had to be revaulted in 1318, the date, also, of the ballflowered tracery in the S aisle windows. The Norman vaulting and carved capitals in the N aisle should be noted, as well as the old glass in the third and fifth windows from the W end and the Perp. door to the cloisters at the E end. Monuments here include the elaborate family one to Mayor Machen (d. 1614) and Flaxman's graceful memorial to Mrs Morley (d. 1784).

The •*Choir* projects one bay into the nave and is separated from it by a 19C screen with the organ above. It is usually entered from the S aisle, near Abbot Seabroke's Chantry (1547). Both choir and *Transepts* look pure Perp., as the walls were veiled with tracery and the massive piers pared down when the Norman choir was transformed in the mid 14C. The design is a perfect unity from floor to ceiling. The tall clerestory windows; the rectilinear tracery made necessary by the size of the end windows; the one-storey design of the tracery, carried up by unbroken vaulting shafts, that covers the Norman triforium and pier arcades; the lierne •vaulting, in the complicated patterns of the choir roof, with its angel

**Gloucester Close**

Abbey Wall (remains of)  PITT  STREET

ST MARY'S STREET

Bishops Palace

MILLERS GREEN

Abbey Wall (course of)

Roman Wall (course of)

CLOISTERS

Gate

Deanery

Kings School House

War Memorial

COLLEGE GREEN

Roman Wall (course of)

Cathedral House

Wall (course of)

Abbey Wall (course of)

COLLEGE STREET

COLLEGE COURT

Maverdine House

N

WESTGATE  STREET

Tower Recess

Lavatorium

Undercroft

CLOISTERS

CHAPTER HOUSE

Treasury

St Paul's Chapel

9

10

St Edmund's Chapel (War Memorial)

17  13

Bp Goldsborough's Chantry

4

5

6  7

14

12

Lady Chapel

Bridge

Nave Altar

Screen (Organ over)

16

High Altar

3

2

8

15

Chantry Chapel (Mothers' Union)

St Stephen's Chapel

SOUTH PORCH

11

St Andrew's Chapel

Col. Carne's Cross

Key to Numbers
1 Sir Onesiphorus Paul
2 Robert Raikes
3 Sir Hubert Parry
4 Edward Jenner
5 Sarah Morley
6 Thomas Machen
7 Ivor Gurney
8 Abbot Seabroke
9 Reliquary
10 John Bower
11 Ald. Blackleech
12 King Edward II
13 Osric of Mercia
14 Abbot Parker
15 Abbot Foliot (?)
16 Robert Curthose
17 Col. Carne's Cross

0 _____ 100 ft
0 _____ 30 ms

**GLOUCESTER CATHEDRAL**

bosses, and the simpler but more subtly skilled roof of the S transept: all these are the quintessence of Perp. architecture. The S transept, remodelled in 1331–37, forestalls by some 20 years the evolution of Perp. elsewhere in England. On its E wall is the so-called Prentice Bracket, in the form of a mason's square; beside it is the Chapel of St Andrew, with a huge diagonal strut. The latest part is the N transept (restored 1368–74). On its E side is St Paul's Chapel, with a fine, restored altar screen; against its N wall is a beautiful arcaded EE structure known as the Reliquary, now forming the door to the Treasury.

The great *E Window, the largest in the country, is said to have been donated by Lord Bradeston c 1352 to commemorate the Battle of Crécy. The light tone of the glass is as innovative as the architecture, and the walls have been made slightly wider than the chancel by tilting them outwards. The reredos is Victorian, as are the sub-stalls. The restored 14C *stalls have vigorous misericords. The W window of the choir—an unusual feature made possible by the difference in height between choir and nave—contains old glass from other windows.

Of the various tombs in the choir, the most beautiful is the *tomb of Edward II, erected by Edward III. It stands under the N arcade of the presbytery, between the monument of Osric of Mercia (founder of the first abbey in 681) and the tomb prepared for the last abbot (1539) but occupied by two bishops. The bracket tomb on the S has been assigned to Serlo, the first Norman abbot, but the figure with the church in his hand is probably Abbot Foliot (d. 1243). In the centre of the presbytery is the tomb of Robert Curthose (d. 1134), William the Conqueror's eldest son, with a curious coloured effigy in bog oak (c 1290) resting on a 15C mortuary chest. In front of the altar are well-preserved encaustic tiles of 1455. The NE Chapel, the Chapel of St Edmund the Martyr, also has good tiles, and fragments of a reredos of c 1450. The SE chapel is dedicated to St Stephen.

The *Lady Chapel was the last great work at Gloucester (1457–98). It is detached from the E end of the choir to avoid obscuring the E window, and its W end diminishes in height and breadth to form a gracefully vaulted vestibule. Open tracery fills the upper part of the W arch. The exquisite lierne vaulting with leaf bosses, the crisply carved tracery of the windows and the narrow wall spaces between, the vaulting shafts, the ruined reredos, the sedilia and the remaining 15C tiles all contribute to the chapel's architectural harmony. The side chapels, with oratories or music galleries in their upper storeys, are delicately vaulted. The late 15C E window of nine lights contains old glass, some of it not designed for this window, which represented the Tree of Jesse. There are several charming monuments.

The *Choir Triforium*, reached from the N transept, contains an exhibition of the building's history. Its two halves are linked by the Whispering Gallery, running outside the E window and across the W end of the Lady Chapel.—The Norman Crypt, entered from the S transept, consists of an apse and five chapels.

The *Cloisters (c 1370–1410), entered from the N aisle of the nave, are remarkably beautiful and well preserved. The fan-tracery vaulting, certainly the first of any extent in Britain, is claimed as an invention of the Gloucester masons. The S side has 'carrel' recesses for desks; on the N side is the lavatorium, with a towel recess in the wall opposite. The Chapter House on the E is restored Norman with a Perp. E window bay. On the W side of the cloisters a medieval undercroft has been turned into the cathedral shop. From here a door leads out into College Green, on the other side of which is the medieval *St Mary's Gateway*, formerly the main gateway for provisioning the abbey.

The gate leads into St Mary's St. Opposite is the memorial to Bishop Hooper, who was martyred here in 1555, watched (so the story goes) by Bishop Bonner from the little window over the gateway. The nearby church of *St Mary-de-Lode*, with its low Norman chancel, stands on the site of a Roman building. Priory Rd to the N has four 11–12C arches marking the site of *St Oswald's Priory*, founded in 909 and destroyed during the siege of Gloucester in 1643.

We return to Westgate St. and, instead of continuing back to the Cross, take Berkeley St. beside the Shire Hall and opposite College St. A series of good 18C houses culminates in *Bearland House* at the end, *Bearland Lodge* on Longsmith St. to the left and *Ladybellegate House* (1705), facing the head of Ladybellegate St. Off Ladybellegate St. is *Blackfriars* (English Heritage, summer standard opening, but closed on Tuesdays and on Wednesday mornings), the church and part of the E range of a 13C Dominican friary, with a fine timber roof.

Beyond Blackfriars we reach Southgate St., opposite the partly 12C church of *St Mary-de-Crypt*. It has some good brasses and the tomb of Robert Raikes, whose house on the other side of the street is now the Golden Cross Inn. George Whitefield preached his first sermon here. Behind St Mary's is *Greyfriars* (English Heritage, open at any reasonable time), the remains of the early 16C church of a Franciscan friary, with a Georgian house added to the W end. Greyfriars Walk continues past the *Eastgate Market* to Brunswick Rd.

To our left on Brunswick Rd is the **City Museum and Art Gallery**. It has a good collection of local archaeological finds, including a 1C bronze mirror from Birdlip, a group of Romano-British sculptures (AD 100–250) from Lower Slaughter, and Roman altars, coins, etc. from the city itself. The foundations of the Roman city wall on which the building stands have been exposed to view. Natural history exhibits include a beehive and aquarium, while the art gallery upstairs has Georgian furniture, barometers, glass, ceramics, silver and English landscape paintings from the 17C onwards.

Beyond the museum Brunswick Rd continues to the junction with Eastgate St. Part of the Roman defences have been excavated by the corner of Constitution Walk, to the left, and on King's Walk, opposite (both open at limited times in summer). We return up Eastgate to the Cross.

The **Docks** lie SW of the Cross, reached via Southgate St. and Commercial Rd, with the *Gloucestershire Regimental Museum*. The whole area is now being redeveloped. The old Albert Warehouse (1851) contains *The Robert Opie Collection* of shopping goods, packaging and advertising from the 19C onwards. Further SW, between the river and the canal, are the remains of the 12C *Llanthony Abbey*, a daughter house of the famous Welsh monastery.

The **Severn Bore**, a wave caused by the incoming tide, is best seen not in Gloucester itself but below the city at places like *Epney* (see below) on the E bank or *Minsterworth* on the W bank (5m W; see also Rte 45B). The larger waves usually come in spring and autumn between 07.00 and 11.00 and the same hours in the evening.

FROM GLOUCESTER TO BERKELEY, 17m by A38, the Bristol road, down the Vale of Severn.—9m. *Frampton-on-Severn*, a charming village 1m to the right of A38, has a church with a Romanesque lead font, one of six identical ones in Gloucestershire. Beyond the canal a winding road follows the Severn back towards Gloucester, passing (2¹/2m) *Epney*, known for its elvers, or young eels. See also the Severn Bore, above.—13m. By the Severn beyond *Slimbridge* is the famous *Wildfowl Trust* (open) founded by Sir Peter Scott in 1946, where many thousands of waterfowl may be seen.—16m. The little town of *Berkeley* lies 1m to the right. *Berkeley Castle* (open), entered by a bridge over the moat, still looks the feudal stronghold. Part of the circular keep and inner bailey belong to the mid 12C; the rest is mainly 14C. Edward II was murdered here in 1327. Medieval rooms include the kitchen, the Great Hall (with the original timber roof, a painted 16C screen and 17C Oudenarde tapestries) and the chapel, later converted to a living room. The fine EE *Church* has a good 15C screen and monuments to the Berkeley family. Swift wrote the epitaph on the jester Dicky Pearce (d. 1728) in the churchyard. The house nearby where Edward Jenner (1749–1823) was born and died is now a museum devoted to his memory. There is a nuclear power station by the river (its closure has been announced recently), and another at *Oldbury-on-Severn*, 8m S. At *Sharpness*, 1¹/2m beyond Berkeley, the Gloucester canal joins the Severn.—For the rest of the way by A38 from Berkeley to Bristol, see Rte 20.

FROM GLOUCESTER TO LEDBURY, 17m. A40 heads W towards Ross-on-Wye, crossing the Severn at 1m. *Over Bridge* (English Heritage, open at any reasonable time) was built by Telford in 1825–30. The direct way to Ledbury (another 15m) is by A417, passing W of *Ashleworth* on the Severn, with a tithe barn (NT). A more interesting route keeps on A40 for another mile and then branches right on B4215, up the pretty Leadon valley.—9m. *Newent* is a little town with timbered houses and a good 16C market hall.—12³/4m. *Dymock*, known for its orchards and daffodils, has a large and interesting church with a S doorway of c 1130. At *Kempley*, 2m W, the little Norman church (English Heritage, open at any reasonable time) has a magnificent series of 12–14C *frescoes on its walls and vault.—17m. Ledbury*, see Rte 44.

From Gloucester to *Worcester*, see Rte 42; to *Hereford*, see Rte 43. For the *Wye Valley* and the *Forest of Dean*, W of Gloucester, see Rte 45.

# B.  Via the Vale of the White Horse and Cirencester

Total distance 109m. To (47½m) *Wallingford*, see Rte 36A.—A4130, A417 to (62½m) *Wantage*.—A417, A420 to (72m) *Faringdon*.—A417 to (78m) *Lechlade*.—A417 to (91m) **Cirencester**.—A417 directly to (109m) **Gloucester** (Rte 38A), or alternative way (8m longer) on A419 via *Stroud*.

Maps: OS Landranger 176, 175, 174, 163, 162.

This route goes through the S Cotswolds. Rte 38A, where the region is characterised more fully, cuts across the centre, and the N fringes are described in the journeys from Oxford to Stratford (Rte 40) and Oxford to Worcester (Rte 41). The detours from Faringdon and Cirencester described below make useful connections between the Cotswolds and SW England (Rte 20).

An alternative way of starting the journey goes via (38½m) *Reading* (Rte 20) and A329 along the S bank of the Thames to (47½m) *Streatley* (Rte 36A). It then branches left on A417.—53½m. *Blewbury*, 3m S of *Didcot*, is a pleasant place. In recent years it has enterprisingly taken to commissioning and staging operas, with amateur performers, in its church. The painter Sir William Nicholson (1872–1949) died here.—55m. *Upton* has a small primitive Norman church.—At (57m) *Harwell*, we join the main route described below.

From London via Henley to (47½m) *Wallingford*, see Rte 36A. A4130 continues to (53m) *Didcot*, with a large power station, a railway junction familiar to travellers on the Oxford and Swindon lines. The Railway Centre (open) has large collection of steam engines, rolling stock, etc., from Brunel's Great Western Railway. *East Hagbourne*, 1½m S on the way to Blewbury, is a notably pretty village.—A4130 meets A34 at the roundabout S of Abingdon (Rte 36A), then loops round to join A417 ½m W of *Harwell*, with a large 13–14C church. The sprawling Atomic Energy Research Establishment is on A4185 1½m S.—We follow A417 past (58½m) *East Hendred*, which has a curious early 14C wooden lectern in the church and a Perp. wayside chapel with priest's house attached.—60½m. *Ardington House* (limited opening), also in the lea of the downs S of A417, is a baroque house built in 1719–20, with a handsome staircase hall.

62½m. **Wantage** (8800 inhab.), in the Vale of the White Horse, was the birthplace of Alfred the Great (849–99), whose statue stands in the market place. The parish church has fine brasses and the 14C tomb of Sir William Fitzwarren, who, with his wife Dame Alice, is a leading character in the pantomime 'Dick Whittington'.

The **Vale of the White Horse** lies between Wantage and Faringdon. It is bounded on the S by the *Berkshire Downs, with the Ridgeway connecting a series of important prehistoric sites along their breezy top. This ancient British trackway follows the curve of the hills from Streatley in the E, veers S of Swindon, crosses the upper Kennet valley 1½m E of Avebury (Rte 20) and joins the Wansdyke—a distance of some 40m. The Countryside Commission's 'Ridgeway Path' follows its course as much as modern roads permit, connecting with the Icknield Way in the E.

B4507 running W from Wantage, with the vale on its right and the Ridgeway on its left, gives a good introduction to the landscape and its major points of interest.—½m. A sideroad leads left to (2m) *Letcombe Bassett*. The Iron Age

*The Vale of the White Horse: an illustration by Richard Doyle in Thomas Hughes's 'The Scouring of the White Horse' (1859)*

*Segsbury Camp* by the Ridgeway above the village gives a fine view.—2¼m. The church at *Childrey* (right) has a notable lead font and good brasses.—3¼m. Sparsholt (right) has a church with a 12C doorway and 14C effigies of knights in oak and stone.—5m. Left of the road is a perforated sarsen stone known as the *Blowing Stone. Kingston Lisle Park* (limited opening), to the right, is partly 17C but the most dramatic feature, the entrance hall with its flying staircase, dates from the early 19C. The village church has 14C wall paintings. *Uffington*, 2m NW of Kingston Lisle, has a good EE church. Thomas Hughes (1822–96), who describes the vale in the opening chapters of 'Tom Brown's Schooldays', was born here.—6m. Cut into the turf of *White Horse Hill* (656ft) is the horse which gives its name to the region (English Heritage, open at any reasonable time). Popularly associated with Alfred's victory over the Danes at the Battle of Ashdown, fought somewhere along these downs in 871, it belongs in fact to the 1C BC—certainly the oldest white horse, and perhaps the oldest chalk figure, in Britain. On the W side of the hill is the hollow known as the *Manger* and the natural mound known as *Dragon Hill*, from the local tradition that St George slew the dragon here. *Uffington Castle* (English Heritage, open at any reasonable time), the Iron Age earthwork on top of the hill, has a splendid ˙view. From here the Ridgeway leads SW to (1½m) *Wayland's Smithy* (English Heritage, open at any reasonable time), a neolithic burial mound used at two different dates.

A417 heads across the vale.—64½m. *West Challow*, to the left, has a small, restored 12C church.—We change briefly to A420, the Oxford–Swindon road, before rejoining A417 to enter the market town of (72m) **Faringdon** (seasonal Tourist Information), with a 17C market hall and several old inns. The interesting *Church* has a Trans.

Norman core (note the S doorway and the clustered piers of the crossing) and many good details: six-light Perp. windows in the N aisle, sedilia, monuments. *Faringdon House* was built by Henry Pye (1745–1813), the undistinguished Poet Laureate, who also planted the conspicuous Faringdon Clump. The folly on the hill to the E was built by Lord Berners in 1935, perhaps the last folly in England.

*The Great Coxwell tithe barn*

The great early 13C Cistercian *tithe barn (NT) at *Great Coxwell*, 2m SW, was called by William Morris 'the finest piece of architecture in England'.

A420 leads NE toward Oxford.—5m. *Pusey House* (gardens open) was the birthplace of Edward Pusey (1800–82), leader of the Oxford Movement.—8m. *Kingston Bagpuize* has a church of 1799–1800 by the entrance to *Kingston House* (limited opening). This handsome red-brick building with stone dressings looks early 18C, though the family date it from 1670. There are good panelling and fireplaces inside, and an early 18C gazebo in the pleasant gardens. For *Longworth*, 1m NW, see Rte 36B.

FROM FARINGDON TO CHIPPENHAM, 32m by A420, A3102 and A4.—12m. **Swindon** (91,000 inhab.; Tourist Information) was created by the railway, which made it the site of a major junction and carriage works. It incorporated the market town of *Old Swindon*, on the hill 1m S. Now a business and commercial centre, it has become an important road junction for routes linking SW England with the Cotswolds and the Midlands. The *Great Western Railway Museum* on Faringdon Rd has old locomotives. The birthplace of the writer Richard Jefferies (1848–87) at *Coate Farm*, 1½m SE, is now a museum. The church at *Lydiard Tregoze*, 6m W, has notable monuments to the St John family, who lived at *Lydiard Park* (open), a mansion largely rebuilt in the 1740s, with rich decorative plasterwork inside. The grounds cover more than 260 acres.—17m. *Wootton Bassett*, with modern development, has a half-timbered town hall. *Brinkworth*, 4m NW, has a 15C church with contemporary wall paintings. *Dauntsey*, 2m SW of Brinkworth, was a favourite resort of the poet George Herbert.—Beyond (22m) *Lyneham* the Chippenham road has been demoted to B4069.—32m. *Chippenham*, see Rte 20.

Beyond Faringdon A417 continues NW to (75m) *Eaton Hastings* (Rte 36B) and (76m) *Buscot Park* (NT). Built about 1780 and restored in the 1930s, the house has a fine collection of furniture and paintings, with work by Rembrandt and Burne-Jones, who also designed the E window in the church by the Thames. For *Kelmscott*, on the opposite bank, see Rte 36B.—We cross the river and enter Gloucestershire. —78m. **Lechlade**, a small market town with a large Perp. wool church, marks the upper limit of navigation on the river.—82½m. **Fairford** is a small and attractive town on the Coln. The late Perp. church of *St Mary*, decorated on the outside with sculpture, contains a wonderful array of 16C painted glass *windows, probably from the same Anglo-Flemish workshop that made the glass for King's College Chapel, Cambridge. The series of 28 is complete, telling the Biblical story from the Creation to the Last Judgement. There are handsome merchants' houses in the High St., and in London Rd is the birthplace of John Keble (1792–1866), a leader of the Oxford Movement.

A charming sideroad goes up the Coln valley to (2m) *Quenington*, where the church has a Norman doorway, and (5m) **Bibury**, one of the most popular of all Cotswold villages. Arlington Row (NT but not open) is a much photographed group of stone-built cottages. The 17C Arlington Mill is open as a rural museum. The sideroad continues up the valley beyond the village to join A429, the Foss Way (Rte 38A). A433 leads left from Bibury to Cirencester, passing (2m) *Barnsley House* (gardens open).

91m. **Cirencester** (pronounced 'Siren-sester, 'Sisister' or 'Sisitter'; 16,000 inhab.; Tourist Information) is the most interesting town in the Cotswolds. Once *Corinium*, a Roman provincial capital second in size only to London by the end of the 1C AD, it later became an important market centre for the wool trade. Its medieval prosperity is shown by the parish church of *St John the Baptist*, one of the largest in England, originally Norman but largely rebuilt in the Perp. style. Externally it is notable for the fine W tower (begun in 1400) and the large three-storied *S porch (c 1490), internally for the Trinity Chapel (1430) with many brasses, the fan vaulting of St Catherine's Chapel (1508) and the 'wineglass' pulpit of 1515, one of the few pre-Reformation pulpits to survive in England. The *Corinium Museum has a large and well-presented collection of Roman remains: mosaics, tombstones, painted wall plaster, and fragments of stone carving which include a charming limestone relief of three fertility goddesses.

Excavation has revealed much of the grid system of the Roman streets, with a forum and basilica in the centre. The *Amphitheatre* (English Heritage, open at any reasonable time), one of the largest in Britain, is near the bypass on the W of town. Earthworks at *Bagendon*, off A435 3m N, mark the site of Corinium's predecessor, the Belgic capital Dobunni.

Spitalgate Lane has some arches of the *Hospital of St John* founded by Henry II, but the only relic of the Augustinian abbey which he refounded is a gateway (c 1180) in Grove Lane beyond.

Immediately W of the town is *Cirencester Park* (open, with polo matches on summer weekends), laid out in a series of avenues and rides by the first Earl Bathurst in 1714. Pope's Seat, a rusticated pavilion, recalls the frequent visits of the poet, who may have helped with the landscaping.

A419 follows the course of the Roman Ermin Way SE from Cirencester to (7½m) *Cricklade* on the upper Thames (Rte 36B). Of Cricklade's two interesting churches, St Mary's dates mainly from the early 12C while St Sampson's is a mixture of EE, Dec. and Perp. The Perp. parish church at *Purton*, 4m S, is one of the few in England to have both a central and W tower. *Down Ampney*, 3m N of Cricklade, was the birthplace of Ralph Vaughan Williams (1872–1958).

FROM CIRENCESTER TO BRISTOL, 37m by A433, A46, A432.—2m. A429 bears left for Malmesbury (see below). We keep on A433, through (3m) *Thames*

*Head,* generally regarded as the source of the Thames.—6m. Near *Rodmarton,* to the right, is the *Windmill Tump Long Barrow* (English Heritage, open at any reasonable time).—10m. **Tetbury** (Tourist Information), a small market town on a hill, has always been popular with visitors and attracts even more now that the Prince and Princess of Wales have taken a country house in the neighbourhood. The town hall dates from 1655, and the fine church (1777–81) has tall wooden pillars and contemporary pews and galleries. *Chavenage* (open), 2m NW, is a 16C house with a lovely frontage, tall windows in its great hall and 17C tapestries in the upstairs rooms. The 18C chapel, separate from the house, incorporates earlier stone carving.—13m. *Westonbirt Arboretum* (open), part of a large Forestry Commission estate on the right, has rare trees.—16m. *Didmarton* church has an 18C interior. We pass the Worcester Lodge of Badminton Park (see below).—18m. We join A46, continuing S.—24m. *Old Sodbury* is at the junction with A432, which we follow W. *Badminton Park* (open by written appointment), 3m NE, was begun in 1682 and completed by Kent in 1740. It has splendid Kent interiors and 18C furniture. For *Dyrham Park,* beyond M4 3m further S, see Rte 20.—25m. *Chipping Sodbury* is an old market town with a splendid broad stone-built street and a good church. At the 16C *Little Sodbury Manor* (open by written appointment), to the N, William Tyndale translated the Bible. *Horton Court* (NT), further N, has a Norman hall and late Perp. ambulatory.—37m. *Bristol,* see Rte 20.

FROM CIRENCESTER TO CHIPPENHAM, 21m. We start on A433, as in the route to Bristol above, but branch left at 2m on A429.—11m. **Malmesbury** (2600 inhab.; Tourist Information) is a pleasant little town above the Avon. Of the abbey founded here in the 7C, later one of the most powerful Benedictine foundations, only the nave of the *Abbey Church* (c 1115–40) survives. Its most striking feature is the richly sculptured S porch. Inside is the alleged tomb of King Athelstan (d. 940). The historian William of Malmesbury (c 1090–1143) was a monk of the abbey, as was a certain Oliver, who in the 11C made himself wings and jumped from the tower; miraculously, he was only lamed. The philosopher Thomas Hobbes (1588–1679) was born here, and Joseph Addison was MP for Malmesbury in 1710–19. The market place has a cross of c 1500, and at the foot of the hill is the late 12C *St John's Hospital.* About 2m NE is *Charlton Park House* (limited opening), visited by Dryden but substantially rebuilt by the younger Matthew Brettingham in the 1770s. The church at *Garsdon,* 2m E of Malmesbury, has Washington tombs.—21m. *Chippenham,* see Rte 20.

From Cirencester A417 follows the straight course of the Roman Ermin Way across the Cotswolds to (109m) Gloucester.—99m. *Elkstone,* ¹/₂m to the right, has the best Norman *church in the region.—Beyond (100m) *Birdlip* a sharp detour to the right avoids the steep descent of Birdlip Hill, with a famous *view.

*Great Witcombe,* on the left halfway down the hill, has a small partly Norman church. In the S part of nearby Witcombe Park is *Great Witcombe Roman Villa* (English Heritage, open at any reasonable time) with fine mosaic floors.

A more interesting way of making the journey from Cirencester to Gloucester (8m longer) goes W on A419 past Cirencester Park and along the Stroudwater valley.—97m. *Sapperton,* about 1m N of the road, has a church largely rebuilt in the Queen Anne period, with good 16–18C monuments.—103m. **Stroud** (20,900 inhab.; Tourist Information), at the meeting point of five deep valleys, was the centre of the wool trade and the West of England cloth industry, though few mills now remain. Its history is traced in the local *Museum.*

A46 runs S down the Nailsworth valley, past (2m) *Woodchester* where the Roman pavement is uncovered every ten years, to (4¹/₄m) *Nailsworth,* where the poet and 'super-tramp' W.H. Davies (1871–1940) died. The *Nailsworth Ladder,* a local freak hill, has a gradient of 1 in 2¹/₄. *Avening,* 2¹/₂m SE on B4014 towards Tetbury, has a well-preserved partly Norman church.—Nailsworth and Avening can also be reached from Stroud by the sideroads that run across the uplands E of the valley. Much of the land is owned by NT. We climb to (1m) *Rodborough Common* and (3m) *Amberley,* where Mrs Craik wrote 'John Halifax, Gentleman'. Beyond *Minchinhampton Common* to the E is (4¹/₂m) *Minchinhampton* (671ft), with a pillared market house.

The attractive, winding B4066 leads SW from Stroud.—4¹/₂m. We pass *Nympsfield Long Barrow* (English Heritage, open at any reasonable time). —5¹/₂m. *Uley Tumulus* (English Heritage, open at any reasonable time), popularly known as *Hetty Pegler's Tump*, is a neolithic long barrow on a commanding hill top site.—6¹/₂m. *Owlpen Manor* (open by written appointment to parties only) is a picturesque 16–17C house in the valley E of *Uley*.—9m. *Dursley* has good 18C buildings, including the town hall. William Tyndale (1484–1536), translator of the Bible, is claimed as a native of *Nibley*, 2m S. For *Wotton-under-Edge*, 4m S of Dursley, see Rte 20.

We follow A46 N up the Painswick valley. On the left rises *Haresfield Beacon* (713ft; NT), with a *view over the Severn.—107m. *Painswick* (Tourist Information), a typical Cotswold town with stone-built houses, is famous for its churchyard with 18C *table-tombs and 99 trimmed yews. The *Painswick Rococo Garden* (open), ¹/₂m N, has recently been restored.—110m. *Cranham Woods* lie beneath an earthwork called *Kimsbury Castle* (view).

In a hollow to the left lies *Prinknash Abbey* (open), occupied since 1928 by Benedictine monks and famous for its pottery. The site once belonged to the Abbot of Gloucester but the buildings (by F. Goodhart-Rendel and F.G. Broadbent) date mainly from the 1930s onwards. At *Upton St Leonards*, 1¹/₂m NW of Prinknash, the church has a Norman doorway and EE chancel.

Commanding fine views of the Vale of Severn and the Malvern Hills, A46 descends to join A417 at (111m) *Brockworth*. Cheltenham is 6m straight ahead and Birdlip 3m E by the main road. We turn W for (117m) **Gloucester** (Rte 38A).

# 39   London to Coventry

## A.   Via Banbury and Warwick

Total distance 100m. We follow A41 most of the way.—To (18¹/₂m) Watford (bypassed).—To (21¹/₂m) Hemel Hempstead (bypassed).— To (39m) Aylesbury.—To (56m) Bicester.—To (71m) **Banbury**.—To (90m) **Warwick** (and **Leamington Spa**).—A46, A452 to (94m) Kenilworth.—A429 to (99m) **Coventry**.

Maps: OS Landranger 176, 166 (briefly), 165, 164 (briefly), 151, 140.

A useful central route through the Midlands, dull in its early stages, but connecting easily with Birmingham from Warwick or Coventry. Note the alternative ways from London to Aylesbury and from Aylesbury to Banbury, and the convenient detours from Banbury or Warwick to Stratford-upon-Avon.

A404 and A413 provide an alternative route (40m) to Aylesbury, leaving London via Harrow (see 'Blue Guide London') and the commuter suburb of (20m) *Rickmansworth* (30,000 inhab.). To the right of A404 before we enter Rickmansworth is *Moor Park* (open), now a golf club-house, a mansion of the 1720s variously attributed to Giacomo Leoni and the painter Sir James Thornhill. Mural paintings include work by Verrio belonging to the earlier house built for the Duke of Monmouth in the 1680s.—24¹/₂m. *Chenies*, on the right, is a 19C 'model' village with *monuments of the Dukes of Bedford in its church. Their former home, *Chenies Manor* (open), is a 16C brick house with magnificent chimneys and pleasant formal gardens.—26¹/₂m. The old part of **Amersham** (17,500 inhab.), S of the railway line, has a brick market hall (1682) and almshouses (1657) and an attractive High St. The church contains 17–19C monuments of the Curwen and Drake families. The new town is 1m N at *Amersham-on-the-Hill*. At *Chesham Bois*, 1m beyond, the gardens (open under NGS) have rare and unusual plants. *Chesham*, 2m N of Amersham-on-the-Hill, is a pleasant town in the valley of the Chess.

We change from A404 to A413, which crosses the Chiltern Hills (cf. Rte 38A).—29m. *Little Missenden*, on the left, has a 12C church with 14C wall paintings.—31m. *Great Missenden* lies to the left in a beautiful valley. Its Dec. and Perp. church has a monument to Lady Boys (1638) by Nicholas Stone. Just beyond the village a pleasant road heads left towards Princes Risborough (Rte 38A), passing (on the right at 2m) the turning for *Little Hampden*, where the tiny church has 14C wall paintings.—35m. **Wendover** (8,600 inhab.) is a handsome little town on the Icknield Way. *Coombe Hill* (852ft; NT), the highest of the Chilterns, rises 1½m W.—We descend into the fertile *Vale of Aylesbury* and pass (37½m) *Stoke Mandeville* with its famous hospital for paraplegics before entering (40m) *Aylesbury*.

The main route leaves London through the NW suburbs on A41, with the M1 relieving it between Hendon and M25 near King's Langley. —12m. Between *Bushey* (left) and *Elstree* (right) we enter Hertfordshire.—Leaving the commuter suburb of (18½m) *Watford* (76,000 inhab.) on our left and crossing M25, we join the line of the Grand Union Canal (cf. Rte 39B) just short of (20m) *King's Langley*. The village takes its name from the royal palace where Edmund de Langley (1341–1402), son of Edward III, was born. The church contains the heraldic tomb used for him and his wife Isabella of Castile (d. 1394), though probably designed for Richard II. Richard lay buried elsewhere in the church from 1399 to 1413. Only a fragment remains of the Dominican friary where Edward II's favourite Piers Gaveston was buried in 1315.

The hamlet of *Bedmond*, 1m E, was the birthplace of Nicholas Breakspear (d. 1159) who, as Adrian IV, became the only English pope. There is a tablet remembering him in the 12–13C church of *Abbot's Langley*, ½m S.

A41 bypasses (21½m) **Hemel Hempstead** (79,600 inhab.; Tourist Information), developed as a New Town after the Second World War. The town centre, built mainly in the 1950s and 1960s, has a pleasant water-garden. The good Norman church, with a lead spire, adjoins the old High St., 1½m NE.—27m. **Berkhamsted** (15,500 inhab.; Tourist Information) has the large but scanty remains of the 11C *Castle* (English Heritage, standard opening) where William the Conqueror received the submission of Edgar Atheling in 1066 and John II of France was imprisoned after the Battle of Poitiers (1356). Natives of the town include William Cowper (1731–1800) and Graham Greene, whose father was headmaster of the boys' school founded here in 1541.

About 3m N is **Ashridge**, a Gothick mansion of 1808–1814 by James Wyatt, now a management training centre (limited opening). It stands on the site of a monastery of Bonhommes, founded in 1283, famous for possessing a drop of Christ's blood. The future Queen Elizabeth was arrested here in 1554 by order of Queen Mary. The adjoining park and downland (4000 acres; NT) include a monument to the third Duke of Bridgewater (1736–1803), the canal-builder, and Ivinghoe Beacon (see below).

At (30m) *Cowroast Lock*, the summit lock of 44 from the Thames, we branch left from the Grand Union Canal.—32m. *Tring* (10,600 inhab.), with a motorway bypass to the S, is an ancient town at the foot of the Chilterns. The baptismal register of the handsome 14–16C flint church contains entries referring to the Washington family. Along Akeman St. is the *Zoological Museum*, a collection begun by the second Lord Rothschild and now a department of the Natural History Museum in London. Beyond is *Tring Park*, formerly a seat of the Rothschild family.

From the station, 1³/₄m E of the town, the railway enters Robert Stephenson's great cutting (1834–38) through the summit of the hills. *Aldbury*, a charming village 1m further E, is the burial place of Mrs Humphry Ward (1851–1920), who lived at Stocks.—About 1¹/₄m W of Tring is *Drayton Beauchamp*, where the judicious Hooker was rector in 1584–85. The church has 14C glass in its E window.

B488 and B489 run NE to (10m) Dunstable (Rte 39B), following the course of the Icknield Way and passing (3¹/₂m) *Ivinghoe*, from which Scott derived the title of 'Ivanhoe'. It has a striking 13–14C church and a post windmill of 1627 (NT), one of the oldest in Britain. *Ivinghoe Beacon* (756ft; NT) has an early Iron Age hill-fort; the view across to Whipsnade (Rte 39B) is marred by a radio station.

Beyond Tring we enter Buckinghamshire.—39m. **Aylesbury** (48,200 inhab.; Tourist Information), the county town, has lost much of its historic character to insensitive modern development. From the ring road Great Western St. passes beneath *Friar's Square* market, a new precinct in harsh and restless concrete incorporating at different levels the bus station, County Library and municipal offices. It emerges in the old Market Square, with the original *County Hall* of 1723–40 by Thomas Harris and the *Bull's Head*, 15C behind its Victorian exterior; just off it is the *King's Head* (NT), also 15C, with a fine mullioned window. Good 17–18C houses survive, notably in Temple St. and Church St., where the former grammar school (15C but rebuilt in 1720) houses the *County Museum*, with a good collection of local antiquities.

*Dinton*, off A418 4¹/₄m SW of Aylesbury on the way to Thame, has a church with an elaborate Norman ˙S doorway and some good brasses. *Nether Winchendon House* (limited opening), in a pretty village 2¹/₄m W of Dinton, is a Tudor building with 18C Gothick alterations.

FROM AYLESBURY TO BANBURY VIA BUCKINGHAM, 34m by A413 and A422, an alternative to the main route, via Bicester, described below.—10m. *Winslow* is a handsome place, with *Winslow Hall* (open by appointment), a brick town house of 1700 almost certainly by Wren. 3m W is ˙*Claydon House* (NT), partly late Tudor and partly built by Sir Thomas Robinson in 1760–80 for the second Earl Verney. It contains many rococo apartments designed by Lightfoot (otherwise unknown), including an amazing 'Chinese Chippendale' room; a magnificent staircase with plasterwork by Joseph Rose; good family portraits; and memorials of Florence Nightingale, who frequently visited her sister here. The adjoining church of *Middle Claydon* has monuments of the Verneys and previous owners, the Giffards.—17m. **Buckingham** (8000 inhab.), a quiet old town, has long been superseded as county town by Aylesbury. Built round the market place, with a Georgian town hall at the S end and the 18C jail further N, it is notable for the 15C *Chantry Chapel* (NT), with a Norman doorway. The high-lying parish church was built in 1771–81 but completely altered in the 1860s by Sir Gilbert Scott, who was born at *Gawcott*, 1¹/₂m S. The *University of Buckingham*, opened in 1976 and granted its royal charter in 1983, is Britain's only independent university. The Hunter St. campus has restored old buildings.

The remote Perp. church of *Hillesden*, beyond Gawcott 4m S of Buckingham, is one of the best in the county, while the church at *Chetwode*, about 3m further W, is the chancel of an Augustinian priory, founded in 1245, with a beautiful five-light E window. Both have good stained glass.—The church at *Maids' Moreton*, 1¹/₂m N of Buckingham, is a beautiful example of mid 15C work.

An avenue leads N from Buckingham to (3m) **Stowe**, formerly the home of the Dukes of Buckingham and now a public school (state rooms and grounds open at Easter and during summer holidays). The house, originally late 17C, was altered and enlarged during the ownership (1697–1749) of Sir Richard Temple, later Viscount Cobham, and again in the 1770s, when Robert Adam designed the imposing S front. The ˙grounds, among the supreme achievements of 18C picturesque landscaping, were designed for Temple on the grandest scale by Vanbrugh, Bridgeman, Kent and Capability Brown, with Gibbs also contributing to the numerous garden buildings. The scenery by the Octagon Lake, with the Palladian Bridge near its NE tip, is particularly charming.

A422 runs NW from Buckingham and enters the S tip of Northamptonshire just before (24m) **Brackley** (6600 inhab.), a pleasant old town on A43 halfway between Oxford and Northampton. The *Town Hall* (1706) stands in the middle of the broad High St. *Magdalen College School*, founded in 1548 in buildings acquired for his Oxford foundation by William of Waynflete, incorporates the much altered chapel of a Hospital of St James and St John. This, like the low-lying parish church of *St Peter*, still has medieval statues in the niches of its tower.—A422 continues NW, leaving Northamptonshire for Oxfordshire beyond (31m) *Middleton Cheney*, where the church has splendid stained glass by Morris and Co., particularly the *E window of 1865.—34m. *Banbury*, see below.

The main route follows A41 from Aylesbury to (45m) *Waddesdon*. ***Waddesdon Manor** (NT) contains one of the finest private art collections in the country.

The mansion was built for Baron Ferdinand de Rothschild in 1874–80 by Hippolyte Destailleur in the style of a French château, with motifs copied from Blois and Chambord. It stands in splendid grounds landscaped by Lainé.

Many of the rooms have boiseries, or carved wooden panelling, brought from 18C French houses. The furniture is also mainly 18C French, with masterpieces made by Riesener for Marie Antoinette and the future Louis XVIII in 1777–90, and a bureau (1779) belonging to Beaumarchais, with inlay alluding to his works. The Savonnerie carpets, Sèvres porcelain, sculpture (by Lemoine, Clodion, Falconet and others), snuff boxes, musical instruments, etc. are of the same period. The collection of paintings includes, in the Morning Room, work by Rubens, de Hooch (*'The Game of Ninepins'), Cuyp, Dou, van der Heyden, Metsu, Terborch, Teniers and Gainsborough. Elsewhere are paintings by Watteau, Lancret, Pater and Boucher, portraits by Reynolds and Romney, and portraits of Perdita Robinson by both Gainsborough and Reynolds.

The *Bachelors Wing (open on Fridays only) displays 16–17C armour; 15–17C painting and sculpture; miniatures (including Anne of Denmark, by Hilliard); Renaissance jewellery; 16–17C glass; Limoges enamel; and illuminated manuscripts.

1½m N is *Quainton Railway Centre*, former depot of the Grand Central Railway, with vintage steam locomotives. *Quainton* church, 1m beyond, has many fine 17–18C monuments.

51m. A sideroad leads S from A41 to (4m) *Brill*, on an isolated hill enjoying a wide *view, with an interesting 11–14C church and an old windmill.

*Wotton House* (limited opening), 3m NE of Brill, is early 18C with alterations to the interior by Sir John Soane in 1820.—*Boarstall*, 2m W of Brill, has a 14C fortified gatehouse (NT, open by written appointment) and an 18C duck decoy in natural woodland (also NT).

We enter Oxfordshire before reaching (56m) **Bicester** (pronounced 'Bister'; 17,200 inhab.), a dull town. The big church has a stained glass window (1866) by Morris and Co.—65m. *Aynho*, at the S tip of Northamptonshire, is a charming village built in creamy stone. *Aynhoe Park* (limited opening) is a 17C house altered by Sir John Soane in 1800–05.—We cross the Cherwell, marking the border of Oxfordshire, and join the Oxford road at the handsome village of (67½m) *Adderbury*. The large 14C *church, with a 15C chancel, has notable carving on the outside. Adderbury House was the home of the Earl of Rochester (1647–80).

The neighbourhood has several interesting churches. *King's Sutton*, 1½m E across the Cherwell, has an elaborate Perp. steeple. *Bloxham*, a large, well-built village 2m W, has a magnificent *church, mainly 14C, with carving by the same masons who worked at Adderbury and stained glass by Morris and Co. *South Newington* church, 1½m beyond Bloxham, has wall paintings dating from c 1360.

71m. **Banbury** (38,200 inhab.; Tourist Information) is a busy town with several 17C houses. It is famous for its cakes and ale and for

'Banbury Cross', destroyed by Puritans in 1602 and replaced by a new one in 1859. The large neo-classical church (1790–1822) is by S.P. and C.R. Cockerell, the citizens having blown up the medieval one with gunpowder.

*Broughton Castle* (open), on B4035 3m SW, is a moated building of c 1300 remodelled as a Tudor mansion. The interior has 16C plaster ceilings, panelling and chimneypieces, including a superb one in the French style in the room known as the Star Chamber. The chapel survives from the 14C, while the Gallery is the most notable of 18C Gothick alterations.—*Warkworth*, 2m E of Banbury, has the mid 14C tomb of (?) Sir John de Lyons in its church.—For *Middleton Cheney*, see the alternative route from Aylesbury to Banbury, above.

FROM BANBURY TO COVENTRY VIA SOUTHAM, 27m via A423. This alternative to the main route described below heads directly N from Banbury, avoiding Warwick and Leamington.—4¹/₂m. *Mollington*. Charles I defeated Waller in 1644 at *Cropredy*, on the Cherwell 2m E. We enter Warwickshire.—6m. *Farnborough Hall* (NT) is a 17–18C building, notable for its rococo plasterwork and attractive grounds.—9m. *Wormleighton*, 1¹/₂m to the right, has a church with a Perp. screen and Jacobean woodwork, and the remains of an early 17C manor house, half destroyed after Prince Rupert's stay here before Edgehill. —14m. *Southam* is a small town with an inn on the site of the 14–18C mint where trade tokens were made. The church, mainly 14–15C, has a fine clerestory and 16C timber roof.—27m. *Coventry*, see below.

FROM BANBURY TO STRATFORD-UPON-AVON. The direct route, 20m by A422, runs via the steep *Sun Rising Hill*.—3m. The 17C *Wroxton Abbey*, once the home of Lord North, Prime Minister during the American War of Independence, is now owned by Fairleigh Dickinson University (limited opening).—5m. At *Alkerton*, left of A422, the gardens of Brook Cottage are open by appointment under NGS.—Near the top of the hill is (8m) *Upton House* (NT), a 16–17C building with an important collection of paintings by El Greco, Rembrandt, Bosch (\*'Nativity'), Hogarth and Reynolds, as well as Brussels tapestries, porcelain and furniture.

A better route to Stratford (21m) follows A41, the Warwick and Birmingham road, to (5m) the pleasant village of *Warmington* and branches left on B4086. —Below (7¹/₂m) *Edge Hill* (1 in 7) the first, indecisive battle of the Civil War was fought in 1642. The village has a sham castle built by Sanderson Miller in the 1740s, now a pub, overlooking the battlefield.—13m. *Compton Verney* (not open) is an 18C house, with work by Robert Adam, standing near a large lake. We cross the Foss Way.—Beyond (16m) *Wellesbourne* we change to B4086 and pass *Charlecote Park* on the way into (21m) *Stratford-upon-Avon* (both Rte 40).

FROM BANBURY TO NORTHAMPTON, 25m. From A422 2m E of Banbury we branch NE on B4525.—7¹/₂m. *Sulgrave Manor* (open) is the English home of George Washington's ancestors, rebuilt by Lawrence Washington after he acquired the property in 1539. The porch bears the family coat of arms, dubiously regarded as the origin of the 'Stars and Stripes'. The house has been heavily restored as a Washington museum, with 16–17C furnishings and portraits of the President by Gilbert Stuart, Charles Willson Peale and Archibald Robertson. The village of *Sulgrave* has an interesting church with memorial brasses of Lawrence Washington (d. 1584) and his wife.—11m. At *Canons Ashby* the church is a relic of an Augustinian priory. *Canons Ashby House* (NT), the seat of the Dryden family, is mid 16C with Jacobean and Queen Anne alterations, and pleasant formal gardens. Inside, the Jacobean plaster ceiling of the drawing room is outstanding.—At 17m B4525 crosses A5 (Rte 39B) and becomes B452, and at 21m we join A45, heading E to (25m) *Northampton* (Rte 46).

Beyond Banbury A41 soon crosses into Warwickshire.—76¹/₂m. *Warmington*, see the detour from Banbury to Stratford above.—The *Dassett Hills* rise on the right. At 83¹/₂m we see the windmill at *Chesterton*, 1¹/₂m to the right. Built in 1632, this curious structure has been variously attributed to the landowner Sir Edward Peyto, Inigo Jones and Nicholas Stone. Stone was certainly responsible for the monument (1639) to Sir William Peyto and his wife in the handsome Dec. and Perp. parish church.—We cross the Foss Way.

90m. **WARWICK** (22,000 inhab.), an ancient county town famous for its medieval castle, stands on a rocky hill overlooking the N bank of the Avon. It owes much of its handsome and unified appearance to rebuilding after a disastrous fire in 1694.

**Tourist Information Centre**: The Court House, Jury St.

**Car Parks**: The Butts, Market Place, Warwick Castle (Castle Lane and Stratford Rd), St Nicholas Park, Priory Rd, New St. and Puckerings Lane. Multi-storey car park in Bowling Green St.

**Railway Station**: Off Coventry Rd, NE of the centre.

**Buses**: from Market Place.

We begin at the *East Gate*, a relic of the old town walls, crowned with a Gothick chapel of 1788. Warwick Castle, to the S, is described at the end of this tour. Smith St. heads E, passing the birthplace of the poet Walter Savage Landor (1775–1864) on the left. *St John's House*, on the right beyond, is a picturesque 17C building on the site of a Hospital of St John. It is now a branch of the County Museum, with costumes, domestic scenes, musical instruments and a regimental collection. From the East Gate the dignified Jury St. leads towards the centre of town. Outstanding among its buildings are the Georgian *Pageant House* on the left and, at the central crossing, the *Court House* (1725–28) by Francis Smith, now containing the Town Council offices and Tourist Information Centre.

In Castle St., to the left, is the 16C house of Thomas Oken (d. 1573), now the *Warwick Doll Museum*.

Church St., on the right, leads to the collegiate church of **St Mary**. After the original building was largely destroyed in the fire of 1694, the tower, nave, aisles and transepts were rebuilt by Sir William Wilson in a curious mixture of Gothic and Renaissance styles.

Inside, the main points of interest are survivals from the earlier church. The tall chancel, completed in 1392, has a noteworthy vault. In the centre stands the *tomb, with recumbent effigies, of Thomas Beauchamp, Earl of Warwick (d. 1369), the founder of the choir, and his wife. In front of the altar is a brass to Cecilia Puckering (d. 1626) with an anagram on her name. The former chapter house, N of the choir, contains the pretentious tomb of Fulke Greville, Lord Brooke (see Warwick Castle, below). The Norman crypt has massive piers.

From the S transept we enter the *Beauchamp Chapel, a wonderful example of Perp., built in 1443–64. The bear and ragged staff of the Warwicks are much in evidence in the decoration. Outside the entrance (a convincing pastiche of 1704) is the brass of Thomas Beauchamp, Earl of Warwick (d. 1401), who finished the choir, and his wife. In the centre of the chapel is the tomb of its founder, Richard Beauchamp, Earl of Warwick (d. 1439), and his wife, with a brass effigy surmounted by a guard of unusual design. By the N wall is the gorgeously painted monument of Robert Dudley, Earl of Leicester (d. 1588), friend and Councillor to Elizabeth I, and his wife Lettice (d. 1634); his infant son, Robert Dudley (d. 1584), lies by the S wall. To the SW of the founder's tomb is the altar tomb of Ambrose Dudley, Earl of Warwick (d. 1590). The windows have contemporary glass and the stalls date from 1449. Over the W door is a painted Last Judgement of 1678, damaged in the fire. Between the chapel and the chancel is the so-called Little Chantry with rich fan vaulting and niches, and a curious wooden piscina.

Returning to the main thoroughfare, we follow the High St. past the *Aylesford Hotel* (1696) and the *Warwick Arms Hotel* (1790), the vista being closed by the *West Gate*. The chapel above the gate belongs to the **Lord Leycester Hospital** (open), whose half-timbered buildings make a picturesque group on the right.

The Hospital was founded by Robert Dudley, Earl of Leicester, in 1571, combining the buildings of several religious guilds to provide an asylum for aged or infirm retainers and their wives. The brethren, now ex-servicemen, wear black gowns on state occasions and still retain the original silver badges of 1571. The Guildhall (c 1450) in the S range contains a small museum, while the Great Hall of King James in the W range, dating from soon after 1383 but named after a royal visit in 1617, has a fine oak roof. The Chapel of St James over the gateway was founded in 1383; the tower was added in 1450 and the E window in the 19C. A malthouse and the former Anchor Inn, both 17C, are now flats for the brethren.

Fragments of the town walls survive N of the West Gate, and can be seen from Friars St. and Bowling Green St. From Bowling Green St. we may reach the Market Place, with the 17C Market Hall housing the *County Museum*. Its collection of local geology, natural history and history includes the 17C Sheldon tapestry map of Warwickshire.

To reach *Warwick Castle* (open), which stands above the Avon on the S side of the town, we return to the East Gate and follow Castle Hill to the right. From the outside the castle has the satisfyingly picturesque look of a 14C fortress, while its state rooms are those of a 17–19C mansion. It is extremely popular with visitors.

Although 'The Anglo-Saxon Chronicle' records that Ethelfleda, daughter of Alfred the Great, established a fortification at Warwick in 914, the mound to the W of the present castle is a Norman motte. This Norman fortress, an earth and timber structure built at the behest of William the Conqueror, was strengthened in stone in the 12C. The Earls of Warwick reconstructed the castle in the 14C, building outer walls and adding stong towers and gateways. In 1604 it was granted by James I to Sir Fulke Greville, later Lord Brooke (1554–1628), who spent large sums on its repair. His 17–19C descendants, Earls of Warwick in the second creation, were largely responsible for the present appearance of the state rooms and private apartments. In 1978 the castle was bought by Madame Tussauds, who have carried out repairs and added to the displays with the aim of increasing the already large number of visitors.

A winding approach cut through solid rock leads to the entrance via the Clock Tower and Barbican, with historical displays. To its left is the entrance to the Armoury and the massive, irregular Caesar's Tower, with dungeons in the lower storey; to its right is the 12-sided Guy's Tower, with a good view of the castle buildings from the top. On the other sides of the turfed Inner Court are the Bear and Clarence Towers (right), the Norman mound (in front) and the range of domestic buildings overlooking the river (left).

The Great Hall, originally 14C but with much 19C reconstruction, contains arms and armour, a huge 14C cooking pot, a bust of Charles I by Rysbrack and the grotesque 'Kenilworth Buffet' of 1851. The state rooms (mostly decorated in 1770–90) contain portraits by Van Dyck, Lely and Kneller, sculpture, furniture and china. Noteworthy objects include the Adam fireplace in the Cedar Drawing Room, the Italian inlaid table in the Green Drawing Room and the Delft tapestries in the Queen Anne Bedroom. The private apartments contain a reconstruction, with tableaux of wax figures, of a royal weekend party in 1898.

The gardens, laid out by Capability Brown in 1753, have pretty walks, peacocks and a conservatory, now housing a 'spectacle' devised by the present management.

Mill St., with some attractive old houses, descends from the castle gate to the river, giving a view of the castle and the broken 14C bridge. The main Banbury road leads to the stone bridge of 1790, which gives a better *view of the castle. On the left is the pleasant *St Nicholas's Park*. Beyond the river is Bridgend, with some timbered buildings and, in Myton Rd to the left, *Warwick School*, in 19C buildings but claiming a continuous existence since 1100.

**ROYAL LEAMINGTON SPA** (56,500 inhab.), only 2m E of Warwick, owes its Regency and Victorian buildings and its handsome gardens to the former popularity of its chalybeate and salt springs.

They first attracted attention towards the end of the 18C and the first bath was opened in 1786, but real prosperity came in the 19C, when Dr Henry Jephson was the leading physician and Queen Victoria bestowed the prefix 'Royal' on Leamington Spa.

**Tourist Information Centre**: Jephson Lodge, The Parade.

**Car Parks**: Clement St., Bath St., Radford Rd and by Royal Spa Centre in Newbold St.

**Railway Station**: Old Warwick Rd (A425), SW of town centre.

**Buses**: from The Parade.

**Theatre**: Royal Spa Centre, Newbold St.

**Famous visitors**. Ruskin was taken by his solicitous parents to consult Dr Jephson in 1841. The same year brought Cobden to Leamington, to urge the recently bereaved John Bright to work for the repeal of the Corn Laws. Dickens, who later gave public readings here, made Leamington the scene of Mr Dombey's introduction to Mrs Skewton and Edith Granger, his future second wife. Nathaniel Hawthorne stayed here while writing 'Our Old Home' in 1858.

In the middle of the town, where the Victoria Bridge crosses the river Leam, stands the *Royal Pump Room*, with a colonnade of 1813–14 but otherwise rebuilt in 1926. Physiotherapy and hydrotherapy treatments are still given here, and it is the last remaining place in the country where the waters can be taken under the National Health Service. Behind it are the *Royal Pump Room Gardens*; on the other bank of the river, York Walk leads ³/₄m to the large *Victoria Park*. Opposite the Pump Room are the beautiful *Jephson Gardens*, with the *Mill Gardens* further away, S of the river.

Bath St. leads S towards the railway station, passing the odd church of *All Saints*, begun in 1843 to the design of its vicar and extended by Blomfield. The *Art Gallery and Museum* is in Avenue Rd, to the right. Its collection includes Dutch and Flemish paintings (Bloemaert), 19–20C English paintings, ceramics (Delft, Wedgwood) and 18C drinking glasses.

N of the Pump Room runs the spacious Parade, with many early 19C buildings. More of Leamington's characteristic architecture can be seen in Clarendon Square, further N, and Lansdowne Crescent and Lansdowne Circus (NE), reached by turning right along Warwick St.

*Offchurch*, 3m E, has a 13C church with Norman details.

FROM WARWICK TO STRATFORD-UPON-AVON. The direct way (8m) is by A429 and A46. A more interesting route, 1¹/₂m longer, stays on A429, crossing the Avon just before (3m) *Barford*.—5³/₄m. We branch right on B4088, skirting the edge of *Charlecote Park* (Rte 40), and turn right on B4086 for (9¹/₂m) *Stratford-upon-Avon* (Rte 40).

FROM WARWICK TO BIRMINGHAM, 20m by A41.—6m. *Baddesley Clinton*. For *Packwood House*, 2m W, see the detour from Stratford to Birmingham in Rte 40.—10m. *Knowle* has a long-bodied Perp. church.—11m. We cross M42.—13m. *Solihull* (107,100 inhab.; Tourist Information), now a suburb of Birmingham, has a restored 13–15C church.—20m. *Birmingham*, see Rte 48.

The main route leaves Warwick by the Coventry road, heading N past a statue of Guy and the boar by Keith Godwin (1964) to (91m) *Guy's Cliffe*, where a 15C chantry with a gigantic statue of the knight is romantically situated above a pool of the Avon. Here, according to legend, Guy of Warwick lived the life of a hermit after killing the Dun Cow and the giant Colbrand and performing heroic deeds in the Holy Land. Nearby is the picturesque so-called Saxon Mill, often painted by David Cox and others.—91¹/₂m. We join A46 near

Gaveston's Cross (1832), marking the spot where Edward II's favourite, Piers Gaveston, was executed in 1312.

94m. **Kenilworth** (19,300 inhab.; Tourist Information), left of A46, has the scanty remains of a 12C Augustinian priory and a fine Norman doorway, perhaps from the priory, inserted in the tower of the over-restored parish church. The town is usually visited for **˙Kenilworth Castle** (English Heritage, standard opening and summer Sunday mornings), a magnificent ruin in red sandstone, with Norman, 14C and Elizabethan work and historic associations made famous by Sir Walter Scott.

It was founded soon after 1120 by Geoffrey of Clinton, Treasurer of England. The keep was built in 1170–80 and the outer wall and its towers in 1203–16. John of Gaunt, Earl of Lancaster, added the Strong Tower, the Great Hall and the southern rooms in the 1390s. The castle passed to his son, Henry IV, and remained royal until Queen Elizabeth granted it to Robert Dudley, Earl of Leicester, in 1563. He improved and enlarged the building, and entertained Elizabeth here in 1565, 1568, 1572 and 1575. The lavish pageants of the last year are described by Scott. In 1648 the castle was awarded to the Parliamentarian Colonel Hawkesworth, who began the process of destruction.

Visitors can enter by Castle Green on the N side, but the better approach is from the S, crossing the causeway which once dammed the artificial lake to Mortimer's Tower. The curtain wall and towers of the Outer Ward belong to the early 13C; the stables and gatehouse at the N entrance, the only part of the castle still habitable, are the Earl of Leicester's additions. To the right as we enter the Inner Court is the massive Norman keep. Adjoining it on the same side are the scanty remains of the kitchens, beyond which is the Strong Tower (1390), with the room of Amy Robsart, Leicester's first wife. The W side of the Inner Court is occupied by John of Gaunt's Great Hall, with two fine oriels at its S end. On the S side are the White Hall, or Great Chamber, and the Second Chamber, ending John of Gaunt's work. In the SE angle are Leicester's Buildings, containing the rooms where Queen Elizabeth stayed in 1575. Henry VIII's Lodgings, on the E side, have practically disappeared. The Garden was on the N side of the keep.

**Stoneleigh Abbey** (open), by the Avon 3m E of Kenilworth, is a baroque mansion (1714–26) by Francis Smith of Warwick. The 14C gatehouse and some Norman doorways with fine mouldings survive from the Cistercian monastery founded here in 1154, while the E wing (not open) belongs to the Elizabethan house built after the Dissolution. In Smith's W range, the Card Room and Dining Room preserve their contemporary wood panelling, while the Saloon and Chapel have plasterwork decoration added later in the 18C. The Royal Agricultural Show is held in the park in early July. The parish church of *Stoneleigh* has Norman work, including the font, and monuments of the Leigh family.

From Kenilworth A429 heads directly N to Coventry. On the left shortly before we cross (97m) A45 is the *University of Warwick*, founded in 1961 and opened in 1965. The Arts Centre (1974, enlarged in 1981 and 1986) contains a theatre, smaller studio theatre, cinema, concert hall and the Mead Gallery, with a permanent collection and temporary exhibitions.

99m. **COVENTRY** (318,000 inhab.) looks wholly modern at first sight. It is dominated by Sir Basil Spence's cathedral, the shopping precinct, the inner ring road and all the other fruits of the rebuilding programme which followed the disastrous German bombing raid in 1940. In fact, the city has a long history, particularly as a centre of trade and manufacturing. The ruins of the old cathedral have been lovingly preserved next to its successor but elsewhere, with the medieval street plan all but effaced, the relics of Coventry's past—its parish churches, and the remains of its powerful religious houses and guilds—are disjointed fragments which need seeking out among the post-war development.

**Tourist Information Centre**: Central Library, Smithford Way

**Car Parks**: at many points near the inner ring road. Roof-top parking in the shopping precinct.

**Bus Station**: Pool Meadow, near the inner ring road, NE of the centre.

**Railway Station**: Eaton Rd, S of the centre and the inner ring road.

**Theatres**: Belgrade Theatre, Corporation St.; Arts Centre, University of Warwick.

**History**. *Coventre*, the *Couentrev* of the Domesday Book, may derive from a Saxon convent, but its practical history begins with the foundation of a Benedictine priory in 1043 by Leofric, Earl of Mercia, and his wife Godgyfu. The legend of how Lady Godiva averted her husband's anger from the town by riding naked through its streets is first found in permanent form in the 'Flores Historiarum' of 1235; the episode of Peeping Tom dates only from the 17C.

After the Conquest the town prospered so greatly, as a centre of the wool trade and then of cloth-making, that by 1377 it ranked next to London, York and Bristol in industrial importance.

After the cloth industry declined at the end of the 16C, Coventry became famous for woollen caps, silk ribbons, watches and (in the 19C) sewing-machines. Its bicycle industry was established in the 1870s and its motor industry in the 1890s. An important armaments centre during both World Wars, Coventry suffered the German air raid which devastated its old cathedral, much of its centre and many of its factories on the night of 14 November 1940. Rebuilding began in post-war years under the supervision of the City Architect, Sir Donald Gibson.

**Famous natives and residents**. George Eliot (1819–79) attended boarding school at Nantglyn, No. 29 Warwick Row, W of Greyfriars Green, and lived with her father in 1841–49 at Bird Grove in the Foleshill Rd. The actress Ellen Terry (1847–1928) was born in either Market St. or Smithford St. The poet Philip Larkin was born here in 1922.

The centre of Coventry is Broadgate, an open space attractively laid out as a garden with a statue of Lady Godiva on horseback by Reid Dick (1949). Under the Godiva Clock is a mosaic memorial to 16C Coventry martyrs by René Antonietti (1953). The reliefs on the steel doors of the National Westminster Bank are worth noting. To the W of Broadgate extends the shopping precinct, the dreariest part of Coventry's post-war rebuilding programme.

To the E rise two of Tennyson's 'three tall spires' of Coventry. The nearer belongs to *Holy Trinity*, a good Perp. church which has a notable roof and tower-lantern (1667), a remarkable Perp. stone pulpit, and stalls with misericords from Whitefriars. The W window is by Hugh Easton (1955). The actress Sarah Siddons was married here

*The old Coventry Cathedral after the bombing raid of 1940*

in 1773. Priory Row, N of the church, has some pleasant old houses and fragments of the priory church demolished in 1539.

Just to the S the splendid Perp. steeple dominates the remains of the old cathedral, built as the parish church of St Michael, raised to cathedral status in 1918 and largely destroyed in 1940. The ruined shell has been rededicated as a memorial shrine and vestibule to the new **Cathedral**. Its moving desolation is heightened by the altar cross of charred roof beams (now a replica). Set against the S wall is Sir Jacob Epstein's brooding figure of Christ, 'Ecce Homo' (1935). In a gesture of reconciliation, the vestries were rebuilt as an international centre by German students and apprentices.

The new cathedral, designed by Sir Basil Spence and built in 1954–62, extends towards the N at right angles to the old. (Thus its 'E end' in fact faces N, but in the description below the liturgical rather

COVENTRY CATHEDRAL

Down to Undercroft
Chapel of Christ in Gethsemane
Sutherland Tapestry
LADY CHAPEL
High Altar
Chapel of Christ the Servant (Industry)
Ruins of Priory Church
Chapel of Unity
Baptistry Window
Bethlehem Font
Epstein 'St Michael'
St Michael's Avenue
Porch
Ruins of Medieval Cathedral
Charred Cross
Epstein 'Ecce Homo'

than geographical points of the compass are used.) Benjamin Britten's 'War Requiem' was written for its rededication.

The exterior, with an alternating screen of wall (in pink sandstone) and window set saw-toothed to the line of the building, gives marked contrasts according to one's viewpoint. The roof is topped by a gilded bronze flèche, locally nicknamed 'Radio Coventry'. On the nave wall facing Priory St., by the steps leading up to the porch, is Epstein's bronze of St Michael subduing the Devil. The extended roof of the porch links old and new buildings together. Their unity is further emphasised by the enormous glass screen, engraved with translucent figures of saints and angels by John Hutton, which takes the place of a W wall.

Since the side windows are hidden from view when the cathedral is entered from the W end, attention is immediately drawn towards the altar by the immensity of Graham Sutherland's tapestry. The *Nave* has a floor of polished black and white marble, contrasting with the plain walls. The ceiling, carried on two rows of slender concrete columns, is made up of concrete ribs which form an unbroken diamond pattern, filled in with wooden louvres. The weight of the roof above is carried wholly by the outer walls. The *Baptistery*, to the right, is a shallow alcove bounded by an immense stained-glass *window, by John Piper and Patrick Reynties, extending from floor to ceiling. The font is a rough sandstone boulder from the valley of Barakat outside Bethlehem. Opposite is the entrance to the *Chapel of Unity*, an undenominational place of worship shaped like a crusader's tent. Its mosaic floor was designed by the Swedish artist Einar Forseth; the windows, by Margaret Traherne, were paid for by donors in the German Federal Republic.

At the foot of each section of nave wall are the carved stone *Tablets of the Word, by Ralph Beyer. As we advance down the nave, each pair of the ten nave windows comes successively into view, throwing light from their abstract colour schemes towards the altar. They were designed by Lawrence Lee, Geoffrey Clarke and Keith New.

The *Chancel* is not distinguished structurally from the nave but formed by the traditional placing of lectern (with bronze eagle by Elizabeth Frink), pulpit and stalls. These and the bishop's throne on the left have canopies which suggest, not too happily, flocks of doves in flight. The uncased organ is built on either side against the end walls of the aisles. The unadorned stone altar stands alone in front of a huge silver-gilt cross by Geoffrey Clarke, which cradles another cross of nails. Beyond is the *Lady Chapel*, its structural simplicity forming a foil for the vast *tapestry by Graham Sutherland which fills the whole E wall. Woven at Felletin, near Aubusson, in France, it depicts Christ in Glory with man at his feet. A lower panel showing Christ crucified gives the effect of a reredos to the Lady Chapel altar and, when seen from the nave, to the high altar.

To the right of the Lady Chapel is the theatrical *Chapel of Christ in Gethsemane*, separated from the aisle only by a wrought-iron crown of thorns designed by Sir Basil Spence. Behind the asymmetrically placed altar a kneeling angel in bronze relief is silhouetted against a rich gold mosaic, by Stephen Sykes. A short passage leads to the *Chapel of Industry* (Chapel of Christ the Servant), combining the functions of the former guild chapels. Its plain glass windows give glimpses of industrial Coventry. To the left of the Lady Chapel, steps lead down to the visitors' centre in the *Undercroft*.

*John F. Kennedy House*, a residential youth centre in the precincts, was opened in 1965 by Herr Willy Brandt, then Chief Burgomaster of Berlin and later Chancellor of West Germany.

In Priory St., flanking the cathedral, rises the *Coventry (Lanchester) Polytechnic* (1955–65). S of the cathedral is *St Mary's Hall (open when not in civic use), founded in 1342 for the Merchant Guild, enlarged c 1400 for the Trinity Guild and since 1552 the property of the Corporation.

Above the kitchen and vaulted crypt is the Great Hall, with the Coventry Tapestry, an early 16C Flemish work probably commemorating the visit of Henry VII and Elizabeth of York in 1500. Two small chambers opening off the hall have panelling from old Coventry inns. On the S rises the 13C Caesar's Tower, perhaps a relic of the Earl of Chester's vanished castle. The only part of the building to be destroyed in 1940, it has been reconstructed with the old material. Mary, Queen of Scots, was imprisoned for a while in 1569 on its second floor.

Greyfriars Lane leads S from High St. past *Ford's Hospital* (1509), a half-timbered almshouse for five poor men and their wives, restored after bomb damage. Further S is the third of the three spires of Coventry, the octagonal steeple (c 1350) of *Christ Church*, the only part of the church to survive the bombing of 1940.

Warwick Rd goes on to Greyfriars Green, with its charming gardens and a statue of Sir Thomas White (1492–1567), founder of St John's College, Oxford. Eaton Rd, on the other side of the inner ring road, continues to the station.

## The **Herbert Art Gallery and Museum** is in Jordan Well.

On the Ground Floor is the Bates Room, with natural history displays including a vivarium and aquarium; there is a particularly good section containing live reptiles and amphibians. Also on the ground floor are the main social history rooms, which tell the story of Coventry with Anglo-Saxon and medieval objects and reconstructed rooms showing silk ribbon-weaving and watch-making. There are numerous representations of the Godiva story.

The First Floor contains the temporary exhibition galleries. In addition, there is a fine display of mainly English 18C furniture and silver. The large painting of Bacchus and Ariadne by Luca Giordano has recently been restored. There is a representative collection of Graham Sutherland's preparatory sketches for the tapestry in the cathedral, and an excellent display of Chinese art, the foundation of a permanent exhibition of non-European art.

By Whitefriars St. and a subway under the ring road, we reach the **Whitefriars Museum**, comprising the E cloisters, chapter house and dormitory of a Carmelite friary founded in 1342, with a small explanatory display. The building is often used for special sculpture exhibitions and for concerts, plays, etc.

Hales St., N of the centre, begins near the inner ring road and the Pool Meadow bus station with a section of the old *City Wall* (1356, dismantled 1662), skirted by a pleasant garden, connecting the small Swanswell Gate and Cook St. Gate. Around the corner is the *Museum of British Road Transport*, with cars, motor cycles and bicycles by famous Coventry manufacturers (Daimler, Jaguar, Singer, Standard, Triumph, etc.). Corporation St. leads from the W end of Hales St., passing the *Belgrade Theatre*, whose name recalls the wartime exchange of aid between the two bombed cities. In Hill St., on the right, *Bond's Hospital* and the former buildings of *Bablake School*, both originally 16C, make a picturesque group. Close by, at the corner of Corporation St. and Fleet St., is the mid 14C *St John's Church*, with a lantern tower. The phrase 'to send to Coventry' may derive from the fate of defeated Royalist troops imprisoned in the church during the Civil War and shunned by the local inhabitants. Spon St., continuing Fleet St. to the W, was a centre of the watch-making industry and still has some medieval cottages.

*Wyken*, in the NE suburbs, has a Norman church with a 15C wall painting of St Christopher.—*Coombe Park*, about 3m E of Coventry, has formal gardens and woods. Coombe Abbey (not open) stands on the site of a Cistercian monastery and incorporates part of its 13–15C cloisters.—At *Baginton*, beyond A45 3m S of Coventry, the Lunt (open) is a reconstructed Roman fort of the 1C AD. The parish church has a good brass of Sir William Bagot (d. 1407), a minor character in Shakespeare's 'Richard II'.

FROM COVENTRY TO BIRMINGHAM, 17m by A45. We leave Coventry to the NW and join A45.—6m. *Meriden* has a cross said to mark the centre of England. *Berkswell*, 2m S, is a pleasant village in a rural pocket now threatened by development of the coalfield. The interesting church has a Norman chancel and Saxon and Norman crypts. *Great Packington*, 1m NW of Meriden, has a remarkable church (1789–90) on a Greek-cross plan by Joseph Bonomi.—8m. We cross M42.—10m. *Elmdon*, with Birmingham Airport, is near the National Exhibition Centre.—We approach (17m) *Birmingham* (Rte 48) through the E suburbs of Yardley and Small Heath.

From Coventry to *Chester*, see Rte 51.

# B.  Via St Albans and Rugby

Total distance 91m. We follow A5 for most of the way.—A5, A5183 to (19m) **St Albans**.—A5183, A5 to (32m) Dunstable.—A5 to (45m) Milton Keynes.—A5 to (59m) Towcester.—A5 to (67m) Weedon Bec.—A5, A428 to (81m) **Rugby**.—A428 to (91m) **Coventry** (Rte 39A).

Maps: OS Landranger 176, 166, 165 (briefly), 152, 140.

M1 provides a quick alternative, with easy access to the major towns along the way.

A5 runs NW from London, following the course of the Roman Watling Street, and changes its name to A5183 beyond (11m) *Elstree*.

19m. **ST ALBANS** (72,300 inhab.), on a hill by the little river Ver, is an ancient place with the remains of the Roman city of Verulamium and a largely Norman abbey church, now the cathedral. There are some good old houses and inns in the streets around the market centre.

**Tourist Information Centre**: No. 37 Chequer St.

**Car Parks**: near the Civic Centre, E of St Peter's St., and, for Verulamium, near St Michael's (best approached from A414).

**Bus Station**: St Peter's St.

**Railway Stations**: City Station (Watford line), NE of the centre; Abbey Station (St Pancras line), S of the centre.

**Theatre**: Amateur productions at Abbey Theatre, Holywell Hill.

**Events**: International Organ Festival held biennially in July (1989, etc.) in the cathedral.

**History**. St Albans is the successor of the Roman *Verulamium* (see description below). It owes its name to St Alban, a Roman soldier and the first Christian martyr in England, beheaded here in AD 209 for sheltering Amphibalus, the priest who had converted him. The hill where he was executed became the site of a Roman shrine, a Saxon church and a Benedictine abbey founded c 793 by Offa, King of Mercia. The abbey rose to great wealth and power, its head being the premier abbot of England between 1154 and 1396. Two important battles took place at St Albans during the Wars of the Roses: Henry VI was defeated and captured at the first, near Holywell Hill in 1455, and released after Queen Margaret's victory at the second, on Bernard's Heath N of St Peter's church in 1461. The abbey church became cathedral of a new diocese in 1877.

**Famous natives and residents**. Nicholas Breakspear, who became Pope Adrian IV in 1154, was educated at St Albans. The chronicler Matthew Paris (d. 1259) was a monk here. The composer Robert Fayrfax was organist in the abbey church from 1498 until his death in 1521. Sir Francis Bacon (1561–1621) lived and died at Gorhambury (see below) and is buried in St Michael's church (see below). The dramatist James Shirley (1596–1666) taught at the Grammar School. Sarah, Duchess of Marlborough (1660–1774), was born at St Albans and lived at Holywell House, which stood at the foot of Holywell Hill, until Blenheim Palace was built. The poet William Cowper (1731–1800) was a patient at Dr Cotton's Collegium Insanorum in 1764–65.

The *Clock Tower* (limited opening), dating from 1411, in the High St. is the centre of the town. In front of it stood an Eleanor Cross, destroyed in 1702. The old French Row leads N, past a 15C inn, to the *Town Hall* of 1830. The broad, tree-shaded St Peter's St., where a market is held on Wednesdays and Saturdays, goes on to *St Peter's*, a late Perp. church with old glass and a tablet to Edward Strong (d. 1723), Wren's master mason.

Nearly opposite the W end of St Peter's are *Pemberton's Almshouses* (1624); the bus station lies beyond. Hatfield Rd to the E has another fine group of almshouses, founded by Sarah, Duchess of Marlborough in 1736. The *City*

*Museum*, opposite, displays craft tools, workshops and period rooms, and a natural history collection. Off the E side of St Peter's St. is the *Civic Centre* with the *City Hall* (1968).

Passages from High St. or the attractive Holywell Hill lead to the massive, inelegant **Cathedral**, commanding higher ground than any other English cathedral. The central tower with its striking arcade and part of the N side of the long, narrow nave are Norman, built from Roman bricks and tiles. The ugly W front and transeptal facades are mainly 19C.

**St Albans Cathedral**

Reference
1 Ramryge's Chantry
2 Wallingford's Chantry
3 St Alban's Shrine
4 Watching Loft
5 Duke of Gloucester's Tomb
6 Shrine of St Amphibalus

The central part of the cathedral, standing on the site of Alban's martyrdom and Offa's Saxon abbey, is still substantially the church built by Paul of Caen, the first Norman abbot, in 1077–88 and dedicated in 1116. The nave was lengthened to the W in 1200–35 and the E end, which seems originally to have finished with seven apses just E of the transepts, rebuilt with presbytery, retrochoir and Lady Chapel between 1235 and 1326. Restoration was begun by Sir Gilbert Scott in 1856 and completed, after the church had been raised to cathedral status in 1877, by Sir Edmund Beckett (later Lord Grimthorpe) who designed and paid for the W front and transept windows.

The plain but graceful W end of the *Nave* is EE, abruptly joining the severe Norman work on the N side •nd continued on the S side by five Dec. bays of 1323. The W and S sides of the Norman piers have 13C and 14C •wall paintings; the westernmost, showing the Crucifixion, is probably by Walter of Colchester (c 1220), whom Matthew Paris called 'an incomparable painter'. A stone rood screen (c 1350) separates the nave from the Norman ritual *Choir*, which is continued to the E by the Presbytery. The fine choir ceiling, divided into square painted panels, dates from the late 15C; the tower ceiling was renewed in 1952, when one original panel was removed to the N aisle. A larger panel of c 1530 from the N transept, showing St Alban's martyrdom, is preserved in the S choir aisle. Here, too, is the magnificent •brass of Abbot Thomas de la Mare (d. 1396). Most of the presbytery and retrochoir was rebuilt in 1235–60; the unique wooden vault was painted c 1450. The elaborate stone reredos behind the high altar dates from 1484 but is marred by 19C statues; the altarpiece of the Resurrection is by Sir Alfred Gilbert. On the N side of the presbytery is the chantry of Abbot Ramryge (d. 1520), on the S side the chantry of Abbot Wallingford, donor of the reredos.

The *Transepts* are the best preserved part of the Norman church. The arches on their E sides led into apsidal chapels. The N transept has a 15C fresco of Doubting Thomas. The large rose window on the N wall is by Lord Grimthorpe. In the S transept the blind •triforium on the E wall has arches separated by small circular shafts which, though fitted with Norman capitals and bases, are assumed to be from Offa's Saxon church. The S wall was rebuilt by Lord Grimthorpe, who incorporated in it some late Norman arcading.

Immediately E of the presbytery is *St Alban's Chapel*, with the elaborately carved marble base of the saint's early 14C shrine, pieced together from more than 2000 fragments in 1872. On the N side is the unusual •watching loft of c 1400, with a relic cupboard below and carvings on the back. On the S side is the •monument to Humphrey, Duke of Gloucester (d. 1447), Henry V's brother; it has a tall canopy with statuettes of English kings and a grille of Sussex ironwork. On either side of the retrochoir are chapels, to St Michael (N) and Our Lady of the Tapers (S), and beyond is the *Lady Chapel* (1308–26).

A door from the S transept leads to the slype and the new red-brick *Chapter House* (1982; William Whitfield).

Most of the other monastic buildings were destroyed after the Reformation but the *Abbey Gatehouse* (1361), now part of St Albans School, survives a few yards W of the cathedral. Abbey Lane leads down to a bridge over the Ver, near the little *Fighting Cocks Inn*, probably on the site of a boathouse of the Saxon monastery.

Beyond the river and ornamental lake are the park and playing fields on the site of the Roman **Verulamium**.

Prae Wood, on the hill to the SW, was site of a Belgic settlement of the late 1C BC. Verulamium itself was founded soon after the Roman conquest of AD 43 and became a 'municipium', the only one in Britain, two years later. Sacked by Boudicca (Boadicea) in 61, it was rebuilt on a larger scale and flourished until c 410.

To the S is part of the early 3C city wall (English Heritage, open daily 10.00 to dusk), which enclosed over 200 acres. A hypocaust with mosaic floor (AD 150 and 300) has been preserved under cover. The foundations of the basilica have been marked out beside the •*Museum* to the W. The splendid collection of finds from the site includes mosaics, wall paintings on plaster, burial urns, lead coffins and a well-preserved 2C bronze figurine of Venus. On the other side of A414, further W, is the •*Roman Theatre*, built c 140 and enlarged several times, the last in c 300.

*The Roman theatre at Verulamium (St Albans)*

**St Michael's Church**, near the museum, has the tomb of Sir Francis Bacon, with a statue showing him in a characteristic attitude ('sic sedebat'; 'thus he used to sit'). The church, founded in 948, has traces of Saxon work and a Jacobean pulpit.

St Michael's St. leads back to the town centre via Fishpool St. (with several 15–16C inns and 18C houses), Romeland Hill (the old burial ground of the abbey) and the attractive George St.

*Gorhambury* (limited opening), beyond the Roman theatre about 1½m W, is a late 18C house with part of Sir Francis Bacon's library, portraits and busts of the Bacon family and two fireplaces by Piranesi. In the hall are two enamelled windows from the Tudor house where Sir Francis lived and died; its ruins (English Heritage, open at any reasonable time) lie ¼m W.—At *Chiswell Green*, about 2m S of St Albans on the Watford road (B4360), are the *Gardens of the Rose* (open), the showground of the Royal National Rose Society and site of the British Rose Festival in early July.—Beyond *London Colney*, 3m SW of St Albans, there is an exhibition of de Haviland aircraft (limited opening) in the grounds of *Salisbury Hall*. The house itself (not open) is a medieval manor remodelled by Charles II for Nell Gwynne. The architect Nicholas Hawksmoor (1661–1736) is buried in the churchyard of St Botolphs at *Shenley*, 2m S of London Colney.

From St Albans to *Bedford, Oundle* and *Stamford*, see Rte 47B.

A5183 changes its name back to A5 after it crosses M1 at 25m. *Flamstead*, ½m S of our road, is a pretty village.—We enter Bedfordshire shortly before (32m) **Dunstable** (35,700 inhab.; Tourist Information). The church of *St Peter*, incorporating the remains of an

Augustinian priory founded by Henry I, is a grand example of Norman and EE work. Cranmer pronounced sentence of divorce against Catherine of Aragon here in 1555. Pupils of Dunstable School include Gary Cooper (1901–61).

For *Luton*, to the E, see Rte 47B.—At *Whipsnade*, on the Chilterns 3m SW of Dunstable, the 500-acre *Zoo* run by the Zoological Society of London is a pioneer venture in keeping wild animals in uncaged freedom within enclosures and paddocks.

36m. *Hockliffe*, at the junction with A4012.

3m W is **Leighton Buzzard** (30,600 inhab.), an old town now united with its neighbour *Linslade* on the opposite bank of the Ouse. The EE church has a beautiful spire, good 13C ironwork on the W door and interesting carvings on the crossing piers. The basilican *church at *Wing*, 2½m SW, has a Saxon apse, crypt and nave arches; among 16–17C Dormer monuments is the unusual classical tomb (1552) of Sir Robert. *Ascott House* (NT), set in a charming garden, has the Anthony de Rothschild collection of paintings (Cuyp, Hobbema, Gainsborough, Stubbs), furniture and Chinese porcelain. *Mentmore Towers* (limited opening), 2½m S of Wing, is a neo-Jacobean mansion built for Baron Meyer de Rothschild in 1852–54 by Sir Joseph Paxton, the architect of the Crystal Palace. It is now administrative headquarters of the Maharishi University of Natural Law. *Stewkley*, 3m NW of Wing, has a richly decorated late Norman *church (c 1150).

A4012 runs N from Hockliffe past (2m) *Milton Bryan*, the birthplace of Sir Joseph Paxton, to (4m) *Woburn*, a handsome little town. **Woburn Abbey** (open) was a pioneer among stately homes in the campaign to attract large numbers of visitors. Its atmosphere has suffered in the process. Built on the site of a Cistercian foundation, the house is largely by Henry Flitcroft (W range, 1747–61) and Henry Holland (S range, 1787–90). The sumptuous interior has an outstanding collection of paintings, with rooms devoted to Canaletto and Reynolds, work by 16–17C Dutch masters and George Gower's portrait of Elizabeth I. The grounds have various amusements, several species of deer, including the unique Père David herd, and a famous safari park.

We enter Buckinghamshire.—45m. **Milton Keynes** (Tourist Information), developed as a new city since 1967, has absorbed several older towns and villages, notably *Fenny Stratford*, *Bletchley*, *Wolverton* and *Stony Stratford*. Its population is expected to reach 150,000 by 1990. A grid of roads and roundabouts spreads out from the large central shopping area just N of A5 to enclose separate developments. Walton Hall, SE of the shopping centre, is headquarters of the *Open University*.

From Milton Keynes to *Northampton* via *Newport Pagnell*, see Rte 46.

We cross the Great Ouse and enter Northamptonshire.—51m. From the roundabout A508 leads N to (13m) Northampton via Stoke Bruerne (Rte 46). A422, heading S to (7m) Buckingham (Rte 39A), passes at 1m the turning for *Passenham*, where the church has misericords of 1628 and wall paintings. The remnants of Whittlewood Forest lie to the W of A5.

59m. **Towcester** (5000 inhab.) is an old town, once important for its coaching inns, on the site of the Roman *Lactodorum*. The church of *St Lawrence* contains the tomb of Archdeacon Sponne (d. 1449), a local benefactor.

*Easton Neston*, to the E (public drive to the church), is a mansion remodelled by Wren and Hawksmoor.—The church at *Slapton*, 4m SW of Towcester, has remarkable 14C wall paintings. Edith Sitwell (1887–1965) is buried at *Weedon Lois*, about 4m further W.

A43 to (11m) *Brackley* (Rte 39A) passes (4m) *Silverstone* with its motor-racing track.

67m. *Weedon*, properly *Weedon Bec*. At *Stowe Nine Churches*, 2m S, the church has a Saxon tower and good monuments, including one of 1617–20 to Elizabeth Lady Carey by Nicholas Stone. There are

brasses and medieval monuments in the church at *Dodford*, 1¼m W
of Weedon.

FROM WEEDON TO COVENTRY VIA DAVENTRY, 23m by A45.—4m. **Daventry**
(17,000 inhab.) is an ancient town with a handsome church of 1752–58 by David
Hiorne. Charles I spent the week before Naseby at the Wheatsheaf. A BBC
transmitter is prominent on the outskirts. A361, the Banbury road, leads S to the
source of the Cherwell at (4½m) *Charwelton*. The church, 1m E, has fine 15–
16C brasses and tombs of the Andrews family.

7m. *Braunston* is an important waterway junction on the **Grand Union Canal**.
Formed in 1929 by the union of the Grand Junction, the Regent's and six other
canals (all still navigable), the Grand Union links Braunston with the Thames
(S), the Nene (E) and the Trent (N) and with most centres of the Midlands. The
old Grand Junction Canal, built in 1793–1805, leaves the Thames at Brentford
and runs a 94m course via Watford, Berkhamsted, Tring, Leighton Buzzard,
Wolverton and Weedon, closely followed by the Midland railway, to join the
Oxford Canal (Rte 36B) here. It has tunnels between Blisworth and Stoke
Bruerne (Rte 46) and E of Braunston (2042yds long). From Braunston, the N
reach of the Oxford Canal connects via (23m) the Hawkesbury junction with the
Coventry Canal.—From the *Norton* junction, 4½m E of Braunston, the old
*Grand Union* (24½m; 1814), which now forms part of the 'Leicester Arm', runs
N to the Leicestershire and Northamptonshire Union Canal at Gumley near
Market Harborough, threading Crick and Husbands Bosworth tunnels and
descending Foxton locks; from here the Trent may be reached.—From the
*Napton* junction, 5m W of Braunston, the Oxford Canal goes S to Oxford via
Banbury and the 'Birmingham Arm' of the Grand Union runs via Warwick and
Kingswood (Rte 40) to Birmingham.

We enter Warwickshire and cross M5.—12m. *Dunchurch* lies 3m S of Rugby
(see below).—18m. *Ryton*, with a Police. At (20m) *Willenhall* we approach the
suburbs of Coventry. *Wolston*, 3½m E, has a church with Norman work, and
some remains of an old priory.—23m. *Coventry*, see Rte 39A.

Beyond Weedon A5 continues along the line of the old Watling
Street, closely accompanied by the Grand Union Canal (see above),
the main Midland railway line and the M1.—70½m. Near *Buckby
Locks* on the canal was the Roman settlement of *Bannaventa*. A mile
further N we pass the junction of two arms of the Grand Union on the
left, then cross the Leicester arm and the railway line in the *Watford
Gap*, by the big motorway junction. A5 leaves its Roman line near
(76m) *Kilsby*.

The church at *Ashby St Ledgers*, on A361 2½m S, has 14C wall paintings. The
manor house (not open) belonged to Robert Catesby and was a meeting place
for conspirators in the Gunpowder Plot.

77m. We leave A5, turning left on to A428. Rte 51, from Coventry to
Chester, picks up the A5 further N beyond Nuneaton.—78½m.
*Hillmorton* church has 14C effigies.—81m. **Rugby** (60,400 inhab.;
Tourist Information) is an important railway junction and an indus-
trial centre, with a famous public school.

*Rugby School* was founded in 1567, though it first became eminent under the
headmastership (1828–42) of Dr Thomas Arnold. The mainly 19C buildings are
dominated by the work of William Butterfield. His characteristic emphatic
chapel (1872) has 16C Flemish glass and windows by Morris and Co., as well as
the tomb of Dr Arnold, moved from the earlier chapel which his son Matthew
Arnold made the subject of a famous poem. A statue by Brock commemorates
Thomas Hughes (1822–96), author of 'Tom Brown's Schooldays', and a tablet on
the 'Doctor's Wall' commemorates William Webb Ellis, whose 'fine disregard for
the Rules of Football' originated the game of Rugby. Famous pupils include Sir
Richard Temple, Walter Savage Landor, Dean Arthur Stanley, Matthew Arnold,
Thomas Hughes, Lewis Carroll, Arthur Hugh Clough, Wyndham Lewis and
Rupert Brooke, a native of Rugby and son of a master at the school.

FROM RUGBY TO LEICESTER, 21m by A426.—4m. We cross A5 NE of Rugby. The
Roman station of *Tripontium* lay 1m S. At *Shawell*, 1m E, Tennyson wrote

much of 'In Memoriam'.—The only place of interest further along the way is (7m) **Lutterworth**, where John Wyclif was rector of St Mary's from c 1374 until his death in 1384. His works were condemned in 1414 by the Council of Constance, and his remains were disinterred, burned and thrown into the little river Swift. The church has two fine wall paintings.—21m. *Leicester*, see Rte 46.

FROM RUGBY TO MARKET HARBOROUGH, 18m by B5414 and A427. B5414 crosses A5 and then M6 and M1 near their junction with each other, and follows the Avon, which here divides Northamptonshire from Leicestershire.—5m. *Swinford. Stanford Hall* (open), 1m to the right, is a dignified house of 1690, with additions by Francis Smith of Warwick, in a splendid park. It has a collection of Stuart and Jacobite paintings. The early 14C church of *Stanford*, on the Northamptonshire bank of the river, contains fine 14–16C glass and good 16–17C monuments. The organ, brought from Magdalen College, Oxford, is said by tradition to have come originally from Whitehall Palace.—At (9½m) *North Kilworth* we join A427, heading E from Lutterworth (see above).—Beyond (12m) *Husbands Bosworth* we follow the course of the Welland.—18m. *Market Harborough*, see Rte 46.

From Rugby to *Althorp* and *Northampton*, see Rte 46.

A428 continues W from Rugby to (91m) **Coventry** (Rte 39A).

# 40   Oxford to Stratford-upon-Avon

Total distance 39m. **Oxford**, see Rte 37. We follow A34 throughout.—To (8m) Woodstock.—To (18m) Chipping Norton (bypassed).—To (39m) **Stratford-upon-Avon**.

Maps: OS Landranger 164, 151.

This route passes the N fringe of the Cotswolds, described and explored more fully in Rtes 38A and 38B.

The traveller hardly needs warning that the two major sights along the way, Blenheim Palace and Stratford itself, are among the most popular tourist attractions in England.

**Oxford**, see Rte 37. We leave the city by the Woodstock road, A34. —8m. **Woodstock** (2000 inhab.; Tourist Information) is an attractive little town with Georgian houses and a *Town Hall* (1766) by Sir William Chambers in the High St *Fletcher's House*, in Park St. opposite the church, contains the *Oxfordshire County Museum*, devoted to the archaeology, crafts and industry of the region. Further on, the Triumphal Gate leads to Woodstock's chief attraction for visitors, **Blenheim Palace** (open), the vast baroque mansion Sir John Vanbrugh built for the first Duke of Marlborough.

It stands on the site of the royal manor of Woodstock where, in the 12C, Henry I enclosed a deer park and built a hunting lodge. Henry II enlarged it into a palace and, according to tradition, built a secluded bower for his mistress, 'Fair' Rosamond. Edward the Black Prince (1330–76), son of Edward III, was born here. In 1554–55 the future Queen Elizabeth was confined in the gatehouse by her sister Mary. In 1704 Queen Anne gave the manor to John Churchill, Duke of Marlborough, as reward for his victory over the French at Blenheim that year. The decayed remains of the medieval palace were swept away and in 1705 Vanbrugh, aided by Nicholas Hawksmoor, began to build a new palace—the only building in Britain not intended for royal occupation to bear that title. It was finally completed after the duke's death in 1722 at a total cost of £300,000, of which £240,000 was paid by an increasingly reluctant Parliament.

From the Triumphal Gate the visitors' entrance leads through the *park (2700 acres) landscaped on the grand scale by Capability Brown in 1764–74. The artificial lake, crossed by Vanbrugh's Grand Bridge, was formed by damming a valley of the river Glyme. Near the N shore are Fair Rosamond's Well and the presumed site of the medieval Woodstock Manor. Beyond, the Victory Column

*Blenheim Palace*

(1730) stands at the head of an avenue of trees. Formal gardens are represented by the parterre immediately E of the palace and the water terraces on the W, both added this century.

The palace itself consists of a central block linked by curved colonnades to a kitchen courtyard on one side and a stable courtyard on the other. Vanbrugh conceived it in his heaviest and most elaborate manner, deliberately aiming to create a 'national Monument' rather than a home, even for a Duke and Duchess. To Horace Walpole the result looked like 'the palace of an auctioneer who had been chosen King of Poland'. Sympathetic observers have pointed to the romantic effect of its skyline, more reminiscent of a medieval castle than an 18C country house.

The Great Hall, with stonework by Gibbons and a painted ceiling by Thornhill, makes a restrained introduction to the otherwise lavish interior. A series of drawing rooms have ceilings by Hawksmoor and a distinguished collection of portraits (Kneller, Romney, Reynolds, Sargent, Van Dyck). The Saloon has a painted ceiling by Laguerre and marble doorcases by Gibbons. The State Rooms are hung with Brussels tapestries commemorating the first Duke's campaigns. The Long Library is notable for its stucco ceiling and the statue of Queen Anne and bust of the first Duke by Rysbrack, also responsible (with Kent) for the pompous tomb of the Duke and Duchess in the Chapel. Sir Winston Churchill (1874–1965), born in the bedroom W of the Great Hall, lies beside his ancestors in the churchyard of *Bladon*, on the SE edge of the park.

In the Evenlode valley NW of Woodstock are the little towns of (6m) *Charlbury*, below *Wychwood Forest*, and (12m) *Shipton-under-Wychwood*.

12m. *Over Kiddington. Ditchley Park* (open by appointment), 1¼m left, now an Anglo-American study centre, is by James Gibbs (1720–26) with decorations by Flitcroft and Kent. It stands on the site of the house where the Earl of Rochester (1647–80) was born.—18m. **Chipping Norton** (5000 inhab.; Tourist Information), 1½m W of

A34, is a Cotswold market town. It has a church with Perp. nave and several brasses, and a row of 17C almshouses.

*Great Tew*, 6m E, is a charming village. Lucius Cary, Viscount Falkland (1610–43) made his house here, now vanished, the centre of a literary circle that included Ben Jonson, Suckling, Cowley and Waller. He is buried in the church, which also has a monument by Chantrey to Mary Anne Boulton (d. 1829), wife of the engineer Matthew Boulton who purchased Falkland's estate in 1816. —*Hook Norton* church, 5m NE, has a carved Norman *font.—Warren Hastings (1732–1818) was born at *Churchill*, 3m SW of Chipping Norton, and buried at *Daylesford*, 5m W.—For *Stow-on-the-Wold*, 9m W, see Rte 38A.

From Chipping Norton to *Worcester*, see Rte 41.

We return to A34 and continue N to the boundary between Oxfordshire and Warwickshire.—21m. The *Rollright Stones*, ½m W of the road, are a group of neolithic monuments: the stone circle called the King's Men, the remains of a burial chamber called the Whispering Knights and, across the road, an outlying stone of doubtful significance, the King Stone.—26m. **Shipston-on-Stour** has 17–18C houses.

*Ilmington*, 4m NW, has a good Norman church.—*Barcheston*, 1m SE of Shipston, has a 16C alabaster monument in its church. William Sheldon began tapestry weaving in England here in 1560.—*Compton Wynyates*, the lovely Tudor mansion in a wooded hollow 5m E of Shipston, is unfortunately no longer open to the public.

A34 descends the valley of the Stour, keeping near the river most of the way.—27m. *Honington* is a pretty village and *Honington Hall* (limited opening) a splendid house, late 17C outside and mid 18C inside. The nearby parish church dates mainly from the 1680s.

39m. **STRATFORD-UPON-AVON** (20,900 inhab.), thanks almost entirely to the fact that Shakespeare was born and died here, has developed from a small market town into the most popular tourist attraction in England outside London. The birthplace alone is visited by more than 500,000 people each year. As a result, Stratford—really no more interesting intrinsically than half a dozen or so other Warwickshire towns—has been mummified beyond recognition, and whatever special atmosphere may once have attached to the buildings connected with Shakespeare has vanished altogether. The town can now claim serious attention only as the provincial home of the Royal Shakespeare Company, which, with the opening of the new Swan Theatre in 1986, operates three theatres here.

**Tourist Information Centre**: Judith Shakespeare's House, No. 1 High St.

**Car Parks**: Bridge Foot, Bridge Way, Rother St., Arden St., Windsor St.

**Bus Station**: Bridge Foot.

**Railway Station**: off Alcester Rd, about ½m W of the centre.

**Theatres**: The Royal Shakespeare Theatre and the Swan Theatre on Waterside, and the Other Place on Southern Lane, all administered by the Royal Shakespeare Company. The Stratford season lasts from about mid April to December or January. See walking tour below for further details.

**Annual Events**: Shakespeare Birthday Celebrations (April); Boat Club Annual Regatta (usually 3rd Saturday in June); Stratford-upon-Avon Festival (July), with a wide range of activities; Mop Fair (12 October).

The **Shakespeare Birthplace Trust** administers the Birthplace itself, Hall's Croft, the New Place estate, Anne Hathaway's Cottage (Shottery) and Mary Arden's House (Wilmcote). An inclusive ticket for all five properties is available.

**History**. The poet's father John, native of the nearby village of Snitterfield, had moved to this 'proper little mercate town' (as Camden described it) by the early 1550s and set up business on Henley St. as a glover—though rival traditions also make him a wool merchant or butcher. He achieved local eminence with his appointment as Alderman in 1565 and High Bailiff in 1567, the latter post making him a Justice of the Peace. In 1557 he had married Mary Arden, daughter of a prosperous yeoman from nearby Wilmcote. William was the third of their eight children, and the eldest son. The date of his baptism, 26 April 1564, has given Englishmen a patriotic excuse for celebrating his birthday as 23 April, St George's Day. Virtually nothing can be said of his childhood or youth in Stratford beyond the safe assumption that he attended the local grammar school and the fact that he married Anne Hathaway of Shottery in 1582. His first daughter, Susanna, was born in 1583 and the twins Judith and Hamnet in 1585. Neither the date nor the occasion of his leaving Stratford is known, though it

*Shakespeare's Birthplace before Victorian restoration*

evidently happened during the 'lost years' 1585–92 and is attributed by a stubborn local legend to his poaching adventures at Charlecote Park. He kept close ties with the town, strengthened when he bought New Place in 1597 and inherited the Henley St. house on his father's death in 1601. He retired to New Place in 1611, died at Stratford on 23 April 1616 and was buried at Holy Trinity church, where he had been baptised. His son Hamnet had died in infancy but his wife and both daughters outlived him, continuing the family connection with Stratford. Susanna married Dr John Hall and Judith married Thomas Quiney, a vintner. Shakespeare's last direct descendant was Elizabeth Hall, who married Thomas Nash but left Stratford after his death to become Lady Bernard. She died in 1670.

After Shakespeare's death the history of Stratford became intertwined with the growth of his reputation. The town's status as a national literary shrine was established by David Garrick's Jubilee of 1769—a three-day festival which celebrated Shakespeare's memory in every conceivable way except performing any of his plays. In the 19C Stratford's rise was furthered by the public purchase of the Henley St. house and the building of the first Memorial Theatre in 1877–79. The popular novelist Marie Corelli made the town her home from 1901 until her death in 1924.

The old centre of the town is formed by a gridiron of streets parallel to the river. A convenient walking tour begins at its NE corner near the *Clopton Bridge*, built by Sir Hugh Clopton in 1480–90 and widened in 1925. We follow Bridge St. to its junction with High St., where *Judith Shakespeare's House* is now the Tourist Information Centre. On our right Henley St. leads to the modern *Shakespeare Centre* (1964), with its large library, through which we enter **Shakespeare's Birthplace** (open). This consists of two timber-framed houses, originally part of a row but now detached. Shakespeare is presumed to have been born in the W half, now fitted up in the manner of a 16C family home. The E half is a museum illustrating his life, work and times. The small garden is planted with flowers and trees mentioned in the plays.

The building dates from the late 15C or early 16C. John Shakespeare was living in the W half and apparently using it for his business premises by 1552. He bought the other half in 1556, and at some later point in the century the two houses were connected and a rear wing added. Shakespeare inherited the property in 1601, though his mother and sister, Joan Hart, continued to live in it. On the latter's death in 1646 it passed to Susanna Hall and then to her daughter Elizabeth. When she died in 1670 it returned to the Hart family, who remained owners until the early 19C. During these vicissitudes the E half became an inn known as the Swan and later as the Swan and Maidenhead, while the W half was at one time a butcher's shop. Public interest in the building was first aroused by the 1769 Jubilee, when Garrick arbitrarily identified the first-floor bedroom in the W half as the birthroom itself. The tenants obligingly took to showing visitors an implausible collection of Shakespeare relics. The Shakespeare Birthplace Committee (predecessor of the modern Trust) bought the property in 1847 and reopened it as a museum in 1863, after substantial repairs and alterations charitably described as restoration. The annual number of visitors has grown steadily from a trickle of about 1000 in the early 19C and about 30,000 by the turn of the century to its present overwhelming flood. There are entertaining accounts by early travellers in Washington Irving's 'Sketch Book', Nathaniel Hawthorne's 'Our Old Home' and Henry James's short story 'The Birthplace'.

We return down Henley St. and continue along High St. On the right is *Harvard House* (open), a building of 1596 where John Harvard's mother Katherine Rogers spent her childhood. It was restored under the supervision of Marie Corelli and presented to Harvard University in 1909. The row of half-timbered buildings continues to the corner of Ely St. On the opposite corner, where High St. continues as Chapel St., stands the *Town Hall* (open). The statue of Shakespeare on the N front was presented by Garrick in 1769. Chapel St. has several old inns and, on the left at the end, the **New Place** estate (open), which consists of Nash's House and the site of Shakespeare's New Place next door.

Nash's House, a half-timbered building with a reconstructed streetfront, was inherited by Shakespeare's granddaughter Elizabeth Hall from her first husband, Thomas Nash. It contains a museum of Stratford history. From it we can enter the garden planted on the foundations of New Place, the late 15C house Shakespeare bought in 1597 and retired to in 1611. It was torn down in 1759 by Rev. Francis Gastrell after a dispute about rates with the local Corporation. The gardens of New Place are entered separately from around the corner in Chapel Lane; in the central lawn is a mulberry tree said to be descended from the original tree planted by Shakespeare and cut down by the short-tempered Gastrell in 1756.

Opposite New Place, at the corner of Chapel Lane and Church St., is the *Guild Chapel*, with a late 13C chancel, a nave rebuilt by Sir Hugh Clopton in 1495 and a wall painting of the Last Judgement (c 1500). Beyond lie the *Grammar School* where Shakespeare is assumed to have been educated, in the former Guildhall, and a row of alms-houses once maintained by the Guild. On the opposite side of the street is the 18C *Mason Croft*, once the home of Marie Corelli and now the Shakespeare Institute of the University of Birmingham.

From the end of Church St. we follow Old Town to the left. *Hall's Croft* (open), a Tudor town house on the left, was the home of Shakespeare's daughter Susanna and her husband Dr John Hall. It contains Tudor and Jacobean furniture, and one room has been equipped as a 16C dispensary. Near the end of the road, among lime trees by the bank of the river, is **Holy Trinity Church**, an interesting building in its own right but usually visited because Shakespeare is buried in it.

The tower and transepts are 13C, the nave and aisles early 14C, while the chancel and nave clerestory were rebuilt in the late 15C, when the porch was added. The spire (1765) replaces the original wooden one.

The font where Shakespeare was christened is at the W end of the N aisle. In the chancel (entrance fee) a case displays copies of the registers with entries for his baptism and burial. His grave lies on the N side of the chancel, its slab bearing a famous doggerel inscription. On the wall above is Gheerart Janssen's monument, with an epitaph celebrating Shakespeare's achievement in literature and the (recoloured) bust which has disappointed so many visitors. Close by are the graves of Shakespeare's wife, his daughter Susanna and his sons-in-law Dr Hall and Thomas Nash. The graves of other relatives are unmarked. The chancel also contains the tombs of its builder, Dean Balsall (d. 1491), and of Shakespeare's friend John Combe (d. 1614), while the Clopton Chapel at the E end of the N aisle has monuments of the Cloptons.

We return to the centre of town by Southern Lane and its continuation as Waterside, running alongside the river and past the Royal Shakespeare Company's three Stratford theatres. **The Other Place**, on the left, is the smallest (150 seats) and has the broadest repertoire, ranging from classical to contemporary plays. The **Swan Theatre** (1986; Michael Reardon), on the right, inhabits the shell of the original Memorial Theatre, built in 1877–79 but gutted by fire in 1926. Its auditorium (430 seats) recalls the design of Elizabethan playhouses and is used for staging the work of Shakespeare and his contemporaries. The large **Royal Shakespeare Theatre** (1500 seats) is devoted to Shakespeare's work. The building (1932; Elizabeth Scott) has sculptured decoration by Eric Kennington and a terrace overlooking the Avon.

The *Royal Shakespeare Collection* has the 'Flower Portrait' of Shakespeare, which may be either model for or copy of the Droeshout engraving in the First Folio, and a remarkable collection of theatrical relics.

Beyond the Royal Shakespeare Theatre are the pleasant *Bancroft Gardens*.

The Stratford-upon-Avon Canal, built in 1793–1816, runs N from the Bancroft Gardens to join the Worcester and Birmingham Canal at (25¹/₂m) *King's Norton*. Its long neglected S section, now NT and open to pleasure craft, rises by 36 locks with large aqueducts at *Edstone* and *Wootton Wawen* to (13¹/₂m) *Kingswood* and the Grand Union Canal (Rte 39B).

**Shottery**, the birthplace of Shakespeare's wife, is about 1m W of Stratford, reached by a footpath. *Anne Hathaway's Cottage* (open) is a half-timbered Elizabethan farmhouse with thatched roof, still containing some of its 16C furniture. From Shottery a lane leads NW, crossing A422, to (2¹/₄m more) **Wilmcote**, with *Mary Arden's House* (open), the half-timbered farmhouse where Shakespeare's mother is said to have been born. It contains 16C furniture and the barns have a collection of farm equipment.

The villages, churches and country houses in the surrounding region, several connected with Shakespeare in legend or actuality, can offer some relief from the atmosphere of Stratford itself.—Shakespeare's parents were married in the church at *Aston Cantlow*, beyond Wilmcote 4¹/₂m NW of Stratford. It has a good late 13C chancel.—*Tiddington*, on B4086 1¹/₂m E of Stratford, and *Alveston*, 1m further, are pretty villages. They lie on the way to (4¹/₂m) *Charlecote Park* (NT), a heavily restored Tudor mansion with a fine original gatehouse. A legend insists that the young Shakespeare was caught poaching deer in the park and brought before its owner, Sir Thomas Lucy. The nearby church, rebuilt when the house was altered in the 19C, has three handsome 17C monuments to members of the Lucy family.—*Clifford Chambers*, by A46 1¹/₂m S of Stratford, was visited by Shakespeare's contemporary Michael Drayton (1563–1631). The church has Norman details.

FROM STRATFORD TO BIDFORD-ON-AVON, 7m by A439. We leave Stratford with
Shottery (see above) to our right and, on the left, the turning for (2m)
*Luddington*, where the church is the strongest claimant to be the scene of
Shakespeare's marriage (cf. Temple Grafton below).—4m. *Welford*, 1m S of the
road, is a pretty village with a maypole.—7m. **Bidford-on-Avon** has the former
Falcon Inn, which a stubborn local tradition makes the scene of a drinking bout
by the youthful Shakespeare. The crab tree beneath which he slept off the
effects has long since vanished. *Wixford*, 2m N on the way to Alcester, has a
church with Norman details.

FROM STRATFORD TO ALCESTER, 8m W by A422, partly following the course of
the Roman road. Shottery (see above) lies to the S as we leave the town.—4½m.
The church at *Temple Grafton*, 1m S of the road, is sometimes claimed as the
scene of Shakespeare's marriage (cf. Luddington above).—8m. **Alcester** is an
ancient little town of Roman origin, with a 17C town hall, some Tudor houses
and a church made Gothick outside and classical inside in 1729–30. Off B4089 1
½m NE is the 14C *Kinwarton Dovecote* (NT), with a fine ogee doorway. *Great
Alne*, 1½m further, has an old watermill.—Off A435 2m N of Alcester is
*Coughton Court* (NT), the early 16C house of the Roman Catholic Throckmorton
family. Behind the imposing gatehouse, with wings of 1780, are the half-
timbered N and S wings. The E wing was destroyed by a mob in 1688. The hall,
in the gatehouse, has a lovely fan-vaulted ceiling and other rooms have wood
panelling. The staircase was brought from Harvington Hall. The family portraits
include one by Largillière, and there is a collection of Jacobite relics. Nearby is
the Perp. parish church, with many of its original furnishings and 16C
Throckmorton tombs, and a Roman Catholic church (1857) by Hansom. At
*Studley*, 2m further N, the church has a Norman doorway.—*Ragley Hall* (open),
on A435 1¾m SW of Alcester, was begun by Robert Hooke in 1679–83, altered
and decorated by Gibbs c 1750 and given a portico by James Wyatt in the 1780s.
The handsome interiors, redecorated in recent years, include fine plasterwork
by Gibbs, especially the baroque decoration of the ˙Great Hall. Among the
paintings are work by George Morland, Reynolds (portrait of Horace Walpole),
van Loo, Hoppner and Lely. One staircase has a mural by Graham Rust (1983),
the other a large painting by Ceri Richards (1964).—See above for *Wixford*, 2m
S of Alcester.

FROM STRATFORD TO BIRMINGHAM, 25m by A34, following the last stage of the
old coaching route from London via Oxford and Stratford, and running parallel
to the Stratford-upon-Avon Canal for the first part of the journey.—6m. *Wootton
Wawen*, left of the main road after we cross the canal, has a church with a Saxon
core.—8m. *Henley-in-Arden* is a quaint little town with an old market cross, a
Perp. church, a 15C former Guildhall and the 17C White Swan.—11m. *Lap-
worth*, 1m to the right, has a church with Norman details. *Kingswood*, at the
junction of the Stratford Canal and the Grand Union Canal, lies 1½m further
E.—13m. *Hockley Heath*. 2m E is *Packwood House* (NT), a timber-framed Tudor
building with good furniture and an outstanding collection of tapestries and
textiles. The topiary garden of yew trees dates from the 17C.—We cross M42 at
16m and pass through the suburbs of Hall Green and Sparkbrook on the way
into the centre of (25m) *Birmingham* (Rte 48).

From Stratford to *Banbury* and to *Warwick*, see Rte 39A.

# 41 Oxford to Worcester: The Vale of Evesham

Total distance 58m. **Oxford**, see Rte 37.—A34 to (18m) Chipping Norton, see Rte 40. We then follow A44 throughout.—To (27m) Moreton-in-Marsh.—To (36m) Broadway.—To (42m) Evesham.—To (49m) Pershore.—To (58m) **Worcester**.

Maps: OS Landranger 164, 163 (briefly), 151 (briefly), 150.

Before dropping down into the Vale of Evesham, this route goes across the N fringes of the Cotswolds, explored more fully in Rtes 38A and 38B.

**Oxford**, see Rte 37, and to (18m) *Chipping Norton*, see Rte 40. We leave the town on A44.—22m. A436 leads left to (5½m) *Stow-on-the-Wold* (Rte 38A), passing (2½m) *Daylesford* (Rte 40) and (3m) *Oddington* (Rte 38A). Shortly beyond the turning for Stow a sideroad on the left leads in 1m to *Chastleton House* (open). Built in 1603 of Cotswold stone, it has strikingly handsome exterior, and keeps its great hall and long gallery, together with some original plasterwork and furniture.—27m. **Moreton-in-Marsh** (Tourist Information) is a small market town with the Foss Way as its High St. The Curfew Tower dates from the 16C. *Stow-on-the-Wold* lies 4m S on A429 (the Foss Way).—At (29m) *Bourton-on-the-Hill* we reach the crest of the Cotswolds. *Batsford Park Arboretum* (open), 1m N, has rare trees. At *Sezincote*, 1½m S, the house (limited opening) was built c 1805 by Cockerell and Thomas Daniell in an Indian style anticipating the Royal Pavilion at Brighton; the oriental gardens (open) are by Repton.

About 4m N of A44 is **Chipping Campden** (seasonal Tourist Information), once a centre of the Cotswold wool trade and now popular with visitors for its many handsome stone buildings. The broad, curving *High St.* is a picturesque medley of local styles from the 14C to the 18C. Market Place, the row of buildings in the middle of the street, includes the *Town Hall*, 14C but much altered, and the *Market Hall* of 1627. The *Woolstaplers' Hall* (c 1340) is now a museum of bygones. Further S are the remains of the 17C mansion built by Sir Baptist Hicks, Viscount Campden, and a group of almshouses of 1612. The nearby parish church of *St James*, with its great *W tower* and its tall and airy nave, typifies the Perp. wool churches of the region. The brasses in the chancel include one of the local wool merchant William Grevil (d. 1401). Among the elaborate monuments to the Noel and Hicks families in the S chapel is the tomb of Viscount Campden (d. 1629) and his wife, perhaps by Nicholas Stone.

Off B4081 4m NE of Chipping Campden is the beautiful *Hidcote Manor Garden* (NT), created this century by Lawrence Johnston. Opposite is *Kiftsgate Court Garden* (open). *Mickleton*, on A46 just beyond the end of B4081, is a pretty village at the N fringe of the Cotswolds.

Beyond Moreton-in-Marsh A44 enters the county of Hereford and Worcester and descends Broadway Hill.—34m. *Broadway Tower* (open), in the country park ½m left of the road, was built as a folly by the Earl of Coventry in 1800. It contains exhibitions of the Cotswold wool trade and of work by William Morris, who stayed here; the top floor and roof have a wide view.—36m. **Broadway** (seasonal Tourist Information) has been made overwhelmingly popular with tourists by its reputation as one of the most handsome villages in the country. Among the many 16–18C houses on the broad, stone-built High St. are the *Lygon Arms*, now a hotel but once a manor house used by both Charles I and Cromwell as the tide of battle flowed in the neighbourhood, and the *Tudor House* (1660). The medieval parish church of *St Eadburgha*, largely Perp. despite its ancient dedication, lies 1m S. The sideroad continues another 1¼m to *Snowshill Manor* (NT), a typical Cotswold manor house with Tudor work behind the façade of c 1700. It contains a magpie collection assembled by a previous owner (Japanese Samurai armour, 18C musical instruments, early bicycles, model ships, etc.).

*Buckland*, off A46 2m SW, has England's oldest rectory, with a 15C great hall (open). A46 continues SW to (6m) *Hailes Abbey* and (9m) *Winchcombe* (Rte 38A).

A44 crosses the **Vale of Evesham**, watered by the river Avon and its many tributaries as it winds its way from Stratford (Rte 40) in the NE to join the Severn at Tewkesbury (Rte 42) in the SW. The district is known for its vegetables and fruit, especially plums. *Bredon Hill* (Rte 42), an outlier of the Cotswolds, rises to the left of our road.—39m. *Wickhamford* church, ½m right of A44, has the tomb of Penelope

Washington (d. 1697), bearing the Washington arms.—42m. **Eve-sham** (15,300 inhab.; seasonal Tourist Information) is a pleasant town with tree-lined walks along the banks of the Avon. In the Market Place are the half-timbered 15C *Round House* and the *Town Hall*, built in 1586 but remodelled in the 19C. All that survives of the once large and rich Benedictine *Abbey* founded in the 8C is the Norman and Tudor gateway of the churchyard and the detached 16C *bell tower, a superb example of Perp. at its most ornate. The abbey precinct contains two parish churches: the Perp. *St Lawrence*, now redundant, and *All Saints*, the present parish church, which is Norman beneath Perp. remodelling. The old *Almonry* (open), where pilgrims to St Lawrence were lodged, houses a small museum of local remains from the Romano-British period onwards.

At the Battle of Evesham (1265) the army commanded by the future Edward I defeated Simon de Montfort, who was buried in the abbey church. An obelisk (1845) marks the site of the battlefield about 1m N of the town.—*Middle Littleton*, by B4085 3m NE, has a 13C or 14C tithe barn (NT).—At *Bretforton*, off B4035 4m E of Evesham, the Fleece Inn dates partly from the 14C.—At *Ashton-under-Hill*, 5¹/₂m SW of Evesham, *Bredon Springs Garden* is open under NGS.

At (49m) **Pershore** (Tourist Information), another pleasant town on the Avon, the choir and transepts of the Benedictine *Abbey Church* are preserved as the parish church. The 14C tower, originally over the crossing, now stands at the W end of the building. Inside are the Norman crossing arches and S transept, and a beautiful apsidal E end of the early 13C, with vaulting built after a fire in 1288. *Strensham*, 5m SW near M5, was the birthplace of Samuel Butler (1612–80), author of 'Hudibras'.

58m. **WORCESTER** (pronounced 'Worster'; 75,900 inhab.) stands on the smoothly flowing Severn, looking E across the Vale of Evesham and W to the Malvern Hills. The central tower of its cathedral makes a conspicuous landmark. Many other old buildings survive, but the redevelopment inflicted on much of the city centre in the 1960s is a notorious example of insensitive modern planning.

**Tourist Information Centre**: The Guildhall, High St.

**Car Parks**: Copenhagen St., Dolday and Newport St., Croft Rd, Pitchcroft, Farrier St., Bull Entry, College Precincts, Commandery Rd, and off City Walls Rd. Multi-storey car parks at High St. and Friar St., and at Blackfriars.

**Bus Station**: (town buses) Angel Place; (out-of-town services) Newport St.

**Coach Station**: Croft Rd.

**Railway Stations**: Foregate Street Station, ¹/₄m N of the centre, and Shrub Hill Station, ³/₄m E of the centre.

**Theatre**: The Swan, near Pitchcroft.

**Annual Events**: The Three Choirs Festival (August) rotates annually between Worcester, Hereford and Gloucester cathedrals. It is next held at Worcester in 1990. Founded c 1715 and continuous since 1724, it has given first performances to works by Elgar and Vaughan Williams and is one of the finest choir festivals in the world.

**History**. There are scanty traces of an Iron Age settlement (c 500 BC) and a Roman town, perhaps called *Vertis*, on the ridge where the cathedral now stands. But the real history of Worcester began c 680, when the bishopric was founded in the Saxon *Wigorna Ceaster*. At the Conquest the town was important enough to be made the seat of a Norman castle. Its adherence to the Royalist cause during the Civil War won Worcester the motto 'Civitas in Bello in Pace Fidelis' ('The City Loyal in War and Peace'). It was the first city to declare for Charles I, and the last rallying point for supporters of the young Charles II, defeated at the Sidbury Gate in 1651. Known for its cloth trade in the Middle

Ages, Worcester recovered from the upheavals of the Civil War to become a prosperous manufacturing centre in the 18C and early 19C. Its glove-making factories have virtually disappeared, but the city is still the home of Royal Worcester porcelain, started in 1751, and of Lea and Perrins sauce, begun at a chemist's shop in Broad St. in 1825. Berrow's 'Worcester Journal', probably established in 1690 and certainly in circulation by 1709, is the oldest English newspaper with a continuous history.

**Famous natives and residents**. The novelist Mrs Henry Wood (1814–87) was born and the madrigalist Thomas Tomkins (1572–1656) died here. The composer Sir Edward Elgar (1857–1934), born at the nearby village of Lower Broadheath (see below), spent much of his life at Worcester and died here at a house demolished in 1969. An Elgar Trail follows sites connected with his life and work in the city and surrounding region; a useful accompanying pamphlet is available from the Worcester and Malvern Tourist Information Centres.

Key to Numbers

1 Elgar Window
2 Sir John Beauchamp
3 Bp Bullingham
4 Bp Johnson
5 Stanley Baldwin
6 Bp Hough
7 Bp Philpott
8 King John
9 Prince Arthur's Chantry
10 Bp Cantelupe
11 Bp Blois
12 Charlotte Digby
13 Sir Griffith Rice
14 'Miserrimus' Stone

WORCESTER CATHEDRAL

We approach the **˙Cathedral** from College Yard, where a few 18C houses still survive in pleasant contrast to the bleak modern development nearby. The outside of the cathedral suffered thoroughgoing renewal by A.E. Perkins and Sir Gilbert Scott in 1864–74. Most of it is now Victorian, and only the rich central tower survived relatively unscathed. The real beauty of the cathedral lies within, in the great E end and the unusually interesting collection of tombs and monuments.

The present building is the latest of several to stand on the site. It succeeds two Saxon cathedrals—the first presumably dating from the establishment of the bishopric in c 680, the second erected while Oswald was bishop (961–92)—and Wulstan's cathedral of 1084–89. The chief surviving fragment of this Norman building is the crypt. Wulstan was canonised in 1203, after miracles had begun to happen at his tomb, and the resulting flow of pilgrims encouraged (and paid for) a major campaign of rebuilding. Work on the new E end began with the Lady Chapel in 1224. The remodelling of the nave, started in 1317, was finished only after serious interruptions in the 1370s—the date, too, when the central tower was completed.

We enter by the impressive late 14C N Porch, halfway along the nine piers of the *Nave*. The two W bays (c 1160) are remarkable examples of Trans. work, their capitals foreshadowing later foliage design and their pointed arches already EE in manner. The other seven bays differ entirely from them, and are not uniform. On the N side they are Dec. (1317–27) and on the S very early Perp., probably built immediately before the nave vaulting was completed in 1377. The lofty triforium is also different on the N and S sides. The N aisle has a tablet and memorial window to Elgar (not buried here) in the second bay and, in the sixth, the tomb of Sir John Beauchamp and his wife (c 1400), opposite the altar tomb of Robert Wilde (d. 1607) and his wife. Beyond the Jesus Chapel, further E, is the curious tomb of Bishop Bullingham (d. 1576), not in its original place. In the S aisle the lower part of the wall belonged to the Norman nave. Five Norman recesses face the present pier arches, two of them filled with later monumental arches. The two W bays are contemporary with those of the nave. A monument to Bishop Johnson (d. 1774) by Robert Adam, with a bust by Nollekens, stands at this end of the aisle. The ashes of Stanley Baldwin (1867–1947) lie at the W entrance.

The aisleless *W Transepts* are a mixture of Norman and Perp., with 19C restoration. The E wall of each transept has a fine Norman arch. Below the one in the N transept is Roubiliac's elaborate monument to Bishop Hough (d. 1743); here, too, are tablets to three novelists with local connections, Mrs Sherwood (1775–1851), Mrs Henry Wood (1814–87) and Francis Brett Young (1884–1954). The S transept has the Great Organ; the Little Organ (by 'Father' Smith, 1704), said to have belonged to Handel, is in the choir.

The **˙E end** is second only to that of Beverley Minster as a work of the period 1220–60. Its quality is best seen in the EE *Lady Chapel*, begun in 1224, with tall lancet windows and sculptured arcade below, and in the *E Transepts*. Among the sculptures in the spandrels is the Worcester Crucifix, at the E end of the S aisle, with expressive figures of the Virgin and St John (restored 1862). The piers and arches are taller at the E end than in the *Presbytery*, which is built over the Norman crypt, raising the floor level considerably above that of transepts and Lady Chapel. The detached shafts of Purbeck marble were added by Bishop Giffard (1268–1302). The late Victorian stalls incorporate lively 14C **˙misericords**; the pulpit is 16C and the other furniture 19C.

The tomb of King John (d. 1216) stands in the Presbytery. It still contains his skeleton, though only the Purbeck marble **˙effigy** is contemporary with his death. The lion at the king's feet bites the end of his sword, allegedly a reference to the curbing of royal power by the barons with the signature of Magna Carta. The tomb chest is probably of the same date as the adjacent **˙Chantry of Prince Arthur**, erected in 1504, two years after the prince died at Ludlow aged only 15. Within the screenwork below are two fine effigy tombs, probably of Bishop Giffard (see above) and a kinswoman. The Lady Chapel has the tombs of Bishop Cantelupe (d. 1266) and Bishop Blois (d. 1236). On the N wall is a tablet to Izaak Walton's second wife (d. 1662), with an epitaph by him. To the left is a sensitive monument by Chantrey to Mrs Digby (d. 1820). Opposite the NE transept, now St George's Chapel, is the tomb of Bishop de Cobham (d. 1327), who built the Jesus Chapel and began the new nave. The SE transept, now the Dean's Chapel, has the tombs of Sir William de Harcourt (14C) and Sir Griffith Rice (d. 1523), and a small alabaster Madonna carved c 1470 by Nottingham craftsmen.

The many pillared *Crypt* is entered from the SW transept. Begun by Wulstan in 1084, it is the largest Norman crypt in England and the second oldest of the four apsidal crypts in English cathedrals (Canterbury is earlier, Winchester and Gloucester later). Its complexity and beauty must have been even greater in its original form, extending to the E.

The *Library* (open by prior appointment), in a room over the the S aisle of the nave, has some 4000 volumes, both manuscripts and printed books of the 15–18C.

The late 14C *Cloisters* are entered from the S nave aisle or through the richly moulded late Norman door from College Green. Of the fine roof *bosses, those in the S walk form a Jesse Tree, representing the ancestors of Christ, while in the N walk adoring angels turn towards a central boss carved with the Virgin and Child. The tombstone simply inscribed 'Miserrimus' ('Most wretched man') at the W end of the N walk, which inspired Wordsworth to a speculative sonnet, is said to be that of a Jacobite canon unable to adjust to the rule of William III. The early 12C *Chapter House* on the E side of the cloisters, a circular building with a central shaft, set the pattern for later chapter houses (at Lincoln and Wells, for example). The walls with their Norman blind arcading are made of alternate bands of green and brown stone. The windows and vaulting are Perp. alterations. On the S side of the cloisters is the monks' *Refectory*, on a vaulted Norman undercroft, which became part of King's School after the Reformation. (Both Refectory and Chapter House are open on application to the verger on duty.)

College Green, S of the cloisters, has 18C houses and the *Edgar Tower* (c 1350), once the great gate of the monastery.

The most interesting secular building in Worcester is the *Commandery* (open), off Sidbury SE of the cathedral. Originally founded as the Hospital of St Wulstan in 1085, it became a private house at the Reformation; what survives is mainly 15C. Its rich interior, with a great hall, contains exhibits of the Civil War, local trades, etc.

In Severn St., to the SW, are the *Royal Worcester Porcelain Works* (guided tours), founded in 1751 and occupying this site since 1840. The adjoining *Dyson Perrins Museum* (open) has a comprehensive collection of antique Worcester.

Friar St. and New St. leading N from Sidbury to the Old Cornmarket both have good timbered buildings. In Friar St. are the *Tudor House Museum*, dealing with the social and domestic life of the city, and *Greyfriars* (NT), mainly late 15C. In New St. are the early 16C *Nash House* and, at the Cornmarket end, *King Charles's House* (1577), where Charles II found momentary refuge after the battle of Worcester.

The pedestrianised High St., running N from the cathedral, begins with a statue of Elgar (1981). The former church of *St Helen* on the corner of Fish St. is now the County Records Office, with the marriage contract of Shakespeare and Anne Hathaway. The *Guildhall* (open), on the left beyond, is a splendid building (1721–23) by a local pupil of Wren, Thomas White. The statues of Charles I and Charles II on either side of the entrance reflect the city's politics. The assembly room inside (1791) has portraits of George III and Queen Charlotte by Reynolds. Down Church St. to the right is the church of *St Swithin*, with a Perp. tower but otherwise by E. and T. Woodward (1733–36). The remarkably complete 18C interior includes a magnificent *three-decker pulpit with mayor's chair. In Trinity St., behind, is the restored 16C *Queen Elizabeth's House*.

High St. is continued by The Cross, The Foregate and Foregate St. At the end of The Cross is the church of *St Nicholas* (1732), also by

*The Guildhall, Worcester*

White. The Foregate has *Berkeley's Hospital*, an almshouse of 1703 built in the Dutch style. The *City Museum and Art Gallery* in Foregate St. contains exhibits of geology, natural history and archaeology as well as regimental collections.

Deansway, leading from the cathedral to the Worcester Bridge over the Severn, passes the 18C street frontage of the old *Bishop's Palace* and the distinctive slender spire (1791) of the demolished church of *St Andrew*, known locally as the Glover's Needle. Opposite is the former *Countess of Huntingdon's Chapel* (1804–15), with a Regency interior, currently being restored as a concert hall for the neighbouring *Elgar School of Music*. The church of *All Saints*, at the corner of Deansway and Bridge St., was largely rebuilt in 1739–42; it contains furnishings by Sir Aston Webb and an 18C wrought-iron sword rest from the mayor's stall. The *Worcester Bridge*, built in 1771 and since widened, gives a good general view of the city. *Pitchcroft* racecourse lies to the N. The *County Cricket Ground* is on the far bank, looking across to the cathedral.

At *Lower Broadheath*, off A44 3m W, the cottage where Sir Edward Elgar was born in 1857 is now a museum with photographs, musical scores, etc. —*Wichenford*, near B4204 5½m NW of Worcester, has a half-timbered 17C dovecote (NT).—The gardens (open) of *Spetchley Park*, 3m E of Worcester on A422 towards Stratford, include a deer park.

FROM WORCESTER TO TENBURY WELLS, 23m by A443 and A456. We go up the Severn valley to (6m) *Holt Heath*, where our road turns left. *Holt*, to the right by the river, has a Norman church and the remains of its 14–16C castle (not open). *Holt Fleet*, to the N, has a bridge by Telford (1828).—9m. S of the main road and *Great Witley* stands the ruined shell of *Witley Court* (English Heritage; summer standard opening but closed on Mondays and on Tuesday afternoons), a 17C house remodelled by Samuel Dawkes in the 1860s. The Italianate ˙chapel, now the parish church, has a painted ceiling by Antonio Bellucci brought from the vanished mansion of Canons in 1747 and a monument by Rysbrack to Lord Foley (d. 1732). Abberley Hill rises N of the village.—We follow the Teme

Valley, changing to A456 near its confluence with the Rea, to (23m) *Tenbury Wells* (Rte 52).

FROM WORCESTER TO BIRMINGHAM. M5 is the fast connection between the two cities but A38 makes a more interesting journey (26m).—Beyond (4m) *Martin Hussingtree* it follows a Roman course.—7m. **Droitwich** (18,000 inhab.; Tourist Information) was known to the Romans as *Salinae* because of its salt springs. It was developed as a spa in the 19C by John Corbett, whose buildings give the town its characteristic brick and half-timbered style. The most interesting church is *St Peter's*, ½m S of the centre, where Edward Winslow (1595–1655), one of the Pilgrim Fathers, was baptised. *Hotel Impney* at Dodderhill, off A38 1m NE of the centre, is the château Corbett built for himself in 1869–75. *Hanbury Hall* (NT), off B4090 2½m E of Droitwich, is a charming Queen Anne house of 1701 with staircase and ceilings painted by Thornhill, a collection of English porcelain figures and an orangery.—We cross M5 and pass, on the right at 11m, the salt-working centre of *Stoke Prior*. Just beyond is the turning for the *Avoncroft Museum of Buildings* (open), with many different types of old building reconstructed in an open-air setting.—13m. **Bromsgrove** (43,700 inhab.; Tourist Information) has some gabled houses and a handsome Perp. church. A headstone in the churchyard honours two engine drivers whose locomotive blew up in 1840 while climbing the Lickey Incline (see below). The poet A.E. Housman (1859–1936), who spent part of his childhood in Bromsgrove, was born at *Fockbury*, 1m NW. Near *Tardebigge*, 3m E of Bromsgrove, where the church has a graceful spire of 1776, the flight of locks on the Worcester and Birmingham Canal is the longest in Britain. *Redditch* (66,600 inhab.; Tourist Information), 3m further E, is a dull place.

The road now climbs between the *Clent Hills* (1036ft; NT) on the left and the *Lickey Hills* (900ft).—17m. The large estate of *Chadwich Manor* (NT) near the top is a favourite weekend resort from Birmingham. We pass between *Rubery*, with its large hospitals, on the left and *Rednal*, with the grave of Cardinal Newman (see Rte 48).—26m. *Birmingham*, see Rte 48.

From Worcester to *Gloucester*, see Rte 42; to *Hereford*, see Rte 44; to *Shrewsbury*, see Rte 53.

# 42 Gloucester to Worcester via Tewkesbury

Total distance 25m. **Gloucester**, Rte 38A. We follow A38 throughout.—To (10m) **Tewkesbury**.—To (25m) **Worcester**, Rte 41.

Maps: OS Landranger 162, 150.

M5 runs E of A38 throughout the journey.

**Gloucester**, see Rte 38A. We take A38 N from the city, up the Vale of Gloucester.—7½m. On the left, B4213 and the unclassified road branching from it lead to (1½m) **Deerhurst**, by the Severn, with two outstanding Saxon buildings. The *church of St Mary* belonged to a Saxon monastery with a documented history from 804. The lower half of the tower is Saxon masonry, and later herringbone work can be seen on many parts of the exterior. The nave, with its EE arcades, incorporates the original choir; its Saxon apse, not rebuilt after a 15C fire, can easily be traced outside. The E wall of the tower has a curious two-light triangular-headed window; below it are a triangular opening (like several others in the N and S walls) and a blocked door once leading to a W gallery. The ancient *font has spiral ornamentation, probably earlier than the 9C. A unique feature of the 15C brass of Sir John and Lady Cassey in the N choir aisle is the named figure of their dog, 'Terri'. About 200 yards away, across the road and attached to a fine half-timbered house, is *Odda's Chapel* (English Heritage, open at any reasonable time). According to an inscribed foundation stone now in the Ashmolean Museum at

Oxford, it dates from 1056 and was built by Earl Odda as a memorial chapel for his brother Aelfric.

10m. **Tewkesbury** (9700 inhab.; seasonal Tourist Information), on the Warwickshire Avon close to its meeting with the Severn, is a handsome old town with one of the most magnificent abbey churches in England, many good half-timbered houses and pleasant riverside scenery.

The Yorkists led by Edward IV, the future Richard III and the Duke of Clarence finally defeated the Lancastrians under Margaret of Anjou at the Battle of Tewkesbury (1471), fought in the 'Bloody Meadow' 1/2m S of the town. Dickens's Mr Pickwick dined at the Royal Hop Pole on Church St. The town is also the setting of Mrs Craik's novel 'John Halifax, Gentleman' (1856).

The ***Abbey Church**, almost as large as Westminster Abbey, is remarkable for its blend of Norman and Dec. architecture and for the splendour of its medieval tombs.

The Benedictine abbey was founded in 715. The present church was begun in 1092 by Robert Fitzhamon and consecrated in 1121. Norman work on the building was brought to a close when the upper stages of the central tower were added c 1160. The tower and nave were vaulted and the ambulatory and E end were remodelled in the first half of the 14C. The church today remains substantially as it was when it was reconsecrated after the Battle of Tewkesbury, though neglect and frequent restoration have left their mark both inside and outside. Sir Gilbert Scott's work in 1875–79 provoked William Morris to form the Society for the Protection of Ancient Buildings. The splendid *central tower is the largest Norman tower in existence, with wide views over the surrounding vales and hills. The N Porch is impressively plain, while the W front is almost entirely taken up by a grand recessed arch rising nearly to roof height; the Perp. style window was added in 1686. The fanciful cluster of Dec. chapels at the E end contrast with the austerity of the Norman work.

The interior has an even more varied range of architectural beauty. Although the great pillars of the *Nave dwarf the triforium and the Dec. clerestory and vaulting (c 1340), they justify their predominance by the grandeur of their scale. Along the centre of the nave are vigorously carved roof bosses. The tower vaulting has shields and a circle of suns representing the 'sun of York' triumphant over the Lancastrians at Tewkesbury. A brass in the pavement below marks the traditional site of the grave of Edward, the young Lancastrian Prince of Wales killed in or shortly after the battle. The *Transepts* are Norman with 14C windows. The beautiful S transept contains the apsidal *Lady Chapel* with Raphael's 'Madonna del Passeggio', which once belonged to Madame de Pompadour. The transept also has a memorial tablet to Mrs Craik (1826–87).

The choir is surrounded by an *Ambulatory* with radiating chapels added in 1330–50. On the N side is the St Margaret's Chapel, with the tomb of Sir Guy de Brienne (d. 1390), and St Edmund's Chapel, with bosses showing the saint's martyrdom. Beside it is the cenotaph of Abbot Wakeman (d. 1549), with a startling effigy. Behind the high altar is the vault where the murdered Duke of Clarence and his wife were buried in 1478. The truncated Norman pillars of the *Choir* support pointed arches and a tall superstructure with a richly groined and bossed 14C roof. The brasses, monuments and 14C *windows of the choir commemorate the Fitzhamons, De Clares, Despensers, Beauchamps and other lords of Tewkesbury in its great days. Finest of all is the exquisite Perp. *Beauchamp Chantry (1422), still with traces of its original colouring. Next to it is the Fitzhamon Chantry (1397), and to the E the canopied tomb and effigies of Hugh Despenser and his wife (c 1349), who largely financed the rebuilding of the choir and E end. On the S side of the high altar is the Perp. Despenser Chantry, also called the Trinity Chapel (c 1390, restored 1983), with some of the earliest fan vaulting in England and the kneeling figure of Edward Despenser in the roof. To the E is the tomb of Hugh Despenser's father, also Hugh (d. 1326). The old organ S of the choir stalls is known as the Milton Organ, since the poet is believed to have played it when it was at Hampton Court Palace during the Commonwealth.

The only other monastic building to survive is the 15C *Abbey House*, much altered in the 18C; the nearby gatehouse is a 19C restoration.

The row of half-timbered 15C cottages in Church St. includes a countryside museum in memory of the local author John Moore (1907–67).

**Bredon**, on B4080 3m NE, has a fine Norman and Dec. church and a large 14C tithe barn (NT) restored after a recent fire. Above it is the rounded *Bredon Hill* (961ft), with a *view and an Iron Age hill-fort. *Elmley Castle*, on its NE flank, has an interesting church with the sumptuous tomb of the first Earl of Coventry (d. 1699) by William Stanton.

*Tredington*, off A38 2½m SE of Tewkesbury, has a little Norman church. At *Stoke Orchard*, on the other side of M5 1½m further, the church has five layers of wall paintings, the earliest (early 13C) depicting the life of St James of Compostela. The sideroad continues another 2m to *Bishop's Cleeve* (Rte 38A).

From Tewkesbury to *Ledbury*, see Rte 44.

We leave Tewkesbury via King John's Bridge (c 1200, rebuilt in 1963) over the Avon. The Severn Bridge is by Telford (1826). Our road continues up the Severn valley and passes under M50.—16m. Beyond the river about 1m left is *Upton-on-Severn* (seasonal Tourist Information), a pleasant little place with good 18C houses. The White Lion is usually identified as the scene of a memorable night of errors in Fielding's 'Tom Jones'.—17½m. *Severn Stoke*. Beyond M5 about 1½m E is *Croome Court*, Capability Brown's first building (1751), now a school (not open). The nearby church has 17C monuments of the Earls of Coventry and a graceful wooden font (1760). *Pirton* church, 1m N, has a half-timbered tower.—25m. **Worcester**, see Rte 41.

# 43  Gloucester to Hereford via Ross-on-Wye

Total distance 30m. **Gloucester**, Rte 38A.—A40 to (16m) **Ross-on-Wye**.—A49 to (30m) **Hereford**.

Maps: OS Landranger 162, 149.

**Gloucester**, see Rte 38A. We take A40 W from the city, crossing the Severn at 1m.—At (7m) *Huntley* we reach the outskirts of the *Forest of Dean*, explored in Rte 45B. *May Hill* (969ft), commanding a fine view, rises on the right. Shortly beyond, we enter the county of Hereford and Worcester.—14m. On the left are the Dec. tower of the church at *Weston-under-Penyard* and the woods of *Penyard Park*. Just E of Weston is the site of the Roman *Ariconium*, where iron was smelted.

16m. **Ross-on-Wye** (7200 inhab.; Tourist Information) is an attractive market town on a hill above the E bank of the Wye. The *Prospect*, by the church, gives a good view of the horseshoe bend in the river. *St Mary's Church* itself is a large Dec. and Perp. building, poorly restored in 1743 and again in 1862. The E window has glass of 1430, while the E window in the N aisle has become a trellis for a climbing tree. The many good monuments include those of the Rudhalls (1530–1651). In front of the altar is the grave of John Kyrle (1637–1724), the town's most noted benefactor, praised as the Man of Ross in Pope's third 'Moral Essay'. Kyrle's house, bearing his bust, stands in the market place by the red sandstone *Market House* of 1660–74.

# HEREFORD

| 0 | | | | 300 yards |
| 0 | | | | 300 metres |

The 'Ross Spur', part of the unfinished M50 motorway to South Wales, provides the quickest route to Birmingham, via the junction with M5.

From Ross to the *Wye Valley* and the *Forest of Dean*, see Rtes 45A and 45B.

A49, the direct road to Hereford, crosses the Wye by the *Wilton Bridge* (1597 but widened). To its N is the ruined 13–16C *Wilton Castle* (not open), destroyed by the Royalists in the Civil War.—25m. The road climbs the flank of *Aconbury Hill* (904ft), with an Iron Age hill-fort.

More attractive, and very little longer, are the sideroads which keep closer to the river between Ross and Hereford. On the E bank B4224 goes via (24m) *Fownhope*, between the *Woolhope* hills and the Wye. On the W bank, unclassified roads lead to a charming reach at (21m) *Hoarwithy* and then join B4399 near (27m) *Holme Lacy*, where the interesting church by the river has 16–19C monuments of the Scudamore family. On its way into Hereford B4399 passes (30m) *Rotherwas Chapel* (English Heritage, Saturdays and Sundays in summer only), a curious mixture of 14C, 16C and 19C work.

30m. **HEREFORD** (47,700 inhab.) stands on the Wye near the Welsh marches. Its strategic position gave the city a long and bloody part to play in military history, culminating in its misfortunes during the Civil War. Although the castle—once 'high and stronge, and full of great towres'—has all but vanished, the cathedral, medieval street pattern and several interesting old buildings survive. Hereford today is a market centre for the surrounding countryside, as well as home of a famous cider-making industry.

**Tourist Information Centre**: Town Hall, St Owen's St.

**Car Parks**: Gaol St., off Bath St., off Blueschool St., Blackfriars St., Edgar St., West St., Greyfriars Avenue, between Greyfriars Bridge and Bridge St., Wye St., St Martin's St.

**Bus Station**: Commercial Rd, NE of the centre.

**Railway Station**: off Commercial Rd.

**Theatre**: The Nell Gwynne, Edgar St.

**Annual Events**: The Three Choirs Festival (August) rotates annually between Hereford, Gloucester and Worcester cathedrals. It is next held in Hereford in 1991. Founded c 1715 and continuous since 1724, it has given first performances to works by Elgar and Vaughan Williams and is one of the finest choir festivals in the world.

**History**. The city's name is Saxon, meaning 'army ford', a clear indication that it was from early times a military post along the approaches to southern Wales. The town was laid out toward the end of the 7C, at about the same time the bishopric was founded, and the first earthwork defences built a century later to protect the area between the river and the present East and West streets. In the 10C a meeting here between King Athelstan and the Welsh chieftains fixed the Wye as the border. Ralph, the Norman nephew of Edward the Confessor, built one of the first Norman castles in England on the site now known as Castle Green, but in 1055 the town was sacked and burnt by the Welsh. Under the Normans Hereford grew into an important border garrison and trading centre. It suffered badly during the troubled reign of King Stephen, and again during the struggle between Henry III and Simon de Montfort, when de Montfort held both Henry III and the future Edward I prisoner at Hereford in 1264. Stone city walls and towers, following the course of the modern inner city ring road, had been completed by the end of the 13C. In 1326 Hugh Despenser was hanged here after his capture at Neath, and Owen Tudor was executed at High Town in 1461 after the Battle of Mortimer's Cross. During the Civil War Hereford was twice taken by Parliament and unsuccessfully besieged for a month by a Scottish army in 1645. After this the city stagnated, though in 1774 the walls and other old buildings were demolished in an attempt to modernise what was still a medieval—and notoriously unhealthy—city. But it was only in the 19C, with proper sewage and water supply and the arrival of the railway, that modern Hereford started to develop.

**Famous natives and residents**. The poet Thomas Traherne (1637–74), Charles II's mistress Nell Gwynne (1650–87) and the actor David Garrick (1717–79) were born in Hereford. The artist David Cox was a drawing master here in 1814–26.

The commercial centre of Hereford is the broad pedestrian street known as High Town. The *Old House (open), a black-and-white building of 1621, is furnished in the 17C style. In High St. to the W the church of *All Saints* has a distorted spire, late 14C carved oak stalls and a chained library (open by appointment only). Broad St. leads S from the church to the cathedral close. On the right at the bottom is the *City Museum and Art Gallery*, with a fine Roman altar and tessellated pavements, and a collection of 19C watercolours by local artists.

The ***Cathedral** is a modest building in the local sandstone. Its chief interest is the mixture of different styles and periods, and the unusual treasures it contains. Its chief weakness is the treatment it has suffered in the name of restoration.

The see of Hereford was detached from Lichfield toward the end of the 7C and a stone cathedral later built on the site where, according to legend, the ghost of the murdered St Ethelbert of East Anglia (d. 794) demanded burial. A later Saxon cathedral, ruined in the Welsh invasion of 1055, was rebuilt by the first Norman bishop, Robert de Losinga, beginning in 1079. His work was largely obliterated by Bishop de Reynelm (1107–15), grandly called 'founder of the church' on his tomb. Bishop Robert de Béthune (1131–48) completed the nave and restored the choir. Bishop William de Vere (1186–99) radically altered the E end, originally apsidal, and probably began the Lady Chapel, though this was not finished until c 1220. Later bishops refined details but increased the cathedral's lack of unity. Peter of Aquablanca built the N transept in c 1260, Swinfield (1283–1316) the inner N porch, and Adam of Orleton (1317–27) the chapter house and central tower, rising from Norman piers and arches. Bishop Booth (1516–35) added the outer N porch. The fall of the W tower in 1786 gave James Wyatt the excuse to pull down two W bays and destroy much Norman work in the nave, rebuilding after his own idea of Gothic. In 1856–63 Sir Gilbert Scott restored the whole cathedral, reconstructing what Wyatt had destroyed at the E end. Wyatt's W front was replaced by J. Oldrid Scott's pseudo-Dec. façade in 1908.

Externally, the best view is from the NE, where we can see the handsome 13C N transept and 14C tower as well as the Lady Chapel, choir and NE transept. We enter by the N porch. The 12C *Nave* is one of the richest Norman designs in England, with massive piers and elaborately carved arches. Its upper part was evilly treated by Wyatt (1788), who rebuilt the triforium, clerestory and wooden vaulting. The aisles are late Dec. on Norman lower courses. The N aisle has a monument to Bishop Booth (d. 1535) and the S aisle one to Sir Richard Pembridge (d. 1375); the sculptured Norman font nearby depicts the Apostles (cf. Mitcheldean and Newnham, both Rte 45B).

The *N Transept* was built c 1260 by Peter of Aquablanca, probably to house his own exquisitely arched and pinnacled tomb. Here too is the shrine of St Thomas Cantilupe (d. 1282), notable for its naturalistic foliage and figures of knights. Under the great window, one of the largest examples of Geometrical tracery in England, is the canopied tomb of Bishop Charlton (d. 1344). In striking contrast the *S Transept* keeps its Norman character. The primitive design of the E wall is probably Losinga's work (1079) and thus the oldest part of the cathedral. Three tapestries designed by John Piper now hang here, and there is a triptych of the South German school (c 1530). Bishop Trevenant (d. 1404), who made the Perp. alterations to the transept, lies under the S window. The coloured tomb effigies nearby are of Alexander Denton (d. 1577), his wife and child. The fireplace on the W wall is Norman in origin.

Until 1843 the *Tower Lantern*, with its many shafts and curious gratings, was hidden by a 15C roof.

The *Choir*, originally dedicated in 1110, has a rich Norman triforium below a graceful EE clerestory which, like the vaulting, dates from the 13C. The main arches are supported by massive piers and the capitals of the semi-detached

**HEREFORD CATHEDRAL**

Key to Numbers
1 Bp Booth
2 Sir Richard Pembridge
3 Bp Acquablanca
4 Bp Cantelupe's Shrine
5 Bp Charlton
6 Bp Trevenant
7 Alexander Denton
8 Bp Trilleck Brass
9 'Mappa Mundi'
10 Bp Stanbury
11 Joanna de Bohun
12 Peter de Grandisson
13 Bp Losinga

shafts are elaborately carved. The grand Norman arch to the E, surmounted by
a blind arcade, originally led to the centremost of three apses but is blocked by a
pier of the processional aisle added when the E end was altered in 1186–99. The
stalls and bishop's throne are 14C. A marble slab opposite the throne commemorates St Ethelbert, and there is a 14C statue of the saint on the S side of the
sanctuary. The 12C wooden chair to the left of the altar is said to have been
used by King Stephen in 1138. Under the carpet nearby is a good brass to
Bishop Trilleck (d. 1360).

In the N choir aisle hangs the famous *Mappa Mundi, drawn on vellum
c 1290 by Richard of Haldingham. A typical medieval map, it shows Jerusalem
in the centre and Paradise at the top, with Europe (and Hereford) at the bottom
left. (The outrageous decision to sell the map in aid of cathedral funds was
announced as this Guide was going to press). The *Chained Library (open),
now housed in the former muniments room opposite the map, has nearly 1500
chained books, the largest collection in the world. Its manuscripts include two
pages from a 7C Gospel of St Matthew, the Four Gospels (8C) and the Hereford
Breviary (1265–70). Also opening from the N choir aisle is the Perp. *Chantry

of Bishop Stanbury (d. 1474), with rich fan vaulting and heraldry; his alabaster tomb is across the aisle. The S choir aisle has 14C effigies of early bishops.

The *E Transepts* were built on the site of the Norman apsidal chapels between c 1190 and 1370, most of the work dating from 1290. The SE transept contains a bust by Roubiliac, probably of James Thomas (d. 1757).

The *Lady Chapel* (1220) is a beautiful example of EE work, especially the clustered window shafts and the (restored) lancets at the E end. On the S side is the 15C tomb of Precentor Swinfield, with his swine rebus, and behind a screen of painted stone is the *Chantry of Bishop Audley (1492–1502). On the N side are the effigy tombs of Joanna de Bohun (d. 1327) and Sir Peter de Grandisson (d. 1358). Below the chapel is the EE *Crypt* (open) of c 1220, the last to be built in an English cathedral. It is now the Treasury.

From the SE transept the *Vicars' Cloister*, a covered walk with a carved oak roof, leads to the quadrangular *College of Vicars Choral* (1475). The *Bishop's Cloister*, with two Perp. walks, leads from the S side of the nave. The remains of the ten-sided 14C *Chapter House* can be seen off the E walk, in the garden between the two cloisters. The W walk, demolished in 1760, was partly replaced by a two-storey building in 1897.

The *Cathedral School*, immediately E of the cathedral, dates back to 1381 and includes the cathedral choristers among its pupils.

The *Bishop's Palace* (not open) stands between the cathedral and the river. A tablet on the wall of the bishop's garden in Gwynne St. marks the supposed site of Nell Gwynne's birthplace.

King St. and Bridge St. go on from the cathedral to the *Wye Bridge* (1490 but widened in 1826), which is relieved by the modern Greyfriars Bridge (1966) further upstream. From the neighbouring Greyfriars Avenue we can walk W along the near bank of the river to the *Herefordshire Waterworks Museum*, a 19C pumping station with its machinery in working order. *Bishop's Meadow*, with a river walk, extends E from Wye Bridge along the far bank to the Victoria Footbridge, which crosses to Castle Green.

*Castle Green*, by the river SE of the cathedral, marks the site of Hereford's castle. The pool on its N side was part of the moat. In the middle is a column (1809) to Nelson.

We return to High Town along St Owen's St., passing the *Town Hall* (1904) and Tourist Information Centre, the *Shire Hall* (1819; Smirke) and *St Peter's Church*, with 13C steeple and 15C stalls.

Commercial St. runs NE from High Town and becomes Commercial Rd after it crosses the ring road, marking the line of the old walls. At (c 3/4m) the corner of Venns Lane beyond the railway station is the *Churchill Gardens Museum*, a Regency house exhibiting 18–19C costumes and furniture.—Widemarsh St. runs N from High Town, passing a plaque marking the site of Garrick's birthplace at the corner of Maylord St. and then crossing the ring road and the line of the walls. The *St John and Coningsby Museum*, on the right at c 1/2m, was an almshouse for old soldiers and servants, established in 1614 on the site of a Hospital of the Order of St John. The heavily restored chapel dates from c 1200. The garden has a 14C preaching cross and other relics of a Dominican house founded in 1322.—The pedestrianised Eign Gate leads from the W end of High St. to the ring road. Victoria St., to the left, has some remains of the 13C walls. Eign St., Whitecross St. and Whitecross Rd (A438) continue W, passing (left) the *Museum of Cider* and (right) the *Bulmer Railway Centre* (limited opening), with several historic railway engines. The heavily restored *White Cross*, at 1¼m, was erected in 1361 by Bishop Charlton in thanksgiving for the departure of the Black Death, during which markets were held here.

Beyond *Swainshill*, 5m W on A438 to Hay-on-Wye, *The Weir* (NT) is a garden overlooking the Wye. *Kentchester*, 1/2m N, is the site of the Roman *Castra Magna*, on the road from Wroxeter near Shrewsbury to Caerleon. *Credenhill*, near A480 another 1/2m N, has a tablet to the poet Thomas Traherne in the church where he was rector in c 1657–66. *Brinsop*, 1m further, has a small church with a Norman tympanum (c 1150) and a memorial window to Wordsworth and his sister Dorothy, several times guests at nearby Brinsop Court.—At *Madley*, on B4352 6m W of Hereford, the *church has a 13C nave and 14C apse over a vaulted crypt. The 12C N porch was a transept of an earlier church. *Moccas Court* (limited opening), 5m further, is a plain red-brick house by Robert Adam (1775–81) in a park by Capability Brown (1778).—At **Kilpeck**, 7m SW of Hereford off A465 to Abergavenny, the well-restored *church has some of the richest Norman carving in the country. Especially noteworthy are, on the outside, the S doorway and W window and, inside, the chancel arch and the apse. At *Abbey Dore*, off A465 about 5m W, the *church preserves the mainly EE choir and transepts of a Cistercian abbey church (1180–c 1280). On the opposite bank of the river Dore are the gardens (open) of Abbeydore Court.

From Hereford to *Worcester*, see Rte 44; to *Shrewsbury*, see Rte 52; to *Hay-on-Wye* and *Abergavenny*, see 'Blue Guide Wales'.

# 44  Worcester to Hereford: The Malvern Hills

Total distance 31m. **Worcester**, Rte 41.—A449 to (7m) Great Malvern.—A449 to (16m) Ledbury.—A438 to (31m) **Hereford**, Rte 43.

Maps: OS Landranger 150 and 149.

An alternative, less interesting route from Worcester to (28m) Hereford on A44 and A465 swings N of the Malvern Hills via the high-lying *Bromyard Downs* and (14m) **Bromyard** (Tourist Information), with many half-timbered houses. *Lower Brockhampton House* (NT), 2m NE of Bromyard, is a late 14C moated manor with a half-timbered 15C gatehouse. Only the hall is open.

**Worcester**, see Rte 41. We leave the city on A449, heading SW and crossing the Teme at (2m) *Powick Bridge*. The *Malvern Hills rise sharply from the flat landscape ahead.

*The Malvern Hills, looking north towards the Worcestershire Beacon*

This narrow range of hard Pre-Cambrian rocks, mainly gneiss, runs from N to S for about 9m, separating the Severn Plain around Worcester from the rolling countryside around Hereford. There are about twenty summits, averaging only a little over 1000ft, with intervening faults eroded into hollows. The chief hills, from N to S, are West Hill, North Hill, Sugarloaf Hill, the Worcestershire Beacon (the highest point, 1395ft), the Herefordshire Beacon, Swinyard Hill, Midsummer Hill, Hollybush Hill, Ragged Stone, and the Gloucester Beacon (or Chase End). Most can be climbed by easy paths, with benches. The many springs and wells have made Malvern water famous. The region is intimately connected with the music of Sir Edward Elgar (1857–1934), whose local roots are traced by the Elgar Trail, described in a useful pamphlet available from the Worcester or Great Malvern Tourist Information Centres.

7m. **Great Malvern** (30,200 inhab.; Tourist Information), on the slopes to the left of A449, is the chief of several places which take their name from the hills. St Ann's Well on the side of the nearby Worcestershire Beacon had made the town a fashionable spa by the 1820s, and it still keeps the atmosphere of a genteel inland resort, aided by its many hotels and its public school, Malvern College, founded in 1863. The Malvern Festival, held at the Festival Theatre and Winter Gardens in late May, is largely devoted to Shaw's plays and Elgar's music.

The fine *Priory Church*, with a tower recalling that of Gloucester Cathedral, looks entirely Perp. from the outside but its interior is largely that of the original Norman building (c 1085), with massive round piers in the nave. Much 15C glass survives, notably in the N transept window, with a portrait of Prince Arthur, eldest son of Henry VII. The choir screen is panelled with locally made 15C *tiles, and there are good monuments and misericords.

Above the church stands a restored Perp. gateway of the Benedictine priory where William Langland (1330?–1386?), author of 'Piers Plowman', is thought to have been educated.—The opera singer Jenny Lind (1820–87) is buried in the cemetery near the railway station.
    *North Hill* (1307ft), with a good view of the town and its church, takes about ½hr to climb from Great Malvern. On the other side of the hill, reached by B4232, *West Malvern*, looks across to the Herefordshire hills. The *Royal Well* (1150ft) is nearby.

Beyond Great Malvern A449 swings round to follow the line of hills from N to S.—8m. The *Worcestershire Beacon* (1395ft), on the right, commands a splendid *view that includes 15 counties, the cathedrals of Hereford, Worcester and Gloucester, the abbeys of Malvern, Tewkesbury, Deerhurst, Evesham and Pershore, the Wrekin (N) and the Brecknock Hills (W). B4232 branches right from A449 near the Beacon, making its way S via *Wyche Cutting* and the *Jubilee Drive* to rejoin the main route near (4m) the Herefordshire Beacon.—10m. *Malvern Wells* has the Holy Well (680ft). To the E is the *Three Counties Showground*, where the agricultural fair is held in June. —At (11m) *Little Malvern* the 14C church is a relic of the Benedictine priory founded in 1171. Little Malvern Court incorporates the 14C Prior's Hall (limited opening). Elgar is buried in the Roman Catholic cemetery.—The hills continue S of Little Malvern but A449 veers W to (12m) *Wynd's Point* (830ft), the pass between the main ridge and the *Herefordshire Beacon* (1114ft). On top of the Beacon is a hill-fort with medieval additions where, according to tradition, Caractacus was captured in AD 75.

A449 descends to (16m) **Ledbury** (Tourist Information), a busy little town on the slope of the hill. The 17C *Market House*, perhaps by John Abel, still stands on its original tall chestnut pillars. The *Feathers* and the *Talbot* are late 16C inns with fine interiors. The large *Church* is mainly 13–14C, with a massive detached tower and good monuments, notably the Skynner Tomb (1631) in the chancel and a rare 13C effigy of a priest in the N transept. In the churchyard lies Jacob Tonson (d. 1736), publisher of Dryden and Pope. *Ledbury Park* (not open) is a gabled manor of 1590. William Langland, author of 'Piers Plowman', may have been born at Ledbury; John Masefield (1878–1967) was a native, and Elizabeth Barrett Browning (1806–61) spent much of her early life in the neighbourhood.

*Bosbury*, on B4220 3m N, has many interesting old houses, notably the Crown inn. The church contains two Harford family tombs, one of them (1573; John Guldo) the oldest signed monument in England. *Castle Frome*, by B4214 1½m farther N, has a magnificent *font of c 1150, with a vivid Baptism of Christ of the Hereford school of sculpture.—At *Much Marcle*, 4½m SW of Ledbury, *Hellen's* (limited opening in summer, otherwise by written appointment) is a manor house dating from the 13C. Attractive lanes lead NW over Marcle Hill to Woolhope (see below) and Hereford.

FROM LEDBURY TO TEWKESBURY, 14m by A438.—2m. *Eastnor Castle* (limited opening) is a massive exercise in medievalism by Sir Robert Smirke (1812–15). As well as its collection from Italy, which includes some 17C panelling, the interior is rich in Victoriana, with decoration by Pugin (1849) and George Fox (1860s) and recently installed frescoes by G.F. Watts.—The road continues across the S tip of the Malverns, passing near (7m) *Birtsmorton*, with a delightfully unspoilt 12–16C moated manor (not open) where Wolsey was chaplain c 1503–7.—14m. *Tewkesbury*, see Rte 42.

From Ledbury to *Gloucester*, see Rte 38A.

We follow A438 N and W from Ledbury through a rich countryside of orchards and hop gardens. The wooded hills around *Woolhope*, to the left, command wide views; see also Rte 43.—23m. *Tarrington* church has a fine 12C chancel arch.—31m. **Hereford**, see Rte 43.

# 45   Ross-on-Wye to Chepstow

## A.   The Wye Valley

Distances: 26m on the direct route, 33½m including the detours to Goodrich and Symond's Yat Rock. **Ross-on-Wye**, see Rte 43.—A40 to (11m) **Monmouth**.—A466 to (21m) Tintern.—A466 to (26m) **Chepstow**.

Maps: OS Landranger 162 or OS Outdoor Leisure map (1:25,000 or 2½in to 1m).

The Wye (Welsh *Gwy*, water) rises in Wales on the slopes of Plynlimon, only 2m from the headwaters of the Severn, and flows SE and E via Rhayader, Builth Wells and Hay to Hereford. It then turns S, flowing past Ross-on-Wye and Monmouth to join the Severn just below Chepstow—a total course of 130m. The *valley of the lower Wye between Ross and Chepstow, where the river meanders and loops back on itself between wooded cliffs and gorges, is among the finest inland scenery in Britain. Its natural beauty is enhanced by the border castles at Goodrich and Chepstow and the incomparable Tintern Abbey.

This reach of the river first became popular toward the end of the 18C, when tourists—Wordsworth and Coleridge among them—satisfied their eye for the picturesque by admiring the views which

William Gilpin's influential travel guide (1782) commended and their appetite for Gothic by making moonlit visits to Tintern. The tourists continue to come in large numbers, but except for the obvious beauty spots near the major roads it is not the sort of countryside that can easily be made to feel unpleasantly crowded.

Offa's Dyke, the great earthwork which the Mercian king (757–795) built along the western border of his territory between the Dee and the Severn, ran near the E bank of the Wye from Monmouth to Chepstow. The Offa's Dyke Path established by the Countryside Commission loosely follows its course and incorporates the surviving stretches of the dyke. Another long distance walk, the Lower Wye Valley Walk, follows the river from Hereford to Chepstow (about 50m); further details are available from local Tourist Information Centres. There are also forest trails on both banks.

**Ross-on-Wye**, see Rte 43. We leave the town by Wilton Bridge and join A40, heading S.—4m. An unclassified road leads left to (³/₄m) *Goodrich Castle** (English Heritage, standard opening and summer Sunday mornings), standing on bedrock above the river.

It takes its name from Godric, who built the first fortress at the beginning of the 12C. Of today's ruins, the grey sandstone keep is mid 12C and the other buildings, in red sandstone, are 13C. The castle belonged to the Earls of Pembroke for most of the 13C, passing in c 1326 to the Talbots, later Earls of Shrewsbury. It was slighted after the Civil War, during which it had been held successively by the Parliamentarians and the Royalists. Wordsworth met the little girl who inspired 'We Are Seven' here in 1793.

A farm near Kerne Bridge, ¹/₂m E, preserves some domestic remains of *Flatesford Priory* (1347). Below, the river makes a long loop and the scenery becomes more varied. Its right bank belongs to Herefordshire and its left bank to Gloucestershire.

*Symond's Yat Rock** (pronounced 'Sim-') lies 3m S of Goodrich. The rock (473ft) is a famous beauty spot, rising between two reaches of the Wye only 500 yards apart at their nearest point. Its peak commands a glorious view of the river as it loops through wooded scenery: to the E are the steep *Coldwell Rocks*, where the Wye makes a wide bend to the N, while to the SW the river sweeps round the Great Doward (see below). There is an orientation table, and the log cabin by the Forestry Commission car park has information about geological and forest trails. B4432 leads S into the Forest of Dean (Rte 45B).

We return to A40.—6¹/₂m. *Whitchurch* was the childhood home of the artist Wilson Steer (1860–1942). B4164 leads left to the popular village of (1m) **Symond's Yat** below the rocks which here wall the Wye. Beyond Whitchurch A40 skirts the hills of *Great Doward* (661ft) and *Little Doward* (700ft) to the left. On the S slope of Great Doward is *King Arthur's Cave*, reached by sideroads and paths, where excavation has discovered signs of human use from the late Ice Age (c 12,000 BC) to Roman times as well as fossil remains of mammoth, rhinoceros and hyena. There is an Iron Age hill-fort on Little Doward, between the cave and *Ganarew* on A40.—Shortly beyond Ganarew we enter the Welsh county of Gwent, so named in 1974. It was previously Monmouthshire which, though strongly Welsh in character, had been removed from the jurisdiction of the Lords Marchers and included among English counties by Henry VIII in 1535.

11m. **Monmouth** (7400 inhab.; Tourist Information), county town of the old Monmouthshire, is a pleasant market centre on the W bank of the Wye above its meeting with the Monnow. Probably the site of the Roman *Blestium*, it grew up around the 12C castle and Benedictine priory. For the most part its street plan has been unchanged since the 15C.

The chronicler Geoffrey of Monmouth (d. 1155), born in the town, may have been a monk at the priory. Henry V (Harry of Monmouth; 1387–1422) is thought to have been born in the castle.

Agincourt Square, the old market, is the town centre. The *Shire Hall* (1724) carries a statue of Henry V; in front is one of the Hon. Charles Rolls (d. 1910), one of the founders of Rolls Royce and a native of nearby Hendre. Of the *Castle*, approached by Castle Hill roughly opposite Shire Hall, little survives apart from the early 12C keep (or Great Tower). The adjoining *Great Castle House* (1673) is army property. Priory St., leading N from the square, has the *Market Hall* (rebuilt 1969) with a local history centre and a collection of Nelson relics. *St Mary's Church*, a short way NE, stands on the site of the priory church. Largely rebuilt by G.E. Street (1881), it still has its graceful Dec. spire and, in the baptistery, some 15C tiles and a cresset stone from the earlier church (c 1102). Monnow St. leads S from Agincourt Square to the *Monnow Bridge*, the only example in Britain of a gatehouse actually standing on a bridge. Just beyond is the small, over restored Church of *St Thomas Becket*, with a Norman chancel arch and N door (c 1180).

Across the river 1m E is *Kymin Hill* (850ft; NT), with a 'temple' built in 1800 to honour Nelson's admirals, commanding a *view over the Wye and the Monnow.

For Usk, 13m SW, and for the route W from Monmouth to *Abergavenny* via *Raglan Castle*, see 'Blue Guide Wales'.

From Monmouth to the *Forest of Dean* to the E, see Rte 45B.

We cross the Wye and branch right on A466. The valley narrows, and for the rest of the way road and river run close together.—Beyond (13m) *Redbrook*, the left bank belongs to Gloucestershire and the right to Gwent. A stretch of Offa's Dyke survives on the wooded heights of the Gloucestershire bank.—At (16m) *Bigsweir Bridge* A40 crosses to the Gwent bank.—17¹/₂m. *Llandogo* is beautifully placed in a fold of the steep wooded hills.—20m. Near (20m) *Brockweir*, a former port and shipbuilding centre on the Gloucestershire bank, there is another stretch of Offa's Dyke. For *Hewelsfield*, 2m E, see Rte 45B.

21m. *Tintern Abbey* (Cadw, Welsh Historic Monuments; open) stands on a patch of level ground by the river against a backdrop of tree-covered hills. Despite the ugliness of its immediate surroundings, it is still probably the most romantic Cistercian ruin in Britain.

It was founded in 1131, but little remains of this first abbey and most of what survives today dates from the 13C and 14C. After being dissolved in 1536 the abbey mouldered quietly away until the vogue for ruins at the end of the 18C made it popular with tourists. It inspired a famous poem by Wordsworth and was painted by Turner.

The entrance leads through an excellent exhibition centre. The *Church*, by far the most interesting of the buildings to survive, is on the far (S) side of the precinct. Its chief feature (best viewed from outside the site) is the great W window of seven lights above the W doorway, with its twin trefoil-headed openings. The nave, mostly late 13C, still has its clerestory on the S side. Beyond the four large and beautiful crossing arches that once supported the

*Tintern Abbey*

tower is the huge, superbly proportioned *E window covering almost the whole of the wall.

The remains of the domestic buildings (1220–70) on the N side of the church are relatively unimportant. The size of the Lay Brother's Refectory at the NW corner of the main *Cloister* is a reminder that, with the Cistercian emphasis on agriculture, lay brothers usually outnumbered monks. From the vestry on the E side of the cloister there is a door into the N transept, which incorporates remains of the original 12C church, as well as having the night stairs to the monks' dormitory and a six-light window with much of its tracery. Beyond the *Infirmary Cloister* and its attached buildings to the NE is the *Abbot's Lodging* with his hall, camera and chapel.

The abbey made much use of the river as a waterway, and the neighbouring Anchor Hotel is on the site of the Watergate; a 13C arch leading to the slipway can be seen. Just W of the abbey, beside the car park, the *Guest House* and other buildings have been excavated.

*Chapel Hill Walk* (1½m) and *Barbadoes Walk* (2m) are waymarked walks in Tintern Forest to the W, both starting from the Forestry Commission car park ¼m up the Llanishen road.

For the surviving stretch of Offa's Dyke across the Wye SE of Tintern, see Rte 45B.

Below Tintern the Wye is tidal, making so many loops and bends on its way to Chepstow as almost to double the direct distance of 4m. A40 climbs above the river.—23m. *Wyndcliff* (650ft; the 'y' is pronounced long) is a popular viewpoint, reached either by steps from the car park on the main road or by taking the sideroad to the right $\frac{1}{2}$m beyond and following the path from the car park. The view includes the Severn and the Severn Bridge, prominent to the S, the Mendips beyond and the Cotswolds in the E.—24$\frac{1}{2}$m. On the left is *Piercefield Park* with Chepstow racecourse.

26m. **Chepstow** (9000 inhab.; Tourist Information) is an old market town on the W bank of the Wye above its junction with the Severn. It grew up around the Norman castle, and developed into a prosperous port and shipbuilding centre in the 18C and early 19C.

The *Castle* (Cadw, Welsh Historic Monuments; open), separated from the town by a ravine, is strikingly placed on a steep platform of rock washed by a broad reach of the Wye.

It was founded soon after the Conquest by William FitzOsbern, Earl of Hereford, and is unusual for having been built of stone from the outset. In its present form it dates mainly from the 14C.

We enter through a gatehouse of 1225–45 flanked by drum-towers. On the N of the inner ward are the remains of domestic buildings. This part of the castle, overhanging the cliff, gives a good view down to the river and upwards to the Great Tower. On the SE of this ward is Marten's Tower, so called because the regicide Henry Marten was held here from 1660 until his death in 1680; Jeremy Taylor was also a prisoner, in 1655. Beyond the middle ward is the Great Tower of the original castle (1067–72); its E door and the S and W wall arcades are the oldest part of the building. The upper ward and the barbican lie beyond.

The *Museum*, across Bridge St. from the castle car park, is devoted to local history. Two bridges cross the river nearby; the road bridge dates from 1816 and the railway bridge, although modernised, was originally built by Brunel. *St Mary's Church*, ruthlessly restored in the 19C, belonged to the Benedictine priory. The Norman nave, aisle and W door survive; inside are the tomb of Henry Marten and interesting monuments. The 13C *Port Wall* which enclosed the town to the S and W can be traced for much of its course, one good place being the main car park off Beaufort Square. The W gate spanning the main street, though probably more or less true to the original design, was rebuilt in 1524.

The S end of Offa's Dyke is across the Wye 2m SE, between B4228 and Sedbury Cliffs.

From the *Severn Bridge*, just over 1m S of the town centre, to *Bristol*, see Rte 20.—From Chepstow to *Gloucester* via the *Forest of Dean*, see Rte 45B.

# B.   The Forest of Dean

Maps: OS Landranger 162 or OS Outdoor Leisure map (1:25,000 or 2$\frac{1}{2}$in to 1m).

The **Forest of Dean** is a steeply edged plateau occupying the wedge of land between the lower Wye and the Severn estuary. The average height is about 650ft, though Ruardean Hill in the N rises to 951ft. Its oak and beech woodlands were reserved as a royal forest by Edward the Confessor, and in 1938 the region became the first National Forest Park (34,000 acres). The many forest trails make it an excellent area for walking.

The long history of mining gives the Forest an added interest. The Romans first extracted iron ore from the limestone inner rim of the plateau at the Scowles, near Bream. Iron-mining flourished in the

Middle Ages, with 'free miners' enjoying special rights, and lasted until the 19C. Today the old 'bell pits' are overgrown. Coal-mining was carried on near the centre of the Forest, with large-scale workings in the region between Coleford and Cinderford. It too has been abandoned and replanting by the Forestry Commission has helped conceal the ugliest effects, though an industrial atmosphere still lingers in some of the towns.

The routes suggested below head E across the region from Monmouth and Chepstow (Rte 45A) towards Gloucester (Rte 38A).

FROM MONMOUTH VIA MITCHELDEAN TO A40, 16m on A4136. we leave Monmouth by crossing the Wye and following A4136 NE. The road climbs round the side of *Kymin Hill* (Rte 45A) and (2¾m) the *Buckstone* (951ft), with a rocking stone and a *view.—We reach the outskirts of the Forest of Dean at (3¾m) *Staunton*, where the church is partly Norman, like several on the fringes of the forest. For *Coleford*, 2m SE, see route below.—6m. B4228 and then B4432 head N through *Berry Hill* to (2½m) *Symond's Yat Rock* (Rte 45A). The woodland on the left has several forest trails.—A4136 continues to (11m) *Nailbridge*. At *Ruardean*, 2m NW on B4227, the church has a *carving of St George and Dragon (c 1150) on the tympanum of the porch, by the Hereford school of sculpture. *Ruardean Hill* (951ft) makes a good viewpoint.—13½m. *Mitcheldean*, a recently expanded town, has some half-timbered houses and a 14–15C church with a distinctive slender spire rebuilt in c 1760, a fine carved oak roof and a

*St George and the Dragon, carved on the tympanum at Ruardean church*

Norman font showing the Apostles (cf. Newnham, below, and Hereford Cathedral). At *Abenhall*, ³/₄m S, the church has a 15C font with the arms of local free miners.—16m. A4136 joins A40 near *Huntley* and *May Hill*, on the way from Gloucester to Ross-on-Wye (Rte 43).

FROM CHEPSTOW TO GLOUCESTER VIA COLEFORD AND CINDERFORD, 33m. We leave Chepstow by crossing the river on A48 and branch left at 1m on B4228.—2m. *Wintour's Leap* is a 100ft precipice with a view over the Wye.—3m. A fragment of Offa's Dyke (English Heritage, open at any reasonable time) lies between our road and the river.—4m. There is a picnic site and viewpoint in the woods to the left.—At (6m) *Hewelsfield*, right of B4228, the village church has a Norman tower and nave. For *Brockweir* and Offa's Dyke, left of the road, see Rte 45A.—7¹/₂m. *St Briavels*, in a high position overlooking the Wye valley, has a partly Norman church and a 13C castle, now a youth hostel.—9¹/₂m. B4321 leads left to (³/₄m) *Clearwell*, where Clearwell Castle is a Gothick building of 1727, now a hotel, and the *Caves* (open) are old iron mines, with a museum and geology exhibition. At *Newland*, 1¹/₂m NW, the spacious church is known as the 'Cathedral of the Forest'. It has a Dec. spire and a 15C brass depicting a free miner.—B4228 goes on to (12m) *Coleford*, where we head N and E on B4226 to (15¹/₂m) *Speech House*, in the centre of the Forest. Now a hotel, it was built in 1676 as a courthouse for the Foresters of Dean. There are forest trails in the woods to both N and S; the New Fancy Trail leads to a good viewpoint 2m S.—B4226 continues E to (18m) *Ruspidge* and (19m) *Cinderford* (seasonal Tourist Information), once a coal-mining centre. For the Soudley valley to the S, see route below.—We take A4151 W to (19¹/₂m) *Littledean*. *Littledean Hall* (open) is a 16–17C building, with oak-panelled rooms, on older foundations. The grounds have good views.—A4151 joins A48 at (22m) *Elton*, on the route to (33m) Gloucester described below.

FROM CHEPSTOW TO GLOUCESTER VIA A48, 28m. A dull road following the Severn estuary, with the Forest to the N.—8m. *Lydney* has a fine 14C cross. The grounds (limited opening) of *Lydney Park* contains a deer park and the remains of a 12C castle and Roman temple, with a museum of excavated objects. From *Bream*, on B4231 3m NW, a path leads to the Roman iron workings called the Scowles. The *Norchard Railway Centre* on B4234 1m N of Lydney is headquarters of the Dean Forest Railway, with old steam locomotives.—11m. *Nibley*. A considerable fragment of Roman road has been exposed at *Blackpool Bridge*, on B4431 2¹/₂m NW.—11¹/₂m. *Blakeney*. B4227 leads up the Soudley Valley, with the *Dean Heritage Museum* at (2m) *Lower Soudley*.—15m. *Newnham* is a charming little town on a bend in the river. The rebuilt church has a Norman font depicting the Apostles (cf. Mitcheldean, above, and Hereford Cathedral).—At (17m) *Elton* we are joined by A4151 from Cinderford (see route above).—18¹/₂m. at *Westbury-on-Severn* the church has a detached 13C tower with shingled 14C spire. *Westbury Court Garden* (NT) is a formal water-garden laid out at the end of the 17C.—23m. *Minsterworth* is a good place to see the Severn Bore (Rte 38A).—25m. We join A40, heading E for (28m) *Gloucester* (Rte 38A).

# 46   London to Northampton and Leicester

Total distance 96m.—To (45m) Milton Keynes, see Rte 39B.—A5, A508 to (64m) **Northampton**.—A508 to (82m) Market Harborough.—A6 to (96m) **Leicester**.

Maps: OS Landranger 176, 166, 165 (briefly), 152, 141, 140 (briefly).

Less interesting for the major towns along the way than for the smaller places and the detours.

We follow Rte 39B along A5 to (45m) **Milton Keynes**.

An alternative to the main route to Northampton described below follows A422 N from Milton Keynes to (5m) *Newport Pagnell* (10,800 inhab.). *Chicheley Hall* (limited opening), on A422 2m NE, is a lovely baroque house (1719–23) by Francis Smith of Warwick. The outside has a richly carved frieze, capitals and doorcase. Inside, the hall is by Henry Flitcroft, and there is handsome wood panelling in several rooms. For *Olney*, further N, see the detour from Northampton to Bedford below.—From Newport Pagnell we follow B526 to (7½ m) *Gayhurst*. The elegant *church of c 1728, by an unidentified architect, contains an expressive monument to Sir Nathan Wright and his son. It stands beside the Elizabethan mansion (not open) where the gunpowder conspirator Sir Everard Digby (1578–1606) lived and his son Sir Kenelm Digby (1603–65) was born.—To the left near (9m) *Stoke Goldington* the tall steeple of *Hanslope* church can be seen.—We join A508 shortly before (18m) *Northampton* (see below).

The main route leaves A5 at (51m) the roundabout beyond *Stony Stratford*, heading N on A508.—57m. *Stoke Bruerne*, left of the road, is a charming place on the Grand Union Canal (Rte 39B) near the S end of the Blisworth tunnel. The **Waterways Museum** is devoted to the history of the canal. In *Stoke Park* (limited opening of gardens and exterior) two pavilions and a colonnade survive from the earliest English house on a Palladian plan (1630), attributed to Inigo Jones. —We cross M1.—On the way into Northampton, after (63m) the junction with A45, we pass an *Eleanor Cross, one of three which survive from the series marking the overnight stops in the funeral procession of Queen Eleanor of Castile in 1290. See Lincoln (Rte 72) for further details. Just beyond is the 16–19C *Delapré Abbey*, now the County Record Office (gardens open; limited opening of public rooms), on the site of the Cluniac nunnery where the queen's body lay.

64m. **NORTHAMPTON** (162,000 inhab.), the county town, is a manufacturing centre known for its long history of shoemaking. A dull place with much nondescript modern development, it has little to interest visitors except its fine churches, St Peter, All Saints and St Sepulchre.

**Tourist Information Centre**: No. 21 St Giles St.

**Car Parks**: Victoria Promenade, Commercial St., St Johns, Albion Place, Horsemarket, Upper Mounts. Multi-storey car parks in Mayorhold, Lower Mounts and Grosvenor Centre.

**Bus and Coach Station**: Greyfriars, with access from Grosvenor Centre.

**Railway Station**: Castle Station, W of town centre.

**Theatre**: Royal Theatre, Derngate.

**History**. The castle which Simon de Senlis, first Earl of Northampton, built in this ancient Saxon town soon after the Norman Conquest became a favourite resort of kings and the site of several great councils and parliaments. St Thomas Becket was tried at the castle in 1164, and Shakespeare laid the first scene of 'King John' in the great hall. A decisive battle (1460) in the Wars of the Roses was fought outside the town walls. Northampton sided with Parliament during the Civil War, and one of Charles II's first acts was to raze its castle and walls. It suffered a disastrous fire in 1675.

**Famous natives and residents**. Robert Browne (?1550–?1633), leader of the Brownist sect which founded Congregationalism, died in Northampton jail (see St Giles's church below). Philip Doddridge (1702–51) was minister at the Congregationalist church for the last 22 years of his life. The poet John Clare (1793–1864) was an inmate of the county asylum here from 1841 until his death. Spencer Perceval, the Prime Minister assassinated in 1812, and the rationalist reformer Charles Bradlaugh (1833–91) were MPs for Northampton.

From Castle Station, on the site of the vanished castle, Marefair leads towards the centre of town. On the right is *St Peter, one of the finest late Norman parish churches in England, dating from c 1160. The most interesting features are the richly carved arch on the W front and, inside, the massive W tower arch and the carved capitals of the piers. There is also a fine Saxon cross shaft. The *Congregational Church* in Doddridge St., to the left, dates from 1695. It has a monument to its former minister Philip Doddridge (d. 1751).

Gold St. continues Marefair to *All Saints, handsomely rebuilt after the fire of 1675. Its early 18C Ionic portico, with a statue of Charles II in Roman costume, was a favourite haunt of John Clare when he was allowed out of Northampton asylum. The church is nicely complemented by the *County Hall* (1682) on the opposite side of George Row. The *Guildhall* in St Giles Square is florid Victorian Gothic (1864, enlarged in 1892). The *Museum and Art Gallery* in Guildhall Rd has paintings by 15–18C Italian artists and by the Norwich School, British ceramics, collections of local geology and archaeology, and an interesting display tracing the history of footwear.

St Giles St. leads from the Guildhall to the church of *St Giles*, Perp. with Norman fragments. Robert Browne, founder of the Brownist sect, is buried here.—The RC church of *St John* in Bridge St. uses the converted almshouse and chapel of a medieval hospital of St John. The chapel has a fine Perp. W window.

N of All Saints is the big Market Square, where the main market is held on Wednesdays, Fridays and Saturdays. At the NE corner the rebuilt façade of *Welsh House* (1595) survives the destruction of much of the neighbourhood to make way for the nearby *Grosvenor Centre* and other development in the 1960s and 1970s. From the NW corner Sheep St. leads past the house where Dr Doddridge had his academy to *St Sepulchre, one of only four round churches to survive in England. (The others are at the Temple in London, Cambridge and Little Maplestead in Essex.)

The tower and spire are late 14C. The round part, with its eight Norman pillars supporting late 14C arches, was built c 1100–15 by Simon de Senlis on his return from the Crusades. It resembles its prototype, the Church of the Holy Sepulchre in Jerusalem, more closely than the other English round churches. The present nave is a 13–14C enlargement of the original Norman choir, while the present choir dates from 1860–64. On the N wall is the quaint Coles brass (1640).

Further N, in Barrack Rd, is the *Roman Catholic Cathedral*, much enlarged from a church of 1844 by Pugin.—Abington St., a shopping thoroughfare leading NE from the Market Square, is continued by Wellingborough Rd to the *County Cricket Ground*, on the left, and *Abington Park*, on the right. The manor house contains the *Abington Museum*, with period rooms, Chinese ceramics and Natural History collections. Shakespeare's grand-daughter Lady Bernard (d. 1670) lived here and is buried in the S chapel of the old village church.—In Kettering Rd, branching left from Wellingborough Rd, the 19C church of *St Matthew* has a stone Madonna and Child (1944) by Henry Moore and a painting of the Crucifixion (1946) by Graham Sutherland.

6m NW on A428 towards Rugby is **Althorp** (open), the family home of the Princess of Wales and hence extremely popular with visitors in recent years. The 16C house was remodelled several times, notably in the 1730s by Roger Morris, who designed the splendid entrance hall, and in the 1780s by Henry Holland. It contains a large and distinguished *collection of pictures, furniture and china, part of it inherited from Sarah, Duchess of Marlborough. The portraits include work by Reynolds and Gainsborough in the Marlborough Room and by Van Dyck, Lely and Kneller in the Picture Gallery.

The church of *Great Brington* on the W side of the park contains the *tombs of the Spencers from 1522 onwards and is the burial place of George Washington's ancestors Laurence (d. 1616) and Robert (d. 1622), who moved from Sulgrave (Rte 39A).—Off A428 about 3m beyond Althorp are: *Holdenby House* (limited opening of gardens; house open to parties by appointment), 2m E, a Tudor house where Charles I was held prisoner in 1647; *Coton Manor Gardens* (limited opening), 2m N; and *Guilsborough*, 1m beyond Coton, with glass by Morris and Co. in the church and a former school building of 1668.

FROM NORTHAMPTON TO BEDFORD VIA OLNEY, 21m. A428 crosses *Yardley Chase*, a wide tract of moorland with fine oaks.—7m. *Yardley Hastings*. About 1¹/₂m N is *Castle Ashby House* (open to parties of 25 or more by prior appointment), an Elizabethan mansion with additions in the 1630s, sometimes ascribed to Inigo Jones, including a lettered balustrade. It has a noted collection of furniture and paintings (Reynolds, Kneller, Raeburn). The church has interesting monuments. At *Easton Maudit*, 2m E of Castle Ashby, the antiquarian Thomas Percy of 'Percy's Reliques' was vicar from 1753 to 1782. The church has 17C monuments of the Yelvertons.—Shortly beyond Yardley Hastings we branch right on B5388 to (10¹/₂m) *Olney* (3500 inhab.) a charming little town in the northern tip of Buckinghamshire. In the market place the red-brick house where William Cowper lived with Mrs Unwin in 1768–86 is now the *Cowper and Newton Museum*. It has relics of the poet and his friend John Newton (d. 1807), perpetual curate of Olney, as well as an exhibit of the local lace-making industry. From the river Ouse there are beautiful views of the early Dec. *Church* with its tall spire. The handsome village of *Weston Underwood*, 2m SW, was Cowper's home from 1786 until 1795. The church at *Ravenstone*, 1m further, has good 18C woodwork and the elegant tomb, perhaps by Joseph Catterns, of Lord Chancellor Finch, Earl of Nottingham (d. 1682), founder of the adjoining almshouses.—B565 rejoins A428 just before (13m) *Cold Brayfield*. —14m. *Turvey* has a large, interesting church with an early 14C painted *Crucifixion and fine 16C monuments of the Mordaunts. *Clifton Reynes*, on the Ouse 3m W, has 13–14C wooden effigies in its church.—From (18m) *Bromham* a sideroad leads about 3m NW to *Stevington*, with a restored 18C post windmill. *Stagsden Bird Gardens* (open), on A422 2m SW of Bromham, is a breeding centre for pheasants, waterfowl and owls.—21m. *Bedford*, see Rte 47B.

FROM NORTHAMPTON TO HIGHAM FERRERS, 15m. A45 is the faster road but A4500, the old Wellingborough road, is more convenient for the sightseer. Both run parallel to the Nene.—3¹/₂m. *Great Billing* has a pretentious monument of 1700 by John Bushnell in the church. *Little Billing*, 1m SW, has a remarkable Saxon font.—4¹/₂m. *Ecton* was the home of Benjamin Franklin's ancestors until his father left for New England in 1685.—On the right at 6¹/₂m is *Earls Barton*, where the church is famous for its late Saxon *tower, the most important work to survive from this period in England. *Whiston* church, 1¹/₂m SW, is a lovely example of late Perp. (1534). For *Castle Ashby*, further S, see the detour from Northampton to Bedford above.—10m. **Wellingborough** (39,600 inhab.) is an old town above the Nene. The parish church of All Hallows has good misericords and modern windows by John Piper and Patrick Reyntiens. St Mary's is a florid building (1908–30) by Sir Ninian Comper.—We join A45 for the last part of the journey to (15m) *Higham Ferrers* (Rte 47B).

From Northampton to *Banbury*, see Rte 39A.

A508 continues due N from Northampton, past (70m) the Pitsford reservoir, to (71m) *Brixworth*, with the kennels of the Pytchley hunt. The Saxon *church, originally built c 680 with bricks from local Roman buildings, shows three distinct phases of work before the Conquest. *Spratton*, 2¹/₄m W, has a Norman and Trans. church containing the effigy of Sir John Swinford (d. 1371), with the earliest known example of the SS collar.—73m. *Lamport Hall* (limited open-

*The Saxon tower of Earls Barton church*

ing), right of our road, was built by John Webb in the 1650s and extended by Francis Smith of Warwick and his son in the 1730s. —76m. The battlefield of *Naseby*, where the Parliamentarian army defeated Charles I and Prince Rupert in 1645, lies 4m W of the road beyond *Haselbech*. A column put up in 1936 marks the correct site.

We enter Leicestershire just before (82m) **Market Harborough** (16,000 inhab.; Tourist Information), a fox-hunting centre. The market place has the grammar school of 1614 and *St Dionysius*, a Perp. church with a beautiful Dec. broach spire. Nearby is the house where Charles I is said to spent the night before Naseby. The *Museum* in the Council Offices on Adam and Eve St. is devoted to local history.

From Market Harborough to *Rugby*, see Rte 39B.

We continue N on A6.—88m. *Kibworth* has some 17–18C houses and an old post mill of 1711. Philip Doddridge (see Northampton, above) was dissenting minister here in 1723–25.

96m. **LEICESTER** (282,300 inhab.), the county town, is an unattractive place. The pervasive effects of its industry and manufacturing—in the outer sprawl of 20C housing estates, inner ring of 19C red-brick terraces and ghastly redevelopment of the centre—make it hard to appreciate the real points of interest, chiefly its Roman remains and several good museums.

**Tourist Information Centre**: No. 12 Bishop St.

**Car Parks**: Multi-storey parks in St Peter's Lane (off Vaughan Way), St Nicholas Circle, Lee Circle, Haymarket, etc.; also Abbey St. and Welford Rd.

**Bus Station**: St Margaret's, Abbey St.

**Railway Station**: London Rd, SE of the centre.

**Theatres**: Haymarket Theatre and Studio Theatre, The Haymarket; The Little Theatre, Dover St.; Phoenix Art Theatre, Upper Brown St.

**History**. According to tradition, King Lear and his daughters lived at Leicester. The Romans made it the fortified town of *Ratae Coritanorum*. It was the seat of the East Mercian bishopric from 680 to 869, but soon afterwards became one of the five towns of the Danelagh (hence the suffix 'gate', from the Danish 'gade', which survives in the street names). It was recovered by Ethelfleda, the daughter of Alfred the Great, in 918. After the Norman Conquest it fell to Hugh of Grantmesnil, who built the castle, and in 1239 to Simon de Montfort, Earl of Leicester and a great benefactor of the town. Lancastrian kings acknowledged its importance by holding three parliaments here in the 15C and by making frequent visits to the castle, though Richard III had to sleep at an inn on his way to Bosworth Field in 1485. Prince Rupert besieged and captured Leicester during the Civil War (John Bunyan serving in the defending army), but Parliament recovered it after the Battle of Naseby. Subsequent prosperity came from the hosiery trade, encouraged by the introduction of the stocking frame in the late 17C. In 1800 the population still stood at only 17,000, a reminder (if the visitor needed one) that most of Leicester's growth belonged to the industrial era.

**Famous natives and residents**. Thomas Cooper (1805–92), the Chartist, was born here. Thomas Cook, Secretary of the Leicester Temperance Society, took his first pioneer step as a tour operator when he organised a railway excursion to Loughborough and back in 1841.

The former centre is now virtually closed to traffic and it is difficult to see the *Clock Tower* (1866), with statues of Simon de Montfort and other local benefactors, as the hub of converging main roads which developed outside the Roman E gate. It is approached from the railway station to the SE by Granby St., the chief shopping thoroughfare. From East Gates the Roman main street ran W to the Soar Bridge; the High St. follows the medieval line a little to the N. The High Cross stood where it met the old thoroughfare from N to S, now Highcross St. and its continuation, in St Nicholas Circle.

To the right Highcross St. leads past the site of the Free Grammar School of 1573 (plaque). Beyond the inner ring road are *All Saints*, a well-proportioned early Dec. church with a Norman W doorway, clock of c 1620 and EE font, and, to the E, *St Margaret*, with a noble Perp. tower and chancel and fragments of Saxon masonry at the E end of the N aisle. The fine *Great Meeting* (1708), one of the oldest Nonconformist chapels, survives in East Bond St. behind St Margaret's Baths and the car park on Vaughan Way.

By the intrusive new St Nicholas Circle stands the church of **St Nicholas**, the oldest in Leicester, built partly of Roman materials with an attractive early Norman tower, a primitive Saxon nave and an EE chancel. On the W side of the churchyard rises the **Jewry Wall** (English Heritage, open at any reasonable time), a mass of Roman masonry with bonding courses of brick and four recessed arches. It may have been the W wall of a basilica in the Roman forum, which

# LEICESTER

| 0 | 500 yards |
| 0 | 500 metres |

extended E and N, or part of the later Roman baths, which can be seen in plan to the W. Beyond is the **Jewry Wall Museum**.

A museum of archaeology up to the Middle Ages, its important *Roman exhibits include several mosaic pavements (notably the Peacock mosaic, and Cyparissus and his stag), large wall paintings, a wooden bucket with bronze decoration, and milestones from the Foss Way. The columns outside come from a colonnade in the forum.

The adjoining *Vaughan College* is the University's Department of Adult Education.

Beyond *West Bridge* over the Grand Junction Canal, St Augustine's St. leads to *Bow Bridge* over the Soar, where a plaque records the last resting place of Richard III. Tradition maintains that his body, brought back from Bosworth for burial in the Greyfriars monastery, was thrown into the river at the Reformation but afterwards reburied near here.

Castle St. leads from the opposite side of St Nicholas Circle to *St Mary de Castro, an interesting church with an unusual ground plan. The original Norman collegiate church was enlarged with a chancel in the richest late Norman style (after 1150) and, in the EE period, a massive tower and a wide parochial nave on the S side. Noteworthy features include: the Norman N doorway, arcading in the N aisle, windows and sedilia; the Dec. roof and the original chancel; the EE sedilia; the Perp. roof in the S nave; and the 13C font. The few remains of Leicester's once famous *Castle* are reached through a timber gateway (1445). *Castle House*, on the right, incorporates the domestic buildings. In the secluded Castle Yard, where Wesley used to preach, a facade of c 1698 masks the late Norman hall, divided into three in 1821, so that only the N and S ends are visible. (Now an assize court, it is open when not in use.) A doorway from the hall can be seen in the W wall of the church.

The *Turret Gateway* (1423) leads into the Newarke, the 'new work' added to the castle in 1332. The rebuilt *Trinity Hospital* was founded in 1331 by Henry of Lancaster and enlarged in 1354 by his son Henry, Duke of Lancaster, who died here in 1361. Mary Bohun (d. 1394), mother of Henry V, is buried in the partly original chapel. The *Newarke Houses Museum*, occupying two 16–17C buildings, illustrates the social and industrial history of Leicester since the Middle Ages with 17C panelled rooms, a 19C street scene and collections of clocks and musical instruments. Beyond are the various buildings of the *Polytechnic*. The splendid early 15C *Magazine Gateway*, isolated amid the traffic, houses the Museum of the Royal Leicestershire Regiment.

Southgates or the more peaceful Castle St. lead back N to St Nicholas Circle. *Wygston's House* in the pedestrian Applegate E of the cirle is now a museum of 18–20C costume. The old civic church of **St Martin**, raised to cathedral status in 1926, stands on a cramped site in Peacock Lane. Originally EE, with a Perp. chancel, it was largely refashioned in 1844–67 by Raphael Brandon. To its W is the *Guildhall* (open), a 14–16C building which originally belonged to the Guild of Corpus Christi. The great hall is imposing, and the mayor's parlour has a fine 17C chimneypiece, woodwork and stained glass. The Town Library, whose foundation in c 1587 makes it one the earliest free municipal libraries in England, was first installed here about 1633.

A little to the E of cathedral and Guildhall is the *Market Place*, now under permanent roofing, where the main markets are held on Wednesday, Friday and Saturday. The old *Corn Exchange* has a fine outside staircase (c 1851). To the S are the *Town Hall* (1875) and the

*Central Library.* King St., beyond, leads to the *New Walk*, a long tree-lined pathway laid out in 1785, with the **Museum and Art Gallery**.

It contains impressive displays of geology and natural history, and an ancient Egyptian gallery. The large art collection covers a wide range but is particularly strong in 19–20C English painters (the Bloomsbury circle, L.S. Lowry, Stanley Spencer) and the German Expressionists.

University Rd leads to the right from the end of New Walk and passes *Victoria Park*, with the *De Montfort Hall* and Lutyens's fine *War Memorial*, on the way to the **University of Leicester**, which received its charter in 1957. The main building, originally a hospital, dates from 1837; the Department of Engineering (1959–63; James Stirling and James Gowan) is conspicuous among the modern additions. The neighbouring *Wyggeston Boys' School* can trace its origins to a charitable foundation of 1513.

Haymarket and Belgrave Gate, leading NE from the Clock Tower, are continued beyond the inner ring road by Belgrave Rd. To the left are *Abbey Park*, with a lake, and the remains of **Leicester Abbey**, where Cardinal Wolsey came to die in 1530. His tomb has disappeared, and little is left of the rich Augustinian monastery except the conjectural foundations and the boundary wall. Further N, in Corporation Rd off Abbey Lane, a sewage pumping station with Victorian beam engines is now the *Museum of Technology*. Off Belgrave Rd further N is *Belgrave Hall* (open), a Queen Anne house with charming gardens, now a period museum of coaches and agricultural equipment.

**Charnwood Forest** is a wooded, hilly region of granite and slate rising out of the plain NW of Leicester. A convenient tour leaves the city on A50 and branches left to (4¹/2m) *Groby*. Elizabeth Woodville, later Edward IV's wife, lived at the manor house with her first husband, Sir John Grey. A sideroad leads N, below A50 and past the attractive Groby Pool, descending to (6¹/2m) *Newton Linford*. *Bradgate Park* (open), with old oak trees and herds of red and fallow deer, is the best place to see the natural appearance of the forest. The ruined Bradgate House (open) was the birthplace of Lady Jane Grey, the 'nine days' queen' (1537–1554).—About 2m NW of Newton are the 14C remains of *Ulverscroft Priory* (not open).—We can continue to *Bardon Hill, Mount St Bernard* and *Grace Dieu*, described in the detour from Leicester to Burton below, or return via *Cropton Reservoir, Thurcaston* (where Bishop Latimer was born in 1485) and *Rothley*.

FROM LEICESTER TO BURTON-UPON-TRENT, 25m by A50. The disused line to Swannington was Robert Stephenson's first railway (1832).—4¹/2m. *Groby*, see above. *Kirby Muxloe*, 2¹/2m S, has the remains of a moated, brick-built *castle begun in 1480 by William, Lord Hastings and never completed (English Heritage, standard opening but closed on Wednesday afternoons and on Thursdays in winter).—Beyond (10m) *Bardon Hill* (912ft), a famous viewpoint in Charnwood Forest on the right, we enter the Leicestershire coalfield.—12m. *Coalville* (30,800 inhab.; Tourist Information) is a mining and brick-making town. *Donington-le-Heath*, 1m SW, has a restored 13C manor house (open). The Trappist monastery of *Mount St Bernard*, remotely situated in Charnwood Forest about 3m NE of Coalville, was founded in 1835, the first new abbey in England since the Reformation. Its fine church was begun by A.W.N. Pugin in 1840 (partly open). Beyond Whitwick 3¹/2m N of Coalville is *Grace Dieu*, with the scanty remains of a 13C Augustinian nunnery (seen in a field skirted by A512) and the manor house where Francis Beaumont (1584–1616) was born.

17m. **Ashby-de-la-Zouch** (11,500 inhab.; seasonal Tourist Information) is a pleasant little town. Its ruined *Castle (English Heritage, standard opening but closed on Thursdays and alternate Fridays in winter), originally Norman and 14C, was refortified by William, Lord Hastings in 1474–76 and slighted by the Parliamentarians during the Civil War. The late Perp. church of *St Helen*, nearby, has a rare 15C recumbent effigy of a pilgrim, and the tombs of the second Earl of Huntingdon (d. 1561) and Selina, Countess of Huntingdon (d. 1791), Wesley's friend. The 'Tournament Field' was made famous by Sir Walter Scott's 'Ivanhoe' lies about 1m N of the town. About 2m E is *Coleorton Hall* (National Coal Board), where Wordsworth, his sister Dorothy and Coleridge advised the owner, Sir George Beaumont (d. 1827), on the landscaping of his grounds. *Appleby Magna*, off A453 5m SW of Ashby, has a handsome early 14C church and a moated 15–16C manor house (not open), while *Appleby Parva*, ³/4m beyond, has a grammar school of 1693–97.—From Ashby to *Derby*, see Rte 55, to *Nottingham*, see Rte 57.—A50 passes (20m) *Swadlincote* (23,400 inhab.; Tourist Information).—25¹/2m. *Burton-upon-Trent*, Rte 48.

FROM LEICESTER TO GRANTHAM, 30m. A607 branches right from A46, the Foss Way, shortly before (4¹/₂m) *Syston* and follows the valley of the Wreake. The village names ending in 'by' show Danish occupation.—6m. *Quenborough*, to the right, was Prince Rupert's headquarters during the siege of Leicester.—7m. *Rearsby*. There is a fine early 14C church at *Gaddesby*, 2¹/₂m E.—8¹/₂m. *Brooksby*, where George Villiers, Duke of Buckingham, was born at the hall in 1592, has a beautiful little Perp. church.—15m. **Melton Mowbray**, see Rte 57. —We cross the limestone outcrop of the Leicestershire Wolds, for which (20m) *Waltham-on-the-Wolds* is a good centre. *Sproxton*, 3m E, has a complete 10C cross.—From (26m) *Denton*, with a 13–15C church, we can reach *Belvoir Castle* (Rte 59).—27m. *Harlaxton Manor*, one of the most extravagant 19C mansions in the country, was built to the designs of Anthony Salvin and its owner, Gregory Gregory, in the 1830s. It is now an extension college of the University of Evansville, Indiana.—30m. *Grantham*, see Rte 59.

From Leicester to *Rugby*, see Rte 39; to *Birmingham*, see Rte 48; to *Derby* and *Sheffield*, see Rte 55.

# 47   London to Stamford

## A.   Via A1

Total distance 91m. To (21m) Hatfield.—To (24m) Welwyn Garden City.—To (32m) Stevenage.—To (39m) Baldock.—To (77m) Norman Cross.—To (91m) **Stamford**.

Maps: OS Landranger 176, 166, 153, 142, 141 (briefly).

A1 bypasses the towns—including all those listed above—and becomes motorway for several stretches, though the frequent round-abouts on the non-motorway parts and the heavy lorry traffic make it unpopular with some long-distance travellers. For some of the way it follows a historic route. Ermine Street, the Roman road from London to the North, ran via Ware and Huntingdon (now A10, A14; Rte 68) but coincided with A1 between Alconbury and Colsterworth, N of Stamford, before continuing (as B6403 and A15; Rte 72) via Lincoln and the Humber ferry. The Great North Rd, the old coaching route, began by following the present A1000 through Barnet and Potters Bar to Hatfield and Welwyn, and then B197 between Stevenage and Baldock, but joined the present A1 between Biggleswade and Markham Moor, N of Newark. The journey up A1 is continued in Rte 59 (Stamford to Doncaster) and Rte 85B (Doncaster to Durham, Newcastle and Berwick).

A1 becomes motorway from (15m) the junction with M25 until just short of (21m) **Hatfield** (29,000 inhab.), developed as a 'satellite town' of London after the Second World War. The old town stands on the Great North Road, 1m E. Its church has the striking tomb of Lord Burghley's son Robert Cecil, first Earl of Salisbury (d. 1612), a small 13C effigy of a knight and a monument by Nicholas Stone (1617). In a fine park E of the town is *Hatfield House (open), one of the largest and most splendid Jacobean mansions in the country.

It was built in 1607–12 for the first Earl of Salisbury by Robert Lyminge, architect of Blickling Hall; like the Norfolk house, it uses red brick with stone dressings. The S front, originally the main entrance, has a stone clock tower and loggia (now closed in to form the armoury) which have been attributed to Inigo Jones. Notable inside the house are the screen and minstrels' gallery in the Great Hall, the elaborately carved oak staircase by John Bucke, and the chimneypiece by Maximilian Colt in King James's Drawing Room. The large collection of paintings includes portraits of Elizabeth I by Isaac Oliver and Nicholas Hilliard and a delightfully informal portrait of the first Marchioness of Salisbury by Reynolds. In the grounds stands the surviving part of the old Palace (1497), where Elizabeth I was living in confinement when her sister Queen Mary died in 1558.

24m. **Welwyn Garden City** (pronounced 'Wellin'; 47,000 inhab.; Tourist Information), E of the road, was begun in 1920 on the same principles as Letchworth (see below) and later expanded as a satellite town in conjunction with Hatfield.—27m. *Welwyn* (9000 inhab.), W of A1, is the old town. Edward Young (1683–1765), author of the lugubrious 'Night Thoughts', was rector here. The railway crosses the graceful *Digswell Viaduct* (1848–50), 1m E.

A pleasant stretch of country, missed by the motorway, can be reached by taking B656 via (1½m) *Codicote*. At *Ayot St Lawrence*, 2¾m W, *Shaw's Corner* (NT) was the home of George Bernard Shaw from 1906 until his death in 1950. It remains virtually unaltered since his day.—4½m. **Knebworth House** (open) has been the ancestral home of the Lyttons since 1492. Its fantastic 19C Gothic exterior, impressive only from a distance, conceals the core of the Tudor house within. The Banqueting Hall has a fine early 17C screen and gallery, and later 17C wood panelling in the neo-classical manner. The State Drawing Room, refurbished by Edward Bulwer-Lytton, first Baron Lytton (1803–73), is a spirited piece of Victorian medievalism. The house also preserves the novelist's study, with mementoes of his friend Dickens. At *St Paul's Walden*, 3m NW, the church has a *choir of 1727.—9m. **Hitchin** (30,000 inhab.; Tourist Information) is a handsome market town with narrow streets and old inns. The fine 12–15C parish church has good screens, a 15C font and several brasses. George Chapman (1559?–1634), playwright and translator of Homer, is said to have been born in Tilehouse St., where there are many 16–18C houses. From Hitchin to Bedford, see Rte 47B.—A600 and A6001 lead via (15m) *Henlow*, with its large RAF camp, to rejoin A1 at (19m) *Biggleswade* (see below).

A1, here motorway, continues N past Stevenage and Baldock.—32m. **Stevenage** (74,000 inhab.; Tourist Information), with a wide High St., was developed to the E in the 1950s as another of London's satellite towns. Edward Gordon Craig (1872–1966) was born here. 4m E is the village of *Benington*, with the *Lordship Gardens* (limited opening). —39m. **Baldock** (6700 inhab.), a pleasant old town where the Great North Road crossed the Icknield Way, has a broad High St. and a church with a fine 15C rood screen. The name is a corruption of 'Baghdad', recalling that Baldock stood on land belonging to the Knights Templar.

*Ashwell*, 4½m NE, has a 14C church with a striking tower which preserves a curious graffito of old St Paul's Cathedral. The Town House, now a village museum, is one of many good houses in the attractive main street.

FROM BALDOCK TO LUTON, 14m by A505.—2m. **Letchworth** (31,800 inhab.), the first 'garden city' in England, was founded under the inspiration of Ebenezer Howard in 1903.—5m. *Hitchin*, see above.—8m. *Great Offley* has several monuments by Joseph Nollekens in the church.—14m. *Luton*, see Rte 47B.
  From Baldock to *Cambridge* via *Royston*, see Rte 68.

We enter Bedfordshire before (46m) *Biggleswade* (11,600 inhab.), a dull town to the E.

At *Ickwell*, about 2m W of A1, the clockmaker Thomas Tompion (1638–1713) was born.—The airfield at *Old Warden*, 1m further, has the *Shuttleworth Collection* (open) of historic planes and cars. Nearby is the *Swiss Garden* (open), dating from the 19C. The earlier house on the site of *Southill Park* (not open),

1¹/2m S of Old Warden, was the birthplace of Admiral John Byng (1704–57), shot 'pour encourager les autres' after the loss of Minorca. Henry Holland designed the present house for the Whitbread family in the 1790s.

At (50m) *Sandy*, near the foot of a sandstone ridge, we cross a road from Cambridge to Bedford (Rte 47B).—We cross the Great Ouse beyond (52¹/2m) *Tempsford*.—57m. *Eaton Socon* lies near another route from Cambridge to Bedford. **St Neots** (21,200 inhab.), on the far bank of the Great Ouse 1¹/2m NE, has a fine Perp. church tower.

From St Neots B1043 follows the river via (3m) *Great Paxton*, where the church has Saxon work inside, to (8m) *Godmanchester* and (9m) *Huntingdon*, both Rte 68.

From St Neots to *Higham Ferrers*, see Rte 47B.

62m. *Buckden* has a Perp. church overshadowed by the remains of the 15C brick palace of the Bishops of Lincoln, now belonging to the RC Claretian Missionaries. Catherine of Aragon lived here between her divorce and her retirement to Kimbolton. B661 leads W to the reservoir at *Grafham Water*.—65m. A604 goes E to (1¹/2m) *Brampton* and (3¹/2m) *Huntingdon*, both in Rte 68.—Beyond (67¹/2m) *Alconbury* A1 is joined by A14 from Huntingdon and follows the line of Ermine Street.

At *Little Gidding*, about 5¹/2m NW of Alconbury, Nicholas Ferrar (1592–1637) founded the Anglican community remembered in T.S. Eliot's 'Four Quartets'. Ferrar's tomb stands outside the W door of the little church, largely rebuilt in the 18C.

75m. *Glatton*, W of A1, has a big, handsome church with a Perp. tower.—76¹/2m. *Stilton*, also W, gave its name to the cheese, which was not made in the neighbourhood but brought by waggon from Leicestershire to be taken to London by coach. Its sale at the 17C Bell Inn ceased in 1964 after 170 years.—77m. At *Norman Cross*, now a roundabout, French prisoners were held during the Napoleonic Wars. A15 branches NE to (5m) *Peterborough*, Rte 68.—Beyond (81m) the intersection of A1 with A605 from Peterborough to Oundle stood the important Roman station of *Durobrivae*, from which Ermine Street crossed the Nene and followed a straight line to Stamford. An earlier Roman road, King Street, headed due N.—At (83¹/2m) *Wansford Station* the Nene Valley Railway preserves steam trains and operates a section of the old track running 5m E to Nene Park and Orton Mere. An extension further E towards Peterborough is planned.—At (85m) *Wansford*, with a handsome old inn, Rte 47B joins our route.—87m. *Wittering* church, W of the road, has a Saxon arch.

91m. **STAMFORD** (16,200 inhab.) can fairly claim to be the most handsome town of its size in England. It stands on the Welland, between the fens of Eastern England and the limestone country of the Midlands, from which it takes its building stone. The street plan and parish churches survive from the days of its medieval importance, but Stamford's chief glory is the almost unequalled range of 17–19C houses and civic buildings.

**Tourist Information Centre**: Stamford Museum, Broad St.

**Car Parks**: Bath Row, Wharf Rd, Scotgate, North St.

**Bus Station**: Sheepmarket.

**Railway Station**: off Station Rd in St Martin's, S of the river.

**Annual Events**: Stamford Festival every July. The Stamford Shakespeare Company stages amateur productions at Tolethorpe Hall, off A6121 2m NE, from June to early August. The famous Three-Day Horse Trials are held in the park of Burghley House every September.

**History**. Standing at a convenient crossing of the river Welland, Stamford (the 'stone ford') is a natural centre for settlement. It became one of the five Danelagh towns after the Danish invasion of the 9C, and after the Conquest acquired a castle and town walls enclosing the area N of the river. The Domesday Book (1086) calls it a market, but in the Middle Ages Stamford was chiefly notable for the number of its religious foundations and parish churches. The arrival of seceding students from Oxford in 1333 briefly made it a serious competitor to the older university. After the Reformation the town developed as an important coaching stop and trading centre on the Great North Road, as its 17–19C houses still testify. It was saved from further development in the 19C by the decision to route the main railway line through Peterborough. In 1967 it became the first town in England and Wales designated a Conservation Area under the Civic Amenities Act.

**Famous natives and residents**. Daniel Lambert (1770–1809), who weighed 52 stone 11 lb (739 lb; 335 kg) at his death, is buried in the cemetery of St Martin's. John Clare (1793–1864), who worked at Burghley House in 1809, was first helped to public notice by a local bookseller. The conductor Sir Malcolm Sargent (1895–1967), a native of Stamford, is buried in the cemetery off Little Casterton Rd.

We begin S of the river on St Martin's High St.—a fine, largely 18C streetscape giving equally handsome views toward the centre of town. The late Perp. church of *St Martin* contains the tombs of Lord Burghley (1520–98), Queen Elizabeth's Lord Treasurer, and other members of the Cecil family, and late 15C *glass from Tattershall and other Lincolnshire churches. The *George*, at the foot of the hill, is an old coaching inn with a sign still spanning the roadway.

We cross the Welland and climb the hill towards the prominent EE tower and Dec. *spire of *St Mary*. On the left we pass a Norman archway into St Mary's Passage and on the right the *Town Hall*

(1777). The largely Perp. interior of St Mary's contains the elaborate monument of Sir David Phillips (d. 1506) and his wife. Beyond the church St Mary's St. goes left towards Red Lion Square (see below), but it is worth turning right instead. On the left we pass the former Stamford Hotel, a grand Regency building, and on our right the *Old Theatre* of 1768 where Edmund Kean and Sheridan played, now an Arts Centre. St George's Square, beyond, is a delightful little backwater with the *Assembly Rooms* of 1725 (also used by the Arts Centre) and the church of *St George*. Its chancel and clerestory were rebuilt in 1449 at the expense of Sir William Bruges, first Garter King of Arms, and some of the old glass refers to founder members of the Garter.

Maiden Lane, with 16C buildings, leads N to the pedestrianised High St., where the former church of St Michael, largely 19C, has been made into shops. The *Public Library* opposite is converted from the old meat market (1804). St Paul's St., continuing High St. to the right, has the buildings of *Stamford School*, founded in 1532, with a 12–13C chapel. Lord Burghley, Lord Northcliffe and Sir Malcolm Sargent were pupils. The gateway opposite is the only relic of Brazenose Hall, said to have been built for the Oxford students in 1333 and otherwise demolished in 1688. At the road fork by the hospital further E is the gateway of *Whitefriars*, founded in 1285, where Richard II held council in 1392. Opposite, a plaque commemorates the site of *Greyfriars* monastery, founded in 1220. Joan, Fair Maid of Kent, the wife of the Black Prince, was buried here in 1385.

In Priory Rd, to the SE, the Benedictine *St Leonard's Priory* has remains of c 1090 and a W front of 1150.

We walk back along St Paul's St. and branch right on Star Lane. This brings us into Broad St., with many 18C houses, where the market is held on Fridays. The *Museum* on the left, with the Tourist Informa-

*Stamford in the eighteenth century: a print by Samuel and Nathaniel Buck*

tion Centre, has exhibits of local archaeology and crafts. On the right is the most impressive of Stamford's many almshouses, *Browne's Hospital*, founded c 1480.

Red Lion St. continues Broad St. down into Red Lion Square. *St John*, to the left, is a Perp. church with good woodwork. *All Saints*, immediately to our right, is mainly EE with Perp. additions, including the tower and spire, and curious external arcading. The impressive interior has some fine brasses.

The little Barn Hill, leading beyond All Saints, has some good Queen Anne and Georgian houses, while nearby Scotgate has 17C almshouses.

The old brewery in All Saints St. has been reopened as a *Brewery Museum*. The street and its continuation, St Peter's St., lead W above the bus station and past several almshouses to the site of St Peter's Gate, dismantled in 1770 when more almshouses were built here. Petergate, running N, has the only one of Stamford's defensive towers to survive. Rutland Terrace enjoys a good view of the Welland valley. Several charming old lanes, such as King's Mill Lane and St Peter's Vale, lead down to the waterfront.

**Burghley House** (open), 1¼m SE off B1443 towards Barnack, was built for the great Lord Burghley in 1560–87. The palatial *exterior, and particularly the exuberant and fantastic skyline with its profusion of Renaissance motifs, make a wonderfully dramatic effect in the wide and graceful parkland. The interior, extensively remodelled and redecorated in the 1680s, is disappointing by comparison. The Chapel has an altarpiece by Veronese and, like other rooms, carving attributed to Grinling Gibbons. The State Rooms are dominated by Antonio Verrio's massive, uninspired paintings on ceilings and walls. The very large art collection (for which a full catalogue is available) contains some interesting portraits.

B1443 continues about 2m beyond Burghley to *Barnack*, famous for its building stone. The church has a Saxon *tower (c 1000) and a beautiful EE porch and font.—*Wothorpe*, by A43 1m SW of Stamford, has the remains of the 17C mansion once occupied by George Villiers, second Duke of Buckingham (not open).—*Little Casterton*, on the site of a Roman station 2m N of Stamford, has an EE church.

From Stamford to *Oundle* and *Bedford*, see Rte 47B; to *Rutland Water* and *Nottingham*, see Rte 57; to *Doncaster*, see Rte 59.

# B.  Via Bedford and Oundle

Total distance 93m. A5, A5183 to (19m) St Albans, see Rte 39B.— A1081 to (30m) Luton.—A6 to (49m) **Bedford**.—A6 to (63m) Higham Ferrers.—A605 to (77m) **Oundle**.—A605, B671 to (86m) Wansford.— A1 to (92m) **Stamford**, see Rte 47A.

Maps: OS Landranger 176, 166, 153, 141, 142.

A devious route by comparison to Rte 47A but particularly interesting beyond Bedford, with several different ways of crossing Northamptonshire from Higham Ferrers to Stamford.

From London to (19m) *St Albans*, see Rte 39B.—We take A1081 N via (24m) *Harpenden* (27,900 inhab.), with pleasant green spaces on its High St.

We enter Bedfordshire on the way to (30m) **Luton** (165,000 inhab.; Tourist Information), traditionally a centre of straw-hat making but now with engineering and motor works. There is little of interest except the fine church of *St Mary*, NE of the station. It has a 14C tower and, inside, good Dec. work and the Wenlock Chapel (1461), with a late Perp. screen, remarkable double arch, monuments and brasses. The tabernacled stone font canopy (c 1330–40) was given by Phillipa of Hainault. The *Museum and Art Gallery* in Wardown Park contains exhibits of local history, including the straw-plait and lace industries.

*Luton International Airport*, SE of the town, has passenger services to Amsterdam, Brussels, Connaught, Cork and Dublin, and charter services to holiday resorts in Spain, Italy, the Canary Islands, Malta, Tunisia, Portugal, Morocco and Greece.

**Luton Hoo** (open) stands 2m S of Luton in a fine park by Capability Brown. The house, originally built by Robert Adam in 1767–74 but altered, gutted by fire and reconstructed, is less interesting than its contents. The *Wernher collection includes medieval ivories, Renaissance bronzes and jewellery, tapestries from Beauvais and Gobelins, English porcelain and Fabergé jewellery. Among the many fine paintings are work by Bermejo, Lippi, Altdorfer and the 17C Dutch school (Hobbema, van Ostade, de Hooch, Metsu, Dou, Wouwermans), as well as portraits by John Hoppner and Sargent.

From Luton to *Baldock*, see Rte 47A.

We take A6 N from Luton, passing (40m) *Silsoe*. *Wrest Park* (English Heritage, open in summer season at weekends and Bank Holidays only), ³/₄m E, a house of 1834–39 in the French style, has 18–19C landscaped grounds and garden buildings. Attached to the church at *Flitton*, 1¹/₂m W of Silsoe, is the mausoleum of the de Grey family with 16–19C tombs (English Heritage, open at any reasonable time).—41m. *Clophill* lies 3m E of **Ampthill** (5800 inhab.; Tourist Information), a handsome little town in hilly countryside. The mainly Perp. church has a monument to Richard Nicholls (1624–72), first English governor of New York, with the cannon ball which is said to have killed him at the Battle of Solebay (Rte 60).

*Ampthill Park*, ¹/₂m W on the Woburn road, has a memorial cross with an inscription by Horace Walpole marking the site of Ampthill Castle, where Catherine of Aragon lived during the divorce proceedings in 1531–33.—On a ridge N of the town, by B530, stands the still elegant shell of the early 17C *Houghton House*, built for the Countess of Pembroke, Sir Philip Sidney's sister, and variously attributed to John Thorpe and Inigo Jones (English Heritage, open at any reasonable time). It is sometimes identified with the House Beautiful in Bunyan's 'Pilgrim's Progress'. About 1¹/₂m further N, on its way into Bedford, B530 passes the turning for *Houghton Conquest*, where the church has a 14C wall painting, fragments of good old glass, and brasses.—The church at *Marston Moretaine*, 4m NW of Ampthill, has a detached belfry and a window by Morris and Co.

A6 continues N, bypassing (46m) **Elstow**, the birthplace of John Bunyan (see below). The half-timbered *Moot Hall* on the village green is now a museum illustrating his life and times. In the parish church Bunyan was baptised, rang the bells and heard the sermons which first stirred his conscience. Now over-restored, it incorporates Norman work from the church of a Benedictine nunnery founded in 1078. Over the N door is a Norman group of Christ between St Peter and St John. Inside are fine brasses of Lady Argentein (d. 1427) and Abbess Elizabeth Hervey (d. 1524).

49m. **BEDFORD** (74,000 inhab.), the county town, has connections with John Bunyan and some pleasant scenery by the river, but little else to interest the visitor.

**Tourist Information Centre**: No. 10 St Paul's Square.

**Car Parks**: Castle Lane. Multi-storey car parks in Lurke St., Harpur Centre and by the bus station in All Hallows.

**Railway Station**: Midland Rd, W of the town, for main line and Bletchley services.

**Buses**: from All Hallows to all destinations.

**Famous natives and residents**: John Bunyan (1628–88), born near Elstow, served in the Parliamentarian army during the Civil War and returned to his native area to follow his father's trade of tinker or brazier. In 1653 he joined a Nonconformist group in Bedford, becoming pastor in 1672 and holding the position until his death. Arrested for unlicensed preaching in 1660, he spent most of the next 12 years in the County Gaol, which stood at the corner of High St. and Silver St. Here he wrote 'Grace Abounding to the Chief of Sinners' (1666) and probably began the first part of 'Pilgrim's Progress', completed during a later spell of imprisonment in 1676–77, when he may have been held in the County Gaol again or in the Town Gaol on the old bridge. He died in London and is buried in Bunhill Fields. Bedford's Dissenting tradition was maintained by the philanthropist John Howard (1726–90), whose interest in prison reform was first aroused during his term as High Sheriff of Bedford, and William Hale White ('Mark Rutherford'; 1831–1913), son of a local bookseller.

The Ouse Bridge (1813) stands at the S end of the High St. Upstream is the *County Hall*, while *The Embankment follows the tree-lined N bank of the river downstream to a (1/2m) Russell Park. The church of *St Mary*, S of the bridge, has a Norman tower. Near the bridge are the *Swan Hotel* (1794; Henry Holland) and the *Bedford Museum*, with local history, archaeology, geology and natural history. The mound in the gardens is all that survives of the Norman castle which commanded the ford over the Ouse until its destruction in 1224. Adjoining is the *Cecil Higgins Art Gallery*, with an excellent collection of smaller works of art, including English watercolours and drawings, porcelain and *glass.

In Mill St. behind the Museum, *Howard House* belonged to the prison reformer. Nearby is the *Bunyan Meeting*, built in 1850 on the site of the barn where Bunyan used to preach. The panels on the bronze doors (1876) illustrate the 'Pilgrim's Progress'. The adjacent *Bunyan Museum* has an interesting collection of relics. A plaque in St Cuthbert's St. to the N marks the site of Bunyan's home from 1655.

High St. runs N from the Ouse Bridge through the centre of town. St Paul's Square, to the left, has a statue of John Howard and the principal church, *St Paul*, with the 14C stone pulpit from which Wesley preached his assize sermon in 1758 and the brass of a prominent local benefactor, Sir William Harpur (d. 1573).

Behind are the 18–19C *Town Hall* and the *Civic Theatre* (with amateur productions), and in Harpur St. to the NW the façade (1830; Edward Blore) of the Bedford Modern School now fronts a shopping centre.

Bunyan's statue stands at the N end of High St., facing the site of the County Gaol where he was imprisoned. The church of *St Peter* has a Norman S porch and tower incorporating Saxon work.

*Cardington*, off A603 2½m SE, was the home of John Howard after 1758. The church has a black Wedgwood font and the churchyard a memorial to victims of the R101 airship disaster in 1930; the airship hangars dominate the RAF station.

FROM BEDFORD TO HITCHIN, 17m by A600.—10m. *Shefford. Chicksands Priory* (limited opening), off A507 1¼m W, has the remains of a Gilbertine priory incorporated in an 18–19C house. The site is now marked by a gigantic USAF antenna, likened by Pevsner to a steel Stonehenge. For *Southill Park* and other places N of Shefford, see Rte 47A.—17m. *Hitchin*, see Rte 47A.

FROM BEDFORD TO CAMBRIDGE. The fast route takes A428, a brief stretch of A1 and then A45. A slightly more interesting route (29m) begins on A603.—4m. *Willington* has a 16C dovecote and stables (NT, open by prior appointment) and, in the church, the fine Gostwick tomb (1615).—We cross the A1 (Rte 47A) on the way into (8m) *Sandy*, where we continue E on B1042.—12m. *Potton*. 2m E is *Cockayne Hatley*, with 17C Flemish wood carving in the church.—At 19½m we cross A14 to join A603, passing *Wimpole Hall* (Rte 68) on the way to (29m) *Cambridge* (Rte 69).

From Bedford to *Northampton* via *Olney*, see Rte 46.

We continue N on A6.—50½m. *Clapham* has a Saxon church tower.—55m. *Bletsoe*, to the right, was the birthplace of Lady Margaret Beaufort (1443–1509), Henry VII's mother.—We enter Northamptonshire before (62m) *Rushden* (22,700 inhab.), a shoe-making town where the largely Dec. church has a 'strainer arch' (cf. Finedon below), a 15C screen and 17C alabaster Pemberton tombs. *Hinwick House* (limited opening), 3½m SW, is a Queen Anne building of local stone, with Mortlake tapestries and a good collection of portraits. At *Hinwick Hall* the first school for spastic boys opened in 1943.

63m. **Higham Ferrers** (5200 inhab.) is a handsome stone-built little town. The EE and Dec. *Church has a beautiful spire, double nave, stalls with good misericords and bench ends, and, among several brasses, one of Laurence St Maur (d. 1337). The schoolhouse and bede house in the churchyard belonged to the college of secular canons founded in 1422 by Archbishop Chichele (1362–1443), a native of the town. Nearby, College St. has the surviving fragments of the college's quadrangle, including its chapel (English Heritage, exterior only, open at any reasonable time).

Standing at the junction of A6 with A45 and near the junction with A605, Higham Ferrers is starting-point for several interesting detours and alternative ways to Stamford.

FROM HIGHAM FERRERS TO STAMFORD VIA KETTERING, ROCKINGHAM AND UPPINGHAM, 34m. We start on A6.—1½m. *Irthlingborough* (4900 inhab.), beyond the Nene, has a church with a detached 14C bell-tower crowned by an octagon.—At (4m) *Finedon* the excellent Dec. church has a 'strainer arch' across the nave (cf. Rushden above).—6m. *Burton Latimer* (5400 inhab.) has early 14C paintings of St Catherine's martyrdom in its church. The village of *Pytchley*, 3m W, gave its name to a famous pack of foxhounds, later moved to Brixworth (Rte 46).—8m. *Barton Seagrave* has an early Norman and EE church.—9m. **Kettering** (45,400 inhab.; Tourist Information) is a nondescript industrial town. The late Perp. church has a tall spire and an early Dec. N doorway and E end. The Art Gallery in Sheep St. has travelling exhibitions and a good collection of 19–20C English art, developed from the collection donated by Sir Alfred East (1849–1913), a native of Kettering. The Westfield Museum in West St. has Roman finds and displays about the local shoe making industry. *Rushton Hall*, off A6003 4½m NW, was home of the prominent Catholic landowner Sir Thomas Tresham (1534–1605). Now a school of the Royal National Institute for the Blind, it is open by prior appointment. Nearby stands the wonderful *Triangular Lodge* (English Heritage, summer standard opening) built in 1593–97 by Sir Thomas in symbolic expression of his faith. *Rothwell* (6400 inhab.), on A6 4m NW of Kettering, has a market house with heraldic decorations begun by Sir Thomas in 1578 and a handsome Trans. church with good misericords.

We leave Kettering on A6003.—13m. The church at *Great Oakley*, ¾m E, has stalls with misericords from the vanished Pipewell Abbey.—We pass W of (15m) **Corby** (47,600 inhab.; Tourist Information), an ugly town which has survived the death of the steel industry that first created it in the 1930s.—17m. *Rockingham* is a charming stone-built village. *Rockingham Castle* (open) stands on the escarpment overlooking the Welland valley. William the Conqueror ordered the building of the castle and later kings refurbished it. It passed from royal hands in 1544, and the process of converting Rockingham into a private residence has continued ever since, interrupted only by the Civil War, when Sir Lewis Watson yielded the castle to the Parliamentarian army. The result is a pleasantly eclectic blend of medieval fortress and informal country house. Edward I's gatehouse still stands, and remains of the Norman keep survive in the gardens; the fortified walls have become a terrace with fine views. The flag tower was added by Salvin in 1838. Inside, the Great Hall has been subdivided and the present Hall is mainly Tudor. The Long Gallery has portraits by Reynolds, Zoffany and Angelica Kauffmann, as well as mementoes of Dickens, who used Rockingham as the model for Chesney Wold in 'Bleak House'. Outside, the terrace and formal gardens (whose yew walk is noted in the novel) lead to a 19C wild garden in the ravine below.

A6003 continues N into the former county of Rutland, now part of Leicestershire.—20m. To the W is *Stoke Dry*, overlooking *Eyebrook Reservoir*, with Digby monuments in its church. Sir Everard Digby (1578–1606), executed for his part in the Gunpowder Plot, was born here. *Lyddington*, 1m E of A6003, has a 15–17C Bede House in the surviving part of a manor house belonging to the Bishops of Lincoln (English Heritage, summer standard opening). The beautiful 14C church has communion rails of 1635 which completely surround the altar, an apparently unique design adopted as a compromise during liturgical controversy.—22m. **Uppingham** (2800 inhab.) is a pleasant little town. The church has a pulpit given by its most famous rector, Jeremy Taylor (1613–67). Uppingham School, founded in 1587, first became a leading public school under the headmastership of Dr Edward Thring in 1853–87. Former pupils include the novelist Norman Douglas. *Preston*, 2m N, has a partly Norman church. For Oakham and Rutland Water, further N, see Rte 57.

N of Uppingham we branch E on A47.—At (26m) *Morcott*, where the church is mainly late Norman, we follow A6121. *North Luffenham*, 1¹/₂m NE, has a handsome 13–14C church.—30¹/₂m. *Ketton*, famous for its stone, has ugly cement works by the main road but a fine 13–14C church and some pleasant houses in the older part of the village by the river Chater.—34m. *Stamford*, see Rte 47A.

FROM HIGHAM FERRERS TO STAMFORD VIA GEDDINGTON AND DUDDINGTON, 31m. We follow the detour above to (9m) *Kettering* and then take A43 through the pleasant countryside of *Rockingham Forest*, once a royal deer forest but no longer heavily wooded.—10¹/₂m. *Weekley* has 16–17C Montagu tombs in the church, and a charming almshouse (1611) and school (1624). *Warkton*, 1¹/₂m SE, has later *monuments of the Montagus, including work by Roubiliac and Robert Adam.—12m. *Geddington*, once a royal manor, is notable for its beautiful *Eleanor Cross (English Heritage), one of three which survive from the series marking the overnight stops in the funeral procession of Queen Eleanor of Castile in 1290. See Lincoln (Rte 72) for further details. The interesting church has a late Dec. spire, Saxon remains and fine screens, and there is a heavily repaired medieval bridge. *Boughton House* (limited opening), in fine grounds 1¹/₂m SE, was grandly remodelled in the French style in 1683–1709. The impressive State Rooms have painted ceilings by Chéron and Mortlake tapestries; the fine collection of art includes many sketches by Van Dyck.—20m. *Deene Park* (limited opening), to the left, is a mainly Tudor mansion, still with its Great Hall. The church contains the memorial of the Earl of Cardigan (d. 1868), leader of the charge of the Light Brigade at Balaclava. *Kirby Hall* (English Heritage, standard opening and summer Sunday mornings, but closed on Mondays and Tuesdays in winter), 2m W, is the shell of a mansion begun in 1570 but owing much of its sophisticated appearance to alterations in 1638–40. These have been attributed to Inigo Jones, though Nicholas Stone is a better candidate.—We pass (26m) *Duddington* and (27m) *Collyweston*, both among the best stone-built villages in England. Collyweston is known for its roofing slabs.—29m. *Easton-on-the-Hill*, another handsome village, has an early 16C Priest's House (NT, open by prior appointment).—We cross A1 and enter (31m) *Stamford*, see Rte 47A.

FROM HIGHAM FERRERS TO ST NEOTS, 17m by A45.—9m. *Kimbolton* has a handsome main street. *Kimbolton Castle* (limited opening), now a school, incorporates part of the castle where Catherine of Aragon lived in 1533–36 after her divorce but owes its present, dignified appearance to remodelling by Vanbrugh in 1707–14. The church at *Swineshead*, 4m SW, has a remarkable Dec. choir, with misericords from a vanished priory.—At 16m we cross A1 on the way into (17m) *St Neots*, Rte 47A.

From Higham Ferrers to *Northampton* via *Wellingborough*, see Rte 46.

The main route branches right on A605 just N of Higham Ferrers. —65m. *Stanwick* church has an exquisite octagonal tower and spire. —65¹/₂m. *Raunds* (7400 inhab.), a shoemaking town, has a 13C church with another famous *spire.—70m. *Thrapston* is a quiet little town.

The beautiful Perp. church at *Islip*, on the Nene ³/₄m W, contains a tablet to Mary Washington (d. 1624). *Twywell* church, 2¹/₂m further, has early Norman features. The 15C church at *Lowick*, 1¹/₂m N of Islip, has a remarkable octagonal lantern on the *tower, fine contemporary monuments and good stained glass of the Dec. period.

A604, heading E from Thrapston to Huntingdon, passes (6m) *Molesworth*,

with its USAF base, and (8m) *Leighton Bromswold*, 1m N of the road. The
*church here was rebuilt by George Herbert, incumbent in 1626–30. Nearby is
the gatehouse of a vanished Jacobean mansion.—17m. *Huntingdon*, see Rte 68.

73m. *Thorpe Waterville. Aldwincle*, across the Nene 1½m W, was the
birthplace of the historian Thomas Fuller (1608–61) and John Dryden
(1631–1700). Dryden spent part of his boyhood at *Titchmarsh*, 1½m
SE of Thorpe Waterville, and is remembered by a tablet in the
church, notable also for its handsome Perp. tower. *Lilford Park*
(open), 1½m N of Thorpe Waterville, has aviaries and other attractions; the Jacobean Lilford Hall is rarely open.—75m. *Barnwell*, to the
right, has the ruins of a 13C castle (not open).

77m. **Oundle** (3500 inhab.; Tourist Information) is a handsome
stone-built little town with one of the tall church steeples characteristic of the region, a public school and many good 17–18C houses. The
front of the Talbot Inn (1626) was built with materials from
Fotheringhay Castle (see below), and the oak staircase inside comes
from the same source.

Fine misericords from the demolished choir of Fotheringhay can be seen in the
churches at *Lower Benefield* (3m W), *Hemington* (3m SE) and *Tansor* (2m NE).
The Nene between Tansor and *Cotterstock*, nearer Oundle, is particularly
charming, while *Polebrook*, on the way to Hemington, has one of the finest
churches in the district.—*Southwick Hall* (limited opening), 2½m NW of
Oundle, has 14C, Tudor and 18C work.—A footpath from the Brigstock road,
4m SW of Oundle, leads to *Lyveden Old Bield* (not open) and *Lyveden New
Bield* (NT). The old building was remodelled by Sir Thomas Tresham of Rushton
(see above). His new building is an unfinished shell begun in the 1590s, shaped
like a Greek cross and adorned with esoteric references to his ardent Catholicism.

80m. *Warmington* has a remarkable EE church with its original roof,
groined in wood. *Fotheringhay* lies on the other side of the Nene, 2m
NW. The mound of the great keep (not open) is almost the only
surviving trace of the royal castle where Richard III was born in 1452
and Mary, Queen of Scots, tried and executed in 1587. The early 15C
collegiate church, with a noble lantern tower, lacks the original choir.
It contains two monuments erected by Queen Elizabeth in memory of
Yorkist princes buried here.—At (82m) *Elton* we branch left on B671.
*Elton Hall* (limited opening) is a 15–19C mansion, notable for its
collection of early Bibles and of work by English painters.—At (86m)
*Wansford* we join A1, following Rte 47A to (92m) **Stamford**.

# NORTH MIDLANDS

The previous section of this guide marked the upper limit of the South Midlands by a line drawn roughly from the Severn and the Wye in the SW to the Wash in the NE, passing through the centre of England. The North Midlands, explored in this section by routes starting from the various cities along this line, continue up to the borders of Merseyside, Greater Manchester and South Yorkshire. On the W lies the border with Wales, while in the E the course of the A1 is again used to distinguish the Midlands from Eastern England. The area thus defined includes parts of Hereford and Worcester, West Midlands, Warwickshire, Leicestershire and Lincolnshire and all of Shropshire, Cheshire, Staffordshire, Derbyshire and Nottinghamshire.

Southerners still tend to regard this region, as they do virtually anything N of Watford, as mainly industrial and hence mainly dull. By way of confirmation they can point to cities like Birmingham, Derby or Nottingham, whose brash, ugly vitality helped make England 'the workshop of the world' in the 19C, and to areas like the Potteries or the Black Country, whose very names have a grim, uninviting ring. This picture, of course, is no more accurate than one that makes everything S of Watford green and sleekly prosperous. Industrialism has certainly shaped the landscape throughout much of the Midlands, yet countryside has survived too, and often survived close to the cities and the factories. The Midlands owe a lot of their character to this conjunction of rural with urban, pastoral with industrial—the effect so vividly rendered in D.H. Lawrence's novels. And in recent years we have come to realise that industrial culture itself, rather than being an ugly blot to be wished away, can constitute an instructive, even absorbing part of our history. The canal and the railway viaduct, the factory and the warehouse have begun to take their place beside the castle, the church and the country house as significant monuments.

A look at the basic contours of the landscape helps a more precise understanding of this mixture of countryside and industry which now makes up the North Midlands. We can begin by imagining the region in terms of a roughly marked letter U, the broad strokes of the letter being chiefly plain or vale and their inner and outer edges chiefly hill. At the bottom of the U, in the S, is the limestone belt stretching across southern England from Dorset through Somerset, the Cotswolds and Northamptonshire. It continues up the E fringe of our region to create, in the Leicestershire and Lincolnshire countryside explored in routes from Stamford, the same softly undulating hills and handsome stone-built villages that make Northamptonshire so attractive. Like Northamptonshire, they are also among the least known beauty spots of England. Much better known, as well as more dramatic, is the hilly countryside that marks the W fringe of the region in the Shropshire part of the Welsh Marches. Here limestone is mixed with the ancient Pre-Cambrian rocks of Wales to create famous and sometimes romantically named hills, like Wenlock Edge and the Long Mynd, as well as geological quirks like the extinct volcanic bump of the Wrekin.

If the limestone country around Stamford and the Shropshire hills define the outer edges of the U, its inner edges and central core are the Peak District of Derbyshire and neighbouring counties. The country here is made up of two distinct landscapes, both long popular for the wildness and beauty of their scenery and both now incorporated in the National Park. In the S is the limestone White Peak, with its undulating hills, deep and wooded dales (like Dovedale) and underground caverns; further N, gritstone (or millstone grit) makes the bleaker country of the Dark Peak.

Marking out the strokes of the U itself between these hills is a much flatter landscape of sandstones and marls, which stretches down through the Cheshire plain and N Shropshire, crosses Staffordshire, West Midlands, and the N parts of Warwickshire and Leicestershire, and moves up through Nottinghamshire. Its shape is echoed by the course of the Trent—'the calm and characteristic stream of middle England', as Arnold Bennett called it—as it flows along its broad valley through the Potteries and the brewing town of Burton, swings past Nottingham and turns N through Newark on its way to join the Humber estuary. The red earth ranges from fertile farmland to the thin, sandy soils which support Sherwood Forest in the E and Staffordshire's Cannock Chase in the W.

Most striking of the building materials which characterise this region, and certainly the most surprising to those who would see it as grimly industrial, is the timber from the ancient forests. The forests themselves have largely vanished but have left their permanent trace in the half-timbered buildings throughout the W half of the region, making quite as rich a display as anything the Weald or East Anglia can boast. In a village like Weobley, near Hereford, we can see cottages of ancient cruck construction—with big curved timbers rising from or near ground level to support the walls as well as the roof. Later houses, built on the 'box-frame' principle, show the wealth of decorative ornament and the bold contrast between blackened wood and white infill which have earned them nicknames like 'black-and-white' or 'magpie'. They include country houses like Bramall Hall, near Stockport, and the prodigious Little Moreton Hall in Cheshire, now made famous by a thousand National Trust tea-towels; town houses like the superb Churche's Mansion in Nantwich; and the rich streetscapes of Ludlow, Shrewsbury and Chester. The famous Rows at Chester, too, remind the visitor that it was the 'black-and-white' houses of this region, rather than the less dramatic styles of the Weald or East Anglia, which inspired the 19C half-timbered revival. At Wightwick Manor, near Wolverhampton, we find a 19C half-timbered country house whose Pre-Raphaelite interior perfectly matches the promise of its exterior. The sandstones, inevitably, provide the second traditional building material of the region. Bunter Sandstone can be seen at Nottingham, where the tunnels and caves cut into the rock on which the castle stands demonstrate its softness. The lovely rose-coloured Keuper Sandstone gives Lichfield and Chester cathedrals, as well as innumerable parish churches, their distinctive look.

More characteristic than either timber or sandstone is the red brick, fired from the local marl clays, which has left its mark, for good and ill, on most towns of the Midland sandstone belt. Few English building materials are so various in their effect. It can look sedate and mellow in Georgian houses, vivid and exuberant in 19C civic buildings, and pinched and mean in the soot-covered terraced houses which make up so much of the towns and cities of the Red Midlands. Sadly, it is these seemingly endless 19C streets which can dominate the visitor's first and last impressions of the region.

This is not inappropriate, for they are the most pervasive reminder of the industrial forces which have shaped the history of the

Midlands. Yet this 19C result came toward the end of a long process. Early but now almost forgotten industries had included, for example, the Derbyshire lead-mining of which Wirksworth was a centre in the Middle Ages and the Cheshire salt-mining that gave the suffix '-wich' to its chief towns (Middlewich, Northwich, Nantwich). Of early origin, too, is the pottery industry which gave Stoke-on-Trent its familiar name as the Potteries; it still flourishes, celebrating its history and products in several excellent museums. Its crucial period of growth was the 18C, when Josiah Wedgwood came as close as anyone to realising the age's progressive ideal of uniting art and manufacture. Elsewhere, the crucial developments of the 18C exploited fast-running water to power the textile mills. The silk mill John and Thomas Lombe built on the river Derwent at Derby in 1717–21 (now the site of the city's industrial museum) is important as the first true factory, where dependence on a common energy source brought hitherto dispersed workers into an organised community. Yet its city location is less than typical, for the search for water frequently took industry to places that we might now innocently suppose to be unspoiled and rural. Hence we find Richard Arkwright's cotton mill (1771) also on the Derwent but at Cromford near the fringe of the Peaks and the Quarry Bank Mill (1784) on the aptly named river Bobbin at Styal, near Wilmslow—both of them now among the well-preserved and well-displayed industrial sites of the region. In addition to being a source of power, water also became the chief means of commercial transport. At the end of the 18C and the beginning of the 19C men like James Brindley and Thomas Telford created· the massive canal system which links the Trent with the Thames, the Severn and·the Mersey.

The next phase depended on coal, iron and steam. Coal and iron, of course, are found at many places throughout the region but had previously been exploited only on a small scale. The two were first brought in vital conjunction at Coalbrookdale, in Shropshire's Severn gorge, when the second Abraham Darby began smelting iron ore with coke rather than the traditional charcoal in 1709. The Darbys left a permanent monument to their achievement in the famous iron bridge (1779), which now overlooks a complex of museums and displays giving by far the most imaginative introduction to our industrial heritage. In 1775, at the Soho Manufactory in Handsworth, Birmingham, Matthew Boulton and James Watt began those experiments with steam engines that would free industry from its dependence on fast-running water, encouraging it to concentrate in massive, energetic cities like Birmingham or sprawl in dismal conurbations like the Black Country.

These places have survived later changes, though sometimes only with difficulty—becoming cleaner with the advent of electricity, turning away from the production of coal, iron and steel, and depending increasingly on engineering and metal-finishing connected with the motor industry. And modern forms of power, electricity and the internal combustion engine, have in turn created landmarks in the complex motorway system that includes 'Spaghetti Junction' near Birmingham and in the power stations that line the Trent valley.

# 48 Birmingham

**BIRMINGHAM**, with just over 1 million inhabitants, is the second largest city in Britain as well as England and the capital of the industrial West Midlands. A substantial, bustling and friendly place, it has much to interest the visitor: excellent collections in the City Museum and Art Gallery and in the Barber Institute of Fine Arts at the University, a first-rate Museum of Science and Industry and stained glass by Burne-Jones in the 18C St Philip's Cathedral. Some good 19C buildings and a well-restored canal walk survive modern redevelopment of the centre, and the redevelopment at least has a boldness in tune with Birmingham's big-city energy.

**Tourist Information Centres**: No. 2 City Arcade, between New St. and Corporation St.; Airport Information Desk, Birmingham International Airport; and National Exhibition Centre, 9m SE on A45.

**Car Parks**: at many points around the inner ring road.

**Bus Station**: Bull Ring Centre.

**Coach Station**: Digbeth.

**Railway Stations**: New Street, for London, connecting with Birmingham International, located at the National Exhibition Centre and serving the airport and most major cities. Moor Street, local services to Stratford and Leamington.

**Airport**: Birmingham International Airport at Elmdon, 7m SE on A45. Passenger services to Heathrow, Gatwick, Isle of Man (summer), Manchester, Southampton, Aberdeen, Edinburgh, Glasgow, Prestwick, Belfast, Cork, Dublin, Guernsey, Jersey, Toronto, New York and many European destinations.

**Theatres**: Hippodrome, Hurst St.; Alexandra, John Bright St.; Repertory, Broad St.; Midland Arts Centre, Cannon Hill Park; The Triangle, Aston University.

**Concerts**: City of Birmingham Symphony Orchestra in the Town Hall, about three times weekly.

**Annual Event**: International Motor Show at National Exhibition Centre in October.

**History**. Although a market was held and tolls levied here before the Norman Conquest, Birmingham is chiefly a modern and industrial city. It was known for its metal workers by 1538, when John Leland found 'a great parte of the towne ... mayntayned by smithes'. The abundant local supplies of coal and iron, combined with the presence of 'small masters' skilled in a wide variety of trades, caused its phenomenal growth at the end of the 18C. The population was 35,000 in 1760, 86,000 in 1801, and 233,000 in 1851. Matthew Boulton (1728–1809) formed his famous partnership with James Watt (1736–1819) to make steam engines at the Soho Manufactory, Handsworth, in 1775. The printer John Baskerville (1706–79), the chemist Joseph Priestley (1733–1804) and William Murdock (1754–1839), the inventor of gas lighting, typified the city's contribution to advances in science and learning. De Tocqueville, a visitor in 1835, found Birmingham 'an immense workshop, a huge forge, a vast shop'. Practically everything metal from pen-nibs to railway carriages and armaments was turned out, with jewellery also an important trade. By this time, too, it was a centre of religious Nonconformity and political radicalism, playing a leading part in the Reform agitation of 1832 and the Chartism of 1839. Its continued national importance is shown by the names of the radical philanthropist Joseph Sturge (1793–1859); John Bright (1811–89), MP for the city from 1857; and Joseph Chamberlain (1836–1914), Mayor from 1873 and MP for the city from 1876. Chamberlain's 'civic gospel' made Birmingham a byword for enlightened municipal government, a tradition maintained by his son Neville Chamberlain (1869–1940), Mayor in 1915–17 and Prime Minister in 1937–40.

The enlargement of its boundaries in 1911 made the city the second largest in England; in 1951 it overtook Glasgow to become the second largest in Britain. In the 20C it has kept its variety of trades, but with the motor and motor accessories industry playing an increasingly important role. The post-war years brought a major campaign of redevelopment which has robbed Birmingham of much older architecture and given it distinctively modern landmarks: New Street Station and the Bull Ring Centre, the inner ring road and, amid the

complex motorway system of which the city is now the hub, the notorious 'Spaghetti Junction' on M6.

**Famous natives, residents and visitors** in addition to those mentioned above. The artists David Cox (1783–1859) and Sir Edward Burne-Jones (1833–98) and the novelist J.M. Shorthouse (1834–1903) were natives. John Henry Newman (1801–90) established the Oratory of St Philip Neri in 1847 and lived there for most of the remainder of his life. Gerard Manley Hopkins (1844–89) was received into the Roman Catholic Church at the Oratory in 1866. Hilaire Belloc (1870–1953) attended the school attached to it.

The inner ring road, designed by Sir Herbert Manzoni in the 1940s and responsible for devastating much of the older Birmingham, tightly encloses the centre in an oval of about ½m by ¾m, with an additional cross link by Colmore Circus. It makes life difficult for pedestrians, who have to cross it by steps and tunnels, but the piazzas created by the roundabouts (or 'circuses') are sometimes attractive.

For walking tours of the city we may fix the centre at Victoria Square, just inside the W side of the ring road, by Paradise Circus. Here the statue of the Queen (1901; Thomas Brock) overlooks a group of 19C civic buildings. The **Town Hall** (1831–35), modelled on a Roman temple, is by Joseph Hansom of hansom-cab fame and E. Welch. The *Crown Post Office* (1899; Sir H. Tanner), to the S, contains a statue of the postal reformer Sir Rowland Hill (1795–1879), son of a Birmingham schoolmaster. On the N side of the square stands the elaborate neo-Renaissance *Council House* (1874–79), with its dome. Around the corner in Chamberlain Square is the 1880s façade of the *City Museum and Art Gallery* (see below) with the clock tower known locally as 'Big Brum', connected by a bridge across the street to the Council House Extension (completed in 1919). They face a Gothic monument to Joseph Chamberlain (1880; J.H. Chamberlain, no relation), statues of James Watt and Joseph Priestley, and the **Central Library** (1974; John Madin Design Group), which contains the important Shakespeare Memorial Library and the Boulton and Watt Collection of documents and engineering drawings. It stands on the site of the forerunner of Birmingham University, Mason College, founded in 1875.

The *City Museum and Art Gallery** is one of the best outside London, with rich collections of painting and sculpture, applied art, and archaeology, as well as local history and natural history. The Pre-Raphaelite paintings are outstanding.

From the Chamberlain Square entrance we climb the stairs past the bookstall to the *Round Room*, its walls crowded with canvases in the 19C manner, and the Information Desk.

*Galleries 1–7*, on the right, offer a spectacular vista of Victorian decoration, with cast-iron balconies and staircase and huge gaseliers. They contain applied art: coins and medals, metalwork, ceramics, glass, stained glass, costumes and jewellery. The ceramics collection includes a good representative display of English porcelain and a particularly strong display of pottery and tiles by William de Morgan. The pleasant Edwardian Tea Room at the end of the wing sometimes has music recitals.

From the Round Room a passage leads over the bridge, with its contemporary craft displays, to the Museum Shop and, on the right, the Feeney Galleries with the main collection of painting and sculpture. *Galleries 10–11* display Oriental ceramics and applied art. The English 19C art in *Galleries 12–14* includes the *Pre-Raphaelite collection: Rossetti (Proserpine; Beata Beatrix), Millais (Blind Girl), Hunt (Valentine Rescuing Sylvia from Proteus; Finding of the Saviour in the Temple), Brown (Last of England; fine landscapes), Alexander Munro (sculpture of Paolo and Francesca), Burne-Jones and their followers, including Arthur Hughes (Long Engagement), Henry Wallis (Stonebreaker) and Charles

*'The Last of England' by Ford Madox Brown, in the Birmingham City Museum and Art Gallery*

Rossiter (To Brighton and Back for 3/6d). Other 19C artists represented include Turner (Pass of St Gotthard), Constable, Wilkie, Egg (Travelling Companions), Frith, J.F. Lewis, Leighton, Poynter, Alma-Tadema.

*Gallery 15* has a superb collection of English and Continental silver. Other galleries are devoted to temporary exhibitions.

*Galleries 20–27* display English and European art of other periods, the room numbers running counter to the chronological order. Medieval and Renaissance work in *Galleries 26–27* includes: Simone Martini (triptych), Memling, the Master of San Lucchese, a 15C Florentine Madonna in polychrome terracotta, a large Pentecost from the studio of Botticelli, a terracotta Madonna from the studio of Verrocchio, Giovanni Bellini, Palma Giovane, Garofalo, Scorel, Boccaccio Boccaccino. 17C art in *Galleries 23–25* includes: Rubens (Head of a Man; oil sketch of James I Uniting England and Scotland), Lely (Cromwell; Susannah and the Elders), David Teniers the Younger, Ochtervelt, William van de Velde the Younger, Guercino (Erminia and the Shepherd), Gentileschi (Rest on the Flight to Egypt), Gennari, Crespi, Strozzi, Renieri, Murillo (Vision of St. Anthony of Padua), Castiglione, Pellegrini, Reni, Giordano, Dolci, Francisque Millet, Claude (Landscape near Rome; Embarkation of St Paul), and Gaspard Poussin (Classical Landscape). There are also busts by Roubiliac and Nollekens. 18C work continues in *Gallery 22*, with Gainsborough (Miss Isabella Franks), Reynolds (Roffey Family; Mrs Luther), Allan Ramsay (Mrs Martin), Hogarth (Distressed Poet), Joseph Wright, Lawrence, Fuseli, Loutherbourg, Canaletto (two views of Warwick Castle), Francesco Guardi and Boucher. There is sculpture by Rysbrack (bust of Shakespeare), Chantrey and Girardon.

*Galleries 20–21* contain late 19C and 20C art: Sickert, Sisley, Henry Tonks, Mary Cassatt, Degas, Vuillard, Pissarro, Renoir, Fantin-Latour (L'Aurore et la

Nuit), Mark Gertler, Jack Butler Yeats, Paul Nash, Stanley Spencer, Vlaminck, Rouault, Braque, Modigliani, Ben Nicholson, Francis Bacon, Ceri Richards, Peter Lanyon and more recent figures. Sculptures include works by Degas, Renoir (bust of Mme Renoir), Gaudier-Brzeska, Rodin, Epstein, Hepworth and Moore (Warrior with Shield).

*Galleries 29–30*, at street level by the Charles St. entrance, contain local history. The museum's archaeological collection is on the main and upper floors above, with Mexican and Peruvian antiquities on the staircase. *Gallery 32* has finds from Jericho (reconstructed tomb of c 1800 BC), Ur, Nineveh, Nimrud and Cyprus; also Luristan bronzes, a Greek red-figure stamnos (c 460 BC), Roman tombstones and the marble bust of a young girl (2C AD). *Gallery 34*, the balcony above, has Egyptian archaeology: funerary objects, stelae, mummies and the limestone bust of a nobleman (18th Dynasty, 1412–1376 BC). *Gallery 35* is devoted to the archaeology of Birmingham and the West Midlands. A new ethnographic display is in preparation for *Gallery 33*.

The remaining galleries on the upper floor contain tropical birds, butterflies and shells; the Beale Collection of birds; zoology; palaeontology; geology; and botany. *Gallery 41* has the Pinto Collection of wooden bygones, with an extraordinary range of objects from matches to a ship's figurehead.

EAST FROM VICTORIA SQUARE. Colmore Row, lined with 19C banks and insurance offices, is Birmingham's best street. Stone-fronted palazzi from the 1860s survive on the N side between Newhall St. and Church St., and on the S side W.R. Lethaby's *Eagle Insurance Building* (1900) is outstanding.

**St Philip's Cathedral** was built as a parish church by Thomas Archer in 1709–25 and raised to its present status in 1905. The elegant baroque exterior has a tower topped by a dome and cupola. J.A. Chatwin lengthened the chancel in 1883–84. The cool interior, with Corinthian columns at the E end, makes an ideal setting for the richly glowing *stained glass windows designed by Edward Burne-Jones for Morris and Co. The one at the W end (1897) depicts the Last Judgement; the trio at the E end (1884–90) the Nativity, Ascension and Crucifixion.

Beyond Colmore Circus, Snow Hill Ringway leads past the site of the former GWR station (now redeveloped) to St Chad's Circus, which contains a memorial to President Kennedy with a large mosaic by Kenneth Budd (1969). The red-brick *Roman Catholic Cathedral* outside the ring road was designed by Pugin and built in 1839–41, the first new RC cathedral in England since the Reformation. The spacious interior has 15C stalls from Cologne, a 16C pulpit from Louvain and good glass (1868) by Hardman in the N transept window.

S of St Philip's Cathedral attractive narrow streets lead to New St., the central thoroughfare running from Victoria Square to St Martin's Circus and the Bull Ring. *New Street Station*, off its S side, was transformed with the addition of a tower block and shopping centre in the 1960s.

Corporation St., running N from this point, was laid out in the 1870s and 1880s by Joseph Chamberlain's City Council as part of a slum improvement scheme. The original buildings have largely been replaced by post-war development but at the N end, beyond Old Square, the red-brick and terracotta *Law Courts* (1887–91; Sir Aston Webb and Ingress Bell) and the *Methodist Central Hall* (1903; E. and J.A. Harper) make a handsome group.

New St. meets High St. below the *Rotunda*, a striking circular block of offices (1965; James Roberts). Adjoining is the vast *Bull Ring Centre* (1961–64; Sydney Greenwood and T.J. Hirst), a pioneer inner-city shopping precinct with multi-level shops, offices, car parks, bus station, etc. There are now plans to redevelop the area on a more humane scale. On a terrace above the open-air market stands Westmacott's bronze statue of Nelson (1809). To the S is *St Martin's*, the city's original parish church, largely rebuilt by J.A. Chatwin in

1873–75 on the 14C plan. It contains medieval monuments of the de Birmingham family and a stained glass window (1875–80) by Burne-Jones for Morris and Co. in the S transept.

Digbeth and its continuation, Deritend, follow an old but now dreary course SE from St Martin's. We pass the coach station on the righthand side of Digbeth and the half-timbered *Crown Inn* on the lefthand side of Deritend.

There are several other points of interest scattered about the area E of the ring road. On Stratford Place Bordesley, S of Deritend, *Stratford House* dates from 1601. *St Alban's Church*, on Conybere St., Highgate, further S, is an excellent example of J.L. Pearson's work (1881), in one of the city's first post-war housing redevelopment areas. N of Deritend, the *Curzon Street Station* (1838; Philip Hardwick) has a fine Ionic portico. In Gosta Green, further N, is the **University of Aston in Birmingham**, formerly a College of Advanced Technology, chartered in 1966.

NORTH FROM VICTORIA SQUARE. We go under the bridge connecting the Art Gallery and the Council House Extension. At the corner of Margaret St. is the handsome Gothic *School of Art* (1881–85; J.H. Chamberlain and William Martin). Beyond in Margaret St. is the *Birmingham and Midland Institute*, with a wide range of cultural activities. We continue along Edmund St. to Newhall St., with the the spendid red brick and terracotta of the former telephone exchange (1869; Frederick Martin) on the corner. We turn left and go under the ring road at Great Charles St. to the **\*Museum of Science and Industry**, in an old factory building by the canal. It graphically illustrates the work of Birmingham engineers and craftsmen with working steam, gas and hot air engines (including the oldest working steam engine in the world, made by Boulton and Watt c 1779), electrical equipment, machine tools, mechanical organs and innumerable other items. There are special sections devoted to transport (with a splendid steam locomotive) and aircraft.

From here we can join the canal walk described in the route W from Victoria Square below. Near the museum is the prominent *PO Tower* (1966) in Lionel St. *St Paul's*, in the old jewellery quarter to the N, is an attractive church of 1799.

WEST FROM VICTORIA SQUARE TO THE CANAL. Broad St., running W from the Library and Paradise Circus to Five Ways, begins with a disastrous jumble of buildings which have stubbornly failed to come together as a civic centre. On the righthand corner are the *Hall of Memory* (1925), devoted to the Birmingham dead of the First World War, and, behind, the District Council Offices in *Baskerville House* (1939; Cecil Howitt). Beyond are the *Birmingham Repertory Theatre* and the site where the new convention centre is being built. On the other side are the *Central TV Studios*, the former *Municipal Bank* (1933; Cecil Howitt), an odd-coloured memorial to Boulton, Watt and Murdock (1956; William Bloye) outside the *Register Office*, and the site for a new hotel.

From Gas St., on the left, we can reach the *Gas St. Canal Basin* for a \*walk (about 1½m) along part of the city's canals. The Worcester and Birmingham Canal leads SW from the basin via the attractive wooded scenery of Edgbaston and the King's Norton tunnel (see South-Western Suburbs below). We head in the opposite direction, taking the towpath under Broad St., to *Worcester Bar*, the centre of the English canal system. The straight 'main line', completed by Telford in 1838, continues N via Smethwick to Wolverhampton, with two towpaths and the loops of the previous 'contour' canal on either side. We turn right, where a well-restored stretch of the Birmingham and Fazeley Canal descends through 13 locks, passing the Museum of Science and Industry and the PO Tower (see the walk N from Victoria Square above) on its way to Snow Hill. There is a British Waterways Board information centre at Cambrian Wharf, and there are good views of the city, old and new, at many points along the route.

SOUTH-WESTERN SUBURBS. *Edgbaston*, reached by A456 (Hagley Rd) from the Five Ways junction at the end of Broad St., is a pleasant residential suburb with good mid 19C houses (notably on Wellington Rd). The **Oratory of St Philip Neri** was founded by Newman in 1847. He lived in the Priest's House and is remembered by a tablet in the Italianate church (1903–09; E. Doran Webb). His grave is at Rednal (see below). The *Botanical Gardens* are S of Hagley Rd. The artist David Cox (1783–1859) is buried at *Harbourne*, 1½m SW. See below for the rest of the way by A456 to Kidderminster.

A38 (Bristol Rd) and A441 (Pershore Rd) both run SW from the inner ring road. To the left of A441 are (1¾m) the *Edgbaston Cricket Ground* and (2¼m) *Cannon Hill Park*, the most pleasant of the city's parks. Its imaginative *Nature Centre* has indoor and outdoor enclosures of British wildlife, aquaria, an underwater observation pond, nature trails, etc. The *Midland Arts Centre* is on the N side of the park.

The **University of Birmingham** lies on the right of A38 about 2½m S of the inner ring road. Established in the city centre as Mason College in 1875, it moved here when it received its university charter in 1900. The tall *Chamberlain Tower* (327ft) is the most striking feature of the original buildings, a rigidly planned red-brick complex by Sir Aston Webb and Ingress Bell (1900–09). Recent development, under the supervision of Sir Hugh Casson and Neville Conder, includes University Square, to the N, with their *Staff House* and *University Centre* (both 1962). Further N are the *Sports Centre* (1965–66; Chamberlin, Powell and Bon), the tower of the *Arts and Commerce Building* (1970; Arup Associates) and, at the NE corner, the *Faculty of Education* (1968; Casson and Conder ). W of the campus, beyond the railway and the Worcester and Birmingham Canal, rises the large *Queen Elizabeth Hospital* (1938) with the Medical School.

By the East Gate of the university on Edgbaston Park Rd, near A38, is the **\*Barber Institute of Fine Arts**. A statue of George I on horseback by John Van Nost the Elder (1722), originally on Grattan Bridge in Dublin, stands outside the building by Robert Atkinson (1939). Founded under the will of Lady Barber (d. 1933), the Institute contains a music room and a small but select art collection, normally open to the public as well as to members of the University. Italian painting is represented by Ugolino da Siena (St Francis), Simone Martini (St John the Evangelist), Giovanni Bellini (St Jerome; portrait of a boy), Matteo di Giovanni (Madonna), Cima, Signorelli, Dossi, Beccafumi, Veronese (?) and Guardi. Dutch and Flemish: Rubens (Landscape near Malines), Franz Hals (Man Holding a Skull, one of his earliest works), Van Dyck (Ecce Homo), Cuyp, Steen, Ruisdael and Van Gogh. French: Poussin (Tancred and Erminia), Claude (classical landscape), Watteau (?), Corot, Delacroix, Courbet, Pissarro, Manet (portrait of Carolus-Duran), Monet (Church at Varengeville), Renoir (Young Woman Seated), Gauguin, Toulouse-Lautrec, Bonnard and Magritte. English: Gainsborough (Harvest Wagon; two fine portraits), portraits by Reynolds, Romney and Lawrence, landscapes by Turner and Wilson, and work by Rossetti (Blue Bower), Whistler and Sickert. The collection also includes some fine Italian Renaissance bronzes, and sculptures by Giovanni della Robbia (?), Roubiliac (bust of Pope), Louis Barye, Rodin and Degas; silver, ivories, enamels; Greek and Roman antiquities; Oriental, Indian and African works; miniatures, drawings, prints and illuminated manuscripts; and furniture.

Across Edgbaston Park Rd are the buildings of **King Edward's School** (open by written appointment). Originally founded in 1552, it moved to New St. in 1936. The Upper Corridor of the demolished New St. building, by Charles Barry and Pugin (1833–37) in the same style as their Houses of Parliament, has been re-erected here as the *Chapel.*

*Selly Oak* is ¾m S of the university on A38. The ruined 13C *Weoley Castle* (open) lies 1¼m W.—**Bournville**, 1m S of Selly Oak, is the site of the Cadbury chocolate works and a charming 'model village' first laid out for the Cadbury brothers by W.A. Harvey in the 1890s. It has influenced later garden suburbs and municipal housing schemes throughout the country. Two half-timbered 14C houses, *Selly Manor* and *Minworth Greaves* (open), have been rebuilt on the estate. *King's Norton*, 1½m further S, has an interesting church with 15C spire, an old grammar school (formerly the priest's house) and, to the S, the N portal of the West Hill tunnel (1¹/₂m long) of the Worcester and Birmingham Canal.—From the Selly Oak junction A38 continues 3¹/₂m SW to *Longbridge*, with its motor works. Newman is buried in the little graveyard of the country house of the Oratory Fathers at *Rednal*, 1m S. See Rte 41 for rest of way by A38 to Bromsgrove and Worcester.

EASTERN AND SOUTH-EASTERN SUBURBS. In *Yardley*, 3¹/₂m E of the inner ring road by A45 and A4040, is the half-timbered *'**Blakesley Hall** (open), built between 1573 and 1590. It contains exhibits about half-timbered buildings, rural crafts, etc.—At *Tyseley*, 3m SE on A41 (Warwick Rd), the former GWR depot is now a working *Railway Museum* with steam locomotives etc. —*Sarehole Mill* (open), the last of Birmingham's 18C corn mills, stands on the river Cole about 3¹/₂m SE of the inner ring road via A34. Again fully operational, it has displays of rural life, etc.

NORTH AND NORTH-EASTERN SUBURBS. *'**Aston Hall** (open), a fine Jacobean house, stands in *Aston Park*, 1¹/₂m NE of the inner ring road between A38(M) and A34. A red-brick mansion of 1618–35 with delightful gables and chimney-stacks, it contains a notable staircase, Long Gallery and plaster ceilings. Charles I stayed in the room now named after him in 1642. The Johnson Room contains 18C panelling from the Birmingham home of Dr Johnson's friend Edmund Hector. Other rooms have decoration added by James Watt, son of the engineer, who lived here in the early 19C. The house is the original of Washington Irving's 'Bracebridge Hall'.—*Handsworth*, beyond A34 about 2m W, can also be reached from the inner ring road by A41. Now a depressed suburb made notorious by the 1985 riots, it was the site of the Soho Manufactory where Matthew Boulton and James Watt demonstrated the power of the steam engine in 1775–1800. Boulton, Watt and Murdock all rest in St Mary's Church, the first with a monument by Flaxman, the other two with monuments by Chantrey.—*Perry Bar*, 3m N of the inner ring road by A34, has the church of St Matthew (1964; Robert Maguire and Keith Murray).

FROM BIRMINGHAM TO LICHFIELD AND DERBY, 40m. The quick way to Lichfield is by A38, heading NE from the centre via Aston and (3m) the notorious 'Spaghetti Junction' of M6. A slower but more interesting route takes A5127 from the junction through (4m) *Erdington*. About 1¹/₂m NW is *St Mary's College*, or *Oscott College*, a Roman Catholic seminary with chapel fittings (1837–42) by Pugin. Lord Acton (1834–1902) was a lay pupil.—7m. **Sutton Coldfield** (86,500 inhab.) is a pleasant residential town.The heavily restored church has a Norman font and the monument of Bishop Veysey (d. 1556), a native and local benefactor. *Moat House*, c 1700, is attributed to Sir William Wilson. *New Hall* (not open), 1¹/₂m SE, is a moated mansion partly dating from the 13C. W of the town is *Sutton Park* with the interesting late 19C suburb of *Four Oaks* on its N side.—We cross A5, Watling Street, near the Roman remains at *Wall* (Rte 51). —16m. **Lichfield**, see Rte 51.—A38 follows the course of the Roman Rynkild Street.—20¹/₂m. *Fradley*, to the left, is near the junction of the Coventry Canal with the Trent and Mersey Canal.—21m. *Alrewas* has an interesting church with Norman doorways and an EE chancel. For Elford, beyond the Tame to the SE, see Rte 51.

A38 is flanked by the Trent and the canal.—28¹/₂m. **Burton-upon-Trent** (47,900 inhab.; Tourist Information) is famous for its breweries, which originally flourished here because of the high gypsum content of the local water. The *Bass Museum of Brewing*, in a former joinery warehouse of 1866 in Horninglow St., traces the history and technology of the industry. For *Needwood Forest* and *Hoar Cross*, to the W, see Rte 51. From Burton to Leicester, see Rte 46.

We cross the Dove, here marking the border with Derbyshire.—From (32¹/₂m) *Egginton Common* we can reach **Repton**, 2m SE, once capital of the Saxon kingdom of South Mercia. *St Wystan's Church* has a tall spire, 10C chancel and a crypt which may date from the 7C. The buildings of *Repton School*, founded in 1557, incorporate some fragments of the Augustinian priory. At *Foremark*, 2m E, the church (1662) has outstanding early Georgian ironwork by Robert Bakewell of Derby. Foremark Hall (not open) is a Palladian building of 1759–61 by David Hiorne.—40m. *Derby*, see Rte 55.

FROM BIRMINGHAM TO LEICESTER, 40m. The quick route is by M6 and M42. A more interesting route takes A47 E from the centre.—10m. *Coleshill*, N of the junction of M6 and M42, has a Dec. and Perp. church with a fine spire (rebuilt in the 19C), Norman font and good monuments. We follow B4114.—13m. *Shustoke*, with reservoirs to the N, was the birthplace of the antiquary Sir William Dugdale (1605–1686), who is buried in the church. *Maxstoke Castle* (not open), 1m S, is a moated and fortified mansion of 1346.—We continue on

B4114 through (14m) *Over Whitacre.*—20m. *Hartshill* and (22m) **Nuneaton**, see Rte 51.—We take A47 to (27m) *Hinckley* (55,300 inhab.; Tourist Information). At *Bosworth Field* (with a visitor centre), 4½m N, Henry Tudor became Henry VII by defeating and killing Richard III in 1485. *Stoke Golding*, S of the battlefield, has an early Dec. *church remarkable for the beauty of its details. Dr Johnson worked as an usher in the grammar school at the little town of *Market Bosworth*, 2m beyond the battlefield.—40m. *Leicester*, see Rte 46.

FROM BIRMINGHAM TO KIDDERMINSTER, 19m by A456. We leave the city to the SW.—At (9m) *Halesowen* the poet William Shenstone (1714–63) established a famous garden. He is buried in the church. A fragment of the ruined 13C priory he incorporated into his effects survives.—11m. **Hagley Hall** (open) was built in the 1756–60 by Sanderson Miller for George Lyttelton, first Lord Lyttelton (1709–73). The severe Palladian exterior contrasts with the rich plaster decoration by Francesco Vassali inside. The *grounds, laid out by Lyttelton with Shenstone's help and praised by James Thomson in 'The Seasons', have a sham ruin by Miller and a temple by James 'Athenian' Stuart. The church, rebuilt by Miller and altered by G.E. Street, has a monument to Lyttelton's first wife Lucy by Roubiliac. The *Clent Hills* (1036ft; NT) rise to the S. **Stourbridge** (54,700 inhab.), about 2m N, is the centre of a glass-making industry introduced about 1556 by refugees from Hungary and Lorraine.—19m. *Kidderminster*, see Rte 53.

From Birmingham to *Warwick*, see Rte 39A; to *Coventry*, see Rte 39A; to *Stratford-upon-Avon*, see Rte 40; to *Worcester*, see Rte 41; to *Chester*, see Rte 49.

# 49  Birmingham to Chester via the Black Country

Total distance 72m. **Birmingham**, see Rte 48. We follow A41 throughout.—To (14m) **Wolverhampton**.—To (32m) Newport.—To (52m) Whitchurch.—To (72m) **Chester**, see Rte 50.

Maps: OS Landranger 139, 127, 126 (briefly), 117.

The first part of our journey passes through the **Black Country**, the industrial region NW of Birmingham, which used to belong to Staffordshire but was given to the newly created West Midlands in 1974.

The coal and iron industries, practised on a small scale since the Middle Ages, developed on a large scale in the 19C, expanding the towns of the region into one more or less indistinguishable conurbation. Smoke from the furnaces made it as notorious for its pollution as Staffordshire's other major industrial area, the Potteries. In 'The Old Curiosity Shop', where Little Nell's wanderings follow part of the present route, Dickens described it as a modern hell: 'On every side, and far as the eye could see into the heavy distance, tall chimneys, crowding on each other and presenting that endless repetition of the same dull, ugly form, which is the horror of oppressive dreams, poured out their plague of smoke, obscured the light, and made foul the melancholy air. On mounds of ashes by the wayside, sheltered only by a few rough boards, or rotten pent-house roofs, strange engines spun and writhed like tortured creatures; clanking their iron chains, shrieking in their rapid whirl from time to time as though in torment unendurable, and making the ground tremble with their agonies'. Now that motor accessories, engineering and metal-finishing industries have replaced coal, iron and steel production, the Black Country is at least cleaner, though its towns and cities are largely nondescript.

An alternative to the main route to Wolverhampton described below runs further S, on A4123 and A459, via (9m) **Dudley** (187,200 inhab.; Tourist Information). *Dudley Castle* (open), a ruin dating partly from the 14C but mainly from the 16C, has landscaped grounds with an open-air zoo. The *Black Country*

*Museum*, on the canal basin near the entrance to the Dudley tunnel, has reconstructed chain-making and glass-cutting workshops, period buildings, etc.

The main route takes A41 NW from the centre of Birmingham, via Handsworth to (4½m) **West Bromwich** (154,900 inhab.). The *Oak House* (open) has handsome 16C half-timbering. The Old Manor House in Hall Green Rd, about 2m N, is a moated 14–16C building well-restored as a restaurant.

**Walsall** (178,900 inhab.), beyond the motorway tangle 5½m N, was the birthplace of Jerome K. Jerome (1859–1927), remembered by a museum on Bradford St. The finely placed parish church of *St Matthew*, rebuilt by Francis Goodwin in 1820–21, keeps a set of 15C misericords. The *Museum and Art Gallery* at the Central Library in Lichfield St. has the Garman-Ryan art collection with many works by Epstein.

We continue along A41. At (8m) *Wednesbury* (34,500 inhab.) the museum and art gallery contains exhibits of local history, 19C paintings, etc.—11½m. *Bilston* (33,100 inhab.) has a church of 1825–26 by Francis Goodwin. The museum and art gallery contains interesting, mainly local exhibits of 18–19C enamels, Staffordshire pottery and industrial history. The poet Sir Henry Newbolt (1862–1938) was a native.

14m. **Wolverhampton** (252,400 inhab.), the capital of the Black Country and an iron-making centre since the 18C, is an ancient town, deriving its name from Wulfrun, sister of King Edgar, who endowed a church here in 994. The present *church of St Peter, in the centre near the pleasant Queen Square, is a large and handsome Perp. building which testifies to Wolverhampton's prosperity as a wool town in the Middle Ages.

Apart from some remains of earlier work at the crossing, it belongs mainly to the late 15C; the N transept is slightly later, and the W front and E end were rebuilt by Ewan Christian in 1862–55. The nave has double clerestory windows and a Perp. stone pulpit and font. The gallery at the W end is Jacobean and the inner S porch is modern. The N transept contains a monument, perhaps by Jasper Latham, to Colonel John Lane (d. 1667), who helped Charles II escape after the Battle of Worcester, and the S transept a fine bronze statue of Admiral Sir Richard Leveson (d. 1605) by Hubert Le Sueur. Outside stands the elaborately carved Wolverhampton Cross, probably 9C.

The *Museum and Art Gallery*, in a striking Italianate building (1883; J.A. Chatwin) in nearby Lichfield St., contains temporary exhibitions, Oriental collections and 18–20C paintings, mainly British (Gainsborough, Raeburn, Joseph Wright, Angelica Kauffmann, Fuseli, Cox, Linnell, Danby, Landseer).

*Willenhall*, about 3m E, has a museum with exhibits of the local lock-making industry.—*Moseley Old Hall* (NT), 3m N of Wolverhampton off A449 near M54, is a 17C house clad in 19C brick. Charles II hid here after the Battle of Worcester in 1651. *Penkridge*, 6m further N on the way to Stafford (Rte 51), is an old town with a large 13–15C church containing good Littleton monuments. —*Wightwick Manor* (NT; pronounced 'Witick'), 3m W of Wolverhampton by A454, is a splendid brick and half-timbered house built by Edward Ould for the paint manufacturer Theodore Mander in 1887 and 1893. The interior is a superb expression of late 19C taste, with Morris wallpaper and fabrics, stained glass by Kempe, tiles by William de Morgan and Pre-Raphaelite paintings.—*Chillington Hall* (limited opening) lies 8m NW of Wolverhampton on an unclassified road beyond M54. The Tudor house was rebuilt by Francis Smith of Warwick (1724) and Sir John Soane (1786–89), who created a saloon by covering over the former courtyard with a characteristic domed roof. The grounds, with 18C garden buildings, were laid out by Capability Brown.

From Wolverhampton to *Shrewsbury*, see Rte 52.

Beyond Wolverhampton we leave the Black Country, crossing the S tip of Staffordshire on the way into Shropshire.—A41 bypasses (21½m) *Albrighton*.

The RAF base at *Cosford*, to the W, has an Aerospace Museum with a large collection of historic aircraft.—Unclassified roads lead NE from Albrighton to (c 2½m) *White Ladies Priory* (English Heritage, open at any reasonable time), a small Augustinian foundation, with the remains of the 12C church. After his defeat at the Battle of Worcester Charles II spent the better part of a week hiding here and at *Boscobel House* (English Heritage, standard opening and summer Sunday mornings), a half-timbered 17C hunting lodge about 1m beyond. A descendant of the famous oak tree stands in a field nearby.

At (23½m) *Tong*, just beyond M54, the early 15C *church is famous for the number and beauty of its tombs, chiefly of the Vernons and the Stanleys. The 17C antiquarian Sir William Dugdale names Shakespeare as author of the epitaphs on the ends of the tomb of Sir Thomas Stanley (d. 1576). Dickens had the church in mind as the resting place of Little Nell in 'The Old Curiosity Shop'.—At 26m we cross A5.

*Little Nell among the tombs in Tong church: an illustration to Dickens's 'The Old Curiosity Shop'*

*Weston Park* (open), at *Weston-under-Lizard* 1½m E, is a handsome brick mansion of 1671, with splendid furniture, Aubusson and Gobelins tapestries and a good collection of paintings which includes work by Van Dyck and Jacopo Bassano. Among the garden buildings are a Roman Bridge and Temple of Diana by James Paine (1760); the large park also contains various tourist amusements.—For Oakengates and Wellington, W along A5, see Rte 52.

32m. **Newport** (9000 inhab.; Tourist Information) has a pleasant main street and an impressive *Grammar School* of 1656.

*Aqualate Mere*, 2m E, is the largest lake in Staffordshire.—At *Lilleshall*, off A518 3m SW, the church has a Norman font. *Lilleshall Abbey* (English Heritage, summer standard opening), to the SE, was founded in c 1148 for canons of the Order of Arrouaisians, which later merged with the Augustinians. The beautiful remains include part of the 12–13C church and cloister buildings.

At (43m) *Ternhill* we cross A53.

For the way SW to Shrewsbury, see Rte 52.—The ancient town of **Market Drayton** (8900 inhab.), 3m NE, has half-timbered and Georgian houses and a church with a prominent 14C tower. Lord Clive (Clive of India, 1725–74), who attended the old grammar school, was born at *Styche*, 2m NW, and buried at *Moreton Say*, 2m W. At *Blore Heath*, on A53 about 3m E of Market Drayton, the Yorkists under the Earl of Surrey defeated the Lancastrians under Lord Audley in 1459. A53 continues to Newcastle-under-Lyme (Rte 54).

52m. **Whitchurch** (7200 inhab.; Tourist Information) has a church rebuilt in 1713, with the tombs of John Talbot, 1st Earl of Shrewsbury (d. 1453), and John Talbot (d. 1550), founder of the grammar school. The composer Sir Edward German (1862–1936) was born E.G. Jones at Whitchurch.

Off A49 6m N are the gardens (limited opening) of *Cholmondeley Castle*, a 19C building partly by Robert Smirke.—From Whitchurch to Shrewsbury, Ludlow and Hereford, see Rte 52.

We enter Cheshire on the way to (58½m) *Hampton Heath*. *Malpas*, 1½m SW, was the birthplace of the hymn-writer Bishop Reginald Heber (1783–1826). The Perp. church has a beautiful nave roof and a good collection of monuments.—At (69m) *Rowton Moor*, on the left, the Royalist defeat in 1645 led to the fall of Chester the following year.—69½m. *Christleton*, on the right, has a church (1874–78) by William Butterfield.

72m. **Chester**, see Rte 50.

# 50 Chester

**CHESTER** (58,400 inhab.), the county town on the Dee, has long been popular with visitors both for its convenient position on the way to North Wales and for its own sake. With its well-preserved circuit of walls partly following their Roman course, its famous half-timbered 'rows' and its cathedral, the city keeps much of its medieval appearance. The fact that a lot of the picturesque detail is Victorian does not spoil the effect, though the crowds of tourists and the appallingly congested traffic often threaten to do so.

**Tourist Information Centres**: Town Hall, Northgate St.; Chester Visitor Centre, Vicar's Lane.

**Car Parks**: at many points off the inner ring road.

**Bus Stations**: Princess St. for local and long-distance services; Delamere St. for coach services.

**Railway Station**: off Brook St., NE of the centre and the inner ring road.

**Theatres**: Gateway Theatre, Hamilton Place; Little Theatre Club, Gloucester St.

CHESTER

0    300 yards
0    300 ms

**History**. The Roman *Deva* or *Castra Devana* (the 'camp on the Dee') was founded about AD 48 and became headquarters of the 20th legion. Another name, *Castra Legionum*, evolved into the Welsh *Caerleon* and the Anglo-Saxon *Legaceaster*, shortened to *Ceaster*. After the Romans left (c 380) the town which had grown up around the camp was successively in the hands of the Welsh, the Saxons and the Danes until Ethelfleda, daughter of Alfred the Great, rebuilt it in 907. Chester resisted the Normans longer than any other English city, but in 1070 William the Conqueror granted it to his nephew Hugh Lupus, with as much land as he could win from his Welsh neighbours. As Earl of Chester, he was virtually ruler of an independent territory. The earldom reverted to the Crown in 1237 and since 1254 has been one of the titles held by the sovereign's eldest son. Largely because of its port, the town's prosperity grew during the Middle Ages until, as the river began to silt up in the 15C and 16C, trade gradually shifted to Liverpool. The Chester Cycle, one of four cycles of mystery plays to survive in England, was performed from the 14C to the 17C. In the Civil War the town sided with Charles I, but after his defeat in September 1645 at Rowton Moor (about 3m SE) it was starved into surrender the following February. Its prosperity revived in the 19C with the spread of the railways. In this era, too, it became popular with tourists, particularly as the first historic landmark for American visitors arriving by way of Liverpool.

**Famous natives, residents and visitors**. The chronicler Ranulf Higden (d. 1364) was a monk at St Werburgh's, now the cathedral. The artist Randolph Caldecott (1846–86) was a native. Thomas De Quincey (1785–1859) spent part of his wandering boyhood near St John's church. Also connected with the church is Thomas Hughes (1822–96), author of 'Tom Brown's Schooldays', who passed his last years in nearby Dee Hills Park. Swift used the port on his way between England and Ireland; his friend the poet Thomas Parnell died here while making the same journey in 1718. The impressions of 19C American visitors are captured by Henry James in 'The Ambassadors' (1903) and a delightful essay collected in 'English Hours' (1905).

The city centre is the Cross, at the junction of the Roman roads whose course is now represented by Watergate St., Bridge St., Eastgate St. and Northgate St. The heavily restored *St Peter's Church*, at the corner of Northgate St., stands on the site of part of the Roman praetorium, or camp headquarters. The *Cross* itself is a reconstruction using some fragments of the 15C one destroyed in the Civil War. The main feature of the nearby streets is the *'Rows*, galleries or arcades forming continuous passages along the first floor of the half-timbered houses and shops. Why this curious arrangement developed, probably in the 13C, is uncertain, but the most likely explanation is that the solid Roman ruins encumbered the site at street level. Some buildings are genuinely old and a few have medieval crypts. More belong to the 19C half-timbered revival, though they are not necessarily the worse for that. A particularly spectacular example of 1888 by the chief local exponent, T.M. Lockwood, stands at the corner of Eastgate St. and Bridge St.

WEST FROM THE CROSS. Watergate St., once the main street to the port, has rows on both sides and some of the best buildings in Chester, all on the left. *God's Providence House* is a reconstruction of 1862 incorporating the inscribed beam from the original house of 1652. No. 11 has the finest medieval crypt in the city and the 16C *Leche House* a notable hall. *Bishop Lloyd's House* is the most richly carved in Chester. *Ye Olde Custom House Inn* (1637) stands at the corner of Weaver St. Opposite, the *Guildhall* (open) occupies the 19C former Trinity Church. Nicholas St., part of the inner ring road, marks the W line of the Roman wall. Beyond is the heavily altered *Stanley Palace* (1591), once the residence of the Earls of Derby and now belonging to the English Speaking Union. For the Watergate, see the city walls below.

SOUTH FROM THE CROSS. Bridge St. has rows on both sides and some particularly attractive houses on the right. No. 12, a bookshop, has a vaulted crypt. The *Dutch Houses*, near the corner of Commonhall St., date from the 17C but have 13C or 14C fragments. On the same side beyond are the *Toy Museum* and a building with three old stone arches on its upper storey. In Whitefriars, leading to the right, No. 1 is an attractive house with a gable of 1658. Opposite Whitefriars the former St Michael's church, mainly 19C, is now the **Chester Heritage Centre**, with displays of architecture and conservation in the city. We cross Grosvenor St. to continue down Lower Bridge St. On the corner is the *Falcon*, dating partly from 1626, where Handel stayed in 1741. Further down are the late 16C or early 17C *Tudor House* on the left, and on the right *Ye Olde King's Head*, mainly early 17C, and *Gamul House*, where Charles I stayed in 1645. The *Bear and Billet Inn*, near the Bridgegate at the foot of the street, dates from 1664 and was the town house of the Earls of Shrewsbury until the 19C. For the Bridgegate and the Dee Bridge, see the city walls below.

Castle St., by the King's Head, leads to the former church of St Mary-on-the-Hill, now *St Mary's Centre* (open), with 17C monuments and a timber roof said to have been brought from Basingwerk Abbey. Further on is the entrance to the **Castle**, today a handsome group of neo-classical buildings (1793–1820; Thomas Harrison) serving as Assize Court, County Hall, etc. The equestrian statue of

**CHESTER CATHEDRAL**

Field Marshal Viscount Combermere (d. 1865) outside the main entrance is by
Marochetti. The *Cheshire Military Museum* is at the NE corner. The only
surviving parts of the medieval castle begun c 1070 by Hugh Lupus are a stretch
of the inner bailey wall and the early 13C *Agricola's Tower* (English Heritage,
standard opening), with the vaulted chapel of St Mary de Castro on its first floor.
   Grosvenor St. leads back to Bridge St. and the Cross. It passes the **Grosvenor
Museum**, on the right, notable for its *Roman inscribed stones and other
exhibits of Roman Chester. Upstairs are paintings of local scenes. The well-
furnished *Georgian House* in nearby Castle St. is also part of the Museum.

EAST FROM THE CROSS. Eastgate St., with rows on its righthand side,
is still Chester's main street. Most of its buildings are 19C, though
Brown's of Chester uses a 13C vaulted crypt as one of its departments. St Werburgh's St., on the left, leads to the cathedral. Eastgate,
at the end, is the starting point for a walk around the walls and for
points of interest outside the walls. All these are described below.

NORTH FROM THE CROSS. In Northgate St. the rows are mostly on the
ground floor. Remains of the Roman praetorium survive in the
basement of No. 23. A window in Hamilton Place, off the same side,
allows a view of the Roman strongroom. Beyond, still on the W side of
the street, are the Market Square and the Victorian Gothic *Town Hall*
(1864–69; W.H. Lynn), with the Tourist Information Centre.

There are two interesting old houses on the lefthand side of the street as it
continues to the Northgate: the *Pied Bull Inn*, with an 18C frontage and older
work behind, and the 15C former *Blue Bell Inn*, now a tiny restaurant. For the
Northgate, see the city walls below.

The ***Cathedral** stands opposite the Town Hall, its W front almost
masked by the former buildings of King's School (1875–77; Sir Arthur
Blomfield), now a bank, on the site of the abbot's lodging. We
approach it either from the N, through the 14–15C *Abbey Gateway*
and Abbey Square, or from the S by St Werburgh's St. Both routes
emphasise how its W end is hemmed in by city streets, just as its E
end lies close to the city wall.

The college of secular canons dedicated to St Werburgh (d. c 700) was
refounded as a Benedictine abbey in 1092 by Hugh Lupus, Earl of Chester, with
the help of St Anselm. At the Reformation it became cathedral of the new
diocese of Chester. The chief remains of the Norman church are on the N side.
Beginning with the Lady Chapel (1250–75), the rest of the building reflects all
periods up to the 19C. The choir, largely the work of Edward I's military
engineer Richard of Chester, dates from c 1300; the arcades of the S transept
and the S arcade of the nave from the mid 14C; the rest of the nave, the
clerestory of the S transept and the top stages of the tower from the end of the
15C. The cathedral was several times restored in the 19C, most notably by Sir
Gilbert Scott in 1868–76.
   Externally, the red sandstone has a pleasing effect which makes up for the
modest site and the lack of dramatic features. The two-storied SW porch is
Tudor. Worth searching for on the SE corner of the huge S transept are the 19C
corbels depicting Gladstone and Disraeli. The apsidal E end of the S choir aisle
has a remarkable polygonal roof by Scott. A detached modern bell tower (1975;
George Pace), stands in the SE corner of the precinct. The city wall gives the
best view of the E end.
   From the raised W end of the *Nave* we have a vista of great simplicity and
beauty, enhanced by the warm sandstone. The S arcade is Dec., the N arcade
late Perp. A plain frieze takes the place of a triforium, with a late Perp.
clerestory above. The glass in the W window is by W.T. Carter Shapland (1961).
At the W end of the S aisle, in the base of the unfinished SW tower, is the
Consistory Court of 1636 with interesting wood furnishings. The wall of the N
aisle, now covered by J.R. Clayton's mosaics (1886), is Norman; the base of the
unfinished tower at its W end, now the Baptistery, has a font of Byzantine

*Chester Cathedral: a corbel outside the south transept
portraying Disraeli as defender of the Church of England*

design brought from Italy in 1885. From both ends of this aisle, doors (the E one
Norman of c 1100) lead into the cloisters (see below).

The small *N Transept* was part of the Norman church and is thus the oldest
part of the cathedral. The organ loft over the entrance has a magnificent organ
case by Scott (1876). The windows and roof, with Tudor heraldry, are late Perp.
A monument by Sir Arthur Blomfield (1864) to the 17C theologian Bishop John
Pearson stands in the centre and a wall tablet commemorates the 19C artist
Randolph Caldecott. On the E side a Norman archway with a small row of
triforium arches above leads into the Sacristy, where Trans. work replaces a
Norman apse. The N side gives access to the vestibule of the chapter house (see
below).

The huge *S Transept*, with aisles and sidechapels, is 14C Dec. and 15C Perp.
It served as the parish church of St Oswald from the early 16C to the late 19C.
The great S window (1887) is by Blomfield. There is a charming little monument
to Thomas Greene (d. 1602) and his two wives on the NW pier.

The 13–14C *Choir* has a beautiful triforium. The *stalls (c 1390), with their
spired canopies, bench ends and misericords, are among the best in England.
The bishop's throne is by Scott. Gates of Spanish wrought iron (1558) lead into
the choir aisles. Both were lengthened to the E in about 1500, but the *S Choir
Aisle* has an apsidal end by Scott. The chronicler Ranulf Higden (d. 1364) is
buried in this aisle, and the third window from the W is a fine example of
Pugin's work (1850). The *N Choir Aisle* keeps its Tudor end, now St Werburgh's
Chapel, though the line of the original Norman apse is marked in the pavement.
Near the entrance we can see the base of a Norman column and a capital turned
over and used as a foundation when the choir was rebuilt. The EE *Lady Chapel*
(c 1275–80), reached from the N choir aisle, has the reconstructed fragments of
St Werburgh's shrine and three original ceiling *bosses (recoloured in 1960).

The *Cloisters* are reached from the N aisle of the nave. They were rebuilt
c 1536 and restored by Giles Gilbert Scott in 1911–13, though some Norman
work survives in the wall of the S walk. A graceful vestibule leads from the E
walk to the rectangular 13C *Chapter House*. Along the W walk runs a 12C
undercroft, part of it now housing the bookshop. In the N walk the cafeteria
occupies the large 13C refectory, with 15C windows and a staircase leading to
the *pulpit used for mealtime readings. The hammerbeam roof is modern.

Abbey Square has good Georgian houses. St Werburgh's St. has 19C half-
timbering and, in Music Hall Passage off its W side, the remains of a chapel
originally built c 1280 for the parish of St Oswald, later serving as a wool hall,
theatre and concert hall.

THE CITY WALLS. The walk around the ancient *City Walls begins at the *Eastgate*, dating in its present form from 1769 with a handsome clock added to celebrate Victoria's Diamond Jubilee. The Romans defended their fort with turf ramparts and later with stone. In the 12C the system was extended S and W to protect the castle, and more towers were added in the 13C and 14C. An irregular rectangle, built from 15ft to 25ft high in red sandstone, enclosed the old city. Despite later alteration and rebuilding, particularly of the towers and gates, a remarkable amount of the wall survives today, chiefly medieval but with some Roman work on the N and E sides. It is worth making the full circuit along the top (about 2m), but in any case visitors should be sure to cover the stretches N from Eastgate to Northgate (600yd) and S from Eastgate to Newgate (250yd) and the Roman remains outside the walls.

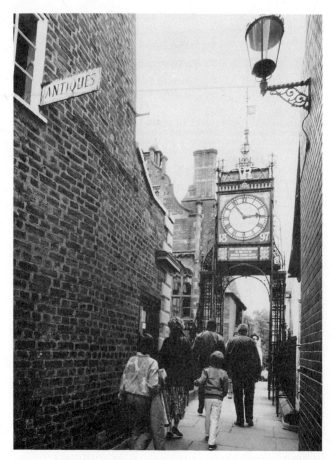

*The Eastgate clock, Chester*

We head N from the top of the steps by the Eastgate, past the modern bell tower and the E end of the cathedral, of which we get a good view. At the *Kaleyard Gate*, a postern at the end of Abbey St., it is worth climbing down and going through the gate to see the remains of the Roman wall to the S. The walk then rounds the choir school playing fields. At the NE corner stands *King Charles's Tower* (restored 1658), so called because the king is said to have watched the defeat of his troops at Rowton Moor from here; its other name, *Phoenix Tower*, comes from the crest of the local guilds who once occupied it. It contains a small Civil War exhibition. The N wall, part of which may be Norman work and which also has stretches of Roman stone, skirts the Shropshire Union Canal on the site of the former moat. Beyond the canal stands the modern *Northgate Arena* sports centre. The *Northgate* was rebuilt by Thomas Harrison in 1808. Stretches of Roman wall can be seen from Northgate Bridge, particularly to the W. On the opposite bank is the former *Bluecoat School* (1717).

We come next to *Morgan's Mount*, a square tower overlooking a flight of canal locks and commanding a view of the Welsh hills. The walk then crosses St Nicholas St. by *St Martin's Gate* (1966) and reaches the semicircular *Goblin Tower*, or *Pemberton's Parlour*, rebuilt in 1894. One wing of the *Royal Infirmary*, to the S, stands on Infirmary Field, first a Roman cemetery and later the burial ground for plague victims. The railway cuts across the NW corner of the walls. *Bonewaldesthorne Tower*, at the angle, is connected by a projecting wall to the *Water Tower*, built to defend the port in 1322.

The walk descends to street level as it runs S past the Royal Infirmary to the *Watergate*, rebuilt in 1788. On the right lies the *Roodee*, a large open space surrounded by the racecourse where the Chester Races have been run since 1540. Near the SW angle of the walls the Dee is crossed by the *Grosvenor Bridge*, built by Thomas Harrison in 1832.

The irregular S wall runs between the river and the castle to the *Bridgegate* (1782). The medieval *Dee Bridge*, widened in the 19C, has seven irregular arches. The causeway or weir to its E is said to have been constructed by Hugh Lupus to serve the mills, remembered by the song 'The Jolly Miller of Dee', which stood here until the 19C. Today salmon fisheries extend downstream. In the suburb of *Handbridge* across the river is the distinctive steeple of *St Mary-without-the-Walls* (1885–87).

Soon turning N, the walls pass the *Recorder's Steps* (1700) and the *Wishing Steps* (1785) on the way to the junction of the medieval and Roman walls at the *Newgate*, built by Sir Walter Tapper in 1932 to replace its neighbour, the narrow *Wolf Gate* (1768). The ruined 14C *Thimbleby's Tower*, or *Wolf Tower*, and Eastgate lie beyond.

OUTSIDE THE WALLS. The main points of interest outside the walls are near Newgate. Foundations of the Roman wall and its SE angle tower (AD 74–96) survive immediately N of the gate. The *Roman Gardens*, to the S, have a reconstructed hypocaust and some Roman columns (none in situ). The *Roman Amphitheatre* beyond dates from c 100 but covers an older wooden site. The largest so far discovered in Britain, it would have seated some 9000 people; it is unusual in having a small temple to Nemesis, immediately W of the N entrance. There is a good plan of the site.

The unpleasantly commercial *Chester Visitor Centre*, in Vicar's Lane, has Tourist Information, restaurant, displays illustrating Chester's history, etc.

*   **St John's Church**, opposite, preserves the crossing tower and part of the nave of a Norman collegiate church.

Founded c 1075, it was for about its first ten years cathedral of the diocese of Mercia, moved briefly from Lichfield; hence early references to a bishopric of Chester 500 years before St Werburgh's became the present cathedral. The NW tower, already rebuilt in 1523, fell in 1573 and destroyed the W end; in 1881 the lofty detached belfry erected on its site fell in its turn, crushing the beautiful N porch. R.C. Hussey, responsible for most of the Victorian restoration, replaced the belfry with an incongruous structure on the NE, but the porch was rebuilt in its original EE form.

The ruined stump of the old belfry still stands outside the W end. Beyond the E end are the ruins of the choir and Lady Chapel, with some good Trans. work.

The vaulted 13C 'crypt', perhaps the chapter house, at one time served as kitchen for a house above in which the young Thomas De Quincey lived briefly.

Inside, the massive pillars and arches of the nave date from c 1095. The triforium of four arches to each bay and the aisles are Trans. (c 1200), while the clerestory is EE. A plaque to the right of the entrance commemorates Thomas Hughes (see below). The NW corner has Saxon crosses and medieval effigies. The Warburton Chapel, on the S side, has the skeleton monument of Lady Warburton (d. 1693).

Below the S wall of the churchyard is the *Hermitage*, an 18C house standing on the site of an anchorite's cell where, so a curious tradition maintains, King Harold retired after the Battle of Hastings. On the river bank below St John's are The Groves, a shady promenade with landing stages. Pleasure cruises leave from here. To the E extends *Grosvenor Park*, where the 13C Shipgate has been re-erected. Thomas Hughes spent the last years of his life at No. 16 Dee Hills Park, immediately E of Grosvenor Park.

OUTSKIRTS. The *Zoo and Gardens* at *Upton*, 2m N, provide natural surroundings for an important collection of animals. The gardens have fine floral displays.—*Eccleston*; 3m S on an unclassified road following the course of the Roman Watling Street from the Dee Bridge, is the chief village of the Grosvenor estate. The church (1899) is by G.F. Bodley. At *Eaton Hall* (not open), further S, most of the pretentious mansion built by Alfred Waterhouse for the 1st Duke of Westminster in 1870–91 has been demolished, though the chapel and stable court survive. In the forecourt is a huge statue of Hugh Lupus by G.F. Watts.

FROM CHESTER TO LIVERPOOL VIA PORT SUNLIGHT, 18m. See Rte 73 for an alternative way to Liverpool via Hoylake. Both routes cross the *Wirral*, the peninsula between the Dee and Mersey estuaries. A5116 runs due N to join A41 at 2m. At **Ellesmere Port** (63,100 inhab.), to the right at 3¹/₂m, the Shropshire Union Canal from Chester joins the Manchester Ship Canal. The *Boat Museum* at the docks has warehouses, workshops, hydraulic steam engines, a collection of over 50 craft, and associated exhibitions. *Stanlow*, to the E, is site of the Shell oil refinery.—A41 continues to (9m) *Eastham*, on the right, where the Manchester Ship Canal joins the Mersey. At the docks tankers discharge their oil for pumping to the Stanlow refinery.—13m. **Port Sunlight** is a model community built in 1888–1914 by W.H. Lever, Lord Leverhulme, around his Sunlight soap factory. The *Lady Lever Art Gallery* has an outstanding collection of English art (Reynolds, Wilson, Constable, Turner) and particularly of work by the Pre-Raphaelites (Ford Madox Brown, Holman Hunt, Millais, Rossetti and Burne-Jones). There is also a superb collection of Wedgwood ware and 18–19C furniture. For *Thornton Hough*, on B5136 3m SW, see the alternative way to Liverpool in Rte 73.—16m. *Birkenhead*, and thence through the Mersey Tunnel to (18m) *Liverpool*, see Rte 73.

FROM CHESTER TO MANCHESTER VIA NORTHWICH, 40m. We follow A51 to (6m) *Tarvin* (Rte 51), then A54 past (8m) *Kelsall*.—We take A556, to the left, shortly before (10¹/₂m) *Delamere*, in the middle of *Delamere Forest* with its quiet meres among pinewoods. *Eddisbury Hill*, on the left, has a well-preserved stronghold attributed to Alfred the Great's daughter Ethelfleda.—17m. **Northwich** (17,100 inhab.), bypassed to the S, now has chemical factories but was once a centre of the Cheshire salt industry also carried on at Middlewich and Nantwich. There is a *Salt Museum* on London Rd, and the Lion Salt Works (open to visitors) survives at *Marston*, 1¹/₂m NE. *Great Budworth*, beyond Marston 3m N, has a Perp. church with 13C stalls and a good 15C font. *Arley Hall* (open), 4m further N, is a 19C neo-Jacobean house with a chapel by Salvin and good gardens.

Beyond Northwich we branch right on A5033, crossing M6, to (24m) **Knutsford** (13,700 inhab.; Tourist Information), an attractive town with several old houses and a church of 1741. It is the 'Cranford' of the novel by Elizabeth Gaskell (1810–65), who spent part of her childhood here and is buried in the old Unitarian graveyard near the station. *Tatton Park* (NT and Cheshire County Council), 3¹/₂m N, is a neo-classical mansion begun in 1780–90 by Samuel Wyatt, brother of James, and finished in 1808–13 by Lewis Wyatt. Much of the furniture was made for the house by Waring of Lancaster. The grounds include a Japanese garden and a deer park. The church of *Rostherne*, on the bank of the lovely mere a little to the N, contains Egerton family monuments. *Peover Hall* (limited opening), off A50 4m S of Knutsford, is an Elizabethan building with fine 17C stables. The nearby church of *Over Peover* contains fine tombs of the Mainwarings. *Lower Peover*, 2m W, has a rare 14C half-timbered *church with a 16C stone tower.

From Knutsford we regain A556 and, after crossing M56, join A56 in the pretty valley of the Bollin.—31½m. *Altrincham*, and on to (40m) *Manchester*, see Rte 75A.

FROM CHESTER TO WARRINGTON, 20m by A56.—10m. *Frodsham*, on a hill overlooking the Weaver marshes, has a partly Norman church. Our road winds back and forth across M56. Runcorn is to the W.—15m. *Daresbury* was the birthplace of Lewis Carroll (Charles Lutwidge Dodgson, 1832–98), commemorated in the church by a window depicting scenes from 'Alice in Wonderland'. —20m. *Warrington*, see Rte 75A.

FROM CHESTER TO WREXHAM. The main road, A483, reaches the Welsh border at (5m) *Pulford*, passes (8m) *Gresford* with its fine church and reaches Wrexham at 12m. A more pleasant route takes B5130 due S from Chester to (9m) *Farndon*, where Edward the Elder died in 924 and the mapmaker John Speed (1552?–1629) was born. *Stretton*, 3m SE, has a working watermill (open). A 14C bridge crosses the Dee to enter Wales at (9½m) *Holt*, with a good church. For (15m) *Wrexham*, and on to *Bala*, *Dolgellau* and *Barmouth*, see 'Blue Guide Wales'.

From Chester to *Bangor*, see 'Blue Guide Wales'; to *Birmingham*, see Rte 49; to *Coventry*, see Rte 51; to *Hereford* via *Ludlow* and *Shrewsbury*, see Rte 52.

# 51   Coventry to Chester

Total distance 97m. **Coventry**, see Rte 39A.—A444 to (8m) **Nuneaton**.—A444, A5, A51 to (22m) **Tamworth**.—A51 to (29m) **Lichfield**.—A51, A513 to (45m) **Stafford**.—A34 to (53m) Stone (bypassed).—A34, A51 to (77m) **Nantwich**.—A51 to (97m) **Chester**, see Rte 50.

Maps: OS Landranger 140, 139, 128, 127, 118, 117.

**Coventry**, see Rte 39A. We head N on A444, crossing M6 at 4m. —5½m. *Griff House* was the childhood home of George Eliot (1819–80), born 2m W at South Farm (see Arbury Hall below). At (7m) *Chilvers Coton*, now a suburb of Nuneaton, the church where she was christened Mary Ann, or Marian, Evans has been rebuilt after wartime bomb damage.—8m. **Nuneaton** (71,500 inhab.; Tourist Information), a dull manufacturing town, has a centre designed by Frederick Gibberd in 1947. The *Library* contains a George Eliot collection and the *Museum and Art Gallery* memorabilia of the novelist. *St Nicholas*, the handsome parish church, is EE and Perp. *St Mary's*, rebuilt in the 19C and 20C, preserves some fragments of the Norman church belonging to the Benedictine nunnery from which the town takes its name.

*Arbury Hall* (limited opening), 2m SW, is notable for the 'Gothick alterations made to the Elizabethan house by Sir Roger Newdigate, founder of the Oxford poetry prize, from the 1740s to the 1790s. Sanderson Miller gave advice and Henry Keene was among the architects employed. There is a good collection of family portraits and furniture. The stables are late 17C. George Eliot's father was agent on the estate, and the house appears as 'Cheverel Manor' in 'Scenes of Clerical Life'.—There is a country park 2m NW of Nuneaton at *Hartshill*, where the poet Michael Drayton (1563–1631) was born.

From Nuneaton to *Leicester* and to *Birmingham*, see Rte 48.

A444 continues N to join A5, following the straight line of the Roman Watling Street, at 11m. *Fenny Drayton*, ½m N, was the birthplace of George Fox (1624–91), founder of the Society of Friends. *Lindley*, 1m E, where the Motor Industry Research Association has its proving ground, was the birthplace of Robert Burton (1577–1640) of 'The Anatomy of Melancholy'. We head W.—13m. *Mancetter*, to the left, was the Roman *Manduessedum*.—14m. *Atherstone* is an old market town with coaching inns. The remains of the Cistercian *Merevale*

*Abbey*, about 1m W, include the 13–14C chapel outside the gate, now the parish church; it contains a plain Perp. screen, early 14C Jesse window and good medieval monuments and brasses.

Beyond (18¹/₂m) the junction with M42, here marking the boundary with Staffordshire, we branch right on A51. For places further W on A5 as it swings past Wolverhampton on its way to Wellington, see Rte 49.—22m. **Tamworth** (64,300 inhab.; Tourist Information) is an ancient town much expanded since the 1960s by overspill population from Birmingham. Offa, King of Mercia, had a palace and a mint here in the 8C, and the town was fortified by Ethelfleda, daughter of Alfred the Great, in the 10C. The oldest part of the present *Castle* (open), near the meeting of the Anker and the Tame, is the Norman shell keep; the great hall and other buildings are largely Jacobean. They contain a local history museum with Saxon coins from Tamworth mint. The light and spacious 14C *Church* has a tower with a double spiral staircase, interesting monuments and stained glass by Morris and Co. The delightful *Town Hall* (1701) was paid for by Thomas Guy, founder of Guy's Hospital in London and MP for Tamworth. A statue of Sir Robert Peel (1788–1850), a later MP for the borough, stands in front. He is buried at *Drayton Bassett*, beyond A5 1¹/₂m S. His house no longer stands but the grounds are now the *Drayton Manor Park and Zoo*.

A513 follows a pleasant route along the Tame valley past (4¹/₂m) *Elford*, where the church has notable 14–16C monuments. *Alrewas*, 3m further, lies on the way from Birmingham to Burton-upon-Trent and Derby (Rte 48).

We continue W on A51, passing (26m) *Packington*, with the Museum of the Staffordshire Regiment outside the Whittington Barracks.

29m. **LICHFIELD** (26,300 inhab.) is the most interesting town in Staffordshire. It has a cathedral in beautiful surroundings and an 18C atmosphere which is fitting reminder of its connection with Dr Johnson and other literary men of the period.

**Tourist Information Centre**: Donegal House, Bore St.

**Car Parks**: between Bird St. and Dam St., The Friary, Lombard St., Tamworth St. and Cathedral Close (for cathedral visitors only).

**Bus Station**: Birmingham Rd.

**Railway Stations**: City station, off Birmingham Rd, for Birmingham; Trent Valley station, 1m E, for London and Stafford.

**Annual Events**: Festival of Traditional Song and Dance (June); Lichfield Festival, with concerts, exhibitions, etc. (July); Johnson Birthday Celebrations and Supper (September).

**Famous natives and residents**. Lichfield enjoyed a remarkably rich intellectual and literary life, particularly in the 18C. The sites connected with its most famous son, Samuel Johnson (1709–84), are commemorated with proper local pride. Two useful guides are available: 'Johnson's Lichfield' and 'The Johnson Trail', the latter tracing his connections throughout the Midland counties. Other distinguished Lichfieldians include: the antiquarian Elias Ashmole (1617–92), born in the same street as Johnson; Joseph Addison (1672–1719), who lived here as a child when his father was Dean of Lichfield; and Johnson's friend David Garrick (1717–79), who spent his childhood here. On his frequent return visits to Lichfield Johnson encountered members of the literary coterie which included Erasmus Darwin (1731–1802), grandfather of Charles Darwin and himself a distinguished scientist; Anna Seward (1747–1809), poetess and 'Swan of Lichfield'; Richard Lovell Edgeworth (1744–1817), educator and father of the novelist Maria Edgeworth; and Thomas Day (1748–89), author of the children's book 'Sandford and Merton'. The playwright George Farquhar was stationed here as a recruiting officer in 1705. Richard Hurd was Bishop of Lichfield in 1775–81.

The market place has statues of Johnson (1838; R.C. Lucas) and Boswell (1908; Percy Fitzgerald). Edward Wightman, the last person burned for heresy in England, was executed here in 1612; and here in 1651 George Fox, founder of the Society of Friends, walked barefoot crying 'Woe to the bloody city of Lichfield'. On the corner of Market St. stands the *Dr Johnson Birthplace Museum*, where Johnson's parents lived over the family bookshop, with interesting personal relics and a valuable library. Johnson's baptism is recorded in the register of St Mary's church opposite, since rebuilt and now the *St Mary's Centre* (open), with displays illustrating Lichfield's history. Johnson and Boswell several times stayed at the former Three Crowns Inn, next door to the birthplace. The house beyond was Elias Ashmole's birthplace.

Bore St., at the S end of Breadmarket, has the Gothic *Guildhall* of 1846, the 18C *Donegal House* (the former Guildhall, now the Tourist Information Centre) and the 16C half-timbered *Lichfield House* (now the Tudor Café).—St John's St.

*The west front and distinctive three spires of Lichfield Cathedral*

leads S towards the railway station, passing the *Hospital of St John Baptist*, built in 1495, with a striking row of chimneystacks. The much altered chapel (open) has an E window of 1984 by John Piper. The *Council Offices* opposite stand on the site of the old Grammar School attended by Ashmole, Addison, Garrick and Johnson, and incorporate the 17C headmaster's house.

The shortest way from the market place to the cathedral is by Dam St., with Georgian houses and, at the corner of the picturesque Quonians Lane, the site of the dame school attended by Johnson. The best way is by Market St. and then Bird St., which has two good 18C inns: the *George*, on the site of the one which Farquhar made the scene of 'The Beaux' Stratagem' (1707), and the *Swan*, where Johnson and the Thrales stayed on their way to Wales in 1774. Beyond the *Arts Centre* (local exhibitions), we cross the bridge flanked by *Minster Pool* and a public garden with Elizabeth Scott's statue of Captain Smith of the 'Titanic'. The *Library and Art Gallery*, also with local exhibitions, stands next door to the site of Garrick's childhood home. It is worth continuing a little beyond the entrance to the cathedral close to the house where Erasmus Darwin lived, on the right, and the 16C *Milley's Hospital*, on the left.

The quiet *Close has half-timbered houses on Vicars' Close at the NW corner, and the *Deanery* (c 1700) and the former *Bishop's Palace* (1687–88), now the Cathedral School, on the N side. It makes a charming setting for the *Cathedral, built of red sandstone from nearby Borrowcop Hill and unique among medieval English churches in having three spires. The central one is a 17C restoration in the style of older W spires, just as the richly decorated *W front is almost entirely a 19C reproduction of the 13–14C original. They are reminders that the building, while still among the most beautiful English cathedrals, has also been one of the most heavily damaged and restored.

Nothing visible survives of the Saxon church built after St Chad, Bishop of Mercia, moved his bishopric from Repton in the 8C, and only doubtful remnants of the Norman church that succeeded it. The earliest parts of the present cathedral are the three W bays of the choir and the sacristy (1195–1208). These, like the transepts and chapter house (1240–50), are EE, while the nave (1280) is early Dec., and the Lady Chapel (1320–36) and presbytery (1337) are in the full Dec. style. The cathedral was twice besieged during the Civil War, in 1643 and again in 1646, when the central spire was destroyed and the interior badly damaged. Repairs began during the Restoration. James Wyatt saved the nave walls from collapse in 1795–98, removing much stone vaulting in the process. A thorough 19C restoration was begun by Sidney Smirke and continued after 1857 by Sir Gilbert Scott and his son John Olrid Scott.

Though long in proportion to its width, the interior is graceful and unified, carrying the eye along the unbroken vista of arches to the stained glass of the Lady Chapel. The *Nave*, built in the transitional period between EE and Dec., is richly ornamented. The fine carved capitals and stone roof bosses are original, but Wyatt substituted wood-and-plaster groining in most of the roof. The beautiful triforium, with dog-tooth moulding, is unusually large; the clerestory windows are of elaborate and uncommon design. Just inside the entrance, in the NW corner, are wall tablets to the poetess Anna Seward and the writer and traveller Lady Mary Wortley Montagu (d. 1762), and in the SW corner, now the bookstall, a monument to Joseph Addison's father (d. 1703).

The *Transepts* (c 1220–40) are earlier than the nave, but their stone-vaulted roofs date from the late 15C and are lower than the originals (so the fine rose window in the S gable cannot be seen inside). The Perp. windows are 17C and the EE ones 19C. The N transept has the skeleton monument of Dean Heywood (d. 1492). The S transept has a war memorial chapel, with busts of Johnson and Garrick (both buried in Westminster Abbey) by Westmacott and, behind the altar, the monument of the last survivor of Nelson's captains, Admiral Sir William Parker (d. 1866). The window above has some of the Herkenrode glass (see below).

Lady Chapel

19

15

16

18

20

17

14

Consistory Court
(St Chad's Head Chapel over)

St Michael's Chapel
( War Memorial )

CHAPTER

HOUSE

Vestibule

Throne

13

12

11

St Stephen's
Chapel

10

5  6

9

7

8

○ Font

4

TOWER

21

1

2

3

Key to Numbers
1 Anna Seward
2 Lady Mary Wortley Montagu
3 Dean Addison
4 Dean Heywood
5 Dr Johnson
6 David Garrick
7 Admiral Sir Wm. Parker

8 Erasmus Darwin
9 Archdeacon Hodson
10 Major Hodson
11 Sir John Stanley
12 Bishop Hacket
13 Bishop Hugh de Patteshull
14 Bishop Walter de Langton

15 Robinson children
16 Bishop Ryder
17 Bishop Lonsdale
18 Bishop Woods
19 Bishop Selwyn
20 Site of St Chad's Shrine
21 Statue of Charles II

# LICHFIELD CATHEDRAL

100 feet
30 metres

The handsome metal crossing screen (1859–63) was designed by Scott and made by Francis Skidmore of Coventry. The *Choir* is deflected 10° to the N from the line of the nave. The first three bays are EE and the oldest part of the cathedral. Here the triforium is replaced by high arcaded window sills with a passage through the piers. The tracery is 17C except for the fine Dec. window on the S side. The *S Choir Aisle* has a small two-storey extension (c 1225): the lower stage, now the consistory court, was the sacristy and the upper, with its charming minstrel gallery, was probably used for displaying St Chad's head to pilgrims. In the same aisle are a medallion to Erasmus Darwin; monuments to Archdeacon Hodson (d. 1855) and Major Hodson (d. 1858) by G.E. Street; the strange effigy of Sir John Stanley (d. 1515), naked to the waist; the tomb of Bishop John Hacket (d. 1670), who restored the cathedral after the Civil War; effigies of Bishop Hugh de Patteshull (d. 1245) and Bishop Walter de Langton (d. 1321); and, at the E end, the finest of Sir Francis Chantrey's early works, his *monument to the Robinson children (d. 1812). The window above contains old Flemish glass. At the E end of the *N Choir Aisle* is one of Chantrey's last works, the monument of Bishop Ryder (d. 1836), beneath another window with old Flemish glass. Nearby are the effigy of Bishop Lonsdale (d. 1867) by G.F. Watts and a bust of Bishop Woods (d. 1953) by Epstein.

The Dec. *Lady Chapel* is a polygonal apse with nine tall windows resting on an arcade. The seven easternmost windows contain *glass (c 1530–40) brought from the Cistercian abbey of Herkenrode near Liège in the 19C. The other two windows have glass of the same period. On the S are three mortuary chapels, one containing the effigy of Bishop Selwyn (d. 1878), after whom Selwyn College, Cambridge, is named.

The exquisite *Chapter House* is connected to the N choir aisle by a vestibule with canopied stalls. Completed in 1249, it is an irregular decagon with beautiful arcading and wonderfully undercut capitals, corbels and bosses. It contains an exhibition of the 8C Lichfield Gospels. The Library above has many rare Bibles, a fine manuscript of 'The Canterbury Tales' and a copy of South's sermons (1694) used by Johnson in compiling his dictionary.

A pleasant walk from the Close skirts Stowe Pool on the way to (1m) *Stowe*, where St Chad's church is the burial place of Lucy Porter, Johnson's step-daughter, and Catherine Chambers, servant to Johnson's parents. The EE doorway, the Dec. E window and the font of 1455 are all worth noting.

At *Wall*, by A5 2m SW, the excavated remains of the Roman settlement of *Letocetum* include the baths and a museum of finds (English Heritage, standard opening, but closed on Mondays and Tuesdays in winter).—*Hanch Hall* (open), 3½m NW of Lichfield off B5104, is 16–19C with a Queen Anne front. The grounds are a bird sanctuary. At *Mavesyn Ridware*, 3m further, the Old Hall has a 14C gatehouse (open by appointment).

From Lichfield to *Birmingham* and to *Burton-upon-Trent* and *Derby*, see Rte 48.

Beyond Lichfield the heights of Cannock Chase appear on the left of A51 and we reach the pleasant valley of the Trent and Mersey Canal runs beside the river.—36m. *Rugeley* (24,300 inhab.), with an interesting old church, was the home of the poisoner William Palmer, executed in 1856. It is dominated by a huge power station.

**Cannock Chase**, about 30,000 acres stretching between Lichfield and Stafford, was once a royal hunting forest and later a centre for coal and iron mining. It is a region of high moorland with bracken, fern, a few surviving oaks, National Forestry Commission plantations of spruce and pine, and herds of fallow deer.

*Abbot's Bromley*, beyond *Blithfield Reservoir* 7m N of Rugeley, has half-timbered houses and a church with a neo-classical tower of 1688. The ancient Horn Dance is held annually on the Monday following the first Sunday after 4 September. *Hoar Cross*, 3m E of Abbot's Bromley, has a splendid Gothic Revival *church (1872–76) by G.F. Bodley. *Hoar Cross Hall* (limited opening) is a neo-Jacobean building of 1862–71 with chapel decorations by Bodley. *Needwood Forest*, with oaks and hollies, lies further E.

A51 continues directly from Rugeley to (15m) *Stone*, passing (4m) *Great Haywood*, with the picturesque Essex Bridge and the junction of the Trent and Mersey Canal with the Staffordshire and Worcestershire Canal, and (10m) *Sandon*, with an extraordinary

monument to Samson Erdeswicke (d. 1603) in the church on the edge
of Sandon Park. Our route makes a detour S to include Stafford,
branching left from A51 at (38m) *Wolseley* along A513 and the N
edge of Cannock Chase.

At (41m) *Milford* is the entrance to **\*Shugborough** (NT and
Staffordshire County Council).

Originally built for the Anson family at the end of the 17C, the house was
several times enlarged, notably in 1745–48 by Thomas Wright of Durham and in
1790–1806 by Samuel Wyatt. Wright added the bow-windowed pavilions and
Wyatt the portico, which together dominate the handsome neo-classical
entrance front. The interior has some rococo plasterwork of the 1740s by Vassali
and Wyatt's splendid Red Drawing Room, with a good collection of French
furniture and memorabilia of Admiral Lord Anson (1697–1762).

The service buildings house the *Staffordshire County Council Museum*, with
exhibitions of domestic life, etc. The *Park Farm*, to the S, is a museum of
agriculture.

Best of all are the \*garden buildings added by James 'Athenian' Stuart in
1764–71, among the first examples of the Greek Revival in England. The route
through the park passes his Lantern of Demosthenes, Triumphal Arch and
Temple of the Winds. His Doric Temple stands in the gardens N of the house,
near the Shepherd's Monument, Chinese House, Chinese Bridge and Admiral
Anson's monument to his cat. At the NE corner is the Essex Bridge (see Great
Haywood above).

From Milford a sideroad leads N to (1½m) *Tixall*, where the 16C gatehouse
survives from the house where Mary, Queen of Scots, was briefly held in 1586.
*Ingestre*, 1½m further N, has a lovely church of 1676, probably by Wren, close
to Ingestre Hall (not open), with a Jacobean front.

**45m. Stafford** (56,000 inhab.; Tourist Information), the ancient
county town of Staffordshire, became a centre of shoemaking in the
18C and of electrical engineering in the 20C. It keeps some
interesting old houses.

The Market Square has the handsome former *Shire Hall* (1795;
John Harvey). The main street, Greengate St., leads S. Set back from
its righthand side is the large and handsome parish church of *St
Mary*, drastically restored by Sir Gilbert Scott in 1841–44, with a
central tower, EE nave and Dec. transepts. It contains a bust of Izaak
Walton (1593–1683), a native of Stafford, who was baptised in the
remarkable Norman font. Outside the W end are the foundations of
St Bertelin's chapel (c 1000) and a replica of the wooden cross found
when the site was excavated in 1954. Continuing along Greengate
St. we pass the half-timbered *High House* (1555), where Charles I
and Prince Rupert lodged in 1642, and the *Swan Hotel*, where
George Borrow was ostler in 1825. *St Chad's*, opposite, another
church restored by Scott, has a Norman nave and elaborate chancel
arch. Further S stands the former *Chetwynd House*, now the Post
Office, where Sheridan used to stay while he was MP for Stafford
(1780–1806). Tipping St., just beyond St Chad's, leads to Eastgate St.,
where the *William Salt Library*, in a beautiful 18C house, has a
valuable collection of books and manuscripts about the county. Izaak
Walton is said to have been born in a house that stood opposite.

The earthworks of the Norman motte-and-bailey castle are 1¼m W, off A518
(the Newport road).

FROM STAFFORD TO UTTOXETER, 15m by A518.—4m. *Hopton Heath* was the
scene of an indecisive Civil War battle in 1643.—At (5m) *Weston* we cross
A51.—6½m. The church at *Stowe-by-Chartley*, on the right, has a monument to
Sir Walter Devereux (d. 1537) and his two wives, and two memorial tablets by
Lutyens.—8m. On the left are the ruined 13C *Chartley Castle* and the 19C
successor to the mansion where Mary, Queen of Scots, was held for eight
months in 1586, immediately before being taken to Fotheringhay.—15m.
*Uttoxeter*, and on to Derby, see Rte 55.

From Stafford to *Manchester* via the *Potteries*, see Rte 54.

A34 runs due N from Stafford and bypasses (53m) *Stone* (12,000 inhab.), where the painter Peter De Wint (1784–1849) was born.

At *Shallowford*, near *Norton Bridge* station about 3½m SW, Halfhead Farm was left to Stafford by Izaak Walton for charitable purposes but later sold. The house known as Izaak Walton's Cottage is preserved as a museum. *Eccleshall*, about 2m further W, has a fine EE church and the remains of a castle of the Bishops of Lichfield. Near *Mill Meece*, 3m N of Eccleshall on the way back to A51, is a steam-powered pumping station of c 1905 (limited opening).

Beyond Stone we branch left on A51.—The *Dorothy Clive Garden* (open), on the right near (66m) *Willoughbridge*, was begun in 1939.—Beyond (68m) *Woore*, in the NE tip of Shropshire, we enter Cheshire.—77m. **Nantwich** (12,000 inhab.; Tourist Information) was once a centre of the salt industry, like Northwich and Middlewich. The handsome 14C *Church* has contemporary *stalls with misericords and a rare stone pulpit. *Churche's Mansion* (1577), a merchant's house with superbly decorated half-timbering in Hospital St., survived the fire which swept the town in 1583. Now a restaurant, it is also open to view. There are many later Elizabethan and Georgian houses in High St. and Welsh Row. The herbalist John Gerard (1545–1612) was a native of Nantwich.

*Dorfold Hall* (limited opening), off A534 1m W, is a brick Jacobean house with original and 18C interiors.

FROM NANTWICH TO CONGLETON, 17½m by A534.—4m. **Crewe** (47,800 inhab.; Tourist Information) is a railway town, brought into being by the engine works of the old LNWR and the junction of the lines to Birmingham, Manchester, Liverpool and Chester. Crewe Hall (not open), to the E, is a 17C mansion rebuilt in the Jacobean style by E.M. Barry after a fire in 1866.—10m. *Sandbach* and (17½m) *Congleton*, see Rte 54.

Beyond Nantwich A51 runs alongside the Shropshire Union Canal, joined at (80m) *Hurlestone* by its Llangollen branch and at (81½m) *Barbridge* by its Middlewich branch.—83m. *Calveley*. *Bunbury*, 2m W, has a fine collegiate church, Dec. and Perp., with the recumbent effigy of its founder, Sir Hugh Calveley (d. 1393), among the monuments. The SE chapel has a notable Perp. screen (1527). Beyond A49 about 2½m further W is *Beeston Castle* (English Heritage, standard opening), built by the Earl of Chester in 1220 and dismantled in 1646. It stands dramatically on a red sandstone crag, and the magnificent *view across the Cheshire plain includes *Peckforton Castle* (not open), built by Anthony Salvin in 1844–50, to the S.—We cross A49 near (87m) *Taporley*, to the right, where the main street has handsome houses and the church good 17C monuments.—At (91m) *Tarvin* the church has 14C woodwork and a 17C nave roof.

97m. **Chester**, see Rte 50.

# 52   The Welsh Marches: Hereford to Chester via Ludlow and Shrewsbury

Total distance 94m. **Hereford**, see Rte 43.—A49 to (13m) Leominster (bypassed).—A49 to (24m) **Ludlow** (bypassed).—A49 to (40m) Church Stretton.—A49 to (53m) **Shrewsbury**.—A49 to (74m) Whitchurch (Rte 49).—A41 to (94m) **Chester**, see Rte 49 and Rte 50.

Maps: OS Landranger 149, 138, 137 (briefly), 126, 117.

A route through the traditional border country of England and Wales, now the W parts of Hereford and Worcester and of Shropshire. Apart from its reminders of the region's violent military past, the route is notable for the combination of lovely countryside and half-timbered houses.

**Hereford**, see Rte 43. A49 runs N, through the Lugg valley.—1m. *Holmer* church has a detached half-timbered belfry.—6m. *Dinmore Manor* (open), just over 1m W, preserves a 12–14C chapel of the Knights Hospitaller. We go over the wooded *Dinmore Hill* to (9m) *Hope-under-Dinmore. Hampton Court* (not open), ³/₄m E, is a castellated mansion built by Sir Rowland Lenthall with the ransom of prisoners taken at Agincourt in 1415. *Bodenham*, 2m further SE, is charmingly placed on the Lugg.

13m. **Leominster** (9100 inhab.; Tourist Information), pronounced 'Lemster', is a market town and centre for light industry on the river Lugg. It has a number of attractive houses, Georgian and earlier, and a large *Church*, once part of a Benedictine priory, illustrating every style from Norman to Perp. The Norman work includes the nave on the N and the fine W doorway. The main nave, added in 1239 as the parish church, has a beautiful Perp. window. The 14C S aisle has lovely ballflower ornamentation. In the park to the S stands the half-timbered *Grange Court*, the best of the town's old houses. It was built in 1633 by John Abel, the 'King's Carpenter', as the Market House and moved to its present site in the 19C. The *Leominster Folk Museum* in Etnam St. just S of Corn Square has local collections.

*Weobley*, 9m SW, is notable for its half-timbered houses, some showing the early method of cruck construction. The fine 13–14C church with a graceful spire contains a memorial to the regicide Colonel John Birch (d. 1691).

FROM LEOMINSTER TO THE WELSH BORDER. A44 leads W to (5m) *Eardisland*, a village on the Arrow with several good half-timbered houses. *Burton Court* (open), c 1m S, is a modest late 18C house preserving the 14C hall from an earlier building. It contains an exhibition of European and Oriental costumes. —7¹/₂m. *Pembridge* is a large village with a 16C market hall, half-timbered houses and a 14C church notable for its detached timber *belfry. Shobdon*, 3m N beyond the airfield, has a Gothick church of 1755.—14m. *Kington* (2000 inhab.) has some Georgian houses and another good church, EE and Dec. Mrs Siddons made her acting début in a barn here in 1772 or 1773. The golf course on *Bradnor Hill* (1284ft; NT), 1¹/₂m NW, is the highest in England. *Hergest Croft Gardens* (open), 1m W of Kington, have rhododendrons, azaleas and maple and birch woodland.—For a continuation of the route to New Radnor and Rhayader, and for other routes from Leominster into Wales, see 'Blue Guide Wales'.

FROM LEOMINSTER TO LUDLOW VIA MORTIMER'S CROSS, 18m. We follow A44, as in the route to the Welsh border above, but turn right at 4m on A4110, partly following the course of the Roman Watling Street.—At (7m) *Mortimer's Cross* the Yorkists led by the future Edward IV defeated the Lancastrians in 1461. At *Aymestrey*, 1m N, the church has a 16C rood screen. From Mortimer's Cross we turn right on B4362, passing an 18C watermill (English Heritage, open summer season, Thursdays, Sundays and Bank Holidays, 14.00–18.00 only).—8m. *Lucton* has a school building of 1708.—9m. *Croft Castle* (NT) keeps its 14–15C walls and corner towers, modified in the 16–17C. The interior was largely remodelled in the 18C, with plasterwork by Thomas Pritchard and a Gothick staircase. The little church in the grounds contains the elaborate tomb of Sir Richard Croft (d. 1509) and his wife. A path (1m) leads NW across the park to the large Iron Age hill-fort of *Croft Ambrey*.—11m. B4362 joins B4361. We head N.—13½m. *Richards Castle*, on the Shropshire border, has a Norman and 14C church with a detached tower, and (1m NW) a dilapidated Norman-style motte-and-bailey castle.—18m. *Ludlow*, see below.

The main route passes (16m) *Berrington Hall* (NT) with a fine park, including an artificial lake, laid out by Capability Brown. The house, built by Henry Holland in 1778–81, has fine marble and plasterwork decoration. It contains several 18C paintings of Admiral Rodney's naval battles. *Eye Manor* (not open), 1m W of Berrington Hall, was built in 1680 for Ferdinando Gorges, a West Indian slave-trader. The nearby church, with a 13C porch, contains two 16C alabaster monuments.

We enter Shropshire just before (20m) *Woofferton*, in the valley of the Teme.

FROM WOOFFERTON TO KIDDERMINSTER, 23m by A456.—4½m. *Burford House Gardens* (open), developed since 1954 in the grounds of an 18C house, have unusual plants and a collection and museum of clematis.—5m. **Tenbury Wells** (2500 inhab.), which enjoyed a brief vogue as a spa in the mid 19C, has half-timbered inns from its days as a coaching stop on the road to Wales. The church contains interesting monuments.—17m. *Callow Hill* has the Visitor Centre for the *Wyre Forest*, 6000 acres stretching N of our road.—19m. **Bewdley** (8700 inhab.; Tourist Information) is a quiet old town on the Severn which lost importance to Stourport (Rte 53) in the canal era. It preserves its fine stone bridge (1795–98) by Thomas Telford and a superb array of *Georgian buildings on the High St., Load St. and Severnside. Load St. has the Town Hall of 1808, the 16C Post Office and, in Butcher's Row, a museum of local crafts and everyday life. The church (1745) is by E. and T. Woodward. The steam service along the *Severn Valley Railway* (Rte 53) between Kidderminster and Bridgnorth stops at the station of the E bank of the river. Stanley Baldwin (1867–1947) was born at Bewdley.—After it crosses the Severn A546 passes (20½m) the *West Midland Safari Park*.—23m. *Kidderminster*, see Rte 53.

24m. **LUDLOW** (7500 inhab.), finely placed on a hill overlooking the rivers Teme and Corve, is an attractive old place with a castle and many half-timbered houses.

**Tourist Information Centre**: (seasonal) Castle St.

**Car Parks**: Castle Square, Upper and Lower Galdeford.

**Railway Station**: Station Drive, off Corve St.

**Annual Event**: Ludlow Festival (music, exhibitions and a performance of Shakespeare in the castle) during last week of June and first week of July.

**History**. Corve St. and Old St. follow the line of the prehistoric and Roman routes which crossed the site. There may have been an ancient settlement, but the present town owed its growth to the castle established c 1086 as a stronghold of the Welsh Marches and made the seat of the Lords President of the Marches in 1475. Built on a grid pattern still apparent today, Ludlow had walls and seven gates by the 14C. The wool trade which made it prosperous in the Middle Ages was later replaced, from the mid 18C to the mid 19C, by glovemaking and a reputation as a social centre for the Shropshire nobility and gentry. The railway, which reached the town in 1851, took society further afield and Ludlow declined until the 20C brought light industry and tourism.

The town centre is marked by the classical *Butter Cross* of 1743–44 by William Baker. The *Museum* in Church St. to the rear of the building has an exhibition of local history.

The large, mainly 15C church of **St Laurence**, to the N, testifies to the prosperity of Ludlow's wool trade in the Middle Ages. Externally, the crossing tower and the early 14C hexagonal porch are notable. There is good 15C glass in the E window, while the reredos, screens and monuments to officials and lords of the Welsh Marches in the chancel all deserve examination. The oldest tomb is that of Ambrosia (d. 1574), sister of Sir Philip Sidney. The Lady Chapel has a 14C Jesse Window.

The ashes of A.E. Housman (1859–1936) are buried in the churchyard beneath the N wall. Opposite the E end of the church stands the picturesque *Reader's House*, a half-timbered Tudor building with a Jacobean porch, incorporating some fragments of a much older stone 'church house' acquired in the 14C or 15C by the ancient Palmers' Guild. In the 18C it was the residence of the 'reader', an assistant to the rector.

High St. leads W from the Butter Cross to Castle Square. The *Castle Lodge* has 16C timberwork above 14C stonework.

The ruined *Castle* (open) stands picturesquely on cliffs overlooking Ludlow's two rivers. Begun c 1086, it was expanded and altered until 1581 and partly dismantled after its capture by Parliament in 1646.

We enter the large *Outer Ward* through a late 12C gateway, above which were the rooms in which Samuel Butler, then steward to the Earl of Carbery, wrote much of 'Hudibras' (1661–62). To the left are battlemented Tudor ruins. Ahead is the 13C *Mortimer's Tower*, allegedly the prison of Henry II's opponent Hugh de Mortimer. Beyond the dry inner moat is the castle's smaller *Inner Ward*. We enter by the 14C gateway, with the arms of Elizabeth I and Sir Henry Sidney, Lord President of the Marches and father of Sir Philip Sidney. To the left of this is the oldest part of the castle, the late 12C Norman *Keep*, with a *view from the top. In the ward stands the exquisite late Norman *Round Chapel*; the foundations of the chancel and apse on its E side have been exposed. The range of 13–14C buildings N of the chapel include, from W to E: the suite of rooms where Henry VIII's older brother Prince Arthur died in 1502, the year after his marriage to Catherine of Aragon; the *Great Hall*, now roofless, where Milton's masque of 'Comus' was performed in 1634 to celebrate the Earl of Bridgewater's appointment as Lord Lieutenant of Wales; a state apartment of unknown function; the *Armoury*; and the *Pendower Tower*, where the young Prince Edward and his brother were held for nearly ten years until 1483, when they were taken to the Tower of London and murdered.

Dinham runs from the SW corner of Castle Square to the 18C *Dinham House*, now a crafts centre, and the former *St Thomas's Chapel*, with some 12C work. —Mill St., running S from Castle Square, has several Georgian houses.

There are excellent walks down the hill from the Butter Cross. King St. leads E to the Bull Ring, a once wide street filled in during medieval times. The *Feathers Hotel* (1603) is the most lavish of all Ludlow's half-timbered buildings. Corve St., partly Georgian and partly Tudor, with *Foxe's Almshouses* (1593) in stone and many half-timbered houses, leads to the 18C *Corve Bridge*. Old St. drops from the Bull Ring to the *Town Preacher's House* (c 1620) and the 14C *Lane's House*. To the right are fragments of the 13C town wall. *Broad St., starting splendidly at the corner of King St. and running S from the Butter Cross, is one of the best streets in England. It descends through *Broad Gate*, the only survivor (much restored) of the town's seven gates, to the 15C *Ludford Bridge* (*view) over the Teme. The back lanes and alleys are worth exploring.

*Leintwardine*, on A4113 8½m W, is the site of the Roman *Bravonium*, a station on Watling Street. The church has 15C stalls and the tomb of General Tarleton (1754–1833), who served in the American War of Independence. We can return via (12½m) *Wigmore*, with the ruin of the 12–14C castle of the Mortimers, and over the wooded *Bringewood Chase*, SW of Ludlow.

*The Feathers Hotel at Ludlow*

The **Clee Hills**, E and NE of Ludlow, can be explored by taking A4117, the Kidderminster road, and branching left at 1½m on B4364 towards Bridgnorth. *Titterstone Clee Hill* (1749ft; *view) rises to the S of this road, *Brown Clee Hill* (1790ft) to the N.—From (10m) *Cleobury North* we swing round Brown Clee Hill on sideroads via (13m) *Ditton Priors* and (15½m) *Abdon*. *Heath*, 2m beyond, has a small but complete Norman chapel.—From here we descend to B4368 at (21m) *Diddlebury* in *Corve Dale*, the broad valley separating the Clee Hills from the long ridge of **Wenlock Edge** (800–950ft). *Aston Munslow*, ¾m to the right, has the *White House Museum of Buildings and Country Life*, with 13–18C buildings, farm equipment, etc. For the rest of the way to Much Wenlock, see Rte 53.—B4368 heads left to (27m) *Craven Arms* (see below), passing B4365 for (28½m) *Ludlow*.

FROM LUDLOW TO KIDDERMINSTER, 23m. We take A4117 along the S side of the Clee Hills via (12m) *Cleobury Mortimer* (2000 inhab.), where the church has a Trans. Norman tower and some good 13C work.—Just before (17m) *Callow Hill* we join the detour from Woofferton described above.—23m. *Kidderminster*, see Rte 53.

26m. *Bromfield* has remains of a Benedictine priory, including the 12C gatehouse and the nave of the church, now part of the parish church. The painted ceiling is 17C.—30½m. *Stokesay Castle

(English Heritage) is the oldest and probably the finest example in England of a moated and fortified manor house.

The picturesque half-timbered gatehouse (1570) leads into the courtyard opposite the main range of buildings, a hall and solar flanked by two towers. This was largely built between 1285 and 1305, though the lower storeys of the N tower date from c 1240. Among the notable features inside are the roof of the great hall, probably including some of its original timbers, and the medieval stone fireplace and 17C Flemish overmantel in the solar.

31¹/₂m. *Craven Arms* (1400 inhab.), named after its coaching inn, later became important as a junction of the railway to central Wales.

*Wenlock Edge* (see above) rises to the NE.—*Clun*, 8¹/₂m W of Craven Arms on B4368, is a remote little town with an old bridge, a ruined 12C castle and a poorly restored Norman church. A good section of *Offa's Dyke* survives to the SW. *Caer Caradoc*, 3m SE of Clun, is one of the many border and Welsh hill-forts bearing the name of Caractacus; it may have been the scene of his defeat by the Romans in AD 50 (cf. Caer Caradoc near Church Stretton below). —*Bishop's Castle*, 10m NW of Craven Arms, is a small town with picturesque houses but no castle. The hilly A488 heads NE to (23m) Shrewsbury, following the Welsh border for some of the way and passing (6m) *Mitchell's Fold Stone Circle* (English Heritage, open at any reasonable time) on the left, the rocky ridge of *Stiperstones* (over 1700ft) on the right, and (12m) *Minsterley*, with a 17C brick church.

36¹/₂m. *Acton Scott*, right of A49, has a working farm museum.—40m. **Church Stretton** (3900 inhab.; seasonal Tourist Information) stands at 650ft, below the moorland ridge of the *Long Mynd* (1700ft) to the W. The church has much Norman work and a powerful 13C roof.

The greater part of the Long Mynd is NT (Information Centre in the Carding Mill valley). There are some 15 prehistoric barrows, many of them either side of the Port Way. This ancient trackway, running the 7m length of the ridge, was used by prehistoric axe traders, became part of the drovers' route from Montgomery to Shrewsbury and still marks the parish boundaries.
    The hill-fort at *Caer Caradoc* (1506ft), NE of Church Stretton, is another claimant to be the scene of Caractacus's defeat by the Romans (cf. Caer Caradoc near Clun above).—The unclassified road branching right from A49 nearby follows the line of the Roman Watling Street, connecting Leintwardine and Wroxeter, through (4¹/₂m) *Frodesley* before veering away from its Roman course to (6m) **Acton Burnell**. The beautiful EE church contains the *brass of Sir Nicholas Burnell (d. 1382), the finest 14C brass in England, and monuments to Sir Richard Lee (d. 1591) and Sir Humphrey Lee (d. 1632), ancestors of the American Confederate general Robert E. Lee. The monument to Sir Humphrey is by Nicholas Stone. *Acton Burnell Castle* (English Heritage, open at any reasonable time) is a ruined fortified manor house built by Edward I's chancellor, Robert Burnell, in 1284. In the timber house which preceded it he had the previous year entertained the king at the first Parliament to which the Commons were directly summoned. *Langley*, 1¹/₂m S, has a Tudor chapel with early 17C fittings (English Heritage, open by prior arrangement). *Pitchford*, 1m N of Acton Burnell, has a church with a remarkable wooden effigy of a knight (c 1250), and a beautiful half-timbered manor house of 1473 (not open). We can rejoin A49 via *Condover*, 3m NW. The church has a late Norman N transept and a 17C nave formed by combining the early nave and N aisle after the fall of the central tower in 1660. The monuments include work by Roubiliac and G.F. Watts. Condover Hall, a fine stone house of 1598, is now a school for handicapped children.

The main route along A49 is less interesting than the detour through Acton Burnell.—48m. *Stapleton*, to the left, has a 13C church originally built with two storeys, later combined.—Mary Webb lived at (49m) *Lyth Hill*, to the left. *Bomere Pool*, to the right of (50m) *Bayston Hill*, is the 'Sarn Mere' of her novel 'Precious Bane' (1924).—51¹/₂m. *Meole Brace*, a suburb of Shrewsbury at the junction of A49 and A5,

SHREWSBURY

400 yards
400 metres

was Mary Webb's home in 1902–12. The 19C church where she was married has superb *stained glass by Morris and Co., especially the apse window (1870–72).

53m. **SHREWSBURY** (87,300 inhab.), generally pronounced 'Shrozebury', is the county town of Shropshire. Its lovely position on a hill almost encircled by a loop of the river Severn made it strategically important as a stronghold of the Welsh Marches. Shrewsbury's special charm for visitors is the wealth of half-timbered houses and picturesque streets, often quaintly named.

**Tourist Information Centre**: The Square.

**Car Parks**: Barker St., Riverside, Greyfriars, Belmont Place, Frankwell, Abbey Foregate.

**Bus Station**: Barker St.

**Railway Station**: Castle Foregate.

**Theatre**: Music Hall, The Square.

**Annual Events**: Shropshire and West Midland Agricultural Show (May); Shrewsbury Regatta (May); International Youth Music Week (July); Shrewsbury Flower Show (August); British Isles Horse and Tractor Ploughing Championships (first Saturday in October).

**History**. Shrewsbury's history reflects the violent instability of the Marches in Saxon and Norman times. It was settled by local chieftains in the 5C and 6C, though it may have been used as a hill-fort before then. Under the name of *Pengwern* it later became the seat of the Princes of Powys. After Offa, King of Mercia, captured the settlement at the end of the 8C it was known by alternative Saxon names, *Scrobesbyrig* (fort in the scrub) and *Sloppesbury*, from which the modern 'Shrewsbury' and 'Salop' evolved. At the Norman Conquest Shrewsbury was made part of the Marcher lordship belonging to Roger de Montgomery. It was captured by Llewelyn the Great in 1215 and 1232 and by rebellious barons in 1234. Edward I used it as the seat of his government during his subjugation of North Wales, executing Dafydd, the last royal Welsh prince, here in 1283. Henry Percy (Hotspur), with his father the Earl of Northumberland a leader of the rebellion against Henry IV, was defeated and killed in 1403 at the Battle of Shrewsbury, fought 3m N (see Battlefield church below). In the stable Tudor era the town traded in wool and flax with the Welsh, and it is from this period of prosperity that most of its half-timbered houses date. During the Civil War Charles I and Prince Rupert briefly made Shrewsbury their headquarters in 1642, and Prince Rupert returned in 1644, but the town fell to Cromwell's troops in 1645.

**Famous natives, residents and visitors**. The Elizabethan poet Thomas Churchyard (1520?–1604), Admiral John Benbow (1653–1702), the poet John Hamilton Reynolds (1794–1852) and Charles Darwin (1809–82) were all natives. George Farquhar wrote 'The Recruiting Officer' (1706), set in Shrewsbury, while staying at the Raven Inn, which stood in Castle St. Lord Clive (Clive of India, 1725–74) was Mayor of Shrewsbury in 1762 and its MP from 1761 until his death. The Shropshire novelist Mary Webb (1881–1927), who lived at Meole Brace and Lyth Hill (see above) and portrayed Shrewsbury as 'Silverton', is buried in the cemetery. See below for famous pupils of Shrewsbury School.

The town centre is The Square, with a statue of Clive of India (1860; Marochetti) and the *Old Market Hall*, a stone building of 1595. On the S side is the *Music Hall* (1840), with the theatre and Tourist Information Centre. College Hill, further S, has the **Clive House Museum**, in the mainly 18C brick house occupied by Clive of India when he was mayor. Its collection is notable for local ceramics (Caughley and Coalport ware).

We begin a walking tour by turning left from The Square into High St., which descends between two of Shrewsbury's best half-timbered buildings, *Ireland's Mansion* (c 1580) on the left and *Owen's Mansion* (c 1592) on the right, to Pride Hill. John Collier's shop, opposite, incorporates remains of the medieval *Bennet's Hall*

probably used as a Mint by Charles I in 1642. Pride Hill climbs to the
*High Cross* (1952; Laurence Gotch), on the site of the earlier cross
where Hotspur's body was hanged, drawn and quartered in 1403.

Pride Hill is continued N by Castle St. and Castle Gates. On the right is the *Old
Council House* (1625), the meeting place of the Council of the Marches,
occupied by Charles I in 1642 and James II in 1687. Just beyond is the entrance
to the **Castle**, now housing the *Shropshire Regimental Museum*. The building
has had a chequered history: first completed by Roger de Montgomery in 1083,
it was rebuilt by Edward I, partly dismantled after its capture by Parliament in
the Civil War, modernised by Thomas Telford in 1790 and twice restored in the
20C. The gateway and part of the main walls survive from the Norman building
and the hall, with alterations, from its Edwardian successor. The *Library* on the
opposite side of the road occupies the old buildings (1630) of Shrewsbury
School; in front is a statue of Darwin. The road goes on to the railway station.

From High Cross, St Mary's St. quickly reaches *St Mary's Church,
with its distinctive tall spire.

Inside, the sedile is Norman, the nave is EE and the N aisle was rebuilt or
restored during the Commonwealth. The *stained glass, collected from many
sources, includes a large 14C Jesse window at the E end, from old St Chad's;
16C glass from St Jacques, Liège, in the Trinity Chapel; and 19 panels made in
1500 by the Master of St Severin of Cologne and brought from the Abbey of
Altenburg, now in the triple lancet on the N side of the chancel and the middle
window of the S nave aisle. The Trinity Chapel has a 14C effigy of a knight and
14C alabaster carvings; the N chapel has a tablet to Admiral Benbow.
    *St Mary's Cottage* and *Draper's Hall*, both attractive half-timbered houses,
stand immediately N and S of the church. Church St., opposite, leads to *St
Alkmund's Church*, rebuilt in 1795. Francis Eginton's striking E window is a
copy of Guido Reni's Assumption. On the corner of Church St. and Butcher Row
is the 15C *Jones's Mansion* (now a hotel), where Prince Rupert lodged in 1644.
Butcher Row has good 15C and 16C houses.

St Mary's St. continues S as Dogpole, with the *Guildhall* (1696) and
the *Old House* (NT, but not open), occupied by Mary Tudor. At the
bottom the street joins Wyle Cop opposite the *Lion Hotel*, a partly
Tudor and partly 18C coaching inn. Its guests have included Thomas
De Quincey, the future William IV, Dickens and Disraeli; Paganini
and Jenny Lind both gave concerts here. Below the Lion is the half-
timbered house where the future Henry VII lodged on his way to
Bosworth Field. We meet the river at *English Bridge*, with handsome
stonework, built by John Gwynn in 1769 and widened in 1927.

Abbey Foregate, on the opposite bank, is the site of the monastery
founded by Roger de Montgomery in 1083. Nothing remains of its
domestic buildings except the elegant little 14C *Reader's Pulpit* of
the refectory, S of the road, but the **Abbey Church** survives.

Built of purple-brown stone, the church has a Dec. W tower with a Norman base
and doorway. The statue above the W window is said to be Edward III. The two
W bays of the nave were rebuilt at the same time as the tower; the rest are
powerful Norman work. The transepts and chancel, built by J.L. Pearson in
1886–88, considerably shorten the original length of the church. Opposite the N
door are fragments from the shrine of St Winifred, showing figures of the saint
with St John the Baptist and St Beuno. The N aisle has a monument to Richard
Onslow (d. 1571), Speaker of the House of Commons, and a 13C effigy of a
lawyer. The tomb in the S aisle is said to be that of Roger de Montgomery. The
war memorial under the tower remembers the poet Wilfred Owen, killed in
1918, as Lieut. W.E.S. Owen, MC.
    The *Coleham Pumping Station* in Longden Coleham, S of Abbey Foregate
near the bridge, is open as a museum of trade and industry, with 19C sewage
pumping engines. In Monkmoor Rd, a little beyond the Abbey Church, are the
*Shire Hall* and *Whitehall*, a stone mansion of 1582. *Lord Hill's Column*, to the E,
was erected in 1816 in honour of Viscount Hill (1772–1842), veteran of the
Peninsular War.

We walk back across the English Bridge into Wyle Cop and branch left into Beeches Lane and its continuation as Town Walls. E.W. Pugin's *Roman Catholic Cathedral* of 1856 is on the right; on the left are fragments and the only remaining tower (NT, but not open) of the old walls. Murivance continues to *New St Chad's*, a strangely planned church by George Steuart (1792), with a Doric façade and tower, and a circular nave. Below is the **Quarry**, a large public park within the loop of the Severn.

**Shrewsbury School** stands on the hill across the river, reached by the Kingsland toll bridge. Founded by Edward VI in 1552, it originally occupied the site of the library, by the castle. The present buildings are mainly by Sir Arthur Blomfield (1882). Famous pupils have included Sir Philip Sidney (whose statue stands in front of the school), Fulke Greville, Judge Jeffreys, Dr Burney (father of the novelist), Charles Darwin, Samuel Butler (of 'Erewhon') and Stanley Weyman.

Claremont Bank brings us round to the *Welsh Bridge* (1795). On the opposite bank of the river Frankwell and The Mount lead to *Darwin House*, birthplace of Charles Darwin in 1809.

We return from the Welsh Bridge to The Square via Barker St **'Rowley's House Museum**, in a dreary position near the bus station, occupies a late 16C half-timbered house and its early 17C brick neighbour. Outstanding among the collection of local history, geology, etc. is the material excavated from the Romano-British city of Viroconium at Wroxeter (see below), which includes Samian pottery, the inscribed tablet which stood over the entrance to the forum and a beautifully decorated silver mirror. We can walk through the modern shopping precinct, *New Market Hall*, to Shoplatch, from which Market St. leads back into The Square.

**Haughmond Abbey** (English Heritage, standard opening but closed on Tuesdays and alternate Wednesdays in winter) stands 4m NE on a rocky escarpment overlooking the Severn. It was founded for Augustinian canons in 1135 and rebuilt towards the end of the century. Little is left of the 12C church, but the remains of the monastic buildings include the 14–15C abbot's lodging, with a graceful oriel window; the infirmary hall of the same dates; and the 12C chapter house, with a 16C ceiling and windows added when the abbey was converted into a mansion.—*Atcham*, on A5 4m SE of Shrewsbury, has a fine sandstone bridge across the Severn (1771; John Gwynn) and the only church in the country dedicated to St Eata, containing 16C glass. *Attingham Park* (NT), N of the village, is a mansion of 1785 by George Steuart in grounds landscaped by Humphry Repton. The handsome interior includes a picture gallery, largely hung with portraits, by John Nash (1807). **Wroxeter**, 1½m further E, is the site of the Romano-British city of *Viroconium* (English Heritage, standard opening). Founded as a military garrison about AD 60, it developed into a tribal centre of the Cornovii before its decay and abandonment sometime after AD 400. A good small museum details its history. The chief visible remains are the 2C public baths and the colonnade of the forum. Wroxeter church has Saxon work using Roman stones and a Norman chancel with fine 16–18C monuments.

FROM SHREWSBURY TO OSWESTRY, 16m.—A5 leads NW, crossing the Severn at (4m) *Montford Bridge*.—8½m. *Nesscliffe* lies at the foot of a wooded hill crowned by an earthwork. The oddly named *Ruyton-XI-Towns*, 2m N, was formerly a borough made up of the 11 towns of the Manor of Ruyton. *Melverley*, on the Severn 4m SW of Nesscliffe, has a fine half-timbered church of the 15C or early 16C. *Adcote* (open) in *Little Ness*, 2¾m E of Nesscliffe, is a country house of 1876–81 by Norman Shaw, now a school.—At (13m) *West Felton* we branch left from A5, passing the Shropshire Union Canal.—16m. **Oswestry** (13,200 inhab.; Tourist Information) is an ancient border town and busy market centre. It is named after St Oswald, King of Northumbria, crucified here in 642 after his defeat in battle by Penda, the pagan King of Mercia. The poet Wilfred Owen (1893–1918) was a native. *Offa's Dyke* lies W of the town. *Old Oswestry* (English Heritage, open at any reasonable time), 1m N, is an impressive Iron Age fort with an elaborate entrance and ramparts. Near *Weston Rhyn*, 4½m N of Oswestry, is *Tyn-y-Rhos Hall* (open), dating in part from 1711. *Whittington*,

3m NE of Oswestry, has the moat and 13C gatehouse of a castle built by the Peverels. *Ellesmere* (2500 inhab.), 5m further NE, lies among several of the small meres that characterise the Shropshire plain.—From Oswestry to *Welshpool*, and from Whittington to *Chirk* and *Llangollen*, see 'Blue Guide Wales'.

FROM SHREWSBURY TO MARKET DRAYTON, 19m. We take A49 N through (3m) *Battlefield* (see below) and then branch right on A53, which we follow for the rest of the way.—7¹/₂m. *Shawbury* has a late Norman church and an airfield. *Moreton Corbet Castle* (English Heritage, open at any reasonable time), 1¹/₂m N, has a ruined 13C castle keep and the shell of a fine house of 1579.—13¹/₂m. *Hodnet* has some good half-timbered houses. The church contains a monument by Chantrey to the hymn-writer Bishop Reginald Heber (1783–1826), rector here for 15 years. *Hodnet Hall*, built for the Heber family by Salvin in 1870, has 60-acre •gardens (open) with a 17C tithe barn and dovecote.—19m. *Market Drayton*, see Rte 49.

FROM SHREWSBURY TO WOLVERHAMPTON, 30m. We follow A5 past (4m) *Atcham* and (5¹/₂m) *Wroxeter*, described above, where it picks up the course of the Roman Watling Street.—11¹/₂m. *Wellington* (Tourist Information), at the end of M54, is one of several older towns absorbed by the new industrial town of **Telford** (103,800 inhab.), designated in 1965, whose centre lies beyond the motorway to the SE. For the Ironbridge Gorge Museums on Telford's S edge, see Rte 53. The **Wrekin**, 2m SW of Wellington, is an isolated extinct volcano with wide views from its summit (1334ft). There are impressive Georgian almshouses (1725) at *Preston-upon-the-Weald-Moors*, 4m NE of Wellington. *Rowton*, off A442 6m N of Wellington, was the birthplace of the Puritan divine Richard Baxter (1615–91).—From (16m) *Oakengates*, on the E fringe of Telford, A464 leads SE.—19m. *Shifnal* is a little town with many good half-timbered and Georgian houses, which may have inspired the romantic description by Dickens in Chapter 46 of 'The Old Curiosity Shop'. Bishop Percy is said to have acquired the manuscript used in his 'Reliques of Ancient Poetry' (1765) here. The church of St Andrew, Norman to Perp., contains many monuments.—At 26m we join A41 and follow Rte 49 to (30m) *Wolverhampton*.

From Shrewsbury to Worcester, see Rte 53.

An attractive alternative to the main route N to Whitchurch described below takes A528 to (6m) *Harmer Hill* and then follows B5476 through (10m) *Wem*, a small market town where William Hazlitt spent much of his youth, and (12m) *Ednaston*, where the church has a fine Norman door. We reach Whitchurch at 18m.

The main route follows A49.—56m. The church at *Battlefield*, left of the road, was founded in 1408 to commemorate the Battle of Shrewsbury, fought in open country to the N and W in 1403. It marked the defeat of the rebellion against Henry IV by the Earl of Northumberland and his son Henry Percy (Hotspur). The church contains an early 15C Pietà in oak, probably from the chapel of the nearby moated mansion of *Albright Hussey*.—57¹/₂m. *Hadnall* church has a monument to the Peninsular War veteran Viscount Hill (d. 1842), who lived at Hawkstone Hall, further N.—63¹/₂m. *Preston Brockhurst* is 1¹/₂m E of *Clive Hall* (not open), birthplace of the playwright William Wycherley (1640?–1716).

At (74m) *Whitchurch* we join Rte 49.—94m. **Chester**, see Rte 50.

# 53   Worcester to Shrewsbury

Total distance 48m. **Worcester**, see Rte 41.—A449 to (14m) Kidderminster.—A442 to (27m) **Bridgnorth**.—A458 to (35m) **Much Wenlock** (for **Ironbridge**).—A458 to (48m) **Shrewsbury**, see Rte 52.

Maps: OS Landranger 150 (briefly), 138, 127 (briefly), 126.

**Worcester**, see Rte 41. A449 runs due N.—3m. *Hawford*, ½m E of the road, has a half-timbered 16C dovecote (NT).—5¾m. *Ombersley* (bypassed) has good half-timbered houses. For Witley Court, 5m W, and Droitwich, 3m E, see Rte 41.—From (9m) *Crossway Green* A4025 bears left for (3m) *Stourport-on-Severn* (19,100 inhab.; Tourist Information), a pleasant town at the meeting of the Severn, the Stour and James Brindley's Staffordshire and Worcestershire Canal (1766–71), which brought it into being. Bewdley (Rte 52) is on the Severn 3m upstream.—11½m. *Hartlebury Castle*, to the left, has been the residence of the Bishops of Worcester since the 13C. The state rooms (limited opening) include the 15C great hall and the handsome 18C library built by Bishop Hurd. The N wing houses the *Hereford and Worcester County Museum* (open), devoted to rural crafts, domestic life, etc.

14m. **Kidderminster** (51,300 inhab.; Tourist Information), known for its carpets, has little of interest except the fine parish *Church*, which contains a large early 15C brass and several good monuments. Outside it stands a statue of the Puritan divine Richard Baxter, minister here from 1641 to 1666. Another statue, beside the town hall, commemorates the postal reformer Sir Rowland Hill (1795–1879), a native of the town. Kidderminster Town Station, next to the BR station on A448 E of the centre, is the S terminus of the *Severn Valley Railway*, which runs a steam service (March to October) along the lovely route through (3½m) Bewdley to (16m) Bridgnorth.

The 16–18C *Harvington Hall* (open), off A448 3m SE, once home of the Catholic Throckmorton family, has priest holes and 17C wall paintings. The pleasant village of *Chaddesley Corbett*, about 1m further, has a Norman font in the church.—*Kinver Edge* (NT), 4m N of Kidderminster, is a natural moorland park.

From Kidderminster to *Birmingham*, see Rte 48; to *Bewdley* and *Woofferton*, and to *Ludlow*, see Rte 52.

We take A442, running parallel to the Severn, and enter Shropshire.—Beyond (23m) *Quatt* is *Dudmaston* (NT), a house of c 1700, perhaps by Francis Smith of Warwick. It contains fine furniture, Dutch flower paintings and modern art. There is a charming garden by a large lake.

27m. **Bridgnorth** (11,100 inhab.; Tourist Information) stands picturesquely on the Severn, which divides it into High Town on the W bank and Low Town on the E bank. The two are connected by steps and the steep Castle Hill Railway. High Town was defended by the *Castle* built in 1098–1101, perhaps on the site of a fort used by Alfred the Great's daughter Ethelfleda and the Danes. It was blown up in 1646 after the siege by Parliamentarian troops, which did much damage and caused much rebuilding elsewhere in the town. The only fragment to survive is the perilously leaning tower in the public park at the S end of High Town; there are lovely views over the valley from here. Nearby is the church of *St Mary Magdalene*, designed by Thomas Telford in 1792–97 but with an apse added by Sir Arthur Blomfield in 1876. East Castle St., with the *Governor's House* of c 1633, leads into the wide and pleasant High St. In the middle stands the handsome *Town Hall* (1650–52), with a half-timbered upper storey on stone arches. Spanning the street beyond is the heavily restored 18C *North Gate*, now housing a local museum. Church St. leads into the little close surrounding the church of *St Leonard*. Damaged in the Civil War, it has a nave roof of 1662 and contains some 17–18C cast-iron monuments but is otherwise largely the result of Victorian rebuilding. *Baxter's House* was home of the

Puritan Richard Baxter while he was rector in 1640. The house (1580) where Bishop Thomas Percy was born in 1729 stands near the bridge.

The station off Hollybush Rd, at the S end of High Town, is the N terminus of the *Severn Valley Railway* (see Kidderminster above). The locomotive sheds are open to visitors.—The grounds of *Stanmore Hall*, on A458 1½m E, house the *Midland Motor Museum*.

From Bridgnorth to *Ludlow* over the Clee Hills, see Rte 52.

We take A458 E from Bridgnorth.—30m. *Morville Hall* (NT, open by prior appointment only) is an Elizabethan house converted in the 18C. *Upton Cresset Hall* (limited opening), 2½m S by a winding sideroad, is a Tudor mansion with delightful chimneys and a detached gatehouse. The roof of the Great Hall can be seen in an upstairs bedroom.—36m. **Much Wenlock** (Tourist Information) is a little town with a good *Church*, Norman to Perp., and a charming half-timbered *Guildhall* (open) resting on wooden pillars. *Wenlock Priory* (English Heritage, standard opening but closed on Thursdays and Fridays in winter) was founded in the 7C as a nunnery with St Milburga as abbess and refounded by Leofric, King of Mercia, in c 1050. It became a priory for Cluniac monks after the Norman Conquest. The substantial remains include a good deal of the EE church and the 12C chapter house, with some well-preserved Norman blind arcading. The 15C prior's lodging is now a private house.

**Ironbridge** (seasonal Tourist Information), on the S edge of Telford 5m NE of Much Wenlock, was the birthplace of the Industrial

*The Iron Bridge*

Revolution and is now the best-preserved site of industrial archaeology in the country. The rich mineral deposits in the narrow gorge of the Severn were exploited by the first Abraham Darby (1667–1717), who smelted iron ore with coke rather than the traditional charcoal at nearby Coalbrookdale in 1709. Fifty years later the second Abraham Darby (1711–63) succeeded in making iron suitable for forging as well as casting. In 1779 the third Abraham Darby (1750–91) spanned the river with the world's first *Iron Bridge (English Heritage, open at any reasonable time). The **Ironbridge Gorge Museum* has restored and recreated the region's industrial past at several different sites. There is an information centre for visitors in the *Severn Warehouse*, W of the bridge. The *Coalbrookdale Museum of Iron*, ³/₄m NW of the bridge, explores the history of iron-making on the site of the first blast furnace. E of the bridge are the 18C *Bedlam Furnaces* and the *Jackfield Tile Gallery*, in the original Craven Dunhill works. The *Coalport China Museum*, 1¹/₂m E, is also devoted to the region's pottery industry, with restored factory buildings, a bottle kiln and displays of Coalport and Caughley ware. *Blists Hill Open Air Museum*, on the Shropshire Canal 1¹/₂m NE of the bridge, has recreated industrial buildings, cottages and shops.

*Buildwas Abbey* (English Heritage, standard opening) stands on the S bank of the Severn 2m W of Ironbridge and 2m N of Much Wenlock. It was founded in 1135 for monks of the Savignac Order, which merged with the Cistercians soon afterwards. The 12C ruins include the church, with sturdy piers in the nave, and the elegant chapter house. Thomas Telford's first iron bridge (1795–96), which stood nearby, has been demolished. The Shropshire novelist Mary Webb (1881–1927) was born at *Leighton*, on the N bank of the Severn 2m further E. —*Benthall Hall* (NT), 4m NE of Much Wenlock off the route to Ironbridge, is a 16C stone house with oak panelling, an elaborate oak staircase and decorated plasterwork. The nearby church was built in 1667 and altered in the 19C.
   B4378 and B4368 head SW from Much Wenlock, following the S flank of *Wenlock Edge* (Rte 52) down Corve Dale to (15m) *Craven Arms*. At 6m we pass *Shipton Hall* (open), a late 16C stone house with 18C remodelling inside. Externally it resembles *Wilderhope Manor* (NT, used as a youth hostel but open), in remote country 2¹/₂m NW.

The main route from Much Wenlock continues on A458, crossing the NE end of Wenlock Edge.—42¹/₂m. *Cross Houses*. Near *Cantlop*, 2m SW, is a cast-iron bridge by Thomas Telford over Cound Brook (English Heritage, open at any reasonable time).—48m. **Shrewsbury**, see Rte 52.


# 54 Stafford to Manchester: The Potteries

Total distance 55m. **Stafford**, see Rte 51. We follow A34 throughout.—To (8m) Stone, see Rte 51.—To (18m) **Newcastle-under-Lyme** (for **Stoke-on-Trent**).—To (30m) Congleton.—To (55m) **Manchester**, see Rte 74.

Maps: OS Landranger 127, 118, 109.

**Stafford** and A34 to (8m) *Stone* (bypassed), see Rte 51. We continue N along the industrial valley of the upper Trent.—13m. *Trentham Gardens* (open), site of the mansion designed by Sir Charles Barry in 1833–42 and largely demolished in 1910, has grounds landscaped by Capability Brown in 1759 and parterres added for the Victorian house by W.A. Nesfield. The striking mausoleum opposite the entrance is by C.H. Tatham (1807).—18m. **Newcastle-under-Lyme** (72,900 inhab.; Tourist Information) is an old industrial town with a wide High St. The *Borough Museum* in Brampton Park has an interesting local history collection.

The *University of Keele*, 3m W on A525, was founded as the University College of North Staffordshire in 1949 and granted its university charter in 1962. The modern buildings grouped around the 19C Keele Hall (by Salvin) include the chapel by George Pace (1964–65).—*Whitmore* is a pleasant place 4m SW on A53, the road to Market Drayton (Rte 49). The church has a half-timbered bell-tower restored in the 19C. The Mainwaring monuments include the alabaster tomb of Edward Mainwaring (d. 1586) and his wife, with part of the date left blank. *Whitmore Hall* (limited opening) is timber-framed, with a handsome brick front added in 1676. The stable block is late 16C.

The **Potteries**, adjoining Newcastle to the E, are famous as the national centre of the industry from which they take their name. Familiarly known as 'The Five Towns', they consist in fact of six large towns stretching for about 8m along the A50: from S to N, Longton, Fenton, Stoke-upon-Trent, Hanley, Burslem and Tunstall. This ungainly sprawl, amalgamated into the borough of **Stoke-on-Trent** in 1910, is now a city of 252,400 people.

Pottery has been made here since the Middle Ages but the industry received its first great impetus when Josiah Wedgwood (1730–95) opened his factory at Etruria in 1769 and, in the words of his epitaph at Stoke, 'converted a rude and inconsiderable manufactory into an elegant art and an important part of the national commerce'. Other famous names established by the late 18C were Davenport, Minton, Spode and Copeland; Doulton came from London in the 19C. They flourished not so much because of the local marl clay, suitable only for the coarsest ware, but because of the Staffordshire coal needed for firing. China clay was brought from Devon and Cornwall, ball clay from Dorset, flints from Norfolk and felspar from Derbyshire. The Trent and Mersey Canal, designed by James Brindley, was complete by 1777. In the 19C the region became notorious for the worst forms of industrial pollution, its landscape scarred by colliery spoil heaps, marl holes, scraff heaps of broken crockery and above all by smoke from the chimney stacks and distinctive bottle kilns of the 'pot banks'. Arnold Bennett (1867–1931), a native of Hanley, vividly paints this picture in his novels and stories. The Potteries today look very different: electric firing has replaced coal, the bottle kilns have all but disappeared, and much of the industrial landscape has been imaginatively reclaimed to make public parks. The chief interest for visitors is the wealth of museums. The Gladstone Pottery Museum at Longton provides an excellent historical introduction, and there are fine collections of pottery, porcelain and ceramics at the City Museum in Hanley as well as at the various factory museums. Many of the factories also have shops and tours; full details are available from the Tourist Information Centre in Stoke.

**Stoke** lies 2m E of Newcastle by A52. The church of *St Peter* (1826–29) contains memorials to Josiah Wedgwood, with a portrait medallion by Flaxman, and Josiah Spode II (d. 1827). Some arches of the medieval church survive outside. The *Minton* works in London Rd has a good museum, and there is another at the *Wedgwood Visitor Centre* in *Barlaston*, 4m S.—**Fenton**, 1m SE, is the smallest of the towns. The *Coalport* works includes a craft centre demonstrating traditional skills. At **Longton**, 1m further SE, the *Gladstone Pottery Museum* occupies a Victorian pot bank with restored bottle kilns, engine house and workshops. Working demonstrations and some good displays bring the history of the industry to life. At *Weston Coyney*, 2m E of Fenton, old sand quarries have been landscaped as the *Park Hall Country Park*, with good views.

**Hanley**, beyond *Hanley Park* N of Stoke, is the centre of the region and the largest of its towns. The *City Museum and Art Gallery* in

*The Gladstone Pottery Museum at Longton, with some of the few surviving bottle kilns in the Potteries*

Broad St. has major collections of pottery and porcelain, chiefly from Staffordshire, and of ceramics from many countries, together with exhibits of local history. English 20C painting and English water-colours are strongly represented in the fine art galleries. Arnold Bennett's childhood home was at No. 205 Waterloo Rd, N of the centre.—At *Etruria*, about 1m SW on the A53 to Newcastle, Josiah Wedgwood opened his factory in 1769 and built his home, Etruria Hall. He chose the name in the mistaken belief that the classical vases which he copied came from Etruria. The lively *New Victoria Theatre* is beyond.

**Burslem**, N of Hanley and the *Central Forest Park*, is called the 'Mother of the Potteries'. Josiah Wedgwood was born here and had his first factory on the site of the *Wedgwood Institute* (1869), with handsome terracotta decoration, in Queen St. It housed the school which Arnold Bennett attended. The *Sir Henry Doulton Gallery* in Nile St. displays the firm's ware since 1815.—*Smallthorne*, about 1¹/₂m NE, has the half-timbered *Ford Green Hall*, now a folk museum.—A50 continues N from Burslem to (1m) **Tunstall**. The *Chatterley Whitfield Mining Museum*, with underground tours, is off A527 2m NE.—The canal-builder James Brindley (1716–72) is buried at *Newchapel*, off A34 2m N of Tunstall.

FROM STOKE TO LIVERPOOL, 49m. A50 goes N from Stoke through Burslem and Tunstall and crosses A34 (see below). At (9m) *Rode Heath* we bear left on A533. For Rode Hall, to the E, see the main route below.—13m. *Sandbach* (14,700 inhab.) is an old town with two reconstructed Saxon *crosses (English Heritage, open at any reasonable time).—18m. *Middlewich* (8200 inhab.) was a Cheshire salt town, like (24m) *Northwich*, described in Rte 50.—36m. *Runcorn* (64,400 inhab.; Tourist Information), greatly expanded since the 1960s, is a chemical manufacturing town on the Manchester Ship Canal and the Mersey, crossed by a railway bridge (1864–68) and road bridge (1961; Mott, Hay and Anderson). The remains of the 12C *Norton Priory* (open), off A558 3m E, were excavated in the 1970s. The site has a good Norman doorway and a museum of finds, including mosaic tiles, and monastic life.—37m. *Widnes*, and on to (49m) *Liverpool*, see Rte 75A.

From Stoke to *Derby*, see Rte 55; to *Ashbourne* via *Alton*, see Rte 56B.

---

Beyond Newcastle A34 crosses the N Staffordshire coalfield and enters Cheshire.—25m. *Scholar Green*.

*Mow Cop* (1091ft; NT), to the E, is crowned with a sham ruin of the early 1750s.—*Rode Hall* (limited opening), ³/₄m to the W, is a much altered house of c 1700 with work by Lewis Wyatt.

27m. *Little Moreton Hall* (NT) is probably the best and certainly the most striking half-timbered manor house in the Midlands. The range with the Great Hall was built in the late 15C and altered in 1559; the other buildings around the courtyard, including the Long Gallery, were added by 1580.—29m. *Astbury* has a noble Dec. and Perp. church with 17C furnishings.—30m. **Congleton** (23,800 inhab.; Tourist Information), a silk and cotton weaving town in the 19C, has old inns. From Congleton to *Nantwich*, see Rte 51.—36¹/₂m. *Capesthorne Hall* (open), on the left, is an 18C house by Francis and William Smith of Warwick rebuilt in the Elizabethan style by Blore in 1837–39 and Salvin in 1861. The chapel of 1720 survives nearby. From the huge park there is a view of the radio telescopes at *Jodrell Bank* (open), 3m W on A535.—38¹/₂m. *Nether Alderley* has a 15C corn mill (NT). —40¹/₂m. *Alderley Edge* was developed as a wealthy residential district in the 19C. Dean Stanley (1815–81) was born at the rectory. The church has a stained glass window (1873) by Morris and Co. The Edge (650ft; partly NT) is a wooded sandstone escarpment with fine views.—42m. **Wilmslow** (30,200 inhab.).

*Styal* (NT), in the pretty valley of the Bobbin 1¹/₂m N, is a wonderfully complete factory community of the early Industrial Revolution centred on the Quarry Bank Mill (1784), now a working museum.—*Lindow Moss*, 1¹/₂m W of Wilmslow, has given its name to 'Lindow Man', an ancient body found preserved in a bog here in 1984.—*Mobberley*, 4m SW of Wilmslow on the way to Knutsford, has a church with a timber roof of 1450, rood screen of 1500 and memorial window to George Leigh Mallory (1886–1924), who died climbing Mount Everest.

At (47m) *Cheadle* we reach the suburbs of Manchester.—55m. **Manchester**, see Rte 74.

# 55 Leicester to Derby and Sheffield

Total distance 63m. **Leicester**, see Rte 46.—A6 to (11m) Loughborough.—A6 to (27m) **Derby**.—A38, A61 to (51m) Chesterfield.—A61 to (63m) **Sheffield**, see Rte 75G.

Maps: OS Landranger 140 (briefly), 129, 128, 119, 120 (briefly), 110 or 111.

A useful connecting route through the centre of the Midlands, dull in itself but giving access to the Peak District (Rte 56). M1, following a roughly parallel course, is the fast alternative.

**Leicester**, see Rte 46. We join A6, via Belgrave Rd or St Margaret's Way from the inner ring road.—4m. At *Wanlip*, near the Soar and the Grand Union Canal to the right, the fine brass of Sir Thomas Walsh (d. 1393) in the church is the earliest with an English inscription.—At (5m) *Rothley*, on the left, the partly Elizabethan Rothley Court Hotel has the chapel of a preceptory of the Knights Templar. Thomas Babington Macaulay (1800–59) was born here. The parish church has Babington monuments and (outside) a 10C cross. A steam service runs along a reopened section of the Great Central Railway via Woodhouse and Quorn to Loughborough (weekends and Bank Holidays).—6¹/₂m. *Mountsorrel* is known for its red granite.—8m. *Quorndon*, or *Quorn* (pronounced 'Corn'), has good 16C tombs in the church.

The kennels of the famous Quorn hunt are now at *Seagrave*, 4¹/₂m E, via (1m) *Barrow-upon-Soar*, where the church has a fine Perp. wooden roof.—From Quorn B591 goes W into *Charnwood Forest* (Rte 46).

11m. **Loughborough** (47,600 inhab.; Tourist Information), a dull red-brick town, is a hosiery and engineering centre. It is also known for the historic Taylor's bell foundry; the *War Memorial Tower* (1922–23), a prominent landmark in Queen's Park, has a carillon of 45 bells. The parish church of *All Saints* is a spacious Dec. and Perp. building much restored by Sir Gilbert Scott. *Loughborough University of Technology*, with modern buildings on the Leicester road, was founded as the College of Technology in 1909 and raised to its present status in 1964.

FROM LOUGHBOROUGH TO NOTTINGHAM, 15m by A60.—We cross the Soar and enter Nottinghamshire beyond (3m) *Hoton*.—8m. The attractive village of *Bunny*, rebuilt by the 'wrestling baronet' Sir Thomas Parkyns (1664–1741), has a fine 14C church with a noble chancel.—10m. *Ruddington* has two museums, one devoted to local history and the other to framework knitting.—15m. *Nottingham*, see Rte 57.

A6 descends the Leicestershire bank of the Soar to (16m) *Kegworth*, an interesting village with a handsome late Dec. church and 19C buildings once used for framework knitting. The church at *Kingston-on-Soar*, on the Nottinghamshire bank to the E, has a 16C chantry displaying the rebus (babe in tun) of the Babington family. From the large junction with M1 N of Kegworth, A453 leads SW to (1¹/₂m)

*East Midlands Airport*, with direct passenger services to Aberdeen, Edinburgh, Glasgow, London (Heathrow), Guernsey, Jersey, Belfast, Dublin, Amsterdam, Malaga and Paris. The Aeropark has aviation exhibits and an information centre. At *Castle Donington*, to the N, is the International Motor Sport Centre with a racing circuit and the Donington Collection of racing cars and motorcycles.—For A453 to *Ashby-de-la-Zouch* and to *Nottingham*, see Rte 57.

17m. *Lockington*, to the left beyond the junction with M1 and A453, has fine woodwork in its church.—We cross the Trent, here marking the Derbyshire border, and the Trent and Mersey Canal to (21m) *Shardlow*, with a museum of canal history.—23m. *Elvaston Castle Country Park* has beautiful gardens, a working estate museum, etc. The County Show takes place here on Spring Bank Holiday Monday.

27m. **DERBY** (215,700 inhab.) is the traditional county town of Derbyshire, though no longer the seat of its administration. Given its historic importance and its size, it has surprisingly little to attract visitors; to many it is simply a convenient gateway to the Peak District (Rte 56). Apart from the cathedral (originally built as a parish church) and a few handsome 18C buildings (chiefly on Friar Gate), the most interesting aspect of Derby is its varied industrial history, to which the recently established Industrial Museum gives a good introduction.

**Tourist Information Centre**: Central Library, Wardwick.

**Car Parks**: Main Centre, Eagle Centre, The Cockpitt, Burton Rd, Bold Lane, Chapel St.

**Bus and Coach Station**: Morledge. City buses also from Market Place.

**Railway Station**: Midland Rd, SE of the centre.

**Theatre**: Playhouse, Eagle Centre. Concerts in Guildhall and Assembly Rooms, Market Place.

**History**. The Roman station of *Derventio* was at Little Chester on the opposite bank of the Derwent. In 854 the town was taken by the Danes, who renamed it *Deoraby* and made it (with Nottingham, Leicester, Lincoln and Stamford) one of the five cities of the Danelagh. Recaptured by the Saxons in 917, it became an important centre in the Middle Ages. In 1745 Prince Charles Edward Stuart penetrated as far south as Derby with his Highland army but after two days was forced to begin the retreat to Scotland, where the disaster of Culloden awaited him. In the 1720s Defoe had found 'gentry rather than trade' in Derby but industry was developing. The silk mill started by John and Thomas Lombe in 1717–21, on the site of the present Industrial Museum, was not just the first to succeed in England but also the first true factory. William Duesbury established the Royal Crown Derby works (now part of the Royal Doulton Tableware Group) in the 1750s. The 19C made Derby a centre of the Midland Railway, with large engineering workshops, and Rolls-Royce Ltd moved here in 1908, two years after its foundation.

**Famous natives and visitors**. The painter Joseph Wright ('Wright of Derby'; 1734–97) was born in Iron Gate, Herbert Spencer (1820–1903) in Exeter St. and John Flamsteed (1646–1719), the first Astronomer Royal, at *Denby*, 6½m N. Samuel Johnson married Tetty Porter at St Werburgh's church in 1735.

London Rd runs toward the centre of the town past Midland Rd, leading to the railway station on the right, and the *Royal Infirmary* (1891) on the left. Beyond the inner ring road lie the heavily restored 14–15C church of *St Peter* on the left and the modern shopping precincts of Main Centre and Eagle Centre on the right. Cornmarket leads straight ahead into the older, largely pedestrianised shopping area around the Market Place. We take a devious route, turning left into Victoria St Between Wardwick and the Strand, beyond, are the

*Library* and Tourist Information Centre, as well as the **Museum and Art Gallery**.

The *Museum*, largely devoted to local history, has a working model showing the development of the Midland Railway, two natural history galleries and a collection of Blue John. The Prince Charlie Room has oak panelling from Exeter House, where the Young Pretender lodged in 1745. The *Art Gallery* has outstanding collections of Derby porcelain and paintings by Joseph Wright of Derby.

Nearby *St Werburgh's* was the scene of Dr Johnson's wedding. Largely rebuilt by Sir Arthur Blomfield in 1894, it contains a wrought-iron font cover of 1716 by Robert Bakewell (see cathedral below). The church stands at the beginning of Friar Gate, whose 18C houses make it the most handsome street in Derby.

We continue N on Bold Lane and turn right into St Mary's Gate, with the handsome *Crown Court*, formerly the *County Hall*, of 1660. At the end rises the lovely Perp. *tower of the **Cathedral**. Originally the parish church of All Saints, it was raised to cathedral rank when the new diocese was separated from Southwell in 1927.

The tower, built c 1510–30, is all that survives of the medieval church. The rest was demolished to make way for James Gibbs's nave (1723–25); the E end, by Sebastian Comper with windows by Ceri Richards and Patrick Reyntiens, was added in 1965–72. The chief feature of the interior is the wrought-iron *screen by the local craftsman Robert Bakewell (d. 1752), stretching the full width of the church. The fine monuments include the effigy tomb of 'Bess of Hardwick' (Elizabeth, Countess of Shrewsbury; d. 1608) in the S choir aisle and, next to it, the figure of Caroline, Countess of Bessborough (d. 1760) by Rysbrack.

Queen St. leads N from the cathedral. Off Full St. to the right is the **Derby Industrial Museum**, in a partly rebuilt version of the silk mill which John and Thomas Lombe opened in 1717–21. The ground floor contains Rolls-Royce aero engines, while the first floor illustrates Derbyshire's wide variety of industries. The first stage of a gallery devoted to railway engineering has been opened. Queen St. continues to the junction with the inner ring road, spanned by a footbridge leading to Pugin's *Roman Catholic Church* (1838). Between the 18C St Mary's Bridge and the modern bridge carrying the ring road across the Derwent is the 14–15C *Chapel of St Mary at the Brygge*, one of the few surviving bridge chapels in England.

Iron Gate leads down the hill from the cathedral to the Market Place. The *Guildhall* (1842) has been renovated as a concert hall, etc. Behind is the huge barrel-vaulted *Market Hall* (1864). On the E side of the square are the *Assembly Rooms* (1970; Casson, Conder and Partners).

The *Royal Crown Derby Works* in Osmaston Rd includes a museum of Derby china dating from the 1750s; factory tours are available by appointment. Behind is the *Arboretum*, landscaped by J.C. Loudon in 1840.

**Kedleston Hall** (NT) stands about 4½m NW of the city. It was built in 1759–65 by Robert Adam, succeeding James Paine and Matthew Brettingham as architect. He modified the original Palladian design to create a masterpiece in his own more sumptuous style, though Dr Johnson found the result ostentatious. The interior, decorated by Adam with plasterwork by Joseph Rose, is particularly notable for the *Marble Hall with columns of local alabaster and the central Rotunda. There are good collections of 18C furniture and of Italian and Dutch 17C painting, and a museum of Indian art collected by Marquess Curzon of Kedleston (1859–1925) while he was Viceroy of India. The large park has buildings by Adam, including a bridge over the lake and a boathouse. The church has Curzon tombs from the 13C onwards.

Notable churches near Derby are at: *Chaddesdon*, a large suburb 2m NE, rebuilt c 1357 with a notable screen and a wall lectern, a local characteristic; *Breadsall*, 2½m NE, rebuilt by Caröe in 1915 after arson by suffragettes but keeping its Norman doorway and splendid 14C spire; and *Morley*, 4m NE, with *monuments and 15C glass from Dale Abbey, near Ilkeston (Rte 57).

FROM DERBY TO NOTTINGHAM, 16m by A52.—At (8m) *Sandiacre*, N of the junction with M1, the church has a fine 14C chancel.—We continue through *Beeston* to (16m) *Nottingham* (Rte 57).

FROM DERBY TO ASHBY-DE-LA-ZOUCH, 14m.—We head S on A514 to (5m) *Swarkestone*, where the long 14C bridge over the Trent was the most southerly point reached by the advance guard of Highland rebels in 1745.—Beyond (6m) *Stanton-by-Bridge* we branch left on B587 for the pleasant small town of (7m) *Melbourne*, where the pioneer travel agent Thomas Cook (1808–92) was born. The church has a fine Norman *interior with mighty arcades. *Melbourne Hall* (limited opening), a 17–18C building with work by Francis Smith of Warwick and his son, was the home of two Victorian Prime Ministers, Lords Melbourne and Palmerston. The formal gardens laid out in 1700, overlooking a lake, include a wrought-iron arbour (1706–11) by Robert Bakewell. At *Ticknall*, on A514 2m SW, is the entrance to *Calke Abbey*, a country house of 1701–03 recently acquired, with its marvellously complete contents, by NT. The park, on the S side of Staunton Harold reservoir, is open; the house is planned to open after restoration in 1989.—B587 continues to (10m) *Staunton Harold*, where the church (NT) is one of the few built during the Commonwealth. It stands picturesquely beside the 18C Hall (now a Cheshire Home) and above a lake. —11m. We join A453 heading SW to (14m) *Ashby-de-la-Zouch* (Rte 46).

FROM DERBY TO STOKE-ON-TRENT, 33m.—W of Derby A516 branches from A38 and joins A50 at (10m) *Hatton*, on the N bank of the Dove. **Tutbury**, on the Staffordshire bank 1½m S, is famous for its alabaster. Mary, Queen of Scots, was a prisoner in the 14–15C castle, now ruined but with 18C additions. The church is the nave of a Benedictine priory founded c 1080, with a magnificent Norman *W door of c 1160.—13m. *Sudbury*, left of A50, has a charming village street. *Sudbury Hall* (NT) is a red-brick Restoration house with good plaster decoration and woodcarving inside, including work by Grinling Gibbons. A servants' wing has been converted into a *Museum of Childhood*. The church at *Hanbury*, 3m SE, claims to have the oldest alabaster effigy in England, of Sir John Hanbury (d. 1303).

We enter Staffordshire before (18m) **Uttoxeter** (9000 inhab.), where Dr Johnson stood bareheaded in the rain in the market place to expiate his refusal to attend his father's bookstall some 50 years earlier. A bas-relief on the conduit depicts the incident. *Checkley*, on the former course of A50 4m NW, has a church with a Dec. chancel, old glass and three late Saxon crosses. From Uttoxeter to *Ashbourne*, see Rte 56B; to *Stafford*, see Rte 51.

A50 continues to (27m) *Blythe Bridge*. At *Dilhorne*, 2m N, the Foxfield Railway Society has a museum of steam locomotives, with trips on a former mineral line.—We enter the Potteries at (29m) *Longton*.—33m. *Stoke*, see Rte 54.

From Derby to *Lichfield* and *Birmingham*, see Rte 48; to *Manchester* via *Matlock*, *Bakewell*, and *Buxton*, see Rte 56A, via *Ashbourne* and *Leek*, see Rte 56B.

We join A38 N of Derby.—At Butterley Station near (37m) *Ripley* (18,700 inhab.) the Midland Railway Centre has steam locomotives and rolling stock from the old LMS railway, with a 3m section of working line.—40m. *Alfreton* (23,100 inhab.; Tourist Information) is a colliery town. A615 leads NW to (8m) *Matlock* (Rte 56A).—A61 continues N via (44m) *Ogston Reservoir*, on the left, and the colliery town of (46m) *Clay Cross* (9300 inhab.).

51m. **Chesterfield** (70,500 inhab.; Tourist Information), an engineering centre, is famous for the twisted spire of its parish church, caused by the warping of the timbers beneath the lead covering. Inside, the building (c 1350) has good window tracery and elaborate 16C tombs. The *Peacock Heritage Centre*, in a half-timbered 16C building on Low Pavement, has local exhibits. George Stephenson (1781–1848), who lived 1m NE at Tapton House, is buried in the 19C church of *Holy Trinity* on Newbold Rd. The *Stephenson Memorial Hall* now houses a civic theatre.

A632 leads E across the colliery-dotted *Scarsdale* to (6m) *Bolsover* (Rte 58A); A617 leads SE to (12m) *Mansfield* via *Hardwick Hall* (both Rte 58A).

At (53m) *Old Whittington*, to the right of A61, the plans for the overthrow of James II in 1688 were arranged in Revolution House (open), formerly an inn.—57m. The church at *Dronfield* (23,300 inhab.) has a fine 14C chancel with the brasses (1399) of two brother priests on the same slab, said to be a unique occurrence.

63m. **Sheffield**, Rte 75G.

# 56   The Peak District

Maps: OS Landranger maps as indicated in the separate routes below, or OS Peak District Tourist map (1:63,360 or 1in to 1m) for the National Park and its fringes. Walkers need OS Outdoor Leisure maps (1:25,000 or 2½in to 1m) for the Dark Peak and the White Peak.

The hilly region known as the *Peak District stands at the S end of the Pennine Chain, bounded roughly by the cities of Derby in the S, Manchester in the NW and Sheffield in the NE. Though it is also often called the Derbyshire Peak, its characteristic scenery extends into Staffordshire in the S and W and, to a lesser extent, into Cheshire in the W, Greater Manchester and West Yorkshire in the N, and South Yorkshire in the NE. About 540 square miles are included in the Peak District National Park, the first National Park to be created under the Parliamentary Act of 1949 and still one of the largest. Its boundaries are marked by the distinctive roadside millstones which greet the many visitors it attracts. On the map the Park forms a large oval shape, slightly dented in the SE to exclude the industrialised country around Matlock and Wirksworth and, for similar reasons, more dramatically deformed in the W to omit the wedge of land from Buxton to Whaley Bridge and New Mills. Buxton, though popular as a touring centre, thus lies outside the Park. The largest town inside its boundaries—indeed, the only town of any size—is Bakewell.

There is no single hill or range of hills known specifically as the Peak. Rather, the whole region belongs to what geologists call the 'Derbyshire Dome', a conical mass of rock forced up from the bed of the warm, shallow sea that once covered it. The upper stratum was gritstone, also known as millstone grit from its most obvious use for making millstones; beneath lay whitey-grey carboniferous limestone. The way that different parts of this dome have weathered largely accounts for the two distinct types of landscape we now find. Millstone grit survives in the Dark Peak of the W, E and N, creating a wild, treeless scenery of heather-clad moorland that rises over 2000ft at a few points, notably Kinder Scout. The hills are often guarded towards their summits by low, black lines of crag locally called 'edges' (e.g. Froggatt Edge in the E, and Axe Edge in the W). This country is particularly attractive to determined walkers and climbing enthusiasts. In the centre and S of the region is the White Peak, still hilly but gentler and more accessible, where the millstone grit has been worn away to expose the underlying limestone. The sweet, green uplands of this plateau are divided by loose stone walls, built without mortar, into an endless chequer of fields. In the valleys, the Dove, the Manifold and the Wye have forced their way through the limestone to create the famous and beautiful Dales: narrow ravines, often pleasantly wooded and fringed by white cliffs and striking rock formations.

Both the desolate country of the Dark Peak and the gentler landscape of the White Peak have been popular with visitors since the 17C, when Thomas Hobbes and Charles Cotton enumerated their 'wonders' and Cotton fished the trout waters of the Dove with his friend Izaak Walton. By the Romantic era the Peak District was valued, like the Wye Valley and the Lake District, as a miniature English equivalent of the Alps. The list of its wonders extended beyond natural features like Mam Tor (the 'shivering mountain' near Castleton), the limestone caverns near Buxton and Castleton, and the spring at Buxton to include the Duke of Devonshire's mansion at Chatsworth. A welcome feature of recent years has been the new awareness of the Peak's industrial heritage: Arkwright's water-powered cotton mill at Cromford, the lead mines around Matlock and Castleton, and the canal and railway systems, including the Monsal Dale railway viaduct. Fittingly, dismantled railway lines now form the High Peak, Tissington and Monsal Trails, which give a pleasant and easy introduction to walking in the region.

The custom of well-dressing, observed or revived in towns and villages throughout the region, probably originated as a pagan thanksgiving for water. The wells are decorated with flower petals pressed into a clay base to form pictures or designs, which are then blessed at a religious service. Ceremonies are held in May at Tissington (Ascension Tide), Etwall, Wirksworth, and Monyash; in June at Ashford (Trinity Sunday), Youlgreave, Hope, Tideswell, Litton, Rowsley and Wyaston; in July at Bakewell, Stoney Middleton, Buxton, Pilsley and Bonsall; in August at Bradwell, Barlow, Eyam and Wormhill; and in September at Whitfield. Exact dates can be obtained from Information Centres and the National Park Office.

There are National Park Information Centres at Bakewell, Castleton and Edale, and seasonal Information Centres at Hartington (open weekends and Bank Holiday Mondays from Easter to end of September) and Fairholmes (open daily Easter to end October and winter weekends). Useful publications listing local events, licensed camping and caravan sites, Youth Hostels, etc. are available from the National Park Office, Aldern House, Baslow Road, Bakewell, Derbyshire DE4 1AE.

# A.   Derby to Manchester via Matlock, Bakewell and Buxton

Total distance 68m. **Derby**, see Rte 55. We follow A6 throughout.
—To (19m) **Matlock**.—To (26½m) **Bakewell**.—To (38m) **Buxton**.
—To (44m) Chapel-en-le-Frith.—To (48m) Whaley Bridge.
—To (59m) Stockport.—To (66m) **Manchester**, see Rte 74.

Maps: OS Landranger 128 (briefly), 119, 110 (briefly) and 109 or OS Peak District Tourist map for National Park area.

**Derby**, see Rte 55. A6 heads N, along the Derwent valley.—4½m. *Duffield* has the excavated foundations of a huge Norman keep razed to the ground in 1266 (NT). Kedleston Hall (Rte 55) is about 3½m SW of Duffield. B5023 goes up the Ecclesbourne valley from Duffield to (8m) Wirksworth (see below).—9m. *Belper* developed as an industrial town with the opening of Jedediah Strutt and Richard Arkwright's cotton mill in 1776. The valley becomes more beautiful beyond (11m) *Ambergate*.—13m. *Whatstandwell* lies beneath *Crich Stand* (955ft; *view), about 2m NE. It is reached via *Crich*, with the National Tramway Museum.

Off B5035 1½m NE of Crich, on a steep knoll overlooking the Amber, is the ruined late 15C *Wingfield Manor* (not open) where Mary, Queen of Scots, was imprisoned in 1584–85.

At (15m) *High Peak Junction* are the restored workshops of the Cromford and High Peak Railway (open).

The High Peak Trail follows the disused railway line 17m W and N towards Buxton. It crosses B5036 near the Black Rocks (see below) after 1½m and, about ½m beyond, passes near *Middleton Top*, with a restored 19C winding engine (open) used for hauling wagons up the steep gradient.—For the junction with the Tissington Trail near *Parsley Hay*, see Rte 56C.

17m. *Cromford* has a rich industrial history. Richard Arkwright established his water-powered cotton mill here in 1771; it is now open, with a small exhibition. Rows of model workers' houses survive in North St. There are trips (summer weekends) by horse-drawn narrow boat along a restored section of the Cromford Canal.

To the W lies the wooded *Via Gellia*, named after the local family of Gell. A sideroad leads to the upland village of *Bonsall*, 1½m NW of Cromford, with a good market cross and a 14C church spire surrounded by curious 'crowns'. A footpath continues N to Masson Hill (see below).
  **Wirksworth** (5500 inhab.), beyond the *Black Rocks* on B5036 1½m S of Cromford, was once a lead-mining centre. It is now a market town, though limestone is still quarried nearby. The 19C Moot Hall in Chapel Lane preserves the 16C dish used as the standard measure for lead ore. The fine 13–14C church has a remarkable Saxon *coffin-lid and, in the S transept, a small carving of a lead miner, apparently 12C. Wirksworth is also connected with George Eliot, who portrayed it as Snowfield in 'Adam Bede'. The *Carsington Reservoir* is being constructed to the SW.

A6 continues N to **Matlock** (20,600 inhab.), the administrative centre of Derbyshire. The general name includes (17m) *Matlock Bath* (Tourist Information), in the narrow limestone ravine of the Derwent, and (19m) *Matlock*, at the open end of the ravine beyond. Matlock proper consists of two distinct parts, Matlock Bridge by the river and Matlock Bank on the steep hill above. The tepid natural springs encouraged its development as a spa town from the Regency onwards but its great popularity dated from 1853, when John Smedley opened his hydropathic treatment centre at Matlock Bank, in buildings now occupied by the County Council. Indiscriminate building, tawdry amusements and crowds of tourists mar the extraordinary natural beauty of the setting, particularly at Matlock Bath.
  The Pavilion at Matlock Bath houses the interesting *Peak District Mining Museum*, with geological displays, tools and machinery; nearby is the *Temple Mine* (open). On the W side of the narrow pass between Matlock Bath and Matlock are the wooded *Heights of Abraham* (open), with cable car, Great Rutland Cavern and Nestus Mine, and a view from the Victoria Prospect Tower. Further W is the commanding height of *Masson Hill* (1110ft). Overhanging the opposite side of the river is *High Tor* (673ft; view).

The grounds of the 19C *Riber Castle*, c 2m SE of Matlock via A615 and Tansley, contain an excellent *wildlife park with British and European birds and animals.—*Dethick*, about 4m SE off A615 beyond Tansley, has a 13C church with a good tower of 1530. *Lea Gardens* (open), S of Dethick, have rhododendrons, etc. in a woodland setting.

Beyond Matlock we enter the broad upper valley of the Derwent.
—21m. The church of *Darley Dale*, 1m left, has a stone parclose
screen, stained glass by Morris and Co., an early 14C effigy of a
knight and two incised 16C slabs of the Rowsley family.

About 2³/₄m SW, up the long hill of B5057, is the pleasant village of *Winster*,
with a 17–18C market house (NT Information Centre and shop).

B5057 heads 3³/₄m N from Winster to rejoin A6 between Rowsley and
Bakewell, flanked by gritstone moors rich in Bronze Age remains. The most
notable is the *Nine Ladies Stone Circle* (English Heritage, open at any
reasonable time) on *Stanton Moor* to the E, reached via (1³/₄m) the sideroad for
*Birchover* or (2¹/₂m) the sideroad for *Stanton-in-Peak*. At 3m a sideroad
branches W for (³/₄m) *Alport*, where the picturesque limestone valleys of the
Bradford and the Lathkill meet. *Monyash*, at the source of the Lathkill 4¹/₂m
NW, can be reached by road from Bakewell (see below) or A515 (Rte 56C).
*Youlgreave*, on the Bradford ³/₄m SW, has a handsome church with a Perp.
tower, a miniature tomb effigy of 1488, a curious 12C font and stained glass by
Morris and Co.

The main route enters the National Park at (23¹/₂m) **Rowsley**, by the
junction of the Derwent and the Wye. The Peacock Hotel is a fine
building of 1652.

4m N is *****Chatsworth** (open), the grand classical mansion of the
Dukes of Devonshire in its vast park. It is popular with visitors and
crowded at holiday times.

The Elizabethan house, begun by Sir William Cavendish and completed by his
widow, 'Bess of Hardwick', was replaced by the present building between 1687
and 1707. William Talman designed the S and E sides; the W side with its
central pediment and the curved N side, through which visitors enter, are
probably by Thomas Archer. Wyatville added the N wing (1820–30).
   The house contains a superb collection of furniture and works of art. The most
striking features of its decoration are the pompous ceiling paintings by
Laguerre, Verrio and others, and the *wood carving, once attributed to Grinling
Gibbons but now known to be largely the work of a local artist, Samuel Watson
(1663–1715). Both are seen throughout the State Apartments and, to their best
advantage, in the *Chapel. Like several other rooms, the State Dining Room has
furniture by Kent. The State Drawing Room contains Mortlake tapestries; the
State Music Room a door with a trompe l'oeil painting by Jan van der Vaart; and
the State Bedroom the bed in which George II died. Beyond the Sketch
Galleries, with Mortlake tapestries, Delft ware and modern family portraits
(including a fine Sargent), are the Chapel, the curious Oak Room, the Library,
Ante-Library and Dome Room. The Great Dining Room has portraits by Van
Dyck; work by Franz Hals and Rembrandt hangs in the Sculpture Gallery.
   The Orangery leads to the formal Gardens, originally laid out when the
present house was built, with a famous cascade and fountains. A maze now
covers the site of the conservatory (1836–39) built by the 6th Duke and his head
gardener, Joseph Paxton, anticipating his design for the Crystal Palace.
   The *Park (11,000 acres) is watered by the Derwent and bounded to the E by
moorland. Just N of James Paine's bridge (1762) is a remnant of the Elizabethan
house, Queen Mary's Bower, named after the captive Mary, Queen of Scots.
   *Edensor* is a 'model village' of 1839 on the W edge of the park. The church
(mainly by Gilbert Scott, 1867) contains a striking classical monument to the 1st
Earl of Devonshire (d. 1625) and a brass inscription to John Beaton (d. 1570),
steward to Mary, Queen of Scots. Joseph Paxton is buried in the churchyard.
—From *Baslow*, a pleasant village on the Derwent beyond the N edge of the
park, A621 heads NE to Sheffield (Rte 75G).

A6 leaves the Derwent at Rowsley and continues along the lovely
winding valley of the Wye.—24¹/₂m. We pass the junction with B5056
from Winster (see above).—25m. *****Haddon Hall** (open), standing on a
wooded slope above the river, is one of the most complete and best
preserved medieval manor houses in England.

About the middle of the 12C Haddon passed from its Norman lords, the
Avenells, to the Vernons. They were united with another powerful local family

in 1558 when Lady Dorothy Vernon married Sir John Manners, though the story of her elopement is probably just a romantic legend. The Manners family, created Dukes of Rutland, moved to Belvoir Castle in Leicestershire about 1700 and left Haddon unoccupied and unaltered for 200 years.

The picturesque stone buildings are grouped around two courtyards on different levels. There is a small museum by the gatehouse entrance. The 12–15C Chapel has contemporary wall paintings. The 14C Hall, dividing the courtyards, has a 15C screen and a restored roof. The Parlour has a rare 16C decorated ceiling and panelling. Above is the 17C Long Gallery added by Sir John Manners. From the ante-room nearby run the steps down which Dorothy Vernon is said to have eloped. The lovely terraced *gardens were laid out in the 17C.

26½m. **Bakewell** (3900 inhab.), an attractive little market town with a five-arched medieval bridge across the Wye, is a popular centre for visitors and walkers in the White Peak. The 17C Market Hall houses the Peak National Park and Tourist Information Centre. The *Church*, with a Saxon cross outside, has a Norman W doorway and a S porch with 9–13C gravestones. It contains an elaborate 14C font and, in the S transept, 15–17C monuments of the Vernons and Manners, including those of Dorothy Manners (d. 1584) and her father, Sir George Vernon (d. 1567). The quaint tomb of Sir Godfrey Foljambe (d. 1377) and his wife is in the S aisle. The *Old House Museum*, in Cunningham Place above the church, has a folk collection in a building of 1534 later leased by Richard Arkwright for his workers. 'Bakewell pudding', different from the so-called 'Bakewell tart' found elsewhere, was first made at the Rutland Arms in the 19C. The Bakewell Agricultural Show is held on the first Wednesday and Thursday in August.

FROM BAKEWELL TO HATHERSAGE, 9m. We cross the Wye and head N on A619, the Baslow road, branching left on B6001 after ¾m.—From (4½m) *Calver*, the road descends into the Derwent valley. Middleton Dale (see below) is to the left, while the millstone grit of *Froggatt Edge* rises on the opposite bank.—6½m. *Grindleford* stands on a lovely reach of the river. For the *Longshaw Estate* (NT), see Rte 56D. About 3m SW of Grindleford by B6521, a hilly road with lovely views, is the large upland village of **Eyam** (pronounced 'Eem'). It preserves touching reminders of its devastation in 1665–66, when the plague killed more than 250 of the 350 inhabitants. Led by the rector, William Mompesson, and the ejected minister, Thomas Stanley, the villagers succeeded in isolating their parish and preventing the spread of the disease. A remembrance service is held on the last Sunday of August on the hillside where the villagers worshipped during the plague. There is a fine Saxon cross, perhaps 9C, in the churchyard. On A623 ½m S is the rocky gorge of *Middleton Dale*, leading E through the village of *Stoney Middleton* back to (2m) Calver.—B6001 continues NW from Grindleford to (9m) *Hathersage* (Rte 56D).

FROM BAKEWELL TO CHAPEL-EN-LE-FRITH VIA TIDESWELL, 14¼m.—We branch right from A6 at (1½m) *Ashford-in-the-Water* (see below), taking B6465 past (3m) *Monsal Head* (see below) to (5½m) *Wardlow*. A623 heads E to Middleton Dale (see above), but we go W to (7m) *Tideswell*, where the large and beautiful 14C *church has a striking W tower, a stone screen behind the altar and the brass of Bishop Pursglove (d. 1579). *Wheston*, 1½m W, has a good 14–15C cross. For Tideswell Dale to the S, see below.—10m. *Peak Forest* has a church of 1657–66 dedicated to King Charles the Martyr. *Tunstead*, 3m S, birthplace of the canal-builder James Brindley (1716–72), has the largest limestone quarry in Europe.—14¼m. *Chapel-en-le-Frith*, see below.

Beyond Bakewell A6 follows the Wye past the pleasant village of (28m) *Ashford-in-the-Water* but leaves the river at (29¾m) *Deep Dale* and does not rejoin it until it has climbed past (30½m) *Taddington Wood* (NT) to (34½m) *Topley Pike*. It thus gives only tantalising glimpses of the beautiful *valley to the N.

*The Monsal Dale railway viaduct*

This is best explored by taking B6465 from Ashford to (1½m) *Monsal Head*, with the viaduct of the disused railway line built in 1863 and denounced by Ruskin for destroying the natural beauty of the scene so that 'every fool in Buxton can be at Bakewell in half-an-hour'. The Monsal Trail follows the course of the line through (1m) *Monsal Dale* and (3m) *Miller's Dale* (NT), with a nature trail leading N up *Tideswell Dale*. About 1½m further, beyond B6049, is the splendid crag of *Chee Tor* in a narrow limestone ravine. The trail ends at (7m) the Wyedale car park on A6 near Topley Pike.

38m. **BUXTON** (20,800 inhab.), outside the National Park, stands on higher ground (about 1000ft) than any town of comparable size in England. Still a popular centre for visitors to the Peak, it has some handsome architecture from its days as a spa.

**Tourist Information Centre**: The Crescent.

**Car Parks**: Market Place (except market days), Cattle Market, Pavilion Gardens, Wye St. and Sylvan Park off Spring Gardens.

**Buses**: from the Market Place.

**Railway Station**: Station Rd, NE of the Crescent.

**Theatre**: Opera House, Water St.

**Annual Events**: Well dressing in July. Buxton International Festival of Music and the Arts, end of July to beginning of August.

**History**. The springs, with their warm (28°C), bluish water, attracted the Romans in about AD 79; they named their settlement *Aquae Arnemetiae*, or 'The Spa of the Goddess of the Grove'. In the Middle Ages the town became a kind of English Lourdes and the Chapel of St Ann grew rich from pilgrims' offerings. Buxton again developed as a spa under the guidance of the 5th Duke of Devonshire at the end of the 18C.

The centre of the old town, Higher Buxton, on the hill to the S, is the Market Place with the 19C *Town Hall*. Nearby is the *Museum and Art Gallery*, with a small but interesting collection of prehistoric bones from bone caverns, a few local Roman antiquities, Blue John ware (see Castleton, Rte 56D) and 17–19C pottery from Stoke. Paintings include work by De Wint, Algernon Newton and Brangwyn. In High St., S of the Market Place, stands the unobtrusive church of *St Ann* (1625).

Higher Buxton is linked with Lower Buxton, the spa to the N, by the Slopes, a landscaped hillside with graded paths where patients taking the waters could exercise. Chief among the spa buildings is the *Crescent (1780–90) designed by John Carr of York to emulate the Palladian architecture of Bath. The *Library* occupies the handsome former Assembly Room. On the edge of the Slopes opposite the Crescent are the drinking fountain known as *St Ann's Well* and the former Pump Room of 1894, now housing the *Micrarium* (open), which displays natural history through microscopes.

Beyond the NE end of the Crescent is the attractive 19C Colonnade with, further N, the huge domed *Devonshire Royal Hospital*, built as stables by Carr in 1790 and converted in 1859. Station Rd leads E to the *Transport Museum* and the *Peak Rail Steam Centre*, home of the local railway preservation society.

Beyond the the SW end of the Crescent is the cloistered Square and the *Opera House*, designed by Frank Matcham and splendidly restored in 1979. The *Pavilion Gardens*, watered by the Wye before it disappears underground, are flanked by a range of 19C spa buildings, including the *Conservatory*, *Octagon* and a swimming pool filled with warm spa water. To the N is Wyatville's church of *St John the Baptist* (1811).

*John Carr's Crescent at Buxton*

**Poole's Cavern** (open), in *Buxton Country Park* almost 1m SW, is a natural limestone cave near the source of the Wye.—The *Cat and Fiddle Inn*, on A537 about 5m W, stands on desolate, high moorland (1690ft). *Macclesfield Forest* and *Macclesfield* (Rte 56B) lie further W. The old road from *Burbage* to the Cat and Fiddle passes the head of the Goyt valley; part of the lower valley is submerged in a reservoir for Stockport.

The bleak millstone grit of **Axe Edge** (1810ft), on A53 2½m SW of Buxton, is the highest point in the neighbourhood. From the surrounding slopes flow the region's major rivers: the Goyt (N), the Wye (N and E), the Dove and the Manifold (SE), and the Dane (SW). *Lud's Church*, a dramatic rock fissure on the Dane 5m further SW, is sometimes identified as the scene of Sir Gawain's encounter with the Green Knight in the medieval poem (but cf. Wetton Mill, Rte 56B). The whole of this neighbourhood, including the Roaches (Rte 56B) and the lower Dane Valley, is the most beautiful near Buxton.

A5002 climbs NW from Buxton directly to (8m) *Whaley Bridge* (see below), passing Combs Moss on the right and the lovely *Goyt Valley* with its reservoirs on the left. It can be explored by walking routes from the car parks at Goyts Lane, The Street, Errwood Hall, Goytsclough Quarry and Derbyshire Bridge. The sideroad linking The Street and Derbyshire Bridge is closed to traffic on Sundays and Bank Holidays between May and September; at all other times the section beyond Errwood is restricted to one-way traffic heading S.

From Buxton to *Ashbourne* via *Dovedale*, see Rte 56C.

The main route follows A6 N of Buxton, passing *Combs Moss* (1662ft) on the left, to (44m) *Chapel-en-le-Frith*, an old-fashioned town with market cross and stocks.

FROM CHAPEL-EN-LE-FRITH TO GLOSSOP, 9m by A624. The road heads along the rugged fringes of the National Park through (4½m) *Hayfield*, with Kinder Scout (Rte 56D) to the E.—9m. **Glossop** (25,300 inhab.; Tourist Information), with 19C cotton mills, stands on A57, the direct road from Sheffield to Manchester (Rte 56D). The Heritage Centre has an exhibition of local history. The *Dinting Railway Centre* (open) is nearby.

From *Chapel-en-le-Frith* to *Sheffield* via *Castleton* and *Hathersage*, see Rte 56D.

A6 continues W to (48m) *Whaley Bridge* (5500 inhab.), with a fine Georgian inn, at the mouth of the Goyt valley (see above).—51m. *New Mills* (9100 inhab.) is a manufacturing town near the Cheshire border. The church at *Mellor*, 2¾m NW, has a good Norman font and a Perp. wooden pulpit. B6101 follows the Goyt from New Mills to (4m) *Marple* (23,900 inhab.), where the restored aqueduct (1796–1801) of the Peak Forest Canal crosses the valley.—52½m. *Disley* is 2m N of **Lyme Park** (NT).

The originally Elizabethan house was superbly remodelled in 1725 by Giacomo Leoni and altered again by Lewis Wyatt in the early 19C. The rooms are a mixture of 17–19C work, with limewood carving that may be by Grinling Gibbons in the Saloon. Beyond the formal gardens is the magnificent *deer park (1320 acres). The Cage, on the ridge to the N, is an Elizabethan hunting tower altered by Leoni; the Lanthorn Tower, in the woods to the E, was removed from the Elizabethan house and rebuilt here in the 18C.

At (57m) *Hazel Grove* A6 is joined by A523 from Leek and Macclesfield (Rte 56B).—59m. **Stockport** (136,500 inhab.; Tourist Information) is dominated by the huge railway viaduct (1839–40) spanning the narrow valley of the Mersey. The high-lying parish church of *St Mary* was rebuilt by Lewis Wyatt in 1813–17 but keeps its Dec. chancel. There is a statue of Richard Cobden (1804–65), Stockport's MP in 1841–47, in St Peter's Square. The church of *St Thomas* on Wellington Rd South is by George Basevi (1822–25). The *War Memorial Art Gallery* has 19–20C British paintings, including work by L.S. Lowry, and Epstein's head of Yehudi Menuhin. The *Museum* in Vernon Park remembers the social and industrial history of the area, including hat-making.

*Bramall Hall** (open), 3m S via A5102, is one of the best black-and-white houses in the country, with a rich display of timber and plaster outside and some handsomely preserved rooms inside. In its present form the house dates from 1500 to 1600, though parts of the S wing are earlier, including the chapel with its wall painting.

66m. **Manchester**, see Rte 74.

# B.   Derby to Manchester
# via Ashbourne and Leek

Total distance 58m. **Derby**, see Rte 55.—A52 to (13m) **Ashbourne**. —A52, A523 to (28m) **Leek**.—A523 to (41m) Macclesfield.—A523 to (49m) Hazel Grove.—A6 to (51m) Stockport and (58m) **Manchester**, see Rte 56A.

Maps: OS Landranger 128, 119, 118 and 109 or OS Peak District Tourist map for National Park area.

A route along the S and W fringes of the Peak District and the National Park.

**Derby**, see Rte 55. We leave the city on A52.—4m. *Kirk Langley* is a pleasant village. Kedleston Hall (Rte 55) is about 2m NE.—6¼m. *Brailsford* has a Saxon cross in the churchyard, left of our road. —10½m. *Osmaston*, to the left, is a 19C 'model village'.

13m. **Ashbourne** (6000 inhab.; Tourist Information), on the S edge of the limestone country of the Peak, is an attractive market town with many good Georgian houses, particularly on St John's St. and Church St. near the little triangular market place. Opposite the Tudor buildings of the *Grammar School* in Church St. is the house where Dr Johnson often visited his friend Dr John Taylor. The 13C *Church* of St Oswald, the best in the county, has a tall spire, beautiful S arcade with notable *capitals and double transepts. The monuments include the touching memorial by Thomas Banks to Penelope Boothby (d. 1791) and medieval tombs of the Cockayne family. A traditional game of football is played in the main street on Shrove Tuesday and Ash Wednesday.

FROM ASHBOURNE TO STOKE-ON-TRENT VIA ALTON, 21m. We take A52 W to (1½m) *Mayfield* (see below) and branch left on B5032.—4¼m. *Ellastone* is identified with 'Hayslope', the chief scene of 'Adam Bede'. George Eliot's father Robert Evans (d. 1849), who spent his childhood in the area, is buried in the churchyard. *Norbury*, on the other bank of the Dove, is the 'Norbune' of the novel. Its church has an impressive 14C chancel with blind arcading and striking tracery, a wealth of 14–15C glass and medieval tombs of the Fitzherberts.—Beyond Ellastone B5030 forks left to Uttoxeter (Rte 55). We continue along B5032 to (8m) *Alton*, in the wooded valley of the Churnet. Perched on a sandstone cliff are the scanty ruins of the castle (c 1175) in the grounds of the Convent of the Assumption, built by Pugin in the 1840s. At *Alton Towers* (open), on the opposite side of the glen, the shell of the 19C mansion (also partly by Pugin) and its lovely formal gardens are surrounded by what the management advertises as 'Britain's only world-rated leisure park'. *Croxden Abbey* (English Heritage, open at any reasonable time), 2m S of Alton, was a Cistercian foundation of 1176; the 13C ruins include the W end of the church.— 12m. *Cheadle* is a pleasantly situated town with a Roman Catholic church (1846) by Pugin and a nature reserve on *Hawksmoor* (NT), overlooking the Churnet to the NE.—A521 leads to (15m) *Blythe Bridge* (Rte 55) and A50 continues to (21m) *Stoke* (Rte 54).

From Ashbourne to *Dovedale* and *Buxton*, see Rte 56C.

Beyond Ashbourne A52 crosses the Dove into Staffordshire at

(14$^1$/$_2$m) *Mayfield.*—17m. At the fork we follow A523 along the S boundary of the Peak District National Park to (20m) *Waterhouses.*

From the car park at the former railway station walkers (and cyclists) can explore the dramatic scenery to the N, following the Hamps river to its junction with the Manifold at (3$^1$/$_2$m) *Beeston Tor* (NT), and continuing up the Manifold valley to: (4$^3$/$_4$m) *Thor's Cave*, where the river begins the underground course ending at Ilam (Rte 56C); (6m) *Wetton Mill*, sometimes identified as the scene of Sir Gawain's meeting with the Green Knight in the medieval poem (cf. Lud's Church, Rte 56A); and (8m) *Hulme End* (Rte 56C). Some of this country can also be reached by the steep and twisting sideroads leading from Waterhouses to (3$^1$/$_2$m) *Grindon*, (6m) *Wetton* and (8m) *Butterton.*

28m. **Leek** (19,700 inhab.; Tourist Information) is a little industrial town, once known for silk-weaving, among good scenery. The *Brindley Water Mill* (open) was designed by the canal-builder James Brindley in 1752. From the churchyard (with Saxon cross shafts) there is a fine view of the *Roaches*, a range of hills about 5m N, perhaps the best example in the country of tumbled masses of millstone grit.

*Cheddleton*, 3m S, has a flint mill (open) on the Churnet. There are trips along the canal in narrow boats.

30m. *Rudyard Lake*, from which Kipling took his name, is a long reservoir which has almost the charm of a natural lake.—We cross the Dane, marking the Cheshire border, shortly before (35$^1$/$_2$m) the junction with A54, leading SW to (4$^1$/$_2$m) *Congleton* (Rte 54) and NE to (12m) *Buxton* (Rte 56A), with the lower Dane valley and *Lud's Church* (also Rte 56A) to the right.—41m. **Macclesfield** (46,800 inhab.; Tourist Information) was once the centre of the English silk industry. The largely rebuilt church of *St Michael* contains the Legh and Savage Chapels, with medieval effigies and the 'indulgence brass' of Roger Legh (c 1506).

A537 leads past the wild *Macclesfield Forest* and the lonely *Cat and Fiddle Inn* to (12m) *Buxton* (Rte 56A).—*Gawsworth Hall* (open), in a pretty village off A536 4m SW, is a lovely half-timbered manor house of the late 15C, with later additions. The interesting church has 17C monuments of the Fittons, including Mary Fitton (d. c 1620), once thought to be the 'Dark Lady' of Shakespeare's sonnets.

43$^1$/$_2$m. The pretty village of *Prestbury* lies to the left. The churchyard of St Peter's, the 13–15C mother church of Macclesfield, has a Norman chapel with a beautiful doorway; a half-timbered priest's house stands opposite the church.—45m. *Adlington Hall* (limited opening), to the left, is a 'black and white' house with Georgian brick additions. The late 15C Great Hall has a fine hammerbeam roof and an organ (c 1670) by 'Father' Bernard Smith.

At (49m) *Hazel Grove* we join A6 and follow Rte 56A through (51m) *Stockport* to (58m) **Manchester**.

# C.  Ashbourne to Buxton via Dovedale

Total distance 22m. **Ashbourne**, see Rte 56B.—A515 to (22m)
**Buxton**, see Rte 56A.

Maps: OS Landranger 119 or OS Peak District Tourist map.

The direct route along A515, passing E of Dovedale, is much less
interesting than the alternatives and detours by sideroad or
footpath suggested below.

The Tissington Trail, a footpath along a dismantled railway line
closely following the course of A515, runs from Ashbourne to join
the High Peak Trail (Rte 56A) at (12¹/₂m) Parsley Hay.

**Ashbourne**, see Rte 56B. The Buxton road leads due N past the
pleasant village of (2¹/₂m) *Fenny Bentley*. The church contains the
Beresford tomb (c 1550) showing two shrouded adult figures in
alabaster with 21 children below. *Bradbourne* church, 2¹/₂m NE, has
interesting Norman and Saxon carving.—4m. *Tissington*, on the
right, is an attractive village with a Norman church tower.—6m.
*Alsop-en-le-Dale*, to the right, has a partly Norman church. The
Norman church tower at *Parwich*, 2¹/₂m E, has a striking tympanum.

A much more attractive way of making this part of the journey
takes the sideroad leading NW from Ashbourne across the Bentley
Brook to (1¹/₂m) *Mapleton*, on the Dove. It then climbs past (3¹/₂m)
*Thorpe*, with the Peveril of the Peak Hotel, and (4m) the *Izaak Walton
Hotel* to (5m) *Ilam*, where the church has a Norman font, the EE
shrine of the local St Bertram, a group by Chantrey and two Saxon
cross shafts outside. The 19C *Ilam Hall* (now a Youth Hostel) has
beautiful grounds (NT, with Information Centre) where the Manifold
rises from the underground course begun at Thor's Cave (Rte 56B).

Thorpe and Ilam stand at the S end of *•Dovedale*, the narrow and
wooded limestone ravine through which the Dove forces its way from
Milldale, about 3m N. It is the most popular beauty spot in the
Derbyshire Dales.

Dovedale was fished by Izaak Walton (1593–1683), author of 'The Compleat
Angler', and his friend and collaborator, Charles Cotton (1630–87) of Beresford
Hall. Among later generations, it was praised by travellers with tastes as
different as Dr Johnson ('he who has seen Dovedale has no need to visit the
Highlands') and Byron ('there are things in Derbyshire as noble as in Greece or
Switzerland'). The National Trust now owns about 2500 acres of land in the
Dove, Manifold and Hamps valleys, with covenants protecting nearly 3000
more.

The entrance lies between the bare summits of *Thorpe Cloud* (E; 942ft) and
*Bunster Hill* (W; 1000ft). The footpath up the dale follows the E (or Derbyshire)
bank from the stepping stones on the Dove. *Dovedale Castle*, on the W (or
Staffordshire) bank, is the first of the fancifully named limestone crags which
mark the route, though in summer the trees can make them hard to distinguish.
Others include the *Lover's Leap* (E), the *Twelve Apostles* (W) and the jagged
*Tissington Spires* (E). Beyond the caves known as *Dove Holes*, we reach the end
of Dovedale proper at (c 3m) *Milldale*.

It is worth following the river about 4m further to *Hartington* (see below),
through a series of ravines ending with *Wolfscote Dale* and, most striking of all,
the densely wooded *Beresford Dale*. This includes the pool frequented by Izaak
Walton and Charles Cotton. Cotton's fishing lodge (1674) stands on private land
at the exit from the dale. His pew is among the 17C woodwork in *Alstonefield*
church, ³/₄m NW of Milldale.

Beyond Alsop-en-le-Dale A515 climbs through green countryside
intersected in all directions by loose stone walls.—After (9¹/₂m)
*Newhaven*, with a famous coaching inn, we pass the roads for
Youlgreave and Matlock (Rte 56A) on the right.

B5054, branching left about $\frac{1}{2}$m beyond, offers an interesting alternative way into Buxton via (2m) *Hartington* (seasonal National Park Information Centre, open weekends and Bank Holiday Mondays from Easter to end of September), on a high plateau near Beresford Dale (see above), and (3m) *Hulme End*, on the Manifold (Rte 56B). Shortly beyond, we turn N on B5053 for (8m) *Longnor*, an excellent centre for the upper Manifold and Dove, and rejoin A515 at 11m.

12m. *Parsley Hay* is near the junction of the Tissington Trail with the High Peak Trail (Rte 56A). *Arbor Low* (English Heritage, open at any reasonable time), $\frac{3}{4}$m E, is a fallen stone circle surrounded by a ditch and earth rampart (2500–1700 BC).—22m. **Buxton**, see Rte 56A.

# D.   Sheffield to Manchester
# via Hathersage and Castleton

Total distance 46m. **Sheffield**, see Rte 75G.—A625 to (11m) **Hathersage**.—A625 to (17m) **Castleton**.—A625, interrupted at Mam Tor, to (24m) Chapel-en-le-Frith.—A6 to (28m) Whaley Bridge, (39m) Stockport and (46m) **Manchester**, see Rte 56A.

Maps: OS Landranger 110 and 109 or Peak District Tourist map.

A hilly, scenic route along the boundary between the White Peak and the Dark Peak. A57, the direct road from Sheffield to (37m) Manchester, runs via (10m) *Ladybower Reservoir*, (24m) *Glossop* and (30m) *Hyde*. For the section between Ladybower Reservoir and Glossop, see the detour from Bamford below. For an alternative way from Sheffield to Manchester via Penistone, see Rte 75G.

**Sheffield**, see Rte 75G. A625 quits the suburbs beyond (3m) *Ecclesall* and enters the Peak District National Park before (8$\frac{1}{2}$m) *Fox House Inn*, on the serpentine course of the border between South Yorkshire and Derbyshire.

*Carl Wark*, an impressive fort on the moor 1m NW, may be late Iron Age or post-Roman.—The *Longshaw Estate* (NT; Information Centre), 1500 acres of moor and woodland with nature trails, stretches S of A625. Sheepdog trials are held here in September.

9$\frac{1}{2}$m. *Millstone Edge* commands a surprise *view of the upper Derwent valley.—11m. **Hathersage**, beautifully situated, is the 'Morton' of Charlotte Brontë's 'Jane Eyre' and the reputed birthplace of Robin Hood's lieutenant, Little John, said to be buried in the churchyard above the village. The church, mostly 14C, has good 15C brasses of the Eyre family. From Hathersage to *Bakewell*, see Rte 56A.

Near (13m) *Bamford*, to the right, A625 leaves the Derwent, which flows down from the moorlands of N Derbyshire.

The huge *Ladybower Reservoir* and *Derwent Reservoir* N of Bamford were constructed in 1937–39, drowning the lower Ashop valley and part of the Derwent valley, including the village of Ashopton. There is a seasonal National Park Information Centre (open daily from Easter to end of October and weekends in winter) at *Fairholmes* near the Derwent Dam. From (9$\frac{1}{2}$m) the *Slippery Stones*, a packhorse bridge higher up the Derwent, the Cal-Der-Went Walk continues NE to (16m) *Langsett* (Rte 75F) across wild moors whose highest point, near the top of *Margery Hill* (1791ft), commands a *view S and W unrivalled in England for savage desolation.—Langsett can also be reached from Bamford by a sideroad (16$\frac{1}{2}$m), less wild but very beautiful, leading N from A57 past (7$\frac{1}{2}$m) *Strines Reservoir* and (12$\frac{1}{2}$m) *Broomhead Hall* to (15m) *Midhopestones*.

FROM BAMFORD TO GLOSSOP, 16m by A6013 and A57, including the tricky Snake Pass. A6013 climbs past *Win Hill* (1523ft; view) on the left. A57 heads left across the reservoir and follows its N shore to the deep and narrow valley of the Ashop, with the savage N escarpment of Kinder Scout (see below) on the left and the moorland of *Hope Forest* (16,555 acres) to the right.—From (8¹/₂m) *Snake Inn* (1070ft) a well-defined path leads 6¹/₂m SW to *Hayfield* (see below and Rte 56A), with fine views from the highest point (1670ft). Beyond the Snake Inn A57 gives a view of the craggy *Fairbrook Naze*, the most striking summit of Kinder Scout. *Lady Clough Forest* (nature trail) fringes the road.—11¹/₂m. We reach the flat summit of *Snake Pass* between *Featherbed Top* (1785ft) on the left and *Higher Shelf Stones* (2039ft) on the right, with *Bleaklow* (2060ft) beyond, and then make the steep and winding descent to (16m) *Glossop* (Rte 56A).

Beyond Bamford A625 follows the valley of the Noe, which flows from Edale. In front rise Mam Tor and the other hills round Castleton.—15¹/₂m. *Hope* has a 10C churchyard cross.

Near the old lead-mining village of *Bradwell*, in the limestone-quarrying area to the S, is the *Bagshawe Cavern* (open), with stalactites. *Brough*, between Bradwell and the main road, has scanty remains of the Roman *Navio*.—The green and open valley of Edale (nearly 2000 acres NT), NW of Hope, is bounded on the S by Mam Tor and Lose Hill and on the N by the moorland edges of Kinder Scout. *Edale* (National Park Information Centre), 5m from Hope, is surrounded by the wildest scenery in Derbyshire. From here the Countryside Commission's Pennine Way runs 250m N to the Scottish border.

The broken-edged plateau of **Kinder Scout** (2088ft; NT), NW of the village, is the highest ground in Derbyshire. The Pennine Way crosses it but the route can be difficult and should be tried only in good weather. An easier but still attractive walk W to (7¹/₂m) Hayfield uses part of the alternative course of the Pennine Way. We follow the valley from Edale to (2m) *Upper Booth* and the end of the lane 1m beyond. A path climbs steeply up *Jacob's Ladder* to (4m) *Edale Cross* (c 1750ft) on the neck between Kinder Scout (right) and *Brown Knoll* (left; 1804ft). The Pennine Way continues N but we head W, descending a charming moorland valley to (7¹/₂m) *Hayfield*. The walk from Hayfield around the NW side of Kinder Scout to the Snake Inn is described on the detour from Bamford to Glossop above.

17m. **Castleton** (National Park Information Centre) is popular with tourists for the caverns and mines in the neighbourhood. The ceremony of 'Riding the Garland', now connected with the restoration of Charles II but older in origin, is held on the evening of 29 May, Oakapple Day. Perched on the summit of the limestone crag to the S is the small late Norman keep (c 1176) of *Peveril Castle* (English Heritage, standard opening and summer Sunday mornings), originally founded by William of Peveril in 1068. Part of the enceinte wall also survives. At the foot of the precipice is the spectacular mouth of Derbyshire's largest natural cave, the *Peak Cavern* (open), once known as the Devil's Arse, with 400-year-old rope walks. *Cavendish House* (open) has a collection of articles made from Blue John, a local variety of fluorspar with a purple or yellowish colour ('bleu jaune').

A landslide from *Mam Tor* (1700ft; NT), appropriately called the Shivering Mountain, has blocked the course of A625 W of Castleton. We take the sideroad climbing steeply through the limestone ravine of *Winnats Pass* ('Wind-gates'; NT) to rejoin A625 at (19m) the bottom of the hill. The *Speedwell Mine* (open), an old lead mine at the entrance to the pass, has a gallery and a natural pothole of unfathomable depth reached by steps and an underground boat trip. At the top of the pass are the famous *Blue John Cavern* (open), and the *Treak Cliff Cavern* (open), now the richest source of Blue John.

A625 crosses the flank of *Rushup Edge*.—At (24m) *Chapel-en-le-Frith* we join Rte 56A for (44m) **Manchester**.

# 57  Stamford to Nottingham via Rutland Water

Total distance 39m. **Stamford**, see Rte 47A. We follow A606
throughout.—To (11m) **Oakham**.—To (20m) Melton Mowbray.
—To (39m) **Nottingham**.

Maps: OS Landranger 141, 130 (briefly), 129.

**Stamford**, see Rte 47A. We head W on A606, crossing A1 and
entering the former county of Rutland, now absorbed into
Leicestershire.—Just beyond (5m) *Empingham* we reach the NE
corner of *Rutland Water.

It has the largest surface area (3100 acres) of any man-made lake in northern
Europe, though Kielder Water in Northumberland exceeds it in capacity. Begun
in 1971 to supply water to the expanding towns of the E Midlands, it was formed
by damming the shallow valley of the Gwash near Empingham and pumping
water from the Nene at Wansford and the Welland at Tinwell. The pleasantly
landscaped result, about 5m long and with an irregular perimeter of 24m, also
serves as a popular centre for leisure and recreation. There is an information
centre at Sykes Lane, SW of Empingham, with car parks and picnic sites there
and at Whitwell, Barnsdale and Normanton. There are many miles of perimeter
footpath for walkers, a nature trail connecting the Whitwell and Barnsdale
picnic sites, and a nature reserve at the W end of the Water with a visitors'
centre in the public section at Lyndon. Dinghies and sailboards can be launched
from the Day Sailing Centre at Whitwell, where a few hire craft are also
available; the Rutland Sailing Club is near Edith Weston. Permits for trout
fishing are obtained from the Whitwell Fishing Lodge or in advance by post
from The Old Hall, Whitwell, Oakham, Leicestershire LE15 8DW; anglers also
need an Anglian Water Regional or Divisional Rod Licence.

As well as the main route along the N shore suggested below, it is worth
taking the longer way by sideroads round the S shore.—At (2m) *Normanton*,

*Normanton church, half in and half out of Rutland Water*

with a car park and picnic site, the neo-classical church standing on a short causeway at the edge of the reservoir makes a striking landmark. Now deconsecrated and housing a water museum, it was built in 1764, extended in 1826 and partly rebuilt in 1911.—3m. *Edith Weston* takes its name from Edith, widow of Edward the Confessor.—4m. By the shore N of *Lyndon* is the visitors' centre for the public section of the nature reserve.—Beyond (5¹/₂m) *Manton* we join A6003 heading N to Oakham.—7¹/₂m. At *Egleton*, to the right, the church has a *S doorway in the Saxo-Norman style with a carved tympanum believed to be Saxon.—9m. *Oakham*, see below.

The main route from Empingham follows A606 along the N side of the Water past (6¹/₂m) *Whitwell*, with car park, picnic site, Day Sailing Centre, Fishing Lodge and nature trail leading 1m W to the car park and picnic site at *Barnsdale*. The pleasant village of *Exton*, 1¹/₂m N of Whitwell, has a fine park and a church with a splendid group of 16–18C *monuments which includes work by Grinling Gibbons and Nollekens.—9¹/₂m. A sideroad to the left leads along a spur of land jutting out into the middle of the reservoir to (1¹/₂m) the little village of *Upper Hambleton*.

11m. **Oakham** (9100 inhab.; Tourist Information), the former county town of Rutland and a famous fox-hunting centre, is a handsome little place built of the local limestone and ironstone. Natives include Sir Jeffrey Hudson, Queen Henrietta Maria's dwarf (1619–82), and Titus Oates (1649–1705), who fabricated the Popish Plot against Charles II.

The chief relic of the *Castle* (open) is the late Norman *great hall. Nailed to its walls is a remarkable collection of horseshoes presented, in obedience to the local custom, by visiting peers to the lord of the manor. Nearby are the handsome, mainly 14–15C church of *All Saints*, the original building of *Oakham School* (founded in 1584), refitted as a Shakespeare centre, and the old *Buttercross* and stocks. *Flore's House* in the High St. dates from the late 14C. The *Rutland County Museum* in Catmose St. occupies a former riding school of the Rutland Fencibles, a volunteer cavalry regiment raised in 1794. It contains Iron Age finds from the Rutland Water site, Roman remains unearthed at Great Casterton, agricultural equipment, etc.

The Rutland Agricultural Show is held on the first weekend in August at *Burley-on-the-Hill*, a late 17C–early 18C mansion 1¹/₂m NE.
There are interesting churches at *Teigh*, 4m N, with furnishings of 1782; *Market Overton*, 6m NE, with a Saxon tower arch; *Whissendine*, 4m NW, where the lovely late 13–15C building has part of the old rood screen (1516) from St John's College, Cambridge; and *Brooke*, 2¹/₂m S, with an Elizabethan interior (c 1579).

A606 leads NW to (20m) **Melton Mowbray** (23,600 inhab.; Tourist Information), another quiet country town which is also a fox-hunting centre. The EE and Dec. *St Mary's*, one of the finest parish churches in Leicestershire, has a beautiful effigy of a lady (c 1400) in the S transept. Opposite the church is a 17C bede house. The *Melton Carnegie Museum* is devoted to the history of the area, including its famous connection with pork pies and Stilton cheese.

The surrounding Leicestershire Wolds are also explored in the detour from Leicester to Grantham in Rte 46.

A606 follows a hilly course into Nottinghamshire.—30m. We cross A46, the Foss Way, running from Leicester to Newark-on-Trent. *Willoughy-on-the-Wolds*, off A46 3m SW, has 14–15C tombs of the Willoughby family in its church. The regicide Colonel Hutchinson (see below) is buried at *Owthorpe*, off A46 4m NE.

39m. **NOTTINGHAM** (271,000 inhab.) is unusual among Midland cities in having a medieval and an industrial past of equal import- ance. It is more typical in having treated neither very well, leaving the visitor to seek out their fragments among the inner ring road and modern shopping centres. The site of the castle and the old Lace Market are of most interest. The unusual man-made caves, cut into the sandstone rock on which the city stands, lie mainly beneath private houses but are included in the tours organised by the Tourist Information Centre.

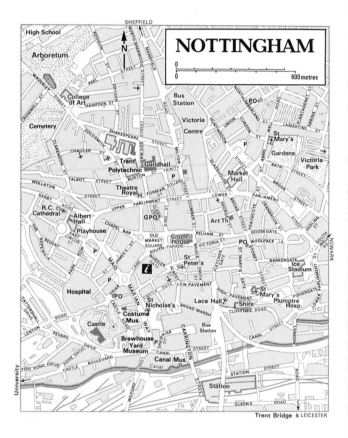

**Tourist Information Centres**: No. 16 Wheeler Gate; County Hall, Loughborough Rd, West Bridgford.

**Car Parks**: Trinity Square, Wollaton St., Maid Marian Way, Victoria and Broad Marsh shopping centres.

**Bus Stations**: Victoria and Broad Marsh shopping centres.

**Railway Station**: Carrington St., ½m S of the centre, beyond Broad Marsh shopping centre.

**Theatres**: Nottingham Playhouse, East Circus St.; Theatre Royal, Theatre

Square, with Royal Concert Hall adjoining; Arts Theatre, George St.; Lace Market Theatre, Halifax Place.

**Annual Events**: Nottingham Festival in June. The Goose Fair is held on the first Thursday, Friday and Saturday of October at the Forest Recreation Ground, N of the Arboretum. Now a fun fair, it originated as a trading fair in the Middle Ages.

**History**. The Saxon *Snotingaham* was occupied by the Danes in 868 and became (with Derby, Leicester, Lincoln and Stamford) one of the five cities of the Danelagh. It was recaptured in 918 by Edward the Elder, who built the first bridge at the strategically important crossing of the Trent. The castle added after the Norman Conquest became the key to the Midlands and a favourite royal residence. In 1642 Charles I opened the Civil War by raising his standard N of its walls on what is now Standard Hill, but the castle was soon seized for Parliament by Colonel John Hutchinson and demolished on his orders in 1651.

In the 14–15C Nottingham was famous throughout Europe for its alabaster carvings. Its industrial prosperity as a centre of lace- and hosiery-making dated from the invention of the stocking-frame by the Rev. William Lee of nearby Calverton in 1589. Hargreaves came to the town with his spinning jenny in 1768, and Arkwright opened his first mill the following year. The Luddite riots of 1811–16, organised by starving weavers bent on machine-breaking, were at their most violent in Nottingham.

**Famous natives and residents**. Natives include Colonel John Hutchinson (1615–64), the artists Thomas and Paul Sandby (1721–98 and 1725–1809), the poets Henry Kirke White (1785–1806) and 'Festus' Bailey (1829–1912), founder of the Salvation Army. The painter Richard Bonington (1801–28) was born at *Arnold*, 3m NE. Lord Byron lived in Nottingham as a boy (plaque in St James St. between the Old Market Square and Maid Marian Way). The Chartist leader Feargus O'Connor (1794–1855) was MP for Nottingham in 1847–48. D.H. Lawrence attended the High School and University College in its old building on Shakespeare St. (see below).

We begin in the large, sterile Old Market Square, its E side filled by Cecil Howitt's *Council House* (1928). Cheapside, S of the Council House, has the over-restored *Flying Horse Hotel* with pargeting; the old *Bell Inn*, off the NW corner of the square, is more interesting. Several streets climb from the N side of the Square to Upper Parliament St., which has the *Theatre Royal* (1865) with the new *Royal Concert Hall* (opened in 1982) immediately behind.

South Sherwood St. leads N between the *Guildhall* (1888) and the buildings of *Trent Polytechnic*, including the original University College (1881), which D.H. Lawrence attended, in Shakespeare St. beyond. Shakespeare St. continues NW to the *Arboretum*, a handsome park with aviaries and a statue of Feargus O'Connor. On the S side is the *College of Art and Design*, with a statue of Bonington; on the N side the 19C buildings of the *High School* (founded 1513), where Lawrence was a pupil. The Goose Fair (see above) is held on the Forest Recreation Ground, beyond.

The dreary Lower Parliament St., continuing Upper Parliament St. to the E, goes under a walkway from the huge *Victoria Shopping Centre*. The narrow streets to the S still have their medieval names and courses. We take Broad St. and its extension, Stoney St., into the old *Lace Market with its red-brick mid 19C warehouses, the most interesting survival of Nottingham's industrial past. The church of *St Mary*, mainly late 15C, has a massive central tower, wide nave and rich Perp. windows; there is a painting by Fra Bartolommeo in the N aisle.

At the corner of Fishergate, a little to the E, is *Plumptre Hospital* (1823; founded 1392) for 13 widows.

High Pavement leads W from St Mary's, past the *Shire Hall* (1770), the *County Record Office* (formerly the Judge's Lodgings) with a façade of c 1833, and the former *Unitarian Chapel* (1876), now being converted into a lace museum. It replaces the building where Bonington was baptised, Coleridge preached and the youthful Byron worshipped. A plaque opposite marks the site of Henry Kirke White's home. Beyond Weekday Cross we continue along Middle and Low Pavement, with good 19C houses. The *Broad Marsh Shopping Centre* lies to the S; hemmed in by Marks and Spencer to the N is the church of *St Peter*, partly rebuilt in the 15C.

Castle Gate crosses the ugly Maid Marian Way, part of the inner ring road, with the attractive 17–18C church of *St Nicholas* to the S and the 15C *Salutation Inn* to the N. On the right of the approach to the castle is *Newdigate House*, where the French general Marshal Tallard was held after his capture at Blenheim in 1704. On the lefthand side of Castle Gate a row of 18C houses now contains the *Museum of Costume and Textiles*, with period rooms. A half-timbered 16C building moved from Middle Pavement houses the *Lace Centre*.

The grounds of the **Castle** (open) spread up the sides of a steep sandstone rock. Outside the walls are a modern statue of Robin Hood and reliefs depicting episodes from the legends connected with him. The heavily restored late 13C gatehouse is the only major relic of the fortress begun by William Peveril soon after the Conquest. The rest was dismantled in 1651 after Colonel Hutchinson had captured it from the Royalists during the Civil War. The Italianate mansion which the Duke of Newcastle built on the site in 1674–78 suffered a similar fate when it was gutted by fire during the Reform riots of 1831. Restored in 1875–78, it reopened as England's first municipal **Museum and Art Gallery** outside London.

The ground floor displays glass (including the Bles Bowl of c 1685), silver and English ceramics (good Wedgwood), as well as ethnographic and regimental collections. There is an exhibit of local history downstairs. The mezzanine floor has finds excavated at Nemi, near Rome, by Lord Savile in 1885. The picture gallery upstairs is notable for works by Bonington and a range of 18–20C English artists (Richard Wilson, John Crome and other members of the Norwich school, Rossetti, Stanley Spencer) and for alabaster carvings of the Nottingham school.

There are conducted tours of the passages in the rock beneath the castle, including *Mortimer's Hole*, said to have been used by the young Edward III in 1330 when he came to arrest Roger Mortimer, lover of the king's mother Queen Isabella. The *Trip to Jerusalem Inn*, claiming to be the oldest inn in England, adjoins the entrance to another passage at the foot of the rock to the SE. The nearby *Brewhouse Yard Museum*, illustrating Nottingham's domestic and commercial life, occupies a group of restored 17C houses and the caves in the rock behind them.

Canal St. leads E from the bottom of Maid Marian Way to the *Canal Museum*, in a converted 19C warehouse.

The *Park Estate*, W and N of the castle, is a handsome 19C residential area which repays exploration. In the Derby Rd, on its N side, stands the *Roman Catholic Cathedral of St Barnabas*, an impressive building of 1840–42 by Pugin. Close by are the Methodist *Albert Hall* (1909) and the *Nottingham Playhouse* (1959–63; Peter Moro).

**Trent Bridge** (1869–71), about 1m S of the city centre, crosses the river to the famous *County Cricket Ground* (left) and the *County Hall* (right) in *West Bridgford*. The Victoria Embankment gardens have pleasant scenery. The grounds of Notts County and Nottingham Forest fooball clubs are on opposite banks of the river. Downstream (E) are the racecourse and park at *Colwick*. Colwick Hall, now a restaurant, was the home of Mrs Musters, Byron's Mary Chaworth (d. 1832). See below for A453, heading SW from the ring road at West Bridgford to Ashby-de-la-Zouch.

A6005, beginning as Castle Boulevarde at the S end of Maid Marian Way, heads W from the city via (1m) *Lenton*, where the modern church has a carved Norman \*font from Lenton Priory. About 1m further is the **University of Nottingham**, founded as University College in 1881 and incorporated in 1948. It moved to buildings by Morley Horder in this pleasantly landscaped park in 1928. *Beeston*, a former textile village 1m beyond, has striking Boots factory buildings by Sir Owen Williams (1930–32 and 1937–38).

**Wollaton Hall** (open), 2½m W on A609, was built for Sir Francis Willoughby in 1580–88 by Robert Smythson. Its *exterior combines a symmetrical plan with elaborate ornament in a triumph of Elizabethan bravado. The central tower, containing the hall and rising above the four corner towers, is a conspicuous and unusual feature. Inappropriately, the building now houses a *Museum of Natural History*. The large park has an *Industrial Museum* in the 18C stable block and a cast-iron camellia house of 1823.

A609 continues beyond Wollaton Hall to (7m) *Ilkeston* (33,000 inhab.; Tourist Information), a mining and lace-making town in the industrial Erewash valley. The church has an early 14C stone screen and sedilia. There is a local museum in a late 18C house on the High St. At *Dale*, on the moor 3½m SW off A6096, a single arch survives from the Premonstratensian abbey. *Eastwood* (11,700 inhab.), off A610 and A608 4m N of Ilkeston, is famous for its connections with the early life and work of D.H. Lawrence (1885–1930). His birthplace on Victoria St. is open as a museum.

FROM NOTTINGHAM TO ASHBY-DE-LA-ZOUCH, 22m by A453, heading SW from the ring road at West Bridgford (see above).—7m. On the right is the Jacobean *Thrumpton Hall* (open to parties of 20 or more). The village of *Gotham*, about 2m E, was famous in traditional jokes for the naivety of its inhabitants. Washington Irving and the Superman comics borrowed the name for New York.—10m. We cross M1 and A6 near *Kegworth*, the *East Midlands Airport* and *Castle Donington* (all in Rte 55).—16m. *Breedon-on-the-Hill* has a fine church with a remarkable sculptured frieze and a cross shaft of the 8C.—22m. *Ashby-de-le-Zouch*, see Rte 46.

FROM NOTTINGHAM TO SOUTHWELL, 13½m by A612.—5m. *Stoke Bardolph* lies by the Trent 1m to the right. The main road commands wide views across the valley, which it follows as far as (10m) *Thurgarton*, where the church preserves a W doorway and other remains of a 13C priory.—13½m. *Southwell*, see Rte 59.

From Nottingham to *Loughborough* and to *Derby*, see Rte 55; through Sherwood Forest to *Doncaster* via *Ollerton* and *Worksop*, see Rte 58A; through the Forest via *Mansfield* to *Worksop*, see Rte 58B.

# 58  Sherwood Forest

**Sherwood Forest**, in the Middle Ages a region of oak woodland, dense bracken and heath held by the Crown under forest law, occupied roughly the whole western part of Nottinghamshire. History has not treated it kindly. Private enclosure, the reclamation of land for farming, the growth of Nottingham and, above all, the development of the Nottinghamshire coalfield have reduced it to a narrow strip lying mainly between A60 and A614, N of Nottingham. Here, among the depressing towns and the insensitive plantations of Corsican pine, some lovely woodland has been preserved through its inclusion in the so-called 'Dukeries': the great parks of Welbeck (formerly Duke of Portland), Clumber (formerly Duke of Newcastle), Worksop (formerly Duke of Norfolk) and Thoresby (formerly Duke of Kingston). Worksop and Welbeck are closed to the public but Clumber and Thoresby, and also the park at Rufford, are open. The oak trees here and at Birklands and Bilhaugh nearby are some of the noblest survivors of the ancient British forests.

The outlaw Robin Hood is celebrated in medieval ballads, also making the occasional appearance in folk drama and contemporary chronicles. These place his exploits in Yorkshire and Cumberland as well as Sherwood Forest. He became inseparably linked with

Nottinghamshire only in later centuries, when attempts were also made to find a historical basis for the legend. The antiquary Joseph Ritson, who published the first collection of the Robin Hood ballads in 1795, identified him as Robert Fitz-Ooth, born at Locksley in 1160 and reputed to be the Earl of Huntingdon—doubtful claims which have frequently been challenged and amended. Scott's 'Ivanhoe' (1819) and Thomas Love Peacock's 'Maid Marian' (1822) consolidated the romantic image of the outlaw and his merry men who outwit the Sheriff of Nottingham as they rob the rich to help the poor. Preserved for later generations on film and television, it remains a firm favourite of the local tourist industry.

Of the routes suggested below, the first takes A60 along the W fringe of the region and heads beyond it to Doncaster, while the second goes through the heart of the forest, passing near the Sherwood Forest Visitor Centre at Edwinstowe.

# A. Nottingham to Doncaster via Mansfield and Worksop

Total distance 42m. **Nottingham**, see Rte 57. We follow A60 throughout.—To (14m) Mansfield.—To (26m) Worksop.—To (42m) **Doncaster**, see Rte 81.

Maps: OS Landranger 129, 120, 111.

**Nottingham**, see Rte 57. We leave the city on A60.

An alternative to the main route below branches left at 1m and follows A611 to (6m) *Hucknall* (28,100 inhab.), a mining town where Byron is buried in the family vault of the church. *Annesley Hall* (not open), 2m further N, was the early home of the cousin with whom he fell in love, Mary Chaworth. We can rejoin A60 by taking B6011 E from Hucknall through (1m) *Linby*, a pretty place with two village crosses, and branching left on B683 at *Papplewick*, 1m beyond.

We continue N on A60 past (5m) the turning for A614, followed in Rte 58B, to (10m) the *Pilgrim Oak*. On the left is the entrance to Lord Byron's ancestral home, *Newstead Abbey* (open).

The 12C Augustinian priory which Henry II founded was converted into a house by Sir John Byron in 1540 but had largely fallen into decay by the time the poet inherited it in 1798. He made fitful repairs and lived here at intervals between 1808 and 1818, when debts forced him to sell the property.

A long drive flanked by rhododendrons leads through the park to the lake and the buildings. They owe their present appearance outside to repairs by Byron's successor, Colonel Wildman, though part of the lovely late 13C W front of the priory church is still intact. At the core of the house is the old cloister square with the chapter house which the Byrons made a chapel and the poet used for his menagerie. The main apartments upstairs have mementoes of him.

14m. **Mansfield** (58,900 inhab.) is a dull town with hosiery mills and collieries, spanned by a large railway viaduct. The 13–15C *Church* has a beautifully proportioned interior.

**•Hardwick Hall** (NT), off A617 6m NW, is one of the finest Elizabethan mansions in the country. It was built in the 1590s, probably by Robert Smythson, for 'Bess of Hardwick', as Elizabeth, Countess of Shrewsbury, was popularly known. Her initials decorate the balustrades above the vast display of windows which prompted the rhyme 'Hardwick Hall, more glass than wall'. Inside, a superb stone staircase rises from the Hall to the High Great Chamber, with a painted plaster frieze, and the Long Gallery, with handsome chimneypieces and a portrait of Mary, Queen of Scots. There is good contemporary furniture and a famous •collection of tapestries and embroidery. The grounds preserve the original layout of walled courtyards; nearby are the ruins of *Hardwick Old Hall* (English Heritage, exterior open at any reasonable time).—To the N lies the curious little church of *Ault Hucknall*, with early Norman details, where Thomas Hobbes (1588–1679), the author of 'Leviathan', is buried.—*Sutton Scarsdale Hall*, beyond M1 about 6m NW of Hardwick, is a ruined building of 1724 by Francis Smith of Warwick (English Heritage, exterior open at any reasonable time).

*Hardwick Hall*

*Bolsover* (11,100 inhab.; Tourist Information), on A632 about 4m N of Hardwick, stands on the lip of a ridge of magnesian limestone with views W to the distant Peak. **•Bolsover Castle** (English Heritage, standard opening and summer Sunday mornings), originally built by William Peveril in the 11C, was rebuilt and enlarged by Sir Charles Cavendish in 1613–17. He reconstructed the Norman keep on its old foundations in an interesting mixture of the Gothic and Renaissance styles, with some heavily decorated marble chimneypieces. The long gallery, now partly ruined, and the riding school were added c 1620–30.

A60 continues N from Mansfield through (15½m) *Mansfield Woodhouse* (26,700 inhab.) and (18m) *Warsop*, with a good 12–13C church.—From (21m) *Cuckney* A616 leads SE to Thoresby and Ollerton (Rte 58B) and NW to *Creswell Crags*, a limestone ravine where the caves have yielded rich finds of early Stone Age occupation; there is a display in the Visitor Centre. Beyond Cuckney we pass *Welbeck Abbey* (not open), now an Army training school.

The 3000-acre park is one of the chief survivals of the ancient Sherwood Forest. The house, on the site of a 12C Premonstratensian abbey, dates mainly from the 17C; the strangest of its later additions is the extraordinary series of underground rooms and tunnels built by the disfigured 5th Duke of Portland (d. 1879).

We pass *Worksop Manor* (not open), where a grand 17C house and its 18C successor once stood, on the way into (26m) **Worksop** (36,900 inhab.; Tourist Information), an industrial town on the edge of the coalfield. The church of *Worksop Priory*, an Augustinian foundation of 1103, has a splendid Norman *nave (c 1150–60), EE Lady Chapel (c 1240) and S door with elaborate ironwork of c 1260. The transepts and crossing were rebuilt in 1929–35 and the new E end completed in 1965–74. A 14C gatehouse survives S of the church.

*Steetley Chapel*, a little apsidal building off A619 1½m W, is rich mid 12C Norman work.—*Thorpe Salvin*, 4m W, has an elaborate carved *font in the Norman church.

We continue N on A60 beyond the Forest.—29m. *Carlton-in-Lindrick* has a Norman church.—At (32m) *Oldcotes*, just before we enter South Yorkshire, we cross A634.

*Blyth*, 2m SE, see Rte 59.—**Roche Abbey** (English Heritage, summer standard opening and weekends in winter) lies 3m W of Oldcotes. The ruins of the Cistercian monastery founded in 1147 include the transepts of the church. They stand on a beautiful site landscaped in the 18C by Capability Brown as part of the grounds of Sandbeck Park. The church of *Laughton-en-le-Morthen*, 2m SW, has a fine Perp. spire and a Saxon N doorway.

34m. *Tickhill* (5000 inhab.) has a ruined Norman castle, a Perp. church of c 1360 containing one of the earliest Renaissance monuments in England (1478), and a domed 18C market hall.
   We cross A1, here motorway, and M18 on the way into **Doncaster** (Rte 81).


# B.   Nottingham to Worksop via Ollerton

Total distance 28m. **Nottingham**, see Rte 57.—A60, A614 to (19m) Ollerton.—A616, B6034 to (28m) **Worksop**, see Rte 58A.

Maps: OS Landranger 129, 120.

**Nottingham**, see Rte 57. We leave the city on A60, as in Rte 58A, but branch right from it at 5m on A614.—15½m. *Rufford*, on the right, has a Country Park (open) and the remains of an Elizabethan and Jacobean house on the site of a Cistercian monastery (not open).

Shortly beyond, B6034 branches left to (1½m) *Edwinstowe* with the Sherwood Forest Visitor Centre. The church has a good 13C tower with a later spire and, in the chancel, the fragment of an EE pillar piscina. Signposted footpaths and trails lead into the surrounding woodland. We can rejoin the main route 1¼m N, through the beautiful forest tract of *Birklands*, where the famous *Major Oak* is reputed to be over 1400 years old.

19m. **Ollerton**, to the right, is an old market centre with *New Ollerton* to its N.—We take A616 through the lovely forest of *Bilhaugh*, where B6034 from Edwinstowe joins us on the left. *Thoresby* (not open), on the right beyond, is an extravagant mansion by Anthony Salvin (1865–71) in a handsome park. Lady Mary Wortley Montagu (1689–1762) was born in an earlier house on the site.

Beyond (22m) *Budby*, a 'model village' of 1807, we branch right on B6034 through a lovely tract of countryside.—23½m. A sideroad on the right leads via *Carburton* and its Norman chapel to **Clumber Park** (NT; Information Centre), 3800 acres of park and woodland with a serpentine lake and an *avenue of lime trees 3m long.

The demolition of the house in 1938 spared the *chapel, one of the great achievements of Victorian Gothic, built by Bodley and Garner in 1886–89. The interior is of softly tinted red Runcorn stone, with stained glass by Kempe.

28m. **Worksop**, see Rte 58A.

# 59   Stamford to Doncaster

Total distance 72m. **Stamford**, see Rte 47A. We follow A1, which bypasses the towns.—To (21m) **Grantham**.—To (35m) **Newark** (for **Southwell**).—To (49m) Markham Moor roundabout.—A638 to (54m) East Retford.—A638 to (72m) **Doncaster**, see Rte 81.

Maps: OS Landranger 141 (briefly), 130, 121 (briefly), 120, 111.

See beginning of Rte 47A for a note on the history of A1.

**Stamford**, see Rte 47A. To the N of the town we enter the former county of Rutland, now part of Leicestershire, and join A1. The church of (2m) *Great Casterton* is 13C. At (3m) *Tickencote*, on the left, the church has a rich late Norman *chancel arch and a vaulted choir with boss (c 1160). The elaborate exterior arcading (restored 1792), 13C font and 14C wooden effigy of a knight should also be noted. —Beyond (8m) *Stretton* we re-enter Lincolnshire. The oolite of *Clipsham* quarries, 1½m E, makes a famous building stone.—Just to the left of (13m) *Colsterworth* is the modest little *Woolsthorpe Manor* (NT), where Sir Isaac Newton (1642–1727) was born.—17m. *Great Ponton* has a conspicuous church tower (1509). At *Boothby Pagnell*, 3m E, the late 12C *manor house (open by appointment) is the most complete surviving example of a Norman domestic building in England. A1 bypasses Grantham to the W.

21m. **Grantham** (30,100 inhab.; Tourist Information), an ancient town that became a railway centre, keeps some of its old character near the N end of the High St. Here we find the *Angel and Royal Hotel*, one of the finest medieval inns in the country, with a rich late 15C façade. King John is said to have held a court here in 1213, and Richard III signed the Duke of Buckingham's death warrant here in 1483. The 18C *George Hotel*, nearly opposite, is praised by Dickens in 'Nicholas Nickleby'. In the nearby market place are the 16C conduit and an old market cross. Grantham's Eleanor Cross (see Lincoln, Rte 72) once stood on St Peter's Hill, to the S, where there is now a statue of Sir Isaac Newton. The *Museum* near the statue has local archaeological finds and a Newton collection.

Vine St. branches to the right from the N end of High St., with the medieval *Blue Pig* inn at the junction with Swinegate. The largely 13C parish church of *St Wulfram*, beyond, has a striking crocketed *spire; the light and spacious interior is notable for its varied window tracery. A library (1598) over the S porch has chained books, and the 14C crypt was probably once St Wulfram's shrine. To the NE of the church is the old schoolroom (1497) of *King's School*, which Newton attended; to the E is the 14–15C *Grantham House* (NT, open by written appointment), with grounds stretching down to the river Witham.

**Belvoir Castle** (open), pronounced 'Beever', lies beyond *Denton* (Rte 46) about 7m SW of Grantham. A coarse exercise in Gothic begun by James Wyatt in the early 19C, it nevertheless makes an impressive silhouette and commands a wide view across the Vale of Belvoir. The *Picture Gallery contains work by Holbein, Poussin, Gainsborough and Dutch and Flemish masters. There are good family portraits, including work by Reynolds, elsewhere in the house, with collections of tapestry, armour, etc. and a regimental museum of the 17th/21st Lancers.

FROM GRANTHAM TO NOTTINGHAM, 22m by A52 across the Vale of Belvoir.—At (7m) *Bottesford* the fine early Perp. church has a tall crocketed spire and a chancel crowded with *monuments to successive owners of Belvoir. The church of *Orston*, 2½m NW, has a Restoration font in the Gothic style.—11m. *Aslockton*, to the right, was the birthplace of Archbishop Cranmer (1489–1556).—13m. *Bingham* has an interesting church in a mixture of EE, Dec. and Perp.—From (17m) *Radcliffe-on-Trent* the river winds N to *Shelford*, where the church has memorials of the Stanhopes. W of the town are the National Water Sports Centre and *Holme Pierrepoint Hall* (open), an early Tudor manor house with 17C and 19C work. The nearby church has 17C work in a mixture of classical and Gothic styles, and a memorial to the poet John Oldham (1653–83).—22m. *Nottingham*, see Rte 57.

FROM GRANTHAM TO LINCOLN, 25m by A607.—2m. *Belton House (NT) is a magnificent late 17C building of Ancaster stone. Several rooms keep their contemporary woodwork and plaster ceilings, while the Library and Boudoir were altered by James Wyatt in the 1770s. Also of interest are the wall paintings in the Hondecoeter Room, the unusual 18C painted floor in the Tyrconnel Room and the collection of tapestries. The park was landscaped by William Eames in the 18C. The church of *Belton* has good monuments.—From (5m) *Honington* A153 heads via (2m) *Ancaster* to (8m) *Sleaford* (Rte 72). A607 continues N, skirting the *Cliff* (right), an oolite escarpment crowned by a series of interesting churches.—8m. *Caythorpe* has an unusual Dec. church, partly rebuilt.—12m. *Leadenham* has a good late Dec. church. For A17, leading across the escarpment to (9m) *Sleaford*, see Rte 72.—16½m. *Navenby* has the finest church on the Cliff.—At (22½m) *Bracebridge Heath* we join A15 and follow Rte 72 into (25m) *Lincoln*.

*Belton House*

From Grantham to *Leicester*, see Rte 46; to *Boston* via *Sleaford*, see Rte 72.

At (31m) Shire Bridge we enter Nottinghamshire. The graceful spire of *Claypole* church rises to the right.

35m. **Newark-on-Trent** (24,600 inhab.; Tourist Information), bypassed to the E by A1, is an ancient town at the junction of the old Great North Road and the Foss Way. Its natives include the painter Sir William Nicholson (1872–1949) and the actor Sir Donald Wolfit (1902–68). Gladstone first entered Parliament in 1832 as the member for Newark.

The 12–15C *Castle* (not open) guards the river crossing. Now only an impressive shell, it was dismantled in 1646 after three sieges by Parliamentarian armies in the Civil War. King John died here in 1216. In the large *Market Place are the *Town Hall* (open) of 1774–76 by John Carr of York, the restored *Old Town Hall* (1708), two big 18C inns (one now a bank and insurance company) and the 14C *White Hart Inn*, with carved and painted timberwork. Prince Rupert was living in the half-timbered *Governor's House* in Stodman St. at the time of his disastrous quarrel with Charles I. The stately parish church of *St Mary Magdalene* is notable outside for its Dec. spire and EE tower. The interior is mainly Perp.

The oak rood screen dates from 1505, the choir stalls from c 1525, and the Meyring and Markham chantry chapels, flanking the altar to N and S respectively, from 1500 and 1506. The Markham chantry has a double squint and two painted panels showing a Dance of Death. In the N choir aisle is the large Flemish brass of Alan Fleming (d. 1373).

Wilson St., NW of the church, has good Georgian houses. The *Town Museum* in Appleton Gate, to the NE, has a good collection of local archaeological finds. It occupies the former Magnus Grammar and Song School, with a Tudor hall (1529), which the composer John Blow (1649–1708) attended. The *Beaumond Cross* at the S end of Carter Gate is thought to be a 15C wayside preaching cross. In Devon Park, S of the town, is the *Queen's Sconce*, a star-shaped earthwork built as a platform for cannon in the Civil War.

At *Hawton*, 2m S, the church has one of the finest *Easter Sepulchres in England, with sedilia and piscina to match (c 1330).—*East Stoke*, on A46 (the Foss Way) 4m SW, is the site of the Roman station *Ad Pontem*. The Battle of Stoke (1487), at which Henry VII captured the pretender Lambert Simnel, was fought at nearby Stoke Fields.—*Holme*, off A1133 about 4m N of Newark, has a church rebuilt in 1485 by John Barton, a woolstapler of Calais, with contemporary fittings and stained glass.

---

**Southwell** (6350 inhab.; pronounced 'Suthall') lies about 7m W of Newark via A617 and A612. A dignified little town, it is dominated by the *Minster** which, though raised to cathedral status only in 1884, equals the greatest English cathedrals in beauty.

A church is said to have been founded here c 630 by Paulinus, the first Bishop of York, but the first authentic reference is in a charter of c 956 granting Southwell to Oskytel, Archbishop of York. He established a college of secular canons which, though temporarily suspended under Henry VIII and again under Edward VI, survived until 1840. The new diocese of Southwell was created in 1884 by removing Nottinghamshire from the see of Lincoln and Derbyshire from the see of Lichfield; Derby became a diocese in its own right in 1927.

The minster superbly illustrates three successive styles of architecture. The severe W towers, the low central tower, and the nave and transepts with circular clerestory windows, are all Norman (early 12C), and on the N side is a rare late Norman porch. The choir is a beautiful example of EE (c 1234–50), while the Dec. chapter house (1295–1300) is the chief glory of the building.

The magnificent *Nave, with its massive Norman piers and big triforium, is brilliantly lit by the Perp. W window and the Perp. windows inserted in the aisles. The tower arches have cable moulding. The *N Transept* has the fine alabaster tomb of Archbishop Sandys (d. 1588) and, over the door in the W wall, a sculptured tympanum from the Saxon church. The outline of the Norman apse is marked on the floor of the Airmen's Chapel. The *S Transept* has a wooden sculpture of the Virgin and Child (1952) by Alan Coleman.

The graceful EE *Choir* is separated from the nave by a Dec. stone rood screen (c 1335) with the organ over it. The screen is elaborately carved with miniature human heads (many restored in the 19C), and the stalls behind it have misericords. The capitals of the arch above are carved in what looks a Saxon rather than Norman style. The clerestory and triforium of the choir are ingeniously combined to increase the impression of height. Two heads on corbels on the N side are said to represent Walter de Gray and Henry III, the archbishop and king under whom the choir was built. The E window has two rows of four lancets instead of the more usual three or five; the Flemish glass in the lower lights comes from the old Temple Church in Paris. The splendid brass lectern (c 1500) was recovered from the lake at Newstead Abbey, where the monks had thrown it at the Dissolution. The sedilia on the S side are in the same style as the rood screen (and were likewise restored in the 19C). The S choir aisle has a patchwork window of old glass, perhaps from the chapter house, and a fragment of Roman tessellated pavement, probably from the Saxon church.

A corridor leads N from the choir to the exquisite octagonal **Chapter House (1295–1300). Oak, maple, hawthorn, vine, ivy and hop, among other types of leaf and blossom, luxuriate over the capitals of the entrance doorway and the canopies of the arcading within. Apart from being the earliest sculpture of this kind in England, this naturalistically carved foliage is also one of the supreme achievements of the mason's art. The building itself is unique among stone-vaulted chapter houses of this type in not being supported by a central pillar.

S of the minster are the remains of the *Palace* (c 1380) belonging to the Archbishops of York, with the 20C Bishop's Manor built inside them.

On the Old Market Place W of the minster stands the *Saracen's Head*, a half-timbered coaching inn where Charles I surrendered to the Scots Commissioners in 1646. Byron lived with his mother in 1803–08 at *Burgage Manor*, a Georgian house on the Green beyond King St. to the N.

From Southwell to *Nottingham*, see Rte 57.

---

The main route rejoins A1 N of Newark.—47m. *Tuxford*. The medieval field system survives at *Laxton*, 3m SW. The architect Nicholas Hawksmoor (1661–1736) was born at *Ragnall*, 5m NE of Tuxford. —From (49m) *Markham Moor* roundabout A1 swings W and then becomes motorway as it bypasses Doncaster. The church at *Blyth*, 10m beyond the roundabout and just short of the motorway, has the early Norman *nave of a Bendictine priory church. A better way from Markham Moor to Doncaster follows A638, the route of the old Great North Road.—From (51m) *Gamston* B6387 leads 3m S to the *National Mining Museum* at Lound Hall, near Bevercotes colliery.—54m. **East Retford** (19,300 inhab.; Tourist Information) is a market town and railway centre. *North Leverton*, 4m E, has a working windmill of 1813.—57m. *Barnby Moor*. Blyth (see above) lies 3m NW.—61m. *Scrooby* claims a connection with William Brewster (1560?–1644), one of the Pilgrim Fathers.—At (63m) *Bawtry* we enter South

Yorkshire. *Austerfield*, 1½m NE on A614, with an interesting Norman church, was the birthplace of William Bradford (1590–1657), the second governor of Plymouth in New England. Near *Mattersey*, off B6045 4m SE of Bawtry, are the scanty remains of a priory of Gilbertine canons founded c 1185 (English Heritage, open at any reasonable time).—67½m. *Rossington*, left of our road, has a church with a Norman S doorway and chancel arch and a 15C pulpit.

72m. **Doncaster**, see Rte 81.

# EASTERN ENGLAND

Eastern England is roughly defined to its W by the course of the A1 as it connects London and the South Yorkshire border, and more exactly to its S by the Thames estuary. Its long seaboard, flat for the most part and without deep-water harbours, stretches from the Thames up past the Wash to the Humber in the N. Inside these boundaries lie six counties, starting with Essex in the S and continuing up the coast with Suffolk and Norfolk, the true heart of what is traditionally called East Anglia. To their W lies Cambridgeshire, enlarged in 1974 to swallow up the former Huntingdonshire and to reach as far as Peterborough. Above the Wash is Lincolnshire, still one of the largest and most varied English counties even after administrative changes gave its northern tip to a new creation, Humberside.

This region has its own distinct character. Historically, the coastline gave access to the seas of northern Europe and the ports of the Netherlands. Coastal villages became fishing centres, while the hinterland grew fat on the Flemish wool trade. Eastern England grew into a place of affluent small towns, rather than great cities or great estates, and these communities maintained a sturdy independence in religion and politics. Already the home of Queen Boudicca's Iceni, as well as the breeding ground of Kett's rebellion and the Pilgrimage of Grace, Eastern England became in the 17C a centre for radical dissent. Oliver Cromwell was a native of Huntingdonshire, while the Eastern Counties Association—formed of Essex, Suffolk and Norfolk—was a stronghold of the Parliamentary cause. Boston in Lincolnshire, a town connected with the Pilgrim Fathers, was only one of many places in the region to give its name to the map of New England.

Today, now that fishing has declined in the face of foreign competition and wool is no longer a staple, Eastern England is still mainly rural and agricultural. A visitor's impression of Essex in 1594 as 'fatte, fruteful, and full of profitable things' could still apply not only to that county but to most of its neighbours as well. In the S, to be sure, the London suburbs continue their march into Essex and will no doubt be encouraged to advance further as Stansted is developed into the capital's third airport. Humberside is largely industrial, and the recent opening of the controversial Humber Bridge must surely have an impact on adjoining Lincolnshire, if only by increasing N–S traffic through the county. Felixstowe on the Suffolk coast flourishes as a container port, while in the W Peterborough continues to grow at a rate its authorities assure us is planned. But despite these things, the region still lacks major industrial or even commercial centres—Norwich, traditionally its largest city, has only about 122,000 inhabitants—and stands apart from the great traffic routes of England.

On the whole, Eastern England has suffered the same happy neglect from tourists as well as industrialists and planners. Because it is not on the way to anywhere, it does not lend itself to inclusion in those brisk circuits by which foreign visitors review the pleasures of England: they proceed W from London to Oxford, Stratford-upon-Avon and Bath, or N to York and Durham. Because it lacks National Parks, those officially designated areas of outstanding natural beauty, and perhaps because it enjoys a reputation with strangers for being merely a flat, wet place, Eastern England is sometimes ignored even by more leisurely travellers. It is symptomatic that Cambridge, the most obvious tourist attraction in the area, has never been able to rival Oxford in popularity.

This is not to say that Eastern England does not reward the visitor. Cambridge apart, it has much to offer in a conveniently small compass. In Norwich it has preserved a true regional capital of great antiquity; in Lincoln and Colchester it has two major Roman settlements that continued to flourish in later periods. The great Saxon monastic foundations and their Norman successors have left major landmarks at Ely and Peterborough. These centres are connected by a network of towns and villages which together can boast perhaps the richest array of parish churches in any English region. And they stand amid a landscape more varied than the popular image of the region admits—a landscape that has left its imprint on the history of English painting in the work of Constable, Gainsborough and the Norwich School.

If Eastern England seems something of a quiet corner, a place separate as well as distinct from the rest of the country, then this is no recent accident but largely the result of its natural situation. Its southern boundary, the Thames estuary, was once enforced by the dense Essex forests of which Epping Forest is the only surviving reminder. W and N lay the Lea marshes, now so thoroughly absorbed into the dull outskirts of London that the traveller is hardly aware of their existence. The western boundary dividing the region from the Midlands, now prosaically defined by the course of the A1, was in former times marked by the discouraging barrier of the Fens.

This flat marshland—it is only occasionally more than 20ft above sea level—stretches N from near Cambridge and Peterborough up to the Wash and continues into that part of Lincolnshire aptly named Holland. Its inland reaches are peat fen, progressively reclaimed since the Duke of Bedford called in the Dutch engineer Cornelius Vermuyden in the 17C. High-banked roads follow mathematically straight irrigation canals and rivers through a bleak landscape where the dark earth is fertile for bulbs, vegetables and grain. Near the coast the Fens become saltmarsh, made by the silting up of great river estuaries. Here the work of reclamation may date back to the Romans and had certainly been undertaken before the Norman Conquest. The tussocky grass, almost devoid of trees, makes good grazing land.

Low-lying, bounded on one side by the Fens and on the other by a sea that continually erodes its coastline, Eastern England has at its core a long outcrop of chalk running NE in modest continuation of the Chilterns in central England. Rising sharply out of the Fens in the W, it tilts down towards the coast. Nowhere flat, it is never hilly—rising above 400ft at only a few points in Suffolk and not reaching even 300ft in Norfolk. Yet it provides several distinct types of good farmland and gently rolling scenery: the Gog Magog Hills in Cambridgeshire, the open heath country of Breckland around Thetford and the fertile uplands of Norfolk. N of the Wash, it resumes in the more dramatic landscape of the Lincolnshire Wolds and continues beyond the Humber.

This varied scenery offers much to cheer the eye of both the farmer and the traveller, but it leaves the region poor in one striking respect. Eastern England has no building stone. Chalk—or clunch, as it is called when quarried for building—is too soft to withstand the weather for long. Indeed, it is too soft to wear well even indoors, as the condition of the Lady Chapel at Ely cathedral bears heartbreaking witness. Proper stone to grace the cathedrals and churches, the

Norfolk country houses and the Cambridge colleges, had to be imported. So Barnack limestone, from near Stamford, was ferried by barge down the rivers and through the Fens.

For humbler, everyday purposes the region has had to make do with local alternatives, which combine to create the characteristic appearance of its townscapes and parish churches. Flint, of course, is the oldest. It was being quarried with highly industrialised efficiency at Grime's Graves in Norfolk from about 2100 BC, and was still being knapped (or chipped into usable shape) at nearby Brandon within living memory. The round flint church towers, usually built in the 10C or 11C, are particularly distinctive: there are 114 in Norfolk, 41 in Suffolk and 8 in Essex, making 168 out of the total 180 in England as a whole. Their simple, functional air contrasts sharply with the local style of flushwork, where flint is used in combination with dressed stone to create decorative patterns. It can be seen on church porches and towers throughout the region, as well as on the civic buildings of Norwich and King's Lynn.

Thatching makes a durable roof from reed or grass. There are about 50 thatched churches in Norfolk and about 20 in Suffolk, in addition to the thousands of houses where thatch makes a pleasant contrast with walls brightly painted in orange, yellow or pink. Timber from the Essex forests created the characteristic weather-boarding throughout the county. Further N, in Suffolk and Norfolk, it enriched the domestic architecture of towns like Lavenham and Long Melford, and was carved into the magnificent angel roofs which are the glory of so many churches. Brick, too, was being used from a very early date—at Coggleshall in Essex, for example, and Little Wenham Hall in Suffolk—and could create impressively elaborate effects at Layer Marney, Oxburgh and Tattershall. In the 19C Fletton, now a suburb of Peterborough, gave its name to one of the most famous and widely used English bricks. In Cambridgeshire and Suffolk the local brick is a yellowish white, while in Norfolk it is a warm red that contrasts cheerfully with the ubiquitous grey flint. Such modest combinations of local material, like the gentle variety of the landscape, are typical of a region that makes up in quiet charm what it may lack in the dramatic or the sublime.

# 60 London to Colchester, Ipswich and the East Coast

Total distance 124m. The route follows A12 throughout.—To (15m) Gallows Corner.—To (31m) **Chelmsford** (bypassed).—To (53m) **Colchester** (bypassed).— To (71m) **Ipswich** (bypassed).—To (79m) Woodbridge (bypassed).—To (114m) **Lowestoft**.—To (124m) **Great Yarmouth**.

Maps: OS Landranger 177, 167, 168, 155 (briefly), 156, 134.

A12 is slow and congested for much of the way, particularly at summer weekends; likewise the detours to Southend, Harwich, Clacton and Felixstowe. Rte 62 describes a quieter but less direct way to the coast.

A12 runs NE from London through monotonous suburbs to (15m) *Gallows Corner*.

A127 leads E to Southend.—9m. *Laindon*, engulfed by *Basildon New Town* (152,300 inhab.), has a church with a unique 15C priest's house of timber against its W end. B1007 goes S over the *Langdon Hills* (387ft), with fine views of the Thames estuary (see below).—21½m. *Prittlewell* has a good 13C church and, in a delightful park, the refectory and prior's house of a 12C Cluniac priory, now a museum of local and natural history with a large collection of communications equipment. It is the 'south end' of the old village, standing near the mouth of the Thames, that grew into the seaside resort of **Southend-on-Sea** (156,700 inhab.; Tourist Information). The pier, 1½m long, is the longest in the world. Southend's more select part is known as *Westcliff-on-Sea*. Southchurch Hall (open) is a moated 14C manor house, with appropriate furnishings and displays of local history and medieval life. From *Southend Airport*, 2m N, passenger services fly to Guernsey, Jersey, Basle, Billund, Brussels and Ostend. To the W of Southend is *Leigh-on-Sea*. *Hadleigh*, 2m further, has a Norman church and a ruined castle, rebuilt in 1359–70 as a residence of Edward III and made the subject of a famous painting by Constable (English Heritage, open at any reasonable time). To the S is the low-lying *Canvey Island*, protected by a sea-wall, with the methane gas terminal on its S side.—A13 continues W along the estuary, passing N of *Coryton* (10m from Southend), with its huge oil refineries, and (15m) **Tilbury**, with its container port and passenger ferry to Gravesend on the Kent shore. *Tilbury Fort* (English Heritage, standard opening) was first constructed by Henry VIII in 1539. Here Elizabeth I made her famous speech to the camp assembled in anticipation of the Armada in 1588 ('I know that I have the body of a weak, feeble woman, but I have the heart and stomach of a king, and of a king of England too'). Replacing the Henrician fort is a superb example of military engineering built for Charles II in 1670–83.

To the E of Southend the front extends past *Thorpe Bay* to (3½m) *Shoeburyness*. The flat deserted island of *Foulness*, overlooking *Maplin Sands* to the NE, was once chosen as the site of London's third international airport, a dubious honour later transferred to Stansted (Rte 63).

*Rochford*, 4m N of Southend, has a Tudor mansion (not open), rebuilt by Anne Boleyn's father, and a fine brick church tower (c 1500). *Great Stambridge* church, 1½m E, partly pre-Conquest, was scene of the marriage of Governor Winthrop of Massachusetts and Mary North in 1605. *Ashingdon*, 2m N of Rochford, is the probable site of the Battle of Assandun, at which Edmund Ironside was defeated by Canute (1016).

20m. *Brentwood* (bypassed; 55,800 inhab.) was the first staging post on the old coaching road out of London, as the fine inn on the High St. testifies; opposite are some typical Essex weatherboarded houses. Brentwood School, founded in 1557, retains one block of 16C buildings. Adjoining *Shenfield*, where the church contains a remarkable oak arcade, grew round the railway junction on another road to Southend (A129; 21m). This runs via (4½m) *Billericay*, with a Chantry House where the Pilgrim Fathers assembled before embarking for America, and (15½m) *Rayleigh*, with a good example of a Norman castle mound (NT).

The brick towers and massive timberwork in the village churches are reminders of the absence of building stone and of the great forest that covered Essex in the Middle Ages. At (23½m) *Mountnessing* (left) the church has huge timber struts supporting the tower.—At (25m) *Ingatestone* (right) the church contains 16–17C tombs of the Petre family, builders of the Hall nearby.—At (27m) *Margetting* (right) the oak steeple and 15C Jesse window are noteworthy.

31m. **Chelmsford** (58,200 inhab.), the county town of Essex, became a bishop's see in 1913. *St Mary*, now the *Cathedral*, was completed in 1424 but nearly the whole body of it collapsed in 1800 and had to be rebuilt. Its chief features are the beautiful flintwork S porch and the massive tower with its flèche spire (1749). In the N wall of the chancel is a curious double or 'fan' arch (early 15C). The monument to Thomas Mildmay (1571) is also interesting. The *Shire Hall*, by John Johnson, is an Ionic building of 1789–92. Marconi developed his early wireless at Chelmsford and the town has a large electronics industry.

The *Museum* in Oaklands Park at Moulsham, 1m S, contains Roman and other antiquities, the Tunstill collection of English drinking glasses and a wing devoted to the Essex Regiment.

FROM CHELMSFORD TO MALDON AND BURNHAM-ON-CROUCH.—Beyond (5m) · *Danbury*, which has a pleasant sandy common and a church with three 13C wooden effigies, the road forks. A414 continues NE to (10m) **Maldon** (13,900 inhab.; Tourist Information), a picturesque old port and yachting resort on the Blackwater. The interesting church of *All Saints*, at the N end of the High St., has a triangular EE tower, Dec. S aisle and 18C nave. Nearby is the 15C *Moot Hall* (open by appointment), with quaint porch and tower, used from 1556 until 1974 as the centre of local government. Attached to the tower of *St Peter* is the · *Library* (open) of Dr Thomas Plume, a fine collection of 17C books bequeathed to the town on his death in 1704. *St Mary*, overlooking the attractive harbour at the S end of the High St., has the remains of a 12C nave and a 17C brick tower with a white wooden steeple added a century later. By following the course of the river and the sea-wall towards Northey Island and the Causeway, we reach the site of the Battle of Maldon (991), described in the Anglo-Saxon poem, where Brihtnoth was defeated by the invading Vikings. From *Heybridge*, with a massive church tower, a canal and footpath lead to (³/₄m) *Heybridge Basin*, frequented by yachtsmen and eel boats. *Langford*, beyond the river 1¹/₂m NW of Maldon, has the only church in England with a W apse.

From the Danbury fork B1010 leads SE. At (9¹/₂m) *Purleigh* Laurence Washington, great-great-grandfather of George Washington, was rector in 1623–43. The church tower has been restored as a Washington memorial with contributions from America.—19m. **Burnham-on-Crouch** (6,300 inhab.), on the estuary of the Crouch, is a centre for yachting and oyster-breeding. —*Southminster*, 2¹/₂m N, has a large Perp. church. *Bradwell-juxta-Mare*, 5m further N, has a church with 14C details. The former rectory, Bradwell Lodge (open by appointment), is a 16C house with an 'Adam' wing. On the coast, 2m further NE, is the chapel of *St Peter-on-the-Wall*, erected by St Cedd in the 7C on the ruins of the Roman fort of Othona, one of the castles of the 'Saxon Shore' (cf. Burgh Castle, below, and Brancaster, Rte 67). In striking and unwelcome contrast is the nuclear power station.

From Chelmsford to *Bury St Edmunds* and *Cromer*, see Rte 61.

36¹/₂m. *Hatfield Peverel* (right) has a partly Norman church. —39¹/₂m. *Witham* (left; 25,400 inhab.) is an ancient town with a fine 13–15C church, 1m W, beyond the station. A plaque at No. 24 Newland St. marks the house where Dorothy L. Sayers lived from 1929 until her death in 1957.—43m. *Kelvedon*, on the left, has a High St. with a wealth of old houses ranging in style from local weather-boarding to Georgian brick; more than 20 are 17C.

B1024 runs NW to *Coggleshall* (Rte 63). B1023 runs SE to the Blackwater.—3m. *Tiptree* is famous for its jam.—7m. *Tolleshunt D'Arcy*, a pretty village, has a 16C moated hall with a bridge of 1585. At *Tolleshunt Major*, 2m W, by the church, is the 16C brick gatehouse and fortified wall of Beckingham Hall, a house rebuilt in the 18C (open by appointment).—9m. *Tollesbury* preserves some old sail-drying sheds.

At (47m) *Marks Tey* the road is joined by A120.—48m. *Copford* has a fine Norman *church, 1m S, with an apse and a magnificent series of mural paintings showing Christ in Majesty, the raising of Jairus's daughter, signs of the Zodiac, and the Virtues (c 1150; restored). A12 swings left to bypass Colchester; we follow the old Roman alignment of the road into the city.

53m. **COLCHESTER** (140,700 inhab.) stands on a commanding ridge above the Colne which has attracted settlement since the earliest times. It is England's oldest recorded town, and shows its historic importance in the wealth of remains from different periods: the Romano-British city walls, the Norman castle and St Botolph's priory, and the many old houses, including some 200 Georgian ones.

**Tourist Information Centre**: No. 1 Queen Street.

**Car Parks**: Osborne St., Priory Rd, St Botolph's, Sheepen Rd, Middleborough. Multi-storey car park at Queen St., St John's, St Mary's.

**Bus Station**: High St.

**Railway Stations**: North Station (1m N of the centre); St Botolph's, Magdalen St. (branch line to coast only).

**Theatre**: Mercury, Balkerne Gate.

**Annual Events**: Rose Show and Carnival in July; Oyster Feast in October.

**History**. There was a Bronze Age settlement (c 1100 BC), sited on the ancient ridgeway, and its strategic position led Cunobelin (Cymbeline), ruler of the Trinovantes, to make his capital here c AD 10. The Emperor Claudius captured it in AD 44 and established the *Colonia Camulodunum*, the first Roman *colonia* in Britain. This was stormed by Boudicca, queen of the Iceni, and after her defeat was re-established as a Roman garrison. Tradition has it that the Emperor Constantine was born here. On the departure of the Romans it became the Saxon stronghold of *Colneceaster*. William the Conqueror built the castle, whose keep is the largest in Europe; from the years that followed are seven surviving medieval churches within the walls and the remains of three abbeys. In the 14–17C the town was a centre of the cloth trade, its prosperity boosted by the influx of Flemish weavers in 1570. In the Civil War Colchester was staunchly Royalist, holding out against Fairfax's siege for 11 weeks.

The *'**City Walls** are the most striking witness to Colchester's Roman past. Nearly 2m in extent, and enclosing an oblong area in which the city centre still lies, they are best seen from the W side.

Probably begun in the time of Vespasian but afterwards strengthened and extended, the wall seems to have been over 20ft high, and parts are still over 10ft. The W section includes the ruined *Balkerne Gate*, most of which lies beneath the Hole-in-the-Wall inn. *St Mary-at-the-Wall* (now an arts centre) retains only the tower of the church slighted by Cromwell. Nearby is the obtrusive *Water Tower* (1882), the dominant feature of the Colchester skyline, affectionately known to the inhabitants as 'Jumbo'.

We turn N by Head St., past the former King's Head inn where the Royalists surrendered in 1648, to meet North Hill with its old houses, near the civic church of *St Peter*. Partly classicised in 1758, it retains 13C ironwork on its (blocked) S door and unusual 16C brasses. The broad High St. runs W and E on the line of the ancient ridgeway and the Roman road. To the left is the *Town Hall* (1898–1902) by John Belcher; to the right the fine 15C *Red Lion Hotel*. On the left, further on, is the entrance to the park surrounding the *'**Castle**, a Norman building constructed in part of Roman materials (open).

The massive keep (151½ft by 110ft, with walls 12ft thick) is half as big again as the White Tower at London but lost its upper storey in 1683. Built on the platform of a Roman temple to Claudius, it contains a *Museum* notable for a fine collection of late Celtic and *'**Roman antiquities. The *Castle Park* includes a section of the Roman wall and affords a pleasant view of the Colne valley. An obelisk on the N side of the castle marks the spot where Lucas and Lisle, the Royalists defenders of the town, were shot by Fairfax in 1648. Adjoining the park is *Holly Trees*, a mansion of 1718, now containing a good collection of bygones. A *Natural History Museum* occupies an old church opposite.

High St. now passes between the pargeted *East Lodge* and the *Minories Art Gallery*, a Georgian house displaying contemporary arts and crafts. Its continuation, East Hill, descends past *St James* (with a good monument of 1727) to the Colne. *Siege House*, occupied by Fairfax as his headquarters, and the *Rose and Crown* inn are the most striking of the timbered buildings beyond the bridge.

Priory St. leads S from the junction of High St. and East Hill along the wall to the ruined church of *St Botolph's Priory*, an Augustinian foundation of c 1100 built mainly of Roman brick (English Heritage, open at any reasonable time). The arcaded W front has three portals, the fine one in the centre receding in five orders. By Stanwell St. we reach St John's Green, with *St John's Abbey Gateway*, the stately Perp. relic (c 1415) of a Benedictine house (English Heritage, open at any reasonable time).

We may now return to the centre of town, crossing the line of the wall by Scheregate steps. On the righthand side of Trinity St. is *Holy Trinity Church*, with a Saxon tower built of Roman brick and a Saxon doorway. It is now a museum of rural crafts. A plaque marks the house opposite where the composer John Wilbye died in 1638; he lived for many years at Hengrave Hall (Rte 63). *Tymperleys*, a fine half-timbered mansion next door, was the birthplace of Dr William Gilberd (1544–1603), physician to Elizabeth I. In West Stockwell St., N of the High St., are the disused Dec. church of *St Martin* and many fine old houses, including the home of Ann and Jane Taylor, verse writers for children in the early 19C. *St Helen's Chapel* (not open), a little further to the E, dates from c 1290. It stands in the Dutch Quarter, where the Flemish weavers made their home when they arrived in Colchester in the 16C.

About 2m W of the city is *Lexden*, possibly the site of Cunobelin's capital. The pre-Roman earthworks effectually bottle up the peninsula between the Colne and the small stream known as the Roman river. Considerable remains are still visible (English Heritage, open at any reasonable time).—The *University of Essex*, founded in 1962, is in *Wivenhoe Park*, 2m SE.—About 6m SW, off B1022, and 3m from Tiptree, is *Layer Marney Tower* (open). This enormous brick gatehouse, built c 1525, is medieval in plan but Renaissance in ornament. The adjoining church contains the *tombs of the Lords Marney (c 1525–30), the first purely Renaissance tombs in England (cf. Oxborough, Rte 61).

On the NE bank of the Colne estuary, below Colchester, are (4½m) *Wivenhoe*, with notable pargeting in East St., S of the church, and (10m) *Brightlingsea*, with a good church 1m inland. Opposite Brightlingsea, between the estuaries of the Colne and the Blackwater, is the island of *Mersea* with its yachting resort of *West Mersea*, 9m from Colchester via B1025. *Bourne Mill* (1591; NT), with a wild extravaganza of gables, lies on B1025, and a little further on is *Cannock Mill*, still in working trim.

FROM COLCHESTER TO CLACTON AND WALTON. A133 leads E to (10m) *Weeley* and then SE to (16m) **Clacton-on-Sea** (43,600 inhab.; Tourist Information), one of the most crowded resorts in Essex. It is flanked by *Jaywick* to the W and *Holland-on-Sea* to the E. About 4½m W is the pleasant old village of *St Osyth*, where Osyth, queen of the East Saxons, was murdered by the Danes c 870. A *Priory (open) on the site preserves a fine 15C gatehouse, with a collection of paintings, and other monastic buidings in a pleasant garden. On the creek below are a restored tide mill and a boating lake.

From Weeley (see above) B1033 heads E via *Thorpe-le-Soken* to the quiet seaside resort of (17m) **Frinton-on-Sea** and its homelier neighbour (17½m) **Walton-on-the-Naze** (joint population 14,700; seasonal Tourist Information in Walton). The *Naze* is a headland to the N. Oysters are cultivated in the muddy creeks of Walton Backwaters, to the NW.

FROM COLCHESTER TO HALSTEAD. From Lexden (see above) A604 ascends the pleasant *Colne Valley.—At 8m the former Chappel and Wakes Colne railway station has been restored as the *Stour Valley Railway Centre*, with locomotives from the old Great Eastern Railway.—10m.*Earls Colne* church has a fine 16C tower, partly of brick.—13½m. *Halstead*, see Rte 61.

FROM COLCHESTER TO HARWICH, 19m via A137 and B1352.—At (10m) *Mistley* the 'Towers' are a fragment of the only church in England by Robert Adam, built in 1776 (English Heritage, open at any reasonable time).—19m. **Harwich** (15,500 inhab.; seasonal Tourist Information) is an old port and naval base on the broad estuary of the Stour and Orwell, with many 16–18C buildings. Among them is the red-brick *Guildhall* (1769), with an eccentric Gothick door. On the Green is the 17C Naval Treadmill Crane. The Low Lighthouse in 'Chinese' style contrasts with the resplendent white brick High Lighthouse of 1818. Nelson stayed several times at the Three Cups inn, while Captain Jones of the 'Mayflower' was married in Harwich and lived in King's Head St. Ferry services run to the Hook of Holland, Hamburg, Esbjerg, Kristiansand, Gothenburg, Hirtshals and Oslo; there is also a local service (passengers only) to Felixstowe (see below).

From Colchester to *Bishop's Stortford*, see Rte 63.

A12 leads NE from Colchester, and at (59½m) *Stratford St Mary* we cross the border into Suffolk and enter East Anglia. The Perp. church with excellent flushwork is an appropriate introduction to the area. The *N porch has an interesting window, and inside is a fine roof and 15C stained glass. There are some good 16C houses in the village. The surrounding region, with its pleasant woodlands by the banks of the Stour, is associated with the painter John Constable (1776–1837).

Constable's birthplace in *East Bergholt*, 3m NE, does not survive but nearby are many of the scenes which, he said, 'made me a painter'. Among his favourite local subjects were: the watermills of Stratford St Mary itself; the picturesque *Flatford Mill* and *Willy Lott's Cottage*, 1m S of Bergholt (both NT but used by the Field Studies Council); and the fine 15C tower of *Stoke-by-Nayland* church, 4m W of Stratford. **Dedham** (seasonal Tourist Information), a dignified village 1½m E of Stratford, attracted both Constable and Sir Alfred Munnings, who lived from 1919 until his death in 1959 at *Castle House* (open). The fine church was built in 1492–1520 and many houses of the 16–18C survive.—According to local legend the church of East Bergholt was deprived of its steeple by the devil, and so its bells are hung in a timber cage (1531) in the churchyard.—*Nayland*, on the Stour 1½m S of Stoke, preserves some painted panels from a 15C rood screen.

*Little Wenham Hall* (not open), 1½m N of (64m) *Capel St Mary*, is a very early example of Flemish brickwork (c 1250).—At (67½m) *Washbrook* and *Copdock*, both with good churches, the Roman road swings N towards *Venta Icenorum* (Caistor St Edmund, Rte 64). A12 drops into the valley of the Orwell and bypasses Ipswich.

71m. **IPSWICH** (120,400 inhab.), the county town of E Suffolk, stands at the head of the estuary. A thriving port and farming centre, known also for its agricultural machinery and printing works, Ipswich has too often torn down its past without putting much of worth in its place. The visitor today finds a patchwork of attractive historic buildings and unattractive modern town planning.

**Tourist Information Centre**: Town Hall, Princes St. (by Cornhill).

**Car Parks**: Tacket St., Foundation St. and Civic Centre.

**Bus Station**: Turret Lane.

**Railway Station**: Burrell Rd (S of the river).

**Theatre**: Wolsey Theatre, Civic Drive.

**History**. A prehistoric settlement grew up at the ford where the Gipping becomes navigable as the Orwell. It received its name, *Gipeswic*, from the Anglo-Saxons, was an important burgh by Domesday, and flourished for centuries as an agricultural centre and port. Chaucer's Merchant 'wolde the see were kept for anything/ Bitwixe Middleburgh and Orewelle'. It has more medieval parish churches than any English town of comparable size. From the peak of its proserity in the 18C it remained a busy market town, its large Wet Dock handling North Sea traffic and the great Thames barges.

**Famous natives and residents**. Cardinal Wolsey (1475?–1530) was born at Ipswich, the son of a butcher. Clara Reeve (1729–1807), Gothic novelist, was born and died here. Jeremy Collier (1650–1726), the clergyman who wrote 'A Short View of the Immorality and Profaneness of the English Stage', and H. Rider Haggard (1856–1925), the adventure novelist, attended Ipswich School.

The scale of Ipswich has been greatly changed by the building of its new Civic Centre. Cornhill, the traditional centre with the old *Town Hall* of 1867, lies to the E and is the natural place to start a walking tour. Tavern St., one of several central shopping streets now closed to traffic, runs E. From it Dial Lane leads right, past the handsome tower of *St Lawrence*, to Butter Market. Here we find *Sparrowe's* or the

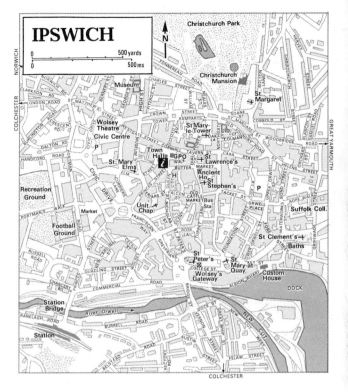

# IPSWICH

NORWICH

COLCHESTER

0    500 yards
0    500 ms

Christchurch Park

N

NORWICH RD

CLARKSON ST

LONDON ROAD

Museum

CHARLES    STREET

HIGH ST

CROWN    STREET

Christchurch Mansion

FONNEREAU ROAD

ST MARGARET ST

St Margaret

GREAT YARMOUTH

BURLINGTON RD

CRESCENT RD

DALTON RD

HANDFORD ROAD

CIVIC DRIVE

PORTMAN'S WALK

ST MATTHEW ST

GEORGE ST

WESTGATE STREET

Wolsey Theatre
Civic Centre

St Mary Elms

Recreation Ground

Market

Football Ground

RAMPARTS

TOWER

Town Hall

ELM ST

PRINCES STREET

ST NICHOLAS STREET

St Mary-le-Tower

CORNHILL

GPO

BUTTER MARKET

CULLIERS

FRANCISCAN WAY

St Lawrence's

Ancient Ho.

St Stephen's

OLD CATTLE MARKET

Bus Sta.

TAVERN ST

OAK LANE

COLMAN'S RD

CARR STREET

ST HELEN'S STREET

COBBOLD ST

WOODBRIDGE ROAD

ORWELL PLACE

TACKET ST

ROPE WALK

Suffolk Coll.

BLANCHE ST

CHRISTCHURCH ST

BOLTON LANE

SOANE ST

Unit. Chap.

CECILIA ST

GREYFRIARS

ROSE LANE

ST PETER'S

FOUNDATION STREET

St Clement's

Baths

WATERWORKS ST

GRIMWADE

RUSSELL ROAD

CHANCERY Ln.

QUADLING STREET

COMMERCIAL ROAD

St Peter's

COLLEGE ST

Wolsey's Gateway

BRIDGE ST

St Mary-at-Quay

ALBION WHARF

Custom House

DOCK

Station Bridge

RANELAGH ROAD

Station

BURRELL ROAD

River Orwell

COCK ST

MENNT

DOCK ST

AUSTIN STREET

FELAW STREET

NEW CUT WEST

COLCHESTER

Ancient House (1567), with a splendidly elaborate pargeted façade added in the reign of Charles II. Tavern St. continues E to the old *Great White Horse Hotel*, on the left, where Dickens stayed and Mr Pickwick had his embarrassing encounter with the lady in yellow curl papers.

Northgate St., with old houses and a 15C gateway, leads N past the *Library* (important Suffolk collections) to St Margaret's Plain. To the right is the noble flint church of *St Margaret*, with a double hammer-beam roof and a 15C clerestory. In a pleasant park adjoining stands *Christchurch Mansion* (open), built in 1548–50 and altered after a fire in 1675.

It now houses a large collection (36 rooms) of local antiquities and paintings. Especially notable are the Pownder brass of 1525 (from St Mary-at-Quay, see below), part of a Tournai marble font, an early Tudor wing (re-erected here) and the Wingfield Room, with 16C panelling from an inn in Tacket St., once the house of Sir Anthony Wingfield (d. 1552). The Wolsey Memorial Art Gallery, added in 1931, has works by the Suffolk painters Gainsborough and Constable.

We may return to the centre by taking Oak Lane from Northgate St., past the rebuilt civic church of *St Mary-le-Tower*, with a conspicuous spire (176ft).

A second excursion from Cornhill starts by going W on Westgate St. In High St., to the right, is the *Ipswich Museum*, with important

*Sparrowe's House (sometimes called the Ancient House) in Ipswich*

collections illustrating local geology and fauna, the prehistoric and Roman periods in East Anglia (including replicas of the Sutton Hoo and Mildenhall treasures now in the British Museum), etc. Museum St., leading left from Westgate St., has buildings fronted with Suffolk white brick. Behind the 15C church of *St Mary Elms* stands a row of medieval cottages. Off Friars St., beyond the junction with Princes St., is the handsome *Unitarian Chapel* of 1699. We go through the courtyard to St Nicholas St., which leads S. At the corner with Silent St. is a striking group of half-timbered houses, one identified by a plaque as the birthplace of Cardinal Wolsey. St Peter's St. continues S to the church of *St Peter*, which contains a font of Tournai marble (c 1100) and the Knapp brass of 1604.

Hard by stands *Wolsey's Gateway*, the sole relic of a college of secular canons founded by the Cardinal in 1527, one of 'those twins of learning, Ipswich and Oxford', that 'fell with him,/ Unwilling to outlive the good that did it' (Shakespeare's 'Henry VIII', IV,ii). College St. leads E past *St Mary-at-Quay*, now the local headquarters of the Boys' Brigade, and the fine classical *Custom House* (1844) by J.M. Clarke, overlooking the Wet Dock of 1842.

We continue to Fore St. and head N, back towards the centre, passing the *Neptune Inn* and *Lord's* coal wharf, both 17C. In St Clement's Lane, to the right, the church of *St Clement* has a slender Perp. tower. From the N end of Fore St. Orwell Place leads into Tacket St. Here the Salvation Army Citadel occupies the site of the theatre where David Garrick made his debut as an actor proper in 1741, under the name of Lyddal, in Southerne's 'Oronooko'. A kiln discovered in 1961 in nearby Cox Lane is believed to have manufactured the late Saxon pottery known as 'Thetford ware'.

At *Holbrook*, on B1080 6m S, is the Royal Hospital School, moved from Greenwich in 1933, where the sons of sailors and marines are trained for the Navy. On the way there the road passes *Freston Tower* (c 1640) and *Woolverstone Hall*, a boys' boarding school. Beyond the school, on the bank of the Orwell 7m from Ipswich, is *Pin Mill*, a favourite mooring for yachts.

FROM IPSWICH TO FELIXSTOWE, 12m via A45 across *Nacton Heath*, or 15m by the more interesting sideroad which keeps closer to the Orwell. It passes *Nacton* church; *Orwell Park*, the home of Admiral Vernon ('Old Grog'), now a school; and *Broke Hall* (not open), the home of Admiral Sir Philip Broke (1776–1841), commander of the 'Shannon' in her memorable encounter with the 'Chesapeake' (1813).—**Felixstowe** (20,900 inhab.; Tourist Information), a pleasant resort, stands on a cliff between the Orwell and the Deben. Its esplanade, 2¹/₂m long, was the starting-point of the romantic swim described in Meredith's 'Lord Ormont and His Aminta'.—About 2m S is Felixstowe Dock, with a container port and car-ferry service to Zeebrugge and Rotterdam. The 18C Landgnard Fort (English Heritage) stands on the site of earlier defences. —Across the Deben, about 2m N of Felixstowe, is *Bawdsey*, site of the first radar station (1936).

FROM IPSWICH TO SUDBURY, 21m via A1071.—5m. *Hintlesham Hall*, now a restaurant.—10m. **Hadleigh** (5900 inhab.), a well-built old centre of the woollen trade, has a large late 14C church. The fine Deanery Tower (1495) was the gatehouse to the palace of Archbishop Pykenham. The Guildhall (open) has a timber roof and an 18C assembly room. Thomas Woolner (1825–92), sculptor and Pre-Raphaelite, was born here. The Oxford Movement was started by the vicar of Hadleigh, Hugh Rose, in 1833. *Kersey*, 1¹/₂m NW, one of the Suffolk weaving villages, gave its name to 'Kerseymere' ('Cashmere'). The pretty *street, with many fine timbered houses, dips down to a ford across the Brett. The *church has a lovely flushwork S porch and a fine hammerbeam roof, and there are also remains of a 13C Augustinian priory. *Lindsey*, another weaving village 1m further W, gave its name to the cloth 'Lindsey-woolsey'. The 14C church has a tie-beam roof and wall paintings. *St James's Chapel*, ¹/₂m S, dates from the 13C and has tiny lancet windows (English Heritage, standard opening).—15¹/₂m. *Boxford* has pretty timbered houses and a wooden late Dec. porch to its church. In 1828 William Corder committed the 'Murder in the Red Barn' at *Polstead*, 2m SE.—21m. *Sudbury*, see Rte 61.

FROM IPSWICH TO NORWICH, 43m. Leaving A45 at (4m) *Claydon* (Rte 63), we continue on A140, following the line of the 'Pye Road', the Roman way from Colchester to Caistor St Edmund, to (10m) *Earl Stonham* (see Rte 62). On the former airfield of *Mendlesham* (14¹/₂m; left) is a memorial to the men of the USAF. The Perp. church has a splendid flushwork tower; it contains a good collection of 15–17C armour, a Jacobean font cover and pulpit, and a brass to John Knyvet (1417). Hakluyt was rector of *Wetheringsett*, ³/₄m E of the road, from 1590 until his death. The village has some good timbered cottages.—At (19m) *Yaxley* church is a 'sexton's wheel', used to determine voluntary fast days, one of only two in England (cf. Long Stratton below). **Eye**, 1¹/₂m E, is an attractive litte town with a 16C timber-framed Guildhall. The church, with good flintwork, particularly in the tall *tower, preserves a richly painted rood screen of c 1500. To the W are the remains of the Norman castle of the Malets. —Crossing the Waveney, we enter Norfolk at (23m) **Scole**, which was an important staging post midway between Ipswich and Norwich at the crossing of the Great Yarmouth and Bury St Edmunds roads. The White Hart is a stately building of 1655 with Dutch gables. Remains of a Roman posting station, *Villa Faustina*, have been found at Scole House and at Waterloo, on the Waveney. **Diss** (5400 inhab.), 2¹/₂m W, is an attractive little town built round a 6-acre mere. Among its important buildings are the Dolphin Inn and Saracen's Head, timber-framed with overhangs, and the Victorian 'Shambles'. The church has a tall flushwork tower with processional arches at its base. John Skelton (1460–1529), poet and tutor to Henry VIII, was given the living here in 1498 and held it until his death.

The *Bressingham Steam Museum*, 3m W of Diss on A1066, has a superb collection of traction engines and locomotives, including the Royal Scot. The church at *South Lopham*, 1½m further W, has a good Norman tower. *Hoxne* (pronounced 'Hoxen'), 3m SE of Diss, is a pretty village. Abbey Farm, to the S, is the traditional site of the death of St Edmund, killed fighting the Danes in 869 and for many years the patron saint of England. The church has a fine tower and ˙wall paintings of St Christopher, the Seven Deadly Sins, and the Seven Works of Mercy.

A140 continues N from Scole to (28½m; left) *Tivetshall St Margaret*, where the church has a large Royal Arms (Elizabeth I).—32m. *Long Stratton* church has a 'sexton's wheel' (cf. Yaxley above) as well as a Jacobean font cover and pulpit. *Shelton* ˙church, 2m E, is a fine Perp. building with good brickwork (1480) by Sir Ralph Shelton. In the graceful interior is a well carved Royal Arms (William III).—34m. *Tasburgh* (on the left), a stronghold of the Iceni, has an Iron Age settlement and hill-fort. The bridge over the Tas at (35½m) *Newton Flotman* is partly medieval. *Saxlingham Nethergate* church, 1½m E, has fine 13C glass.—*Venta Icenorum* and *Caistor St Edmund* (Rte 64) lie ½m N of (39m) *Dunston*.—43m. *Norwich*, see Rte 64.

From Ipswich to *Bury St Edmunds* and *Newmarket*, see Rte 63.

Beyond (76m) *Martlesham* A12 swings left to bypass Woodbridge. The old road, narrow and congested, descends to (79m) **Woodbridge** (7200 inhab.), a charming old town on the Deben. The fine Perp. church has excellent flushwork and a famous peal of bells in the tower (108ft). Inside are a 15C font and a monument to Thomas Seckford (d. 1587). The neighbouring Market Hill is dominated by the Shire Hall, originally built in 1575 though much changed. Tennyson stayed at the Bull Hotel when visiting his friend Edward FitzGerald (1809–93), who came to live at Woodbridge in 1860 and lodged over a shop on the N side of Market Hill. The surrounding streets have several more handsome inns, and New St. has a curious 18C steelyard. To the left of the main road, further on, is Little Grange, where FitzGerald spent his declining years. The walk along the Deben, with its yachts and tide mill, is pleasant.

FitzGerald lived in 1837–53 in a thatched cottage, still standing, at *Boulge*, 2½m N. He is buried in the churchyard of St Michael in the grounds of the demolished Boulge Hall nearby. On his grave blooms a descendant of the rose bush brought from Omar Khayyám's tomb in Persia.—The village of *Grundisburgh*, 3m W of Woodbridge, is grouped round a green through which a small stream flows. In the church beautiful double hammerbeam ˙roofs with a multitude of angels cover the nave, S aisle and chapel. There is also a 13C wall painting of St Christopher.

FROM WOODBRIDGE TO ORFORD, 12m. From *Melton*, 1m NE of Woodbridge, A1152 crosses the Deben. To the right, on B1083 to Bawdsey, is *Sutton Hoo* (open summer weekends for guided tours), where a tumulus excavated in 1938–39 yielded the remarkable ship burial of a Saxon chieftain (c 650–70) of the Wuffingas, who ruled East Anglia at that time. The gold, silver and enamel treasures are now in the British Museum; replicas are displayed in Ipswich Museum (see above). B1084 diverges right from A1152 and crosses *Rendlesham Forest*, with fine oaks.—8m. *Butley* still has the 14C gatehouse (now a private house) of an Augustinian priory, 1m S. Oysters are bred in the Butley river. —12m. **Orford** is a picturesque decayed seaport with a castle built by Henry II in 1165–67 (English Heritage, standard opening but closed on Thursdays and on Friday mornings in winter). Its massive keep and three towers together form an irregular polygon of 18 sides. The ruined chancel of the church has a double row of Norman columns. The river Ore here runs nearly parallel with the coast for 10m, separated from the sea by a narrow shingly spit. At Orfordness in 1935 Robert Watson-Watt carried out the practical experiments that gave birth to radar defence.—The lonely church of *Iken*, 4½m N of Orford, commands a good view of the Alde estuary.

81m. *Utford* church (13C) has a superb tabernacled *font cover, and good benches with poppy heads and deep carving.—84m. *Wickham Market*, where the Dec. church with a tall spire stands to one side of the pleasant little market square.—86m. *Little Glemham* church has a Norman doorway. Just beyond, the road skirts the park of *Glemham Hall* (not open), an 18C house on Elizabethan foundations.—91½m. *Saxmundham* is a small market town with a Dec. church containing 16C Flemish stained glass.

For *Leiston*, 4½m E, and *Aldeburgh*, 7½m SE, see Rte 62.—Beyond (95m) *Yoxford* an unclassified road on the right leads via *Westleton* to (5½m) *Dunwich*, now merely an attractive coastal village but an important seaport before the sea swept it away. It was the seat of the first East Anglian bishopric, established c 630, merged with that at North Elmham and transferred successively to Thetford and Norwich. Little is left of its ancient glory except the remains of a 13C Franciscan friary and the ruins of a 12C chapel near the present church, which includes materials from the last surviving old church. The local Museum tells the story of Dunwich's decline.

101m. *Blythburgh*, on the tidal Blyth, was once a bustling port before the retreat of the sea and the silting up of the river closed it. It lies beneath one of the finest *churches in Suffolk, built in 1442–73, containing original woodwork and a painted tie-beam roof with angels, used as targets by William Dowsing's infamous crew of iconoclasts but relatively unharmed.—**Southwold** (1800 inhab.; Tourist Information), 5m E, is a charming old town, seaside resort and North Sea fishing port with pretty, colourful houses. Its harbour at the mouth of the Blyth is backed by open heathland. George Orwell (1903–50) used to visit his parents' home on the High St. The great Perp. *Church* has a notable rood screen, a panelled roof and canopied stalls.

*Walberswick*, 1m S across the river, has a half-ruined church as large as those at Blythburgh and Southwold.
An unclassified road running W from Blythburgh leads via (2m) *Wenhaston*, with an interesting panel picture of the Last Judgement dating from c 1480 in its church, to (5½m) *Halesworth*, where the Perp. church has good 15C brasses. About 4m SW on B1117 is *Heveningham Hall* (limited opening), built in 1777–80 by Sir Robert Taylor and decorated by Wyatt, with its park landscaped by Capability Brown. It is still undergoing repairs after a serious fire.

N of Blythburgh A12 skirts the fine park of *Henham* and reaches (106m) *Wrentham*. A sideroad leads 1m E to *Covehithe*, like Dunwich a port destroyed by the encroachment of the sea. Its fine ruined church has a smaller structure inside it, put up in 1672 to serve the needs of the reduced population. Offshore in the same year the indecisive Battle of Solebay (i.e. Southwold Bay) was fought between the Dutch fleet and the English and French under the Duke of York, later James II.

114m. **LOWESTOFT** (55,200 inhab.), the most easterly town in England, is a popular seaside resort with a sandy beach, and a flourishing fishing port and ship-building centre. Thomas Nashe (1567–1601?) and Benjamin Britten (1913–76) were born here.

**Tourist Information Centre**: The Esplanade.

**Car Parks**: Esplanade, Belvedere Road, Clapham Rd, etc. Multi-storey car park in Battery Green.

**Bus Station**: London Rd North.

**Railway Stations**: Station Square (by the harbour); also at Oulton Broad North and South.

**Theatre**: Sparrow's Nest, North Lowestoft.

**Annual Event**: Oulton Regatta Week in late August.

In the centre are the railway station and the harbour, the latter protected by the *South Pier*. Suffolk Rd, opposite the station, leads to the *Fish Market* and the trawler basin. A bascule bridge leads to the S part of town, with the long Esplanade and the *Claremont Pier.*—We reach the N part of Lowestoft by London Rd North. In the old town, where a few old houses preserve their bright red pantiles, is the High St., from which narrow lanes called 'Scores' lead down toward the shore. *Lowestoft Ness* is the dreary easternmost point of Britain (long. 1° 45′ E). At the N end of the High St. stand the *Lighthouse* and, beyond, the *Lowestoft and East Suffolk Maritime Museum* and the *Royal Naval Patrol Service Museum.*—The parish church of *St Margaret* at the NW edge of town, reached from the High St. by B1074 towards Somerleyton, is a spacious 15C flint building with an older tower. Thomas Nashe was baptised here.

The inner harbour, known as *Lake Lothing*, communicates by Mutford Lock with (1¹/₂m) Oulton Broad, a favourite centre for fishing and boating, with a yacht station. *Oulton* church, with a Norman chancel arch, is 1m N of the Broad. George Borrow (1803–81) wrote most of his books at his home on Oulton Broad, but the house no longer stands The *Lowestoft Museum* in the adjoining park has displays of local archaeology and history and a collection of Lowestoft china.
  *Blundeston*, 3¹/₄m NW, gave Dickens the name, though not the spelling, for David Copperfield's childhood home and was often visited by the poet Gray. At *Lound*, 1¹/₂m further N the church has a Perp. screen with a rood by Sir Ninian Comper (1914). From Blundeston we may go W to (3m) *Somerleyton Hall* (open), built by John Thomas for the railway entrepreneur Sir Morton Peto in 1844, around an old 17C manor. It has fine panelling and carving, and a maze in the gardens. The church and village were built at about the same time in an amusing eclectic style. Beyond is (4m) *Herringfleet*, with a partly Norman church and 17C hall and barn. For (5m) *St Olave's Priory* and (6m) *Fritton Decoy*, see below.

FROM LOWESTOFT TO SCOLE, 30m. A146 crosses the Waveney between Lake Lothing and Oulton Broad.—9m. **Beccles** (8900 inhab.; seasonal Tourist Information), a town on the Waveney noted for its crayfish, has a fine Perp. church with a detached tower 92ft high. In 1794–97 Chateaubriand lived here as an émigré and fell in love with the daughter of the parson at Bungay. At *Gillingham*, 1¹/₂m NW, is a pure early Norman church divided into five parts: Galilee, tower space, nave, chancel and apse.—B1062 continues to (15m) **Bungay** (4100 inhab.), with an octagonal market cross and two interesting churches, one of which has a pre-Norman round tower. The ruined Norman *Castle*, built by Hugh Bigod, Earl of Norfolk, in c 1165, has the remains of a keep and fore-building, and a twin-towered gatehouse added in 1294. About 2¹/₄m SE of (19¹/₂m) *Homersfield*, at *South Elmham*, are the pre-Norman ruins called the Old Minster and wrongly claimed as the site of the East Anglian cathedral of Elmham (cf. North Elmham, Rte 66A).—22m *Harleston. Mendham*, 2m S, was the birthplace of Sir Alfred Munnings (1878–1959). At *Wingfield*, 5m SW of Harleston, the *church (1362) contains fine monuments of the Wingfield and de la Pole families. The de la Poles, Earls and Dukes of Suffolk, built the *Castle* (not open), with a handsome three-storied gatehouse of 1384 and a Tudor house behind. The Wingfields built the *College* (open), where the 18C façade conceals an older building. *Fressingfield*, 4m S of Harleston, has the 16C Fox and Goose inn, a church with fine *bench ends, roof and a Willis organ (from the Chapel Royal of the Savoy), and the grave of Archbishop Sancroft (1616–93).—30m. *Scole*, see above.

A12 runs N to (121¹/₂m) *Gorleston*, now included in the borough of Yarmouth, a seaside resort on a low cliff at the mouth of the Yare. Its sands are broad and clean and the large Dec. church, inland, has a good 15C font. From South Town, where Cotman lived as a drawing master in 1812–23, we cross the Yare by Haven Bridge.
  124m. **GREAT YARMOUTH** (48,300 inhab.) is the chief town and the most popular seaside resort on the Norfolk coast. It stands on a peninsula formed by the Yare as it combines with the Waveney and

the Bure to flow south from Breydon Water into the sea through a narrow mouth. Seaside Yarmouth fills the eastern edge of the peninsula, though its atmosphere makes itself unpleasantly felt throughout the whole town. Beside the Yare is the port whose herring fleets and curing houses made 'Yarmouth bloaters' famous, though nowadays its trade is mainly in supplies for North Sea oil and gas exploration. The most interesting part, the old town, lies to the N where the Bure and the Yare meet to pass under Haven Bridge. Originally enclosed by walls built between 1261 and 1400, it is made distinctive by the 'Rows', a system of extremely narrow lanes running at right angles to the river and the sea to form a gridiron. Despite heavy bombing in the Second World War, a large number of its flint cottages and 18C houses survive.

**Tourist Information Centres**: South Quay; (seasonal) Marine Parade.

**Car Parks**: North Quay, The Conge, Market Place, Marine Parade. Multi-storey car park off Market Rd, near Market Gates Shopping Precinct.

**Bus Station**: Wellington Rd, near Marine Parade.

**Railway Station**: Vauxhall Station, reached from North Quay and Vauxhall Bridge.

**Ferry services**: Continental passenger service daily from Atlas Wharf to Scheveningen; local passenger service across the Yare to Gorleston from just S of the Fish Wharf.

**Amusements**: all the usual seaside attractions on Marine Parade.

**Famous natives and visitors**. Anna Sewell (1820–78), author of 'Black Beauty', was born on Priory Plain (see below). Dickens stayed at the Royal Hotel on Marine Parade in 1848, and readers of 'David Copperfield' will remember Yarmouth's connection with the Peggottys. In the 1850s George Borrow often visited No. 169 King St., finishing 'Romany Ry' there in 1857.

On Hall Quay, by Haven Bridge, are the *Town Hall* and the *Star Hotel*, a restored Elizabethan house, once the residence of John Bradshaw, President of the Court of Commissioners for the trial of Charles I. The Town Hall contains perhaps the best authenticated portrait of Nelson, painted from life in 1801 by Matthew Keymer, a Norfolk artist. The fine South Quay has many houses of great charm, among them No. 4, a refronted Tudor house which tradition claims as the scene of the conference at which Cromwell and his officers decided on the fate of Charles I. It is now the *Elizabethan House Museum*. On Greyfriars Way behind the museum are the scanty remains of the 13C *Greyfriars Cloisters* (English Heritage, summer season Mondays to Fridays 09.30–18.00). The local museum nearby incorporates the walls and basement cells of the 14C *Tolhouse* (or jail). Continuing down South Quay, we come to the *Old Merchant's House* and the *Row 111 Houses*, good specimens of Yarmouth's 17C town houses (English Heritage, summer season Mondays to Fridays 09.30–18.00).

The walk between Hall Quay and the large, busy Market Place is rich in reminders of the old town, particularly on Market Row. King St. leads S from the Market Place through the town and past *St George's* (1714), an ingeniously planned church with a nice cupola, now an arts centre. On Blackfriars Rd, beyond the S end of King St., are two surviving towers from the *Tower Walls*.

At the NE corner of the Market Place are the interesting almshouses called *Fishermen's Hospital* (1702). No. 26 Priory Plain, just beyond, was the birthplace of Anna Sewell. *St Nicholas*, one of the largest parish churches in England, was completely gutted in 1942. Though the outside preserves its ancient appearance, with 12C

Norman tower and EE W front, the interior was completely restored in 1957–61 by Stephen Dykes Bower. The Norman font came from the deserted church of Highway in Wiltshire, the pulpit from St George's. The ironwork, furnishing and stained glass by Brian Thomas, and the screens (1969) by Stephen Dykes Bower, are noteworthy. The adjoining *Priory Hall*, on the S side, now a school, was originally the guesthouse of a Benedictine foundation established by Bishop Losinga. A large section of the *Town Walls* bounds the churchyard of St Nicholas; the *NW Gate* survives from North Quay.

The *Maritime Museum for East Anglia* is on Marine Parade in the centre of seaside Yarmouth. Beyond the S end of the Parade are the *South Denes*, home of Dickens's Peggotty family but now an ugly rash of caravans. The *Nelson Monument*, a Doric column of 1819, gives good views.

About 3m W of Yarmouth is **Burgh Castle** (English Heritage, open at any reasonable time). A Roman fortress on the Saxon Shore (c AD 300), it commanded the large harbour at the confluence of the Yare and Breydon Water. The three remaining landward walls are still held together by Roman mortar, though they lean at acute angles. The church to the NE has a Norman round tower, using Roman material from the castle.

FROM YARMOUTH TO BECCLES, 15m via A143 and A146. The road goes through an area whose churches have 12C round flint towers and 15C lion fonts. The one at (7m) *Fritton*, with a beautiful Norman apse, overlooks the *Fritton Decoy*, the most charming of the East Anglian lakes.—7½m. *St Olave's* has a ruined 13C Augustinian priory (Engish Heritage, open at any reasonable time).—9½m. *Haddiscoe* has a Norman S portal and striking Saxon work in the tower.—15m. *Beccles*, see above.

From Yarmouth to *Norwich*, see Rte 64; to *Cromer* and *King's Lynn*, see Rte 67.

# 61   London to Bury St Edmunds and Cromer

Total distance 142m. A12, slow and congested, to **Chelmsford**, see Rte 60.—A130, A131 to (42m) Braintree.—A131 to (57m) Sudbury.—A134 to (74m) **Bury St Edmunds**.—A134, B1106 to (89m) Brandon.—A1065 to (103½m) Swaffham.—A1065 to (119½m) Fakenham (Rte 66A).—A148 to (142m) **Cromer** (Rte 67).

Maps: OS Landranger 177, 167, 168 (briefly), 155, 144, 132, 133.

We follow Rte 60 to (31m) **Chelmsford**. Leaving the town by the station, we take A130 3½m N and turn NE on A131. At *Pleshey*, 2¾m NW of the junction, the village is enclosed in an earth rampart, with a huge motte and bailey on the S preserving a brick arch bridge.—38m. *Great Leighs* has the Essex showground. *Little Leighs* priory (not open), ¾m W of our road, has two gatehouses and part of a quadrangle of c 1550.—42m. **Braintree** (31,100 inhab.), at the junction of two Roman roads, was a medieval wool town. Nicholas Udall, author of 'Ralph Roister Doister', was vicar here from 1537. Bank St. leads past old houses and inns to *Bocking*, adjoining on the N, with a good 15C church.

*Black Notley*, 1¾m SE, was the birthplace of the naturalist John Ray (1628–1705), who is buried in the churchyard. *Cressing Temple*, 3m SE, has two huge barns, one 15C and the other perhaps partly pre-Conquest.—From Braintree to *Bishop's Stortford* and to *Colchester*, see Rte 63.

49m. *Halstead* (9300 inhab.), in the upper valley of the Colne, has an unexpectedly steep High St. The mill set up by the Courtaulds in 1826 is by the stream. *Gosfield Hall* (limited opening), 2½m W, has a brick Tudor court and panelled long gallery. It was Louis XVIII's first English home in 1807–09.

A604 leads NW towards Haverhill via (3½m) *Sible Hedingham*, where the church is the probable burial place of the condottiere Sir John Hawkwood, who was born here and died at Florence in 1394. *Castle Hedingham*, 1½m NW, has a beautiful late Norman church and a massive Norman keep of c 1100 (open).

From Halstead to *Colchester*, see Rte 60.

At 51½m. *Little Maplestead* (left) the church, mainly early 14C, is the latest and smallest of the four medieval round churches to survive in England. (The others are at Cambridge, Northampton and the Temple in London.)—57m. **Sudbury** (9900 inhab.; Tourist Information) has half-timbered houses from its prosperous days of silk weaving, and three striking Perp. churches. All have good woodwork, and *St Gregory* has a splendid font cover. In the vestry of St Gregory's is preserved the head of Simon of Sudbury, Archbishop of Canterbury in 1375–81, beheaded by Wat Tyler during the Peasants' Revolt. The town was the birthplace of Thomas Gainsborough (1727–88), commemorated by a statue in Market Hill. His house in Stour St. (open), with 18C furnishings, has a collection of paintings by him and his contemporaries.

*Edwardstone*, 6m E, was the birthplace of John Winthrop (1588–1649), first Governor of Massachusetts. His son John (1606–76), Governor of Connecticut, was born at *Groton*, 1m further, which has given its name to a famous American school.—From Sudbury to *Ipswich*, see Rte 60.

60m. *Long Melford*, see Rte 62.—67m. *Bradfield Combust* was the family home and burial place of Arthur Young (1741–1820), agriculturist and traveller, who attended school at nearby Lavenham. *Rushbrooke*, 2½m, NE, has a charming little church.

74m. **BURY ST EDMUNDS** (28,900 inhab.), the historic centre of West Suffolk, has won praise from visitors over many centuries for its neat and prosperous appearance. Cobbett thought it 'the nicest town in the world'. It takes its name from the shrine of St Edmund, last king of East Anglia (d. 869). The abbey, founded in 945 and rebuilt in the 11C, became one of the noblest and wealthiest in England; it now lies ruined. The town has been the seat of the Bishop of St Edmundsbury and Ipswich since 1914.

**Tourist Information Centre**: Abbey Gardens, Angel Hill.

**Car Parks**: Angel Hill, Chequer Square, St Andrews St. South, St Andrews St. North and Parkway.

**Buses**: from Angel Hill and Cornhill.

**Railway Station**: Northgate St.

**Theatre**: Theatre Royal, Westgate St.

**History**. The town owes its grid pattern to Abbot Baldwin (1065–97) who laid out round the abbey the first planned town of Norman Britain, with Churchgate, the main street, in line with the high altar. In 1214 the barons, headed by Archbishop Langton, drew up the 'Petition of the Barons', the basis for Magna Carta, at the abbey church. Nowadays the town is noted for brewing and processing sugar beet.

**Famous natives and visitors**. The landscape gardener Humphry Repton (1752–1818), the diarist Henry Crabb Robinson (1775–1867) and the novelist 'Ouida' (Louise de la Ramée; 1840–1908) were natives. Edward FitzGerald attended the King Edward VI School. Other writers who visited Bury include Defoe, Dickens ('The Pickwick Papers') and Carlyle ('Past and Present'). William Corder, the murderer of Maria Marten, was hanged here in 1828.

The existing remains of the **Abbey** (English Heritage) are approached from Angel Hill, on the E side of the town, in which is the *Athenaeum*, a building in the Adam style, and the fine *Angel Hotel* (18C, with 13C cellars), where Sam Weller first met Job Trotter.

The imposing *Abbey Gateway* (1327, rebuilt after fire in 1347) is now the entrance to a well-kept public garden in which are the formless ruins of the refectory, the abbot's house, etc., and the *Abbot's Bridge* (13C) across the Lark. Beyond the river are the modern buildings of *King Edward VI School*, where Edward FitzGerald was a pupil. To the S are the ruined E end and transepts of the abbey church. The W front is now incorporated into a row of houses. The *Norman Tower* is a magnificent example of early Norman work, executed with the axe and not with the chisel. Beside it is the *Cathedral of St James*, with a noble nave begun in 1438, and good 19C windows and roof; a new NW porch and cloister walk were dedicated in 1960–61 and a new chancel, by Stephen Dykes Bower, replaces that by Gilbert Scott. Across the huge graveyard is *St Mary*, a beautiful 15C church, with a magnificent hammerbeam *roof, and a fine waggon roof in the choir. In the S aisle are the tomb (with skeleton effigy) and chantry ceiling of John Baret (1467) and the brass of Jankyn Smith and his wife (1487), while S and N of the choir are the imposing Drury and Carew tombs (1536 and 1501). The N or Notyngham Porch (1437) has an elaborate vault and pendant. In the NE corner of the sanctuary is a plain slab marking the grave of Mary Tudor (1496–1533), sister to Henry VIII.

The Queen Anne house (NT) at No. 8 Angel Hill contains the small but excellent Gershom-Parkington collection of clocks and watches. In Northgate St. is the ruined gatehouse of *St Saviour's Hospital*, where Humphrey, Duke of Gloucester, died in 1447.

Abbeygate St. (with Georgian shopfronts), or Churchgate St., in which is a notable Independent Chapel of 1711, lead to Cornhill, the business centre of the town. In the Traverse is *Cupola House* (1693), a dignified town mansion, the best of many 17–18C houses in Bury. Many streets have earlier houses and inns. A little below the *Market Cross*, remodelled by Adam in 1774, is the 12C *Moyses Hall* (now a museum), which may have been a Jewish merchant's house. In Guildhall St. at the other end of Cornhill is the *Guildhall*, with a porch of c 1480, and in Westgate St. is the *Theatre Royal* (NT) by William Wilkins (1819; restored 1962–64).

*Ickworth* (NT), 3m SW, a mansion built in 1794–1830, recalls by its unusual plan the eccentricity of its owner, Frederick Hervey, Earl of Bristol and Bishop of Derry (1730–1803). The rotunda with flanking wings looks unattractive outside and creates awkwardly shaped rooms inside, but the collection of furniture, silver, porcelain, paintings and sculpture (Flaxman's 'The Fury of Athamas') is distinguished. The park has pleasant walks.—At *Ampton*, 5m N of Bury, Jeremy Collier was rector in 1679–84.

FROM BURY TO NORWICH, 39½m. We take A143 to (6½m) *Ixworth*, where the main street may be the start of the Peddars' Way (Rte 67). The Abbey (open by prior appointment) incorporates the remains of a 12C priory and 15C prior's lodging, recently restored. *Stowlangtoft* church, 2m SE, contains *bench ends and misericords, and Flemish panelling at the E end.—Near (10m) *Stanton* we branch left on B1111, and beyond (16m) *Garboldisham* we branch right on B1114.—At (19½m) *Kenninghall* stood a palace of the Howards, Dukes of Norfolk, demolished in 1650. It was the birthplace of the poet, Henry Howard, Earl of Surrey (1517–47), and Mary I took refuge here in 1553 before going to Framlingham. We follow B1113.—21½m. *Banham* has a zoo and a collection of vintage cars and motorcycles.—23½m. *New Buckenham* has a Perp. church, the scanty remains of a Norman chapel and a quaint market hall with pillory, while *Old Buckenham*, to the W, has a thatched church.—We join A140 on the way into (39½m) *Norwich*, see Rte 64.

From Bury to *Newmarket* and to *Ipswich*, and to *Hengrave* and *Icklingham*, see Rte 63.

The main route follows A134 towards Thetford (Rte 63), but soon branches left at (76½m) *Fornham St Martin* on B1106. We cross A11 (Rte 63) at (86m) *Elveden*—89m. *Brandon* was for long a centre of flint knapping, one of the oldest trades in the world.—We cross the Little Ouse into Norfolk.

*Weeting*, 1m N on B1106, has a 12C castle with a good keep and square moat (English Heritage, open at any reasonable time). *Methwold* church, 5½m further on, has a Perp. crocketed steeple (120ft) and a brass to Sir Adam de Clifton (d. 1367).

We follow A1065 across Thetford Chase.—At 91½m B1108 branches right to (1m) *Grime's Graves*, an area of neolithic flint quarries (English Heritage, standard opening and summer Sunday mornings). Nearly 400 shafts and pits have been discovered closely clustered together, and one has been opened so that visitors can descend to the galleries radiating from the bottom.—103½m. **Swaffham** (4800 inhab.), a market town with good Georgian buildings. The elegant Rotunda crowned with a figure of Ceres was erected by the Earl of Oxford in 1783. The large Perp. church has a double hammerbeam roof and carvings of the peddlar who, tradition says, built it after finding treasure nearby.

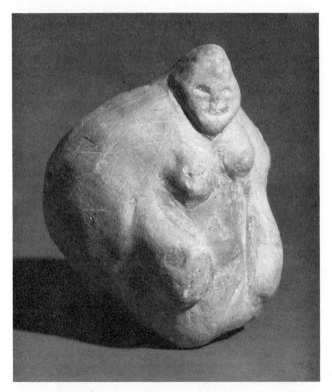

*Chalk idol found at Grime's Graves (now in the British Museum)*

*Cockley Cley*, 3m SW, has a folk museum and reconstruction of an Iceni encampment on its original site.—At *Oxborough*, another 4m SW, the church steeple fell in 1948 and destroyed most of the nave but spared the Bedingfield Chapel, with terracotta *monuments of c 1520 in the Italian style (cf. Layer Marney, Rte 60).

Nearby is *Oxburgh Hall (NT), still partly occupied by the Bedingfields. In the 1480s Sir Edward built not a castle but a square brick mansion defended by a moat and splendid castellated gatehouse. A descendant pulled down the S range in 1778 but the loss was tactfully made good in the 1830s, when the SE tower was also added and most of the windows renewed. So the outside of Oxburgh has kept its picturesque appearance. Another 19C addition, the formal French parterre by the moat, makes a pleasing contrast. Inside, notable features are the 19C library with fireplace by A.W.N. Pugin and, particularly, the turret rooms and spiral staircase of the gatehouse. Its roof offers a wide view of the flat countryside around. Furnishings incude: 17C embossed leather covering two staircase walls; needlework panels signed by Mary, Queen of Scots, and Bess of Hardwick; and the Sheldon tapestry, a vividly detailed map of Berkshire, Oxfordshire and parts of neighbouring counties woven c 1647.

107½m. **Castle Acre** (left) with the fine remains of a large Cluniac *Priory founded by William de Warenne in 1090 (English Heritage, standard opening and summer Sunday mornings). Its chief feature is the beautiful late Norman W front of the church, but the prior's lodging and chapel (remodelled in Tudor times and later used as a farmhouse), the reredorter and the Tudor entrance gatehouse are also noteworthy. The castle which gave its name to the village stood on huge earthworks, probably Roman. Its main remnant is the N

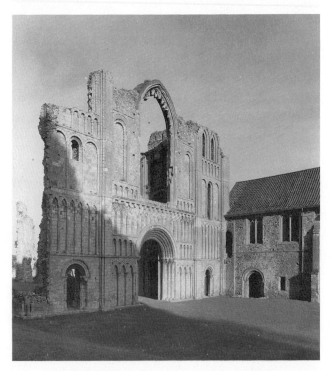

*Castle Acre Priory, the west front of the church*

gateway spanning the street. The church, between castle and priory, contains painted 15C woodwork. The Peddars' Way (Rte 67) can be seen to the N.

*South Acre* church, just to the S, contains a brass to Sir John Harsick (d. 1384) and his wife, the tomb of Lord Mayor Barkham (1621), a 14C wooden effigy and a delicately carved 14C screen. At *West Acre*, 2¼m W, the gatehouse and barn of another priory have survived near the church (with a wide 14C chancel arch). *Narborough* church, 2½m further SW, has a fine standing effigy of Clement Spelman, Recorder of Nottingham (d. 1679), as well as good brasses (one a palimpsest). A 14C gatehouse is the chief relic of the priory of *Pentney*, 1m beyond.

At 108m is the tiny Saxon church of *Newton*.—113m. *Weasenham St Peter* has a small church with elaborate flushwork. A sideroad beyond leads to (1m) *Wellingham* church, with a fine painted screen (1532).

The church of *Tittleshall*, 2m E, has striking *monuments to Sir Edward Coke (d. 1634) by Nicholas Stone; to Coke's wife, Bridget Paston (d. 1598); to Thomas Coke, Earl of Leicester (d. 1759) and his wife, with bust by Roubiliac; and to other members of the family.

116m. The road passes the lodge gates of *East Raynham Hall*, sometimes ascribed to Inigo Jones, home of the agricultural pioneer 'Turnip' Townshend (Charles, 2nd Viscount Townshend; 1674–1738).—117m. The church at *Toftrees* has a Norman font of local type.—119½m. *Fakenham*, see Rte 66A.

We take A148 NE via *Thursford* (Rte 66B) to (130m) *Letheringsett*, with a round church tower and a watermill, recently restored to working order (open).—132m. **Holt**, an attractive and colourful village, the birthplace of Sir Thomas Gresham (1519–79), Lord Mayor of London and founder of the Royal Exchange, who propounded 'Gresham's Law'. Gresham's School here was founded by his uncle in 1555.—At 136½m we pass the entrance to *Sheringham Hall* (see Rte 67). A sideroad leads right to (3m) *Baconsthorpe Castle* (English Heritage, open at any reasonable time), a moated and fortified manor house built by the Heydon family in the 15C. The surviving ruins include walls, towers and a gatehouse with flint facing.—142m. **Cromer**, see Rte 67.

# 62  London to Aldeburgh

Total distance 110½m. A11, A113 to (21m) Chipping Ongar. —A11, A1060, B184 to (34m) Great Dunmow.—B1057 to (49m) Steeple Bumpstead.—B1054, A604 to (52m) Wixoe.—A1092 to (55½m) **Clare.**—A1092 to (63m) **Long Melford.—Unclassified road to (67m) Lavenham.**—A1141 to (70m) Monks Eleigh.—B1115, B1078 to (80m) **Needham Market.**—B1078, A140 to (85m) Earl Stonham. —A1120 to (94m) Saxtead Green.—B1119 to (96m) **Framlingham.** —B1119 to (103m) Saxmundham (Rte 60).—B1119 to (107½m) Leiston.—B1122 to (110½m) **Aldeburgh.**

Maps: OS Landranger 177, 167, 154 (briefly), 155, 156.

This alternative to the A12 (see Rte 60) passes by secondary roads through some of the finest Essex and Suffolk countryside to the E coast. It is not for the hurried motorist.

We take A11 through the E suburbs and at (7m) the Green Man, Leytonstone, pick up A113.—11m. *Chigwell* retains a village centre with 15C church, grammar school and 17C inn, the 'Maypole' of Dickens's 'Barnaby Rudge'.—16m. We cross M25. —21m. *Chipping Ongar* ('Chipping' meaning 'market') has a Norman church and Saxon castle mound. *Greensted-juxta-Ongar*, 1m W, has a *church (c 845) with a remarkable nave of split oak tree trunks set upright on a sill. The body of St Edmund rested here for a night in 1013 on its return from London to Bury St Edmunds, whence it had been removed in fear of the Danes. The brick choir dates from c 1500.

*Stondon Massey*, 2m SE of Ongar, was the residence of William Byrd ('father of musick') in 1595–1623. It has an early Norman church. *Blackmore*, 2m further E, has a church with a fine timber tower, and Jericho House, built on the site of a favourite manor of Henry VIII.

B184 from Ongar follows the ridge above the valley of the Roding, an ancient trackway known by its Saxon name of 'The Rodings' (or 'clearings', hence 'road').—23½m. *Fyfield* church has a 12C font and unusual sedilia with sculptured heads. The parishes of *Willingale Doe* and *Willingale Spain*, 2m E across the valley, have churches sharing one churchyard; St Andrew's is part Norman, and St Christopher's has good brasses.—26m (½m left) *Abbess Roding* church is 14C, with a Norman font and an 18C pulpit with fine tester.—At 27½m we turn right on A1060 to (28m) *Leaden Roding* church with a weatherboarded belfry, and Norman nave and chancel. To the E lie the Easters; *High Easter* church has a fine timber roof. B184 turns N and joins a Roman course (disused nearer London) on which stands (30½m) *High Roding*, with a 13C church (15C pulpit). *Great Canfield* church, 1m W, has a Norman chancel arch, and, above the altar, a 13C *wall painting of the Madonna and Child.—34m. *Great Dunmow* (4500 inhab.), a pleasant old market town, stands above the Chelmer.

The church at *Stebbing*, 3m NE, has a fine stone rood screen (cf. Great Bardfield below).—*Little Dunmow*, off A120 2½m SE of Great Dunmow, has the remains of *Dunmow Priory*, where by an old custom a'flitch of bacon could be claimed by any married couple who had 'not repented them, sleeping or waking, of their marriage in a year and a day'. The oath was originally taken kneeling before the Prior; the 'jury' of the present-day revival is an innovation. *Felsted*, 1m further, a Jutish settlement, has a partly Norman church. It contains a 17C monument by Epiphanius Evesham to the first Lord Rich (d. 1568), founder of the school, which originally stood next to the church. Richard Cromwell was a pupil.

FROM GREAT DUNMOW TO THAXTED, 6½m by B184.—3m. *Great Easton* has the remains of a motte and bailey castle. *Little Easton* church, about 1½m SW, contains 12–15C *wall paintings, 17C German glass and fine 15–18C monuments. H.G. Wells lived here in 1912–30.—6½m. **Thaxted** is a picturesque little town with old houses and a Jacobean Guildhall on wooden pillars (limited opening). The spacious 14–15C *church has a fine crocketed spire, pinnacled buttresses and grotesque gargoyles. The font, pulpit, N and S porches, timber roofs and organ (1703; John Harris) are all worth noting. The tower windmill, with its main machinery still intact, is now a rural museum. Thaxted was the birthplace of Samuel Purchas (1577?–1626) of the 'Pilgrimes'. Gustav Holst composed 'The Planets' while organist at the church in 1916. *Chickney*, 3½ m SW, has a primitive Norman church.

From Great Dunmow to *Bishop's Stortford* and to *Colchester*, see Rte 63.

B1057 winds NE from Great Dunmow through two notably attractive villages whose much publicised charms often make them crowded in summer. At (41½m) *Great Bardfield* a number of local crafts have been revived. The church has a 14C stone rood screen (cf. Stebbing above).—43m. *Finchingfield* is nicely grouped round a village green and duckpond below the squat Norman tower of the church, topped by an 18C cupola.—49m. *Steeple Bumpstead* church has a good monument to Sir Henry Bendysshe (d. 1717) and his baby son. *Haverhill* (17,100 inhab.), now a London 'overspill' town, lies 3m N. —We take B1054, join A1092 to cross the Stour into Suffolk at (52m) *Wixoe* and follow the valley.—53½m. *Stoke-by-Clare* is a pretty village with a large Perp. church containing a pulpit of 1498 and a wall painting of 1550.—55½m. **Clare** preserves many beautiful houses, some pargeted, and remains of the Augustinian priory founded in 1248, where Edward III's son Lionel, Duke of Clarence (d. 1368) was buried. Of the castle, only part of the keep still stands. The church is Perp., with much early Tudor work; the N chancel door has notable tracery. All the glass was destroyed by the notorious Parliamentarian, William Dowsing. A timber-framed house in the High St. contains a local museum.—58m. *Cavendish*, with a spacious green, has a church with a fine flint clerestory. It contains tombs of the Cavendish family, including Sir John (d. 1381), who built the chancel. The 15C Nether Hall is now a museum and gallery; the adjoining vineyard is also open. Across the Stour is the church of *Pentlow*, with a round tower, opposite a timbered manor house (c 1500).

*A Suffolk village: Cavendish*

63m. **Long Melford** is strikingly arranged, having both church and hall around the large, attractive green at the N end and, leading S, a High St. over 2m long with many good half-timbered and Georgian houses. The late Perp. *Church* is a magnificent example of the Suffolk style, with elaborate flushwork, long nave and tall windows, and tall clerestory above. It is spacious and handsomely proportioned inside. The aisles and N chapel have 15C *stained glass. The Clopton Chantry, off the N aisle, contains good monuments and brasses. The Lady Chapel, attached to the E end of the church, has an ambulatory with fine wooden ceiling and sculptured corbels. E of the green is *Melford Hall* (NT).

It was built in the 1550s and 1560s by Sir William Cordell, Speaker of the House of Commons and Master of the Rolls, who was visited here by Elizabeth I. Its Tudor character is still shown by the exterior, a brick three-sided courtyard facing away from the green, and by the position of hall and gallery inside. Otherwise, the interior has been greatly altered, mainly by Thomas Hopper in the early 19C. His Regency library is charming.

*Flushwork at Long Melford church*

¹/₂m N of the green is *Kentwell Hall* (open), approached by a long avenue of lime trees planted in 1678. The moated house has the same plan as Melford Hall and a similar date (shortly before 1563). Most of the interior was refurbished after a fire in the 1820s, again by Hopper. Several rooms have recently been restored.

By the timbered *Bull Hotel* we take a sideroad E to (67m) **Lavenham**. The village is the most picturesque in Suffolk and, like Long Melford, bears witness to the comfortable prosperity that the wool trade brought East Anglia in the late Middle Ages. Many streets have half-timbered houses, with carved angle posts and pargeting. In the Market Place is the *Guildhall* of 1529 (NT), with a corner post representing the 15th Earl of Oxford; nearby is the *Little Hall* (open), a 15C hall house. In Water St. another hall house, the *Priory* (open), belonged to a Benedictine Order before it was enlarged into the home of a wool merchant. The *Angel Hotel* has a 16C plaster ceiling and 14C wall paintings, while the *Swan* incorporates the old Wool Hall. The *Church*, magnificently sited, is of the same style as Long Melford: tall tower, long nave, generous clerestory, flushwork throughout. It was built (1480–1520) in friendly rivalry by the 14th Earl of Oxford and Thomas Spring, a wealthy clothier. It has a fine S porch, the *Spring Chantry (1523) and the Oxford Chantry, and good misericords.

*Acton* church, c 3m SW, contains the *brass of Sir Robert de Bures (d. 1302), one of the oldest and best in England, and a monument to Robert Jennens (d. 1722), aide-de-camp to Marlborough. *Little Waldingfield*, c 2m E of Acton, has a fine 15C church.

We take A1141 to (68½m) *Brent Eleigh* where the church has 14C wall paintings.—70m. *Monks Eleigh* has good houses, a mill, and a large Perp. church. *Lindsey* and *Kersey*, 2m and 3m, SE, see Rte 60.

B1115 continues E to (71m) *Chelsworth*, an attractive village on the Brett (bridge of 1754). The church contains a decorated tomb recess and a wall painting.—At (72m) *Bildeston*, with good timber cottages, we fork right on B1078.—75½m. *Great Bricett* church, with a Norman door, is all that remains of an Augustinian priory.—78m. *Barking* has a Dec. church with an early tie-beam roof, and parclose and *rood screens.—80m. **Needham Market** (3900 inhab.) is a pleasant town with old houses (some dating from the 14C) lining the High St. The church contains a splendid *roof, covered with angels.

We leave the town on B1078 and, at the junction with A45, turn N on A140 to (85m) *Earl Stonham*. The *church has a spectacular double hammerbeam roof with angels. The Jacobean pulpit is equipped with four hour glasses, for sermons from ¼hr to 2hr. We follow A1120 E to (86m) *Stonham Aspal*, whose large church has a Dec. tower. The chancel of *Crowfield* church, 2m SE, is timber-framed, the only one in Suffolk.

At 89½m B1077 leads S, passing *Framsden* (windmill) on the left, to (2m) *Helmingham Hall*, where the gardens and deer park are sometimes open in summer. B1079 forks left to (4m) *Otley*. The Hall (limited opening), ¼m NE, is a lovely 15–16C house, moated and timber-framed, with herringbone brick and pargeting. Bartholomew Gosnold, a descendant of the builders, settled and named Cape Cod and Martha's Vineyard in Massachusetts.

92½m. *Earl Soham* has an attractive green.—94m. *Saxtead Green* has a windmill in full working trim (English Heritage, summer standard opening except Sunday).

*Dennington*, 2½m NE, has an impressive church with notable *parclose screens. The benches have carved ends, one of a 'sciapod' (a one-legged man using his foot as a sunshade). There is a rare pyx canopy and the tomb of Lord Bardolph, who fought at Agincourt.

We branch right on B1119.—96m **Framlingham**, grouped round the triangular Market Hill, has an imposing ruined *Castle (English Heritage, standard opening and summer Sunday mornings). Built mainly during Edward I's reign, it is one of the earliest castles to use not a central keep but a surrounding curtain wall with towers at intervals. Queen Mary found refuge here with the Howards during the attempt to place Lady Jane Grey on the throne. Within the shell stands the Poor House (1636), and the towers are adorned with Tudor chimneys. The battlements look across the Meres to the *College*, Suffolk's memorial to Prince Albert (1864), on the opposite hill. The stately *Church, Perp. with Dec. survivals, has a covered hammer-beam roof. It contains the magnificent *monuments of the Howard family—including Henry Howard, Earl of Surrey, the poet, executed in 1547—and of Sir Robert Hitcham (d. 1636), with fine supporting angels. In the sanctuary is the Flodden helmet, worn at the battle by the English commander, the 2nd Duke of Norfolk. The organ has some pre-Commonwealth pipes.

103m. *Saxmundham*, see Rte 60.—At 107½m we reach *Leiston* (5100 inhab. with Sizewell), where Richard Garrett built the railway engineering works and workers' cottages, and commissioned the striking church by E.B. Lamb (1853).

About 1m N are the ruins of the Premonstratensian *Leiston Abbey* (English Heritage, open at any reasonable time), which transferred here from Minsmere in 1363. The church at *Theberton*, 1m further on, has a round tower, thatched roof and Norman doorway. C.M. Doughty (1843–1926) of 'Arabia Deserta' was born at Theberton Hall. To the E of Theberton, in a wild sandy area extending to low sea cliffs, is the *Minsmere* nature reserve.—*Sizewell* nuclear power station, on the coast 2m E of Leiston, is being expanded by the addition of a second reactor. *Thorpeness*, on the coast 3m SE of Leiston, is a holiday village with a pleasant boating lake.

We take B1122 S to (110½m) **Aldeburgh** (2900 inhab.; seasonal Tourist Information), a seaside resort and fishing village. It was a favourite haunt of Edward FitzGerald, while George Meredith and Wilkie Collins spent holidays here. The local atmosphere was tell-ingly evoked in 'The Borough' by the native poet George Crabbe (1754–1832). There is a memorial to him in the Perp. church. The *Moot Hall*, a half-timbered 16C building now standing amid the encroaching shingle, was the town hall of the old town washed away by the sea.

Since the 1945 production of Benjamin Britten's 'Peter Grimes', based on a poem by Crabbe, Aldeburgh has been a centre for musical activity. Many of Britten's later operas were composed for local performance. The Aldeburgh Festival is held in June at the Maltings in *Snape*, about 5m W, converted into an opera house in 1967 and restored again after a fire in 1969.

# 63 London to Newmarket and Norwich

Total distance 105m. A104, B1393 to (16½m) Epping.—B1393 to (23m) Harlow.—A1184 to (29½m) Bishop's Stortford.—B1383 to (44m) Stump Cross.—A11, A1304 to (56m) **Newmarket**.—A1304, A11 to (76m) Thetford.—A11 to (105m) **Norwich** (Rte 64).

Maps: OS Landranger 177, 167, 154, 143 (briefly), 144, 134 (briefly).

M11, the London–Cambridge motorway, provides a direct route from Wanstead/South Woodford to (38m) Stump Cross. The route suggested here follows the course of the old A11, now relieved of heavy traffic after Harlow but irritatingly relabelled as several separate roads until Stump Cross.

We leave London on A104, passing through *Woodford* and *Epping Forest*, described in 'Blue Guide London'. We change to B1393 near the N edge of the Forest and pass M25.—16½m. *Epping* (12,300 inhab.) has a long High St. with a church of 1899 by Bodley and Garner.—23m. At **Harlow** (79,800 inhab.) the New Town to the left of the old village was developed from 1947 onward under the architectural supervision of Sir Frederick Gibberd. The town centre incorporates some good sculptures (Rodin, Moore, etc.). The Georgian *Passmores House* is now a museum of local history, including objects unearthed during building operations.—A1184 heads N to (15½m) *Sawbridgeworth* (7800 inhab.), where the church contains good brasses.—29½m. **Bishop's Stortford** (22,800 inhab.; Tourist Information), a Hertfordshire market town almost declined into a dormitory suburb, has a fine church of c 1400 with contemporary woodwork, a few good buildings in the old centre, and a public school. The old vicarage in South Rd where Cecil Rhodes (1853–1902) was born is now a museum.

FROM BISHOP'S STORTFORD TO COLCHESTER, 32m by A120, the Roman Stane Street. The road skirts the N side of *Hatfield Forest* (1049 acres; NT), once part of the ancient royal forests of Essex, with hornbeams and a boating lake. *Stansted Airport*, to the N, once mainly used for charter flights, is now being developed as London's third airport.—4m. *Takeley* church has a decorative font cover and Roman material in its walls. At *Hatfield Broad Oak*, 3m S, the church contains a fine mailed effigy of Robert de Vere, Earl of Oxford (d. 1221).—We continue through (9m) *Great Dunmow* (Rte 62) and (17m) *Braintree* (Rte 61). —At *Coggleshall*, bypassed at 23m, the church has good brasses of the Paycocke family. \*Paycocke's House (NT) is a richly ornamented merchant's dwelling of c 1500. Near the Blackwater, ¾m S, a farmhouse incorporates the remains of a Cistercian abbey (1140), perhaps the earliest medieval brick building in England.—At (27m) *Marks Tey* we join A12 for (32m) *Colchester* (Rte 60).

From Bishop's Stortford to *Ware* via *Much Hadham*, see Rte 68.

B1383 continues N to (33½m) *Stansted Mountfitchet*, with a modern reconstruction (open) of its wooden motte-and-bailey castle and Norman village.—38m. **Newport** is a typical West Essex town with a long street, an old Grammar School and many 16–17C houses, some with pargeting. It has a fine Perp. church; even better is the one at *Clavering*, an attractive village on the Stort, 3½m SW.

At *Widdington*, 2m SE of Newport, is \*Prior's Hall Barn (English Heritage, summer season weekends only), the most impressive medieval aisled barn to survive in the area.

40m. \***Audley End** (English Heritage, open afternoons from Good Friday to mid October) is a palatial Jacobean mansion on the site of the Benedictine Walden Abbey.

Audley End was built in 1603–16 for Thomas Howard, 1st Earl of Suffolk, but reduced to about a third its original size in the 1720s by Vanbrugh, who demolished the inner and outer courtyards. With its two grand porches, the wing that survived is still imposing. Several of the rooms have furnishings lent by Lord Braybrooke, who sold the house to the government in 1948. Noteworthy are: the huge hall with splendid wood screen and plaster work; the drawing room and dining room by Robert Adam (recently restored); the Gothick chapel of 1768; and the saloon with Jacobean ceiling. Among the paintings, Hans Eworth's portrait of Margaret Audley (1562) is outstanding. The park, ornamented with monuments, temples and bridges, was landscaped by Capability Brown in the 1760s. The Tea Bridge overlooks a charming waterside scene.

About 1½m E is the charming little town of **Saffron Walden** (12,500 inhab.; Tourist Information), with a fine Perp. church and some picturesque timbered buildings, including the Sun Inn (NT), a notable 15C house with 17C pargeting, used as a headquarters by Cromwell and Fairfax. In the grounds of the interesting little Museum, which contains a pillory and an Anglo-Saxon sword, are the ruins of the 12C castle. The pleasant Bridge End gardens (open) at the N end of the town belonged to a house destroyed by fire; the Victorian maze has recently been replanted.—At *Hempstead*, 6m E, the highwayman Dick Turpin (1705–39) was born. In the Harvey Chapel of the church lie William Harvey (1578–1657), who discovered the circulation of the blood, and Sir Eliab Harvey (1758–1830), commander of the 'Téméraire' at Trafalgar.

At (43m) *Great Chesterford* we curve sharply right across the Cam and enter Cambridgeshire, almost immediately joining the Romanised Icknield Way, on straight alignments all the way to Thetford. *Ickleton*, 1m NW, has a church with Roman monolithic columns, late Saxon details and a 'sacring' bell outside the spire.

At (44m) *Stump Cross* A1301 bears left for (14m) Cambridge (Rte 69).
  *Duxford*, W of the road at 2m, is home of the Imperial War Museum's collection of aircraft and military vehicles (open). Near *Whittlesford* station, ³/₄m N, is Duxford Chapel, once part of a Hospital of St John (English Heritage, open at any reasonable time).—6m. *Great Shelford* church has traces of a 15C painting of Judgement Day over the chancel arch.

From *Stump Cross* the main route follows A11, crossing in succession the line of the Via Devana (Rte 69), the Fleam Dyke and, on Newmarket Heath, the Devil's Ditch. The last two belong to a rampart system raised by the Angles and Mercians during the wars waged in the 6–8C for control of East Anglia.—At (49¹/₂m) *Six Mile Bottom* we take A1304.

56m. **Newmarket** (16,200 inhab.) is the headquarters of English horseracing. Begun under James I, the sport has been more or less regularly practised here since the time of Charles I. On the otherwise disappointing High St. is the *Jockey Club* (1840, restored by Richardson and Gill in 1936). The *National Horseracing Museum* is devoted to the history of the sport and displays some good sporting art.

The most important races decided on the famous racecourse at *Newmarket Heath*, 1¹/₂m SW, are the Two Thousand Guineas (spring), the Cesarewitch (October) and the Cambridgeshire (October). Special permission is needed to visit the training stables, but the horses can often be seen exercising on the Heath in the early morning.
  At *Westley Waterless*, 5m SW, the church has wonderfully delicate *brasses of Sir John Creke and his wife (c 1325).—At *Kirtling*, 4¹/₂m SE of Newmarket, the church has a fine 12C doorway and monuments to the Norths. The gatehouse (1530) of their mansion survives to the S.

FROM NEWMARKET TO IPSWICH, 41m. B1506 forks NE to (5m) *Kentford*, with a Dec. church containing 14C wall paintings. *Moulton*, 1¹/₂m SW, has a little hump-backed bridge over the Kennet marking the ancient route from Bury St Edmunds to Cambridge (English Heritage, open at any reasonable time). We join A45.—*Risby* church, on the left at 10m, has a round Norman tower, Norman chancel arch, a good screen and an extensive series of wall paintings. *Little Saxham*, 2m S, has a round church tower.—At 15m we bypass *Bury St Edmunds* (Rte 61).—19m. *Beyton* church, on the right, has a round Norman tower and (21m) *Woolpit* church has a magnificent S porch and a fine double hammerbeam *roof.—At 23m the road skirts the large *Haughley Park*, with a rebuilt Jacobean mansion and good gardens (limited opening). *Haughley*, 1¹/₂m E, has the remains of a large motte-and-bailey castle and a church with a timber roof.—27m. **Stowmarket** (10,900 inhab.) trades in barley, and manufactures chemicals and agricultural implements. The *Museum of East Anglian Life* is an open-air display of buildings and machinery, including a 19C drainage windmill. The *Church* has a wooden spire above a square flint tower. Milton often used to visit his tutor Thomas Young (d. 1665) at the old vicarage. The neighbourhood is rich in interesting churches: at *Combs*, 1¹/₂m S, and at *Bacton* and *Cotton*, 5m N, with notable roofs.—A45 follows the valley of the

Gipping through (31m) *Needham Market* (Rte 62) to (35m) *Claydon*, with large cement works, and (41m) *Ipswich* (Rte 60).

The main route rejoins A11 N of Newmarket. We cross the Lark at (65m) *Barton Mills*, where the church has 14C stained glass and a Jacobean pulpit. Beyond the village is a large five-way roundabout.

A1101 goes W to (1m) *Mildenhall* (9800 inhab.), a pleasant town with a Georgian High St. and a 15C timber market cross. The *church, whose lovely E window dominates the street, has a Lady Chapel over the N porch and a superb hammerbeam *roof, carved with angels. The 'Mildenhall Treasure', a hoard of 4C Roman silver now in the British Museum, was found in 1946 at *Thistley Green*, W of the USAF base.—A1101 continues into the Fens, joining (11m) A10 between Ely and Downham Market (Rte 70).

From the Barton Mills roundabout A1065 leads N, passing (3m) the USAF base at *Lakenheath*. The good Norman and Dec. church, W of the base, contains a memorial to Lord Kitchener (d. 1916), some of whose 17–18C ancestors lie in the churchyard. In *Hockwold Fen*, 3m N, the Roman town of *Camboritum*, overwhelmed by floods in the 2C, was discovered in 1961. Many military airfields were established in the neighbourhood in 1939–45, and memorials to the men who fell in the war have been set up at *Feltwell*, 1½m N of Hockwold, and at Elveden (see below).—9m. *Brandon* and thence to *Cromer*, see Rte 61.

From the Barton Mills roundabout A1101 runs SE through (2m) *Icklingham*, where the large thatched church has a Norman nave, Jacobean pulpit, 14C chest and stained glass.—7m. *Hengrave* church has a Norman tower and is crammed with monuments to the Kytson family, who built the neighbouring *Hengrave Hall* (now a conference centre), completed in 1538. The ornate bay window by John Sparke over the entrance is one of the best of its date. The arms of the Washington family, connected to the Kytsons, appear in a window.—10m. *Bury St Edmunds*, see Rte 61.

A11 now enters *Breckland*, the heath with gnarled Scots pines and small meres described in George Borrow's 'Lavengro'. Although much of it has been altered by forestry or enclosed for military training and airfields, an abundant bird life still inhabits the more isolated ponds and rushes.—71½m. *Elveden* church is a bizarre jumble of Gothick and Art Nouveau, created by the owners of Elveden Hall (not open), an elaborate 'Moghul–Gothick' fantasy grafted on to the 18C building by the Maharaja Duleep Singh in the 1860s and extended by Lord Iveagh at the turn of the century. From Elveden to *Bury* and to *Brandon*, see Rte 61.—The road now skirts the edge of Thetford Chase and enters Norfolk.

**76m. Thetford** (Tourist Information) has been enlarged to 19,600 inhab. by ugly development which makes it hard to appreciate its ancient importance as seat of the Kings of East Anglia and of its bishops in 1075–94. *Castle Hill*, at the E end of the town, is the finest castle mound in the country, a Norman motte surrounded by Iron Age earthworks. Three of Thetford's five monasteries have left scanty remains: the *Cluniac Priory*, founded in 1104, near the station (English Heritage, open at any reasonable time); a 12C priory of the *Canons of the Holy Sepulchre* (English Heritage, open at any reasonable time) on the Brandon road; and a *Dominican Friary* of 1340. The Friary lies behind the old *Grammar School*, which claims descent from a 7C choir school, where Tom Paine (1737–1809) was educated. He was born in a cottage behind White Hart St. (tablet), near the *Ancient House Museum*. A statue (1964) stands before the *Guildhall*.

*Euston Hall* (limited opening), 4m SE, was built c 1670 for the Earl of Arlington, a member of the Cabal, and enlarged by Matthew Brettingham in 1750–56. Its collection of paintings includes works by Van Dyck, Lely, Kneller and Stubbs. John Evelyn and William Kent both played a part in laying out the grounds. Euston gave its name to the London railway station built on the estate of the

Dukes of Grafton, then owners of the Hall.—The 14C church of *East Harling*, 7m
E of Thetford, has fine medieval Norwich glass and 15–17C monuments.

A1075 leads NE from Thetford to (23m) *East Dereham* (Rte 66A) via (14m)
*Watton*. Near Watton are *Wayland Wood* (2m S), said to be the scene of the
'Babes in the Wood', and *Griston House* (2m SE; not open), said to be the
residence of their wicked uncle.

At 90m the A11 bypasses the pleasant town of *Attleborough* (6000
inhab.), where the Norman and Perp. church has wall paintings and a
magnificent *rood screen of 1475.—96m. **Wymondham** (pronounced
'Windham'), an old market town (9800 inhab.), has one of the finest
*Churches in Norfolk, originally belonging to the priory (afterwards
abbey) of St Mary and St Alban (1107). In 1349 the nave (mainly
Norman) and N aisle (Perp.) were assigned for the use of the
parishioners, who added the W tower about 1450. The E tower and
the original choir, of which only fragments remain, were retained by
the monks. The nave has a hammerbeam roof with angels and large
bosses; part of the ceiling has been removed to show the timbering. It
has a terracotta monument to Elisha Ferrers. Outstanding among the
many timbered houses is the *Green Dragon*. A library occupies the
15C *Chapel of St Thomas Becket*. The *Market Cross* is a timber
building of 1616. Robert Kett, leader of the brief agrarian rebellion of
1549, was a tanner of Wymondham.

About 3½m W is **Hingham**, where the fine Dec. *church has a hammerbeam
roof. The Morley *monument, perfectly preserved, is a triumph of deeply
carved 15C work, with statues of the family. The stained glass is German
(c 1500). There is a bust (1919) of Abraham Lincoln. Hingham was the home of
Robert Lincoln (d. c 1540), generally accepted as the earliest known ancestor of
Abraham Lincoln. Richard Lincoln of Swanton Morley (Rte 66A), buried in 1620
at Hingham, disinherited his son Edward, as a result of which his grandson
Samuel emigrated from Hingham in 1637, to become the first American
ancestor of the President. There was an Abraham Lincoln of Norwich
(b. c 1685).

105m. **Norwich**, see Rte 64.

# 64   Norwich

**NORWICH** (122,300 inhab.), the county town of Norfolk and regional
capital of East Anglia, is situated in a loop of the Wensum and
commanded by its massive castle. It preserves an extremely irregular
plan inherited from its Saxon origins, having neither a main street
nor a central square. Surviving monuments everywhere reflect its
historic importance from the Middle Ages until the Industrial
Revolution, when it was the second city in England. Many of the old
buildings use local flint in flushwork or chequerboard patterns.
Famous for its cathedral, Norwich also boasts more than 30 pre-
Reformation churches: some have already become redundant, and a
total of 20 are scheduled to do so, but their preservation is
guaranteed and various secular uses are being found for them (see
below for details of access). The city's appeal has been greatly
enhanced by the closing of some streets to traffic.

**Tourist Information Centre**: Guildhall (in the Market Place).

**Car Parks**: Cattle Market (by the castle), Castle Meadow, Bethel St. (by the
library). Multi-storey car parks in Malthouse Rd, Duke St., St Giles St. and
Mountergate.

**Buses**: from Surrey St.

**Railway Station**: Thorpe Rd.

**Airport**: Horsham St Faith (3¹/₂m N via A140). Direct services to Aberdeen, Edinburgh, Humberside, Leeds-Bradford, London (Heathrow), Teesside, Frankfurt.

**Theatres**: Maddermarket Theatre, St John's Alley; Theatre Royal, Theatre St.; Whiffler Open-air Theatre, Castle Gardens; Norwich Puppet Theatre, St James Cowgate; Sewell Barn Theatre, Constitution Hill.

**Access to churches.** The following are redundant but may be visited by arrangement with the Tourist Information Centre: *St Gregory*, Pottergate; *St Laurence*, St Benedict St.; *St Margaret*, St Benedict St.; *St Mary-at-Coslany*, St Mary's Plain; *St Michael-at-Coslany*, Colegate; *St Michael-at-Plea*, Redwell St.; *St Saviour*, Magdalen St. The following are usually locked but may be visited by arrangement with the vicar or other custodian: *St Augustine*, St Augustine's St.; *St George*, Colegate; *St John Maddermarket*, Pottergate; *St John de Sepulchre*, Ber St.; *St Martin-at-Palace*, Palace Plain; *St Stephen*, Rampant Horse St. Details are posted outside or may be had from the Tourist Information Centre. A handful of churches, indicated in the walking tour below, are permanently closed. The remainder (whether still devoted to their original purpose or now in secular hands) are open, though in some cases only during limited hours.

**History**. A settlement near the crossing of the Wensum (Fye Bridge) above its confluence with the Yare grew by 850 into a borough trading with the Rhineland. *Northwic* appears on coins minted for Athelstan. In the Danish wars it was destroyed by Sweyn Forkbeard, but by the Conquest it had grown to be one of the largest boroughs in the kingdom, the fief of Gyrth Godwinsson, brother of King Harold, who was immediately replaced as Earl of East Anglia by a Norman. A large motte-and-bailey castle was built, driving a Norman wedge between the English areas. In 1094, when the see of Norwich was created, Bishop Losinga commandeered and razed much of the Anglo-Saxon borough to build his cathedral and moved the market site from Tombland to W of the castle. By 1140 a large community of Jews lived here freely, not confined to a ghetto. The city acquired its charters in 1194 and 1256, and the circuit wall (2¹/₄m) built of stone in 1294–1320 compares in extent with that of London. In the 14C an influx of Flemish weavers helped to make Norwich the centre of the worsted trade. The city was occupied by the rebels during the Peasants' Revolt (1381) and social unrest continued (see the Paston Letters), so that again in 1549 many in Norwich sympathised with the insurrection of Robert Kett, paying the penalty with him on the castle gallows. The advent of the power loom, the banking activities of the Society of Friends, and the foundation of the Norwich General Assurance brought the city into the industrial era. With the coming of the railway the vast cattle market supplied more than half the meat for London. Sporadic air attacks during the Second World War were followed in 1942 by the destructive 'Baedeker raids' on historic targets.

In post-war years the city has suffered changes in the cause of progress, while also fostering pioneer schemes of conservation and restoration. In 1970 the City Council designated seven Conservation Areas, including most buildings of historic and architectural interest; by 1984, there were 15 such areas, and four more are planned. Chief manufactures now are machinery and electrical equipment, boots and shoes, mustard and starch, sweets and beer, though the majority of the working population is employed in service industries. The city is known also for fine printing.

**Famous natives and residents**. Dame Julian of Norwich (c 1342–c 1416), anchoress and mystic; members of the Paston family, authors of the 'Letters' (c 1420–1504); Robert Greene (1560–92), poet and dramatist; Sir Thomas Browne (1605–82); Admiral Lord Nelson (1768–1805); Elizabeth Fry (1780–1845), prison reformer; John Crome ('Old Crome'; 1786–1821), John Sell Cotman (1784–1842) and other painters of the Norwich School; Harriet Martineau (1802–76), author and feminist; George Borrow (1803–81); Rajah Brooke of Sarawak (1803–68).

FROM THE CASTLE TO THE CATHEDRAL. A visit to Norwich may conveniently start at the *Castle, to the E of which a large car park occupies the former Cattle Market. The castle mound was raised just after the Conquest, the great stone keep being built by Henry I after the model of that at Falaise. It is unique among English castles in having an exterior decoration of blank Norman arcading; this was

FAKENHAM

CROMER

Station (Goods)

BAKERS ROAD

ST AUGUSTINE ST

SUSSEX STREET

OAK STREET

St Augustine

GOLDENGROET

PITT STREET

ST GEORGE

ANGLIA

HEIGHAM STREET

LANGLEY ST

DEVONSHIRE

RUSSELL STREET

DERBY STREET

SAYER ST

MARTIN LANE

CRISPIN ROAD

ST MARTIN AT

St Martin's

St Mary's

MUSPOLE

Octagon Chapel

OLD PALACE ROAD

SWAFFHAM & KING'S LYNN

MIDLAND

EXETER ST

MANCROFT ST

ORCHARD STREET

LOTHIAN STREET

NAPIER ST

MILLS YARD

STATION ROAD

WESTWICK STREET

ST MARY'S PLAIN

COSLANY STREET

ST MARY'S

DUKE STREET

COLEGATE

St George

WYMER

DEREHAM ROAD

ASHFORD STREET

DISTILLERY ST

GOLDING STREET

WILLIAM STREET

VALENTINE

St Michael's

St Philip Heigham

WEST POTTERGATE

BARN ROAD

ST SWITHINS ROAD

WELLINGTON LANE

THREE KING LANE

St Swithin

ST BENEDICTS STREET

St Margaret

St Miles Bridge

St Laurence

Dukes Palace Bridge

Blackfriars Bridge

CHARING CROSS

ST ANDR

Car Park

EARLHAM ROAD

HEIGHAM GROVE

DRAGON ST

COW HILL

WILLOW LANE

POTTER GATE

St Gregory

Maddermarket Th

Strangers Hall

St John's

BEDFORD

GRAPES HILL

GILES STREET

St Giles

EXCHANGE ST

LONDON

Heigham Grove

St John the Baptist (R.C.)

CHAPEL FIELD NORTH

BETHEL STREET

Guildhall

City Hall

ST PETER

MARKET

DAVEY PLACE

ROYAL ARCADE

CLARENDON ROAD

NEVILLE STREET

BATHURST

GROSVENOR ST

CHAPEL FIELD ROAD

Chapel Field Gardens

THEATRE STREET

St Peter Mancroft

Library

Car Park

HAYMARKET

GENTLEMENS WALK

WHITE LION ST

RAMPANT HORSE ST

RED LION ST

TRORY STREET

VAUXHALL STREET

KIMBERLEY ST

Theatre Royal

Assembly Rooms

St Stephen

CHANTRY ROAD

MALTHOUSE ROAD

WESTLE

UNTHANK ROAD

ZAMPTILL STREET

OXFORD STREET

SOMERLEYTON ST

NORFOLK PLACE

SUFFOLK STREET

CRESCENT ROAD

BRISTOL

CHAPEL FIELD EAST

ST STEPHEN STREET

SURREY

ESSEX STREET

TRINITY

CAMBRIDGE

UNION STREET

Car Park

Bus Station

QUEEN'S ROAD

GLOUCESTER ST

CHESTER ST

YORK STREET

WILLIAM ST

BRUNSWICK ROAD

NEWMARKET

Hospital

STEBBINGS

KINGSLEY RD

WOOD STREET

VICTORIA STREET

GROVE ROAD

SOUTHWELL ROAD

GROVE AVENUE

N

# NORWICH

| 0 | | 300 yards |
| 0 | | 300 metres |

IPSWICH

accurately reproduced in 1834–39, though in an alien stone, by Salvin.

It now houses a *Museum*, notable for its fine *collection of paintings by such masters of the Norwich School as Crome, Cotman, Stannard, Stark and Vincent. There are informative displays of local history; local antiquities, including the Iron Age hoard of gold and coins unearthed at Snettisham in 1948; and collections of Norwich silver and Lowestoft porcelain.

Below the castle, on the NE, the Anglia Television Centre stands at the city's busiest traffic junction. Bank Plain and its continuation Redwell St. lead N, passing (right) *St Michael-at-Plea*, with a two-storied porch entered above by a Jacobean gallery. Within, the roof has carved angels and the font cover is Jacobean.

Across Prince's St. is the cobbled *Elm Hill, one of the finest medieval streets in England. It was saved and restored by the Norwich Society and the Civic Trust. At the top is *St Peter Hungate*, rebuilt in 1460 by John and Margaret Paston, with a cruciform hammerbeam roof and 15–16C glass. It is now a museum of church art with notable medieval woodwork, vestments, MSS, and bells. Beyond the bend are (left) the *Strangers' Club* (the 'strangers' were the immigrant weavers), early 16C with some 17C work, and (right) *Pettus House*, and beyond (left) the 17C *Flint House*. At the foot, on the corner of Wensum St., the church of *St Simon and St Jude*, aisleless with flint walls, and fine monuments to the Pettus family; it is now the headquarters of the Norwich Boy Scouts (open).

Wensum St. leads to the right past the Maid's Head Hotel to Tombland, the old Saxon market place displaced by the Normans. *Samson and Hercules House* (1657) takes its name from the benign giants supporting the porch; the rest of the square is Georgian and pleasantly tree shaded, with the lofty tower of *St George's Tombland* rising above the trees at the top. The 15C church has a good roof, and a relief and statuette of St George on the 17C font cover.

The *Erpingham Gate* (1420), with beautifully preserved sculpture, leads into the spacious, tree-lined cathedral *Close*.

To the NE of the Erpingham Gate is *Norwich School*, refounded by Edward VI, including the Chapel of St John (c 1316). Among its famous pupils were Robert Greene, Lord Nelson, George Borrow and Rajah Brooke. 'Old Crome' was for a time drawing master here. On the N side of the cathedral is the former *Bishop's Palace*, opened in 1962 as an extension of the school. The Upper Close, running E from *St Ethelbert's Gate* (c 1300; modern parapet), is continued by the Lower Close, leading to *Pull's Ferry*, the picturesque old water-gate of the cathedral precincts (restored 1948). The line of the old canal that passed beneath it, and up which the barges brought the Caen stone to build the cathedral, can still be clearly seen.

The *Cathedral does not dominate the city as at Lincoln or Ely, but leaves that honour to the castle and occupies low ground near the river. Seen from the Close, it is nevertheless a majestic building, mainly Norman, with a soaring spire (315ft) exceeded only at Salisbury.

Building started under Bishop Losinga in 1096, two years after the see of East Anglia was moved from Thetford, and its first phase was complete by c 1145. The clerestory of the choir was rebuilt in the Dec. style by Bishop Percy (1355–69). Bishop Alnwick (1426–36) altered the W front and completed the cloisters, begun 130 years earlier. The present spire and the stone vault of nave and choir were built by Bishop Lyhart (1446–72) and Bishop Goldwell (1472–99).

The Norman style predominates, externally in the *tower and internally in the nave, aisles and transepts. The *Nave* has 14 bays with massive columns,

*An aerial view of Norwich Cathedral*

clerestory and a triforium whose arches, most unusually, are almost as wide as those in the arcade below. The rhythmic unity of the effect is accentuated by the light colour of the stone and the absence of monuments. The majestic lierne-vaulted roof is 15C, and its *bosses, telling the story of the Bible, repay close study (with the mirror trolleys provided or binoculars). The circular hole was used for letting down a thurible, or censer. Two bays of the S aisle near the pulpit were made into a Perp. chantry by Bishop Nykke (d. 1535). The Monks' Door and the Dec. Prior's Door lead from the same aisle to the cloisters. Off the *N Transept* is St Andrew's Chapel, with 15C stained glass; the effigy in the *S Transept* may represent Bishop Losinga.

The *Choir* begins W of the central tower and ends in a semicircular apse with ambulatory and radiating chapels—a French arrangement uncommon in English churches. The presbytery, E of the tower, has been altered but preserves a plan typical of the Christian sanctuary until c 1100. The Bishop's Throne behind the high altar is 8C or earlier and may come from the Saxon cathedral at Dunwich. In the S aisle the Chapter Room has Renaissance panelling and the Bauchun Chapel remarkable roof bosses. At the E end are St Luke's Chapel (S, see below) and the Jesus Chapel (N), each curiously formed out of two segments of a circle. Between them two fine EE arches, from the 13C Lady Chapel, lead into the modern St Saviour's Chapel (1930–32). It contains fine 14C painted panels from St Michael-at-Plea. Even finer is the painted *retable in St Luke's Chapel, probably presented as a thank-you offering for the suppression of the Peasants' Revolt (1381). Together they form a rare survival of masterpieces of the East Anglian school. The so-called Bridge Chapel in the aisle was probably used for displaying relics; the vault above has paintings of 1275.

The *Cloisters*, the only two-storied monastic cloister in England, were rebuilt in 1297–1430. The vault **bosses are even better than those in the nave: nearly 400 in all, they illustrate the life of Christ and the Book of Revelation, as well as depicting the Evangelists, delicate foliage patterns, scenes of contemporary life and several Green Men. Notable also is the tracery of the cloister windows. At the SW corner are the Monks' Lavatories and on the E side is the beautiful Dec. entrance of the vanished Chapter House. Ruins of the Infirmary and Refectory (S side) and Guest Hall (W side) may be seen from the Close.

In May 1919 the body of Nurse Edith Cavell, shot by the Germans in 1915, was brought from Brussels and interred just E of St Luke's Chapel. A bust in Tombland commemorates her heroism.

Palace St., skirting the N wall of the precincts, gives a view through an imposing gateway of c 1430 (good bosses) of the new *Bishop's Palace* and of a surviving 14C porch of the old. Outside the gate stands the little church of *St Martin-at-Palace* with a 14C font and chandelier of 1726. Opposite is *Cotman House*, the home of J.S. Cotman. Further on, in Bishopgate, is the *Great*

site of 13c Lady Chapel

St Saviour's Chapel

Jesus Chapel

St Luke's Chapel

Bridge Chapel

Bauchun Chapel

St Andrew's Chapel

High Altar

Vestry

site of Chapter House (now under road)

PRESBYTERY

CHAPTER ROOM

Throne

Pulpit

Door

Prior's Door

SLYPE (destroyed)

Screen

Chapel of St William

Nave Altar

CLOISTER

Site of Refectory

Pulpit

Monks' Door

Washing Bays

Shop

Key to Numbers
1 Bp Nykke's Chantry
2 Bp Bathurst
3 Ancient Bishop's Throne
4 Bp Goldwell
5 Sir Thomas Erpingham's Chantry
6 Edith Cavell

# NORWICH CATHEDRAL

*Hospital* founded in 1249 by Bishop Walter de Suffield. The original infirmary building, much altered but keeping its Gothic chancel roof, is still in use as wards. The attached church of *St Helen*, rebuilt c 1480, may be visited. Next to the hospital is the house Thomas Ivory built for himself.—The 13C *Bishop Bridge*, at the foot of Bishopgate, is one of the oldest bridges in England still used for traffic. To the left is the brick *Cow Tower*, where the cathedral authorities collected river tolls.

Further N is St James's Hill where there is a splendid view over the river valley to the cathedral, castle and city hall, and beyond, on *Mousehold Heath*, is the best view of Norwich (eloquently described in Chapter 14 of 'Lavengro'), overlooking the city on the NE. Here Kett's followers encamped. The heath was a favourite subject of John Crome's brush, but the famous windmill burned down in 1933.

From the cathedral we may return towards the Market Place by Queen St. Here *St Mary-the-Less* (13C; the 'French Church'), hidden in a huddle of buildings, gives a good idea of medieval conditions. A guild church, it was taken over in turn by Walloons, French Protestants, Swedenborgians, and the Scottish Apostolic Church, and is now a furniture store (not open).

FROM THE CASTLE TO THE MARKET PLACE. From Castle Meadow, to the N of the Castle Hotel, Davey Place leads into the Market Place. Expanded to its present bounds only in the last century, it is splendidly enclosed by civic grandeur of all ages, dominated by a great parish church, and filled with the colour and bustle of the stalls. The E side is Gentleman's Walk, from which *Royal Arcade* runs through to Castle St. where it presents an Art Nouveau façade by Skipper.

Closing the S side is *St Peter Mancroft, an admirable Perp. church with an elaborate tower (the turrets, crenellations, and flèche are additions by the Streets, father and son, in 1881–95). From this tower the first complete peal of 5040 changes was rung in 1715.

The light and lofty arches of the arcade and the arrangement of the clerestory are the epitome of Norfolk Perp., though the double hammerbeam roof is hidden behind ornamental coving. Notable are the font canopy, a 15C alabaster panel, good brasses, and a tomb chest with effigy of Francis Windham (d. 1592). In the chancel is a memorial to Sir Thomas Browne (1605–82), author of 'Religio Medici', who is buried here. The E window is filled with 15C *glass. The sacristy contains admirable church plate and illuminated MSS (13–14C). Outside the church is a statue of Browne, who lived from 1637 to his death in a house near the Lamb Inn yard opposite.

The *City Hall* (1932–38; James and Pierce) matches the scale of square with a tower 202ft high; the bronze lions are by A. Hardiman. The civic regalia, which includes some fine Tudor craftsmanship, is displayed inside. To the S is the *Central Library and Record Office* (1963) with an open court and memorial to men of the US 8th Air Force lost from East Anglian bases in 1941–45. The *Guildhall* (1407–13), of flint, was rebuilt in 1535 with a gable of chequered flushwork; the 16C council chamber within has contemporary panelling and fittings and much 15C stained glass.

NORTH FROM THE MARKET PLACE ACROSS THE RIVER. By London St., made pedestrian and tastefully embellished, and Bedford St. (left) we reach Bridewell Alley. Here the *Bridewell*, a flint-faced house on a vaulted undercroft of 1325 built (c 1370) by Bartholomew, father of William Appleyard, first mayor of Norwich, houses a *museum of local industries. Almost opposite is *St Andrew's Church* (1506), where John Robinson, pastor of the Pilgrim Fathers, was curate. It contains the tombs of Sir John Suckling's mother and other ancestors of the poet. *Suckling House*, adjoining, is a fine 16C town house. **St Andrew's Hall** and **Blackfriars' Hall** (open), built in 1440–70, together constitute the only surviving Dominican church in England. St Andrew's (the nave) has been the city's place of assembly since the Dissolution, while Blackfriars' Hall (the chancel) served as the Dutch church from the 16C to the mid 19C. The Dec. and Perp. windows are notable; the S walk of the cloister and the vaulted vestibule of an earlier, 13C church also survive.

The Wensum (to the N) is crossed by Blackfriars Bridge (1783; Soane). Beyond, in the ancient 'Ward of Over-the-Water', stands *St George Colegate*, a church built in 1459–1513 by rich local weavers. It retains 18C fittings. John Crome is buried here.

To the W along Colegate is *St Michael-at-Coslany*, a fine church covered with flushwork tracery. Further N in St Mary's Plain, *St Mary-at-Coslany* has an Anglo-Saxon round tower; the 15C roof has been beautifully restored to show the diagonal bracing. *St Martin at Oak* in St Martin's Lane is now a night shelter (not open to public). Further N still stands *St Augustine* with Perp. nave and chancel in flint and a brick tower (1687).

To the E along Colegate is the *Octagon Chapel*, originally Presbyterian, now Unitarian, by Thomas Ivory (1755), with an impressive interior. A little further on, a narrow alley leads to the *Old Meeting House* (1693), a fine old Congregational building with a mellow exterior, and the interior perfectly preserved. At the end of the street, *St Clement* has a slender flint tower. It contains many tablets to the Ives and Harvey families, both of whom supplied mayors for the city. To the left is Magdalen St., the first to be comprehensively tidied up and beautified by the shopkeepers under the guidance of the Civic Trust. Along it is *Gurney Court*, where Elizabeth Fry and Harriet Martineau were born. *St Saviour* contains a Georgian W gallery with organ, 15C font, and sword rests. Beyond, Anglia Square is an ambitious modern shopping centre, with offices and a cinema. Further E is *St James Cowgate*, flint, with a brick tower perched on the W roof, a sculptured font, a screen with painted figures (1505), and 15–16C stained glass. It now houses the puppet theatre. From here we may cross Whitefriars Bridge to Palace St. (above), or branch right along Fishergate past the Perp. *St Edmund*, now a store, to Fye Bridge (1822), probably the oldest crossing place of the river, and so to Tombland.

NORTH AND WEST FROM THE MARKET PLACE, AND BACK TO THE CASTLE. Dove St. leads N from the Market Place to *St John Maddermarket*, as its name suggests the centre of the dyeing trade. The fine Perp. tower has the four evangelists on the top battlements. Inside are a superb 18C reredos, many brasses, and monuments to the Sayers and the Sothertons, mayors in the 16C and 17C. The *Maddermarket Theatre* is an 18C building reconstructed as an Elizabethan theatre with apron stage. In Charing Cross is the *Strangers' Hall* (open), a merchant's house with a 15C hall over a 13C undercroft. It was the centre for immigrant weavers, then the assize judge's lodging, and is now a museum of English domestic life.

Westwards along St Benedict St. are five churches. *St Gregory* has a sculptured font, a brass eagle lectern (1496), a 14C sanctuary knocker on the vestry door and a 15C wall painting. *St Laurence* has a tall Perp. tower with two reliefs over the W door, and a 15C font. The Dec. *St Margaret* has an 18C painted reredos above the S door and a brass to Anne Rede (d. 1577) which is a triple palimpsest. The small *St Swithin*, with a charming Victorian bell turret, is now an arts centre. Turning S up the narrow Three King Lane we can see the round Norman tower, with an octagonal 15C upper stage, of the destroyed *St Benedict*.

Across Pottergate (left) is Cow Hill, where *St Giles* has the tallest of the Norwich towers (120ft), used as a beacon. The churchyard is beautifully planted with wisteria trees. Inside are an early hammer-beam roof with angels, brasses and memorials to local doctors.

In Willow Lane, close by, is the house where George Borrow spent his youth. St Giles St. continues W to the *RC Cathedral of St John the Baptist*, built in 1882–1910 by George Gilbert Scott Jr and John Oldrid Scott in a convincing EE style, with rich marbles and fine glass.

*Chapel Field Gardens* leads back to Theatre St., with the *Theatre Royal* and the *Assembly Rooms* (now a restaurant and concert hall), the finest 18C building in Norwich, built by Thomas Ivory in 1754 on the foundations of the college of St Mary. Beyond, in Rampant Horse St., *St Stephen* has a good flushwork tower and an impressive Perp. and Tudor interior with large clerestory windows. The E window has 16C German stained glass. Among good memorials is one in Coade stone to Elizabeth Coppin (d. 1812), with a weeping putto. In Westlegate, across Red Lion St., is *All Saints* in a rural setting. The font is carved with 24 figures of prophets and apostles. Just N is *St John Timberhill*, in whose churchyard prisoners from the castle jail were buried. The chandelier (1500) is German. Timberhill leads N to the castle.

SOUTH FROM THE CASTLE. King St. runs SE from the Prince of Wales Rd. Partly industrialised, it retains some good old buildings, including the town house of the Howards. *St Peter Parmentergate* (not open) stands in a shaded churchyard. The *Barge Inn* is 14–15C. *St Julian* (rebuilt) preserves three Saxon windows in the N wall. A Norman doorway (from the bombed church of *St Michael at Thorn*, to the S) leads into the reconstructed cell of the anchoress Dame Julian. On the left is the *Old Music House* with Norman vaulting (crypt) and 15C timber roof, at one time (1633) the house of Lord Chief Justice Coke. *St Etheldreda* (now an art studio), in another lovely churchyard, has a round tower with a brick and flint octagonal upper stage. Further on, King St. passes between the *Boom Towers*, on either side of the river, and the *Black Tower* (right) where the city walls follow Carrow Hill. Their line can be traced NW to Chapel Field Gardens (see above). The direct return is along Ber St. where *St John de Sepulchre* has a prominent Perp. tower, a two-storied N porch, good flushwork, and East Anglian 'lion' font, and a palimpsest brass. Thence to Timberhill, see above.

SOUTHERN OUTSKIRTS. **Caistor St Edmund**, or *Caister*, about 3m S, was the Roman *Venta Icenorum*, the chief town in the territory of the Iceni. Inside the 2C Roman enclosure of about 34 acres, which seems to have been burnt by the Saxons, is the parish church. Perp., with an EE chancel, it contains a fine carved font of c 1410 and a wall painting of St Christopher.

WESTERN OUTSKIRTS. At *Earlham*, 1½m W, is the **University of East Anglia**, opened in 1963. *Earlham Hall*, once the home of Elizabeth Fry, is now an administrative building. The *buildings by Denys Lasdun, with 'ziggurat' residence blocks, use the varying levels of the fine site in the Yare valley to maximum effect. The *Sainsbury Centre for Visual Arts*, housed in a striking building by Norman Foster (1976), displays a collection of modern and ethnographic art, pre-Columbian, Asian and European antiquities and Art Nouveau.

FROM NORWICH TO YARMOUTH, 20m. A47 at first skirts the Yare.—6m. To the right, on the Yare, is the boating resort of *Brundall*.—11m. *Acle*, with a round-towered 14C church, is a convenient starting-point for the Norfolk Broads (Rte 65). We keep to the right on A47 and skirt Breydon Water.—20m. *Yarmouth*, see Rte 60.

From Norwich to *Ipswich*, see Rte 60; to *Bury*, see Rte 61; to *Newmarket* and *London*, see Rte 63; to the *Norfolk Broads*, see Rte 65; to *King's Lynn*, see Rte 66.

# 65  The Norfolk Broads

Maps: OS Landranger 134, or OS Tourist map (1:50,000 or 1¼in to
1m), or Hamilton's 'Broads Navigation Charts and Index'.

**Broadland**, or the district of the **Norfolk Broads**, forms a triangle on
the map, its apex at Norwich and its base along the coastline
between Lowestoft and Sea Palling. Roads bordered by willows and
streams fringed with reeds cross the level countryside. As both its
shape and its flatness would suggest, the region was once an estuary,
eventually closed at the seaward end by deposits of silt. There are
about a dozen large broads and twice as many smaller ones, shallow
lagoons formed not by the widening of rivers, from which they are
separated by narrow channels, but by the flooding of medieval peat
quarries. Together with the placid and sluggish streams—the chief
being the Yare, the Waveney and the Bure, all meeting ultimately in
Breydon Water—they provide about 200m of navigable water. The
villages are often charming, with interesting churches; there are
some fine old manor houses and a few ruined abbeys and castles.

The main gateways to the Broads are Norwich, Yarmouth,
Lowestoft, Wroxham, Stalham and Potter Heigham. The boatyards
listed in the details of hiring arrangements below make convenient
starting-points for a tour of the waterways. Long popular with
smooth-water sailors and anglers, the Broads get extremely crowded
in the summer.

**Boats.** Yachts, motor cruisers and houseboats may be hired from Blake Holidays
at their headquarters in Wroxham or at Acle, Beccles, Brundall, Burgh Castle,
Horning, Loddon, Oulton Broad, Potter Heigham, Reedham, St Olaves, Somerleyton, South Walsham, Stalham, Sutton, Thorpe and Wayford Bridge; or from
Hoseasons Holidays of Lowestoft at Acle, Beccles, Belaugh, Brundall, Burgh
Castle, Hickling, Horning, Loddon, Ludham, Martham, Oulton Broad, Potter
Heigham, Reedham, St Olaves, Stalham, Thorpe and Wroxham. Inns are
generally available for those who prefer not to sleep on board. Small excursion
steamers ply on the Yare and Bure in summer. The trading wherry, once the
characteristic vessel of the Norfolk rivers, has all but disappeared from these
waters.

**Angling.** The Norfolk Broads and their connecting waterways are best known
for bream and roach, though pike, perch and rudd are also found. All anglers
must hold an Anglian Water rod licence but fishing on most waters is free, apart
from some privately controlled Broads (Wroxham Broad and Hickling Broad, for
example) where day permits are required. Information should be obtained
locally, at boatyards and public houses, or directly from the Recreation and
Conservation Officer, Anglian Water, Norwich Division, Yare House, 62 Thorpe
Road, Norwich NR1 1SA.

A TOUR OF THE BROADS BY ROAD FROM NORWICH, 51m. **Norwich**, see
Rte 64.—Leaving the city by A1151, which skirts Mousehold Heath,
we pass through the suburb of *Sprowston*, where the 14C church has
a brick tower and fine monuments, to reach Broadland at (8m)
**Wroxham**, with a bridge over the Bure. Adjoining *Hoveton* has a
seasonal Tourist Information Centre. *Coltishall*, 2m NW on B1354,
has a picturesque lock marking the limit of navigation on the Bure.
The attractive village has many good 18C houses, and the church has
Saxon windows and a Norman font.—Right of the main road 2m N of
Wroxham and Hoveton is *Beeston Hall* (open), a Gothick house of
1787. Before this, we may take a detour on the right to (11½m)
*Neatishead* and (12½m) *Barton Turf*, where the church has a good
rood screen, for a glimpse of Barton Broad.—Returning to the A1151,
we cross the Ant at (16m) *Wayford Bridge* and pass (18m) *Stalham*,

where the Maid's Head is a 14C inn with 18C façade, and (19m) *Sutton*. From here a left turn leads to (21m) *Hickling*, connected by a lane (³/₄m) with its broad.—From (24m) *Potter Heigham*, which has 14–15C paintings in its church, we can return to Wroxham (8¹/₂m) by Ludham and Horning.—A longer route follows the Yarmouth road across Heigham Bridge, on the Thurne, to (28m) *Rollesby Bridge* between Rollesby Broad and Ormesby Broad. On reaching (30m) *Ormesby* we turn right, then right again through (31¹/₂m) *Filby* and follow A1064 SW across Filby Broad and over the Bure to (37m) *Acle* (see Rte 64). Here we turn right on B1140 for (40m) *South Walsham*, with two churches in one churchyard, and take an unclassified road on the right for (41¹/₂m) *Ranworth*, with glimpses of broads beyond. Ranworth church has a magnificent painted *rood screen and lectern (both early 15C).—Unclassified roads continue via (44¹/₂m) *Salhouse* back to Norwich.

A TOUR OF THE WATERWAYS FROM WROXHAM. Perhaps the most characteristic series of broads are those strung along the river Bure, and **Wroxham** (see road route above) is a favourite starting-point for a tour, though the river is navigable up to *Coltishall* to the NW. About 1¹/₂m below the bridge a dyke on the right leads to *Wroxham Broad (private moorings), sometimes called the 'Queen of the Broads'. On the right is *Salhouse Broad*. On the left, *Hoveton Great Broad* is a nature reserve under the auspices of the Nature Conservancy Council. Access is by river and, on payment, a nature trail can be followed on foot. Below these is (5m) *Horning*. To the right are (6³/₄m) *Ranworth Broad*, a bird sanctuary which cannot be entered by boat, though the Norfolk Naturalist's Trust Centre may be visited, and (9¹/₂m) the Fleet Dyke, leading into *South Walsham Broad*. The tributary Ant, joining the Bure nearly opposite Fleet Dyke, leads via (³/₄m) *Ludham Bridge* and *Irstead* church, with good woodwork, to (4m) *Barton Broad*, a large but shallow lagoon (1¹/₂m long) with wooded banks. About 2m N of this broad, reached via the Ant and a dyke, is *Stalham* (see road route above).—Returning to the Bure, we see on its left bank the ruins of *St Benet's Abbey* (founded in 1020) from which the Bishop of Norwich, the only abbot in the Church of England, takes the style of 'Abbot of St Benet's at Holme'. From *Thurne Mouth*, 11³/₄m from Wroxham, we may ascend the Thurne to (3¹/₂m) *Potter Heigham Bridge*, very crowded in summer, and (5m) *Heigham Sound*, communicating with the shallow *Hickling Broad*, the largest of all (3m in circumference) and a noted bird sanctuary. At its N end is *Hickling Staithe*. To the NE of Heigham Sound, and connected with it by Meadow Dyke is (1¹/₂m) *Horsey Mere* (NT), 1¹/₂m S of which is *Martham Broad*, on the opposite side of the Thurne. —A dyke, 1¹/₂m above the mouth of the Thurne, leads to (³/₄m) *Womack Water* and (1¹/₄m) *Ludham*, with an interesting church.—The lower course of the Bure, from the mouth of the Thurne to (19¹/₂m) *Acle Bridge* and (31¹/₂m) **Yarmouth** (Rte 60), flows through duller country.

The Bure flows into the E end of **Breydon Water** (beware of low tides). At the SW end, near Burgh Castle, is the mouth of the Waveney, whose winding course can be followed to (18m) *Beccles* and (21m) Geldeston Lock. It passes within 1m of *Fritton Decoy* (see Rte 60). The New Cut, beginning near this point, connects it with the Yare at (3¹/₂m) *Reedham* (see below). Oulton Dyke, c 5m above the New Cut, connects it with (1¹/₂m) *Oulton Broad* (see Rte 60) and so with **Lowestoft**.

The Yare enters **Breydon Water** near the Waveney, and can be followed all the way to Norwich. Beyond (6m) *Reedham*, with a fine 17C inn, we pass on the left (1½m) *Hardley Dyke*, the mouth of the Chet, which can be navigated to (4m) *Loddon*, a tiny old market town with a very ancient alms box in its 15C church. Nearby are the churches of *Chedgrave* and *Heckingham*, both with Norman work, and *Hales Hall*, a late medieval manor house and barn, recently restored (limited opening of barn and garden).—9m. *Cantley Red House*, a favourite anglers' inn. About 1m beyond and to the left are the remains of *Langley Abbey* (c 1200).—13m. *Buckenham Ferry*, another gathering place for anglers. A dyke on the left leads to (¾m) *Rockland Broad*, with reed beds rich in wildfowl.—14½m. *Coldham Hall* is known for its large 'baskets' of roach and bream. About ½m off is *Brundall*, and on the left at 16¼m is the entrance to *Surlingham Broad*. The scenery from here to (21m) **Norwich** is very attractive.

# 66 Norwich to King's Lynn

## A. Via Fakenham

Total distance 47m. **Norwich**, see Rte 64.—A1067 to (26m) **Fakenham**.—A148, A1078 to (47m) **King's Lynn** (Rte 70A).

Maps: OS Landranger 133, 132.

A47, the direct road (43m) via East Dereham and Swaffham, is fast but featureless. *North Tuddenham* (13m) was the birthplace of Matthew Vassar (1791–1868), founder of Vassar College, New York.

**Norwich**, see Rte 64.—A1067 ascends the Wensum valley, with the pleasant *Ringland* hills on the left. The church has a magnificent Perp. hammerbeam *roof, disguised by ribbed panelling with angels, and good stained glass. *Weston Longville* church, 2m NW, has a fine 14C wall painting of a Tree of Jesse. The diarist James Woodforde was rector from 1774 until his death in 1803.—On the right beyond (9m) *Attlebridge* is *Great Witchingham*, where the *Norfolk Wildlife Park* contains a notable collection of European mammals in their natural habitat, as well as exotic pheasants, etc.—The main road continues through the pretty hamlet of *Lenwade* and (13m; right) *Sparham*, whose 14C church has a good roof, to (15m) *Bawdeswell*, the home of Chaucer's Reeve. Its church (1955) is by Fletcher Watson. At *Elsing*, 2¾m S, is a good Dec. church with the brass of its founder, Sir Hugh Hastings (d. 1347).

A detour may be taken NE on B1145 to (4m) *Reepham*. St Michael's, with a tall Perp. tower, dominates the little market place. A vestry connects it with a second church, St Mary's, with a Norman font and fine monument to Sir Roger de Kerdiston (d. 1337). A third church has been ruined since 1543. *Booton*, c 1½m SE, has an ambitious Gothic Revival church built in 1875–91 by the incumbent, Whitwell Elwin.—At (5m) *Salle* (pronounced 'Saul') the *church is spectacular. It has a tall, decorated tower, two-storied N and S porches, an arch-braced roof with angels, good bosses in the transepts, finely carved stalls and misericords, and a 15C 'wineglass' pulpit with Jacobean canopy. The church was built by the three local families of Brigge, Fontayne and Boleyn; Anne Boleyn is reputedly buried here. *Heydon*, 2m N of Salle, boasts a pretty village green and church with wall paintings. Heydon Hall (not open) is Tudor with 18C additions.—(7m) *Cawston* church has a high tower and a superb *roof. It was built in the early 15C by Michael de la Pole, Earl of Suffolk.—(11m) *Aylsham*, see Rte 66B.

The main route continues via (17m) *Twyford*, with a Norman church, to (19m) *Guist*.

B1110 leads S to (3m) *North Elmham*, the seat of a bishopric founded in 673 and the only see in East Anglia from 965 to 1075, when it was transferred to Thetford and thence to Norwich. N of the present church stand the ruins of the 11C Saxon cathedral and bishop's palace (English Heritage, open at any reasonable time).—At *Gressenhall*, W of B1110 at 5m, the 18C workhouse now contains the *Norfolk Rural Life Museum*.—9m. **East Dereham**, a market town of 11,800 people, has a fine parish church with painted Perp. ceilings in the N and S chapels, an 18C Flemish chest, and the tomb of William Cowper (1731–1800). Close to the unfinished 16C belfry a ruined chapel covers the site of the tomb of St Withburga, foundress of the church. The site of Cowper's house in the market place is occupied by the Cowper Memorial Church. Bishop Bonner's cottage (1502), with coloured pargeting, is now a museum. George Borrow (1803–81) was born at *Dumpling Green*, 1½m S. At *Shipdham*, 5m SW of Dereham, the 13C church has a two-stage lantern on its tower and contains a wooden *lectern (c 1500). In *Swanton Morley*, a pretty place 5m SW of Dereham, the Angel Inn (NT) incorporates the remains of the house where in 1615 Richard Lincoln made the will that caused his grandson Samuel, direct ancestor of Abraham Lincoln, to leave England for America (cf. Hingham, Rte 63). In the beautiful church (c 1370) a large E window remembers the men of the adjoining RAF station.

26m. **Fakenham** (5800 inhab.; seasonal Tourist Information), a pleasant little market town, has a Dec. and Perp. church with a fine high tower, containing a notable font.

B1105 leads N via (3m) *East Barsham*, with a good early Tudor manor house, to (5m) **Walsingham**, or *Little Walsingham* (seasonal Tourist Information), noted for the ruins of an Augustinian Priory (open) which once owned the famous and wealthy shrine of Our Lady of Walsingham, commemorating the apparition of the Blessed Virgin to the lady of the manor in 1061. The pre-Reformation pilgrimage was revived in 1921 and there are now two shrines: the Anglo-Catholic shrine (1931, enlarged 1938), with a tall red brick tower, where the image of Our Lady of Walsingham was transferred from the parish church in 1931; and the Roman Catholic *Slipper Chapel*, 1½m S, a 14C building reconsecrated in 1938, with a modern *Chapel of Reconciliation* beside it. In the village are also the ruins of a late 13C *Franciscan Friary* (not open) and the parish church (restored after a fire in 1961), containing a fine Perp. font. The *Shirehall Museum* preserves an 18C court room and houses an exhibit about the history of the pilgrimage. The church at *Great Walsingham*, 1m NE, has good bench ends.—About 3½m NE of Walsingham are the remains of the Benedictine *Binham Priory* (English Heritage, open at any reasonable time). The nave (1091) is now the parish church. The *W front remains exquisite despite the crude bricking-up of the great window. It was apparently built before 1244 and is thus the earliest example of bar tracery in England. A medieval wayside cross stands on the green nearby.

From Fakenham to *Bury St Edmunds* and to *Cromer*, see Rte 61.

28m. *Sculthorpe* has a Norman font of a local type.—At (34m) *Harpley* we turn 1m N to ***Houghton Hall** (open), the grandest country house in Norfolk and perhaps the finest example of Palladian architecture in England.

Houghton was built in 1722–31 for Sir Robert Walpole as tangible expression of the wealth and position his career as Prime Minister to George I had won him. Colen Campbell's design followed the plan of Palladio's villas with grand simplicity: an oblong central block with rusticated ground floor and tall piano nobile above, flanked on each side by colonnades leading to servants' wings. It was elaborated in the building, most obviously by the happy addition of James Gibbs's domes, replacing the pedimented corners Campbell had intended for the central block (cf. Holkham). William Kent was mainly responsible for the

*Houghton Hall*

state rooms. They begin with the Stone Hall, a 40ft cube with lavish decoration, among which the ceiling by Artari and the chimneypiece by Rysbrack are outstanding. The grand proportions and rich detail set the note for the rooms that follow, culminating in the splendid saloon. Noteworthy along the way are Kent's painted ceilings, Rysbrack's chimneypiece in the dining room, and the wood carving in the common parlour (presumably from the earlier house on the site and perhaps by Grinling Gibbons). The park was landscaped by Bridgeman.—In the little church are buried Sir Robert (1676–1745) and his son, Horace Walpole (1717–97).

Beyond Harpley A148 crosses the *Peddars' Way* (Rte 67), coming from Castle Acre and Massingham Heath in the S and leading N to Ringstead and the coast.—38¹/₂m. *Hillington* (left) has a manor house of 1627 (not open). For *Sandringham*, 2m NW, see Rte 67.—At 43m a sideroad leads NW to (1m) **Castle Rising**, perhaps the most interesting of Norfolk villages. It has a massive Norman *Castle* of c 1150, with a keep similar to the one at Norwich and huge earthworks covering more than 12 acres (English Heritage, standard opening and Sunday mornings all year). Also a beautiful late Norman church (12C) and the Jacobean *Trinity Hospital* (open), built by Henry Howard before 1614, a charity for ten elderly women who still wear a quaint Stuart costume on Sundays.—45m. *South Wootton* church has a fine Norman font.—47m. **King's Lynn**, see Rte 70A.

# B.   Via Aylsham and Fakenham

Total distance 54m. **Norwich**, see Rte 64.—A140 to (14m)
**Aylsham**.—B1354 to (27m) Thursford.—A148 to (33m) **Fakenham**
(Rte 66A).—A148, A1078 to (54m) **King's Lynn** (Rte 70A).

Maps: OS Landranger 133, 132.

**Norwich**, see Rte 64.—A140 heads N, passing the airport on the
right, to (14m) **Aylsham**, an old market town with handsome 18C
houses. The churchyard of its Dec. church has a monument to
Humphry Repton (1752–1818), the landscape gardener, who lived at
Sustead Hall nearby.

**North Walsham**, 6m NE, is a market town (7900 inhab.) dominated by the
ruined tower of its church, which contains a fine alabaster monument to Sir
William Paston (d. 1608), founder of the Paston School which Nelson attended.
*Worstead*, 3m SE of Walsham, gave its name to a woollen fabric first made here
in the 12C by Flemish immigrants. The 14C church has good flushwork and 15C
screens. *Gunton Hall*, 5¹/₂m NW of Walsham, has a fine park (open to cars).

The main route continues NW from Aylsham on B1354, passing the
lovely *Aylsham Old Hall* of 1689 (NT, open by appointment). At
15¹/₂m it reaches **˙Blickling Hall** (NT), one of the great Jacobean
houses of England.

It was built in 1619–27 for Sir Henry Hobart by Robert Lyminge, the architect of
Hatfield House in Hertfordshire, and altered by the Ivorys of Norwich in
1765–70, about the time when it passed by marriage to the Marquess of Lothian.
The Ivorys' work on the exterior kept close to the spirit of the original, and so

*Blickling Hall*

the predominating effect of Blickling is still a homely Jacobean style untouched by the neo-classicism becoming fashionable in court circles. It is nowhere better displayed than by the S entrance front, a long façade of red brick with a lively skyline of gables, turrets and chimneys. Inside, the fine 17C staircase survives, though in a changed position. The dining room on the ground floor and the south drawing room above have their original fireplaces, and the latter room its original ceiling by Lyminge. But the great showpiece of Blickling is the *gallery, 127ft long, with a magnificent plaster ceiling whose fanciful emblems repay the closest study. The gardens have undergone several transformations. A formal parterre, originally 19C but redesigned in 1930, leads via an avenue of splendid rhododendrons to a little classical temple by the Ivorys, who also built the orangery. The huge mausoleum 1m NW is by Joseph Bonomi (1793). Anne Boleyn spent her childhood in the earlier house on the site. Her family, as well as the Hobarts and Lothians, are remembered in the *Church* by the entrance; the monument to the 8th Marquess of Lothian (d. 1878) by G.F. Watts is outstanding. The Perp. font has cheerful lions.—The church at *Erpingham*, 3m NE, has 15C–17C stained glass brought from Blickling.

From (19½m) *Saxthorpe*, we may turn N to (2m) *Mannington Hall*, a 15C moated house altered in the 19C by the eccentric 2nd Earl of Orford, with a ruined Saxon church in its lovely grounds (gardens open; house open by appointment).—27m. *Thursford*. At *Thursford Green*, c 1m NW, the *Thursford Museum* displays a collection of antique machinery (traction engines, steam engines, Wurlitzer organ, etc.).—33m. **Fakenham**, see Rte 66A.—54m. **King's Lynn**, see Rte 70A.

# 67  Great Yarmouth to Cromer and King's Lynn

Total distance 87m. **Great Yarmouth**, see Rte 60.—A149 to (3m) Caister-on-Sea.—A149, B1159 to (32m) **Cromer**.—A149, A1078 to (87m) **King's Lynn** (Rte 70A).

Maps: OS Landranger 134, 133, 132.

The first leg of the journey avoids the main road to Cromer (34m), via Potter Heigham and North Walsham, and takes a devious but interesting route along the coast.

**Great Yarmouth**, see Rte 60.—The main road leads N to (3m) **Caister-on-Sea**, the site of a Roman harbour. Part of the town wall, gateway and buildings have been excavated (English Heritage, open at any reasonable time). The moated *Castle*, built c 1432, belonged to Sir John Fastolf (Shakespeare's Falstaff) and later to the Pastons (many of the 'Letters' were written here). It now contains a motor museum.—Further N we keep to the right on B1159 via *Hemsby* and (7½m) *Winterton*, with a fine 15C church tower. We turn inland to (8½m) *East Somerton*, with a ruined church in woods, and *West Somerton* church, which has a Norman round tower and 14C wall paintings.—At (10m) *Horsey*, near Horsey Mere (Rte 65), a huge barrier has been erected against the sea to prevent a repetition of the floods of 1938. It has a fine drainage mill (NT).—Through (12m) *Waxham* and (13m) *Sea Palling* we skirt the sandy shore, regaining the coast at (18m) *Happisburgh* (pronounced 'Hazeburgh'), a pretty village with a lighthouse. The fine church has a tall tower, notable font and good Perp. screen.—22m. *Bacton* has the remains of *Broomholm Priory*, now part of a farm, a Cluniac foundation of 1113 mentioned in Chaucer's 'Reeve's Tale' and Langland's 'Piers Plowman'. The attractive village is overshadowed by the terminal of the gas pipeline from the North Sea.—24m. *Paston* is a name familiar from the 15C 'Paston Letters'. A fine flint *barn is all that remains of their manor. The thatched church contains Paston monuments, including two by Nicholas Stone.—26m. *Mundesley* has fine sands and cliffs.

*Knapton* \*church, 1¹/₂m inland, has a double hammerbeam roof with nearly 140 angels, and a fine font cover. *Trunch*, 1m W, has another good roof, a magnificent Perp. \*font cover (one of only four in England) and a good screen.

The road skirts the coast via (28m) *Trimingham*, with a notable painted choir screen, and (30m) *Overstrand*.

32m. **Cromer** (6200 inhab.; seasonal Tourist Information), in a high but sheltered situation, is the most charming of the East Anglian seaside resorts. It became fashionable in Edwardian times, but still keeps its fishing industry, famous for crabs. The 15C church is notable for its splendid tower and for the height of its piers and arches.

3m SW via A148 is \***Felbrigg Hall**, now NT but for 300 years previously the home of the Windham family and its successors. Part of Felbrigg's history is written in the pleasantly inconsistent exterior, where the S range (c 1620) is vigorously Jacobean, with the motto 'Gloria Deo in Excelsis' cut in the balustrade over its three bays, and the W range (1674–87) is quiet and restrained. The story is completed inside by James Paine's alterations of 1750. His library in the Gothick style is particularly notable. Of the outbuildings, the attractive brick orangery dates from 1704–05 and the stables by Donthorne were added in the 1820s. Beyond the walled garden lies fine wooded parkland. The church nearby has a series of \*brasses (1351–1608) and monuments by Grinling Gibbons (to William Windham, d. 1686) and by Nollekens (to the politician William Windham, d. 1813).—A148 continues W from Felbrigg to (1¹/₂m) the delightful wooded *Beacon Hill* (NT), which includes the highest point in Norfolk.—For *Holt*, 5m beyond, see Rte 61.

From Cromer to *Bury St Edmunds* and *London*, see Rte 61.

The main route continues through *East Runton* and *West Runton* above cliffs which have been mostly preserved from permanent building by 'Half-Year Rights', the continuing medieval claim to common grazing; the caravans are removed in the 6-month winter period.—35m. *Beeston Regis* has a fine church on the cliff edge. The 13C priory, to the W, is much ruined.—36m. *Sheringham* (5500 inhab.; seasonal Tourist Information) is a resort known for the North Norfolk Collection of railway relics, etc., at the Victorian station. Steam locomotives run along a restored stretch of the branch line to Weybourne and beyond. *Sheringham Hall* (NT, park but not hall open at time of writing) was built in 1812–17 by Humphry Repton and his son. Repton also laid out the gardens, well preserved and with magnificent rhododendrons.—At (39m) *Weybourne* there are the ruins of an Augustinian priory next to the church. The high ground now recedes and the salt marshes, with their abundant bird life, begin. A shingle barrier was built along the shore after the disastrous flood of 1953.—43m. *Cley* (pronounced 'Cly'), once a busy port, has a fine windmill (NT) and an 18C custom house. The large 13–15C church, ³/₄m inland, has an elaborate clerestory and S porch, and ruined transepts. It contains interesting brasses.

44¹/₂m. **Blakeney** is a delightful sailing village (regatta in August). The *Church* has a slender beacon tower at the E end, fine EE vaulting in the chancel, and a double hammerbeam roof in the nave. A steep High St. with some charming houses leads down to the hard. The undercroft of the 14C *Guildhall* survives (English Heritage, open at any reasonable time). *Blakeney Point* (NT) and the foreshore to the N are noted bird sanctuaries.

*The quay at Blakeney*

At *Langham*, 2m S, Captain Marryat wrote several of his novels.—B1156 follows the Glaven via (1m) *Wiveton*, with a medieval bridge and a good Perp. church, to (2m) *Glandford*, a pretty village with a shell museum beside the interesting church.

48½m. *Stiffkey* is known for its cockles ('Stewkey blues') and for a scandalous vicar in the 1930s.—52m. *Wells-next-the-Sea* (2400 inhab.; seasonal Tourist Information) is an attractive small seaport with a rebuilt Perp. church. For *Binham* and *Walsingham*, see Rte 66A.

About 1m S of (54m) *Holkham* is **'Holkham Hall** (open), seat of the Earls of Leicester and one of Norfolk's grandest country houses.

William Kent built Holkham in 1734–61 for Thomas Coke, the 1st Earl, the owner's choice of the Palladian style being no doubt influenced by nearby Houghton. The plan consists of a central block of state apartments with corridors leading to four lower blocks of rooms for ordinary use; the material is a light-grey brick resembling stone. The most striking room inside is the Marble Hall, where Kent used coloured alabaster to sumptuous effect. Holkham is famous for its art collection: classical sculptures, paintings by Van Dyck, Rubens, both Poussins, Claude, and Gainsborough, and a copy of the lost 'Bathers' cartoon by Michelangelo. The park, with its huge lake, was landscaped by Capability Brown in 1762 and the formal terraces were laid out by Nesfield in 1854. To the N a monument remembers the agricultural improvements of 'Coke of Norfolk' (Thomas William Coke, 1st Earl of Leicester by the second creation; 1754–1842). The tall column, supported by four cows and crowned by a wheatsheaf, was erected by his tenants in 1845. The church, restored and rebuilt in 1870, has two monuments by Nicholas Stone.

57½m. *Burnham Overy Staithe* is a pleasant little resort. Lord Nelson (1758–1805) was born in the old rectory (since demolished) of *Burnham Thorpe*, 1m S. The church contains the font at which he was christened and a lectern and rood made of wood from the 'Victory'; also the fine brass of Sir William Calthorp (d. 1420). About 1m S of Burnham Thorpe is the Augustinian *Creake Abbey*, founded in 1206, with remains of the 13C church and a 14C chapel (English Heritage, open at any reasonable time). The churches of *North Creake* and

*South Creake* are both interesting.—59m. *Burnham Norton* has a church with a lofty circular tower and vestiges of a Carmelite friary (1241).—The font at (60m) *Burnham Deepdale* has 11C carving of the 'labours of the months'.—The resort of (62m) *Brancaster* is on the site of the Roman fort of *Branodunum*, guarding the 'Saxon Shore'. Offshore is *Scolt Head* (NT), a sandy and shingly island with a famous ternery (strictly preserved).—The church at (67m) *Holme-next-the-Sea* contains the earliest brass with an English inscription (c 1400). Here the *Peddars' Way*, a prehistoric trackway improved by the Romans, reaches the sea. It ran inland to Castle Acre and Ixworth (Rte 61).

**71m. Hunstanton** (4100 inhab.; Tourist Information), facing W across the Wash, is a favourite resort, with coloured stratified cliffs. Just S of the old lighthouse are the ruins of a chapel of St Edmund. At *Old Hunstanton*, 1½m N, the church contains a Norman font and Le Strange monuments, including a *brass to Sir Roger (d. 1506).—In the church of (73½m) *Heacham* is a portrait medallion (1933) of Princess Pocohontas (1595–1617), wife of John Rolfe of Heacham Hall, whose parents are buried here.—76m. *Snettisham* and (78½m) *Dersingham* both have fine churches, the former with a tall steeple. *Shernborne*, 2m E, is noted for its Norman font.

1½m S of Dersingham is **Sandringham House**, the country home of the Queen, more interesting for its royal connection than its architecture. It is not open when members of the Royal Family are in residence. Queen Victoria bought the estate for her son, the future Edward VII, and he commissioned the unknown A.J. Humbert to design the present Jacobean-style building of 1870. It was expanded by the addition of a ballroom in 1883 and partly rebuilt in its upper storey after a fire in 1891. The elaborate Norwich Gates by Thomas Jekyll, at the main entrance, were a wedding present from the County of Norfolk to Edward VII (1863). In the pleasant grounds the old stables have been made into an eclectic museum. George VI (1895–1952) was born at York Cottage and died at the House. Sandringham *Church* (late Perp.) contains memorials of Edward VII and members of the Royal Family.—At *Wolferton*, 2¾m W, the railway station built to serve Sandringham is now a museum. The church contains some good screens.

82½m. *Castle Rising*, see Rte 66A.—87m. **King's Lynn**, see Rte 70A.

# 68 London to Cambridge and Peterborough

Total distance 88m. A10 to (20m) Hoddesdon (bypassed).—A1170 to (24m) **Ware**.—A1170, A10 to (41m) Royston.—A10 to (54m) **Cambridge** (Rte 69).—A604 to (70m) **Huntingdon** (bypassed).—A14, A1 to (83m) Norman Cross.—A15 to (88m) **Peterborough**.

Maps: OS Landranger 177, 166, 154, 153, 142.

The fast road to Cambridge is M11; for another way, via Bishop's Stortford, see Rte 63. For A1 to Peterborough, see Rte 47A.

A10 goes N from London, crossing the North Circular Rd at (7m) *Edmonton* and M25 at (12m) *Waltham Cross*, both described in 'Blue Guide London'.—20m. *Hoddesdon* was once an important stage on the coaching route. Despite alterations the High St. keeps some spacious houses and inns, including the Golden Lion (c 1600), with good timbering. John Loudon Macadam lived here in 1825–36. To the E, astride the river Lea, is the *Lee* [sic] *Valley Regional Park* (6500 acres), salvaged from the derelict land and gravel workings of 'the backyard of London' as the result of a plan prepared by the Civic Trust in 1964. Within the confines of the park, 1m NE of Hoddesdon, is *Rye House*, where an abortive plot to assassinate Charles II and his brother James was hatched in 1683; only the late 15C gatehouse survives.

B1197 leads NW to (4m) Hertford, described below, via (2m) *Hertford Heath*. *Haileybury College*, a boys' school founded in 1862, occupies the buildings (by Wilkins) of the College established in 1805 by the East India Company but dissolved in 1858. Clement Attlee was a pupil at Haileybury.

A10 continues N, passing between Ware and Hertford on a high and windy bridge across the valley.

The main route takes A1170 to (22½m) *Great Amwell*, on the right. Its church has a Norman apse. A monument of 1800 (by Robert Mylne) to its creator, Sir Hugh Myddleton, stands in a romantic setting beside one of the springs of the New River.—24m. **Ware** (14,200 inhab.) has reverted to its old character since the bypass opened. In High St. is the *Priory* (Council Office), the remains of a 15C Franciscan foundation (17–18C additions). The river Lea is lined with pleasant houses. The over-restored church has a tablet to Charles Chauncey, the vicar, who became President of Harvard College in 1654. Off East St. in *Bluecoat Yard* are the old Bluecoat School buildings; the original Manor House is 15C with 16–17C alterations. The row of cottages (1698) was used until 1761 for the younger boys of Christ's Hospital (see below) and their 'nurses'. Among many fine 17–18C industrial buildings are Canons Maltings and Albany Corn Stores. The Grammar School occupies *Amwell House* (c 1730), originally the home of John Scott, the Quaker poet; his 'Grotto' is in Scott's Rd. Ware was the limit of John Gilpin's unwilling ride.

B1004 leads NE to (4m) *Widford*, with Blakesware Park, the 'Blakesmoor' of Lamb's 'Essays'. 3m further N is the long Georgian street of *Much Hadham*, for 900 years a manor of the Bishops of London, with a partly 15C 'Palace' and many good 16–18C houses.

About 3m W of Ware via A119, and now almost joined to it, is **Hertford** (21,400 inhab.; Tourist Information), an ancient county town on the Lea, with a *Shire Hall* (1769) by James Adam and some fine old buildings in Fore St. The scanty remains of the *Castle*, where King John of France was held in 1359, include a Norman motte and a gatehouse of 1461–65, 'gothicised' in 1787. On the Ware road are the interesting buildings used by *Christ's Hospital School* until it moved to Horsham in 1985. Beyond the gateway of 1695 is (left) the original girls' school, a long building of 1778. Coloured figures of boys (1721) and girls adorn the street front, and another boy (from the old school at Ware) the School Hall entrance. The fine bust of Treasurer Lockington (c 1716) is from a demolished London church.

At *Bengeo*, in a secluded site on the N bank of the Lea, is a small apsidal Norman church.

A414 goes SE from Hertford, rising above the Lea valley; an alternative road, B158, passes below the *County Hall* of 1939 and keeps nearer the river.—2m *Hertingfordbury* is a pretty village with a church containing Cowper monuments and one to Anne (d. 1622), wife of Lord Baltimore, founder of Maryland.—7½m. *Hatfield*, see Rte 47A.

We rejoin A10 N of Ware. Beyond (26m) *Wadesmill* a roadside obelisk commemorates Thomas Clarkson (1760–1846), who at this spot in 1785 resolved to devote his life to the abolition of slavery.

—27m. *High Cross* church, by Salvin (1846), has a surprising W window of 1893.—At 28½m a sideroad leads right to (¾m) *Standon* church, with an impressive W porch and detached tower. The chancel is raised above the nave under a fine arch (restored in the 19C). The good *brasses include one of John Field (d. 1474), a merchant of the Staple.—At (30m) *Puckeridge* we keep left.

An alternative route from Puckeridge (B1368; 1m shorter) runs via: (32m) *Braughing*, an important Roman road junction; (34m) *Litte Hormead* (left), where the church has 12C *ironwork on its N door; (38m) *Barkway* and (40m) *Barley*, where the inn sign spans the roadway. At 49m we join A10 S of the junction with M11 and Trumpington.

34m. *Buntingford* has a brick church of 1614–26 and a long street of 17–18C houses, notably Ward's Hospital, an almshouse founded in 1684 by Bishop Seth Ward of Salisbury, a native.—At (41m) *Royston* (11,800 inhab.), a dull town, we quit the line of Ermine Street.

Ermine Street continues N as A14 to (21m) *Huntingdon*.—6m. *Arrington* adjoins the park of *Wimpole Hall* (NT), the most important country house in Cambridgeshire.

*Sir John Soane's Yellow Drawing Room at Wimpole Hall*

Wimpole is noteworthy for both its size and the contributions made by several generations of distinguished architects and gardeners. The park was landscaped by Bridgeman, Capability Brown and Humphry Repton; its delightful sham ruin (1768) is by Sanderson Miller. The S entrance avenue over 2m long, laid waste by Dutch Elm Disease, has recently been replanted with limes. Apart from the unfortunate 19C stables, the house is restrained by comparison but equally various in its history. The central block was begun c 1640 for Sir Thomas Chicheley, expanded later in the century and refronted by Henry Flitcroft in 1742–45. The wings were added by James Gibbs in 1719–21. Among the rooms shown, Gibbs's library and chapel (with trompe l'oeil paintings by Sir James Thornhill) and Sir John Soane's *yellow drawing room and bath house (added in the 1790s) are outstanding.

The poet Matthew Prior died here in 1721 while visiting his patron, Edward Harley, Earl of Oxford. The last private owner was Mrs Elsie Bambridge, Rudyard Kipling's daughter. Since 1976 the National Trust has restored *Wimpole Home Farm* (separate fee), built by Soane (1794). The Great Barn houses a display of farming equipment; rare breeds of livestock can be seen in the paddock and grounds.

The parish *Church*, rebuilt by Flitcroft in 1749, has a fine array of monuments to the Chicheley and Hardwicke families.

*Papworth Everard*, 7½m further N on A14, has a famous hospital and a 'village settlement' known for its pioneering work in the training and employment of the disabled.

A10 bears NE and enters Cambridgeshire.—44m. *Melbourn* has a 13C church with an early 16C rood screen.—49m. *Harston* has an imposing flint church.—50m. *Hauxton*, a pretty village, has a church with a Norman nave and chancel, and a 13C painting of St Thomas Becket.

We cross M11 and pass through (52m) *Trumpington* on the way into (54m) **Cambridge**, Rte 69.

We leave Cambridge by the Huntingdon road, which passes Girton College and becomes A604, following the line of the Roman Via Devana.—64m. *Fenstanton* has a little 17C lock-up on the green. The church has a monument to Capability Brown, who lived here from 1767 until his death in 1783.

Shortly beyond Fenstanton, A1096 leads to (2m) **St Ives** (12,300 inhab.), which claims as its founder St Ivo, a Persian missionary bishop of the 6C. On the old bridge spanning the Ouse is a 15C chapel, partly rebuilt in 1689. Oliver Cromwell, who lived here for five years, is remembered by a statue in the market place. *All Saints*, where Laurence Sterne held his first curacy, is a good 15C church. The *Norris Museum* nearby has an interesting local collection. There is charming scenery on the Great Ouse from St Ives to Huntingdon, particularly at the pretty village of *Hemingford Grey* and the 17C *Houghton Mill* (NT and Youth Hostels Association).

68m. *Godmanchester* was a Roman settlement on Ermine Street. The large 13C church, built mainly of cobbles, has a 17C stone tower, a 13C mass dial and good 15C misericords. The medieval Causeway has excellent houses and there is a Chinese Bridge (1827) leading to islands in the river. Island Hall (limited opening) is an 18C house. The 14C *bridge over the Great Ouse was built from both banks at once (reputedly without consultation), which accounts for the misalignment in the centre. **Huntingdon** (17,500 inhab. with Godmanchester; Tourist Information), on the N bank, is the former county town of Huntingdonshire and the birthplace of Oliver Cromwell (1599–1658). The *Cromwell Museum*, in the former grammar school which he and Samuel Pepys (1633–1703) attended, incorporates the W end of a 12C Hospital of St John. To the NW the High St. passes *Cromwell House*, incorporating the house in which Cromwell was born. In the other direction the street leads past the house where William Cowper lived with the Unwins in 1765–67 to *St Mary*, with a Perp. tower rebuilt in 1620.

George St. leads SW past the station to *Hinchingbrooke House* (now a school but sometimes open). Originally an Augustinian nunnery, it was turned into a dwelling after the Reformation by Cromwell's ancestors and expanded again in the late 17C. Its charm survived 19C restoration by Blore. Near the roundabout at *Brampton*, 1m beyond, is the family home of Samuel Pepys (open by written appointment).

*Ramsey* (11800 inhab.), 11m NE of Huntingdon, has a partly Norman church and the ruined late 14C gatehouse (NT) of an important Benedictine abbey founded in 969. The 13C Lady Chapel is now incorporated in the Grammar School.

From Huntingdon to *Thrapston*, see Rte 47B; to *Ely* via *Sutton*, see Rte 70B.

A14 leads NW from Huntingdon past the *Stukeley* villages with their airfield to join A1 at 76m. See Rte 47A for the stretch of road from here to (83m) *Norman Cross*, where we branch right on A15.—84m. *Yaxley*, a pretty village with timbered buildings and brick and tile cottages, has a church with a tall Perp. steeple, medieval wall paintings and a 15C chancel screen.—87m. *Fletton*, famous for the pale bricks made here since the 1880s, is an untidy suburb. Its church has excellent Saxon *carving, perhaps from the monastery at Peterborough.

88m. **PETERBOROUGH**, an ancient city known to the Saxons as *Medeshamstede*, grew up round a great monastery founded c 650 and has been a bishop's see since the Reformation. William Paley, of the 'Evidences', was born here. The city owed its 19C development to railway workshops and Fletton bricks, and is now undergoing 'planned expansion' which has dramatically changed its character and raised its population to 125,500. The figure is intended to reach 150,000.

**Tourist Information Centres**: Town Hall, Bridge St.; Central Library, Broadway.

**Car Parks**: Horse Fair Meadow, Pleasure Fair Meadow, Rivergate, Bishop's Rd, etc. Multi-storey car parks in Queensgate and Northminster.

**Bus Station**: Queensgate.

**Railway Station**: Bourges Boulevard.

**Theatre**: Key Theatre, Embankment Rd.

**Annual Event**: East of England Show (agricultural) in July.

Bridge St. leads from the Nene Bridge (1933) to the market place, passing the *Town Hall* (1929–33; Berry Webber). In Priestgate, opposite, are some good Georgian houses and a *Museum* interesting for its Roman remains, objects found in Whittlesey Mere and *model ships carved in bone by French prisoners at Norman Cross (see above and Rte 47A). From the market place, with 17C *Guildhall*, Cowgate leads W past the Perp. church of *St. John Baptist* (1401–07). In Queensgate, N of Cowgate, is the modern shopping centre (1982).

On the other side of the square the *Western Foregate* (late 12C but much altered) leads into the *Minster Close*, in front of the W façade of the cathedral. The 13C *King's Lodging*, to the right, is now a bookshop. To the left, the chancel of the late Dec. *Becket Chapel* (c 1370) is now the song-school. On the right (S) of the close is the *Abbot's Gateway* (c 1302), leading to the *Bishop's Palace*. The figures are probably Edward I, Abbot Godfrey of Croyland, and his prior. *Abbot Kirkton's Gateway* (1515), to the left, led to the Abbot's Park.

The ***Cathedral** belongs to the splendid series of Fenland

New Building

6

Altar

4        5

3

Pulpit   Throne

St Oswald Chapel

St Benedict Chapel

St Kyneburgha &
St Kyneswitha Chapel

Site of
Lady Chapel
destroyed 1651

Site of Saxon Church

Sacristy

Site of Chapter House

Well
CLOISTER

Site of Refectory

Washing Bays

Nave Pulpit

Lectern

2

Font

1

St Sprite
Chapel

Bishop's
Palace

Trinity Chapel (now Treasury & Library over Porch)

Key to Numbers

1  Portrait of Old Scarlett
2  Edith Cavell
3  Abbot Benedict
4  Burial Place of Catherine of Aragon
5  Burial Place of Mary Queen of Scots (up to 1612)
6  Hedda Stone

# PETERBOROUGH CATHEDRAL

0                    100 feet
0                    30 metres

monasteries, originally Saxon in their foundation and rebuilt after the Conquest. It is one of the most important Norman buildings in England.

Founded by Peada, sub-king of Mercia (d. 656), the first monastery and its church were sacked by the Danes in 870 but rebuilt in the 10C. This second church was burned down in 1116. The present building was begun the following year and substantially completed by 1199. All this Norman work survives except for the central tower, replaced in the 14C and again replaced by J.L. Pearson's tentative imitation of the original in 1884–86. Indeed, apart from its rough handling by Cromwell's troops, Peterborough has been unusually lucky in its later history and preserves a remarkably complete Norman church.

The visitor will first be struck by the grand exception, the W façade. Really a vast porch of three tall bays masking the original front, it was built c 1200–10; confusion was added to the richness of its effect by the central entrance porch, late 14C and Perp. in style. The *Nave recalls us to the forthright simplicity of the original conception, emphasised by the lack of monuments or stained glass and the uninterrupted view to the rounded apse at the E end. The painted wooden ceiling, dating from c 1220 (repainted c 1750 and 1834), is a unique survival. To the N of the W door is an 18C copy of a naive portrait of 'Old Scarlett' (d. 1594), who 'interd two queenes within this place' (see below). On the sixth pier in the S nave a tablet remembers Nurse Edith Cavell, who went to school in Peterborough.

In the wall of the S Transept is the tombstone of two Saxon bishops, discovered in the foundations of the early Saxon church, which can be seen beneath. The timber ceilings of both transepts (restored) are the original Norman ones.

The *Sanctuary is the oldest part of the church, though its wooden roof is Perp. except over the apse, where the original flat roof (painted in 1834) was kept. The apse stands in the so-called 'New Building'—a square-ended retrochoir added to the E end in the late 15C. Its intricate fan vaulting makes a striking contrast to the plain ceilings elsewhere in the cathedral. In the N choir aisle is the tomb of Abbot Benedict (d. 1192), who built the nave; further E is a memorial stone to Queen Catherine of Aragon (d. 1536), whose tomb was demolished by the Puritans. Behind the altar and seen from the retrochoir is the *Hedda Stone; traditionally said to be a memorial for the monks slaughtered by the Danes in 870, it may date from a century earlier. The effigies of 12–13C abbots, brought from the ruined chapter house, are claimed as the finest Benedictine memorials in England. In the S choir aisle a slab marks the supposed burial place of Mary, Queen of Scots (executed at Fotheringhay in 1587), moved to Westminster Abbey in 1612.

The ruined Cloister, S of the cathedral, has 14C washing bays on its S side. From the SE corner a passage (once vaulted) with a blind arcade leads to the two fine EE arcades of the Infirmary, now incorporated in more recent buildings.

Thorpe Hall (occasionally open), a handsome mid 17C house 1m W of Peterborough, has been acquired by the city for use as a cultural and leisure centre. The panelling from one of its rooms has been reconstructed at Leeds Castle in Kent. Longthorpe Tower, 1m beyond, has a remarkable series of early 14C domestic *murals (English Heritage, standard opening but closed on Mondays and on Tuesday mornings). Castor, 2½m further W, has a beautiful Norman *church dedicated to St Kyneburga, daughter of King Peada. It has a richly decorated central tower and a wall painting of St Catherine.

Excursions from Peterborough can also be made E and N into the Fens. Whittlesey, 5m E via A605, is an old town with fine 15C church tower and spire. Thorney, 6½m NE via A47, was the site of a Benedictine abbey founded in 972. The abbey church (1108) is now the parish church and the cloister has become a village green surrounded by houses built from monastic stone. Crowland, see Rte 71A.

From Peterborough to Lincoln and the Humber, see Rte 72.

# 69  Cambridge

**CAMBRIDGE** (101,200 inhab.) is famous as the seat of one of the great English universities. It lies, nowhere more than 50ft above sea level, on the southern edge of the Fens—'a low dirty unpleasant place', wrote the diarist John Evelyn scornfully. The disadvantages of its natural setting, more apparent to a graduate of Oxford than to the disinterested visitor, are offset by the handsome buildings of the colleges. Cambridge is distinguished not just for individual triumphs like King's College Chapel but for its array of the best in English architecture from the late medieval period through the ages of Wren and of Gibbs up to the present day. The college gardens, public commons and avenues of stately trees all increase the beauty of the effect, particularly on the Backs, where the river Cam makes its way behind several of the older colleges.

Though often crowded, and not just during the summer, Cambridge has always attracted fewer tourists than Oxford. Several days are needed to get to know the city properly. Even the most cursory inspection should include King's, St John's, Trinity, Queens' and Jesus Colleges, the Round Church and the Fitzwilliam Museum. The series of walks from the centre suggested below take in all the chief points of interest; the tours of the outskirts that follow are for the more leisurely visitor.

**Tourist Information Centre**: Wheeler St.

**Car Parks**: Corn Exchange St. (entered from Downing St.), Park St., Parker's Piece (Gonville Place), Grafton Centre.

**Bus Station**: Drummer St.

**Railway Station**: 1¼m SE of the city centre (buses·from St Andrew's St.).

**Theatres**: Arts Theatre, Peas Hill; ADC, Park St. Plays are often staged in the colleges, especially during May Week.

**Annual Events**: May Week (actually about 10 days in June), with college balls, plays, concerts and the May 'Bumps' (boat races on the lower river). The Lent 'Bumps' take place in late February. The Cambridge Festival is held in late July, with music, exhibits, plays, feasts etc. Festival of Nine Lessons and Carols in King's College Chapel on Christmas Eve.

**Access to colleges**: In recent years the pressure of tourism has made the colleges adopt more stringent policies about opening to the public. Most of the older, river colleges now restrict access or close altogether during the Lent Term (mid April to the last week of June) and particularly during its examination period (mid May to late June). Precise details, which vary from college to college and year to year, are available from the Tourist Information Centre. Otherwise, the main courts, gardens and chapels are usually open, though King's College Chapel is sometimes closed for rehearsals and recording sessions. Halls are normally closed to the public. Visitors may not enter staircases and working libraries, or walk on the lawns, traditionally sacred to the feet of Fellows.

**History**. Excavations in the Castle Hill area, N of the present centre, have revealed Belgic settlements pre-dating the arrival of the Romans and the establishment of a Roman camp here. Soon after the Conquest the Normans built a castle, a market centre grew up S of the river and the annual trading fair on Stourbridge Common became famous. Their significance was soon eclipsed by that of the University, which probably first developed around the religious establishments of the 12C and was recognised as an important seat of learning in a writ of Henry III (1231). Friction between Town and Gown culminated in the riot of 1381, when the townsmen sacked several colleges and destroyed many documents. Cambridge achieved a European reputation with the advent of Erasmus in 1510. Its wealth and well-being were increased rather than lessened by the great religious change of the 16C; it lost little during the Civil War except the plate melted down for the war chest of Charles I.

Even after the coming of the railway in 1845 Cambridge never grew into an industrial centre as Oxford did, but kept its character as a Fen market town. Of late the city (as it formally became in 1951) has expanded to absorb many surrounding villages, and has gained a reputation for the pioneering computer businesses which flourish in proximity to the research activities of the University.

Early names for the river were the Rhee and, more frequently, the Granta (now usually applied to the two branches above Cambridge). This gave the forms Grantebrycge (Grantabridge) and later Cantebrigge, eventually softened into Cambridge. The present name of the river Cam was thus derived from the town, not the other way about.

**Famous natives**. The cricketer Sir Jack Hobbs (1882–1963). The literary critics E.M.W. Tillyard (1889–1962) and F.R. Leavis (1895–1978) were both born in Cambridge as well as pursuing their careers at the University.

**The University**: The Oxbridge system is described under the entry for Oxford (Rte 37). Cambridge has 25 colleges, the oldest being Peterhouse (1281–84) and the newest being Robinson, which received its first students in 1979. Together they educate over 9000 undergraduates. The smallest colleges are Peterhouse and Corpus Christi, with just over 200 students each, while Trinity, with over 600 undergraduates, is the largest in Cambridge or Oxford. All the colleges originally founded for men now admit women, Magdalene being the last to make the change (1987); of the colleges founded for women only Girton is co-residential. Not incorporated with the University are six foundations for postgraduates (Hughes Hall, Darwin College, St Edmund's College, Wolfson College, Lucy Cavendish College and Clare Hall) and four theological colleges (Westminster College, Ridley Hall, Westcott House and Wesley House).

The centre of the city is *Market Hill*, in fact a square rather than a hill, where a lively open market is still held. The *Guildhall* of 1936–37 fills its S side.

From the SE corner lead Guildhall St. (with a sculpture by Michael Ayrton, the curiously named Petty Cury (perhaps 'petite curye' or 'little cookery') and Lion Yard—all once a pleasant network of sidestreets but now a covered shopping precinct. In Peas Hill, at the SW corner of the Guildhall, is the 12C and 14C church of *St Edward King and Martyr*, where Latimer preached the Reformation. It is entered from St Edward's Passage, which has some good old houses. The nave has fine slender piers; the chancel was enlarged after 1446 to make chapels for Clare College and Trinity Hall. Peas Hill ends at the *Arts Theatre*, built and presented to Cambridge by the economist John Maynard Keynes (d. 1946). In Wheeler St., opposite, are the Tourist Information Centre and the 19C *Corn Exchange*, recently restored as a concert hall.

On the W side of Market Hill is **St Mary the Great** (Great St Mary's), the University church as well as the main parish church of Cambridge. Although a church has stood here since at least the 12C, the present building dates mainly from 1478 and 1608, which saw completion of the tower (good view from the top). The nave has tall, elegant arches, a Tudor roof and fine galleries (1735). The organ, by 'Father' Smith was brought with its case from St James's, Piccadilly, in 1697. Opposite the tower end of the church is \***Senate House**, scene of the degree ceremonies and other public functions of the University. A masterly blend of Baroque ornament and Palladian restraint, it was built in 1722–30, the only part of James Gibbs's plan for a forum of University buildings to be realised. The interior (open only for special exhibitions and events) has a plaster ceiling by Artari and Bagutti, woodwork by the two James Essexes, father and son, and statues of the Duke of Somerset (by Rysbrack) and Pitt (by Nollekens). The Senate House makes an admirable foil to the heavier outline of the former **Old Schools** (i.e. lecture rooms) and the old court of King's College, now housing University offices. Its main E façade, facing the green and King's Parade, was finished by

# CAMBRIDGE

0        400 yards
0        400 metres

N

Girton College & HUNTINGDON

Fitzwilliam College

New Hall

St Edmund's College

Lucy Cavendish College

Westminster College

HUNTINGDON ROAD

VICTORIA ROAD

ST PETER'S STREET

POUND HILL

NORTHA

Observatory & ST NEOTS

Sports Ground

Churchill College

STOREY'S WAY

MADINGLEY ROAD

ROAD

Sports Ground

CLARKSON ROAD

Sports Ground

WILBERFORCE ROAD

GRANGE

ROAD

Sports Ground

ADAMS ROAD

Fellows Garden

BURRELL'S WALK

GARRE

University Library

Clare College

Robinson College

HERSCHEL ROAD

Clare Hall

Fellows' Garden

King's College Choir School

King's Hostel

QUEEN'S

CRANMER ROAD

WEST ROAD

Harvey Court

Selwyn College

University Arts Buildings

SIDGWICK AVENUE

SELWYN GDNS

GRANGE ROAD

Newnham College

Ridley Hall

NEWNHAM WALK

MALT

Wolfson College

Sports Ground

SOMMERFIELD

CLARE RD

NEWNHAM

Sports Ground

BARTON

Recreation Ground

ROAD

GRANTCHESTER

Stephen Wright in 1758 but the courts behind date from c 1350–1473. The N side (1837–40; C.R. Cockerell) houses the law library.

SOUTH FROM MARKET HILL. King's Parade, the wide street that is the heart of visitors' Cambridge, begins immediately S of the Senate House and its adjoining buildings, its lefthand side a pleasant medley of shops and domestic architecture. On the right is **King's College** (340 undergraduates), founded on the Old Schools site by Henry VI in 1441 as 'The King's College of Our Lady and St Nicholas' and re-established here four years later, in connection with Eton College.

The street frontage consists of a lodge and stone screen added in 1828 by William Wilkins. On the S side of the *Great Court*, with its fountain, is the *Hall* (also by Wilkins, 1824–28). On the W is the stately *\*Fellows' Building* by Gibbs (1724), with a lovely lawn sloping down to the river beyond; the S side is bounded by the *Library* and *Bodley's Building* (1894, completed 1928) and the N by Clare College. There is a fine view from the bridge (see also The Backs below).

FAMOUS MEMBERS: Christopher Tye, Walsingham, Phineas and Giles Fletcher, Orlando Gibbons, Edmund Waller, Sir Robert and Horace Walpole, Sir William Temple, 'Turnip' Townshend, M.R. James, Roger Fry, E.M. Forster, Maynard Keynes and Rupert Brooke.

On the N side of the Great Court is *\*\*King's College Chapel*, the centrepiece of Henry VI's plan for his foundation and still the crowning glory of Cambridge architecture. Work began in 1446–61 but was not resumed until 1506–15, when the stone fabric was finished under the patronage of Henry VII; the windows and wood-work were added by Henry VIII. The late Perp. style thus makes the transition from the last great era of medieval churchbuilding to the more secular age of the Renaissance. The rectangular plan is bold and simple, allowing for rich ornamentation of the interior, where the Tudor rose and portcullis are much in evidence among the carved emblems. (The rose and crown motif is probably also the Rosary and Corona of Our Lady.) Outstanding features are the 25 *\*stained-glass windows (all 16C except for that by Clayton and Bell at the W end), the wonderfully delicate *\*fan vaulting of the roof, the wooden organ screen (1533–36) and case (1688), and the stalls. The altarpiece is The Adoration of the Magi by Rubens, donated in 1959, which greatly impairs the effect of the lovely E window.

Each of the chantries, opening between the buttresses, contained an altar. The chantry at the SE corner, with Flemish glass of 1530, is a War Memorial Chapel; the one at the NE corner, with a lierne vault, was completed by 1461. The chantries N of the choir now house an exhibition of the building's history.

In Bene't St., opposite the S range of King's, is *St Bene't's* (i.e. Benedict's) *Church*, with a Saxon tower and tower arch. It was the original chapel of Corpus Christi and is connected to the College by a gallery of finely toned red brick. **Corpus Christi College** (220 undergraduates) is now entered from Trumpington St., the southern continuation of King's Parade. It was founded in 1352 by the united religious guilds of Corpus Christi and the Blessed Virgin.

The *\*Old Court*, reached from the NE corner of the first court, is the earliest example in England of a complete medieval academic quadrangle. The *First Court* itself is a neo-Gothic but ruthlessly symmetrical exercise by William Wilkins (1823–27). The *Chapel* has stall-backs of c 1580 from the previous chapel on the site and some 16C German glass. The *Hall*, with a richly painted roof, contains a fine collection of portraits, among them one of 1584 which may depict Christopher Marlowe. The *Old Library* has a priceless manuscript collection bequeathed by Matthew Parker, Master in 1554 and later Archbishop of Canterbury.

FAMOUS MEMBERS: Matthew Parker, Sir Nicholas Bacon, Christopher Marlowe, John Fletcher, John Cowper Powys, Sir George Thomson, Christopher Isherwood.

S of Corpus Christi is *St Botolph's Church*, its dedication to the patron saint of travellers indicating that the S gate of the city, the Trumpington Gate, once stood nearby. The heavily restored 14–15C building contains a 15C painted rood screen, a handsome 17C font case and cover, and a curious monument to Dr Thomas Plaifer (d. 1609).

On the opposite side of the road a modern development by Fello Atkinson spans King's Lane and discreetly links the S end of King's with the façade of the former Bull Hotel, now part of **St Catharine's College** (380 undergraduates). The College was founded in 1473 by Robert Wodelarke, Provost of King's, but rebuilt in 1674–1757 by Robert Grumbold and James Essex, and extended in 1932–51. Its three-sided front court, of mellow brick, is separated from Trumpington St. only by iron railings (1779).

FAMOUS MEMBERS: Archbishop Sandys, Bishop Lightfoot, James Shirley, Benjamin Hoadly, J.B. Dykes (author of the hymn 'For Those in Peril'), Malcolm Lowry, Sir Peter Hall, Ian McKellen, Howard Brenton.

Behind St Catharine's, reached by King's Lane and Queens' Lane, is **'Queens' College** (430 undergraduates). The plural form in its name indicates the several stages of its foundation, first by Andrew Dokett in 1446, then again two years later under the patronage of Margaret of Anjou (whose husband, Henry VI, had just founded King's College) and finally in 1465 by Elizabeth Woodville, wife of Edward IV. Although modest in scale and ambition, the architecture of Queens' is perhaps the most picturesque of all Cambridge colleges.

The magnificent *'Gatehouse* leads into the 15C red-brick Old Court. To the right are the *Old Chapel*, with a sundial on its wall, and the *Library*, with Jacobean bookcases; straight ahead is the *Hall*, remodelled by James Essex in 1732–34 and restored by G.F. Bodley in 1862–75. Beyond lies the charming *'Cloister Court*. On its N side, to the right, is the half-timbered *'President's Lodge* (c 1595) with a beautiful panelled gallery of c 1604. The famous *Mathematical Bridge*, built in the 18C and reconstructed several times since, leads across the Cam to *Fisher Court* (1936), *Cripps Court* (1972–74; Powell and Moya) and the riverside scenery of The Grove. In the small *Pump Court*, left of the Cloister Court, is the *Erasmus Tower*, above the rooms occupied by Erasmus when he taught Greek here in 1510–13. A passage from the corner of the President's Lodge leads into *Walnut Tree Court* (1617–19) and *Friars Court*, with the large *Chapel* (1890–91; Bodley) between them. Almost opposite the Chapel is the *Erasmus Building* (1959–61; Basil Spence).

FAMOUS MEMBERS: Erasmus, St John Fisher, Sir Thomas Smith, Thomas Fuller (who moved to Sidney), Isaac Milner, Osborne Reynolds, Charles Stanford, T.H. White, Gilbert Harding.

Queens' is bounded to the S by Silver St., from which the little Laundress Lane leads left to the waterside at the end of Mill Lane. The mill pool and weir mark the division between the upper and lower river, which here changes its name to the Granta. Punts can be taken along the Backs or up to Grantchester (see below). The bulk of the *University Centre* (1964; Howell, Killick, Partridge and Amis), usually known as the Graduate Centre, does not improve the scenery on the nearside bank.

For the continuation of Silver St., see Western Outskirts below.

We now return along Silver St. to Trumpington St. and continue S. On the right is the *Pitt Building* of the University Press, a conspicuous

Tudor Revival building (1831–33; Blore) erected from the surplus of funds collected for a statue of Pitt in London. The new buildings of the Press flank the railway line to London.

On the opposite side of the road stands **Pembroke College** (340 undergraduates), founded by the Countess of Pembroke in 1347 but largely modernised or rebuilt.

The *Chapel* (1663–65) was Wren's first major work and the first major classical building of its century in Cambridge. It has a fine plaster ceiling and woodwork, and the serenity of its proportions were only a little altered by the lengthening of the E end in 1880. The *Old Library* on the lefthand side of the first court was originally the first college chapel in Cambridge (1366). *Ivy Court* (c 1614–59) was restored in 1964; to the SE is *New Court* (1882) and *Orchard Building* (1957). The fine *Gardens* contain a statue of Pitt.

FAMOUS MEMBERS. Pembroke has produced many bishops (Ridley, Grindal, Whitgift, Andrewes, etc.) and poets: Spenser, Crashaw, Gray (see Peterhouse for the story of his migration to Pembroke), Mason and Ted Hughes. Pitt the Younger, Sumner Maine, Sir G.G. Stokes, H.S. Guggenheim and Peter Cook were also Pembroke men.

On the right of Trumpington St. is the church of *St Mary the Less* (Little St Mary's), 14C and keeping its exquisitely flowing Dec. tracery despite later alterations. It served as the chapel of adjoining Peterhouse from its foundation until 1632, and the backs of the College's buildings are well seen from the pleasantly overgrown churchyard. **Peterhouse** (210 undergraduates) is the oldest college in Cambridge, founded by Hugh of Balsham, Bishop of Ely, in 1281. It is properly styled 'St Peter's College' and is never called 'Peterhouse College'.

In the first court is the *Chapel*, an attractive example of Laudian Gothic (1628–32), connected with the main buildings by galleries (1709–11). The E window has its original glass and in the reredos is a 15C Pietà of wood. On the right is the dignified *Fellows' Building* by Burrough (1738–42). On the left are the *Old Library* (c 1590, extended in 1633) and the *Hall*, much altered but still substantially the original building of c 1290. The Hall contains portraits, and stained glass by Morris, Burne-Jones, and Madox Brown, who also designed the windows of the *Combination Room* (1460). Beyond the Hall a path leads to the *Garden*. At the back of the second or *Gisborne Court* (1825) is *Fen Court* (1939; Hughes and Bicknell) and, to the N, the new *Library* in the former Museum of Classical Archaeology (1884). The *Master's Lodge*, a handsome Queen Anne house of 1702, stands on the other side of Trumpington St.

FAMOUS MEMBERS. Cardinal Beaufort, Thomas Campion, Crashaw, Gray, Henry Cavendish, Charles Babbage, Clerk Maxwell, Lord Kelvin, James Mason, Gray's rooms in the Fellows' Building, overlooking Little St Mary's, may be identified by the iron bars the poet installed to support a rope ladder in case of fire. Roused by a false alarm, he left Peterhouse in annoyance at the practical joke and became a member of Pembroke.

Just beyond Peterhouse is the **Fitzwilliam Museum**, a massive classical building designed by George Basevi and C.R. Cockerell (1837–47) for the valuable collections Viscount Fitzwilliam left to the University in 1816. The original building was finished in 1875 by E.M. Barry, who designed the entrance hall; since 1924 the Marlay Galleries, on the S side, and further extensions in 1966 and 1975 have been added to house later bequests. The upper galleries (open Tuesday to Sunday afternoons) contain major collections of European paintings, strongly representative of most periods and schools. The pictures are handsomely displayed among sculpture, furniture, ceramics, etc. of the appropriate periods. The lower galleries (open Tuesday to Saturday mornings and Sunday afternoons) contain West Asiatic, Egyptian, Greek and Roman antiquities; Islamic and Far

Eastern art; European ceramics and other applied arts; literary and musical manuscripts; armour; and a medieval collection.

**Lower Floor**

Butler Reading Room (Students only)

Music MS

Lobby Museum Shop

Mellon Rare Books

A. de Rothschild Manuscripts

Small Henderson Glass & Pewter

Armour

Textiles Korean Wares

Oriental

Glaisher European Pottery

Chinese

Near Eastern

Study Room

Lower Marlay European Porcelain & Manuscripts

Coins & Medals

Silver

Founder's Library (not normally open)

Roman

West Asiatic

W.C.

Greek

Egyptian

Entrance

**Upper Floor**

Hamilton Kerr

Adeane Special Exhibitions

20th Century Painting & Sculpture

Charrington Print Room

Dutch Painting

Octagon

Students' Room & Offices

Courtauld Galleries Later Italian Paintings & Majolica

Flemish & Spanish

Broughton Flower Paintings

Upper Marlay Early Italian Paintings & Majorca

Graham Robertson Room

French Painting & Sculpture Mid 17C-20C

V

IV

16C-19C British Paintings & Paintings of Englishmen in Italy

III

I

British School

II

Sculpture Furniture

19C-20C Paintings

# FITZWILLIAM MUSEUM

UPPER GALLERIES. From the entrance hall the staircase leads to the large *Room III*, devoted to English works. They include: portraits by Hans Eworth (•Mary Tudor), Van Dyck (Archbishop Laud), Lely, Hogarth, Allan Ramsay, Romney, Reynolds, Gainsborough (John Kirby, Mrs John Kirby), Wright of Derby (Viscount Fitzwilliam, aged 19), Stubbs (Self Portrait), Raeburn, Batoni and Carlo Dolci; genre scenes by Highmore and Hogarth; landscapes by Richard Wilson and Gainsborough; sporting paintings by Wootton and Stubbs (Gimcrack). The bust of William Pitt is by Nollekens, and the clock beside the door is by Thomas Tompion (c 1700). The gallery above contains paintings from the reserve collection.

*Room II*, to the right, has 19–20C English works by Madox Brown (version of Last of England), Millais, Rossetti, Holman Hunt, Edward Lear (View of the Temple of Apollo at Bassae in Arcadia), G.F. Watts, Etty, George Richmond,

Augustus John (Thomas Hardy, George Bernard Shaw), Sargent, Whistler; also landscapes by Constable (Hampstead Heath, Hove Beach, Salisbury), Turner, John Martin, Inchbold, Bonington, James Stark, Joseph Stannard, John Brett and John Linnell. There are bronzes by Ricketts and furniture by Morris and Co. *Room I* has 20C French and English paintings by Vuillard, Spencer Gore, Gilman, Bonnard, Braque (Reclining Nude, Cubist Still Life), Picasso, Matisse, Paul Nash, Sir William Nicholson, Stanley Spencer (Self Portrait) and Sickert; also furniture by Hans Poelzig and bronzes by Epstein.

In *Room IV*, beyond Room III, are the French schools, with works by Delacroix (Odalisque, The Bride of Abydos), Géricault (Wounded Soldiers in a Cart), Corot (La Châtaigneraie, The Dyke), Fantin-Latour, Courbet, Decamps, Fabre, Vouet, Poussin, Lebrun and Oudry; also a statuette of Voltaire by J.A. Houdon. French painting continues in *Room V* with examples of Boudin, Degas (David and Goliath, Danseuses aux Jupes Violettes, Au Café), Renoir (*Place Clichy, Le Retour des Champs, Le Coup de Vent), Monet (The Cliffs at Etretat, Port-Coton, Les Peupliers, Le Printemps), Signac, Seurat, Cézanne (The Under-growth, Landscape, Head of Uncle Dominique), Gauguin, Pissarro and Sisley; also bronzes by Degas, Rodin and Medardo Rosso.

Room IV leads to the *Upper Marlay Gallery* (Room VI), devoted to Italian paintings, with particularly fine works by masters of the 13–15C Florentine, Sienese and North Italian schools. They include: Simone Martini (*St Geminianus, St Michael and St Augustine), Lorenzo Monaco, Filippo Lippi (Virgin and Child), the Master of the Castello Nativity, Giovanni del Ponte, Domenico Veneziano, Francesco Botticini, Ghirlandaio, Cosimo Tura, Crivelli (Virgin and Child), Cima (St Lanfranc of Pavia) and Pintoricchio. There is also an important group of cassone panels. The *Courtauld Gallery* (Room VII) continues the Italian schools, with Renaissance and Baroque works by Ludovico Carracci, Sassoferrato, Zuccaro, Annibale Carracci, Titian (*Tarquin and Lucretia, *Venus and Cupid), Tintoretto (Adoration of the Shepherds), Salvator Rosa, Francesco Guardi, Canaletto, Pittoni, Guido Reni (Ecce Homo), Maratti, Jacopo Bassano, Veronese (*Hermes, Herse and Aglauros) and Palma Vecchio.

To the right of the Courtauld Gallery is the *Flemish and Spanish Gallery* (Room VIII), with works by Pieter Brueghel the Younger (Village Fete), Murillo and Van Dyck, and *oil sketches by Rubens. The *Graham Robertson Room* and the little *Octagon*, both adjoining, are used for temporary exhibitions.

The room to the left of the Courtauld Gallery, at the head of the staircase, displays the Broughton Collection of flower paintings, as well as terracotta busts by Rysbrack, Roubiliac, and Bushnell. *Room XI*, beyond, has Dutch paintings by Ruisdael, Jan Steen, Wouwermans, Franz Hals, Hobbema (*Wooded Landscape), Cuyp and Van Ostade. From it leads the *Print Room*, which usually houses temporary exhibitions, and the *Hamilton-Kerr Room*, with prints and engravings. The *Adeane Gallery* is used for temporary exhibitions and the *20C Gallery* beyond displays paintings by Léger, Picasso, Rouault, Ben Nicholson, Graham Sutherland and Peter Blake, with sculptures by Henry Moore and Barbara Hepworth.

LOWER GALLERIES. At the foot of the stairs is the small *West Asiatic Gallery*, with superb Assyrian reliefs (9–7C BC). The *Egyptian Collection* is to the right. Room I has exhibits from the pre-Dynastic period to the Coptic period, including the shrine of the goddess Nekhbet, a granite head of Sesostris III (King of Egypt, 1878–1843 BC) and the superb portrait of Ammenemes III (King of Egypt, 1842–1797 BC). Room II contains the *Gayer-Anderson Collection, the coffin of Nekhtefmut (early 9C BC), Roman mummy-portraits, and the huge *sarcophagus lid of Ramesses III (King of Egypt, 1198–1166 BC). The *Greek Room* has representative examples of pottery, seals, bronze and terracotta statuettes, sculpture including the fine Attic gravestones of Theokles and Hegemon, and a colossal caryatid head from the Inner Propylaea at Eleusis (1C BC). Among the exhibits in the *Etruscan and Roman Room* are: the Pashley sarcophagus; a head of Antinöus (AD 110–130); a child's sarcophagus (early 2C AD); a mosaic fountain niche from Baiae (c AD 50); the *cinerarium of Aelia Postumia (AD 25–50); and exquisite *seals and engraved gems. The *Lower Marlay Gallery* contains fine porcelain, silver and watches, together with literary autographs (including Keats's 'Ode to a Nightingale') and musical manuscripts (among them the Fitzwilliam Virginal Book and works by Handel). At the end is the *Glaisher Gallery* with European stoneware and earthenware. Beyond are the *Chinese Collection* of ceramics and jade, and the *Gompertz Collection* of Korean ceramics. An adjoining room displays textiles and costumes. Returning through the Glaisher Gallery we come to the *Islamic Collection* and, beyond, the fine *Henderson Collection* of armour. The adjoining small room has European glass and pewter. The *Rothschild Gallery* contains a miscellaneous but highly interesting medieval collection: ivories and enamels; church plate; an exquisite capital (c 1150) from Avignon; a head of Mary Magdalen in wood (late 15C Italian); and illuminated manuscripts, notably the Breton Gospel Book (9–10C), the Grey-Fitzpayn Book of Hours (c 1300) and the *Metz Pontifical, produced for a Bishop of Metz at the beginning of the 14C, the most sumptuous French liturgical manuscript of its date.

Opposite the museum is a building of 1737, formerly occupied by Fitzwilliam House (now in Huntingdon Rd; see Northern Outskirts below).

Trumpington St. ends at *Hobson's Conduit*, moved here in 1856 from its original site in Market Hill, where it had been erected in 1616, partly at the expense of Thomas Hobson (d. 1631).

A 'carrier between Cambridge and London, and a great benefactor to this University and town', Hobson is the subject of two short poems by Milton. The phrase 'Hobson's choice' embalms his rule of letting out his horses for hire in strict rotation.

In Lensfield Rd, to the left, is the *Scott Polar Research Institute and Museum*, with letters, diaries and photographs from Captain Scott's journey to the South Pole among its exhibits. The Fen Causeway leads right, to the *Engineering Laboratories* and the bleak, low-lying Coe Fen. For Trumpington Rd, to the S, see South-Western Outskirts below.

NORTH FROM MARKET HILL. Immediately N of the Senate House is **Gonville and Caius College** (440 undergraduates), shortened to 'Caius' and pronounced 'Keys'. It was founded by Edmund Gonville in 1348 and refounded by Dr Caius in 1557.

The S side of *Tree Court* (1868–70; Alfred Waterhouse) towers inappropriately over the group formed by the Senate House and Great St Mary's. It is entered from Trinity St. On its opposite side the *Gate of Virtue*, part of the symbolic 'academic path' devised by Dr Caius, leads into *Caius Court* (1565–67). On the left is the *Gate of Honour* (1575), a charmingly eclectic little gateway leading into Senate House Passage. On the right of the court is the *Chapel* (1375, modernised in 1718), with monuments to Dr Caius (d. 1573), Dr Legge (d. 1607) and Dr Perse (d. 1615). A passage by the chapel connects Caius Court with *Gonville Court*, built in the 15C and refaced in 1753. To the left is the *Hall*, rebuilt by Anthony Salvin in 1853.

Second- and third-year students at Caius are still known as 'Junior' and 'Senior Sophs' (i.e. 'Sophisters'), an old Cambridge term that has been adopted in American universities as 'sophomores'. The undergraduates wear distinctive blue gowns with black facings.

FAMOUS MEMBERS: Thomas Gresham, William Harvey, Jeremy Taylor, William Wilkins, J.R. Seeley, Sir Charles Sherrington, James Elroy Flecker, David Frost.

The narrow, usually crowded Trinity St. continues N. Among the medley of buildings on its righthand side, facing the frontage of Caius, is the small 14C church of *St Michael*, now converted into a meeting room.

*Trinity College** is the largest college in either Cambridge or Oxford (640 undergraduates), as well as one of the most handsome. It was established by Henry VIII in 1546, replacing the earlier foundations of King's Hall (1317) and Michaelhouse (1324).

The turreted brick *Great Gatehouse* (1490–1535) belonged to King's Hall. It bears the name of Edward III and the royal coat of arms; the statue of Henry VIII on the street side and the statues of James I, Anne of Denmark and their son, the future Charles I, were added in 1615. The spacious *Great Court* was created from the jumble of buildings belonging to the two earlier foundations by Thomas Nevile, Master from 1593 to 1615, who also placed the fountain in the centre. On the S side (left) is the *Queen's Gate* (1597), with a statue of Elizabeth I. On the N side stands the *Chapel*, completed in 1561, with good 18C woodwork. In the *Ante-Chapel* are statues of *Newton

*The Gate of Honour at Caius College, Cambridge*

(by Roubiliac), Bacon (by Weekes), Barrow (by Noble), Macaulay and Whewell (by Woolner) and Tennyson (by Thornycroft). W of the Chapel are *King Edward III's Tower* (1428–32), a gatehouse of King's Hall rebuilt in this position by Nevile, and the quaint little *King's Hostel*. The W side is dominated by the *Hall*, built by Nevile in the Perp. style; its portraits include one by Reynolds of the Duke of Gloucester, aged six.

The screens passage leads past the Hall into *Nevile's Court*, built c 1605–12 but extended to join Wren's *Library* of 1676–95, which fills the entire W side of the court. Wren placed the library itself on an upper floor and left an open arcade at ground level—an elegant and practical solution to the problem of storing books in the damp atmosphere by the river. On the balustrade are statues (by Cibber) representing Divinity, Law, Physics and Mathematics. The interior has few rivals among English libraries, with limewood bookcases by Grinling Gibbons and busts of Newton, Bacon (both by Roubiliac) and Tennyson (by Woolner). The statue of Byron by Thorvaldsen, at the far end, was meant for Westminster Abbey but refused a place there. The display cases contain illuminated manuscripts, autograph writings by Milton, Byron, Tennyson, Thackeray and Housman, and relics of Newton.

S of Nevile's Court is *New Court* (1825; William Wilkins), to the E of which is *Bishop's Hostel*, a separate building of 1678–71. From its W side we enter the beautiful *'College Grounds*, extending across to the Backs (see below). The view from the bridge (1764–68) is charming.

The College buildings extend across Trinity St. with the two *Whewell's Courts* (1860; Salvin) and the *Wolfson Presidential Building* (1971).

FAMOUS MEMBERS: Essex, Francis Bacon, Coke, Herbert, Cowley, Marvell, Dryden, Newton, Judge Jeffreys, Porson, Melbourne, Byron, Macaulay, Kinglake, Tennyson, Arthur Hallam (of 'In Memoriam'), Edward FitzGerald, Thackeray, Galton, Clerk Maxwell, Lord Acton, Balfour, F.W. Maitland, Charles Stanford, Sir James Frazer, A.E. Housman, Baldwin, Rutherford, Rayleigh, Eddington, Jeans, Pandit Nehru, G.E. Moore, Wittgenstein, Clive Bell, Vaughan Williams, Bertrand Russell, A.A. Milne, Vladimir Nabokov, Enoch Powell, Kim Philby, Guy Burgess, Anthony Blunt. Also members of the royal family, including Edward VII, George VI and Prince Charles. Masters of Trinity have included Archbishop Whitgift, Bishop Pearson, Dr Isaac Barrow, Richard Bentley, William Whewell, Montagu Butler, J.J. Thomson, G.M. Trevelyan, Lord Adrian and Lord Butler.

N of Trinity the street changes its name to St John's St. in deference to *'St John's College* (530 undergraduates), second in size among Oxbridge colleges only to its immediate neighbour. It replaced the 13C Hospital of St John and was founded in 1511 by Lady Margaret Beaufort, mother of Henry VII and foundress of Christ's College, with St John Fisher as her executor.

The *'Gatehouse* was built in 1510–16. Recent cleaning and repainting have greatly enhanced its lavish decoration: a statue of St John, the Beaufort 'yales' supporting the royal arms, Tudor rose and portcullis, forget-me-nots punning on the Beaufort motto ('Souvent me souvient'). The *First Court* was built by St John Fisher, but its S side (left) was rebuilt in 1772 and the large, inappropriate *Chapel* on the N side added by Sir Gilbert Scott in 1864–69. Between the first and second courts is the *'Hall*, with fine panelling, a hammerbeam roof and a portrait of Wordsworth (by Pickersgill). The *'Second Court* (1598–1602; Ralph Symons), built in lovely plum-coloured brick and practically unchanged, justifies Ruskin's praise of it as one of the most perfect in the university. The *'Combination Room* on its N side is one of the finest panelled galleries in England, with a rich plaster ceiling. The *Third Court* was built between 1623 and 1674. The *Old Library*, on its NE side, contains autograph letters, manuscripts and early printed books, including Lady Margaret's Book of Hours (early 15C French) and a vellum copy of Cranmer's Bible (1539).

From this court two bridges cross the river: Robert Grumbold's *Old Bridge* (1696–1712), to the left, and the picturesque *Bridge of Sighs*, connecting with the Gothic *New Court* (1826–31; Rickman and Hutchinson) on the opposite bank. The large and beautiful *College Grounds* make a good approach to the Backs (see below). Beyond New Court is the *Cripps Building* (1966; Powell and Moya), using its position by the river and its inlet to great effect. At its N tip, near the College's back gateway into Northampton St., is the 16C *Merton Hall* (taking its name from the Oxford college which owned it until 1959) and the *School of Pythagoras* (c 1200), one of Cambridge's oldest buildings. Both have been converted to modern use.

Behind the chapel and reached from Second Court is the partly Victorian *Chapel Court*, extended in 1932 by Sir Edward Maufe, who also built *North Court*, facing Bridge St. beyond.

FAMOUS MEMBERS: Sir Thomas Wyatt, Roger Ascham, Lord Burghley, Robert Greene, Thomas Nashe, Strafford, Lord Falkland, Fairfax, Herrick (who moved to Trinity Hall), Matthew Prior, Sir John Herschel, Charles Churchill, Erasmus Darwin, Horne Tooke, Thomas Clarkson, Wilberforce, Wordsworth, Patrick Brontë (father of the novelists), Palmerston, William Barnes, Samuel Butler, Sir Edward Appleton, Sir John Cockcroft, Louis Leakey, Sir C. Aubrey Smith, Cecil Beaton, Jonathan Miller, Derek Jacobi.

Still flanked by the buildings of the College, St John's St. runs N to the junction with Bridge St. and Sidney St. On the Sidney St. corner stands the **'Round Church**, as the Church of the Holy Sepulchre is usually known. Dating from c 1130, it is one of only four medieval round churches to survive in England; the others are at Northampton, Little Maplestead in Essex and the Temple in London. The Norman appearance of its circular part, like the conical roof, is almost entirely due to the ruthless restoration by Salvin and the Cambridge Camden Society (the 'Ecclesiologists') in 1841. The chancel was added in the 15C, also probably the angel roof of the N aisle and choir.

Behind the Round Church are the buildings of the *Cambridge Union Society* (1866; Alfred Waterhouse), founded as a debating club in 1815.

We follow Bridge St. to the N, passing on the right *St Clement's Church*, EE but much altered. Beyond the bridge is **Magdalene College** (pronounced 'Maudlen'; 350 undergraduates), the only one of the older colleges to have its main buildings across the river. It was founded by Lord Audley in 1542, but its history goes back further to the Benedictine hostel established c 1428 by the four great local abbeys of Crowland, Ely, Ramsey and Walden, and later known as Buckingham College (c 1480–1539).

The earlier part of the College stands on the right of Magdalene St., a narrow, crowded thoroughfare with some good medieval buildings. A gateway of 1585 leads to the modest, brick-built *First Court*, which preserves much of the original monastic fabric, especially on the side by the river. The *Chapel*, on the left, still has its 15C timber roof but otherwise bears heavy marks of 19C renovation. The *Hall* was built in 1519, though the elegant interior with a double staircase leading up to the gallery dates from 1714. In the *Second Court* is the *'Pepys Library*, its odd mixture of styles reflecting the sixty years it took to build (c 1640–1700). Since 1742 it has housed the great collection of books left to Magdalene by Samuel Pepys (d. 1702), still kept in their original shelves and their original order. The chief treasure is the cipher manuscript of the famous 'Diary'; among the many other items are both parts of Caxton's manuscript translation of Ovid, the first collected by Pepys and the second donated to the College in 1966. The pleasant *Fellows' Garden* adjoining the library has sculptures by Henry Moore and Gaudier-Brzeska.
  On the opposite side of the road are *Benson Court* (1931–32; Sir Edwin Lutyens and *Mallory Court* (converted to college use in 1925), skilfully brought together in an informal landscape with the addition of new buildings and the conversion of the medieval buildings fronting Magdalene St. (1952–58; David Roberts). *Buckingham Court* (1970), facing the Cripps Building of St John's, is also by Roberts.

FAMOUS MEMBERS: Henry Dunster (first President of Harvard), Pepys, Charles Kingsley, Parnell, A.C. Benson, I. A. Richards, George Leigh Mallory, C.S. Lewis, Sir William Empson, Sir Michael Redgrave.
  For continuations of this route, see Northern, North-Eastern and North-Western Outskirts below.

WEST FROM MARKET HILL. We follow Senate House Passage, between the Senate House and Caius, past the College's Gate of Honour to **Trinity Hall** (300 undergraduates). It was founded in 1350 by William Bateman, Bishop of Norwich, with special provisions for students of law.

The main court is among the oldest in Cambridge, but its 14C buildings were given a new façade in 1730–45 by Sir James Burrough. The *Ante-Chapel* to the left (S) has three 16C brasses. Beyond the *Hall* to the W is the *'Old Library* (c 1600), a lovely brick building with crow-step gables; the chained books inside are of a still earlier date. The charming *Gardens* overlook the river.

FAMOUS MEMBERS: Sir John Paston, Thomas Tusser, Holinshed, Bishop Gardiner, Lord Howard of Effingham, Herrick (who moved from St John's), Lord Chesterfield, Bulwer-Lytton, F.D. Maurice, Sir Leslie Stephen, Ronald Firbank, J.B. Priestley, Donald Maclean.

Trinity Lane leads S from the gateway of the College towards King's College Chapel. On the left it passes the back of the Old Schools and the *Gatehouse* once belonging to King's College, its lower part 15C but its upper part not completed until the 19C. On the right stands **Clare College** (380 undergraduates), founded as University Hall in 1326 and refounded by Lady Elizabeth de Clare in 1338. The elegant simplicity of its architecture and the beauty of its river setting make it one of the most attractive colleges.

The *Chapel* (1763–69; Sir James Burrough and James Essex) is on the right of the lawn leading to the gateway. The main court, rebuilt in 1638–1715 by John Westley and the Grumbold family of local craftsmen, is a wonderfully complete example of its period, its strong and simple unity varied by the small shifts of taste during the years of its building. Its W range opens on to *Clare Bridge* (1640; perhaps by Thomas Grumbold), with a splendidly picturesque *view in virtually every direction. The *Fellows' Garden*, beyond, is among the best in Cambridge. See also The Backs below.

The avenue leads to Queen's Rd and, on the opposite side, Clare's *Memorial Court* (1923–34; Sir Giles Gilbert Scott), with a large War Memorial Arch. The new building in the centre (1986; Sir Philip Dowson), containing the *Library* and other amenities, is designed to harmonise with the blend of monumental and domestic of Scott's original design. In the garden is a bronze Fallen Warrior by Henry Moore.

FAMOUS MEMBERS: Bishop Latimer, Nicholas Ferrar, Lord Cornwallis, Paul Mellon, J.D. Watson.

Behind Memorial Court is the **University Library**, also by Scott (1930–34), with a lofty tower which dominates the prospect for much of the walk from the river, and with an extension added to the rear in 1971. With over 4 million volumes, almost 1 million maps and over 15,000 manuscripts, the library ranks, with the Bodleian, next in order of importance to the British Library in London. Founded in the early 15C and a copyright library since 1709, it includes among its principal treasures: many fine Caxtons, among them his 'Historyes of Troye' (1475–76, the first printed book in English) and the only known perfect copy of his 'Golden Legend' (1483); the Book of Deer (a 10C Gaelic manuscript); and the Codex Bezae of the 6C, one of the five great uncial manuscripts of the Gospels. It also contains the world's largest Charles Darwin archive, the collections of the Bible Society and the library of Sir Geoffrey Keynes. Exhibitions are always on public display in the entrance hall, and there are guided tours of the building each weekday at 15.00.

For Grange Rd, beyond the Library, see Western Outskirts below.

*THE BACKS. This is the familiar name for the tree-shaded grounds on the W bank of the river and, more generally, for the scenery either side of the Cam as it flows past the colleges. The most pleasant tour is by punt, from near the Silver St. bridge in the S or near Magdalene College in the N. A short excursion on foot leaves King's College by its back gateway and follows the path by the side of the Queen's Rd N to the back gateway of Clare College, whose bridge enjoys particularly charming views. The walk may be extended either by continuing up the Queen's Rd to the back gateway of Trinity College, or by entering Trinity College and St John's College through their main gateways.

SOUTH AND EAST FROM MARKET HILL. We follow Petty Cury to St Andrew's St. and head right (S). The church of *St Andrew the Great*, now disused and not usually open, has a monument to Captain Cook (d. 1779) and his family. Opposite is **Christ's College** (360 undergraduates), established in 1505 by Lady Margaret Beaufort, mother of Henry VII and foundress of St John's College, with the assistance of St John Fisher. It replaced God's House, a small college founded by William Byngham in 1436 on the site of King's College Chapel and refounded by Henry VI on the present site in 1448.

The *Gatehouse* is decorated with Beaufort insignia in even richer profusion than the gatehouse of St John's. The pleasantly irregular *First Court*, also built in 1505, was refaced in 1758–69 by James Essex, though the Master's Lodge opposite the main entrance still has its oriel window. The small *Chapel*, to the left, incorporates stone walls from the days of God's House. Panelled in 1701, it contains a fine monument by Joseph Catterns (1684) to Sir John Finch and Sir Thomas Baines. High up on the S wall is the window of Lady Margaret's oratory, now in the Master's Lodge. The *Hall* was rebuilt in 1876; its predecessor saw the earliest certain use of stage scenery in England, at a play in 1551. The *Second Court* is dominated by the *Fellows' Building* (1642), a lively piece of neo-classicism ascribed to Thomas Grumbold, one of the architects of Clare College. It opens on to the beautiful *Fellows' Garden*, which includes a mulberry tree associated (rather doubtfully) with Milton. The third court dates from 1889 to 1953, with Denys Lasdun's *New Court* (1970) reaching N to King St.

FAMOUS MEMBERS: John Leland, Sir Walter Mildmay, Denzil Holles, Milton, Edward King ('Lycidas'), John Cleveland, Francis Quarles, Paley, H.W. Betty (the 'Infant Roscius'), Charles Darwin, Calverley, J.R. Seeley, Walter Besant, Lord Mountbatten, C.P. Snow.

We continue S on St Andrew's St. to **Emmanuel College** (390 undergraduates), founded in 1584 by Sir Walter Mildmay, Elizabeth I's Chancellor of the Exchequer, primarily to train learned clergy for the Church of England. It became famous for its Puritan leanings, providing many of the philosophers and theologians called the 'Cambridge Platonists' and many early emigrants to New England. The College occupies the site and incorporated the buildings of a 13C Dominican priory.

The attractive garden front and main court are by Ralph Symons (1584–89), though the entrance wing and *Hall* (left) were transformed by James Essex (1760–75), while the *Westmorland Building* (right) is a notable work of 1719–22. Facing the entrance is the *Chapel*, flanked by an arcade with a gallery above, all by Wren (1677). It contains an altarpiece by Amigoni (1734), a good plaster ceiling and a memorial window to John Harvard. To the S extends the brick-built *Old Court* of 1633–34; the residential *South Block*, beyond, was completed in 1964. Despite its name, *New Court* to the N is the oldest part of the College except for the N range (1824). Beyond the large *Gardens* are the red-brick Gothic *Hostel* and *Emmanuel House* (1886–94). The stone *North Court* (1913) stands on the other side of Emmanuel St.

FAMOUS MEMBERS: John Harvard, Archbishop Sancroft, Sir William Temple, William Law, Thomas Young, Sir F. Gowland Hopkins, Lord Birkett, Fred Hoyle. Captain Lemuel Gulliver of Swift's 'Gulliver's Travels' attends Emmanuel.

Opposite the main entrance to Emmanuel, Downing St. leads W, flanked by ponderous 19–20C buildings of the science faculties. In the *Downing Site* to the left (S) are the *Museum of Archaeology and Anthropology* and the *Sedgwick Museum*, named after Adam Sedgwick, Woodwardian Professor from 1818 to 1873. Its large fossil collection includes specimens bought by the professor from Mary Anning of Lyme Regis and Britain's oldest intact geological collection, that of Dr John Woodward (1665–1728), in its original cabinets. In the *New Museums*, the name given to the crowded and depressing medley on the right (N), is the *Museum of Zoology*. On Free School Lane, a right turn after Downing St. continues as Pembroke St., are the *Whipple Museum of the History of Science* and the original

*Cavendish Physical Laboratory*, famous for the work of J.J. Thomson, Rutherford, Chadwick and Cockcroft.

Further S, just after St Andrew's St. has changed its name to Regent St., is **Downing College** (360 undergraduates). It was endowed by the will of Sir George Downing (d. 1749), though its foundation was delayed until 1800 by legal complications.

William Wilkins's design proposed buildings in the severest Greek Revival manner surrounding a huge lawn, an effect more reminiscent of a campus than a traditional Cambridge court. In the event, only parts of the E and W ranges (1809–20) were built exactly to his plan. Their N ends were added by E.M. Barry in 1875. The N range was begun by Sir Herbert Baker (1930–31) in a badly debased version of Wilkins's style and completed, with the addition of the central *Chapel*, by A.T. Scott (1951–53). The court remains open to the S, with spacious grounds and a striking view of the *Roman Catholic Church* (1885–90) on the nearby corner of Hills Rd and Lensfield Rd. The *Combination Room* (1970) at the SW corner has a blending design in stone and pre-stressed concrete. The *Howard Building* (1987; by Quinlan Terry), near the NW corner is highly traditional.

FAMOUS MEMBERS: J.M. Neale, C.M. Doughty, F.W. Maitland, C.S. Kenny, F.R. Leavis, Trevor Nunn, John Cleese.

Opposite Downing College is *Parker's Piece*, a large common named after Edward Parker, cook of Trinity College, who leased the land in 1587. Park Terrace, on the N side, has Regency houses. To the S lies the *University Cricket Ground*, known as 'Fenner's'. In Wollaston Rd nearby is *Hughes Hall*, a graduate college (140 students) originally founded as a women's teaching-training college in 1885.

For a continuation of this route, see South-Eastern Outskirts below.

NORTH AND EAST FROM MARKET HILL. We leave Market Hill by Market St. at the NE corner. The church of *Holy Trinity*, on the right at the junction with Sidney St., has a Regency Gothic gallery in its S transept. Jeremy Taylor was baptised here, and the Evangelical leader Charles Simeon (d. 1836) was vicar for 54 years.

We turn left on Sidney St. and head N to **Sidney Sussex College** (300 undergraduates), established on the site of a Franciscan convent by the will of Frances Sidney, Countess of Sussex (d. 1589).

The original buildings by Ralph Symons were completed in 1598, but the present Gothick appearance of the College is the work of Sir Jeffry Wyatville (1831–32), who spared only the oriel windows on the garden front. In *Hall Court*, to the left of the Porters' Lodge, the 18C *Hall* has a portrait of Oliver Cromwell which may be the one he instructed should represent him 'warts and all'. To the N is *Cloister Court*, leading to the wide and beautiful *Gardens*. Right of the Porters' Lodge is *Chapel Court*, with *Sir Francis Clerke's Building* (1628) on its S side and the *Chapel* (rebuilt by T.H. Lyon, 1912–23) on the E. A tablet in the ante-chapel records that Oliver Cromwell's head found its final resting place here in 1960. Beyond the Chapel are *Garden Court* (1923; Lyon) and *South Court* (1938–39; E.R. Barrow); a covered way skirting the Master's Garden leads to *Blundell Court* (1969; Howell, Killick, Partridge and Amis). In King St., leading E from the back gate, is *Cromwell Court* (1983; David Roberts and Whitworth, Hall and Thomas).

FAMOUS MEMBERS: Thomas Fuller (who moved from Queens'), Oliver Cromwell, Thomas Rymer, David Owen.

Beyond Sidney Sussex we pass the Whewell's Courts of Trinity, on the left, and turn right into Jesus Lane. At the corner of Park St. to the left, beyond the classical portico of the *Pitt Club*, stand the *Amateur Dramatic Club* (ADC), founded in 1855 by Francis Burnand, and the fine early 18C 'Little Trinity' guest hostel. Jesus Lane continues past *Wesley House*, a Methodist training college, on the left. Beyond is

**'Jesus College**, founded in 1496 by John Alcock, Bishop of Ely, on the site of the suppressed nunnery of St Radegund. He adapted part of the conventual buildings, making the architecture among the most interesting in Cambridge.

*The gateway of Jesus College*

We approach by a long passage known as 'The Chimney' and enter by Alcock's fine, three-storied *Gatehouse*. The cock perched on a globe, above the central niche, is Alcock's rebus and appears throughout the College. From the 17–18C first court an ogee doorway (again with Alcock's rebus) leads into *'Cloister*

*Court*, created by enlarging the nunnery's cloisters. The old entrance to the Chapter House (c 1210) survives on the E side. The cruciform *Chapel* on the S side keeps the core of the nunnery church. It is a lovely piece of EE work, with traces of Norman in the N transept and Perp. windows added by Alcock. The *stained glass is by Pugin and Hardman, and Madox Brown and Burne-Jones for Morris and Co. On the N side of the cloister is Alcock's *Hall*, with stairs leading from its vestibule to the *Old Library*. The buildings behind the chapel are by Waterhouse (1870) and Morley Horder (1929–35). *North Court*, attractively placed in the spacious grounds, was added in 1964 to designs by David Roberts.

FAMOUS MEMBERS: Cranmer, Sterne, Coleridge, Malthus, Humphry Davy, Quiller-Couch, Alistair Cooke.

Opposite Jesus College is the fine church of *All Saints* (1864), by G.F. Bodley with stained gass and interior decoration by Morris and Co. It is now disused and not normally open. Next door is *Westcott House*, a Church of England training college. Jesus Lane continues to the wide space of *Midsummer Common*, stretching to the river with the college boat houses on the opposite bank.

On Riverside, leading E from the Common towards Stourbridge Common, the old sewage pumping station is now the *Cambridge Museum of Technology* (limited opening), with steam, gas and electric pumping engines.—For a continuation of this route, see Eastern Outskirts below.

SOUTH-WESTERN OUTSKIRTS. The favourite short excursion is to **Grantchester**, a pretty village made famous by its connection with Rupert Brooke. It is best reached by the upper river (about 2m from the mill pond at the end of Mill Lane) or on foot through Grantchester Meadows (about 2m, by following Silver St., Newnham Rd and Grantchester St. from the end of the walk S from Market Hill, above). The poet is remembered in the church, which has a fine chancel and a Norman font. The *Old Vicarage* (not open), where Brooke lodged, is below the church near the river. *Byron's Pool*, 1/2m S, is named after Lord Byron. Walkers should continue an extra 1m from Grantchester to **Trumpington**, associated with Chaucer's 'Reeve's Tale' and still keeping its village character in the centre. The church, early 14C but heavily restored, has a *brass to Sir Roger de Trumpington (d. 1289), the second oldest in England (cf. Stoke d'Abernon, Rte 13B). The drive from Cambridge goes to Trumpington first, following Trumpington Rd from the end of the walk S from Market Hill (above). It passes the *University Botanic Gardens* on the left at 1/4m; they can also be entered from Hills Rd at its junction with Station Rd.

NORTHERN OUTSKIRTS. We follow Castle St. from the crossroads N of Magdalene College (at the end of the walk N from Market Hill above). On the left are the *Cambridge and County Folk Museum*, in the 16C former White Horse Inn, and the church of *St Peter*, with a Norman doorway and font surviving its rebuilding in 1781. The artificial mound of *Castle Hill*, by the *Shire Hall* to the right, was the site of pre-Roman and Roman settlements and of a castle (now demolished) built by William the Conqueror in 1068. It offers good views of the city. Castle St. continues N as Huntingdon Rd. On the left is **New Hall**, founded in 1954 as Cambridge's third college for women and still admitting women only (300 undergraduates). The stark white buildings (1962–66; Chamberlin, Powell and Bon) include a domed hall approached by four staircases. Beyond is **Fitzwilliam College** (420 undergraduates), started in 1887 as a centre for non-collegiate students. It moved from Trumpington St. to its present buildings (by Denys Lasdun) in 1963 and became a full college in 1966.

1m further N is **Girton College**, founded by Emily Davies in 1869 as Britain's first residential college providing a university education for women. It began at Hitchin 'to avoid scandal' but moved to its present site in 1873, still safely remote from the older colleges. Since 1979 it has also admitted men (now 470 undergraduates). The brash red-brick buildings were begun by Alfred Waterhouse; the fine grounds extend to 46 acres. Famous members include Rosamond Lehmann, Muriel Bradbrook, Q.D. Leavis, Baroness Wootton, Baroness Warnock.

Rte 68 continues N to Huntingdon.

NORTH-EASTERN OUTSKIRTS. From the crossroads beyond Magdalene College, at the end of the walk N from Market Hill (above), we follow Chesterton Lane and its continuation as Chesterton Rd. At (1m) the roundabout junction with Elizabeth Way stands the former *Chesterton Hall*, a much-altered Jacobean brick mansion. *Chesterton*, about 1/2m further E, has some pleasant river scenery and a few relics of the days before it became a suburb.

NORTH-WESTERN OUTSKIRTS. We follow Northampton St. from the crossroads N of Magdalene College (at the end of the walk N from Market Hill, above). On the right we pass *Kettle's Yard Art Gallery*, with a good 20C collection including work by Gaudier-Brzeska and Ben Nicholson, and on the left the back entrance to St John's College, with Merton Hall, the School of Pythagoras and the Cripps Building. At the roundabout beyond is *Westminster College*, a Presbyterian training college. We head W on the Madingley Rd. On the right, Lady Margaret Rd leads to *Lucy Cavendish College*, founded in 1965, a women's college admitting graduates and mature undergraduates (80 students). In Mount Pleasant, further N, is *St Edmund's College*, mainly for graduates (70 students in all), founded in 1965. 1/4m beyond is **Churchill College** (380 undergraduates), founded in 1960 as a memorial to Sir Winston with the aim of encouraging the sciences and technology in particular. The buildings by Richard Sheppard and Robson add spaciousness to the traditional Cambridge plan of courts. The *Hall* has a bust of Churchill by Oscar Nemon; sculptures by Henry Moore and Barbara Hepworth are on the lawns.

We may continue W along the Madingley Rd past the *American Military Cemetery* to (3m) *Madingley*, a pretty village with the Tudor mansion where Edward VII lived while keeping his terms at Cambridge (now a hostel and study centre).

WESTERN OUTSKIRTS. We begin on Silver St., passed on the walk S from Market Hill (above), and cross the Cam. Newnham Grange (left), once the home of the Darwin family, is now the nucleus of **Darwin College** (330 students), founded in 1964 as a graduate college by Caius, St John's and Trinity. Sensitive new buildings (1968) were added to the Hermitage and the Granary, extending up to the corner of Newnham Rd. At this junction we follow Sidgwick Avenue straight ahead. On the left are *Ridley Hall*, an Anglican training college, and **Newnham College**, founded in 1875 as the second women's college and still admitting women only (300 undergraduates). The original buildings, in red brick with handsome gables, are by Basil Champneys. Famous members include Constance Garnett, Sylvia Plath, Margaret Drabble and Germaine Greer. Opposite Newnham are the *University Arts Faculties*, laid out from 1952 onwards by Sir Hugh Casson and Neville Conder in a deliberately picturesque and informal manner. The *University Museum of Classical Archaeology* has a large display of plaster casts of Greek and Roman sculpture. To the N the *History Faculty Building* (1965; James Stirling) stands in aggressive contrast. The interesting *Harvey Court* of Caius College (1960; Sir Leslie Martin) is at the NE corner of the site. Sidgwick Avenue ends at **Selwyn College** (330 undergraduates), founded in 1882 for Church of England students 'willing to live economically' and recognised as a college in 1958. The original buildings are by Sir Arthur Blomfield. Famous members include Malcolm Muggeridge.

By turning left on Grange Rd, past some handsome 19C houses of the Queen Anne Revival, and then right on Barton Rd, we reach *Wolfson College*, founded in 1965 as University College and renamed in 1973. It is principally a graduate foundation (50 undergraduates, 200 postgraduates).

The main route turns right from Selwyn and goes N along Grange Rd. In Herschel Rd to the left is *Clare Hall*, a graduate establishment (100 students) founded in 1966 by Clare College but now independent. Again to the left of Grange Rd, looking out on the tower of the University Library, is **Robinson College** (270 undergraduates). It is Cambridge's newest college, endowed in 1975 by a local businessman, David Robinson, with the largest single gift the University has ever received and opened to undergraduates in 1979. The red-brick, L-shaped buildings designed by Gillespie, Kidd and Coia (and at a later stage by Yorke, Rosenberg and Mardall) are more in the style of a castle than a traditional Cambridge college. The Chapel has stained glass windows by John Piper.

N of Robinson College are college sports grounds and, on the left, *Wolfson Court* of Girton College (1969; David Roberts). Grange Rd ends at Madingley Rd (see North-Western Outskirts above).

SOUTH-EASTERN OUTSKIRTS. We begin at the large road junction beyond Downing College (the end of the walk S and E from Market Hill above). Hills Rd goes S and crosses the railway line. Cherry Hinton Rd leads left to (2m) *Cherry Hinton*, where the church has a fine EE chancel. The main route continues on

Hills Rd, passing (1m) **Homerton College** (250 undergraduates), originally a separate teacher training college but now fully affiliated with the University. Beyond (2m) *Addenbrooke's Hospital* we remain on A1307, with the *Gog Magog Hills* beginning to rise on our left, only 222ft high but giants indeed in the flat landscape of Cambridgeshire. The Roman *Via Devana* crosses them and on top is (4m) *Wandlebury Camp*, an Iron Age fort (open).

It is worth continuing the drive to (10½m) *Linton*, with its zoo. At *Balsham*, 3½m N, the church is Dec. and Perp., with two 15C brasses. At *Hadstock*, 2m S, the church is partly 11C with a remarkable N doorway.—For Haverhill, beyond Linton at 19m, see Rte 62.

EASTERN OUTSKIRTS. We continue beyond the end of Jesus Lane (reached in the walk N and E from Market Hill above) along Maid's Causeway and its extension as Newmarket Rd. On the left just after the railway bridge is (1m) *Stourbridge Chapel*, the little Norman chapel of a hospital for lepers. *Stourbridge Common* to the N was for centuries the site of a great trading fair famous throughout Europe; it is now a dreary wasteland.

FROM CAMBRIDGE TO MILDENHALL, 22m. The route continues the drive through the Eastern Outskirts above. We follow the Newmarket Rd to its junction with A45 at the large roundabout, where we head N for (4½m) *Stow-cum-Quy*. The name is probably a corruption of 'Cow Ey' (island). We take B1102 left.—6m. At **Anglesey Abbey** (NT) the crypt of an Augustinian abbey is incorporated into a manor house variously owned by two important men, Thomas Hobson (see Hobson's Conduit above) and Sir George Downing, whose will endowed the college bearing his name. Today the house is badly disfigured by 20C alterations. Much more impressive are the grounds laid out by Lord Fairhaven on an ambitious scale. At *Bottisham*, 1¼m SE, the early Dec. church has fine screens.—7½m. *Swaffham Bulbeck* has an EE church with carved bench ends, and good 16–17C houses clustered round its green; the Commercial End built on a tributary of the Cam is a 19C development, dominated by the Merchant's House.—8½m. *Swaffham Prior* has two churches in the same churchyard; the earlier one has a Norman octagonal tower and the derelict one (restored in 1809) a good Perp. tower.—11m. *Burwell* was a 'long street' village, and its chief glory is the late Perp. *church, with a clunch interior and a palimpsest brass of c 1542. *Wicken Fen* (NT), 3m N, is an untouched fenland area reserved as a sanctuary for the characteristic insects and flowers.—15m. *Fordham* church has an interesting two-storied Lady Chapel on the N side. *Isleham* church, 3m NE, has a good roof, an eccentric Jacobean Communion rail and a charming brass to Thomas Peyton (d. 1484) and his two wives. The little Priory Church (English Heritage, open at any reasonable time) is Norman, with herringbone masonry. *Landwade* church (1445), 2m SW of Fordham, is remote and practically unrestored, with 16–18C monuments to the Cotton family. *Chippenham*, 2½m SE of Fordham, is a model village built by the Thorpes of Chippenham Park. The church has ancient wall paintings. Chippenham Fen (NT, open by special application) is another preserved, undrained fen.—22m. *Mildenhall*, see Rte 63.

From Cambridge to *Bedford*, see Rte 47B; to *London* via *Stump Cross*, *Audley End* and *Bishop's Stortford*, see Rte 63; to *London* via *Royston* and *Ware*, see Rte 68; to *Huntingdon* and *Peterborough*, see Rte 68; to *Ely* and *King's Lynn*, see Rte 70.

# 70   Cambridge to Ely and King's Lynn

## A.   Via Downham Market

Total distance 44m. **Cambridge**, see Rte 69. The route follows A10 throughout.—To (16m) **Ely** (bypassed).—To (33m) **Downham Market** (bypassed).—To (44m) **King's Lynn**.

Maps: OS Landranger 154, 143, 132.

**Cambridge**, see Rte 69.—At (4m) *Milton*, on the right, the church has a Norman chancel arch, 17C altar rails, and monuments by Flaxman and Chantrey.—At (5½m) *Waterbeach* we cross a section of the Car Dyke, the Roman canal dug to transport the Fenland corn to the garrisons of Lincoln and the north, then join for 2m the conspicuous alignment of the Roman Akeman Street.—7m. *Denny Abbey*, on the right, was founded in 1160 by the Benedictines from Ely, taken over a century later by the Knights Templar and, after their suppression, used by the nuns of St Clare. Fragments of the church and refectory building survive (English Heritage, summer standard opening but closed on Mondays and Tuesdays).—11m. *Stretham* is a well-preserved village with a 15C cross, 16–18C houses and a Dec. church. On the Old West River to the SE is a fine Pumping House with the original Butterfly Beam Engine of 1830 (open).

16m. **ELY** is a small city (10,300 inhab.) built on a hill whose modest height of 70ft is made to seem greater by the noble cathedral that tops it and the flatness of the surrounding Fens.

**Tourist Information Centre**: The Library, Palace Green.

**Car Parks**: Barton Rd, Broad St., Ship Lane (by the river).

**Buses**: from Market St.

**Railway Station**: SE of the centre.

**History**. According to Bede, the city acquired its name—'eel island'—from the eels in the Great Ouse, flowing E of the hill. The old 'Isle of Ely' (7m by 4m) was surrounded by marshland that only the 'Fen slodgers' who knew the firm tussock paths could penetrate. On this island Hereward the Wake, 'Last of the English', held out against the invading Norman armies until 1071, when a road was floated across the marsh on bundles of faggots.

The ***Cathedral** belongs to the great series of Fen monasteries established by the Saxons and rebuilt by the Normans. It differs from a sister foundation like Peterborough in the wealth and variety of post-Norman work, particularly the Octagon and Lady Chapel.

The first building, a 7C Benedictine abbey, was sacked by the Danes in 870; its successor was used as headquarters by Hereward the Wake. The present church was begun in 1083 by Abbot Simeon and was substantially complete when the nave was finished in 1189, by which time it had also been raised to cathedral rank.

The most immediately striking part of the exterior, the W front, belongs to this period and is hence in the Norman Trans. style. Its castellated tower has two later additions: an EE Galilee Porch at the base and a Dec. octagonal top with side turrets. The asymmetrical appearance of the front was caused by the fall of the NW tower during a storm in 1701.

The *Nave* is a fine piece of late Norman work and, though the piers of its 12 bays are massive, seems light by comparison with the earlier naves at Durham and Gloucester. Its narrowness is emphasised by the height of the clerestory and triforium arcades. The painted ceiling is 19C but the four E bays of the S aisle keep their original 12C colouring. In this aisle, too, we find: the Prior's Doorway (c 1140), richly ornamented outside; a Saxon cross in memory of Ovinus, vassal to Queen Etheldreda, foundress of the original abbey; and at the E end, another elaborate doorway, used by the monks entering from the cloisters. The lower parts of the *Transepts* show the oldest work in the cathedral (1083–1107). In the E aisle of the N transept is the Chapel of St Edmund, with a 14C screen and a 12C wall painting of the saint's martyrdom. From this transept we reach the *Stained Glass Museum* and the Lady Chapel (see below).

At the junction of transepts and nave is the **Central Octagon**. The sacrist Alan de Walsingham and his carpenter, probably William Hurley, were given the chance to build it in 1322, when the original tower fell and wrecked part of the choir. The octagon takes the entire breadth of nave, transepts and choir as its base, rising on four larger and four smaller arches; above it, the wooden lantern is set with its angles against the faces of the stone walls. The effect,

**Ely Close**

WEST FEN ROAD
ST MARY'S STREET
HIGH STREET
MARKET STREET
High Steeple Gate
Cathedral
Museum
FOREHILL
St Mary's
Bishop's Palace
CHURCH LANE
GALLERY
INFIRMARY
Prior's House
Chapel
King's School
SILVER STREET
Ely Porta
The Park
BROAD

0 _____ 200 yds
0 _____ 200 ms

---

**ELY CATHEDRAL**

Key to Numbers
1 Ovin's Stone
2 Alan de Walsingham
3 David Wynne sculpture
4 Bp Hotham
5 Earl of Worcester
6 Bp William de Luda
7 Sir Robert Steward
8 Sir Mark Steward
9 Bp Northwold
10 Bp William of Kilkenny
12 Dean Caesar
13 Site of St Ethelreda's Shrine
14 Cardinal Louis de Luxembourg
15 Bp Nigel
16 Bp Allen

St Etheldreda's Chapel
Bishop West's Chantry
Bishop Alcock's Chantry
Lady Chapel
PRESBYTERY
St Dunstan's Chapel
LIBRARY
St Edmund's Chapel
St George's Chapel
OCTAGON
Vestry
Ruined Cloister
Monks Door
Prior's Door
St Catherine's Chapel
NORTH WEST TRANSEPT (destroyed)
SOUTH WEST TRANSEPT
Font
GALILEE

0 _____ 25 yards
0 _____ 25 ms

*The Octagon, Ely Cathedral*

writes Nikolaus Pevsner, is 'a delight from beginning to end for anyone who feels for space as strongly as for construction'.

A 19C screen separates the Octagon from the *Choir, which shows a clearly marked division between the three W bays (by Alan de Walsingham) and the delicate EE part beyond (1234–52). Of the choir stalls, the upper ones are 14C with good misericords but the other furnishings are the worst fruit of Gilbert Scott's restoration of the cathedral in the 19C. The aisles contain a series of interesting monuments to medieval bishops. At the E end of the S aisle is the Chantry of Bishop West (d. 1533), combining medieval and classical motifs; the corresponding end of the N aisle is filled by the Chantry of Bishop Alcock (d. 1500), an example of the Perp. style at its most luxuriant.

NE of the N transept is the *Lady Chapel (1321–c 1353), another of Alan de Walsingham's happy additions. The simple rectangular shape is made airy and spacious by the complex lierne-vaulted roof (at 46ft the widest medieval vault in England) and the clear glass of the broad windows. The richly carved foliage and statuettes of the wall seats are still impressive despite their badly damaged state, a result of the softness of the clunch (chalk) in which they are made as much as the vandalism of Lord Protector Somerset's men in 1547.

The *Cloisters* are now represented mainly by the E walk, which forms the S entrance to the nave. Parts of the *Infirmary* are incorporated in Firmary Lane, running E. The *Bishop's House*, S of the cloister, was adapted from the old guest hall and includes remains of the 12C kitchen. The other conventual buildings to survive lie further S and are now used by the *King's School*, refounded at the Dissolution in 1541 but descended from the monastic school where Edward the Confessor (d. 1066) was a pupil. The most interesting group is formed by the *Prior's Hall* and *Prior Crauden's Chapel* (open), another exquisite building by Alan de Walsingham, with its original mosaic tiled floor. *Ely Porta* (the great gateway of the monastery, built c 1394) leads into a street called The Gallery and so back to the cathedral. The *Bishop's Palace*, on Palace Green to the left, is mainly late 17C but preserves wings built by Bishop Alcock and a long gallery added by Bishop Goodrich (d. 1554).

The church of *St Mary*, a little W of the palace, dates from 1215. The half-timbered vicarage next to its churchyard was Oliver Cromwell's home in 1636–47, when he was farmer of the cathedral tithes and MP for Ely.

The *Sacrist's Gate* on the N side of the cathedral now houses a small local museum. Beyond is the High St., which leads right and continues as Forehill down to the banks of the Ouse, pleasantly cluttered with boats in summer. A riverside walk between the two bridges passes the 19C *Maltings*, well restored as a public hall.

FROM ELY TO NEWMARKET, 13m. A142 runs SE across the Fens.—1½m. *Stuntney* was a Bronze Age settlement, and a timber trackway of that period connecting it with Ely has been traced.—5m. *Soham*, a large and attractive village of brick houses, was the site of a cathedral built by St Felix, the 'Apostle of East Anglia' (d. 634). The present church is 12C, with a Perp. tower and good flushwork. There are still many windmills in this area.—8½m. *Fordham* (Rte 69).—We enter Suffolk near (11½m) *Exning* (right), a pleasant old village and the mother parish of Newmarket.—13½m. *Newmarket*, Rte 63.

A10 runs NE from Ely.—21m. *Littleport* has a Perp. church with 19C additions.—At (25m) *Brandon Creek*, where the Little Ouse meets the Great Ouse, we enter Norfolk.—31m. *Hilgay* church has a brick tower (1794).—33m. *Denver* has a 13C church, a fine tower-mill and a series of sluices; the Old Denver Sluices (1825) are by Rennie. Dorothy L. Sayers (1893–1957) used the name of this village for the ducal family of her detective, Lord Peter Wimsey, and the Fenland atmosphere is evoked in 'The Nine Tailors'.—34m. **Downham Market** (4700 inhab.) is a compact market town; the EE church has a high tower and an excellent peal of bells.

A1122 runs E from Downham Market.—4m. *Stradsett* church, with good German stained glass of 1540, is set in the grounds of the Hall, which is Elizabethan with a Georgian façade.—5½m. *Fincham* has a Perp. church with a Norman font.—The road crosses the Devil's Dyke before (10m) *Swaffham* (Rte 61).

35m. *Stow Bardolph* church has 17–19C monuments of the Hare family.—38m. *Tottenhill*.

An unclassified road leads left via Magdalen Rd Station to (2½m) the Great Ouse, across which is the attractive and lonely village of *Wiggenhall St Mary Magdalen* with a Perp. church and 13C tower, containing good painted screens, benches, and Jacobean panelling. *Wiggenhall St Mary the Virgin* lies c 2m NW in beautiful country and has a brick church with excellently carved early 16C benches and a good eagle lectern (1518). On the E bank of the Ouse lies the church of *Wiggenhall St Germans* (also with good benches), where the village has large 16–18C houses. Just to the S is *Wiggenhall St Peter* with an impressive ruined Perp. church standing at the 'Eau Brink'.

44m. **KING'S LYNN** (33,300 inhab.) is an old and attractive port on the Great Ouse, 3m above its outflow into the Wash. The original parish of St Margaret grew up round the Saturday Market; a new town was laid out across the creek to the N in c 1160, with the Tuesday Market and the church of St Nicholas at its centre. Lynn has kept a splendid townscape of buildings—domestic, civic and industrial—from the 14C to the early 19C, particularly between its two market places and by the water. Its affinity with the Netherlands is apparent everywhere.

**Tourist Information Centre**: The Old Gaol House, by the Saturday Market.

**Car Parks**: Saturday Market, Tuesday Market, Baker Lane, Chapel St., Old Cattle Market, etc.

**Bus Station**: Market St.

**Railway Station**: Blackfriars Rd, E of the centre.

**Theatre**: St George's Guildhall, King St.

**Annual Event**: Festival of music and drama at the end of July.

**Famous natives and residents**. Fanny Burney (1752–1840), the novelist, born while her father, Dr Charles Burney, was organist at St Margaret's. Arthur Young (1741–1820), agriculturist and travel writer, married at Lynn in 1765. George Vancouver (1758–98), sailor and explorer, born in a Tudor house behind the Friends' Meeting House in New Conduit St. Eugene Aram, the murderer, was arrested while working as an usher at the corporation school in 1758.

The church of *St Margaret* in the Saturday Market was founded c 1100 by Bishop Losinga of Norwich and rebuilt in the 13C. It contains 14C screens, misericords, an early Georgian pulpit, an organ by Snetzler (1754), and two of the most elaborate *brasses in England, Flemish or German in origin. The Walsoken brass (Adam de Walsoken, d. 1349) has a border of country scenes; that of Robert Braunche (d. 1364) is known as the 'Peacock Brass' from its picture of the feast that Braunche gave for Edward III. Opposite the church, in the direction of Queen St., is a fine group of buildings: the *Gaol* of 1784; the *Guildhall*, built in 1421, beautifully chequered in flint and stone, with an Elizabethan addition in the same style to the left; and the *Town Hall* (1895).

The old streets S of the Saturday Market are worth exploring, especially Nelson St., Bridge St. and Friars St. In the first is *Hampton Court*, a monastic building of c 1400 considerably altered, and in Bridge St. is the restored Jacobean *Greenland Fishery*. Further on are the 14C *Whitefriars Gateway* and the only remaining town gate, the 16C *South Gate*.—E of the Saturday Market, in St James St., is the Perp. *Greyfriars Tower*. In The Walks, beyond, are a fragment of the town wall and the *Red Mount Chapel* (1482), an octagonal brick building probably for the use of pilgrims to Walsingham.

From the Saturday Market, Queen St. and King St. lead N to the Tuesday Market. On the left of Queen St. are *Thoresby College*, a 15C monastic house with 17C front, and *Clifton House*, a 16–17C merchant's house with a tall brick watch tower, a 15C undercroft and a façade remodelled by Henry Bell in c 1708. King's Staithe Lane, leading to the Quay, has fine 16–17C warehouses and 17–18C houses, and King's Staithe Square has the 17–18C *Bank House*, with a statue of Charles I. On the Quay stands the *Custom House* (1683; Henry Bell), perhaps the most graceful composition among the buidings of Lynn. The statue is of Charles II.

Purfleet St. leads right and, after crossing the pedestrianised High St., continues as New Conduit St. On Market St., beyond Paradise Court, are the bus station and the *Lynn Museum* of local history. Its exhibits include medieval pilgrims' badges.

King St. has a wealth of good buildings. They include the *Museum of Social History* in a Georgian house and the 15C *St George's Guildhall*, used as a theatre in the 18C and now restored to this function. The Tuesday Market Place beyond is spacious and dignified, with the *Duke's Head* (1683–89) by Henry Bell. *St Nicholas*, off the NE corner, was built as a chapel of ease in 1146. It has a splendid S porch, good benches, a 15C brass lectern and a tie-beam roof. The neighbouring streets repay exploration.

From King's Lynn to *Norwich*, see Rte 66; to *Cromer* and *Yarmouth*, see Rte 67; to *Boston* and *Grimsby*, see Rte 71.

*The Custom House, King's Lynn*

## B.   Via March and Wisbech

Total distance 59m. **Cambridge**, see Rte 69.—A10 to (16m) **Ely**
(bypassed), see Rte 70A.—A142 to (28m) Chatteris.—A141 to (36m)
**March** (bypassed).—A141, A47 to (46m) **Wisbech** (bypassed).—A47
to (59m) **King's Lynn** (Rte 70A).

Maps: OS Landranger 154, 143, 131 (briefly), 132.

**Cambridge**, see Rte 69.—A10 to (16m) **Ely**, see Rte 70A.—A142 runs
W to (22½m) *Sutton*, on a ridge above the Fens surrounded by
orchards. It has a large and light Dec. church of c 1370.

From Sutton B1381 leads SW to (5m) *Earith*, the point from which the New
Bedford River and the Old Bedford River were cut to Denver (Rte 70A). On their
smooth waters, with floating objects lined up at 3m intervals, experiments in the
17C first demonstrated the curvature of the earth's surface.—A1123 continues
to (6½m) *Bluntisham*, where Dorothy L. Sayers spent her early life at the
rectory.—For (9m) *St Ives* and (154m) *Huntingdon*, see Rte 68.

The road turns NW to (24m) *Mepal*, where it crosses the Bedford
Rivers.—At (28m) *Chatteris* (6200 inhab.) we join A141 from
Huntingdon. Further on, this crosses the Forty Foot Drain, dug in the
17C by Cornelius Vermuyden.—32m. *Doddington* church, left of the
road, has stained glass by Morris and Co., and a Dutch carving of
Christ and the Woman of Samaria.—36m. **March** (14,500 inhab.) has
been an important Fen town since Roman times. It declined when a
new cut allowed the Nene to flow directly from Wisbech to
Peterborough, but flourished again in the 19C as a railway junction.
Its varied history has not given it beauty except for the church of *St
Wendreda*, S of the present centre. The tower is topped with a fine
spire, the building style is a mixture of Dec. and Perp., and the
double hammerbeam *roof with triple ranks of angels is one of the
best in the region.—At (40m) *Guyhirn* we join A47 and follow the
new course of the Nene.

46m. **Wisbech** (17,300 inhab.; Tourist Information), a town of
unexpected distinction, grew up when the new cut of the Nene made
it the port for Peterborough. Fine old warehouses stand by the Nene
quay and two remarkably handsome Georgian streets, *North Brink
and *South Brink, line the banks of the river. The general effect
recalls the tranquil landscapes of the Netherlands, while the variety
of the buildings makes close inspection worthwhile. In North Brink is
*Peckover House* (NT), built in 1722, with a splendid rococo interior.
The garden has a working orangery. E of the memorial to Thomas
Clarkson (1760–1846), campaigner against slavery and a native of
Wisbech, is the *Castle Estate*, a development begun during the 1790s
in emulation of fashionable spa towns. It takes its name from the
castle of 1072, replaced c 1658 by the mansion of John Thurloe,
Secretary of State during the Protectorate; only the entrance gates
and garden walls of Thurloe's house remain, and the present
building is early 19C. The *Church* has, curiously, a second N aisle
added in the 14C; also 15C stained glass, some good monuments and
a brass to Thomas de Braunstone (d. 1401) over 7ft long. *Walsoken
*church, in the Norfolk suburb, has one of the finest Norman
interiors in East Anglia and some notable 17C sculptures.

*West Walton* *church, 1½m further N has an EE interior with beautifully carved
capitals and arcades like those at Lincoln. The 17C Prayer board asks for
delivery from floods, and the detached bell tower to the S of the church dates
from the 13C.—*Emneth* church, 2¼m SE of Wisbech, is Norman, EE and Perp.;

*Leverington* church, 2m NW, is built of clunch; it has an impressive EE tower, a 14C porch, a 15C Jesse window and, in the NE corner, the tomb of Oliver Goldsmith's Tony Lumpkin.

A47 runs NE across the Fens passing (left at 51m) *Terrington St John*, where the 14C church is connected to a later tower by a series of rooms, a staircase and passages. The font cover dates from 1632. —55m. *Tilney All Saints* (left) has a 12C church with much Norman work, a fine Dec. hammerbeam roof, misericords and two fonts. We cross the Great Ouse into (59m) **King's Lynn** (Rte 70A).

# 71  King's Lynn to Boston and Grimsby

## A.  Via Louth

Total distance 90m. **King's Lynn**, see Rte 70A.—A17 to (15m) Long Sutton.—A17, A151 to (17m) Holbeach.—A151 to (25m) Spalding. —A16 to (41m) **Boston**.—A16 to (57m) Spilsby.—A16 to (73m) **Louth**.—A16 to (90m) **Grimsby**.

Maps: OS Landranger 132 (briefly), 131, 122, 113.

**King's Lynn**, see Rte 70A.—A17 runs W through the flat saltmarshes below the Wash, a wide shallow bay gradually being silted up by the rivers that flow into it—the Nene, the Ouse, the Welland and the Witham. It was here that King John was overtaken by the tide, losing his baggage and treasure. The bleak landscape is relieved by a series of splendid churches, noble in scale and often rich in woodwork. —The *church at *Terrington St Clement*, N of our road at 6m, is one of the best, with many interesting details. It has a detached Perp. tower (characteristic of the area), a good 18C chancel screen and a font cover with paintings inside, including one of the Baptism of Christ. The lovely church of *Walpole St Andrew* lies 2½m SW, and nearby is that of *Walpole St Peter*, with beautiful Perp. tracery and ornament. It has a tie-beam roof, 17C screens, misericords and a pulpit of 1620. Under the chancel is a richly groined passage, a public right of way.—10m. *Sutton Bridge* is a small river port on the Nene, over the Lincolnshire border.—13m. *Long Sutton* is a nice little market town whose *church has one of the oldest lead-covered spires in the country (EE), and a 15C porch.—14½m. *Gedney* has a fine EE *church. The tower has a Perp. spire, and the two-storied S porch a turret stair. Inside are 14–15C stained glass and coloured alabaster monuments to the Welby family. Over the S door is an ivory plaque of the Crucifixion. The desolate expanse of the Wash is well seen at *Gedney Drove End*, 5m NE.—15½m. *Fleet* church (14C) has a detached tower with spire and a Perp. W window.—We take A151 left to (17m) **Holbeach** (4800 inhab.), a market town since the 13C and a centre of the bulb-growing district of Lincolnshire. The Trans. church has a tower and spire which dominate the surrounding country.—19½m. *Whaplode *church has a Norman chancel arch and a fine Irby monument (c 1620). The 12C tower stands at the E end of the S aisle. *Moulton*, ½m S, has an early Perp. rood screen, and a steeple 160ft high (c 1380). 22m. *Weston *church is EE with 14C transepts and a Perp. tower; the S porch is notable. About 1½m

N are the ruins of *Wykeham Chapel* (early Dec.).—24m. *Springfield Gardens* (open) has a fine show of bulbs in April and May.

25m. **Spalding** (18,200 inhab.; Tourist Information), an ancient market-gardening town, stands on the river Welland in the very heart of the Fens. As at Wisbech, the flat and spacious townscape creates an atmosphere more characteristic of the Low Countries than England. From the Market Place there are walks to the river, whose banks are lined with good Georgian houses. *Ayscoughfee Hall*, a much altered 15C mansion with a beautiful garden, is open as a museum of agriculture and horticulture. It was the home of Maurice Johnson, founder of the 'Gentlemen's Society of Spalding', the oldest scientific and literary association in England (1710). The church of *St Mary and St Nicholas*, founded in 1284, has been much extended and its tower, with an early Perp. spire, looks small for the double-aisled building.

The pumping stations and other drainage works in the surrounding Fens are of great interest. The boilerhouse of the former pumping station at *Pode Hole*, 2m W, is now a drainage museum. See also Pinchbeck below.

FROM SPALDING TO CROWLAND, 9m via A1073.—3m. *Cowbit* (pronounced 'Coubitt') is a great centre for Fen skating. The road now crosses the fertile *Bedford Level*, named after the reclamation work of the Earl of Bedford and the Dutch engineer Vermuyden (d. 1677) in 1650–53.—9m. **Crowland** (or *Croyland*) is a pleasant town with tree-lined streets, and the seat of an *Abbey which was, with Ely and Peterborough, one of the great Saxon foundations in Eastern England. Originally established c 716 by King Ethelbald of Mercia over the cell of the hermit St Guthlac, it was sacked by the Danes in 870, rebuilt, and burned down in 1091. What survives today is a grand fragment of the Norman church raised in the early 12C by Abbot Joffrid (1109–70): the N aisle (altered in the 15C and now the parish church), the lofty arch of the central tower, the W fronts of the aisles and the attached font. Among the many details worth attention are the relief statues over the W door portraying the life of St Guthlac, the monumental slab to the master-mason William of Wermington in the W tower, and the parclose screen of 1413. The rest of the abbey church suffered harshly after the Reformation, its E part being pulled down in 1540 and the nave and S aisle being destroyed in a bombardment by Cromwell's troops (1643).

27m. *Pinchbeck* has a large church with a 14C tower and much Perp. and Dec. work; the good E window is a 19C restoration by Butterfield. The alloy known as 'pinchbeck' (copper; 'false gold') is named, not from this village, but from Christopher Pinchbeck, the London watchmaker who invented it c 1720. There is a beam engine of 1833 in the *Pinchbeck Marsh* pumping station (open).—31m. *Gosberton* has another fine early Perp. church.

*Donington*, 3¹/₂m NW, was the birthplace of Matthew Flinders (1774–1814), the Australian navigator, who is commemorated in the fine late Dec. and early Perp. church.

The churches of (35m) *Sutterton*, *Algarkirk* (³/₄m E) and (38m) *Kirton-in-Holland* are all interesting.

41m. **BOSTON** (i.e. 'St Botolph's Town'), a seaport and market town (26,400 inhab.) standing near the mouth of the Witham, still has both a handsome church and a lingering atmosphere to remind the visitor of the time, in the Middle Ages, when it grew rich on the wool trade with Flanders. Its great namesake in America acknowledges Boston's proud connection with the Pilgrim Fathers.

**Tourist Information Centre**: Assembly Rooms, Market Place.

**Car Parks**: Bargate Bridge, Bargate End, Bargate Green (not Wednesday), Market Place (not Wednesday or Saturday), Pump Square, South Square, South End.

**Bus Stations**: St George's Rd and London Rd (both W of the river).

**Railway Station**: Station St. (W of river).

**Entertainments**: Theatre and Arts Centre in Blackfriars, Spain Lane; Sam Newsom Music Centre, South St.

**Annual Events**: May Fair, a pleasure fair replacing the old sheep fair, in the week following 3 May; Boston Festival (music and arts) in the first two weeks of June.

**Famous natives and residents**. John Foxe (1517–87), the martyrologist, Jean Ingelow (1820–97), the poetess, and John Conington (1825–69), translator of Virgil, were natives of Boston. The musician John Taverner lived here from 1537 to his death in 1545, dissolving the four local priories in his capacity as Thomas Cromwell's personal agent.

*St Botolph*, one of the largest parish churches in England, testifies to the affluence of the Boston guilds and merchants. It is made conspicuous for 20m around, both on land and sea, by its lofty Perp. tower and beautiful octagonal lantern (cf. Ely). The nickname of 'Boston Stump', which almost universally replaces the church's official dedication, may come from its truncated appearance when seen from a distance or from the belief that a spire was meant to crown the lantern. A few other Perp. additions aside, the building is an almost pure example of the richest period of flowing Dec. The

*'Boston Stump': the church of St Botolph*

oldest part is the lower section of the tower (1309), where a tablet commemorates George Bass, surgeon of the town (born in 1771 at *Aswarby*, 4m S of Sleaford), and other Lincolnshire men who played their part in the exploration of Australia. There are fine misericords, a pulpit (1612) and several interesting tombs, including the fine slab of a Hanse merchant (1340) brought from the destroyed Franciscan church, an effigy of a knight from the church of St John, and one of a lady with charming puppies playing round her feet (early 14C). The SW chapel was restored in 1857 by New England Bostonians in memory of John Cotton (1584–1652), who was vicar here in 1612–33 before he went to America.

Boston has no other building of the first rank, but its streets and houses make a very agreeable walking tour. They are redolent of the sea, with warm brick, bright paintwork and 'flood steps' in front of many doors. We begin in the Market Place, where the lively general market is held on Wednesdays and Saturdays, with the *Corporation Buildings* (1772) and the *Assembly Rooms* (1826) making a handsome display on the W side. In the little Mitre Lane, leading from the N end, is *Pescod Hall*, a restored 15C wool merchant's house, now a shop. In South St., leading from the market to the port, we come first to *Shodfriars Hall*, a Victorian copy of a timbered 16C building. Spain Lane, also on the left, has *Blackfriars*, part of a 13C Dominican friary, now housing a theatre. The 15C *Guildhall* on the corner (left) contains the court (much altered) where Brewster and other Pilgrim Fathers were tried in 1607 for seeking to flee the country: also shown are the cells in which they were imprisoned, and a fine old kitchen. Next door is *Fydell House* (open), a building of 1726 with a lovely carved staircase. It is now owned by the Boston Preservation Trust and houses Pilgrim College, an outpost of the University of Nottingham. The *Grammar School*, by Haven Bridge further on, preserves its original hall of 1567. *Hussey Tower*, behind, is a relic of a mansion of c 1500. Small lanes lead to the sea bank from which the views extend far over the Wash and inland to a superb panorama of church towers.

The marsh villages near Boston have fine churches. That of *Skirbeck*, 1m SE, has an Elizabethan pulpit. Here, too, dyer's woad (Isatis tinctoria) was last grown in England; the old mill for grinding it stopped work in 1932. *Fishtoft*, 1½m beyond, has its village stocks and traces of Norman work in the chancel of its church. The church at *Freiston*, 3½m E, is the nave of a 12C priory church. For churches NE of Boston on A52, see Rte 71B.

FROM BOSTON TO LINCOLN VIA HORNCASTLE, 39m. B1183 runs due N across the Fens to (11m) *Revesby*, the 'model' village attached to Revesby Abbey, named after the Cistercian house that was founded here from Rievaulx in 1142. The present house (not open) is Victorian and little remains of the abbey church. *East Kirkby* church, 2½m E, has fine Dec. and Perp. details.—At (16m) *Scrivelsby* is a late Perp. gatehouse, the last intact remnant of *Scrivelsby Court* (open by appointment), ancient home of the Dymokes who succeeded the Marmions as lords of the manor, a position carrying the right to serve as King's Champion. The church has memorials of the Marmions and the Dymokes. —18m. **Horncastle** (4200 inhab.) stands on the site of the Roman *Banovallum*, at the junction of the rivers Bain and Witham, by the foot of the Wolds (see below). Part of the walls of the fort have been incorporated into the *Library*. In the church of *St Mary* are the brass of Sir Lionel Dymoke, King's Champion (1519), and the monument of Sir Ingram Hopwood, 'who paid his debt to nature ... in the attempt of seizing the arch-rebel [Cromwell] in the bloody skirmish near Winceby' (1643). The scythes blades and hay knives over the door are said to have been fastened to staves for use in the battle. There was a famous August horse fair here, described by George Borrow in 'Romany Rye'. The old rectory at *Somersby*, 6m NE, was the birthplace of Tennyson (1809–92). The church has a memorial to him and a remarkable churchyard cross. *Bag Enderby* church, ½m E, of which Tennyson's father was also rector, has a notable font; there is another, and good monuments, at *Harrington*, 1m further. *Harrington Hall* (limited opening) is a 17C house with Tudor fragments and medieval foundations. Its walled garden is sometimes claimed as the 'High Hall Garden' of Tennyson's 'Maud'. From Horncastle to Sleaford, see Rte 72.

B1190, the shortest road from Horncastle to Lincoln, runs W, crossing the Witham at (29m) *Bardney*, where excavations have laid bare the ground plan of the once wealthy Benedictine abbey and brought to light pillar bases, tomb slabs and other relics. St Oswald (d. 642) was buried here. The church of St Lawrence has an old altar slab with seven crosses.—35m. *Branston* has a late Saxon church tower.—As we approach (39m) *Lincoln* (Rte 72) from the S there are fine views of the cathedral standing over the Fens.

From Boston to *Sleaford*, see Rte 72.

Beyond Boston the Grimsby road runs due N across the Fens, passing at 45m through *Sibsey*, where the Norman church has an EE tower. The *Trader Windmill*, ¹/₂m W of the village, is a brick Victorian tower mill with its machinery still intact (English Heritage, summer standard opening but closed on Tuesdays and on Wednesday afternoons).—57m. **Spilsby** (1600 inhab.; Tourist Information) was the birthplace of the explorer Sir John Franklin (1787–1847), whose statue is next to the medieval *Market Cross*. The 14C *Church* has Franklin's flag and 14–16C monuments of the Willoughby and Bertie families. The one to Richard Bertie (d. 1582) and his wife is splendidly elaborate.

Spilsby stands on the edge of the Fens, with the Wolds of South Lincolnshire rising beyond. These chalk uplands, dramatic continuation of the same chalk scarp that gives Cambridgeshire its gentle Gog Magog hills and Norfolk its fertile plateau, stretch from a western escarpment by the rivers Witham and (further N) Ancholme to the flat coastal strip of marsh and sand in the east. Villages here hug the valleys, while big farms spread over the high ground.

*Halton Holegate*, 1¹/₂m E, has a spacious Perp. church. *Gunby Hall* (NT), 4m further NE, is a plain red-brick house of 1700 in the style of Wren. It has a contemporary oak staircase, portraits by Reynolds and a walled garden. At *Old Bolingbroke*, 4m W of Spilsby via *Mavis Enderby*, only a few mounds remain of John of Gaunt's castle, where Henry IV was born in 1399 (English Heritage, open at any reasonable time). For Somersby and the other places W of Spilsby associated with Tennyson, see the detour from Boston to Lincoln above.

59m. *Partney*, with its pleasant church, was a favourite haunt of Dr Johnson when he stayed with his friend Bennet Langton at nearby Langton Hall (no longer standing).—From (63m) *Ulceby Cross* A1104 leads NE to (3m) *Alford*, a small town (2600 inhab.) with a good Dec. church and a museum of Lincolnshire life in the old Manor House.

*Markby*, 3m NE of Alford, has a thatched church and *Willoughby*, 3m S of Alford, was the birthplace of Captain John Smith of Virginia (1580–1631).—For *Mablethorpe*, on the coast 6m NE of Alford, see Rte 71B.

73m. **Louth** (13,300 inhab.) is dominated by its *Church*, with one of the most beautiful steeples in England (1501–15). The well-proportioned interior has a magnificent high tower arch. It contains paintings and the 'Sudbury Hutch', a chest of c 1500 with portraits of Henry VII and Elizabeth of York. The town centre has good buildings of the 17–19C, harmoniously grouped, especially in Westgate, with a lovely series of 18C doorways, and in Upgate, 16C with additions from every succeeding century. John Smith of Virginia and Sir John Franklin, as well as Tennyson and his brothers, attended the grammar school (rebuilt), and the 'Poems by Two Brothers', containing Tennyson's first published work, was printed in 1827 by a Louth bookseller. The village churches in the neighbourhood are worth attention, but only scanty traces remain of *Louth Park Abbey*, a Cistercian foundation of 1139, 1½m E.

A16 follows the E edge of the Wolds and enters South Humberside.—90m. **GRIMSBY** (92,100 inhab.; Tourist Information), or *Great Grimsby*, has been a fishing and trading port since the 11C, receiving its charter in 1202. It remains the chief fishing port in England, though the size of the catch has greatly declined in recent years. The *Royal Docks*, built in the early 1850s, are dominated by the *Victoria Flour Mill* (1906) and the *Dock Tower* (1852), a copy of the tower on the town hall in Siena. *St James's Church* is a much altered 13C building; its most notable feature is the curious combination of clerestory and triforium.

*Clee*, or *Old Clee*, 1m S, has a restored church whose W tower is a fine example of Saxon work. The nave and font are Norman. For *Cleethorpes*, on the coast further S, see Rte 71B.—The deep-water dock at *Immingham*, 6m up the Humber from Grimsby, was first built in 1912 to handle coal from Yorkshire. It now also has an oil terminal, with oil-refining and chemical industries. A monument at *South Killingholme Haven* marks the site of the Pilgrim Fathers' embarkation for Holland in 1609.

*Ashby-cum-Fenby* is a pretty village 6m S of Grimsby, whose EE church has good Dec. windows and a screen. At *East Ravendale*, 1m SW, are the remains of a Premonstratensian priory, and 2½m W of Ashby lies *Hatcliffe*, beautifully situated above a valley.

From Grimsby to *Lincoln*, see Rte 72.

## B.   Via the Coast

Total distance 108m. **King's Lynn**, see Rte 70A.—To (41m) **Boston**, see Rte 71A.—A52 to (63m) Skegness.—A52 to (81m) Mablethorpe.—A1031 to (108m) **Grimsby** (Rte 71A).

Maps: OS Landranger 132 (briefly), 131, 122, 113.

**King's Lynn**, see Rte 70A.—To **Boston**, see Rte 71A. That route goes N into the Wolds, while the present one heads NE on A52 along the flat coastal tract. The small villages through which it passes continue the fine series of marshland churches seen in the earlier part of the route: (45½m) *Benington*; (47m) *Leverton*, Perp. with good tracery outside and a Dec. interior; (48½m) *Old Leake*, with Norman arcading; and (49½m) *Wrangle*, Perp. with good 14C glass.—At (53m) *Friskney*, to the left, the church is Perp., with some Norman work and later additions. It has a Jacobean pulpit, 14C wall paintings and, in the graveyard, a 17C cross and graveside shelter.—58m. *Wainfleet All Saints*, a large, pleasant village, was the birthplace of William of Waynflete (1395–1486), Bishop of Winchester and founder of Magdalen College, Oxford. He built the Magdalen School, a fine brick building of 1484 with Victorian additions, to supply students for his college. At *Croft*, 2m NE, the Dec. 'church has an early 17C pulpit, good screens and benches, a fine lectern and one of the earliest brasses in England (c 1300).

63m. **Skegness** (14,500 inhab.; seasonal Tourist Information) is a popular resort with good sands. The *Church Farm Museum* has recreated interiors and displays of agricultural equipment. On A158 4½m inland is the Perp. church of *Burgh-le-Marsh*, with a fine tower, screens and 17C pulpit. For *Gunby Hall*, 2m further, see Rte 71A.— Billy Butlin opened his first holiday camp in the 1930s at (66m) *Ingoldmells*. A52 here turns inland to (69m) *Hogsthorpe*, with an EE church, and (73m) *Huttoft*, where the church has a 13C tower, good corbels, a richly carved Perp. font and a 14C chest.—78m. *Sutton-on-Sea* and (81m) **Mablethorpe** (joint population 7,500; seasonal Tourist Information) are less brash than Skegness. D.H. Lawrence stayed at Mablethorpe in his boyhood and remembered the holiday in 'Sons and Lovers'.

We turn inland again and take A1301.—At (85m) *Theddlethorpe All Saints*, to the left, the church is built of colourful stone, with traces of every period from the early Norman. Its interesting contents include a funerary helm. The three *Saltfleetby* villages lie c 1¹/₂m N on the banks of the Great Eau, all with fine churches.—At (89m) *Saltfleet* the manor house (not open) has been identified as Tennyson's 'Locksley Hall, that in the distance overlooks the sandy tracts', but a better candidate is the house so named in (92m) *North Somercotes*. Here the road veers inland to another series of fine churches: (95m) *Grainthorpe*, Perp. with a brick floor, 18C gallery and panelling made from old pews; (96¹/₂m) *Marshchapel*; (101m) *Tetney*, with a high Perp. limestone tower; and (104m) *Humberston*, 18C brick with a Perp. stone tower.—107m. *Cleethorpes* (35,500 inhab.; Tourist Information), now a suburb of Grimsby, developed as a resort round the railway station (1863) built on the front.—108m. **Grimsby**, see Rte 71A.

# 72 Peterborough to Lincoln and the Humber

Total distance 86m. **Peterborough**, see Rte 68.—A15 to (15m) Bourne.—A15 to (33m) Sleaford.—A15 to (50m) **Lincoln**.—B1398, B1206 to (70m) Redbourne.—A15, A18 to (75m) Brigg.—A18, A15 to (86m) **Barton-upon-Humber**.

Maps: OS Landranger 142, 130, 121, 112.

We leave **Peterborough** (Rte 68) by A15.—5¹/₂m. *Glinton. Peakirk*, 1¹/₂m NE, is worth visiting for the 14C wall paintings in the church of St Pega. *Helpston*, 3m W of Glinton, was the birthplace of John Clare (1793–1864).—7m. *Northborough*, the home of Clare's later years, preserves much of its 14C manor house.—We cross the Welland into Lincolnshire just S of (8m) *Market Deeping*, a town with some fine old houses and a 12–13C church, but no longer a market. Its rectory, dating from the 13C is the oldest inhabited parsonage in England. The composer Robert Fayrfax (1464–1521) was born here. At *Deeping St James*, to the E, the church was part of a Benedictine priory, a cell of Thorney. It has a fine 12C nave, Norman font, and a graveside shelter. The RC church near the Welland at *Deeping Gate* has two good sculptures: a 14C Crucifixion and a 15C Virgin.—15m. **Bourne** (8100 inhab.), a typical Lincolnshire market town, is the apocryphal birthplace of Hereward the Wake. In the Priory Robert Mannying (Robert of Brunne, fl. 1300) made the translations from the Norman which laid the foundations for the English language. Lord Burghley (1520–98) was born here, in the house now the Burghley Arms, as was Monsieur Charles F. Worth of Paris (1825–95). The *Priory Church* has Norman arcades. The *Town Hall* (1821) has an unusual exterior staircase. In South St. are good 17C cottages and the Tudor *Red Hall*.

At *Edenham*, 3m NW on A151, the church has a fine roof and monuments of the Bertie family. 2m further on is *Grimsthorpe Castle* (open), a huge building of various dates in spacious parkland laid out by Capability Brown. Most interesting are King John's Tower, a fragment of the 13C castle, and the N front and great hall by Vanbrugh, his last work. The fine collection of art includes works by Holbein. The church at *Irnham*, 3¹/₂m further NW, has an Easter Sepulchre (cf. Heckington below).

20m. *Rippingale*, on the right, has a church with good Geometric windows (14C) and a rare effigy of a deacon.—24m. *Folkingham*, once a town of some importance with its own quarter sessions, has a large and handsome square with a coaching inn. The church is Perp. with an excellent oak screen. Part of the early 19C House of Correction survives in the Billingborough road. At *Pickworth*, 2¹/₂m W, the church has 14C wall paintings.

To the E are (2³/₄m) *Billingborough* church, with a tall tower, splendid flying buttresses and florid windows, and (1m N) *Horbling*, a Georgian village with interesting church and a votive well. *Sempringham*, 1¹/₂m S of Billingborough, was the birthplace of St Gilbert (d. 1189), founder of the only English order of monks and nuns; a Norman doorway and the nave of their church survive.

At 26m we cross A52. *Threekingham*, 1m E, has a Norman church with a fine spire and Dec. windows.—31m. *Silk Willoughby* church (Dec.) has good pews and bench ends, and a Norman font.—33m. **Sleaford** (8500 inhab.) is an old and thriving market town. The *Maltings* (1892–1905), over 1000ft long, is a fine industrial building. The church of *St Denys* is noted for its flowing Dec. window tracery and ornamentation, and a 15C screen with a rood added by Sir Ninian Comper in 1918. It stands on one side of the bustling Market Place in a harmonious group of buildings: the 15C *Vicarage*, the *Sessions House* (1831), the fine Georgian *Bristol Arms*, and the *Corn Exchange* (1857).

*Ancaster*, 6m SW on A153, has given its name to a famous building stone. There are a few traces of the Roman fortified station, *Causennae*, on Ermine Street. *Honington*, 2m further, lies on A607 from Grantham to Lincoln (Rte 59).—A17 leads NW from Sleaford towards Newark-on-Trent across the deserted uplands of the *Cliff* (see below and Rte 59). *Rauceby*, S of the road at 4m, has a conspicuous church with fine tower and 13C broach spire. N of the road at 6m is *Cranwell RAF College*, founded in 1920. *Temple Bruer*, 2m N, with a massive Norman tower, is all that remains of a preceptory of the Knights Templar.

FROM SLEAFORD TO BOSTON, 20m.—A17 leads E to (5m) *Heckington* (Tourist Information), which has a handsome windmill with eight sails. The *church is a fine example of pure late Dec. (1345–80), with exquisite flowing tracery, a magnificent Easter Sepulchre and a fine E window. *Ewerby*, 3m NW, has a noteworthy 14C church with a broach spire, and *Helpringham*, 2¹/₂m S, has a fine Dec. steeple.—We follow A17 right to (12m) *Swineshead*, which has an interesting church, the old stocks and the base of a market cross. *Swineshead Abbey*, where King John stayed in 1216 after crossing the Wash, lay 1m E.—1m S of Swineshead A52 leads left to (20m) **Boston**, see Rte 71A.

FROM SLEAFORD TO HORNCASTLE, 23m via A153. We cross Fenland, through (4¹/₂m) *Anwick* and (9m) *Billinghay*, both with notable church steeples. *South Kyme*, a remote fen village S of the road, has a 13C keep, while its church is a fragment of a 12C priory. We cross the Witham.—13m. **Tattershall** has the tall keep of a *Castle (NT) built c 1440 by Baron Cromwell, Lord High Treasurer to Henry VI, a fine example of a fortified dwelling and perhaps 'the grandest piece of brickwork in the kingdom' (Viscount Torrington). Its walls are in places 16ft thick. There is one large main room on each floor, with some splendid fireplaces. The large collegiate *Church*, late Perp., has many 15–16C brasses, much glass of c 1500 in the E window and a stone choir screen. *Tattershall College* (English Heritage, standard opening) was founded by Baron Cromwell as a choir school. The village cross is 15C.—14m. *Coningsby* is supposed to have given Disraeli the title for his novel. The church has a processional path under its 15C tower. About 4m N is *Woodhall Spa* (2400 inhab.;

seasonal Tourist Information) among pines and firs. At *Kirkstead*, 1m S of Woodhall, is a fragment of a Cistercian abbey (13C) and the isolated *Chapel of St Leonard, now the parish church, a gem of EE architecture with a choir screen of 1210.—23m. *Horncastle*, see Rte 71A.

A15 continues N from Sleaford, climbing the ridge of the oolite limestone escarpment known as the Cliff (see also Rte 59) and passing (43¼m) *Dunston Pillar*, now ruined, built by Sir Francis Dashwood in 1751 as a land lighthouse for travellers across the heath.—47m. *Bracebridge Heath*. The church of All Saints at *Bracebridge*, by A46 to the W, has a Saxon nave and an 11C tower, perhaps pre-Norman, resembling those of St Mary-le-Wigford and St Peter-at-Gowts in Lincoln.

50m. **LINCOLN** (76,700 inhab.), dominated by its superbly placed cathedral, stands mainly on a rocky hill rising from the river Witham on the NW edge of the flat Fens. Despite the growth of industry, it has kept its character and atmosphere as one of the most ancient towns in England.

**Tourist Information Centres**: Castle Hill and Cornhill.

**Car Parks**: Westgate, Danesgate, Saltergate and Cattle Market; multi-storey car park in Flaxengate.

**Bus Station**: off Melville St., by Pelham Bridge.

**Railway Station**: Central Station, St Mary St.

**Theatre**: Theatre Royal, Clasketgate.

**History**. The pre-Roman settlement guarding the gap in the oolite cliff was occupied by the Romans in AD 47, and c 80–86 it became a colony under the name of *Lindum Colonia*. The Saxons also have left their traces, and a little later it became one of the Danelagh towns. Christianity was reintroduced by St Paulinus in 627; the bishopric dates from 1072, when Remigius transferred his bishop's stool from Dorchester-on-Thames to Lincoln. At the time of the Norman Conquest London, Winchester and York alone outranked Lincoln in importance among the cities of England, and in the 13C it was the fourth 'seaport' of the realm. The castle, built by William I was captured about 1140 by Stephen, whose conflict with Matilda surged round the city. Henry II had a second coronation here in 1158.

Lincoln today is important for its heavy engineering works and for agricultural machinery. In the First World War (1916) it was the birthplace of tanks.

In 1290 Queen Eleanor of Castile, wife of Edward I, died at *Harby*, 8m W of Lincoln. The successive stages of the funeral procession that bore her body to Westminster Abbey were marked by the beautiful Eleanor Crosses, erected between 1291 and 1294. The list varies, but began at Lincoln (see Castle and High St. below) and apparently continued with Grantham, Stamford, Geddington, Northampton, Stony Stratford, Woburn, Dunstable, St Albans, Waltham, and Cheapside and Charing Cross in London. The only ones still standing are at Geddington, Northampton and Waltham.

**Famous natives and residents**. William Byrd (1543–1623), the composer, served as organist at the cathedral from 1563 to 1572. Peter de Wint (1784–1849), the painter, lived for many years at Hilton House, Drury Lane (plaque).

A visit to Lincoln should start on Castle Hill, the high plateau marking the centre of the ancient city. On its E side the 14C *Exchequer Gate* leads to the **Cathedral**, outstanding among English churches for its wonderfully soaring position (surpassed only by Durham) and for the richly unified design that made it, in Ruskin's eyes, 'out and out the most precious piece of architecture in the British Isles'.

Its history falls into three main phases. The first began in 1072, when Bishop Remigius moved his see from Dorchester to Lincoln. Consecrated some 20 years later, this Norman cathedral was shattered by an earthquake in 1185, leaving only the central core of its W front as part of the structure we see today. Its fall gave Bishop Hugh (1186–1200), later St Hugh of

CHAPTER
HOUSE

Holy Trinity
Chapel

N E
PORCH

ANGEL
CHOIR

7
10
11
9

St Blaise
Chapel

SOUTH
PORCH

Longland
Chantry

6   4 5

Vestry
St Peter &
St Paul
Chapel

Easter
Sepulchre   3

N E
TRANSEPT

S E
TRANSEPT

Vestries

LIBRARY
(over)

CLOISTER

Treasury

NETTLE
COURT

Vestry

2

A   B   C

D   E   F

N W
TRANSEPT

CENTRAL
TOWER

S W
TRANSEPT

1

Nave Altar

GALILEE
PORCH

Chapels
A   St Michael (Airmen)
B   St Andrew (Seamen)
C   St George (Soldiers)
D   St Edward (Works Chantry)
E   St John Evangelist (Guilds)
F   St Anne (Women)

Morning Chapel
(St Mary Magd.)

Font

CONSISTORY
COURT

Wickham
Annexe

Ringers'
Chapel

0                    100 feet
0                    30 metres

Key to Numbers
1   Bp King
2   Little St Hugh
3   Katherine Swynford
4   Bp Fuller
5   Bp Gardiner
6   St Hugh
7   Queen Eleanor Cenotaph
8   Burghersh Tombs
9   St Hugh's Head Shrine
10  Sir Nicholas Cantilupe
11  Archdeacon Wymbyssh

# LINCOLN CATHEDRAL

*The Angel Choir of Lincoln Cathedral*

Lincoln, the chance to rebuild and extend, with Geoffrey of Noiers in charge of operations. Their work, and the work continuing under their inspiration until c 1250, was responsible for most of the present building. The third and last important stage came in 1255–80 with the addition of the Angel Choir.

The impressive *W front (currently being restored) consists, roughly, of a block of the original Norman work encased in a screen façade of EE lancet work. Above the richly moulded central doorway are 11 statues of kings. The much weathered frieze of carved panels (c 1145), perhaps copied from Modena Cathedral, illustrates the Old Testament on the S side and the New Testament on the N. The SW turret is topped by a statue of St Hugh, while on the NW turret is the 'Swineherd of Stow', who contributed his savings to St Hugh's building work. The W towers belong in their lower stages to a late Norman restoration of c 1141; their upper part is late Dec. (c 1420). The magnificent *central tower, housing 'Great Tom of Lincoln', a bell weighing almost 5½ tons, rises to 271ft and commands a panoramic view. Its upper stages date from 1307–11 (Geometric Dec.).

Walking round the S side, we come first to the Galilee Porch, leading into the SW transept, and then to the Judgement Porch, taking its name from the striking picture of the Last Judgement in its richly decorated arch. Among the interesting gargoyles on this part of the building is one known as the 'Devil looking over Lincoln'. The figures on the buttresses are apparently Edward I and his two wives, Queen Eleanor and Queen Margaret. The clear space beyond offers a good view of the E end, with its noble window, deep buttresses, lines of arcading, enriched gable and crocketed pinnacles. At the top of the gable is a sculpture of the Virgin and Child.

We enter by the doorway in the W front. The *Nave* belongs to St Hugh's rebuilding and is unusually wide, with delicately clustered columns. The effect would be grander if the organ over the rood screen did not block a view of the E end. The late Norman font, in the second bay of the S aisle, is one of only seven in England made from Tournai marble. The *Great* or *W Transepts*, begun by St Hugh and finished between 1220 and 1235, between them house six chapels but are most notable for their lovely rose windows, still with their original glass. The *Dean's Eye,* on the N, is EE (c 1220); the *Bishop's Eye, to the S, is Dec. of c 1325–50 with gracefully flowing tracery.

Elaborately carved doorways and a Dec. stone screen (c 1300) separate the nave from the fine EE *Choir.* We enter by the S aisle, passing the shrine of Little St Hugh, once said to have been ritually murdered by Jews in 1255. The magnificent canopied *choir stalls (early Perp., c 1380) are among the best in England. The wide variety of subjects in the misericords includes the parable of the fox preaching to geese (W end of N range). The N choir aisle has a tablet to

LINCOLN

0 _____ 200 yards
0 _____ 200 metres

the composer William Byrd. The *Lesser* or *E Transepts* are remarkable for their piers with detached crocketed shafts, known as the 'Trondheim Pillars' from their similarity to those at Trondheim in Norway. The Treasury by the NE transept has a magnificent collection of plate, chalices and patens.

The chief glory of the interior is the * *Angel Choir*, built to replace the apsidal end of St Hugh's church when the crowds of pilgrims attracted by the saint's shrine needed more space. Queen Eleanor attended its consecration in 1280. It forms the five E bays of the present choir, and takes its name from the 30 carved angels in the spandrels of the triforium. The refined delicacy of these details, the richness of the bosses and the lovely use of Purbeck marble put it among the greatest achievements of Gothic architecture in England. The famous 'Lincoln Imp' is a grotesque figure at the top of the last complete column on the N side. The monuments include: St Hugh, behind the altar on the N side; the battered 14C shrine of St Hugh's Head, near the Burghersh Chapel in the NE corner; and the cenotaph of Queen Eleanor (destroyed 1644, rebuilt 1891) at the E end. The great E window in the Geometric style, filled with Victorian glass, is the largest and earliest eight-light window in England.

We enter the 13C *Cloister* from the NE transept. In its E walk is the graceful polygonal *Chapter House*, with a single central shaft supporting the vaulted roof. It was the scene of the earliest meetings of the English Parliament, in the reigns of Edward I and II. The N walk, rebuilt as a Doric colonnade by Wren (c 1674), gives fine views of the cathedral. Above is the *Chapter Library* (open), with one bay of the medieval library burned in 1609 but mainly built by Wren to house Dean Honywood's remarkable and varied collection.

The Galilee Porch takes us out of the cathedral into the *Close* or *Minster Yard*. At the corner nearly opposite is the 14C *Cantilupe Chantry House*; below and behind this is the arched entrance to the ruined *Old Bishop's Palace* (English Heritage, summer standard opening but closed on Tuesdays and on Wednesday afternoons), founded in the 12C, with 13–15C additions. Next comes the gatehouse of the *Vicars' Court*, built 1300–80 for a college of priest-vicars. To the E of the cathedral are the *Chancery* (14–15C) and the *Choristers' House*, and further N is the *Priory Gate*, an arch of an old gateway destroyed in 1815. On the green stands a statue of Tennyson by G.F. Watts. On the N side are several old houses, including the present *Bishop's House*.

On the W side of Castle Hill stands the **Castle** (open), one of the eight known to have been founded by William the Conqueror himself. It was started in 1068 and the walls have the herringbone masonry typical of early Norman work built near Roman remains (cf. the tower of St Albans). Unusually, the bailey wall incorporates two mottes.

We enter through the *Eastern Gate*, a massive piece of 14C work on top of a Norman tunnel vault; on the right is a delicate oriel window brought from a house which stood in the High St., popularly but mistakenly known as 'John of Gaunt's Palace'. The walls enclose a pleasant garden of about six acres; on the lawn a fragment of an Eleanor Cross (see above) is preserved. To the left is the *Observatory Tower* on its motte, a Norman base with 14C upperworks and a 19C turret. Steep ladders inside lead to the roof and a dramatic *view. On the second and later motte beyond, the *Lucy Tower*, a shell keep, has the graves of prisoners from the brick *City Prison* by Carr of York and William Lumby, in use from 1787 to 1878 but now courts and a repository for archives. The prison *Chapel* (open) with coffin-like pews, probably dating fromf the 1840s, keeps its oppressive atmosphere. The NE tower, *Cobb Hall*, is 13C and vaulted on two levels; it was the place of execution until 1868. Smirke's *Assize Courts* (1826) stand in the western part of the grounds, behind which is the *West Gate* (not open), beside the W gate of the Roman fortress.

Bailgate, the centre of the Roman town, leads N from the square, with the Tourist Information Centre housed in a fine half-timbered building on the corner. Circles mark the spots where the bases of Roman pillars have been found. The site of *St Paul in the Bail*, at the corner of Westgate, has recently been excavated to reveal the Roman forum (open). Bailgate ends at *Newport Arch*, the N gate of the Roman city, probably dating from the early 2C. In Burton Rd, to the NW, the *Museum of Lincolnshire Life* houses a display of local history during the past 200 years.

Returning down Bailgate, we may follow East Bight to the left. This reveals a part of the Roman Wall, bends round to the right and leads into Eastgate. To our left, in front of the Eastgate Hotel, foundations of a tower of the Roman *East Gate* have been exposed. Descending beyond this, we pass through the Priory Gate (see above) and the early 14C *Potter Gate* and reach the busy Lindum Rd. On the right, in a pleasant setting, is the **Usher Art Gallery**. Its distinguished collection of paintings includes watercolours by *Peter de Wint and other artists with local connections; topographical paintings of Lincolnshire include views of the cathedral by Thomas Girtin and Turner, the latter also represented by his view of Stamford. Also on display are watches, miniatures, porcelain and Tennyson memorabilia.

Monks Rd, to the left further on, leads to the main entrance of the *Arboretum*. Beyond, on the right, is *Monks Abbey*, a small park with the remains of an EE chapel (with Perp. windows), a 'cell' of St Mary's Abbey at York.

From the S end of Lindum Rd Broadgate leads S to the **City and County Museum**, which occupies the 13C *Grey Friars Priory* and contains a fine collection of local antiquities; the upper room has a 'barrel' roof. Melville St. goes on to *Pelham Bridge* (1958).

Turning down St Mary St. we come to the church of *St Mary-le-Wigford* in the High St. It has a Saxon tower, on the outside of which is a Roman memorial slab with a later Saxon inscription. The nave, chancel and N aisle are EE (c 1225). *St Mary's Conduit*, in front of the church, was built in the 16C with stones from the White Friars monastery.

In High St., just to the S, in Akrill's Passage, is a 15C timbered house. Further on is (left) *St Mary's Guildhall*, an interesting 12C building. Beyond is the church of *St Peter-at-Gowts*, with a Saxon tower resembling St Mary-le-Wigford and a Romanesque font. About 1/3m further on stood the *Bar Gate*, the S entrance to the medieval city, near which rose the Eleanor Cross.

High St. leads N, passing the church of *St Benedict*, with a short late Saxon tower and a rustic 13–14C interior, to the *High Bridge*, one of the few bridges in England on which houses still stand. The original ribs can be seen from the riverside path which leads left to *Brayford Pool*, with its old quay. Here we find the *National Cycle Museum*. A short step N of the High Bridge is a fine 15C town gate, the *Stonebow*. Its upper room, still used as the Guildhall, has a fine timber roof and contains the civic insignia (open first Saturday of each month).

High St. ends just beyond the 15C *Cardinal's Hat* at the Strait, which leads upwards to the right. At the top is the *Jew's House, one of the oldest examples of domestic architecture in England (Norman, early 12C). Steep Hill continues the ascent and a step across it forms the so-called *Reader's Rest*. Above this are *Harding House* and other timbered houses, and, on the right, the *House of Aaron the Jew*, a late Norman building with a round-headed window. Michaelgate (to the left) and Danesgate (to the right) are interesting old streets.

FROM LINCOLN TO GRIMSBY, 37m via A46.—8½m. *Snarford* church has fine monuments of the St Poll family.—Under a mile E of (10½m) *Faldingworth* lies *Buslingthorpe*, with a church containing one of the earliest brasses in England (Sir Richard de Boselyngthorpe, c 1310).—Near (16m) *Market Rasen* (2700 inhab.) many traces of Roman and pre-Roman occupation have been found. —24m. *Caistor* stands on the site of a Roman camp and has an interesting church. *Pelham's Pillar*, on top of the Wolds above Caistor, commemorates a plantation scheme by the Earl of Yarborough (1840).—37m. *Grimsby*, see Rte 71A.

From Lincoln to *Grantham*, see Rte 59; to *Horncastle* and *Boston*, see Rte 71A.

The main route from Lincoln to the Humber heads NE for the Humber Bridge; for an alternative route NW via Gainsborough to Goole, see below.

A15 continues N from Lincoln, arrow-straight across the Fens, following the line of the Roman Ermine Street until just before Redbourne. A much more interesting road, B1398, runs parallel and clings to the crest of the Cliff, giving wide views W across the Trent valley, especially at (54m) the junction with the Roman road from *Sturton-by-Stow*.—61m. *Glentworth* has an 11C church tower.—68m. *Kirton-in-Lindsey* is a large village with a fine EE church tower. By the windmill to the N is the *Lincolnshire and Humberside Railway Museum*. We turn right on B1206 to rejoin A15 at (70m) *Redbourne*.—Just before (71½m) *Hibaldstow* an unclassified road leads left to the deserted medieval village of *Gainsthorpe* (English Heritage, open at any reasonable time).—75m. *Brigg* (5400 inhab.; Tourist Information) is a small market town which grew prosperous with the draining of the Fens.

At *Broughton*, 3½m NW, the church has an 11C Saxon tower.—6m W of Brigg is the iron and steel town of **Scunthorpe** (66,400 inhab.; Tourist Information). The Borough Museum and Art Gallery on Oswald Rd has displays of local history and an important collection of prehistoric, Roman and later archaeology. 4m N via B1430 is *Normanby Hall* (open), an experiment in the 'cubic' style built in 1820 by Sir Robert Smirke, architect of the British Museum.

A18 continues NE from Brigg to (79m) the junction with M180 and A15. *Barnetby-le-Wold*, to the right, has a remarkable late Norman lead font in its 20C church. *Humberside Airport*, off A18 2½m further E, has passsenger flights to Heathrow, Norwich, Teesside, Aberdeen, Edinburgh, Glasgow, Belfast, Amsterdam and Esbjerg.—A15 climbs the northern spur of the Wolds, passing (80m) *Elsham Hall Country Park* (open), before dropping down to (86m) **Barton-upon-Humber**

*The Humber Bridge*

(8500 inhab.), a market town and decayed port chiefly interesting for its two churches. *St Peter (English Heritage, open Monday to Friday 14.00–16.00 and by appointment only at weekends) has one of the earliest church towers in England, with characteristic Saxon arcading and panels divided by strips of stone. The narthex, or W porch, is of the same date (c 1000) and its circular lights still have fragments of the original oak shutters. The rest of the building is Dec. and Perp. *St Mary*, close by, is mainly EE with some Trans. work. It has a fine brass to Simon Seman, Sheriff of London in 1433. N of the town the **Humber Bridge** (toll; Tourist Information at North Bank Viewing Area), opened in 1981, joins the two parts of Humberside and leads to *Hull* (Rte 82A).

At *Goxhill*, 4m SE of Barton-upon-Humber, the church has a fine Perp. tower and contains a cross-legged effigy in chain armour (c 1300).—*Thornton Curtis*, 4m SE of Barton-upon-Humber, has a Norman and EE church with a Tournai marble font. 2m E are the remains of **Thornton Abbey**, founded in 1139 for Austin Canons and rebuilt after 1264 (English Heritage, summer standard opening). They include a magnificent brick *gatehouse (1382) with five of its original statues, its oak doors and a charming oriel window, and two sides of the chapter house (1282–1308). At *Brocklesby*, 6 m SE of Thornton Curtis, the church has monuments of the Pelhams, Earls of Yarborough. In the park near the village is a circular mausoleum (1787–94) by James Wyatt.

An alternative route from (50m) Lincoln to the Humber takes A57 NW past the racecourse, with a good grandstand of 1826. The road follows the Foss Dyke cut by the Romans to connect the Trent with the Witham.—3½m S of (55m) *Saxilby* is ***Doddington Hall** (open).

It was built between 1593 and 1600 for Thomas Tailor, the self-made Registrar of Lincoln, and has never changed hands by sale. In all probability the architect was Robert Smythson, who built Hardwick Hall, Worksop Manor and Wollaton Hall. Modest in scale and simple in design by comparison with these great houses, Doddington is nevertheless satisfyingly confident and is lent great charm by its mellowed brickwork. The interior was remodelled in 1760–65 by Thomas Lumby, the Lincoln carpenter also responsible for the nearby village church.

At 56m we branch right on A156 to (59m) *Torksey*, where the Foss Dyke joins the Trent. There was a Saxon mint here. At (61m) *Marton*, we cross Till Bridge Lane, a branch from Ermine Street. The church tower has early Norman herringbone work, and in the chancel is a 13C crucifixion. *Stow* church, 2m E, is one of the largest and oldest pre-Conquest churches in England, with huge 10C crossing arches. It contains an EE font and 13C wall paintings. *Cotes-by-Stow* church, 2m further E, has a fine rood loft.—At (63m) *Knaith* Thomas Sutton, founder of Charterhouse, was born in 1532.—64m. *Lea* church has 14C glass and a 15C Crucifixion.

66m **Gainsborough** (18,700 inhab.) is an old market town and river port on the Trent, crossed by a fine bridge of 1787. Sweyn Forkbeard, King of Denmark, died here in 1014 after conquering England. Ugly red brick has largely triumphed over the picturesque charm George Eliot evoked in her portrait of the town as 'St Ogg's' in 'The Mill on the Floss'. The church of *All Saints* has a Perp. tower and a nave and chancel rebuilt in 1736–44. The *Old Hall* (open) is a manor house rebuilt in the 1480s to entertain Richard III and rebuilt again a century later. The kitchen and great hall of the earlier building survive. The 'eagre', or tidal wave on the Trent, ascends above Gainsborough.—For *Bawtry*, 12m W, see Rte 59.

We follow A631 to the W, turning N at (69m) *Beckingham* on A161.

The road runs through the alluvial **Isle of Axholme**, drained by
Vermuyden and his Dutch workmen (1626–28). Much of the land has
been reclaimed by the flooding process known as 'warping'. Near
(77$\frac{1}{2}$m) *Haxey*, which has a dignified 14C church, the system of strip
cultivation is much in evidence. The 'Haxey Hood', a traditional
game, is played in costume on 6 January.—80$\frac{1}{2}$m. *Epworth* is a large
pleasant village. On the road leading to Owston Ferry stands the Old
Rectory (open), built in 1709 to replace an earlier building that
burned down. John and Charles Wesley (1703–91 and 1707–88),
founders of Methodism, spent their childhood here.—82m. *Belton*
church has a 14C effigy of a knight made from a Saxon gravestone.
The *Sandtoft Transport Centre*, 3m W has trolleybuses, etc.—At
(87$\frac{1}{2}$m) *Crowle* the church has Norman traces, including a good
doorway, and a Saxon cross shaft.—99m. **Goole**, see Rte 81.

# NORTHERN ENGLAND

Northern England, as defined in this section, stretches from the Mersey estuary across to the Humber estuary and up the 'narrowing strand' of England to the Scottish border. Its southern boundary thus runs from Liverpool through Manchester, Sheffield and the complex of industrial towns on the slopes of the Pennines to Hull. In the N, the border runs through wild and often remote countryside between the Solway, near Carlisle, to Berwick-upon-Tweed. The county map, greatly complicated by the boundary changes and new creations of the 1970s, embraces: in the S, Merseyside, Greater Manchester, West Yorkshire, South Yorkshire and the northern half of Humberside; above them, Lancashire, North Yorkshire and County Durham, with Cleveland and Tyne and Wear on the coast; and, bordering Scotland, Cumbria and Northumberland.

Equally intricate, the map of the region's natural contours is dominated by hills and rivers. The Pennine Chain forms a central upland mass, stretching like a backbone from the northern Peak District to the Tyne. The change from millstone grit to mountain limestone along its course typifies the geological variety which makes the other hilly regions of the North, like the Lake District and the North York Moors, distinct and complex units. Their specific composition is described in the separate routes below. Here it is enough to note that chalk, whose smooth and fertile contours so perfectly express the gentle character of most southern landscapes, appears only in the Yorkshire Wolds above Hull. Elsewhere, the northern hills are more rugged than their southern neighbours, often rich in coal or mineral deposits but usually unsuited to arable farming. Their slopes are drained by a network of rivers which help to swell the great estuaries punctuating the coastline—the Mersey in the W and the Humber, the Tees and the Tyne in the E.

Such a landscape lends itself to low-density agriculture or intense industrialisation. The hill may be used for sheep pasture or exploited as a mine. The valley may remain a secluded dale or foster a town crammed by the banks of a vital power source and communication artery. The river's mouth may be marked by a compact fishing harbour or a sprawling industrial port. All these various possibilities have been realised, with the result that nowhere else in England is the juxtaposition of the rural and the urban, the pastoral and the industrial, so strikingly apparent. On the one hand, the North preserves remote and beautiful countryside; four of the best and largest tracts—the Lake District, the North York Moors, the Yorkshire Dales and much of Northumberland's hills and forests—are now National Parks. On the other, the region is crowded with towns and cities which burst into energetic, ungainly life during the Industrial Revolution of the 18–19C and are now often withering in the harsher economic climate of the 20C.

The very sharpness of the contrast which greets the traveller who heads from the cities and towns near the S end of the Pennines into the Yorkshire Dales, or approaches the Lake District by way of the decayed ports and coalfields on the Cumbrian coast, or enters the North York Moors from the Teesside region, can obscure the length and subtlety of the process which has gone into its making. However emphatically it may have left its stamp, the Industrial Revolution was by no means the only determining event in the region's long and varied history. In Northumberland and Cumbria the ruins of

Hadrian's Wall still mark the northern limit of Roman Britain. The medieval castles stretching down Northumberland's coast—at Bamburgh, Dunstanburgh, Alnwick and Warkworth—are monumental evidence of its later history as the disputed outpost of English territory. The medieval 'pele towers' found here and elsewhere in the North provide humbler but equally eloquent reminders of the hazards of border life. These small defensive structures, two or three storeys high and usually with only one room to each storey, survive either by themselves or as the core of buildings expanded into country houses in later, more peaceful times.

In one aspect a stern and remote frontier, Northumberland and its southern neighbour County Durham were also a vital centre: the place where Celtic Christianity first established itself on English soil. From Holy Island (or Lindisfarne), where St Aidan founded his bishopric in 635, it spread to monasteries at Hartlepool, Jarrow and Monkwearmouth. The crosses which still stand at Bewcastle and Gosforth, the church at Escomb and the Saxon crypts at Hexham and Ripon are witness to its wider diffusion. At Whitby the EE ruins of a later monastery now occupy the marvellous cliff-top site of the Saxon foundation where the Celtic and Roman churches conferred at the Synod in 664, and at Durham the great cathedral rebuilt soon after the Conquest marks the final resting place of St Cuthbert, the most revered saint of the early Church, and of Bede, its chronicler.

If Durham, probably the most romantic of all the northern cities, stands as the great summative achievement of the Church in its first phase, then York testifies to the power and splendour it achieved later in the Middle Ages. Its minster and parish churches, with their superb stained glass, are famous beyond the need for special praise or introduction. Indeed, their fame has unfairly overshadowed the merits of other Yorkshire churches like Ripon, Selby and, particularly, Beverley. And certainly no part of England is richer in monastic remains or in natural settings which display their ruined glory to such poignant effect. The Cistercian abbeys of Rievaulx and Fountains, in particular, are unrivalled in Europe.

The wealth of Yorkshire's ecclesiastical foundations and its market towns was partly derived from wool. The trade became a staple of the region's economy and made cloth centres of towns like Leeds, Wakefield and Bradford long before industrialisation set in. The size and dignity of the late 18C Piece Hall at Halifax shows the importance that such industries could attain even in their cottage phase. Elsewhere in the region, many of the other activities that came to typify the Industrial Revolution can also boast a long pre-industrial history. Lead-mining is one of the oldest: the moors around Pateley Bridge, for example, bear traces of Roman and medieval workings. The hills of the Lake District were being mined for silver, iron, copper and other minerals as well as lead several centuries before tourists began seeking them out for their picturesque beauty: the Keswick pencil industry goes back to the German immigrants who arrived to work the local 'plumbago' mines in the 16C. Sheffield cutlery was known to Chaucer, and by the 17C the folly of carrying coals to Newcastle was becoming proverbial. In the 18C Captain Cook made his first voyage round the world in ships built at Whitby.

The processes which transformed these industries in the 18–19C have already been sketched in the introduction to the North Midlands. In the North, they are summed up by the rise of Manchester. With its wealth and squalour, its brashness and sophistication, it was more completely a child of the Industrial Revolution than any other

English city. Fed by the supply of cotton which arrived from America via Liverpool, and stimulated by the advances in spinning and weaving associated with the names of Arkwright, Crompton, Hargreaves and Kay, it grew into the regional capital of an industry which gave life to the mill towns of Pennine Lancashire. Its canal system spanned the entire history of that era in communications and transport, with the Bridgewater Canal begun by James Brindley in 1759 signifying its modest beginning and the Ship Canal of 1887–94 its ambitious finale. The Liverpool and Manchester Railway—the first line of more than local importance—opened in 1830, some five years after its engineer George Stephenson had pioneered his famous Stockton–Darlington line.

In their own age the cities and towns that grew with the industrial boom of the North simultaneously excited and alarmed contemporaries. Today, they inspire equally mixed reactions, though often of a more melancholy sort. As the introduction to the North Midlands has already noted, we have at last begun to cherish the industrial heritage which previous generations regarded as merely functional or downright ugly. Manchester's Liverpool Road Station is now the centre of an ambitious and expanding museum complex, for example, and Liverpool's Albert Dock has been restored to its former grandeur. By the same token, we have at last begun to value the architectural achievements of the 19C city, though in many cases the change of taste has come too late to save Victorian centres from a dreadful battering at the hands of post-war planners and developers. Mercifully, the ring roads and shopping centres and gimmicky tower blocks have not swept away the work of John Dobson in Newcastle, or Cuthbert Brodrick in Leeds, or the great town halls of Manchester and Liverpool. Yet admiration for this legacy has come at precisely the time when the cities are also undergoing deep economic and social crisis. The virtual disappearance of the cotton industry and the decline of industries like coal, steel and shipbuilding have bred the familiar 20C problems of urban decay in their most urgent form. So the northern cities now present a curious mixture of conservation and dereliction. It remains to be seen if the Urban Development Corporations, Task Forces, Enterprise Zones and other remedies proposed by the 1980s can restore them to anything like health or wholeness.

# **73** Liverpool

**LIVERPOOL** (510,300 inhab.) has become a city of contrasts. St George's Hall, Liverpool Museum, the Walker Art Gallery, and the abundance of good 19C banks, office buildings and residential streets all remind the visitor of its days as a great Atlantic seaport and a great Victorian city. They testify to an energy, confidence and civic pride that continued into the 20C long enough to produce the Edwardian grandeur of the waterfront and to give the city its two cathedrals, one Anglican and the other Roman Catholic. Yet these monuments now stand among urban decay that speaks all too eloquently of Liverpool's decline in recent years. Even the restoration of the splendid Albert Dock, welcome though it is on aesthetic grounds, looks more like cosmetic surgery than genuine revitalisation.

INGSWAY TUNNEL

EVERTON

ISLINGTON

ERSKINE STREET

WAY

Mus. of Labour Hist.

Walker Art Gal

iverpool Mus

Libraries

Wellington Mon.

St John's Gardens

St Georges Hall

Empire Th.

Royal Court

St John's Shopping Centre

acon

Neptune h.

Lyceum

Central Station

Lime St. Station

Bus Station

LONDON ROAD

PEMBROKE PLACE

University

BROWNLOW

Metropolitan Cathedral (RC)

University

MOUNT PLEASANT

OXFORD STREET

Everyman Th.

CAMBRIDGE SQUARE

LEECE STREET

HARDMAN

St Luke's

Philharmonic Hall

Liverpool Inst.

CANNING

Baths

St James Cathedral

Cemetery

HUSKINSSON

PARLIAMENT

FALKNER STREET

FALKNER SQUARE

WAVERTREE

PRINCES ROAD

PRINCES AVENUE

N

ST JAMES PLACE

WARWICK STREET

DINGLE

**LIVERPOOL**

0      400 yards
0      400 metres

**Tourist Information Centres**: No. 29 Lime St.; Atlantic Pavilion, Albert Dock.

**Car Parks**: Albert Dock. Multi-storey car parks in Paradise St., Hanover St., St John's Centre, Mount Pleasant.

**Bus and Coach Stations**: The main bus terminus is at Pier Head, but most buses stop on Roe St., by St John's Centre. The National Express travel office is in Skelhorne St., near Lime Street Station.

**Railway Stations**: Lime Street Station for London and most destinations; Central Station for Merseyrail underground system; Northern Line to Southport, Ormskirk and Hunts Cross; Wirral Line via James Street Station and Birkenhead (Hamilton Square Station) to New Brighton, West Kirby and Rock Ferry (junction for Chester).

**Ferries**: Mersey ferries to Birkenhead (Woodside) and Wallasey (Seacombe) and ferries to Douglas, Isle of Man, from Pier Head. Ferries to Belfast and Dublin from terminal at Brocklebank Dock, 3m N of Pier Head.

**Airport**: At *Speke*, 7m SE of centre via A561. Passenger services to Heathrow, Isle of Man, Jersey, Belfast, Dublin.

**Theatres**: Empire, Lime St.; Everyman, Hope St.; Playhouse, Williamson Square; Neptune, Hanover Square; Royal Court, Roe St. The Royal Liverpool Philharmonic Orchestra gives regular concerts at Philharmonic Hall, Hope St.

**Annual Events**: Festival Parade in city centre (early June); Woolton Show (August Bank Holiday).

**History**. Although King John built a castle and founded a settlement here to serve as a point of departure for Ireland, Liverpool's real growth as a port dates from the 17C to the 19C. The first cargo from the Americas arrived in 1648. Throughout the 18C Liverpool traded with Virginia and the West Indies in sugar, tobacco, cotton and rum, and increased its wealth by the slave trade between Africa and America. The first dock was opened in 1715, and after 1734 further docks spread W into the neighbouring town of Bootle until they stretched 7 miles in an unbroken line. With the abolition of the slave trade and the introduction of steam Liverpool inherited Bristol's position as England's chief Atlantic seaport, importing cotton from America for the Lancashire mills and exporting the finished goods to the world market. From the 1840s it also became the point of arrival and departure for Transatlantic passenger liners. In the process its population rose from about 6000 in 1700 to about 80,000 in 1800 and about 685,000 in 1900. A city that grew great with the Industrial Revolution and the Empire, Liverpool has suffered inevitable decline in the 20C. The collapse of the cotton trade, the loss of markets provided by the Empire, the rise of Southampton as a passenger port and the development of air transport: all these factors have conspired against it. It briefly won itself a fashionable reputation as a centre for popular culture in the 1960s, the era of the Beatles and the 'Liverpool sound'. Otherwise, its vitality, resilience and good humour have been sorely tested in recent years by unemployment, declining population, housing problems and urban dereliction, as well as financial crises and political confrontation in its civic government.

**Famous natives, residents and visitors**. Liverpudlians include the painter George Stubbs (1724–1806), the poets Felicia Hemans (1793–1835) and Arthur Hugh Clough (1819–61), W.E. Gladstone (1809–98), the architect Alfred Waterhouse (1830–1905) and the Beatles, who first appeared at the Cavern, since demolished, on Matthew St. in January 1961. Sir Francis Bacon (1561–1626), the local solicitor and philanthropist William Roscoe (1753–1831) and William Huskisson (1770–1830) were all MPs for the city. Richard Mather (1596–1669), father of Increase and grandfather of Cotton Mather, was minister of the Unitarian church in Park Rd, Toxteth Park. Cobbett arrived at Liverpool from his second visit to America in 1819 with the disinterred bones of Tom Paine among his luggage. Nathaniel Hawthorne served as US Consul here in 1853–57 and was visited by Herman Melville in 1856. Matthew Arnold died here of a heart attack in 1888. Famous local murders include the Maybrick case of 1889 and the Wallace case of 1931.

THE WATERFRONT AND DOCKS. The finest view of the city is from the Mersey, on one of the ferries or the landing stage at Birkenhead. The waterfront is dominated by the Edwardian office buildings which show Liverpool at the height of its prosperity and by the pinnacled steeple of St Nicholas; the city rises behind them to a skyline crowned with the two cathedrals.

The landing stage for the Mersey and Isle of Man ferries is the surviving fragment of what was once the world's largest floating quay, connected to the river wall by ten hinged bridges and an inclined roadway. The upper deck of the bus station and ferry terminal buildings gives a fine view of the river scene. Pier Head, the open space behind the terminal, was formed by covering over the old St George's Dock. The *Royal Liver Building* (1910) has two 295ft towers topped by the legendary 'Liver birds' (pronounced 'Lye-ver') which are supposed to have given their name to the city. Next to it are the less ambitious *Cunard Building* (1913–16), now the *Custom House*, and the *Dock Offices* (1907), with a neo-Renaissance dome.

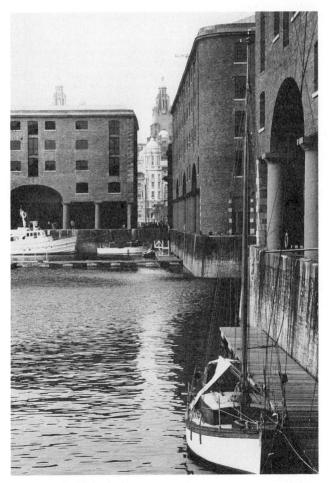

*The Albert Dock*

Behind the offices is the ventilating station of the Mersey Tunnel, rebuilt in 1951–52 after wartime damage.

The docks, stretching for several miles either side of Pier Head, are in their present form mostly the work of Jesse Hartley, dock engineer from 1824 to 1860, who built the massive river wall and boundary wall, pierced by gates and lodges of colossal proportions. Many docks are becoming disused and derelict but S of Pier Head the magnificent *Albert Dock, with the adjoining docks, has been restored as a centre for shops, restaurants, offices, museums, etc. Built by Hartley in 1841–45, the Albert Dock has five-storied brick warehouses on huge pillars forming a colonnade round the basin. The *Merseyside Maritime Museum occupies one warehouse and some of the buildings around *Canning Half-Tide Dock*. Its displays include full-size craft, models, paintings, marine equipment, etc., with special exhibits about the Port of Liverpool, the dock system and emigration from Liverpool in the 19–20C. The *Tate Gallery, Liverpool*, with selections of modern art from the Tate's permanent collection in London, opened in another warehouse in 1988. Canning Place, across the inner ring road from *Canning Dock* and *Salthouse Dock*, occupies the site of Liverpool's first dock, built in 1715 and filled up in 1829. Restoration work has begun in the docks continuing S to *Queen's Dock*.

In the memorial garden overlooking the N end of Pier Head stands the church of *St Nicholas*, Liverpool's original parish church, founded in 1360 as a chapel of ease to the mother church at Walton. Only the distinctive steeple (1815; Thomas Harrison) survived an air raid of 1941; the rest is modern Gothic (1952; Edward C. Butler). Opposite the church is the Dock exit from the Mersey Tunnel. New Quay has the *Large Objects Collection* (summer opening only) of the Mersey-side museums and galleries, with 19–20C vehicles driven by horse, steam and motor, industrial machinery, specimens of local architecture, scientific equipment and one of the few remaining examples of the Blue Streak rocket.

FROM THE WATERFRONT TO THE CENTRE (ST GEORGE'S HALL). Water St. leads up from the Cunard Building past some good 19C buildings, notably the remarkable *Oriel Chambers* (1864; Peter Ellis) on the left. The Georgian **Town Hall** was designed by John Wood the Elder in 1749–54, with a dome (1802) and portico (1811) added by James Wyatt and John Foster. It is open to the public once a year, usually in August. The quadrangle behind, known as Exchange Flags, was the meeting place of cotton brokers before the opening of the Cotton Exchange. A monument to Nelson (1813) stands in the centre.

Castle St., opposite the Town Hall, is lined with Victorian banks and office buildings, notably Norman Shaw's *Westminster Bank* (1901–02), on the right, and C.R. Cockerell's *Bank of England* (1845–48), now a TSB branch, on the left. It leads to Derby Square, on the site of King John's castle, pulled down in 1659, with a statue of Queen Victoria and the *Queen Elizabeth II Law Courts* (1984).

Water St. is continued beyond the Town Hall by Dale St., with a fine range of 19C buildings culminating in the *Municipal Buildings* (1866). The scene beyond is violently disrupted by flyovers and, on the right, the entrance to the **Mersey Tunnel**, or *Queensway Tunnel*, built in 1925–34 to carry road traffic the 2¹/₂m journey under the river to Birkenhead. *Kingsway*, a second road tunnel added in 1971, connects Scotland Rd to the N with Wallasey. Facing the Queensway tunnel entry are *St John's Gardens*, with a collection of statues, overlooked on the E by St George's Hall and on the N by the impressive civic buildings of William Brown St.

The **Liverpool Museum**, in a much altered building of 1857–60 near the lower end of William Brown St., has grown from the natural history collection bequeathed by the Earl of Derby in 1851 to fill five floors of wide-ranging exhibits.

They include an aquarium and vivarium; a natural history gallery with plant room; a land transport gallery; sections devoted to the social, industrial and maritime history of Merseyside; and a planetarium with associated displays of time-keeping and space exploration.

The collections of archaeology and the decorative arts on the first floor include Egyptian, Roman and Greek antiquities, notably the double coffins of Ditamunpaseneb, Attic Red Figure pottery and the Ince Blundell Hall marbles; Anglo-Saxon jewellery, notably the 7C *Kingston Brooch, one of the finest examples of cloisonné work of its period; Chinese cloisonné enamels; classical and medieval ivories; and tribal art from New Guinea and Africa, notably Benin bronzes from Nigeria.

The *County Libraries* next door are housed partly in Cornelius Sherlock's delightful circular *Picton Reading Room* (1875–79). This links the Museum building with the *Walker Art Gallery, home of one of the most important art collections outside London. The early Italian and Flemish paintings are outstanding.

Though the original building (1874–77; Sherlock and H.H. Vale) has twice been enlarged, the gallery still does not have enough space to exhibit all its treasures. A selection of the paintings, arranged chronologically on the first floor, is given below.
  *Room 1*, almost the furthest from the foyer, contains Italian painting, 1300–1500: Simone Martini (Christ Discovered in the Temple), Ercole de' Roberti (Pietà), Master of Forli (Christ on the Cross), Pietro Perugino (Birth of the Virgin), Cosimo Rosselli (St Lawrence), Bartolommeo di Giovanni, Spinello Aretino and (?) Vecchietta (St Bernardino Preaching). *Room 2* displays Italian, German and French schools, 1400–1600: Francesco Granacci (Life of St John the Baptist), Isenbrandt (Virgin and Child), Lucas Cranach the Elder (Nymph at Fountain), Florentine School (Virgin and Child with St John), Signorelli (Virgin and Child), Master of Aachen (Scenes from the Crucifixion), Master of Frankfurt (Holy Family), Joos van Cleve (Virgin and Child with Angels), Master of the Virgo inter Virgines (Entombment), Jan Mostaert (Portrait of a Man), French School (Portrait of a Lady with Parakeet), Hans Baldung Grien (Mercenary Love), Rosso Fiorentino (Portrait of a Young Man). *Room 3* displays Venetian and North Italian Schools, 1400–1750: Bartolommeo Montagna (Virgin and Child with Saint), Giovanni Mazone (St Mark Enthroned), Giovanni Bellini (Young Man), Girolamo da Santa Croce (Resurrection), (?) Palmezzano (Virgin and Child with Saints), Vicentino (Court of Heaven), Procaccini (Marriage of St Catherine), Studio of Veronese (Finding of Moses), Bonifazio Veronese (Virgin and Child with Saints), Vincenzo Catena (Virgin and Child). *Room 5* displays other European schools, 1600–1800: Paulus Bor (Magdalen), Solimena (Birth of St John the Baptist), Ciro Ferri (Rest on the Flight into Egypt), Pittoni (Solomon and Queen of Sheba), Carel Fabritius (Portrait), Anton Raffael Mengs (Self-portrait), Govaert Flinck (Portrait of an Oriental), Van Schuppen (Guitar Player), Rembrandt (*Self-portrait, c 1629), Van Dyck (Infanta Isabella, one of several versions), Ruysdael (River Scene), School of Rembrandt (Betrothal), Rubens (*Virgin and Child with St Elizabeth and St John), Nicolas Poussin (*Landscape with Ashes of Phocion), Murillo (La Vierge Coupée). The Poussin was acquired in 1983. The Murillo was cut in two during the Pensinular War and not reunited until 1862.
  Rooms 6–10 display the British Schools. *Room 6*, 1500–1800, contains a portrait of Henry VIII (School of Holbein) and the Pelican Portrait of Elizabeth I (after Nicholas Hilliard), as well as work by Hogarth (Garrick as Richard III), Stubbs (Molly Longlegs; Horse Frightened by Lion), Richard Wilson (Snowdon; Valley of the Mawddach), Gainsborough (Isabella, Countess of Sefton), Kneller, Lely, Reynolds, Romney, Arthur Devis and Wright of Derby. *Room 7*, 1800–1850, displays work by Turner (Linlithgow Castle; Landscape), Lawrence (Thomas Coke), Benjamin West (Death of Nelson), Constable, Cox and Landseer. *Room 8* has work by the Pre-Raphaelites: Millais (Lorenzo and Isabella), Holman Hunt (Eve of St Agnes) and John Brett (Stonebreaker). The Liverpool artists also represented here include John J. Lee (Sweethearts and

Wives). *Room 9* contains High Victorian work by Holman Hunt (Triumph of the Innocents), Maclise, Poynter, Watts and W.F. Yeames (And When Did You Last See Your Father?).

*Room 10* has paintings of 1870–1930, including work by Luke Fildes, Tissot (Mrs Chapple-Gill and her Daughters), Atkinson Grimshaw, Stanhope Forbes (Street in Brittany; Off to the Fishing Grounds), Sir George Clausen and Edward Hornel. *Room 11* has work by the Impressionists and Post-Impressionists, 1850–1930: Degas (Woman Ironing), Cézanne (The Murder), Monet, Seurat, Matisse, Vuillard, André Derain and Vlaminck. The British paintings of 1910–60, displayed in *Room 4* and downstairs, include work by Sickert, Augustus John, Paul Nash, Matthew Smith, Stanley Spencer, Ivon Hitchens, Lowry, Lucien Freud and David Hockney. Among the sculptures are interesting examples of the 16–18C and works by Epstein, Rodin, Barye, Gaudier-Brzeska, Renoir and Henry Moore (Falling Warrior).

The long row of public buildings ends with the former County Sessions House of 1884, now the **Museum of Labour History**, with displays illustrating Merseyside working-class life from the 19C and a collection of trade union banners.

The *Wellington Monument* (1863) stands at the head of Lime St. Beyond is the main façade of *'St George's Hall* (open), one of the best Greek Revival buildings in England. It was designed by Harvey Lonsdale Elmes in 1839, at the age of twenty-four, and completed after his death in 1847 by Sir Robert Rawlinson and C.R. Cockerell. The Great Hall inside has a tunnel vault of hollow blocks, a Minton tile floor, a huge organ and statues of local celebrities, including one of William Roscoe by Chantrey. Off the hall is an interesting court-room and (not open at the time of writing) a concert room with a balcony supported by caryatids.

On the plateau in front of the hall are the *Cenotaph* (1930; Lionel Budden) and statues of Victoria and Albert, both on horseback, and Disraeli. The best view of the building is from the terrace of *Lime Street Station* opposite. When it was built in 1867, the cast-iron span of the station's train shed was the largest in the world. Alfred Waterhouse's railway hotel (1868–71) is now used as offices. The view to the S is closed by the modern shopping precinct of *St John's Centre* with its tall concrete tower.

FROM THE CENTRE (ST GEORGE'S HALL) TO THE ANGLICAN CATHEDRAL. We continue SE on Lime St. to Ranelagh Place. Brownlow Hill, on the left, climbs past the *Adelphi Hotel* (1912) to the RC cathedral and the University (see below). We follow Ranelagh St. past the *Central Station* to its junction with Bold St.

Hanover St. continues straight ahead from the junction. School Lane, to its right, has the attractive building of the former *Bluecoat School* (1716–17), now an arts centre. Seel St., left of Hanover St., has a museum of the Beatles, *Beatle City*.

The attractive Bold St., now partly pedestrianised, begins with Thomas Harrison's *Lyceum Club* (1802), now disused and boarded up. It ends at the church of *St Luke*, built in 1831 and gutted during World War II. Leece St. climbs to Rodney St., one of the best of the city's late 18C and early 19C residential streets. The poet Arthur Hugh Clough was born at No. 9 and Gladstone at No. 62.

The Anglican **Cathedral** stands high on the ridge of St James's Mount overlooking the city and the Mersey. It was completed after almost 75 years of continuous work in 1978. The architect, Sir Giles Gilbert Scott, was in his early twenties when his design was adopted in 1902 and he worked on the building until his death in 1960—a longer time than Wren spent on St Paul's. Scott's ideas changed greatly as the building progressed, but he held to his original concept

# LIVERPOOL ANGLICAN CATHEDRAL

of 'a vast hall' quarried out of the local sandstone: the cathedral is the largest church in Britain, and is exceeded in Europe only by St Peter's in Rome and by Milan and Seville cathedrals. Though its Gothic Revival style may seem a hopeless anachronism in the 20C, the building has a strikingly original plan.

It is built N and S, following the line of the rock ridge, but in the description that follows the points of the compass are used in the ecclesiastical sense, with the actual S end referred to as E, etc.

Externally the dominating feature is the huge central tower (1949), resting, unusually, on the outer walls of the building. At its base are the short double transepts and N and S porches. We enter by the W front, the last part to be built and finished more simply than originally planned.

The *Nave* (1948–78) is only three bays long, the two W ones forming a well reached by steps from the side aisles and the E one spanned by the Dulverton Bridge (1961), a huge stone arch supporting a musicians' gallery. They are deliberately subordinate to the huge central space formed by the undertower and the two transept crossings, unobstructed by pillars and capable of seating 4000 people. Particularly striking is the tremendous height of the arches of the undertower, with its superb vaulting. The windows (by James Hogan) form two groups of triple lancets surmounted by a rose. The SW transept, the Bapistery, has a marble font by Carter Preston. The S porch contains a brass-rubbing centre. The NW transept is enclosed as a bookstall and the N porch as a cafeteria.

The tall *Choir* (1924), matching the nave in length, has a triforium but no clerestory. The stone reredos, with carved panels by W. Gilbert and L. Weingartner, is unusual in forming an integral part of the E wall. The E window, the largest in England, has stained glass on the theme of 'Te Deum'. The choir aisles, with the two parts of the great organ above their W ends, are connected by an ambulatory. The octagonal *Chapter House* (1924) opens off the NE corner. The *Lady Chapel*, SE of the choir and on a lower level, was the first part to be completed (1910). Its elaborate Dec. Gothic, rising to a stone traceried vault, is markedly different from the rest of the building. The altarpiece is by Scott and Bodley, appointed joint architect during the early stages of the building.

Outside the W end is John Foster's Greek Revival *Oratory* (limited opening), recently restored. Nearby is the entrance to *St James's Cemetery*, romantically laid out in an old quarry below the cathedral. It contains the mausoleum, now appallingly neglected, of the politician William Huskisson, killed at the opening of the Liverpool and Manchester Railway in 1830.

FROM THE ANGLICAN CATHEDRAL TO THE RC CATHEDRAL AND THE UNIVERSITY. The direct route goes N from the Anglican cathedral on Hope St., with the *Philharmonic Hall*. A roundabout but more interesting way explores the early 19C streets which extend E and N of the Anglican cathedral toward Abercromby Square (see below). Huskisson St., Percy St., Canning St. and Falkner Square are all worth the detour.

The RC **Metropolitan Cathedral**, on top of Mount Pleasant, was designed by Sir Frederick Gibberd and built in 1962–67. Locally nicknamed the 'Mersey Funnel', it consists of a circular skeleton of concrete trusses and flying buttresses, faced with Portland stone and white mosaic, rising up to a glass-panelled lantern tower with a crown of slender pinnacles. It stands over the vast crypt which is the only completed part of Sir Edwin Lutyens's ambitious design for the cathedral, projected in the 1930s and abandoned after World War II. Gibberd's scheme ingeniously uses the crypt to create an open piazza as well as a podium for his own building.

We enter from the S by the porch under the sharply angled belfry, ferociously decorated by William Mitchell. The open pavilion of the interior, lit with stained glass by John Piper and Patrick Reyntiens, has a central sanctuary below a canopy of hanging tubes. The high altar is a slab of white marble from Skopje; the crucifix is by Elizabeth Frink. The spaces between the buttresses form a ring of chapels around the perimeter. Immediately to the right of the entrance is the simple circular Baptistery; diagonally opposite is the Lady Chapel, with glass by Margaret Traherne. The Blessed Sacrament Chapel on the far side from the entrance has windows, tabernacle and altar painting by Ceri Richards.

Lutyens's crypt is entered separately by stairs at the N corners of the piazza. Built of brick in a Renaissance style, it has massive pillars, cavernous vaults and maze-like aisles, with a series of chapels.

The **University** stretches N and E of the RC cathedral on either side of Brownlow Hill. Founded as University College in 1881 and made a constituent college of the Victoria University of Manchester in 1884, it became an independent university in 1903.

Alfred Waterhouse's original *Victoria Building* (1889–92) on Brownlow Hill is surrounded by buildings mostly added since 1950, each by a different architect, showing neither remarkable individuality nor any attempt at cohesion, and prompting the accusation from one unkind critic of 'trying to live down to Waterhouse'. On the opposite corner is the *Students' Union*, the pleasant N end designed by Sir Charles Reilly (1910–13). Of some note are the *Harold Cohen Library* (1936–38; Harold A. Dod) and, next to it, the *Electrical Engineering Building* (1962–65; Yorke, Rosenberg and Mardall); the *Civil Engineering Building* (1958–59; E. Maxwell Fry) in Brownlow St.; the *Chadwick Physics Laboratory* (1957–59; Sir Basil Spence), facing the Green; and Denys Lasdun's striking *Sports Centre* (1963–66) on the corner of Abercromby Square. The E side of the square is filled by the *Senate House* (1966–68; Tom Mellor). Among the early 19C houses opposite is the **University of Liverpool Art Gallery**. Its collection includes English watercolours (Turner, Girtin) and oils, and English porcelain and silver.

See the beginning of this walk for the streets stretching S from Abercromby Square towards the Anglican cathedral.

SUBURBS. As the city plan inset shows, Liverpool's suburbs stretch from *Everton* in the N, known for its toffee and its football team based at Goodison Park, to *Speke* airport in the S. (Speke Hall is described in Rte 75A.)

They are well provided with parks and open spaces which, with other points of interest, can be combined into an easy drive of about 15m. From near the Anglican cathedral Princes Rd leads SE to *Prince's Park* (1842), one of the earliest Victorian public parks and Joseph Paxton's first, and the much larger *•Sefton Park*, with a lake and superb palm house (1896). Off Hesketh St. on its SW side is the *Lark Lane Motor Museum* with vintage cars and motorcycles. By the waterfront, on ground reclaimed by using the spoil from the first Mersey Tunnel, is the attractive *Otterspool Park* and the *Festival Park*, laid out for the International Garden Festival in 1984.

From nearby *Aigburth* we can join the Queen's Drive, a handsome boulevard (7m long) encircling the city. In Mossley Hill Rd (right), opposite the parish church, is the **Sudeley Art Gallery**, with a good collection of British paintings including fine works by Gainsborough and Turner. On the E side of Mossley Hill the *Botanic Gardens* at Harthill adjoin *Calderstones Park*. Inside the circuit of Queen's Drive are *Wavertree Playground* and *Newsham Park*, with a lake. To the right of the road at *West Derby*, 5m NE of the centre, is **Croxteth Hall and Country Park** (open). The Jacobean house, with additions of 1702 and 1902, contains period displays, Sefton family portraits, etc. Outside are displays of crafts and carriages, a walled garden, a home farm and 530 acres of parkland with woodland walks. In *Anfield*, to the left, are Liverpool's football ground and *Stanley Park*, enjoying fine views. Beyond Walton Hall Park, on the right, Queen's Drive meets the road leading out to *Aintree*, 5m N, Liverpool's racecourse. The Grand National, the chief event of the steeplechasing season, has been run here in March/April since 1839.

THE WIRRAL: WEST BANK OF THE MERSEY. **Birkenhead** (123,900 inhab.; Tourist Information), on the W bank of the Mersey opposite Liverpool, can be reached by Merseyrail, road tunnel or ferry. Now badly depressed, it developed as a port and shipbuilding town in the 19C. The first iron ship in England was built by Laird & Co. (now Cammell Laird) in 1829 and the famous Confederate privateer 'Alabama' was launched in 1862. The docks, begun in 1844–47, were amalgamated with Liverpool docks in 1855 after a period of intense rivalry. The painter Wilson Steer (1860–1942) was a native and the poet Wilfred Owen lived here from 1900–07.

The stately Hamilton Square was designed in 1825–44 by J. Gillespie

Graham, one of the architects of Edinburgh's New Town. The *Town Hall* was added in 1887. Close to the derelict 19C *St Mary's Church* in Priory St. are the ruins of *Birkenhead Priory* (open), established in 1150, with a chapter house and refectory. The vault of the 19C shipbuilders William and John Laird stands in the churchyard. The *Williamson Art Gallery and Museum* in Slatey Rd has a collection of 18–19C English watercolours and 19C English oil paintings, including work by Wilson Steer; also Liverpool and other porcelain, Della Robbia pottery, and local history displays, including ferry models. *Birkenhead Park* was beautifully laid out by Joseph Paxton in 1843–47 with handsome villas and lodges around the perimeter.

The borough of **Wallasey** (90,100 inhab.), beyond the Great Float N of Birkenhead, comprises the towns of New Brighton, Wallasey, Egremont, Seacombe, Liscard and Poulton. *Seacombe*, connected with Liverpool by ferry and the Kingsway tunnel, and *Egremont* are residential suburbs on the Mersey. A riverside promenade leads to *New Brighton* (Tourist Information), a resort at the mouth of the Mersey. Sibelius's music was first publicly heard in England at a concert conducted by the composer here in 1899. The battery (1827) at Perch Rock, built to guard the approach to Liverpool, now contains an aircraft museum.

FROM BIRKENHEAD TO CHESTER VIA HOYLAKE, 30m by A553 and A540. For an alternative route to Chester via Port Sunlight, see Rte 50. The present route takes A553 inland across the Wirral via (2m) the village of *Bidston*. Bidston Hill is a favourite viewpoint.—8m. **Hoylake** (32,900 inhab.), at the mouth of the Dee, has the Royal Liverpool golf course. William III embarked from here on his way to the Battle of the Boyne (1690).—9¹/₂m. *West Kirby* is a more sheltered resort. The *Hilbre Islands* off the coast are a nature reserve (access by foot at low tide; permit required). Caldy Hill is another good viewpoint. Between West Kirby and Neston the former coastal railway line now makes a fine walk through the *Wirral Country Park*.—11¹/₂m. *Thurstaston* has the Visitor Centre for the Country Park, as well as a 200-acre common (NT) with heathland and a good hilltop view. The church (1883–86) is by J.L. Pearson. *Arrowe Park*, 2¹/₂m NE, was site of the first Boy Scouts' world jamboree in 1929.—15m. *Heswall*. —18¹/₂m. *Neston* (18,400 inhab.), ³/₄m to the right of A540, was the birthplace of Emma Lyon, Lady Hamilton (1763–1815). Nearby *Parkgate*, now stranded by saltmarsh, was once the starting-point of the Dublin packet, used by Handel, Swift and John Wesley. At *Ness*, S of Neston, are the splendid *University of Liverpool Botanic Gardens*, with familiar and unusual plants in a parkland setting. *Thornton Hough*, on B5136 2m NE of Neston, is a 'model village' created by Lord Leverhulme of Port Sunlight after he bought the estate in 1891.—30m. *Chester*, see Rte 50.

FROM LIVERPOOL TO SOUTHPORT, 20m by A565. We head N along the bank of the Mersey, past the docks which stretch to (3m) *Bootle* (62,500 inhab.).—At (4m) *Seaforth*, with a container port, Gladstone spent part of his boyhood at his father's country house.—5m. *Waterloo* is a resort founded in 1815.—6¹/₂m. *Great Crosby* has the Merchant Taylor's School.—The road continues inland, past (12¹/₂m) *Formby* (25,800 inhab.).—20m. **Southport** (89,700 inhab.; Tourist Information) is a resort with a 19C promenade and a pier of 1859, the first in Britain built for pleasure rather than as a landing stage. The handsome Lord St. has Regency villas and late 19C iron verandahs in front of the shops. The Royal Birkdale is notable among its golf courses. The old parish church of *Churchtown*, adjoining to the N, contains magnificent woodcarving (c 1704) from the demolished church of St Peter, Liverpool. The botanic gardens have a museum of local history. *Meols Hall* (limited opening) is a 17C house with later additions. *Scarisbrick Hall* (now a school), 4¹/₂m SE by the Orsmkirk road, is an astonishing Gothic Revival mansion by A.W.N. and E.W. Pugin (1836–68). *Halsall*, 1¹/₂m S of Scarisbrick on A567, stands near the attractive Leeds and Liverpool Canal.

From Liverpool to *Chester* via *Port Sunlight*, see Rte 50; to *Stoke-on-Trent*, see Rte 54; to *Manchester*, see Rte 75A; to *Preston, Blackburn, Burnley* and *Halifax*, see Rte 75B; to *Lancaster* and *Carlisle*, see Rte 76.

# 74 Manchester

**MANCHESTER** (448,900 inhab.) is the financial, business and cultural centre of a sprawling conurbation of some 3½ million people which embraces its immediate W neighbour Salford, still anomalously a separate city, and a dozen surrounding towns (Bolton, Oldham, Rochdale, Stockport, etc.). Despite its ancient origins the city is essentially a creation of the Industrial Revolution, when, as 'Cottonopolis', it became regional capital of the Lancashire cotton-manufacturing district. Some great landmarks of its 19C prosperity survive but, thanks to wartime bomb damage, wholesale demolitions following closure of the huge railway yards and bad modern development, the city centre now lacks coherence. For the visitor, Manchester's strength lies in the cultural tradition expressed in its concerts, libraries, museums and galleries.

**Tourist Information Centres**: Town Hall Extension, Lloyd St.; International Arrivals Hall, Manchester International Airport.

**Car Parks**: Collier St., Faulkner St., George St., Lower Mosley St., Watson St., Whitworth St., Whitworth St. West. Underground car parks in Cateaton St. and York St. (Piccadilly Plaza). Multi-storey car parks in Chorlton St., Church St., Gartside St., High St., King St. West, Market Place.

**Bus Stations**: Piccadilly and Arndale Centre. Coach station in Chorlton St.

**Railway Stations**: Victoria Station (Inter-City), connecting with Salford; Piccadilly Station (Inter-City), connecting with stations at Oxford Rd, Deansgate and Old Trafford.

**Airport**: Manchester International Airport, the chief airport for Northern England, 10m S between Altrincham and Wilmslow (connecting spur from junction 5 of M56). Passenger services to Heathrow, Gatwick, Barrow, Birmingham, Ipswich, Isle of Man, Southampton, Aberdeen, Dundee, Edinburgh, Glasgow, Belfast, Cork, Dublin, Guernsey, Jersey, Toronto, New York and many European and world-wide destinations.

**Theatres**: Opera House, Quay St.; Palace Theatre, Oxford St.; Royal Exchange Theatre, St Ann's Square; Library Theatre, St Peter's Square; Green Room, Whitworth St. West; University Theatre, Devas St., off Oxford Rd; Forum Theatre, Civic Centre, Wythenshawe. Concerts by the Hallé Orchestra in the Free Trade Hall, Peter St.

**History**. *Mancunium*, or *Mamucium*, a walled Roman fort on the military road from Chester to York, stood in the Castlefield area at the S end of Deansgate. The later Saxon town, garrisoned against the Danes in 923, lay further N near the present cathedral.

Manchester's industrial prosperity had its beginnings in Edward III's settlement of Flemish weavers here in 1375. They worked in wool and linen, though cotton was being imported from the Levant by the 17C. The rise of the Lancashire cotton industry dates from the middle of the 18C, fostered by the moist climate, improvements in machinery and a convenient local coal supply. The first Manchester cotton mill opened in 1781 and Arkwright's mill, established on Miller's Lane in 1783, became the first to use steam power. The transport of raw cotton, coal and the finished goods was aided by a system of waterways which began with the Duke of Bridgewater's historic canal in the mid 18C and, by the early years of the 19C, linked the city with Ashton and Oldham, Bolton and Bury, and Rochdale. The huge Ship Canal (1894), stretching to the Mersey estuary, made Manchester a major inland port. Meanwhile, the era of steam transport had been introduced with the opening of George Stephenson's Liverpool and Manchester Railway in 1830.

To the rest of Victorian England, Manchester became the chief example not only of the prosperity but also of the hardship brought about by the Industrial Revolution, notorious for the unchecked evils of its factory system and the plight of its millhands. At the 'Peterloo Massacre' (1819) the yeomanry killed 11 people in dispersing a mass protest by workers at Peter's Field. The sufferings of later decades were described by Friedrich Engels in 'The Condition of the

# MANCHESTER

0 — 300 yards
0 — 300 metres

N

PRESTWICH

Chetham's Hospital

Cathedral

Victoria Bridge

Blackfriars Bridge

Salford Station

Albert Bridge

Irwell Bridge

River Irwell

Royal Exchange

Arndale Shop Cen

St Ann's

Law Courts

John Rylands Library

Opera House

County Courts

Police

Free Trade Hall

Town Hall

Library

Gt. Manchester Mus. of Science & Industry

Air & Space Gallery

Roman Fort

Castlefield Visitors' Centre

G-Mex

Hotel

Bridgewater Canal

Rochdale Canal

Deansgate Station

LIVERPOOL

SALFORD  ECCLES

URMSTON  SALE

Working Class in England' (1845) and Elizabeth Gaskell in 'Mary Barton' (1848) and 'North and South' (1855). Opposition to government intervention was a central tenet of the 'Manchester School', led by Richard Cobden (1804–65) and John Bright (1811–89), which played a central role in shaping 19C Liberal politics. Its pressure aided the passage of the 1832 Reform Act which gave the city, until then 'the largest village in Europe', its first parliamentary representation. The Anti-Corn Law League, founded in Manchester, helped bring about repeal of the restrictive corn tariffs in 1846. The modern 'Guardian' newspaper is the descendant of the 'Manchester Guardian', founded in 1821 to advocate the Liberals' belief in parliamentary reform, free trade and non-intervention in foreign affairs.

**Famous natives.** Mancunians include Thomas De Quincey (1785–1859), William Harrison Ainsworth (1805–92), Frances Hodgson Burnett (1849–1924), David Lloyd George (1863–1945) and L.S. Lowry (1887–1976). For famous residents, see the Portico Library, Chetham's Hospital and the University, below.

*Thomas Gainsborough's 'Peasant Girl Gathering Faggots', City Art Gallery, Manchester*

THE CITY CENTRE. Manchester's most prominent civic building is Alfred Waterhouse's Gothic **'Town Hall** (1867–76) with its tall central tower. The great hall, included in guided tours of the interior, has a double hammerbeam roof and mural paintings by Ford Madox Brown illustrating the history of the city. The tower overlooks Albert Square, with the Albert Memorial (1862) and statues of Gladstone and John Bright. To the S are the *Town Hall Extension*, connected to the main building by bridges over Lloyd St., and the rotunda of the **Central Library**, both designed by E. Vincent Harris in the 1930s. The largest municipal library in the world, with a reading room second in size to that of the British Library, it houses nine specialised libraries and the *Library Theatre*. The main entrance faces St Peter's Square, with a war Cenotaph by Lutyens (1934).

Mount St. leads S to the former Central Station, now converted into *G-Mex*, the city's new exhibition centre. Peter St. leads W from Mount St. with an impressive line of buildings on its S side: the *Midland Hotel* (1898), the *YMCA* (1909) and the former *Theatre Royal* (1845), followed by the handsome Italianate façade of the **Free Trade Hall**, designed by Edward Walters in 1856 and well restored after wartime bomb damage. The home of the Hallé concerts, it stands on the site of Peter's Field where the Peterloo Massacre took place in 1819 and of the hall where Cobden and Bright delivered their speeches against the Corn Laws.

Mosley St., running NE from St Peter's Square, soon meets Princess St., running SE from Albert Square alongside the Town Hall. On the corner stands the **'City Art Gallery**, in a severely handsome classical building designed by Sir Charles Barry for the Royal Manchester Institution in 1825–29. It houses the city's chief collections of paintings, sculpture, silver, glass and pottery; the remainder are in the branch galleries listed below. The Pre-Raphaelite paintings are outstanding among the rich collection of British art displayed here.

The *Entrance Hall* and *Balcony* have been restored to their original neo-classical splendour, with gilded and stencilled decoration on the ceiling and walls. The displays include sculptures by Thorvaldsen and Edward H. Baily and paintings by Etty, Watts, Val Prinsep, Albert Moore, Leighton, Tissot, Poynter and Alma-Tadema. The *Assheton-Bennett Galleries* contain Chinese jades, sculpture and ceramics; Japanese prints; early English earthenware; English and French ceramics, silver and glass; 17C Dutch genre paintings; and work by the Manchester-born L.S. Lowry, with reconstructions of the studio and livingroom of his home at Mottram-in-Longdendale.

The picture galleries continue upstairs. *Room 1* has early Italian paintings, including a Virgin and Child with Goldfinch (c 1380) by a member of the Florentine School and a Crucifixion by a follower of Duccio; a Virgin and Child by the Flemish Master of the Magdalen Legend; Dutch paintings by van Ruisdael, Cuyp, van Goyen and Ochtervelt; and British paintings by John Souch (Sir Thomas Ashton) and Lely. *Room 2* and *Room 3* display work by Turchi (Flight into Egypt), Bernardo Bellotto (View of the Castle of Konigstein), Claude Lorrain (Adoration of the Golden Calf), Stubbs (Cheetah and Stag with Two Indians) and Gainsborough (Peasant Girl Gathering Faggots). *Room 4* has paintings by Bonington, Crome, Cotman, Cox, Constable, de Wint, Etty, Linnell, Samuel Palmer and Turner (Thomson's Aeolian Harp; Now for the Painter) among other Engish artists. *Room 5* displays Pre-Raphaelite paintings, furniture and decorative arts in a splendidly recreated 19C setting. The artists represented include Ford Madox Brown (Work; Stages of Cruelty), Rossetti (Bower Meadow; Astarte Syriaca; Joli Coeur), Holman Hunt (Hireling Shepherd; Shadow of Death; Lady of Shalott; versions of Light of the World and Scapegoat) and Millais (Autumn Leaves; Winter Fuel). *Room 6* has paintings by Corot, Courbet, Fantin-Latour, Pissarro, Sisley and Gauguin and sculpture by Rodin. *Room 7* and *Room 8* have paintings by Briton Rivière, Leighton, Burne-Jones, Maclise, Watts, Frith and Sir George Clausen, with High Victorian sculpture and decorative art.

The **Athenaeum Gallery**, in Barry's Manchester Athenaeum Club building (1839) next door on Princess St., houses a changing programme of temporary exhibitions. The other branches of the City Art Galleries, described in the tours of Outer Manchester, are the Gallery of English Costume at Platt Hall, Rusholme; the Fletcher Moss Museum and Art Gallery, Didsbury; Wythenshawe Hall, Northenden; and Heaton Hall, Heaton Park.

Mosley St. continues NE from the City Art Gallery. The *Portico Library* (by Thomas Harrison), on the corner of Charlotte St. to the right, opened in 1806 as a social and literary institution. Its first secretary was the Manchester doctor Peter Mark Roget, remembered for his 'Thesaurus' (1852), and its early readers included De Quincey and Elizabeth Gaskell. Mosley St. ends at Piccadilly, with one of the city's few public gardens and some of its many insensitive modern buildings (1959–65; Covell, Matthews and Partners). The busy Market St. leads left to the Exchange (see below).

NORTH FROM THE CENTRE TO THE CATHEDRAL, AND BACK BY DEANSGATE AND CASTLEFIELD. The busy Cross St. leads N from Albert Square to the Royal Exchange. On the way it is intersected by King St., with a pleasant pedestrianised shopping stretch to the left and some of Manchester's best buildings among the banks and offices to the right. C.R. Cockerell's former *Bank of England* (1845–46), now a TSB branch, and Lutyens's *Midland Bank* (1929) are outstanding. In St Ann St., left of Cross St. beyond the King St. junction, is the lovely church of *St Ann* (1709–12) with a contemporary pulpit and font and Carracci's 'Descent from the Cross'. De Quincey, born in a house that stood at the corner of Cross St. and John Dalton St. nearby, was baptised here. On the right of St Ann's Square, with its statue of Cobden, is the **Royal Exchange** (1914–21), the latest of the city's several cotton exchanges, transformed in 1976 into a restaurant and theatre with a spectacular auditorium.

The *Wellington Inn*, a 16C half-timbered house, survives in the otherwise redeveloped Market Place. John Byrom (1692–1763), Jacobite poet, author of 'Christians Awake' and inventor of a system of shorthand, was born here.

Victoria St. continues N to the **Cathedral**, dwarfed by modern tower blocks and looking across the grimy waters of the Irwell towards Salford. The old parish church of Manchester was made collegiate in 1421 by a charter of Henry V which also licensed the lord of the manor and rector, Thomas de la Warre, to rebuild. The present church is thus largely Perp., dating mainly from 1422–1520. It was raised to cathedral status in 1847. The square tower was resurfaced and heightened when the building was restored in 1867; further restoration was carried out after damage to the E end in World War II.

The *Nave* is made disproportionately wide by the double aisles, the outer aisles having originally accommodated chantries to Henry V, the founder, etc. The tall and graceful tower arch is a relic of the earlier church. The tower fan vaulting is 19C, and the stained glass in the W window is by Anthony Holloway (1980). In the NW corner is a 19C statue of Humphrey Chetham (see below). The main beams of the 15C roof are supported by angels with musical instruments, typical of the superb woodwork throughout the church. The beautiful Perp. choir screen is also 15C.

The *Choir* has elaborately carved •stalls of c 1485–1506, with a full set of misericords, by the Ripon school of craftsmen who also made the stalls there and at Beverley. Like the splendid 15C panelled roof, they suffered from blast in 1940 and have been well restored. Also notable in the choir are the brass of Warden Huntington (d. 1458), the 17C chandeliers and the 18C ironwork.

In the retrochoir a restored screen of c 1440 leads into the *Lady Chapel*, destroyed in 1940 and rebuilt by Sir Hubert Worthington. There is a Madonna by Sir Charles Wheeler on the outside. S of the choir are the *Bishop Fraser*

*Chapel* (1885), the octagonal *Chapter House* (1485) and the *Jesus Chapel*, founded in 1506, with a 16C screen. At the NE corner of the church is the *Chapel of the Manchester Regiment*, built by Bishop Stanley in 1513 and restored after the landmine fell outside its E window in 1940. The modern glass is by Margaret Traherne.

Beyond the cathedral is ***Chetham's Hospital**, originally built in 1421 by Thomas de la Warre as a residence for the warden and fellows of his collegiate church. The astrologer John Dee (1527–1608) was warden here. Under the will of Humphrey Chetham (1580–1653) the buildings were converted into a charity school for the maintenance and education of 40 poor boys. In 1969, after a period as a grammar school which supplied the choristers of the cathedral, it became a school for young musicians. The fine collegiate buildings, with 15C refectory and screens passage, are in use by the school. The old dormitory wing is occupied by the foundation's *Library* (open).

It claims to be the oldest surviving public library in England, its books having been chained until c 1740. It now comprises some 85,000 volumes (90 incunabula) and many manuscripts, and specialises in the topography of the North-west. The Reading Room contains the 17C portrait of Chetham on which his statue in the cathedral is based, a chained library dated 1655 and a desk used by Marx and Engels.

Chapel St., beginning opposite Chetham's Hospital, is the main street of Salford, explored in Outer Manchester: West, below. N of Chetham's Hospital are *Victoria Station* and the beginning of Cheetham Hill Rd, followed in Outer Manchester: North, below.

Deansgate leads SW. On the right is Basil Champneys's handsome neo-Gothic Deansgate Memorial Building of the ***John Rylands University Library of Manchester** (open), endowed and built by Mrs Rylands in memory of her husband and opened in 1900 as the John Rylands Library. In 1972 this merged with the Manchester University Library, on the University campus in Oxford Rd, and the Deansgate Memorial Building is now the rare printed books and manuscripts division of the Library.

The watermarking of the red Penrith sandstone in the entrance hall is remarkable. A public exhibition of rare items from the library's collections, changed at intervals throughout the year, is on display. The collection of about 1 million printed books (from a total of over 3 million in the John Rylands University Library of Manchester) includes the Althorp Library of 40,000 volumes collected by the 2nd Earl of Spencer (d. 1834) and the Christie Collection of 8000 volumes bequeathed to Manchester University by Professor Richard Copley Christie (d. 1901). The superb collection of early printed books includes the 'St Christopher' block-print (1423), the earliest dated piece of European printing extant; about 4000 incunabula; Bibles in over 400 languages; an outstanding Aldine collection; and many fine bindings. The manuscript collection includes the major portion of the Bibliotheca Lindesiana bought from the 26th Earl of Crawford (d. 1913), some 20,000 items representing around 65 different language groups; the 'St John Fragment' (c AD 120), the earliest New Testament manuscript extant, and the 'Deuteronomy Fragment' (2C BC); and about ³/₄ million documents and charters.

Hardman St., on the right, leads to the *Law Courts* (1961; Leonard Howitt). Quay St., to its S, has the *Opera House* (1912) and the *County Courts*, built c 1770, Cobden's residence and later the first home of Owens College (see University, below). St John's St., also on the right of Deansgate, has good Georgian houses.

We can return to the centre by following Peter St., to the left, past the Free Trade Hall to St Peter's Square. Before doing this, it is worth continuing S on Deansgate to Castlefield, site of the Roman fort and of Manchester's early canal and railway systems. The neighbourhood has been partially rescued from its subsequent decay to become an 'Urban Heritage Park', with some interesting displays and an excellent museum. At the corner of Liverpool Rd, on the right, stands the *Castlefield Visitors' Centre*, in the same building as the *Urban Studies Centre*, with further exhibitions and displays. Next door is the *Castlefield Gallery*, devoted to contemporary art.

On the left of Liverpool Rd is a modern reconstruction of the N gateway of the *Roman Fort*, with displays about Roman Castlefield in the adjoining gardens. On the opposite side of Liverpool Rd the splendid cast-iron market hall (1877) houses the *Air and Space Gallery*, whose exhibits about the history of flight include material on loan from NASA. It is part of the *Greater Manchester Museum of Science and Industry*, which displays its main exhibits in the former Liverpool Road Station, the world's oldest surviving railway station, built in 1830 as the terminus of George Stephenson's Liverpool and Manchester Railway.

Galleries include the Power Hall, a converted goods shed with the world's largest collection of working stationary steam engines as well as vintage cars, steam locomotives, etc.; the Electricity Gallery; the Lower Byrom St. Warehouse, with displays about the textile industry, printing and papermaking; and the restored station platform and First Class Booking Hall, with an exhibition and audio-visual show about the history of the railway. There are also exhibitions about the history of Greater Manchester and 'Underground Manchester'.

S of the museum and the railway lines is the terminus of the **Bridgewater Canal**, begun in 1759 by James Brindley for the 3rd Duke of Bridgewater, the first canal in England to be cut through open country rather than following the course of an existing river. The first section, opened in 1761, runs NW from the city to the duke's coal mine at Worsley (see Outer Manchester: West, below); a later extension runs from Stretford to (26m) Runcorn. Reclamation work has begun on the decayed canal basin, and there is a worthwhile walk along the towpath of the Rochdale Canal (1804), leading E to Princess St. See Salford (in Outer Manchester: West, below) for the Manchester Ship Canal.

SOUTH-EAST FROM THE CENTRE TO THE UNIVERSITY. Oxford St., leading SE from St Peter's Square, is continued by Oxford Rd, the main thoroughfare of South Manchester. It passes under the Mancunian Way, part of the ring road.

After 1m we come to the **University of Manchester**, spreading on both sides of Oxford Rd with a characteristic building by Waterhouse (1873, later enlarged) as the centrepiece of its campus.

Historically the first and today the largest of Britain's civic universities, it developed out of Owens College, founded under the will of John Owens and opened on Quay St. in 1851. The Victoria University was founded in 1880 with Leeds and Liverpool as constitutent colleges. By 1904 these were independent, and Owens College was incorporated as the Victoria University of Manchester. The *John Rylands University Library of Manchester* owns editions of Francis Thompson and George Gissing, both students, and of Elizabeth Gaskell, who lived locally (see below). Ernest Rutherford discovered the nuclear structure of the atom at Manchester, and the world's first computer was produced here in 1948. Several departments have exhibitions in their foyers illustrating their work, and the *University Theatre* houses a professional company.

The University's **Manchester Museum**, on the right of the entrance, contains a famous collection of Egyptian antiquities found by Sir

William Flinders Petrie (1853–1942), a rare archery collection, fine Japanese ivories, and a large natural history collection and vivarium.

Elizabeth Gaskell, married to a Unitarian preacher and lecturer at Owens College, lived after 1850 at No. 84 Plymouth Grove, to the E, leading to the Stockport road. The house is now the University Overseas Centre. Charlotte Brontë several times visited her future biographer here and had earlier begun 'Jane Eyre' (1847) at a house, since demolished, in Boundary St.

Further along Oxford Rd, on the left, is the *Royal Infirmary*, founded in 1752 and moved here in 1908. Set back from the opposite side of the road is the **Whitworth Art Gallery**, a bequest of Sir Joseph Whitworth (d. 1887) and since 1958 part of the university.

It contains superb collections of *English watercolours from the 18C to the present day, including work by Turner, Constable and Blake, and European drawings, including work by Picasso, Van Gogh and Pissarro. The collection of *textiles includes 1–10C Coptic robes and cloths; a 15C German altar frontal; 16–18C Spanish, Italian and Near Eastern embroideries and 18–19C Far Eastern work; 16–17C English embroideries; 18–19C English and French printed cottons; and costumes of the Diaghilev Russian Ballet. The wallpaper collection is one of the best in the country, with impressive French scenic panels as well as work by William Morris, Charles Voysey and Kate Greenaway. The large collection of contemporary art includes work by Andy Warhol, Lucien Freud, Francis Bacon, Howard Hodgkin and Anthony Caro. A regularly changing exhibition programme continues throughout the year. Items not on display may generally been seen on request.

OUTER MANCHESTER: SOUTH. Oxford Rd continues S from the university and the Whitworth Art Gallery and becomes Wilmslow Rd. On the right at 1m is **Platt Hall**, a red-brick Palladian building of 1764, now a branch of the City Art Galleries and home of the *Gallery of English Costume*. The collection, ranging from the 17C to the 20C, is the largest and most comprehensive outside the Victoria and Albert Museum in London. *Platt Fields Park* lies to the S. *Hollings College*, opposite, has a gimmicky building by Leonard Howitt (1957–60). Nearby Old Hall Lane leads to the buildings of *Manchester Grammar School*, founded in 1515 by Hugh Oldham, Bishop of Exeter, and moved here from beside Chetham's Hospital in 1931. Pupils have included John Bradford, Humphrey Chetham, De Quincey, Harrison Ainsworth, the playwright Stanley Houghton (1881–1913) and the novelist Louis Golding (1895–1958).

*Withington*, 1m S, has the interesting church of St Christopher (1935; B.A. Miller). *Didsbury*, about 1½m further, is a well-to-do suburb above the Mersey. The church of St James has a fine monument to Sir Nicholas Mosley (d. 1612), Lord Mayor of London. The 19C parsonage with its pleasant garden and parkland is now the *Fletcher Moss Museum and Art Gallery*, another branch of the Manchester City Art Galleries, containing late 19C and early 20C paintings etc. with local associations and an Arts and Crafts room.

*Wythenshawe Hall*, also administered by the City Art Galleries, is by A5103 in *Northenden* about 3m W of Didsbury and 5m S of the city centre. Partly dating from the 16C but several times remodelled, it is furnished as a country house, with displays of 16–17C paintings, furniture, weapons, etc. The *Wythenshawe Estate* is a garden suburb developed by the Manchester Corporation from 1931 onwards and designed by Barry Parker. It has two outstanding modern churches: St Michael's, Orton Rd, by Caichemaille-Day and Lander (1937), and the William Temple Memorial Church, Simonsway, by George Pace (1954–65).

OUTER MANCHESTER: WEST. Chapel St., beginning opposite Chetham's Hospital, is the main street of **Salford** (98,000 inhab.), Manchester's immediate neighbour on the W bank of the Irwell but still technically an independent city. Among its buildings are the RC *Cathedral of St John* (1844–48) in Chapel St., and the neo-classical *St Philip's Church* (1825; Sir Robert Smirke). The Crescent has some good Georgian houses, including the home of the scientist James Prescott Joule (1818–89). The *Art Gallery and Museum* at the entrance to *Peel Park* contains a reconstructed 19C street and the largest collection in the country of paintings by L.S. Lowry, born in Manchester and a resident of Salford for much of his life. The nearby *University of Salford* was opened as a technical college in 1896.

*'Coming from the Mill' by L.S. Lowry, from the collection of the City of Salford Art Gallery and Museum*

The *Salford Mining Museum*, on Eccles Old Rd (A576) NW of the centre, has displays and reconstructed scenes from the history of coal-mining. It is housed in a Greek Revival villa of 1825–29 by Sir Charles Barry.

*Ordsall Hall* (open), S of Salford's centre, is a half-timbered 16C building with appropriate furniture and exhibits of local history. Further S are the docks of the **Manchester Ship Canal**, built in 1887–94, running a 35½m course which connects Manchester with the Mersey at Eastham. Part of the dockland is now being redeveloped after its decline in recent years. On the S bank are the industrial estate of *Trafford Park*, also being redeveloped, and the county cricket ground at *Old Trafford*.

*Eccles* (37,200 inhab.) lies 2m W of Salford by A57. *Monks Hall Museum*, in a partly 16C building, has collections of childrens' toys, games and dolls. Industrial exhibits include a Nasmyth steam hammer from the old Britannia Iron Foundry in neighbouring *Patricroft*. At *Barton*, S of A57, a remarkable swing aqueduct carries the Bridgewater Canal over the Ship Canal. The RC church on the opposite bank is a splendid building by E.W. Pugin (1867–68). *Worsley*, near M62 about 2½m NW of Eccles, marks the start of the Bridgewater Canal (see also Castlefield, above). Near the parish church (1846; Gilbert Scott) are the canal basin and the tunnel entrance to the underground system for bringing coal from the duke's mine to the surface. Worsley Old Hall, formerly the home of the Bridgewater family, was almost entirely rebuilt in the 19C and is now a restaurant.

OUTER MANCHESTER: NORTH. From the roundabout beyond Victoria Station we head N on Cheetham Hill Rd (A665). The old bus garage near (1¼m) the junction with Queen's Rd (A6010) is now the *Museum of Transport*, with a large collection of buses, coaches and memorabilia. **Heaton Hall**, in its park off A576 2½m further N, is a handsome neo-classical house largely built by James Wyatt in 1772. Now administered by the City Art Galleries, it has been restored and furnished in the appropriate style. The Music Room has an organ by Samuel Green (1790) and the Cupola Room superb *painted decoration by Biagio Rebecca.

From Manchester to *Stafford* via the *Potteries*, see Rte 54; to *Derby* via the *Peak District*, see Rtes 56A and 56B; to *Sheffield* via the *Peak District*, see Rte 56D; to *Liverpool*, see Rte 75A; to *Bolton, Blackburn* and *Settle*, see Rte 75C; to *Bury, Burnley* and *Skipton*, see Rte 75D; to *Rochdale, Halifax* and *Bradford*, see Rte 75E; to *Huddersfield* and *Leeds*, see Rte 75F; to *Sheffield* via *Penistone*, see Rte 75G.

# 75 The Manufacturing Towns of Lancashire and Yorkshire

This densely populated region stretches from Liverpool to Manchester and across the Pennines to Sheffield and Leeds, taking in a host of other cities and towns along the way. Formerly belonging to Lancashire and the West Riding of Yorkshire, it is now divided between Merseyside, Greater Manchester, Lancashire, South Yorkshire and West Yorkshire. Its traditionally industrial character has changed, too. Historically, the great activities fostered by the Industrial Revolution were centred here: coal-mining in the southern part of Lancashire and in South Yorkshire, textile production from cotton in Lancashire and wool in West Yorkshire, and steel production in the Don valley. Now the cotton industry has vanished or declined into a much smaller industry dependent on artificial fibre. Steel and coal have both suffered upheavals of which the miners' strike of 1984–85 is the latest dramatic reminder. The woollen industry alone has proved fairly resilient. The result, where it has not simply been the economic depression which has left its mark on much of the region, has been diversification, particularly into engineering and chemical works.

Perhaps tourism should be added to the list of new industries. Its traditional image was hardly inviting, but the region has at last begun to establish itself on the tourist map. It certainly has much to offer. The industrialisation of the landscape never completely despoiled its often rugged scenery, and great natural beauty survives in places like Pendle Hill, the Calder valley, Rossendale, the Ryburn valley, the moors near Rochdale and Oldham, and the Colne valley. The towns and cities, however meanly unimaginative most of their ordinary housing might be, expressed their civic pride in grand 19C town halls and public buildings, and in museums and art collections of more than merely local importance. Industrial history, particularly the history of textile production, is now remembered in some excellent museums.

## A.  Liverpool to Manchester

Maps: OS Landranger 108, 109.

The direct roads are (34m) M62 and M602, its extension into Salford, and (33m) A580. The routes suggested below pass through the intervening towns.

VIA WARRINGTON 35m by A57. **Liverpool**, see Rte 73.—We cross M57 on the way to (8m) *Prescot* (11,000 inhab.), a centre of the watch trade in the 18–19C, with a Museum of Clock and Watchmaking in the High St. The parish church has a classical exterior (1729) and Jacobean roof. The seat of the Earls of Derby at Knowsley Hall, to the N, is not open but its grounds contain the large *Knowsley Safari Park*, entered from the eastbound carriageway of the Prescot bypass.—At (10m) *Rainhill* A57 crosses the original Liverpool and Manchester Railway. Stephenson's 'Rocket' won the trial of locomotives held here in 1829, the year before the line opened. In commemoration, Rainhill was the first stop made by the last scheduled steam passenger train to run in Britain (from Liverpool to Carlisle) in 1968. The RC church of *St Bartholomew* (1840) is an Ionic temple with a rich interior.—18m. **Warrington** (57,400 inhab.; Tourist Information), on the N bank of the Mersey, is an old town which has become a centre for foundries, chemicals and soapworks. The *Town Hall* occupies a mansion built in 1750 by Gibbs, probably also the architect of *Holy Trinity* in 1760. The parish church of *St Elphin*, further E, was rebuilt with a handsome tall spire by Frederick and Horace Francis in 1859–67. The *Museum and Art Gallery* in Bold St. has collections of local history, natural history, antiquities, firearms, etc., as well as 19C paintings.

Academy St. is named after the Warrington Academy of higher education for the sons of Dissenters, which flourished between 1757 and 1783. Joseph Priestley was a tutor in 1761–67, and Thomas Malthus a pupil. Its first premises were in Bridge St., where John Howard also lodged in 1777–89 while printing his book on prison reform. Both Independent and Primitive Methodism started in Warrington.

From Warrington to *Chester*, see Rte 50.

Beyond Warrington A57 crosses M6 and runs close to the Manchester Ship Canal.—31m. *Eccles*, (33m) *Salford* and (35m) **Manchester**, see Rte 74.

VIA ST HELENS, 33m by A57, A58 and A572. From Liverpool to (8m) *Prescot*, see above.—A58 bears left for (11½m) **St Helens** (98,800 inhab.), a centre of the British glass-making industry since 1773. The *Pilkington Glass Museum*, in the headquarters of the Pilkington glassworks, illustrates the history, manufacture and technology of glass in all forms. The *Museum and Art Gallery* in College St. has bottles and displays of other local industries, as well as local natural history, and a good collection of English watercolours. The conductor Sir Thomas Beecham (1879–1971), a member of the family which manufactured Beecham's Pills, was a native of St Helens.

A58 goes on to (5m) *Ashton-in-Makerfield* (29,300 inhab.), with the racecourse at *Haydock Park* to its S, and continues through (9m) *Hindley* (25,500 inhab.) to (16m) *Bolton* (Rte 75C).
  **Wigan** (79,500 inhab.) lies 4m N of Ashton by A49. Its reputation as the typical Northern manufacturing town was summed up by the old joke about 'Wigan Pier', made popular by the Wigan-born music-hall comedian George Formby Senior and perpetuated in the title of George Orwell's study of industrial depression in the 1930s, 'The Road to Wigan Pier'. The name is now used for the buildings by the basin of the Leeds and Liverpool Canal, on A49 S of the town centre. Currently being restored, they include a Heritage Centre, with exhibits and performances by actors bringing to life the history of the area, and Trencherfield Mill, with the world's largest working mill steam-engine and textile and rope-making machinery. The church of *All Saints*, rebuilt in 1845–50, has a partly 13C tower and a S aisle window by Morris and Co. (1868). There are two RC churches in Standishgate, the classical *St John's* (1819) and the Gothic *St Mary's* (1818).

From St Helens we take A572 through (16m) *Newton-le-Willows* (19,700 inhab.), and cross A49 and M6 on the way to (22m) *Leigh* (45,300 inhab.).—27m. *Worsley* and (33m) **Manchester**, see Rte 74.

VIA WIDNES AND ALTRINCHAM, 40m by A561, A562, A50 and A56. **Liverpool**, see Rte 73. We take A561, passing Liverpool airport at (7m) *Speke*. *Speke Hall* (NT and Merseyside Council), also to the right, is one of the finest half-timbered manor houses in the country. Built for the Norris family between about 1492 and 1612, it has four large wings surrounding a cobbled courtyard. Inside, the Great Hall has splendid 16C Flemish panelling and the Great Parlour a carved overmantel and Jacobean plaster ceiling.—A561 continues past the motor car works of *Halewood*.—The churchyard of (10m) *Hale*, on the right, has the grave of John Middleton (1578–1623), the 'Childe of Hale', said to have been 9ft 3in tall. Shortly afterwards A561 joins A562.—13m. **Widnes** (54,400 inhab.; Tourist Information) stands on the N bank of the Mersey opposite Runcorn (Rte 54). Its long connection with the alkali and chemical industry is recorded in the *Halton Chemical Industry Museum*, housed in an office building of 1860 on Spike Island.

20m. **Warrington**, see above. We cross the Mersey on A50, and at (21m) *Latchford* cross the Manchester Ship Canal before turning left on A56.—25m. *Lymm* (10,400 inhab.), on the Bridgewater Canal, is a pleasant old place with a 17C market cross and replica wooden stocks.—31m. *Bowdon* (4900 inhab.), birthplace of the composer John Ireland (1879–1962), has 19C villas and a parish church of 1858 with interesting monuments from its predecessor. *Dunham Massey* (NT), about 1½m W, is a red-brick house of 1732 arranged round an open courtyard, like the Tudor building it replaced. It contains good collections of 18C paintings and furniture and Huguenot silver. The garden has recently been replanted, and the large deer park has ancient trees.—32m. **Altrincham** (39,600 inhab.) is a dormitory town on the fringes of Manchester. Beyond the twin towns of (35m) *Ashton-upon-Mersey* and *Sale* we cross the Mersey a second time and then M63.—40m. **Manchester**, see Rte 74.

# B.  Liverpool to Preston, Blackburn, Burnley and Halifax

Total distance 71m. **Liverpool**, see Rte 73.—A59 to (31m) **Preston**.—A59, A677 to (41m) **Blackburn**.—A679 to (46m) Accrington.—A679 to (50m) **Burnley** (bypassed; Rte 75D).—A646 to (64m) Hebden Bridge.—A646 to (71m) **Halifax**.

Maps: OS Landranger 108, 102, 103, 104.

**Liverpool**, see Rte 73. We leave the city by Scotland Rd (A59), passing (2½m) *Walton* and (5½m) .the racecourse at *Aintree*, described in Rte 73. The church of *Sefton*, to the left at 7m, has interesting monuments and magnificent 16C screens and stalls.—At (12m) *Ormskirk* (27,800 inhab.) the church, mainly Perp. with Norman remains, has a tower and steeple side by side. It contains the burial chapel of the Stanleys, Earls of Derby.—17½m. *Rufford Old Hall* (NT) is a late 15C half-timbered building, with a brick wing added in 1662 and altered in 1821. The Great Hall has a fine hammerbeam roof and a fantastically carved movable screen, apparently the only one to survive complete. There are also collections of 17C oak furniture and 16C arms, armour and tapestries.

31m. **Preston** (125,800 inhab.; Tourist Information), once capital of the ancient duchy of Lancaster, is the administrative centre of Lancashire. Engineering and other industries have replaced the cotton-weaving on which it once depended, and new uses have been found for many of its red-brick mill buildings.

Though it has little to show for its early history, 'Proud Preston' has always been important because of its strategic position on the Ribble astride the lowland route from Scotland. It received its first charter in 1179; the Guild Festival, which dates from that time, is celebrated every 20 years (next in 1992). The town was sacked by Robert Bruce in 1323, captured by the Parliamentary armies in 1643, and occupied by the Old Pretender in 1715 and by the Young Pretender in 1745. Like much of S Lancashire, it remains an important stronghold of Roman Catholicism.

Famous natives include the painter Arthur Devis (1711–87) and the poets Francis Thompson (1859–1907) and Robert Service (1874–1958), the 'Canadian Kipling'. The house where Sir Richard Arkwright (1732–92), another native, developed his water frame in 1768 survives on Stoneygate. Dickens's visit during the cotton workers' strike in 1854, when he stayed at the Bull and Royal Hotel in Church St., gave him useful material for 'Hard Times'.

The town has several modern shopping centres as well as older covered markets. The *Harris Museum and Art Gallery*, in a striking classical building (1882–93; James Hibbert) overlooking the Flag Market, displays local archaeology and social history and 18–20C paintings, etc., including work by the Devis family. Winckley Square, S of Fishergate, is the centre of a pleasant late Georgian quarter. *Avenham Park* and *Miller Park*, further S, slope down to the Ribble. The *County and Regimental Museum*, with regional and military exhibits, occupies the Old Sessions House on Stanley St., E of the centre.

The singer Kathleen Ferrier (1912–52) was born at *Higher Walton*, 3m SE on A675. About 3m further is *Hoghton Tower* (limited opening), pronounced 'Hawton', a 16C fortified house where James I is said to have knighted the loin of beef ('sirloin') on a visit in 1617.
B6243 follows the N side of the Ribble valley through (7m) the high-lying *Longridge* and (12m) *Hurst Green*, passing near Stonyhurst College, to (18m) *Clitheroe* (Rte 75C). *Chingle Hall* (open), on B5269 3¹/₂m W of Longridge near *Goosnargh*, is a small medieval manor house with old beams (said to be Viking), secret rooms and a reputation for ghosts. St John Wall (1620–79), one of the English martyrs canonised in 1970, was born here. There is a country park 5m NW of Longridge at *Beacon Fell* (873ft), with fine views. *Chipping*, a pleasant stone-built village 5m NE of Longridge, makes a good centre for walks in the fell country further N. *Ribchester*, by the Ribble 3m SE of Longridge on B6245, has remains of the Roman fort of *Bremetennacum* with a museum of finds from the site. The 13–15C church and the village centre, with the 18C White Bull inn, are attractive. There are pleasant river walks, with a fine bridge of 1774 1¹/₂m upstream. *Stidd*, ¹/₂m NE, has a little Norman chapel and early 18C almshouses.
From Preston to *Bolton*, see Rte 75C; to *Blackpool* and to *Lancaster*, see Rte 76.

We leave Preston by New Hall Lane (A59) and cross the river and M6.—35m. A59 bears left for Clitheroe (Rte 75C); we follow A677. *Samlesbury Hall* (open), shortly beyond the junction, is a half-timbered 14–16C manor house much altered in the 19C, now a centre for sales and exhibitions of antiques, collectors' items, etc. It was originally built by the Southworth family, best known of whom is St John Southworth (1592–1654), another of the English martyrs canonised in 1970. The hall contains a reconstructed fragment of a carved screen like the one at Rufford.

41m. **Blackburn** (109,000 inhab.; Tourist Information) was once the greatest cotton-weaving centre in the world. It now depends on engineering more than textiles but mill buildings and chimneys survive, notably by the Leeds and Liverpool Canal. The Liberal politician John Morley, later Viscount Morley of Blackburn (1838–1923), was a native.

The *Cathedral* was built as a parish church in 1820–31 and raised to its present status in 1926. John Palmer's Gothic building was enlarged between 1938 and 1967 by new transepts, crossing and E end, with Laurence King succeeding W.A. Forsythe as architect. King designed the corona and needle spire, John Hayward the stained glass in the lantern and also the huge statue of Christ (1965). The *Museum and Art Gallery* in Museum St. contains medieval illuminated manuscripts and early printed books; Greek, Roman and English coins; local antiquities; and a regimental gallery. The pictures include Japanese prints, 19–20C watercolours and Victorian oil paintings. The adjoining *Lewis Textile Museum* in Exchange St., illustrating the development of the industry, has working machinery. *Witton Country Park* is 1m W of the town.

B6234, an alternative to the main route below, runs E to Accrington via (2m) *Stanhill* and (2½m) *Oswaldthistle*. James Hargreaves invented the spinning jenny in 1764 at what is now the Post Office in Stanhill; after the mob destroyed his home and machinery, he moved to Nottingham.

From Blackburn to *Bolton* and *Manchester* and to *Settle*, see Rte 75C.

A679 leads E to (46m) **Accrington** (35,900 inhab.), another former cotton-weaving town. 'Accrington Bloods', the harsh red engineering bricks popular with late 19C and early 20C builders, are not much in evidence in the local architecture. The *Town Hall* (1857) was built in tribute to the politician Sir Robert Peel, descended from a powerful family of local manufacturers. The *Haworth Art Gallery* has the largest collection of Tiffany glass in Europe, with 19–20C English watercolours and oil paintings.—At 50m we leave A679 and bear right on A646, bypassing the centre of **Burnley**, described in Rte 75D. The road passes Towneley Hall (also Rte 75D), climbs the moors and enters West Yorkshire at (57m) *Cornholme.*

At (60m) *Todmorden* (14,700 inhab.), a former cotton-spinning town, the imposing neo-Renaissance Town Hall (1870) spanned the Yorkshire–Lancashire border when it was built. Natives include the cotton manufacturer John Fielden (1784–1849), MP and prime mover of the 1847 Act limiting the working day to ten hours, and Sir John Cockcroft (1897–1967), pioneer of radar and atomic energy.

The walkers' route known as the Calderdale Way links some fine scenery in a 50m circuit of the region, from Todmorden in the W to Brighouse beyond Halifax in the E, with connecting paths to the main centres in the valley.—A681 leads W from Todmorden to (4½m) Bacup and Rossendale (Rte 75D).

We follow A646 along the valley of the Calder, where the Rochdale Canal runs alongside the river. The Pennine Way crosses our route by the prominent Stoodley Pike obelisk.—64m. *Hebden Bridge* (Tourist Information) is a typical West Riding mill town, jammed into the narrow valley bottom. The community of weavers from which it sprung was at *Heptonstall* on the shoulder of the moor above; the two are still connected by a steep packhorse way. Hebden Bridge has a working clog mill (open) and a museum of pre-1939 cars, motorcycles and bicycles. Heptonstall has a ruined church, an octagonal Wesleyan chapel of 1764, some handsome houses and an interesting local museum in the old grammar school. Sylvia Plath (1932–63) is buried in the new churchyard. *Hardcastle Crags* are in the NT woods of Hebden Dale, 3m NW. *Haworth* (Rte 75H) is 7m N by A6033.—Our road follows the Calder to (65m) *Mytholmroyd*, with the pleasant *Cragg Vale* to its S. To the NE are (1m) *Midgley*, one of the villages where the traditional 'Pace Egg Play' is acted at Easter, and (2m) *Luddenden*, with cottages, mills and cobbled streets in a steep little valley. Branwell Brontë, brother of the novelists, drank at the Lord Nelson inn at Luddenden while working as a railway clerk nearby in 1841–42.—A646 then climbs out of the Calder valley above *Sowerby Bridge* (Rte 75E), passing the distinctive *Wainhouse Tower* of 1877 (limited opening).

71m. **Halifax** (87,500 inhab.; Tourist Information Centre), rising steeply on the slopes of the Hebble valley, has been moulded by the

*The Piece Hall, Halifax, with the spire of the Congregational church behind*

cloth trade. Its best monument is the *Piece Hall* (1779; Thomas Bradley), a vast trading market with 315 rooms opening on to a colonnaded courtyard. An open-air market is held on Fridays and Saturdays. Restored in 1976, the building houses shops, the Tourist Information Centre, an *Art Gallery* with changing exhibitions, and the *Pre-Industrial Museum*, tracing the history of the cottage wool industries. The *Calderdale Industrial Museum* in the adjoining 19C mill has early textile and engineering machinery, much of it working, and other relics of the region's past.

The Piece Hall is overlooked from the E by the tall spire which survives from the burnt *Congregational Church* (1857). The low-lying 15C parish church, further E, has oak furnishings and a life-size wooden beggar by the poor box.—Market St., to the W of the Hall, has the ornate *Borough Market* (1891–98). Princess St. and Crossley St., to the N, have some handsome 19C buildings culminating in the *Town Hall* (1859–62; Sir Charles Barry and E.M. Barry), with its extraordinary spired tower.

The *National Museum of the Working Horse* is in the old station goods yard off South Parade, S of the church.—Gibbet St., W of the town centre, has the base and a replica of the Halifax Gibbet, a precursor of the guillotine, used until 1650 for executing cloth thieves ('From Hell, Hull, and Halifax, good Lord deliver us!').—In Haley Hill (A647), to the N, is *All Souls* (1857–59), which Sir Gilbert Scott considered his best church. Higher up, in Akroyd Park, the *Bankfield Museum* contains a good collection of English costumes and textiles from the Balkans, Burma, etc., toys, natural history and the museum of the Duke of Wellington's Regiment.

**Shibden Hall** (open), off A58 1m NE of the centre, is a partly half-timbered 15–17C house standing in an attractive park with a lake in the valley below. It contains a good collection of period furniture and late 16C wall paintings behind the panelling in the dining room. The fascinating *Folk Museum of West Yorkshire* in the outbuildings and 17C barn has a brewhouse and dairy, agricultural implements and horse-drawn vehicles, and craft workshops.

*Brighouse* (35,200 inhab.), 5m SE of Halifax, has the *Smith Art Gallery*, with temporary exhibitions drawn from a permanent collection of 17C Dutch and Flemish and 19C English paintings.

From Halifax to *Rochdale* and *Manchester* and to *Bradford*, see Rte 75E.

# C.  Manchester to Bolton, Blackburn and Settle

Total distance 53m. **Manchester**, see Rte 74.—A6, A666 to (11m) **Bolton**.—A666 to (24m) **Blackburn** (Rte 75B).—A666, A59 to (35m) Clitheroe (bypassed).—A59 to (42m) Gisburn.—A682, A65 to (53m) **Settle** (Rte 86C).

Maps: OS Landranger 109, 103, 98 (briefly).

**Manchester**, see Rte 74. The Bolton road begins as A6, leaving the city by Chapel St., Salford. At 3¼m we bear right on A666 towards the Irwell valley.

11m. **Bolton** (147,100 inhab.; Tourist Information), now with engineering and chemical works, was a texile manufacturing centre specialising first in wool and later in cotton goods. It was the home town of Samuel Crompton (1753–1827), who was born at Firwood Fold and invented the spinning mule at Hall i' th' Wood in 1779, and of the soap magnate William Hesketh Lever, later Lord Leverhulme (1851–1925).

The imposing classical *Town Hall* was completed in 1873; its interior has been refurbished after a disastrous fire in 1981. The nearby *Civic Centre* (1939) contains a *Museum and Art Gallery*; the *Octagon Theatre* is opposite. Churchgate, E of the centre, has Bolton's oldest pub, the Man and Scythe, where the Earl of Derby spent the night before his execution in 1651. Richard Arkwright worked as a barber on Churchgate in the 1760s before returning to his native Preston. N of the centre, the redundant church of *St George* (1769) has become a craft centre and the first town hall, known as *Little Bolton Town Hall*, a museum of local history.

The *Textile Museum*, 2m N on Tonge Moor Rd, displays early machinery including Crompton's mule, Hargreaves's spinning jenny and Arkwright's water frame.— *'Hall i' th' Wood* (open), off Crompton Way about 2m N of the centre, is a stone and half-timbered manor house dating from the 15C to the 17C, restored and presented to the town by Lord Leverhulme. It contains 17C furnishings and relics of Crompton, who invented the spinning mule while living here in 1758–82.—*Turton Tower* (open), 4m N of Bolton on B6391, is a 15C pele tower with later alterations and additions. It contains a museum of furniture and weapons.

FROM BOLTON TO PRESTON. A675, the direct road (18m), leads across some fine moorland via Belmont, Hoghton and Higher Walton (Rte 75B). Another way, 1m longer, begins by taking A673 to (5m) *Horwich* (18,000 inhab.). To the N are *Rivington Reservoir*, supplying Liverpool, and *Rivington Pike* (1190ft; fine view). The country park on the slopes of the moor includes the splendid *Lever Park*, part of the Rivington Hall Estate laid out by Lord Leverhulme for the public in 1904. The village of *Rivington*, beyond the park, has a good 16–17C church and a Unitarian chapel of 1703.—We cross M61 and pass through (8m) *Adlington* before joining A6.—11m. **Chorley** (34,700 inhab.) was the birthplace of Miles Standish (1584–1656), one of the Pilgrim Fathers, and the sugar magnate Sir Henry Tate (1819–99), donor of London's Tate Gallery. *Astley Hall* (open), 3/4m NW of the centre, has an impressive 17C façade added to an earlier half-timbered building. It contains extravagant plaster ceilings and interesting collections of furniture and Leeds pottery. *Leyland* (26,700 inhab.), off A49 4m NW of Chorley, has motor works and a museum of commercial vehicles. The old grammar school building houses a local museum.—19m. *Preston*, see Rte 75B.

Beyond (15m) *Egerton* A666 crosses bleak moors diversified by ravines.—19m. *Darwen* (30,000 inhab.) has petrochemical and plastics works, and the prominent brick chimney of the India Mills (1859–67).—24m. **Blackburn**, see Rte 75B.

We leave the industrial district and emerge into the valley of the Ribble, joining A59 at 29m.—31m. *Whalley*, a pleasant village on the Calder, has an interesting church with Anglo-Saxon crosses outside and fine woodwork inside, including 15C stalls with misericords. These come from nearby **Whalley Abbey** (open), founded by Cistercians who moved from Stanlow on the Wirral in the 1280s. Its last abbot, John Paslew, was executed in 1537 for his part in the Pilgrimage of Grace against Henry VIII's religious reforms the previous year.

The early 14C outer gateway (English Heritage, open at any reasonable time) lies outside the modern precincts, to the NW. We enter from the the NE by the late 15C inner gateway. Only the foundations of the large church (1330–80) remain, with a modern high altar marking the place of the medieval one, but more survives of the cloister. The lay brothers' quarters in its W range are used as a Roman Catholic church hall. In the E range is the entrance to the octagonal chapter house. Behind it are some remains of the abbot's lodging, most of which was converted into a private house and is now a diocesan conference centre (not open).

John Mercer (1791–1866), textile chemist and inventor of 'mercerising', was born at *Dean*, 13/4m S.—*Great Mitton* (or *Mitton*), 2m NW on B6246, is beautifully situated above the junction of the Hodder and Calder with the Ribble. The church has a 15C rood screen, Jacobean pews and 16–18C

Shireburn monuments. Near *Hurst Green*, on B6243 2¹/₂m further W, is *Stonyhurst College*, a Roman Catholic school founded by the Jesuits at St Omer in 1593 and moved here in 1794. The nucleus of its buildings is the Elizabethan mansion built by Sir Richard Shireburn in 1594–1606. The road continues W via Longridge to *Preston*, see Rte 75B.

A59 continues NE, bypassing (35m) **Clitheroe** (13,600 inhab.; Tourist Information), the northernmost of the cotton towns. It is dominated by the limestone outcrop with the shell of its Norman *Castle* (open). The *Castle House Museum* displays local geology, archaeology and history. E of the town rises *Pendle Hill* (1827ft), associated with the 17C 'Lancashire Witches' and George Fox's mission of 1652.

From the pretty village of *Downham*, 3m NE of Clitheroe, a steep sideroad runs across the flank of the hill via (7¹/₂m) *Newchurch-in-Pendle* towards (11m) *Nelson* (Rte 75D).
   A fine moorland route, beginning as B6243, leads W from Clitheroe across the Ribble and then branches N on the unclassified road to Whitewell.—5m. *Browsholme Hall* (limited opening) is a Tudor and Jacobean house with later additions; the interesting contents include oak panelling, original furniture and family portraits.—8m. *Whitewell*, in the wooded valley of the Hodder.—At (10m) *Dunsop Bridge* we join the road leading through the Trough of Bowland from Lancaster (Rte 76).
   Another good route leads NW from Clitheroe on B6478 via (1¹/₂m) *Waddington* and (6¹/₂m) *Newton*, with views over Waddington Fell.—8m. *Slaidburn*, a remote village in beautiful country, has a handsome inn, 18C grammar school and a church with Jacobean rood screen and 18C pews and three-decker pulpit. We can go on to rejoin the main route at (18m) *Long Preston* (below), passing through (13m) *Tosside*, with its bleakly situated little 18C church, on the edge of *Gisburn Forest*.

The main route follows A59, passing (38¹/₂m) *Sawley Abbey*, or *Salley Abbey*, the scanty remains of a Cistercian house founded in 1148 (English Heritage, open at any reasonable time).—At (42m) *Gisburn* the church, adjoining Gisburn Park, has a 13C doorway and 15C chancel screen. The village is the starting-point of the Ribble Way, a walkers' route (42m) following the river SW to its estuary near Preston.

At the charming village of *Bolton-by-Bowland*, 3m W, the church has a Perp. font and the tomb of Sir Ralph Pudsey (d. 1481).—*Bracewell*, 2m E of Gisburn, has a church with Norman work. For *Barnoldswick*, 1¹/₂m further, see Rte 75D.

We head N on A682. At (49¹/₂m) *Long Preston*, we join Rte 86C and follow A65 to (53m) **Settle**.

# D.   Manchester to Bury, Burnley and Skipton

Total distance 41¹/₂m. **Manchester**, see Rte 74.—A56 to (8¹/₂m) **Bury**.—A56 to (16¹/₂m) Rawtenstall.—A56 to (23m) **Burnley**.—A56 to (27¹/₂m) Nelson.—A56, A59 to (41¹/₂m) **Skipton** (Rte 86C).

Maps: OS Landranger 109, 103.

**Manchester**, see Rte 74. A56 heads N, crossing M62 on the way to (8¹/₂m) **Bury** (67,500 inhab.), known for its open-air market and its black pudding. The market place has a statue of the politician Sir Robert Peel (1788–1850), born near Bury, whose grandfather introduced calico-printing into Lancashire. There is a monument at the S end of Market St. to John Kay (1704–64), inventor of the fly shuttle (1743), who was mobbed by his fellow townsmen and died a pauper in France. The *Art Gallery and Museum* has 19C English paintings and watercolours, and displays of local history.

A56 now follows the narrowing valley of the Irwell, 'the most long-suffering stream in the kingdom'.—12½m. *Ramsbottom* (17,800 inhab.), on the left, had the printing works belonging to the Grant brothers, originals of the Cheerybles in Dickens's 'Nicholas Nickleby'.—15m. To the left of A56 are *Haslingden* (15,900 inhab.), where the paving stones known as 'Haslingden Flags' used to be quarried, and *Helmshore*, with the Higher Mill Museum and Museum of the Lancashire Textile Industry. Housed in old mill buildings, it contains early textile machines, including a water wheel and fulling stocks, and exhibits of cotton processing and spinning.—A56 bears right, climbing through the moorland *Forest of Rossendale* to (16½m) **Rawtenstall** (22,200 inhab.), with 19C buildings from the days when it was developed as a mill town by the Whitehead brothers. The Rossendale Museum, in a former mill owner's house, has exhibits of local history.

A681 leads to (4m) **Bacup** (15,200 inhab.), near the E end of Rossendale, where the *Natural History Society Museum* has a large collection of domestic and industrial bygones as well as natural history. A681 continues to (4½m) *Todmorden* (Rte 75B) and A6066 follows the Whitworth valley S to (6m) *Rochdale* (Rte 75E).

A56 heads N.—18m. *Crawshawbooth* has a Friends' Meeting House built in 1716 and enlarged in 1736.—18½m. *Goodshaw* has an 18C Baptist chapel with furnishings of c 1800 (English Heritage, open Monday to Friday 10.00–16.00 and weekends by appointment). —23m. **Burnley** (69,900 inhab.), in a pretty region blackened by its industries, was the centre of Lancashire cotton weaving by the end of the 19C. The most interesting survival is the *Weavers' Triangle*, along the Leeds and Liverpool Canal S of the centre, with weaving sheds, warehouses, mills, foundries and weavers' cottages. The *Canal Toll House Heritage Centre* provides an introduction to its history.

*Towneley Hall* (open), in a large park off A671 1½m SE of the centre, has work of most periods from the 15–19C. Particularly interesting are the plasterwork (1725–30) by Vassalli in the hall and the early 16C chapel, moved to its present position in 1712. The house is now an art gallery and museum with wide-ranging collections which include pottery, vestments from Whalley Abbey and 18–19C English paintings, notably Zoffany's portrait of Charles Towneley. The old brewhouse is a museum of local crafts and industries.—*Gawthorpe Hall* (NT), on the outskirts of *Padiham* 3m NW of Burnley, is a Jacobean mansion built around a pele tower and remodelled by Sir Charles Barry in 1849–51. It has a striking long gallery, and contains the Rachel Kay-Shuttleworth Collection of textiles.—At *Harle Syke*, 3m NE of Burnley, the *Queen Street Mill* (open) is a steam-powered cotton-weaving mill of 1894 preserved in working order.—The pretty village of *Hurstwood*, 3¼m E of Burnley, is said to have been the poet Spenser's home while he was writing 'The Shepheardes Calender' (1579).

From Burnley to *Preston* and to *Halifax*, see Rte 75B.

27½m. **Nelson** (30,400 inhab.; Tourist Information) is named after the Admiral. Pendle Hill (Rte 75C) rises to the W, and the Haworth moors (Rte 75H) stretch to the E.—29½m. **Colne** (18,200 inhab.), once a centre of the wool trade, has a museum about the British in India. —A56 branches N to (34m) *Earby*, near the North Yorkshire border, with a museum of lead-mining in the 17C former grammar school (limited opening). At *Barnoldswick*, 3m W, the Bancroft Mill engine of 1922 which drove 1000 looms has been preserved (limited opening). The secluded church of St Mary-le-Ghyll has Jacobean box pews and a three-decker pulpit.

We join A59 at 37m and continue to (41½m) **Skipton** (Rte 86C).


# E. From Manchester to Rochdale, Halifax and Bradford

Total distance 36m. **Manchester**, see Rte 74.—A664 to (11m) **Rochdale**.—A58 to (27½m) **Halifax** (Rte 75B).—A58, A6036 to (36m) **Bradford**.

Maps: OS Landranger 109, 110 (briefly), 104.

M62 crosses the Pennines between Rochdale and Oldham, passes over the holding dam of Scammonden Reservoir, SE of Ripponden, and runs between Halifax and Huddersfield, serving Bradford and Leeds by spurs.

**Manchester**, see Rte 74. We leave the city by A664.—6m. *Middleton* (51,700 inhab.), formerly a silk and cotton town, now has plastics and chemical industries. The commanding church, with a curious tower, contains a 16C rood screen, brasses of the Asshetons and a stained-glass window commemorating Flodden (1513).

11m. **Rochdale** (92,700 inhab.), both a wool town and a cotton town in its day, has a handsome *Town Hall* (1866–71; W.H. Crossland) modelled after the Flemish cloth halls. The parish church of *St Chad* contains glass by Morris and Co. (1872) in the W window. The *Rochdale Museum*, in the 18C former vicarage, has displays of local history paying particular tribute to two famous natives, the Liberal politician John Bright (1811–89) and the singer Gracie Fields (1898–1979). The *Art Gallery* on the Esplanade has 19–20C British paintings. The building in Toad Lane where the Society of Equitable Pioneers opened its grocery shop in 1844, thus beginning the Co-operative Movement, has been restored as the *Rochdale Pioneers Memorial Museum*. There are attractive moors to the E and NW, with many reservoirs.

From Rochdale to *Bacup* via the Whitworth valley, see Rte 75D.

We follow A58, climbing to the moors beyond (14½m) *Littleborough*. Just before the summit (1269ft), where we cross the Pennine Way, a *Roman road carries straight on over *Blackstone Edge*. A long stretch of paving keeps the central gutter in which turf was probably placed to give the horses added foothold on the hill.—We enter West Yorkshire, descending from Rishworth Moor to (22m) *Ripponden* (5100 inhab.), with an 18C packhorse bridge, in the wooded Ryburn valley. The Ryburn Farm Museum occupies a farmhouse and its adjoining barn.—We follow the river to (25½m) *Sowerby Bridge* (15,500 inhab.; Tourist Information) with the canal basin of the Calder and Hebble Navigation. A rush-bearing ceremony, dating back to the 17C, is held on the first weekend in September.

27½m. **Halifax**, see Rte 75B.—Beyond *Shibden Hall* (also Rte 75B) A6036 branches left from A58 and climbs steeply via (31½m) *Shelf*, once known for its damask and worsted.

36m. **BRADFORD** (280,700 inhab.) has traditionally been the centre of the worsted trade. Its connection with wool dates back to the 16C, but it is essentially a Victorian city and keeps handsome 19C civic buildings, warehouses and mills. Of late Bradford has been surprisingly successful in attracting tourists, and some good new museums have opened.

**Tourist Information Centre**: City Hall.

**Car Parks**: Kirkgate/Arndale Centre, Charles St., Interchange Station, Westgate, Chester St., Hall Ings, Balme St., Forster Square Station, Cheapside.

**Railway Stations**: Interchange Station, Bridge St., for main line trains. Forster Square Station for Ilkley, Keighley, etc.

**Bus Station**: Interchange.

**Theatre**: Alhambra, Morley St.

**Airport**: Leeds–Bradford Airport at *Yeadon*, 6¹/₂m NE. For services, see Leeds (Rte 75F).

**Famous natives** etc. Frederick Delius (1863–1934), J.B. Priestley (1894–1984) and John Braine (1922–86) were natives, and Sir Henry Irving died here after a performance of Tennyson's 'Becket' in 1905.

The Gothic **City Hall** (1869–73), with its striking campanile, is by the local firm of Lockwood and Mawson; the extension to the S is by Norman Shaw (1902–09). The neo–classical *St George's Hall* (1851–53) on the corner of Bridge St., to the E, is also the work of Lockwood and Mawson. SW of the City Hall, on the opposite side of Princes Way, are the *Alhambra Theatre* (1914), with recent alterations outside and an Edwardian auditorium inside, and the excellent **National Museum of Photography, Film and Television** in a building originally designed as a cinema. It has a huge IMAX screen (the biggest in Europe) and exhibits which include the Kodak Collection of photographs and television galleries with a TV studio.

Great Horton Rd leads W to the *University of Bradford*, in the buildings of the former Technical College, raised to university status in 1966.—Grattan Rd, off Westgate to the N, has the inventive *Colour Museum*, in a former wool warehouse, with exhibits about the science of colour and the history of dyeing and textile-printing.

Market St. heads NE from the Town Hall to the Venetian Gothic **Wool Exchange** (1864–67), also by Lockwood and Mawson, on the corner of Bank St. The city's request for advice from Ruskin about the design of the Exchange provoked the magnificent rebuke in his lecture 'On Traffic'. From the end of Market St. we turn right on Cheapside to Forster Square. Above it stands the **Cathedral**, the 14–15C former parish church, raised to its present status in 1919 and greatly extended by Sir Edward Maufe in 1951–63. It contains a beautiful 15C font cover, good monuments and some early stained glass by Morris and Co. (1862) reset in the modern Lady Chapel. The streets to the S make up the merchant quarter known as 'Little Germany', with some splendid 19C warehouses.

NW of Forster Square, Cheapside continues as Manor Row, Manningham Lane and Keighley Rd (A650) to Lister Park, about 1m from the centre. The *Cartwright Hall* (open) is an ornate building of 1904 named after Edmund Cartwright (1743–1823), inventor of an early power loom. It contains a good collection of 19–20C British painting and sculpture, with some earlier English and Continental paintings which include Reynolds's 'Brown Boy'. In Heaton Rd nearby is the grandest of Bradford's mills, the huge *Manningham Mill*, or *Lister's Mill* (1871–73), with its Italianate chimney. Like several other mills in the area, it has a shop open to the public.—Church Bank, leading NE from the cathedral, is continued by Otley Rd and Harrogate Rd (A658). Otley Rd passes the interesting 19C *Undercliffe Cemetery*, now being restored. Moorside Rd, off

Harrogate Rd 2¹/₂m from the city centre, has the *Bradford Industrial Museum* in a former spinning mill, tracing the development of the worsted industry. There are working demonstrations of the steam engines which powered the mill, and the adjoining mill owner's house has been restored. The transport gallery contains locally made cars and motorcycles and the city's last tram.

*Manningham (or Lister's) Mill, Bradford*

The old Ludlam St. bus depot in Mill Lane, off Manchester Rd to the S of the city centre, is now the *West Yorkshire Transport Museum* (limited opening), with buses, trams, fire engines, etc. It is the first stage of a project to convert a 5m stretch of railway running through the Spen valley to Heckmondwike into an operating tramway.—*Bolling Hall* (open), 1¹/₂m SE of the centre on A650 towards Wakefield, is a 15–18C manor house. Now a museum, it contains 17C panelled rooms and oak furniture and, in the Georgian wing by John Carr of York, some pieces by Chippendale.

At *Thornton*, 4m W of the centre by B6145, a house in Market St. was the birthplace of Charlotte, Emily, Anne and Branwell Brontë.—*Fulneck*, 4m E of Bradford and 1m S of *Pudsey*, has the oldest Moravian church in England (c 1742–50). Benjamin Latrobe (1764–1820), architect of the Capitol in Washington DC, was born here.

*Leeds* (Rte 75F) is 9m W of Bradford by A647; *Shipley*, in Airedale (Rte 75H), is 3m N.

# F. Manchester to Huddersfield and Leeds

Total distance 40m. **Manchester**, see Rte 74. We follow A62 throughout.—To (7m) **Oldham**.—To (25m) **Huddersfield**.—To (40m) **Leeds**.

Maps: OS Landranger 109, 110, 104.

For M62, the fast alternative, see Rte 75E.

**Manchester**, see Rte 74. A62 heads NE through dreary suburbs. —7m. **Oldham** (95,500 inhab.; Tourist Information) once boasted the largest number of spindles of any cotton town in the world. Several cotton mills are still at work, together with many other textile mills, although the great textile machinery works of Platt Brothers has closed down. The *Town Hall* (1841; Joseph Butterworth: enlarged 1879 and 1917) is modelled on the Temple of Ceres near Athens. It stands at the top of Yorkshire St., opposite the *Parish Church* (1823–27; Richard Lane). Cobbett became MP for Oldham in 1832, and Sir Winston Churchill first entered Parliament as the member for Oldham in 1900.

A669 heads E to join A635, the Barnsley road, which runs to (15m) *Holmfirth* (see below) across the N tip of the Peak District National Park and the bleakly impressive *Saddleworth Moor*, associated with the Moors Murders of the 1960s.

Beyond Oldham A62 climbs over the Pennines.—11½m. We cross the river Tame. The once important cloth-making centres of *Delph* and *Dobcross*, N and S of the road, have old cobbled streets and weavers' stone houses.—At (14½m) *Standedge*, the summit of the moor (1271ft), we cross the Pennine Way and the West Yorkshire border. Beneath Standedge run railway tunnels and the Huddersfield Narrow Canal tunnel (1811), over 3m long, the highest and the longest canal tunnel in Great Britain. It emerges in the Colne Valley at (17½m) *Marsden*, where the tunnel keepers' cottages have been converted into a Canal and Countryside Centre. The Standedge Trail is a 12m circular walk linking this end of the tunnel with the S end at Diggle. The canal has been restored from Marsden to (20m) *Slaithwaite*, and the towpath can be walked all the way to Huddersfield. —A62 follows the river, the canal and the railway to (22m) *Golcar*, on the left, where a group of 19C weavers' cottages have been restored as the Colne Valley Museum (limited opening). The 12m circuit of the Colne Valley Walk starts and finishes here.

25m. **Huddersfield** (123,200 inhab.; Tourist Information), one of Yorkshire's great cloth towns, is strikingly placed among the hills and generously laid out with wide streets. The *Railway Station* (1847–48; J.P. Pritchett) has a handsome neo-classical façade looking out on St George's Square, the centrepiece of Huddersfield's mid-19C development. To the N is the *Brook St. Market* (1887–89) and to the S, on Westgate, the *Byram Arcade* (1880–81), with an elegant entrance. The *Town Hall* (1878–84), further S, contains a concert hall where the famous Huddersfield Choral Society performs. The Huddersfield Contemporary Music Festival is held in November.

The *Library and Art Gallery*, in Princess Alexandra Walk nearby, has
a collection of mainly 20C British art.

Off Wakefield Rd (A629), on the E side of the ring road, is the *Apsley Basin* of
the Huddersfield Broad Canal, or Sir John Ramsden's Canal (1776), which runs
N via a curious vertical lift bridge to join the Calder and Hebble Navigation at
Cooper Bridge (see below). The Huddersfield Narrow Canal (see above) heads
S. *Ravensknowle Park*, about 1m further E on the Wakefield road, contains the
re-erected entrances of the old Cloth Hall (1776) and a hypocaust from Slack
(the Roman Cambodunum, 3¹/2m W). The *Tolson Memorial Museum*, also in the
park, has displays of natural history, local and social history, transport and
textiles. Beyond the park A629 turns S, past the Tudor *Woodsome Hall* (now a
golf club). B6116 branches left to (4m) *Kirkburton*, with an early 13C church
containing the remains of a Saxon cross. *Skelmanthorpe* church, 2¹/2m further
on, has an 11C font. The area is dominated by the fine TV mast by Ove Arup on
*Emley Moor*.
   NW of the city centre, off Halifax Rd (A629), are the interesting 19C suburbs
of (1¹/4m) *Edgerton* and (2m) *Lindley*, with a striking clock tower (1900–02;
Edgar Wood).—*Castle Hill*, 2m S of Huddersfield, has an early Iron Age fort and
the 19C Jubilee Tower (open).—*Almondbury*, E of the hill and 2m SE of the city
centre, has a good late Perp. church.

FROM HUDDERSFIELD TO SHEFFIELD, 26m by A616.—From (3¹/2m) *Honley* A6024
climbs to (2¹/2m) *Holmfirth* (21,800 inhab.; Tourist Information), a grim little
town made famous as the location of TV's 'Last of the Summer Wine', with a
postcard museum based on cards produced by the local firm of Bamforths.
A6024 continues another 7m over bleak moors to Woodhead (Rte 75G), with a
fine view near the *Holme Moss* TV mast on the Derbyshire border.—A616
crosses the Don at (10¹/2m) *Hazlehead Bridge* and the Manchester–Barnsley
road (Rte 75G) at (11¹/2m) *Flouch Inn*, skirting the fringe of the Peak District
National Park as far as (12¹/2m) *Langsett* (Rte 56D).—At (17¹/2m) *Deepcar* we
reach the attractive *Wharncliffe Woods*, also entered from (21m)
*Oughtibridge*.—26m. *Sheffield*, see Rte 75G.

A62 continues to (28m) *Cooper Bridge*, where the Huddersfield
Broad Canal (see above) meets the Calder and Hebble Navigation.

A644 leads left to (2m) *Brighouse* (Rte 75B). To the right, it passes through the
main centres of the heavy woollen industry, with many mills.—1¹/2m. *Mirfield*
(18,700 inhab.). Charlotte, Emily and Anne Brontë were pupils, and Charlotte a
teacher, at Miss Wooller's school in *Roehead* to the N.—At (4¹/2m) **Dewsbury**
(48,300 inhab.) the church, rebuilt in the 18C and 19C, has fragments of a Saxon
cross and some 13–14C stained glass. The Dewsbury Museum in Crow Nest
Park is largely devoted to the theme of childhood. There is a small canal
museum at the basin of the Calder and Hebble Navigation. **Batley** (42,600
inhab.), 1¹/2m N, originated the manufacture of shoddy, heavy cloth made from
reprocessed material. It has a 13–15C church and the Bagshaw Museum, with
local displays and Egyptian and Oriental collections, in an eccentric house built
by a local woollen merchant in 1875. *Thornhill*, 2¹/4m S of Dewsbury, has a
church with much 15C stained glass, 15–20C monuments of the Savile family
and fragments of Saxon crosses.

The main Leeds road goes on through (31m) *Heckmondwike* (9700
inhab.), a centre of the blanket industry, and (33m) *Birstall*.

This is the district connected with Charlotte Brontë's 'Shirley' (1849). The
Elizabethan *Oakwell Hall* (open), ³/4m NW, with panelling and oak furniture, is
the heroine's home ('Fieldhead'). The 18C Red House (open) at *Gomersal*, ³/4m
W of Birstall, was the home of Charlotte Brontë's friend Mary Taylor and the
model for 'Briarmains' in the novel.—*Morley* (44,100 inhab.), another cloth
town, 3m NE of Birstall, was the birthplace of the politician Herbert Asquith
(1852–1928).

40m. **LEEDS** (448,500 inhab.), built across a basin of the river Aire, is
the commercial capital of Yorkshire and a busy industrial town,
traditionally a centre of the textile trade. Its industries are concentrated on the flat ground S of the river, while the residential suburbs
are on the heights that ring the city to the N. Modern development

has left the centre with little sense of history, though some good 19C
buildings survive, notably the splendid Town Hall.

**Tourist Information Centre**: No. 19 Wellington St.

**Car Parks**: Quarry Hill (St Peter's St.) and Wellington St. Multi-storey car parks
in Woodhouse Lane and Albion St.

**Bus Station**: New York St.

**Railway Station**: City Station, by City Square.

**Airport**: Leeds/Bradford Airport at *Yeadon*, 8m NW. Passenger services to Heathrow, Stansted, Isle of Man (summer), Cardiff, Edinburgh, Glasgow, Belfast, Dublin, Amsterdam.

**Theatres**: Leeds Playhouse, Calverley St.; Grand Theatre (the home of English National Opera North), New Briggate; City Varieties (music hall), The Headrow; Civic Theatre, Cookridge St.

**Events**: The Leeds International Concert Season runs from October to June each year. The City of Leeds Open Brass Band Championships are held each May. The Leeds Conductors' Competition is held biennially (next in 1990). The Leeds Musical Festival and the Leeds International Pianoforte Competition are held triennially (next in 1990). The Musical Festival, established in 1858, was conducted by Sir Arthur Sullivan in 1883–98 and heard the first performance of Walton's 'Belshazzar's Feast' in 1931.

**History**. The monks of Kirkstall Abbey began a trade in wool which was consolidated by Flemish workmen in the reign of Edward II. By the 18C the Leeds cloth market was the finest in the country, Defoe finding it 'a prodigy of its kind and not to be equalled in the world'. With the advent of steam power the city also became a centre for ready-made clothing, concrete and engineering. Leeds Pottery was once famous.

**Famous natives, residents and visitors**. Charles I was confined in Red Hall, formerly in Upper Headrow, for a few days while being led captive to London in 1847. The painter Atkinson Grimshaw (1836–93) was born and died at Leeds. The caricaturist Phil May (1864–1903) was born in Wallace St., New Wortley (near the Pudsey road) and Louis le Prince (1842–90), pioneer of the cinema, had his workshop in Woodhouse Lane.

City Square, outside the railway station, is the hub of several busy streets. The statuary in its central triangle includes the Black Prince on horseback (1899; Brock), eight bronze maidens (1899; Drury) and statues of Joseph Priestley, James Watt, John Harrison and Dean Hook. On the E side, overshadowed by tower blocks, is the Gothic *Mill Hill Chapel* (rebuilt in 1847), where Priestley was minister in 1767–78.

Boar Lane leads E to the Georgian church of *Holy Trinity* (1721–27) and, beyond Briggate, the splendid glass-domed *Corn Exchange* (1861–63) by the local architect Cuthbert Brodrick who was also responsible for the Town Hall and the Civic Theatre. *Kirkgate Market* (1904), to the N, has a baroque exterior and a good display of iron and glass inside. Kirkgate runs SE under the railway to the parish church of *St Peter*, rebuilt in 1837–41 for Dean W.F. Hook (1798–1875), the High Church vicar and 'Apostle of the West Riding'. It contains a restored Saxon *cross.

The busy Park Row, with some good 19C buildings, leads N from City Square to the broad thoroughfare of The Headrow. In Victoria Square to the left is the classical ***Town Hall** (1853–58), Cuthbert Brodrick's masterpiece and one of the best civic buildings in the North.

The nearby **City Art Gallery** shows 19C and 20C paintings and sculpture. The Old Masters and decorative arts belonging to the city are housed at Temple Newsam and Lotherton Hall (see below). The gallery was expanded in 1982 by the addition of a sculpture gallery and a centre for the study of sculpture named in honour of Henry Moore, who, with Barbara Hepworth, was a student at Leeds College of Art under Jacob Kramer.

The gallery is probably best known for its fine *collection of English water-colours, prints and drawings. 19C French and British landscapes include work by Courbet, Sisley, Signac, Derain, Constable, Crome, Corot and Daubigny. Victorian canvases include work by Leighton, Lady Butler and Atkinson Grimshaw. The Sam Wilson collection contains an amazing Alfred Gilbert fireplace and murals by Sir Frank Brangwyn. The strong collection of 20C

British art includes paintings by Sickert, Nash, Spencer, Piper, Bacon, Hitchens, Wyndham Lewis and Kramer, and sculptures by Moore, Hepworth, Epstein, Arp and Paolozzi. There is a changing exhibition programme, supported by educational activities, films and performance.

The adjoining *City Museum* has collections of geology, natural history, ethnography and archaeology, including Egyptian mummies, Greek and Roman marbles, and local finds, together with a display of coins and medals.

Calverley St. leads N to the twin-towered *Civic Hall* (1933; E. Vincent Harris) and the huge buildings of *Leeds Polytechnic* (by Yorke, Rosenberg and Mardall, begun in 1953).—Cookridge St., continuing Park Row N beyond The Headrow, has the Roman Catholic *St Anne's Cathedral* (1904), with a Lady Chapel altar of 1842 by Pugin from the previous cathedral, and the *Civic Theatre* (1865–68; Brodrick), originally built as the Mechanics' Institute.

The Headrow prolongs Westgate eastward across Briggate to Vicar Lane. **St John's** in New Briggate is a fine example of Laudian Gothic, built by the local cloth merchant John Harrison in 1632–34. Its superb woodwork includes the original *screen, pews and pulpit. Beyond Vicar Lane, Eastgate continues to the monumental *Quarry Hill Flats* (1935–41; R. Livett), the largest such estate in England when it was first built.

The **University of Leeds** is in Woodhouse Lane, beyond the inner ring road NW of the centre. Incorporated in 1904, it grew out of the Leeds School of Medicine (1831) and the Yorkshire College of Science (1874), and was for a time affiliated to the Victoria University (see Manchester, Rte 74). The largely undistinguished buildings, begun by Alfred Waterhouse in 1877, include the large *Parkinson Building* (1951; T.A. Lodge). The *Brotherton Library* (open by appointment with the Librarian), with its fine circular reading room, was the gift of Lord Brotherton (1856–1930). It contains his personal library (the Brotherton Collection, rich in early books and manuscripts, particularly of English literature) amongst some two million volumes in one of the largest academic library systems in the country.

The main residential areas lie to the N of the city, in the neighbourhood of *Headingley*, *Chapel Allerton* and *Roundhay*. Adel, about 2¼m N of Headingley, has a beautiful little Norman *church with interesting sculptures on the S porch and the chancel arch. The large *Golden Acre Park*, 1m beyond, has gardens, woodland and a lake. See below for the continuation of A660 to Otley.—In Roundhay Rd, the approach to *Roundhay Park*, one of the finest public parks in the country, is the remarkable Romanesque church of *St Aidan* (1894) with splendid mosaics by Sir Frank Brangwyn.

A65 follows the river Aire NW from the centre to (1½m) *Leeds Industrial Museum* in the impressive Armley Mills building of 1806. Its displays illustrate the development of the city's major industries, including textiles, clothing, optics and heavy engineering, with reconstructed industrial settings. There is a collection of railway engines, and a 1920s picture palace.—*Kirkstall Abbey* (open) lies about 1½m further, in a park by the river. A Cistercian house founded by monks from Fountains in 1152, its ruins are better preserved than those of any other great northern abbey. The chief remains are the impressive church, with its collapsed Perp. tower; the late Norman and EE chapter house, which is almost intact; and the abbot's lodging, a splendid piece of 13C domestic architecture. The restored 12C gatehouse N of the road is now the *Abbey House Museum*, with folk collections including toys and games, and reconstructed Victorian streets with shops, cottages and an inn.

FROM LEEDS TO SELBY, 21m by A63. The road crosses the ancient district of *Elmet*, stretching NE towards Tadcaster.—5m. **Temple Newsam** (open) is a

Jacobean house altered in the 18C, now containing the *collections of decorative art belonging to the Leeds City Art Galleries. The former house on the site was the birthplace of Lord Darnley in 1545 and the original of 'Templestowe' in Scott's 'Ivanhoe'. The Georgian long gallery and library, and the Chinese drawing room, are outstanding among the interiors. The rich art collections include English pottery, silver and 16–18C furniture; the paintings include work by Paul van Somer, Pellegrini, Reynolds and Morland. Outside are a home farm, seven specialist gardens and a large park laid out by Capability Brown in 1762. See Rte 85B for *Lotherton Hall*, by A1 6m NW, also belonging to Leeds City Art Galleries.—10m. A63 meets A1 (Rte 85B), which is followed S for 1¹/2m before A63 resumes its eastward course.—13m. *South Milford*, N of A62 on A162, and (14m) *Monk Fryston*, see Rte 85B.—21m. *Selby*, see Rte 81.

FROM LEEDS TO DONCASTER, 28¹/2m by A639, branching left from A61 S of the city.—7¹/2m. *Methley* church contains interesting 15–17C tombs and effigies of the Waterton and Savile families, and a lectern with an elaborate 16C base. —10m. *Castleford* (36,000 inhab.), a grimy colliery and bottle-making town at the junction of the Aire and the Calder, was the important Roman station *Lagentium*. Finds, together with locally made glassware and pottery, are displayed in the small museum in the library. The sculptor Henry Moore (1898–1986) was born here.—13¹/2m. **Pontefract** (32,000 inhab.) is a market town famous for its racecourse and for the liquorice lozenges known as 'Pomfret cakes' which take their name from the old pronunciation of its name. Richard II died in the Norman castle in 1400, either murdered by Sir Piers Exton (as in Shakespeare's play) or starved to death. Other prisoners included James I of Scotland and Charles, Duke of Orleans, after his capture at Agincourt. The castle was razed to the ground in 1649 and only a few fragments survive in the recreation ground which now covers its site. *Ackworth School*, 3m S on A628, a Quaker boarding school opened in 1779, occupies the buildings of a Foundling Hospital of 1758. It is open by appointment during the vacations. Nostell Priory lies 2¹/2m W of Ackworth on the way to Wakefield (Rte 75H).—At (20m) *Barnsdale Bar* we join A1 (Rte 85B), 8¹/2m N of *Doncaster* (Rte 81).

FROM LEEDS TO OTLEY, 11m by A660. We quit the city via Headingley and Adel and Golden Acre Park (see above).—7m. *Bramhope* has a Puritan chapel of 1649 with contemporary fittings in the grounds of the former Bramhope Hall. —11m. *Otley*, in Wharfedale, see Rte 86A.

From Leeds to *Sheffield* and to *Airedale* and *Skipton*, see Rte 75H; to *Harrogate*, *Ripon* and *Thirsk*, see Rte 80; to *York*, see Rte 81.

# G.   Manchester to Penistone
# and Sheffield

Total distance 41m. **Manchester**, see Rte 74.—A57 to (9¹/2m) Mottram-in-Longdendale.—A628 to (27m) **Penistone**.—A629, A61 to (41m) **Sheffield**.

Maps: OS Landranger 109, 110.

The direct way (37m) from Manchester to Sheffield is by A57. For another route via Hathersage and Castleton, see Rte 56D.

**Manchester**, see Rte 74. A57 runs E, crossing the Tame beyond (5¹/2m) *Denton* (37,700 inhab.).—7m. *Hyde* (35,600 inhab.) is one of a group of cotton and coal towns in the once beautiful Tame valley.

The oldest and most important is *Ashton-under-Lyne* (44,700 inhab.), 2m N, with some magnificent *glass of c 1500 in its church. *Dukinfield* (18,100 inhab.) and *Stalybridge* (26,400 inhab.) are nearby, with *Mossley* (10,100 inhab.) further upstream.

9¹/2m. *Mottram-in-Longdendale*, where the painter L.S. Lowry (1887–1976) spent the later years of his life, has a fine Perp. church. A57 heads S via Glossop (Rte 56A). We take A628, entering Derbyshire and the Peak District National Park, and following *Longdendale*, watered by the Etherow and almost filled with reservoirs.—Beyond (16½m) *Woodhead*, a deserted site where the moorland road to Holmfirth (Rte 75F) bears left, we see the mouth of the Woodhead Tunnel, which pierces the hard millstone grit of the Pennines and emerges over 3m away in South Yorkshire. The digging of the first tunnel (1840–46), one of the great feats of Victorian railway-building, killed 32 navvies and injured 250 more. This tunnel is disused; the second twin tunnel (1847–52) has been reopened to carry electricity cables. A new twin-track tunnel has carried the railway since electrification in 1954.—We cross the border into South Yorkshire. A long descent past (23m) the *Flouch Inn* (Rte 75F) brings us to the rocky valley of the Don and (27m) **Penistone** (9000 inhab.), a bleak little town with steel works and a fine Dec. church.

A628 continues E through pleasant country to the South Yorkshire coalfield. —3m. *Silkstone* has a church with fine woodwork, a monument to Sir Thomas Wentworth (d. 1675) and a memorial to the hydraulic engineer Joseph Bramah (1748–1814). For *Cawthorne* and *Cannon Hall*, to the N, see Rte 75H.—7m. *Barnsley*, see Rte 75H.

Beyond Penistone we take A629 S.—From (32m) *Wortley* we can reach Wharncliffe Woods (Rte 75F). Beyond Wortley we join A61.

41m. **SHEFFIELD** (542,700 inhab.), the largest city in Yorkshire and the fourth largest in England, has been a centre for the production of cutlery since the Middle Ages and of high-quality steel since the 18C. Standing at the foot of the Derbyshire hills, where the river Sheaf meets the river Don, it had become 'the foulest town in England in the most charming situation' when Horace Walpole visited it in 1760. It now claims the cleanest air of any manufacturing city in Europe, and has a centre transformed by imaginative planning and architecture. In recent years it has also become an important venue for conferences.

**Tourist Information Centre**: Town Hall Extension, Union St.

**Car Parks**: Union St., Union Lane, Eyre St., Eyre Lane, Surrey Place, Broad St., Wheel Hill, Sheaf St., Park Goods Station, Moorfoot. Multi-storey car park in Pond St./Arundel Gate.

**Bus Station**: Pond St.

**Railway Station**: off Sheaf Square, E of the centre.

**Theatres**: Crucible Theatre, Norfolk St.; Library Theatre, Tudor Place. Orchestral concerts at City Hall, Barker's Pool.

**History**. *Hallam* or *Hallamshire*, the ancient manor which embraced Sheffield and its neighbouring parishes, was already famous for its cutlery in the 14C, when the miller in Chaucer's 'Reeve's Tale' carried a 'Sheffeld thwitel' (knife) in his hose. By the end of the 16C the town had about 60 hallmarks. In 1740 Benjamin Huntsman invented the crucible process of steel production, and in 1742 Thomas Boulsover discovered that silver could be bonded to copper and then rolled into sheets, producing the famous Old Sheffield Plate, later superseded by electroplate. By the 19C the great steel works stretched in an unbroken line down the valley of the Don, NE through the suburbs of Attercliffe, Brightside and Tinsley to Rotherham.

**Famous natives and residents**. Mary, Queen of Scots, spent most of her captivity from 1570 to 1584 in the custody of the Earl of Shrewsbury at Sheffield, partly in the castle and partly in Sheffield Manor. The sculptor Sir Francis Chantrey (1781–1841), born and buried at nearby Norton, had his portrait studio in Paradise Square. The 'Corn Law Rhymer' Ebenezer Elliott (1781–1849), born at Masborough, near Rotherham, established his Sheffield iron foundry in 1821. Joseph Locke (1805–60), the railway engineer, and John Stringfellow (1799–1883), who flew the first heavier-than-air machine, were born at Attercliffe.

The crocketed spire of the Anglican **Cathedral** in Church St., at the W end of High St., marks the centre of the old town. The diocese was created in 1914, and the core of the building is still the 15C Perp. parish church. Already heavily restored in the 19C, it was enlarged in the 1930s and 1940s by Sir Charles Nicholson, who added the chapels and chapter house on the N side, and in the 1960s by Arthur Bailey, responsible for the narthex tower and the W end of the nave. The Wilkinson monument (1805) on the N side of the chancel is Chantrey's first important commission. The Lady Chapel, or Shrewsbury Chapel, contains the tombs of the 4th Earl of Shrewsbury (d. 1538) and the 6th Earl (d. 1590), Bess of Hardwick's husband and keeper of Mary, Queen of Scots. The Chapter House has stained-glass windows depicting scenes from Sheffield's history.

High St., continuing Church St. to the E, leads to the roundabout of Castle Square, with its underground shopping concourse. The ingeniously planned *Castle Market* (1960–65) by the city architect J.L. Womersley on Waingate, to the N, occupies the site of the castle, of which just a few fragments remain. This was the main fortress where Mary, Queen of Scots, was held captive.—The remnants of the Georgian quarter N of the cathedral include the quiet oasis of Paradise Square. John Wesley preached to his largest weekday congregation here in July 1779, and Chantrey had his studio at No. 24 in 1802.

Facing the cathedral on the S side of Church St. stands the Greek Revival *Cutlers' Hall* of 1832, the third building erected on this site for the Cutler's Company, incorporated in 1624. Open by appointment, it contains the Company's collection of silver. The annual feast given by the Master Cutler is held here.

Fargate, a pedestrianised street which includes the newly completed Orchard Square shopping complex, leads S to the **Town Hall** (1890–97; E.W. Mountford), a gabled Renaissance building with a prominent tower topped by a statue of Vulcan, symbol of the city's chief industries. To its S are the *Peace Gardens*, flanked by the *Town Hall Extension* (1977). Facing Barker's Pool, further W, is the **City Hall** (1932), a classical building by E. Vincent Harris with decorations by G. Kruger Gray. Surrey St. heads E from the Town Hall to the *Central Library*, whose top floor houses the *Graves Art Gallery.

Its collections are held in common with the Mappin Art Gallery (see below) and items are subject to removal from one gallery to the other. They include a wide range of European art (Murillo, Procaccini, Ruisdael, Van der Neer); a strong collection of British watercolours (Turner, Girtin); 19C British painting (Turner, Burne-Jones); 20C British painting (Sickert, Nash, Gwen John, David Bomberg); and Chinese ivories. The ivories and, in general, most of the works on paper are kept at the Graves. The Victorian collection is usually displayed at the Mappin. Any visitor wishing to see specific works or groups of works should call the galleries to ensure that they are on show or make an appointment to view. There is also an energetic programme of temporary exhibitions.

Norfolk St. leads N from Surrey St. The *Ruskin Gallery*, opened in 1985, is housed in an imaginatively converted 19C wine shop. It brings together in a new display the contents of the Guild of St George museum which Ruskin established at Sheffield in the 1870s to provide a liberal education for local workmen—a wonderfully eclectic assembly of geological specimens, watercolours, photographs, plaster casts of architectural fragments, etc. The *Crucible Theatre*, further N, houses two auditoria. The World Professional Snooker Championships are held here each year.

Rising up the steep slope E of the railway are the spectacular *Park Hill* and *Hyde Park* estates (1958–62) by J.L. Womersley. Among the most influential post-war experiments in high-density housing, they have raised streets and connecting bridges. The same architect's estate (begun in 1955) at *Gleadless*, 2m S, sets low houses into the hillside.

The **University of Sheffield** is about 1m W of the city centre in Western Bank. Incorporated in 1905, it had its origin in Firth College, founded in 1879, and the Sheffield School of Medicine, founded in 1828. Modern additions to the original red-brick neo-Tudor buildings (1903–05; E.Mitchel Gibbs) include the dominating *Arts Tower* (1960–65; Gillins, Melvin, Ward and Partners). Just beyond is the beautiful *Weston Park*, with an observatory and a statue of Ebenezer Elliott, the 'Corn Law Rhymer'. The *City Museum, in the park, has superb collections of Old Sheffield Plate and Sheffield cutlery, together with local silver and ceramics, and archaeological and geological collections. The adjoining *Mappin Art Gallery* holds its collections in common with the Graves Art Gallery (see above); the 19C paintings are usually displayed here. The university church of *St Mark* in Broomfield Rd was rebuilt in 1958–63 by George Pace, with a W window by John Piper and Patrick Reyntiens.

The *Kelham Island Industrial Museum*, in a former generating station by the river Don NW of the centre, is reached via Corporation St. and Alma St. Exhibits include operational steam and gas engines. Reconstructed workshops are manned by craftsmen demonstrating the skills of the 'little mesters' who once sustained the city's cutlery trade.

A625 leads SW, past (1½m) the handsome *Botanical Gardens* with conservatories of 1837–38 by Joseph Paxton. *Whiteley Wood*, off A625 about 2½m further SW, has the *Shepherd Wheel* (open), a water-powered grinding works on the river Porter.—A621 also leads SW from the city to (3½m) *Beauchief*, on the left. The chapel, with its 14C tower and arches, is a relic of a Premonstratensian abbey founded in 1183. The nearby *Abbeydale Industrial Hamlet* (open) preserves an 18–19C water-powered scythe works, with crucible furnace, forges, grinding workshops, office buildings, etc. The road continues to (6m) *Totley*, with the mouth of the Totley Tunnel (3½m), the second longest in England, and to (13½m) *Baslow* in the Peak District (Rte 56A).—A61, heading S, passes (2m) *Meersbrook Park* with the so-called *Bishops' House* (open), in fact a half-timbered yeoman's house dating originally from the late 15C. At *Norton*, about 2m further S, an obelisk commemorates Sir Francis Chantrey (1781–1841), born and buried here.

Norfolk Rd goes SE from the centre to *Norfolk Park*. To the E are the remains of *Sheffield Manor*, a 16C mansion occasionally occupied by Mary, Queen of Scots, during her captivity. The well-preserved *Turret House* houses a small museum which is normally open during the summer.

FROM SHEFFIELD TO DONCASTER, 18m by A6109 or A6178 and A630.—6½m. **Rotherham** (82,000 inhab.) is a murky coal and iron town on the Don. The altered 15C bridge has an ancient chantry. The parish church is one of the finest Perp. churches in the North, with a crocketed spire, Jacobean pulpit and delightful poppy-heads on the chancel stalls. Rockingham china (made at *Swinton*, 3½m N) is displayed at the Art Gallery in Walker Place and at the Clifton Park Museum, in a charming 18C house. The museum also has finds from the Roman fort at *Templeborough* to the SW, now obliterated by steel works. The suburb of *Masborough*, to the W, was the birthplace of the 'Corn Law Rhymer' Ebenezer Elliott (1781–1849). About 3½m NW is the grandiose mansion of *Wentworth Woodhouse* (not open), begun by Henry Flitcroft in the 1730s for the 1st Marquis of Rockingham.—A630 to (12½m) *Conisbrough* and on to (17½m) *Doncaster*, see Rte 81.

From Sheffield to *Derby* and *Leicester*, see Rte 55; to *Manchester* via *Hathersage* and *Castleton*, see Rte 56D; to *Huddersfield*, see Rte 75F; to *Leeds*, *Airedale* and *Skipton*, see Rte 75H.

# H.   Sheffield to Leeds, Airedale and Skipton

Total distance 60½m. **Sheffield**, see Rte 75G.—A61 to (13½m) Barnsley.—A61 to (23½m) Wakefield.—A61 to (33m) **Leeds** (Rte 75F).—A647, A657 to (43½m) Shipley.—A650 to (51½m) Keighley (for **Haworth**).—A629 to (60½m) Skipton (Rte 86C).

Maps: OS Landranger 110 (or 111), 104, 103 (briefly).

**Sheffield**, see Rte 75G.—A61 heads nearly due N through the South Yorkshire coalfield.—At (12m) *Worsborough* the Mill Museum (open) has a 17C and a 19C mill, both restored to working order.—13½m. **Barnsley** (73,600 inhab.; Tourist Information) is the centre of the coalfield. The *Cooper Gallery* in Church St. contains a good collection of 19–20C English watercolours and work by Eugène Isabey.

At *Cawthorne*, off A635 4½m W, the church has glass by the Pre-Raphaelite Spencer Stanhope in the W window and by Morris and Co. in the N chapel, and two fonts, 11C and Perp. The village adjoins *Cannon Hall* (open), an 18C house mainly by John Carr of York, in landscaped parkland. It is now a country house museum with 17–19C furniture, English, Dutch and Flemish paintings, and good collections of pottery and glassware. In the parkland of *Bretton Hall*, 3½m further N, is the *Yorkshire Sculpture Park* (open), with work by Henry Moore and Barbara Hepworth.—At *Woolley*, 4½m NW of Barnsley, the church has interesting bench ends.—At *Royston* (8,900 inhab.), 3½m N of Barnsley, the Perp. tower of the church has a five-sided oriel.—*Monk Bretton Priory* (English Heritage, standard opening), off A628 2m E of Barnsley, was a Cluniac foundation of c 1154 which later became Benedictine. Remains include the 14C gatehouse and 13–14C buildings around the cloisters, but little of the 12C church.

From Barnsley to *Penistone* and *Manchester*, see Rte 75G.

23½m. **Wakefield** (58,500 inhab.; Tourist Information), an ancient city above the river Calder, is the county town of West Yorkshire as it was of the West Riding. A centre of the cloth trade before the Industrial Revolution, it keeps some prosperous Georgian houses (in South and West Parade, for example) and has never become as industrialised as its neighbours.

The medieval Wakefield Cycle, one of four cycles of mystery plays to survive in England, includes the famous 'Second Shepherd's Play' by the so-called Wakefield Master. The Battle of Wakefield (1460), at which Richard, Duke of York, was killed by the Lancastrians, was fought near Sandal Castle, 1¾m S. Famous natives include Dr John Radcliffe (1652–1714), the physician and Oxford benefactor; George Gissing (1857–1903), born in Westgate; and Dame Barbara Hepworth (1903–75).

The public buildings on Wood St. include the interesting *Court House* (1810), *County Hall* (1894–98; Gibson and Russell) and *Town Hall* (1880; T.E. Collcutt), and the *Museum*, mainly of local history. The *Art Gallery* on Wentworth Terrace to the N has a good collection of 20C painting and sculpture, including work by Barbara Hepworth and Henry Moore.

Kirkgate leads E to the **Cathedral**, with its tall crocketed spire. Dating mainly from c 1470, it was the parish church until the new diocese was created in 1888. Sir Gilbert Scott rebuilt the spire in the course of heavy restoration in 1858–74, while J.L. and F.L. Pearson added the new E end in 1901–05. Inside, the most striking features are the fine wooden rood screen of 1635 (with additions by Sir Ninian Comper, 1950), the organ case (1743) and the display of church treasures in the N choir aisle, and the stained glass by Kempe (1872–1900). Kirkgate continues SE from the cathedral down to the Calder and the medieval bridge with its *Bridge Chapel*, originally built c 1350 (open by appointment). Despite substantial rebuilding by Sir Gilbert Scott in 1847, it is the most important of the handful of medieval bridge chapels surviving in England.

**Nostell Priory** (NT), off A638 6m SE, was begun in the Palladian style by James Paine in 1733–50 and continued by Robert Adam in 1765–80. The interior, superbly decorated by Paine and Adam, has ˙furniture designed for the house by Chippendale, who was for many years the estate carpenter. The dolls' house (1735) is probably his earliest surviving work. The paintings include Holbein's portrait of Sir Thomas More's family. In the park stands *Wragby* church, where Paine was married in 1741, with a wealth of Swiss glass (1514–1751) and a Norman font brought from the vanished church of Auburn on Yorkshire's E coast. Nearly opposite is the site of the Augustinian priory, founded c 1119, which gave its name to the house.—At *West Hardwick*, 2½m NE, is the *Top Farm Agricultural Museum*.

*Normanton* (17,300 inhab.), on A655 about 4m E of Wakefield, is a grimy town with a large 14–15C church.—*Horbury* (9100 inhab.), on A642 3m SW of Wakefield, was the birthplace of John Carr (1723–1807), who is buried in the church he built at his own expense in 1791–93.

At *Overton*, 6m SW on A642, the Huddersfield road, the redundant Caphouse Colliery has been re-opened as the *Yorkshire Mining Museum*.

Beyond Wakefield A650 heads NW, bypassing Leeds, to Bradford (Rte 75E) and Shipley (below). A61, the main route, goes due N.

33m. **Leeds**, see Rte 75F.—We leave the city on A647, branching right on A657 to follow the largely industrialised lower reaches of **Airedale** to (43½m) *Shipley* (27,900 inhab.).—44½m. *Saltaire* is named after the river and Sir Titus Salt (1803–76), who moved his mohair and alpaca mills from Bradford in 1853 to create a model industrial settlement with sturdy terraced housing. He is buried in the mausoleum by the Congregational Church. The Victoria Hall contains a museum of 19C reed organs and harmoniums. We join A650, which has come directly from Wakefield.—47m. *Bingley* (28,100 inhab.), a mill town, has a five-rise staircase of locks on the Leeds and Liverpool Canal.—50½m. *East Riddlesden Hall* (NT) is a 17C house in a vigorous local style, with a rose window over the porch and an elaborate fireplace in the hall. The medieval tithe barn has a collection of farm vehicles and implements. A track leads N across *Rombald's Moor* to (5m) *Ilkley* in Wharfedale (Rte 86A).—51½m. **Keighley** (pronounced 'Keethley'; 57,500 inhab.), another mill town, has the *Cliffe Castle Museum and Art Gallery*, with local geology, natural history, social history, pottery, crafts, etc. The *Worth Valley Railway* runs to Haworth and Oxenhope.

**Haworth** (Tourist Information) is 4m SW by A629 and A6033. Imperishably associated with the Brontës, this bleak village on the shoulder of the moors has become a popular tourist centre and is often unpleasantly crowded in summer. The cobbled main street climbs precipitously to the tiny square by the church. The chief attraction is the *Brontë Parsonage* (open), where the Rev. Patrick Brontë brought his family in 1820 and where his children, Charlotte (1816–55), Emily (1818–48), Anne (1820–49) and Branwell (1817–48), spent the majority of their lives. The Georgian building has been restored to its appearance in the Brontës' day, with items of their furniture and many memorabilia, of which the most interesting are the books and manuscripts in the Bonnell Room. The library is open for research by prior arrangement. The *Church*, where Charlotte married the curate Mr Nicholls in 1854, contains the vault of all the family except Anne, who died in Scarborough. Only the tower survives from their time; the rest was rebuilt in 1879–81. The Black Bull inn was the haunt of the unfortunate Branwell. Walks can be taken across the moors, which exercised so great an influence on the sisters, W to (2m) the *Brontë Waterfall* and (3m) *Top*

*Withens,* perhaps 'Wuthering Heights', or to (2½m) *Ponden Hall,* perhaps the 'Thrushcross Grange' of 'Wuthering Heights', (6½m) the ruined *Wycoller Hall,* perhaps the 'Ferndean Manor' of 'Jane Eyre', and (10m) *Colne* (Rte 75D). Top Withens and Ponden Hall are linked by the Pennine Way.—A6033 continues S from Haworth to (7m) *Hebden Bridge* in the Calder valley (Rte 75B).

From Keighley A629 follows Airedale to (56m) *Glusburn.* Charlotte Brontë was governess in 1839 at the 18C Stonegappe Hall (not open), the 'Gateshead Hall' of 'Jane Eyre', about 2m W. *Kildwick,* 1m N across the Aire, has a 14C stone bridge and a Perp. church.—60½m. **Skipton,** see Rte 86C.

# 76 Liverpool to Lancaster and Carlisle

Total distance 118m. **Liverpool,** see Rte 73.—A59 to (31m) **Preston,** see Rte 75B. We then follow A6 for the rest of the route.—To (52m) **Lancaster.**—To (74m) Kendal.—To (99m) Penrith.—To (118m) **Carlisle.**

Maps: OS Landranger 108, 102, 97, 90, 86 (briefly), 85.

M6, intertwined with A6, offers a fast alternative for most of the way.

**Liverpool,** see Rte 73. We take A59, following Rte 75B to (31m) **Preston.**

FROM PRESTON TO BLACKPOOL, LYTHAM ST ANNES AND FLEETWOOD. *The Fylde,* the plain between the estuaries of the Ribble and the Wyre, separates Preston from the coastal resorts to its W. It is crossed by M55 and A583, both going directly to Blackpool (16½m by either road). A584 branches left from A583 to (12m) Lytham St Annes, then follows the esplanade leading to (20m) Blackpool and (24m) Thornton Cleveleys and continuing as A587 to (29m) Fleetwood.
    **Lytham St Annes** (39,700 inhab,; Tourist Information) is a quiet residential resort stretching along the shore from Lytham, facing S at the mouth of the Ribble estuary, to the more open St Annes, looking SW. It has several major golf courses and *Lytham Hall* (not open), a Jacobean house altered by John Carr in 1764.
    **Blackpool** (147,900 inhab.; Tourist Information), 'famous for fresh air and fun', is the leading resort in the North-West and one of the most popular resorts in the country, drawing over 16 million visitors a year. Its attractions include the famous Illuminations; the Tower (1894) with its ballroom, aquarium and indoor circus; three 19C piers; the 40-acre Pleasure Beach; the 300-acre Stanley Park with boating lake and sporting facilities as well as superb gardens and conservatories; and several golf courses. It is the only town in England where trams are still in public service. Blackpool Airport has passenger services to the Isle of Man, Belfast, Dublin and Jersey.
    *Thornton Cleveleys* (26,100 inhab.; seasonal Tourist Information) is a resort on the way from Blackpool to Fleetwood. *Rossall Hall,* 1m N, is a public school where Sir Thomas Beecham was a pupil.
    **Fleetwood** (28,500 inhab.; Tourist Information), looking N across Morecambe Bay from the mouth of the Wyre, is one of the largest fishing ports in England as well as a resort. The history of its industry is told in the museum on Dock St. There is a local ferry across the Wyre to *Knott End,* and a seasonal ferry service (primarily for day excursion passengers) to Douglas, Isle of Man.
    A585, the road from Fleetwood to (22½m) Preston, passes near (6m) *Poulton-le-Fylde* (17,600 inhab.), a market town with an old cross and stocks and an 18C church.

Beyond Preston A6 runs N through pleasant country.—42m. *Garstang,* a market town on the Wyre and the Lancaster Canal, lies between the plain of the Fylde and the fell country of the Forest of Bowland.—50m. *Bailrigg* makes an attractive site for the *University of Lancaster*, founded in 1964, in mainly low-rise buildings which form a pedestrian precinct (begun by Bridgwater, Sheppard and Epstein).

52m. **Lancaster** (46,300 inhab.; Tourist Information), a historic place, was for centuries the county town of Lancashire until the rise of Preston.

The Duchy of Lancaster, originating in the earldom given by Henry III to his son Edmund in 1265, has been royal since it passed to Henry IV from his father John of Gaunt, Shakespeare's 'time-honoured Lancaster', in 1399. The office of Chancellor of the Duchy of Lancaster is a political appointment normally held by a member of the Cabinet. In the 18C the town became a prosperous port for the West Indies trade and an important centre of cabinet-making, known particularly for the work of the Gillow family. The scientist Sir Richard Owen (1804–92), educated at the grammar school, and the poet Laurence Binyon (1869–1945) were natives. George Fox was imprisoned in the castle in 1664.

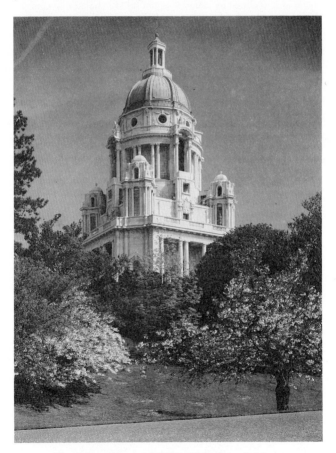

*The Ashton Memorial (1906–09) by John Belcher, Lancaster*

The *Castle* (open for guided tours), high above the river on the site of the Roman fort, is a much altered building which includes the prison, Shire Hall and Crown Court added by Thomas Harrison and Joseph Gandy in 1788–1823.

The chief medieval remains are the *Gatehouse* (c 1400) and the Norman *Keep*, restored c 1585. One of its turrets is known as 'John of Gaunt's Chair'. The 13C *Hadrian's Tower* contains a miscellaneous collection of prison equipment. The *Shire Hall* and *Crown Court* (not included on the tour when in session) have splendid Gothick interiors and coats of arms.

To the NE of the castle is the *Priory Church of St Mary*. The priory became a cell of the Benedictine abbey at Sées in 1094 and was placed under the jurisdiction of the Bridgettines in 1414. The present building is mainly Perp., but the SW entrance doorway belongs to the 12C church and a doorway in the W wall may be Saxon. The rebuilt tower was designed by Henry Sephton (1754). The interior contains exquisitely carved oak *stalls (c 1340).

From the W end there is a fine view and a path leading down to St George's Quay, with Georgian warehouses and the Old Custom House (1764; Richard Gillow), now Lancaster's *Maritime Museum*.

Good Georgian houses, still a feature of the town generally, mark Castle Park and Castle Hill. The *Cottage Museum* on Castle Hill has an interesting period interior. At the top of Church St., the *Judge's Lodging* (c 1630) contains furniture by the local firm of Gillow and a museum of childhood with the Barry Elder doll collection.

The old centre, to the SE, is well documented in the *City Museum* occupying the Old Town Hall (1781–83) in Market Square. It contains models of Lancaster in 1610, 1778 and 1821; a well-arranged collection of antiquities, with 1–4C Roman pottery and fragments from Cockersand Abbey; and the museum of the King's Own Royal Lancaster Regiment. To its NE, near the bus station, is the redundant church of *St John* (1754) with a tower added by Thomas Harrison in 1784. Harrison also designed *Skerton Bridge* (1783–88), further NE. In Dalton Square, S of the City Museum, stand the *Town Hall* (1906–09; E.W. Mountford) and the *Victoria Memorial* (1907), given by the linoleum tycoon Lord Ashton. To the E, beyond the *Roman Catholic Cathedral* (1859), is another of his gifts, Williamson Park; on the crest of its hill stands John Belcher's splendid *Ashton Memorial* (1906–09), recently restored and open to the public.

A588 runs SW to (4m) *Conder Green*, beyond which B5290 branches right to (4³/4m) *Glasson*, an 18C dock on the Lune estuary, where salmon are taken by 'whammelling' with the drift-net or by the stationary haaf-net. The next right-hand turning off A588, at (5m) *Upper Thurnham*, leads in about 3m to a farm on the coast beside which, in a wild and romantic position, is the finely vaulted 13C chapter house of *Cockersand Abbey* (not open), with a few fragmentary remains nearby.

FROM LANCASTER TO MORECAMBE AND HEYSHAM, 5¹/2m by A589, heading NW from the city.—3¹/2m. **Morecambe** (41,200 inhab. with Heysham; Tourist Information), named after its bay, is a seaside resort long known for its shrimps, with an 'oceanarium' (performing dolphins), Wild West theme park, etc. For the walk across the bay, see Hest Bank below and Grange-over-Sands, Rte 77. —5¹/2m. **Heysham** (pronounced 'Heesham') has a nuclear power station, oil refineries and a ferry service to Douglas, Isle of Man from its harbour. The old village to the N has some interesting houses and a 12–14C church with a carved 'hog-back' tombstone and a fragment of a Saxon cross in its churchyard. On the promontory above is the ruin of St Patrick's Chapel (9C?); nearby are some early Saxon rock graves with holes for a post or cross.

FROM LANCASTER TO KIRKBY LONSDALE, 16m by A583 along the S bank of the
Lune.—1m. A fine aqueduct (1797; John Rennie) carries the Lancaster Canal
over the Lune on its way to Kendal.—2¼m. The churchyard at *Halton*, on the N
bank, has an early 11C *cross showing episodes from the saga of Sigurd the
Volsung.—We enter the *Crook o' Lune*, the loveliest part of the green valley of
Lonsdale, painted by Turner.—8½m. *Hornby* is a centre for anglers. The castle
(not open) has a 13C pele tower with additions by Sir Edward Stanley
('Monteagle'; d. 1523), who also built the octagonal tower of the church in
thanks for his safe return from the Battle of Flodden. A pleasant alternative way
to Kirkby Lonsdale crosses the Loyn Bridge and follows the N bank of the Lune
via *Gressingham* and *Whittington*.—At (10½m) *Melling* the 15C church has a
raised chancel.—12½m. *Tunstall*, see Rte 86C. On the left about 1½m beyond
the village is the site of a Roman fort, perhaps *Galacum*.—16m. *Kirkby
Lonsdale*, see Rte 86C.

From Lancaster a fine moorland road leads SE to (12m) the *Trough of
Bowland* (1000ft), the pass between the Bleasdale Moors on the right and the
Forest of Bowland, and then follows the Hodder valley to (15½m) *Dunsop
Bridge* (Rte 75C). From here we can turn S to *Clitheroe* or N via *Slaidburn* to
*Long Preston*.

The main route continues N on A6.—55m. *Slyne* lies ¾m E of *Hest
Bank*, the S end of the 'road' across the sands of Morecambe Bay (see
Grange-over-Sands in Rte 77).—56½m. *Bolton-le-Sands* gives a good
view of the bay.—At (58½m) *Carnforth* (4800 inhab.) the old station
yards and sheds now house the *Steamtown Railway Centre*, which
displays a large collection of British and Continental steam locomotives and coaches as a memorial to one of the last homes of steam
in Britain, closed in 1968. There are regular train rides in summer
along short stretches of standard and 15in gauge track, and occasional special excursions on the British Rail line.

Unclassified roads run N and NW to (1½m) *Warton*, below the limestone
Warton Crag, with a ruined 14C rectory (English Heritage, standard opening)
and the Washington arms on its church tower; (4½m) *Silverdale*, overlooking
Morecambe Bay, where Elizabeth Gaskell did some of her best work; and (8m)
*Arnside*, once a busy port and now a quiet resort on the sandy estuary of the
Kent. *Arnside Knott* (NT), 1m S, gives good views of Morecambe Bay and the
Lake District mountains.—*Leighton Hall* (open), in a fine park 1½m N of
Warton, has a Gothic façade added by Thomas Harrison in 1800 and contains
furniture by the Gillow family, who bought the house in 1822.

A6 enters Cumbria.—65m. *Beetham* has a fine old bridge.—66m.
*Milnthorpe* was the birthplace of the regional novelist Constance
Holme (1881–1955).—At (69m) *Levens Bridge* A590 heads left for the
Cumbrian coast (Rte 77). For Levens Hall, see below.—A6 then joins
the course of A591 and passes Sizergh Castle (see below) before
A591 branches left for *Windermere* and the Lake District (Rte 78A).

**74m. Kendal** (23,400 inhab.; Tourist Information), pleasantly situated on the Kent, is an old town known for making shoes and once
known for its cloth. 'Kendal Green' was a kind of heavy serge.
Narrow 'yards' or alleys lead off the long main street. Catherine Parr
(1512–48) was born in the ruined Castle on the hill to the E. The
painter George Romney worked in Kendal before going to London in
1762 and returned in 1798 to die at a house near the bridge at the S
end of the town. He is commemorated by a tablet in the *Parish
Church*, notable for the five aisles which enlarge the Perp. nave into a
rectangular forest of pillars. The Bellingham Chapel has a 13C coffin
lid with foliated cross, sword and shield. The *Abbot Hall Art Gallery*,
in a handsome building (1759) by John Carr of York overlooking the
river, displays portraits by Romney (notably 'The Gower Family'),
his pupil Daniel Gardner (1750–1805), a native of Kendal, and other
18C artists, with 18C furniture (Gillow of Lancaster), porcelain,

silver and glass. There is also a fine collection of watercolours (Turner, Ruskin), and, shown from time to time, a wide-ranging collection of modern art. The *Museum of Lakeland Life and Industry* in the converted stables has a farming display and reconstructions of craft workshops, period rooms and a Victorian street. The *Kendal Museum*, in a wool warehouse by the railway station at the N end of the town, traces the natural history, archaeology and human history of the region.

*Scout Scar* (752ft), a limestone ridge on the edge of the National Park 2½m SW, commands a fine view.—*Sizergh Castle* (NT), about 3m S of Kendal, the home of the Strickland family since 1239, consists of a magnificent and well-preserved 14C pele tower, a much altered 15C Great Hall and 16C wings. The delicate Elizabethan panelling and carved chimneypieces are outstanding. Contents include Elizabethan furniture, family portraits and Stuart relics. The grounds have a large rock garden established in the 1920s.—*Levens Hall* (open), 2m further S, is famous for the *topiary garden laid out by Guillaume Beaumont in 1692. The house, an Elizabethan mansion added to a medieval pele tower, has splendid plasterwork, panelling and chimneypieces; Cordova leather wall hangings (1692); 17–18C furniture (including pieces by Gillow of Lancaster); a good collection of paintings; and a rare piece of 18C patchwork made from Indian chintz. Mrs Humphry Ward made the house and its surrounding dales the scene of 'Helbeck of Bannisdale' (1898).

From Kendal to *Whitehaven* and *Carlisle* via the Cumbrian coast, see Rte 77; to *Windermere*, *Ambleside*, *Grasmere* and *Keswick*, see Rte 78A; to *Settle*, *Skipton* and *Ilkley* via Ribblesdale, Craven and Upper Airedale, see Rte 86C; to *Hawes*, *Leyburn* and *Ripon* via Wensleydale, see Rte 86D; to *Kirkby Stephen*, see Rte 86E.

Beyond Kendal A6, increasingly intertwined with M6, begins the long climb up *Shap Fells*, reaching (83m) the summit at 1304ft. The road is as notorious for winter snows as the railway was in the days of steam for the necessity of 'banking' locomotives and 'doubleheading'. The Shap granite quarries have yielded stone for many famous buildings, including the Albert Memorial in London. To the left there are views of the High Street range and, later, of Blencathra (Saddleback) as we descend to (88¾m) *Shap*.

In the Lowther valley 1m SW stands *Keld Chapel* (NT, key available in village), a small 16C monastic building. About ½m downstream are the ruins of *Shap Abbey* (English Heritage, open at any reasonable time), a foundation for Premonstratensian canons moved here c 1199, with a splendid 16C W tower. A fine road leads from Shap to (10m) Pooley Bridge (Rte 78B) via (3½m) *Bampton Grange*, 2m from Haweswater, and the charming village of (7m) *Askham*.

94m. *Hackthorpe*. Beyond *Lowther* to the NW are the ruins of *Lowther Castle* (not open), built in 1806–11 by Sir Robert Smirke for the Earl of Lonsdale, Wordsworth's patron, and demolished in 1957. The church nearby was partly rebuilt in 1686.—At (96½m) *Clifton* a 15C pele tower survives from the old hall (English Heritage, standard opening).—97½m. *Eamont Bridge* has two neolithic sites, the henge fancifully known as *Arthur's Round Table* and *Mayburgh Earthwork*, with a single stone still in place (both English Heritage, open at any reasonable time). B5320 branches left for *Ullswater* (Rte 78B).

99m. **Penrith** (12,200 inhab.; Tourist Information) is an old market town built in red sandstone. Its ruined 14–15C *Castle* (English Heritage) stands in the park opposite the railway station. Outside the dignified church of *St Andrew* (1720–22) are two ancient slabs known as the Giant's Grave and the Giant's Thumb, probably c 1000, and the old 16C grammar school briefly attended by William and Dorothy Wordsworth, whose mother came from Penrith. In Great Dockray the *Gloucester Arms* may have been a residence of Richard

III and the 16C *Two Lions Inn*, once the town house of the Lowthers, has a notable plaster ceiling. *Hutton Hall* in Friargate incorporates a 15C pele tower.

*Penrith Beacon* (937ft), NE of the town, commands a magnificent view.—By A66 1½m SE of Penrith stand the ruins of *Brougham Castle*, pronounced 'Broom' (English Heritage, standard opening and summer Sundays from 11.00; closed Mondays and alternate Fridays in winter). The fine late 12C–13C keep and later buildings, restored by Lady Anne Clifford in the 17C, stand near the site of the Roman station of *Brocavum*. The *Countess Pillar* (English Heritage, open at any reasonable time), by the road about 1m further E, was erected by Lady Anne in 1656 in memory of her parting from her mother, the Countess of Cumberland, in 1616.—*Hutton-in-the-Forest* (open), 6m NW of Penrith by A6 and B5305, is a 17–19C house built around a 14C pele tower. It has an early 17C Laudian Gothic gallery wing and a late 17C central façade. The interior, much altered by Anthony Salvin, preserves the splendid late 17C Cupid Staircase. The pleasant grounds are open all year.

From Penrith to *Ullswater* and *Windermere*, see Rte 78B; to *Keswick*, *Derwentwater*, *Borrowdale*, *Buttermere* and *Cockermouth*, see Rte 78C; to *Scotch Corner*, see Rte 86F; to *Alston*, see Rte 86G.

A6 continues N past (101½m) the turning for Hutton-in-the-Forest (see above) and (112m) the turning for *Wreay*, 1½m W, where the remarkable church was designed by Sara Losh in 1842 on the plan of a Roman basilica, enriched with carving by the local mason William Hindson.

A more attractive route from Penrith to Carlisle follows A686, the Alston road, to (5m) *Langwathby* by the Eden and then takes the unclassified road to the left. —At (6¾m) *Little Salkeld* the old watermill has been restored to working order. Less than 1m beyond are the monolith and stone circle known as *Long Meg and Her Daughters*, with 65 stones, 27 of them still upright. *Little Meg*, ½m NE, is a circle of 11 standing stones.—11m. *Kirkoswald*, a beautifully situated village, has scanty remains of a castle and a church with a detached tower. The College has a fine entrance of 1696. *Lazonby*, just over 1m SW, is reached by a fine bridge of 1763 over the Eden. The attractive village of *Great Salkeld*, 2m further S, has a 14C fortified tower and a Norman doorway.—We continue N on sideroads from Kirkoswald to (26¼m) *Carlisle* via (12½m) *Staffield*, with the enchanting Nunnery Walks beside the Croglin Water, and (15¾m) *Armathwaite*, where we cross a lovely stretch of the Eden.

118m. **CARLISLE** (71,500 inhab.), the county town of Cumbria as it was of Cumberland, is an ancient Border fortress with a chequered history remembered in many of the Border ballads. Though the cathedral, castle and fragments of the city wall survive, the city's atmosphere now owes more to its 19C industrial growth and its modern role as the region's centre of trade and commerce.

**Tourist Information Centre**: Old Town Hall, Green Market.

**Car Parks**: William St., Cecil St., Upper Viaduct, Lower Viaduct, Town Dyke Orchard, The Lanes, Devonshire Walk (by the castle), The Sands (beyond the Civic Centre).

**Bus Station**: Lowther St.

**Railway Station**: Citadel Station, S of the Market Square.

**Annual Events**: Cumberland Agricultural Show on the third Thursday of July; Carlisle Great Fair in the third week of August.

**History**. Hadrian's Wall ran through the suburb of Stanwix (*Petriana*) on the N bank of the Eden. An important military station was established on the S bank during the earlier Roman occupation. It later became a small town, *Luguvalium*, which survived into Saxon times, though sacked by the Danes in 875 and constantly beleaguered by the Scots. William Rufus recaptured it from them and began the castle in 1092, though the city was again under Scottish control in 1136–57. During the Civil War it surrendered to the Scottish army under General Leslie after a siege of nine months in 1644–45. Bonnie Prince Charlie entered Carlisle in 1745, proclaiming his father king at the market cross, but the city was retaken by the Duke of Cumberland a few weeks later. Carlisle's industrial development began after the defeat of the rebellion with the establishment of calico-printing works and cotton mills. In the 19C it exchanged its earlier role as a port for that of railway centre, with the Newcastle–Carlisle line opening in 1836 and Citadel Station becoming the terminus for seven railway companies. The 'Carlisle Experiment' in the state ownership of licensed premises, started during the First World War to control the sales of liquor to munition workers, ended in 1972.

From Court Square outside *Citadel Station* we enter the city by English St., passing between the two huge drum-towers of the *County Buildings* and *Court House*, designed by Thomas Telford and Sir Robert Smirke in 1807–12 but incorporating part of the old *Citadel* founded by Henry VIII. At the end of English St. is the large market square with the *Market Cross* (1682) and the rather rustic-looking 18C *Town Hall*, housing the Tourist Information Centre. The half-timbered 15C *Guildhall* is now a museum devoted to the history of the city and its guilds.

Scotch St., with the *Lanes Shopping Centre* on the right, and Rickergate lead to the *Civic Centre* (1956–64; Charles B. Pearson and Partners), with a striking octagonal Council Chamber raised on stilts.

Castle St. leads to the beautiful E end of the cathedral, passing No. 81, where Charlotte Charpentier lodged before her marriage to Sir Walter Scott in the cathedral in 1797.

The *'**Cathedral**, built mainly of red sandstone, dominates the city. The destruction of most of the nave in the 17C has given it a permanently lop-sided appearance, as well as making it the smallest English cathedral, but it contains many fine points of detail.

The church of the Augustinian priory founded after the Conquest became a cathedral in 1133—the only Augustinian church in England that was also the seat of a bishop. The original Norman building survives in the two W bays, the crossing, and the S transept. Replacement of the original presbytery began c 1225 in the EE style, and continued, after a fire in 1292, in the Dec style. Bishop Strickland (1400–19) rebuilt the N transept and added the central tower. The original nave was drastically truncated during the Civil War when General Leslie's Scots tore down six of its eight bays for the building stone.

The two surviving bays of the *Nave*, serving as a memorial chapel to the Border Regiment, are plain Norman work of 1123. Their arches were distorted by settlement in the 13C. The window over the N door contains fragments of old glass. The small Norman *S Transept* has a Runic inscription on the wall. Bishop Strickland's *N Transept* contains the *'Brougham Triptych, a Flemish altarpiece depicting the Passion, probably carved at Antwerp c 1505 and installed here in 1979.

The original E end, only two bays long, was greatly extended in the 13–14C to form the present *Choir* and *Chancel*. The piers of the EE arcade have superb 14C capitals showing the labours of the months. The special glory of the choir is the magnificent Dec. *'E Window* (c 1340–45, restored 1983–84). Its tracery lights hold glass of c 1360 showing the Last Judgement; the glass in the main lights is by John Hardman (1861). Below is a monument to the theologian Archdeacon Paley (1743–1805), buried in the N choir aisle. The splendid wooden barrel-vaulted ceiling (c 1360) was restored in the 19C and repainted in 1970. The choir stalls, with good misericords, date from c 1420. Their backs were painted c 1484–1507 with the Apostles, and scenes from the lives of St Anthony and St Cuthbert (N) and St Augustine (S). Other notable woodwork includes the lovely Flamboyant screen of St Catherine's Chapel at the W end of the S choir aisle and Prior Salkeld's *'screen (1542) between the presbytery and N aisle. The splendidly carved 16C Flemish *'pulpit was brought from Cockayne Hatley in Bedfordshire in 1964. In the centre of the choir is the brass to Bishop Bell (d. 1496).

Some remains of the monastic buildings survive in the precinct called The Abbey, to the SW. The *Deanery*, once the Prior's Lodging, incorporates a 13C pele tower; the first floor has a fine early 16C painted ceiling and the second floor contains the *Prior's Tower Museum*, devoted to the history of the cathedral and its site. The hall known as the Fratry (13C, rebuilt 1482) is now the *Chapter Library*. The *Gateway* was rebuilt in 1527.

Further along Castle St. is Tullie House (1689), now the *Carlisle Museum and Art Gallery*. It contains prehistoric and Roman antiquities, notably finds from Luguvalium and Hadrian's Wall; displays of local geology, natural history and social history; 18–19C English porcelain; 19–20C English paintings; and toys, dolls, costumes and musical instruments. Abbey St., behind, has Georgian and 19C houses.

A pedestrian subway leads under Castle Way to the **Castle** (English Heritage, standard opening and summer Sunday mornings), founded in 1092 but many times altered during centuries of military use. It stands at the NW end of the city between the Eden and its tributary the Caldew, guarding the Anglo-Scottish border. To the N and W its walls are identical with the city walls, which continue along either side of the strip of land in front of the outer gates.

The impressive *Ireby Tower* leads into the outer ward, where the barrack blocks include the *Alma* (1819). In the inner ward, reached by the 14C *Captain's Tower*, is the massive Norman *Keep, one of the finest examples of its kind in England, though probably built during the Scottish occupation of 1136–57. It was originally entered by a doorway on the first floor, over a forebuilding whose foundations can be seen. On the second floor are 14–15C carvings made by prisoners. Later prisoners included the cattle thief or 'reiver', William Armstrong ('Kinmont Willie'), who escaped in 1596, and the defeated Scottish rebels in 1745. The restored remnant of the 14C *Queen Mary's Tower*, also in this ward, recalls the confinement here of Mary, Queen of Scots, for two months in 1568. The *Museum of the Border Regiment and the King's Own Royal Border Regiment* is housed in the medieval former royal palace. There is a fine view from the ramparts.

Returning through the subway and turning right into Annetwell St., we can follow the city wall past the back of the Deanery to the *Sallyport Steps*. The 15C tithe barn in Heads Lane, opposite, is the only English tithe barn inside a city wall; it has been restored as the parish hall of *St Cuthbert's Church* (rebuilt 1778). St Cuthbert's Lane leads back into the market square.

*Wetheral*, on the Eden 5m to the E, has the 15C gatehouse of a Benedictine priory founded in 1106 (English Heritage, standard opening). On the opposite bank of the river stands *Corby Castle* (not open), a 17–19C house built on to a 13C pele tower.—*Burgh-by-Sands* (pronounced 'Bruff'), 5m NW of Carlisle, is on the line of Hadrian's Wall, which continued 7½m further NW to the Solway Firth at *Bowness-on-Solway*. On the marsh about 1¼m N of Burgh-by-Sands a monument marks the spot where Edward I died in 1307 on his way to crush Robert Bruce's rebellion.—Beyond *Rockcliffe*, 5m NW of Carlisle between A74 and the estuary, is the late Georgian *Castletown House* (limited opening).

FROM CARLISLE TO THE SCOTTISH BORDER. A7 heads N through flat country to (8m) *Longtown* (Tourist Information), an ancient town on the Esk about 3m S of the border. About ¾m S of the town is the early 17C parish church of *Arthuret*.—Before Longtown A74 branches left from A7 to cross the border at *Gretna*, on the Sark 9m NW of Carlisle. *Gretna Green*, just beyond, was a famous destination for runaway couples seeking immediate marriage under the liberal terms of Scottish law.—The country between the Esk and the Sark was the 'Debatable Land', long disputed by England and Scotland. At *Solway Moss*, 3m W of Longtown, the Scots under James V were crushingly defeated in 1542. The present border was agreed in 1552.—From Gretna to *Glasgow* or *Edinburgh* and from Longtown to *Edinburgh*, see 'Blue Guide Scotland'.

From Carlisle to *Whitehaven* and *Kendal* via the Cumbrian coast, see Rte 77; to *Cockermouth*, see Rte 78C; to *Newcastle* via *Tynedale* and *Hexham*, see Rte 87A; to *Newcastle* along *Hadrian's Wall*, see Rte 87B.

# 77   The Cumbrian Coast: Kendal to Whitehaven and Carlisle

Total distance 118m. **Kendal**, see Rte 76.—A6 to (5m) Levens
Bridge.—A590 to (30m) Dalton-in-Furness (for
**Barrow-in-Furness**).—A595 to (77m) **Whitehaven**.—A595, A596
to (85m) Workington.—A596 to (91m) Maryport.—A596, A595 to
(118m) **Carlisle**, see Rte 76.

Maps: OS Landranger 97, 96, 89, 85.

Closely following the coastal railway for much of the way, this
route takes in a mixture of fine views, industry, post-industrial
decline and small seaside resorts, with access to the Lake District
(Rte 78) from several points.

**Kendal**, and A6 S to (5m) *Levens Bridge*, see Rte 76. We turn right on
A590, which enters the S tip of the Lake District National Park on the
way to (11¹/₂m) *Lindale*.

B5277 leads to Morecambe Bay at (2m) the resort of **Grange-over-Sands** (3600
inhab.; seasonal Tourist Information). From *Kent's Bank*, 2m SW, a 'roadway'
leads across the sands of the bay to (9m) Hest Bank (Rte 76). The Cartmel monks
guided travellers this way, and coaches later used it as a shortcut. It is now a
popular walk but, since the bay and the route change with each tide, should not
be attempted without the services of the guide at Guides Farm, Cart Lane,
Grange.

2m W of Grange, the charming little town of **Cartmel** has a beautiful 12C
priory •church, now the parish church. The diagonal upper stage was added to
its Norman tower in the 15C, when the Perp. nave and fine E window were also
built. The S choir aisle is Dec. The choir stalls, with misericords, date from
c 1440; the choir screen and stall canopies were installed c 1620. Memorials
include the fine Harrington tomb (1347) and Thomas Woolner's monument to
Lord Frederick Cavendish, assassinated in Phoenix Park, Dublin, in 1882. The
14C priory gatehouse (NT) survives in the square. *Holker Hall* (pronounced
'Hooker'; open), near *Cark* 2¹/₂m SW of Cartmel, was partly rebuilt by Paley and
Austin after a fire in 1871. Its grounds have formal and woodland gardens, a
deer park, a motor museum and a rural crafts exhibition.

From Lindale A590 heads inland, climbing to (13¹/₂m) *High Newton*
on the way to the Leven valley at (16¹/₂m) *Newby Bridge*, near the
foot of Windermere (Rte 78A). Our road then follows the Leven,
crossing it before (19m) *Haverthwaite*. In summer a steam railway
runs to Lake Side, connecting with the motor launch service up
Windermere to Bowness and Waterhead.—21¹/₂m. *Greenodd*.

An attractive route goes up the Crake valley to (10¹/₂m) Coniston (Rte 78A) via
(8m) *Torver*. A5092, leaving the valley at (2m) *Lowick Green*, makes a shortcut
with fine views to (8¹/₂m) *Broughton* (see below).

A590 leaves the National Park and heads down the Furness peninsula to (25m) the market town of **Ulverston** (12,000 inhab.; Tourist
Information). Natives include Sir John Barrow (1764–1848), founder
of the Royal Geographical Society, remembered by the monument on
*Hoad Hill* to the NE, and Stan Laurel (1890–1965), remembered in
the *Laurel and Hardy Museum*. George Fox (1624–91) lived at the
Elizabethan *Swarthmoor Hall* (open), ¹/₂m S.

The church at *Pennington*, 2m SW, has a reset Norman tympanum with a runic
inscription.—A5087 takes a pleasant route along the shore of Morecambe Bay
to (12m) *Rampside* and (13m) *Roa Island* (see below). It passes (3m) the little
resort of *Bardsea*, just S of the early 19C mansion of *Conishead Priory* (now a
Manjushri monastery, but open), and (7m) *Aldingham*, where the church stands
inside its own sea wall.

30m. **Dalton-in-Furness** (11,000 inhab.), in the middle of the Furness peninsula, has the 14C *Dalton Tower* (NT, open on application to the local custodian). The painter George Romney (1734–1802) was born and buried at Dalton.

A590 continues down to (4m) Barrow at the tip of the peninsula. Hidden away in the 'Vale of Deadly Nightshade', to the left at 1½m, are the lovely sandstone ruins of *Furness Abbey (English Heritage, standard opening and summer Sunday mornings from 11.00). Founded in 1123 by the future King Stephen, it became second only to Fountains among the great Cistercian abbeys of the

*The ruins of Furness Abbey: an engraving from Charles Mackay's 'The Scenery and Poetry of the English Lakes: A Summer Ramble' (1846)*

North. We enter through a small exhibition centre. Little remains of the church's Norman nave. The transepts, with a fine N doorway, are late Norman and EE work with 15C windows; the beautiful sedilia and piscina in the choir are Perp., like the W tower. The E wall of the cloister is pierced by rich arches of c 1230, and the elegant chapter house is EE. The two 13C effigies of knights in armour in the vaulted 14C infirmary chapel are perhaps the oldest in England.—To the SE the Mill Beck is crossed by the medieval *Bow Bridge* (English Heritage, open at any reasonable time).

**Barrow-in-Furness** (61,700 inhab.; Tourist Information) was developed from 1846 onwards as an iron and steel town by Sir James Ramsden of the Furness Railway. Its port has Vickers shipbuilding and engineering yards, and dock terminals operated by British Nuclear Fuels and British Gas, whose pipeline from the Morecambe Field in the Irish sea comes ashore here. A bridge leads across to the suburb of *Vickerstown* on the long *Walney Island*, sheltering the harbour, with nature reserves at its N and S ends.—To the SE, reached by A5087, are (4m) *Rampside* and (5m) *Roa Island*. A ferry serves *Piel Island*, about 1/2m offshore, with the ruins of the castle built in 1327 (English Heritage, open at any reasonable time). Lambert Simnel, pretender to Henry VII's crown, landed here in 1487.

A595 runs N from Dalton, making a wide loop round the Duddon Sands.—From (41m) *Broughton-in-Furness* A593, a charming road, branches right for Coniston (Rte 78A), and from (42m) *Duddon Bridge* sideroads go up both sides of the Duddon valley to Ulpha (Rte 78A).—From (44½m) *Hallthwaites* A5093 branches 3½m S to *Millom* (7000 inhab.; seasonal Tourist Information), developed as an iron-working town in the 19C but with an interesting church and remains of a 14C castle. The poet Norman Nicholson (1914–87) lived here.

A595 sweeps round the base of *Black Combe* (1857ft), a distant outlier of the Skiddaw slates which make up the mountains in the N and NW of the Lake District. It then runs parallel to the sandy coast, crossing the Esk just before (59m) *Muncaster Castle* (open), incorporating a 14C pele tower but largely rebuilt by Anthony Salvin in 1862–66.

It contains Elizabethan chimneypieces and 16–17C furnishings. The terrace commands a superb view over the Esk; the grounds have azaleas and rhododendrons and a bird garden.

60m. *Ravenglass* (seasonal Tourist Information) is a pleasant place at the junction of the Esk, the Mite and the Irk. Remains of a bath house survive from the Roman fort of *Glannaventa* (English Heritage, open at any reasonable time). The former station of the Furness Railway is now a railway museum, with a narrow-gauge railway service via Muncaster Mill to (7m) *Dalegarth* in Eskdale (Rte 78D). The nature reserve offshore has sand dunes with natterjack toads; visitors should contact the County Land Agent and Valuer, Property Services Department, Cumbria County Council, 15 Portland Square, Carlisle CA1 1QQ.

For *Eskdale*, *Wastwater* and *Scafell*, and *Ennerdale*, reached from A595 between Ravenglass and Whitehaven, see Rte 78D.

A595 crosses the Mite, near the restored *Muncaster Mill* (open), and then the Irt on the way to (62½m) *Holmrook*. B5344 leads along the coast to the little resort of (3¼m) *Seascale*.—At (65m) *Gosforth* (Lake District National Park local information point) the churchyard has a famous Anglo-Danish •cross of c 1000, 14½ft high, apparently mixing Norse legend with Christianity in its decoration. The Gosforth Show is held on the third Wednesday in August.—To the right of (67½m) *Calder Bridge* is the ruined Cistercian *Calder*

*Abbey* (not open). Near the coast is the *Sellafield* site of British Nuclear Fuels, consisting of Calder Hall, the world's first industrial-size nuclear power-station (opened in 1956), and the Sellafield nuclear reprocessing plant (called Windscale when it was opened in 1951). There is an exhibition centre by the N Gate.—71½m. *Egremont* (Tourist Information) has a ruined 12–13C castle with a gatehouse on a high mound (open). The Egremont Crab Fair is held on the third Saturday in September; it includes a curious 'gurning' competition, in which a prize is awarded to the person pulling the ugliest face with his head through a horse collar.

The resort of *St Bees*, 2½m NW, has a boys' school founded by Archbishop Grindal in 1583 and an interesting collegiate church of c 1120, restored by Butterfield in 1855–58, with a fine but weatherbeaten W doorway. Further NW is *St Bees Head* (462ft), the starting point of A. Wainwright's 190m Coast-to-Coast Walk, ending at Robin Hood's Bay (Rte 84).

We reach the coastal region, now suffering post-industrial decline, where coalmines and ironworks were established in the 17–19C. The last Cumbrian colliery closed in 1986.—77m. **Whitehaven** (26,700 inhab.; Tourist Information), developed as a coal port in the 17C and laid out in a grid pattern in the 18C, keeps some good Georgian and 19C buildings. The *Museum* in the former Market Hall (1880) has exhibits of local geology, archaeology, trade and industry, and a collection of ship models. The church of *St James* (by the engineer Carlisle Spedding, 1752–53) contains galleries, a fine plaster ceiling, an elegant pulpit and an altarpiece by Procaccini. The Sir Nicholas Sekers Theatre at *Rosehill*, 2m NE, presents plays, concerts, etc.

From Whitehaven to *Cockermouth*, see Rte 78C.—For *Eskdale*, *Wasdale* and *Scafell*, and *Ennerdale*, reached from A595 between Whitehaven and Ravenglass, see Rte 78D.

Beyond (81m) *Distington* we bear left on A596.—85m. **Workington** (27,600 inhab.), at the mouth of the Derwent, had coalmines reaching under the sea. Mary, Queen of Scots, landed here on her flight to England after the Battle of Langside (1568) and was taken to Carlisle Castle. The church of *St John* (1823; Thomas Hardwick) in Washington St. is a handsome neo-classical building. —91m. **Maryport** (11,600 inhab.; Tourist Information) is a decayed coal and iron port, with a *Maritime Museum*.

FROM MARYPORT TO CARLISLE VIA SILLOTH, 34½m. B5300 continues up the coast via (5m) the resort and fishing village of *Allonby* to (12½m) **Silloth** (seasonal Tourist Information) on the Solway Firth.—B5302 turns inland to (18m) *Abbeytown*, where the parish church occupies part of the nave of the Cistercian church of Holme Cultram, an abbey founded in 1150 by Henry, son of David I of Scotland. The original work includes the W doorway, massive clustered pillars and newel stair.—B5302 joins the main route below near (23½m) *Wigton*.

A596 turns inland for (98½m) *Aspatria*, where the church has a hog's back tombstone and fragments of Anglo-Danish sculpture.—107m. *Wigton* (4800 inhab.) is an old market town with an 18C church and a market fountain with fine reliefs by Thomas Woolner (1871). Horse sales are held on the last Wednesday in October.—At (112m) *Thursby* we join A595 again.—118m. **Carlisle**, see Rte 76.

# 78 The Lake District

Maps: OS Landranger as indicated in the separate routes below or OS Lake District Tourist map (1:63,360 or 1in to 1m) for the National Park and its fringes.

The **'Lake District** contains some of the best-loved scenery in England. For almost two centuries its combination of craggy mountains, serene lakes and green valleys has attracted probably more praise and more visitors than any other region. Yet it is actually quite small—a mere corner of North-West England tucked between the A6/M6 and the Cumbrian coast, measuring about 35m across. Windermere, the largest of the 16 lakes, is just 10½m long; Scafell Pike, though it is the highest mountain in England, reaches only 3210ft. The Lake District's appeal comes from the astonishing variety concentrated in its small compass, and from the wildness and even grandeur achieved by its apparently modest dimensions.

To understand the forces which have shaped this landscape and created its underlying structure we cannot do better than follow Wordsworth's advice in his guidebook to the Lakes. There, in a memorable passage, he recommends that the reader join him in imagination on top of Great Gable or Scafell—or, better still, on a cloud midway between these two mountains and a few feet above their summits. From this vantage point the continually changing vistas which can delight but almost bewilder the visitor to the valley floor fall into a distinct pattern. The lakes and valleys stretch out below like the spokes radiating from the hub of a great wheel. Beginning in the SE and moving clockwise, Wordsworth notes: Langdale and Windermere; Coniston Water, 'a broken spoke sticking in the rim'; the Duddon valley; Eskdale; Wastwater; Ennerdale; Buttermere, Crummock Water and Lorton Vale; and Borrowdale and Derwentwater. These last run due N and, as Wordsworth admits, the NE sector that follows does not conform neatly to his image. But from the top of Helvellyn to the E a fragment of another wheel is represented by: Thirlmere and St John's in the Vale; Ullswater; Haweswater (though it is not actually visible from the top of Helvellyn); and finally, the vale of Grasmere and Rydal Water, bringing us back to Windermere in the S.

As this configuration so obviously suggests, the central Lake District was once a great dome, thrust up to a greater height than any of the present mountains. Water found its way down the fissures in the slopes, establishing the course that the valleys still follow today. With the coming of the Ice Ages glaciers gouged the watercourses into deeper troughs and, where these were blocked by glacial material, the lakes formed. Dry valleys like St John's in the Vale once held lakes which later drained or became silted up. The strip of land which now separates Buttermere and Crummock Water is a clear example of silt deposit that has divided one original lake into two. The tarns on the sides of the fells are meltwater pools filling the scooped-out hollows left at the glacier's head.

These forces were at work not on a homogeneous unit but on several types of rock: their differing reactions gave further variety to the landscape. The oldest rocks are the Skiddaw slates whose softness rounds and blunts the massive outlines of the northern fells overlooking Keswick. In the S another but much younger slate—Silurian slate—makes the peaceful and undramatic scenery of Windermere which forms so many visitors' first impression of the Lakes.

The central area is hard volcanic rock—the Borrowdale Volcanic Series—which does not erode smoothly but breaks into peaks and crags or shatters into scree. Its rugged effects can be seen in Borrowdale itself, by the wild shores of Wastwater, and in the great fells which stretch from the Scafell range and Great Gable in the W through Bowfell, the Langdale Pikes, Coniston Old Man (formally The Old Man of Coniston), Helvellyn and the Fairfield range, to the High Street range in the E.

Archaeologists point to significant evidence of early human settlement: neolithic stone axes in Langdale, the Castlerigg stone circle, and the Roman ways over High Street and the Hardknott Pass, with its fort perched above Eskdale. Etymologists note the strong Scandinavian element still apparent in the local place-names, introduced by the Norse settlers who arrived in the 10C from Ireland, Scotland and the Isle of Man. Yet for centuries the human history of the Lake District was unremarkable enough, remote from the public life of the nation. Sheep-farming was the mainstay of the rural economy, as it still is today. From the 16C to the 19C the hills were mined with increasing thoroughness for silver, iron, copper, lead and other minerals. The Keswick pencil industry, originally dependent on local sources of graphite, and the shafts and quarries which mark Coniston Old Man are the most obvious of many reminders of the region's industrial history. So, too, is the loss of the ancient forests consumed as charcoal for smelting.

Far from holding any special appeal, the Lake District could disgust outsiders for whom remote hills and valleys merely signified difficult or dangerous travel, backward customs and bad farmland. Defoe spoke for his age when he dismissed the region as 'the wildest, most barren and frightful in England'. Yet he wrote just before the shift of taste, beginning with the Picturesque Movement in the later years of the 18C and continuing into the 19C with the Romantic Movement, that reversed the judgement of previous generations and made these very qualities attractive. The poet Gray's journal of his visit, published in 1775, shows the first stirrings of this new sensibility. The first guidebook, by Thomas West in 1778, proclaims it as doctrine: 'Such as spend their lives in cities, and their time in crowds, will here meet with contrasts that enlarge the mind, by contemplation of sublime objects and raise it from nature to nature's first source'. The poetry of Wordsworth, most local of the so-called 'Lake Poets', confirmed that the need for nature felt by the new city-dwellers of the Industrial Revolution could best be satisfied by the Lake District. His presence at Grasmere and then Rydal, like that of Ruskin at Coniston in the half century following Wordsworth's death, reinforced the region's intimate bond with literature and landscape art. The list of famous natives, residents and visitors at the end of this introduction shows in summary fashion how the Lake District, geographically marginal, became almost central to the artistic life of the nation from the late 18C until the end of the 19C.

Such popularity brought obvious dangers. Wordsworth himself lived to deplore the glaring new villas which disfigured the view and, memorably but unsuccessfully, to oppose the opening of the Kendal and Windermere railway line in 1847. His protest contained the seed of all the later battles to preserve the region, though their ground would shift from the building of railway lines to the conversion of lakes into reservoirs and the enlargement of local roads into communication arteries. Pioneers in the appreciation of nature gave way to pioneers in its conservation. The National Trust, founded in 1895, grew from the activities of Canon Rawnsley and Ruskin's disciple Octavia Hill, and the generosity of Beatrix Potter, in the Lake District. Since it bought Brandelhow Woods by the shore of Derwentwater in 1902 it has become the largest property-holder in the region, owning more than 120,000 acres with about 12,000 more protected by covenants. It was fitting, too, that the Lake District should have become the largest of the ten National Parks created in England and Wales after the Second World War.

The four routes described below tour the region by the main roads, though the detours which branch from them sometimes tackle narrow or steep sideroads. They take in all the most popular, and often overcrowded, tourist attractions: Windermere, Ambleside, Grasmere and Langdale; Ullswater and Helvellyn; Derwentwater, Borrowdale and Buttermere. They also include less crowded areas like the Skiddaw fells and the western lakes and valleys. Major fells are described briefly and starting points for popular walking routes are indicated; shorter and easier walks are described in detail when they are the only way of reaching a place that should tempt even the short-winded motorist out of the car. Fellwalkers, rockclimbers, etc. need more detailed advice than the present guide can attempt; hints for obtaining it are given under the appropriate headings below.

**Famous natives and residents**. William Wordsworth (1770–1850), born at Cockermouth, brought up partly at Penrith and educated at Hawkshead, lived with his sister Dorothy Wordsworth (1771–1855) at Grasmere in 1799–1813, mainly at Dove Cottage, and then at Rydal Mount until his death; he is buried at Grasmere. Samuel Taylor Coleridge (1772–1834) lived at Greta Hall, Keswick, in 1800–03 and with the Wordsworths at Grasmere in 1808–09. Robert Southey (1774–1843) lived at Greta Hall, Keswick, from 1803 until his death; he is buried at Keswick. The painter J.C. Ibbetson lived at Ambleside and Troutbeck in 1799–1805. The journalist and critic John Wilson ('Christopher North') lived at Windermere in 1807–15. Thomas De Quincey was tenant of Dove Cottage, Grasmere, in 1808–30. The scholar and critic James Spedding (1808–81) lived at Mirehouse, Bassenthwaite. Shelley and Harriet Westbrook lived at Keswick in 1811–12. Felicia Hemans lived near Ambleside in 1829–31. Dr Thomas Arnold lived at Ambleside after his retirement from Rugby until his death in 1842. Harriet Martineau lived at Ambleside from 1845 until her death in 1876. John Ruskin lived at Coniston from 1871 until his death in 1900. Canon Hardwicke Rawnsley was incumbent of Crosthwaite, near Keswick, in 1883–1917. Beatrix Potter lived at Near Sawrey from 1905 until her death in 1943. Sir Hugh Walpole lived near Derwentwater from 1932 until his death in 1941; he is buried at Keswick.

**Famous visitors**. Thomas Gray in 1767 and 1769; William Gilpin in 1772; Gainsborough in 1783; Turner in 1797 and several times later; Constable in 1806; Charles Lamb, Coleridge's guest, in 1802; Keats in 1818; Sir Walter Scott on his birthday in 1825 and other occasions; Edward FitzGerald in 1835, Tennyson in 1835 and 1851 and Carlyle several times, all as guests of James Spedding; Charlotte Brontë, Harriet Martineau's guest, in 1850. Charles Dickens and Wilkie Collins had a dreadful time on Carrock Fell in 1857.

**National Park Information Centres**. The main visitors' centre is at Brockhole, near Windermere. Other information centres · are at Bowness, Coniston, Glenridding, Grasmere, Hawkshead, Keswick, Pooley Bridge, Seatoller, Waterhead and Gosforth (Rte 77). In addition, there are local National Park information points in Post Offices or shops at Dalehead (Thirlmere), Elterwater, Far Sawrey and High Lorton. Written inquiries should be addressed to the visitors' centre at Brockhole.

**Walking**. With 1500 miles of public right of way, the Lake District is ideal walking country. Walkers need the four OS Outdoor Leisure maps (1 to 25,000 or 2½in to 1m). The best guidebooks are A. Wainwright's seven-volume 'Pictorial Guide to the Lakeland Fells' (1955–66) and its various supplementary volumes, which include 'A Coast-to-Coast Walk' (1973), describing a route from St Bees Head to Robin Hood's Bay, and 'Fellwalking with Wainwright'

(1984), detailing 18 favourite walks. Two guides by 'John Parker' (the pseudonym of John Wyatt), 'Walk the Lakes: 40 Easy Walks' (1983) and 'Walk the Lakes Again: 38 Easy Walks' (1985), stick to lower ground. The National Park Authority publishes a useful pamphlet, 'Enjoy the Hills in Safety', which includes estimates of how long it takes to climb the major fells.

**Rockclimbing.** The sport was pioneered on Pillar Rock (Ennerdale), Napes Needle (Great Gable), Scafell Crag, Pavey Ark (Langdale Pikes) and Dow Crag (Coniston), and is particularly popular in Langdale and Borrowdale. New routes of extreme technical difficulty are still being opened up. The local Fell and Rock Climbing Club publishes a series of six guidebooks.

**Boating.** Subject to the necessary permission, boats can be launched on Bassenthwaite Lake, Buttermere, Coniston Water, Crummock Water, Derwentwater, Esthwaite Water (rowing boats only), Grasmere (small boats), Thirlmere, Ullswater and Windermere. Power boats are permitted, subject to speed limits, on Coniston Water, Derwentwater, Ullswater and Windermere. Water ski-ing is allowed on Windermere. The National Park publishes a useful pamphlet, 'Enjoy Water in Safety'.

**Sports and Shows.** These often preserve interesting Lakeland traditions, with displays of the hardy local breed of Herdwick sheep, Cumberland and Westmorland wrestling, hound trailing and fell running. The largest is Grasmere Sports, held on the Thursday nearest 20 August. Others include: Ambleside Sports on the Thursday before the first Monday in August; Ennerdale Show on the last Wednesday in August; Eskdale Show on the last Saturday in September; Hawkshead Show on the third Tuesday in August; Keswick Show on August Bank Holiday Monday; Patterdale Sheep Dog Trials on August Bank Holiday Saturday; and the Wasdale Head Shepherds' Meet and Show on the second Saturday in October. Also the Egremont Crab Fair, Gosforth Show and Wigton Horse Sales, all in Rte 77.

**Glossary of local terms.** *Band*, raised terrace or ridge between two lower tracts; *beck*, stream; *combe*, hollow; *dodd*, lower spur or foothill, generally rounded; *fell*, hill or mountain; *force* or *foss*, waterfall; *gill* or *ghyll*, narrow mountain stream; *hause*, top of a pass (French 'col'); *holme*, island; *how* or *howe*, low rounded hill; *knott*, rocky knob; *nab* or *neb*, projection; *pike*, peak; *pitch*, steep ascent; *raise*, pile of stones, cairn; *rigg*, ridge; *scar* or *scarth*, crag, steep rock face; *scree*, steep slope of loose rocks; *stickle*, sharp peak; *tarn*, small mountain lake; *thwaite*, clearing; *trod*, sheep path; *wyke*, bay.

**Books.** Since Thomas West's guide in 1778, travel literature about the Lakes has grown to make a list probably longer than any other English region can boast. Wordsworth's 'Guide to the Lakes' still makes a good travelling companion, particularly in the illustrated edition by Peter Bicknell (1984). In the 20C Norman Nicholson, another poet who lived in the region, wrote several studies, including 'Portrait of the Lakes' (revised as 'The Lakes', 1977). John Wyatt, who also writes as 'John Parker', provides a crisp general introduction in the official Countryside Commission guide to the National Park (1987). A. Wainwright's books, already mentioned above, have a charm and good sense that commend them even to walkers of limited energy. The best-rounded general book is 'The Lake District' (revised edition 1974) by Roy Millward and Adrian Robinson in 'The Regions of Britain' series.

# A.   Kendal to Windermere, Ambleside, Grasmere and Keswick

Total distance 28m. **Kendal**, see Rte 76. We follow A591 for most of the way.—To (8m) **Windermere**.—To (12½m) **Ambleside**.—To (16m) **Grasmere**.—To (28m) **Keswick** (Rte 78C).

Maps: OS Landranger 97 and 90 or OS Tourist map for the National Park.

A591 is probably the most popular way of entering the Lake District, with many of the most crowded tourist attractions on its course.

**Kendal**, see Rte 76.—The main route takes A5284 to join A591 at the edge of the National Park 1¹/₂m NW of the town. The road closely follows the course of the Kendal–Windermere railway line, opened in 1847 despite protests from Wordsworth ('Is then no nook of English ground secure/ From rash assault?').—From (5m) *Staveley* a sideroad goes N up the charming little valley of the Kent to (4m) *Kentmere*, with a pele tower and restored 16C church, backed by the High Street range of fells which separate it from Haweswater (Rte 78B). Its sister valley of *Longsleddale*, watered by the Sprint, is explored by the sideroad running E from Staveley via (4m) *Garnett Bridge* to (9m) *Sadgill*.

An alternative way of starting the journey takes B5284 via (4m) *Crook* to (7¹/₂m) the lakeside road, A592, just S of Bowness and the pier for the Windermere ferry.—A third and much more devious route takes the steep sideroad which enjoys marvellous views on its way to (3¹/₂m) *Underbarrow* and (6m) *Crosthwaite*, and then strikes SW across the Levens Bridge–Bowness road. Beyond (8m) *Bowland Bridge* the road climbs to an unexpected view before descending to (13m) *Newby Bridge* at the S tip of Windermere. The turning on the left beyond Bowland Bridge leads in 1m to *Cartmel Fell*, above the lovely Winster valley. The church of St Anthony (c 1504) contains good woodwork, a mutilated pre-Reformation Crucifixion, a three-decker pulpit and 15C *glass which may come from Cartmel Priory.

8m. **Windermere** (Tourist Information), transformed from a little hamlet by the arrival of the railway, merges with its older neighbour, **Bowness-on-Windermere** (National Park Information Centre; 8600 inhab. together), on the E shore of the lake from which they take their name. They are a popular starting point for tours, though the crowds and resort atmosphere hardly make a promising introduction to the Lakes. The *Windermere Steamboat Museum*, by the lakeside road from Windermere to Bowness, has a fine collection of old craft. In Bowness the parish church of *St Martin*, consecrated in 1483, contains late 15C stained glass from Cartmel Priory in its beautiful E window and a memorial by Flaxman to Bishop Watson of Llandaff (d. 1816) in its S aisle.

**Windermere** ('Vinandr's lake'), 10¹/₂m long but almost as narrow as a river, is the largest lake in England as well as the best known one in the Lake District. In summer its surface is often crowded with yachts and power boats. The shores are beautifully wooded and the surrounding hills much gentler than the dark volcanic crags which overhang the northern and western lakes. *Orrest Head* (784ft), just N of Windermere railway station, and *Queen Adelaide's Hill* (259ft; NT), W of the station, make good viewpoints. Sightseeing launches cruise the length of the lake from Bowness, Waterhead and Lake Side. They pass the wooded *Belle Isle*, with the circular neo-classical house built by John Plaw in 1774 which became a favourite subject with picturesque painters. It is now a conference centre, and open only to groups by prior arrangement. A car ferry crosses regularly to the W shore from the pier S of Bowness.

FROM BOWNESS TO LAKE SIDE AND THE W SHORE. A592 heads S on a well-wooded route keeping fairly close to the shore.—2m. *Storrs Point* was the scene of a regatta celebrating Sir Walter Scott's birthday in 1825, attended by Wordsworth, John Wilson, George Canning and Southey. Storrs Temple (NT, but not open), on the lake, was built in honour of Admirals Duncan, St Vincent, Howe and Nelson in 1804.—There is a car park and a good view across the lake

*Windermere: an aquatint by William Gilpin from his
'Observations, Relative Chiefly to Picturesque
Beauty, Made in the Year 1772, On Several Parts of
England' (1786)*

near (3¼m) the *Beech Hill Hotel*.—5½m. We pass beneath *Gummer's How*
(1054ft), another splendid viewpoint.—6½m. The sideroad from Bowland
Bridge and Kendal (see above) joins A592. By the lake is the *Fell Foot Park*
(NT).—7¼m. *Newby Bridge* (also on Rte 77) lies just beyond the foot of
Windermere. We join A590 but almost immediately turn right again to cross the
Leven for (8½m) *Lake Side*, with the pier for the Windermere cruises and the
station served by the steam railway from Haverthwaite (Rte 77).—Sideroads
continue up the much quieter W shore of the lake, passing (9½m) the *Stott Park
Bobbin Mill* (English Heritage, summer standard opening), built in 1835 and
restored to working order, and (11m) the 19C gardens (open) of *Graythwaite
Hall*.—At 14m we join B5285 just W of the ferry pier. A footpath leads through
the wooded *Claife Heights* (NT), N of the road, returning down the shore.

FROM BOWNESS TO HAWKSHEAD AND CONISTON. We reach B5285 on the W
shore either by the detour just described or by the car ferry from the pier S of
Bowness to *Ferry House*, now the laboratory of the Freshwater Biological
Association.—Skirting Claife Heights, the road climbs to (1m) *Far Sawrey*
(National Park local information point).—At (1½m) *Near Sawrey* is *Hill Top*
(NT), the 17C farm cottage where Beatrix Potter lived intermittently in 1905–13
and wrote some of her best-loved books. One of the most popular attractions in
the Lake District, the little house gets very crowded.—B5285 continues along
the E side of *Esthwaite Water*, one of the smaller lakes (1½m long and about
¼m wide), and passes the pool known as the *Priest Pot*.—We park outside (4m)
**Hawkshead** (National Park Information Centre), a picturesque little town with
half-timbered houses, narrow streets and a network of little squares, often
overrun by tourists. Herdwick sheep can be seen at the agricultural show held
on the third Tuesday in August. On a hillock stands the 15–16C church, with
plain, low-arched arcades, 17–18C murals and interesting monuments. In
1779–87 Wordsworth was a pupil at the old grammar school (open) founded by
Archbishop Sandys of York in 1585. The poet apparently lodged, not at the
cottage in Hawkshead marked with a plaque, but at the hamlet of *Colthouse*,
½m NE. *Grizedale Forest*, owned by the Forestry Commission, lies S of
Hawkshead between Esthwaite Water and Coniston Water. A sideroad runs
down to (2¾m) *Grizedale*, with a Visitor Centre and the Theatre in the Forest,
and (4m) *Satterthwaite*, where the forest trails include one leading NE to the
Windermere ferry.

N of Hawkshead B5285 is joined by the road from Ambleside at (4½m)
*Hawkshead Courthouse* (NT), a 15C gatehouse where the manor courts were
held, once the property of Furness Abbey.—Beyond (5¼m) *Hawkshead Hill*,
where a sideroad on the right leads to Tarn Hows (see below), we reach the

highest point of our journey at *High Cross* (647ft) and get a marvellous view of Coniston Water as we descend.

7¹/₂m. The village of **Coniston** (National Park Information Centre), beautifully situated at the foot of Coniston Old Man and the other Coniston Fells near the head of Coniston Water, is as closely associated with John Ruskin (1819–1900) as Grasmere is with Wordsworth. His home, Brantwood, is described on the drive round the Water, below. He is buried in the NE corner of Coniston churchyard beneath an Anglo-Saxon style cross. The nearby *Ruskin Museum*, opened the year after his death, has paintings, drawings, manuscripts, geological specimens from his collection and personal relics from Brantwood. *Coniston Old Man* (formally *The Old Man of Coniston*, perhaps from the Welsh *Allt Maen*, 'steep or high rock'; 2631ft), usually climbed from the village, is impressive despite the marks of copper mines and slate quarries on its sides. *Dow Crag* (2555ft), beyond the tarn to its W, is a favourite with rockclimbers. **Coniston Water**, just over 5m long and ¹/₂–¹/₄m wide, is a smaller and quieter version of Windermere. *Peel Island*, one of three islets, is the 'Wild Cat Island' of Arthur Ransome's 'Swallows and Amazons' (1931). Donald Campbell set a world water speed record of 260.35 mph here in 1959 and died attempting to raise it in 1967. The steam yacht 'Gondola', originally launched in 1859 and renovated by NT, makes passenger cruises to Park-a-Moor and back. There is a superb view down the lake from near *Tarn Hows*, a popular viewpoint in NT land 2¹/₂m NE of Coniston village, reached by taking B5285 back towards Hawkshead and branching left through the woods up to the tarn.

A drive round the Water, with views dominated by the Old Man, also begins by taking B5285 but soon branches right, round the head of the lake, to join the road down the E shore at (1¹/₂m) *Tent Lodge*.—2¹/₂m. On the left is *Brantwood* (open), which Ruskin bought in 1871 and made his chief home until his death in 1900. There are splendid views from the grounds and from his bedroom in the turret. Though it has lost most of the extraordinary art collection he assembled, the house still contains work by Burne-Jones, Samuel Prout and William Henry Hunt, as well as many paintings and drawings by Ruskin himself, with personal relics, furniture, etc. His boat 'Jumping Jenny' is in the coach house.—3m. There is a fine view from the lakeside picnic site across to the Old Man. —Beautiful woodland, most of it NT, flanks the shore almost as far as (6³/₄m) *High Nibthwaite*, at the foot of the lake. About ¹/₂m beyond we turn right to cross the Crake and join A5084 from Greenodd (Rte 77). The view up the lake is superb, backed by Fairfield and Helvellyn.—At (11¹/₄m) *Torver* we join A593 from Broughton-in-Furness (Rte 77).—13¹/₂m. *Coniston*.

From Windermere to *Ullswater* and *Penrith*, see Rte 78B.

From Windermere the main route follows A591 up the shore of the lake, with a fine vista of fells opening up ahead and to our left. A592, branching right for Ullswater, and the sideroad for Troutbeck branching right at (9m) *Troutbeck Bridge* are both described in Rte 78B.—10m. *Brockhole*, by the lake shore, is the main National Park Information Centre, with gardens, exhibitions, lectures and a wide range of activities.—11m. *Dove Nest*, on the slopes of Wansfell to the right, was home of the poet Felicia Hemans in 1829–31. Beyond are the wooded *Jenkin Crag*, with a view over the lake, and *Stagshaw Garden* (both NT).—12m. *Waterhead* (National Park Information Centre), with the pier for the sightseeing launches which cruise up and down the lake. In Borrans Field W of the car park are the fragmentary remains of the Roman fort of *Galava* (English Heritage, open at any reasonable time).

12¹/₂m. **Ambleside** (2900 inhab.; seasonal Tourist Information and NT Information Centre), in the Vale of Rothay beyond the head of Windermere, is a popular little centre which grew with the influx of tourists in the 19C. The sports festival held on the Thursday before the first Monday in August includes fell running, hound trailing and Cumberland and Westmorland wrestling. The July rushbearing ceremony is depicted in a mural in the church (1850–54; Gilbert Scott), which also contains a Wordsworth memorial chapel. The painter J.C. Ibbetson, who married at Ambleside in 1801, lived here and at Troutbeck in 1799–1805. Harriet Martineau lived at The Knoll, by A591 on the way to Rydal, from 1845 until her death in 1876.

The fells which overlook the little vale include *Wansfell Pike* (1851ft), to the E, with the **Stock Ghyll Force**, a 70ft waterfall, near its foot about ¹⁄₂m from the town. Beyond the Rothay, to the W, rises *Loughrigg Fell* (1099ft). Dr Thomas Arnold of Rugby retired to Fox How, near its foot, in 1834 and his son Matthew Arnold kept up the family connection with the house. To the N, almost encircling the valley of Rydal Beck, is the distinctive horseshoe range which takes its name from the tallest fell, *Fairfield* (2863ft), on the NW of the arc; three of its neighbours, *Dove Crag*, *Hart Crag* and *Great Rigg*, exceed 2500ft. Fellwalkers make the circuit from Ambleside via High Sweden Bridge and *Low Pike* (1657ft) or from Rydal via *Nab Scar* (1450ft).

FROM AMBLESIDE TO CONISTON AND HAWKSHEAD. A593, the direct road to Coniston, heads SW across the Rothay and runs between the foot of Loughrigg Fell and the attractive Brathay river on its way through (1m) the hamlet of *Clappersgate* to (2¹⁄₂m) *Skelwith Bridge*, near the waterfall of *Skelwith Force*. It then crosses the river and climbs to the top of (4m) *Oxenfell Pass* (526ft), with a fine view of the Langdale Pikes. At 5¹⁄₂m the road joins *Yewdale*, beneath the *Yewdale Fells*, and at 7¹⁄₂m it reaches *Coniston*, described on the detour from Bowness, above.—An alternative route, taking in Hawkshead, branches S on B5286 at Clappersgate and joins B5285, the Bowness–Coniston road, at (4¹⁄₂m) Hawkshead Courthouse.

A TOUR OF THE LANGDALES FROM AMBLESIDE. We follow a 16m circuit recommended by Wordsworth in his 'Guide' past fells now very popular with fellwalkers and rockclimbers.—We start by taking A593, the Coniston road. Just short of (2¹⁄₂m) *Skelwith Bridge* B5343, the easy road to Great Langdale, branches right. However, we follow A593 across the Brathay and branch right at 3¹⁄₂m, just beyond the top of the hill.—The little sideroad twists and turns down to (4m) *Colwith Bridge*, where we fork left for the valley of **Little Langdale**, with its waterfall, village and tarn. *Lingmoor Fell* (1530ft; partly NT), to the N, separates it from Great Langdale.—At (6m) the fork in the road at the head of the dale, the left branch goes over Wrynose Pass (see below). We take the right branch, which becomes narrow and steep as it crosses the W slope of Lingmoor. A striking view of the Langdale Pikes opens out in front. *Blea Tarn* ('dark tarn'), on the left, is the setting of Wordsworth's 'The Excursion' (1814). From the top of the pass the road drops abruptly down to (8¹⁄₂m) the Old Dungeon Ghyll Hotel at the head of the lovely valley of *Great Langdale*.

To the N the view is dominated by the rugged flanks and crags of the *Langdale Pikes*, a range of five fells with *Pike o' Stickle* ('the peak with the sharp summit'; 2323ft) at the W end and Harrison Stickle (2415ft) near the E end chief among them. *Pavey Ark* (2288ft) at the E end is a favourite with rockclimbers.—To the W rises the mass of **Bowfell** (2960ft).—*Crinkle Crags* to the SW are more easily reached from the road over Wrynose Pass, described below.

B5343 follows Great Langdale from the Old Dungeon Ghyll Hotel, soon passing near *Dungeon Ghyll Force*, a waterfall of 65ft framed by the walls of a picturesque gorge, on the slopes to the left.—From (11m) *Chapel Stile* a hilly sideroad branches left to (3m) Grasmere past the Youth Hostel at *High Close* (523ft; NT) and down *Red Bank*, with a lovely view of Grasmere lake.—B5343 leaves Great Langdale at (11³⁄₄m) the village of *Elterwater* (National Park local information point), taking its name from the smallest of the lakes, and joins A593 at (13¹⁄₄m) *Skelwith Bridge*.

FROM AMBLESIDE TO ESKDALE OVER WRYNOSE PASS AND HARDKNOTT PASS. A 14¹⁄₂m route to the western lakes and fells along a steep, narrow and twisting road, sometimes impassable in winter. It follows the Roman way from the fort of Galava at Waterhead to the fort of Glannaventa at Ravenglass.—We take the tour of the Langdales described above as far as (6m) the road fork at the head of Little Langdale. The road to the left climbs up to (7¹⁄₂m) the top of **Wrynose Pass** (1270ft), where the Three Shires Stone marks the old meeting point of Cumberland, Westmorland and Lancashire. To the N is *Pike o' Blisco* (2304ft) and beyond, to the NW, the five **Crinkle Crags**, with their highest summit at 2816ft.—The road drops down to (9¹⁄₂m) *Cockley Beck*, in the upper part of the Duddon valley. See below for the road following the river to the S.—We climb again to (10³/₄m) the **Hardknott Pass** (1292ft), between *Hard Knott* (1803ft) to the N and *Harter Fell* (2129ft) to the S. On the right, about ¹/₂m beyond the top of the pass, stand the interesting remains of the Roman fort of *Mediobogdum* (English Heritage, open at any reasonable time), superbly placed on a shelf of rock overlooking Eskdale.—At 12¹/₂m we cross the Esk and at 14¹/₂m we reach *Boot* (Rte 78D).

At Cockley Beck, between Wrynose Pass and Hardknott Pass, a road heads S down the lovely \***Duddon Valley**, or *Dunnerdale*, quieter than better known valleys like Langdale or Borrowdale. Wordsworth praised it in a popular series of sonnets (1820).—From the stony levels near Cockley Beck the river winds through (2m) the wooded cleft at the picturesque *Birk's Bridge* and another fine gorge just before (4m) *Seathwaite*. The churchyard here contains the grave of 'Wonderful Walker', the 18C rector and benevolent despot of the parish.—From (7m) *Ulpha* a steep sideroad makes a 5m journey over *Birker Fell* (889ft), near *Devoke Water*, to Eskdale (Rte 78D).—Beyond Ulpha sideroads follow both sides of the valley to (c 11m) *Duddon Bridge* (Rte 77).

From Ambleside to *Ullswater* and *Penrith*, see Rte 78B.

From Ambleside A591 continues to (14m) *Rydal*, on the right of the road. The church has memorials to Thomas and Matthew Arnold. *Rydal Mount* (open) was Wordsworth's home after leaving Grasmere in 1813 until his death in 1850. He laid out the large, pleasant garden and named the nearby *Dora's Field* (NT), which he bought in 1826, after his daughter. W of the hamlet is *Rydal Water*, a charming little lake less than 1m long and about ¹/₄m across, connecting with Windermere by the Rothay.—A591 skirts its N bank, passing *Nab Cottage*, where Thomas De Quincey lived in 1806 and Hartley Coleridge, son of the poet, from 1840 until his death in 1849. Above rises *Nab Scar* (1450ft), which some walkers make the first ascent in their round of the Fairfield horseshoe (see Ambleside, above). —Beyond Rydal Water the road turns N to follow the shore of its sister lake, Grasmere, with pleasant views of the vale of Grasmere and its surrounding fells.

16m. The village of **Grasmere** (National Park Information Centre and NT Information Centre), left of the main road, is another popular centre for tourists. Its sports festival, held on the Thursday nearest 20 August, is the largest in the Lake District and includes fell running, hound trailing and Cumberland and Westmorland wrestling. The rush-bearing ceremony also takes place in August.

Grasmere, however, is chiefly famous for its connection with William Wordsworth (1770–1850). He is commemorated with a medallion by Thomas Woolner in the church and buried in the churchyard near his sister Dorothy (d. 1855), his wife Mary (d. 1859) and other members of their family. Here also are the grave of Hartley Coleridge (d. 1849) and a memorial to the poet Arthur Hugh Clough, who died in 1861 at Florence. From 1799 to 1808 Wordsworth lived at *Dove Cottage* (open), a little 17C building S and E of the village and main road. A converted barn opposite houses the *Grasmere and Wordsworth Museum*. Thomas De Quincey took over the tenancy, holding it for more than 20 years, when the cottage became too cramped to hold the poet, his sister, wife and growing family. The Wordsworths moved first to *Allan Bank*, NW of the church, and then in 1811 to the *Parsonage*, which they left for Rydal Mount in 1813.

\***Grasmere** lake is the roundest in the Lake District, barely 1m long and fully ¹/₂m wide, with a little island in the middle. There is a favourite view from the so-called *Wishing Gate*, less than ¹/₂m S of Dove Cottage on the old road to Rydal. A pleasant walk round the lake (4m) follows the road on the W shore to *Red Bank*, with a good view, and then takes the lane leading left to *Loughrigg Terrace* (about 300ft; NT), with more good views. We return by taking the footbridge across the Rothay between Grasmere and Rydal, and following either A591 or, better, the old road to Dove Cottage.

Beyond Grasmere A591 climbs, with the Fairfield range on the right, to (19m) the top of *Dunmail Raise* (782ft), the dip between *Seat Sandal* (2415ft) on the right and *Steel Fell* (1811ft) on the left. Tradition maintains that Dunmail, the last king of Cumbria or Strathclyde, was buried here after his defeat by the Saxon King Edmund in 945; in fact, Dunmail died some 30 years later. Below lies **Thirlmere** ('lake in a hollow'), a narrow sheet of water nearly 4m long. It lost much of its character when Manchester Corporation raised its level to make a reservoir in 1894, against the opposition of Canon Rawnsley and others concerned to preserve the Lake District. Both shores are planted with conifers. A sideroad winds around the W bank, with rocky crags and a forest trail.—A591 takes the E bank, passing (20m) the church from the drowned village of *Wythburn* and skirting the tree-shrouded base of Helvellyn (Rte 78B). It can be climbed from various points along the way, notably Wythburn and (22½m) *Thirlspot*, though the popular routes approach it from the Ullswater side.—23¼m. Beyond *Dalehead* (National Park local information point) the wooded *Great How* (1092ft) cuts off the view of the foot of Thirlmere, where the sideroad to the W bank crosses the dam.

B5322 branches right for the lovely \*St John's in the Vale, with the *Castle Rock* (about 1000ft) of Sir Walter Scott's 'Bridal of Triermain' on the right and a fine view of Blencathra ahead.—At (4m) *Threlkeld* we join A66 (Rte 78C), heading W for Keswick.

A591 crosses St John's Beck.—26¼m. At the top of *Castlerigg* (702ft) a sideroad leads ½m right to the neolithic or Bronze Age \***Castlerigg Stone Circle** (English Heritage, open at any reasonable time), set against a fine panorama of fells. A smaller rectangle of stones stands inside the 100ft circle.—28m. **Keswick**, see Rte 78C.

# B. Penrith to Ullswater and Windermere

Total distance 26m. **Penrith**, see Rte 76. We follow A592 for most of the way.—5m. Pooley Bridge.—13m. Glenridding.—14m. Patterdale.—26m. **Windermere**, see Rte 78A.

Maps: OS Landranger 90 and 97 (briefly) or OS Tourist map for the National Park.

A scenic route, very popular with tourists.

**Penrith**, see Rte 76.—From the M6 roundabout SW of the town we head W on A66 but soon branch left on A592, joining the Eamont as we enter the National Park.—3m. *Dalemain* (open), on the right, has Elizabethan work and the remains of a 12C pele tower behind its 18C façade. The 16C panelling, Jacobean plaster ceiling, Chinese drawing room and the gardens are notable.—5m. We reach the head of Ullswater and **Pooley Bridge** (National Park Information Centre), left of the main road.

An alternative way from Penrith starts by following Rte 76 down A6 to (1½m) *Eamont Bridge* and then turns right on B5320, reaching Pooley Bridge in 5¾m.

The road passes (2½m) *Yanwath*, where the Hall incorporates an old pele tower; (3m) *Tirril*, where the Roman road coming down from the High Street reaches the Eamont valley; and (4m) a turning on the right for *Barton*, where the church has late 13C–early 14C arches strengthening the original Norman arches of its tower.

A detour leads S from Yanwath via (2½m) *Askham* and (6m) *Bampton* (Rte 76) to (8m) the foot of **Haweswater** ('Hafr's water'). In 1937 Manchester Corporation made the original, much smaller lake into a reservoir about 3½m long by flooding the valley, church and village of Mardale. The result has very little charm, though there are good views across to the High Street range from the road along the E shore and a fine grouping of fells at the head.

**High Street** (2718ft) is the tallest of the long line of fells, mainly above 2000ft, which separate Haweswater from Ullswater. The name, also used for the range as a whole, refers to the Roman road connecting Windermere and Penrith which still runs in a clearly defined path for 11m along the ridge.

*Ullswater** ('Ulfr's water'), 7½m long, is second in size to Windermere but quite as popular, its shores often crowded with tourists and its surface with boats. Yet it remains the grandest of the lakes, given a special beauty by the winding course which divides it into three distinct reaches, the scenery growing lovelier towards the head at the S end. A passenger service by motor yacht connnects Pooley Bridge and Glenridding with *Howtown* on the E shore, which can also be reached by the sideroad from Pooley Bridge. A splendid walk (6m) follows the shore from Howtown to Glenridding; this can be varied or made into a circuit of about 9½m from Howtown by following the road inland to (¾m) *Martindale*, with its tiny 17C church, continuing to (3m) the head of *Boardale* and rounding the slopes of *Place Fell* (2154ft) to return along the shore.

A592 follows the W shore, with increasingly fine views across the lake, and skirts **Gowbarrow Park** ('windy hill'; NT), entered from the foot of the Dockray road, A5091, at 10½m.

The park, which covers the whole Ullswater side of *Gowbarrow Fell* (1578ft), is inseparably associated with the daffodils of Wordsworth's 'I wandered lonely as a cloud', whose descendants still bloom here. To the right stands *Lyulph's Tower*, a small 18C shooting lodge. A path climbs from the entrance to the park ½m up to one of the most beautiful waterfalls in the Lake District, *Aira Force*, 65ft high, romantically situated in a deep winding ravine. The path continues past another pretty little fall, *High Force*, to (1¼m) *Dockray*, where a fine high-level walk leads S through Glencoyne Park.

Beyond Dockray A5091 climbs past *Matterdale End*, 2½m from the lakeshore, and reaches its highest point at 1124ft, W of *Great Mell Fell* (1760ft), before descending to (5m) *Troutbeck* and A66 (Rte 78C).

A592 continues to skirt the lake, passing *Glencoyne Park* (NT) and *Stybarrow Crag* (NT), with the ancient oaks of *Glencoyne Wood* (NT) above it.—13m. **Glenridding** (National Park Information Centre), at the mouth of its valley, has the pier for the motor launches which cruise the length of the lake. We pass a well, on the right, with misty traditions of baptisms by St Patrick, and cross the mouth of *Grisedale*.—14m. The village of **Patterdale** ('Patrick's Dale') is just beyond the head of Ullswater. Sheepdog trials take place here on August Bank Holiday Saturday.

*Helvellyn** (3118ft), rising W of Glenridding and Patterdale, is the tallest of the range which separates Ullswater from Thirlmere. Though Scafell Pike and Scafell are higher, Helvellyn is the most famous of the Lake District mountains and the one most likely to tempt tourists up from the valley floor. It can be climbed from the Thirlmere side (Rte 78A) but the most popular ways to the top start from the road between Glenridding and Patterdale and follow *Striding Edge* or *Swirral Edge*. They both pass *Red Tarn* (2356ft), the

*Aira Force: an engraving from Charles Mackay's 'The Scenery and Poetry of the English Lakes: A Summer Ramble' (1846)*

highest of the Lake District tarns. Near the summit, with its wide views, stands a memorial to Charles Gough, who fell to his death from Striding Edge in 1805 and whose body was guarded by his dog until its discovery several months later; both Wordsworth and Scott wrote poems about the incident. Another memorial nearby records the landing of the first aeroplane on Helvellyn in 1926.

The fells at the head of Grisedale include *Dollywagon Pike* (2810ft) at the end of the Helvellyn range, *St Sunday Crag* (2756ft) and, to the S, *Cofa Pike*, the N spur of Fairfield.

A592 crosses the Deepdale Beck, Goldrill Beck and Pasture Beck, where it turns right to follow the E side of (16m) *Brothers Water* (NT), popularly supposed to be named after the drowning of two brothers. There is a view back to Place Fell by the head of Ullswater.—It then becomes the highest road in the National Park as it mounts rapidly to (19m) the top of **Kirkstone Pass** (1489ft), celebrated in an ode by Wordsworth. Just short of this point, on the right, is the stone whose supposed resemblance to a church gives the pass its name. Just beyond, to the right, a sideroad follows the Stock Ghyll valley to Ambleside (Rte 78A).—A592 swings to the left and makes its descent above the beautiful Troutbeck valley.—At 22m a sideroad on the right leads to Windermere through the village of *Troutbeck*. At its S end is *Townend* (NT), built about 1626, a finely preserved example of a house belonging to a Lake District 'statesman' or yeoman farmer. As well as the range of household equipment typical of such a farm, it contains a magnificent array of intricately carved built-in furniture. —A592 keeps to the left, crossing the river beyond (23m) the village church, with a stained-glass window by Morris, Ford Madox Brown and Burne-Jones.—26m. **Windermere**, see Rte 78A.

## C.   Penrith to Keswick, Derwentwater, Borrowdale, Buttermere and Cockermouth

Total distance 40¹/₂m. **Penrith**, see Rte 76.—A66 to (17¹/₂m) **Keswick** (bypassed).—B5289 to (30¹/₂m) Buttermere.—B5289, B5292 to (40¹/₂m) **Cockermouth**.

Maps: OS Landranger 90 and 89 or OS Tourist map for the National Park.

A66, originating at Scotch Corner (Rte 86F) and ending on the Cumbrian coast at Workington (Rte 77), is a fast modern road heavily trafficked by holidaymakers touring the northern and central Lake District. This route abandons it at Keswick for more interesting, though not always less crowded, roads.

**Penrith**, see Rte 76.—A66 leads W, soon entering the National Park. A more interesting start, adding 2m to the journey, follows B5288 via *Greystoke*, a pleasant village with a rebuilt castle. St Andrew's, founded as a collegiate church in the 14C, has misericords and 15C glass in its E window.—9m. For A5091 leading S to Dockray and Ullswater via *Troutbeck* (not to be confused with the Troutbeck near Windermere), see Rte 78B.—10¹/₂m. The turning on the right leads to *Mungrisdale*, *Mosedale* and *Caldbeck*, on the drive round the Skiddaw Fells described below.—From (12m) *Scales* hardy fellwalkers tackle Blencathra (see below); the easier route starts from *Blencathra Centre*, NW of (13³/₄m) *Threlkeld*. For St John's in the Vale, opening to the S of Threlkeld, and the nearby Castlerigg Stone Circle, see Rte 78A.—A66 joins the valley of the Greta, before swinging right to bypass Keswick by a viaduct over the Greta Gorge, part of the road enlargement carried out in the 1970s despite opposition from the National Park Authority and other conservation groups. We take A5271 for the town centre.

17¹/₂m. **Keswick** (5600 inhab.; National Park Information Centre), beneath the Skiddaw Fells and just N of Derwentwater, is a popular tourist centre. The Keswick Show, with cattle, sheep and horse classes, hound trailing and Cumberland and Westmorland wrestling, takes place on August Bank Holiday Monday.

The main streets converge on the narrow market place where the *Moot Hall* (1813) stands on an island in the road. To the S is the prominent spire of *St John's* church (1813; Anthony Salvin). Sir Hugh Walpole (1884–1941) is buried in the SW corner of the churchyard, which commands a fine view. Station St. leads NE to the delightful *Fitz Park*, bounded by the river. The *Museum* contains wide-ranging collections notable for geological specimens; manuscripts and other material relating to Wordsworth, Southey and Sir Hugh Walpole; and Flintoft's scale model of the Lake District (1867).

To the right of Main St., leading NE from the market place, is *Greta Hall* (now part of Keswick School), where Coleridge lived from 1800 to 1803 and Southey from 1803 until his death in 1843. Near Greta Bridge is the *Pencil Museum*, tracing the history of the local industry which began in the 16C. Plumbago or 'wad' was mined at Seathwaite in Borrowdale.—At *Crosthwaite*, near the bypass about 1/2m further on, the late Perp. church stands on the site of the church built by St Kentigern in 553. It contains a brass to Sir John Ratcliffe (d. 1527) and his wife, and a monument to Southey (with an inscription by Wordsworth), who is buried in the churchyard. Canon Hardwicke Rawnsley (1851–1920) was vicar of Crosthwaite in 1883–1917.—Shelley lived with Harriet Westbrook in the winter of 1811–12 in a cottage on Chestnut Hill.

N of the town rises the bold mass of the Skiddaw range of fells. Though the name comes from the Old Norse for 'craggy hill', their soft slate gives them gentler, more rounded contours than the jagged Borrowdale Volcanic hills to the S. **•Skiddaw** itself, the highest (3054ft), overlooks Bassenthwaite Lake at the W end of the range. Fellwalkers usually approach it round the side of its 'cub', *Latrigg* (1203ft), beyond A66 just NE of Keswick; stiffer routes go from Millbeck or Mirehouse, off A591, by way of *Carl Side* (2400ft). Further E in the Skiddaw range is **•Blencathra** (2847ft), also called *Saddleback* because of its distinctive shape, best seen from St John's in the Vale (Rte 78A) and climbed from Blencathra Centre or Scales, off A66.

•A DRIVE ROUND THE NORTHERN FELLS, 31m. The route takes narrow and sometimes steep sideroads through the fine, remote country at the back of Skiddaw.—We return E along A66 and at 7m turn N on the sideroad running alongside *Souther Fell* (1713ft) to the pleasant hamlets of (9m) *Mungrisdale* and (10m) *Mosedale*. The summit of *Carrock Fell* ('rocky fell'; 2174ft) has a hill-fort, perhaps Brigantian. Dickens and Wilkie Collins described their misfortunes climbing it in 'The Lazy Tour of Two Idle Apprentices' (1857).—We continue along the N fringe of the National Park via (15m) *Hesket Newmarket* to (16 1/2m) **Caldbeck** (also on the detour from Cockermouth to Carlisle, below). The churchyard contains the grave of the fox-hunter John Peel (d. 1854), immortalised in the song.—We follow B5299 to the W, branching left on the Uldale road and left again for (21m) *Longlands*, (22 1/2m) *Over Water* and (22 1/2m) *Orthwaite*. Here we cross the valley to join A591 at (25 1/2m) *High Side*.—31m. *Keswick*.

**•Derwentwater**, an oval about 3m long and 1m wide, lies between the Skiddaw Fells and the rugged 'Jaws of Borrowdale'. One of the loveliest lakes, it is also, with Windermere, Ullswater and Buttermere, one of the most popular. The shores blend abrupt crags, green fells and wooded slopes, while little islands dot the surface of the lake. The chief ones (all NT) are *Derwent Island*, site of the colony established by the German miners who settled at Keswick in the 16C; *Lord's Island*; the smaller *Rampsholme*; and *St Herbert's Island*, where St Cuthbert's disciple St Herbert (d. 687) is thought to have lived as a hermit. The 'floating island' which periodically surfaces near Lodore is a tangled mass of weeds buoyed up by marsh gas. The NT owns the W half of the lake itself, as well as large stretches of its shore. There are good footpaths on the W shore, served by the motor launches which link the landing at Keswick with jetties at various points around the lake.

*ROUND DERWENTWATER BY ROAD, 10m. B5289 leads S.—We soon turn left on Lake Rd, passing the landing stages at the foot of Derwentwater and *Cockshott Wood* (NT) on the way to *Friar's Crag* (NT, with Information Centre), a famous viewpoint. It was bought in memory of Canon Rawnsley, a founder of the NT, in 1922. The crag has a memorial to Ruskin, who eloquently recalled his childhood memories of the spot in 'Modern Painters'. *Calf Close Bay* is ¹/₂m S.—B5289 follows the E shore, passing (³/₄m) the wooded *Castle Head* (529ft; NT), commanding perhaps the best view of the lake.—We pass through the *Great Wood* (NT), with *Walla Crag* (1234ft) rising to the left; beyond it is *Falcon Crag* (1050ft).—2m. The lane on the left leads to Watendlath (see the detour below). In the grounds of *Barrow House*, now a Youth Hostel, to the left, are waterfalls descending over 100ft.—3m. *Lodore Falls*, despite Southey's rhapsodic verses, are disappointing except after heavy rain.—B5289 continues S through Borrowdale (see the main route below), but we cross the Derwent for (4¹/₂m) the popular village of *Grange*.—From (5m) *Manesty* footpaths lead up the W shore, giving open views of the lake.—On the left, beneath the ridge of *Cat Bells* (1481ft), are the woods of *Manesty Park* and *Brandelhow Park*. They are both NT and Brandelhow, bought in 1902, was the first NT property in the Lake District. The bay between them, where the Brandley lead mine survived into the 19C, gives a good view of the lake. *Brackenburn* was the home of Sir Hugh Walpole.—Near (6³/₄m) *Hawes End* a fine view opens across the Newlands valley to the W.—Beyond (7¹/₂m) *Swinside* Forestry Commission plantations mainly hide the lake from view. *Lingholm Gardens* (open) are down by the shore.—10m. *Keswick*.

The detour to Watendlath branches left from the drive round the lake just before Barrow House.—After ¹/₂m we cross the Barrow Beck by *Ashness Bridge*, an old packhorse bridge with a famous view of Skiddaw, and climb through woods, skirting the Watendlath Beck for much of the way.—3m. *Watendlath* is a popular hamlet on a small tarn, the setting for much of Sir Hugh Walpole's 'Judith Paris' (1931) in his 'Herries Chronicle'. Walkers may follow the track SW another 1¹/₂m to *Rosthwaite* on the Borrowdale road.

FROM KESWICK TO COCKERMOUTH BY A66, 13m. A busy road, best avoided. —B5289 heads NW to join A66 at ³/₄m, just beyond the Derwent.—A66 crosses the Newlands and turns N at 2m to avoid *Braithwaite*. The sideroad which now runs parallel to A66 on the left is more pleasant, skirting the foot of the fells of Thornthwaite Forest and passing beneath *Barf* (1536ft), with the rock known as *The Bishop*, usually painted white.—4¹/₂m. The sideroad rejoins A66 on the W shore of **Bassenthwaite Lake** ('Bastun's lake'), 4m long and ¹/₂m wide, the northernmost of the lakes. There is a good view across the water to Skiddaw but otherwise the traffic on A66, enlarged in the 1970s despite opposition from the National Park Authority and other conservation groups, destroys enjoyment of the shore.—7m. Just before *Dubwath* A66 leaves the lake and branches E. —13m. *Cockermouth*, see the main route below.

FROM KESWICK TO COCKERMOUTH BY A591, 15m. Better than A66.—From the A66 roundabout N of Keswick we take A591 for the E shore of Bassenthwaite. Just beyond the roundabout a sideroad branches right for *Ormathwaite*, *Applethwaite* and *Millbeck*, rejoining A591 at (2¹/₂m) *Dodd Wood*. Southey maintained that 'the terrace between Applethwaite and Millbeck' offered the best view of Derwentwater. Skiddaw can be tackled from here or from Mirehouse.—4m. *Mirehouse* (open) is a predominantly late 18C–early 19C house between the foot of Skiddaw and the lake. The scholar James Spedding (1808–81) entertained Tennyson, Carlyle and Edward FitzGerald here. The closing scene of Tennyson's 'Idylls of the King' is said to have been inspired, during his visit in 1835, by the lakeside view near the little, partly Norman church of St Bega. There are good walks in the nearby wood and along the shore.—At (5¹/₂m) *High Side* the drive round the Skiddaw Fells, described above, joins A591.—At (7¹/₄m) *Castle Inn* we turn left on B5291 and cross the Derwent by the Ouse Bridge (good view).—9m. Beyond *Dubwath* we join A66 for (15m) *Cockermouth*, described at the end of the main route below.

FROM KESWICK TO COCKERMOUTH VIA THE NEWLANDS VALLEY AND BUTTERMERE, 19m.—We take B5289 and A66 W for (2½m) *Braithwaite*, at the entrance to the little *Coledale*.—We then follow the sideroad which heads S along the slopes of the fells flanking the lovely *Newlands* valley. It was the site of the old Goldscope copper mine, which closed in 1864, perhaps a corruption of *Gottesgab* ('God's gift'), the name used by the German miners who settled here in the 16C.—Beyond (5¼m) *Gillbrow* we climb to (6¼m) the high-lying *Keskadale*, with an ancient oak wood on the right, and then (7¾m) *Newlands Hause* (1096ft), between *Robinson* (2417ft) on the left and *Whiteless Pike* (2159ft) and *Wandope* (2533ft) on the right.—There is a good view as we drop down to (9m) the village of *Buttermere*, where we join the main route to (19m) *Cockermouth* described below.

FROM KESWICK TO COCKERMOUTH VIA THE WHINLATTER PASS, 11½m.—As in the route through the Newlands valley, we begin by taking B5289 and A66 to (2½m) *Braithwaite*.—We then follow B5292 as it climbs through *Thornthwaite Forest*, with woodland trails and a Forestry Commission Visitor Centre near (5m) the top of the **Whinlatter Pass** (1043ft), between *Lord's Seat* (1811ft) on the right and *Grisedale Pike* (2593ft) on the left.—We descend, with *Whinlatter* (1696ft) to our right, via (7¼m) *High Lorton* (National Park local information point) into (8¼m) *Lorton Vale*. Here we join the main route to (11½m) *Cockermouth* described below.

From Keswick to *Grasmere*, *Ambleside* and *Windermere*, see Rte 78A.

The main route from Keswick follows the drive round Derwentwater as far as (22m) the S end of the lake but, instead of turning right for *Grange*, keeps on B5289 along the bank of the Derwent and into the 'Jaws of Borrowdale'. On the left are *Grange Fell* (1363ft; NT) and the *Bowder Stone* (NT), a marvellously balanced mass of metamorphic rock weighing about 2000 tons, which fell from the neighbouring cliffs. Immediately opposite is the wooded *Castle Crag* (900ft; NT). Further S over Rosthwaite rise *Glaramara* (2560ft) and *Allen Crags* (2572ft) and, to their W, Great End, the N buttress of the Scafell group (Rte 78D).—The road clings to the river until \***Borrowdale** ('valley of the fortress') suddenly opens out, its level green floor ringed by crags and fells. Ever since early tourists sought it out as the most picturesque valley in the Lake District, it has remained the most popular.—23½m. The village of *Rosthwaite* stands on the pretty *Stonethwaite Beck*, flowing down a little dale with the finely shaped *Eagle Crag* at its head. From Rosthwaite a bridlepath leads NE between Watendlath and Grange Fells to (1½m) Watendlath (see above).—At (25m) *Seatoller* (National Park Information Centre) B5289 leaves the Derwent, which flows down the dale from *Seathwaite*, about 1¼m S, near the disused plumbago mines which once served the Keswick pencil industry.—We climb to (26½m) the top of the **Honister Pass** (1176ft), with a noble view back into Borrowdale.

\***Great Gable** (2949ft) rises to the S, though the best view of the mountain is from Wasdale Head (Rte 78D). The summit, more or less at the centre of the Lake District, commands a panoramic view. Walkers reach it from the car park at the top of the pass via *Grey Knotts* (2287ft), *Brandreth* (2344ft) and *Green Gable* (2603ft). A more difficult route goes from Seathwaite via the *Sty Head Pass* (1600ft), which the hardy walker can also follow to Wasdale Head or via the Corridor Route to Scafell Pike.

From the top of the pass B5289 drops sharply through wild and bleak country beneath *Honister Crag* (1750ft), scarred by slate quarries, and *Fleetwith Pike* (2126ft) on the left.—From (28½m) *Gatesgarth*, at the bottom, a demanding walkers' route leads to the left over the *Scarth Gap Pass* (1410ft), the saddle between *Haystacks* (1750ft) and *High Crag* (2443ft), to Ennerdale (Rte 78D).—Ahead, the green beauty of Buttermere is suddenly revealed. Our road follows the NE shore of the lake to (13½m) the village of *Buttermere*, where it is joined by the route from Keswick via the Newlands valley (see above).

*Buttermere ('dairy pasture lake'; NT), a favourite spot with tourists, and its larger, wilder neighbour **Crummock Water** ('crooked water'; NT) were once united in a single lake about 4½m long. A strip of land formed by alluvial deposits now divides them. On the W the mountains rise abruptly from the water's edge, with High Crag, *High Stile* (2644ft) and *Red Pike* (2479ft) above Buttermere. Paths encircle the lake. At its NW corner, opposite the village, are the thread-like cataracts of *Sour Milk Gill*, flowing down from *Bleaberry Tarn*. In a small ravine SW of Crummock Water is *Scale Force (NT), a striking waterfall with a sheer leap of at least 120ft.

Loweswater ('leafy lake'; NT), reached by the sideroad which branches left from B5289 around the N end of Crummock Water, is a charming little lake about 1m long. A path goes through *Holme Wood* (NT) on its SW shore. —Beyond Loweswater sideroads continue around the edge of the National Park via (2½m) *Lamplugh* to (7½m) Ennerdale Water (Rte 78D).

Beyond (34m) *Brackenthwaite* and the turning for Loweswater our road enters *Lorton Vale*, watered by the Cocker, and beyond (36½m) *Low Lorton* joins B5292, which has come from Keswick over the Whinlatter Pass.—39m. We cross A66 and leave the National Park.

40½m. **Cockermouth** (7100 inhab.; seasonal Tourist Information) is a pleasant little town at the meeting of the Derwent and the Cocker, marked by the ruined 13–15C castle of the Percys. *Wordsworth House* (NT), a handsome 18C building at the W end of the main street, was the birthplace of the poet in 1770 and his sister Dorothy in 1771. Their father, John, is buried in the church.

Fletcher Christian, the 'Bounty' mutineer, was born in 1764 at *Moorland Close*, 1½m SW. *Eaglesfield*, ¾m further on, was the birthplace of the scientist John Dalton (1766–1844) and of Robert de Egglesfield, chaplain to Queen Philippa of Hainault and founder of The Queen's College, Oxford.—At *Bridekirk*, 2½m N of Cockermouth, the largely 19C church incorporates two Norman doorways and a remarkable *font of c 1140, decorated with Norse motifs and signed in runic letters by the artist.

FROM COCKERMOUTH TO CARLISLE, 24½m by A595.—We follow A595 via (9m) *Mealsgate*; (13m) *Red Dial*, on the Roman road near *Olenacum*, which is mistakenly known as *Old Carlisle*; and (17½m) *Thursby* where we are joined by A596.—24½m. *Carlisle*, see Rte 76.

A pleasant and hilly alternative way from Mealsgate, 5½m longer, follows B5299.—1½m. *Boltongate* church has an unusual tunnel-vaulted 15C nave. —The road continues along the side of the fell, entering the N tip of the National Park before (8m) *Caldbeck* (also on the drive round the Skiddaw Fells from Keswick) and striking NE via (17m) *Dalston* to (21m) *Carlisle*.

FROM COCKERMOUTH TO WHITEHAVEN, 13m.—We follow A66 W along the Derwent valley and branch left on A595 for (9m) *Distington* and (13m) *Whitehaven* (Rte 77). We can reach the western lakes and fells from various points along A595 between Whitehaven and Ravenglass.

# D.   Eskdale, Wastwater and Scafell, and Ennerdale

Maps: OS Landranger 96 (briefly) and 89 or OS Tourist map for the National Park.

The western lakes and fells are the least crowded but not the least beautiful part of the region. Motorists reach them most easily from various points along A595, the coastal road between Ravenglass and Whitehaven (Rte 77). Sideroads also connect Eskdale and Ennerdale with the heart of the Lake District.

**Eskdale** runs SW to the coast from its source between the Scafell range and the Bowfell range. It has no lake on its floor, but its mountains and waterfalls repay a visit. The Eskdale Show takes place on the last Saturday in September.

The narrow-gauge railway mentioned in Rte 77 brings us from *Ravenglass* via (1m) *Muncaster Mill* and (4m) *Eskdale Green* to (7m) *Dalegarth*, halfway up the dale.—Motorists can take the sideroad up the S bank of the Esk from near *Muncaster Castle* or the sideroad from near *Holmrook*. About 1¼m E of Holmrook a turning on the left leads to *Irton* church, with a fine 9C cross shaft.—However, the best routes (both described in Rte 78A) come from the E, over Hardknott Pass and Wrynose Pass from Little Langdale and Ambleside, and from the S, over Birker Fell and past Devoke Water from the Duddon valley. Both take steep and twisting roads which are not for timid drivers.

*Boot*, about ¼m above the railway terminus, is a little village on the Whillan Beck shortly before it joins the Esk on its way down from *Burnmoor Tarn*.—The chief attraction nearby is \*Stanley Force, over the Esk 1¼m S, a 60ft waterfall made particularly charming by its wooded setting. There is a fine view from the open fell above.—To see something of Upper Eskdale we take the road to the foot of the Hardknott Pass, about 2½m from Boot, and then follow the path along the bank of the Esk, passing the *Esk Falls* after another 2m. Experienced fellwalkers can continue up the Esk, with the Scafell range on their left and Bowfell and *Esk Pike* (2903ft) on their right. The passes from Wasdale, Langdale and Borrowdale meet near the summit of *Esk Hause* (2490ft).

\*Wastwater, the deepest, grimmest and most savage of all the lakes, is approached by the sideroad from *Gosforth* on A595 (Rte 77).—We reach the woods by the foot of the lake at 5¼m and continue the 3m length of its N shore. The astonishing range of screes on the opposite side rises almost vertically from the water's edge, culminating in *Illgill Head* (1983ft).—The road ends at (9½m) *Wasdale Head*, in a remote hollow surrounded by mountains. The Shepherds' Meet and Show takes place on the second Saturday in October.

The magnificent views from Wasdale Head are dominated to the SE by the Scafell group, the most impressive in the Lake District. The name, pronounced 'Scorefell', means 'bare fell'. The slopes above 2000ft are NT. \*Scafell Pike (3210ft) is the highest point in England, and in clear weather the view from its summit includes Snowdon to the S and the Isle of Man and the Mourne Mountains in Ireland to the W. Fellwalkers usually climb it from here or from Seathwaite in Borrowdale (Rte 78C) via the Sty Head Pass and the Corridor Route. The summit of \*Scafell (3162ft), its neighbour to the S, is reached ʿrom Wasdale via Lord's Rake or from Eskdale via Burnmoor Tarn.

*Great End* (2984ft) forms the N buttress of the group.—*Great Gable* (2949ft), NE of Wasdale Head, can be climbed from Wasdale Head or, more popularly, the Honister Pass or Seathwaite (Rte 78C). The best view is from here. *Napes Needle* on its S flank and *Scafell Crag* on the N face of Scafell were among the first challenges tackled by rockclimbers in the Lake District in the 19C.

**Ennerdale Water**, the westernmost of all the lakes, lies E of A595 between Egremont and Whitehaven (Rte 77), though it can also be reached by the detour from Crummock Water via Loweswater and Lamplugh (Rte 78C). The Ennerdale Show takes place on the last Wednesday in August.

From *Egremont* we take A5086 NE to (3m) *Cleator Moor* and then follow sideroads to (6m) *Ennerdale Bridge*, where the churchyard is the scene of Wordsworth's 'The Brothers', and (10m) the car park at *Bowness Knott*.

The lake, about 2½m long, is stern and solemn, encircled by mountains whose lower slopes have Forestry Commission plantations. The North-West Water Authority discreetly uses it as a reservoir; a proposal in 1978 to raise its water level was rejected. There are forest trails, and a footpath leads round the Water. It is worth walking along the track which goes up the dale from Bowness Knott to (about 4½) the fine combination of *Steeple* (2687ft) and *Pillar* (2927ft), to the S. The famous *Pillar Rock*, a vertical crag almost 600ft high, was first climbed by John Atkinson, an Ennerdale cooper, in 1826 and is still popular with experienced rockclimbers. The track continues another 1½m to the remote Youth Hostel between the Scarth Gap Pass and the Black Sail Pass.

# 79  The Isle of Man

Maps: OS Landranger 95.

The **Isle of Man** (64,300 inhab.) lies almost in the centre of the Irish Sea, midway between England and Ireland (about 30m from both) but closer to the Scottish than the Welsh coast. The nearest land is 16m N at Burrow Head in Dumfries and Galloway. The island itself is about 33m long and 13m broad. Except for the northern plain, it is largely mountainous, with slate uplands reaching their highest point at Snaefell (2036ft). The wooded river glens and the cliff-bound coast make for some particularly attractive scenery. The chief coastal towns were developed as resorts in the 19C, when the island added tourism to its traditional occupations of crofting and fishing. Several picturesque railways survive from this period.

The wide range of antiquities extends from megalithic ritual and burial sites of c 3500 BC to some impressive 19C mining remains. The *crosses decorated with scenes from Norse mythology and interlaced patterns testify to the Celtic and Viking influences which shaped Manx culture. There are more runic inscriptions (usually displayed in the parish churches) than in the whole of Norway. However, a Scandinavian flavour survived chiefly in personal and place names, the Manx language being akin to Irish and Scottish Gaelic. It now has only about 50 fluent speakers and is preserved largely in ceremonial.

**History.** *Ellan Vannin* or *Mannin* (perhaps 'middle isle') was first settled by hunter-gatherers using microlithic flint implements by about 6000 BC. At the time of conversion to Christianity the Manx apparently spoke a Brythonic Gaelic, and were then increasingly subject to Norse influence. Godred Crovan, a Norseman and perhaps the 'King Orry' of Manx legend, won a decisive victory in 1079 and united the island with the Hebrides. It was handed over to Scotland in 1265 but Edward I's intervention soon brought it under English control. Its first viceroys, the Montacutes, Earls of Salisbury, called themselves 'Kings of Man'. In 1406 Henry IV bestowed the island on the Stanleys, Earls of Derby; the 4th changed his title to 'Lord of Man' in 1505, on the ground that he would rather be a great lord than a petty king. The 7th Earl's wife held the island on his behalf for the king during the Civil War, but after the Earl's execution in 1651 it was surrendered by the receiver-general, William Christian, the Illiam Dhône ('brown-haired William') of Manx history. In 1765 the Duke of Atholl, descendant and successor of the Earls of Derby, sold his sovereignty to the Crown. The Three Legs device was probably adopted by the 13C, though the earliest example to survive is on the 14C Maughold cross; the motto 'Quocunque jeceris stabit' ('Wherever you throw it, it stands') appeared on the earliest known Manx coinage (1668).

**Administration.** The Isle of Man is constitutionally separate from the United Kingdom. Its legislative and executive authority is the Court of Tynwald, the world's oldest parliament with continuous traditions. The name comes from the Old Norse 'thing' and 'völlr', meaning 'assembly' and 'field'. It consists of the House of Keys (24 elected members) and the Legislative Council (the Attorney General, the Bishop of Sodor and Man, and eight members elected by the House of Keys); their collective monthly meetings are headed by the Lieutenant Governor, representing the Crown. British Acts of Parliament do not apply to the Isle of Man unless expressly so enacted, but the laws of Tynwald require Crown approval and must be proclaimed on Tynwald Hill.

**Practical Details.** The Isle of Man government issues its own notes and coins, though English, Scottish and Northern Irish money is equally accepted. Some shops, etc. accept Eire currency at the appropriate exchange rate. The island has had its own postal authority since 1973; UK stamps are not valid. Customs duties and VAT are in line with Westminster.

**Annual Events.** The open-air assembly of Tynwald is held at Tynwald Hill, near St John's, on 5 July (old Midsummer Day). Peel has a Viking Festival in the first week of July. The Isle of Man TT (Tourist Trophy), an international motor-cycling competition, takes place in late May/early June. Dating from 1907, the races now cover a mountain course of c 38m beginning and ending at Douglas. The Southern 100 road races take place in July, and the Manx Grand Prix (the Manx Amateur Motorcycle Road Races) in late August/early September. The Tudor Webasto Manx International Rally in September is one of the top ten rallies in Europe. The Isle of Man International Cycling Week is held in June.

**Ferry Services.** By Isle of Man Seaways to Douglas from Heysham, the chief point of departure, throughout the year; from Liverpool, Fleetwood, Stranraer, Belfast and Dublin between May and September.

**Air Services.** Passenger flights, chiefly by Manx Airlines, to the Isle of Man (Ronaldsway) Airport, 1½m NE of Castletown, from Blackpool, Heathrow, Liverpool, Manchester, Glasgow, Belfast and Dublin throughout the year; from Birmingham, Bristol, Leeds/Bradford, Newcastle, Edinburgh and Jersey in summer.

**DOUGLAS** (20,400 inhab.), on the E coast, is the island's capital and its chief resort. It stands on a wide bay backed by a range of hills, just below the confluence of the Awin Dhoo and Awin Glass (the 'dark' and 'light' rivers).

**Tourist Information Centres**: No. 13 Victoria St., and Sefton Information Bureau, Harris Promenade.

**Car Parks**: off Victoria St., and in North Quay and Athol St. Multi-storey car park in Chester St.

In the bay rises Conister (or St Mary's) Rock with its *Tower of Refuge* (1832) for shipwrecked sailors. The **Sea Terminal** where the ferries arrive and depart is at Victoria Pier, with the *Bus Station* 1/4m W in Lord St. and the *Railway Station* 1/2m W in North Quay. The chief attraction of Douglas is the seafront, a 2m promenade stretching from the pier to the *Derby Castle* terminus of the Manx Electric Railway (see Douglas to Ramsey, below) and the *Summerland* indoor leisure, sports and entertainment complex. The promenade passes many of the town's main hotels and entertainment centres, including the restored *Gaiety Theatre* (1900; Frank Matcham). The journey can be made by the Douglas Horse Tramway, opened in 1876.

The oldest part of town, W of Victoria Pier, has some handsome terraces of Victorian houses and the chief public buildings, including the *Town Hall* (1899) and the *Legislative Buildings* (1894; guided tours), with the chambers of the Legislative Council, the House of Keys and the Tynwald Court. *St George's* church stands a little SW.

The **Manx Museum** in Crellin's Hill, above the junction of the Loch and Harris Promenades, is the island's national museum.

Its contents are wholly Manx and cover a wide range: natural history, archaeology, social history (including costume and a reconstructed 19C farmhouse, barn and dairy), fine arts and applied arts. They are currently being redisplayed, and a large extension will open in 1989. The building also houses national archives and a reference library.

Further N in Upper Douglas is *Noble's Park*, with the grandstands overlooking the start and finish of the Isle of Man TT. The distinctive tailless Manx cat is bred at the *Cattery* (open).

On *Douglas Head* (view), reached by the swing bridge at the end of Parade St., are a lighthouse, the Manx Radio station and a *Camera Obscura* (open). The lifeboat station at the foot stands near the site of the house owned by Sir William Hillary (1771–1847), founder of the Royal National Lifeboat Institution. The *Marine Drive* along the cliffs to (3½m) *Port Soderick*, with its pretty glen, has been closed to vehicles because of rock falls but is still open to walkers.

The N suburb of *Onchan* (7900 inhab.), beyond the official residence of the Lieutenant Governor at *Government House*, has a 19C church with a pretty spire. Captain William Bligh of the 'Bounty' was married in its predecessor in 1771.—At *Kirk Braddan*, 1½m NW of Douglas, a number of runic crosses are kept in the old church, 18C with an earlier tower. The churchyard contains interesting monuments and the grave of the painter John Martin (1789–1854). —*Braaid*, about 4m W of Douglas, has *St Patrick's Chair*, an early Christian monument, and the so-called *Stone Circles*, in fact an exceptionally large Norse boat-shaped house with subsidiary building and a large, presumably earlier, round house.

FROM DOUGLAS TO PORT ERIN, 14½m by road. Between May and September the journey can also be made by the Steam Railway, originally opened in 1874.—We take A5 to (5m) *Santon*. On the coast 1m S is the pretty bay of *Port Grenaugh*, with a Viking promontory fort on the clifftop.—5¾m. The *Fairy Bridge* gets its name from the local superstition that travellers should greet the fairies as they pass over it.—At (8m) *Ballasalla* the modest ruins of *Rushen Abbey*, an offshoot of Furness Abbey founded by Olaf I in 1135, stand in the pleasure gardens by the Silverburn river. Upstream are the medieval monks' bridge and the pretty *Silverdale Glen*, partly a national glen and partly Manx NT.

A5 continues W to (6m) Port Erin via (3½m) *Colby*, about 1/2m S of the pretty *Colby Glen*.

A8 branches S from Ballasalla, skirting the *Isle of Man (Ronaldsway) Airport*. On its edge is *King William's College*, the island's chief independent school, founded in 1668. Pupils have included the Manx poet T.E. Brown (1830–97) and Dean Farrar (1831–1903), author of 'Eric: or Little by Little'.

10m. **Castletown** (3100 inhab.; Tourist Information), the capital of the island until 1869, is a compact old town with attractive shopping streets and a tidal harbour. *Castle Rushen* (open), dating perhaps from the time of Magnus (1252–65) or somewhat earlier, was developed by successive kings and Lords of Man. Bridge St. has the interesting *Nautical Museum* (open seasonally), with an 18C armed yacht in her original boat cellar.

*Scarlett*, to the S, has a visitors' centre and geological nature trail, with a footpath leading round the point to the Iron Age/Norse promontory fort at *Poyllvaaish*.—On the E side of Castletown is *Hango Hill*, where William Christian was 'shot to death' in 1663 for his surrender of the island. Further on is *Derbyhaven*, a small village at the neck of *Langness*, the promontory which forms the E side of Castletown Bay and has a golf course and great wildlife interest.

A7 heads W from Castletown to (11½m) *Balladoole*, where the fortified hilltop at Chapel Hill is an important archaeological site, with Bronze Age burials and a 9C Viking ship burial overlying early Christian graves. The site also includes a 12C 'keeill', or chapel.—At (13¾m) *Gansey*, A7 continues directly to Port Erin (see below). We branch ¾m left to **Port St Mary** (1600 inhab.; Tourist Information), a fishing village and centre for golf, watersports and yachting on the W side of *Bay ny Carrickey*, with a harbour and breakwater 400 yds long.

A lovely *coast walk (3m) heads down the SW tip of the island, with its splendid perpendicular cliffs and caves, via *Perwick Bay*; the remarkable series of fissures known as the *Chasms*; *Black Head* and *Spanish Head* (Manx NT), where the cliffs rise to a height of 400ft; the *Burroo Ned* promontory fort; and *Calf Sound*, with earthworks.—A31, the direct road to the Sound, passes through (1½m) *Cregneash*, with the *Cregneash Village Folk Museum* (open seasonally) in the characteristic old houses of a crofting and fishing community, centred on the cottage of Harry Kelly (d. 1934).—Offshore is the *Calf of Man* (616 acres; Manx NT), reached by boat from Port St Mary or Port Erin, a bird sanctuary and observatory, also with grey seals. About ¾m to its SW is the automatic lighthouse on the *Chicken Rock*.

15m. **Port Erin** (2900 inhab.; Tourist Information), one of Man's oldest and most attractive towns, stands among fine scenery on a square bay protected by a ruined breakwater. It has excellent bathing and golfing. The Steam Railway terminus contains a *Railway Museum* and the *Marine Biological Station* an aquarium (open). There is a fine view from Milner's Tower, crowning *Bradda Head* on the N side of the bay. A footpath continues along the coast c 2m N to *Fleshwick Bay*.

FROM PORT ERIN TO PEEL, 14m, an interesting route by A36 and A27.—A36 passes close to (4m) *The Stacks*, with a good cliff view. —6½m. *South Barrule* (1585ft) has a huge late Bronze Age hill-fort and a fine view over the S half of the island. A36 continues round the hill, with interesting mining remains to the N and more traces of silver and lead mines at (4m) *Foxdale*.—A27 branches left for (9m) *Dalby*, a quiet village about ½m inland of *The Niarbyl*, commanding the best coastal view on the island.—11m. *Glen Maye* is a delightful wooded spot with pretty waterfalls. A walk leads up the coast to Peel via *Contrary Head* and the folly on *Corrin's Hill*.—14m. *Peel*, see below.

FROM DOUGLAS TO PEEL, 11½m by A1.—Beyond (5m) *Crosby*, on the slopes of *Greeba Mountain* (1383ft) to the right, are *Greeba Castle*, where the writer Sir Hall Caine died in 1931, and the ruins of *St Trinian's Church*.—8½m. *St John's*, where the Tynwald Mills produce and sell the traditional Manx tweed.

On the right is **Tynwald Hill**, a tiered artificial mound where, in accordance with ancient Scandinavian custom, new laws are proclaimed in Manx and English at the open-air assembly held on 5 July.

From St John's to *Ramsey*, see below.

11½m. **Peel** (3700 inhab.; Tourist Information), the most attractive town on the island, has grown up around the fishing village at the mouth of the Neb. It is the main centre for curing Manx kippers. The Viking Festival in the first week of July, commemorating the invasion of AD 798, features replica longships. 'Odin's Raven', which made the crossing from Trondheim to Peel in 1979, is on display at the *Viking Longship Museum*.

On *St Patrick's Isle*, connected by a causeway to the W arm of the harbour, \***Peel Castle** (open) stands inside a stout 16C wall.

To the right, beyond the *Keep* and the *Guard Room*, are the roofless 13–14C ruins of *St German's Cathedral*, founded by Bishop Simon (1230–48). Other remains include the *Old Palace* of the bishops, with a banqueting hall; *Fenella's Tower*; the *Round Tower*, resembling those in Ireland; and the roofless 9C *St Patrick's Chapel*. Recent work by the St Patrick's Isle Excavation Trust has yielded interesting results, including the rich contents of a woman's grave of the Viking period, now in the Manx Museum at Douglas.

From Peel to *Port Erin*, see above.

FROM PEEL TO RAMSEY.—Beyond (3m) *St John's* on the way into Peel from Douglas (see above), we branch N up the valley of the Neb on A4.—5m. We pass the mouth of the wooded \**Glen Helen* with the *Rhenass Falls*.—The road descends to the coast at (9½m) *Kirk Michael*, where the conspicuous parish church has exceptionally fine Norse cross slabs.—A3 heads N, passing (11m) *Bishopscourt*, formerly the residence of the Bishop of Sodor and Man, with a theological college and a chapel which is the official pro-cathedral. —12¼m. *Ballaugh*, pronounced 'Ballaff', lies about 1½m S of its old 17C church, with an 11C cross and a curious font.—A3 continues inland, passing (13¾m) the *Curraghs Wildlife Park* (open), where the collections include rare species of otters, deer and many water birds.—From (14½m) *Sulby* A14 runs up the narrow \**Sulby Glen*, the 'Manx Switzerland', to the *Tholt-y-Will Inn* in beautiful grounds with waterfalls.—15½m. *Sulby Bridge* is a favourite anglers' resort.—17m. *Lezayre* is near the site of the battle which won Godred Crovan ascendancy·over the island in 1079.—19½m. *Ramsey*, see below.

FROM DOUGLAS TO LAXEY AND RAMSEY BY THE \***MANX ELECTRIC RAILWAY**. Opened in successive stages between 1893 and 1899, this 3ft gauge electric railway runs in summer (May to September) from the Derby Castle Station at the N end of Douglas promenade. It passes through scenery offering a superb combination of coastal views, mountains and glens.—Beyond *Banks Howe* (393ft) we reach the beautiful (2½m) *Groudle Glen*. From May to September the recently reconstructed miniature *Groudle Glen Railway* (1896) connects *Lhen Coan* with the coast at 'Sea Lion Cove'.—4¾m. *Garwick Glen* and the megalithic *Cloven Stones*, to the E.—7m. **Laxey** (1300 inhab.), now a popular resort, was once a centre of lead, zinc and copper mines. The huge *Laxey Wheel* (1854), for pumping water from the mines, survives in working order and the area is being revitalised as an industrial archaeology park. The St George's woollen mill, producing Manx tweed, can be visited.

In summer the *Snaefell Mountain Railway*, opened in 1895, climbs from Laxey to (5m) the top of **Snaefell** (2036ft), the island's highest mountain. The line crosses the mountain road from Douglas to Ramsey at (3½m) the Motorcycle Museum (see below). The summit, with a café and gift shop, commands a *view which takes in the whole of the island and, in good weather, the Lake District peaks in England, the Mull of Galloway in Scotland, the Mourne Mountains in Ireland and the Snowdon group in Wales.

The Ramsey line returns to the coast along the N side of the valley, passing on the left the so-called *King Orry's Grave*, a neolithic chambered cairn of c 3500 BC. We then get a superb *view of *Bulgham Bay*, 400ft below.—There are pretty waterfalls at (10½m) *Dhoon Glen*, (12m) *Glen Mona* and (13m) the unspoilt *Ballaglass Glen*. About ½m S of Ballaglass Glen is *Cashtal yn Ard*, a chambered cairn contemporary with King Orry's Grave.—*North Barrule* (1860ft) appears on the left, *Maughold Head* (373ft) on the right.—18m. *Ramsey*, see below.

FROM DOUGLAS TO RAMSEY BY THE MOUNTAIN ROAD, A18.—We branch left from the Laxey road at (1½m) *Governor's Bridge* and make the laborious climb past (4½m) *Keppel Gate*, with magnificent views, to (8m) the foot of Snaefell at the junction with the Snaefell Mountain Railway (see above). The *Motorcycle Museum*, near the highest point on the TT course, has a large collection of old bikes and memorabilia. From here we can descend to the left, by A15 through *Sulby Glen*, and join A3 at (15m) *Sulby* (see Peel to Ramsey, above). Or we can follow A18 to the right, crossing the E slopes of Snaefell and the W slopes of North Barrule. Ramsey is 20m from Douglas by the former route, and 15m by the latter.

**Ramsey** (5800 inhab.; Tourist Information), on a magnificent bay, is the second holiday resort on the island, after Douglas. It has a sandy beach, a long pier and *Mooragh Park*, with a boating lake etc. 'The Grove' Rural Life Museum (open seasonally), near the N edge of the town, is an early 19C house with Victorian furnishings and, in the outbuildings, a collection of agricultural equipment appropriate to larger Manx farms, including a horse-powered threshing machine.

The background of mountains makes the surroundings of Ramsey very attractive. Walks can be taken to the *Albert Tower*, with a view, about ¾m S; and SW via *Glen Auldyn* or over *North Barrule* and along the ridge to (c 4m) *Snaefell*.

A15 runs SE along the coast via *Ballure Glen* and *Port Lewaigue* to (3½m) *Maughold* (pronounced 'Mack'ld'), where a coastal footpath (Manx NT) leads past St Maughold's Well. The churchyard contains three separate early chapels, or 'keeills', as well as the site of a fourth, the parish church; also a large collection of early cross slabs and a 14C standing cross with the earliest version of the Isle of Man's Three Legs emblem. The path continues to the lighthouse at *Maughold Head*, with good sea birds.—A10 heads N from Ramsey to (4½m) *Bride*, with a *cross carved with the image of Thor. A16 branches right to (7½m) the *Point of Ayre*, the N tip of the island, with a lighthouse. A visitors' centre near *Ballaghennie* explains the wildlife value of this unique area of heathland. Nesting birds include terns.—A9 heads NW from Ramsey to (4m) *Andreas*, where the collection of Celtic and Viking crosses in the church includes *Sandulf's Cross, with beasts and inscriptions.—There are more Viking crosses at *Jurby*, 8m NW of Ramsey, mainly by A13. The former World War Two aerodrome nearby has secondhand shops, etc.

# 80  Leeds to Harrogate, Ripon and Thirsk

Total distance 37¹/₂m. **Leeds**, see Rte 75F. We follow A61
throughout.—To (8m) Harewood (see Rte 86A).—To (15m)
**Harrogate**.—To (26m) **Ripon** (for **Fountains Abbey** and
**Studley Royal**).—To (37¹/₂m) **Thirsk** (Rte 85A).

Maps: OS Landranger 104, 99.

**Leeds**, see Rte 75F. A61 runs N through *Chapel Allerton* and climbs
to (5m) *Alwoodley*, passing near the *Moortown* golf course. It then
descends to cross Wharfedale at (8m) *Harewood*, described in Rte
86A, and enters North Yorkshire.

15m. **HARROGATE** (66,500 inhab.), with large hotels, public
gardens and good shops, was once the leading spa town in the North
and has now become an important conference venue. It makes a
convenient base from which to tour the surrounding countryside.

**Tourist Information Centre**: Royal Baths Assembly Rooms, Crescent Rd.

**Car Parks**: Royal Baths Assembly Rooms, Royal Hall, International Centre,
Railway Station, Odeon Cinema, East Parade, Princes Square, Valley Drive,
Harlow Moor Drive. Multi-storey car parks in Tower St. and Union St.

**Bus Station and Railway Station**: Next to each other in Station Parade, E of the
war memorial.

**Theatre**: Harrogate Theatre, Oxford St. Concerts in International Centre;
morning coffee concerts in Royal Baths Assembly Rooms.

**Annual Events**: The Great Yorkshire Agricultural Show in July at Harrogate
Showground, SE of the town; International Festival of music and arts in July/
August.

**History**. Harrogate has nearly 90 springs in all, 30 of them in Bogs Field (Valley
Gardens), where sulphur and iron wells occur close together and yet are quite
distinct. They seem to have been used locally in earlier times, but the town's
development as a spa began with the rediscovery of the Tewit Well by William
Slingsby in 1571 and St John's Well by Dr Michael Stanhope in 1631. Smollett's
'Humphry Clinker' testifies to its vogue in the 18C. Harrogate reached the
height of its popularity in the Victorian and Edwardian era, and its reputation
began to fade after the First World War. Agatha Christie spent most of her much
publicised ten-day disappearance in 1926 at the Hydropathic Hotel.

The 200-acre common known as *The Stray* lies immediately S of the
town centre and is connected to it by West Park. The *Royal Baths
Assembly Rooms* (1897, with later additions), facing Crescent
Gardens, house Turkish Baths and the Tourist Information Centre. In
Kings Rd to the N is the *Royal Hall* (1903) with its modern adjunct,
the *International Centre*. To the W is the *Royal Pump Room* (1842),
now a museum of local history with costumes, pottery and Victoriana.
Water from the old sulphur well in the basement can be tasted.
Further W are the *Valley Gardens*, with formal floral displays and a
path leading to (1m) *Harlow Car Gardens*, the ornamental gardens
and woodlands of the Northern Horticultural Society. *Birk Crag* is to
the N.

*Almscliff Crag* (750ft), a good viewpoint, lies off A658 about 4m SW.—*Spofforth*,
off A661 about 5m SE of Harrogate, has a ruined 14C castle of the Percy family
(English Heritage, standard opening). A661 continues via (6m) *Stockeld Park* to
(8m) *Wetherby* (Rte 85B).

W of Harrogate A59 runs over the moors via (9m) *Blubberhouses*, in the
Washburn valley, to (16¹/₂m) *Bolton Abbey* (Rte 86A). At about 3m the road
passes the turning for *Hampsthwaite*, 1m N, the home of W.M. Thackeray's
ancestors.

From Harrogate to *York*, see Rte 81.

A61 crosses the Nidd just before (19m) *Ripley*, on Rte 86B through Nidderdale from Knaresborough to Grassington.

26m. **RIPON** (12,000 inhab.; seasonal Tourist Information) is a pleasant little cathedral city which claims to have been granted its first charter by Alfred the Great in 886. St Wilfrid's Feast is celebrated, with a procession through the streets, on the first Sunday in August.

The spacious Market Place has a 90ft obelisk erected as a monument to himself by William Aislabie of Studley Royal in 1781. The *Town Hall* (1801; James Wyatt) bears the city's motto, referring to the 'waker an', or watchman, who lived in the timber-framed but much altered *Wakeman's House*, now the museum and Tourist Information Centre. The ancient custom of sounding curfew on a horn is still observed at 21.00, and a handbell still announces the opening of the market at 11.00 each Thursday.

Kirkgate leads to the **Cathedral**, small and not particularly impressive at first sight, but of great interest for its variety of building styles (Saxon to Perp.) and for its beautiful choir stalls.

# RIPON CATHEDRAL

A monastery was founded c 660 at Ripon, which Bede calls *Inhrypum*. St Wilfrid (634–709) built a church about ten years later, and for a short time (681–86) Ripon was a bishop's see. It became a cathedral again in 1836, when the diocese was separated from York. The crypt of Wilfrid's Saxon church survives, though the Danes destroyed the rest of the building in the 9C. The second Saxon church was destroyed by the Normans in 1069. They soon built a third church, part of which survives in the apsidal chapel at the E end of the chapter house and the undercroft below it. The present church, the fourth on the site, was begun by Archbishop Roger of York (1154–81) as a church for secular canons. His plan, unique in England, included an aisleless nave, an aisled choir, transepts with E aisles only, and a central tower. Archbishop Walter de Grey (1215–55) probably built the present W front, with its twin towers and rows of lancet windows. It is the only EE example of a twin-towered façade of its kind in England, for at Wells the towers stand clear of the aisles. Some have found its severe restraint flat and lifeless but, like the whole outside of the church, it must have had more impact before the loss of the leaded spires to all three towers in the 1660s. The E end of the choir is a Dec. reconstruction of the last quarter of the 13C. The SE corner of the central tower collapsed c 1450, and the S and E sides were rebuilt in the Perp. style, leaving the Trans. work of the N and W sides unaltered. Finally, the nave was enlarged by the addition of aisles at the end of the 16C.

The *Nave* and aisles are now unusually wide, the Perp. alterations contrasting with the much older work from Archbishop Roger's time at the E and W ends. The base of a pillar from the 10C cathedral survives in the N aisle. The pulpit is a fine work of 1913. The *Transepts* keep Archbishop Roger's design in fair completeness but the rebuilt Perp. S and E tower arches give the crossing an unfinished look. The Gothic pulpit in the N transept was originally above the rich stone screen (c 1480, with later statues). The organ case above the screen is by Sir Gilbert Scott (1860).

The *Choir, with its unusual glazed triforium (or double clerestory), is a remarkable mixture of three building periods: Trans., Dec. and Perp. The Geometric tracery of the great E window, and the naturalistic foliage of the capitals in the two E bays, are characteristic of the finest Dec. work. The roof has some superb gilded bosses (c 1300). The stalls,.with their excellent set of *misericords, were carved c 1489–94 by the local school which also made the stalls at Manchester and Beverley. Scott restored them in the 19C. The ornate reredos is by Sir Ninian Comper (1922). The choir aisles end in chapels; that of St Wilfrid, on the N, is believed to have contained the saint's shrine.

On the S side of the choir is the apsidal Norman *Chapter House*. The undercroft below was restored in 1948–60 as a chapel and choir vestry. The Dec. Lady Chapel, or Lady Loft, in a very unusual position above the Chapter House, now houses the *Chapter Library* (open by request).

The *Crypt, one of the half-dozen Saxon crypts in the country, was built by St Wilfrid, like the one at Hexham. Now containing church treasures, it has a central chamber for displaying relics and wall niches for holding lights. The narrow hole on the N side is known as 'St Wilfrid's Needle'; the ability to crawl through it was once taken as a proof of chastity.

The pleasant buildings in Minster Rd on the N side of the cathedral include remains of the medieval Canon Fee Court, with the 19C *Courthouse* behind, and the *Old Deanery*, a much altered 16C building now a hotel.—Bedern Bank leads from the W end of the cathedral down to the river Skell. High St Agnesgate, on the left, has the ruined 15C chapel of *St Anne's Hospital*. Low St Agnesgate and St Marysgate lead N from the end of the street to the chapel of the *Hospital of St Mary Magdalen*, founded for lepers by Archbishop Thurstan (d. 1140), near the Ure bridge.

The landscaped gardens of ***Studley Royal** and the lovely ruins of ***Fountains Abbey** lie off B6265 to the W of Ripon, with sideroads

*Fountains Abbey: a woodcut from Thomas Gent's 'The Antient and Modern History of the Loyal Town of Rippon' (1733)*

leading to entrances at 1½m and 3m respectively. First linked together as one great estate in the 18C, they have been reunited since 1983 in a single NT property of 680 acres.

We visit the abbey first, starting at the W entrance. Close by stands *Fountains Hall* (open), a handsome Jacobean mansion built mainly of monastic stone. The ruins beyond, among the largest and best preserved in England, are beautifully sited in the wooded valley of the little river Skell. The abbey was founded in 1132 by a breakaway group of Benedictines from St Mary's, York, but taken over by the Cistercians in 1135. It had become the wealthiest Cistercian found-

Key to Numbers
1 Kitchen
2 Chapel
3 Misercord
4 Pentise
5 Prison
6 Sacristy

**FOUNTAINS ABBEY**

ation in England by the middle of the next century. The buildings, on a scale which everywhere reflects the abbey's importance, belong to four main periods. To the first (1135–47) belong the nave and transepts of the church; to the second (1147–79), the gradual reconstruction of the domestic buildings; to the third (1220–47), the rebuilding of the church's E end; and to the fourth (1498–1526), the addition of the church's tall Perp. tower.

Substantial remains of the *Church* survive, notably the nave, 11 bays long and complete to ceiling height, a grand example of austere Cistercian architecture. Note the pointed arcade above the solid Norman piers. The *Chapel of the Nine Altars at the extreme E end is a miracle of delicate design, close in date to the similar chapel at Durham cathedral. The Perp. tower stands in an unusual position, at the end of the N transept. In the vestry off the S transept is the tomb of a knight (c 1300) of the Percy or Mowbray family.

The most remarkable of the buildings around the cloister is the *undercroft of the *Lay Brothers' Dormitory* on the W side, supported on a central row of 19 pillars, Now open from end to end, it was originally divided into the *Lay Brothers' Refectory*, storerooms, etc. The size of the refectory, the dormitory above, its extension across the river, and the *Lay Brothers' Infirmary*, spanning the river further W, are all reminders of how large a lay community was attached to Cistercian monasteries. On the E side of the cloister is the *Chapter House*, with three fine entrance arches and abbots' tombstones. Next to it are the parlour and undercroft of the *Monks' Dormitory*. On the S side are, from the E: the *Warming Room* with its huge fireplace, the only heated room in a Cistercian monastery; the fine *Monks' Refectory*, with tall lancet windows and a laver outside the door; and the small *Kitchen*. Above the Warming Room is the *Muniment Room*, reached by the monks' day stairs. E of the cloister buildings, and built partly across the Skell, are the foundations of the huge *Monks' Infirmary*.

A lovely walk along the valley E of the ruins brings us to the landscaped gardens of Studley Royal, developed by John Aislabie, MP for Ripon and Chancellor of the Exchequer, after his involvement in the South Sea Bubble forced his retirement from public life in 1720. His designs, on the grand scale and in the formal Dutch manner, exploited the picturesque prospect of the ruins and in 1767 his son William Aislabie, who continued the work, added Fountains to the estate.

The Skell is canalised to supply a series of striking water gardens: the *Crescent Pond*, the *Moon Pond*, cascades and a lake. The *'surprise view' of the abbey is the best of several contrived vistas. The garden buildings artfully dotted about the landscape include the *Temple of Piety*, the *Octagonal Tower* and the *Banqueting House*—the last, like the stables, probably by Colen Campbell, the pioneer of English Palladianism. Beyond the water gardens are the deer park and the sumptuous *St Mary's Church* (1871–78; William Burges), looking along the avenue of limes to the towers of Ripon cathedral. Aislabie's house does not survive.

Beyond Fountains B6265 continues SW to (9m) *Pateley Bridge* (Rte 86B).

There are several good country houses near Ripon. *Markenfield Hall* (limited opening), off A61 3½m SW, is an early 14–16C manor house with a moat. *Newby Hall* (open), off B6265 4m SE, is a Queen Anne house remodelled by Robert Adam in 1767–80. His lovely *interior contains plasterwork by Joseph Rose, one of only five sets of Gobelins tapestries made for an English house, and a sculpture gallery housing the collection of the dilettante William Weddell. There are pleasant gardens and grounds, with *Skelton* church (1871–72; William Burges), the counterpart to his church at Studley Royal. *Norton Conyers* (open), off A61 3½m N, is medieval in origin but largely 17–18C in appearance, with a fine park and walled garden. The family legend that a madwoman had been confined in the attic during the 18C may have suggested the fate of the first Mrs Rochester to Charlotte Brontë, who visited the house in 1839.

From Ripon to *Wensleydale*, via *Leyburn*, *Hawes* and *Kendal*, see Rte 86D.

The main route continues on A61 from Ripon, crossing the Ure, then (30m) A1 (Rte 85B), and finally the Swale at (32½m) the pleasant little village of *Skipton-on-Swale*.—37½m. **Thirsk**, see Rte 85A.

# 81 Doncaster to York

Total distance 34m. We follow A19 throughout.—To (20m) Selby.
—To (34m) **York**.

Maps: OS Landranger 111, 105.

Doncaster is at the end of Rte 59, up the A1 from Stamford.

**Doncaster** (81,600 inhab.; Tourist Information), by the river Don on
the site of the Roman *Danum*, has been known for horseracing since
the 17C and for railway engineering since the Great Northern
Railway established its workshops here in the 19C. The racecourse
still flourishes, though the Plant Works (as they are known locally) no
longer play a major part in the town's industry.

The parish church of *St George* (1854–58), replacing a medieval
church destroyed by fire, is one of Sir Gilbert Scott's grandest works.
The *Mansion House* (1745–48; James Paine), is one of only three
official Lord Mayor's residences in the country; the other two are in
York and London. The *Museum and Art Gallery* on Chequer Rd has
collections of local history, geology and natural history; glassware
and ceramics, including Yorkshire pottery; Dutch paintings; horseracing exhibits; and a gallery of the King's Own Yorkshire Light
Infantry Regiment.

The racecourse, on the Town Moor to the E, has a modern
grandstand and exhibition centre. Its oldest classic race, the St Leger,
was established in 1776 and is run during the second week of
September; tradition has it that 'winter comes in with the tail of the
last horse in the Leger'. The William Hill Lincoln Handicap in March
begins the flat-racing season in Britain.

*Cusworth Hall Museum*, off A638 about 2¹/₂m NW, occupies a mid-18C house
by George Platt and James Paine set in its own parkland. Its collections
illustrate the everyday life of local people over the last 200 years. The chapel
and billiard room have plasterwork by Joseph Rose.—The interesting church at
*Sprotbrough*, 3m W of Doncaster, has good woodwork and a curious stone seat
in the chancel, apparently 14C and perhaps a sanctuary chair.

At **Conisbrough**, in the valley of the Don 5m SW of Doncaster by A630, the
Norman castle built c 1180 by Hamelin, half-brother of Henry II, has perhaps
the best circular *keep in England (English Heritage, standard opening). The
parish church has fine capitals and a carved 12C tomb chest.—A630 continues
to (11m) Rotherham and A6109 or A6178 to (17¹/₂m) *Sheffield*, both in Rte 75G.

FROM DONCASTER TO HULL. The quick way, avoiding Goole, is by M18 and
M62. The slower way (46m) takes A630 NE from Doncaster to join A18.
—7¹/₂m. Hatfield, with a good 12–15C church, is in *Hatfield Chase*, part of the
district known as the 'Levels', mostly under water until drained by Cornelius
Vermuyden in 1626.—A18 joins A614 on the way to (10¹/₂m) *Thorne*, a small
town with a church of c 1300, on the W edge of a great peat moor. The large
church at *Fishlake*, 2m W, has a lavishly decorated late Norman S *doorway of
c 1170.—A614 skirts the Don, canalised lower down by Vermuyden as the Aire
and Calder Navigation, and touches the Aire at (17¹/₂m) *Rawcliffe*.—20¹/₂m.
**Goole** (18,400 inhab.; Tourist Information), brought into existence by the
opening of the docks in 1826, stands at the meeting of the Don and the Ouse not
far from the point where the Ouse joins the Trent to form the Humber. The Aire
and Calder Navigation Company built the conspicuous church in 1843–48.
From Goole to Lincoln, see Rte 72.—22m. *Boothferry Bridge* crosses the Ouse.
—23m. *Howden* and on to (47m) *Hull*, see the detour from Selby below.

From Doncaster to *Nottingham* via *Mansfield* and *Worksop*, see Rte 58A; to
*Stamford*, see Rte 59; to *Leeds*, see Rte 75F; to *Sheffield*, see Rte 75G; to
*Durham*, *Newcastle* and *Berwick*, see Rte 85B.

After crossing the Don we bear right on A19 and continue N across a system of rivers and canals to (18½m) *Brayton*, where the 14–15C church has a fine tower, chancel arch and S doorway with notable carving of c 1150.

20m. **Selby** (10,700 inhab.; Tourist Information), a market and manufacturing town by the tidal Ouse, is a dull place except for the magnificent *'Abbey Church*, one of the most perfect monastic churches in England.

The Benedictine abbey was founded in 1069. The first stage of church building took place in c 1100–c 1230, embracing the transition from Norman to EE; the choir was rebuilt on a grander scale and the nave windows enlarged, in the Dec. style, in c 1280–1340.

The W front has a superb Norman doorway with EE blind arcading above; the W window is a Perp. insertion and the two W towers were raised a storey by J. Olrid Scott in 1935. The Nave displays several distinct periods of building. Norman work (c 1100–1123) appears in the four E bays on the N side and two on the S side, and the four tower arches. At the W end the architecture becomes Trans., with pure EE in the S triforium and both clerestories. The *S Transept* was rebuilt by Scott in 1912 on the site of the old transept ruined by the fall of the central tower in 1690. The *N Transept* has a lofty Perp. window with 20C glass.

The *'Choir* is Dec. throughout, though of more than one period, with the remains of rich sculpture and a charming triforium balustrade. The sedilia were almost certainly designed c 1380 by Henry Yevele, architect of the nave at Canterbury. The great *'E window* (c 1340) is a Jesse window with a fine Doom in its beautiful Flamboyant tracery. The arms of the Washington family appear in a window of the S choir clerestory. The War Memorial Chapel S of the choir contains a 15C alabaster *'Deposition* by the Nottingham School. The N porch has a Norman doorway as good as the one on the W front; its upper storey is decorated with EE blind arcading.

*Drax*, off A1041 6½m SE, is dominated by its huge power station. The partly Norman church is notable for its carved figures and its 16C bench ends. A1041 continues to (6m) *Carlton Towers* (limited opening), a 17C house transformed into an extravagant Gothic mansion in 1873–77 by E.W. Pugin and John Francis Bentley, architect of Westminster Cathedral. *Snaith*, 1½m further, has a 13–15C church with Dawnay tombs.

FROM SELBY TO HULL, 34m. We take A63, branching E from A19.—At (5m) *Hemingbrough* the 12–15C church has a tall *'spire*, good woodwork and a set of bench ends.—*Wressle*, to the left beyond (7m) the Derwent bridge, has the ruins of a 14C castle belonging to the Percys, Earls of Northumberland.—10m. **Howden** *'church*, one of the most important in the region, was rebuilt after it was made collegiate in 1267. It is thus Dec., but of different dates. The *'W front* (1306–11) is a beautiful composition, and the crossing tower (completed in the 15C) is one of the finest in Yorkshire. The nave and crossing are used as the parish church. The Saltmarsh Chapel contains family tombs from the 14C to the 20C. The 14C choir and early Perp. chapter house are ruined but keep many beautiful details. The chronicler Roger of Hovedon (d. 1201?) was rector of Howden, and his statue stands in front of the market hall. The novelist Nevil Shute (1899–1960) worked with Barnes Wallis on the design of the R100, Britain's last successful airship, here in 1923.—Beyond Howden A63 continues as B1230, running alongside M62 past (11½m) the turning for *Eastrington*, with an interesting church. At (19m) the end of M62, we join A63 again and bear S near the foot of the Wolds.—24m. **Brough**, to the right, is the site of the Roman station of *Petuaria*, one of the few in England identified by an inscription found on the actual site. The fort guarded the ferry by which Ermine Street crossed the Humber.—34m. *Hull*, see Rte 82A.

From Selby to *Leeds*, see Rte 75F.

B1223 and B1222, heading N from Selby, offer an alternative to the main route to York described below.—4½m. *Cawood* has the 15C gatehouse to the palace of the Archbishops of York, where Wolsey was arrested in 1530.—7½m. *Stillingfleet* church has a Norman *'S doorway*, with ironwork on the door showing Viking influence, and the 14C effigy of a knight.—14½m. *York*, see below.

The main route crosses the Ouse by the Selby toll bridge and continues N on A19 through flat countryside.

34m. **YORK** (99,800 inhab.) is one of the most attractive old cities in England, despite dull patches of 19C and 20C development close to the centre and despite the hordes of tourists who have made its historic quarters increasingly self-conscious. The city walls, themselves among York's main attractions, enclose streets which follow their narrow and irregular medieval course, with overhanging rows of old buildings and parish churches whose stained glass echoes the chief glory of the city's great Minster. The local purple-grey brick is used to particularly handsome effect in the 18C houses which evoke York's prosperity in a later age.

**Tourist Information Centres**: De Grey Rooms, Exhibition Square; Railway Station, Station Rd.

**Car Parks**: Marygate, Esplanade, Leeman Rd, Nunnery Lane, Bishophill, St George's Field, Paragon St., City Mills, Foss Bank, Heworth Green, Union Terrace.

**Bus Station**: Rougier St.

**Railway Station**: Station Rd, S of the river.

**Theatre**: Theatre Royal, St Leonard's Place.

**History**. The Brigantian settlement was garrisoned by Vespasian's nephew Quintus Petillius Cerialis in AD 71 and, as *Eboracum*, became headquarters of the 6th Legion and capital of the province of Lower (i.e. Northern) Britain. Stone city walls replaced earth ramparts in the early 2C. Hadrian was the first emperor to visit York, in AD 121, while Septimius Severus and Constantius Chlorus both died in the city (211 and 306). On the latter's death Constantine the Great was proclaimed Emperor of Western Rome here, the only time an emperor was proclaimed in Britain. *Eoforwic*, the Saxon town which emerged after the Romans' withdrawal in AD 407, took a leading role in the spread of Christianity throughout Northern England. Paulinus baptised King Edwin of Northumbria here in 627 and York became one of the chief centres of European learning while Alcuin (734–802) was 'Magister Scholarum'. Danish invaders captured the city in 867, naming it *Jorvik* and making it an important port and trading centre. As in other English cities, the suffix '-gate' in street names is a legacy of their presence (cf. the modern Danish '-gade').

William the Conqueror established two castles; city gates and walls were built in the 12–14C. As capital of Northern England, York was favoured by the Plantagenets: Henry I granted its first charter, Henry II and Edward II held parliaments here and in 1328 Edward III married Philippa of Hainault in the Minster. The Duke of York became the title of the sovereign's second son. The Minster and several monastic foundations made York a religious centre, while its prosperity as a port and a staple town of the wool trade fostered powerful guilds. These were responsible for the York Mystery Cycle, 48 plays dating from about 1340 and making up one of the four surviving cycles in England. They are still performed in York about every three or four years.

During the Civil War the city surrendered to the Parliamentary forces under General Fairfax after the Royalist defeat at Marston Moor in 1644. The 18C made York a fashionable social centre, where the gentry of the North maintained town houses. George Hudson, the fraudulent 'Railway King', was Lord Mayor in the 1830s and 1840s, and his influence made York headquarters of the North-Eastern Railway. In the 19C, too, the chocolate-making firms of Rowntree's (recently taken over by Nestlés) and Terry's expanded to occupy their present importance in the city's industrial life.

**Famous natives, residents and visitors**. Natives include the conspirator Guy Fawkes (1570–1606); the sculptor John Flaxman (1755–1826); the painters William Etty (1787–1849) and Albert Moore (1841–93); the architect and inventor of the hansom cab J.A. Hansom (1803–82); and the poet W.H. Auden (1907–73). Margaret Clitherow, canonised as St Margaret of York in 1970, was pressed to death in 1586 after being accused of sheltering Jesuit priests. Laurence Sterne lodged here in the 1740s and a Stonegate printer first issued 'Tristram Shandy' (1760–67). The highwayman Dick Turpin was tried and hanged at York in 1739, and the murderer Eugene Aram in 1759. Turpin's famous ride to York was in fact made by Swift Nick (William Nevinson) in the 17C and added to the Turpin legend by William Harrison Ainsworth in his novel 'Rookwood' (1834).

YORK

0 _____ 200 yards
0 _____ 200 metres

N

EAST END

St Stephen's Chapel

All Saints' Chapel

11

10

Lady Chapel

7

High Altar

12

Entrance to Crypt

8

PRESBYTERY

Zouche Chapel

CHAPTER HOUSE

Vestry

CONSISTORY COURT

VESTIBULE

St Nicholas' Chapel

9

1

2
3

4

5

6

Screen

CENTRAL

PORCH

Stairs down

'Five Sisters' Window

TOWER

Nave Altar

St George's Chapel

St John's Chapel

Minster Shop

Plan of Undercroft

Pulpit

Choir Practice Room (Above)

Emergency Exit

Down from South Transept

St Cuthbert's Chapel

Undercroft Museum Floor

Foundation strengthening

Key to Numbers
1 Astronomical Clock
2 Abp Greenfield
3 Admiral Cradock
4 Abp Walter de Grey
5 Dean Duncombe
6 Abp Thomson
7 Site of Shrine of St William of York (?)
8 Abp Savage
9 William de Hatfield
10 Abp Bowet
11 Abp Scrope
12 Abp Dolben

WEST FRONT

0                    100 ft

0          30 ms

# YORK MINSTER

THE MINSTER AND ITS ENVIRONS. ***York Minster**, in the N corner of the old city, is the largest English medieval cathedral and ranks second only to Canterbury in ecclesiastical importance. The Archbishop of York holds the title Primate of England (Canterbury is Primate of All England), and his sway extends over 14 dioceses in the North Midlands and the North. Though called a minster (from the Latin *monasterium*), the cathedral was never monastic and so lacks a cloister or domestic buildings. Its architecture covers three periods: EE (transepts), Dec. (nave and chapter house), and early and late Perp. (choir and towers). As at Canterbury, the atmosphere suffers from the large number of visitors.

The present Minster is the latest of several to stand on the site. The first was the wooden chapel put up for the baptism of King Edwin of Northumbria and his court by Paulinus on Easter Day 627. Its stone successor was destroyed in the troubles following the Norman Conquest. Thomas of Bayeux, the first Norman archbishop, began rebuilding c 1080, though his choir was soon rebuilt again by Archbishop Roger of Pont-l'Evêque (1154–81). The building we see today gradually replaced this Norman church. Archbishop Walter de Grey (1215–55) rebuilt the S transept (c 1220–40) and began the new N transept (1240–60). A new nave was started in 1291 and completed c 1345. The Norman choir was replaced by the present one in 1360–1405. The W towers were complete by 1474 and the central tower by c 1480, bringing to an end the labour of nearly 250 years.

Structural investigation in 1967 showed that the central tower and the E and W ends were in danger of collapse. The foundations of the four columns supporting the central tower were encased in reinforced concrete, and repairs made to the W towers and E end. The Minster has also suffered several damaging fires: in the choir (1829), nave (1840) and the roof of the S transept (July 1984).

The best view of the exterior is from the city walls (see below). Its finest parts are the *W façade, particularly the great window and finely sculptured portal; the N transept, especially the façade and 'Five Sisters' window; the octagonal chapter house; and above all the great *central tower.

The glory of the Minster inside is its * *stained glass, mainly by a well-defined local school of artists and craftsmen. The *Nave* is unusually tall and broad, with widely spaced piers and the triforium virtually suppressed to create the largest possible space for the glass. The design presupposes a stone vault which was never built, and the present wooden roof (part of Sydney Smirke's restoration after the 1840 fire) continues the earlier deception by being painted to look like stone. There is superb tracery in the large clerestory windows and particularly in the great *W window (1338), where the upper part suggests the shape of a heart. Unlike the nave, the unusually wide aisles are stone vaulted. Their W windows have fine glass, and the second window from the W in the N aisle contains a panel of the oldest glass in England (c 1150). Besides the 14C glass elsewhere in the aisles, the remains of 12–13C glass in the clerestories are worth studying. All round the nave and choir, below the triforium, are painted stone shields of Edward II and the barons who met in parliament at York in 1309–10.

The tall Perp. lantern at the crossing and the spacious transepts, with aisles on their W as well as their E sides, create an impression of size which is hardly lessened by the obtrusive triforium and correspondingly meagre clerestory. The *S Transept*, with its rose window of c 1500 and the tomb of Archbishop de Grey, has been restored after the fire of 1984. The *N Transept* is dominated by the tall lancet lights of the *'Five Sisters', with their wonderful 13C grisaille glass. The wooden vaulting dates from 1934–51 but incorporates many bosses and ribs from the 15C ceiling. The astronomical clock (1955; Sir Albert Richardson) is a memorial to the airmen based in North-East England who died in World War II.

From the E aisle of the N transept a *vestibule leads to the *Chapter House* (fee). Built in 1260–1300, both are among the supreme examples of Dec. work in England, second only to their counterparts at Southwell Minster. They preserve contemporary glass of rare quality set in lovely tracery, and over 250 carved stone heads and almost 300 foliage capitals and pendants. The octagonal chapter house is unsupported by any central column, though (unlike Southwell) the vaulting is of wood rather than stone.

In the SW corner of the S transept is the entrance to the *Undercroft Museum* (fee) in the space excavated during the repairs of 1966–72. The reinforced concrete encasing the foundations of the central piers contrasts powerfully with the exposed foundation walls of the present Minister, its Norman predecessor and the Roman headquarters building. Pre-Conquest sculpture and capitals from Archbishop Thomas's cathedral, unearthed during the repairs, are on display. The adjoining treasury in part of the original Norman crypt contains, among its magnificent collection of church plate and domestic silver, the 11C Horn of Ulph and the mazer bowl traditionally connected with Archbishop Scrope (see below).

The *Choir* is separated from the nave by an elaborate stone rood screen, traditionally dated c 1475–1500, with life-size statues of English kings (all original except Henry VI). The vaulted entrance has a central boss of the Assumption of the Virgin (c 1150), Byzantine in manner. The glass in the great *E window, by John Thornton of Coventry (1405), forms the largest expanse of medieval glazing in England and probably in the world. The soaring windows of the E transeptal bays contain 15C glass showing the lives of St Cuthbert and St William of York, whose miracle-working shrine is believed to have stood behind the high altar. All the woodwork in the choir was destroyed in the fire of 1829, and the stalls, by Sir Robert Smirke, are an approximate reproduction of the originals. The traceried altar screen (1831) is a free copy of its 15C predecessor.

The N choir aisle has the monument of Archbishop Savage (d. 1507), with a restored chantry, and the damaged but finely wrought effigy tomb of William of Hatfield (d. 1336), Edward III's son. The *Lady Chapel* has the splendid tomb of Archbishop Bowet (d. 1423); opposite is the plain, restored monument of Archbishop Scrope, beheaded in 1405 (see Shakespeare's 'Henry IV, Part 2'). The S choir aisle has monuments of Archbishops Dolben (d. 1686) and Lamplugh (d. 1691) by Grinling Gibbons and of William Burgh (d. 1808) by Westmacott. Steps lead down from this aisle to the Zouche Chapel (1352).

The late Norman *E Crypt*, entered from the choir aisles, holds great archaeological and architectural interest. Its structure shows the extent of Archbishop Roger's choir and the pillars, probably dating from the time of Archbishop Thomas (c 1080), have capitals with intricate Romanesque carving. The font marks the site of Paulinus's original wooden chapel. Beneath a trapdoor is the base of a pillar of the Roman praetorium.

In Dean's Park, N of the Minster, there is a fragment of the cloister belonging to Archbishop Roger's Norman *Archbishop's Palace*. Its 13C chapel, built by Archbishop de Grey, has been used since the 19C as the *Minster Library* (open), now connected with the University of York. The exhibition of its main treasures includes the baptismal entry for Guy Fawkes from St Michael-le-Belfrey (see below).

Immediately E of the Minster is *St William's College* (open when not in use). Originally a prebendal house, it was enlarged c 1461 for the chantry priests attached to the Minster and much altered after the Dissolution. Restored in the 20C as the meeting place of the Northern Convocation, it is now used for meetings of all kinds. It keeps a fine timbered roof and carved figures. To the left in Minster Yard stands the *Treasurer's House* (NT), a 17C building on a site used since Roman times, with good 17–18C furniture.

Opposite the S transept of the Minster a Roman column from the headquarters of the 6th Legion has been re-erected. The late Perp. church of *St Michael-le-Belfrey* has some magnificent 14C and 16C *stained glass; Guy Fawkes, probably born at what is now Young's Hotel in Petergate, was baptised here in 1570. Nearby Stonegate, reached by the alley between the column and the church, is one of York's prettiest streets of old buildings. A passage leads from it to the remnant of a Norman house, now an open courtyard. Low Petergate leads from the beginning of Stonegate to Goodramgate and the 13–14C *Holy Trinity*, York's quaintest church, with box pews and a fine E window of 1470–80. The mid 14C houses of Lady Row further along Goodramgate are the oldest in York.

THE CITY WALLS. Goodramgate continues NE to Monk Bar and the *City Walls*, among the finest surviving examples of medieval city fortification in Europe. Much restored in their present form, they date mainly from the reign of Edward III (1327–77), though the gates (or bars) incorporate Norman work and the N section of the walls follows the line of the smaller Roman system built in the 2C. The full circuit of about 2¹⁄₂m is worth making, and the stretch between Monk Bar and Bootham Bar is particularly attractive.

*Monk Bar* (open), probably taking its name from a nearby monastic house, is the tallest of the four main gates and, like the others, has a Norman core. It was encased in the 14C, when the portcullises were added. We mount the wall and follow it to the left, round the N angle, with lovely views of the Minster more than compensating for the dull prospect outside the wall. *Bootham Bar*, the only gate on the site of a Roman one, was rebuilt in the 18C and 19C but keeps its Norman archway.

Museum Gardens, with its fragment of the Roman wall, is described later in the tour of the city. For the moment, we leave the wall and follow St Leonard's Place and Museum St. to Lendal Bridge, with the *Lendal Tower*, largely rebuilt in the 19C. We rejoin the wall at the *North St. Postern* on the opposite bank of the river. There is a good view back to the Minster from the stretch leading to *Toft Tower* at the W corner. *Micklegate Bar* (open), shortly beyond, is the chief of the four original gates. Richard of York's head was displayed here in 1460–61 and those of Jacobite rebels in 1746. Beyond the 19C *Victoria Bar* and the S angle of the walls we skirt the mound of *Baile Hill*, site of one of William the Conqueror's two castles. We cross the river by the iron *Skeldergate Bridge*, pass the *Castle* (see below), cross the Foss or canal, and regain the wall at *Fishergate Postern* (c 1505), in a dreary neighbourhood. From here we follow the top of the wall past *Fishergate Bar* to *Walmgate Bar*, the only one which still has its barbican or outwork. The stretch between the brick 16C *Red Tower* and *Layerthorpe Bridge* was never walled, as the city was protected here by a marsh. At the bridge we remount the wall; beyond the *Merchant Taylors' Hall* on the left (see below) is the foundation of the Roman E bastion.

THE CITY ART GALLERY AND MUSEUM GARDENS. We begin at Bootham Bar, reached on the walk along the city walls or by taking High Petergate from the W end of the Minster, past the house where the Cavalier and traveller Sir Thomas Herbert (1606–82) died.

The **City Art Gallery** dominates Exhibition Square. Its wide-ranging collection illustrates most developments in Western European painting from the 14C to the present.

Continental painting is displayed in the *Main Gallery* on the ground floor. Among the Italian pictures are a group of good early Florentine and Sienese panels, including two scenes from the life of St Clement by Fungai, and work by Foschi (Agony in the Garden), Parmigianino (Portrait), Domenichino (Monsignor Agucchi) and Bellotto (View in Lucca). Among the Northern European pictures are some good early panels, including Bernhard Strigel's Sleeping Soldier, and work by Baburen (Roman Charity), van Streek (Vanitas), van Goyen (Peasants and Horsemen) and Snyders (Game Stall). Spanish painting is represented by Valdés Leal (Jesuit Conversion) and Melendez (Still Life); French painting by J.F. Millet (Nobleman of Capernaum), Watteau (Le Defilé) and Gravelot (Le Lecteur).

British painting is displayed in the *South Gallery* on the ground floor. The interesting collection of early portraits includes work by George Gower (?), Edward Bower and Lely. The 18C section includes work by Francis Cotes, de Loutherbourg, William Marlow, Philip Mercier and Reynolds. A room is devoted to nude studies and historical subjects by William Etty, born in York.

The *Burton Gallery* on the first floor has a wide range of 19–20C art: apocalyptic landscapes by John Martin and Francis Danby; genre pictures by Thomas Faed and others; canvases by G.F. Watts and Albert Moore; late 19C French paintings, including Barbizon School landscapes and work by Ribot, Bonvin and Fantin-Latour; and paintings by most important British artists of the period 1900–50, notably Sickert, Gilman, Gore, Gwen John and Nash.

The *Pottery Gallery* on the first floor contains the finest holding of Staite Murray's work, and important examples by Bernard Leach, Shoji Hamada and other potters of the period 1920–60. There is a continuous programme of temporary exhibitions, mostly shown in the *Exhibition Gallery* on the first floor.

Next door is the lovely **King's Manor**, originally the abbot's lodging
of St Mary's Abbey (see below) and assigned after the Dissolution to
the Lord President of the Council of the North. Founded c 1270 but
dating mostly from an enlargement of 1485–90, it was visited by
Henry VIII, James I, Charles I and occupied by Strafford while he was
Lord President in 1628–40. The artist Francis Place (1647–1728) lived
here, and Dickens and 'Phiz' stayed with the cathedral organist on
their way back from Teesdale in 1838. The building is now used by
the University of York; its courtyards and public rooms are open.

Across St Leonard's Place are the De Grey Rooms, with the Tourist
Information Centre, and the *Theatre Royal*, opened on this site as the
New Theatre in 1740. The building, several times altered since the
18C, incorporates the 12C vaulted crypt of St Peter's Hospital,
founded by Athelstan and rebuilt by William Rufus.

At the end of St Leonard's Place we turn right, into Museum St., for
Museum Gardens. Stretching down to the river, these pleasantly
laid-out grounds of the Yorkshire Museum contain an interesting
medley of ruins and old buildings. On the right as we enter are the
remains of *St Leonard's Hospital*, founded by Archbishop Thomas
(d. 1116) to replace Athelstan's 10C hospital. The ruined passage,
undercroft and chapel date from the 13C. At the corner of the city
wall beyond is the *Multangular Tower*, medieval in its upper stages
and 4C Roman below. The inside, with a collection of Roman coffins
unearthed in various parts of the city, can be seen from the grounds
of the *Public Library*.

The **Yorkshire Museum** is housed in William Wilkins's building for
the Yorkshire Philosophical Society (1827). It contains displays of
geology and natural history together with an outstanding *collection
of archaeology.

The Roman Life gallery has the central fragment of Trajan's gateway (AD
107–08), some fine mosaics, tombstones, altars, the preserved hair of a Roman
lady and a reconstructed Roman kitchen. The Anglo-Saxon and Viking Life
gallery has an impressive array of Viking artefacts, including the 8C silver gilt
Ormside Bowl and the Gilling Sword. There is also a large display of Yorkshire
pottery. Regular special exhibitions are held in addition to the permanent
galleries.

The museum's basement is built around the fireplace and part of the
chapter house of the Benedictine **St Mary's Abbey**, founded c 1080
by Stephen of Lastingham and enlarged by William Rufus. The ruins
of the *Abbey Church* begun by Abbot Simon of Warwick in 1259
consist chiefly of the N wall and part of the W front. The foundations
of the E end of the original Norman church, with seven apses, have
been partly excavated. The N door of the nave looks into the
churchyard of *St Olave's*, with Etty's tomb. The church has some 15C
glass. The *Abbey Gatehouse* (not open) adjoins it and the precinct
wall runs from the river around the N corner of the gardens,
originally meeting the city walls at Bootham Bar. The abbey's 16C
*Hospitium*, or guest house, by the river is administered by the
Yorkshire Museum and is open for special exhibitions as advertised.
A fragment of the water gate stands nearby.

SOUTH FROM MUSEUM GARDENS TO THE CASTLE AND BACK. Lendal
and Blake St both lead S from Museum St. to St Helen's Square. The
former *Judge's Lodging*, now a hotel, in Lendal is a fine building of
1718–25. The *Assembly Rooms* (open except when in use for functions) in Blake St. were built in 1732–36 by the 3rd Earl of Burlington,
the patron of Palladianism in England. Inside is an Egyptian Hall,

with double rows of columns, as derived by Palladio from Vitruvius. The mural paintings of Roman York in the Rotunda endow Constantine the Great with Burlington's features. St Helen's Square, the centre of modern York and site of the main gate to the Roman city, is overlooked by the church of *St Helen*, which preserves some 15C glass. The *Mansion House* (open by prior arrangement), facing the church, was built in 1725–26 as the official home of the Lord Mayor; the only other Mansion Houses in England are at Doncaster and London. The 15C *Guildhall* (open), by the river behind the Mansion House, has been rebuilt on the old lines since World War II bomb damage.

Coney St. heads S from the square, passing *St Martin-le-Grand*, a late Perp. church partly rebuilt by George Pace after wartime bomb damage. In Spurriergate, beyond, the 12–15C church of *St Michael* was sadly truncated by road widening but still has some medieval glass inside. Spurriergate is continued by Nessgate.

In the shopping centre off Coppergate, to the left, the hugely popular **Jorvik Viking Centre** occupies the site of the Danish Viking neighbourhood excavated by the York Archaeological Trust. It contains interesting displays of the objects unearthed and the archaeological techniques employed, but the gimmicky presentation—with journeys by electrically operated train through a reconstructed Viking street—cheapens its subject.

We continue S along Castlegate. The redundant 13–15C church of St Mary on the lefthand side has become a heritage centre, the *York Story*. *Fairfax House** (open), built by John Carr for Viscount Fairfax of Emley in 1755–62, has been well restored by the York Civic Trust. It has superb plaster ceilings and wrought ironwork, and now houses the outstanding Noel Terry collection of 18C furniture, paintings, porcelain and clocks. Carr also built *Castlegate House* (1763) opposite.

The **Castle**, one of the two established at York by William the Conqueror, is now largely replaced by John Carr's Assize Courts (1773–77) and the Museum. The chief remaining medieval fragment is the 13C *Clifford's Tower* (English Heritage, standard opening and summer Sunday mornings), with its remarkable quatrefoil ground plan, on the mound thrown up by the Conqueror. The wooden Norman keep was destroyed during the anti-Jewish riots of 1190, in which 150 Jews who had fled here for sanctuary were killed. The **Castle Museum** (open) is housed in the former Female Prison (1780; John Carr) and the old Debtors' Prison (1705). Its rich folk collections were begun by the enterprising Dr J.L. Kirk of Pickering (d. 1940).

The outstanding feature is Kirkgate, a reconstructed 19C street with cobbles, shops and a hansom cab. There are also 17–20C interiors, an 18C automaton clock and, among the Victoriana, royal commemorative ware. The Debtors' Prison has the condemned cell where Dick Turpin and Eugene Aram were held; a reconstructed Edwardian street; craftsmen's workshops; costumes and toys; and a military collection. The mill outside is open and working in summer. Part of the castle's outer wall, protecting the city between the Ouse and the Foss, survives behind the museum and the assize courts.

From the castle we return N along Castlegate and turn right into Coppergate for The Pavement. *All Saints*, at its W end, is a partly rebuilt 15C church with an elegant octagonal lantern on its square tower and a curious brass knocker on the N door. In The Pavement itself stands the half-timbered Jacobean house where Sir Thomas Herbert was born in 1606.

*The drawing room ceiling of Fairfax House in York*

The *Merchant Adventurers' Hall* in Fossgate, leading S from the E end of The Pavement, was built by York's most powerful guild, which controlled the northern cloth-export trade in the 15–17C. The Great Hall (1357–68) has splendid timberwork. Underneath is the Hospital, occupied by the guild's pensioners until 1900, with massive wooden piers and a 15C chapel, altered in the 17C. There is a pleasant garden. Beyond the bridge Fossgate is continued by Walmgate, with two interesting churches: *St Denys*, with a Norman S doorway moved from its original place and good 14C glass, and *St Margaret* (not open), rebuilt in the 19C but with an elaborate *porch of c 1160 brought from the demolished church of St Nicholas.

The Stonebow, leading E and N from The Pavement, is continued by Peasholme Green with the half-timbered 17C *Black Swan Inn*. Opposite is the partly 15C *St Anthony's Hall*, built by the ancient Guild of St Anthony and now headquarters of the Borthwick Institute of Historical Research, part of the University of York. The main hall, with a good timber roof and bosses, is open. The nearby church of *St Cuthbert* (not open) incorporates Roman stones. Aldwark leads back to the Minster via another guild hall, the *Merchant Taylors' Hall* (open when not in use), with a 14C roof behind the 17–18C exterior.

There are two ways, both interesting, of making the walk N from The Pavement. The Shambles, York's narrowest and quaintest street, leads to the pleasant little King's Square at the bottom of Low Petergate. Parliament St., the only wide street in the centre of York, leads via Davygate to St Helen's Square. It passes through St Sampson's Square, where the *Roman Bath Inn* takes its name from the the Roman remains in its basement.

WEST OF THE RIVER. There are some interesting churches across the Ouse, best reached by following High and Low Ousegate W from The Pavement. *St John the Evangelist*, beyond the bridge, is now an arts centre. The late 12–15C *All Saints*, North St., has *stained-glass windows in the N aisle depicting the Fifteen Last Days, in illustration of the 14C poem 'The Pricke of Conscience', and the Corporal Acts of Mercy, besides other glass of great beauty. The angel corbels have been well restored. Micklegate, continuing W, has good Georgian houses and two more churches: *St Martin-cum-Gregory*, with good glass, and *Holy Trinity*, the much altered fragment of a great priory church, with a memorial to Dr John Burton (d. 1771), the original of Dr Slop in Sterne's 'Tristram Shandy'. Performances of the medieval mystery plays began their circuit of the city outside the gateway of the priory. *St Mary*, in Bishophill Junior to the S, has a tower with Saxon work. The stones of its demolished sister church, St Mary in Bishophill Senior, were used by George Pace to build a new church (1965) in the NW suburb of *Acomb*. Beyond Micklegate Bar (see the city walls, above) the Georgian architecture continues in Blossom St., where the *Bar Convent* (1760; Thomas Atkinson) has a museum of 13–19C church embroidery, plate and illuminated manuscripts.

The *National Railway Museum* is W of the railway station in Leeman Rd. A branch of the Science Museum in South Kensington, it brings together a wide range of relics in a former steam locomotive shed. The main hall contains steam locomotives from 1829 onwards restored in their original liveries, including the record-breaking 'Mallard', and rolling stock from 1797 onwards, with special emphasis on royal carriages. Other galleries display smaller items, models and a collection of railway posters, paintings, photographs, etc.

SOUTH-EASTERN OUTSKIRTS. The **University of York**, opened in 1963, is 1½m SE of Walmgate Bar at *Heslington*. Attractively laid out around an artificial lake, the campus incorporates the 19C Heslington Hall (now administrative offices) among new buildings mostly in the modular system, CLASP. The university also uses several buildings in the city centre, notably King's Manor and St Anthony's Hall (see above).

SOUTH-WESTERN OUTSKIRTS. The racecourse, at the *Knavesmire*, about 2m SW of the city by A1065 (the Leeds road), is one of the finest in the country, with a history dating from 1731. Flat-race meetings are held between May and October, and the racing museum in the grandstand is open on race days. The city gallows, where Dick Turpin and Eugene Aram were executed, stood at the Knavesmire until 1801.

FROM YORK TO HARROGATE, 19½m by A59. The road follows a Roman course to (8m) the Skip bridge over the Nidd. To the S lies *Marston Moor*, where Cromwell won his decisive victory over the Royalists in 1644. To the left, just beyond the river, is *Kirk Hammerton*, where a Saxon church forms the S aisle of the 19C church. *Nun Monkton*, 3m NE at the meeting of the Nidd and the Ouse, has a beautiful little conventual church (Trans. and EE) with glass by Morris and Co. (1873) in a pleasant village setting.—13m. We cross A1 (Rte 85B).—16m. *Knaresborough*, see Rte 86B.—19½m. *Harrogate*, see Rte 80.

FROM YORK TO LEEDS, 23m. A1065 leads past the racecourse (see above) to join A64, which we follow for the rest of the way.—10m. *Tadcaster* (5900 inhab.) is a brewing town on the Wharfe. The church has an E window with stained

-glass (1875–80) by Morris and Co. *Towton*, 2¹/₂m S, is near the battlefield
where the Lancastrians were defeated in 1461. *Bolton Percy*, 3¹/₂m SE of
Tadcaster, has a good church of 1424 with fine original glass in the E window
and an Elizabethan sundial in the churchyard. The manor house of *Nun
Appleton* (not open), on the Wharfe 1¹/₂m further SE, has been rebuilt since it
was the home of General Fairfax (1612–71) and the subject of Andrew Marvell's
'Upon Appleton House'. Fairfax's tomb is preserved in the 19C church at
*Bilbrough*, 4m NE of Tadcaster.—At (13m) *Bramham Moor* A64 crosses A1 (Rte
85B).—At 15m a sideroad leads left to *Barwick-in-Elmet* (1¹/₂m), with some
remarkable Norman mounds.—23m. *Leeds*, see Rte 75F.

From York to *Hull*, see Rte 82A; to *Bridlington*, see Rte 82B; to *Scarborough*,
see Rte 83; to *Whitby*, see Rte 84; to *Durham, Newcastle* and *Berwick*, see Rte
85A.

# 82 The Yorkshire Wolds

The **Yorkshire Wolds**—as they are usually still called, despite the
1974 county changes which eliminated the East Riding of Yorkshire
and assigned them largely to Humberside—are the northernmost
chalkland in Britain, the last outpost of the belt originating in
Salisbury Plain and reaching up through East Anglia and Lincolnshire. Here they form a crescent shape which extends from the
Humber estuary a few miles W of Hull to the cliffs between Flamborough Head and Filey. They are at their steepest on the western
and northern escarpments which rise out of the York plain and the
Vale of Pickering, but their highest point, Garrowby Hill, is only 807ft
and their characteristic landscape is gentle and undulating. Many of
the villages in these dry uplands feel surprisingly remote. In the S
and E the Wolds trail off into the plain of Holderness and the boulder-
clay coastline between Spurn Head and Bridlington.

## A.   York to Hull

Total distance 38m. **York**, see Rte 81.—A1079 to (19¹/₄m) Market
Weighton.—A1079, A1035 to (29¹/₄m) **Beverley**.—A1174, A1079
to (38m) **Hull**.

Maps: OS Landranger 105, 106, 107.

**York**, see Rte 81. From Walmgate Bar we head E on A1079, passing
the junction with A64 and A166·(the Bridlington road, Rte 82B) at
(3¹/₄m) *Grimston*.—Beyond (6³/₄m) *Kexby* we cross the Derwent,
marking the boundary between North Yorkshire and Humberside.—
At (11¹/₄m) *Barmby Moor* B1246 branches left for (2m) *Pocklington*, a
small town where William Wilberforce (see Hull, below) went to
school. The fine 13–14C church, with a Perp. tower, contains a 14C
cross head. Stewart's Gardens and Museum, in the grounds of
Burnby Hall, are named after their creator Major P.M. Stewart
(d. 1962): the gardens include lakes with an abundance of water lilies
and the museum houses sporting trophies and an interesting ethnographical collection. A sideroad runs 5¹/₂m N from Pocklington via
Bishop Wilton to A166 (Rte 82B).

19¹/₄m. **Market Weighton** (3800 inhab.; pronounced 'Weeton') is at
the foot of the Wolds.

About 1½m NE is *Goodmanham*, the 'Godmundingaham' of Bede, where the partly Norman church probably stands on the site of the pagan temple destroyed after the Great Council of 626. It is notable for its chancel arch and its 16C font.—*Nunburnholme* church, 4¾m N of Market Weighton, has an interesting 10C cross. *Kiplingcotes*, 3¾m E of the village, is the starting-point of the Kipingcotes Derby, the oldest and longest horserace in England, run yearly since 1519 on the third Thursday in March. The present 4m course has been used since 1667. A peculiarity of the race is that the winner usually receives less prize money than the runner-up.—*North Newland*, 4m SE of Market Weighton, has perhaps the finest Norman *church in the region.

Beyond (26¾m) *Bishop Burton* A1079 swings S to bypass Beverley. A1035 continues into the town.

29¼m. **Beverley** (16,400 inhab.; Tourist Information), once the county town of the East Riding of Yorkshire and now the administrative centre of Humberside, is an old-fashioned market town with a racecourse, many attractive houses and two splendid churches. The martyr Bishop John Fisher (1459–1535) was born here.

Within the restored red-brick *North Bar* (1409), the only survivor of the five town gates, stands *St Mary's Church. Its Dec. chancel dates from c 1300, while the nave and tower were rebuilt in the Perp. style after the original tower collapsed in 1520.

The W front (c 1380–1411) spans the transition from Dec. to Perp., while the great S porch has an outer EE arch (perhaps not in situ), surmounted by a Dec. canopy, and an inner Norman arch. The nave was carefully restored by Sir Gilbert Scott; its roof was renewed in 1937. The hoodmould stops in the N aisle arcade record the contributors to rebuilding in the 1520s: note particularly the delightful group of minstrels. The panelled ceiling of the chancel was painted with the figures of English kings in 1445; George VI was added when it was restored in 1939. The rood screen and misericords (c 1445) deserve attention. The NE chapel (1330–49) has elaborate vaulting and flowing window tracery. The rich sculpture throughout is well preserved, and includes a rabbit which is said to have inspired Lewis Carroll's White Rabbit.

The Saturday Market, the town's main square, has a charming *Market Cross* of 1711–14. The main street leads S to the Minster past the Georgian *Guildhall* (limited opening). Its courtroom has a fine stucco ceiling. Above the *Library* in Champney Rd, to the right, is the *Museum, Art Gallery and Heritage Centre*, with local history exhibits and a permanent collection of work by the local artist Frederick Elwell (1870–1958).

**Beverley Minster** equals some English cathedrals in size and outstrips many in splendour. As well as its superb early 16C choir stalls, it boasts a great achievement in stone-carving from each of the main Gothic eras: the EE choir and transepts, the Dec. Percy tomb and the Perp. W front.

In 721 John of Beverley, Bishop of Hexham and later of York, was buried at the monastery he had founded here on the site of a chapel of St John the Evangelist. He was canonised in 1037 and kings, from Athelstan to Henry V, conferred benefits on the church in gratitude for victories won after pilgrimages to his shrine. The first minster was destroyed by the Danes in 866, and its successor disfigured by fire in 1188 and the fall of the central tower in 1213. Rebuilding began soon afterwards and continued for two centuries—spanning the EE, Dec. and Perp. styles but keeping a remarkable unity of design. The Perp. *W front with its slender twin towers, probably the finest of its kind in England, marked the completion of work in c 1420. Hawksmoor's restoration saved the church from ruin in the 18C; further work was carried out by Sir Gilbert Scott in 1866–68 and another major restoration began in 1977.

In the *Nave* the W bay is Perp. and the two E bays are EE; the rest is fine Dec. work of c 1300–50. Here, as throughout the church, the exquisite stone-carving deserves careful attention: note, for example, the musicians on the hoodmould stops in the N aisle. The W doors are decorated with figures of the Evangelists added during Hawksmoor's restoration. The S aisle has the massive late Norman font of Frosterley marble, with an elaborate cover of 1726, and the

*Beverley Minster, the west doorway*

canopied Dec. 'Sisters' Tomb'. St John of Beverley is buried at the E end of the nave. The central tower above the crossing still houses the medieval treadwheel crane used for lifting stones. The Snetzler organ (1769) was restored when Scott designed the screen in 1880. The EE *Great Transepts* have both E and W aisles, like the transepts at York. In the S arm is an early 17C painting of Athelstan, and in the E aisle of the N arm a remarkable 14C tomb with the effigy of a priest, possibly Gilbert de Grimsby (d. 1306).

Like the Great Transepts, the *Choir* and its E transepts are EE work at its purest and loveliest. The N choir aisle has a rare double staircase, which led to the Chapter House (since destroyed). The *Stalls* (c 1520–24) are superb woodcarving by the school whose work also survives at Ripon and Manchester; the array of 68 misericords is the largest, and one of the best, in England. The canopies were much renovated in the 18C. The front of the Dec. altar screen was renewed in 1826 and adorned with statues and mosaics in 1897. On the N side stands the magnificent *Percy Tomb*, lacking a chest or effigy on its slab but thought to be the tomb of Lady Idoine Percy (d. 1365). Its richly carved canopy, with figures, foliage and heraldic emblems, is one of the masterpieces of medieval art. Also on the N side of the altar is the 'Fridstol', or sanctuary chair, said to date from Athelstan's time (924–39). The lovely *Retrochoir* has an E window inserted in 1416 which contains fine 13–15C glass, some collected from other windows. The back of the reredos has vaulting and blind arcading (c 1340), with Flamboyant tracery. The small 15C *Northumberland Chapel*, to the N, holds the mutilated tomb of the 4th Earl of Northumberland (d. 1489).

Lady
Chapel

Altar

Site of Chapter House

Staircase

6

5
4

War Memorial
Chapel

3

NORTH

TRANSEPT

Screen
(Organ over)

2

SOUTH

TRANSEPT

NORTH
PORCH

1

Font

SOUTH
PORCH

Key to Numbers

1 Sisters' Tomb
2 St John of Beverley
3 Unknown priest's tomb
4 Fridstol
5 Percy tomb
6 4th Earl of Northumberland

0                                              100 feet
0                                              30 metres

# BEVERLEY MINSTER

In Friars Lane beyond the E end of the Minster stand the restored buildings of the Dominican friary founded in c 1240, now partly used as a Youth Hostel but also open to other visitors.—Flemingate, leading SE from the Minster, has the *Museum of Army Transport*, with over 100 vehicles of different types on a 5-acre site.

S of Beverley A1174 rejoins A1079.

38m. **HULL** (268,300 inhab.), officially *Kingston upon Hull*, stands where the river Hull flows into the Humber. For centuries it has been the leading port on the estuary. The old town, centred on the splendid parish church near the meeting of the rivers, has much more character than the modern centre and, despite the loss of Queen's Dock and now of Prince's Dock, the surviving town dockland and wharves are being rescued from the neglect they suffered in previous decades.

**Tourist Information Centres**: Central Library, Albion St.; City Hall, Queen Victoria Square; King George Dock, Hedon Rd; North Bank Viewing Area of Humber Bridge, Ferriby Rd, Hessle.

**Car Parks**: Off Northern Orbital Way, Ferensway and Castle St., and in Albion St. and Dock St. Multi-storey car parks in Pryme St., Osborne St., George St. and Market Place.

**Bus and Coach Station**: Ferensway.

**Railway Station**: Paragon Station, Ferensway.

**Theatres**: New Theatre, Kingston Square; Spring St. Theatre. Concerts in the City Hall and Middleton Hall (University).

**Ferries**: From King George Dock to Rotterdam (Europoort) and Zeebrugge.

**History**. Originally called *Wyke*, the town was refounded and laid out as a seaport by Edward I in 1293–99—hence the 'King's Town' in its official name. Defended by walls and ditches, it outstripped its rivals on the Humber and became England's chief seaport by the 14C. Its refusal to admit Charles I in 1642 was the first overt act of rebellion in the Civil War, and it resisted Royalist sieges in 1643 and 1644. In the late 18C and early 19C the medieval ditches were replaced by the chain of Town Docks, whose course across the angle between the two rivers thus marks the extent of Hull before its expansion.

**Famous natives and residents**. Natives include the anti-slavery crusader William Wilberforce (1759–1833), the poet William Mason (1724–97), the pioneer aviator Amy Johnson (1903–41) and the poet Stevie Smith (1902–71). Andrew Marvell (1621–78), born at nearby Winestead, was educated at the old Grammar School and served as MP for Hull from 1658 until his death. Philip Larkin (1922–85) worked as librarian at the University.

THE CITY CENTRE: QUEEN VICTORIA SQUARE AND QUEEN'S GARDENS. From the handsome *Paragon Station* (1848) the broad and attractively planted Paragon St. leads E to Queen Victoria Square, the centre of Victorian and modern Hull, with the *City Hall* (1903–09; J.H. Hirst).

On the S side is the **Ferens Art Gallery**. A lively programme of special exhibitions means that items are frequently rearranged; works not on show can be seen by appointment.

The collection includes Humberside marine paintings, 20C British art (Moore, Hepworth, Hockney), a group of portraits by 20C British painters and popular works by the Beverley artist Frederick Elwell (1870–1958). Earlier English painting is represented by Hoppner, Constable and Bonington. One gallery is permanently devoted to Netherlandish Old Masters, including portraits by Frans Hals and van der Helst; works by Volmarijn (Supper at Emmaus) and Barent Fabritius (Dismissal of Hagar); still-life paintings by C.N. Gysbrechts and P.J. Elinga; and interiors by de Blieck and Eglon van der Neer. Other foreign schools are represented by an early Canaletto and works by José Ribera, Guardi and Maffei. An extension S towards Prince's Dock is due to open in 1990.

On the E side is the *Town Docks Museum, housed in a prominent, triangular building with three domes, the former offices of the Hull Dock Company (c 1868–78; C.G. Wray). Displays show the history of whaling, trawling and Hull's mercantile past, with notable collections of scrimshaw, maritime paintings and ship models. The splendid, many-columned court room of the former Dock Company survives. Its view takes in Queen's Gardens, to the E, and Prince's Dock, to the S, derelict for many years but now being redeveloped as a shopping centre and leisure complex with a margin of water on three sides.

Queen's Gardens is a spacious square created in the 1930s on the site of Queen's Dock and slowly being surrounded by modern development. On the N side are *Portcullis House* and the *Police Headquarters*. At the E end is the *Wilberforce Monument* (1834), backed by the *Humberside Colleges of Further and Higher Education*. The *Nautical College* is in George St., behind a multi-storey car park, and the skyline to the N is dominated by the tower of *Kingston House*.

The RC church of *St Charles Borromeo*, on Jarratt St. just S of Kingston Square, has baroque late 19C decoration.

FROM QUEEN VICTORIA SQUARE TO HOLY TRINITY AND THE OLD TOWN. The pedestrianised Whitefriargate leads SE. Parliament St., on the left, preserves some 18C façades. We turn right on Trinity House Lane past the 18C *Trinity House*, founded for distressed sailors in the 14C, rebuilt in 1753 and used for training seamen since 1787. Just beyond is **\*Holy Trinity**, one of the largest and longest parish churches in England.

The transepts and chancel, begun c 1300, are important for their early use of brick. The nave was added c 1400 and the fine central tower c 1500. The interior has interestingly varied window tracery, with stained glass by Walter Crane (1897 and c 1907) in the S aisle. The font and some of the bench ends in the choir are c 1370. A tomb in the S choir aisle is thought to belong to Sir William de la Pole (d. 1366), first mayor of Hull and ancestor of the Earls and Dukes of Suffolk. The retrochoir has a fine communion table of 1770.

In King St. at the W end of the church an open-air market is held on Tuesdays, Fridays and Saturdays. SW of the church is Hull's oldest secular building, the *Old Grammar School* (1583), where Andrew Marvell and William Wilberforce were pupils. It has recently been restored as a Heritage Centre. The E end of Holy Trinity looks out on Market Place, with a gilt statue of William III (1734; Peter Scheemakers).

THE OLD TOWN: SOUTH FROM MARKET PLACE. From the statue we follow Queen St. S to *Victoria* or *Corporation Pier*, where the Hull flows into the Humber. Nearby is a statue of William de la Pole. The *Minerva Pier* makes a good lookout point for the Humber, the riverside docks and the distant Humber Bridge. To the E, the Hull is spanned by the *Tidal Surge Barrier* (1980) just below the *Myton Bridge*; a riverside walk, parallel to High St. (see below), continues up past the wharves to *Drypool Bridge*. To the W, the Humber Dock (1803–09; John Rennie) and Railway Dock (1846; Jesse Hartley of Liverpool) have been reclaimed as the *Hull Marina*. The old *Spurn Lightship* (1927) is moored here. A promenade with marine artefacts and modern sculpture is being created on the E side; the lockkeeper's cottage survives at the S end and a seven-storey warehouse by the junction of the two docks, to the W.

THE OLD TOWN: NORTH FROM MARKET PLACE. Lowgate continues Market Place to the N, past the *Market Hall* (1902–04) and the *Hepworth Arcade* (1894) on the left. Beyond, on the right, the pavement cuts through the tower of the Perp. church of *St Mary* (enlarged by Sir Gilbert Scott in 1861). The narrow Bishop Lane leads to High St., once the city's main street, between Lowgate and the river. *Maister House* (NT), a merchant's house of 1744, has a Palladian entrance hall and \*staircase, decorated by Joseph Page with ironwork by Robert Bakewell of Derby; the rest of the building, let as offices, is not open.

Opposite in the former Corn Exchange is the **Transport and Archaeology Museum**, with horse-drawn vehicles, early motor cars and motor bicycles. The \*collections of prehistoric, Roman and Saxon antiquities include an Iron Age log boat discovered near Holme-on-Spalding Moor, late Bronze Age/early Iron Age images from Roos

Carr and a Viking sword from Skerne. The Roman collection is shown with a display of Romano-British mosaics from both sides of the Humber, notably the mosaic from Horkstow and pavements from Rudston and Brantingham.

Further on are the *Nelson Mandela Gardens*, a walled enclosure planted with herbs and shrubs around a pool containing a statue of Minerva. A new *Transport Museum* is being built behind the garden; the first phase (opened in 1988) houses Hull's only surviving tram, the Kitson steam tram (c 1882), and the Ryde Pier tram (1871). N of the garden is *Wilberforce House, a 17C brick merchant's house where Charles I was entertained in 1639, Georgianised shortly before William Wilberforce was born here in 1759. It contains displays about the history of slavery and the campaign for its abolition. The museum extends into the neighbouring Georgian houses, both beautifully restored after wartime damage; the complex includes period rooms with displays of Hull silver, costumes, arms and artefacts. A yard at the rear of Wilberforce House, with a chemist's shop (c 1900) removed from Leeds, leads to a garden giving on to the riverside wharves.

Further N in High St. a section of the old wood-block paving has been renewed. The ranges of warehouses (now converted into flats) include the city's earliest industrial building, *Pease Warehouse* (1759). We can return to the modern centre along Alfred Gelder St. to the left, past the site of the new Crown Courts and the imposing *Guildhall* (1907–16; Sir Edwin Cooper).

In High St. N of Alfred Gelder St. stands the Georgian *Blaydes House* (open by appointment). Remains of the medieval town walls have been excavated in North Walls, opposite. The citadel (1541), one of the last defensive works carried out by Henry VIII, has been excavated on the E bank of the Hull close to the site of the old *Victoria Dock*, filled in during the 1970s, and the remains will be included in future development plans.—High St is continued N by Dock Office Row and, beyond North Bridge, Wincolmlee. Charterhouse Lane, on the left, has the *Charterhouse Chapel* (open) in the 18C almshouses.

WESTERN OUTSKIRTS. In Cottingham Rd, 2¼m NW of the centre, is the **University of Hull**, founded as University College in 1925 and raised to university status in 1954. The red-brick buildings blend well. *Middleton Hall* contains the University Art Collection, largely of British art 1890–1940. Further W, the old village of *Cottingham* has a fine Dec. and Perp. church with the over-restored brass of Nicholas de Luda (d. 1384), the rector who built the chancel.

A63, the Selby road, leads W from Hull to (4½m) *Hessle* and (7½m) *North Ferriby*, the starting point of the Wolds Way, a long-distance footpath leading to (79m) Filey (Rte 82B). From Hessle the **Humber Bridge** (toll; Tourist Information at North Bank Viewing Area), opened in 1981, crosses to *Barton-upon-Humber* (Rte 72).

HOLDERNESS. This flat region stretches S and E of Hull between the Humber and the North Sea, with resorts at *Withernsea* (6000 inhab.), 20½m E, and *Hornsea* (7200 inhab.; seasonal Tourist Information), 18½m NE. There is a bird sanctuary at *Hornsea Mere*.

A1033, the main road to Withernsea, runs via (6m) *Hedon* (4500 inhab.), a famous port before Hull was dreamt of, and (16m) *Patrington*, each with an excellent church. Hedon *church, known as the 'King of Holderness', has a Dec. nave, EE choir and transepts, and a noble Perp. tower. The tracery in the windows of the three E bays of the nave is exceptionally fine. Patrington *church, the 'Queen of Holderness', with a tall central spire, is a beautiful example of Dec. work. The W window, the vaulted Lady Chapel in the S transept, the Easter Sepulchre and the exquisite capitals should all be noted. Andrew Marvell (1621–78) was born at the rectory in *Winestead*, 1½m NW of Patrington.—From Patrington B1445 goes on to (6m) *Easington*, where the North Sea gas pipeline comes ashore. The coast ends in *Spurn Head*, 13m from Patrington or Withernsea, a causeway of sand and pebbles overgrown with sharp-pointed rushes. The last 4m of the road runs through a nature reserve, with a bird migration observatory. No trace has survived of the port of

*Ravenspur*, where the future Henry IV landed 'upon the naked shore' in 1399 and Edward IV arrived on his return from exile in 1471, nor of its Danish predecessor *Ravenscar*, the 'Hrafnseyrr' of Icelandic saga, from which Olaf, son of Harald Hardarda, set sail after his father's defeat at Stamford Bridge in 1066. The medieval cross of *Kilnsea*, another eroded village, still stands at Hedon.

B1238 branches E from A165, the main Hull–Bridlington road, to (8m) *Sproatley* and (12m) *Aldbrough*, where B1242 continues up the coast to Hornsea. *Burton Constable Hall* (open), 1½m N of Sproatley, is an Elizabethan house altered in the 18C, with work by Thomas Lightoler, Thomas Atkinson and James Wyatt inside.—Beyond Hornsea the coast road continues to (14m) Bridlington (Rte 82B) via (5½m) *Skipsea*, with a large motte-and-bailey castle (outer bailey English Heritage, open at any reasonable time).

From Hull to *Lincoln* and *Peterborough* via the *Humber Bridge*, see Rte 72; to *Selby* and to *Doncaster*, see Rte 81.


# B.   York to Bridlington


Total distance 40m. **York**, see Rte 81.—A1079 to (3¼m) Grimston.—A166 to (28m) Great Driffield.—A166 to (40m) **Bridlington**.

Maps: OS Landranger 105, 106, 101.


**York**, see Rte 81. From Walmgate Bar we head E on A1079, branching left on A166 at (3¼m) *Grimston*. The *Yorkshire Museum of Farming*, occupying an 8-acre site at *Murton* on the left, has live-stock, exhibitions, crafts and a programme of special events.—8m. *Stamford Bridge*, over the Derwent and the Humberside border, was the scene of King Harold's victory over Harald Hardrada of Norway shortly before his defeat at Hastings in 1066.—A166 reaches the Wolds. The sideroads leading N to Malton (Rte 83) and S to Pocklington (Rte 82A) run through out-of-the-way country and quiet villages. There is interesting Norman work in the local churches, for example at *Bishop Wilton*, a charming village in a combe 1m S of (12½m) *Garrowby Hill*, and at (19m) *Fridaythorpe*, on top of the Wolds.

B1251 branches NE from Fridaythorpe to (5½m) *Sledmere*. Sledmere House (open) was begun in 1751 and completed by the agricultural reformer Sir Christopher Sykes in the 1780s. The plaster decoration by Joseph Rose was restored after a fire in 1911, when the Turkish room was also added. There is a good collection of 18C furniture and paintings. In the fine park laid out by Capability Brown stands the parish church (1898; Temple Moore) and in the village, a memorial to the Yorkshire Waggoners, the regiment raised by Sir Mark Sykes in 1912, and an imitation Eleanor Cross (1900; Temple Moore) converted into a war memorial.

Several interesting routes lead over the Wolds from Sledmere.—B1253, continued by B1248, heads N to (11½m) Malton (Rte 83). At 4m we pass *Duggleby*, about 3m NE of the deserted medieval village and church of *Wharram Percy* (English Heritage, open at any reasonable time). At (7m) *North Grimston* the church has one of the crudely carved Norman *fonts for which the district is noted.—B1253 heads E to (16½m) Bridlington (see below). At 2½m it passes the turning on the right for *Cowlam*, with another Norman font. At 5m it crosses B1249, about 1½m N of *Langtoft*, with the Norman font from the disused church at nearby Cottam. At 10½m it passes *Rudston*, with an early Norman church tower and, in the churchyard, a huge menhir 25ft high.—B1252 goes SE to rejoin A166, passing (2½m) a good viewpoint at the striking memorial to Sir Tatton Sykes (d. 1863) on *Garton Hill*.

The church at (25m) *Garton-on-the-Wolds* was rebuilt by J.L. Pearson (1856–57) and G.E. Street (1871–80), with frescoes by Clayton and Bell. It is perhaps the most impressive result of the church building and restoration campaign by Sir Tatton Sykes and his son, also Sir Tatton.—28m. **Great Driffield** (9100 inhab.), often just called *Driffield*, is a pleasant agricultural town with a fine 15C church tower.

*Kirkburn*, 3½m SW, has a Norman *church with rich carvings, a Norman font and an unusual tower staircase (c 1200). *Bainton*, about 2m further SW, has a notable church of 1335 with the elaborate tomb of Sir Edmund de Mauley (d. 1314).

At (33¼m) *Burton Agnes* the interesting church contains the extraordinary monument of Sir Henry Griffith (d. 1654). He built *Burton Agnes Hall** (open), a lovely red-brick mansion designed by Robert Smythson, in 1598–1610.

We enter via the splendid turreted gatehouse. The house itself contains a Great Hall with carved stone screen, a fine oak staircase, a recently restored Long Gallery, and throughout the house, good ceilings, panelling and chimneypieces. The interesting collection of paintings is particularly strong in Impressionist and Post-Impressionist work. Nearby stands the original Norman manor house, altered in the 17C and 18C (English Heritage, standard opening).

40m. **Bridlington** (29,300 inhab.; Tourist Information), on the wide sweep of Bridlington Bay, is a resort with fine sands and a small harbour where a regatta is held in August. William Kent (1685–1748) was born here. The *Parish Church* in the old town to the N uses the impressive EE to Perp. nave of the old priory church, founded for Augustinian canons in 1113. Notable features are the W façade, the N porch and the elegant arcades. The neighbouring *Bayle Gate* dates from c 1388.

FROM BRIDLINGTON TO THE FLAMBOROUGH PENINSULA. B1255 runs NE past the turning for (2m) *Sewerby Hall* (open), on the cliffs to the S, a Georgian mansion in a fine park.—3½m. The *Danes' Dyke*, in fact a pre-Roman earthwork, runs across the peninsula.—4m. *Flamborough* church, partly Norman and EE, has a 16C *rood loft.—B1259 continues to the headland at the sheer chalk cliffs of (6m) **Flamborough Head**, a sanctuary for sea birds during the breeding season. The best scenery (rock stacks, caves, etc.) is on the N side, reached by B1255 from Flamborough village. It was off Flamborough Head that the American privateer Paul Jones captured the British ship 'Seramis' after a bloody fight in 1779; his own ship, the 'Bonhomme Richard', sank the next day. From the village we can join the Bridlington–Scarborough detour described below by following B1229 along the cliffs via (3m) *Bempton* and (6m) *Speeton*.

FROM BRIDLINGTON TO FILEY AND SCARBOROUGH, 17m by A165.—The road leaves Humberside for North Yorkshire, and is joined by the road from Flamborough Head just before (6½m) *Reighton*, where the church has a fine Norman font.—10½m. **Filey** (5700 inhab.; seasonal Tourist Information), to the E, is a resort on Filey Bay at the NE tip of the Wolds. Two long-distance footpaths meet here: the Wolds Way (79m), heading S to North Ferriby and Hessle Haven on the Humber (Rte 82A), and the Cleveland Way (93m), heading up the coast and round the North York Moors National Park to Helmsley (Rte 84). The sandy beach stretches below the cliffs to the low rocky spit of *Filey Brigg*. The interesting church of St Oswald mixes EE with traces of Norman work. At Hunmanby, a large and attractive village 3m SW, the partly Norman church has 19C furnishings.—There are good sea views on the way to (17m) *Scarborough* (Rte 83).

From Bridlington to *Hull*, see Rte 82A.

# 83  York to Scarborough

Total distance 41m. **York**, see Rte 81. We follow A64 throughout.
—To (17½m) Malton (bypassed).—To (41m) **Scarborough**.

Maps: OS Landranger 105, 100, 101.

**York**, see Rte 81. We leave the city by Monkgate and follow A64
across the York plain.—10½m. *Barton Hill* lies 1m SE of *Foston*,
where Sydney Smith was rector in 1809–29.

The unclassified road going N from Barton Hill is continued by the
five-mile avenue of *Castle Howard (open), the vast baroque
mansion which Sir John Vanbrugh, helped by Nicholas Hawksmoor,
built for Charles Howard, 3rd Earl of Carlisle.

Vanbrugh produced his first designs in 1699 and finished the main body of the
house by 1712, though he was still at work on the grounds and garden buildings
when he died in 1726. The fact that he came to the project apparently without
architectural experience has provoked speculation about the extent of
Hawksmoor's contribution. The N and S fronts and the striking central dome
show the same combination of monumentality and exuberance as Blenheim
Palace, the other great fruit of Vanbrugh and Hawksmoor's collaboration. The
W wing, through which visitors now enter, was completed in a much more
restrained Palladian style by Sir Thomas Robinson of Rokeby Park (Rte 86G) in
1753–59.

Inside, the magnificent Great Hall has an elaborate chimneypiece and a
painting by Giovanni Pellegrini in the dome. The room was restored after the
fire which badly damaged the S front in 1940, though the Music Room and the
Tapestry Room also keep some of their original decoration. The impressive
collection of pictures and furniture is shown to its best advantage in the Orleans
Room, with paintings by Rubens and Domenico Feti, and the Long Gallery,
added in 1800, with portraits by Holbein (Henry VIII; the 3rd Duke of Norfolk),
Van Dyck, Lely and Kneller. The Chapel, altered in 1870–75, has a bas-relief by
Sansovino and stained glass by Morris and Burne-Jones.

The stable block (1781–84; John Carr) to the W of the house contains the
largest private collection of historic costume in Britain, with original specimens
mainly from the early 18C to the present day; also costumes from the Diaghilev
Russian ballet.

With its magnificent avenue, obelisks, gatehouses and lakes, the park creates
a formal 18C landscape on the grandest scale. The garden buildings include,
both SE of the house, Vanbrugh's Temple of the Four Winds and Hawksmoor's
*Mausoleum.

*Sheriff Hutton*, 4m W of Foston, has the ruins of its 14C castle. The church
contains 14–15C effigies, one of them probably of Richard III's son Edward
(1471–84), and the brass of two babies (1491).

11½m. *Whitwell-on-the-Hill* is to the left. To the right, in an attractive
setting on the opposite bank of the Derwent, are the scanty but
beautiful ruins of *Kirkham Priory*, an Augustinian foundation of 1122
(English Heritage, standard opening). They include the sculptured
gatehouse and the exquisite *lavatorium in the cloister, both late
13C, and the Romanesque refectory doorway.—To the left of A64
further on is another turning for (3m) Castle Howard, via *Welburn*.

17½m. **Malton** (4100 inhab.; seasonal Tourist Information),
bypassed by A64, is a market town on the Derwent, with two partly
12C churches. It stands on the site of the Roman station of *Derventio*,
and the *Museum* occupying the 18C former Town Hall in the market
place has a good Roman collection. Across the river is *Norton* (5900
inhab.). At *Old Malton*, 1m NE, the late Norman and EE parish
church with a beautiful W front and aisleless nave is a relic of the
Gilbertine priory founded c 1150.

Castle Howard, 6m SW, is reached by the sideroad which passes (3m) *Easthorpe
Hall* (not open), the home of Dickens's friend Charles Smithson (d. 1844), who
entertained the novelist here while he was writing 'Martin Chuzzlewit'.

A169 heads N to (7m) Pickering (Rte 84), past (4¹/₂m) the turning for *Flamingo Land*, a zoo and amusement park at *Kirby Misperton*, 1¹/₂m W.

FROM MALTON TO HELMSLEY, 15m by B1257.—4¹/₂m. *Barton-le-Street* has a rebuilt church with good Norman carving and (6m) *Slingsby* the ruins of a fine early 17C country house.—8m. *Hovingham*, a pleasant village, has a church with a Saxon tower, cross and sculptured stone panel which may have been part of an altar or tomb. *Hovingham Hall* (open to parties only, by appointment) is a Palladian house designed c 1750 by its owner, Sir Thomas Worsley. *Nunnington Hall* (NT), by the Rye 2¹/₂m N, is a 16C and late 17C manor house with a fine staircase, panelling and chimneypieces. It contains a collection of miniature rooms furnished in the style of different periods.—At (12m) *Oswaldkirk* we join Rte 84 for (15m) *Helmsley*.

From Malton to *Sledmere* and *Great Driffield*, see Rte 82B.

A64 skirts the northern escarpment of the Wolds, with the flat Vale of Pickering on our left.—Beyond (22¹/₂m) the attractive spire of *Rillington* church we pass, on the left, the park of *Scampston Hall* (1803; Thomas Leverton).—27¹/₂m. *East Heslerton* church was built in 1877 by G.E. Street for Sir Tatton Sykes of Sledmere (Rte 82B). The spire has statues of the Four Latin Fathers designed for Bristol Cathedral but rejected as un-Protestant.—There is a fine view from the Wolds escarpment above (33¹/₂m) *Staxton*. Shortly beyond, A1039 branches right for Filey (Rte 82B). We head N on A64 via (36¹/₂m) *Seamer*.

41m. **SCARBOROUGH** (41,800 inhab.), the most popular seaside resort in the North-East, is splendidly situated on two sandy bays separated by a rocky headland crowned with the ruined castle. The seafront is laid out with pleasant irregularity, and the cliffs of both bays are covered with delightful gardens.

**Tourist Information Centre**: St Nicholas Cliff.

**Car Parks**: Brook Square, Castle Rd, Eastborough, Falconers Rd, Vernon Rd. Westwood, Marine Drive and Royal Albert Drive; also Albion Rd, Esplanade and Weaponess Valley Rd in South Bay, and Burniston Rd, Friarsway and Upper and Lower Northstead in North Bay.

**Coach Stations**: Westwood and William St.

**Bus Station**: Junction of Valley Bridge Parade and Somerset Terrace.

**Railway Station**: Junction of Valley Bridge Rd and Westborough.

**Theatres**: The Spa (see below); Royal Opera House (repertory drama), St Thomas St.; Open Air Theatre, Northstead Manor; Futurist Theatre, South Bay; Library Theatre, Vernon Rd; and Theatre in the Round, Valley Bridge Parade, known for its premieres of plays by Alan Ayckbourn.

**History**. The headland has been the site of an Iron Age settlement, a Roman beacon, Saxon and Norman chapels, and the castle, built in a seemingly impregnable position 300ft above the sea. The fishing village developed as a spa town after the discovery of mineral springs in 1620 and as a seaside resort in the second half of the 18C—probably the first place in England where sea bathing became fashionable. Smollett's 'Humphry Clinker' (1771) and Sheridan's 'A Trip to Scarborough' (1777) testify to its early popularity.

**Famous natives etc**. The painter Lord Leighton (1830–96) and Dame Edith Sitwell (1887–1964) were born here and the painter Atkinson Grimshaw lived here after 1876. Anne Brontë (1820–49) died at a house on the site of the Grand Hotel and is buried in the detached churchyard of St Mary.

The main street, known as Westborough, Newborough and East-borough, descends NE from the *Railway Station* to the old fishing harbour on **South Bay**. Nearby are the house (c 1350), now a café, where Richard III is said to have stayed and the 17C *Three Mariners Inn* (open).

To the N the broad Marine Drive sweeps round the base of the headland and continues as Royal Albert Drive to (1¹/₂m) the quieter **North Bay**, with

*Northstead Manor Gardens*. Above are *Alexandra Gardens* and *Peasholm Park*, with a boating lake and glen.

The only way that a Member of Parliament may resign his seat is by accepting the stewardship of the Manor of Northstead, or that of the Chiltern Hundreds in Buckinghamshire, which are both offices of profit under the Crown and hence incompatible with parliamentary duties.

Immediately above the harbour the steep streets of the old town climb to Castle Rd. Here stands the parish church of *St Mary* (c 1180), with four vaulted 14C chapels opening off the S aisle. Its choir and N transept were destroyed during the siege of the castle in 1645. Anne Brontë is buried in the detached part of the churchyard, E of the church. Of the ruined **Castle** (English Heritage, standard opening and summer Sunday mornings), the chief remains are the keep (1158–64) and the 13C barbican by which it is approached across the moat. On the cliff are foundations of the 4C Roman signal station.

Piers Gaveston was besieged and captured here by the Earl of Pembroke in 1312. Parliamentarian sieges during the Civil War starved the castle into surrender in 1645 and 1648. It was slighted after its final capture, and further damaged when a German battleship bombarded it in 1914. George Fox, the Quaker, was imprisoned here in 1665–66.

SW of the headland and the harbour the sweep of South Bay begins with *St Nicholas Cliff* and its gardens, and continues with the steep ravine of the *Valley Gardens*. St Nicholas St.., on top of the cliff, has the *Town Hall* in a converted mansion (1852; H.J. Wyatt). Further inland, the early 19C Crescent has the *Art Gallery*, with local scenes and work by Lord Leighton and Atkinson Grimshaw, and the *Natural History Museum* in Woodend, once the Sitwell family's villa. The *Rotunda Museum* in the Valley is an early purpose-built museum (1829), with displays of local archaeology and social history. Overlooking the sea stands the monumental *Grand Hotel* (1863–67; Cuthbert Brodrick of Leeds).

The Valley is spanned by *Valley Bridge* and, nearer the sea, *Spa Bridge*, leading to the *Spa* and its gardens at the foot of the South Cliff. It includes a concert hall, theatre, restaurant and ballroom. The pretty *South Cliff Gardens* (views) and *Holbeck Gardens* stretch along the cliff face. The church of *St Martin-on-the-Hill* (1863; G.F. Bodley) has a splendid Morris and Co. interior, with stained glass, pulpit, altar and reredos by Morris, Burne-Jones, Rossetti and Ford Madox Brown and a huge organ case by Bodley himself.

Off the Filey Rd, further S, is *Oliver's Mount* (500ft) with a prominent War Memorial and wide views.

The Cleveland Way passes through Scarborough on its way up the coast from Filey (Rte 82B). To the S, *Cornelian Bay* (2½m), *Cayton Bay* (3½m) and *Gristhorpe Cliff* (5m) lie on its course; to the N, *Cloughton Wyke* (4½m) and *Hayburn Wyke* (6m; see also Rte 84).

From Scarborough to *Filey* and *Bridlington*, see Rte 82B; to *Pickering* and to *Whitby*, see Rte 84.

# 84 The North York Moors: York to Whitby

Total distance 57½m. **York**, see Rte 81.—B1363 to (20m)
Oswaldkirk.—B1257, A170 to (23½m) Helmsley.—A170 to (36½m)
Pickering.—A169, A171 to (57½m) **Whitby**.

Maps: OS Landranger 105, 100, 94 or OS Tourist map for the
National Park (1:63,360 or 1in to 1m). Walkers need the two OS
Outdoor Leisure maps (1:25,00 or 2½in to 1m).

The **North York Moors** stretch from the sharply defined western
escarpment of the Hambleton Hills and Cleveland Hills across to the
coast between Scarborough and Staithes, N of Whitby. The central
hills, covered with heather, rise to about 1400ft and create an open
landscape with wide views. The drainage has run off in deep parallel
valleys—long to the S, where all the streams eventually join the
Derwent, and short to the N, where they flow into the Esk. In these
dales the scenery is greener and sometimes wooded. Here, too, the
sandstone and limestone which predominate among the moorland
rocks can be seen to advantage in the houses which line the
characteristically wide village streets and in the ruined abbeys which
are among the region's chief attractions. Both the dales and the
moors above make excellent walking country. As well as many
shorter excursions, there are several popular long-distance routes:
the Cleveland Way (93m), starting at Helmsley, the Lyke Wake Walk
(40m) from Osmotherley to Ravenscar, and the eastern part of
A. Wainwright's Coast-to-Coast Walk, from Osmotherley to Robin
Hood's Bay.

Since 1952 the region has been designated a National Park, with a
visitors' centre at Danby and information centres at Sutton Bank and
Pickering. Further information can be obtained by post from the
North York Moors National Park Information Service, The Old
Vicarage, Bondgate, Helmsley, York YO6 5BP.

**York**, see Rte 81. We leave the city by Gillygate and take B1363 due
N to (8m) *Sutton-on-the-Forest*, whose name recalls the vanished
royal Forest of Galtres. Sutton Park (open) is an early Georgian house
with good plasterwork, furniture, pictures and porcelain. Laurence
Sterne was vicar from 1738 and lived here until 1759. In 1741 he also
acquired the living of (10½m) *Stillington*.—The road climbs to
(15½m) the summit of the *Howardian Hills* and then drops down to
(18m) *Gilling*, or *Gilling East*. The castle (hall and Great Chamber
open) stands on medieval foundations but is chiefly interesting for its
Tudor and Georgian alterations. The *Great Chamber (c 1575–85)
has a decorated plaster ceiling, painted frieze, wood panelling and
chimneypiece, and painted glass.—At (20m) *Oswaldkirk* we join the
detour from Malton in Rte 83 and reach the edge of the National
Park.

An unclassified road leads W beneath the limestone escarpment of the
Hambleton Hills to (2m) *Ampleforth*, where there is a Benedictine priory
founded in 1802, with a well-known boys' public school.—5m. **Byland Abbey**
(English Heritage, standard opening), one of the great Cistercian foundations of
Yorkshire, moved to its present site in 1177. The chief remains are the striking
W front, with the fragment of a rose window above the row of lancets, and the S
transept of the church, which contains fine 12–13C *tiles. The museum has a
display of carved stones and tiles.—6½m. *Coxwold* is a delightful village,
popular with visitors. Laurence Sterne was perpetual curate here from 1760
until his death in 1768, writing part of 'Tristram Shandy' and 'A Sentimental

Journey' at the house he renamed Shandy Hall (open). The building dates from c 1450. Sterne's pulpit still stands in the Perp. church, with its unusual octagonal tower. His body was reburied near the S wall in 1969. *Newburgh Priory* (limited opening), just SE, is a 16–18C house on the site of a 12C Augustinian foundation. It preserves a tomb said to contain the headless body of Oliver Cromwell. *Kilburn*, 2¼m NW of Coxwold beneath Roulston Scar and the 19C White Horse, is known for the village workshop of Robert Thompson (d. 1955) whose woodcarving, 'signed' with a mouse, adorns many Yorkshire churches.

B1257 and A170 lead N from Oswaldkirk to (23½m) **Helmsley** (1400 inhab.; seasonal Tourist Information, and National Park office), a pleasant little town at the foot of the Cleveland Hills and a popular centre for visitors to the moors. To the W of the large market place are the ruins of the 12C *Castle* (English Heritage, standard opening and summer Sunday mornings), with large earthworks and a range altered in the 16C. The gardens of the 18–19C *Duncombe Park*, under 1m SW, are open; the house itself may open in 1990.

   ***Rievaulx Abbey** (English Heritage, standard opening and summer Sunday mornings) stands in a beautiful setting in *Ryedale*, off B1257 2½m NW of Helmsley. Its name, pronounced 'Reevo', preserves the Anglo-Norman form of the valley's name. Founded in 1132, the earliest of Yorkshire's Cistercian houses, it grew to become one of the greatest. Its ruins are as substantial and well preserved as those of Fountains and Kirkstall, and perhaps more beautiful.

The slope of the valley forced the monks to build their church on a N–S, rather than W–E, axis; the following description uses the ecclesiastical rather than the actual compass points. Of the Norman nave (c 1140), which had a galilee porch at the W end and side chapels in the aisles, little remains except the base of the outer walls and the stumps of the pillars. The transepts combine Norman with EE work, while the *choir (c 1230) is EE at its finest and purest.

Of the domestic buildings to the S, the most interesting are grouped around the main cloister, where a fragment of the original arcade has been reconstructed. The late 12C Chapter House in the E range is apsidal, an unusual feature in a Cistercian foundation; the shrine of the first abbot, William (d. 1148), is by the entrance. Between the warming house and kitchen in the S range stands the massive EE Refectory, with remains of a lavatorium on either side of the door and a pulpitum inside.

*Rievaulx Terrace* (NT), entered separately from B1257, was laid out as part of Duncombe Park in the 1750s to command a magnificent *view of the dale and abbey ruins. There are two classical temples, one with a permanent exhibition about 18C English landscape design.

Beyond Rievaulx B1257 skirts Ryedale on the E and continues up *Bilsdale*, at the head of which *Urra* earthwork runs along the crest of the hill for c 3m. We cross the Cleveland Hills to (20m) Stokesley, on the detour from Whitby to Teesside described below. At 1½m a sideroad on the left leads across the valley to (4½m) *Hawnby*, at the E foot of the Hambleton Hills.

A charming lane climbs W from Rievaulx to join A170, the main Helmsley–Thirsk road, a little short of (4m) the top of *Sutton Bank* (car park and National Park Information Centre), where a wide and sudden view extends across the York plain to the Pennines. The descent to Thirsk (Rte 85A) is notoriously steep and perilous.

The Cleveland Way, a long-distance footpath (93m), takes a circuitous route from Helmsley along the W and N escarpment of the moors to Saltburn-by-the-Sea and then down the coast through Whitby and Scarborough to Filey (Rte 82). Its first stage passes Rievaulx on the way to Sutton Bank; here it turns N to join the old drove road across the Hambleton Hills via *Hesketh Dike* and many earthworks and standing stones to (c 10m) *Osmotherley*, near Mount Grace Priory (Rte 85A). Osmotherley is also the starting-point of the Lyke Wake Walk to Ravenscar and the North York Moors section of A. Wainwright's Coast-to-Coast Walk to Robin Hood's Bay.

From Helmsley to *Malton*, see Rte 83.

At Helmsley the main route turns E on A170, skirting the S fringe of the moors and the National Park.—Beyond (26¾m) *Nawton* a sideroad branches ½m N to the prettily wooded *Kirkdale*, where St Gregory's Minster has a *sundial commemorating the rebuilding of the church in the reign of Edward the Confessor (c 1050). In the quarry face by the ford stood the Kirkdale Cave, discovered in 1821, which yielded a rich haul of lion, hyena, rhinoceros and mammoth bones of the pre-glacial period.—29½m. *Kirkbymoorside* has a handsome high street off the main road.

A sideroad runs N to (3m) *Gillamoor*, with a surprise view of the moors just beyond the church, and continues up the W side of *Farndale*, noted for its daffodils. Beyond (7m) *Low Mill* the route is one-way and can be crowded in spring. There is also a pleasant riverside walk (3m) from the car park at Low Mill to Church Houses. Motorists can return down the E side of the valley to *Hutton-le-Hole* (seasonal Tourist Information), a charming village popular with visitors. The Ryedale Folk Museum has exhibits illustrating daily life in the region, and a splendid open-air section with reconstructed buildings (medieval cruck house, 16C manor, 18C cottage, etc.).

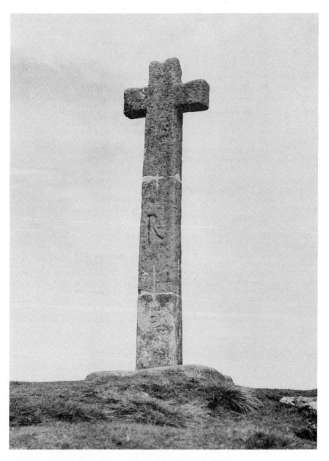

*The Ralph Cross on the North York Moors*

*Lastingham*, c 2m E of Hutton-le-Hole, is a pretty village beneath Staunton Moor. Its church, begun c 1078, has a remarkable early Norman *crypt with a collection of pre-Conquest stonecarving. Beneath the crypt is buried St Cedd, founder in 654 of the original Saxon monastery destroyed by the Danes. *Appleton-le-Moors*, 2m S of Lastingham, keeps its medieval plan; while *Cropton*, 2m SE, has a ruined castle with a view of Rosedale.

A fine *road heads N from Hutton-le-Hole along *Blakey Ridge* to (13m) Castleton (see below), keeping above 1000ft for much of the way. At (8m) the crossroads, with wide views, stands Ralph Cross, one of the traditional crosses which mark boundaries and routes on the moors. Another, the curious Fat Betty, stands on the Rosedale Abbey road just to the right.

*Rosedale Abbey*, 4m NE of Hutton-le-Hole by the direct road, is another popular village. Its churchyard has a fragment of the Cistercian nunnery founded here in the mid 12C. The crests of the surrounding hills were worked for ironstone in the 19C and early 20C, and the course of the railway line which linked the mines makes an interesting walk. Particularly impressive mine ruins can be seen on the path leading from Hill Cottages, 1½m up the dale from Rosedale Abbey.

35m. *Middleton* church has three 10C wheel-head crosses.—36½m. **Pickering** (5900 inhab.; National Park Information Centre) is a plain little town with a *Castle* (English Heritage, standard opening and summer Sunday mornings) where Richard II was held for a time after his abdication. It has a 13C shell keep and 14C curtain wall. The Norman and Dec. *Church* has a Norman font, but its chief interest is the remarkable series of wall paintings (c 1450) in the nave, too drastically restored in the 19C. The *Beck Isle Museum*, in a Regency house, has exhibits of local history and folk life.

Between April and October the privately owned *North Yorkshire Moors Railway* operates a regular steam and diesel service up the narrow, wooded *Newtondale* to (18m) Grosmont in Eskdale (see the detour from Whitby to Middlesbrough, below). It stops at Levisham, Newtondale Halt and Goathland, and connects at Grosmont with the BR service between Whitby and Middlesbrough. The moors railway was built as a horse-drawn tramway by George Stephenson in 1836 and converted to steam by George Hudson, the Railway King, in 1845.

FROM PICKERING TO SCARBOROUGH. A170, the direct road, takes 17m.—6m. *Ebberston Hall* (open), on the left, is a little villa by Colen Campbell (1718).—At (9¼m) *Brompton* Wordsworth married Mary Hutchinson in 1802.—10½m. *Wykeham* has a church by Butterfield (1853).—17m. *Scarborough*, see Rte 83.

A more interesting alternative route branches N from A170 at (2½m) the charming village of *Thornton Dale* and takes the forest drive (toll) via (5¾m) *Low Dalby* (Forestry Commission Visitor Centre), (11m) *Bickley* and (13m) *Langdale End* to (15m) *Hackness*. By the late 18C Hackness Hall (not open) stands the interesting Norman and EE parish church, with a Saxon cross bearing inscriptions in Latin and what is apparently a variant of Ogham, a Perp. font cover, a Jacobean pulpit, and a monument by Chantrey to Mrs Johnstone (d. 1819).—There are several ways of completing the journey from Hackness to Scarborough. The shortest (21m in all) goes E to (16m) *Suffield* and then descends, with a superb view, to join A171 at (18m) *Scalby*. A second route (23½m) follows the Derwent and the lovely wooded *Forge Valley* to rejoin A170 at 19m, between *West Ayton* and *East Ayton*. A third route (22m) branches E from the Forge Valley to A171 via Lady Edith's Drive.

From Pickering to *Malton*, see Rte 83.

A169 heads N from Pickering and climbs to the open moor.—42m. A steep sideroad leads left to the moorland villages of (½m) *Lockton* and (1½m) *Levisham*, with unusual views of the deep dales below them. Levisham church, with a Saxon chancel arch, stands by the Beck.—45½m. *Saltergate Inn* stands on the old pack route by which Whitby salt was taken to Pickering market for distribution throughout Yorkshire, and near the head of the *Hole of Horcum*, where the moor has been eroded by the springs that rise on its slopes.—On the descent to (47½m) *Eller Beck Bridge* the ominous white radar domes of the Ballistic Missile Early Warning Station (1963) dominate *Fylingdales Moor* to the right.

Beyond the bridge a road branches left across the moor to (2½m) *Goathland*, a good centre for walking. The village maintains a tradition of folk dancing by the Plough Stotts (sword dancers). The 70ft drop of *Mallyan Spout* is 1m SW, and on *Wheeldale Moor*, 3m SW, over a mile of a *Roman road has been exposed (English Heritage, open at any reasonable time).

A long, steep descent leads to (53m) *Sleights*, where the main road quits the National Park. In a wooded setting on the Little Beck 3½m SE is the 40ft waterfall of *Falling Foss*. For the network of sideroads leading W through Eskdale, see the detour from Whitby to Middlesbrough below.—We cross the Esk and, at 55m, turn E on A171.

57½m. **WHITBY** (13,800 inhab.; Tourist Information), a fishing port and once a centre for whaling and ship-building, is probably the most handsome town on the NE coast. Red-tiled houses rise up the steep banks of the Esk above the busy harbour. The East Cliff is crowned by the superb combination of parish church, graveyard and abbey ruins, the West Cliff by the holiday resort developed in the 19C.

The two William Scoresbys, father (1760–1829) and son (1789–1857), were both natives. Another famous navigator, Captain Cook (1728–79), served his apprenticeship with a local shipping firm and made his first voyage round the world in Whitby-built ships. Elizabeth Gaskell made Whitby the 'Monkshaven' of 'Sylvia's Lovers' (1863), while in Bram Stoker's novel (1897) Count Dracula makes his landfall in England during a storm in the harbour and takes refuge in St Mary's churchyard. The novelist Storm Jameson (1891–1986) was born at Whitby.

The road from York passes Pannett Park, where the *Museum* contains a good collection of local geology, archaeology and natural history, a section devoted to Captain Cook and other Whitby sailors, and a display of Whitby jet ornaments. The neighbouring *Art Gallery* has local paintings. We follow Baxtergate past the Post Office and cross the Esk by the swing bridge (1908). In Grape Lane, on the right, the *Captain Cook Memorial Museum* occupies the late 17C house where the navigator served as an apprentice. The picturesque Church St. is the main thoroughfare of the old fishermen's quarter. From its N end a flight of 199 steps climbs to *St Mary's Church* on top of the East Cliff, its interior a charming muddle of 17–18C galleries and box pews and a three-decker pulpit. The Cholmley Pew (c 1700) almost obscures the Norman chancel arch. The churchyard contains weatherbeaten 18C tombstones and a 19C cross commemorating the poet Caedmon (d. c 680), a monk at the abbey.

*Whitby Abbey (English Heritage, standard opening and summer Sunday mornings) lies beyond the churchyard, romantically placed on the cliffs 200ft above the sea.

The house for monks and nuns founded in 657 by St Hilda of Hartlepool became important enough to serve as host to the Synod of Whitby (664), at which representatives of the Roman and Celtic churches met to discuss differences in custom and practice. The abbey was destroyed by the Danes in 867 but refounded for the Benedictines in 1078.

Nothing visible survives of the Saxon abbey, which lay slightly to the N of later buildings; the outline of the apsidal Norman church is marked within the walls of the present ruin. This is largely EE, begun c 1220, though the change to Dec. (in the 14C) can be seen toward the W end. The central tower and much of the S side have vanished, and the W end was further damaged by a German battlecruiser in 1914. However, the N side of the nave, the N transept and the E end, with its rows of lancets, testify to the magnificence and delicacy of the building. A row of arches from the nave has been re-erected by the boundary wall to the N. The domestic buildings, which stood to the S, have gone but part of their site is occupied by the late 17C mansion of the Cholmleys, now derelict.

The West Cliff, its top marked by whalebones and a statue of Captain Cook, is the holiday quarter of Whitby, with a promenade, sandy beach and the so-called *Spa* (concert hall, theatre, etc.). East Terrace (c 1850; John Dobson of Newcastle) is part of the early development of the resort undertaken by George Hudson, the Railway King.

FROM WHITBY TO SCARBOROUGH, 19½m by the hilly A171.—From (2½m) *Hawkser* B1447 leads left to the coast at (2m) **Robin Hood's Bay**, a picturesque fishing village on a steep slope, overrun with tourists in summer. A. Wainwright's Coast-to-Coast Walk via Osmotherley from St Bees Head ends here. —A171 crosses *Fylingdales Moor*, with its radar domes conspicuous on the right (see above).—From (14m) *Cloughton*, on the edge of the National Park, a sideroad leads N via (1½m) *Hayburn Wyke*, a wooded dell laid out with a labyrinth of walks, and over *Staintondale Moor* to (5½m) *Ravenscar*, a resort at the N end of a range of fine cliffs. The Lyke Wake Walk from Osmotherley ends here.—19½m. *Scarborough*, see Rte 83.

FROM WHITBY TO MIDDLESBROUGH VIA ESKDALE. A171, the main road, goes via Guisborough and misses Eskdale, which lies to the S. We turn S from it on A169 to (4½m) *Sleights* and then head W on hilly and meandering sideroads.—7m. *Grosmont* is the terminus of the North Yorkshire Moors Railway from Pickering (see above), connecting with the BR line from Whitby to Middlesborough. —Near (9m) *Egton Bridge* is the ornate Roman Catholic church of St Hedda (1866). It was the parish of Father Postgate, executed for his faith in 1679 at the age of 83.—11½m. *Glaisdale* stands at the mouth of a beautiful side valley. The Beggar's Bridge (1619) crosses the Esk nearby.—We cross the Esk at (13m) *Lealholm* to reach (17m) *Danby*, with the North York Moors National Park centre. To the NE rises *Danby Beacon* (981ft); to the SE lies the ruined 14C *Danby Castle* (not open but visible from the road), near the medieval Duck Bridge over the Esk.—19m. *Castleton*, a good centre for moorland walks, stands at the N end of the road along Blakey Ridge from Hutton-le-Hole (see above). The church (1924–26) has woodcarving by Thompson of Kilburn.—21½m. *Commondale* is another good starting-point for walks.—We continue W to (24m) *Kildale*, where we leave the Cleveland Hills, and (26m) *Easby*, beyond the boundary of the National Park. The church at *Ingleby Greenhow*, 2m S, is Georgian with Norman fragments.—29m. *Stokesley* is a little market town with a fine wide street. A173, the Guisborough road, leads 3m NE to *Great Ayton*, near the conical *Roseberry Topping* (1051ft). Captain Cook attended the village school here and the schoolhouse, rebuilt in 1785, now contains a museum. The site of his cottage, removed to Melbourne in 1934, is marked by an obelisk of Australian granite. A 60ft obelisk erected in his honour in 1827 stands on Easby Moor. B1257 heads S from Stokesley to Rievaulx and Helmsley (see above). —A172 heads N from Stokesley and enters Cleveland on the way into (38m) *Middlesbrough* (Rte 85B).

FROM WHITBY TO MIDDLESBROUGH VIA THE COAST, 32m by A174.—3m. *Sandsend* is a little resort.—4m. *Lythe* has a superb view S over Whitby and the bay, and a church with many Saxon fragments. *Mulgrave Castle* lies in a wooded valley 1m S.—From (9m) *Hinderwell* a sideroad runs 1m SE to *Runswick* on Runswick Bay.—10½m. *Staithes*, set partly at the bottom of a deep ravine, is a pretty fishing village which attracts tourists. Captain Cook was apprenticed to a draper here before he moved to Whitby. *Boulby Cliff* (666ft), to the W, is the highest cliff on the E coast of England.—We leave the National Park on the way to (14½m) *Loftus* (8500 inhab.), a beautifully situated but grimy town.—19m. *Saltburn-by-the-Sea* and on to (32m) *Middlesbrough*, see Rte 85B.

# 85 York and Doncaster to Durham, Newcastle and Berwick

## A. From York

Total distance 143½m. **York**, see Rte 81.—A19 to (23m) Thirsk.
—A168 to (32m) Northallerton.—A167 to (48m) **Darlington**, and on
to (66½m) Durham, (81m) Newcastle and (143½m) Berwick, see
Rte 85B.

Maps: OS Landranger 105 (briefly), 100, 99, 93.

**York**, see Rte 81. We head N on A19.—3½m. *Skelton* has a beautiful
little EE church of c 1247.—From (5¼m) *Shipton* a sideroad leads
2½m W to *Beningbrough Hall* (NT), built for the Bourchier family in
1716. It contains a fine staircase, woodwork and plaster; a well-
preserved Victorian laundry; and a collection of portraits on loan
from the National Portrait Gallery.—12½m. *Easingwold* has a pleasant market place away from the main road.

At *Alne*, 4m SW, the 12C *doorway of the church is carved with animals from
the bestiary.—*Raskelf*, 2m NW, has the only wooden church tower in the
county.—For *Stillington* and *Sutton-on-the-Forest*, E of Easingwold, see Rte 84.

23m. **Thirsk** (6800 inhab.; seasonal Tourist Information) is a traditional Yorkshire market town with a good Perp. church, a racecourse
and a local museum in the birthplace of Thomas Lord (1755–1822),
founder of Lord's Cricket Ground. The country vet stories of 'James
Herriot' are set in Thirsk and its surrounding region; several 'Herriot
trails' follow the locations.

FROM THIRSK TO MIDDLESBROUGH OR STOCKTON-ON-TEES.—A19 runs N, skirting the foot of the *Hambleton Hills* and the *Cleveland Hills* and the edge of the
North York Moors National Park (Rte 84).—Shortly before (11m) the Cleveland
Tontine Inn we pass the turning on the right for *Mount Grace Priory** (NT and
English Heritage, standard opening), founded in 1398, the most perfect Carthusian monastery in England. Its ground plan—two large courts with the church
between them—reflects the fact that Carthusians led a solitary rather than
communal life, each monk having a small house and garden. Part of the
domestic buildings were converted into a private house in the 17C.—At 17m we
enter Cleveland and approach the depressed industrial region along the Tees
estuary. A19 bears right for (25m) *Middlesbrough* (Rte 85B). A67 bears left to
(20m) *Yarm*, a quaint old town on a loop of the Tees, dominated by the brick
arches of its railway viaduct (1849). It keeps a broad High St. and many inns
from the days when it was an important stage on the coaching route. The
first meeting of the promoters of the Stockton and Darlington Railway, opened in
1825, was held at the George and Dragon. We cross the river by a 14C bridge to
*Egglescliffe* and follow A135, passing the Preston Hall Museum on the way into
(24m) *Stockton-on-Tees* (Rte 85B).
   Thirsk lies W of the *North York Moors*, reached by following A160 up the
perilous Sutton Bank, at the edge of the Hambleton Hills, to *Helmsley* (Rte
84).—From Thirsk to *Ripon*, *Harrogate* and *Leeds*, see Rte 80.

N of Thirsk we join A168.—32m. **Northallerton** (9600 inhab.) is the
county town of North Yorkshire. A large market is held in its broad
High St. on Wednesdays and Saturdays. The fine church, mostly
12–13C, has a striking Perp. tower.

A684 heads SW, crossing the A1 near *Leeming Bar* (Rte 85B) and joining
Wensleydale at *Leyburn* (Rte 86D).

We follow A167, passing (34½m) the site where King Stephen defeated the Scots at the Battle of the Standard in 1138.—At (44½m) *Croft-on-Tees* we cross the winding river and enter County Durham. The Old Rectory was the boyhood home of Lewis Carroll.

Byron spent his honeymoon at *Halnaby Hall*, now demolished, 3m SW. —*Sockburn*, with a ruined church containing Anglian fragments, is attractively placed on the Tees 5m SE. Wordsworth and Coleridge stayed here in 1799.

48m. **Darlington**, and on to (66½m) *Durham*, (81m) *Newcastle* and (143½m) *Berwick*, see Rte 85B.

# B.   From Doncaster

Total distance 175m. **Doncaster**, see Rte 81.—A1 to (15½m) Ferrybridge.—A1 to (32m) Wetherby.—A1 to (44m) Boroughbridge.—A1 to (71m) Scotch Corner.—A1, A1(M), A66(M), A66 to (79½m) **Darlington**.—A167 to (98m) **Durham**.—A167 to (104m) Chester-le-Street.—A6127 to (112½m) **Newcastle**.—A6125 to (119½m) Seaton Burn.—A1 to (127m) Morpeth.—A1 to (145m) Alnwick.—A1 to (175m) **Berwick**.

Maps: OS Landranger 111, 105, 99, 93, 88, 81, 75.

This route continues the journey up the A1 begun in Rte 47A (London to Stamford) and Rte 59 (Stamford to Doncaster). A1 bypasses the villages and towns, including Doncaster, that lined the former *Great North Road*, and crosses many of the transverse roads by flyovers or underpasses. Beyond Scotch Corner a short section of the old alignment is designated motorway but, beginning with the Darlington bypass, the motorway follows a new alignment: bypassing Durham to the E, briefly coming close to its old course near Chester-le-Street, and then veering E again to avoid Newcastle and cross the Tyne by the tunnel below Jarrow. It returns to its old alignment at Seaton Burn. The present route follows the course of the Great North Road, successively relabelled A167, A6127 and A6125, where most of the points of interest lie.

**Doncaster**, see Rte 81. We cross the Don and head NW on A638. *Adwick-le-Street*, right of the road at 3½m, has a 12–16C church with the tomb of James Washington (c 1580).—5½m. We join A1 at the end of the Doncaster bypass. A638 continues to Wakefield (Rte 75H).—At (8½m) *Barnsdale Bar* A1 quits the Roman line, which runs to the W as A639 and A656 through Pontefract and Castleford (Rte 75F). *Robin Hood's Well* (rebuilt by Vanbrugh), 1m S, marks the centre of the former forest of Barnsdale, which legend makes a favourite haunt of the outlaw.—10¾m. *Wentbridge* is bypassed to the E by a fine viaduct (1962).—12½m. *Darrington* church has a remarkable Lady Chapel with a small gallery above its entrance and 15C stained glass.—At (15½m) **Ferrybridge** A1 crosses the Aire by a modern bridge, leaving John Carr's bridge of 1797 for foot traffic. We enter an ugly industrial area dominated by the eight huge cooling towers of (16m) *Brotherton*. Particularly unpleasant are the stagnant scummy pools used for chemical settlement.

A162 branches right for Tadcaster and York (Rte 81) through the ancient district of *Elmet*.—3m. We cross the Selby road, A63, just W of *Monk Fryston*, where Richard Monckton Milnes, Baron Houghton (1809–95), entertained Swinburne, Sir Richard Burton and Charles Kingsley and employed the American Henry

Adams as his secretary at the Hall, now a hotel.—4m. *South Milford*. To the W is the 14C gatehouse of *Steeton Hall* (English Heritage, open at any reasonable time).—At (5½m) *Sherburn-in-Elmet* the partly Norman church contains a 15C •cross head, foolishly cut in half in the 19C.

The little •church at *Birkin*, 3½m E of Brotherton, is an unspoilt late Norman building (c 1140) with a good carved doorway and capitals and a vaulted apse.

19m. *Ledsham*, to the W, has a church with Saxon and Norman work and *Kippax*, 3m further W, a Norman church.—24m. *Aberford*, ¼m W, stands on the line of the Roman road shortly before it veers towards York. Parlington Park has an arch built by Sir Thomas Gascoigne in 1783 to celebrate 'liberty in North America triumphant'.

**Lotherton Hall**, 1m E of A1, is a museum of the decorative arts administered by the City of Leeds. It contains the Gascoigne family's collection of silver, porcelain, racing cups, jewellery, furniture and paintings (Pompeo Batoni's portrait of Sir Thomas Gascoigne); 18–20C costume; English 19C porcelain and furniture; 19–20C arts and crafts, including pottery by Bernard Leach and his school; early Chinese ceramics and other Oriental works.

At (26½m) *Bramham Moor* A1 crosses A64, the Leeds–York road (Rte 81).—28½m. *Bramham*. To the SW is *Bramham Park* (open), a Queen Anne house restored early in the 20C, with a good collection of pictures and furniture. The early 18C garden is a rare survival of the formal French style.—32m. **Wetherby** (10,200 inhab.; Tourist Information), bypassed to the E, is a dull market town on the Wharfe. Its racecourse lies off B1224, the York road, E of A1.

A661, the Harrogate road, passes (2m) *Stockeld Park* (limited opening), a fine small Palladian house of 1758–63 by James Paine.—3m. *Spofforth* and on to (8m) *Harrogate*, see Rte 80.

From Wetherby to *Ilkley*, *Grassington* and *Hawes* through Wharfedale, see Rte 86A; to *Knaresborough* and *Grassington* through Nidderdale, see Rte 86B.

At (35½m) *Walshford* we cross the Nidd, and at 39½m the A59 from York to Harrogate (Rte 81).—(44m) **Boroughbridge**, now bypassed, was once the major crossing point of the Ure, where the Roman road rejoined its N line after branching E to York. Edward II defeated the Duke of Lancaster here in 1322; and in 1569 the Rising of the North, the Catholic rebellion against Elizabeth I, came to an abortive end at the Crown, then the Tancreds' manor house. The *Devil's Arrows*, three Bronze Age monoliths, stand about ¼m SW of the village.

**Aldborough**, ¼m E, occupies the site of *Isurium Brigantium*, a Brigantian settlement developed by the Romans as a camp for the 9th Legion in the 1C and as a major town in the 2C. Part of the Roman wall and two mosaic pavements survive, with an exhibition of finds (English Heritage, summer standard opening and at any reasonable time from October to March). The 14–15C church has a large 14C brass.—For *Newby Hall*, 2½m NW of Boroughbridge, see Rte 80.

50½m. We cross (Rte 80), the road from Leeds, Harrogate and Ripon to Thirsk.—60m. *Leeming Bar*, on the right. There is a Tourist Information Centre at the A1 service area. Northallerton (Rte 85A) is 6m NE by A684.

A684 heads W to Wensleydale.—7³⁄₄m. *Bedale* has a good church, mainly 13–14C, with a defensive tower and 14C Fitzalan tombs. The 18C Bedale Hall contains a local museum. *Thorp Perrow Arboretum* (open), off B6268 about 2½m S, contains many rare trees and shrubs. *Snape*, ½m further, has the remains of a 15–16C stronghold of the Nevilles and the Cecils.—11¼m. *Patrick Brompton* church has a beautiful 14C chancel.—15m. *Constable Burton Hall* is a handsome Palladian house of 1762–68 by John Carr, set in large informal gardens (open more frequently than the house).—12½m. *Leyburn* in Wensleydale, see Rte 86D.

66m. *Catterick*, on the right, has a good 15C church.—67m. *Catterick Bridge*, also on the right, has a racecourse and a 15C bridge over the Swale.

On the moor 3m W is *Catterick Garrison*, the 'Aldershot of the North'. The road to it passes some traces of the Roman military camp of *Cataractonium* and (2¹/₂m) *Hipswell*, probably the birthplace of John Wyclif (c 1330–84).

71m. **Scotch Corner** (seasonal Tourist Information) is a major junction. Rte 86E takes A6108 SW to *Richmond* and then follows Swaledale to *Kirkby Stephen* and *Brough*. Rte 86F takes A66 over the Pennines to *Penrith*. We keep on the A1, which soon becomes motorway and bears right. The Roman road continues as B6275 through Piercebridge (Rte 86G).—75¹/₂m. We branch right on A66(M), crossing the Tees into County Durham and following A66 into Darlington.

79¹/₂m. **Darlington** (99,700 inhab.; Tourist Information) is a market town which grew into a centre for heavy industry after the opening of Edward Pease and George Stephenson's Stockton to Darlington Railway, the world's first passenger line, in 1825. The *Darlington Railway Centre and Museum* in the North Road Station (1842) displays Stephenson's No. 1 'Locomotion', which drew the first train at a rate of 10–13mph, the 'Derwent' engine (1845), and other early relics. The former *Town Hall* and *Market* are by Alfred Waterhouse (1861–64). The *church of *St Cuthbert*, originally collegiate, is a fine EE building (1180–1250) with a 14C spire. It contains a curious stone rood screen added to strengthen the central tower, stalls and misericords of the time of Bishop Langley (1406–37) and a 17C Gothic font cover. Church Lane to the N is a relic of old Darlington.

From Darlington to *Barnard Castle* and through Teesdale to *Alston*, see Rte 86G.—*Bishop Auckland*, 11m NW, is the starting-point for Rte 86H through Weardale to *Alston*.

*Teesside Airport*, 6m E of Darlington on A67, has passenger flights to Gatwick, Heathrow, Humberside, Norwich, Aberdeen, Glasgow, Belfast and Amsterdam.

FROM DARLINGTON TO STOCKTON-ON-TEES, MIDDLESBROUGH AND SALTBURN. —The suburb of *Haughton-le-Skerne*, 1¹/₂m NE of the town centre, has an attractive green and a Norman church containing good 17C woodwork.—A66 heads E and enters (6m) the county of Cleveland, a creation of the 1974 boundary changes, dominated by the heavily industrial and now badly depressed towns along the Tees estuary. They developed, thanks to the Stockton and Darlington Railway, as ports handling coal from the Durham coalfield and then, with the discovery of iron in the Cleveland Hills, as steel and ship-building centres. The 20C added oil refineries, petrochemical works and, near the N tip of the estuary, the Hartlepool nuclear power station, which came fully on stream in 1983. The last shipyard closed in 1987.

11m. **Stockton-on-Tees** (86,800 inhab.) keeps some of its Georgian character in the broad High St. with the parish church (1710–12) and Town Hall (1735). The *Green Dragon Museum*, off Finkle St. by the Georgian theatre, has displays of local history. The cabinetmaker Thomas Sheraton (1751–1806) was born in Stockton; John Walker invented the friction match here in 1827; and Harold Macmillan, Earl of Stockton (1894–1986) took his title from the borough he represented in Parliament for most of the years between the wars. The *Preston Hall Museum*, off A135 2¹/₄m SW, has Victorian interiors and a recreated Victorian street with working craftsmen; also pewter, arms and armour, and toys. A135 continues to Yarm (Rte 85A). *Norton*, on the Hartlepool road 2m NE of Stockton, keeps much of its character as a prosperous village, with 18–19C houses around the green and pond; the church, Stockton's parish church until the 18C, has a Saxon crossing and the 14C effigy of a knight. *Billingham*, further on, is a modern industrial town with ICI petrochemical works. The church, enlarged in 1939, has a fine 10C Saxon tower.

Beyond Stockton we cross the river to (12m) *Thornaby.*—15m.
**Middlesbrough** (149,800 inhab.; Tourist Information) developed in the 19C as a
port and an iron and steel town. The *Dorman Gallery*, with natural history, local
history and Linthorpe Pottery, and the *Middlesbrough Art Gallery*, with
changing exhibitions from its collection of 20C British art, are in Linthorpe Rd.
The *Cleveland Gallery* in Victoria Rd mounts changing exhibitions from
collections which include decorative art, maps, geology and contemporary art.
The *Newport Bridge* (1934), the first vertical lift bridge in England, crosses the
river to Billingham. The *Transporter Bridge* (toll), opened in 1911, crosses to
*Port Clarence* for Hartlepool. *Ormesby Hall* (NT), off A171 about 3m SE, is a mid
18C house with good plaster ceilings and a stable block by John Carr. *Marton*,
1¹/2m to its W, has the *Captain Cook Birthplace Museum* in Stewart Park near
the site of the cottage where the explorer was born in 1728. *Newham Grange
Farm Museum*, off A174 another 1m W, is part of a working farm.

A1085 continues past the Wilton ICI petrochemical works and the Redcar
British Steel works to the coast, with A174 following a parallel course to the S.
—24m. **Redcar** (36,700 inhab.; seasonal Tourist Information) is a 19C resort with
a racecourse in the centre and a lifeboat museum on the seafront. *Kirkleatham*,
2¹/2m S, has a fascinating array of 18C buildings. The *Old Hall Museum*, a free
school endowed by Sir William Turner (d. 1692) and built in 1710, has displays
about the region's social and industrial history. The Turner Hospital, founded
by Sir William in 1676 and rebuilt in the 1740s, contains a fine chapel by James
Gibbs (open on request). The church of St Cuthbert has Gibbs's mausoleum of
Marwood William Turner (d. 1739) with good 18C monuments, including work
by Scheemakers.

A1085 skirts the dunes to (25¹/2m) *Marske-by-the-Sea* and then turns inland to
join A174 on the way to (28¹/2m) **Saltburn-by-the-Sea** (20,000 inhab.; Tourist
Information), developed as a resort in the 19C. A hydraulic lift (1884) connects
the town at the top of the cliff with the seafront and pier. *Hunt Cliff* (549ft) rises
to the E. *Skinningrove*, 3¹/2m down the coast, has the *Tom Leonard Museum* on
the site of an old ironstone mine. To Whitby, see Rte 84.

The return to Middlesbrough can be made on A174 to (1¹/2m) *Brotton* and
A173 to (4m) *Skelton* (16,200 inhab. together), where the 18C Gothick castle
was a favourite haunt of Laurence Sterne and the 'Demoniac Club'. There is a
truncated little Norman church near *Upleatham*, 2m NW, and a working
watermill at *Tocketts Mill*, on A171 1¹/2m W of Skelton. A171 continues to (8m)
*Guisborough* (19,900 inhab.; Tourist Information), at the foot of the Cleveland
Hills. *Guisborough Priory* (English Heritage, standard opening but closed on
Fridays and alternate Thursdays in winter) was founded for Augustinian canons
c 1119; the scanty ruins include the beautiful Dec. E end of the early 14C
church. For A171 to Whitby, see Rte 84.—A171 heads N to (18m) Middlesbrough via Ormesby Hall.

From Stockton A19 and A689 lead to **Hartlepool** (pronounced 'Hartleepool';
94,400 inhab.; seasonal Tourist Information), which developed during the 19C
into England's third largest port and a major ship-building centre. The novelist
Sir Compton Mackenzie (1883–1972) was born here. The *Gray Art Gallery and
Museum* in Clarence Rd has collections of archaeology, local history, natural
history, Chinese porcelain and 19–20C paintings, with reconstructed buildings
in the grounds. The original and much more interesting settlement, NE of the
docks, dates from the foundation of a Saxon convent c 640. St Hilda was its
abbess c 649–57. A headstone from her time is preserved in the EE parish
church of *St Hilda*, which has a heavily buttressed tower. Towards the sea a
gateway and section of the 13C town walls survive. The *Hartlepool Maritime
Museum* traces the port's history.
From Stockton to *Durham*, and to *Sunderland* and *Newcastle*, see below.

Beyond Darlington A167 follows the course of the old Great North
Road.—84¹/2m. *Aycliffe*, on the Skerne just after we cross A1(M), has
a 13C church and two carved Saxon crosses (one with St Peter, head
downwards). *Newton Aycliffe* (24,700 inhab.), beyond, is a new town
developed since 1947.—91m. *Ferryhill* is on the edge of the coalfield
centred on *Spennymoor.*—There is a good view as we cross the Wear
at (94m) *Croxdale*. We can then branch right on A1050 to enter
Durham by New Elvet, or we can continue on A167 to (97m) *Neville's
Cross*, where the Nevilles and the Percys defeated David II of
Scotland in 1346. A right turn brings us into Durham by Crossgate,
past the partly Norman church of *St Margaret*.

98m. **DURHAM** (26,400 inhab.), in romantic contrast to the often depressed and depressing industrial region that surrounds it, is the most beautiful city between York and Edinburgh. It stands on a bold peninsula of rock almost encircled by the Wear, its great cathedral and castle towering above the steep and richly wooded banks.

**Tourist Information Centre**: Market Place.

**Car Parks**: Railway station, Framwelgate Peth, Claypath. Multi-storey car parks in Milburngate and Leazes Bowl.

**Bus Station**: North Rd.

**Railway Station**: Above the city to the NW.

**Annual Events**: Miners' Gala in July; Folk Festival and City Carnival in August.

**History**. Durham grew up, somewhat like St Albans, round the nucleus of a cathedral built on virgin soil in 995 (see below). Its name first appears as *Dunholm* ('hill-island') about 1000, developing its final form through Norman influence. The prince-bishop held his own courts of law and ruled with the powers of a petty sovereign, in return for defending the northern marches of the kingdom, so that the city had, almost from the first, a double aspect—'half church of God, half castle 'gainst the Scot'.

The railway station, high above the city on the NW, gives a magnificent *view across the river to the cathedral and the castle. North Rd, below the impressive railway viaduct (1857), descends to the Wear at *Framwelgate Bridge*, with a famous *view, rebuilt by Bishop Skirlaw c 1400 and widened in 1856. We climb Silver St. to the triangular Market Place, with the church of *St Nicholas* (1857), the *Town Hall* (1851) and a spirited equestrian statue of the 3rd Marquess of Londonderry (d. 1854).

The direct route then follows Saddler St. and Owengate up to the lovely Palace Green, where the cathedral and castle confront each other. The 17C buildings by Bishop Cosin on the other sides include, on the W, the former Grammar School (now the *University Music School*) where the poet Christopher Smart, Shelley's friend Thomas Jefferson Hogg, and R.S. Surtees, the creator of Jorrocks, were pupils.

A longer route branches left from Saddler St. and crosses the Wear by the 13C *Elvet Bridge*, widened in 1804–05 but keeping a few old bridge-houses. On the farther side is the 18C 'suburb' of Elvet. Old Elvet, with the *Royal County Hotel*, the 19C *Old Shire Hall* (now the University's administrative offices) and several fine houses, leads to the *Courthouse* (1809–11), near an unexpected view of the cathedral. We follow New Elvet, to the right, past *Elvet Riverside* (1962–66; Architects' Co-Partnership), housing the University's arts and modern language faculties, and *Dunelm House* (1961–65; Architects' Co-Partnership), with the Students' Union and the Staff Club. *Kingsgate Footbridge* (1962–63; Ove Arup), crosses the river. Hallgarth St. leads left to the *Prison*; some medieval tithe barns near it have been converted into a social club. We continue by Church St. to *St Oswald*, a late 12C–15C church partly rebuilt in 1834, with a Morris and Co. W window by Ford Madox Brown (1864–65). The path across the churchyard gives a magnificent *view of the cathedral and continues beside the river along the delightful 'Banks' to *Prebends' Bridge* (1772–78), with another *view. On the outer bank the path continues N up to Framwelgate Bridge, with a branch leading left up to a *view of the W end of the cathedral from South St. On the inner bank a path also continues N to Framwelgate Bridge past the *Old Fulling Mill* (open), housing a museum of local archaeology.

**DURHAM**

0 _____ 300 yards
0 _____ 300 metres

Another follows the loop of the river round to Elvet Bridge. We climb steeply to the cathedral via South Bailey.

The **'Cathedral** is beyond doubt the greatest piece of Norman work in the British Isles and commands the best site of any English cathedral, unrivalled even at Lincoln.

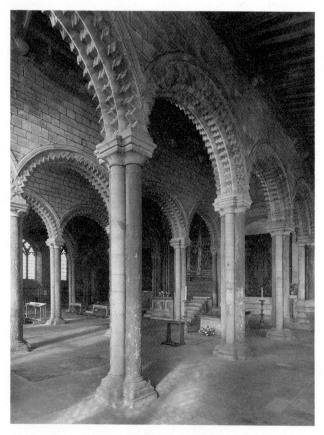

*The Galilee Chapel, Durham Cathedral*

The monks of Lindisfarne fled when the Danes raided their island in 875, taking with them the body of their bishop, St Cuthbert (d. 687). They settled at Chester-le-Street in 883 and found a final refuge at Durham in 995. Little or nothing remains of the Saxon cathedral built by Bishop Aldhun and consecrated in 998. Bishop William of St Carileph (or St Calais) began the present great Norman church in 1093 with the choir, transepts and crossing; Bishop Ranulph Flambard (1099–1128) finished the nave. The rib vaulting of the choir may be the first in Western architecture; its main vault (c 1104) was rebuilt in the early 13C, but original work (before 1096) survives in the choir aisles. The pointed transverse arches of the nave, probably the earliest (c 1130) in a high vault anywhere in Europe, mark another approach toward Gothic, though again without compromising the massively Romanesque character of the building. The Galilee at the W end was added as a Lady Chapel by Bishop Pudsey (or Le Puiset; 1153–95), while the two W towers were probably built between 1150 and 1226. The original three apses at the E end were replaced between 1242 and 1279 by the Chapel of the Nine Altars, paralleled only at Fountains Abbey. The great central tower (c 1260) was partly rebuilt c 1464–88.

Though the building has kept most of its Norman glory undiminished, later hands did not always treat it well. 18C restorers pared down the walls (N side, E end, W towers) by several inches, removing much detail in the process. In the 1790s the most barbarous of James Wyatt's suggested changes—adding a spire, knocking down the Galilee—were successfully opposed by the London Society of Antiquaries. Anthony Salvin misguidedly cleared out Bishop Cosin's 17C woodwork in the 1840s, though most of it has been put back again. Sir Gilbert Scott's restoration (1870–77) added the present choir screen.

The figure of a cow, outside at the NE end, perpetuates the legend that a

Key to Numbers
1 Sanctuary Knocker
2 Miners' Memorial
3, 4, 5 Neville Tombs
6 Bp Langley
7 Venerable Bede
8 Bp Shute Barrington
9 Prior Castell's Clock
10 Bp Hatfield (Bp's Throne over)
11 Neville Screen
12 St Cuthbert's Shrine

# DURHAM CATHEDRAL

woman looking for her dun cow guided Bishop Aldhun in choosing the site for his church. We enter by the NW porch, spoilt when its upper storey was removed in the 18C. The famous mid 12C sanctuary knocker (replica here, *original in the Treasury) is a reminder that Durham was a place of sanctuary throughout the Middle Ages.

Inside, the uninterrupted view from the W end makes a powerful impression. No other great English church keeps its original Norman bulk so comparatively untouched, and nowhere else is the Norman work so strongly individualised—an effect due largely to the great circular columns (7ft in diameter, 22ft in circumference) with their incised ornament and to the abundance of zigzag moulding. The *Nave alternates single circular columns with clustered ones. Quadripartite rib vaulting spans each bay, and the pointed transverse arches spring from the clustered piers. The W window is an insertion of c 1346. The towering tabernacle of the Renaissance font is part of the magnificent wood-work with which Bishop John Cosin (1660–72) endowed his cathedral. The Frosterley marble in the pavement to its E marks the point beyond which women could not enter. The S aisle has the case of the organ built by Father Smith (1683) to stand on the choir screen, the Miners' Memorial (1948) and two battered effigies surviving from the former Neville chantry.

The graceful, many-pillared *Galilee, entered from the W end of the nave, is a remarkable example of Trans. work, begun by Bishop Pudsey in 1175 and altered by Bishop Langley (d. 1437), who built his altar tomb in front of the W door. It contains the tomb of the Venerable Bede, who died at Jarrow in 735 and whose remains were brought to Durham in 1020. The 12C wall paintings in the bay of the E wall may be of St Cuthbert and St Oswald.

The open lantern above the crossing is unusually tall and dignified. The original Norman ends of the *Great Transepts* were altered in the 14C (N) and 15C (S) by the insertion of the present windows, but the vaulting of both transepts is original (c 1105). The S transept has Sir Francis Chantrey's statue of Bishop Barrington (d. 1826) and Prior Castell's Clock (c 1500, several times restored).

The *Choir is separated from the crossing by a light, open screen of coloured marbles by Sir Gilbert Scott, replacing Bishop Cosin's mid 17C screen which Salvin removed. Cosin's fine stalls, however, survive. On the S is the Bishop's Throne, the 'highest in Christendom'; its lower part serves as the monument of Bishop Hatfield (1345–81), who erected it. The magnificent stone *Altar Screen* (c 1375), with its lofty open pinnacles, was the gift of John, Lord Neville.

Though wholly different in style, the *Chapel of the Nine Altars* (1242–78) harmonises admirably with the choir. Its slender polished shafts are of Frost-erley marble. The tracery of the great E rose window is neo-Gothic tampering by Wyatt (1795). The rich Bede Altar in the central chapel was designed by Stephen Dykes Bower (1935). The fine 13C stone cross, to the S, came from the vanished abbey of Neasham, near Darlington. St Cuthbert's shrine behind the High Altar was destroyed at the Reformation and the saint now rests beneath a simple marble slab with candlesticks and tester by Sir Ninian Comper (1949). The plan of the original Norman apse is outlined on the floor.

Durham was established as a secular church, but Bishop St Carileph made it monastic in 1083 by bringing Benedictines from Jarrow and Monkwearmouth. The monastic buildings are grouped round the *Cloister* (c 1388–1418), S of the nave. Both doorways from the church are noteworthy, especially the Monks' Door (W) with splendid ironwork of c 1130. The W range consists of the *Monks' Dormitory* (open), built by Bishop Skirlaw (1388–1404), still with its original timber roof. It contains a fine display of 7–11C sculptured stones, mainly crosses, from Durham and the surrounding region (Hexham, Hartlepool, Jarrow, Monkwearmouth, Escomb, etc.). The *Treasury* (open) in the 13C under-croft displays fragments of *St Cuthbert's carved wooden coffin, made before 698, in which his body was carried on its wanderings, and the relics found inside it: an exquisite mid 7C pectoral cross, 7C portable altar, 10C vestments, and 11C(?) comb. Also on view are the original *sanctuary knocker and the cathedral's collection of illuminated manuscripts, seals, documents, plate and vestments. The refectory on the S side was rebuilt c 1684 as the *Chapter Library* (open to scholars only). The *Chapter House* (not open) in the E range was completed under Bishop Geoffrey Rufus (1133–41), partly destroyed in 1796 and restored in 1895.

From the cathedral cloisters we cross The College to the *Gatehouse* (c 1500), leading to the attractive houses and college buildings of North and South Bailey. In South Bailey St Mary-the-Less (rebuilt 1847) contains a fine 13C Majesty. In North Bailey St Mary-le-Bow (1685), with a screen of 1707, is now a Heritage Centre.

*St Cuthbert's coffin, Durham Cathedral*

The **•Castle** stands opposite the cathedral on Palace Green, guarding the exact neck of the peninsula. Begun in 1072, it served as the palace of the prince-bishops until the 1830s, when it became the University College of the newly founded university (see below). It has kept the motte-and-bailey plan of a Norman fortress through all its mutations. Guided tours are given throughout the year, but during longer hours in the Easter and summer vacations.

The outer arch of the main *Gateway* is Norman but its upper floors, like the outer walls of the castle, were rebuilt by James Wyatt. The *Keep* (not open), on the mound to the right of the courtyard, was rebuilt in the 1830s. On the left of the courtyard, Bishop Cosin's Ionic porch leads into the screens passage. The *Kitchen*, with its huge fireplaces, was adapted from the 12C building by Bishop Fox in 1499. The *Great Hall*, now the college's dining hall, keeps its original 14C roof among alterations by virtually every succeeding age. We climb the splendid *Black Staircase* added by Bishop Cosin in the 1660s to *Tunstal's Gallery* (1530–39). The *doorway surviving from Bishop Pudsey's 12C hall is a supreme example of richly decorated Norman work. It now leads into the state rooms (not open). *Tunstal's Chapel* (c 1542) at the end of the gallery contains fine woodwork. We climb next to the *Norman Gallery*, with open wall-arcades and decorated arches belonging to the upper floor of Pudsey's hall. A spiral staircase leads down to the earliest part of the castle, the *Norman Chapel* (c 1080), with interesting capitals.

The **University of Durham**, England's third oldest university, was founded in 1832 by Bishop Van Mildert, the last episcopal count palatine, who gave up the castle and part of his princely revenue for the purpose. Its organisation modifies the Oxbridge system, with residential colleges responsible for the students' social and domestic life and faculties responsible for their teaching.

After *University College*, in the castle and neighbouring buildings, the other early foundations were also in the heart of the city: *Hatfield College* (1846) in 17–20C buildings in North Bailey and *St Cuthbert's Society* (1888) in a 19C building in South Bailey. Later growth has extended beyond the peninsula. S of the river are: *St Mary's College* (1899; main buildings by E. Vincent Harris, 1952); *St Aidan's College* (1947; buildings by Sir Basil Spence, 1964); *Grey College* (1959; buildings by T. Worthington, 1960–61); *Van Mildert College* (1965; buildings by Middleton, Fletcher and Partners, 1966); *Trevelyan College* (1966; buildings by Stillman and Eastwick-Field, 1967); and *Collingwood College* (1972; buildings by Richard Sheppard, Robson and Partners, 1973). The *College of St Hild and St Bede*, off Leazes Rd N of the river, was formed by a merger of two independent Colleges of Education and fully integrated into the university in 1979. It has a fine chapel (1939; Mottistone and Paget). *St Chad's College* (1904) in North Bailey and *St John's College* (1909) in South Bailey are Church of England Colleges which also admit students to the full range of university courses. All the colleges are co-residential except St Mary's and Trevelyan, which admit women only. King's College, Newcastle, was part of Durham University from 1937 until 1963, when it became the University of Newcastle in its own right.

Views of the cathedral and castle from Grey College and St Aidan's are worth seeking out. The *Oriental Museum*, on Elvet Hill below St Aidan's, has notable collections of art and archaeology. The *Botanic Garden*, off Hollingside Lane near Collingwood College, has 18 acres of worldwide trees, shrubs, cacti, etc., with a tropical collection and a Visitors' Centre.—The church of *St Giles*, off Gilesgate near St Hild and St Bede, contains early and late 12C work and an unusual 16C effigy. Off Gilesgate a 14C gatehouse survives from *Kepier Hospital*, founded by Bishop Flambard in 1122.

Near the *County Hall*, 1m NW of the centre by Framwelgate on the way to A167, is the *Durham Light Infantry Museum and Arts Centre*, with a lively programme of exhibitions.—*Finchale Priory* (English Heritage, standard opening), pronounced 'Finkle', is charmingly situated on the bank of the Wear about 4m N of the city, reached by lane and footpath or by the sideroad branching E from A167. It was founded c 1195 by Benedictines from Durham on the site of the cell where St Godric had spent his last years and died in 1170. The ruins include the 13C church, with the tomb reputedly belonging to the saint, and the 14C cloister buildings, notably the refectory and its undercroft.

*Sherburn Hospital*, 2½m E of the city, has the contemporary gatehouse of the hospital founded by Bishop Pudsey in 1181.—*Ushaw College* (not open), beyond Neville's Cross 4m W, was founded in 1808 in direct succession to the dispossessed seminary for Roman Catholic priests at Douai. The chapel (1884; Dunn and Hansom) incorporates furnishings from the earlier chapel by Pugin.—*Brancepeth* lies on A690 3½m SW of Neville's Cross. Its castle (not open), mostly rebuilt in the 19C, was the seat of the Neville family until 1569. In the grounds stands the 12–14C church of *St Brandon*, with remarkable Neville monuments and *woodwork by the future Bishop John Cosin, rector here in 1626–44.

*Bishop Auckland*, 11m SW of Durham by A167 and A688, is the starting-point for Rte 86H through Weardale to *Alston*.

FROM DURHAM TO STOCKTON-ON-TEES, 19m by A177.—We cross the Wear near (1¹/₂m) *Shincliffe*, with a pleasant main street.—5¹/₂m. *Coxhoe*, where Elizabeth Barrett Browning (1806–61) was born at the Hall, since demolished.—10¹/₂m. *Sedgefield*, with the 18C grounds of Hardwick Hall Country Park and the racecourse to the right of the road. The church has a Perp. tower and a good 17C screen and stalls in Bishop Cosin's manner.—19m. *Stockton*, see above.

FROM DURHAM TO SUNDERLAND, 13m by A690, or 20m by A690, A182 and A1293.—1m. A sideroad leads from the roundabout to (2¹/₂m) *Pittington*, right of A690, where the church has an interesting N arcade of c 1175.—2m. We cross A1(M).—7m. *Houghton-le-Spring* (31,000 inhab.), in Tyne and Wear, has good 16–18C houses and a fine 13C church containing the tomb of Bernard Gilpin (d. 1583), the 'Apostle of the North'.—A690 continues straight to (13m) *Sunderland* (see below).

The longer route, adding 7m, takes A182 N from Houghton to (13m) **Washington** (50,900 inhab.), developed as a colliery New Town and now the site of the Nissan motor works. The *Old Hall* (NT) in Washington Village is an early 17C building incorporating fragments of the medieval house of the Washington family. The *Washington 'F' Pit Museum*, in the winding house of the former colliery, has an 1888 steam engine. The *Waterfowl Park* designed by Sir Peter Scott, on the Wear to the E, has a view across the river to the *Penshaw Monument* (NT), a Greek temple built in 1844 to commemorate 'Radical Jack', the 1st Earl of Durham.—A1231 heads along the N bank of the Wear, passing near the airport and Hylton Castle on the way into (20m) *Sunderland* (see below).

FROM DURHAM TO NEWCASTLE BY THE DERWENT VALLEY, 27m, a pleasant alternative to the main route below. We leave the city on A691.—7¹/₂m. *Lanchester* has a good Norman and EE church with Roman columns in the N arcade and a Roman altar (AD 244) in the porch, and, ¹/₂m SW, remains of the Roman *Longovicium*.—11¹/₂m. We continue straight ahead on B6309, following the Roman road. *Consett* (33,400 inhab.), a steel town until the works closed in 1980, is 2m W.—14m. *Ebchester* stands on the site of the fort of *Vindomara* above the Derwent, and has Roman stones in its church tower. R.S. Surtees (1803–64), the creator of Jorrocks, is buried here.—A694 goes E along the Derwent valley to (15m) *Hamsterley*. Surtees spent much of his life at the 18C *Hamsterley Hall* (not open), in the woods about 2¹/₂m SE.—A694 crosses the river for (19m) *Rowlands Gill*, on the Derwent Walk Country Park which follows the route of the former Derwent Valley Railway between Consett and the visitors' centre at Swalwell, near A69. Just beyond Rowlands Gill it offers views of the ruined home of the Bowes family and the tall Liberty monument (1757) in the Gibside estate (not open). Off B6314 S of Rowlands Gill is the beautiful *Gibside Chapel* (NT), designed as the Bowes family mausoleum by James Paine in 1760 and converted in 1809, with a three-decker pulpit.—22¹/₂m. We join A69 and the Tyne near *Swalwell*.—27m. *Newcastle*, see below.

We leave Durham by Framwelgate, past the Durham Light Infantry Museum (see above) and the County Hall, and join A167 at (99m) *Framwellgate Moor*.—104m. *Chester-le-Street* (20,500 inhab.) is a colliery town on the site of the Roman fort of *Concangium*. The monks of Lindisfarne came here with the body of St Cuthbert in 883, moving on to Durham in 995. The church is notable for its spire, Lumley monuments (mostly Elizabethan imitations of medieval work) and anchorite's cell, now housing local history exhibits.

The *North of England Open Air Museum at *Beamish*, 3m W on A693, illustrates the everyday life of the North-East in the late 19C and early 20C. The reconstructed buildings on its 200-acre site include a 1920s high street with Co-op store, pub, offices and shops; a railway station; a pithead, drift mine and miners' cottages; and a working home farm. The *Causey Arch* (1725–26), about 1¹/₂m NW of the museum, was built for the horsedrawn wooden waggonway that linked Tanfield colliery with the Tyne at Gateshead and so is arguably the world's oldest surviving railway bridge. The course of the metal railway that replaced it runs N to (½m) the junction with the Bowes Railway (see below), near the *Tyneside Locomotive Museum*, with locally built engines. In summer steam locomotives haul passenger trains along the stretch between Marley Hill and Sunniside.

About 1m E of Chester-le-Street is *Lumley Castle* (now a hotel), a fine example of the local type of 14C castle, altered by Vanbrugh.

The old road continues N as A6127, with A1(M) running alongside. We enter the county of Tyne and Wear, created in 1974 from the once great North-East coalfield and the Tyneside and Wearside ship-building region, now badly depressed, which used to belong to County Durham and Northumberland. Shortly beyond (107½m) *Birtley* the road crosses relics of the old Bowes Railway, a rope-hauled colliery line whose first section was designed by George Stephenson in 1826. The *Bowes Railway Heritage Museum* at *Springwell*, 2m NE of Birtley, has locomotives, rolling stock, displays of rope-haulage and steam rides along a short stretch of track. —112m. **Gateshead** (81,400 inhab.; Tourist Information) has lost its former industrial base as a port for the Tyne coalfield and a centre of heavy engineering, particularly railway workshops. The *Metro Centre* (1986–88), said to be the largest drive-in shopping centre in Europe, is the latest attempt to help revive the region's depressed economy. The *Shipley Art Gallery* has changing displays from a permanent collection notable for the Dutch school and 19C British painting. The parish church of *St Mary* was gutted by fire in 1979. The National Garden Festival will be held here in 1990. From Gateshead to Jarrow and South Shields, and to Sunderland and Stockton, see below.—The road enters Newcastle by the Tyne Bridge.

112½m. **NEWCASTLE UPON TYNE** (192,500 inhab.), never hyphenated and usually abbreviated to *Newcastle*, is the county town of Tyne and Wear as well as Northumberland and, unofficially, the capital of the North-East. It keeps a lively big-city atmosphere despite the economic problems of recent years. The quayside and river, where coal-exporting for centuries gave Newcastle its identity, now combine picturesque decay with signs of redevelopment—a familiar picture throughout Britain's dockland and waterways. The city centre that rises up the steep N bank of the Tyne has its share of insensitive modern replanning, but also a continually surprising skyline and, above all, the superb streets built by the speculator Richard Grainger (1798–1861) with John Dobson (1787–1865) and other local architects.

**Tourist Information Centres**: Central Library, Princess Square; Blackfriars, Monk St.; Newcastle Airport.

**Car Parks**: New Bridge St. (park and ride), Claremont Rd. Multi-storey car parks in John Dobson St., New Bridge St. and Greenmarket (Newgate St.).

**Railway Station**: Central Station, Neville St.

**Bus and Coach Stations**: Eldon Square Bus Concourse, Haymarket, Marlborough Crescent, Worswick St., Gallowgate.

**Metro**: Monument Station is the main interchange for the new rapid transit system (opened in 1981), using former British Rail suburban lines and an underground section to link the centre of the city with the suburbs and the coast. There are BR interchanges at Central Station and at Heworth, on S Tyneside.

**Ferry services**: Local ferries across the Tyne between South Shields and North Shields. Passenger ferries from Tyne Commission Quay, about 7m downstream near Percy Main, North Shields, to N European ports (Esbjerg, Gothenburg, Bergen, Stavanger).

**Airport**: At Woolsington, 6m NW. Direct passenger flights to Gatwick, Heathrow, Humberside, Isle of Man (summer), Teesside, Aberdeen, Belfast, Dublin, Amsterdam, Bergen, Oslo, Paris, Stavanger.

**Theatres**: Theatre Royal, Grey St.; Newcastle Playhouse, Barras Bridge; New Tyne Theatre, Westgate Rd; People's Theatre, Stephenson Rd. Annual visit by Royal Shakespeare Company to Theatre Royal and other theatres each spring. The City Hall, Northumberland Rd, is the home of the Northern Sinfonia Orchestra and the main venue for concerts.

**Annual Events**: The Hoppings, a travelling fair, on Town Moor (N of the centre) in last full week of June; Tyneside Summer Exhibition in July/August; Newcastle Festival in November.

**History**. Newcastle was the Roman station of *Pons Aelius* on Hadrian's Wall. It took its present name from the 'new castle' Robert Curthose, eldest son of William the Conqueror, built in 1080. The city suffered more than once at the hands of the Scots, and held out against them on behalf of Charles I for ten weeks in 1644. Two years later the Scots surrendered Charles to the English Parliament here. At first a centre of the wool trade, Newcastle flourished on coal-mining and coal-exporting from the Middle Ages onwards: the sarcasm 'to carry coals to Newcastle' was already familiar by the 17C. The 19C added shipbuilding, steel production and engineering; the 'Rocket' was built at George Stephenson's Newcastle works.

**Famous natives and residents**. The poet Mark Akenside (1721–70), Admiral Collingwood (1750–1810), the politician Lord Eldon (1751–1838), the arms manufacturer Lord Armstrong (1810–1900), Dickens's friend and biographer John Forster (1812–76) and Hugh Stowell Scott (1862–1903), who wrote historical novels as Henry Seton Merriman, were all born in here. The engraver Thomas Bewick (1753–1828), born near Eltingham (Rte 87A), worked in Newcastle and died at his home in Gateshead.

FROM THE CATHEDRAL SOUTH TO THE TYNE AND BACK. The **Cathedral** stands in Mosley St., midway between the Tyne Bridge and Central Station. Formerly one of the largest parish churches in England, it was raised to cathedral status in 1882. The W tower with its famous *spire delicately supported in mid-air by flying buttresses is the chief landmark of central Newcastle. The earliest and best example of a 'crown spire' in Britain (c 1448 but since rebuilt), it set the pattern for similar spires, notably at St Giles's, Edinburgh.

The interior is mainly 14–15C. Unusually, the columns of the nave (1330–60) lack capitals. Beneath the striking lierne vault of the tower stands the font; its superbly carved *canopy (c 1500) has a miniature vault and boss inside. Nearby is a bust of Admiral Collingwood, Nelson's second-in-command at Trafalgar, who was baptised and married here. St Margaret's Chapel, interrupting a series of low arched recesses in the S aisle, has a roundel of 15C glass. The lectern dates from c 1500, and the upper part of the organ case survives from the original Renatus Harris organ of 1676. The S transept has an elaborate 17C monument of the Maddison family. The magnificent *Flemish brass commemorating Roger Thornton (d. 1429) and his wife, one of the best and largest in the country, now hangs on the wall of the S choir aisle—too high to be properly appreciated. The crypt has 14C rib vaulting and a small internal 'wheel' window. The cathedral's treasures (seen on request) include the so-called Hexham Bible of c 1220. Thomas Bewick had his workshop at the SW corner of the churchyard.

St Nicholas St. leads S to the remains of the *Castle (open), on a site cruelly cut in two by the railway.

The *Black Gate*—named after a person, not its colour—is a fine barbican of 1247 with a 17C upper part. It houses the *Bagpipe Museum*, with a large collection of Northumbrian pipes. The handsome though not very big *Keep*, on the other side of the railway, was built by Henry II in 1172–77 on the site of Robert Curthose's 'new castle' (1080). An outside staircase over the forebuilding mounts to the restored entrance (1848) at second-floor level. This arrangement is paralleled only at Dover and may be the work of the same mason. The *Hall* occupies most

*The crown spire of Newcastle Cathedral*

of the interior of the keep. Stairs lead up to the restored battlements (with a good view of the city and river) and down to the beautiful though much restored *Chapel* (c 1168–78) in the forebuilding, and the so-called *Garrison Room*, with its central pillar. Chambers and passages in the thickness of the walls can also be explored.

We cross Castle Garth and, passing the *Moot Hall* (1810) on our left, go through the S postern gate to descend the steep Castle Stairs to the river by the *Swing Bridge* (1876), on the site of the Roman and medieval bridges. Downstream is the *Tyne Bridge* (1925–28; Mott, Hay and Anderson). Upstream are the superb *High Level Bridge* (1845–49; Robert Stephenson and John Dobson), with the road suspended beneath the railway, and the new *Queen Elizabeth II Bridge* carrying the Metro.

Handsome 16–17C houses rise to four or five storeys in Sandhill, to the left. A tablet on No. 41 marks the window through which Bessy Surtees eloped in 1772 to marry the future Lord Chancellor Eldon. The *Guildhall*, opposite, was rebuilt by Robert Trollope in 1658, classicised in the 18C and given its rounded E end by Dobson in 1823. Quayside, where an open-air market is held on Sunday mornings, leads under the Tyne Bridge. There is a fine view up the river bank to *All Saints' Church* (1786–96; David Stephenson) with its striking steeple and elliptical nave. Shortly beyond stands the *Custom House* (1766, altered by Sydney Smirke in 1838). Broad Chare has the *Trinity Maritime Centre* (open) and *Trinity House* (not open), a foundation of 1492, with 16–19C buildings.

Milk Market leads into City Rd and an area several times battered by change. Opposite are the Dutch-style buildings of the *Keelmen's Hospital* (1701). Further E is *St Ann's Church* (1764–68; William Newton). We head up City Rd towards the Swan House roundabout, passing a corner tower of the medieval city walls on the left. Hemmed in by later development stands the Holy Jesus Hospital, an arcaded and Dutch-gabled almshouse of 1681–83, restored as the *John George Joicey Museum*.

Devoted to the social history of Newcastle, it contains audio-visual displays, 17–19C period rooms, swords and sporting guns made in the North-East, and regimental collections.

Pedestrian passages lead to Mosley St. below the monstrous and barren *Swan House* (1970; Robert Matthew, Johnson-Marshall and Partners in association with George Kenyon), entombing Dobson's fine *Royal Arcade* (1831).

FROM THE CATHEDRAL NORTH TO THE CIVIC CENTRE AND THE UNIVERSITY, AND BACK. *Grey St., climbing N from Mosley St. in a gentle curve of classical façades, is John Dobson's masterpiece (1835–38) and one of the finest streets in England. On the right stands the *Theatre Royal* with its splendid portico (1837; Benjamin Green). On the left is the entrance to the well-preserved Edwardian *Central Arcade* (1905). At the top of the street stands the *Grey Monument*, also by Green, commemorating the 2nd Earl Grey (1764–1845), the Liberal Prime Minister responsible for the Reform Bill of 1832. His statue is by Edward H. Baily. *Monument Station* is the main interchange for the Metro, the city's rapid transit system.

Grainger St. and the Eldon Square Shopping Precinct, to the left, are visited later in this walk. Now we take New Bridge St. to the right, passing Northumberland St. and the Art Nouveau *Pearl Assurance Building* (1904) on the way to the modern John Dobson St. This leads N between the *Central Library* (1968; Sir Basil Spence), with the main Tourist Information Centre, and the **Laing Art Gallery** in a neo-baroque building of 1904.

It contains wide-ranging collections of British art from the 18C to the present, including paintings by Gainsborough, Reynolds, Landseer, Burne-Jones (Laus Veneris), Holman Hunt (Isabella and the Pot of Basil), Stanley Spencer and John Hoyland, and a good display of work by John Martin. Also on exhibit are British textiles; British and local ceramics and silver; and British and Newcastle glass, including 18C enamelled glass by William Beilby. There is a continuous programme of temporary exhibitions.

In Croft St., opposite, is the *Plummer Tower*, a relic of the medieval wall altered in 1742.

Northumberland St., a busy shopping street, continues Pilgrim St. N to Barras Bridge, where Dobson's Gothic Revival church of *St Thomas* (1825–30) forms the focal point between the Civic Centre and the University.

The **Civic Centre** (1960–68; George Kenyon) has a quasi-monastic plan in the shape of a cross, with a central tower, and an arcaded cloister or quadrangle enclosed by the administrative wings.

A *Ceremonial Way*, lined with tall flambeaux and dominated by a huge bronze symbolising the Tyne, leads to the elliptical *Council Chamber*. A pool in the quadrangle is embellished with bronze swans in flight (by David Wynne), reflecting Newcastle's ties with the Scandinavian countries. At the N end stands the plain and massive *Banqueting Hall*, with deep-set slit windows. The *Tower* has a copper lantern, decorated with sea horses and crowned by the three castles of the city's arms; its carillon plays traditional Newcastle tunes.

The **University of Newcastle** grew out of the College of Medicine (1834) and the school of engineering, Armstrong College (1871). They amalgamated in 1937 to form King's College, part of Durham University until granted university status in its own right in 1963. Among the new buildings are the *Physics Laboratories* (1961; Sir Basil Spence), the *University Library* (1982; Faulkner-Brown), and the *Medical School* (1984; Robert Matthew, Johnson-Marshall). The campus has several good museums.

The *Museum of Antiquities* contains a splendid collection, particularly of finds from Hadrian's Wall.

It includes: the late Bronze Age Whittingham sword; Iron Age finds from Ryton; the Celtic Aesica brooch (AD 75–80) from Hadrian's Wall, and other similar brooches; a gladiator and the *Bear cameo (3C), both from South Shields, and a set of bronze Roman military cooking vessels (2C) found near Ponteland; Roman altars, inscriptions and relief sculpture; an Anglo-Saxon hanging bowl (the most northerly in England); the Falstone Latin/Runic inscription (8–9C); and part of a 10C cross from Alnmouth. Notable also are the scale models of Hadrian's Wall; original and reconstructed Roman body armour; a reconstruction of the Carrawburgh Mithraeum; and a facsimile of the Corbridge Lanx (original in British Museum).

The *Hatton Gallery* has 16–18C European paintings, a large relief by Kurt Schwitters and African sculptures.—The *Greek Museum*, open on application to the Department of Classics, houses a small but important collection of Mediterranean antiquities. Of particular note are the Greek arms and armour; the Greek and Etruscan ceramics, including some fine pieces of Corinthian black-figure and Athenian red-figure; and the series of architectural terracottas from Sicily and Magna Graecia.—The *Mining Museum* in the Department of Mining Engineering has a good collection of miners' lamps.—The *Hancock Museum*, in Barras Bridge to the N, has large collections of geology and natural history, with a Thomas Bewick Room.

Further N is the large *Town Moor.*—Beyond the little *Brandling Park*, on the E side of the Great North Road (subway), stands the *Royal Grammar School.* —Overlooking the pleasant *Leazes Park*, SW of the university, is the dignified Leazes Terrace (1829–30; Thomas Oliver). The St James's Park ground of Newcastle United Football Club adjoins it.

From Barras Bridge the busy Haymarket (with a Metro station and bus station), Percy St. and Newgate St. lead SW, passing the huge *Eldon Square Shopping Precinct* (1976; Chapman, Taylor and Partners) on the left. *St Andrew's Church*, on the right, has a good chancel arch and a marvellously carved 15C font cover like the one in the cathedral.

The remains of the medieval *City Walls* (1265–1307) begin in the churchyard and continue, with towers, along West Walls and Bath Lane to Westgate Rd. *Blackfriars*, between Friars St. and Monk St. inside the angle of the walls, houses a Tourist Information Centre, local history displays and craft workshops in the restored buildings of the Dominican friary founded before 1239 and later used by craft guilds. Nearby Fenkle St. has the *Old Assembly Rooms* (1776; William Newton).

Newgate St. curves SE to the junction with Grainger St., which has a handsome stretch of buildings (partly by John Wardle, 1835–39) leading up to the Grey Monument. The *Grainger Market* (1835; Dobson) on its lefthand side is a good covered market. We can reach Westgate St. and Neville Rd, on the walk W from the cathedral (below), by taking Grainger St. to the right from Newgate St. Or we can complete the walk by following Bigg Market and Cloth Market to Mosley St. and the Cathedral.

WEST FROM THE CATHEDRAL. Mosley St. is continued W by Collingwood St., with *Lloyd's Bank* (1891) and the *Literary and Philosophical Society* (1822–25), where George Stephenson demonstrated his miners' safety lamp in 1815 and Sir Joseph Swan his electric light bulb in 1879. J.G. Lough's statue (1862) of the engineer Robert Stephenson stands at the fork of Neville St. and Westgate Rd. **Central Station** (1848–63) is a fine building by Dobson, with elegantly curved train sheds behind its classical entrance.

The 14–15C church of *St John the Baptist*, at the junction of Westgate Rd and Grainger St., has a Jacobean pulpit and beautiful font cover. Thomas Bewick was married here.—The Old Assembly Rooms, Blackfriars and the medieval walls, all described above, can be reached from Westgate Rd.

We follow Neville St. to the junction with Clayton St. and Pugin's *Roman Catholic Cathedral* (1844) with a spire added by J.A. Hansom. Westmorland Rd continues to Blandford Square and the **Museum of Science and Engineering**. Its permanent displays illustrate the history of motive power, with working models; the history of the Tyne, with a model of the river in 1929; and Tyneside's industrial pioneers, including George and Robert Stephenson, Sir Joseph Swan and Lord Armstrong.

SOUTH TYNESIDE: FROM NEWCASTLE/GATESHEAD TO JARROW AND SOUTH SHIELDS, 10$\frac{1}{2}$m. by A184, A185. From Gateshead we skirt the S bank of the industrial Tyne.—7m. **Jarrow** (27,200 inhab.; Tourist Information), whose name recalls unemployment and the Hunger March of 1936, has ship-repair yards and oil installations. The *Tyne Tunnel* (1967; toll) takes the A1 under the river to Willington Quay and North Shields. Part of the basilica founded here by Benedict Biscop in 682 survives as the chancel of *St Paul's Church*, with its 11C tower, to the E of the town. The dedication stone of 685 can be seen above the chancel arch inside; the N aisle has interesting displays of pre-Conquest sculptured stones. The Venerable Bede ('the monk of Jarrow') lived in the adjoining monastery from 682 until his death in 735, writing his 'Historia Ecclesiastica' here. The chair in the chancel is traditionally said to be his, though dendrochronology has shown it to be only about 800 years old. The *Bede Monastery Museum*, in a late 18C mineowner's house, displays Saxon and medieval finds, as well as temporary exhibitions. Its grounds and herb garden are also open. The popular novelist Catherine Cookson was born at Jarrow in 1906, and much of the South Tyneside region advertises itself to tourists as 'Catherine Cookson Country'.

10$\frac{1}{2}$m. **South Shields** (87,200 inhab.; Tourist Information), at the head of the estuary, developed as a coal port and resort in the 19C. The local ferry crosses the Tyne to North Shields. The *Old Town Hall* (1768) has been restored after the wartime bomb damage which laid waste much of the old Market Square. Near the seafront the Roman fort of *Arbeia* has been excavated and its gateway rebuilt. The *Roman Museum* displays building, military, household and personal items from the site. The *Central Museum and Art Gallery* has local history exhibits, including a section about the invention of the lifeboat at South Shields. The author and naturalist Ernest Seton Thompson (1860–1946) was born here, but went to Canada at the age of five.

FROM NEWCASTLE/GATESHEAD TO SUNDERLAND AND STOCKTON, 11½m. From Gateshead we follow A184, relabelled A1 for part of the way, through (7m) *East Boldon*, beyond which we turn S on A1018.—10½m. **Monkwearmouth** is an unattractive suburb of Sunderland. *St Peter's Church* preserves the tower, W wall and porch from the Saxon church of the monastery founded by Benedict Biscop in 674. Bede entered the monastery in 680 at the age of seven, moving to Jarrow in 682. *Monkwearmouth Station* (1848), with a lovely neo-classical façade, is now a museum of land transport. The booking office and other parts of the building have been restored to their original condition. *Roker*, an Edwardian seaside suburb 1m NE, has an excellent church by E.S. Prior (1906–07) with Arts and Crafts furnishings which include an altar tapestry by Burne-Jones and tablets by Eric Gill.—We cross the Wear by a bridge (1929; Mott, Hay and Anderson) replacing one of 1793–96, then the boldest iron bridge of its time.

11½m. **Sunderland** (196,200 inhab.; Tourist Information), at the mouth of the river, developed as a coal port and a centre of ship-building and engineering in the 19C. Sir Joseph Swan (1828–1917), who in 1878 narrowly anticipated Edison in inventing the electric light bulb, was born here. George Hudson, the fraudulent 'Railway King', became its MP in 1845, and Sir Henry Irving made his first stage appearance here in 1856. The *Town Hall* and *Civic Centre* (1968–70) were designed by Sir Basil Spence, Bonnington and Collins. The *Museum and Art Gallery* in Mowbray Park has exhibits of local and maritime history, Sunderland glass and pottery, English silver and 18–20C British painting. *St Michael's Church* (enlarged by W.D. Caröe, 1932–35) in High St. West and the parish church of *Holy Trinity* (1719) near the docks are worth seeking out. The *Grindon Museum*, off A183 3m SW, has reconstructed 19–20C interiors. *Hylton Castle* (English Heritage, standard opening), off A1290 3m NW, is a 15C gatehouse-keep with the arms of the Washington family on its front.—From Sunderland to Washington and Durham, see above.

We continue S on A1018 through the coalfield.—At (14½m) *Ryhope* the Pumping Station Museum has the original beam engines of 1868. *Seaham* (21,100 inhab.), 2½m S, is a coal port with a badly polluted coastline. In 1815 Byron was married at Seaham Hall, to its N.—A1018 turns inland and joins A19 at (16½m) *Seaton*.—At (20½m) *Easington*, with a 13C church, the Hartlepool road bears left. It passes the mining town of *Peterlee* (22,800 inhab.; Tourist Information), founded in 1948 and named after the miners' leader Peter Lee (1864–1935).—A19 continues to (36m) *Billingham* and (39m) *Stockton*, both described in the detour from Darlington, above.

NORTH TYNESIDE: FROM NEWCASTLE TO TYNEMOUTH AND WHITLEY BAY. The quickest route (9½m) takes A1058, leaving Newcastle via (1½m) *Jesmond Dene*, a lovely park in the Ouseburn valley. The route below (11m) takes A193, linking up the industrial towns on the N bank of the Tyne.—3½m. *Wallsend* (44,700 inhab.) is so called because Hadrian's Wall reached the Tyne here. The recently excavated site of the fort of *Segedunum* lies near the Heritage Centre and Swan Hunter's ship-building yard. We cross the N approach to the Tyne tunnel and pass the road for Tyne Commission Quay, with the passenger ferry terminal (seasonal Tourist Information).—7½m. *North Shields*, with a local ferry service across the Tyne to South Shields.—At (8½m) **Tynemouth** (60,000 inhab. with North Shields) the head of the estuary was guarded by the *Castle and Priory* (English Heritage, standard opening and summer Sunday mornings, but closed on Tuesdays and alternate Wednesdays in winter). There was a monastery here by the 7C, refounded c 1090 as a Benedictine priory. The ruins consist chiefly of the EE presbytery and 15C Percy Chapel, enclosed by the castle wall and 14C gatehouse.—A193 continues up the coast past (9½m) the former fishing village of *Cullercoats* to (11m) the resort of **Whitley Bay** (37,100 inhab.; seasonal Tourist Information). On its way further N to (7m) *Blyth* (see below) the coast road passes (3¼m) *Seaton Sluice*. To its W stands *Seaton Delaval Hall* (limited opening), built by Vanbrugh in 1718–29 and, though gutted by fire in 1822, still ranking as one of his masterpieces. The little church is Norman.

FROM NEWCASTLE TO THE SCOTTISH BORDER AT CARTER BAR, 45m by A696 and A68, a lovely route through some remote countryside.—We pass Newcastle Airport on the way to (7½m) *Ponteland* (10,700 inhab.) in Northumberland.—13½m. *Belsay Hall and Castle* (English Heritage, summer standard opening and summer Sunday mornings; also weekends in winter), to the left, consist of a 14C pele tower attached to a ruined 17C mansion, and a Greek Revival house of 1810–17 built by the owner, Sir Charles Monck, with the help of the antiquary Sir William Gell and John Dobson.—We pass (17m) *Shaftoe Crags*, on the right. *Capheaton Hall* (not open), 1m left, is a beautiful house of 1668 by Robert Trollope of Newcastle, where Swinburne spent part of his childhood with his grandfather.—19m. *Kirkhale*, to the left, was the birthplace of Capability Brown (1716–83). **\*Wallington** (NT), 2m N in lovely grounds landscaped by Brown, is a late 17C house with good 18C plasterwork inside. The Central Hall, added for Lady Pauline Trevelyan by John Dobson in 1855, has painted decoration by William Bell Scott, Ruskin and others. There are good collections of paintings, furniture, needlework and dolls' houses, and a superb collection of fine porcelain.—21m. *Kirkwhelpington*, on the edge of the wild Northumbrian moors.—30m. **Otterburn** was the scene of the Scottish victory over the English in 1388, remembered in the English ballad of 'Chevy Chase' and the Scottish ballad of 'The Battle of Otterbourne'. Douglas, the Scottish leader, was killed and Hotspur, the English leader, captured.—At (31½m) *Elishaw* we join A68, the Roman Dere Street from Corbridge (Rte 87A), and enter the Northumberland National Park (see note to Rte 87). The road follows the wild valley of *Redesdale* past (34½m) *Rochester*, with the Roman station of *Bremenium* ½m right, and (42m) *Catcleugh Reservoir*. Between the two, A68 is joined by the drive (11m; toll) through the Border Forest Park from Kielder (Rte 87A).—We reach the border at (45m) **Carter Bar** (1371ft), at the SW end of the Cheviot Hills. The last Border skirmish, the Raid of Reidswire, took place here in 1575.—From Carter Bar to Edinburgh via Jedburgh and Melrose, see 'Blue Guide Scotland'.

From Newcastle to *Carlisle* via *Tynedale* and *Hexham*, see Rte 87A; via *Hadrian's Wall*, see Rte 87B.

Beyond Newcastle A6125 skirts the W edge of the coalfield.—At *Killingworth*, E of (117m) *Gosforth Park* racecourse, George Stephenson built his first locomotive in 1814.—At (119½m) *Seaton Burn*, on the Northumbrian border, we join A1.—127m. **Morpeth** (14,500 inhab.; Tourist Information) is a pleasant little market town on the Wansbeck. The 14C church of *St Mary* contains a restored Jesse window, and an adapted 15C gatehouse survives from the *Castle*. The 13C *Chantry* near the river has been converted to house a local history museum and the Tourist Information Centre. Vanbrugh's *Town Hall* (1714) in the Market Place was altered in 1869–70. The 15C *Belfry* in Oldgate rings a curfew at 20.00 every evening.

*Mitford*, 2m upstream where the Font flows into the Wansbeck, and *Bothal*, 3m downstream, both have ruined castles and interesting churches.

Roads run SE from Morpeth to (5m) *Bedlington*, with an attractive High St., and (9m) the colliery and ship-building port of *Blyth* (36,500 inhab.); and E to (9m) the small seaside resort of *Newbiggin-by-the-Sea* (12,100 inhab.). N of Newbiggin are the colliery towns of (2½m) *Lynemouth* and (3½m) *Ellington*, with the world's largest undersea mine.—The winding B roads leading SW from Morpeth to (26m) *Corbridge* (Rte 87A) pass (6m) *Whalton* and (16m) *Stamfordham*, two good villages enhanced by their long greens. Whalton church contains good 13C work. *Belsay*, where the route crosses A696 between Walton and Stamfordham, lies on the detour from Newcastle to Carter Bar, above.

FROM MORPETH TO COLDSTREAM, 45m. About 2½m N of Morpeth we turn left on A697.—At (9m) *Weldon* we cross the Coquet, explored in the detour from Felton below, and beyond (10½m) *Longframlington* we climb over the moors of *Rothbury Forest*.—15m. We cross B6341, heading SW to Rothbury and NE to Alnwick via Edlingham, all described later in this route.—19m. *Bridge of Aln Inn*. The church at *Whittingham* (pronounced 'Whittinjam'), 1½m W, has traces of Saxon work. *Cally Castle* (not open), 2m SW of Whittingham, is a 17–19C mansion built round a pele tower.—Beyond (22m) *Powburn* we can follow the valley of the Breamish W into the Northumberland National Park (see note to Rte 87), with a seasonal Information Centre at (2½m) *Ingram*. Beyond lies the prehistoric settlement of *Greaves Ash*, scattered over about 20 acres, and, 4m from Ingram, the fall of *Linhope Spout* in the heart of the desolate Cheviot

Hills.—31m. **Wooler** (seasonal Tourist Information) is a small, grey market town on the edge of the Northumberland National Park and the Cheviots. *Humbleton Hill*, where Hotspur defeated Earl Douglas in 1402, rises 1½m W. *The Cheviot* (2674ft), about 6m SW, is the highest hill in the group, with a wild and desolate view. *Chillingham Castle* (open), 6m SE of Wooler, keeps the square corner towers of the 14C fortress, with 15–19C additions including an Elizabethan Long Gallery. It is currently being restored. The grounds include formal gardens, landscaping by Sir Jeffry Wyatville (1753) and lovely woodland. The small church contains the elaborate table-tomb of Sir Ralph Grey (d. 1443). *Chillingham Park* (open) has a unique *herd of wild white cattle.—From (33¼m) Akeld B6351 heads W along the valley of the Glen past *Yeavering Bell* (1182ft; *view), on the left, above the site of Edwin of Northumbria's 7C palace. Beyond (2¾m) *Kirknewton* it crosses the College Burn and beyond (5m) *Kilham* a sideroad goes on up the Bowmont Water to (11m) *Kirk Yetholm* in Scotland, at the end of the Pennine Way.—Beyond Akeld A697 follows the valley of the Till past (38m) *Ford*, with its partly 14C castle (not open), on the opposite bank. The village was improved in the 19C by Ruskin's pupil Louisa, Marchioness of Waterford, whose paintings are displayed in the former village school. *Etal* (pronounced 'Eetle'), a pleasant little place 1½m NW of Ford, has the remains of a 14C castle (English Heritage, open at any reasonable time).—39¼m. *Crookham*. About 1½m W is the battlefield of *Flodden*, where the English defeated the Scots in 1513. A monument to 'the brave of both nations' stands near *Branxton* church on the spot where James IV of Scotland is supposed to have fallen.—43m. *Cornhill* and (45m) *Coldstream*, see below.

Beyond Morpeth A1 crosses the Coquet near (137m) *Felton*.

For *Warkworth*, on the river about 7½m E, see below.—To follow the river W we take B6345 from Felton to (4m) *Longframlington*, turn S on A697 to (5½m) *Weldon*, and then head W again on B6344.—6½m. *Brinkburn Priory* (English Heritage, summer standard opening and summer Sunday mornings from 11.00), founded c 1130 for Augustinian canons, stands on a lovely site by the river. Its handsome late 12C church spans the transition from Norman to EE. The nearby Georgian house incorporates part of the cloister buildings.—11½m. **Rothbury** (1700 inhab.; seasonal National Park Information Centre) is an attractive market town. The church font stands on part of a 9C cross. *Cragside* (NT), splendidly sited on a hillside 1m NE, was largely designed by Norman Shaw in 1869–85 for the Newcastle arms manufacturer Lord Armstrong. The fine interiors contain work in the Pre-Raphaelite taste, including pottery and tiles by William De Morgan and paintings by Evelyn De Morgan, as well as Victorian technology (central heating, electric light, hydraulic lift, etc.). The wooded grounds run to 900 acres. The heather-clad *Simonside Hills* (1447ft) rise SW of Rothbury.

B6341 continues through the beautiful moorland scenery of *Coquetdale*. —4m. The sideroad to the right enters the Northumberland National Park beyond (6½m) *Sharperton*. Near *Holystone*, about 1m S, is a well (NT) in which Paulinus is said to have baptised 3000 Northumbrians in 627. Beyond (9m) *Harbottle* (seasonal National Park and Northumberland Wildlife Trust Information Centre), with the remains of a late 12C castle, and (10½m) *Alwinton*, the sideroad reaches the boundary of the vast Redesdale Firing Range (closed during firing practice) and continues to (19½m) *Blindburn*, 3m from the Roman camp of *Chew Green* on Dere Street, near the Scottish border.—After the turning for Sharperton B6341 crosses the Coquet and goes through (12m) *Elsdon*, with a pele tower near the church and the earthworks of a Norman castle, on the way to (15m) *Otterburn* (on the Newcastle–Carter Bar detour, above).

145m. **Alnwick** (7200 inhab.; seasonal Tourist Information), pronounced 'Annick', is an unspoilt old town above the Aln. The 15C *Hotspur Gate*, with *Pottergate* near the church, is the only relic of the medieval walls. *St Michael's Church* contains good capitals, 14–15C effigies and a fine Flemish chest in the vestry.

*Alnwick Castle* (open), overlooking the river, makes a marvellously romantic spectacle. This is largely the result of 19C rebuilding, though the medieval plan and some good details survive.

The original 12C shell-keep and curtain wall were strengthened and enlarged when the Percys, later Earls and then Dukes of Northumberland, bought the castle in 1309. Robert Adam rescued it from disrepair in the mid 18C but his work was expunged a century later, when Anthony Salvin gave the exterior its present baronial appearance and Italian workmen created the ornate interior.

We enter near the *Barbican* and *Gatehouse* (c 1440). The early 14C *Abbot's Tower* in the Outer Bailey contains a regimental museum. The 14–15C *Middle Gateway* leads into the Middle Bailey, where the *Constable's Tower, Hotspur's Seat* and *Postern Tower* are early 14C. The Postern Tower houses a good museum of prehistoric and Roman archaeology, with Celtic and Viking material. We enter the *Keep* by the mid 14C *Octagonal Towers,* with a Norman arch beyond. The 19C state rooms, in the style of a Renaissance palace, contain a fine collection of paintings (Andrea del Sarto, Tintoretto, Titian, Claude Lorrain, Van Dyck, Canaletto, Turner). The grounds are by Capability Brown.

Only a 14C gatehouse remains of *Alnwick Abbey,* beyond the Aln, founded in 1147 for Premonstratensian canons.—*Hulne Priory,* on a hill above the river 3m NW, is reached on foot through the beautiful grounds of Hulne Park either from Alnwick or from B6346 (admission pass from the Estate Office, Alnwick Castle). It is privately occupied but can be seen with the tenant's permission. Founded c 1240, Hulne is the earliest example of a Carmelite friary in England, and the ruins are the most perfect of their kind.

B6341, the Rothbury road to the SW, passes near (6m) *Edlingham,* where the castle ruins include a handsome 15C tower (English Heritage, open at any reasonable time).

A1068 leads E to (4¹/₂m) **Alnmouth**, a resort on the estuary of the Aln. B1339, heading N, passes the turnings for (4¹/₂m) the beautiful gardens (open) of *Howick Hall* and (5¹/₂m) the fishing village of *Craster,* known for its kippers, with a tiny harbour and a medieval tower. Near Dunstanburgh Castle B1339 joins B1340, on the alternative route from Alnwick to Belford, below. —Beyond Alnmouth A1068 continues another 3m down the coast to *Warkworth,* a lovely village on a loop of the Coquet, with a medieval bridge and a partly Norman church. The spectacularly sited *Warkworth Castle* (English Heritage, standard opening and summer Sunday mornings) was founded in the 12C and became a stronghold of the Percys in 1332. The ruins include the walls, gatehouse and vestiges of the great hall (all before 1215), the Lion Tower (c 1400) with the lion emblem of the Percys, and the marvellous 15C keep. About ¹/₂m upstream is the remarkable 14C *Hermitage* cut into the cliff (English Heritage, summer season, weekends only).—2m beyond Warkworth we reach *Amble-by-the-Sea* (5400 inhab; seasonal Tourist Information), a port at the mouth of the Coquet. About 1m offshore is *Coquet Island,* the site of a cell of Tynemouth Priory, with a lighthouse.

A1 from Alnwick to (160m) *Belford* is not interesting and the alternative route nearer the coast, described below, is recommended. *Preston Tower* (open), right of A1 at 153m, is a late 14C pele tower with tunnel-vaulted rooms.

---

The alternative way from Alnwick to Belford, 8m longer than the main route, takes B1340 to (7¹/₄m) *Christon Bank.* About 2m E is *Embleton*, with a vicar's pele tower (14C). On the rocky headland 2m beyond, and 1m from the end of the road, are the striking ruins of **Dunstanburgh Castle** (English Heritage, standard opening and summer Sunday mornings). One of the largest Border castles, it was begun in 1314 and strengthened by John of Gaunt, then Lieutenant of the Scottish Marches, in 1380–84. The Wars of the Roses hastened its ruin. The Lilburn Tower and parts of the curtain walls survive but the boldest feature, dominating the beautiful coastline, is the twin-towered *gatehouse-keep.* For Craster, to the S, see above.—B1340 joins the coast at (13m) *Beadnell* and continues to (14¹/₂m) the resort of *Seahouses* (seasonal Tourist Information).

In summer there are boat trips from the harbour to the *Farne Islands* (NT), an archipelago of about 28 small islands forming the E tip of the dolerite scarp known as the Great Whin Sill. They are a breeding place for the grey seal and about 20 species of seabirds. The *Inner Farne,* c 2m from the coast, is the nearest and largest. St Aidan often withdrew here from Lindisfarne for prayer and contemplation, and St Cuthbert lived from 676 to 684 in a hermitage whose site is marked by a 14C chapel, returning to die here in 687. The *Longstone Lighthouse*, on one of the remotest islands, was the scene of the rescue by Grace Darling (1815–42) and her father of the survivors of the 'Forfarshire' in 1838.

17½m. **Bamburgh** was the Saxon capital of Bernicia and, for a time, of the united kingdom of Northumbria. The *Castle* (open), romantically placed on a dolerite crag by the shore, served for generations as a royal fortress. The magnificent keep is Norman and much of the curtain walling dates from before 1250, but the Newcastle arms tycoon Lord Armstrong rebuilt most of the remainder in the late 19C. There is a fine view of the coast from the ramparts. The *Church* on the opposite side of the village has a lovely 13C choir. St Aidan died here in 651, though he was buried on Holy Island. The tomb of Grace Darling stands in the churchyard and her lifeboat is preserved in the museum named after her.

B1342 heads inland past the S tip of *Budle Bay* to join A1 just before (23m) *Belford*.

---

A1 continues past *Beal*, to the right at 166½m on the direct route. *Holy Island*, or **Lindisfarne**, can be reached from here by a causeway (about 3m) uncovered at low tide. The tables posted at each end should be consulted.

King Oswald of Northumbria gave the island to St Aidan (d. 651), a missionary from Iona, who became the first Bishop of Lindisfarne in 635. Under him and his successors, who included St Cuthbert (d. 687), Holy Island became one of the earliest and most shining centres of Christianity in England. A glorious relic survives in the famous Lindisfarne Gospels (c 698), now in the British Museum. When the Danes descended in 875, the monks fled with the body of St Cuthbert, finding a final refuge at Durham in 995.

Nothing remains of this first monastery. The existing *ruins (English Heritage, standard opening and summer Sunday mornings) belong to the Benedictine priory founded as a cell to Durham in 1083. Despite erosion by nine centuries of sea weather, the red sandstone church remains a superb example of Norman work, remarkable for its fortified character and very like the mother church at Durham. Note the incised decoration of the nave pillars and the diagonal rib vault between the crossing piers. The domestic buildings to the S are 13–14C. Nearby are a small museum displaying carved stones and other remains from the priory, and the EE parish church with its massively buttressed bell tower.

The fine view from the ruins takes in Bamburgh Castle on the mainland to the S and, on a dolerite rock E of the priory, *Lindisfarne Castle* (NT), a small 16C fort ingeniously converted into a private house by Sir Edwin Lutyens in 1903. It contains a good collection of 17C oak furniture, and the grounds include a walled garden by Gertrude Jekyll.

At (174m) *Tweedmouth* we cross the Tweed by the high concrete New Bridge (1925–28), supplementing the 15-arched Old Bridge (1611–34). To the left is Robert Stephenson's Royal Border Bridge, built for the railway in 1850.

175m. **Berwick-upon-Tweed** (12,200 inhab.; seasonal Tourist Information) is an ancient border town at the mouth of the Tweed.

Alternately English and Scottish for centuries, Berwick had changed hands at least 13 times when it was finally surrendered to England in 1482. It was then made a bastion against the Scots and organised as a kind of extra-territorial community with a government of its own. This autonomy was recognised until the 19C.

The town centre is enclosed by *Ramparts* (English Heritage, open at any reasonable time) begun in 1555, among the earliest northern

European examples of the new military engineering pioneered in Italy. The N front was complete in 1569; the rest is a later extension, not finished until 1747. They enclose a much smaller area than Edward I's wall, of which only traces survive. The *Castle* where Edward judged in favour of John Balliol's claim to the Scottish crown in 1291 was largely demolished to make way for the railway station in the 19C, but a few fragments still stand nearby (English Heritage, open at any reasonable time). The fine *Ravensdowne Barracks* (English Heritage, summer standard opening and summer Sunday mornings from 11.00), built in 1717–21, are perhaps by Vanbrugh. They contain the local museum and art gallery, an exhibition about the history of the British infantry soldier from 1660 to 1880, and the regimental museum of the King's Own Scottish Borderers. *Holy Trinity* (1648–52) is one of the few churches built during the Commonwealth; the outside is marred by 19C turrets, but the inside has good woodwork and a reredos by Lutyens. The church-like *Town Hall* (1754–60) preserves its original jail cells on the upper floor. In the grounds of the early 18C Governor's House, overlooking the pleasant Palace Green, is the *Lindisfarne Wine and Spirit Museum*.

At *Halidon Hill* (537ft), 2m NW, a Scottish army attempting to raise the English siege of Berwick was defeated with great slaughter in 1333.

FROM BERWICK TO KELSO, 23m by A698 and B6350. We follow the S bank of the Tweed, marking the Scottish border.—6½m. **Norham** lies in a bend of the river 1¾m NW. Its ruined *Castle* (English Heritage, standard opening but closed on Tuesdays and alternate Mondays in winter) was the Border stronghold of the prince-bishops of Durham. Bishop Pudsey built the fine Norman keep (c 1160). In the church (with a Norman chancel) Edward I opened the assembly to decide the rival claims of Bruce and Balliol to the Scottish throne in 1290.—9¾m. We cross the deep ravine of the Till by the 15C *Twizel Bridge*, over which the English vanguard passed safely before the Battle of Flodden (1513). The 'castle' above is a ruined folly (1770).—At (13m) *Cornhill-on-Tweed* our road is joined by A697, which crosses the river into Scotland at *Coldstream*.—B6350 continues along the S bank via (15½m) *Wark-on-Tweed*, with the scanty remains of its once formidable castle, and enters Scotland shortly beyond (17½m) *Carham*. —23m. *Kelso*, see 'Blue Guide Scotland'.

From Berwick to *Edinburgh* via *Dunbar* and *Haddington*, see 'Blue Guide Scotland'. A1 crosses the border 3m N of Berwick at *Lamberton Bar*, where the tollkeeper performed the same good offices for runaway couples as the Gretna Green blacksmith.

# 86 The Dales

Maps: OS Landranger maps as indicated in the separate routes below. Walkers need OS Outdoor Leisure maps (1:25,000 or 2½in to 1m) for the Yorkshire Dales (three sheets) and Teesdale (one sheet).

The Pennine Chain, the loosely linked series of hills forming the so-called 'backbone of England', stretches N from the Peak District to the river Tyne in Northumberland. It is never very broad, avoided by the A1 on the E and the A6, intertwined with M6, on the W. Nor is it particularly high, its hills rarely exceeding 2000ft; the tallest rise in the W, where Cross Fell (between Appleby and Alston) achieves 2930ft. Its geological structure shows the same mixture of gritstone, or millstone grit, and limestone as the Peak District, already described in the introduction to Rte 56. Millstone grit predominates in the S, sometimes weathered into fantastic shapes which enliven the moorland scenery. The limestone region begins near Skipton and the Aire Gap, where the Craven Faults create dramatic effects like Malham Cove and the local 'scars'. Further N, in Teesdale, we find the S edge of the Whin Sill (or Great Whin Sill), the intrusive scarp of hard igneous rock over which the waterfall at High Force hurls itself.

This upland landscape of fell, moor and rock is varied by the dales, the winding valleys of the rivers which make their way down the Pennine slopes. Most flow eastwards, though the Ribble perversely heads S before issuing into the sea on the W coast near Preston. The southern reaches of the dales have proved a natural breeding-ground for industry since the 18C; they are toured on the way through the Yorkshire and Lancashire manufacturing towns in Rte 75. The present section follows the largely agricultural dales further N—Wharfedale (Rte A below), Nidderdale (Rte B), the upper stages of Airedale and Ribblesdale (Rte C), Wensleydale (Rte D) and their many tributary dales—where the countryside remains wild or wooded or just pleasantly green. Bolton Abbey in Wharfedale is the best-known example of the picturesque combination of water, wood and ruin which the dales can offer, just as Grassington, higher up the same valley, typifies their charming stone-built towns and villages. Leadmining has left its trace further N, in Swaledale (Rte E) and Teesdale (Rte G), but only in Weardale (Rte H) do we again encounter the real scars of industry.

These routes repeatedly interconnect and, in their possible combinations with each other, offer the motorist a choice of many different ways over the Pennines, linking points on or near the A1 (Rte 85B) with points on or near the A6 (Rte 76). But the character of the landscape, with its often steep and narrow roads, hardly suits long-distance travellers or car-bound sightseers: they are better advised to cross the Pennines by the high-lying A66 (Rte F) between Scotch Corner and Penrith, or to follow A69 (Rte 87A) along the Tyne valley from Newcastle to Carlisle. The dales attract climbers, pot-holers and, above all, walkers. In addition to the various short walking detours suggested in the routes that follow, several long-distance footpaths are worth noting here. The Dales Way (81m) connects both Leeds and Bradford with Bowness-on-Windermere in the Lake District, following Wharfedale, Dentdale and the valleys of the Lune and the Kent. The central section of A. Wainwright's Coast-to-Coast Walk, 190m from St Bees Head to Robin Hood's Bay, follows Swaledale. The central section of the Pennine Way, which starts at Edale in the Peak District and ends at Kirk Yetholm over the Scottish border, goes via Malham (Upper Airedale), Horton-in-Ribblesdale, Hawes (Wensleydale), Keld (Swaledale), Middleton-in-Teesdale and Alston.

Most of the Yorkshire Dales toured in Rtes A–E are part of the National Park established in 1953 and covering 650 square miles. There are National Park Information Centres at Aysgarth Falls, Clapham, Grassington, Hawes, Malham and Sedbergh, with smaller local information points in village shops, Post Offices, cafés, etc., at Askrigg, Bolton Abbey, Buckden, Burnsall, Grassington, Dent, Gunnerside, Hebden, Horsehouse, Horton-in-Ribbesdale, Kettlewell, Langcliffe, Litton, Muker, Reeth, Stump Cross Caverns and Thoralby. Further details can be obtained from the Information Service, Yorkshire Dales National Park, Colvend, Hebden Rd, Grassington, Skipton, North Yorkshire BD23 5LB.

# A. Wharfedale: Wetherby to Ilkley, Grassington and Hawes

Total distance 58m. **Wetherby**, see Rte 85B.—A58 to (1½m)
Collingham.—A659 to (14m) Otley.—A660, A65 to (20m) **Ilkley**.
—A65 to (23m) Addingham.—B6160 to (26m) Bolton Abbey.
—B6160 to (36½m) **Grassington**.—B6160 to (46½m) Buckden.
—Unclassified roads to (58m) **Hawes** (Rte 86D).

Maps: OS Landranger 105 (briefly), 104, 98.

**Wetherby**, see Rte 85B. We take A58 SW to join A659 near (1½m)
*Collingham*, which can also be reached directly from A1. The parish
church has the remains of 9C Saxon crosses.

*Bardsey*, off A58 2¼m SW, was the birthplace of William Congreve (1670–1729)
and has a late Norman church with a Saxon tower.
    We head W along the broad and not very interesting valley of **Lower
Wharfedale**, where the river divides West Yorkshire from North Yorkshire.
—6m. *Harewood*, in the sharp bend where the Leeds road joins A659, is a model
village by John Carr of York (1760) outside the walls of *Harewood House
(open).

The mansion was built in 1759–72, with Robert Adam modifying Carr's original,
severely Palladian design. Sir Charles Barry remodelled the S façade and added
a third storey in 1843. Inside, only the Entrance Hall is decorated by Carr; the
rest of the house keeps some of the best Adam interiors in England, reaching a
superb climax in the Gallery. The plasterwork is by Joseph Rose and the
painted wall panels are by Angelica Kauffmann, Antonio Zucchi and Biagio
Rebecca. Much of the *furniture was made for Harewood by Chippendale (see
Otley, below). The paintings include work by Turner, Thomas Girtin, Bellini,
Catena, Pollaiuolo, El Greco, Titian, Veronese and Tintoretto, and family
portraits by Gainsborough, Reynolds, Hoppner, Romney and Lawrence. There
are also good collections of Sèvres porcelain and Chinese porcelain.
    Outside, the formal terrace and parterre by Barry and Nesfield, to the S,
contrasts with the landscaped park by Capability Brown which extends to the
N. It contains a *Bird Garden* with exotic species, the ruins of *Harewood
Castle*, and the Perp. *Church*. Among the fine series of monuments here is the tomb of
Chief Justice Gascoigne (d. 1419), who is said to have committed the future
Henry V for contempt of court (see Shakespeare's 'Henry IV, Part 2').
    From Harewood to *Leeds* and to *Harrogate*, *Ripon* and *Thirsk*, see Rte 80.

14m. **Otley** (13,800 inhab.; Tourist Information) is an industrial
market town on the Wharfe. The cabinetmaker Thomas Chippendale
(1711–79) was born here. The restored Perp. church contains 17–19C
monuments of the Fairfax and Fawkes families, and fragments of
9–11C Saxon crosses. The churchyard has a monument with a scale
model of the Bramhope Tunnel, in memory of the railway navvies
killed during its construction in 1845–49. The *Chevin* (841ft), rising to
the S, gives a good view of the Wharfe valley and the hills to the NW.

The view from the Chevin takes in *Farnley Hall* (not open), about 1½m NE of
Otley, an Elizabethan house with a wing added by John Carr in 1786–90.
Turner frequently visited his friend Walter Fawkes (a descendant of Guy
Fawkes) here, and used a view of the Chevin during a thunderstorm in his
painting of 'Hannibal Crossing the Alps'.—To the E of Farnley Park is the
village of *Leathley*, with its early Norman church tower and 18C Hall and
almshouses.—Beyond Farnley B6451 follows the Washburn valley, partly filled
by reservoirs, to (7m) *Blubberhouses* on the Harrogate–Bolton Abbey road (Rte
80).
    *Guiseley*, 2½m S of Otley, has a gabled rectory (1601) and an interesting
partly Norman church, where the parents of the Brontë sisters were married in
1812. Ancestors of the American poet Longfellow are buried in the churchyard.
    From Otley to *Leeds*, see Rte 75F.

We join A660 as we leave Otley and A65 as we enter (16½m) *Burley-in-Wharfedale*. On the other side of the Wharfe beyond the village we can see *Denton Park* (not open), rebuilt by John Carr in 1778, where General Fairfax was born in 1612.

20m. **Ilkley** (24,100 inhab.; Tourist Information), once a popular spa town, spreads from the S bank of the Wharfe up towards the high moorland made famous by the Yorkshire song. The late Perp. parish church of *All Saints* has three Anglian crosses in the churchyard. The *Manor House Museum* behind it is a 15–17C building on the site of the W gate of the Roman fort of *Olicana*. Part of the Roman wall has been exposed nearby. The collection includes many archaeological finds as well as 17–18C farmhouse furniture.

The neighbourhood is also rich in Bronze Age remains. The *Panorama Stone*, a fine example of a rock carved with the distinctive 'cup and ring' motif, can be seen in the public gardens opposite the 19C *St Margaret's Church* in the S part of the town. The most famous of the Bronze Age stone circles on the breezy moors further S is the *Twelve Apostles*, beyond the *White Wells* about 1½m from Ilkley. The *Swastika Stone*, on *Addingham High Moor* about 2m SW of Ilkley, may be of Iron Age date.—The *Cow and Calf*, above Ben Rhydding about 1m SE of Ilkley, are blocks of millstone grit weathered into fantastic shapes.

The track from Ilkley to (5m) East Riddlesden Hall and (6m) Keighley (Rte 75H) crosses the highest part of *Rombald's Moor* (1321ft), 2m S.—A pleasant little road follows the N bank of the Wharfe from Ilkley via *Nesfield* and *Beamsley* to (5½m) Bolton Abbey (see below).

From Ilkley to *Skipton*, *Settle* and *Kendal*, see Rte 86C.

At (23m) *Addingham*, with the small shaft of a late Anglian cross in its church, A65 goes on to Skipton (Rte 86C). We bear right on B6160 for the Yorkshire Dales National Park and *Upper Wharfedale*, one of the loveliest valleys in England.—At (25m) *Bolton Bridge* we cross the Skipton–Harrogate road (A59).

At *Beamsley*, off A59 ¾m E, the hospital founded by the Countess of Cumberland in 1593 provided accommodation in almshouses opening off a little circular chapel. The *Beamsley Beacon* (1314ft), a good viewpoint, rises across the valley of the Kex Beck.

26m. *Bolton Abbey* (National Park local information point) is the misleading name for the village which includes *Bolton Priory* (open). The ruin stands on a promontory of level parkland in a loop of the Wharfe, with craggy hills on the opposite bank—a setting which inspired a famous watercolour by Turner and which Ruskin thought the most beautiful of any English ruin. Inevitably, it is a favourite spot with visitors.

The priory of Augustinian canons was founded at Embsay, outside Skipton, by Cecily de Romille in 1120 and moved here by her daughter, Lady Alice, in the 1150s—to commemorate the drowning of her son in the Strid (see below), claims a sentimental legend. The nave of the *Church* has been used as the parish church since c 1170 and so was spared at the Dissolution. It is entered by the magnificent Perp. W front, added by Prior Moon in 1520 and intended as the base of a tower which was never completed. This masks the 13C front. The EE nave and its single aisle inside end at the blocked-up crossing arch. Outside, the transepts, choir and E window (minus its tracery) survive nearly to roof level, but the monastic buildings to the S have almost entirely disappeared. The 19C *Bolton Hall*, W of the ruins, incorporates the medieval gatehouse.

The lovely wooded banks of the Wharfe stretching N of the priory are well worth exploring. A footbridge and stepping stones cross from the ruins to the E bank, with its fine views, where paths and tracks can be followed up to (3m) Barden Bridge (see below). At 1¼m a charming detour on the right follows the Posforth Beck, with its waterfalls, to (¾m) the *Valley of Desolation*. The nature trail along the W bank is reached from the right fork in the road at the Cavendish Fountain, about 200yds beyond the entrance to the priory ruins. It passes (2m) the narrow and dangerous cleft of the Wharfe known as the Strid (i.e. 'Stride').

B6160 also continues along Wharfedale to (29m) *Barden Bridge*. High up on the left is *Barden Tower* (i.e. 'Boarden Tower'), which Henry, Lord Clifford, the 'Shepherd Lord', rebuilt in Henry VII's reign and used for alchemical studies. It was restored in 1658–59 by Lady Anne Clifford, who added the little parish church attached to the cottage on the S. From the bridge an unclassified road follows the E bank to Burnsall, passing *Simon's Seat* (1529ft; view) and, near *Appletreewick*, the striking gully of *Troller's Gill*.—B6160 takes the W bank to (33m) **Burnsall** (National Park local information point), on a lovely reach of the Wharfe. It has an old Grammar School (1602) and an interesting church with a Norman font and Jacobean pulpit. —35½m. *Linton*, to the left, is a pretty village with a packhorse bridge and an old clapper bridge across the stream, and Fountain's Hospital (1721) in the style of Vanbrugh. The partly 12C church stands beside the Wharfe ¾m NE.

We cross the river to (36½m) **Grassington** (1300 inhab.; 650ft; National Park Information Centre), a charming little town apt to get crowded with visitors during the tourist season. In the tiny square on the hill two former leadminers' cottages now house the *Upper Wharfedale Folk Museum*.

From the E end of the bridge a path leads ½m upstream to *Ghaistrill's Strid*. —B6265 crosses the Wharfe to *Threshfield* and leads via Linton and (3¾m) *Cracoe* to (9½m) Skipton (Rte 86C).

From Grassington via *Stump Cross Caverns* to *Pateley Bridge* in Nidderdale, see Rte 86B.

39½m. *Conistone*, on the E bank of the Wharfe, has a heavily restored old church with pews by Robert Thompson of Kilburn. A fine limestone gorge lies to the E.—Recrossing the Wharfe we reach (40m) *Kilnsey*, at the base of the overhanging *Kilnsey Crag*, part of the Mid Craven Fault (see Rte 86C) and a notorious challenge for rockclimbers.

FROM KILNSEY TO MALHAM TARN OR STAINFORTH. There are several ways leading W, by small and sometimes perilous roads, to Malham Tarn and Stainforth in Ribblesdale (both in Rte 86C). Walkers can reach the Tarn by Mastiles Lane, the old drovers' road running across *Kilnsey Moor* (about 5½m). Motorists should take the unclassified road which branches left from B6160 beyond Kilnsey and follows the Skirfare to (4m) *Arncliffe*, attractively laid out around its village green. From here a steep moorland road swings left to (9m) Malham Tarn. The name of *Fountains Fell*, to the right of the road, recalls that it marked the W boundary of the land in Wharfedale belonging to Fountains Abbey.—Another road continues from Arncliffe up the E bank of the Skirfare through the lovely *Littondale* to (6m) *Litton* (National Park local information point) and (8½m) *Halton Gill*, where a steep moorland road heads left, passing between Fountains Fell and *Pen-y-Ghent* on the way to (16m) Stainforth.

B6160 crosses the Skirfare.—42½m. **Kettlewell** (700ft; National Park local information point), a large village on the E bank of the Wharfe, is a good centre for anglers and walkers.

*Great Whernside* (2308ft; view) rises to the E. A steep and rough road skirts its N flank and that of *Little Whernside* (1984ft) on the way to Coverdale, with a National Park local information point at (8m) *Horsehouse*, and (13m) Coverham in Wensleydale (Rte 86D).

B6160 continues up the E bank to (44½m) *Starbotton* and (46½m) **Buckden** (780ft; National Park local information point).

FROM BUCKDEN TO AYSGARTH, 8m by B6160. Beyond Buckden the road bears right and climbs rapidly along the Cray Beck, with waterfalls and a good view back, to (1½m) *Cray* (1050ft). About 1½m further on a track, unsuitable for cars, bears left via the *Stake Pass* (1832ft) for Semer Water and (10½m) Bainbridge (both in Rte 86D).—B6160 climbs to about 1390ft before descending into *Bishopdale*.—5m. *Newbiggin* lies on the opposite side of the dale from *Thoralby*, with a National Park local information point and a traditional forge in working order.—6½m. *West Burton* is an attractive village with a large green, a 19C cross and an old packhorse bridge below Walden Beck waterfall.—8m. *Aysgarth*, see Rte 86D.

The final stage of the way to Hawes is by unclassified roads, which grow progressively rough and steep. From Buckden we cross the Wharfe and continue up the dale, here called *Langstrothdale*. —47¾m. *Hubberholme* has a small 12C church with a rood loft of 1558 bearing the arms of the Percy family. The stalls are modern work by Robert Thompson of Kilburn.—At (50m) *Deepdale* we cross the river.—At (51m) *Beckermonds* (970ft) two streams unite to form the Wharfe. The cloudberry is so abundant on the hills here that its berries redden the ground. Our road turns sharply to the right, climbs to (53¾m) the summit of *Fleet Moss* (1934ft) and then drops down to (58m) **Hawes** in Wensleydale (Rte 86D).

# B.   Nidderdale: Wetherby to Knaresborough and Grassington

Total distance 32m. **Wetherby**, see Rte 85B.—B6164 to (7m) **Knaresborough**.—B6165, B6265 to (22m) Pateley Bridge.—B6265 to (32m) **Grassington** (Rte 86A).

Maps: OS Landranger 105 (briefly), 104 (briefly), 99, 98 (briefly).

**Wetherby**, see Rte 85B. We follow B6164 NW, crossing into North Yorkshire and joining the valley of the Nidd at (4½m) *Little Ribston*.

7m. **Knaresborough** (13,400 inhab.; seasonal Tourist Information), where a railway viaduct crosses the steep ravine of the Nidd, is an old-fashioned town with 18C houses. High above the river in Castle Gardens (*view) are the remains of John of Gaunt's *Castle*, where Richard II was imprisoned in 1399. Its best preserved part is the 14C keep, which (uniquely) also served as a gatehouse between the inner and outer wards. The *Old Court Museum* has local history displays. The church of *St John*, EE to Perp., contains 17C monuments of the Slingsby family and stained glass by Morris and Co.

To the N of High Bridge is the public park of *Conyngham Hall*, with a zoo. High Bridge leads across to some delightful walks on the opposite bank of the river. In the *Dropping Well Estate* (open) to the S are *Mother Shipton's Cave*, where the prophetess is said to have been born in 1488, and the *Dropping Well*, famous for its petrifying properties. On the other bank, below Low Bridge, is the curious *Chapel of Our Lady of the Crag* (open), a shrine cut into the rock c 1408, with a roughly carved figure of a knight at its entrance. Above is a late 18C house, also partly cut into the limestone cliff.

About 1m downstream, near Grimbold Bridge, is *St Robert's Cave*, or *Eugene Aram's Cave*, where Aram hid the corpse of his victim Daniel Clark in 1745. Aram's body was returned to Knaresborough and hung in chains after his execution at York in 1759.—At *Farnham*, 2m N of the town, the church has a Norman apse.

From Knaresborough to *York*, see Rte 81.

We follow B6165, which crosses the Harrogate–Ripon road (Rte 80) on the way into (11¹/₂m) *Ripley*, a 'model' estate village built by Sir William Amcotts Ingilby in 1820–30. The churchyard has the remains of a curious cross with niches for kneeling at the base, perhaps 13C. *Ripley Castle* (open) has a 15C gatehouse, 16C tower, late 18C additions, and a serpentine lake in the park. Cromwell spent the night here after the Battle of Marston Moor.—B6165 rejoins the course of the river before (18¹/₂m) *Summer Bridge*. On the moors 2m N are *Brimham Rocks* (NT), grotesquely shaped crags of millstone grit scattered over 60 acres.

B6165 joins B6265 shortly before (22m) **Pateley Bridge** (1900 inhab.; seasonal Tourist Information), a pleasant little town set among beautiful scenery. The ruined church of *St Cuthbert*, high above the town, has wide views. The *Nidderdale Museum*, in the Council Offices opposite the 19C church of St Mary, has exhibits of local life. The Nidderdale Agricultural Show takes place here on the Monday nearest 20 September.

**Nidderdale** proper lies to the N, reached by steep and narrow sideroads. Part of the dale is filled by *Gouthwaite Reservoir* between (1¹/₂m) *Wath* and (4¹/₂m) *Ramsgill*. The murderer Eugene Aram (1704–59) was born at Ramsgill and kept school at Gouthwaite Hall, now submerged.—6¹/₂m. *Lofthouse*, with the *How Stean* gorge and caves (open) to the W.—7¹/₂m. *Middlesmoor* has a good view of the dale.—Rough tracks (no cars) continue to the head of the dale, 6m further on, at *Angram Reservoir* beneath *Little Whernside* (1984ft) and *Great Whernside* (2308ft), also seen on the way from Kettlewell through Coverdale in Rte 86A.

About 1¹/₂m S of Pateley Bridge, beyond *Bewerley*, is the 19C Yorke's Folly. From Pateley Bridge to *Fountains Abbey*, *Studley Royal* and *Ripon*, see Rte 80.

We cross the Nidd and follow B6265 W over the steep *Greenhow Hill* to the Yorkshire Dales National Park and Wharfedale. The hill has been mined for lead since the time of the Brigantes, and traces of Roman and medieval workings survive on either side of the road. —26¹/₂m. *Stump Cross Caverns* (open; National Park local information point), discovered by lead-miners in the 19C, have fine stalactites and stalagmites.—30¹/₄m. *Hebden*, with another National Park local information point.—32m. **Grassington**, see Rte 86A.

## C.   Upper Airedale, Craven and Ribblesdale: Ilkley to Skipton, Settle and Kendal

Total distance 54m. **Ilkley**, see Rte 86A. We follow A65 throughout.—To (9¹/₂m) **Skipton**.—To (25m) **Settle**.—To (41m) Kirkby Lonsdale.—To (54m) **Kendal** (Rte 76).

Maps: OS Landranger 104, 103, 98, 97.

**Ilkley**, see Rte 86A. We follow A65 to the W, skirting the S edge of the Yorkshire Dales National Park, which we explore on several of the excellent detours this route offers. We stay on A65 beyond (3m) *Addingham*, where Rte 86A turns right to follow Wharfedale, and leave West Yorkshire for North Yorkshire. The road crosses the watershed into the upper reaches of **Airedale**, whose lower, largely industrialised course is followed on the journey N from Leeds via Keighley to Skipton in Rte 75H.

9½m. **Skipton** (13,200 inhab.; Tourist Information) is a fine old market town with a broad main street leading up to *Skipton Castle* (open).

*The Conduit Court at Skipton Castle*

The Norman castle built by Robert de Romille in 1090 was rebuilt by Robert de Clifford in the early 14C. A Tudor range (not open) was added in 1536. Beginning in the 1650s, Lady Anne Clifford restored the whole building after it had been besieged and then slighted by Parliamentarian troops during the Civil War. Her additions include the lettered balustrade above the entrance display-ing the Clifford motto 'Désormais' ('Henceforth'). With their six round towers, the main buildings survive in remarkably good condition, roofed and floored throughout. In the centre is the pleasantly irregular *Conduit Court, created by Henry, Lord Clifford, the 'Shepherd Lord', in Henry VII's reign and restored by Lady Anne, who planted the yew tree. The archway leading into the court is a relic of the Norman castle.

The parish *Church* contains Clifford tombs, with heraldic decoration, and a fine screen of 1533. The *Craven Museum* in the Town Hall illustrates local geology, archaeology and social history.—The old railway station at *Embsay*, 1½m NE, is now headquarters of the *Yorkshire Dales Railway*, with a collection of steam locomotives and goods vehicles. Visitors can make a 3m round trip on a preserved stretch of the Skipton–Ilkley line.

Skipton is the capital of the Mountain Limestone region of **Craven**, stretching from the sources of the Wharfe and the Ribble to the borders of Lancashire. The upland scenery to the N is some of the finest in Yorkshire, particularly wild and dramatic at the crags, scars and broken limestone 'pavements' of the escarpments known as the Craven Faults, which run from Wharfedale (see Kilnsey, Rte 86A) past Malham and Settle to Kirkby Lonsdale.

FROM SKIPTON TO MALHAM, 11m. We follow A65 to (4¹/2m) *Gargrave* (see below), where we turn right.—9³/4m. *Kirkby Malham*, birthplace of the Parliamentarian general John Lambert (1619–83), has an interesting Perp. church. A narrow road, with a fine *view, leads over the moor (1272ft) past (3¹/4m) the beautiful waterfall of *Scaleber Force* to (5m) Settle.—11m. **Malham** (National Park Information Centre), set among wild hill scenery near the source of the Aire, is an attractive village which gets overcrowded at summer weekends and Bank Holidays.

Two of the most dramatic features of the Mid Craven Fault lie beyond. *Gordale Scar*, about 1¹/4m NE by road and footpath, is a deep ravine (about 300ft) formed by the collapse of a cave system. Energetic walkers can climb the rocks by the side of the waterfall to reach the upper valley. Across the road to the S of the Scar is the charming waterfall of *Janet's Foss* (NT), with a nature trail nearby. *Malham Cove*, ³/4m N of the village by road and footpath, is a limestone amphitheatre, 300ft high, with markings on the pavements of its upper level showing where a waterfall once flowed over its lip. A stream—not the Aire, as is sometimes supposed—issues fully grown from its base. The little country road passing near the Cove continues almost to the secluded upland lake of *Malham Tarn* (NT), another 2¹/2m N, where Charles Kingsley set the opening scenes of 'The Water Babies' (1863). Tarn House, on the N shore, is used by the Field Studies Council. The Tarn nurses the river Aire, for the stream which drains it to the S and disappears underground a little way beyond at Water Sinks reappears at Aire Head, just S of the village of Malham. From the crossroads W of the Tarn steep and narrow routes lead W to (5m) Settle and N to (5m) Arncliffe in Littondale (Rte 86A). Walkers can take Mastiles Lane, the old drover's road, E from the Tarn across Kilnsey Moor to (c 5¹/2m) Kilnsey in Wharfedale (Rte 86A).

From Skipton to *Burnley*, *Bury* and *Manchester*, see Rte 75D; to *Leeds* and *Sheffield*, see Rte 75H; to *Grassington* in Wharfedale, see Rte 86A.

We continue NW from Skipton to (14m) *Gargrave*, where the road, the railway and the Leeds and Liverpool Canal meet in the Aire Gap. The detour to Malham described above branches right.—A65 crosses into **Ribblesdale**.—At (21m) *Long Preston* it is joined by the roads from Clitheroe and Slaidburn, both described in Rte 75C.

25m. **Settle** (2300 inhab.; seasonal Tourist Information) is a pleasant little market town which makes an excellent centre for exploring the wild surrounding country. The *Shambles* in the market square is partly 17C, and the distinctive local style of 17–18C building, with its curious doorway arches and playfully shaped columns, is splendidly illustrated by the *Folly* (1694), now an antique shop. The *Museum of North Craven Life* is in Chapel St. Natives of Settle include George Birkbeck (1776–1841), founder of the Mechanics' Institutes and the London University college which bears his name, and Benjamin Waugh (1839–1908), founder of the National Society for the Prevention of Cruelty to Children.

*Giggleswick*, about ³/4m W on the opposite bank of the Ribble, has a boys' public school founded in 1512. Its domed chapel (1897–1902) is the masterpiece of Sir T.G. Jackson.

The Mid Craven Fault marks the landscape from Settle E to Malham. The best and most accessible of the caves in *Langcliffe Scar*, about 2m above the town, is the *Victoria Cave* which, with the nearby *Jubilee Cave*, has yielded traces of occupation from mesolithic to Roman times.

FROM SETTLE UP RIBBLESDALE TO HAWES, 21¹/2m by B6479 and B6255. This *route crosses the wildest corner of Yorkshire. Its first stage follows the Ribble to its source and runs alongside the Settle–Carlisle line (1875), the most arduous stretch of railway building in England.—³/4m. *Langcliffe* (National Park local information point).—2¹/2m. *Stainforth*, where the Ribble flows through a narrow gorge, has a waterfall and single-arched 17C bridge (NT) on the old drovers' road from York to Lancaster. *Catrigg Force* is about 1m E above the village. A sideroad branches NE to (7¹/2m) Halton Gill and (12m) Arncliffe in Littondale (Rte 86A).—6m. *Horton-in-Ribblesdale* (Tourist Information and National Park local information point), in a region scarred by quarrying, is a popular centre for walkers, cavers and potholers in the 'Three Peaks': *Pen-y-Ghent* (2273ft) to the E, *Ingleborough* (2373ft; see below) to the W, and Yorkshire's highest point, *Whernside* (2419ft; see also Rte 86D), beyond. Horton church is mainly Norman. We cross the Ribble as we leave the village.—At (11¹/2m) *Ribblehead* the railway crosses the barren moor by a breathtaking *viaduct (24 arches; ¹/4m) before disappearing into the Blea Moor Tunnel (1¹/2m long). For B6255 heading left to Ingleton, see below. We take B6265 to the right.—We pass (15m) the turning on the left for Dentdale and Sedbergh (Rte 86D), and descend *Widdale* to (21¹/2m) *Hawes* (Rte 86D).

From Settle to *Blackburn, Bolton* and *Manchester*, see Rte 75C; to *Malham*, see above.

Beyond Settle A65 climbs past *Giggleswick Scar*, on the South Craven Fault, with the *Ebbing and Flowing Well*.—31m. **Clapham** (National Park Information Centre), an attractive village at the S foot of Ingleborough, is a popular starting-point for excursions into the hills.

*Ingleborough Cave* (open), 1¹/2m N through the pleasant *Clapdale Woods*, has a series of chambers and passages 800yd long, filled with glittering stalactites and stalagmites. Another 1m further up the hillside is the mouth of *Gaping Gill*, a cavern 350ft deep, into which a waterfall flings itself. From here it is an easy climb of 1¹/2m to the top of **Ingleborough** (2373ft), the most striking though not the highest of the Yorkshire hills, with a panoramic *view. On the level summit are the remains of an Iron Age fort, with part of the walls still standing, and the foundations of circular huts of the 1C. We can descend N to (2m) Chapel-le-Dale or SW to (3m) Ingleton.

35m. **Ingleton** (seasonal Tourist Information), another attractive village and popular centre for visitors, stands where two streams unite in a ravine spanned by a railway viaduct (1859, now disused). A lovely walk of about 4m follows the wooded banks of the streams, with their waterfalls.

B6255 heads NE to (6m) Ribblehead (see above) around the flank of Ingleborough and past limestone scars and caves which include (1¹/2m) *White Scar Cave* (open) and *Weathercote Cave*, a rocky chasm with a waterfall, at (4m) *Chapel-le-Dale*.

A65 crosses the NE corner of Lancashire.—At (39¹/2m) *Cowan Bridge* Charlotte and Emily Brontë entered the Clergy Daughters' School in 1824 but were withdrawn the following year after their elder sisters, Maria and Elizabeth, died of typhus contracted here. Part of the building survives N of the bridge over the Leck and is marked by a plaque. It appears in 'Jane Eyre' as 'Lowood' and its headmaster, the Rev. William Carus Wilson, as 'Mr Brocklehurst'. An 'exposed and hilly road' leads SW to (2¹/4m) *Tunstall*, 'Brocklebridge' in the novel, with the church attended by the pupils of the school. From Tunstall to *Lancaster*, see Rte 76.—We enter Cumbria and cross the Lune just below the 15C *Devil's Bridge*.—41m. **Kirkby Lonsdale** (1500 inhab.; Tourist Information) is an ancient town in a beautiful spot by the river, painted by Turner and praised by Ruskin as 'one of the loveliest scenes in England'. *Ruskin's View* is near the churchyard; the church has good Norman work.

A683, a beautiful road, goes up Lonsdale via (1m) *Casterton* to (11m) *Sedbergh* (Rte 86D).—From Kirkby Lonsdale to *Lancaster*, see Rte 76.

47m. A65 crosses M6.—54m. **Kendal**, see Rte 76.

# D.   Wensleydale: Ripon to Leyburn, Hawes and Kendal

Total distance 61m. **Ripon**, see Rte 80.—A6108 to (14m) Jervaulx Abbey.—A6108 to (19½m) **Leyburn**.—A684 to (26¼m) Aysgarth. —A684 to (35m) **Hawes**.—A684 to (50m) Sedbergh.—A684 to (61m) **Kendal**, see Rte 76.

Maps: OS Landranger 99, 98, 97.

**Ripon**, see Rte 80. A6108 heads up the valley of the Ure, which beyond Kilgram Bridge becomes *\*Wensleydale*. Broad and green in its lower stages, with tributary rivers creating side valleys to the N and S, it runs among wilder fells near its head beyond Hawes.

We cross the Ure at (5½m) *West Tanfield*, a pleasant village with the Perp. gatehouse of the Marmions' castle (English Heritage, standard opening). The church contains Marmion effigies, including those of Sir John (d. 1387) and his wife under an iron hearse; there is also modern woodcarving by Robert Thompson of Kilburn.—We meet the river again at (9m) *Masham*, with a large market place once used for sheep fairs and an interesting 12–16C church with Danby tombs.—14m. **Jervaulx Abbey** (open) was founded by Cistercians who moved here from Aysgarth in 1156. The name, pronounced 'Jervo', is Norman French for 'Yoredale', or 'Ure valley'.

The picturesquely overgrown ruins look confusing from the entrance, but the foundations of the large church can be traced at the N of the site. The monastic buildings are arranged around the cloister to its S in the usual Cistercian pattern, with the chapter house and monks' dormitory (two-storied wall) on the E side.—*Kilgram Bridge*, about 1½m E of the abbey, marks the point where the Ure valley becomes Wensleydale.

From (15½m) *East Witton* a sideroad leads W to (2m) the 17C *Braithwaite Hall* (NT, open by appointment with the tenant) and (3m) the slight remains of *Coverham Abbey*, a Premonstratensian house moved c 1212 to this beautiful site near the foot of *Coverdale*. From here to Kettlewell, see Rte 86A.—17½m. *Middleham* has racing stables and the imposing ruins of *Middleham Castle* (English Heritage, standard opening), once the stronghold of Warwick the Kingmaker and a favourite residence of Richard III, whose son Edward died here in 1484. The space between the large Norman keep (c 1170) and the 13C curtain wall is extraordinarily narrow. To the SW is the site of an earlier castle on higher ground.

We cross the Ure again on the way to (19½m) **Leyburn** (675ft; seasonal Tourist Information), an old market town high up on the N bank and a popular centre for excursions in E Wensleydale. It is the venue for the Wensleydale Agricultural Show in August and two fairs, in May and October.

A footpath which begins just N of the Bolton Arms leads ¼m W to the *\*Leyburn Shawl* (800ft), a green terrace running along the N side of the valley and giving an exceptionally fine view of Wensleydale. About halfway along the walk is the *Queen's Gap*, where Mary, Queen of Scots, is said to have stopped during her attempted escape from Bolton Castle.

FROM LEYBURN TO RICHMOND. The direct way to (9m) *Richmond* (Rte 86E) takes A6108 to (3½m) Halfpenny House and branches right across *Hipswell Moor*, past (4½m) *Hartleap Well*, the scene of Wordsworth's poem, and the firing ranges in the military training area W of *Catterick Garrison* (Rte 85B). A better way, about 1m longer, stays on A6108 to reach Richmond via an attractive stretch of Swaledale.

From Leyburn to A1 at *Leeming Bar*, see Rte 85B.

20¹/₂m. *Wensley*, once a market town but now only a village, gave its name to the dale. It has a 13C bridge and an interesting 13C church containing a Flemish *brass of a priest, Sir Simon de Wenslaw (d. 1394), choir stalls with carved poppyheads (1527), and fragments of 14C wall painting. The Bolton pew incorporates an old parclose (1506–33) from the Scrope chantry at Easby Abbey, and near the door is a unique wooden reliquary (of St Agatha?), also from Easby. On the opposite side of the village green from the church are the entrance gates of *Bolton Hall* (not open), 1m W.

Roads follow both sides of the dale to Aysgarth, in the Yorkshire Dales National Park beyond Wensley. A684, on the S, goes through the pretty village of (22¹/₂m) *West Witton* and under *Penhill* (1792ft; view).

The route along the N side of the dale, about 3m longer, is more interesting. We pass below *Scarth Nick*, which gives a superb *view, and descend to (3¹/₄m) *Redmire*. About 1m NW is *Bolton Castle* (open), the late 14C fortified manor house of the Scropes. Mary, Queen of Scots, was held here in 1568–69. The battlements give a lovely view of Wensleydale. At (6¹/₂m) *Carperby* we turn left to cross the river.

26¹/₄m. **Aysgarth** (National Park Information Centre at the Falls) stands on a hill above some charming scenery where the Ure, crossed by a 16C bridge, flows over a series of flat limestone edges, forming the *Upper Falls* above the bridge and the *Lower Falls* ¹/₂m below. The nearby church has a superb rood screen and two carved pew ends, apparently from Jervaulx Abbey. The old mill displays a collection of horse-drawn carriages, etc.

The *Walden Valley* and the pleasant *Bishopdale* open to the S. Buckden (Rte 86A) in Wharfedale can be reached by a good road through Bishopdale or a rough track from Bainbridge.

31¹/₂m. *Bainbridge*, at the foot of the flat-topped *Addlebrough* (1564ft), is a pleasant village with a large green. A horn is blown here every evening at 21.00 from Holy Rood (28 September) to Shrove Tuesday to guide travellers benighted on the fells. Brough Hill, to the E, is the site of the Roman fort of *Virosidum*.

The river Bain leads 2¹/₂m SW to Yorkshire's only natural lake, **Semer Water**, beautifully situated at the foot of *Raydale*. The local legend of a submerged village may derive from the Iron Age settlement which stood here. A track leads from Semer Water over the Stake Pass to Bishopdale (see above).—N of Bainbridge a bridge crosses the Ure for (1¹/₂m) **Askrigg** (National Park local information point), once a centre of hand-knitting and clockmaking, with a late Perp. church, market cross and 17–18C houses. *Nappa Hall* (not open), 1¹/₄m E, is a fortified farmhouse of c 1460. For the fell road to Muker, see Rte 86E.

35m. **Hawes** (1300 inhab.; 800ft; seasonal Tourist Information and National Park Information Centre), a popular centre for visitors to Upper Wensleydale, is a grey little town with a big livestock market and the Duerley Beck cascading through its E end. The *Upper Dales Folk Museum* is housed in the former railway station. About 1¹/₂m N is *Hardrow Force*, painted by Turner, with a path under the 90ft waterfall.

From Hawes to *Wharfedale*, see Rte 86A; to *Settle* and *Ingleton*, see Rte 86C; to the *Buttertubs* and *Muker*, see Rte 86E.

Beyond (36m) *Appersett* we pass the pretty waterfall of *Cotter Force*, on the right.—At (40¹/₂m) the *Moorcock Inn* (1063ft) A684 leaves the Ure, which rises to the N.

B6259, the Kirkby Stephen road, heads this way. It passes (2¼m) *Lunds Fell* (2186ft), with the source of the Ure, and (2¾m) the striking ravine of *Hell Gill*, where the river Eden begins as Hell Gill Beck, and descends *Mallerstang*, the green valley of the Eden, between *Wild Boar Fell* (left; 2324ft) and *Mallerstang Edge* (2328ft). Between the road and the river lies *Pendragon Castle* (open), a 12C pele tower restored in the 17C by Lady Anne Clifford, which legend says was built by Uther Pendragon, father of King Arthur.—10m. *Kirkby Stephen*, see Rte 86E.

A684 enters Cumbria and descends *Garsdale*, with *Baugh Fell* (2216ft) to the N. A more interesting way to Sedbergh follows the moorland road on the left through the parallel *Dentdale*, the valley of the Dee, and the pleasant village of *Dent* (National Park local information point), with narrow cobbled streets, once famous for its cottage knitting industry. The Cambridge geologist Adam Sedgwick (1785–1873) was born here. The fine fells on the left culminate in *Whernside* (2419ft; *view), Yorkshire's highest point and the northernmost of the 'Three Peaks' (Rte 86C).—50m. **Sedbergh** (seasonal Tourist Information and National Park Information Centre) is a popular place, in a beautiful mountain site. Its public school was founded in 1525 by Roger Lupton, Provost of Eton. *Briggflatts*, 1¼m SW, has an early Friends' meeting house (1675).

From Sedbergh to *Kirkby Lonsdale*, see Rte 86C.

A684 crosses the Lune, marking the W boundary of the Yorkshire Dales National Park, and then (56m) M6.—61m. **Kendal**, see Rte 76.

# E.  Swaledale: Scotch Corner to Richmond, Kirkby Stephen and Brough

Total distance 40½m. **Scotch Corner**, see Rte 85B.—A6108 to (4m) **Richmond**.—A6108, B6270 to (14½m) Reeth.—B6270 to (23m) Muker.—B6270 to (36m) **Kirkby Stephen**.—A685 to (40½m) **Brough** (Rte 86F).

Maps: OS Landranger 93 (briefly), 92, 99 (briefly), 98, 91.

**Scotch Corner**, see Rte 85B. A6108 leads SW to (4m) **Richmond** (7700 inhab.; seasonal Tourist Information), a splendid old town on the Swale with much to remind the visitor of both its medieval and its 18C prosperity. It has given its name to many other places, including Richmond-upon-Thames.

The *Castle (English Heritage, standard opening and summer Sunday mornings) stands on a precipice sheer above the river.

Originally built c 1071 by Alan Rufus, the 1st Norman Earl of Richmond, it keeps many features from this period: curtain wall, gatehouse, chapel and Scolland's Hall, a rare survival of a Norman great hall ('very probably the oldest in England', says Pevsner). The magnificent keep over the gatehouse was added in 1171–74; there is a good view from the top.

The large cobbled market place has a cross of 1771 and several good 18C buildings around its sides. The former church of Holy Trinity is now the *Green Howards Museum*, devoted to the North Yorkshire regiment. The *Georgian Theatre* to the N is one of the oldest theatres in the country, built in 1788 and reopened in 1963 after 100 years of disuse. It is open in summer when a play is not being staged, and contains a theatre museum. The Perp. *Tower in Friary Gardens, off Victoria Rd, is the only relic of the Greyfriars' monastery founded in 1258. The Richmondshire Museum, in Ryder's Wynd to the E, has local history exhibits which include carved Saxon stones, craftsmen's tools, etc. The heavily restored parish church of St Mary, which stood outside the town walls, has Perp. choir stalls with misericords brought from Easby Abbey. Frenchgate and Pottergate both have good Georgian houses. Hill House was the home of Frances l'Anson, the 'Lass of Richmond Hill' in the 18C song.

*Easby Abbey (English Heritage, summer standard opening and at any reasonable time in winter), in a beautiful setting by the Swale 1m SE, can be reached by B6271 or a pleasant riverside walk. It was founded for Premonstratensian canons in 1155 and dedicated to St Agatha of Sicily. The picturesque ruins have an unusual and irregular ground plan. Very little remains of the church, but the 13C refectory on the S side of the cloister still stands almost to its full height. On its W side are the monks' dormitory and guests' solar. The 14C gatehouse, to the SE, is substantially intact.

Hudswell, 2m SW of Richmond, can be reached by a pleasant walk through NT woods along the S bank of the Swale.—The old road climbing the N bank to (5m) Marske (see below) gives good views and passes between (2½m) broadcasting aerials and Whitcliffe Scar, with Robert Willance's monument (1606) giving thanks for his lucky escape when his horse went over the escarpment.

From Richmond to Leyburn, see Rte 86D.

A6108 follows the winding course of *Swaledale, the deepest, wildest and one of the loveliest of the Yorkshire Dales. Norse influence lingers in many of the place names, and there are traces of its industrial past as a centre of lead-mining.—5½m. We cross the river and enter the National Park.—8½m. The picturesque Dunnerholme Bridge leads across the Swale to Marske, 1m NW, with an 18C Hall (not open) and a 15C bridge across the Marske Beck.—At 9m A6108 heads left to Leyburn (Rte 86D). We follow B6270, passing (11m) the scanty ruins of two nunneries: (11m) the Cistercian Ellerton Priory and, on the opposite bank 1m beyond, the Benedictine Marrick Priory, now part of a Youth Centre.—13½m. Grinton has the mother church of Upper Swaledale, with Norman to Perp. work. We cross the river again.—14½m. Reeth (seasonal Tourist Information and National Park local information point) has an attractive green and the Swaledale Folk Museum.

A hilly road goes up the side valley of Arkengarthdale, with disused lead mines, and crosses the moors via (11m) Tan Hill Inn (1732ft), the highest pub in England, to (20m) Brough (see below). Another road branches right from Arkengarthdale at 4m and leads via the forested ridge of the Stang (1677ft), with good walks, to (15m) Barnard Castle (Rte 86G).

Though still dotted with villages, Swaledale grows wilder beyond Reeth and the road becomes hilly.—17½m. Feetham.—We cross the river at (20m) Gunnerside (National Park local information point). Ivelet, 1m W, has pretty falls.—23m. Muker (National Park local information point) is a quaint village in a beautiful situation. The Swaledale Agricultural Show takes place here in September.

There are two steep sideroads to Wensleydale (Rte 86D) from this part of Swaledale. One starts about ¾m E of Muker and leads over the fells (1633ft) to (5m) Askrigg. The other, more interesting and with excellent *views, starts 1m beyond Muker, passes the four deep holes in the limestone known as the Buttertubs and makes its way over the Buttertubs Pass (1726ft) to (6½m) Hawes.

At Muker B6270 quits the Swale and follows the Muker Beck to (24½m) Thwaite and (26½m) Keld, where it rejoins the Swale.

Walkers can follow the track along the W bank of the Swale past
*Kilsdon Force*, in a romantic site ¹/₂m below Keld.—The head of
Swaledale beyond Keld is much less impressive, but B6270 commands a fine view of the Eden valley from (32¹/₂m) the top of the pass,
where we leave the National Park and cross into Cumbria.

36m. **Kirkby Stephen** (1500 inhab.; Tourist Information) is a
pleasant town on the Eden. The church, with a Perp. tower, contains
15–16C tombs of the Musgraves and Whartons and an Anglo-Danish
cross shaft showing Satan in bonds.

A685 leads to (23¹/₂m) *Kendal* (Rte 76) via (4¹/₂m) *Ravenstonedale* (pronounced
'Rassendale') and (11¹/₂m) *Tebay*.—From Kirkby Stephen to the *Moorcock Inn*
and Wensleydale, see Rte 86D.

A685 leads to (40¹/₂m) **Brough**, where we join Rte 86F.

# F.   Scotch Corner to Penrith

Total distance 49m. **Scotch Corner**, see Rte 85B. We follow A66
throughout.—To (9m) Greta Bridge (for Barnard Castle, Rte 86G).
—To (15m) Bowes.—To (28m) Brough.—To (36m) Appleby.
—To (49m) **Penrith** (Rte 76).

Maps: OS Landranger 93 (briefly), 92, 91, 90 (briefly).

Not a Dales route as such, but a useful cross-Pennine route
connecting with the Dales to the N (Teesdale from Greta Bridge)
and S (Swaledale from Brough) and offering a fine contrast of
scenery between Pennine moorland and the Eden valley.

**Scotch Corner**, see Rte 85B. A66 follows the line of the Roman road
connecting the garrisons at York and Catterick with those at Penrith
and Carlisle. For *Stanwick Fortifications*, N of the road at 2m, see Rte
86G.—We leave North Yorkshire for County Durham.—9m. *Greta
Bridge*, *Rokeby Park* and, 3¹/₂m NW, *Barnard Castle*, see Rte 86G.
—15m. **Bowes** has the ruined Norman keep of its castle within the
earthworks of the Roman fort of *Laventrae* (English Heritage, open at
any reasonable time). The school which was Dickens's main model
for 'Dotheboys Hall' in 'Nicholas Nickleby' occupied the low stone
building at the W end of the village.

We follow the upper valley of the Greta, spanned at 17¹/₂m by the
natural limestone formation called *God's Bridge*. The desolate waste
of *Stainmore Forest* reaches its summit (1436ft) at (21m) the Roman
camp of *Rey Cross*, where we enter Cumbria. A magnificent *view
now opens across the rich valley of the Eden to the distant mountains
of the Lake District, and the road descends rapidly.—28m. **Brough**
(670 inhab.; Tourist Information) has a ruined castle, built c 1170
within the Roman fort of *Verterae* and restored in the 17C by Lady
Anne Clifford (English Heritage, standard opening but closed on
Wednesdays and alternate Tuesdays in winter).

From Brough to *Kirkby Stephen* and Swaledale, see Rte 86E; through Lunedale
to *Mickleton* in Teesdale. see Rte 86G.

36m. **Appleby** (2400 inhab.; Tourist Information), properly *Appleby-
in-Westmorland* and formerly the county town of Westmorland, is a
charming place with a steep High St. The castle (open), overlooking
the Eden, was restored by Lady Anne Clifford in the 17C but still has

its fine Norman keep. The church contains monuments to Lady Anne (d. 1676) and her mother, the Countess of Cumberland. The organ was brought here from Carlisle Cathedral in 1684. For *High Cup Nick*, see Rte 86G.

We follow the beautiful valley of the Eden, with the Lake District fells in the distance on the left and the Pennine Chain on the right. *Cross Fell* (2930ft), the highest point of the Pennines, rises NE of (42m) *Temple Sowerby*. The gardens of *Acorn Bank* (NT), 1m N of Temple Sowerby, include orchards and an important herb garden. The 16–18C manor house is open by arrangement.—Beside (47½m) *Brougham Castle* (Rte 76) we cross the Eamont.—49m. **Penrith**, see Rte 76.

# G.   Teesdale: Darlington to Barnard Castle and Alston

Total distance 48½m. **Darlington**, see Rte 85B. A67 to (16m) **Barnard Castle**.—B6277 to (26½m) Middleton-in-Teesdale.—B6277 to (48½m) **Alston**.

Maps: OS Landranger 93 (briefly), 92, 91, 87 (briefly).

**Darlington**, see Rte 85B. A67 runs W up the valley of the Tees.—5m. *Piercebridge* lies within the Roman fort on Dere Street, now B6275, extending N from Scotch Corner to Bishop Auckland. The remains of a drainage system (NW of the green) and some mounds of the walls survive, together with some fragments of the abutment and piers carrying the 2C timber bridge across the Tees (English Heritage, open at any reasonable time).—8m. *Gainford* has a good 13C church beautifully situated above the Tees.—10m. *Winston*, with a fine bridge of 1764, is 2¼m S of Staindrop (see below).

*Stanwick Fortifications* (English Heritage, open at any reasonable time) lie 4m SE of Winston and 3½m SW of Piercebridge. The earthworks, enclosing 850 acres, were built by the Brigantes in the 1C AD and used as a rallying point against the Romans.

16m. **Barnard Castle** (6000 inhab.; Tourist Information) is an attractive little market town with wide streets, in a lovely site on the N bank of the stony Tees. Below the quaint *Market Cross* (1747) stands the 16C *Blagraves House*. Dickens stayed at the *King's Head Hotel* in 1838 on a flying trip with Phiz to investigate the northern private schools. A little watchmaker's shop nearly opposite sugggested his 'Master Humphrey's Clock'.

The ruined *Castle* (English Heritage, standard opening but closed on Wednesday afternoons and on Thursdays in winter) from which the town takes its name is strikingly placed above the Tees near the old *County Bridge*.

The castle was founded c 1125–40 by Bernard Balliol and confiscated in 1296 after the revolt by John Balliol, King of Scotland, against Edward I. Its best preserved features are the 12–14C Mortham Tower, the 13C hall range partly improved by Richard III (bearing his emblem of the boar) and the 13C Round Tower.

The *Bowes Museum*, off Newgate E of the centre, looks unexpectedly like a French château. It was built by the colliery owner John Bowes of Streatlam and his wife Josephine, Countess of Montalbo, in

1869–76 as a museum for their art collection. Durham County Council now administers it.

The Bowes' collection is notably strong in Spanish painting (El Greco, Goya), porcelain (Chantilly) and French 18C furniture and works of art. The mechanical silver swan makes a prominent exhibit. Later additions include paintings by Canaletto and displays of dolls, toys, costumes, English decorative art and archaeological finds from the county.

FROM BARNARD CASTLE TO BISHOP AUCKLAND, 14¹/₂m by A688, partly following the line of the Roman road.—6m. *Staindrop* has an interesting 11–14C *church with monuments of the Neville and Vane families. Close by is the entrance to *Raby Castle (open), a superb 14C castle modified by later generations but keeping its romantically medieval silhouette. It passed to the Vanes from the Nevilles after the leading role played by Charles Neville, Earl of Westmorland, in the Rising of the North against Elizabeth I in 1569. Particularly impressive are the Neville gateway; the magnificent Barons' Hall, lengthened by William Burn in the 1840s; the medieval kitchen; Burn's octagonal drawing room; and the Gothick entrance hall, part of John Carr's alterations in 1768–88. There are good collections of pictures, particularly portraits, and French 19C furniture. Outside are walled gardens, a collection of carriages in the stables and a large deer park.—14¹/₂m. *Bishop Auckland*, see Rte 86H.

From Barnard Castle to *Reeth*, see Rte 86E.

*Teesdale stretches from the meeting of the Greta and the Tees, 3m below Barnard Castle, to Cauldron Snout, 20m above it. Before continuing N on the main route it is well worth making the detour S described below.

FROM BARNARD CASTLE TO GRETA BRIDGE, a 10¹/₂m round. Crossing the river to the suburb of *Startforth*, we follow the S bank of the Tees to (1³/₄m) the picturesque ruins of **Egglestone Abbey** (English Heritage, open at any reasonable time), a daughter house of Easby Abbey founded for Premonstratensian canons in 1195–98. A good deal of the EE church still stands.—2m. The *Abbey Bridge* (1773) commands a lovely view in both directions. About 1m further on a lane leads left to the superbly romantic *meeting of the Greta and the Tees, painted by Cotman and Turner, and *Mortham Tower*, a 14C pele tower with later additions.—We join A66 (Rte 86F) as we skirt *Rokeby Park* (limited opening), a Palladian house which the amateur architect Sir Thomas Robinson built for himself in 1735. It contains good furniture, paintings and needlework pictures. Sir Walter Scott's visits in 1809 and 1812 inspired his poem 'Rokeby'. —3³/₄m. *Greta Bridge*. A pleasant walk follows the river SW via (2¹/₂m) the wooded *Brignall Banks* to (7m) *Bowes* (Rte 86F).—The return to Barnard Castle can be made via *Whorlton*, 2¹/₂m NE of Greta Bridge and 1m W of *Wycliffe*, where the church has 13–15C glass. John Wyclif's family may have taken its name from the village, though the reformer himself was probably born at Hipswell (Rte 85B), near Richmond.

The main route goes N up Teesdale, following B6277 along the SW bank and passing *Deepdale* on the left.—20m. *Cotherstone*, a Quaker village at the foot of *Baldersdale*, had a school of the 'Dotheboys' Hall' type where Richard Cobden was a pupil in 1814–19.—22m. *Romaldkirk* is an attractive village with the 12–15C mother church of this side of Teesdale.—24m. Beyond *Mickleton* we cross the foot of *Lunedale*.

B6276 follows the dale towards (14m) *Brough* (Rte 86F). On the right beyond (7m) *Grains o' th' Beck* the Lune flows from its source on the slopes of *Mickle Fell* (2591ft; view), the highest hill in County Durham.

We cross the Tees to (26¹/₄m) the former lead-mining town of **Middleton-in-Teesdale** (1200 inhab.; 750ft) and follow the narrowing valley into the wilder landscape of upper Teesdale.—29¹/₂m. *Bowlees* has a Visitor Centre and picnic area. Behind the village the Causeway Sike tumbles over several waterfalls, notably at *Gibson's Cave*, about ³/₄m N. *Low Force* is S of the village on the Tees. We can cross to the S bank by Wynch Bridge, just below the falls, and follow a stretch of the Pennine Way 1½m up the river to *High Force, not the highest but perhaps the most majestic waterfall in England, where the Tees hurls itself over a 70ft cliff into a wooded valley. The dolerite rocks here are the exposed S edge of the igneous scarp known as the Whin Sill (or Great Whin Sill) which stretches up into Northumberland to form the landscape of Hadrian's Wall and the Farne Islands. A shorter but less interesting approach to High Force, via the N bank, is from B6277 at (31m) the *High Force Hotel.*—At (33½m) *Langdon Beck* a track leads across the Tees to (2¾m) *Cow Green Reservoir.* A nature trail follows the shore to (1½m) the dam at its S end and, just beyond, *Cauldron Snout*, also part of the Whin Sill, where the Tees descends a wild dolerite ravine in a series of cascades. Mickle Fell (see above) rises to the S.

In good weather walkers can follow the Pennine Way over the fells W of Cauldron Snout to (5m) *High Cup Nick*, a savage ravine between the dolerite cliffs of the Whin Sill. The Pennine Way then descends to (9m) the pleasant village of *Dufton*, from which footpaths continue S to (12½m) *Appleby* (Rte 86F).

Just beyond Langdon Beck a steep unclassified road heads N over the fells to (5m) *St John's Chapel* in Weardale (Rte 86H).

B6277 becomes one of the highest roads in England after it leaves Teesdale, climbing over (40m) *Yad Moss* (1962ft) on the Cumbrian border. The infant waters of the South Tyne flow down the other side of the fell through (44m) *Garrigill*, on the left.—48½m. **Alston** (1900 inhab.; Tourist Information), at about 950ft, is the highest market town in England. The highest point of the Pennines, *Cross Fell* (2930ft), lies on the Pennine Way to the S.

The *South Tynedale Railway*, a narrow-gauge tourist line on the trackbed of the old BR line to Haltwhistle, runs excursions from Alston station along the valley to (1½m) Gilderdale Halt. An extension is planned.

A686 heads SW to (20m) *Penrith* (Rte 76) via (5¾m) *Hartside Cross* (1903ft; *view).—A686 heads NE to (15½m) *Langley Castle* and (17m) *Haydon Bridge* (both Rte 87A), past (11m) the head of *West Allen Dale* and *East Allen Dale* (Rte 86H).—A689 follows the wooded South Tyne Valley N to (19m) *Brampton* (Rte 87A). It passes (2m) *Whitley Castle*, on the left, with the remains of a Roman fort on Maiden Way, here joined by the Pennine Way.—For A689 SE from Alston to Weardale and *Bishop Auckland*, see below.

# H.    Weardale: Bishop Auckland to Alston

Total distance 38m.—A689 and unclassified road to (5½m) Witton-le-Wear.—A68, A689 to (18m) Stanhope.—A689 to (38m) **Alston** (Rte 86G).

Maps: OS Landranger 93 (briefly), 92, 87.

Bishop Auckland is roughly equidistant between Darlington and Durham (both Rte 85B) and Barnard Castle (Rte 86G).

The colliery town of **Bishop Auckland** (32,600 inhab.) has been the chief country residence of the Bishops of Durham since the 12C. Their palace, *Auckland Castle* (limited opening of staterooms and chapel), is mainly 17–18C but its beautiful *chapel was built from the ruins of the late 12C banqueting hall by Bishop Cosin (d. 1672), who is buried here. The attractive Bishop's Park (open) has an 18C gatehouse and a deer shelter.

About 1¼m SE is the large and handsome 13C mother church of *St Andrew Auckland*, with a fine 19C Northumbrian cross reconstructed from fragments. —*Escomb*, on the S bank of the Wear about 3m W of Bishop Auckland, has a small and simple 7C *church, one of the earliest in England. It was built partly with stones from the Roman fort of *Vinovia* (open) at *Binchester*, 1m N of Bishop Auckland. The site includes an excavated bath system.—*Shildon*, 3m S of Bishop Auckland, has the *Timothy Hackworth Museum* in the restored home and workshop of the engineer to the Stockton and Darlington Railway.

From Bishop Auckland to *Barnard Castle*, see Rte 86G.

We follow the N bank of the Wear as closely as possible, taking A689 to (3¾m) *High Grange* and then branching left on the unclassified road to (5½m) the attractive village of *Witton-le-Wear*. Its striking but altered castle of 1410 stands S of the river; the grounds are a public park with a camping and caravan site.

*Hamsterley Forest*, beginning about 4m W, has 1100 acres of Forestry Commission land open to the public, with a Visitor Centre, forest drive and forest walks.

We follow A68 N and at 8½m rejoin A689.—At (12½m) *Wolsingham* (2800 inhab.) we rejoin the river where the valley narrows to form **Weardale**. Its natural beauty has been scarred by a long industrial history of stone quarrying, mining for lead and iron ore, and steel and cement works.—15m. *Frosterley* is known for its 'marble', really a black fossil-rich limestone, used in the North (in the Chapel of the Nine Altars at Durham Cathedral, for example) as Purbeck 'marble' is in the South.—18m. **Stanhope**, among limestone quarries, is the centre of upper Weardale and a good headquarters for walks over the moors. The church, mainly 13C, contains a Roman altarstone found on nearby Bollihope Common. Bishop Joseph Butler, author of the 'Analogy', was rector in 1725–40.—The landscape grows wilder and industry less intrusive as we follow the dale through (20½m) *Eastgate* and (23¼m) *Westgate*, marking the boundaries of the hunting park which belonged to the Bishops of Durham.—A689 crosses to the S bank of the river shortly before (25m) *St John's Chapel*, a charming little place. A steep fell road leads S to (5m) *Langdon Beck* in Teesdale (Rte 86G).—At (26¼m) *Irehopesburn* the minister's house attached to the 18C Methodist chapel is now the *Weardale Museum*, with reconstructed period interiors and a collection of minerals.—We cross back to the N bank at (27m) *Wearhead*, where Burnhope Burn and Killhope Burn unite to form the Wear. —28m. *Cowshill*.

B6295, heading N, follows the wooded *East Allen Dale*.—3¼m. *Allenheads* is a delightfully secluded village, and (10½m) *Allendale Town* a good centre for walks in the dale and nearby *West Allen Dale*.—14½m. We join A686, which heads NE via *Langley Castle* to (16½m) *Haydon Bridge* (Rte 87A). The lovely NT woodland where the Allen meets the South Tyne is most easily reached from A69 (Rte 87A).

30½m. *Killhope Wheel* (open) is a well-preserved 19C lead-mining site, with a large water wheel driven by the burn.—Surrounded by bleak hills, A689 becomes the highest main road in England as it climbs over (32m) *Killhope Cross* (2056ft; fine views) on the Cumbrian border.—The river Nent flows down the side of the fell from (33¼m) the former leadmining village of *Nenthead* to join the South Tyne.—38m. **Alston**, see Rte 86G.

# 87  Newcastle to Carlisle

The **Northumberland National Park** covers much of the county from Hadrian's Wall in the S to the central Cheviot Hills in the N, and from the Simonside Hills in the E to Kielder Water and the Forestry Commission's Border Forest Park in the W. Its wild and remote border country, almost roadless in its northern reaches, includes the upper valleys of the Rede, the Coquet and the North Tyne. The Pennine Way enters the Park at Greenhead and follows the line of the Roman Wall before heading N via Bellingham to end at Kirk Yetholm.

Rte 87B follows the S fringe of the Park along Hadrian's Wall, while Rte 87A includes a detour up the valley of the North Tyne from Hexham via Bellingham. The detours from Newcastle to Carter Bar, from Morpeth to Coldstream and from Felton along Coquetdale, all in Rte 85B, also cross the Park.

There are seasonal National Park Information Centres at Twice Brewed, Rothbury and Ingram; jointly operated centres at Housesteads (with NT, open April to October and weekends in March and November) and Harbottle (with the Northumberland Wildlife Trust, open weekends and Bank Holidays from Spring Bank Holiday to September); and an information van at Cawfields (open weekends and Bank Holidays from May to September and daily in August). Further information can be obtained by writing to the Northumberland National Park, Eastburn, South Park, Hexham, Northumberland NE46 1BS.

## A.  Via Tynedale and Hexham

Total distance 58¹/₂m. **Newcastle**, see Rte 85B.—A695 to (17¹/₂m) Corbridge.—A695 to (21m) **Hexham**.—A69 to (48¹/₂m) Brampton. —A69 to (58¹/₂m) **Carlisle**, see Rte 77.

Maps: OS Landranger 88, 87, 86, 85 (briefly).

**Newcastle**, see Rte 85B. We follow A695 along the N bank of the Tyne to (3m) *Scotswood*, where we cross the river.—7¹/₂m. *Crawcrook*. At *Wylam*, 1¹/₂m NW, the former school house is now a railway museum; the cottage (NT) where George Stephenson was born in 1781 lies about ¹/₂m E of the village, by the river and near the course of the 18C waggonway.—10m. *Prudhoe* (11,800 inhab.) has a ruined 12C castle on a cliff (English Heritage, standard opening but closed on Wednesdays and alternate Fridays). *Ovingham* (pronounced 'Ovinjam'), across the Tyne ³/₄m NW, has an EE church with a Saxon tower. At its foot lies the engraver Thomas Bewick (1753–1828). His birthplace at Cherryburn House near the hamlet of *Eltringham*, about 1m W of Prudhoe, has been opened as a museum.—The valley becomes more attractive. Opposite (13m) *Stocksfield* is *Bywell*, a beautifully situated village with a 15C gatehouse, an 18C Hall by James Paine and two fine 11–13C churches, one with a Saxon tower.

17¹/₂m. **Corbridge** (3100 inhab.; seasonal Tourist Information) is a pleasant old town on the N bank of the Tyne, here spanned by a bridge of 1674. The church, rebuilt in the 13C, has an 8C Saxon 'porch tower' and windows and a Norman S doorway. The Tourist Information Centre occupies a 13C vicar's pele tower. Like the tower arch in the church, it is built of stones from *Corstopitum* (English Heritage, standard opening), ¹/₂m NW, a Roman garrison town and supply depot that grew from a late 1C fort guarding their main crossing of the Tyne.

The remains include two granaries; a fountain and aqueduct; two military compounds whose walls were later combined with a defended gateway; the remains of earlier temples; a headquarters building with a strongroom like the one at Chesters and, over it, an unfinished storehouse with rusticated masonry, one of the largest Roman buildings to survive in Britain. The first-class collection in the museum includes the *Corbridge Lion, a 3C sculptured fountainhead.

*The Corbridge Lion*

At *Newton*, off A69 3½m E, the *Hunday National Tractor and Farm Museum* has probably the largest collection of vintage tractors in Europe, as well as engines, a narrow-gauge railway, crafts and animals.—*Aydon Castle* (English Heritage, summer standard opening), off A68 or B6321 1m NE of Corbridge, is a 13–14C fortified manor house.

A68, roughly on the line of the Roman Dere Street, runs N from Corbridge through lonely country, crossing the Wall at (2¾m) *Stagshawbank* (Rte 87B). —At (16½m) *West Woodburn*, on the edge of the National Park, we cross Redesdale near the Roman fort of *Habitancum.*—22½m. *Elishaw* is on the way from Newcastle to Carter Bar (Rte 85B).

From Corbridge to *Morpeth*, see Rte 85B.

18½m. The ruined *Dilston Castle*, on the Devil's Water to the left, was the original seat of the Earls of Derwentwater, the last of whom was executed for his part in the Jacobite rising of 1715.

21m. **Hexham** (9600 inhab.; Tourist Information) is an ancient and attractive town. Next to the Market Place with its 18C *Shambles* stands the magnificent ***Priory Church**, larger than some cathedrals and one of the finest achievements of EE architecture.

The first church was built by St Wilfrid in 674. The foundations of its apse and some fragments of its nave survive, together with the *crypt, among the best

Saxon crypts in England; inscribed Roman stones from Corstopitum can be seen in its walls. The cathedral of a bishopric from 681 until 821, this Saxon church was sacked by the Danes in 876. It was succeeded by an Augustinian priory, founded in 1114, whose canons built the beautiful choir and long transepts (c 1175–1225). The S transept still has the canons' night stair from the dormitory. The nave, destroyed by the Scots in 1290, was rebuilt by Temple Moore in 1907–09.

The church contains rich furnishings of several periods. The rood screen with its painted panels commemorates Prior Smithson (d. 1524). In the choir are 15C misericords and also the stone Saxon *Bishop's Chair, which later served as a sanctuary chair (cf. Beverley Minster). On the N side of the chancel is the 15C Leschman Chantry and on the S side the Ogle Chantry with a triptych altarpiece; a 15C screen in the sanctuary has painted panels showing bishops and a Dance of Death. In the S transept are the sculptured tombstone of the Roman standard-bearer Flavinus and the Saxon *Acca Cross (c 740).

Some partly restored priory buildings survive to the S, while Cowgarth, off Market St. to the NW, has the ruins of the late 12C gateway.

E of the Market Place stands the 15C *Moot Hall*. Beyond are the *Manor Office* (open), built as a prison in 1330 and now containing displays of border history, and the former *Grammar School* (1684). Fore St. and Market St. are also rewarding.

Hexham makes a good base from which to explore Hadrian's Wall. In the school summer holidays a special bus service runs from Hexham to Haltwhistle via the Military Road (B6318), stopping at or near the major Roman sites along the way.

B6306 runs SE from Hexham, crossing the Devil's Water above the gorge of Swallowship Hill and the Dilston woods, and passes near the site of the Battle of Hexham (1464), at which the Yorkists defeated the Lancastrians. It then climbs across the moors to (10m) **Blanchland**, a charming village in the secluded Derwent valley. The parish church preserves the choir and N transept of the church belonging to the Premonstratensian abbey founded in 1165. The late 15C abbey gateway leads into the unusual square, centrepiece of the model village laid out on the site of the monastic buildings by Lord Crewe in the 1750s.

FROM HEXHAM TO BELLINGHAM, KIELDER WATER AND THE SCOTTISH BORDER. After crossing the Tyne, we follow A69 W and A6079 N past (4m) *Wall* and the Roman Wall. Then we bear left on B6318 across the North Tyne to (5m) *Chollerford* (Rte 87B). Here we take the sideroad to the right for (5½m) *Humshaugh*, pronounced 'Humshalf', and follow the beautiful wooded valley past (6½m) the partly 13C *Haughton Castle*. Leaving the river, we join B6320 and continue N, passing the 18C *Nunwick House* and, on the opposite bank, *Chipchase Castle* with its 14C tower and 17–18C additions, on the way to (11½m) *Wark*.—The road climbs to a view of the wild *Redesdale* before crossing the North Tyne for (17m) *Bellingham*, pronounced 'Bellinjam', on the Pennine Way and the edge of the National Park. The church has a curious 17C stone-vaulted nave. B6320 continues N to Otterburn on the Newcastle–Carter Bar road (Rte 85B).—We follow unclassified roads up the lonely valley of the North Tyne towards its source on the desolate slopes of *Peel Fell* (1975ft).—21m. The sideroad branching right for *Greenhaugh* continues to (3m) *Black Middens Bastle House* (English Heritage, open at any reasonable time), a fortified 16C farmhouse near the junction of the Tarset and Black Burns.—26m. We reach **Kielder Water** and the *Border Forest Park*, with a visitors' centre run by the Northumbrian Water Authority at *Tower Knowe*. Kielder Forest, developed by the Forestry Commission over the last 60 years, is the largest man-made forest in Europe. Kielder Water, completed in 1982, has the largest capacity (44 billion gallons) of any man-made lake in northern Europe, though Rutland Water has a larger surface area. As well as supplying water for the North-east and generating a small amount of electricity for the National Grid, it also serves as a recreational centre, with ferry cruises, boating, water sports, fishing, etc. The road leading across the dam near Tower Knowe gives access to forest trails along the N shore of the Water.—34m. *Kielder Castle*, an 18C former hunting lodge at the N tip of the reservoir, houses an information and exhibition centre run by the Forestry Commission. A forest drive (11m; toll) leads NE to join the Newcastle–Carter Bar road (Rte 85B).—We cross the Scottish border beyond (36m) *Deadwater* and join the Carlisle–Jedburgh road at (40m) *Saughtree*.

The main route follows A69 past (23½m) *Warden*, at the meeting of the North and South Tyne rivers ¾m to the right. The 11C church tower has a Roman arch.—28½m. *Haydon Bridge*, on the opposite bank, was the birthplace of the painter John Martin (1789–1854).

A686 heads SW to (17m) *Alston* (Rte 86G). It passes (1½m) the mid 14C *Langley Castle* (not open) and (2m) the junction with B6295, which follows *East Allen Dale* (Rte 86H).

31½m. From the car park S of the road and river we can explore the lovely NT woodland on the banks of the Allen near its meeting with the South Tyne.—32½m. *Bardon Mill* is 3½m S of Housesteads (Rte 87B).—37m. *Haltwhistle* (seasonal Tourist Information) is a pleasant little town with an EE church.

*Unthank Hall* (not open), 2m SE, was the birthplace of the martyr Bishop Ridley (1500–55). *Featherstone Castle* (not open) is splendidly situated by the bank of the stony South Tyne, 3¼m SW.

A69 quits the South Tyne and, beyond (40½m) *Greenhead* (Rte 87B), follows the line of the old military road into Cumbria.—47m. **Naworth Castle** (limited opening), on the right, was built around a central courtyard in 1335 and tactfully restored by Anthony Salvin after a fire in 1844. It contains a large Great Hall hung with French tapestries, a Long Gallery and a library with a gesso relief by Burne-Jones.

Beyond Naworth the sideroad continues N past the medieval bridge spanning the Irthing to (2m) *Lanercost Priory (English Heritage, summer standard opening) in remote countryside near the Roman Wall. It was founded c 1166 for Augustinian canons. The S and E cloister buildings and the choir and transepts of the church are ruined, but the EE nave has survived as the parish church. Its N aisle has stained glass by Morris and Co. The W front is particularly fine, with elegant arcading and tall lancets. The W range of the cloister is known as Dacre Hall, after Sir Thomas Dacre, who converted it in the 16C.—For *Banks*, 1m NE of the priory, see Rte 87B.—From Banks the moorland road continues about 7m N to *Bewcastle*, where the remote church and ruined castle are built on the site of a Roman fort. The church is famous for its late 7C *cross, 14½ft high, richly decorated with figures, beasts, birds and vine scrolls and bearing a runic inscription.

49¼m. **Brampton** (seasonal Tourist Information) is an old-fashioned market town, with a Country Park at *Talkin Tarn*, 2m SE. A689 follows the wooded South Tyne Valley E and S to (19m) *Alston* (Rte 86G).—A69 completes the journey to (58½m) **Carlisle** (Rte 77).

# B.   Along Hadrian's Wall

Total distance 60½m. **Newcastle**, see Rte 85B.—A69 to (4¼m) West Denton.—B6528 to (7½m) Heddon-on-the-Wall.—B6318 to (23m) **Chesters**.—B6318 to (31m) **Housesteads**.—B6318 to (33½m) Twice Brewed (for **Chesterholm/Vindolanda**).—B6318 to (42m) Gilsland. —B6318 and unclassified road to (43½m) Birdoswald.—Unclassified roads to (50½m) Brampton (Rte 87A).—A69 to (60½m) **Carlisle**, see Rte 87A.

Maps: OS Landranger 88, 87, 86, 85 (briefly), or OS special Hadrian's Wall map (1:31,680 or 2in to 1m).

*Hadrian's Wall**, the most impressive monument to the Roman Empire in Britain, stretches 73 miles from Wallsend on the Tyne estuary, E of Newcastle, to Bowness-on-Solway, W of Carlisle. Building started in AD 122 following the Emperor Hadrian's visit, and the Wall was still being modified when he died in 138. Its purpose was to control the movement of people in and out of the province, to enforce regulations governing entry to the Empire and to prevent petty raiding. Made of local stone with rubble and mortar or clay infill, it probably rose to a height of about 14ft. As building work progressed, its thickness was reduced from 9$\frac{1}{2}$ft (10 Roman feet) to 6–8ft; for some stretches this narrow wall stands on broad foundations. The section W of the river Irthing at Willowford was originally made of turf but replaced in stone; near Birdoswald the turf and stone walls follow different courses. The Wall was patrolled from milecastles built a Roman mile (1875 yards) apart, with two smaller observation turrets regularly spaced between each pair. In the course of building it was decided to replace the forts that already stood to the S with forts astride the Wall itself, placed at roughly 7m intervals and together capable of holding about 10,000 men. The purpose of these regiments was to defend the province in the event of a major invasion. N of the Wall runs a ditch about 27ft wide, missing only where natural features like the Whin Sill made it unnecessary or the rock proved too hard to dig out. At varying distances to its S run the so-called Vallum, in fact a flat-bottomed ditch 20ft wide between mounds 80ft apart, and the military way linking the forts along the Wall. The Vallum was apparently designed to control access to the military zone. A little further S lay the earlier road which the Saxons called the Stanegate. A chain of coastal watch-towers and mile fortlets extended the line of the Wall SW along the Solway Firth, certainly to Maryport and perhaps as far as St Bees Head.

Shortly after Hadrian's death the Romans again moved N, establishing a new frontier on the Antonine Wall between the Forth and the Clyde. This was abandoned about 163 and Hadrian's Wall recommissioned. Though some bases were still held to its N into the 4C, it remained the frontier of the Empire until the end of Roman Britain in 409. Modifications were carried out after the barbarians had crossed it in the 180s and by Constantius Chlorus in 297 after the defeat of Carausius and Allectus's bid for power. Theodosius made a final restoration after the barbarian conspiracy of 367.

The most interesting and popular sites are the forts and civil settlements at Corbridge (Corstopitum), Chesters (Cilurnum), Housesteads (Vercovicium) and Chesterholm (Vindolanda). Though the Wall itself nowhere stands to full height, many long sections survive; the finest stretches march across the countryside of the Whin Sill between Sewingshields and Birdoswald. The Vallum is visible for much of the way. The sites of two important forts lie E of Newcastle: Segedunum at Wallsend and Arbeia, with a reconstructed gateway, beyond the Tyne at South Shields (both in Rte 85B). There is little to see W of Carlisle.

The best way to explore the Wall is on foot, with the help of the special OS map. During the school summer holidays a special bus service runs between Hexham and Haltwhistle via the Military Road, stopping at or near the major sites along the way. The brief itinerary below is designed for motorists and takes in all the major points of interest; unless otherwise noted, it can be assumed that they are administered by English Heritage and are open at any reasonable time. The Roman collections in the Museum of Antiquities at the University of Newcastle and the Tullie House Museum at Carlisle make an excellent start and finish to the trip.

Useful books include 'Hadrian's Wall' (3rd edition 1987) by David J. Breeze and Brian Dobson.

**Newcastle**, see Rte 85B. We leave the city by A69.—2m. *Benwell*, site of the fort of *Condercum*, has a small apsidal temple to the god Antenociticus and a causeway, the only one now visible, across the Vallum.—3½m. *Denton Burn* has a turret (7b), with fragments of the Wall to the W.—At (4¼m) *West Denton* we change to B6528 and pass another stretch of the Wall on the way to (7½m) *Heddon-on-the-Wall*, which has a church with Norman work. Here B6318 follows the course of the Wall to the right. This is the Military Road which General Wade built by quarrying the Wall in 1751 after its predecessor had proved inadequate to bear his artillery during the 1745 rebellion.—9m. *Rudchester*, site of *Vindovala* fort, on the left. Further on, S of the reservoirs, is the pele tower of Welton.—16½m. *Halton Chesters*, site of *Onnum* fort. To the S is the border stronghold of *Halton Castle*.—There are magnificent views at (17¼m) *Stagshawbank*, or *Portgate*, where the Military Road and the Wall are crossed by A68, following the line of the Roman Dere Street. *Corbridge*, 2¾m S, and a detour 19¾m N to *Elishaw* are described in Rte 87A.—21m. *Planetrees* is near *Heaven Fields*, where St Oswald recovered the throne of Northumbria by defeating the heathen King Cadwallon of Gwynedd in AD 633. Beyond Planetrees the road passes a section of the Wall which includes a point where the broad wall is reduced in width and then, near *Brunton House*, a well-preserved turret (26b) with another stretch of the Wall.

We cross the North Tyne at (22¼m) *Chollerford*. The 'abutment of the Roman bridge and, when the river is low, the bases of some piers can be seen about ½m S of the present bridge. The church of *Chollerton*, 1½m NE, has Roman columns in the S arcade and a Roman altar converted to a font. For *Hexham*, 5m S, and the detour N from Chollerford to *Bellingham*, the National Park and the Scottish border, see Rte 87A.—In (23m) the park of **Chesters** are the excavated remains of 'Cilurnum*, claimed as the best surviving example of a Roman cavalry fort in the whole Empire (English Heritage, standard opening and summer Sunday mornings). The headquarters building has a well, protected by a carved phallic stone, and the strongroom keeps its vaulted roof. Also exposed are the commandant's house, parts of three barrack blocks, and several gates and towers. Near the river is a well-preserved 'bath house. The 'museum has an excellent collection of sculptures, inscriptions and everday objects from the Wall.—B6318 enters the Northumberland National Park and passes (25m) *Black Carts* turret (29a), with a stretch of wall, ditch and the Vallum.—26m. *Carrawburgh*, site of the fort of *Brocilitia*, with a 3C temple to Mithras outside its walls.

At (28¼m) *Sewingshields*, with a turret (33b), the Military Road crosses the Vallum and quits the Wall, which now becomes fairly continuous, mounting the crest of the dolerite Whin Sill and commanding wide views. The ditch ends at Sewingshields farm, and along this section turrets and a milecastle (35) are visible. The Vallum diverges considerably to the S of the Wall.—At (31m) **Housesteads**, with a seasonal Information Centre jointly run by NT and the National Park Authority, are the considerable remains of the infantry fort of 'Vercovicium* (NT and English Heritage, standard opening and summer Sunday mornings). They include the headquarters building, commandant's house, granaries, barrack blocks, hospital, flush-water latrine and four impressive gates, The museum contains finds and displays about the history of the fort. To the S stood a large *vicus*, or civil settlement; six buildings are now on display. A good walk leads W along the Wall towards the Steel Rigg

*Vercovicium fort at Housesteads*

car park, passing the well-preserved milecastles 37 and 39 (NT). To
the N are the small Northumbrian lakes, in desolate moorland
crossed by the Pennine Way.—33½m. *Twice Brewed*, with the Once
Brewed Youth Hostel and a seasonal National Park Information
Centre. At *Peel Gap* an extra tower has recently been excavated
between turrets 39a and 39b. The Wall reaches its highest point
(1230ft) on *Winshield Crags* to the W. At **Chesterholm**, 1½m SE of
B6318, are the well-preserved remains of the 3C fort of **Vindolanda**
(English Heritage, standard opening; access controlled by the Vindolanda Trust), with the headquarters building, a bath house and a
Roman milestone still in situ on the Stanegate. The *vicus* or civil
settlement outside its walls, excavated by the Vindolanda Trust, is
particularly interesting, with an inn, houses, workshops, etc.; also a
replica of a section of the Wall at its full height and a good
˙museum.—36m. *Cawfields* milecastle (42) about ½m to the N, near
the car park with the seasonal National Park information van. To its
W is *Great Chesters*, the site of *Aesica* fort. *Haltwhistle* (Rte 87A) is
about 1½m S of B6318.—The Wall crosses the broken dolerite cliffs
known as the *Nine Nicks of Thirlwall*; a good stretch survives at
*Walltown*, with an unusual turret (45a) from a signal system pre-
dating the Wall.—39½m. *Carvoran*, the site of the fort now identified
as *Magnis*, with the interesting *Roman Army Museum*.

We leave the Northumberland National Park just before (40m)

*Greenhead*. From here A69 heads directly to (58m) Carlisle, as described in Rte 87A. However, Wall enthusiasts should continue on B6318, which follows a winding course to the right.—42m. *Gilsland*, near the Cumbrian border in the Irthing valley, was a small but fashionable spa in the days when Sir Walter Scott first met his future wife here. He described the neighbourhood in 'Guy Mannering' (1815). By the railway bridge to the S is the *Poltross Burn* milecastle (48), one of the best preserved examples on the Wall; a section of narrow wall on broad foundations continues about 1m W, through the former vicarage garden and past turrets 48a and 48b, to the abutment of the *Willowford* bridge which carried it across the Irthing (English Heritage, open at any reasonable time; access controlled by Willowford Farm). *Upper Denton* church, about 1¼m SW of Gilsland, has an ill-fitting chancel arch of Roman stones.—From B6318 1m beyond Gilsland we turn left on the unclassified road to (43½m) *Birdoswald*, where one of the largest and most interesting forts on the Wall, traditionally identified as *Camboglanna* but more probably *Banna*, is being excavated (partly English Heritage, open at any reasonable time). From *Harrow's Scar* milecastle (49), by the Irthing about ¼m E of the fort, the turf wall and the stone wall which replaced it follow different courses for about 2m.—The road passes stone-wall turret 49b, turf-wall turrets at *Piper Sike* (51a) and *Leahill* (51b), a signal turret at *Pike Hill* and another turf-wall turret at *Banks East* (52a) on the way to (46½m) *Banks*. A fragment of wall stands 9ft high about ¼m W of the village. The detour N from Banks to *Bewcastle* is described in Rte 87A.

From Banks we can rejoin the main course of Rte 87A by taking the road SW via *Lanercost* and the turning for *Naworth Castle* to (50½m) **Brampton**, from which A69 continues to (60½m) **Carlisle**.

# INDEX TO PEOPLE

Saints, kings, queens, popes and people who take their names from a place (Geoffrey of Monmouth, William of Waynflete, etc.) are indexed under their first names. People best known by their pen- or stage-names (George Eliot, Cary Grant, etc.) are indexed in this form.

# INDEX TO PLACES

This index uses the following abbreviations for counties, etc, in those cases where it is necessary to distinguish between two or more places of the same name or very similar names:

| | | | |
|---|---|---|---|
| Beds | Bedfordshire | IOW | Isle of Wight |
| Berks | Berkshire | Lancs | Lancashire |
| Bucks | Buckinghamshire | Leics | Leicestershire |
| Cambs | Cambridgeshire | Lincs | Lincolnshire |
| Ches | Cheshire | Mers | Merseyside |
| Cleve | Cleveland | Norf | Norfolk |
| Corn | Cornwall | Northumb | Northumberland |
| Cumb | Cumbria | Northants | Northamptonshire |
| Derbys | Derbyshire | Notts | Nottinghamshire |
| Dors | Dorset | Oxon | Oxfordshire |
| Dur | County Durham | Salop | Shropshire |
| Glos | Gloucestershire | Som | Somerset |
| G Man | Greater Manchester | Staffs | Staffordshire |
| Hants | Hampshire | Suff | Suffolk |
| H & W | Hereford and | Susx | Sussex |
| | Worcester | T & W | Tyne and Wear |
| Herts | Hertfordshire | Warw | Warwickshire |
| Humb | Humberside | W Mid | West Midlands |
| IOM | Isle of Man | Wilts | Wiltshire |
| IOS | Isles of Scilly | Yorks | Yorkshire |

# Key to Route Maps

## Key to Counties
### ENGLAND
1 Avon
2 Bedfordshire
3 Berkshire
4 Buckinghamshire
5 Cambridgeshire
6 Cheshire
7 Cleveland
8 Cornwall
9 Cumbria
10 Derbyshire
11 Devonshire
12 Dorset
13 Durham
14 East Sussex
15 Essex
16 Gloucestershire
17 Greater London
18 Greater Manchester

19 Hampshire
20 Hereford & Worcester
21 Hertfordshire
22 Humberside
23 Isle of Wight
24 Kent
25 Lancashire
26 Leicestershire
27 Lincolnshire
28 Merseyside
29 Norfolk
30 Northamptonshire
31 Northumberland
32 North Yorkshire
33 Nottinghamshire
34 Oxfordshire
35 Shropshire
36 Somerset
37 South Yorkshire
38 Staffordshire
39 Suffolk
40 Surrey
41 Tyne & Wear
42 Warwickshire
43 West Midlands
44 West Sussex
45 West Yorkshire
46 Wiltshire

SCOTLAND

Isle of Man

WALES

ENGLAND

Scale of Route Maps
0 miles        10        20        30

2

Ilfracombe
Mortehoe
Woolacombe
Com
Mart

Braunton
Barnstaple
Bideford

Clovelly

Morwenstowe
Kilkhampton
Gt. Torrington
Stratton
Bude
Holsworthy

Okehampton

Boscastle
Tintagel
Camelford
Lydford
Moretonl
Altarnun
Launceston
Polzeath
DARTMOO
Padstow
BODMIN MOOR
Tavistock
Two
Wadebridge
Princetow
Brid
Yelverton
St Mawgan
St Columb
Bodmin
Buckland
Major
Lanhydrock
Cotehele
Abbey
Newquay
House
Liskeard
Buckfas
Roche
Perranporth
CORNWALL
Lostwithiel
Plymout
St Agnes
St Austell
Redruth
Looe
Ivybridge
Fowey
Polperro
St Ives
Camborne
Truro
Newton
Ferrers
Zennor
Mevagissey
Hayle
Thurlestone
Penzance
Portscatho
St Just
Newlyn
St Michael's
St Mawes
LAND'S
Mount
Helston
END
Mousehole
Falmouth
Porthleven
Porthcurno
Helford

Kynance Cove

LIZARD POINT